ASPLOS XVII

Seventeenth International Conference on Architectural Support for Programming Languages and Operating Systems

March 3–7, 2012

London, England, UK

Sponsored by:

SIGARCH

SIGOPS

SIGPLAN

Association for Computing Machinery

With Support from:

ALTERA, AMD, ARM, Bromium, DE Shaw & Co, Google, Hewlett-Packard, HiPEAC, IBM Research, Intel, Microsoft Research, NSF, and VMware

Association for
Computing Machinery

Advancing Computing as a Science & Profession

The Association for Computing Machinery
2 Penn Plaza, Suite 701
New York, New York 10121-0701

ISBN: 978-1-4503-0759-8

Additional copies may be ordered prepaid from:

ACM Order Department
PO Box 30777
New York, NY 10087-0777, USA

Phone: 1-800-342-6626 (USA and Canada)
+1-212-626-0500 (Global)
Fax: +1-212-944-1318
E-mail: acmhelp@acm.org
Hours of Operation: 8:30 am – 4:30 pm ET

ACM Order Number: 415125

Printed in the USA

Message from the Chairs

Welcome to the seventeenth edition of the ASPLOS conference series, and the first to be held outside of North America. We have assembled what we believe to be an outstanding technical program, and are delighted to be presenting it in the historic chambers of the Royal Society in the UK. The program continues and reinforces the ASPLOS tradition of publishing innovative multidisciplinary research spanning the boundaries of hardware, computer architecture, compilers, languages, operating systems, networking, and applications.

We received 172 full paper submissions, which was 13% higher than last year's 152, and 5% lower than the record of 181 set in 2010. 14 submissions had program committee members as co-authors. Once again, the dominant technical theme was parallelism: 70% of both the submitted and accepted papers explicitly indicated a technical keyword specific to parallel processing. The single most popular keyword was "multicore systems," selected by 35% of both the submitted and accepted papers. Interestingly, not one of the 172 submissions selected "VLSI or process technology." There was a nice mixture of submissions across operating systems (34%), compilers and programming languages (28%), and core topics in computer architecture (37%), with 23% of submissions spanning more than one of these. (Most submissions had something to do with computer architecture; the characterization of "core areas" is somewhat arbitrary.)

As in recent years, we employed two rounds of reviewing. An External Review Committee, preselected by the Program Chair, assisted in round one. All submissions received at least three round one reviews. Based on these, we eliminated 71 papers whose average overall score was below 3.5 (on a scale of 1–6), and whose maximum score was below 5 (i.e., no better than "weak accept"). The remaining 101 papers received two additional (PC-only) reviews in round two. This process allowed the program committee to focus the bulk of its attention on papers with a significant chance of being accepted. The typical member of the External Review Committee completed six reviews; the typical Program Committee member did 14.

Almost all reviews were completed by early October, at which point authors had several days to compose a formal response, if they desired (most did). After this rebuttal period, PC members took the author comments into account as they discussed the papers online and, in some cases, updated their scores accordingly.

The PC gathered in Rochester, NY, for a full-day meeting on October 20th, 2011. 74 papers were discussed at the meeting. PC authors stepped out of the room for discussion of their papers; those with conflicts of interest remained in the room, but did not participate in discussion. Papers on which the Program Chair had a conflict of interest (4 in number) had been reviewed in a separate process managed by Jim Larus, and were discussed when the Chair was not present.

At the end of the day, 37 papers were accepted for presentation at the conference, for an acceptance rate of 21.5% — a slightly larger number than last year, but almost the same percentage. Four of the accepts have PC members as co-authors. Nine papers were assigned a "shepherd" to make sure that final versions addressed issues (not necessarily weaknesses) of concern to the program committee.

The logistics behind organizing this conference have been handled by the tireless effort of a team of volunteers: Luis Ceze (University of Washington), Alexandra Fedorova (Simon Fraser University), Steven Hand (University of Cambridge), Timothy Jones (University of Cambridge), Paul Kelly (Imperial College), Mikel Luján (University of Manchester), Robert Mullins (University of

Cambridge), Onur Mutlu (Carnegie Mellon University), and Derek Murray (Microsoft Research). Each member of this team played an important role in making ASPLOS a success.

The ASPLOS Steering Committee gave us valuable assistance over the last year, and Todd Mowry (CMU) was particularly generous with his advice from ASPLOS 2010 and ASPLOS 2011. In addition, Jean Bacon (University of Cambridge), Andrew Herbert, Graham Hutton (University of Nottingham), and Joe Sventek (University of Glasgow) provided advice on organizing a conference in the UK. As always, the support and guidance of the ACM staff was very valuable.

ACM SIGARCH, SIGOPS, and SIGPLAN are the conference sponsors. We want to thank them for their continued support of this unique and important venue that weaves together the interests of multiple SIGs. In addition to the SIGs, and the US National Science Foundation, Google provided generous industrial support for student travel grants. Altera, AMD, ARM, Bromium, D. E. Shaw Group, IBM Research, Intel, Microsoft Research, and VMware have provided financial support to this conference. We thank them for their generous contribution and for their vote of confidence in this premier conference.

Finally, we want to thank all of you for attending ASPLOS in London, UK. We are privileged to have had the opportunity to put together this year's conference. We hope you will find inspiration from the technical program and from interactions with your colleagues from around the world. On behalf of the organizers, we also hope you have an enjoyable visit.

Tim Harris
ASPLOS 2012 General Chair
Microsoft Research

Michael L. Scott
ASPLOS 2012 Program Chair
University of Rochester

Table of Contents

ASPLOS 2012 Organization

General Chair: Tim Harris, *Microsoft Research*

Program Chair: Michael L. Scott, *University of Rochester*

Sponsorship Chair: Steven Hand, *University of Cambridge*

Workshops & Tutorials Chair: Robert Mullins, *University of Cambridge*

Poster Session Chair: Mikel Luján, *University of Manchester*

Provocative Ideas Session Chair: Alexandra Fedorova, *Simon Fraser University*

Doctoral Workshop Chairs: Timothy Jones, *University of Cambridge*
Onur Mutlu, *Carnegie Mellon University*

Student Volunteers Chair: Paul Kelly, *Imperial College, London*

Travel Grants Chair: Derek Murray, *Microsoft Research*

Program Committee: Chris Batten, *Cornell University*
Rastislav Bodik, *University of California, Berkeley*
Angela Demke Brown, *University of Toronto*
Evelyn Duesterwald, *IBM T.J. Watson Research Center*
Dawson Engler, *Stanford University*
Alexandra Fedorova, *Simon Fraser University*
Antonio Gonzalez, *Intel and UPC*
Dan Grossman, *University of Washington, Seattle*
Rebecca Isaacs, *Microsoft Research*
Idit Keidar, *Technion – Israel Institute of Technology*
Hyesoon Kim, *Georgia Tech*
James Larus, *Microsoft Research*
Jan-Willem Maessen, *Google, Inc.*
Evangelos Markatos, *University of Crete*
Margaret Martonosi, *Princeton University*
Kathryn S. McKinley, *Microsoft Research*
Pablo Montesinos, *Qualcomm, Inc.*
Onur Mutlu, *Carnegie Mellon University*
Kunle Olukotun, *Stanford University*
Xipeng Shen, *College of William & Mary*
Tatiana Shpeisman, *Intel Labs*
Daniel Sorin, *Duke University*
Per Stenström, *Chalmers University of Technology*
Steven Swanson, *University of California, San Diego*
Christoph von Praun, *Georg Simon Ohm University, Nuremberg*

External Review Committee:

Ali-Reza Adl-Tabatabai	Galen Hunt
Anastassia Ailamaki	Engin Ipek
Krste Asanović	Kim Keeton
David Bacon	Terence Kelly
Rajeev Balasubramonian	Martha Kim
Luiz Barroso	Konrad Lai
Ricardo Bianchini	Alvin Lebeck
Michael Bond	Ben Lee
George Candea	Milo Martin
John Carter	Andreas Moshovos
Călin Caşcaval	Eliot Moss
Luis Ceze	Ashwini Nanda
Jaewoong Chung	Jason Nieh
Lawrence Crowl	Mark Oskin
Brian Demsky	Keshav Pingali
Stephan Diestelhorst	Lori Pollock
Chen Ding	Feng Qin
Sandhya Dwarkadas	Kishore Ramachandran
Babak Falsafi	Krithi Ramamritham
Pascal Felber	Steve Reinhardt
Bryan Ford	Mothy Roscoe
Guang Gao	Martin Schulz
Maria Garzaran	Marc Shapiro
Garth Gibson	Kai Shen
James Goodman	Chris Stewart
Thomas Gross	Mike Swift
Rajiv Gupta	Josep Torellas
Steve Hand	Emmett Witchel
Maurice Herlihy	Peng Wu
Matthew Hertz	Antonia Zhai
Anne Holler	Yutao Zhong
Michael Huang	Yuanyuan Zhou

ASPLOS 2012 Sponsors & Supporters

Sponsors:

Supporters:

PocketWeb: Instant Web Browsing for Mobile Devices

Dimitrios Lymberopoulos, Oriana Riva, Karin Strauss, Akshay Mittal[‡], Alexandros Ntoulas
Microsoft Research, Redmond, WA, USA
[‡]Indian Institute of Technology, Kanpur, India
{dlymper,oriana,kstrauss,antoulas}@microsoft.com, amittal@iitk.ac.in

Abstract

The high network latencies and limited battery life of mobile phones can make mobile web browsing a frustrating experience. In prior work, we proposed trading memory capacity for lower web access latency and a more convenient data transfer schedule from an energy perspective by prefetching slowly-changing data (search queries and results) nightly, when the phone is charging. However, most web content is intrinsically much more dynamic and may be updated multiple times a day, thus eliminating the effectiveness of periodic updates.

This paper addresses the challenge of prefetching dynamic web content in a timely fashion, giving the user an instant web browsing experience but without aggravating the battery lifetime issue. We start by analyzing the web access traces of 8,000 users, and observe that mobile web browsing exhibits a strong spatiotemporal signature, which is different for every user. We propose to use a machine learning approach based on stochastic gradient boosting techniques to efficiently model this signature on a per user basis. The machine learning model is capable of accurately predicting future web accesses and prefetching the content in a timely manner. Our experimental evaluation with 48,000 models trained on real user datasets shows that we can accurately prefetch 60% of the URLs for about 80-90% of the users within 2 minutes before the request. The system prototype we built not only provides more than 80% lower web access time for more than 80% of the users, but it also achieves the same or lower radio energy dissipation by more than 50% for the majority of mobile users.

Categories and Subject Descriptors H.4.m [*Information Systems*]: Information Systems Applications—Miscellaneous

General Terms Algorithms, Human Factors, Experimentation

1. Introduction

With recent advances in large touch screens and widespread data networks, smartphones are rapidly gaining popularity. They are the most convenient device to access the web, and according to a recent study [22], mobile devices are expected to surpass desktop web browsing in the next 4 years. Mobile phone user's experience has come a long way in the past decade, but such devices still face high network latencies and limited battery life, which can make the mobile experience frustrating.

ASPLOS'12, March 3–7, 2012, London, England, UK.

Luckily, memory capacity is still experiencing healthy improvements [15], and can be used to mitigate the two previous limitations. Surplus memory can be used to store data that is brought to the mobile device when network conditions are favorable. The data can be later accessed at low latency and low energy cost. Based on this observation we have proposed the concept of Pocket Cloudlets [19], *i.e.*, bringing part of cloud services into mobile phones to reduce latency and energy consumption, with the added benefit of significantly reducing the load on the server side as well. We demonstrated the concept using a search service: a set of popular search queries and results is loaded onto the phone at night, when the phone is charging, to speed up searches during the next day. However, in that work we limited ourselves to search and did not address actual web content. While search results change slowly (they can be considered static on a daily basis), web content can change quickly during a single day.

To enable a faster mobile web browsing experience on the currently available mobile infrastructure, this paper proposes an intelligent web content prefetcher that downloads web content on the mobile device at appropriate times, anticipating a user's future web accesses. Perhaps the biggest challenge with prefetching web content compared to search queries and results is that web content is *dynamic*. While the mapping of search queries to search results remains relatively stable over days or even weeks, web content changes frequently. News and social network web sites change continuously, such that the nightly update approach does not work as well as it does for search.

A naïve approach to achieving high prefetching accuracy is to prefetch as much content we can as often as possible. However, this approach is not practical due to constraints in battery capacity and limited network bandwidth. Downloading all frequently accessed web pages of a user every 2 minutes might ensure a lightning-fast web browsing experience, but the battery would not last very long. At a high level, we can consider a prefetch of a web page as unsuccessful or "wasted" either because it happened too long ago (and thus the content on the device is stale), or because the user did not end up explicitly requesting the web page at all. In either of these cases, we end up using some phone's resources without realizing any gains. Therefore, our goal is to achieve timely prefetches without increasing (and possibly decreasing!) energy consumption.

We first analyze the web access traces from roughly 8,000 mobile users over a period of 3 months and show three well-defined patterns. First, users often visit a small set of web pages from their phones, which they tend to repeatedly visit over time. Second, user accesses are often periodic and happen at given time windows. For example, a user may check the Facebook updates every 30 minutes and the CNN news right when she wakes up and during an afternoon break. Third, users often access content in bursts. For example, when the user checks the news, she may also check the weather forecast and current stock prices.

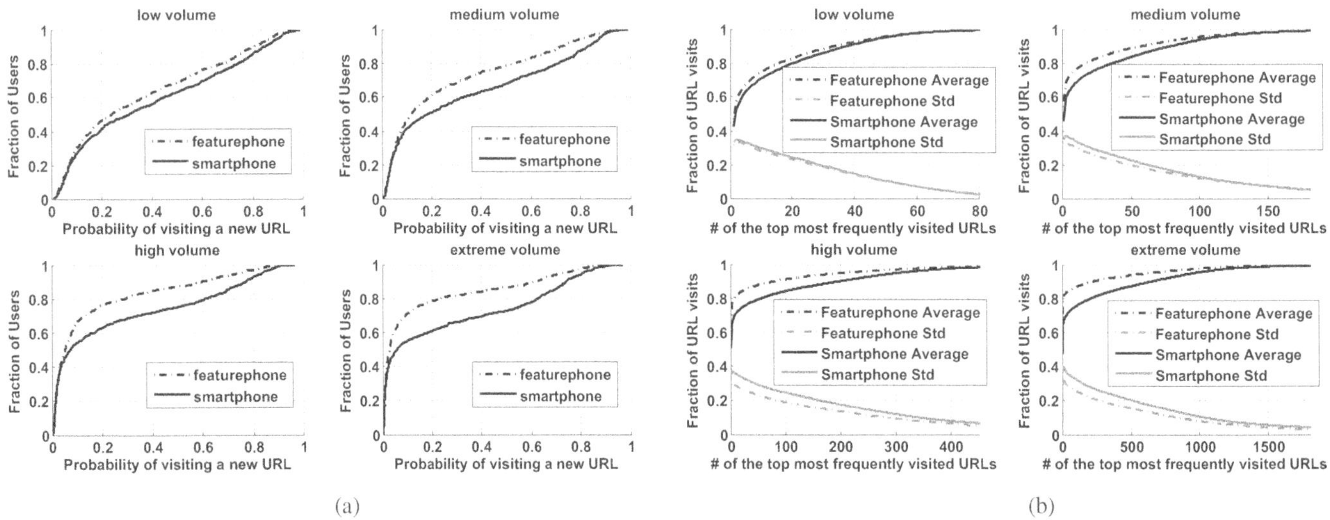

Figure 1. (a) Repeatability of mobile URL visits. (b) Average and standard deviation of the cumulative URL volume that the top most frequently visited URLs are accountable for.

Prior work in web content prefetching has focused on simply correlating sets of web sites accessed together and using this information to prefetch the set when the first page of a set is accessed. In this work, we study properties of mobile web accesses that go beyond these sequential features. We take advantage of the spatiotemporal access patterns obtained from our analysis and use machine learning techniques to create a model that can be used to predict both *what* web pages a user is likely to request as well as *when* these requests are likely to occur. By learning how each individual user accesses the web over time, the phone can proactively download web content before the user explicitly attempts to access it, thus enabling an instant mobile browsing experience.

Our experimental evaluation with real user datasets shows that we can accurately prefetch 60% of the URLs for about 80-90% of the users within 2 minutes before the request. Furthermore, the proposed approach not only provides more than 80% lower web access time for more than 80% of the users, but it also achieves the same or lower radio energy dissipation by more than 50% for the majority of mobile users.

In summary, this paper makes the following contributions:

- Provides a detailed analysis of web browsing on mobile phones from 8,000 users, showing widely disparate behaviors from user to user but a strong spatiotemporal structure for individual users.
- Formulates the problem of web content prefetching as a binary access prediction problem in machine learning, where the features are derived from the observable structure of mobile web browsing. We use stochastic gradient boosting techniques for this purpose, which allow us to provide insight into which features are the most relevant to access prediction.
- Experimentally evaluates the accuracy of the proposed approach for each user by creating individual user models with a portion of the accesses in each trace, and testing their performance with the remaining portion. Quantifies, using a prototype implementation, the impact of the proposed approach on the web access time and radio power consumption with respect to the state-of-the-art.

2. Mobile web Browsing Analysis

Central to our work is the ability to understand and model effectively the user browsing behavior. We start our study by first providing a description of the data set that we used, and continue with the results of our analysis both *on aggregate* across users and *individually* per user.

2.1 Data Set

We used the mobile web access logs of 8,000 users across the United States over a 3-month period. The users were randomly selected among a larger number of users that opted to download and install the Bing application or to enable the pre-installed Bing toolbar on their mobile phones. Users' phones varied from high-end smartphones (*e.g.*, iPhone, Android, Blackberry) to low-end featurephones (*e.g.*, LG and Samsung devices with custom operating systems). From the total of 8,000 users in our dataset, half are smartphone users and half are featurephone users. To get a deeper understanding on user behavior, each of the two sets of users was further split into 4 different classes (low, medium, high, and extreme volume classes) based on the monthly volume of web accesses ([20-40), [40,140), [140,460), [460,∞) respectively). In the logs we analyzed, the information on each web access included unique user identifier, full path of accessed URL, and access timestamp.

2.2 Repeatability of Mobile Web Accesses

We first study the repeatability of mobile web accesses. We compute the number of times that any user will be visiting a new unique URL (*i.e.*, a full path URL that has not been visited before) in the next access. We show the results in Figure 1(a) across volume classes and device types. Approximately 40% to 60% of the smartphone users, for the low and extreme volume classes, are likely to visit a new URL 20% of the time. In other words, 80% of the URL visits are repeated visits for roughly half of the smartphone users. We also observe that users in higher volume classes are more likely to repeat visits than users in lower volume classes. Finally, although the trends are similar for featurephones, the overall repeated visits are higher when compared to smartphone users. Intuitively, featurephone users that have to interact with devices with constrained

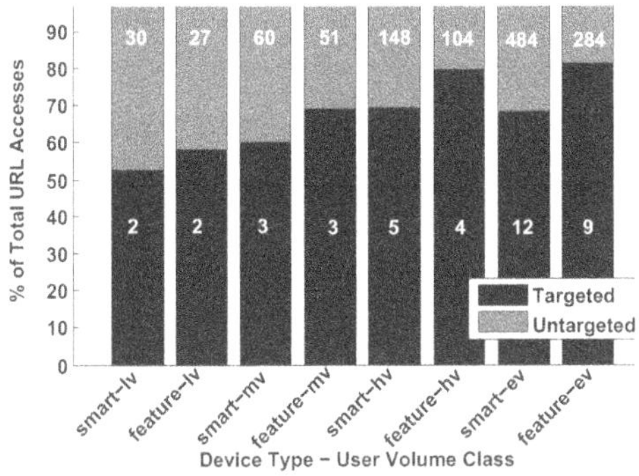

Figure 2. Breakdown of total URL accesses into targeted (URLs that have been accessed at least 5 times in a month) and untargeted. The white numbers in each bar plot represent the average number of unique targeted/untargeted URLs.

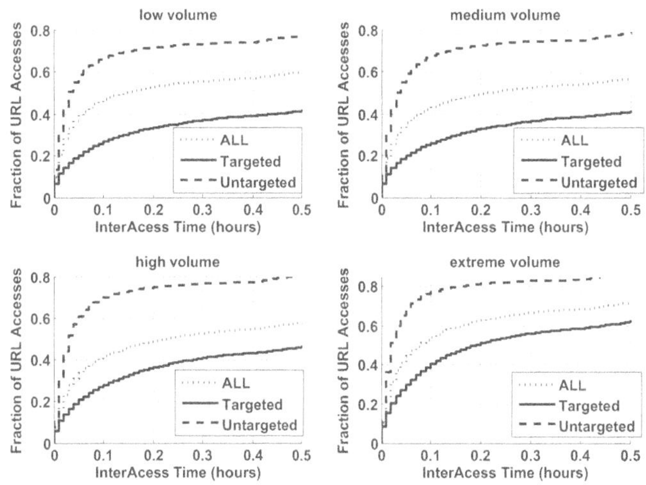

Figure 3. Time elapsed between consecutive smartphone web accesses when all, targeted, or untargeted URLs are considered. The trends are identical for featurephones (not shown).

user interfaces and hardware capabilities are more likely to access the web in a more conservative way compared to smartphone users. They tend to explore the web less and focus more on accessing web content they really need to access.

To examine the repeatability of URL visits in more detail, we also compute, for each user, the cumulative URL volume for the top URLs that the user accesses. The result is shown in Figure 1(b). The numbers on the horizontal axis represent the top most frequently visited URLs (these URLs might be different across users). The vertical axis shows the cumulative fraction of the total URL visits that the number of the most frequently visited URLs is responsible for across users. Notably, across user classes, the most frequently visited URL accounts for about 50% of the overall user's URL visits. In other words, a single URL is responsible for approximately half of a typical user's URL requests. However, we also observe that the overall URL volume varies across users. More specifically, there are users for whom more than 90% of their total URL volume can be attributed to a single URL, and users for which the most frequent URL corresponds to less than 10% of their total volume. It is therefore important for any prefetching technique to take into account the individual characteristics of every user.

2.3 Targeted vs. Untargeted web Accesses

From the analysis so far we infer that the URLs that a user visits fall into two classes: there is a small number of frequently visited URLs, and a long tail of infrequently visited URLs. In order to investigate the properties of these two kinds of URLs we classify them as *targeted* and *untargeted* URLs. We define a *targeted* URL to be one which was visited by the user at least 5 times in a month. We chose this threshold by closely analyzing the user web access logs. We found that smaller thresholds, such as 3, could be too permissive and cause 50% of the extreme volume users to have more than 50 targeted URLs. On the other hand, higher thresholds such as 10 could be too aggressive and cause 30% of the low volume users to have 0 targeted URLs.

We analyze the volume of web accesses generated by targeted and untargeted URLs. As Figure 2 shows, although the targeted accesses are only slightly more than the untargeted accesses for the low volume users, the URL accesses are dominated by targeted accesses for the remaining classes of users. For example, for high volume users, targeted accesses account for 70% of the total smartphone URL accesses.

Figure 2 also provides more insight on the average number of *unique* targeted URLs across the different volume classes and device types (number indicated inside the bars in Figure 2). For low and medium volume users and for both featurephones and smartphones, the average number of unique targeted URLs is roughly 2 and 3 respectively. For high and extreme volume classes, it increases to 9 and 12 for featurephones and smartphones respectively. In other words, 2 to 12 unique URLs are, on average, responsible for more than 70% of a user's web accesses. Hence, enabling the mobile device to properly model *when* and *which* of the small number of targeted URLs will be accessed by the user is of paramount importance for an effective prefetching policy.

2.4 Timing of Mobile Web Accesses

Web pages are constantly updated. For a prefetching technique to be effective, it needs to predict *when* the user's web accesses will take place. Hence, we study the temporal access patterns of our users. Figure 3 shows the elapsed time between consecutive smartphone web accesses for targeted, untargeted and combined (targeted and untargeted) URL visits. Approximately 35% to 50% of targeted URL visits across the 4 volume classes occur within 12 minutes (0.2 hours in Figure 3) of the last targeted URL visit. Additionally, 25% to 40% (depending on the volume class) of targeted URL visits take place within 6 minutes (0.1 hours in Figure 3) of the last targeted URL visit. Hence, a targeted URL access can serve as a good predictor of the time at which a next targeted URL access will occur.

According to Figure 3, untargeted URL visits tend to be more concentrated in time when compared to targeted URLs. Approximately 70% to 80% of untargeted URL visits (as opposed to 35% to 50% of targeted URL visits) take place within 12 minutes of the last untargeted URL visit. In other words, when mobile users explore the web, they tend to visit many more URLs within a short amount of time as compared to when visiting targeted content. We can leverage this information to improve the accuracy of prefetching and save battery resources by not prefetching targeted content when the user is about to visit untargeted URLs.

2.5 A Peek into Individual Users

In addition to relative timing, we also study the role of absolute timing in mobile web browsing (*e.g.*, time of day when URL accesses occur). In general, knowing when to expect URL accesses can drive content prefetching. Figure 4 shows the timestamps within a day of all URL accesses that 4 random smartphone users performed over 3 months.

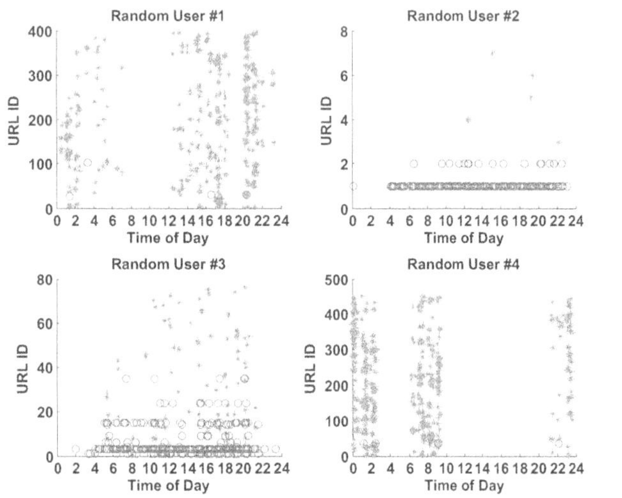

Figure 4. Web accesses of 4 representative smartphone users in the high volume class. All accesses over the 3 months are projected into a single day. The red stars represent untargeted URL visits. The blue circles represent targeted URL visits.

The variance in mobile web access patterns across the 4 users is striking. The URL visits of users 1 and 4 are dominated by untargeted URLs. Most likely, a web content prefetching technique will have difficulty in modeling these users' web browsing patterns accurately, as it has no way of predicting the untargeted accesses. Interestingly, however, users 1 and 4 access web pages from their phones at given time intervals within the day (*e.g.*, user 4's accesses are only between 6am and 9am, 9pm and 11pm, and midnight and 2am). On the other hand, for users 2 and 3, web accesses are dominated by a small set of targeted URLs (2 targeted URLs for user 2 and 7 for user 3). More importantly, the single most frequently visited targeted URL is responsible for the majority of that user's URL visits. Additionally, both users 2 and 3 tend to continuously access this single targeted URL periodically throughout the day. If a prefetching policy can predict *when* the targeted URL will be accessed by the users based on their periodic accesses, it can be very effective in providing an instant mobile browsing experience.

2.6 Summary and Key Findings

The analysis of real web access logs from 8,000 users has highlighted different aspects of mobile web browsing behavior that are critical to content prefetching:

- A small number of targeted URLs is responsible for the majority of a user's URL visits. Predicting these targeted URL accesses can have a huge impact on the user's browsing experience.
- Targeted URL accesses are clustered in time. Mobile users tend to access them in batches within short time windows. Hence, recent targeted URL accesses can be strong indicators of future URL visits.
- Untargeted URL accesses are significantly more clustered in time than targeted URL accesses. Recent untargeted URL accesses can help us decide about the type of future URL accesses (targeted vs. untargeted).
- URL accesses exhibit strong temporal properties that help us prefetch content in a *timely* manner. Prefetching based only on past sequences (or, more generally, sets) of web accesses can be inefficient as it might not provide enough information to decide *when* to prefetch.
- Mobile web browsing behavior across users can vary greatly in the type and number of accessed URLs as well as the timing of URL accesses.

Thus, a data-driven content prefetching technique that takes advantage of the underlying spatiotemporal patterns of each individual user's web browsing behavior is required to enable timely and accurate content prefetching.

3. Content Prefetching As A Learning Problem

Mobile web browsing behavior exhibits several spatial and temporal properties. To enable timely prefetching of web content, the prefetching scheme needs to carefully model and learn all these different properties for each individual user. However, optimally combining these properties is not straightforward.

Our approach is inspired by the web search community, where multiple hundreds or thousands of features are combined to rank web documents (*i.e.*, URLs). In a web search scenario, the user submits a query and the search engine ranks a set of URLs to show the most relevant ones higher up in the result page. The ranking problem is often formulated as a click prediction problem, where for every related URL, the engine has to estimate the probability of a user click on that URL. The higher the probability, the higher the rank of the URL. To create the click prediction model, search engines leverage, among other signals, web search click logs. For every URL displayed to the user, various features are computed, encoding information about the user, the query, the URL or all of them. Each feature vector is labeled as a click (if the URL was clicked) or a non-click (if it was not clicked). The click prediction model is then trained using millions of these labeled feature vectors.

In web content prefetching, the web search click logs are replaced by the user's web access logs. The URLs are no longer web search results, but the targeted URLs identified in the user's web access logs. The click prediction model is now turned into a web access prediction model whose role is to assign, at any given time, an access probability to each targeted URL. The higher the probability, the more likely the user is to request access to this URL. The features used to train the prediction model are the most critical elements of the modeling process and are directly extracted from the user's web access logs.

Conversely to web search, in web content prefetching the user does not explicitly submit a query. Thus, to determine *when* the mobile device should make a web access prediction, we follow an event-driven approach where the mobile device makes web access predictions as a result of certain user actions. For instance, the mobile device makes a prediction every time the user unlocks the phone, activates the browser or visits a URL. Depending on the resulting probabilities, the phone decides whether to prefetch any content.

Figure 5 provides an overview of our web access prediction approach. Offline, the mobile device records user web accesses, including automatic page refreshes, and periodically (*e.g.*, weekly, monthly) uses this information to build a web access prediction model for the user. This model can be built on the mobile device itself, but most likely would be built on users' desktops or the cloud. First, a set of features is extracted for every targeted URL in a user's web logs. The role of these features is to encode the underlying structure of mobile web browsing behavior in terms of spatial and temporal properties, as described in Section 2. Then, the web access logs are mapped to a set of feature vectors that are annotated as accesses or non-accesses.

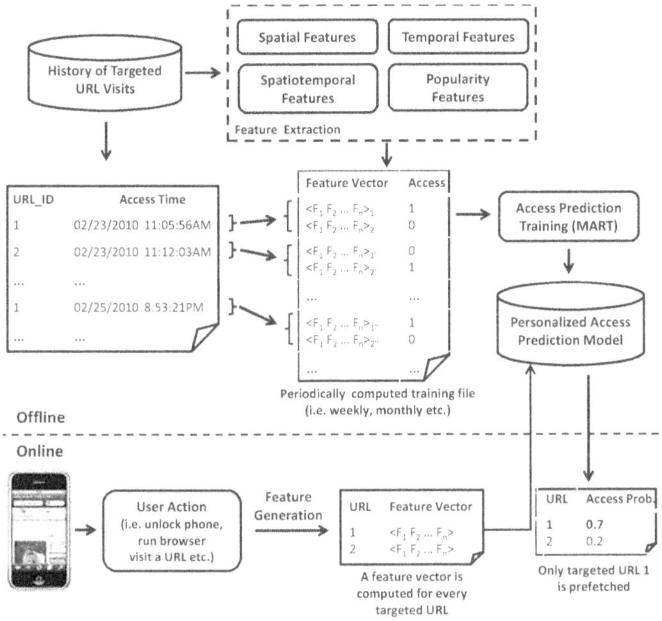

Figure 5. We specify the problem of web content prefetching as an access prediction problem. In this example, the user has two targeted URLs.

Using these labeled feature vector traces, the system trains a model that leverages state-of-the-art stochastic gradient boosting techniques [32], creating a decision tree that supports time ranges, with access probabilities in its leaves. The goal of the training phase is to combine the different features provided as input to enable the model to maximize the number of correct predictions in the test data set. Online, user actions such as unlocking the phone may trigger a prediction. A feature vector is then generated for every targeted URL, and the prediction model is invoked with each of these feature vectors as input. For every feature vector and thus every targeted URL, the model assigns an access probability. Depending on these probabilities and a pre-configured threshold, none, one or more targeted URLs are fetched, along with associated images, css, javascript, etc.

Formulating the problem of content prefetching as a binary access prediction problem and leveraging state-of-the-art stochastic gradient boosting techniques provides a significant advantage. The ability of these modeling tools to consume a large number of features and exploit their dependencies to maximize access prediction enables us to virtually encode any possible information as a feature without being limited by the nature of the modeling tool (*e.g.*, Markov model). More importantly, it allows us to compare the effectiveness of different features in the access prediction task to discover which features best capture mobile web browsing patterns.

3.1 Web Access Prediction with MART

We use MART [32], a learning tool based on *M*ultiple *A*dditive *R*egression *T*rees, widely deployed in commercial systems for web search and advertisement ranking. MART is based on the stochastic gradient boosting approach [14].

To construct the predictive model, MART takes as input historical data on web accesses, which is partitioned into training and validation sets, where the size of the latter is typically $1/5^{th}$ or $1/6^{th}$ of the former. The training data set is used to build the model, while the validation set is used to provide an unbiased error estimate. Each entry contains a set of n features, $\mathcal{F} = \{f_1, f_2, \ldots, f_n\}$,[1] that might be related to a spatial parameter s (*e.g.*, the previously accessed URL), a temporal parameter t (*e.g.*, time of day), a spatiotemporal parameter b (*e.g.*, time since this URL was last accessed), or a popularity feature p (*e.g.*, how popular this URL across all accessed URLs), in conjunction with a label a which records the user's action. The training data is fed into MART to build a classification model, $\mathcal{M}$, which is used to estimate the probability of access $p_{\mathcal{M}}(a|s,t,b,p)$. In our tests, we use the gradient-descent as the optimization technique, and use binary decision trees as the fitting function.

Once model $\mathcal{M}$ is trained, MART reports a relative ordering of all features $\mathcal{F}_q$, which indicates the *"relative feature importance"* when making a prediction. The larger the number of decision tree branches associated to a feature, the higher the importance of that feature. The most important feature has an importance of 1, while other features have a relative importance between 0 and 1. The relative importance of feature values allows us to quantify and compare the impact of different features on the prediction accuracy.

3.2 Feature Generation

Feature generation is one of the most critical steps of the modeling process. Its role is to provide as accurate and discriminative information as possible about the mobile web browsing behavior of individual users. We leverage the findings from our large scale user study to drive the feature generation process. According to our analysis, mobile web browsing behavior exhibits strong *spatial*, *temporal*, and *spatiotemporal* structure. As a result, we introduce 4 sets of features, shown in Table 1, that focus on capturing this structure. Overall, for a user with k targeted URLs, $2 \times k + 11$ features are computed. A detailed description of each feature is provided in Table 1.

The *spatial features* encode sets of mobile web accesses accessed together (Figure 1), and record information about the immediately previously accessed URL (either that it was to an untargeted URL, or to which targeted URL it was). The *temporal features* record the periodicity of targeted web accesses (Figure 4), and the time of day or day of the week in which these accesses occur. The *spatiotemporal features* combine spatial and temporal properties to encode information such as the time elapsed between a targeted URL access and the immediately previous access (Figure 3). These features can provide invaluable information to the model to decide *what* targeted URL and *when* to prefetch, enabling timely prefetches. The *popularity features* encode the popularity of each targeted URL, and can be used to decide which targeted URLs will most likely be accessed. These features can be particularly important, given that the number of targeted URLs varies anywhere from 1 to 10, but usually 2 or 3 of these URLs are responsible for most targeted URL accesses (Figures 2 and 4).

3.3 Training for Timely Prefetches

To understand how features are computed, and training, validation and test files are generated, consider the log of an example user in Figure 6. Web logs are first split into training, validation and test with a data volume ratio of 70%:10%:20%, respectively. We initially process the training data only to identify the targeted URLs of the user, namely $t_1, t_2, \ldots, t_k$ – URLs that have been accessed more than 5 times a month. For the example user in Figure 6, $k = 2$. After having identified the targeted URLs, the training, validation and test data sets are generated as follows.

[1] As the model's goal is to predict targeted web accesses, the feature vectors are generated only for targeted web accesses or non-accesses. However, the feature values encode information about both targeted and untargeted web accesses.

Feature class	Feature name	Definition	Example for $t_x = t_1$ in Figure 6
spatial	t_i_*Targeted**	whether the previous access was to the targeted URL t_i, for $i \in [1, k]$	$t_1 = 0; t_2 = 0$
	Untargeted	whether the previous access was an access to an untargeted URL	1
temporal	*TimeOfDay*	time of day at which the access occurred	$11h15m$
	AvgTime	average access time over all accesses to the same targeted URL t_x	$9h06$
	TimeStdev	standard deviation over all access times for the same targeted URL t_x	$55m$
	Weekend	whether the access happened during a weekend	1
spatio-temporal	*TimeSinceTargeted*	time elapsed since any targeted URL was last accessed	$1d3h15m$
	t_i_*TimeSinceTargeted**	time elapsed since the targeted URL t_i was last accessed, for $i \in [1, k]$	$t_1 = 1d3h15m$; $t_2 = 1d3h14m$
	TimeSinceUntargeted	time elapsed since any untargeted URL was last accessed	$2m$
	TimeSinceAccess	time elapsed since the targeted URL t_x was last accessed	$1d3h15m$
	AvgInterAccessTime	average time between two consecutive accesses to the targeted URL t_x	$1d12h31m$
	InterAccessTimeStdev	standard deviation of inter-access times for the targeted URL t_x	$9h16m$
popularity	*PopAmongTargeted*	popularity of the targeted URL t_x over all k targeted URLs	75%
	PopAmongAll	popularity of the targeted URL t_x over all targeted and untargeted URLs	37.5%

Table 1. Features used for training MART. In the table, we assume the feature vector describes an access to a targeted URL t_x of a user with k targeted URLs. Feature names marked with * correspond to k features, one per targeted URL.

Starting from the first web access in the logs, we divide user's web accesses into multiple *access epochs* with a duration of D minutes each. For instance, Figure 6 shows 4 different access epochs, where $D = 5$. For each access epoch, we compute k feature vectors (Table 1), one for every targeted URL. The vectors for targeted URLs accessed in the epoch are labeled as accessed. All other vectors are labeled as non-accessed.

If a targeted URL is accessed multiple times within an epoch, only one feature vector is computed for the first access to that URL within the epoch. This biases the model towards the first access, which improves timeliness. The duration of the access epoch D defines the freshness of the prediction, and, thus, we call it the *freshness threshold*. Whenever a prediction is made in the beginning of an access epoch and a URL is prefetched, its content is considered fresh for the duration D of the access epoch. In that way, we implicitly assume that the web content update rate is less than 1 update per D minutes.

The labeled feature vectors in the training file are used offline to train the access prediction model. The labeled feature vectors in the test data set are used to evaluate the performance of the model. In particular, for each feature vector in the test file, we retrieve the access probability from the model. An access probability higher than 0.5 corresponds to prefetching the targeted URL (this probability threshold could be adjusted dynamically depending on network and battery conditions). The success or not of the prediction depends on the label of the feature vector in the test file. If it was marked as accessed, the prefetching was successful, otherwise the prefetching was unsuccessful.

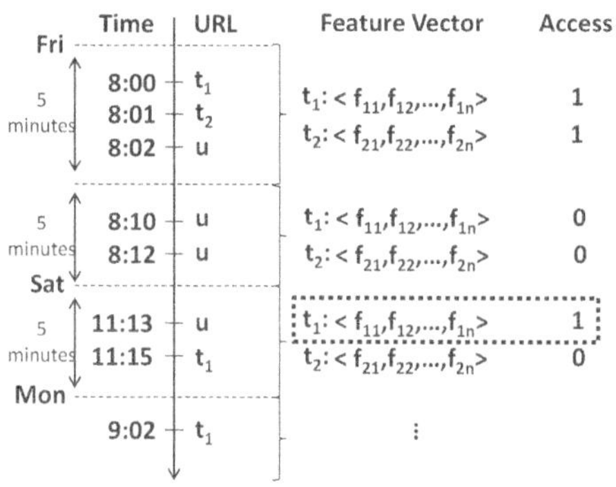

Figure 6. Example of web accesses trace and the resulting web accesses and non-accesses events generated. Dashed lines delimit access epochs. The feature vector values for t_1 in the 3rd access epoch are shown in the last column of Table 1.

4. Evaluation

We evaluate our approach using logs of all 8,000 users in our dataset. We split the dataset into training, validation and test sets, and use the test set to measure the accuracy in predicting both web accesses and non-accesses. To evaluate the freshness of the prefetches, we need to know the content update rate of each web page. Unfortunately, this is hard to reliably estimate because we cannot know all the updates for the pages in our dataset and because several pages require user authentication to be accessed (*e.g.*, Facebook). To provide a notion of prefetch timeliness we leverage the concept of *freshness threshold* previously introduced. Different freshness thresholds allow us to evaluate the ability of the model to timely prefetch content for different time thresholds and, thus, for different content update rates. In the experiments, we use three different thresholds: 2, 5 and 10 minutes. To study the impact of different features on the model's prediction accuracy, we train models with either all or a subset of the proposed features. Overall, for each user we train 6 different models (2 sets of features and 3 freshness thresholds). Across all users, we train a total of 48,000 prediction models.

Finally, we use our prototype implementation of the proposed prefetching approach, shown in Figure 7, to provide an estimate on the power consumption overhead and the web access time gains achieved. The preferred freshness threshold is manually selected by the user.

4.1 Model Prediction Accuracy

We start by evaluating the accuracy of our approach. Our goal is to maximize the number of successful prefetches and minimize the number of unsuccessful prefetches. In all the experiments, we decide to prefetch a web page when the access probability returned by the model is higher or equal to 0.5.

4.1.1 Prefetching Accuracy

Figure 8(a) shows the trained model accuracy in predicting smartphone users' web accesses across different volume classes, and freshness thresholds. We first consider the freshness threshold of 2 minutes. For roughly 80-90% of the users, the prediction model correctly predicts the targeted URL that will be accessed in the next 2 minutes at least 80% of the time. In other words, 80% of the tar-

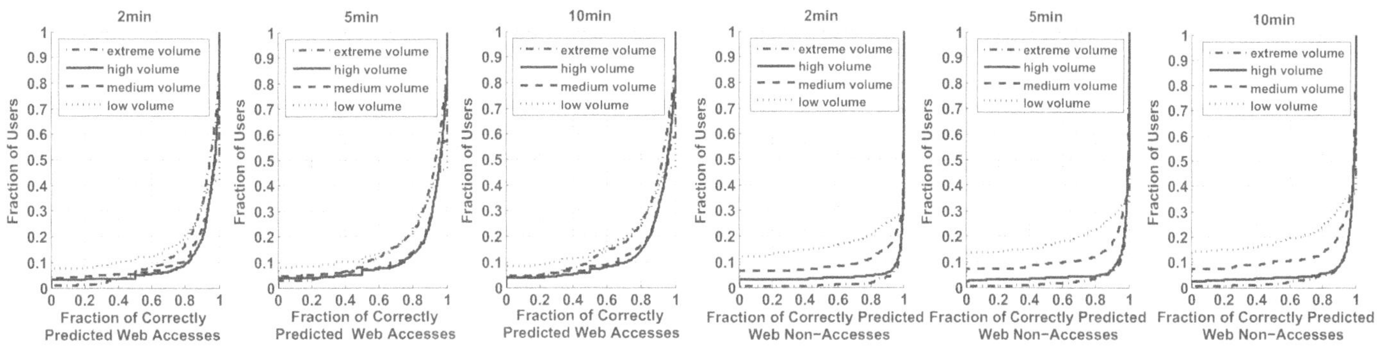

(a) (b)

Figure 8. CDF of successful predictions of (a) web accesses and (b) web non-accesses for smartphone users across different volume classes and freshness thresholds. The results for featurephone users are very similar and are not shown in the interest of space.

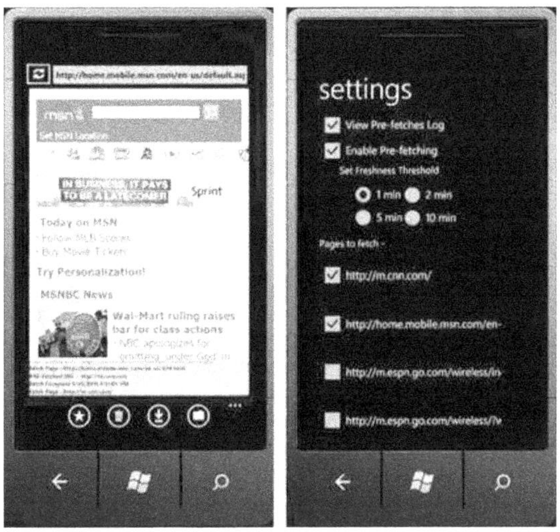

Figure 7. Web access prediction system prototype running on Windows Phone 7.

geted URL accesses of approximately 80-90% of the users can be prefetched within 2 minutes of the user actually accessing them. To put things in perspective, 80% of the targeted URL accesses correspond to 55%-60% of the all URL accesses (targeted and untargeted) for low and medium volume users and to 70% for high and extreme volume users (Figure 2(a)).

The prefetching accuracy across all user volume classes is quite similar. In general, the smaller the web access history, the harder it is to make predictions because the repeatability of URL accesses is lower and low volume users visit the web less frequently, thus not providing enough information for the training phase. Still, the models for low volume users achieve 80% or higher accuracy in 80% of the cases. On the other hand, for high and extreme volume models it is difficult to achieve 100% accuracy in all cases because despite the rich traces of these users, some exhibit a random behavior.

The performance of the prediction model does not vary significantly across freshness thresholds. Higher freshness thresholds (5 and 10 minutes) cause only a slight degradation in the prediction accuracy. For instance, for the high volume class, the percentage of users for which the model successfully predicts at least 80% of their web accesses reduces from 90% (2 minutes) to 87% (10 minutes).

The accuracy for featurephone users (omitted due to space constraints) is consistently slightly better than that for smartphone users. For 95% of the featurephone users (compared to 90% for smartphones) we can successfully predict at least 80% of a given user's web accesses. This is due to the higher repeatability of URL accesses for featurephone users compared to smartphone users (Figure 1).

Overall, across all user volumes, device types and freshness thresholds, at least 80% of a user's targeted accesses can be successfully predicted for approximately 90% of the users. In practice, the proposed content prefetching technique can provide instant browsing experience for 80% of a user's targeted accesses while guaranteeing that the prefetched content will be at most 2 minutes old.

4.1.2 False Positives

Correctly predicting web accesses helps provide an instant mobile browsing experience, but incorrectly predicting non-accesses to web pages can result in unnecessary prefetches (false positives) that can drain the battery of the mobile device. Figure 8(b) shows the fraction of successful non-access predictions of the trained model in the case of smartphone users, across different volume classes and freshness thresholds. For the 2-minute freshness threshold, the model successfully predicts non-accesses at least 80% of the time for anywhere between 90% (high volume class) and 80% (low volume class) of the users. Again, the lower the volume class, the lower the non-accesses prediction accuracy.

Figure 10 provides more insights on the ability of the proposed prefetching technique to accurately predict web non-accesses. It shows the CDF of the actual number of unsuccessful prefetches across smartphone users in the medium and high volume classes for different freshness thresholds. For approximately 90% of the users, the number of false positives (unsuccessful prefetches) is less than 4, 5, 10, and 100 for the low, medium, high and extreme volume classes respectively. Given that the test dataset of every user contained accesses over a period of approximately 20 days, these numbers correspond to less than one (low, medium and high volume classes) and approximately 5 (extreme volume class) unsuccessful prefetches per day. As a result, the proposed prefetching approach has minimal impact on the battery life of the mobile device for the vast majority of mobile users. However, if necessary to limit battery life degradation, the number of prefetches could be throttled by a daily threshold and the probability threshold above which a page is prefetched could be adjusted dynamically.

However, the tail of the CDF plots in Figure 10 can be relatively long, especially for extreme volume users. In general, there is a small percentage of users (less than 2% across all volume classes), for which the number of false positives can significantly increase.

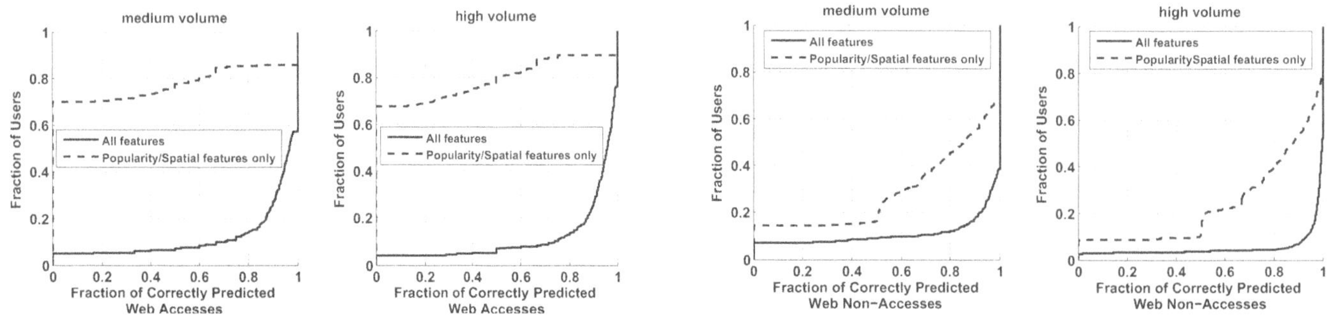

Figure 9. CDF of successful predictions of web accesses, and web non-accesses when all features as well as no temporal or spatiotemporal features are used in the training phase, for the 5-minute freshness threshold and smartphone users. Results are similar across freshness thresholds, device types, and user volume classes, and are not shown in the interest of space.

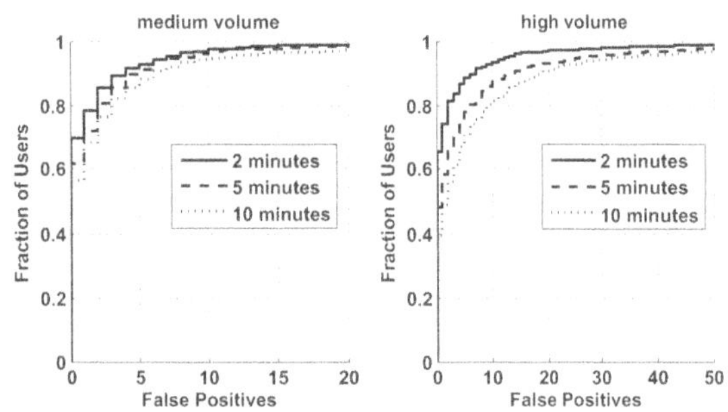

Figure 10. CDF of the number of unsuccessful prefetches for medium and high volume smartphone users, and across different freshness thresholds. The results for featurephones and the rest user volume classes are not shown in the interest of space.

These are users with a random or unpredictable web access behavior. To prevent the number of unsuccessful predictions from negatively impacting the battery life of the mobile device, the prefetching mechanism can monitor, over time, its own access prediction accuracy and accordingly disable any prefetching attempts when the number of false positives exceeds a daily threshold. In that way, even these users will not experience any noticeable degradation in their mobile devices' battery life.

4.1.3 Feature Importance

In this section, we leverage the relative importance of features reported by MART (described in detail in the previous section) to study the impact of different features on the performance of the web access prediction model.

Table 2 shows the relative ranking for the spatial, temporal, spatiotemporal and popularity features for high volume smartphone users (results are similar for other device types and volume classes). Spatiotemporal features have the highest relative importance. For 88% of the high volume users, at least one of the spatiotemporal features is ranked 1st. Popularity features follow next, with 10% of the users having them as the most important features. Pure temporal features are very rarely ranked 1st (2% of the cases), and instead are at the 4th or worse positions in most cases. Spatial features come last: they almost never qualify as one of the top three most important features. This clearly demonstrates the spatiotemporal structure of mobile web browsing behavior. Approaches that predict web accesses solely based on past sequences of web accesses fail to capture the temporal structure of mobile web browsing, one of its most important underlying properties based on these results.

Feat. Class	Feat. Name	Feature Relative Rank				
		1	2	3	4–7	8–14
spat.	*t_i-Targeted*	0.0	0.8	1.4	48.6	49.3
	Untargeted	0.0	0.4	1.1	11.6	86.9
temp.	*TimeOfDay*	2.2	5.8	8.6	82.2	1.2
	AvgTime	0.0	0.0	0.0	0.7	99.3
	TimeStdev	0.0	0.0	0.0	0.4	99.6
	Weekend	0.0	0.0	1.2	42.6	56.2
spat.-temp.	*TimeSinceTargeted*	56.7	22.4	13.8	7.0	0.1
	t_i-TimeSinceTargeted	4.2	6.5	22.5	54.0	12.7
	TimeSinceUntargeted	24.2	46.2	15.1	14.5	0.0
	TimeSinceAccess	2.7	5.9	24.1	66.0	1.4
	AvgInterAccessTime	0.0	0.0	0.0	0.1	99.9
	InterAccessTimeStdev	0.0	0.0	0.0	0.7	99.3
pop.	*PopAmongTargeted*	10.0	11.9	12.2	60.1	5.8
	PopAmongAll	0.0	0.0	0.0	11.6	88.4

Table 2. Feature importance for high volume smartphone users. Each cell reports the % of users for which a certain feature was ranked 1st, 2nd, 3rd, between 4th and 7th or between 8th and 14th. Results are consistent across all volume classes and phone types.

Feature importance is only a relative comparison that indicates the usage frequency of each feature in the prediction model. To better study the impact of different features in prediction accuracy, we trained two different MART models for every user. One uses all the proposed features (Table 1) while the other uses only spatial and popularity features. Figure 9 shows the prediction accuracy for both web accesses and web non-accesses achieved by each model. Across all volume classes, the model that ignores all temporal and spatiotemporal features achieves drastically lower prediction accuracy. Its access prediction accuracy is lower than 5% for more than 60% of the users while the MART model leveraging all the features achieves more than 90% prediction accuracy for the same percentage of users. Similarly, the MART model that leverages all the features is able to always achieve higher non-accesses prediction accuracy. Note that the gap in prediction accuracies between the two models is significantly smaller for non-accesses predictions. This is expected because of the significantly higher number of web non-accesses events in each test file (*i.e.*, for every access epoch, even though no targeted URLs were accessed, a web non-access event is recorded for all targeted URLs).

4.1.4 Comparison to a Naïve Sequential Approach

Figures 1 and 3 suggest that most web accesses are clustered in space and time – most accesses follow shortly after a first access.

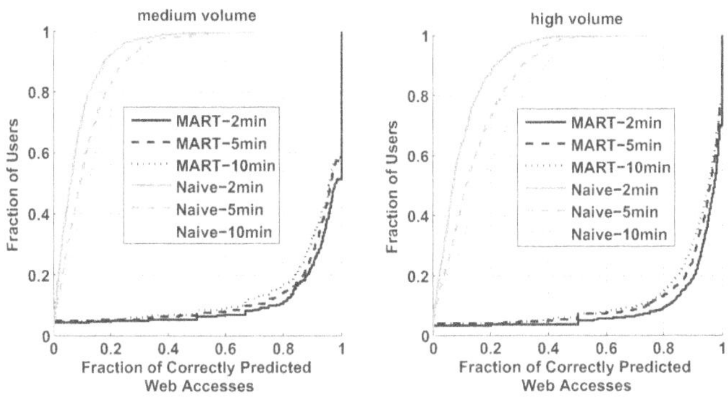

Figure 11. CDF of successful predictions of web accesses for MART and the naïve sequential-based prefetching scheme, for smartphone users. The results for featurephone users and the other volume classes are identical, and are not shown in the interest of space.

For this reason, a naïve approach that fetches all targeted URLs on a periodic basis would be very inefficient from a power consumption point of view. Instead, we consider a naïve approach that prefetches every targeted URL as soon as the user accesses one of the targeted URLs. This approach would avoid the need to build a web access model for every user. To evaluate its effectiveness, we apply it on all 8,000 web access logs in our data set. Similarly to our approach, we use the three different freshness thresholds to indicate the validity of the prefetched data. If a user accesses a targeted URL before the freshness threshold has expired, it does not trigger a new round of prefetches.

Figure 11 shows the web access prediction accuracy achieved by both the naïve sequential approach and MART across different volume classes and freshness thresholds. The MART approach significantly outperforms the naïve sequential approach. For about 80% of the users, the naïve sequential approach achieves a prediction accuracy of less than 20% (medium volume class) and 30% (high volume class). For the same percentage of users, the proposed access prediction model always achieves accuracy higher than 80%.

The difference in performance lies in the fact that a large fraction of users has only 1 or 2 targeted URLs that they constantly visit. For these users, the naïve approach always fails to prefetch the first access, thus missing approximately half of the targeted URL visits. On the other hand, the access prediction model leverages both spatial and temporal information to predict both *which* targeted URL will be accessed and *when*, thus providing for higher performance.

4.2 System Prototype Analysis

We have implemented our prefetching approach in a system prototype running on Windows Phone 7, and is currently being used daily by 10+ people in our research group. On the phone, we built a web browser application (shown in Figure 7) which monitors web accesses and constantly uploads the collected traces to a server running on Windows Azure. The server uses MART to compute the user's prediction model based on the user's logged data, and it periodically updates it as the user's web browsing history grows. The cloud server pushes the MART model to the phone, such that each time a user opens the phone web browser, the local model is invoked and targeted web content is prefetched. In the following, we use the phone prototype to provide an estimate on the power consumed by our approach and the access time gains achieved.

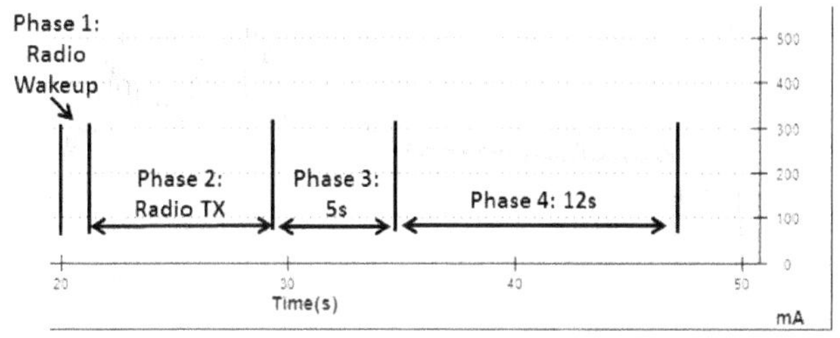

Figure 12. Current consumption (@4.2V) of a Samsung Focus running Windows Phone 7 while transmitting UDP packets. The actual transmission (phase 2) accounts for only a portion of the radio's power consumption (phases 1,3 and 4).

Batch size	Lightweight Avg time (ms) [Stdev]	Heavyweight Avg time (ms) [Stdev]
1	110 [22]	7734 [480]
2	120 [21]	23340 [3026]
3	306 [27]	44452 [1451]
4	382 [19]	51562 [2597]
5	468 [33]	76180 [1129]

Table 3. Time the 3G radio has to spend actively transmitting or receiving data for downloading lightweight and heavyweight web pages with a batch size varying from 1 to 5 pages. Measurements executed on a Samsung Focus running Windows Phone 7.

In order to achieve this, an accurate estimation of both the power consumption model and the radio's transmission/reception time for downloading different web pages is needed. We adopt the power state model of modern 3G radios that has already been studied and extensively measured in the literature [6, 13, 28]. As Figure 12 shows, there are 4 distinct states that the 3G radio can be in. First, the radio incurs an energy overhead every time it has to wake up from the sleep state (phase 1 in Figure 12). Then the actual transmission/reception of data, which is the most power consuming state, takes place (phase 2 in Figure 12). After completion of data exchange, the radio spends approximately 17 seconds in two states with different power profiles (phases 3 and 4 in Figure 12). When the radio starts exchanging data while in phases 3 and 4, no extra energy cost is introduced. Note, however, that with respect to energy, every data transmission incurs a very high energy overhead in terms of the startup cost and especially the 17 seconds tail effect of 3G radios (phase 1 and phases 3 and 4 in Figure 12 respectively). Currently, web accesses that take place more than 17 seconds far apart, will always incur this energy overhead. However, with web content prefetching multiple web pages are simultaneously downloaded at the beginning of each browser session incurring this energy overhead only once. As a result, successful predictions could even lead to reduced energy dissipation.

Besides the power consumed, to accurately estimate energy dissipation, we need to estimate the time it takes to download different web pages (phase 2 in Figure 12). We use lightweight pages such as facebook.com and cnn.com, whose size varies from 5 up to 40 kBytes, and heavyweight pages such as nytimes.com and timesofindia.com, whose size varies from 50 up to 240 kBytes to measure the time that the radio spends transmitting/receiving bytes. As Table 3 shows, fetching 5 lightweight pages of increasing size in a batch takes less than half second, which is much less than the startup time of a regular phone web browser. This means that 5 lightweight web sites can be prefetched by the time the browser is ready for use. Fetching heavyweight sites can take much longer, but also in this case the prefetching approach can help hiding such de-

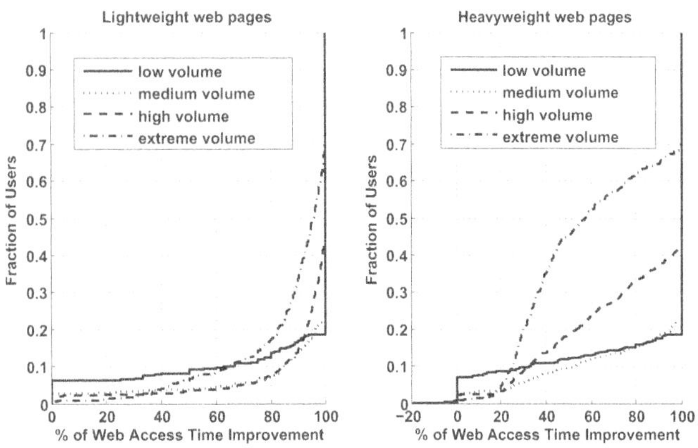

Figure 13. CDF of the web access time (time that the user needs to wait for the radio to download a web page) improvement across all smartphone users when web access prediction is used. Negative values indicate an increase in the user response time. The trends are identical for featurephone users, and are not shown in the interest of space.

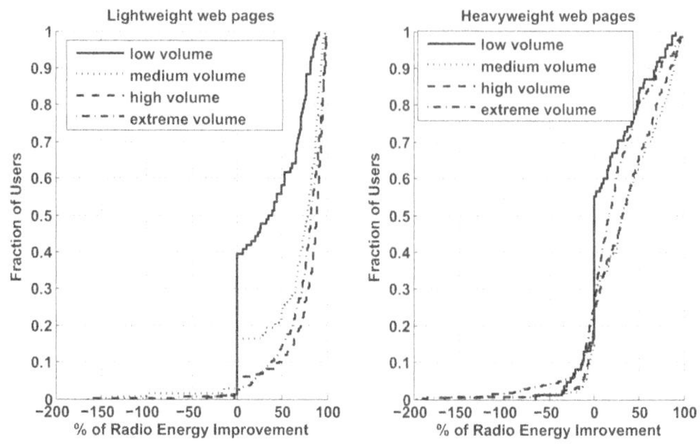

Figure 14. CDF of the radio energy dissipation improvement across all smartphone users when the web access prediction is used. Negative values indicate an increase in radio's energy dissipation. The trends are identical across volume classes and device types, and are not shown in the interest of space.

lay. Assuming a user's targeted sites are all heavyweight pages, if the first accessed page cannot be prefetched by the time the phone browser has loaded, the remaining targets will be still prefetched ahead with large savings in access time. Assuming a user might spend 1 or 2 minutes on the first page, this gives plenty of time for fetching 5 or more heavyweight pages before the user actually requests access to them. Moreover, targeted web sits are fetched in order of MART access probability to minimize the access delay.

In the following we leverage the measurements in Table 3 and Figure 12 to estimate web access times and radio energy dissipation when replaying back user web access logs.

4.2.1 Web Access Time

We define web access time as the time that elapses between a user requesting to visit a web page and the web page being available on the mobile device. Note that web access time here refers to the radio download time (phase 2 in Figure 12) that might be delaying the access to the web page. In all of our experiments, we assume a browser loading time of 3 seconds. We estimated this is roughly the time it takes for the browser to load and the user to make a web page request. As a result, every radio communication delay that takes place within these first 3 seconds is not considered in the computation of web access time.

By replaying back the web access logs of all 8,000 users, we compute the overall web access times in the case of a state of the art browser and in the case of the proposed prefetching scheme. Figure 13 shows the CDF of the web access time improvement achieved by the prefetching scheme for both lightweight and heavyweight pages. In both cases, the proposed prefetching scheme is able to completely eliminate web access time for 30%, 60%, and 80% of the users depending on the different volume class. For all these users, the proposed model was able to prefetch the web pages the user wished to access within the past two minutes, enabling an instant browsing experience. Furthermore, more than 90% of the users across all volume classes, experienced a reduction in their web access times by more than 60%. Only in the case of heavyweight pages, there is less than 2% of users that might experience an increase of up to 20% in their web access times. This is the small set of users where the number of false positives might increase substantially (Figure 10). When many heavyweight pages are simultaneously downloaded, the 3G radio gets congested and the overall web page download might be delayed (the time to simultaneously download 5 heavyweight pages is higher than sequentially downloading the individual pages as shown in Table 3). To prevent the number of unsuccessful predictions from negatively impacting the web access time, the prefetching mechanism can monitor, over time, its own access prediction accuracy and accordingly disable any prefetching attempts when the number of false positives exceeds a daily threshold. In that way, even these users will not experience any noticeable performance degradation.

4.2.2 Radio Energy Dissipation

To quantify the effect of the proposed prefetching scheme on the power consumption of the mobile device, we also compute the total radio energy dissipation due to web accesses for all 8,000 users. Figure 14 shows the CDF of the radio energy improvement achieved by the prefetching scheme when assuming both lightweight and heavyweight pages are accessed by the users. Surprisingly, for anywhere between 75% and 98% of users across volume classes and web page types, the radio energy dissipation remains the same or is reduced when the web content prefetching approach is used. In other words, the proposed approach can enable instant web browsing experience for the majority of the users while maintaining the same or even significantly reducing radio energy dissipation. This is achieved because of the high energy cost that phases 1, 3, and 4 in Figure 12 introduce. When prefetching multiple web pages simultaneously the number of times that the radio needs to wake up from its sleep state and incur these energy costs can be drastically reduced. This can be clearly seen in Figure 15 where the CDF of the radio wake ups is shown when the prediction scheme is used or not used. By bundling web page downloads together, the prefetching scheme needs to wake up the radio significantly fewer times compared to state-of-the-art browsers, resulting in substantial energy savings.

On the other hand, only 2% to 18% of users in the case of lightweight pages, and 15% to 25% of the users in the case of heavyweight pages across different volume classes experience an increased radio energy dissipation. As expected, the impact on radio energy dissipation seems to be higher in the case of heavyweight pages since the false positives incur a higher energy penalty when compared to lightweight pages. For less than 2% of the users the radio energy dissipation can be increased by more than 150% to 200%. To prevent the number of unsuccessful predictions from neg-

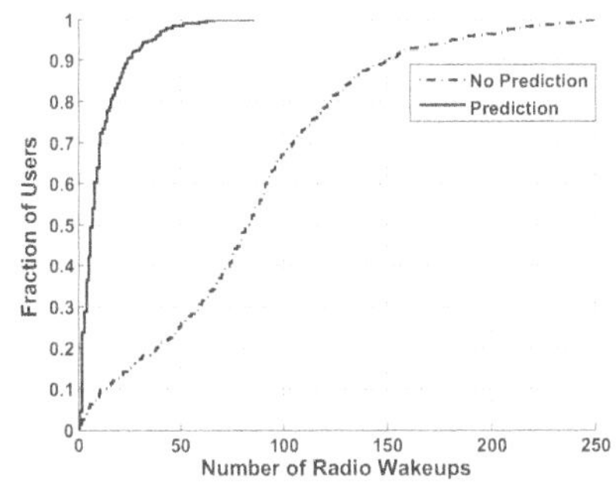

Figure 15. CDF of the number of radio wake ups for high volume smartphone users when the proposed prediction scheme is used or not used. The trends are identical across volume classes and device types, and are not shown in the interest of space.

atively impacting radio's energy dissipation, the prefetching mechanism can disable any prefetching attempts when the number of false positives exceeds a daily threshold.

5. Related Work

Our work is inspired by Pocket Cloudlets [19]. In that work, the authors make the observation that memory capacity can be traded for access time and battery life in online services. It demonstrates the concept with a search cloudlet, where the most popular search queries and results among a large population are transfered to mobile phones at night, when they are connected to the network and charging. In addition, the search cloudlet also caches and ranks higher those pages clicked by the user. However, web content has a much more dynamic behavior than search results, and can be highly personalized. We address these challenges by carefully training an energy-thrifty, personalized web access prediction model capable of doing timely prefetches.

An important contribution of our work is the data analysis we conducted. There have been various studies [3, 7, 11, 26] on characterizing the workload of web clients (session duration, content popularity, size of web responses) with the aim of improving server performance through query caching, server scheduling and TCP channel management. The results of these studies cannot be directly used in our context because *i)* many of these studies are relatively old, *ii)* a large portion of them has focused on improving system performance in wired networks, and *iii)* we analyze web access behavior from a client perspective, rather than a server point of view, to build user-specific models for content prefetching.

Studies in the HCI community on web page revisitation [8–10, 21, 29] are also relevant to our work. The main goal of this body of research is browser and navigation tool design for usability. These studies monitor access behavior on desktop computers, and even more recent work has mostly focused on desktop revisitation patterns [1, 2, 24]. Our data analysis is instead focused on mobile web browsing behavior, which shows distinct access patterns and user intents. We particularly focus on studying how targeted web sites vary across mobile users and how temporal aspects such as absolute time of web accesses and inter-access times can be used in the prediction. Not surprisingly, there are lessons learned from the desktop world analysis that can be used in our context. For instance, Adar et al. [1] observe that revisitation rates for desktops range between 50% and 80% [1], and we found a similar pattern for smartphones. They also study the temporal behavior of revisits to the same page over a large number of websites and correlate the revist time to the type of web content (*e.g.*, fast revisits are common in web pages such as shopping, spam, pornography, while slow revisits are common for pages related to weekend activity, software updates, etc.). A feature related to the category of targeted web sites could be added to our model. Overall, all these studies suggest their findings can be applied to caching and prefetching in browsers, but have not addressed nor implemented and evaluated the problem of effectively modeling the web browsing behavior on a per-user basis.

Web content prefetching has been studied extensively in the context of desktop browsing [17, 20, 23, 25]. However, these approaches are not directly applicable to the mobile world because they do not take into account the constraints of latency and energy consumption imposed by mobile devices. In the context of mobile devices, prefetching has been used to support disconnected operation [18, 33], or to reduce access latency and power consumption [4, 6, 33]. Specifically, to minimize energy consumption when prefetching web content, the content is prefetched more aggressively when the available bandwidth changes to higher rates [6] or content with high access probability, low update rate, a small data size, and a high retrieval delay is fetched with higher priority [33]. Other approaches to reducing power consumption use proxies to push new content to the mobile client only when the portion of the web page of interest to the user is updated, and make use of batch updates [4]. These techniques are orthogonal to our work, in the sense that they look at specific optimizations which could be integrated into our system to reduce power consumption. Our primary goal is not to minimize energy consumption, but proposing a web content prefetching model which respects the power constraints of mobile devices.

There exists a number of techniques for predicting a user's web accesses. Most previous work is based on two assumptions: first the users' behavior can be captured *only* by sequential or set patterns and, second, *all* users show similar behaviors. Hence, most work uses variations of the Markov model [27], *i.e.*, they attempt to determine the probability of a user accessing web content based on previously accessed content. Dependency graph algorithms consider only first-order dependencies [16], while more sophisticated approaches, such as prediction-by-partial match, use higher-order dependencies [23]. Yet, these algorithms are trained with the set of accessed content units only, and do not take the temporal structure of web accesses into account. In our work, we do not focus only on sequential or set patterns, but we also use additional features such as the relative and absolute timing of web accesses, which allow us to achieve much higher prefetching accuracy. Moreover, we show that each user's web access patterns are different, and we address this variability by building personalized models.

Since web content is highly dynamic, timeliness is an important aspect in prefetching it [4, 30, 31]. Most previous approaches that considered timeliness of content delivery rely on subscription-based prefetching. Subscription-based prefetching assumes that the user manually subscribes to content of interest, which is updated at a proxy or the client itself whenever it is modified, and the network and/or battery conditions are favorable [30, 31]. Our work does not rely on the user to provide any information about interests or to create subscriptions. Some approaches operate in a link-based fashion and prefetch content that is linked from the content currently being viewed by the user [12]. Although automatic, these approaches may result in high bandwidth consumption and untimely requests, especially when the currently viewed content has a lot of outgoing links, thus it is not suitable for mobile devices.

Another line of work relies on community-based profiles for content access prediction [5, 6, 17, 23, 25]. Communities is an interesting dimension to prefetching, but in mobile web browsing, the community data is not very helpful due to the high variability of web browsing behavior across users.

6. Conclusions

Trading surplus memory capacity for lower latency and battery life is desirable. Prior work was only capable of taking advantage of this surplus memory for relatively static content. This work provides the missing piece that enables mobile devices to handle dynamic content. We presented a study of web access patterns of 8,000 users over a 3-month period. We found that users do not browse the web randomly from their phones. Instead, we found a strong spatiotemporal signature in mobile web browsing. Based on these observations and the fact that each user behaves differently, we presented a framework for extracting a web access prediction model for each *individual* user. By predicting users' web accesses, we can provide a faster web browsing experience, with the same or lower radio energy dissipation. Our experimental evaluation on real datasets showed that for about 80-90% of the users we can accurately prefetch 60% of the URLs within 2 minutes before the request. Our results demonstrate the great potential of the proposed methodology in empowering users to enjoy an instant mobile web browsing experience.

References

[1] E. Adar, J. Teevan, and S. T. Dumais. Large scale analysis of web revisitation patterns. In *Proc. of CHI*, 2008.

[2] E. Adar, J. Teevan, and S. T. Dumais. Resonance on the web: web dynamics and revisitation patterns. In *Proc. of CHI*, pages 1381–1390, 2009.

[3] A. Adya, P. Bahl, and L. Qiu. Analyzing the browse patterns of mobile clients. In *Proc. of SIGCOMM Workshop on Internet Measurement*, 2001.

[4] T. Armstrong, O. Trescases, C. Amza, and E. de Lara. Efficient and transparent dynamic content updates for mobile clients. In *Proc. of MobiSys*, 2006.

[5] A. Balasubramanian, B. Levine, and A. Venkataramani. Enhancing interactive web applications in hybrid networks. In *Proc. of MobiCom*, 2008.

[6] N. Balasubramanian, A. Balasubramanian, and A. Venkataramani. Energy consumption in mobile phones: a measurement study and implications for network applications. In *Proc. of IMC*, pages 280–293, 2009.

[7] P. Barford, A. Bestavros, A. D. Bradley, and M. Crovella. Changes in web client access patterns: Characteristics and caching implications. *World Wide Web*, 2(1–2):15–28, 1999.

[8] L. D. Catledge and J. E. Pitkow. Characterizing browsing strategies in the world-wide web. In *Proc. of the 3rd World-Wide Web conference on Technology, tools and applications*, pages 1065–1073, 1995.

[9] A. Cockburn, S. Greenberg, S. Jones, B. Mckenzie, and M. Moyle. Improving web page revisitation: Analysis, design and evaluation. *IT and Society J.*, 1:159–183, 2003.

[10] A. Cockburn and B. McKensie. What do web users do? an empirical analysis of web use. *Int. J. Hum.-Comput. Stud.*, 54:903–922, June 2001.

[11] C. Cunha, A. Bestavros, and M. Crovella. Characteristics of www client-based traces. Technical Report TR-95-010, 1995.

[12] D. Duchamp. Prefetching hyperlinks. In *Proc. of USENIX Symp. on Internet Technologies and Systems*, 1999.

[13] H. Falaki, D. Lymberopoulos, R. Mahajan, S. Kandula, and D. Estrin. A first look at traffic on smartphones. In *Proc. of IMC*, pages 281–287, 2010.

[14] J. H. Friedman. Stochastic gradient boosting. *Comput. Stat. Data Anal.*, 38(4):367–378, 2002.

[15] ITRS Working Group. International technology roadmap for semiconductors 2009 report. Technical report, 2009.

[16] Z. Jiang and L. Kleinrock. Web prefetching in a mobile environment. *IEEE Personal Communications*, 5(5), 1998.

[17] F. Khalil, J. Li, and H. Wang. Integrating recommendation models for improved web page prediction accuracy. In *Australasian Conference on Computer Science*, 2008.

[18] A. Komninos and M. Dunlop. A calendar based internet content pre-caching agent for small computing devices. *J. of Personal and Ubiquitous Computing*, 12(7), 2008.

[19] E. Koukoumidis, D. Lymberopoulos, K. Strauss, J. Liu, and D. Burger. Pocket cloudlets. In *Proc. of ASPLOS*, 2011.

[20] E. P. Markatos and C. E. Chronaki. A top-10 approach to prefetching on the web. In *Proc. of INET*, 1998.

[21] B. McKenzie and A. Cockburn. An empirical analysis of web page revisitation. In *Proc. of HICSS*, volume 5, 2001.

[22] Mongoose Metrics. Mobile Devices Surpass Desktop Web Browsing in Five to Ten Years, 2010. http://www.mongoosemetrics.com/press_05012010.php.

[23] A. Nanopoulos, D. Katsaros, and Y. Manolopoulos. A data mining algorithm for generalized web prefetching. *IEEE Trans. on Knowledge and Data Engineering*, 2003.

[24] H. Obendorf, H. Weinreich, E. Herder, and M. Mayer. Web page revisitation revisited: Implications of a long-term click-stream study of browser usage. In *Proc. of CHI*, 2007.

[25] V. N. Padmanabhan and J. C. Mogul. Using predictive prefetching to improve world wide web latency. *SIGCOMM Comput. Commun. Rev.*, 26(3), 1996.

[26] V. N. Padmanabhan and L. Qiu. The content and access dynamics of a busy web site: findings and implications. *SIGCOMM Comput. Commun. Rev.*, 30:111–123, 2000.

[27] J. Pitkow and P. Pirolli. Mining longest repeating subsequences to predict world wide web surfing. In *Proc. of USENIX*, pages 139–150, 1999.

[28] F. Qian, Z. Wang, A. Gerber, Z. M. Mao, S. Sen, and O. Spatscheck. Characterizing radio resource allocation for 3g networks. In *Proc. of IMC*, pages 137–150, 2010.

[29] L. Tauscher and S. Greenberg. How people revisit web pages: empirical findings and implications for the design of history systems. *Int. J. Hum.-Comp. St.*, 47:97–137, 1997.

[30] A. Thawani, S. Gopalan, V. Sridhar, and K. Ramamritham. Context-aware timely information delivery in mobile environments. *The Computer Journal*, 50(4), 2007.

[31] E. Vartiainen, V. Roto, and A. Popescu. Auto-update: a concept for automatic downloading of web content to a mobile device. In *Proc. of Mobility*, 2007.

[32] Q. Wu, C. J. C. Burges, K. M. Svore, and J. Gao. Ranking, boosting, and model adaptation. Technical Report MMSR-TR-2008-109, Microsoft Research, 2008.

[33] L. Yin and G. Cao. Adaptive power-aware prefetch in wireless networks. *IEEE Trans. on Wireless Communications*, 3(5), 2004.

Reflex: Using Low-Power Processors in Smartphones without Knowing Them

Felix Xiaozhu Lin, Zhen Wang, Robert LiKamWa, and Lin Zhong
Rice University
{xzl, zhen.wang, roblkw, lzhong}@rice.edu

Abstract

To accomplish frequent, simple tasks with high efficiency, it is necessary to leverage low-power, microcontroller-like processors that are increasingly available on mobile systems. However, existing solutions require developers to directly program the low-power processors and carefully manage inter-processor communication. We present Reflex, a suite of compiler and runtime techniques that significantly lower the barrier for developers to leverage such low-power processors. The heart of Reflex is a software Distributed Shared Memory (DSM) that enables shared memory objects with release consistency among code running on loosely coupled processors. In order to achieve high energy efficiency without sacrificing performance much, the Reflex DSM leverages (*i*) extreme architectural asymmetry between low-power processors and powerful central processors, (*ii*) aggressive compile-time optimization, and (*iii*) a minimalist runtime that supports efficient message passing and event-driven execution. We report a complete realization of Reflex that runs on a TI OMAP4430-based development platform as well as on a custom tri-processor mobile platform. Using smartphone sensing applications reported in recent literature, we show that Reflex supports a programming style very close to contemporary smartphone programming. Compared to message passing, the Reflex DSM greatly reduces efforts in programming heterogeneous smartphones, eliminating up to 38% of the source lines of application code. Compared to running the same applications on existing smartphones, Reflex reduces the average system power consumption by up to 81%.

Categories and Subject Descriptors D.4.2 [**Operating Systems**]: Storage Management – Distributed Memories; D.4.7 [**Operating Systems**]: Organization and Design

General Terms Design, Experimentation

Keywords Heterogeneous systems, energy-efficiency, mobile systems, distributed shared memory

1. Introduction

An emerging, important category of smartphone applications intend to serve their users in the background by sensing the physical world continuously, e.g., health monitoring, context-aware services, and participatory sensing. They, however, can significantly reduce battery lifetime. The key reason is that existing smartphones only expose their powerful central processors to general-purpose processing, including simple, frequent sensor data processing. Many researchers have shown that it is necessary to add a low-power processor to process simple, frequent tasks [1, 29, 34]. Not surprisingly, emerging mobile Application Processors are including low-power general-purpose cores, e.g., TI OMAP4/5 [37, 38], NVIDIA Tegra 2 [26], and Samsung Exynos 4210 [32]. Moreover, sensors intended for mobile devices are also embracing low-power microcontrollers for in-sensor data processing [27, 36]. The resulting hardware architecture is *asymmetric* with multiple, memory-incoherent cores that differ in processing power by orders of magnitudes. In this work, we refer to a traditional powerful central processor, e.g., Cortex-A9 on OMAP4, as a *central processor* and an added low-power processor, e.g., Cortex-M3 on OMAP4 as a *peripheral processor*. Both central and peripheral processors can be multicore themselves.

ASPLOS'12, March 3–7, 2012, London, England, UK.

Although special APIs and toolkits are available for using peripheral processors, they require developers to not only explicitly treat the resulting system as heterogeneous and distributed, but also explicitly handle inter-processor communication. Not surprisingly, there are very few third-party smartphone applications that actually leverage peripheral processors to save energy.

Our goal is to relieve developers from directly dealing with the heterogeneous, distributed nature of the architecture so that they can easily port legacy applications and develop new ones to leverage peripheral processors for energy efficiency. While this goal is reminiscent of that of programming other heterogeneous, distributed systems, we face a set of unique challenges when dealing with smartphones: extreme architectural asymmetry, energy efficiency, and entrenched operating systems and programming models. Our solution to these challenges is a suite of compiler and runtime techniques, called *Reflex*. With Reflex, a developer only needs to encapsulate the code for a peripheral processor as a special class and limit access to system services in the code. Transformed by the Reflex compiler and assisted by the Reflex runtime, the encapsulated code will be able to run on a peripheral processor with native efficiency and communicate with the rest of the application as if it were also running on a central processor. Reflex is compatible with mainstream smartphone operating systems. Over the past two years, Reflex has been evolving and its evolving path is documented in a technical report [16].

The heart of Reflex is a novel software Distributed Shared Memory (DSM) design. The DSM allows code on multiple heterogeneous processors to easily exchange data, even without a hardware-coherent memory. While numerous software DSM designs have been in use, the Reflex DSM design is unique in its focus on energy efficiency and its support of extreme architectural asymmetry. The Reflex DSM contains multiple technical innovations. First, it maintains architectural energy efficiency by using a peripheral processor to serve coherence requests in order to keep more power-hungry ones in sleep. Second, it creates a shared memory abstraction across processors that differ in processing power by orders of magnitude, and minimizes the disruption in frequent data processing on the peripheral processors. Finally, it employs code instrumentation and aggressive compile-time optimization to greatly improve the DSM performance.

We report a complete implementation of Reflex and its evaluation using smartphone sensing applications that are classic or reported in recent literature. With minor code changes, Reflex works for a TI OMAP4430 development platform as well as a tri-processor mobile platform built with a commercial smartphone and two microcontrollers. We show that Reflex reduces the average power consumption of the applications by up to 81% compared to the same applications running on existing smartphones, where only the central processors are leveraged. The experimental evaluation also highlights the great development ease provided by a shared memory: compared to the message passing paradigm, the DSM reduces the source lines of application code by up to 38%, with less than 5% source code difference from the legacy counterpart. Moreover, the Reflex DSM incurs low overhead even in a 16-bit microcontroller, i.e., 25% of ROM, 2.5% of RAM, and 3% of processing time.

The rest of the paper is organized as follows. We provide the background and overview of Reflex in Sections 2 and 3, respectively. In Sections 4 to 6, we present the design of the Reflex runtime, DSM, and compiler support, respectively. We provide the prototype realization in Section 7 and report evaluation in Section 8. We address related work, discuss how Reflex can be extended, and conclude in Sections 9 to 11, respectively.

2. Background

We next provide the motivations to Reflex and outline the key assumptions made by the Reflex design.

2.1 Smartphone Sensing Applications

Smartphones and similar devices are embracing a variety of sensors. An important, emerging category of applications often continuously use these sensors without user engagement, such as participatory sensing, context-aware and mHealth applications. However, such applications are known to be power-hungry even with very efficient sensors. For example, the accelerometer inside the Nokia N900 consumes less than 1mW itself when active, yet the entire smartphone will consume 50–100mW of power when simply reading the accelerometer at 30Hz, reducing the battery lifetime to barely acceptable.

The key reason for this inefficiency is that current smartphones only expose their powerful central processors to third-party programming. It is well-known that a lightly utilized powerful processor is inefficient [10], because its advanced architectural features, e.g., deep pipeline, can barely benefit light workloads, but introduce high static power consumption and high overhead for power management. On the other hand, frequent tasks featured in sensing applications are typically very light workloads because developers often employ a cascaded design that conditions the execution of a complicated task on the output of a simple task in order to improve efficiency [19, 28].

2.2 Lower-Power Processors in Mobile Systems

Many have proposed to add low-power peripheral processors to mobile devices [1, 29, 34, 42] and to wireless sensor nodes [21, 24] in order to process simple, frequent tasks. Mobile Application Processors are actually embracing low-power cores [26, 30, 32, 37, 38]. Moreover, sensors intended for mobile devices are also embracing low-power microcontrollers for in-sensor data processing [27, 36]. All result in extremely asymmetric hardware architecture with the peripheral processors orders of magnitudes weaker and lower-power than the central processors. This extreme

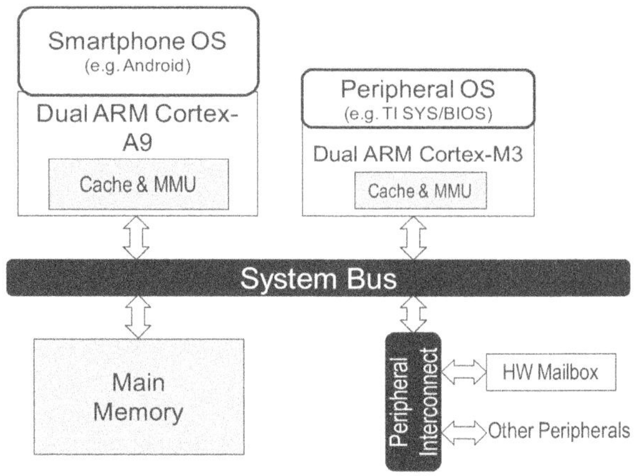

Figure 1. *A TI OMAP4 mobile Application Processor includes two microcontroller cores based on ARM Cortex-M3 in addition to the usual, dual-core ARM Cortex-A9. The M3 cores run their own real-time OS and do not have a coherent memory view with the A9 cores.*

architectural asymmetry is the key to the energy efficiency of accomplishing a wide range of workloads. It also has the following consequences that drive the design of Reflex.

Multiple Microarchitectures: A peripheral processor may have a different microarchitecture than a central processor. This makes solutions relying on a single ISA inadequate. For example, an ultra-low-power microcontroller core like TI MSP430 is necessary in achieving mWatt power consumption for continuous sensing on smartphones [29]. TI OMAP4 employs ARM Cortex-A9 as the central processor but ARM Cortex-M3 as the newly added microcontroller processor. Compared to the Cortex-A9 cores, the Cortex-M3 cores only support a small subset of instructions while lacking many advanced features such as SIMD extensions.

Multiple Kernels: The extreme architectural asymmetry also makes a monolithic kernel impossible to manage all processors. While the central processor usually runs a smartphone OS like Android, peripheral processors often run separate kernels optimized for them. For example, an OMAP4-based system runs SYS/BIOS [39] on its Cortex-M3 cores.

Lack of Hardware-Coherent Memory: Hardware coherence is difficult for smartphones with extremely asymmetric processors. Peripheral processors can barely realize a hardware coherence protocol under tight energy constraint. Furthermore, the microarchitectural difference between strong and weak cores makes hardware coherency even less attractive. For instance, TI OMAP4 Cortex-A9 and Cortex-M3 cores physically share non-coherent memory. To exchange data, the cores of different types need to copy data to and from the memory, and notify each other with the hardware mailbox shown in Figure 1.

2.3 Programming Challenge

The system resulting from extreme architectural symmetry is heterogeneous and distributed. To leverage peripheral processors, a developer not only needs to learn a new programming environment but also needs to carefully manage inter-processor data exchange. This is because simple, frequent tasks of sensor data processing in a sensing application often need to exchange data with the rest of the application. Examples of such data include sensing parameters (static or adaptive), intermediate or final results, and control/status variables. Such data can be read or written by multiple code parts. Furthermore, the sensor data processing

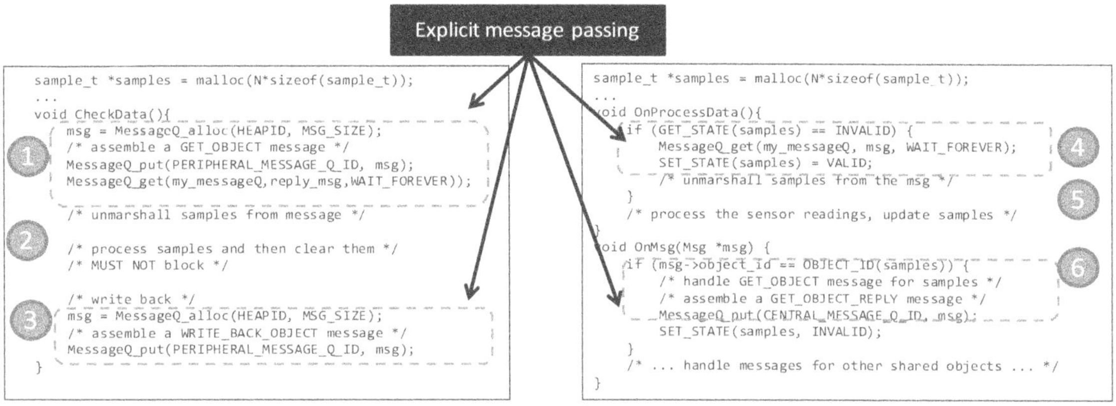

(a) The code for the ARM Cortex-A9 central processor (b) The code for the ARM Cortex-M3 peripheral processor

Figure 2. *Example code based on message passing. The code is written for TI OMAP4 based on the Syslink inter-processor message passing API. To make the list concise, we hide low-level code such as message queue management.*

```
lock m; sample_t *samples; /* global variables */
...
samples = malloc(N*sizeof(sample_t));
...
void CheckData(){
    acquire(m);
    /* process samples and then clear them */
    release(m);
}
```

(a) The code for the ARM Cotex-A9 central processor

```
void OnProcessData(){
    acquire(m);
    /* process the sensor readings, update samples */
    release(m);
}
```

(b) The code for the ARM Cortex-M3 peripheral processor

Figure 3. *Example code based on shared memory. A lock is used to prevent data race.*

task accesses the shared data more frequently than its complicated, infrequent counterpart, often by orders of magnitude, due to the cascaded design mentioned in Section 2.1.

Without hardware coherent memory, all existing programming solutions support data exchange with certain forms of message passing. With systems reported in [1, 34], the developer has to explicitly coordinate the data exchange between central and peripheral processors. To exchange data between a Cortex-A9 core and a Cortex-M3 core on the TI OMAP4, the developer must use an inter-processor message passing API called Syslink provided by TI. Not surprisingly, there are very few third-party smartphone applications that actually use peripheral processors to save energy.

2.3.1 Problems with Message Passing

Message passing is a programming paradigm where distributed code parts communicate by explicitly copying messages, being data or program objects. Programming smartphone sensing with message passing is a nontrivial task. We next use an example based on OMAP4 to illustrate the reasons. Figure 2 shows two code snippets excerpted from a simple sensing application, which uses messages to exchange data with the Syslink API. The two code snippets are executed on two different processors, and both use the `samples` array. The peripheral processor code, running on a Cortex-M3 core, fills `samples` as it acquires sensor readings, and the central processor code, running on a Cortex-A9 core, reads `samples` and clears historical values when necessary.

In the code, message passing exhibits its well-known drawbacks. First, developers need to synchronize distributed copies of the same object with a customized communication protocol, (1) (3) (4) (6) in Figure 2. Due to the discrepancy of ISAs, developers may need to convert `samples` among different data formats. For shared objects containing pointers, e.g., a linked list, the efforts will be more tedious.

The use of message passing is further complicated by the extreme architectural asymmetry. Message-based communication should not interfere with the sensor data processing on the weak, peripheral processors. For example, the computation in (2) should complete in time, because the peripheral processor is stalling its frequent processing task (5) and waiting. Similarly, message handling (6) on the peripheral processor should not be executed so often in order to avoid delaying the frequent data processing. Finally, for energy efficiency, the developer must arrange the communication so that no message should wake up the central processor from a sleep state.

2.3.2 Problems with Software DSM

The archrival to message passing in programming distributed systems without hardware-coherent memory is software DSM. With a software protocol that coordinates multiple distributed memory components to collaboratively serve memory access, software DSM creates the key illusion of a shared address space. Compared to messages, shared memory is a much more familiar abstraction to smartphone developers. The resulting application code is concise and similar to legacy smartphone code, as shown in Figure 3. However, DSM may introduce communication overhead due to thrashing or unnecessary data transfer.

Reflex resorts to DSM in order to conceal the underpinning messages, with the following key rationales. First, compiler and runtime can automate the architecture-dependent mechanics of message passing. Second, overhead of DSM diminishes as access contention decreases [14]. Fortunately, sensing applications tend to have light access contention, since only the data processing task is frequently accessing shared objects. Finally, with compiler techniques, the overhead can be reduced close to what can be achieved by hand-optimized message passing.

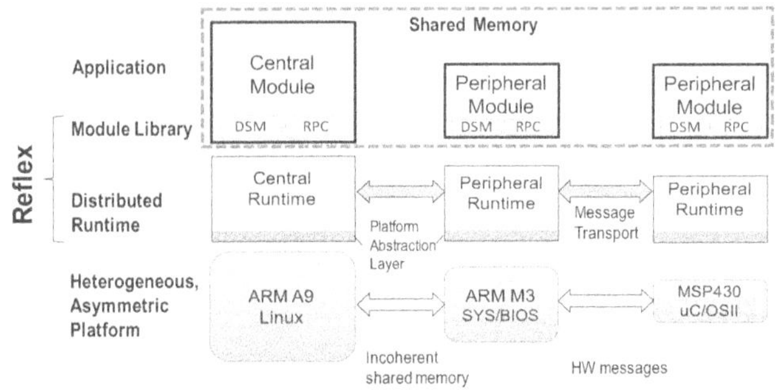

Figure 4. *The structure of Reflex. This example heterogeneous, asymmetric hardware platform is a TI OMAP4-based smartphone with an added MSP430 processor.*

3. Overview of Reflex

Our goal in developing Reflex is to relieve developers from directly dealing with the heterogeneous, distributed platform so that they can easily port legacy applications and develop new ones to leverage the peripheral processors for energy efficiency.

3.1 Programming Constraints

In order to make the system design practical, we require application developers to be aware of peripheral processors in the following two ways. First, developers need to properly encapsulate the code for a peripheral processor as a *peripheral module*. Accordingly, we call the code designated for a central processor a *central module*. To ease the development of peripheral modules, Reflex provides a virtual base class called *ModuleBase*. Developers write a peripheral module as a subclass of ModuleBase.

Second, Reflex restricts system services that a peripheral module can use, since a peripheral processor does not have all the resources available on a central processor, e.g., Internet connectivity. Besides, sensor data processing, according to our observation, only requires limited system services: dynamic memory, timer, and sensor data acquisition.

3.2 How Reflex Works

With an application properly developed as discussed above, the Reflex compiler, the distributed runtime, and the library collectively create an illusion that the application is running on a single processor. The key to this illusion is to support data exchange among modules running on different processors. Reflex recognizes two forms of data exchange: procedure call and shared memory. Reflex automatically translates a procedure call between distributed modules into a synchronous remote procedure call (RPC) and supports the shared memory with software DSM. While the RPC realization is standard and straightforward, the DSM poses significant technical challenges due to the extreme architectural asymmetry.

When the application is launched, Reflex treats the central module as a normal smartphone application and executes it on the central processor. Then, the runtime ships the peripheral module binaries to the proper peripheral processors for execution. When the central module terminates, the Reflex runtime will terminate all running peripheral modules of the application.

3.3 Hardware Requirements

We design Reflex to have minimalist hardware requirements for peripheral processors and their integration with the central processor: at least 8KB of ROM, several KB of RAM, the capability to handle interrupts, and the capability to acquire sensor data without involving the central processor. Reflex only requires a data link capable of interrupt-driven and bi-directional data exchange between peripheral and central processors. The data link can be a low-speed hardware bus, e.g., I^2C; it can also be realized with a physically shared memory and hardware support for inter-processor interrupts, as in TI OMAP4.

Reflex does not require a hardware Memory Management Unit (MMU), although many existing distributed systems leverage MMU to create a shared address space or to trap local memory operations. Despite some peripheral processors indeed have dedicated MMUs, e.g., Cortex-M3 on OMAP4, it is very difficult to implement MMU for even weaker peripheral processors that are necessary for energy efficient sensing applications.

4. Distributed Runtime Design

Figure 4 shows the structure of Reflex, including the distributed runtime and the library. This user-level implementation makes Reflex compatible with existing smartphone operating systems and platforms, although a more disruptive kernel-level implementation is possible.

As shown in Figure 4, the Reflex runtime has one component on each processor: the *central runtime* on the central processor as the coordinator and the *peripheral runtimes* running on the peripheral processors. Locally, a component runtime provides the corresponding module with a unified abstraction of resources. We next describe in detail two important services provided by the distributed runtime.

4.1 Module Execution Model

Unlike many other heterogeneous systems that execute offloaded code synchronously, Reflex executes modules in parallel. To accommodate the DSM and the RPC, the Reflex runtime is enhanced to execute modules with an *event-driven* model, which is implemented with native execution units (e.g., thread or process).

A Reflex event is a formatted data unit sent to a module from either other modules or the local component runtime. These data units can be inter-processor messages (i.e., the primitive used to implement the DSM and the RPC) or can be used in providing local system services. A module has a private event queue to which the local component runtime asynchronously delivers events.

A module must *poll* its event queue to retrieve an event. Polling is non-blocking and lightweight: when the event queue is empty, it only involves checking a flag variable. Such a polling-based model provides the module with the control over exactly when to handle asynchronous events. Polling occurs 1) when the module finishes executing an event handler, its control flow returning into the event loop and 2) according to the instrumentation by the Reflex compiler. In particular, when a module is waiting to receive some DSM or RPC message and stalls the execution of its application code, it also polls its event queue to process DSM and RPC messages that are received but not yet handled. Compared with preemptive event handling, the polling-based model prevents data processing on a weak processor from being overwhelmed by coherence requests sent by stronger processors.

With the event-driven execution model, the code of a module consists of three parts: the event loop as the skeleton of the module, which keeps retrieving and dispatching various events; the application-specific handling of events, as provided by the developer; and functions that support the DSM and the RPC as well as wrapping the system services.

4.2 Message Transport

Globally, all runtime components collectively implement a lightweight message transport as shown in Figure 4. The message transport serves as the only interface for communication among all runtime components as well as the lowest-level primitive of communication among all distributed application modules, a design also adopted by many other heterogeneous systems, e.g., Helios [25] and Barrelfish [3]. A message will be delivered as an event to the destination module.

The message transport is best-effort and does not guarantee reliable delivery. This is because higher-level protocols on top of the message transport, such as the DSM and the RPC, all use messages in request/response pairs between the two communicating modules. Thus, the response message implicitly indicates the delivery of the earlier request message. Furthermore, the higher-level protocols employ message sequence numbers to identify and therefore discard duplicate messages due to timeout and retransmission.

5. Software DSM Design

We now present the design of the Reflex software DSM. The key design objectives are to leverage the architectural asymmetry for energy efficiency while minimizing performance overhead.

5.1 General Design Choices

Overall, the Reflex DSM realizes release consistency and maintains memory coherence at object-level, as will be discussed below.

Memory Consistency Model: To developers, the memory consistency model defines the expected outcome of memory accesses. The Reflex DSM implements release consistency [35]. Release consistency introduces two synchronization operations (`acquire` and `release`) and guarantees that a *correctly* synchronized application will exhibit sequential memory consistency, just as if the application were running on a single processor. By *correctly*, we mean using synchronization operations (`acquire` and then `release`) to construct critical sections to prevent concurrent accesses to the same object, if at least one of these accesses is write.

We choose release consistency for two reasons. First, it is easy for smartphone developers to use. We notice that writing synchronized applications is already a common task in contemporary smartphone development, e.g., Android application development in Java greatly encourages synchronized applications [22]. Second, release consistency is lightweight to implement: it can greatly reduce communication overhead by allowing most communication to happen at synchronization points, a significant benefit to our targeted architecture where the inter-processor communication latency is relatively high.

Coherence Granularity: A DSM design must determine the basic memory unit for which coherence is maintained, i.e., the coherence granularity. A larger unit may better leverage spatial locality to amortize communication overhead, but also increases unnecessary data transfer due to false sharing.

Many DSM solutions support *block-level* granularity, using a fixed-size memory block (or a fixed-size page defined by the MMU) as the basic memory unit for coherence. In contrast, the Reflex DSM uses software objects as the basic memory unit for two reasons. First, Reflex does not assume an MMU. Second, a pre-defined block size leads to a fixed tradeoff between the communication overhead and the false sharing of the resulting DSM. In contrast, *object-level* granularity allows the Reflex DSM to employ compiler-supplied program information to better leverage locality.

The Reflex DSM supports sharing two types of objects: global objects and heap objects. In facing the extremely limited local memory on peripheral processors, a module only caches heap objects it accesses, rather than all heap objects in the application.

The Reflex DSM associates each shared object with an application-wide integer ID that is valid across all modules. The IDs are allocated in ascending order as objects are created, either statically by the compiler (for global objects) or dynamically by the DSM (for heap objects). Each module has its own range to allocate new IDs so it can do so independently. The DSM maintains a table of shared objects in every module; each entry in the table records the metadata of one shared object, including the object ID, type, its local address range, and information about other modules that also share this object.

We next present the *coherence protocol* based on the design choices made above. The protocol specifies how modules sharing an object should behave in accessing the object.

5.2 Protocol Invariant

At the core of our coherence protocol is the following invariant:

Any coherence communication between two processors must be initiated by the stronger one.

This invariant guarantees the energy efficiency of the Reflex DSM: in accessing shared objects, a weak processor will never wake up stronger processors with coherence communication. Such a unique invariant clearly distinguishes our coherence protocol from existing ones, as will be described in detail below.

5.3 Asymmetric Module Roles

Given a shared memory object in an application, we define its *sharing group* as all modules in the application that access it. Each module in a sharing group has a local copy of the shared object. All write/read operations by a module on a shared object are actually performed on the local copy of the object.

In a sharing group, all modules have asymmetric *roles* based on the relative processing power of the processors that these modules are executed with. To facilitate the discussion, we mention a module as strong or weak to refer to the relative processing power of its associated processor. The weakest module in the group is the *home* of the object, while the other modules are *requesters* of the object. Since a module may access multiple shared objects, it can participate in multiple sharing groups and play different roles in them.

While the home of a global object is assigned by the compiler statically, the home of a heap object is determined by the DSM on-the-fly and automatically. Initially, a heap object O allocated by a module M has M as its home; later, if a pointer to O is passed to another module N that is weaker than M, N notifies M that itself will be the new home of O and retrieves the metadata of O from M. After that, M redirects any subsequent requester of O to the new home N, a one-time effort for each requester.

The role asymmetry employed by the Reflex DSM is different from existing heterogeneous DSM solutions in an important way. With performance as the primary goal, most existing heterogeneous DSM solutions employ the most resource-rich (and power-hungry) processor to serve requesters [9, 41]. In contrast, the Reflex DSM greatly favors energy efficiency and, therefore, uses the weakest processor to host the home role. Only if the weakest processor handles memory requests will the protocol invariant (Section 5.2) hold. Therefore, other stronger processors are able to remain in sleep mode as much as possible.

(a) *read_miss* and then *revalidate* from a requester (b) *write_miss* and then *write_back* from a requester

Figure 5. *State transitions in the Reflex DSM coherence protocol. All transitions are triggered by requests from a requester.*

5.4 Finite-state Machine Specification

We now provide details regarding the behaviors of the home and requesters in terms of finite-state machines. A module has a state with regard to any sharing group it participates in; if participating in multiple sharing groups, it will have multiple independent states with regard to each of those groups. A module state can be one of the following two:

- The home can be either `Owned` or `Invalid`.
- A requester can be `Owned`, `Invalid`, or `Shared`.

The states have the same semantics as in most coherence protocols. In a sharing group, conceptually one and only one module is in the `Owned` state. A module in the `Owned` state can read and write to its local copy; a module in the `Invalid` state can neither read nor write to its local copy; a requester module in the `Shared` state can read but not write to its local copy. A module in the `Owned` or `Shared` state has the most updated value of the shared object in its local copy.

Modules in a sharing group change states only by requests sent by a requester. The home module never initiates a change itself. A requester module uses four requests: *write_miss*, *write_back*, *read_miss*, and *revalidate*.

Figure 5 (a) and (b) illustrate the interactions between a requester and the home. In the two cases, the requester needs to read and write to the object, respectively. Before reading the object (Figure 5 (a)), the requester in the `Invalid` state sends a *read_miss* request to the home. The home responds by sending back the most updated value of the shared object. The *read_miss* request will change the state of the requester to `Shared`. Later, when the requester sends a *revalidate* request to the home, the home responds to indicate that the object has not been modified since the last *read_miss* request. Therefore, the requester module remains in the `Shared` state. If the home responds that the object has been modified (not shown in the figure), the requester will transit to the `Invalid` state, and it will need to send a *read_miss* again prior to any further read of the object. Note that *revalidate* is only necessary during synchronization, as we will explain in detail in Section 5.6.

Before writing to the object (Figure 5 (b)), the requester in the `Shared` or `Invalid` state sends a *write_miss* request to the home in order to transit into the `Owned` state; it sends a *write_back* request (along with the latest value from the local copy) to the home in order to transit back into the `Shared` state. Accordingly, the home will transit to `Invalid` and `Owned` after responding to *write_miss* and *write_back* requests, respectively.

The protocol described above introduces two types of latency in applications, namely *home latency* and *requester latency*. Home latency is introduced when a home in the `Invalid` state stalls its execution and passively waits until it is in the `Owned` state. Requester latency is introduced when a requester stalls its execution to wait for responses to *read_miss* or *write_miss* from the home. We will experimentally evaluate the impact of the above latency to applications in Section 8.

5.5 Support for Synchronization

Release consistency defines two synchronization operations for applications: `acquire` and `release`. The Reflex DSM provides *lock* objects to support both operations, implementing a lock as a shared object using the coherence protocol. For example, to `acquire` or `release` a lock, a requester sends the home of the lock object a *write_miss* or *write_back* request of the lock, respectively. To ensure release consistency, Reflex currently requires a lock to have the same home as its protected objects have. We plan to remove the restriction in future work.

According to release consistency, if a module performs `release` and another module subsequently performs `acquire`, the first module must make its updates visible to the second one. In propagating updates during synchronization, homes are *lazy* and requesters are *eager*. When the home `releases` a lock, it performs no coherence communication; it will send an updated value to a requester only when the requester asks for it. In contrast, when a requester `releases` a lock, it writes back all its updated objects that have the same home as the lock has.

Such asymmetric module behaviors are critical to the design goals of the Reflex DSM. The home's laziness guarantees high energy efficiency, as it maintains the protocol invariant stated in Section 5.2. At the same time, the requester's eagerness keeps the home's stalling period small in order to minimize the resulting disruption to frequent processing.

5.6 Notable Design Aspects

We next highlight three notable design aspects that are essential to the objectives of the Reflex DSM. First, a home resolves its access of an unavailable object by passive waiting. This is to maintain the protocol invariant: running on the weakest processor, the home cannot initiate communication to other modules.

Second, to keep an object updated, a requester in the `Shared` state actively revalidates the object with the home. This is unlike most other DSMs where a read-only object is passively invalidated or updated by other hosts. The reason is that the home cannot send out messages to invalidate or update requester's copies. Instead, the home tracks whether a `Shared` requester's copy is still up-to-date, by observing whether the object has been written since the requester's last *read_miss* or *write_back* request. Accordingly, the home responds to *revalidate* requests, as described in Section 5.4.

One may think that the requester-initiated revalidation incurs excessive communication, but actually it does not. In a nutshell, on `acquire` of a lock, a requester will revalidate all its objects that have the same home as the lock has, rather than sending a revalidation request before each read access. This is because release consistency guarantees that a module sees updated values only after each `acquire` operation. In addition, the Reflex DSM piggybacks the communication of revalidation to that of `acquire`, adding no more than one byte per message.

Third, the Reflex DSM aggressively reduces home latency at the cost of increased requester latency. This is achieved by keeping the home in the `Owned` state as much as possible, with the following designs. 1) In propagating updates during synchronization, requesters are eager and the home is lazy, as described in Section 5.5. 2) The home handles coherence requests only when its frequent processing is idle or stalled, supported by the execution model of modules as discussed in Section 4.1. This is because of the extreme resource asymmetry: requesters, running on stronger processors, can produce requests at a much higher rate than the home, running on the weakest processor, can handle. Furthermore, we choose to mitigate requester latency by compiler optimization described in Section 6 below.

6. Compiler Support for DSM

Without assuming MMU support, the Reflex DSM cannot perform coherence operations within trap handlers, as many other DSM systems do. Instead, the Reflex compiler statically automates invocations to coherence operations in developer's code. In addition, the compiler aggregates nearby coherence operations to greatly reduce the DSM overhead.

6.1 Code Instrumentation

In order to realize the coherence protocol specified above, the Reflex compiler analyzes the application code and inserts two types of code: `pre-access` and `post-access`. By design, for each access of a shared object the Reflex compiler inserts necessary `pre-access` code immediately before the access. The `pre-access` code determines the target object of the access and checks the corresponding module state. It does nothing if the state is `Owned` (before read or write access) or `Shared` (before read access). Otherwise, it performs coherence operations that are specific to the nature of the access (read or write) and the role of the module (home or requester). In addition, after a write access in a requester module the Reflex compiler inserts `post-access` code that sends out a *write_back* request and sets the requester back to `Shared`.

6.2 Optimization for Communication

The inserted code introduces overhead in both checking module state and inter-module communication. The Reflex compiler reduces the former overhead by employing a batching technique similar to that of Shasta [33]: if a module state has been checked by an earlier `pre-access` and no related coherence communication has occurred since then, a later `pre-access` can be eliminated. In the following discussion, we will focus on optimizations for reducing the communication overhead.

Batch Prefetching: The Reflex DSM maintains coherence for each shared object. However, fetching each object with an individual message incurs high communication overhead. The Reflex DSM leverages spatial locality to amortize the communication overhead by speculatively fetching multiple objects in a batch.

Once `pre-access` code finds it is necessary to send a *read_miss* or *write_miss* to fetch an object from the home, the DSM also examines objects that have the same home and adjacent IDs. Since object IDs are allocated in ascending order, having adjacent IDs implies potential spatial locality in accessing such objects: they are either global objects defined close to each other in the source code or heap objects allocated consecutively during execution. The DSM adds multiple objects to a batch, fetches them, and receives responses with two single messages, respectively. We will experimentally show the impact of batch parameters in Section 8.

Deferred Write-back: Due to temporal locality, it is common that a shared object is repeatedly accessed in a short period of time, for example, in a loop. By only inserting one `post-access` after all these accesses, the Reflex compiler essentially merges multiple *write_back* requests of the same object, greatly reducing the number of messages.

A requester should defer *write_back* only moderately, in order to keep home latency low. Given that requesters are executed much faster than the home, the DSM leverages release consistency to defer all *write_back*s until the next `release`. The compiler does so by inserting `post-access` right before each `release` to send out all deferred *write_back*s.

To summarize, by design, before each access of shared objects the compiler will insert `pre-access`; however, after optimization only a small, necessary portion of such code is actually emitted. If `pre-access` in requesters finds out that the current module state disallows the memory access, it immediately sends a message of *read_miss* or *write_miss* (with batch-prefetching). In addition, the compiler inserts `post-access` before each call site of `release`. Such code in requesters immediately sends a message of all deferred *write_back*s.

7. Prototype Realization

We have implemented the complete Reflex design in a modular way for portability. In particular, the DSM and the RPC are fully implemented in the module library that is linked into the module code, as shown in Figure 4. The DSM internally uses the message transport supplied by the Reflex runtime. The Reflex compiler instruments the developer's code by inserting invocations of coherence operations defined in the module library. Our Reflex implementation, with minor platform-specific revisions, runs on two platforms, TI OMAP4 and a custom tri-processor platform.

7.1 Reflex Runtime and Library

We realize the Reflex runtime and library with the software structure shown in Figure 4. On the bottom of the runtime is a Platform Abstraction Layer, which wraps all platform-specific functions, such as kernel API and hardware message passing. On top of the Platform Abstraction Layer, we build all major runtime functions and the module library that implements the DSM and the RPC.

The execution model of a module is implemented with the module library, which is dynamically linked with the developer's code during module execution. The module library is implemented with around 1500 lines of commented C/C++ code, consisting of routines that are for the event loop, for the DSM and the RPC, and for wrapping the system services. The Reflex runtime is implemented in around 4000 lines of commented C/C++ code.

7.2 Reflex Compiler Toolkit

We build the Reflex compiler as a transformation pass on top of the LLVM compiler infrastructure [13]. LLVM compiles the source code into LLVM-IR and the Reflex compiler instruments the IR for DSM. Before the module is deployed as part of the application, the module IR is transformed into to a native binary depending on the target processor.

The object-level coherence of the Reflex DSM requires object types to be determined at compile time. To meet such a need, currently Reflex supports application development with a strong-typed subset of C++, by applying rules such as using typed malloc, disallowing pointer arithmetic, and disallowing type-casting, a strategy used in many embedded systems [7]. After compiling the application source code into LLVM IR, the Reflex compiler certifies that the IR is strong-typed; it then outputs descriptions of all types in Interface Description Language (IDL).

Reflex includes a small stub compiler that produces code for (un)marshaling objects across different ISAs. Implemented with around 700 lines of Python code, the stub compiler takes the compiler-generated type descriptions and produces (un)marshaling code used by the DSM and the RPC. The major task of the (un)marshaling code is to convert the formats of typed objects. Most data conversion is straightforward except for pointers. Since processors have separate address spaces, one pointer in a module needs to be converted to be used by another module. To do so, the (un)marshaling code uses a *portable pointer* as the intermediate format among local pointers in separate address spaces.

A portable pointer has 32 bits (the same as the longest local pointer in the system), encoded with the following information: object ID (13 bits), the byte offset within the object (10 bits), type id (6 bits, as used in the compiler-generated IDL), and the home id (3 bits). Before sending out a local pointer in a message, the marshaling code replaces the local pointer with a portable pointer in place. On receiving a portable pointer in a message, the unmarshaling code retrieves the corresponding local pointer based on the encoded object ID and offset. If the unmarshaling code finds the object ID is new to this module (e.g., a heap object newly created by another module), the code allocates an object on the local heap with the type specified in the portable pointer, and adds a corresponding entry in the local object table.

7.3 Hardware Platforms

The Reflex runtime and module library are highly portable, thanks to the layered structure. After changing the marshalling implementation, the message passing implementation, and hundreds of source lines in the Platform Abstraction Layer, we have ported Reflex to two platforms: TI OMAP4 and a custom, tri-processor hardware platform.

7.3.1 TI OMAP4

We have realized Reflex on TI OMAP4. We built the Platform Abstraction Layer to wrap the Syslink inter-processor message passing API, the Linux kernel, and the SYS/BIOS kernel. In particular, the message passing abstraction offered by Syslink enables us to implement the Reflex DSM on OMAP4, despite the fact that message passing is actually using a non-coherent shared memory. Due to page limit, in the rest of the paper we will focus on the implementation and evaluation using the tri-processor hardware platform, which is introduced for the first time by this paper.

7.3.2 Tri-processor hardware platform

We developed the tri-processor hardware platform by extending a Nokia N900 smartphone. As shown in Figure 6, the platform employs the N900's powerful OMAP3630 CPU (OMAP3) as the central processor and employs two ultra-low-power microcontrollers, LPC1343 (LPC) and MSP430F1611 (MSP), as the peripheral processors. Table 1 summarizes the characteristics of these three processors. The platform uses Maemo Linux shipped with the N900 as the central kernel and runs two separated µC/OS-II [12] on two peripheral processors. Built on top of the Platform Abstraction Layer, the peripheral runtime is a set of procedures

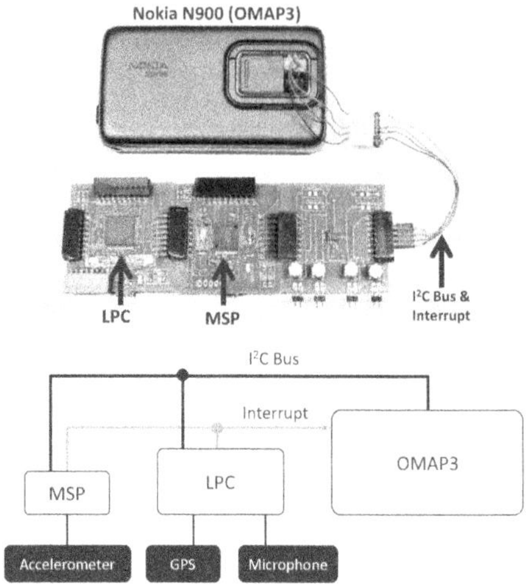

Figure 6. *The tri-processor platform (Top) and its architecture diagram (Bottom)*

Table 1. *The processors used in the tri-processor prototype. At run time, unused processors are turned off to reduce the system idle power.*

	OMAP3	LPC	MSP
Clock Rate	600MHz	72MHz	3MHz
Local Memory	256MB	8KB	10KB
Local Storage	32GB	32KB	55KB
Active Power	~200mW	42.9mW	7.5mW
Idle Power	13.4mW	7mW	3.2mW

linked with the vanilla µC/OS-II kernel. Peripheral modules are executed as µC/OS-II tasks.

I^2C-based interconnect: The three processors are integrated via an I^2C bus at 100KHz and physically share no memory. In order to physically access the I^2C interface and the interrupt line of the OMAP3, we remove the N900's camera module and hijack its connector with the OMAP3. In moving data on the I^2C bus, a byte chunk with a size of typical Reflex messages usually takes tens of milliseconds (6ms for a 48 byte chunk and 18ms for a 176 byte chunk). Built on top of the I^2C bus, the message transport of the Reflex runtime itself incurs little computing overhead, which takes 1500 cycles (MSP), 891 cycles (LPC), and 1800 cycles (OMAP3) in sending a message, and 1560 cycles (MSP), 1612 cycles (LPC), and 1800 cycles (OMAP3) in receiving a message, excluding actual byte sending/receiving. Compared to the tens of milliseconds of interconnect baseline latency, the computing overhead is negligible.

Sensors: The N900, like all commercial mobile devices, tightly integrates its built-in sensors with the central processor (the OMAP3). Therefore, it is very difficult for a peripheral processor to access the built-in sensors without waking up the central processor, violating the hardware requirements of Reflex as outlined in Section 3.3. As illustrated by Figure 6, we add a KXM52 tri-axis accelerometer to MSP through ADC; we add an analog microphone and an MN5010HS GPS receiver to LPC through ADC and UART, respectively.

8. Evaluation

We evaluate Reflex and its DSM with the tri-processor platform reported in Section 7 and four real-world smartphone sensing applications.

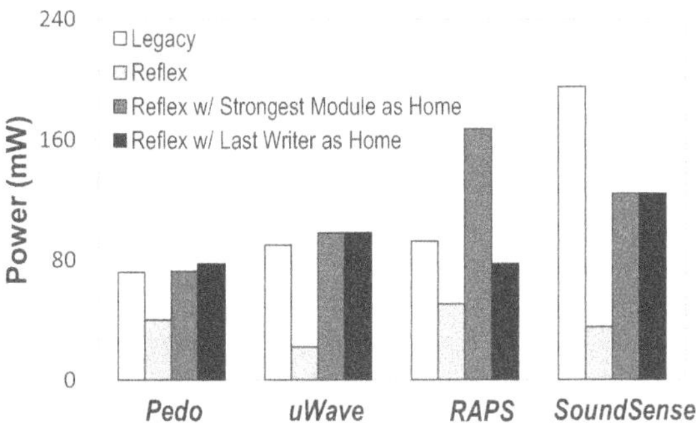

Figure 7. *The average system power consumption of benchmark applications*

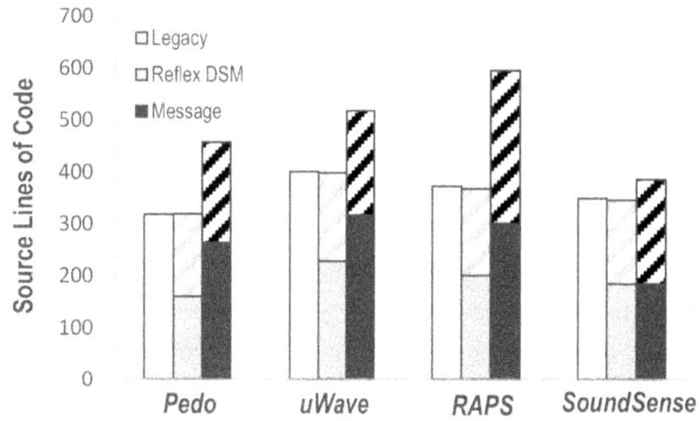

Figure 8. *The source lines of code of benchmark applications. Comment or blank lines are excluded. For a column that consists of two parts, the bottom part shows the source lines of the central module; the top part shows that of the peripheral module(s).*

8.1 Benchmark Applications

Since there is no standard sensing application benchmark, we employ the following four benchmarks, a combination of classic and recently reported smartphone sensing applications. Table 2 provides the typical usage of them used in the reported evaluation.

Pedometer (*Pedo*) uses the accelerometer to count the user steps. *Pedometer* (Reflex) consists of a peripheral module that counts steps and a central module that provides a user interface (UI) to query the step information. The two modules share a few flags and variables that store step count, stride, velocity, distance, and history. The peripheral module can be executed by MSP.

uWave recognizes user gesture with the accelerometer [18]. *uWave* (Reflex) consists of two modules: a peripheral module periodically performs acceleration pattern matching and calls the central module when a gesture is recognized; a central module provides a UI. The two modules share two acceleration templates and a window of recent accelerations, each of which is a 64-element integer array. They also share variables for gesture type, adaptive threshold, and similarity. The peripheral module can be executed by MSP.

Rate-Adaptive Position Sensing (*RAPS*) [28] calculates geo-location uncertainty by comparing current acceleration with context-specific historical averages of velocity and acceleration. When the uncertainty passes a threshold, *RAPS* takes a GPS reading and updates the historical measures. *RAPS* (Reflex) consists of two peripheral modules PA and PB, and the central module. PA monitors acceleration and calculates location uncertainty. When the uncertainty exceeds a threshold, PA calls PB. PB then gathers GPS data, updates the recorded geo-locations, and provides PA with the historical averages. The central module provides a UI to query the recorded geo-locations. PA and PB share information about uncertainty and the historical accelerations. PB and the central module share recent geo-locations with timestamps. PA and PB are executed by the MSP and LPC, respectively.

SoundSense [19] detects sound and analyzes it to determine the mobile user context. *SoundSense* (Reflex) uses a peripheral module to run the frame admission and feature extraction algorithm and a central module to execute simplified context classification. The admission parameters, the window features, and their variances are shared between the two modules. The peripheral module can be executed by the LPC.

We implement each benchmark in three ways: The N900's programming framework (*Legacy*), on the tri-processor platform with message passing (*Message*), and with the Reflex DSM (*Reflex DSM*). A simple UI is implemented for central modules using the Qt framework for N900. Legacy implementations use the N900's built-in sensors while the other two use sensors connected to the peripheral processors. Like most smartphone sensing applications, these benchmark applications spend most time in common scenarios of simple sensor data processing, which determine the overall energy characteristics of the applications.

Table 2. *Benchmark applications used in the evaluation*

Apps	Assumptions of Typical Usage
Pedo	Step detected every 400ms, UI query every 30 sec
uWave	UI activated every 15 min
RAPS	350 new geo-locations per day, GPS on 27% of time [28]
Sound -Sense	Frame sampled every 640ms, 20 events per hour [19]

8.2 Overall Performance of Reflex

We first examine how well Reflex as a whole achieves its goal in saving energy, by measuring the power of the entire system. To do so, we sample current and voltage using USB-2533 (from Measurement Computing) at a measurement rate of 100 HZ. For Legacy implementations, we measure the power of the N900 from its phone-battery hardware interface directly: we physically tap into the interface and simultaneously sample the current (using a 0.1ohm current sense resistor) and the voltage. For the Reflex-based implementations on the tri-processor platform, we additionally include the power of all added hardware. In both cases, we power off unused hardware such as the baseband.

Sensing applications in benchmarks perform periodic processing. We benchmark an application scenario by running it for a given period of time (typically 10 min) with Legacy and Reflex, respectively. During the benchmark period, Legacy and Reflex finish the same amount of sensor data processing. Therefore, the average power over the benchmark period reflects the system energy efficiency.

As expected from the addition of low-power cores, our measurement shows that Reflex reduces the system power consumption by up to 83% for the most common scenarios of each benchmark. Only in scenarios when the central processor is involved do the Reflex-based implementations incur slight power overhead (~3%) from the added peripheral processors. Because such scenarios are relatively rare in real life usage, the Reflex-based implementations will be significantly more efficient than the Legacy implementations. With the per scenario actual power measurement, we emulate the scenario transitions (based on the application usage in Table 2) to compute the application average power. As shown in Figure 7, compared to Legacy implementations, Reflex reduces the average system power consumption by to up to 81% (65% on average).

8.3 Source Code Examination

We investigate how Reflex facilitates application development by examining the source code of the benchmarks. First, how is Reflex different from the legacy development style? As shown in Figure 8, the Reflex-based and the Legacy implementations of the same benchmark have very similar numbers of source lines of code; more importantly, they share most of the source code with 95% identical source lines. Their source code only differs in the way of gluing the programming framework and invoking the system services described in Section 3. This observation validates that Reflex has achieved its goal of maintaining the contemporary programming style and facilitating porting legacy sensing applications to the heterogeneous, distributed architecture.

Second, how does the DSM ease the application development compared to message passing? To make the source code comparison fair, we hand-optimized the message-based code with best efforts, including implementing the commonly-used message manipulations as subroutines and managing objects with a table and iterating over the table to operate the objects. The DSM greatly eases the application development by enabling data exchange in benchmarks to be concisely coded as in the source code of Figure 3. Compared to the message-passing implementations, the DSM reduces the lines of code by 30% on average as shown in Figure 8. In particular, the synchronization operations required by DSM impose a small development burden: they take at most 10 lines per application.

8.4 DSM Performance

We next zoom into the behavior of the Reflex DSM and examine the effectiveness of its important design choices.

8.4.1 Asymmetric Module Role Assignment

The Reflex DSM exploits the weakest processor to host the home module of a shared object and, therefore, keeps more powerful processors in sleep, a strategy that is critical to the energy efficiency goal. We compare this strategy with the following two alternatives that are widely used in other DSM designs: 1) using the strongest processor for the home module and 2) using the module that last wrote to the object as the home module. Based on the per scenario actual power measurement, we show the emulated overall power consumption under both alternative strategies in Figure 7 ('Strongest Module as Home' and 'Last Writer as Home'). With the alternative strategies, the system power consumption is up to five times as much as that of the Reflex DSM, because the strongest processor is woken up to serve coherence requests and therefore unable to remain in sleep mode for a long time.

8.4.2 Storage and Memory Overhead

For a peripheral processor, Reflex introduces a small overhead in storage and memory, i.e., ~8KB ROM and ~0.2KB RAM, due to the runtime and the module library. Of all ROM and RAM equipped by one peripheral processor, the storage (ROM) overhead is less than 25% and the memory (RAM) overhead is less than 2.5%. The Reflex DSM further introduces little storage/memory overhead due to the compiler-inserted code and the object table. All `pre-access` or `post-access` code only increases the ROM usage of a peripheral module by at most 200 bytes. In each central module, the inserted code ranges from 200 to 700 bytes, less than 1.2% of the module storage usage. Each entry in the object table requires 6–8 bytes of extra RAM per module. The increased RAM is up to 119 bytes per module in our benchmarks.

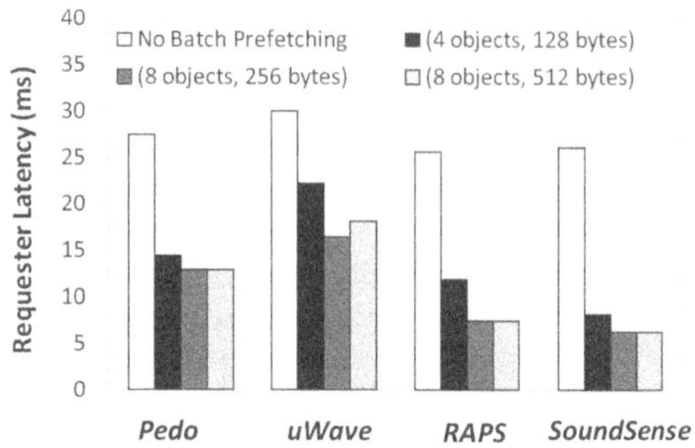

Figure 9. *The average requester latency in fetching an object, without and with batch prefetching*

8.4.3 DSM Execution Overhead

The DSM execution overhead comes from three major sources: module state checking as done by `pre-access`, requester latency, and home latency. In the common application scenarios where no inter-module data exchange occurs, the DSM execution overhead only comes from `pre-access`. With three ISAs in the tri-processor platform, each `pre-access` consists of one bit-shift operation, two to three load instructions and one compare instruction, resulting in only 5–10 extra processor cycles. Furthermore, the Reflex compiler aggressively eliminates `pre-access` for most accesses, using Mod/Ref analysis and object type information. We estimate that the state checking incurs negligible overhead (less than 3%) in the execution time of all benchmarks.

The DSM introduces home latency and requester latency. The measured home latency is 20ms on average, dominated by the message passing delay. Requester latency is effectively amortized over multiple objects by batch prefetching. To demonstrate its benefit, we compare the average requester latency per object without and with the batch prefetching. In the experiment, we vary batch parameters that specify the maximum size and the maximum count of objects that can be fetched with a single message. For example, batch parameters (4 objects, 128 bytes) specify that the DSM will flush a request message to the transport if objects requested by the message are more than 4 or their total size exceeds 128 bytes. As shown in Figure 9, the batch prefetching can reduce the average requester latency by up to 75% compared to the case without batch prefetching. In addition, we experimentally verify that without deferring *write_backs*, the DSM will slow down the execution of benchmark applications by up to 1000 times due to excessive messages, which is prohibitively expensive.

9. Related work

Reflex is the first work that seeks to enable developers to leverage low-power cores in mobile systems easily. The problem of programming heterogeneous, distributed systems is, however, not new. We next discuss the major approaches used to support heterogeneous system programming and in particular data exchange. It is important to keep in mind that Reflex faces a set of unique challenges when dealing with smartphones: *mature programming languages*, *energy efficiency* and *extreme architectural asymmetry*.

Programming with Message Passing: Most heterogeneous systems support inter-processor communication with message-like hardware primitives. Some directly expose message passing to application development. For example, Hydra [43] supports application code distributed on multiple devices communicating with channels. Lime [11] supports code distributed on CPU and FPGA exchanging data through a buffer, a message-passing abstraction. Dandelion [15] supports applications that are distributed across a smartphone and wireless body-area sensors using RPC for message passing. As we analyzed in Section 2.3, programming with message passing can be tedious and error-prone for smartphone sensing applications.

Programming with DSM: Generally, the idea of creating a shared memory illusion by software with messages, or software DSM, is well-known. There is a rich body of software DSM designs for conventional loosely-coupled distributed systems like workstation clusters. Aiming at minimizing the performance overhead of shared memory, these DSM designs have employed OS kernel support [8], compiler techniques [33] and runtime systems [6, 14]. Also, heterogeneity has been addressed [44]. Most of them rely on hardware MMU support. While they inspire the design of the Reflex DSM, none of them is designed for energy efficiency or extreme architectural asymmetry. More recently, Hera-JVM [23] realizes a software cache among heterogeneous cores of the Cell processor. Unlike the Reflex DSM, it implements the cache coherence in a symmetric fashion and with a coarse granularity, by simply flushing the entire cache of a peripheral processor (i.e., SPE) to the main memory during synchronization. This makes Hera-JVM energy-inefficient and improper for smartphone sensing. Partitioned Global Address Space (PGAS) allows multiple processors (many homogeneous ones [2] or a few heterogeneous ones [31]) that share no coherent memory to logically share a window of shared addresses. Unlike Reflex, such a shared window is implemented with symmetric coherence protocols. ADSM [9] provides a software DSM between CPU and GPU by fully implementing the DSM on the CPU, a strategy opposite to the Reflex DSM. Although the strategy is asymmetric, it targets performance instead of energy efficiency and therefore will not work for smartphone sensing applications.

Custom Programming Model: Many programming models have been proposed for heterogeneous systems. Most of them define custom programming interface to bridge the developer's code with the underlying architecture. Qilin [20] provides an API for parallelizable computation so that the computation can be dynamically mapped to heterogeneous resources. Merge [17] defines new language constructs to support the map-reduce pattern. Cell-Ss [4] requires annotations of source code to exploit task-level parallelism. These custom programming models are successful in their targeted applications, mostly scientific or analytic workloads. In contrast, Reflex aims at supporting the mature style of smartphone application development, by providing an object-oriented class and requiring developers to encapsulate the code intended to be executed on peripheral processors.

Hardware-Coherent Memory: While most symmetric multiprocessing (SMP) systems support hardware-coherent memory as exemplified by commercial multicore processors, only a few heterogeneous systems [40, 41] rely on it. As we analyzed in Section 2, hardware-coherent memory is difficult, if possible at all, for the low-power peripheral processors that Reflex is concerned with.

10. Discussion

Type-safe Languages: The Reflex DSM leverages type information to aggressively reduce runtime overhead with static optimization. In the current prototype, we ensure that the type information is statically available by subsetting C++. A more ambitious implementation should directly support modern type-safe languages that are widely used in smartphone development, e.g., Java and C#. We notice that several existing systems already enabled type-safe languages for resource-constrained processors, e.g., Darjeeling [5], the .NET micro framework, and Hera-JVM [23]. We are working towards supporting type-safe languages under extreme resource scarcity.

Reflex beyond smartphone sensing: While Reflex and its DSM design are motivated by smartphones, their technical innovations have a broader impact. Many consumer electronic devices are embracing sensors, from ebook readers to game consoles to tablets. Reflex and its DSM design will allow developers to write efficient applications for such systems with ease. The core ideas of the Reflex DSM can be further extended to high-performance systems with loosely integrated, heterogeneous resources where energy efficiency has become an increasing practical concern.

11. Conclusion

Sensing applications are considered among the emerging killer applications for smartphones. Reflex is the first endeavor toward making programming heterogeneous, asymmetric smartphones easier. Sensing applications on heterogeneous smartphones pose unique systems challenges that were previously not important. In addressing these challenges, we have not only revised known solutions but also devised novel ones in software DSM that exploit extreme architectural asymmetry for high energy efficiency. We note that Reflex still imposes a few constraints in programming due to the requirement of encapsulating a peripheral module and the limit on the peripheral system services. However, our experience suggests such relaxation is necessary: eliminating these constraints would be too expensive to be practical, especially with such an asymmetric architecture.

Acknowledgments

This work was supported in part by NSF CAREER Award #1054693. Robert LiKamWa was supported by a Texas Instruments Graduate Fellowship. The authors are grateful for the useful comments made by the anonymous reviewers and the paper shepherd, Dr. Jan-Willem Maessen.

References

[1] Y. Agarwal, S. Hodges, R. Chandra *et al.*, "Somniloquy: augmenting network interfaces to reduce PC energy usage," in *Proc. USENIX Symp. Networked Systems Design & Implementation (NSDI)*, Boston, Massachusetts, 2009, pp. 365-380.

[2] C. Barton, C. Casaval, G. Almasi *et al.*, "Shared memory programming for large scale machines," in *Proc. ACM SIGPLAN Conf. Programming Language Design and Implementation (PLDI)*, Ottawa, Ontario, Canada, 2006, pp. 108-117.

[3] A. Baumann, P. Barham, P. Dagand *et al.*, "The Multikernel: A new OS architecture for scalable multicore systems," in *Proc. ACM Symp. Operating Systems Principles (SOSP)*, Big Sky, Montana, USA, 2009, pp. 29-44.

[4] P. Bellens, J. M. Perez, R. M. Badia *et al.*, "CellSs: a Programming Model for the Cell BE Architecture," in *Proc. ACM/IEEE Conf. Supercomputing (SC)*, Tampa, Florida, 2006, pp. 86.

[5] N. Brouwers, K. Langendoen, and P. Corke, "Darjeeling, a feature-rich VM for the resource poor," in *Proc. ACM Int. Conf. Embedded Networked Sensor Systems (SenSys)*, Berkeley, California, 2009, pp. 169-182.

[6] J. Carter, J. Bennett, and W. Zwaenepoel, "Implementation and performance of Munin," in *Proc. ACM Symp. Operating Systems Principles (SOSP)*, Pacific Grove, California, United States, 1991, pp. 152-164.

[7] D. Dhurjati, S. Kowshik, V. Adve *et al.*, "Memory safety without runtime checks or garbage collection," *ACM SIGPLAN Notices*, vol. 38, no. 7, pp. 69-80, 2003.

[8] B. Fleisch, and G. Popek, "Mirage: A coherent distributed shared memory design," *ACM SIGOPS Operating Systems Review*, vol. 23, no. 5, pp. 211-223, 1989.
[9] I. Gelado, J. E. Stone, J. Cabezas *et al.*, "An asymmetric distributed shared memory model for heterogeneous parallel systems," in *Proc. ACM Int. Conf. Architectural Support for Programming Languages and Operating Systems (ASPLOS)*, Pittsburgh, Pennsylvania, USA, 2010, pp. 347-358.
[10] C. C. Han, M. Goraczko, J. Helander *et al.*, "CoMOS: An operating system for heterogeneous multi-processor sensor devices," *Technical Report MSR-TR-2006-117, Microsoft Research*, 2006.
[11] S. Huang, A. Hormati, D. Bacon *et al.*, "Liquid Metal: Object-Oriented Programming Across the Hardware/Software Boundary," *ECOOP 2008 - Object-Oriented Programming*, Lecture Notes in Computer Science, pp. 76-103: Springer Berlin / Heidelberg, 2008.
[12] J. J. Labrosse, *MicroC OS II: The Real Time Kernel*: Newnes, 2002.
[13] C. Lattner, and V. Adve, "LLVM: A compilation framework for lifelong program analysis & transformation," in *Int. Symp. Code Generation and Optimization (CGO)*, Palo Alto, California, 2004, pp. 75-86.
[14] K. Li, "Ivy: A shared virtual memory system for parallel computing," in *Proc. Int. Conf. Parallel Processing*, 1988, pp. 94-101.
[15] F. X. Lin, A. Rahmati, and L. Zhong, "Dandelion: a framework for transparently programming phone-centered wireless body sensor applications for health," in *ACM Wireless Health 2010*, San Diego, California, 2010, pp. 74-83.
[16] F. X. Lin, Z. Wang, R. LiKamWa *et al.*, "Transparent Programming of Heterogeneous Smartphones for Sensing," *Technical Report 0310-2011, Rice University*, 2011.
[17] M. D. Linderman, J. D. Collins, H. Wang *et al.*, "Merge: a programming model for heterogeneous multi-core systems," in *Proc. ACM Int. Conf. Architectural Support for Programming Languages and Operating Systems (ASPLOS)*, Seattle, WA, USA, 2008, pp. 287-296.
[18] J. Liu, L. Zhong, J. Wickramasuriya *et al.*, "uWave: accelerometer-based personalized gesture recognition and its applications," *Pervasive and Mobile Computing*, vol. 5, no. 6, pp. 657-675, 2009.
[19] H. Lu, W. Pan, N. D. Lane *et al.*, "SoundSense: scalable sound sensing for people-centric applications on mobile phones," in *Proc. ACM/USENIX Int. Conf. Mobile Systems, Applications, and Services (MobiSys)*, Kraków, Poland, 2009, pp. 165-178.
[20] C.-K. Luk, S. Hong, and H. Kim, "Qilin: exploiting parallelism on heterogeneous multiprocessors with adaptive mapping," in *Proc. IEEE/ACM Int. Symp. Microarchitecture (MICRO)*, New York, New York, 2009, pp. 45-55.
[21] D. Lymberopoulos, N. B. Priyantha, and F. Zhao, "mPlatform: a reconfigurable architecture and efficient data sharing mechanism for modular sensor nodes," in *Proc. ACM Int. Conf. Information Processing in Sensor Networks (IPSN)*, Cambridge, Massachusetts, USA, 2007, pp. 128-137.
[22] J. Manson, W. Pugh, and S. V. Adve, "The Java memory model," in *Proc. ACM SIGPLAN-SIGACT Symp. Principles of Programming Languages (POPL)*, Long Beach, California, USA, 2005, pp. 378-391.
[23] R. McIlroy, and J. Sventek, "Hera-JVM: a runtime system for heterogeneous multi-core architectures," in *Proc. ACM Int. Conf. Object Oriented Programming Systems Languages and Applications (OOPSLA)*, Reno/Tahoe, Nevada, USA, 2010, pp. 205-222.
[24] D. McIntire, K. Ho, B. Yip *et al.*, "The low power energy aware processing (LEAP) embedded networked sensor system," in *Proc. ACM Int. Conf. Information Processing in Sensor Networks (IPSN)*, Nashville, Tennessee, USA, 2006, pp. 499-457.
[25] E. B. Nightingale, O. Hodson, R. McIlroy *et al.*, "Helios: heterogeneous multiprocessing with satellite kernels," in *Proc. ACM Symp. Operating Systems Principles (SOSP)*, Big Sky, Montana, USA, 2009, pp. 221-234.
[26] NVIDIA, *NVIDIA Tegra 2*: http://www.nvidia.com/object/tegra-2.html.
[27] OKI Semiconductor, *ML8953A: MEMS 3-axis accelerometer*: http://www.okisemi.eu/Products/Sensors/mems_accelerometer.html.
[28] J. Paek, J. Kim, and R. Govindan, "Energy-efficient rate-adaptive GPS-based positioning for smartphones," in *Proc. ACM/USENIX Int. Conf. Mobile Systems, Applications, and Services (MobiSys)*, San Francisco, California, USA, 2010, pp. 299-314.
[29] B. Priyantha, D. Lymberopoulos, and J. Liu, "LittleRock: Enabing Energy Efficient Continuous Sensing on Moble Phones," *Technical Report MSR-TR-2010-14, Microsoft Research*, 2010.
[30] Qualcomm, *Snapdragon MSM8660 and APQ8060 Product Brief*: http://www.qualcomm.com/documents/snapdragon-msm8x60-apq8060-product-brief.
[31] B. Saha, X. Zhou, H. Chen *et al.*, "Programming model for a heterogeneous x86 platform," in *Proc. ACM SIGPLAN Conf. Programming Language Design and Implementation (PLDI)*, Dublin, Ireland, 2009, pp. 431-440.
[32] Samsung, *Exynos 4210 Application Processor*: http://www.samsung.com/global/business/semiconductor/productInfo.do?fmly_id=844&partnum=Exynos%204210.
[33] D. Scales, K. Gharachorloo, and C. Thekkath, "Shasta: A low overhead, software-only approach for supporting fine-grain shared memory," *ACM SIGOPS Operating Systems Review*, vol. 30, no. 5, pp. 174-185, 1996.
[34] J. Sorber, N. Banerjee, M. D. Corner *et al.*, "Turducken: hierarchical power management for mobile devices," in *Proc. ACM/USENIX Int. Conf. Mobile Systems, Applications, and Services (MobiSys)*, Seattle, Washington, 2005, pp. 261-274.
[35] D. J. Sorin, M. D. Hill, and D. A. Wood, *A Primer on Memory Consistency and Cache Coherence*: Morgan & Claypool, 2011.
[36] STMicroelectronics, *MEMS motion sensor 3-axis - ± 2g/± 8g smart digital output piccolo accelerometer*: http://www.st.com/stonline/products/literature/ds/12726/lis302dl.htm
[37] Texas Instruments, *OMAP5 Platform - OMAP5430*, http://www.ti.com/ww/en/omap/omap5/omap5-OMAP5430.html.
[38] Texas Instruments, "OMAP4 Applications Processor: Technical Reference Manual," 2010.
[39] Texas Instruments, "TI SYS/BIOS Real-time Operating System v6.x User's Guide (Rev. I)," 2010.
[40] G. Venkatesh, J. Sampson, N. Goulding *et al.*, "Conservation cores: reducing the energy of mature computations," in *Proc. ACM Int. Conf. Architectural Support for Programming Languages and Operating Systems (ASPLOS)*, Pittsburgh, Pennsylvania, USA, 2010, pp. 205-218.
[41] P. H. Wang, J. D. Collins, G. N. Chinya *et al.*, "EXOCHI: architecture and programming environment for a heterogeneous multi-core multithreaded system," in *Proc. ACM SIGPLAN Conf. Programming Language Design and Implementation (PLDI)*, San Diego, California, USA, 2007, pp. 156-166.
[42] R. Want, "Invited Talk: Always-on Considerations for Mobile Systems," in *DAC Wrkshp. Mobile and Cloud Computing*, 2010.
[43] Y. Weinsberg, D. Dolev, T. Anker *et al.*, "Tapping into the fountain of CPUs: on operating system support for programmable devices," in *Proc. ACM Int. Conf. Architectural Support for Programming Languages and Operating Systems (ASPLOS)*, Seattle, WA, USA, 2008, pp. 179-188.
[44] S. Zhou, M. Stumm, K. Li *et al.*, "Heterogeneous distributed shared memory," *IEEE Trans. Parallel and Distributed Systems*, vol. 3, no. 5, pp. 540-554, 2002.

Totally Green: Evaluating and Designing Servers for Lifecycle Environmental Impact

Jichuan Chang Justin Meza Parthasarathy Ranganathan
Amip Shah Rocky Shih Cullen Bash

Hewlett Packard Laboratories, Palo Alto, USA

{jichuan.chang,justin.meza,partha.ranganathan,amip.shah,rocky.shih,cullen.bash}@hp.com

Abstract

The environmental impact of servers and datacenters is an important future challenge. System architects have traditionally focused on operational energy as a proxy for designing green servers, but this ignores important environmental implications from server production (materials, manufacturing, etc.). In contrast, this paper argues for a lifecycle focus on the environmental impact of future server designs, to include both operation and production. We present a new methodology to quantify the total environmental impact of system design decisions. Our approach uses the thermodynamic metric of exergy consumption, adapted and validated for use by system architects. Using this methodology, we evaluate the lifecycle impact of several example system designs with environment-friendly optimizations. Our results show that environmental impact from production can be important (around 20% on current servers and growing) and system design choices can reduce this component (by 30–40%). Our results also highlight several, sometimes unexpected, cross-interactions between the environmental impact of production and operation that further motivate a total lifecycle emphasis for future green server designs.

Categories and Subject Descriptors

C.5.5 [**Computer System Implementation**] Servers

General Terms

Design, Measurement, Performance

Keywords

Environmental sustainability, lifecycle impact, server architecture, datacenter design, disaggregation, dematerialization, green computing, exergy

1. Introduction

Environmental sustainability—the minimization of environmental impact from destruction of natural resources or production of unwanted emissions—is an important social issue that has expanded to include computing systems as well. For example, the carbon footprint from information and communication technology (ICT) is estimated to be more than that of the aviation industry [1]. This impact is likely to grow as other industries adopt computing-based solutions to reduce their carbon footprint (e.g., the use of video conferencing to avoid travel). Recently, the Environmental Protection Agency announced an EnergyStar rating for servers and is legislating stricter requirements and incentives for sustainable solutions. Several companies (including Cisco, Dell, Google, HP, IBM, and Intel) have announced efforts to reduce the environmental footprint of their product offerings. Such trends around environmental stewardship, regulatory compliance, and business differentiation, make it important to design future servers and datacenters to be "green," that is, with reduced environmental impact.

Prior studies in the systems' community to address this challenge have primarily focused on the operational energy as a proxy for the environmental impact. For example, prior work has addressed the electricity consumption of individual servers and clusters as well as the electricity consumption of the power delivery and cooling infrastructure [2, 3, 4, 5, 6, 7, 8, 9, 10, 11, 12]. Such electricity consumption can be significant—a recent study [13] noted that the worldwide datacenter electricity consumption was higher than that of all but four countries in the world! Given that most of this electricity comes from carbon-intensive sources, mitigating this component can significantly address the environmental impact.

However, such focus purely on the operational energy misses additional key components of the environmental impact from other stages in the lifecycle such as the extraction of raw materials, manufacturing, transportation, and recycling. Such sustainability implications from the *production* of the server can be an important contributor to the overall environmental impact and can potentially impact design decisions for sustainability. For example, on small devices such as cell phones, 40–50% of the environmental impact has been attributed to the manufacturing process [14].

It will therefore be important for system architects interested in green designs to study the *lifecycle* environmental impact of their designs. However, a key challenge has been the *absence of good methodologies* to define the net environmental impact of a system design, particularly in a way that can be related back to system design decisions. Additionally, while we can intuitively reason that a server design to address the environmental impact from production would potentially impact other factors such as the operational energy and system performance, *these interactions are not well understood or quantified* for specific designs.

This paper addresses these challenges. Specifically, we make two main contributions. First, we present a methodology that system architects can use to reason about total lifecycle environmental impact of a server design. Our approach is based on the well-studied thermodynamic metric of *exergy* consumption, but

ASPLOS'12, March 3–7, 2012, London, England, UK.

adapted to create models usable from an architectural perspective. Applying our approach, we show that production can contribute significantly to the total environmental sustainability of a server (20% on current servers and higher on future systems).

Second, we use our lifecycle-focused approach to study example designs optimized for environmental sustainability. Our designs include several optimizations such as simpler low-power processors, disaggregation (modular fungible building blocks), dematerialization (reduced-material design), and free cooling (use of ambient outside air). Our results show that system architecture decisions can reduce the environmental impact of production too, by 30–40% for our designs. Also, the environmental impact from production and operation interact in several, sometimes unexpected, ways. For example, reducing the material used in system design reduces the environmental impact from production as intended, but can also improve the operational energy efficiency significantly. Similarly, an energy proportional design, compared to virtual machine consolidation, always achieves better operational energy efficiency, but is not always greener. Overall, our results motivate holistic optimizations across the lifecycle and additional new opportunities to reduce the environmental impact of future designs.

The rest of the paper is organized as follows. Section 2 discusses our methodology to systematically quantify the lifecycle environmental footprint of a server and uses this methodology to quantify the sustainability bottlenecks in existing designs. Section 3 uses our proposed approach to characterize the total environmental impact of sustainability-optimized designs and uses the results to highlight interactions and tradeoffs from a lifecycle-based environmental focus. Section 4 discusses other optimizations and applications for lifecycle analysis and implications for the broader research community. Section 5 discusses related work, and Section 6 concludes the paper.

2. Lifecycle Sustainability Models for System Designers

Below, we describe our proposed methodology for system architects to reason about the total environmental impact of their designs. Section 2.1 provides background on *exergy*, the thermodynamic metric on which our model is based. Sections 2.2 and 2.3 discuss how an exergy-based model can be adapted for system designers to measure the environmental impact from production and operation respectively. Section 2.3 applies the model to understand the lifecycle environmental impact of an existing server design and discusses the validity of our model.

2.1 Exergy to measure sustainability: background

What is exergy? The thermodynamic metric, *exergy*, measures the *available energy* in a system in the unit of joules. This is formally defined as the maximum amount of useful work that can be derived relative to a surrounding reference state. For example, consider a piece of coal or a piston containing highly-compressed gas. Both of these have high exergy due to the potential for useful work. In contrast, the combustion products (e.g., ashes) or the same piston with no compression both have near-zero exergy since little useful work can be derived.

The processes of combustion or piston expansion both *conserve energy* (1st law of thermodynamics) but *consume or destroy exergy* (2nd law of thermodynamics). Such destruction of exergy is typically representative of the irreversibility in a process. For example, the combustion products cannot be reversed to form coal by themselves; this irreversibility is what makes a process or system *unsustainable*: if it were somehow physically possible to reverse the state transitions of coal combustion and associated byproducts, the use of fossil fuels like coal may not be a problem. In this context, a sustainable process may be considered as one that transitions between two physical states *reversibly* (zero exergy destruction). Thus the process irreversibilities captured by exergy destruction can also be used to evaluate sustainability.

Why exergy consumption versus other metrics? Environmental impact has been evaluated along a variety of different metrics, including carbon (greenhouse gas) emissions, energy use, pollution, toxicity, impact to human health, etc. [15]. Often, these metrics do not respond uniformly to a particular design change: for example, replacing one component with another might reduce greenhouse gases, but increase toxic emissions. A large body of research in the environmental sciences is devoted to understanding these different impacts, and developing models that reduce a large number of different environmental impacts into a smaller number of variables [16, 17, 18, 19].

Exergy consumption has recently been shown to be one such metric on which such multi-variable optimizations can be based [15, 20], especially for ICT systems. In particular, empirical studies [15] have showed that optimizing for lifetime exergy consumption leads to similar results to those from more complex environmental models that included resource consumption, ecosystem quality, and human health. Other studies [20] have further clarified the boundary conditions under which exergy consumption can be used as a proxy for sustainability (e.g., the quantity of material and energy used by the system, the number of "energy flows" of material transitioning from one state to another, etc.) and showed that these conditions apply for most classes of IT systems, including those that are the focus of this paper.

An additional advantage with exergy consumption is the availability of a large amount of public data accessible to system designers. For example, several studies document generic mass-specific exergy consumption values of different materials as well as the exergy consumption in various common thermal, chemical, metallurgical, manufacturing, and transportation processes specific to building servers [21, 22, 23, 24, 25].

2.2 Adapting exergy consumption for system designers: environmental impact from production

Limitations of prior exergy-based approaches. Prior work has used *lifetime exergy consumption* to study sustainability but these methods do not provide useful insights for computer architects.

As an illustration, Figure 1(a) shows a breakdown of exergy consumption for an HP DL360 G6 server (two-socket Xeon, four DIMMs, two 72GB HDDs, two 1Gb NICs) following the approach discussed by Hannemann et al. [27]. We focus here on *embedded* exergy consumption, the exergy consumed to "make" the server, namely that spent in materials extraction and manufacturing. To obtain embedded exergy consumption, we systematically disassemble the server and recursively analyze each component further to obtain a mapping of material mass on a per-unit basis (e.g., amount of copper in a server). The resulting data is combined with published exergy consumption values for various materials and manufacturing processes that trace the material flow (from initial extraction through end-of-life) [27], to obtain the total breakdown of embedded exergy consumption (Figure 1(a)).

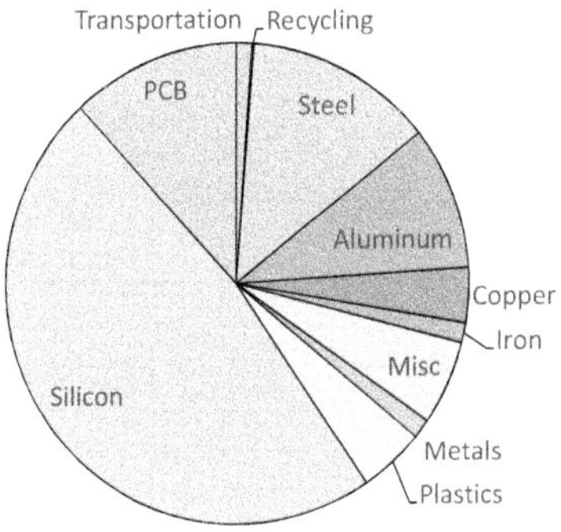

(a)

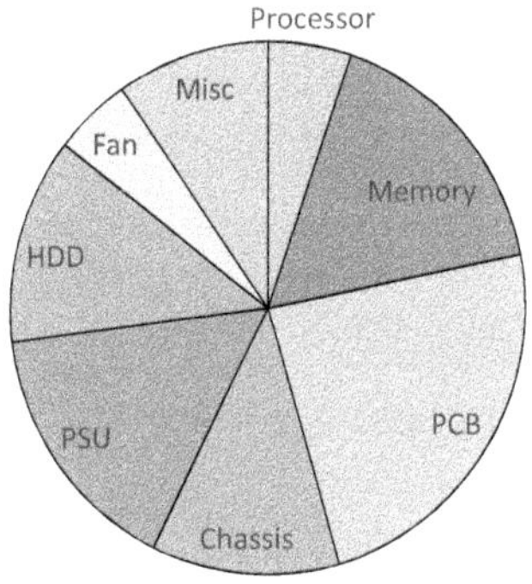

(b)

Figure 1. (a) illustrates the breakdown of embedded exergy consumption from existing sustainability models, which do not provide meaningful insights for systems architects. In contrast, our approach, (b), allows for environmental impact to be defined at the granularity of architectural building blocks. (Total embedded exergy consumption for both approaches is approximately 4.6GJ for a single server.)

Unfortunately, such an approach is not useful for computer architects. First, to study a different server, or a different architectural choice within a server, the entire process has to be repeated. It is impractical to have such disassembly-based exergy analyses for different architectural choices, particularly for future alternative designs that do not yet exist physically. Second, architectural choices span multiple stages of the lifecycle and multiple categories of environmental impact. Optimizations to one system component can result in non-intuitive changes to the total environmental impact by affecting multiple materials. For example, replacing HDDs with flash memory would reduce aluminum and increase silicon, but the designer would have to go to the point in the supply chain where these materials were extracted and retrace the flow of materials across the lifecycle. Similarly, each material category can include contributions from multiple system parts that are hard to separate out. For example, the copper extraction category is influenced by both the PCB traces and the power supply transformer; the silicon category is affected by the CPU, the chipset, and the memory. It is hard to reason about how different system architectures would affect different materials in a system and, in turn, affect the total embedded exergy consumption. Existing approaches to lifetime exergy consumption can thus be laborious and time-consuming for system designers.

Developing exergy consumption models from an architectural perspective. To address these challenges, we modify the above approach to consider lifecycle exergy consumption from an architectural perspective. Specifically, we aggregate exergy analysis at the component level, allowing us to evaluate environmental impact at the granularity of familiar architectural building blocks such as processors, DIMMs, and hard disk drives, as opposed to their associated raw materials and processes. For each component, in conjunction with environmental engineers, we develop a model that normalizes the *exergy-based impact* in terms of physical characteristics that can be related back to the system architecture across both the embedded and operational phases. As an example, DIMMs may be normalized per MB for a given technology, which in turn can be related to the die size; HDDs can be normalized per unit-storage capacity, which in turn can be related to the platter size; and so on. With this approach, understanding the impact of a design optimization at a systems level (e.g., on the die area) can now lead to a corresponding understanding of the impact on embedded exergy consumption.

To determine such architectural *exergy-based impact factors* (the multipliers used to convert from architectural parameter units into embedded exergy consumption), we examine additional published data from system component spec-sheets. As an example, we plot typical mass versus die size for a number of processors and use this plot to convert the typical per-gram estimates of processors into a per-area estimate. This approach is repeated for key parameters of other components (for example, disks are evaluated per unit area; fans are evaluated per unit radius; etc.).

Figure 2 summarizes the impact factors for our model. With our approach, a system architect now only needs to reason about a few (in this case, nine) high-level architecture-specific parameters – the size and number of processor dies, the size and number of memory dies, the size of the disk, the size of the fan and the dimensions of the printed circuit boards, power supplies, and the chassis[1]. The last column of Figure 2 summarizes the sources from which the impact factors were derived. Note that these numbers are based on public exergy consumption data specific to the supply chain assumptions for the (older) G6 server discussed in this paper. However, the methodology and data sources can be easily extended to derive impact factors for other architectural studies with alternate assumptions.

Component	Impact factor	Unit	Sources
Processor			[23, 21, 25]
Pre-fabrication	0.042	MJ/mm^2	
Fabrication	0.7	MJ/mm^2	
Post-fabrication	0.14	MJ/mm^2	
Memory			[21, 25]
Pre-fabrication	0.042	MJ/mm^2	
Fabrication	0.3	MJ/mm^2	
Post-fabrication	0.03	MJ/mm^2	
PCB	3500.0	MJ/m^2	[21, 27]
Chassis	64.0	MJ/kg	[24, 27]
Power Supply Unit (PSU)	341.5	MJ/kg	[21, 27]
Hard disk drive (HDD)	28.4	MJ/in^2	[21, 27]
Fan	0.87	MJ/mm	[24, 27]
Misc. (LEDs, ASICs, etc.)	4200.0	MJ/kg	[22]

Figure 2. An architecture-centric model for embedded exergy consumption. In contrast to materials/manufacturing and disassembly specific exergy consumption, it uses a few architecture-specific impact factors to compute embedded exergy consumption.

[1] The exergy impact factors for the chassis and power supply are still on a weight-basis in our model. However, the weights for these components are usually documented in spec-sheets. For optimizations around new materials-efficient packaging or chassis redesign—such as those that we study later in this paper—dimensional information can be used to compute the new volume, and correspondingly the new weight.

Figure 1(b) illustrates the breakdown of embedded exergy consumption from our model. The embedded exergy consumption computed through our model is consistent with that determined through disassembly-based analysis, but with added flexibility for studying system architecture tradeoffs. Comparing Figures 1(a) and 1(b) illustrate the latter point. Unlike the lack of architectural insights in Figure 1(a), Figure 1(b) now shows that approximately three quarters of the embedded exergy consumption can be traced back to the DRAM memory, PCB boards, chassis, and the power supply unit (PSU).

2.3 Adapting exergy consumption for system designers: environmental impact from operation

Server-operational exergy consumption. Exergy consumption can also be used to quantify the environmental impact from the operational phase of the system lifecycle (*server-operational* exergy consumption). When electricity is consumed by a server, it is converted to heat and loses most of the potential for useful work. Consequently, in most cases (unless the waste heat is harnessed), the exergy consumption during operation can be approximated by the total electricity consumption during operation.

To model such server-operational electricity consumption, prior studies have proposed and validated first-order models that estimate the power consumed across different workloads as a function of workload resource utilization (e.g., [28, 29]). We use a similar approach. For each component, we use its maximum power rating and model how its power varies with utilization. Given workload assumptions on resource usage and the time period of operation, this model can then be used to calculate the operational exergy consumption.

Infrastructure-operational exergy consumption. In most datacenters, the cooling and power delivery infrastructure (air conditioners, power delivery units, etc.) account for a large fraction of the total electricity consumption, and consequently, we account for *infrastructure-operational* exergy consumption as a separate category. (Note that on-board fans are considered part of the server-operational power.) This infrastructure exergy consumption can be modeled using the power usage effectiveness (PUE) multiplier [30],

$$PUE = \frac{\text{operational power} + \text{infrastructure power}}{\text{operational power}}.$$

For many design optimizations, particularly those that just involve changes to the system architecture, a simple pre-determined PUE multiplier can be used over the operational exergy consumption to compute the infrastructure exergy consumption. However, for design optimizations that involve changes to the packaging or cooling architectures, our model uses a thermo-volume based approach developed by Shah et al. [31] to determine the co-efficient of performance of the ensemble (COPG) and in turn, the PUE, to compute the infrastructure exergy consumption. This approach is summarized in Appendix A1. Other approaches such as Mercury [10] can also be used to characterize cooling properties for infrastructure-operational exergy consumption.

2.4 Applying the lifecycle exergy consumption model to an existing server

Benefits of proposed approach. The methodology discussed so far enables high-level *lifetime* analysis of the environmental impact, addressing all stages end-to-end, including raw material extraction, manufacturing, and operation. At the same time, the model is *usable by system designers*, with parameters that can be easily related back to architectural design decisions, and used to derive quick answers for high-level design space exploration. Our approach is also *easily extensible* to address new optimizations and future design choices.

Component	#	Peak power (W)	% idle/peak power
Processor	2	95	10%
Northbridge	1	10	50%
Southbridge	1	5	80%
Memory	4	6	50%
HDD (15K RPM)	2	3	0%
NIC (gigabit)	2	27	0%
Fan	4	4	0%
PSU	1	33	100%
DC conversion	-	15	100%
Misc. (LEDs, ASICs, etc.)	-	10	100%
Total	**-**	**354**	**-**

Figure 3. Number of components, peak power, and idle power factors for the system considered in this study. Power numbers are for a single component. Dashes indicate not applicable data.

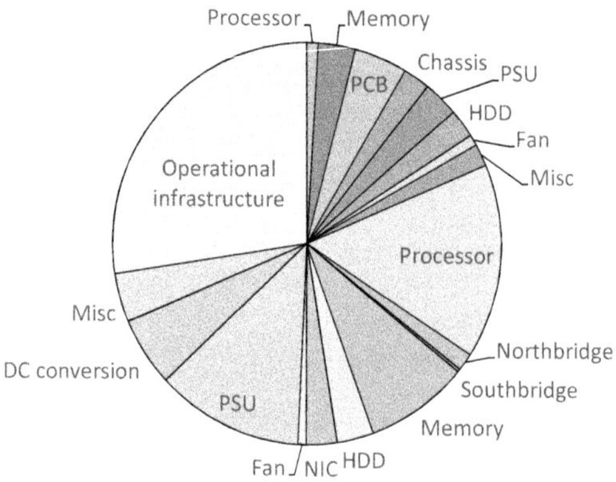

Figure 4. Breakdown of exergy consumption for a traditional server design. Clockwise from the top, the first set of Processor to Misc values are for embedded exergy consumption and the second set of Processor to Misc values are for operational-server exergy consumption.

Sustainability bottlenecks in current server designs. Next, Figure 4 shows the results from applying our methodology to study the total environmental impact of our server, including the operation and production phases. Our choice of parameters for the embedded exergy consumption is detailed in Figure 2, and Figure 3 summarizes the additional model parameters for operational exergy consumption; these are derived from the technical specifications of the server supplemented with additional power characterization experiments. We assume a three year lifecycle and 99.99% uptime, average workload utilization of 25%, and a default PUE of 1.5 (based on [28]).

The overall exergy consumption results show that for a single server, operational exergy consumption dominates the total exergy consumption (54%), followed by infrastructure exergy consumption (27%), and embedded exergy consumption (19%). Notably, the embedded exergy consumption contributes a sizable amount to total system exergy consumption. The components of embedded exergy consumption can be categorized into two broad categories—the silicon electronics in the system (CPU, chipset, memory, ASICs, NICs, etc.) and the physical infrastructure (PCB, chassis, power supplies, fans, etc.). Overall, a datacenter container with a thousand of these servers would consume about 25 terajoules of exergy over a three year period, equivalent to nearly 870 metric tons of coal consumption.

Validation. Section 2.1 discussed the applicability of exergy consumption to measure sustainability. We also performed validation experiments to compare our architecture-focused exergy consumption model with traditional (disassembly-based) exergy consumption models from the environmental community. Comparing the two approaches, we find that the disassembly approach would have suggested a lifetime exergy consumption footprint of around 26.8 GJ per server, while our component-based approach suggests an exergy consumption of approximately 25.4 GJ (a difference of around 5%). In terms of the composition across the lifecycle, both the disassembly-based approach and the architecture-based approach indicate similar breakdown across the server, infrastructure, and embedded phases (within a few percentage points in each category). Thus, we find the two approaches provide quite similar results. However, as discussed earlier, the disassembly-based approach would require on the order of days or even weeks to complete for a new server, while the component-based approach allows for repeated analysis on the order of hours.

3. Lifecycle Sustainability Optimization Insights: Design Studies

This section studies how design tradeoffs change with a lifecycle focus on sustainability. Specifically, how do the various components of the total environmental impact interact with each other? Section 3.1 discusses the sustainability-optimized designs that we consider and Section 3.2 discusses the benefits and insights from evaluating these designs with a lifecycle focus.

3.1 Systems considered

All the designs we consider in this section are container-based solutions. This models a recent trend in the industry where companies like Google, Microsoft, and HP have all built datacenters from shipping containers. A container-based design offers the opportunity to optimize an independent large-sized modular building block in a datacenter, where the only external connections are networking, power, and cooling.

We study three designs—a *baseline* design, similar to containers currently shipping in the market using rack-mounted servers, and two optimized designs, one focusing mainly on *operational energy improvements* using low-power processors in traditional blade servers, and a second *sustainability-optimized* design using more future-looking optimizations around disaggregation, dematerialization, and free-cooling.

Baseline. Figure 5(a) presents our baseline container design, broadly based on the HP POD container design [33]. We assume a standard container size of 12m × 2.33m × 2.35m. The container includes 1056 servers arranged in two aisles of 11 racks each. We assume traditional server designs, specifically using the DL360 server discussed previously in Section 2. The cooling to the container is provided by server-level fans and a container-level direct-expansion heat exchanger unit (DX).

Low-power blade server architectures. The *LP-blade* design is based on proposals in several recent studies [29, 32, 34, 35]. Specifically, these studies argue for low-power server architectures using simpler mobile processors better matched with I/O-bound cloud workloads, and present results showing significant improvements in electricity consumption. We wanted to study the *lifecycle* environmental impact of such operational-energy–optimized designs. Our low-power blade design is based on the HP bc2500 server [36]; the choice of this specific server to derive our parameters was motivated by our access to several of these boards for disassembly for validation. This server uses an Athlon 64X2 3000+ dual-core processor with 2GB DDR2 SODIMM, 80GB SATA drive, and Broadcom 10/100 integrated NIC. We assumed that the server count is scaled to keep the peak throughput performance similar to the baseline (i.e., we benchmarked the performance of both the systems individually and increased the number of *LP-blades* by a factor proportional to the difference in performance). Blades within the enclosure [36] share power and cooling, while outside the enclosure we assume the same container cooling infrastructure.

Dematerialized system architectures. Our final design, *demat,* examines more advanced optimizations targeted at minimizing the environmental impact. Specifically, based on the breakdown of the important sustainability bottlenecks in Section 2, we chose to study three optimization techniques—disaggregation, dematerialization, and free-cooling.

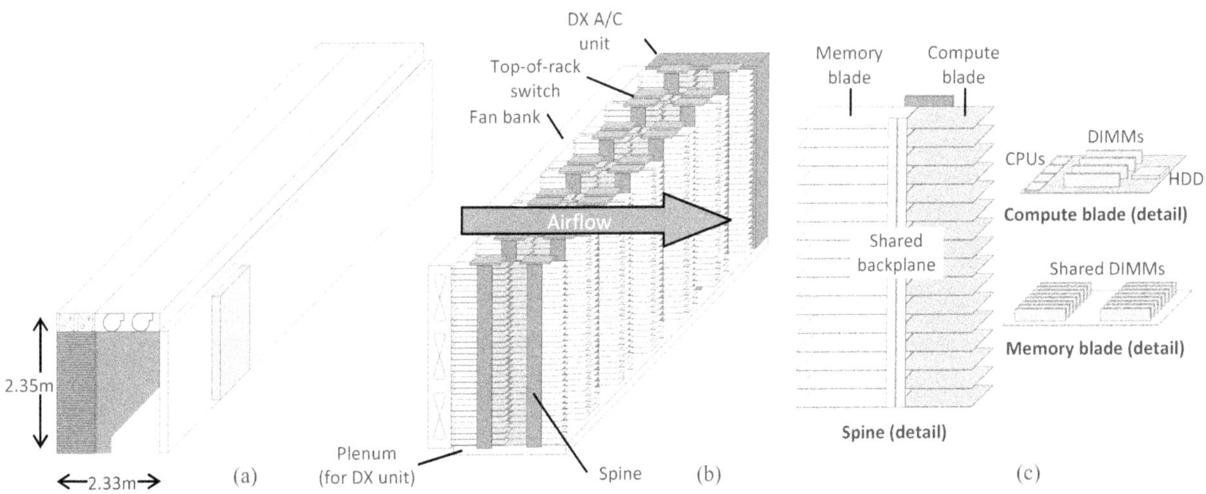

Figure 5: Systems considered. (a) shows the container assumptions for the container design using *baseline* rack-mounted servers; *LP-blade* uses a similar container design except with enclosures of low-power blades instead of rack-mounted servers. (b) and (c) present the design of *demat,* incorporating disaggregation, dematerialization, and free-cooling optimizations.

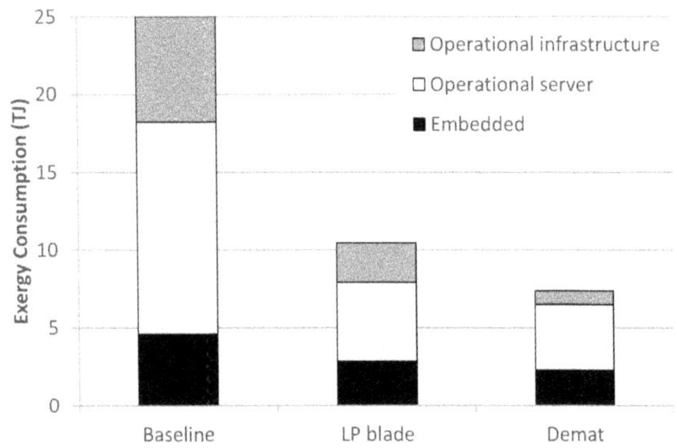

Figure 6. High-level breakdown of total exergy consumption for the three system designs.

A *disaggregated* system architecture separates system functionality into modular fungible blocks—such as a design that uses separate compute blades, storage blades, memory blades, and so on. This improves sustainability by enabling more component-efficient building block designs as well as component reuse across broader ensembles. A *dematerialized* design [1] reduces the amount of material used, particularly around the sheet metal in physical packaging, but also in the size of the printed circuit boards, for example. *Free-cooling* is a technique used in recent datacenters (e.g., those of Facebook, Google, Microsoft) to reuse ambient outside air to cool the datacenter without the infrastructure to chill the air [37].

Figures 5(b–c) present our design incorporating these techniques. The physical packaging and layout of the design consist of multiple "spine" backplanes, with blades attached to the spine. The spines provide communication and power delivery across different elements, and are perforated for air flow. This design reduces sheet-metal, without significantly impacting structural and EMI constraints. We assume two blade types—material-efficient compute blades with low-power processors similar to *LP-blade*, and memory blades that build multi-level memory hierarchies similar to previous proposals [38]. The cooling for the entire container is provided by a single array of shared fans along one side of the container. Blades with similar thermal densities are clustered for improved cooling. The results in this paper assume a location such as San Francisco where typical annual temperatures range between 0 and 30°C.

3.2 Lifecycle sustainability evaluation

3.2.1 Quantification of lifecycle benefits

Our methodology for lifecycle analysis can be used to quantify the total environmental impact of the three designs—*baseline*, *LP-blade*, and *demat*—including both operation and production. Figure 6 summarizes the results. The *baseline* design consumes 25TJ of exergy over its lifecycle. In contrast, *LP-blade* consumes only 10.5TJ, a 58% reduction in the environmental impact (or 2.4× more environmentally sustainable) relative to *baseline*. *Demat* does better, consuming only 7.4TJ, a 71% reduction (and 3.4× better) relative to *baseline*. This translates (using the approach used in [15]) to saving approximately 500–600 metric tons of coal over the system's lifetime.

The overall environmental benefits in the *LP-blade* and *demat* designs come from improvements to the environmental impact from *both operation and production*. Relative to the corresponding numbers for *baseline*, *LP-blade* achieves a 63% reduction in server-operation and infrastructure-operation exergy consumption and a 38% reduction in the embedded exergy consumption for materials and manufacturing. Similarly, relative to the *baseline*, *demat* achieves a 69% reduction in server-operation, 87% in infrastructure-operation, and 51% in embedded exergy consumption.

3.2.2 Cross-category exergy consumption interactions

A further breakdown of the lifecycle environmental impact of the three designs identifies interesting (and in some cases, unexpected) interactions between the different components in the total lifecycle breakdown. Below, we discuss some main results where optimizations to reduce the operation exergy consumption also reduced the embedded exergy consumption and vice versa.

Optimizing operational exergy consumption also benefits embedded exergy consumption. Consider the total exergy consumption benefits of *LP-blade* relative to *baseline*. As expected, the server-operation exergy consumption reduces significantly (63%) due to the use of low-power processors. This is consistent with the 2.3× improvement in performance-per-watt of *LP-blade* over the *baseline*. (There are also some additional, relatively small, improvements in operational exergy consumption due to improved efficiency of shared fans in *LP-blade* relative to *baseline*.) The reductions in the infrastructure-operation exergy consumption are proportional to those in the server-operation exergy consumption (the change from going from rack-mounted servers to blades is relatively minor).

However, in spite of not explicitly targeting the production impact on sustainability, the *LP-blade* design *also reduces embedded exergy consumption by 38%*. To better understand where these benefits come from, Figure 7(a) shows a more detailed breakdown of the embedded exergy consumption across the three designs. Focusing on the *baseline* versus *LP-blade* data first, we can see that the embedded exergy consumption improvements[2] for LP-blade come from two main factors: (1) the shared infrastructure associated with blade servers compared to rack-mounted servers (e.g., PSU, fan), but also (2) the reduced material associated with lower-power servers, both in reduced silicon overhead for the processor and in reduced material overhead for the printed circuit boards. Processor embedded exergy consumption reduces because the lower power processor choice in *LP-blade* leads to smaller total silicon area (in spite of *LP-blade* needing more of these simpler cores to achieve the same performance as *baseline*). The PCB size reduces due to the smaller form-factor *LP-blades*. These results indicate that prior studies that highlighted the environmental advantages of low-power servers [29, 32, 34, 35] primarily from an operational electricity reduction view point are conservative; a lifecycle methodology can identify additional environmental savings from these designs.

Optimizing embedded exergy consumption also benefits operational exergy consumption. Consider the *demat* design. As expected, the benefits in server-operation exergy consumption are not appreciably different from those with *LP-blade*; the additional improvements can be traced back to the energy benefits from memory disaggregation. The embedded exergy consumption reductions are higher compared to *LP-blade* (51% versus 38% relative to baseline). The breakdown in Figure 7(a) shows that these improvements match our intuition about the benefits from shared infrastructure and reduced sheet metal with

[2] Note that there are also (relatively small) degradations in embedded exergy associated with memory and hard disks due to the different parts used in the two real systems we use as reference for this study.

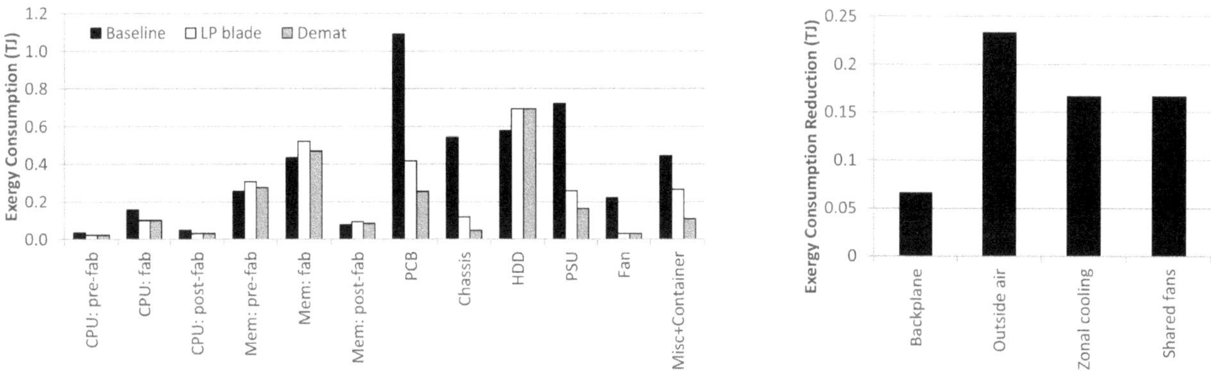

(a) (b)

Figure 7. (a) shows a comparison of embedded exergy consumption across the three evaluated server designs and (b) breaks down the reduction in operational infrastructure exergy consumption due to the cooling techniques employed in the *demat* server design.

dematerialization, and resource savings with memory disaggregation.

However, focusing on infrastructure-operation exergy consumption shows some interesting results. Figure 7(b) shows a breakdown of the attribution of various reasons for the benefits in infrastructure exergy consumption. Interestingly, only 36% of the total infrastructure improvements come from free-cooling's elimination of the thermal work associated with DX heat exchangers. The other benefits in infrastructure-operation exergy consumption actually arise as a consequence of optimizations that originally targeted embedded exergy consumption. For example, removing the backplane yields an 11% reduction in infrastructure exergy consumption (from better air flow); the use of shared fans yields an additional 28% improvement in infrastructure efficiency; and, the ability to cluster blades with similar thermal densities with disaggregation contributes to the remaining 25% improvement in cooling efficiency (by placing a low-density memory zone upstream of a high-density compute zone, air pre-heating is reduced).

A lifecycle-focused approach to understanding total environmental impact can identify and optimize for such interactions across different exergy consumption components.

3.2.3 Other results

To validate the physical aspects of the *demat* design and the cooling methodology, we also prototyped a "miniature dematerialized container" using custom PCB boards with heat sources to model different heat loads. Figure 8(a) shows a photograph of this miniature prototype. As an example validation experiment for the cooling models employed in our results, we used the prototype, in the configuration shown in Figure 8(a), to measure the temperature across the four blades in a cross section of the container. Our prototype doesn't include heat sinks and so is not an exact model of the system in Figure 5(b); nevertheless, the results in Figure 8(b) validate the good fit between our model and actual measurements.

We also studied the impact of our design on performance in the context of web workloads. The two main optimizations in our designs that can potentially impact performance are (1) low-power blades, and (2) memory disaggregation. Both these optimizations have been evaluated in prior studies and shown to not impact performance significantly.

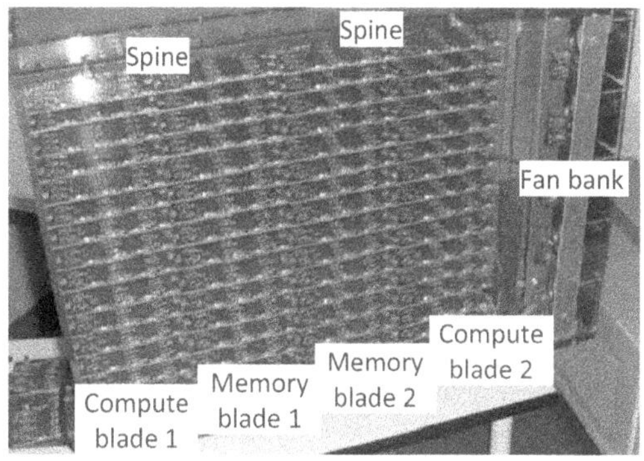

(a)

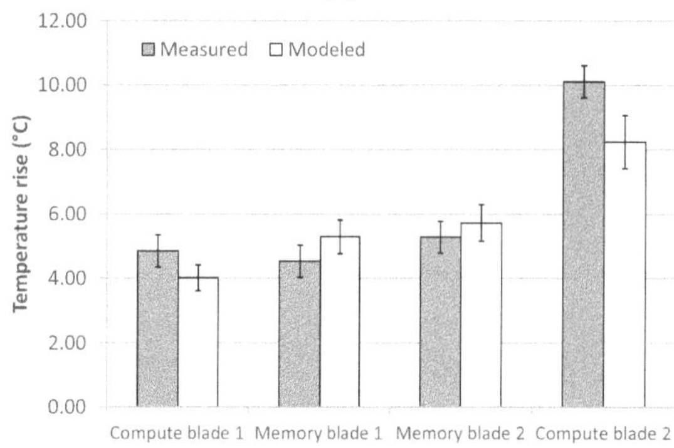

(b)

Figure 8. (a) shows our prototype miniature *demat* design used to validate physical aspects and cooling methodology. Custom PCB boards and fans can be controlled to generate heat and airflow, respectively. (b) shows the results of a validation experiment, comparing the prototype (Measured) to our model (Modeled) in a compute-memory-memory-compute configuration.

For the use of low-power blades, we scaled their number to match the same throughput as the *baseline* and our low-power processors are chosen carefully to not violate latency constraints. For memory blades, we duplicated the simulation-based study in a prior paper on this topic [38]. We specifically considered four web workloads—*indexer*, *search*, *image manipulation*, and *MapReduce-based sort*, and a configuration with four DIMMs of local memory per compute blade supplemented by a shared memory blade. Our results are consistent with prior studies, and show that having such a two level memory hierarchy leads to, on average, only a 2% reduction in performance (with a range of 1–4%).

3.2.4 Discussion

There are several design assumptions we could study further. For example, in this paper, we chose a PUE of 1.5 for our *baseline* based on [28]. If we had instead started with an aggressively-optimized infrastructure having, for example, a PUE of 1.2 (most likely already including optimizations like free-cooling to achieve this), our infrastructure benefits would be different. However, even ignoring infrastructure exergy consumption, *demat* still reduces embedded and operational exergy consumption by 2.3× relative to *baseline* and by 1.2× relative to *LP-blade*. The embedded exergy consumption component improves by 25% going from *LP-blade* to *demat*. Similarly, we also studied systems with longer lifetimes (e.g., 5 years), and our results were qualitatively similar. As discussed earlier, rather than a comprehensive evaluation of the entire design space of specific design assumptions, our main goal in this paper was to understand key insights for computer architects when designing with lifecycle sustainability as a key constraint.

4. Implications of Lifecycle Analysis for System Designers

So far, we have discussed a methodology that system architects can use to reason about the total environmental impact of their designs, and demonstrated the use of this methodology to evaluate specific designs and identify new tradeoffs. Next, we discuss how a lifecycle-based framework can have broader implications for future green server designs. Section 4.1 builds on the results so far and further makes the case for going beyond operational energy efficiency to target the full lifecycle when optimizing environmental impact. Section 4.2 discusses opportunities for new sustainability optimizations that can be evaluated with our framework.

4.1 The case for holistic lifecycle design

The results in Section 3.2 demonstrated positive interactions between different components of exergy consumption. Below we present another example, where optimizing operational energy alone may not yield the greenest design.

Energy proportionality versus consolidation: We compare two commonly-used categories of optimizations to reduce operational energy: (1) energy proportionality (*EP*) [4], optimizations that match power consumption to resource utilization (e.g., P-states); and (2) consolidation (*Con*), packing multiple workloads or virtual machines (VMs) into a smaller number of systems [40, 6]. Given the large body of work in this space, rather than focus on one particular implementation, we study idealized models that extrapolate these optimizations to the future. Such an approach is also better matched with our intent to explore broad tradeoffs between sustainability and operational energy. Therefore, for this experiment, we start with the *baseline* design from before; *EP* assumes ideal proportionality for the server (i.e., we assumed *baseline* hardware parameters from Figure 3, but modified the last column to zero); *Con* assumes perfect bin packing to minimize the number of servers assuming perfect knowledge and divisibility of workload patterns (the server configuration continues to match that of *baseline*).

Figure 9 illustrates the tradeoffs between *EP* and *Con* with data from 11 real-world enterprise clusters from Raghavendra et al. [7], representing a total of 180 servers. Columns 2 and 3 of the table show the operational energy for the *EP* and *Con* designs relative to the *baseline*. For all the traces, energy proportionality is always better than consolidation. This is because EP has perfect scaling of power with workload utilization. However, with *Con*, given that the bin-packing is optimized for the peak of the total utilization (*peak-of-sum utilization*), the average utilization of individual servers is less than 100% in most cases, even after correction for consolidation. Combined with the non-energy-proportional power profile of the *Con* servers, this leads to reduced cluster energy efficiency for *Con* relative to EP. Columns 4 and 5 show the total exergy consumption of the *EP* and *Con* designs relative to the *baseline*. In contrast to the results on operational energy, from a total exergy consumption perspective, *Con* is best for almost half the workloads. In these cases, the reduced server count with consolidation reduces embedded exergy consumption, an effect that *EP* does not have. These reductions (the reduction factor is equal to the reciprocal of the peak-of-sum utilization) offset *Con's* increased operational exergy consumption relative to *EP*, leading to *Con* ultimately being greener than *EP* in these cases. The specific cases where this effect is seen is a function of the workload behavior—its average and peak-of-sum utilizations. (Note that we assume that consolidation leads to lower provisioning of servers; if consolidation just allowed servers to be turned off, we would not get the savings in embedded exergy consumption.)

Workload	Operational-server (% baseline)		Total (% baseline)	
	EP	Con	EP	Con
E-commerce 1	18%	27%	36%	25%
E-commerce 2	48%	66%	57%	63%
Dotcom	37%	52%	49%	49%
Pharmacy	10%	17%	31%	16%
SAP 1	39%	50%	51%	46%
SAP 2	53%	84%	61%	82%
Worldcup 1	27%	61%	42%	60%
Worldcup 2	21%	31%	38%	28%
Consolidation 1	62%	88%	68%	87%
Consolidation 2	59%	88%	66%	86%
Animation farm	98%	100%	98%	100%

Figure 9. Analysis of the tradeoffs between optimizing for operational energy efficiency and optimizing for sustainability. Shaded cells denote the more energy-efficient or more sustainable system.

Co-design of inter-dependent variables: While this example is relatively intuitive, the results illustrate that *the most efficient system design for operational energy does not always correspond to the most sustainable solution*. The best way to optimize for sustainability is to use power-efficient *and* material-efficient systems that scale power with resources and are utilized fully.

More broadly, embedded exergy consumption, server-operation exergy consumption, infrastructure-operation exergy consumption, and performance are not independent variables. As an illustration, consider dematerialization discussed earlier. This optimization targeted at reducing embedded exergy consumption sometimes reduces infrastructure exergy consumption (when removal of sheet metal in the backplane enables better air flow), but in other cases increases infrastructure exergy consumption (when removal of fans in a server increases overall cooling exergy consumption). This optimization also impacts performance, for example, when backplane redesign for dematerialization impacts networking topologies.

Similarly, design optimizations are not independent, with one optimization enabling others. Going back to the dematerialization example, the departure from traditional notions of enclosures allowed us to increase sharing across a larger number of memory blades, and in turn, the disaggregation enables new optimizations

Sustainability opportunity	Why it helps	Possible tradeoffs
CPUs with smaller die areas	Less silicon	Lower operational power, lower performance
Reducing number of CPUs	Less silicon	Lower operational power, lower performance
Upcycling CPUs	Less silicon	Need architectural support, performance implications
Shared CPUs	Shared silicon	Mainly good for consolidation-friendly workloads
Reducing memory	Less silicon/PCB	Lower operational power, lower performance
Shared memory	Shared silicon	Need architectural support, performance implications
Upcycling memory	Less silicon/PCB	Need architectural support, performance implications
Reducing fabrication energy	Less embedded exergy consumption	Need investment in new fabrication technology
Reducing PCB area	Less PCB	Need architectural support, cooling implications
Removing chassis materials	Less steel	Structural issues, need architectural support, cooling impact
Using fewer HDDs	Less copper/other	Lower storage capacity/bandwidth, lower operational power
Upcycling HDDs	Less copper/other	Need architectural support, performance implications
Shared ASICs (e.g., chipset, NIC)	Less silicon	Need architectural support, performance implications
Shared fans	Less materials/power	Potential cooling limitations
Air economizer cooling	Less infrastructure	Limits on heat load, material implications

Figure 10. Some example sustainability opportunities for future system designs and the reasoning from our model as to why they help and the possible tradeoffs involved.

around zones of clustering for optimal thermal density. These examples argue for more holistic optimizations co-designed across system architecture and physical organization. Indeed, our results in Section 3.2 illustrate that the overall improvements in total exergy consumption are achieved through relatively small improvements in multiple components of the system, through several optimizations that work well with one another.

Consequently, when optimizing for sustainability, a *holistic* approach—co-designed across system architecture, physical organization and packaging, and cooling infrastructure—is needed. A lifecycle model can enable such optimizations.

4.2 Opportunities for future research

4.2.1 Targeting embedded exergy consumption

As embedded exergy consumption becomes a more dominant component of total exergy consumption—as it has for mobile systems or when operational exergy consumption is significantly optimized—*new approaches are needed that specifically target embedded exergy consumption.*

Upcyling: For example, the optimizations in the paper so far that target embedded exergy consumption are primarily along the lines of "reduce and reuse". However, there might be benefits from addressing "recycling" in architecture design as well.

Specifically, our *demat* design can potentially benefit from recycling. Compared to a traditional server where all components are decommissioned during an upgrade cycle, the separation of compute, memory, and storage enabled by disaggregation can support incremental upgrading and "upcycling" for lower exergy consumption. This ability to separate the refresh cycle for specific components like memory and disks from the server refresh cycle can amortize material overhead over longer times, enabling greener designs. For example, with separate memory blades, we could upgrade 75% of the memory with every processor upgrade, but upcycle the remaining 25%. Similarly, disks can be upgraded every other processor generation. Plugging such assumptions into our lifecycle model shows that such upcycling optimizations can indeed be beneficial providing an additional 27% reduction in embedded exergy consumption (or about 15% in total exergy consumption).

However, we did not include these optimizations in our *demat* results earlier for two reasons. First, upcycling has potential implications on performance that are hard to model. Memory speed increases every generation, as does memory density. While deferring the upgrades may offer embedded exergy consumption advantages, performance can potentially degrade due to the reduced speed and capacity. In the absence of specific workloads and deployment scenarios, such degradation is hard to characterize. Additionally, the energy efficiency of components has also traditionally changed every generation. The operational exergy consumption benefits from more energy-efficient memory post-upgrade may be important in the total exergy consumption benefits, offsetting upcycling savings. Reliability variations across generations also need to be factored.

Nevertheless, given the potential benefits, upcyling is worthy of further consideration. New architectural designs that enable upcycling, but without these negative effects, is a promising area of future research.

Silicon-efficient designs: One way to reduce the embedded exergy consumption further is to be more material-efficient. New architectures and fabrication processes that maximize the performance-per-exergy-consumption investment in silicon appear a promising area of research to improve the environmental impact from embedded exergy consumption. However, as discussed before, such optimizations need to be considered in the context of their interactions on other aspects of exergy consumption and net performance. Figure 10 lists other potential systems' optimizations to reduce embedded exergy consumption and their tradeoffs.

4.2.2 Targeting operational exergy consumption

Given the large fraction of operational exergy consumption in the overall environmental impact, *reducing operational energy* will continue to be an important way to make future systems greener. Energy-efficient system designs will continue to be important to reduce server-operational exergy consumption; these designs have a multiplicative effect, also reducing infrastructure exergy consumption and in some cases, even embedded exergy consumption. For infrastructure-operational exergy consumption, our results show that *co-designed physical system design and systems architectures* have significant potential. One area that co-designed thermal and system design can particularly help is around recovering exergy from waste-heat that is dissipated.

Renewable sources of energy (e.g., solar power, fuel cells, wind power) are another promising area for future optimizations. A few studies (e.g., [41, 42]) have already considered renewable energy in the data-center and capping approaches for "brown" energy management, but more research opportunities exist. In particular a lifecycle exergy consumption model can also factor the embedded exergy consumption tradeoffs in developing such new energy sources, helping understand net impact on sustainability. New system architectures to leverage alternate energy sources (a few are illustrated in ongoing work around co-designing battery sources with servers [43] or solar power with multicores [44]) will also be important.

4.2.3 Extending the scope of exergy factors

This study focused on the container as the unit of optimization and drew the boundary of exergy consideration at the container level. That is, our current models focus only on the material and energy *directly* related to production and operation of the *evaluated system*. However, a well-known effect within the environmental sciences is that of recursive and cross-dependent flows. For example, when a system requires some metals to be used, beyond the exergy consumption associated with extracting or manufacturing the metals themselves, an entire metals and mining sector of equipment, roads, employees, etc may have be created to support these manufacturing and extraction processes—additional exergy consumption factors that we currently do not model. Understanding how exergy consumption relates to cost is also an important area of future work, particularly when potential environmental costs—such as carbon taxation—are taken into account.

5. Related Work

To the best of our knowledge, our work is the first to study *systems-focused* modeling and optimization of the *total lifecycle environmental impact* including both production and operation.

There are several studies in the environmental community that have studied lifecycle-based exergy analysis for sustainability [20, 27, 45, 26]. Our work builds on these studies, but develops a model better suited from a system architecture perspective. Various industrial approaches to reason about sustainability have been used by different companies (such as Apple, Dell, Google, and HP), but these are primarily based exclusively on metrics like carbon emissions and often do not address the entire lifecycle. Moreover, most of these approaches are not useful in an architectural context.

A few recent systems' studies have examined lifecycle sustainability. In addition to costs analysis, Anagnostopoulou et al. [12] also study the environment impact of the materials in different cooling configurations for large-scale datacenters. They model each configuration with a detailed parts list, and using the spec-sheets for the various parts, identify the weight of the infrastructure and break it down to the usage of major materials. Their results show that larger infrastructures are more materials-efficient than smaller datacenters. Oliver et al. [25] discuss reusing processors across different devices to amortize the production-related environmental impact of silicon over a longer time frame. They use a simple formula for the energy of semiconductor manufacturing, across the die and the assembly. In contrast to our work, neither of these studies have a unified sustainability model that allows comparison and optimization across the embedded and operational aspects.

A large number of prior systems' studies, including recent papers at specialized venues like SustainIT (`www.usenix.org/events/sustainit10`) and IGCC (`www.green-conf.org`), have focused on operational energy efficiency as a proxy for sustainability. In particular, there has been a large body of prior work on reducing the operational electricity consumption of servers [2, 3, 4, 5, 6, 7, 8, 9, 10, 11]. Other studies have examined renewable energy sources for operational energy. Gupta et al. [46] discuss a conceptual framework to reason about renewable energy sources that addresses workload arrival times, energy proportionality support, and environmental conditions. Le et al. [47, 48] and Qureshi [49] study optimization frameworks and policies to tradeoff "brown" and green energy sources. Govindan et al. examine how stored energy can be managed in datacenters [43]. Li et al. [44, 50] have studied the use of renewable energy in processor and datacenter design. However, none of these studies address the lifecycle environmental impact or the tradeoffs between the environmental impact of production and operation.

6. Conclusions

System architects are increasingly required to report on, and optimize, the environmental impact of their designs. Current approaches mainly focus only on operational energy, and miss additional important environmental impact caused by the production of the system. Addressing this limitation, our paper develops a framework for, and motivates optimizations around, a lifecycle focus for server architects designing future green servers. Our framework uses the thermodynamic metric of exergy consumption, adapted and validated for easy reasoning of architectural tradeoffs. Our results using the framework show that production-related impact can be important, contributing to 20% of the total environmental impact on current designs, and that system design choices can improve this component by 30-40%. Our results also demonstrate the need to holistically consider cross-interactions in the sustainability impact from production and operation when evaluating specific green techniques—in some cases, the most (operational) energy-efficient design is not the greenest (e.g., energy proportionality versus consolidation), and in others, optimizations targeting small embedded components of total exergy consumption achieve multiplicative benefits by enabling better environmental impact from operation (e.g., net environmental benefits from dematerialization).

However, this work only addresses the surface of the potential benefits from lifecycle optimizations. In addition to continued improvements in operational and infrastructure efficiencies, promising areas of future research include system architectures designed for renewable energy, architectures to better recover wasted heat, and new architectural approaches for better upcycling and improved performance-per-silicon-investment. Our lifecycle-based model can also be extended to broaden the scope of sustainability to look at the broader impact to society including social and economic costs of high performance in future computing systems. Also, our modeling approach of normalizing environmental impact with respect to of architectural building blocks can be applied to other metrics beyond exergy consumption as well. We hope that the contributions of this paper provide a foundation to study these, and other interesting, research questions for future sustainable and green system designs.

Acknowledgements

Wayne Mack and Tobin Gonzalez assisted in building the prototype discussed in this paper. Ricardo Bianchini, Fred Chong, Kanad Ghose, Anand Sivasubramaniam, Thomas Wenisch, and the anonymous reviewers provided valuable feedback that significantly strengthened this paper.

Appendix A1: Thermo-volume infrastructure modeling for new packaging/thermal designs

To reason about cooling improvements, we employ the method developed and validated by Shah et al. [31]. This approach essentially divides the physical infrastructure into "control volumes" of tractable thermofluidic properties, referred to as "thermovolumes." We use CFD models to model air flow for individual blades, determine thermal and flow resistances for each thermovolume in the spine and datacenter, and perform a closed-form optimization to maximize the coefficient of performance (COPG). COPG is defined as the heat removed per unit amount of work input to a given thermovolume; a larger COPG implies lower cooling power spent in removing heat. In situations (such as ours) when power delivery losses are minimal, PUE is approximately equal to (1 + 1 / COPG).

Cooling power = Q_{dc}/COP_G

- Q_{dc} is the heat dissipation from the datacenter
- COP_G is the coefficient of performance (efficiency of cooling) and is defined as

$$COP_G = (Q_{dc}/W_{comp})/(1 + A + B + C + D)$$

- W_{comp} is the compressor power for thermal work
- $A = \frac{\text{Total power for cooling infrastructure}}{\text{Compressor power}}$
- $B = \frac{\text{Power for blowers and CRAC units}}{\text{Compressor power}}$
- $C = \frac{\text{Pump power}}{\text{Compressor power}}$
- $D = \frac{\text{Cooling tower power}}{\text{Compressor power}}$

(For our free air cooling design, $B = C = D = 0$.)

$W_{comp} = f(\text{supply temp from CRAC efficiency curve})$

$A = g(\text{flow rate, fan operating curve, system pressure } \Delta)$

Figure 11. Key thermal model parameters.

References

[1] Chandrakant Patel. Sustainable information technology ecosystem. FAST Keynote Address, 2008.

[2] David Meisner, Christopher M. Sadler, Luiz André Barroso, Wolf-Dietrich Weber, and Thomas F. Wenisch. Power management of online data-intensive services. In *ISCA '11*, 2011.

[3] Susmit Biswas, Mohit Tiwari, Timothy Sherwood, Luke Theogarajan, and Frederic T. Chong. Fighting fire with fire: modeling the datacenter-scale effects of targeted superlattice thermal management. In *ISCA '11*, 2011.

[4] Luiz André Barroso and Urs Hölzle. The case for energy-proportional computing. *IEEE Computer*, 40(12):33–37, 2007.

[5] David Meisner, Brian T. Gold, and Thomas F. Wenisch. Powernap: Eliminating server idle power. In *Proceedings of the 14th International Conference on Architectural Support for Programming Languages and Operating Systems (ASPLOS '09)*, Washington, DC, March 2009.

[6] Karthick Rajamani and Charles Lefurgy. On evaluating request-distribution schemes for saving energy in server clusters. In *Proceedings of the IEEE International Symposium on Performance Analysis of Systems and Software (ISPASS)*, pages 111–122, Austin, TX, March 2003.

[7] Ramya Raghavendra, Parthasarathy Ranganathan, Vanish Talwar, Zhikui Wang, and Xiaoyun Zhu. No "power" struggles: Coordinated multi-level power management for the data center. In *Proceedings of the 13th International Conference on Architectural Support for Programming Languages and Operating Systems (ASPLOS)*, pages 48–59, March 2008.

[8] Parthasarathy Ranganathan, Phil Leech, David E. Irwin, and Jeffrey S. Chase. Ensemble-level power management for dense blade servers. In *Proceedings of the 33rd International Symposium on Computer Architecture (ISCA 2006)*, pages 66–77, Boston, MA, June 2006.

[9] Xiaobo Fan, Wolf-Dietrich Weber, and Luiz André Barroso. Power provisioning for a warehouse-sized computer. In *Proceedings of the 34th Annual International Symposium on Computer Architecture (ISCA '07)*, pages 13–23, San Diego, CA, June 2007.

[10] Taliver Heath, Ana Paula Centeno, Pradeep George, Luiz Ramos, Yogesh Jaluria, and Ricardo Bianchini. Mercury and freon: Temperature emulation and management for server systems. In *Proceedings of the 12th International Conference on Architectural Support for Programming Languages and Operating Systems (ASPLOS)*, pages 106–116, San Jose, CA, October 2006.

[11] Faraz Ahmad and T. N. Vijaykumar. Joint optimization of idle and cooling power in data centers while maintaining response time. In *ASPLOS*, 2010.

[12] Vlasia Anagnostopoulou, Heba Saadeldeen, and Frederic T. Chong. Quantifying the environmental advantages of large-scale computing. In *First International Green Computing Conference (IGCC)*, 2010.

[13] Greenpeace. "How dirty is your data? A look at the energy choices that power cloud computing." Greenpeace International Report, April 2011.

[14] Mireille Faist Emmenegger, Rolf Frischknecht, Markus Stutz, Michael Guggisberg, Res Witschi, and Tim Otto. Life cycle assessment of the mobile communication system: Towards eco-efficient systems. *International Journal of Life Cycle Assessment*, 11:4, 2006.

[15] Amip J. Shah, Chandrakant D. Patel, and Van P. Carey. Exergy-based metrics for sustainable design. In *Fourth International Exergy, Energy and Environment Symposium (IEEES-4)*, Sharjah, UAE, 2009.

[16] J. Glasson, R. Therivel, and A. Chadwick. *Introduction to Environmental Impact Assessment: Principles and Procedures, Process, Practice and Prospects (3rd Edition)*. Taylor & Francis, 2005.

[17] O. Jolliet, M. Margni, R. Charles, S. Humbert, J. Payet, G. Rebitzer, and R. Rosenbaum. Impact 2002+: A new life cycle impact assessment methodology. *Int. J. Life Cycle Assessment*, 8:324–330, 2003.

[18] M. Goedkoop and R. Spriensma. The eco-indicator 99: A damage oriented method for life cycle assessment. Technical report, PRé Consultants, 2001.

[19] A. Horvath, C. T. Hendrickson, L. B. Lave, F. C. McMichael, and T.-S. Wu. Toxic emissions indices for green design and inventory. *Environment Science & Technology*, 29:86A–90A, 1995.

[20] Amip Shah and Kiara Corrigan. Extending lifecycle exergy analysis beyond resource consumption. In *ASME Energy Sustainability Conference*, Phoenix, AZ, May 2010.

[21] Rolf Frischknecht, Niels Jungbluth, Hans-Jörg Althaus, Gabor Doka, Roberto Dones, Thomas Heck, Stefanie Hellweg, Roland Hischier, Thomas Nemecek, Gerald Rebitzer, and Michael Spielmann. The ecoinvent database: Overview and methodological framework. *International Journal of Life Cycle Assessment*, 10(1):3–9, 2005.

[22] Y. Anny Huang, Chris L. Weber, and H. Scott Matthews. Carbon footprinting upstream supply chain for electronics manufacturing and computer services. In *IEEE International Symposium on Sustainable Systems and Technology (ISSST'09)*, Tempe, AZ, May 2009.

[23] Sarah Boyd, Arpad Horvath, and David Dornfeld. Life-cycle energy demand and global warming potential of computational logic. *Environmental Science and Technology*, 43(19):7303–7309, 2009.

[24] Timothy Gutowski, Matthew S. Branham, Jeffrey B. Dahmus, Alissa J. Jones, Alexandre Thiriez, and Dusan Sekulic. Thermodynamic analysis of resources used in manufacturing processes. *Environmental Science and Technology*, 43:1584–1590, 2009.

[25] John Oliver, Rajeevan Amirtharajah, Venkatesh Akella, Roland Geyer, and Frederic T. Chong. Life cycle aware computing: Reusing silicon technology. pages 58–63, 2007.

[26] David J. Lettieri, Christopher R. Hannemann, Van P. Carey, , and Amip J. Shah. Lifetime exergy consumption as a sustainability metric for information technologies. In *IEEE International Symposium on Sustainable Systems and Technology (ISSST'09)*, Tempe, AZ, May 2009.

[27] Chris R. Hannemann, Van P. Carey, Amip J. Shah, and Chandrakant D. Patel. Lifetime exergy consumption as a sustainability metric for enterprise servers. In *ASME Energy Sustainability Conference*, Jacksonville, FL, 2008.

[28] James Hamilton. Internet-scale service infrastructure efficiency. In *Keynote at the International Symposium on Computer Architecture*, 2009.

[29] Kevin Lim, Parthasarathy Ranganathan, Jichuan Chang, Chandrakant Patel, Trevor Mudge, and Steven Reinhardt. Understanding and designing new server architectures for emerging warehouse-computing environments. In *ISCA*, 2008.

[30] The Green Grid. Green grid metrics: Describing datacenter power efficiency. http://www.thegreengrid.org, 2007.

[31] Amip Shah, Cullen Bash, and Chandrakant Patel. Optimizing data center cooling infrastructure using exergothermovolumes. In *ITherm*, 2010.

[32] James Hamilton. Cooperative expendable micro-slice servers: Low cost, low power servers for internet-scale services. In *CIDR*, 2009.

[33] HP performance-optimized datacenter (POD). http://h71028.www7.hp.com/enterprise/cache/595887-0-0-0-121.html.

[34] A. Caulfield, L. Grupp, and S. Swanson. Gordon: using flash memory to build fast, power-efficient clusters for data-intensive applications. In *ASPLOS-XIV*, 2009.

[35] David Andersen, Jason Franklin, Michael Kaminsky, Amar Phanishayee, Lawrence Tan, and Vijay Vasudevan. Fawn: a fast array of wimpy nodes. In *SOSP*, 2009.

[36] HP bc2500 product page. http://h20000.www2.hp.com/bizsupport/TechSupport/Document.jsp?objectID=c01125713&lang=en&cc=us&taskId=101&prodSeriesId=3436097&prodTypeId=12454.

[37] Eitan Frachtenberg, Ali Heydari, Harry Li, Amir Michael, Jacob Na, Avery Nisbet, and Pierluigi Sarti. High-efficiency server design. In *SC '11*, 2011.

[38] Kevin Lim, Jichuan Chang, Trevor Mudge, Parthasarathy Ranganathan, Steven K. Reinhardt, and Thomas F. Wenisch. Disaggregated memory for expansion and sharing in blade servers. In *ISCA*, 2009.

[39] Rich Miller. Microsoft's chiller-less data center. http://www.datacenterknowledge.com/archives/2009/09/24/microsofts-chiller-less-data-center/, September 2009.

[40] Ripal Nathuji and Karsten Schwan. Virtualpower: coordinated power management in virtualized enterprise systems. In *Proceedings of the 21st ACM Symposium on Operating Systems Principles (SOSP)*, pages 265–278, Stevenson, WA, October 2007.

[41] Kien T. Le, Ricardo Bianchini, Margaret Martonosi, and Thu D. Nguyen. Cost- and energy-aware load distribution across data centers. In *HotPower*, 2009.

[42] Christopher Stewart and Kai Shen. Some joules are more precious than others: Managing renewable energy in the datacenter. In *HotPower 2009*, 2009.

[43] Sriram Govindan, Anand Sivasubramaniam, Bhuvan Urgaonkar. Benefits and Limitations of Tapping into Stored Energy For Datacenters. In *ISCA*, 2011.

[44] Chao Li, Wangyuan Zhang, Chang-Burm Cho, and Tao Li. Solarcore: Solar energy driven multi-core architecture power management. In *HPCA*, 2011.

[45] Chris R. Hannemann, Van P. Carey, Amip J. Shah, and Chandrakant D. Patel. Lifetime exergy consumption of an enterprise server. In *IEEE International Symposium on Electronics and the Environment (ISEE'08)*, San Francisco, CA, May 2008.

[46] Sandeep K. S. Gupta, Tridib Mukherjee, Georgios Varsamopoulos, and Ayan Banerjee. Research directions in energy-sustainable cyber-physical systems. *Elsevier Comnets Special Issue in Sustainable Computing (SUSCOM)*, 2011.

[47] Kien Le, Ozlem Bilgir, Ricardo Bianchini, Margaret Martonosi, and Thu D. Nguyen. Capping the brown energy consumption of internet services at low cost. In *International Green Computing Conference (IGCC 2010)*, 2010.

[48] Kien Le, Ozlem Bilgir, Ricardo Bianchini, Margaret Martonosi, and Thu D. Nguyen. Managing the cost, energy consumption, and carbon footprint of internet services. In *ACM SIGMETRICS*, 2010.

[49] Asfandyar Qureshi, Rick Weber, Hari Balakrishnan, John Guttag, and Bruce Maggs. Cutting the electric bill for internet-scale systems. In *Proceedings of the ACM SIGCOMM 2009 conference on Data communication*, 2009.

[50] Chao Li, Amer Qouneh, and Tao Li. Characterizing and analyzing renewable energy driven data centers. In *International Conference on Measurement and Modeling of Computer Systems*, 2011.

Clearing the Clouds

A Study of Emerging Scale-out Workloads on Modern Hardware

Michael Ferdman[‡], Almutaz Adileh, Onur Kocberber, Stavros Volos, Mohammad Alisafaee, Djordje Jevdjic, Cansu Kaynak, Adrian Daniel Popescu, Anastasia Ailamaki, and Babak Falsafi

[‡]CALCM
Carnegie Mellon University

EcoCloud
École Polytechnique Fédérale de Lausanne

Abstract

Emerging scale-out workloads require extensive amounts of computational resources. However, data centers using modern server hardware face physical constraints in space and power, limiting further expansion and calling for improvements in the computational density per server and in the per-operation energy. Continuing to improve the computational resources of the cloud while staying within physical constraints mandates optimizing server efficiency to ensure that server hardware closely matches the needs of scale-out workloads.

In this work, we introduce CloudSuite, a benchmark suite of emerging scale-out workloads. We use performance counters on modern servers to study scale-out workloads, finding that today's predominant processor micro-architecture is inefficient for running these workloads. We find that inefficiency comes from the mismatch between the workload needs and modern processors, particularly in the organization of instruction and data memory systems and the processor core micro-architecture. Moreover, while today's predominant micro-architecture is inefficient when executing scale-out workloads, we find that continuing the current trends will further exacerbate the inefficiency in the future. In this work, we identify the key micro-architectural needs of scale-out workloads, calling for a change in the trajectory of server processors that would lead to improved computational density and power efficiency in data centers.

Categories and Subject Descriptors C.4 [**Performance of Systems**]: Performance of Systems - Design studies

General Terms Design, Measurement, Performance

1 Introduction

Cloud computing is emerging as a dominant computing platform for delivering scalable online services to a global client base. Today's popular online services, such as web search, social networks, and video sharing, are all hosted in large data centers. With the industry rapidly expanding [15], service providers are building new data centers, augmenting the existing infrastructure to meet the increasing demand. However, while demand for cloud infrastructure continues to grow, the semiconductor manufacturing industry has reached the physical limits of voltage scaling [20, 24], no longer able to reduce power consumption or increase power density in new chips. Physical constraints have therefore become the dominant limiting factor for data centers, because their sheer size and electrical power demands cannot be met.

Recognizing the physical constraints that stand in the way of further growth, cloud providers now optimize their data centers for compute density and power consumption. Cloud providers have already begun building server systems specifically targeting cloud data centers, improving compute density and energy efficiency by using high-efficiency power supplies and removing unnecessary board-level components such as audio and graphics chips [17, 35].

Although major design changes are being introduced at the board- and chassis-level of new cloud servers, the processors used in these new servers are not designed to efficiently run scale-out workloads. Processor vendors use the same underlying architecture for servers and for the general purpose market, leading to extreme inefficiency in today's data centers. Moreover, both general purpose (e.g., Intel and AMD) and traditional server processor (e.g., Sun Niagara, IBM Power7) designs follow a trajectory that benefits scale-up workloads, a trend that was established long before the emergence of scale-out workloads. Recognizing the space and power inefficiencies of modern processors for scale-out workloads, some vendors and researchers conjecture that even using processors built for the mobile space may be more efficient [13, 29, 38, 39].

In this work, we observe that scale-out workloads share many inherent characteristics that place them into a distinct workload class from desktop, parallel, and traditional server workloads. We perform a detailed micro-architectural study of a range of scale-out workloads, finding a large mismatch between the demands of the scale-out workloads and today's predominant processor micro-architecture. We observe significant over-provisioning of the memory hierarchy and core micro-architectural resources for the scale-out workloads. Moreover, continuing the current processor trends will result in further widening the mismatch between the scale-out workloads and server processors. Conversely, we find that the characteristics of scale-out workloads can be leveraged to gain area and energy efficiency in future servers.

We use performance counters to study the behavior of scale-out workloads running on modern server processors. We demonstrate:

- **Scale-out workloads suffer from high instruction-cache miss rates.** Instruction-caches and associated next-line prefetchers found in modern processors are inadequate for scale-out workloads.
- **Instruction- and memory-level parallelism in scale-out workloads is low.** Modern aggressive out-of-order cores are excessively complex, consuming power and on-chip area without providing performance benefits to scale-out workloads.
- **Data working sets of scale-out workloads considerably exceed the capacity of on-chip caches.** Processor real-estate and power are misspent on large last-level caches that do not contribute to improved scale-out workload performance.

ASPLOS'12, March 3–7, 2012, London, England, UK.

- **On-chip and off-chip bandwidth requirements of scale-out workloads are low.** Scale-out workloads see no benefit from fine-grained coherence and high memory and core-to-core communication bandwidth.

The rest of this paper is organized as follows. In Section 2, we provide an overview of the state-of-the-art server processors and scale-out workloads. We provide a detailed description of our benchmarking methodology in Section 3. We present our results in Section 4, concentrating on the mismatch between the needs of scale-out workloads and modern processors. We summarize related work in Section 5 and conclude in Section 6.

2 Modern Cores and Scale-out Workloads

Today's data centers are built around conventional desktop processors whose architecture was designed for a broad market. The dominant processor architecture closely followed the technology trends, improving single-thread performance with each processor generation by using the increased clock speeds and "free" (in area and power) transistors provided by progress in semiconductor manufacturing. Although Dennard scaling has stopped [12, 19, 20, 46], with both clock frequency and transistor counts becoming limited by power, processor architects have continued to spend resources on improving single-thread performance for a broad range of applications at the expense of area and power efficiency.

2.1 Dominant processor architectures

Modern processors comprise several aggressive out-of-order cores connected with a high-bandwidth on-chip interconnect to a deep (three-level) cache hierarchy. While core aggressiveness and clock frequency scaling enabled a rapid increase in computational performance, off-chip memory latency improvements were not as rapid. The "memory wall"—the gap between the speed at which cores could compute and the speed at which data could be delivered to the cores for computation—mandated that the data working set must fit into the on-chip caches to allow the core to compute at full speed. Modern processors therefore split the die area into two roughly equal parts, with one part dedicated to the cores and tightly-coupled private caches and the other dedicated to a large shared last-level cache. The emergence of multi-core processors offered the possibility to run computationally-intensive multi-threaded applications, adding the requirement of fast and high-bandwidth core-to-core communication to allow cores to compute without incurring significant delays when operating on actively shared data.

To leverage the increasing number of transistors on chip for higher single-thread performance, cores are engineered to execute independent instructions out of order (OoO), allowing the processor to temporarily bypass instructions that stall due to a cache access. While OoO execution can improve core resource utilization through instruction-level parallelism (ILP), the core's complexity increases dramatically depending on the width of the pipeline and the size of the reorder window. Large windows require selecting and scheduling among many instructions while tracking all memory and register dependencies. This functionality requires a large and power-hungry scheduler, reorder buffer, and load-store structures. Moreover, the efficacy of growing the instruction reorder window rapidly drops off, resulting in diminishing returns at exponentially increasing area and energy costs with every processor generation. Notably, although wide pipelines and large reorder windows do not harm the core performance, low-ILP applications execute inefficiently because the area and power costs spent on OoO execution do not yield a performance benefit.

The first-level instruction and data caches capture the primary working set of applications, enabling low-latency access to the most-frequently referenced memory addresses. To maintain low access latency, the first-level cache capacity must remain small due to hardware constraints, whereas the last-level caches can have larger capacity, but with a higher access latency. As the size of the last-level cache (LLC) has reached tens of megabytes in modern processors, the access latency of the LLC has itself created a speed gap between the first-level caches and LLC, pushing processor designers to mitigate the gap by inserting an intermediate-size secondary cache. Additionally, to further mitigate the large LLC latency, the number of miss-status handling registers (MSHRs) is increased to allow for a large number of memory-reference instructions to be performed in parallel. Like the core structures for supporting ILP, the mechanisms to support memory-level parallelism (MLP) use considerable area and energy. Increasing parallelism in LLC and off-chip accesses can give a tremendous performance improvement when many independent memory accesses are available to execute, but results in poor efficiency when executing workloads with low MLP.

To increase the core utilization when MLP is low, modern processors add support for simultaneous multi-threading (SMT), enabling multiple software threads to be executed simultaneously in the same core. SMT cores operate like single-threaded cores, but introduce instructions from two independent software threads into the reorder window, enabling the core to find independent memory accesses and perform them in parallel, even when both software threads have low MLP. However, introducing instructions from multiple software threads into the same pipeline causes contention for core resources, limiting the performance of each thread compared to when that thread runs alone.

2.2 Dominant scale-out workloads

To find a set of applications that dominate today's cloud infrastructure, we examined a selection of internet services based on their popularity [2]. For each popular service, we analyzed the class of application software used by the major providers to offer these services, either on their own cloud infrastructure or on a cloud infrastructure leased from a third party. We present an overview of the applications most commonly found in today's clouds, along with brief descriptions of typical configuration characteristics and dataset sizes. Overall, we find that scale-out workloads have similar characteristics; all applications we examined (1) operate on large data sets that are split across a large number of machines, typically into memory-resident shards, (2) serve large numbers of completely independent requests that do not share any state, (3) have application software designed specifically for the cloud infrastructure where unreliable machines may come and go, and (4) use inter-machine connectivity only for high-level task management and coordination.

Data Serving. Various *NoSQL* data stores [5, 10, 43] have been explicitly designed to serve as the backing store for large-scale web applications such as the Facebook inbox, Google Earth, and Google Finance, providing fast and scalable storage with varying and rapidly evolving storage schemas. The NoSQL systems split hundreds of terabytes of data into shards and horizontally scale out to large cluster sizes. Most operations on requested objects are performed using indexes that support fast lookup and key range scans. For simplicity and scalability, these systems are designed to support queries that can be completely executed by a single machine, with all operations that require combining data from multiple shards relegated to the middleware.

MapReduce. The explosion of accessible human-generated information necessitates automated analytical processing to cluster, classify, and filter this information. The map-reduce paradigm [9] has emerged as a popular approach to large-scale analysis, farming out requests to a cluster of machines that first perform filtering and transformation of the data (map) and then aggregate the results (reduce). A key advantage of the map-reduce paradigm is the separation of infrastructure and algorithms [3]. Users implement algorithms using *map* and *reduce* functions and provide these functions to the map-reduce infrastructure, which is then responsible for orchestrating the work. Because of the generality of the infrastructure and the need to scale to thousands of independent servers, communication between tasks is typically limited to reading and writing files in a distributed file system. For example, map tasks produce temporary files that are subsequently read by the reduce tasks, effectively rendering all map and reduce tasks architecturally independent. Whenever possible, the map-reduce infrastructures strive to further reduce communication by scheduling the processing of data on the servers that store that data.

Media Streaming. The availability of high-bandwidth connections to home and mobile devices has made media streaming services such as NetFlix, YouTube, and YouKu ubiquitous. Streaming services use large server clusters to gradually packetize and transmit media files ranging from megabytes to gigabytes in size, pre-encoded in various formats and bit-rates to suit a diverse client base. Sharding of media content ensures that servers frequently send the same content to multiple users, enabling in-memory caching of content by the servers. While in-memory caching is effective, the on-demand unicast nature of today's streaming services practically guarantees that the streaming server will work on a different piece of the media file for each client, even when concurrently streaming the same file to many clients.

SAT Solver. The ability to temporarily allocate compute resources in the cloud without purchasing the infrastructure has created an opportunity for engineers and researchers to conduct large-scale computations. For example, complex algorithms, such as symbolic execution, become tractable when the computation is split into smaller sub-problems and distributed to the cloud where a large number of SAT Solver processes are hosted. However, unlike the traditional super-computer environment with high-bandwidth low-latency dedicated interconnects and balanced memory and compute resources, the cloud offers dynamic and heterogeneous resources that are loosely connected over an IP network. Large-scale computation tasks must therefore be adapted to a worker-queue model with centralized load balancing that rebalances tasks across a dynamic pool of compute resources, minimizing the amount of data exchanged between the workers and load balancers and practically eliminating any communication between workers.

Web Frontend. Web services are hosted in the cloud to achieve high fault-tolerance and dynamic scalability. Although many web stacks are used in the cloud, the underlying service architectures are similar. A load balancer distributes independent client requests across a large number of stateless web servers. The web servers either directly serve static files or pass the requests to stateless middleware scripts, written in high-level interpreted or byte-code compiled languages, which then produce dynamic content. All state is stored by the middleware in backend databases such as NoSQL data stores or traditional relational database servers.

Web Search. Web search engines, such as those powering Google and Microsoft Bing, index terabytes of data harvested from online sources. To support a large number of concurrent latency-sensitive search queries against the index, the data is split into memory-residents shards, with each index serving node (ISN) responsible for processing requests to its own shard. A frontend machine sends index search requests to all ISNs in parallel, collects and sorts the responses, and sends a formatted reply to the requesting client. Hundreds of unrelated search requests are handled by each ISN every second, with minimal locality; shards are therefore sized to fit into the memory of the ISNs to avoid reducing throughput and degrading quality of service due to disk I/O. For performance scalability, ISNs may be replicated, allowing the frontend to load balance requests among multiple ISNs that are responsible for the same shard. ISNs communicate only with the frontend machines and never to other ISNs. In an ISN, each request is handled by a software thread, without communicating with other threads.

Table 1. Architectural parameters.

Processor	32nm Intel Xeon X5670, operating at 2.93GHz
CMP width	6 OoO cores
Core width	4-wide issue and retire
Reorder buffer	128 entries
Load/Store buffer	48/32 entries
Reservation stations	36 entries
L1 cache	32KB, split I/D, 4-cycle access latency
L2 cache	256KB per core, 6-cycle access latency
LLC (L3 cache)	12MB, 29-cycle access latency
Memory	24GB, 3 DDR3 channels, delivering up to 32GB/s

3 Methodology

We conduct our study on a PowerEdge M1000e enclosure [11] with two Intel X5670 processors and 24GB of RAM in each blade. Each Intel X5670 processor includes six aggressive out-of-order processor cores with a three-level cache hierarchy: the L1 and L2 caches are private to each core, while the LLC (L3) is shared among all cores. Each core includes several simple stride and stream prefetchers labelled as *adjacent-line, HW prefetcher,* and *DCU streamer* in the processor documentation and system BIOS settings. The blades use high-performance Broadcom server NICs with drivers that support multiple transmit queues and receive-side scaling. The NICs are connected by a built-in M6220 switch. For bandwidth-intensive benchmarks, two gigabit NICs are used in each blade. Table 1 summarizes the key architectural parameters of the systems.

In this work, we introduce CloudSuite, a benchmark suite of emerging scale-out workloads. We present a characterization of the CloudSuite workloads alongside traditional benchmarks, including desktop (SPECint), parallel (PARSEC), enterprise web (SPECweb09), and relational database server (TPC-C, TPC-E, Web Backend) workloads. For all but the TPC-E benchmark, we use CentOS 5.5 with the 2.6.32 Linux kernel. For the TPC-E benchmark, we use Microsoft Windows Server 2008 Release 2.

3.1 Measurement tools and methodology

We analyze architectural behavior using Intel VTune [26], a tool that provides an interface to the processor performance counters. For all scale-out and traditional server workloads except SAT Solver, we perform a 180-second measurement after the workload completes the ramp-up period and reaches a steady state. Because SAT Solver has no steady-state behavior, we achieve comparable results across runs by re-using input traces. We create SAT Solver input traces that take 45 minutes to execute in our baseline setup and use the first 30 minutes as warmup and the last 15 minutes as the measurement window. We measure the entire execution of the PARSEC and SPEC CINT2006 applications.

For our evaluation, we limit all workload configurations to four cores, tuning the workloads to achieve high utilization of the cores (or hardware threads, in the case of the SMT experiments) while maintaining the workload QoS requirements. To ensure that all application and operating system software runs on the cores under test, we disable all unused cores using the available operating system mechanisms.

We note that computing a breakdown of the execution-time stall components of superscalar out-of-order processors cannot be performed precisely due to overlapped work in the pipeline [14, 28]. We present execution-time breakdown results based on the performance counters that have no overlap. However, we plot memory cycles side-by-side rather than in a stack to indicate the potential overlap with cycles during which instructions were committed. We compute the memory cycles as a sum of the cycles when an off-core request was outstanding, instruction stall cycles contributed by L2 instruction hits, second-level TLB miss cycles, and the first-level instruction TLB miss cycles. Because data stalls can overlap other data stalls, we compute the number of cycles when an off-core request was outstanding using MSHR occupancy statistics,[1] which measure the number of cycles when there is at least one L2 miss being serviced. We do not include L1-D and L2 data cache hits in the computation because they are effectively hidden by the out-of-order core [27].

We perform a cache sensitivity analysis by dedicating two cores to cache-polluting threads. The polluter threads traverse arrays of predetermined size in a pseudo-random sequence, ensuring that all accesses miss in the upper-level caches and reach the LLC. We use performance counters to confirm that the polluter threads achieve nearly 100% hit ratio in the LLC, effectively reducing the cache capacity available for the workload running on the remaining cores of the same processor.

To measure the frequency of read-write sharing, we execute the workloads on cores split across two physical processors in separate sockets. When reading a recently-modified block, this configuration forces accesses to actively-shared read-write blocks to appear as off-chip accesses that hit in a remote processor cache.

3.2 Scale-out workload experimental setup

Data Serving. We benchmark the Cassandra 0.7.3 database with a 15GB Yahoo! Cloud Serving Benchmark (YCSB) dataset. Server load is generated using the YCSB 0.1.3 client [7] that sends requests following a Zipfian distribution with a 95:5 read to write request ratio. Cassandra is configured with a 7GB Java heap and 400MB new-generation garbage collector space.

MapReduce. We benchmark a node of a four-node Hadoop 0.20.2 cluster, running the Bayesian classification algorithm from the Mahout 0.4 library [3]. The algorithm attempts to guess the *country* tag of each article in a 4.5GB set of Wikipedia pages. One *map* task is started per core and assigned a 2GB Java heap.

Media Streaming. We benchmark the Darwin Streaming Server 6.0.3, serving videos of varying duration, using the Faban driver [23] to simulate the clients. We limit our setup to low bit-rate video streams to shift stress away from network I/O.

SAT Solver. We benchmark one instance per core of the Klee SAT Solver, an important component of the Cloud9 parallel symbolic execution engine [6]. Input traces for the engine are produced by Cloud9 by symbolically executing the command-line *printf* utility from the GNU CoreUtils 6.10 using up to four 5-byte and one 10-byte symbolic command-line arguments.

Web Frontend. We benchmark a frontend machine serving Olio, a Web 2.0 web-based social event calendar. The frontend machine runs Nginx 1.0.10 with a built-in PHP 5.3.5 module and APC 3.1.8 PHP opcode cache. We generate a backend dataset using the Cloudstone benchmark [40] and use the Faban driver [23] to simulate clients. To limit disk space requirements, we generate a 12GB on-disk file dataset and modify the PHP code to always serve files from the available range.

Web Search. We benchmark an index serving node (ISN) of the distributed version of Nutch 1.2/Lucene 3.0.1 with an index size of 2GB and data segment size of 23GB of content crawled from the public internet. We mimic real-world setups by making sure that the search index fits in memory, eliminating page faults and minimizing disk activity [38]. We simulate clients using the Faban driver. The clients are configured to achieve the maximum search request rate while ensuring that 90% of all search queries complete in under 0.5 seconds.

3.3 Traditional benchmark experimental setup

PARSEC 2.1. We benchmark the official applications with the *native* input, reporting results averaged across all benchmarks. We present results averaged into two groups, cpu-intensive (cpu) and memory-intensive (mem) benchmarks.

SPEC CINT2006. We benchmark the official applications running with the first *reference* input, reporting results averaged across all benchmarks. Similarly to PARSEC, we separately present cpu-intensive (cpu) and memory-intensive (mem) applications.

SPECweb09. We benchmark the e-banking workload running on the Nginx 1.0.1 web server with an external FastCGI PHP 5.2.6 module and APC 3.0.19 PHP opcode cache. We disable connection encryption (SSL) when running SPECweb09 to allow for better comparison to the Web Frontend workload.

TPC-C. We benchmark the TPC-C workload on a commercial enterprise database management system (DBMS). The database load is generated by 32 clients configured with zero think time and running on a separate machine. The TPC-C database has 40 warehouses. The DBMS is configured with a 3GB buffer pool and direct I/O.

TPC-E. We benchmark the TPC-E 1.12 workload on a commercial enterprise database management system (DBMS). The client driver runs on the same machine, bound to a core that is not used by the database software. The TPC-E database contains 5000 customer records (52GB). The DBMS is configured with a 10GB buffer pool.

Web Backend. We benchmark a machine executing the database backend of the Web Frontend benchmark presented above. The backend machine runs the MySQL 5.5.9 database engine with a 2GB buffer pool.

3.4 I/O infrastructure

Data-intensive scale-out workloads and traditional database server workloads exhibit a significant amount of disk I/O, with a large fraction of the non-sequential read and write accesses scattered throughout the storage space. If the underlying I/O bandwidth is limited, either in raw bandwidth or in I/O operation throughput, the I/O latency is exposed to the system, resulting in an I/O-bound workload where the CPU is underutilized and the application performance unnecessarily suffers.

To isolate the CPU behavior of the applications, our experimental setup over-provisions the I/O subsystem to avoid an I/O bottleneck. To avoid bringing up disk arrays containing hundreds of disks and flash devices, as it is traditionally done with large-scale database installations [44], we construct a network-attached iSCSI storage array by creating large RAM disks in separate machines and connect the machine under test to the iSCSI storage

1. In the processors we study, we measure the occupancy statistics of the *super queue* structure, which tracks all accesses that miss in the L1 caches.

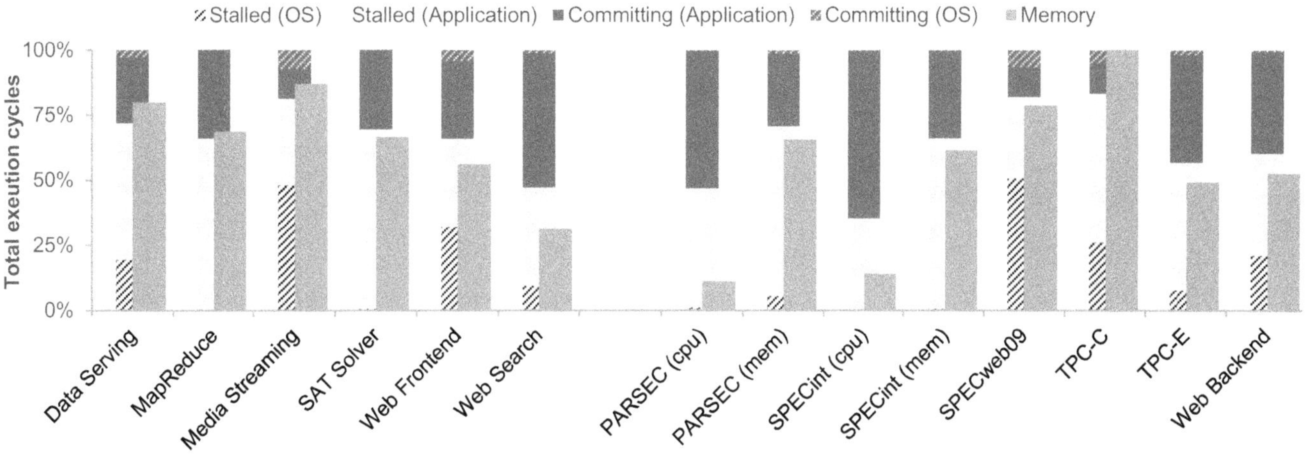

Figure 1. Execution-time breakdown and memory cycles of scale-out workloads (left) and traditional benchmarks (right).

via the high-speed ethernet network. This approach places the entire dataset of our applications in the memory of the remote machines, creating an illusion of a large disk cluster with extremely high I/O bandwidth and low latency.

4 Results

We begin exploring the micro-architectural behavior of scale-out workloads through examining the commit-time execution breakdown in Figure 1. We classify each cycle of execution as *Committing* if at least one instruction was committed during that cycle or as *Stalled* otherwise. Overlapped with the execution-time breakdown, we show the *Memory* cycles bar, which approximates the number of cycles when the processor could not commit instructions due to outstanding long-latency memory accesses.

The execution-time breakdown of scale-out workloads is dominated by stalls in both application code and operating system. Notably, most of the stalls in scale-out workloads arise due to long-latency memory accesses. This behavior is in contrast to the cpu-intensive desktop (SPECint) and parallel (PARSEC) benchmarks, which stall execution significantly less than 50% of the cycles and experience only a fraction of the stalls due to memory accesses. Furthermore, although the execution-time breakdown of some scale-out workloads (e.g., MapReduce and SAT Solver) appears similar to the memory-intensive PARSEC and SPECint benchmarks, the nature of the stalls of these workloads is different. Unlike the scale-out workloads, many PARSEC and SPECint applications frequently stall due to pipeline flushes after wrong-path instructions, with much of the memory access time not on the critical path of execution.

Scale-out workloads show memory system behavior that more closely matches traditional online transaction processing workloads (TPC-C, TPC-E, and Web Backend). However, we observe that scale-out workloads differ considerably from traditional online transaction processing (TPC-C) which spends over 80% of the time stalled due to dependent memory accesses.[2] We find that scale-out workloads are most similar to the more recent transaction processing benchmarks (TPC-E and Web Backend) that use more complex data schemas or perform more complex queries than traditional transaction processing. We also observe that a traditional enterprise web workload (SPECweb09) behaves differently from the Web Frontend workload, representative of modern scale-out configurations. While the traditional web workload is dominated by serving static files and a small number of dynamic scripts, modern scalable web workloads like Web Frontend handle a much higher fraction of dynamic requests, leading to higher core utilization and less OS involvement.

Although the behavior across scale-out workloads is similar, the class of scale-out workloads as a whole differs significantly from other workloads. Processor architectures optimized for desktop and parallel applications are not optimized for scale-out workloads that spend the majority of their time waiting for cache misses, resulting in a clear micro-architectural mismatch. At the same time, architectures designed for workloads that perform only trivial computation and spend all of their time waiting on memory (e.g., SPECweb09 and TPC-C) also cannot cater to scale-out workloads. In the rest of this section, we provide a detailed analysis of the inefficiencies of running scale-out workloads on modern processors.

4.1 Frontend inefficiencies

- *Cores idle due to high instruction-cache miss rates*
- *L2 caches increase average I-fetch latency*
- *Excessive LLC capacity leads to long I-fetch latency*

Instruction-fetch stalls play a critical role in system performance by preventing the core from making forward progress due to a lack of instructions to execute. Frontend stalls serve as a fundamental source of inefficiency for both area and power, as the core real-estate and power consumption are entirely wasted for the cycles that the frontend spends fetching instructions.

Figure 2 presents the L1-I and L2 instruction miss rates of our workloads. We find that, in contrast to desktop and parallel benchmarks, the instruction working sets of many scale-out workloads considerably exceed the L1-I cache capacity, resembling the instruction-cache behavior of traditional server workloads. Moreover, the instruction working sets of most scale-out workloads also exceed the L2 cache capacity, where even relatively infrequent instruction misses incur considerable performance penalties.

We note that the operating system behavior differs between the scale-out workloads and traditional server systems. Although many scale-out workloads actively use the operating system, the functionality exercised by the scale-out workloads is more restricted. Both L1-I and L2 operating system instruction cache miss rates across the scale-out workloads are lower compared to traditional server workloads, indicating a smaller operating system instruction working set in scale-out workloads.

Stringent access-latency requirements of the L1-I caches preclude increasing the size of the caches to capture the instruction working set of many scale-out workloads, which is an order of magnitude larger than the caches found in modern processors. We

2. In addition to instructions and data, TPC-C includes 14% Request-For-Ownership memory cycles. These accesses are not on the critical path, but are part of the memory cycles that appear in Figure 1.

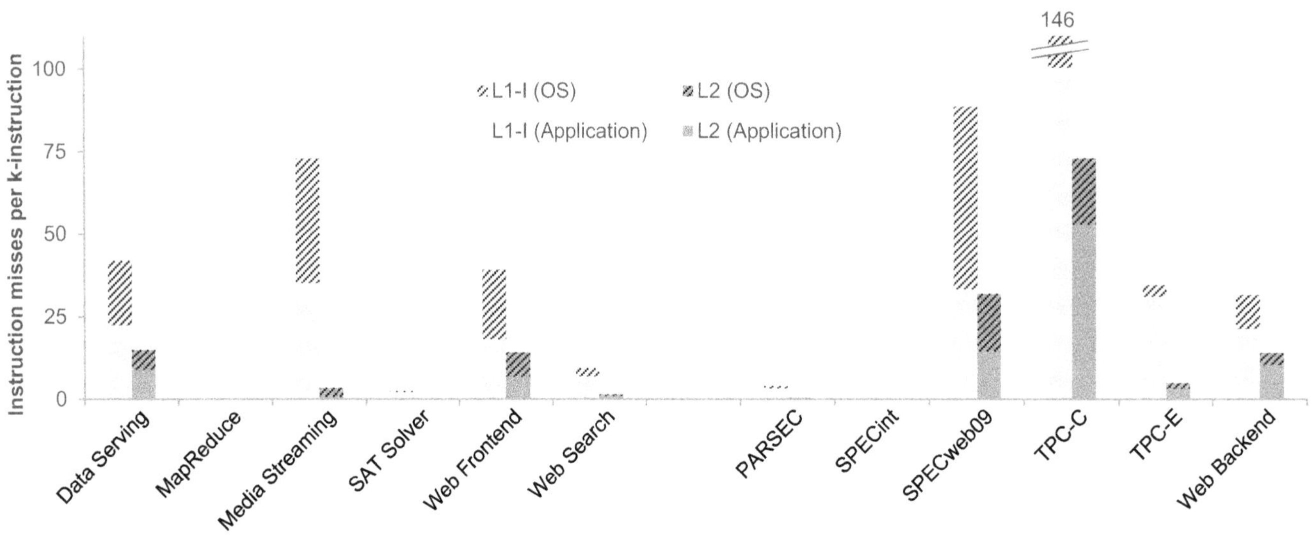

Figure 2. L1-I and L2 instruction cache miss rates for scale-out workloads (left) and traditional benchmarks (right). The OS bars present the instruction cache miss rates of the workloads that spend significant time executing operating system code.

find that modern processor architectures cannot tolerate the latency of L1-I cache misses, avoiding frontend stalls only for applications whose entire instruction working set fits into the L1 cache. Furthermore, the high L2 instruction miss rates indicate that the L1-I capacity experiences a significant shortfall and cannot be mitigated by the addition of a modestly-sized L2 cache.

The disparity between the needs of the scale-out workloads and the processor architecture are apparent in the instruction-fetch path. Although exposed instruction-fetch stalls serve as a key source of inefficiency under any circumstances, the instruction-fetch path of modern processors actually exacerbates the problem. The L2 cache experiences high instruction miss rates, increasing the average fetch latency of the missing fetch requests by placing an additional intermediate lookup structure on the path to retrieving instruction blocks from the LLC. Moreover, the entire instruction working set of any scale-out workload is considerably smaller than the LLC capacity. However, because the LLC is a large cache with a large uniform access latency, it contributes an unnecessarily large instruction-fetch penalty (29 cycles to access the 12MB cache).

Implications To improve efficiency and reduce frontend stalls, processors built for scale-out workloads must bring instructions closer to the cores. Rather than relying on a deep hierarchy of caches, a partitioned organization that replicates instructions and makes them available close to the requesting cores [21] is likely to considerably reduce frontend stalls. To effectively use the on-chip real-estate, the system would need to share the partitioned instruction caches among multiple cores, striking a balance between the die area dedicated to replicating instruction blocks and the latency of accessing these blocks from the closest cores.

Furthermore, although modern processors include next-line prefetchers, high instruction-cache miss rates and significant frontend stalls indicate that the prefetchers are ineffective for scale-out workloads. Scale-out workloads are written in high-level languages, use third-party libraries, and execute operating system code, exhibiting complex non-sequential access patterns that are not captured by simple next-line prefetchers. Including instruction prefetchers that predict these complex patterns is likely to improve overall processor efficiency by eliminating wasted cycles due to frontend stalls.

4.2 Core inefficiencies

- *Low ILP precludes effectively using the full core width*
- *ROB and LSQ are underutilized due to low MLP*

Modern processors execute instructions out of order to enable simultaneous execution of multiple independent instructions per cycle. Additionally, out-of-order execution elides stalls due to memory accesses by executing independent instructions that follow a memory reference while the long-latency cache access is in progress. Modern processors support up to 128-instruction windows, with the *width* of the processor dictating the number of instructions that can simultaneously execute in one cycle.

In addition to exploiting ILP, large instruction windows can exploit memory-level parallelism (MLP) by finding independent memory-accesses within the instruction window and performing the memory accesses in parallel. The latency of LLC hits and off-chip memory accesses cannot be hidden by out-of-order execution; achieving high MLP is therefore key to achieving high core utilization by reducing the data access latency.

Modern processors use 4-wide cores that can decode, issue, execute, and commit up to four instructions on each cycle. However, in practice, instruction-level parallelism (ILP) is limited by dependencies. The *Baseline* bars in Figure 3 (left) show the average number of instructions committed per cycle when running on an aggressive 4-wide out-of-order core. Despite the abundant availability of core resources and functional units, scale-out workloads achieve a modest application IPC, typically in the range of 0.6 (Media Streaming) to 1.1 (Web Frontend). Although workloads that can benefit from wide cores exist, with some cpu-intensive PARSEC and SPECint applications reaching an IPC of 2.0 (indicated by the range bars in the figure), using wide processors for scale-out applications does not yield significant benefit.

Modern processors have 48-entry load-store queues, enabling up to 48 memory-reference instructions in the 128-instruction window. However, just as instruction dependencies limit ILP, address dependencies limit MLP. The *Baseline* bars in Figure 3 (right) present the MLP, ranging from 1.4 (Web Frontend) to 2.3 (SAT Solver) for the scale-out workloads. These results indicate that the memory accesses in scale-out workloads are replete with complex dependencies, limiting the MLP that can be found by modern aggressive processors. We again note that while desktop and parallel applications can use high-MLP support, with some PARSEC and SPECint applications having an MLP up to 5.0, support for

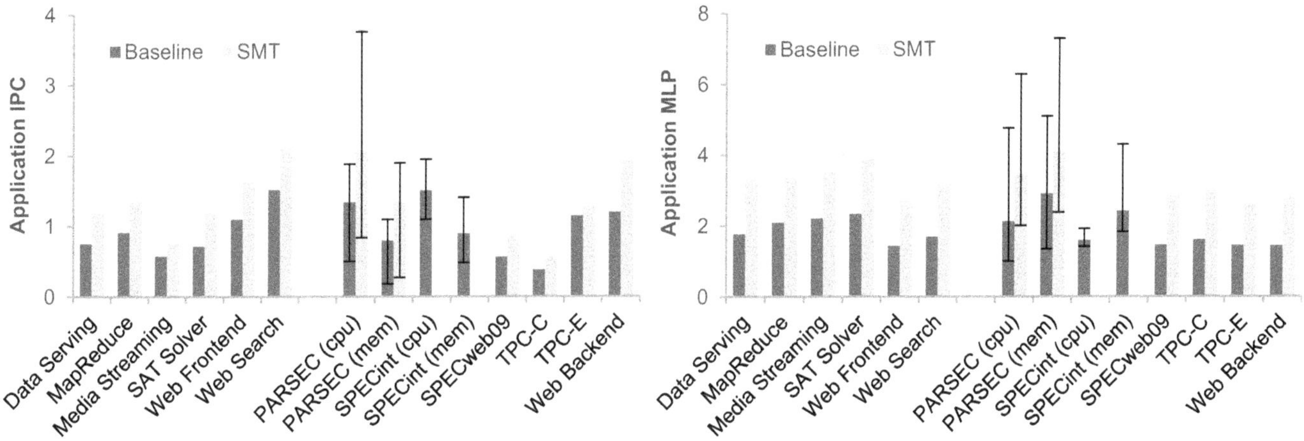

Figure 3. Application instructions committed per cycle for systems with and without SMT, out of a maximum IPC of 4 (left) and memory-level parallelism for systems with and without SMT (right). Range bars indicate the minimum and maximum of the corresponding group.

high MLP is not useful for scale-out applications. However, we find that scale-out workloads generally exhibit higher MLP than traditional server workloads.

Support for 4-wide out-of-order execution with a 128-instruction window and up to 48 outstanding memory requests requires multiple-branch prediction, numerous ALUs, forwarding paths, many-port register banks, large instruction schedulers, highly-associative reorder buffers (ROB) and load-store queues (LSQ), and many other complex on-chip structures. The complexity of the cores limits core count, leading to chip designs with several cores that consume half of the available on-chip real-estate and dissipate the vast majority of the chip's dynamic power budget. However, our results indicate that scale-out workloads exhibit low ILP and MLP, deriving benefit only from a small degree of out-of-order execution. As a result, the nature of scale-out workloads cannot effectively utilize the available core resources. Both the die area and the energy are wasted, leading to data-center inefficiency. Entire buildings are packed with aggressive cores, designed to commit 4 instructions per cycle with over 48 outstanding memory requests, but executing applications with an average IPC of 0.8 and average MLP of 1.9. Moreover, current industry trends point toward greater inefficiency in the future; over the past two decades, processors have gradually moved to increasingly complex cores, raising the core width from 2-way to 4-way and increasing the window size from 20 to 128 instructions.

The inefficiency of modern cores running applications without abundant IPC and MLP has led to the addition of simultaneous multi-threading (SMT) to the processor cores to enable the core resources to be simultaneously shared by multiple software threads, thereby guaranteeing that independent instructions are available to exploit parallelism. We present the IPC and MLP of an SMT-enabled core in Figure 3 using the bars labeled *SMT*. As expected, the MLP found and exploited by the cores when two independent application threads run on each core concurrently is nearly doubled compared to the system without SMT. Unlike traditional database server workloads that contain many inter-thread dependencies and locks, the independent nature of threads in scale-out workloads enables them to observe considerable performance benefits from SMT, with 39-69% improvements in IPC.

Implications The nature of scale-out workloads makes them ideal candidates to exploit multi-threaded multi-core architectures. Modern mainstream processors offer excessively complex cores, resulting in inefficiency through waste of resources. At the same time, our results corroborate prior work [38], indicating that niche processors offer excessively simple (e.g., in-order [8, 29]) cores that cannot leverage the available ILP and MLP in scale-out workloads. We find that scale-out workloads would be well-suited by architectures offering multiple independent threads per core with a modest degree of superscalar out-of-order execution and support for several simultaneously-outstanding memory accesses. For example, rather than implementing SMT on a 4-way core, two independent 2-way cores would consume fewer resources while achieving higher aggregate performance. Furthermore, each narrower core would not require a large instruction window, reducing the per-core area and power consumption compared to modern processors and enabling higher compute density by integrating more cores per chip.

4.3 Data-access inefficiencies

- *Large LLC consumes area, but does not improve performance*
- *Simple data prefetchers are ineffective*

More than half of commodity processor die area is dedicated to the memory system. Modern processors feature a three-level cache hierarchy where the last-level cache (LLC) is a large-capacity cache shared among all cores. To enable high-bandwidth data fetch, each core can have up to 16 L2 cache misses in flight. The high-bandwidth on-chip interconnect enables cache-coherent communication between the cores. To mitigate the capacity and latency gap between the L2 caches and LLC, each L2 cache is equipped with prefetchers that can issue prefetch requests into the LLC and off-chip memory. Multiple DDR3 memory channels provide high-bandwidth access to off-chip memory.

The LLC is the largest on-chip structure; its cache capacity has been increasing with each processor generation due to semiconductor manufacturing improvements. We investigate the utility of growing the LLC capacity for scale-out workloads in Figure 4. We plot the average system performance[3] of scale-out workloads as a function of the LLC capacity, normalized to a baseline system with a 12MB LLC. Unlike in the memory-intensive desktop applications (e.g., SPECint mcf), we find minimal performance sensitivity to LLC size above 4-6MBs in scale-out and traditional server workloads. The LLC captures the instruction working sets of scale-out workloads, which are less than two megabytes. Beyond this point, small shared supporting structures may consume another one to two megabytes. Because scale-out workloads operate on massive data sets and service a large number of concurrent requests, both the dataset and the per-client data are orders of magnitude larger than the available on-chip cache capacity. As a result,

3. User-IPC has been shown to be proportional to application throughput [47]. We verified this relationship for the scale-out workloads.

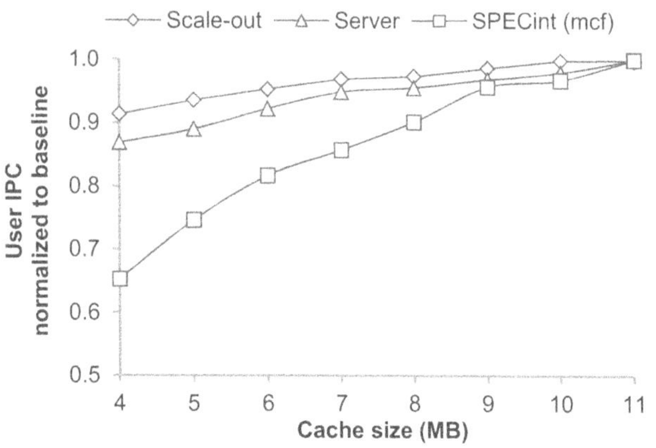

Figure 4. Performance sensitivity to LLC capacity.

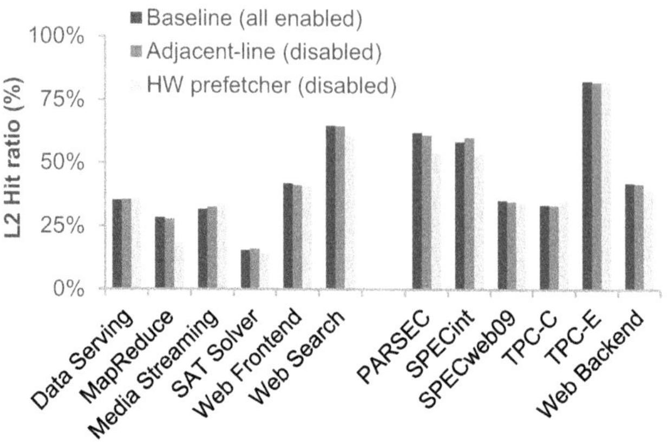

Figure 5. L2 hit ratios of a system with enabled and disabled adjacent-line and HW prefetchers.

an LLC that captures the instruction working set and minor supporting data structures achieves nearly the same performance as an LLC with double or triple the capacity.

Our results show that the on-chip resources devoted to the LLC are one of the key limiters of cloud-application compute density in modern processors. For traditional workloads, increasing the LLC capacity captures the working set of a broader range of applications, contributing to improved performance due to a reduction in average memory latency for those applications. However, because the LLC capacity already exceeds the cloud-application requirements by 2-3x, whereas the next working set exceeds any possible SRAM cache capacity, the majority of the die area and power currently dedicated to the LLC is wasted. Moreover, prior research [22] has shown that increases in the LLC capacity that do not capture a working set lead to an overall performance degradation—LLC access latency is high due to its large capacity, not only wasting on-chip resources, but also penalizing all L2 cache misses by slowing down LLC hits and delaying off-chip accesses.

In addition to leveraging MLP to overlap demand requests from the processor core, modern processors use prefetching to speculatively increase MLP. Prefetching has been shown effective at reducing cache miss rates by predicting block addresses that will be referenced in the future and bringing these blocks into the cache prior to the processor's demand, thereby hiding the access latency. In Figure 5, we present the hit ratios of the L2 cache when all available prefetchers are enabled (Baseline), as well as the hit ratios after disabling the prefetchers. We observe a noticeable degradation of the L2 hit ratios of many desktop and parallel applications when the adjacent-line prefetcher and L2 HW prefetcher are disabled. In contrast, only one of the scale-out workloads (MapReduce) significantly benefits from these prefetchers, with the majority of the workloads experiencing negligible changes in the cache hit rate. Moreover, similar to traditional server workloads (TPC-C), disabling the prefetchers results in an increase in the hit ratio for some scale-out workloads (Media Streaming, SAT Solver). Finally, we note that the DCU streamer (not shown) provides no benefit to scale-out workloads, in some cases marginally increasing the L2 miss rate because it pollutes the cache with unnecessary blocks.

Implications While modern processors grossly over-provision the memory system, data-center efficiency can be improved by matching the processor design to the needs of the scale-out workloads. Whereas modern processors dedicate approximately half of the die area to the LLC, scale-out workloads would likely benefit from a different balance. A two-level cache hierarchy with a modestly sized LLC that makes special provision for caching instruction blocks would benefit performance. The reduced LLC capacity along with the removal of the ineffective L2 cache would offer access-latency benefits while at the same time freeing up die area and power. The die area and power can be practically applied toward improving compute density and efficiency by adding more hardware contexts and more advanced prefetchers. Additional hardware contexts (more threads per core and more cores) should linearly increase application parallelism, while more advanced correlating data prefetchers could accurately prefetch complex access data patterns and increase the performance of all cores.

4.4 Bandwidth inefficiencies

- *Lack of data sharing deprecates coherence and connectivity*
- *Off-chip bandwidth exceeds needs by an order of magnitude*

Increasing core counts have brought parallel programming into the mainstream, highlighting the need for fast and high-bandwidth inter-core communication. Multi-threaded applications comprise a collection of threads that work in tandem to scale up the application performance. To enable effective scale-up, each subsequent generation of processors offers a larger core count and improves the on-chip connectivity to support faster and higher-bandwidth core-to-core communication.

We investigate the utility of the on-chip interconnect for scale-out workloads in Figure 6. We plot the fraction of L2 misses that access data most recently written by another thread running on a remote core, breaking down each bar into *Application* and *OS* components to offer insight into the source of the data sharing.

In general, we observe limited read-write sharing across the scale-out workloads. We find that the OS-level data sharing is dominated by the network subsystem. Multi-threaded Java-based applications (Data Serving and Web Search) exhibit a small degree of sharing from the use of a parallel garbage collector that may run a collection thread on a remote core, artificially inducing application-level communication. Additionally, we found that the Media Streaming server updates global counters to track the total number of packets sent by the server; reducing the amount of communication by keeping per-thread statistics is trivial and would eliminate the mutex lock and shared-object scalability bottleneck. We note that the on-chip application-level communication in scale-out workloads is distinctly different from traditional database server workloads (TPC-C, TPC-E, and Web Backend), which experience frequent interaction between threads on actively shared data structures that are used to service client requests.

The low degree of active sharing indicates that wide and low-latency interconnects available in modern processors are over-provisioned for scale-out workloads. Although the overhead with a small number of cores is limited, as the number of cores on chip increases, the area and energy overhead of enforcing coherence becomes significant. Likewise, the area overheads and power con-

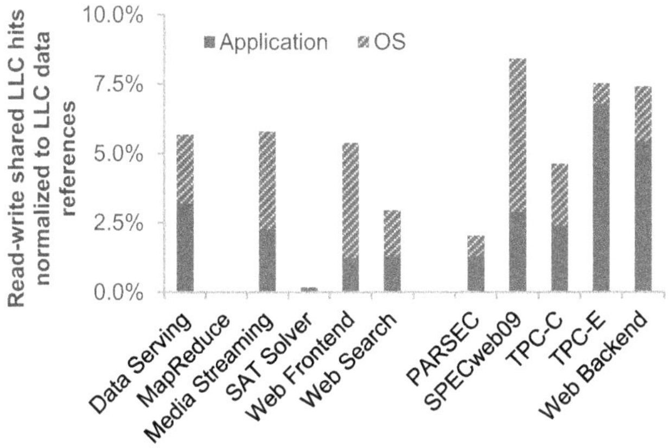

Figure 6. Percentage of LLC data references accessing cache blocks modified by a thread running on a remote core.

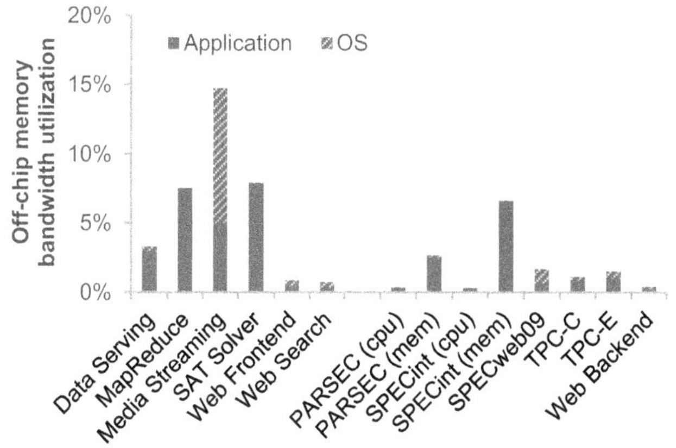

Figure 7. Average off-chip memory bandwidth utilization as a percentage of available off-chip bandwidth.

sumption of an over-provisioned high-bandwidth interconnect further increase processor inefficiency.

Beyond the on-chip interconnect, we also find off-chip bandwidth inefficiency. While the off-chip memory latency has improved slowly, off-chip bandwidth has been improving at a rapid pace. Over the course of two decades, the memory bus speeds have increased from 66MHz to dual-data-rate at over 1GHz, raising the peak theoretical bandwidth from 544MB/s to 17GB/s per channel, with the latest server processors having four independent memory channels. In Figure 7, we plot the per-core off-chip bandwidth utilization of our workloads as a fraction of the available per-core off-chip bandwidth. Scale-out workloads experience non-negligible off-chip miss rates, however, the MLP of the applications is low due to the complex data structure dependencies, leading to low aggregate off-chip bandwidth utilization even when all cores have outstanding off-chip memory accesses. Among the scale-out workloads we examine, Media Streaming is the only application that uses up to 15% of the available off-chip bandwidth. However, we note that our applications are configured to stress the processor, demonstrating the worst-case behavior. Overall, we find that modern processors significantly over-provision off-chip bandwidth for scale-out workloads.

Implications The on-chip interconnect and off-chip memory buses can be scaled back to improve processor efficiency. Because the scale-out workloads perform only infrequent communication via the network, there is typically no read-write sharing in the applications; processors can therefore be designed as a collection of core islands using a low-bandwidth interconnect that does not enforce coherence between the islands, eliminating the power associated with the high-bandwidth interconnect as well as the power and area overheads of fine-grained coherence tracking. Off-chip memory buses can be optimized for scale-out workloads by scaling back unnecessary bandwidth. Memory controllers consume a large fraction of the chip area and memory buses are responsible for a large fraction of the system power. Reducing the number of memory channels and the power draw of the memory buses should improve scale-out workload efficiency without affecting application performance.

5 Related Work

Previous research has characterized the micro-architectural behavior of traditional commercial server applications when running on modern hardware, using real machines [1, 28] and simulation environments [21, 22, 34, 36]. We include traditional server applications in our study to compare them with scale-out workloads and to validate our evaluation framework.

The research community uses the PARSEC benchmark suite to perform experiments with chip multiprocessors [4]. Bienia et al. characterize the PARSEC suite's working sets and the communication patterns among threads [4]. In our work, we examine the execution time breakdown of PARSEC. Unlike the scale-out and traditional server applications, PARSEC has a negligible instruction working set and exhibits a high degree of memory-level parallelism, displaying distinctly different micro-architectural behavior compared to scale-out workloads.

Previous research analyzed various performance or power inefficiencies of modern processors running traditional commercial applications [8, 19, 22, 29, 37, 45, 46]. Tuck and Tullsen showed that simultaneous multithreading can improve performance of scientific and engineering applications by 20-25% on a Pentium4 processor [45]. Our results show similar trends for scale-out workloads. Kgil et al. [29] show that, for a particular class of throughput-oriented web workloads, modern processors are extremely power inefficient, arguing that the chip area should be used for processing cores rather than caches. A similar observation has been made in the GPU domain [18]. Our results corroborate these findings, showing that, for scale-out workloads, the time spent accessing the large and slow last-level caches accounts for more than half of the data stalls [22], calling for resizing and reorganizing the cache hierarchy. We draw similar conclusions to Davis et al. [8] and Hardavellas et al. [22] who showed that heavily multithreaded in-order cores are more efficient for throughput-oriented workloads compared to aggressive out-of-order cores. Ranganathan and Jouppi motivate the need for integrated analysis of micro-architectural efficiency and application service-level agreements in their survey of enterprise information technology trends [37]. To address the power inefficiencies of current general-purpose processors, specialization at various hardware levels has been proposed [19, 46].

As cloud computing has become ubiquitous, there has been significant research activity on characterizing particular scale-out workloads, either micro-architecturally [38, 42], or at the system level [7, 30, 31, 32, 41]. To the best of our knowledge, our study is the first work to systematically characterize the micro-architectural behavior of a wide range of cloud services. Kozyrakis et al. [30] presented a system-wide characterization of large-scale online services provided by Microsoft and showed the implications of such workloads on data-center server design. Reddi et al. [38] characterized the Bing search engine, showing that the computational intensity of search tasks is increasing as a result of adding more machine learning features to the engine. These findings are consistent with our results, which show that web search has the highest IPC among the studied scale-out workloads.

Much work focused on benchmarking the cloud and datacenter infrastructure. The Yahoo! Cloud Serving Benchmark (YCSB) [7] is a framework to benchmark large-scale distributed data serving systems. We include results for the YCSB benchmark and provide its micro-architectural characterization running on Cassandra, a popular cloud database. Fan et al. discuss web mail, web search, and map-reduce as three representative workloads present in the Google datacenter [16]. Lim et al. extend this set of benchmarks and add an additional media streaming workload [33]. They further analyze the energy efficiency of a variety of systems when running these applications. Our benchmark suite similarly includes workloads from these categories.

CloudCmp [31, 32] is a framework to compare cloud providers using a systematic approach to benchmarking various components of the infrastructure. Huang et al. analyzed performance and power characteristics of Hadoop clusters using HiBench [25], a benchmark that specifically targets the Hadoop map-reduce framework. Our MapReduce benchmark uses the same infrastructure. However, we provide the micro-architectural, rather than a system-wide, characterization of the map-reduce workload. For benchmarking modern web technologies, we use CloudStone [40], an open source benchmark that simulates activities related to social events.

6 Conclusions

Cloud computing has emerged as a dominant computing platform to provide hundreds of millions of users with online services. To support the growing popularity and continue expanding their services, cloud providers must work to overcome the physical space and power constraints limiting data-center growth. While strides have been made to improve data-center efficiency at the rack and chassis-levels, we observe that the predominant processor micro-architecture of today's data centers is inherently inefficient for running scale-out workloads, resulting in low compute density and poor trade-offs between performance and energy.

In this work, we used performance counters to analyze the micro-architectural behavior of a wide range of scale-out workloads. We analyzed and identified the key sources of area and power inefficiency in the instruction fetch, core micro-architecture, and memory system organization. We then identified the specific needs of scale-out workloads and suggested the architectural modifications that can lead to dense and power-efficient data-center processor designs in the future. Specifically, our analysis showed that efficiently executing scale-out workloads requires optimizing the instruction-fetch path for multi-megabyte instruction working sets, reducing the core aggressiveness and last-level cache capacity to free area and power resources in favor of more cores each with more hardware threads, and scaling back the over-provisioned on-chip and off-chip bandwidth.

Acknowledgements

The authors would like to thank the anonymous reviewers for their feedback and suggestions. We thank the PARSA lab for continual support and feedback, in particular Pejman Lotfi-Kamran and Javier Picorel for their assistance with the SPECweb09 and the SAT Solver benchmarks. We thank the DSLab for their assistance with Cloud9, Emre Özer and Rustam Miftakhutdinov for their feedback and suggestions, and Aamer Jaleel and Carole Jean-Wu for their assistance with understanding the Intel architecture and configuration. We thank the EuroCloud project partners for advocating and inspiring the CloudSuite benchmark suite. This work was partially supported by EuroCloud, Project No 247779 of the European Commission 7th RTD Framework Programme – Information and Communication Technologies: Computing Systems.

References

[1] Anastassia Ailamaki, David J. DeWitt, Mark D. Hill, and David A. Wood. DBMSs on a modern processor: where does time go? In *Proceedings of the 25th International Conference on Very Large Data Bases*, September 1999.

[2] Alexa, The Web Information Company. http://www.alexa.com/.

[3] Apache Mahout: scalable machine-learning and data-mining library. http://mahout.apache.org/.

[4] Christian Bienia, Sanjeev Kumar, Jaswinder Pal Singh, and Kai Li. The PARSEC benchmark suite: characterization and architectural implications. In *Proceedings of the 17th International Conference on Parallel Architectures and Compilation Techniques*, October 2008.

[5] Fay Chang, Jeffrey Dean, Sanjay Ghemawat, Wilson C. Hsieh, Deborah A. Wallach, Mike Burrows, Tushar Chandra, Andrew Fikes, and Robert E. Gruber. Bigtable: a distributed storage system for structured data. In *Proceedings of the 7th USENIX Symposium on Operating Systems Design and Implementation*, volume 7, November 2006.

[6] Liviu Ciortea, Cristian Zamfir, Stefan Bucur, Vitaly Chipounov, and George Candea. Cloud9: a software testing service. *ACM SIGOPS Operating Systems Review*, 43:5–10, January 2010.

[7] Brian F. Cooper, Adam Silberstein, Erwin Tam, Raghu Ramakrishnan, and Russell Sears. Benchmarking cloud serving systems with YCSB. In *Proceedings of the 1st ACM Symposium on Cloud Computing*, June 2010.

[8] John D. Davis, James Laudon, and Kunle Olukotun. Maximizing CMP throughput with mediocre cores. In *Proceedings of the 14th International Conference on Parallel Architectures and Compilation Techniques*, September 2005.

[9] Jeffrey Dean and Sanjay Ghemawat. MapReduce: simplified data processing on large clusters. In *Proceedings of the 6th Conference on Symposium on Operating Systems Design & Implementation*, volume 6, November 2004.

[10] Giuseppe DeCandia, Deniz Hastorun, Madan Jampani, Gunavardhan Kakulapati, Avinash Lakshman, Alex Pilchin, Swaminathan Sivasubramanian, Peter Vosshall, and Werner Vogels. Dynamo: Amazon's highly available key-value store. In *Proceedings of the 21st ACM SIGOPS Symposium on Operating Systems Principles*, October 2007.

[11] PowerEdge M1000e Blade Enclosure. http://www.dell.com/us/enterprise/p/poweredge-m1000e/pd.aspx.

[12] Hadi Esmaeilzadeh, Emily Blem, Renee St. Amant, Karthikeyan Sankaralingam, and Doug Burger. Dark silicon and the end of multicore scaling. In *Proceeding of the 38th Annual International Symposium on Computer Architecture*, June 2011.

[13] EuroCloud Server. http://www.eurocloudserver.com.

[14] Stijn Eyerman, Lieven Eeckhout, Tejas Karkhanis, and James E. Smith. A performance counter architecture for computing accurate CPI components. In *Proceedings of the 12th International Conference on Architectural Support for Programming Languages and Operating Systems*, October 2006.

[15] Facebook Statistics. https://www.facebook.com/press/info.php?statistics.

[16] Xiaobo Fan, Wolf-Dietrich Weber, and Luiz André Barroso. Power provisioning for a warehouse-sized computer. In *Proceedings of the 34th Annual International Symposium on Computer Architecture*, June 2007.

[17] Google Data Centers. http://www.google.com/intl/en/corporate/datacenter/.

[18] Zvika Guz, Oved Itzhak, Idit Keidar, Avinoam Kolod, Avi Mendelson, and Uri C. Weiser. Threads vs. Caches: modeling the behavior of parallel workloads. In *International Conference on Computer Design*, October 2010.

[19] Rehan Hameed, Wajahat Qadeer, Megan Wachs, Omid Azizi, Alex Solomatnikov, Benjamin C. Lee, Stephen Richardson, Christos Kozyrakis, and Mark Horowitz. Understanding sources of inefficiency in general-purpose chips. In *Proceedings of the 37th Annual International Symposium on Computer Architecture*, June 2010.

[20] Nikos Hardavellas, Michael Ferdman, Anastasia Ailamaki, and Babak Falsafi. Toward Dark Silicon in Servers. In *IEEE Micro*, 31(4):6–15, July-Aug, 2011.

[21] Nikos Hardavellas, Michael Ferdman, Babak Falsafi, and Anastasia Ailamaki. Reactive NUCA: near-optimal block placement and replication in distributed caches. In *Proceedings of the 36th Annual International Symposium on Computer Architecture*, June 2009.

[22] Nikos Hardavellas, Ippokratis Pandis, Ryan Johnson, Naju Mancheril, Anastassia Ailamaki, and Babak Falsafi. Database servers on chip multiprocessors: limitations and opportunities. In *The 3rd Biennial Conference on Innovative Data Systems Research*, January 2007.

[23] Faban Harness and Benchmark Framework. http://java.net/projects/faban/.

[24] Mark Horowitz, Elad Alon, Dinesh Patil, Samuel Naffziger, Rajesh Kumar, and Kerry Bernstein. Scaling, power, and the future of CMOS. In *Electron Devices Meeting, 2005. IEDM Technical Digest. IEEE International*, December 2005.

[25] Shengsheng Huang, Jie Huang, Jinquan Dai, Tao Xie, and Bo Huang. The HiBench benchmark suite: characterization of the MapReduce-based data analysis. In *26th International Conference on Data Engineering Workshops*, March 2010.

[26] Intel VTune Amplifier XE Performance Profiler. http://software.intel.com/en-us/articles/intel-vtune-amplifier-xe/.

[27] Tejas S. Karkhanis and James E. Smith. A first-order superscalar processor model. In *Proceedings of the 31st Annual International Symposium on Computer Architecture*, June 2004.

[28] Kimberly Keeton, David A. Patterson, Yong Qiang He, Roger C. Raphael, and Walter E. Baker. Performance characterization of a quad Pentium Pro SMP using OLTP workloads. In *Proceedings of the 25th Annual International Symposium on Computer Architecture*, June 1998.

[29] Taeho Kgil, Shaun D'Souza, Ali Saidi, Nathan Binkert, Ronald Dreslinski, Trevor Mudge, Steven Reinhardt, and Krisztian Flautner. PicoServer: using 3D stacking technology to enable a compact energy efficient chip multiprocessor. In *Proceedings of the 12th International Conference on Architectural Support for Programming Languages and Operating Systems*, October 2006.

[30] Christos Kozyrakis, Aman Kansal, Sriram Sankar, and Kushagra Vaid. Server engineering insights for large-scale online services. *IEEE Micro*, 30(4):8–19, July-Aug, 2010.

[31] Ang Li, Xiaowei Yang, Srikanth Kandula, and Ming Zhang. CloudCmp: comparing public cloud providers. In *Proceedings of the 10th Annual Conference on Internet Measurement*, November 2010.

[32] Ang Li, Xiaowei Yang, Srikanth Kandula, and Ming Zhang. CloudCMP: Shopping for a cloud made easy. In *Proceedings of the 2nd USENIX Conference on Hot Topics in Cloud Computing*, June 2010.

[33] Kevin Lim, Parthasarathy Ranganathan, Jichuan Chang, Chandrakant Patel, Trevor Mudge, and Steven Reinhardt. Understanding and designing new server architectures for emerging warehouse-computing environments. In *Proceedings of the 35th Annual International Symposium on Computer Architecture*, June 2008.

[34] Jack L. Lo, Luiz André Barroso, Susan J. Eggers, Kourosh Gharachorloo, Henry M. Levy, and Sujay S. Parekh. An analysis of database workload performance on simultaneous multithreaded processors. In *Proceedings of the 25th Annual International Symposium on Computer Architecture*, June 1998.

[35] Open Compute Project. http://opencompute.org/.

[36] Parthasarathy Ranganathan, Kourosh Gharachorloo, Sarita V. Adve, and Luiz André Barroso. Performance of database workloads on shared-memory systems with out-of-order processors. In *Proceedings of the 8th International Conference on Architectural Support for Programming Languages and Operating Systems*, October 1998.

[37] Parthasarathy Ranganathan and Norman Jouppi. Enterprise IT trends and implications for architecture research. In *Proceedings of the 11th International Symposium on High-Performance Computer Architecture*, February 2005.

[38] Vijay Janapa Reddi, Benjamin C. Lee, Trishul Chilimbi, and Kushagra Vaid. Web search using mobile cores: quantifying and mitigating the price of efficiency. In *Proceedings of the 37th Annual International Symposium on Computer Architecture*, June 2010.

[39] SeaMicro Packs 768 Cores Into its Atom Server. http://www.datacenterknowledge.com/archives/2011/07/18/seamicro-packs-768-cores-into-its-atom-server/.

[40] Will Sobel, Shanti Subramanyam, Akara Sucharitakul, Jimmy Nguyen, Hubert Wong, Arthur Klepchukov, Sheetal Patil, Armando Fox, and David Patterson. Cloudstone: multi-platform, multi-language benchmark and measurement tools for web 2.0. In *the 1st Workshop on Cloud Computing and Its Applications*, October 2008.

[41] Vijayaraghavan Soundararajan and Jennifer M. Anderson. The impact of management operations on the virtualized datacenter. In *Proceedings of the 37th Annual International Symposium on Computer Architecture*, June 2010.

[42] Lingjia Tang, Jason Mars, Veil Vachharajani, Robert Hundt, and Mary Lou Soffa. The impact of memory subsystem resource sharing on datacenter applications. In *Proceeding of the 38th Annual International Symposium on Computer Architecture*, June 2011.

[43] The Apache Cassandra Project. http://cassandra.apache.org/.

[44] Transaction Processing Performance Council. http://www.tpc.org/.

[45] Nathan Tuck and Dean M. Tullsen. Initial observations of the simultaneous multithreading Pentium 4 processor. In *Proceedings of the 12th International Conference on Parallel Architectures and Compilation Techniques*, September 2003.

[46] Ganesh Venkatesh, Jack Sampson, Nathan Goulding, Saturnino Garcia, Vladyslav Bryksin, Jose Lugo-Martinez, Steven Swanson, and Michael B. Taylor. Conservation cores: reducing the energy of mature computations. In *Proceedings of the 15th International Conference on Architectural Support for Programming Languages and Operating Systems*, March 2010.

[47] Thomas F. Wenisch, Roland E. Wunderlich, Michael Ferdman, Anastassia Ailamaki, Babak Falsafi, and James C. Hoe. Simflex: Statistical sampling of computer system simulation. *IEEE Micro*, 26:18–31, July 2006.

Iterative Optimization for the Data Center

Yang Chen
SKL Computer Architecture [*], China;
ICT and Graduate School, CAS, China
chenyang@ict.ac.cn

Shuangde Fang
SKL Computer Architecture[*], China;
ICT and Graduate School, CAS, China
fangshuangde@ict.ac.cn

Lieven Eeckhout
Ghent University
Belgium
lieven.eeckhout@elis.UGent.be

Olivier Temam
INRIA, Saclay
France
olivier.temam@inria.fr

Chengyong Wu
SKL Computer Architecture[*], China;
ICT, CAS, China
cwu@ict.ac.cn

Abstract

Iterative optimization is a simple but powerful approach that searches for the best possible combination of compiler optimizations for a given workload. However, each program, if not each data set, potentially favors a different combination. As a result, iterative optimization is plagued by several practical issues that prevent it from being widely used in practice: a large number of runs are required for finding the best combination; the process can be data set dependent; and the exploration process incurs significant overhead that needs to be compensated for by performance benefits. Therefore, while iterative optimization has been shown to have significant performance potential, it is seldomly used in production compilers.

In this paper, we propose Iterative Optimization for the Data Center (IODC): we show that servers and data centers offer a context in which all of the above hurdles can be overcome. The basic idea is to spawn different combinations across workers and recollect performance statistics at the master, which then evolves to the optimum combination of compiler optimizations. IODC carefully manages costs and benefits, and is transparent to the end user.

We evaluate IODC using both MapReduce and throughput compute-intensive server applications. In order to reflect the large number of users interacting with the system, we gather a very large collection of data sets (at least 1000 and up to several million unique data sets per program), for a total storage of 10.7TB, and 568 days of CPU time. We report an average performance improvement of 1.48×, and up to 2.08×, for the MapReduce applications, and 1.14×, and up to 1.39×, for the throughput compute-intensive server applications.

Categories and Subject Descriptors D.3.4 [*Processors*]: Compilers

General Terms Design, Performance

Keywords iterative optimization, compiler, MapReduce, server, data center

[*] State Key Laboratory of Computer Architecture

1. Introduction

Compilers embed a vast set of optimizations, implemented as separate passes of the global optimization strategy. Due to complex interactions among these optimizations as well as with the application software and the underlying architecture, it is exceedingly difficult to find the best combination and parameterization of compiler optimizations. The most aggressive default optimization level, e.g., `-O3` in the GNU C compiler, corresponds to a pre-set combination of compiler optimizations, with each optimization parameterized using simple analytical models or heuristics. However, it has been widely observed that there exist combinations of compiler optimizations that outperform the default optimization levels for many programs by a significant margin. This observation led to iterative optimization [1, 6, 8, 9, 13, 14, 20, 31], which is based on a simple but powerful concept: run a program multiple times, each time compiled with different combinations of compiler optimizations, in order to find the best combination. In spite of the great potential offered by iterative optimization and the significant amount of research done in this area over the past decade, it is still not widely used in (both commercial and public) production compilers, because it is plagued by at least three practical hurdles. (1) In order to find the best combination of compiler optimizations for a given program, many so-called recompilations (for different combinations of compiler optimizations) and training runs (running the recompiled binaries) are required. (2) The costly overhead of recompilation and training runs can easily wipe out the performance benefits of iterative optimization. (3) In most iterative optimization studies, the training runs are performed using the same data set(s), even though, in practice, there is no point for a user to run the same data set multiple times.

In this paper, we demonstrate that servers and data centers offer a context in which all of these hurdles can be overcome, paving the way for practical use of iterative optimization in the data center. We propose Iterative Optimization for the Data Center (IODC), a framework which, to the best of our knowledge, is the first to implement the idea of iterative optimization for the server and warehouse-scale computing domain. The key idea behind IODC is to carefully manage a cost versus benefit trade-off: IODC compensates for the cost of recompilations and training runs through the performance benefist of better performing combinations of compiler optimizations. The strategy operates automatically in the background, and is transparent to the end user, i.e., the user is not aware that training runs nor recompilations occur in the background.

We demonstrate the general applicability of IODC for both MapReduce-style as well as contemporary throughput compute-intensive server applications. We find the MapReduce framework [11] to be a natural fit for IODC. The basic idea is to distribute different combinations of compiler optimizations across *workers*, which perform the recompilations and training runs, and which send performance statistics back to the *master*, which then in turn determines which combination yields the best performance. This process is done repeatedly until the system evolves to the best combination of compiler optimizations. Our experimental results using five MapReduce applications demonstrate an average speedup of 1.48×, and up to 2.08×.

As a second step in the paper, we extend IODC towards non-MapReduce, contemporary throughput compute-intensive server applications. The basic idea here is that the IODC run-time continuously applies the iterative optimization strategy as the program is repeatedly run on the server, possibly over long periods of time. Considering six benchmarks representative of throughput compute-intensive server applications, our strategy achieves an average speedup of 1.14×, and up to 1.39×.

Next to proposing and implementing iterative optimization for the data center, we believe this paper is the first to create realistic conditions for the evaluation of iterative optimization by avoiding data set reuse. We emulate data center operation by considering unique data sets across successive recompilations and training runs, which reflects many independent users interacting with the data center, all leading to different input data sets. In particular, for the MapReduce applications, we consider a very large number of unique data sets, varying between 1.55 million and 310 million unique records; for the server applications, we consider between 28,000 and 177,000 unique data sets, and we use each data set only once through the exploration process. By doing so, we emulate distinct production runs in a real data center.

In this paper, we make the following contributions:

- We propose iterative optimization for the data center (IODC). We believe that this paper is the first, to the best of our knowledge, to implement iterative optimization for warehouse-scale computing.
- We propose a novel online iterative optimization strategy that balances overhead versus benefit, alike a savings account. According to our experimental results, IODC achieves average performance improvements of 1.48×, and up to 2.08×, for a set of MapReduce applications, and 1.14×, and up to 1.39×, for a set of contemporary throughput compute-intensive server applications.
- We emulate realistic conditions in the experimental setup by considering unique data sets, and we demonstrate that IODC can learn good combinations of compiler optimizations across unique data sets. We believe this is the first paper to do so.

The remainder of this paper is organized as follows. In Section 2, we illustrate the performance potential of iterative optimizations and the challenges for applying iterative optimization in practice. In Section 3, we present the IODC strategy. This is done in two steps: we first implement IODC within the MapReduce framework, and we then extend the strategy towards contemporary throughput compute-intensive server applications. After explaining our experimental setup in Section 4, we present the evaluation in Section 5. Finally, we discuss related work in Section 6 and we conclude in Section 7.

2. Motivation

Iterative optimization is a compiler technique that can be applied to any program. Hence, it has the potential of being widely applicable and having broad impact. In particular, given that servers and data centers run the same set of workloads over and over again for many different users, improving performance and/or efficiency by only a small margin may lead to significant performance, energy and cost gains. However, successfully applying iterative optimization in practice is non-trivial. In order to find a good combination of compiler optimizations, many combinations may need to be evaluated because of the complex optimization space. Moreover, for some programs, the best combination may vary across data sets, making it even harder to find a good 'average' combination. Finally, in spite of its high performance potential, the benefits of iterative optimization are not sufficient to tolerate the overhead of a massive number of recompilations and training runs, hence, a careful trade-off between recompiling and training runs versus enjoying performance speedups from iterative optimization is required. In this section, we illustrate and quantify the most important challenges in iterative optimization.

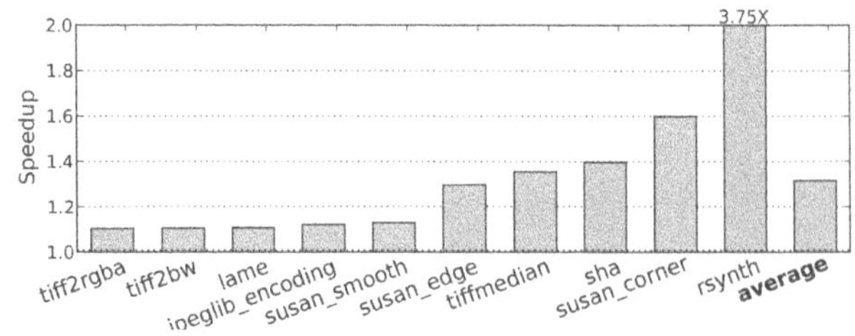

Figure 1. *The performance potential of iterative optimization: The average best performance speedup across 1000 data sets, relative to GCC* `-O3`.

2.1 Iterative optimization: Terminology

However, before doing so, we first introduce some terminology related to iterative optimization. As stated before, iterative optimization tries out a number of combinations of compiler optimizations to find out the best possible combination, or at least a combination that outperforms a compiler's best default optimization level, e.g., GCC's `-O3`. Trying out a combination involves compiling the program with the combination of optimizations, which we refer to as a *recompilation*, and running the compiled binary on real hardware with a given data set, which we refer to as a *training run*. We refer to the *evaluation* of a combination as the process of recompiling, doing the training run, and comparing performance against the compiler's best default optimization level. As will become clear later in the paper, evaluations are done in a way transparent to the end user. To make a distinction between training runs that drive iterative optimization on the one hand, and runs of a program that actually produce user output on the other hand, we refer to the latter as *production runs*.

2.2 Potential of iterative optimization

The performance potential of iterative optimization is substantial, as we will illustrate with the following experiment. We consider a set of 300 combinations, 10 benchmark applications, each with 1000 distinct data sets, and we apply all combinations to all data sets for all benchmark applications, 3 million runs in total. (We refer to Section 4 for a detailed description of the experimental setup.) Then, for each benchmark application and each data set, we select the combination that provides the best performance; subsequently, for each benchmark application, we compute the average best performance across all data sets. The results are reported in Figure 1; the benchmarks are ranked on the horizontal axis by increasing average best performance. The speedup ranges from 1.10× to 3.75×, with an average of 1.31×. These results illustrate the maximum performance that can be achieved using iterative optimization if we had an oracle indicating, for each program and each input data set, what would be the best possible combination of compiler optimizations. The difficulty now is to achieve similar performance improvements in practice.

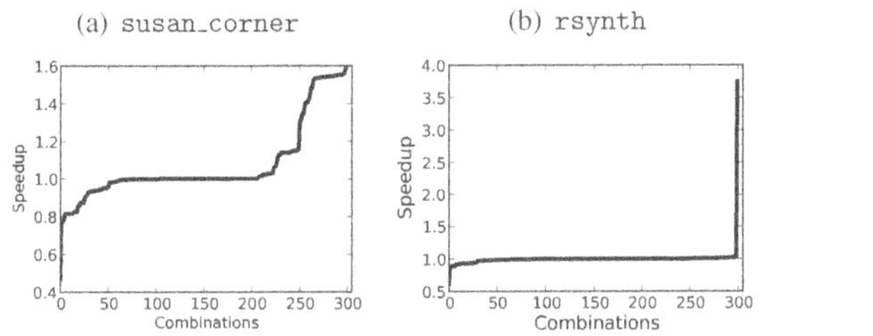

Figure 2. *Cumulative distribution of the average speedup for combinations of compiler optimizations ranked by increasing speedup for (a)* `susan_corner` *and (b)* `rsynth`.

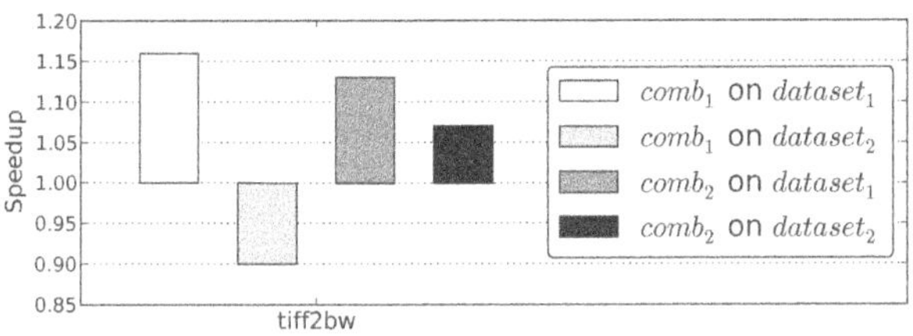

Figure 3. *Demonstrating data set sensitivity for iterative optimization: Applying combinations selected using a data set to another data set for* `tiff2bw`.

2.3 Iterative optimization requires many runs

For some programs, the number of good combinations can be rare, and thus difficult to find, requiring a possibly large number of combinations to evaluate in order to identify the best possible combination(s). Figure 2 illustrates that the number of 'good' combinations varies significantly across programs. For each combination, we average the speedup over 1000 data sets, and we then rank the combinations by increasing average speedup. For `susan_corner`, more than 15% of the combinations yield a speedup of at least 5%, and a few combinations even yield a speedup of 60%. For `rsynth` on the other hand, less than 0.4% of the combinations yield a substantially large speedup. In other words, only a few combinations yield the best possible performance, hence, finding them may require a large number of recompilations and training runs.

2.4 Data set sensitivity

Not only do different programs favor different combinations, also different data sets for the same program may favor different combinations. We illustrate this point in Figure 3 for `tiff2bw`, and two data sets $dataset_1$ and $dataset_2$. For each of these two data sets, we determine the best combination among a set of 300 combinations. $comb_1$ is the best combination for $dataset_1$ (see '$comb_1$ on $dataset_1$'); $comb_2$ is the best combination for $dataset_2$ (see '$comb_2$ on $dataset_2$'). We subsequently apply each combination to the other data set. In some cases, the same combination works (fairly) well for more than one data set, see '$comb_2$ on $dataset_1$' versus '$comb_2$ on $dataset_2$'. However, in other cases, a combination that performs best for one data set may even induce slowdowns for other data sets, see '$comb_1$ on $dataset_2$' versus '$comb_1$ on $dataset_1$'. These results suggest that it is challenging to find a combination that performs well on average across a broad set of data sets. Also, it is to be expected that the 'average' data set changes over time as users come and go and solve different problems. Hence, the best combination that performs well on the average data set must be carefully selected, and the choice must be constantly revisited.

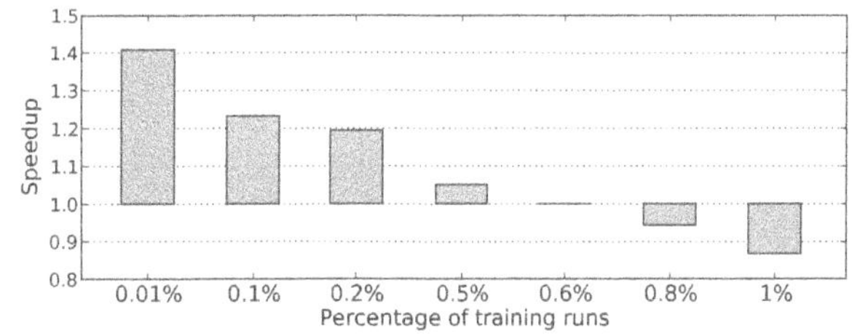

Figure 4. *Impact of training runs on the strategy for* `ann`.

2.5 Overhead/benefit trade-off

In order to explore and compare different combinations of compiler optimizations, programs must be recompiled followed by a training run. While the benefits of iterative optimization can be significant, as demonstrated in the previous sections, they are not sufficient enough to compensate for a careless use of training runs and recompilations. In fact, in order to get any overall performance benefit from iterative optimization, it is essential to find the best possible trade-off between exploring combinations and minimizing training runs and recompilations. In Figure 4, we apply our proposed IODC strategy and vary the total number of evaluations (recompilations plus training runs) as a percentage of the total number of production runs, from 0.01% to 1% for `ann`. Even 0.6% of training runs are enough to wipe out any benefit from iterative optimization, and 1% of training runs results into a slowdown over no iterative optimization by 13%.

2.6 Summary

In conclusion, iterative optimization has significant performance potential, however, achieving it in practice is non-trivial for a number of reasons. (1) A potentially large number of combinations of compiler optimizations may need to be evaluated. (2) Iterative optimization can be data set dependent. (3) A careful balance between benefits and costs is required for iterative optimization to yield overall performance benefits in practice. The data center provides a context in which each of these challenges can be addressed, as will become clear in the next section.

3. Iterative Optimization for the Data Center

We now introduce Iterative Optimization for the Data Center (IODC) which can be applied to both MapReduce-style workloads as well as throughput compute-intensive server workloads. We first introduce IODC for MapReduce workloads, followed by IODC for throughput compute-intensive server workloads.

3.1 MapReduce vs. iterative optimization

MapReduce is a paradigm and framework for processing huge data sets on a distributed system [11]. MapReduce splits up computation in a Map and a Reduce stage. In the Map stage, the *master* partitions the input into smaller sub-problems, and distributes those to the *workers*. Each worker node works on a sub-problem which in itself consists of a number of so-called *records*. In our setup, the entire problem consists of millions of records which are partitioned across the workers in sub-problems, each consisting of on the order of at least thousands of records. The *Map function* represents the work done by the worker in the Map stage; the worker nodes produce intermediate files. In the Reduce stage, the master assigns reduce tasks to the worker nodes, which then produce the final output from the intermediate files. The *Reduce function* specifies what a worker needs to do during the Reduce stage.

This general concept and organization seems to be a natural fit with how iterative optimization operates. Iterative optimization requires that a program be executed many times, albeit compiled differently, in order to understand which combination of compiler

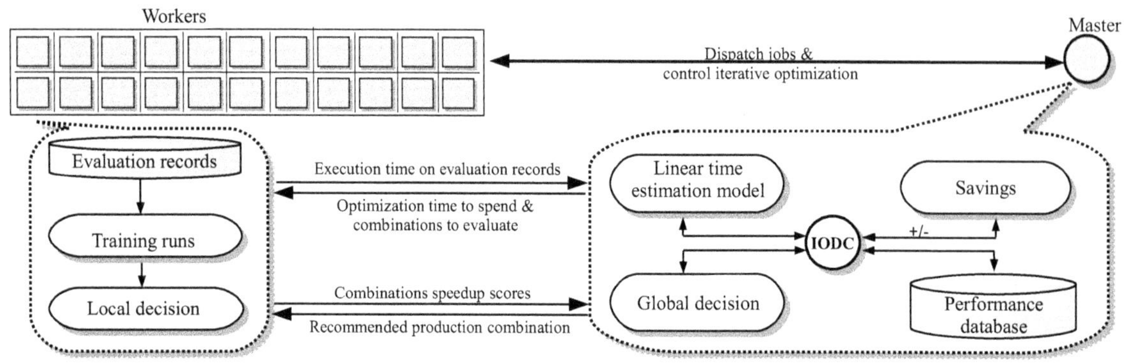

Figure 5. *IODC for MapReduce workloads.*

optimizations yields optimum performance. In MapReduce terminology, the master is running the iterative optimization strategy, while the workers evaluate different combinations of compiler optimizations (recompilations and training runs), and send performance statistics back to the master. Based on the aggregated performance statistics, the iterative optimization strategy running on the master then propagates recommendations to the workers about which compiler combinations to employ in the future.

3.2 IODC for MapReduce

Although the overall concept of IODC seems to be an intuitive fit for MapReduce workloads, designing an efficient strategy is challenging. The main difficulty is to make sure that the overhead of training runs, recompilations and communication overhead between the master and the workers do not outperform the benefits of iterative optimization. The key principle of our approach is to manage costs and benefits carefully. As mentioned before, evaluations of combinations of compiler optimizations are done on-the-fly, in a way that is transparent to the user. Further, iterative optimization continuously searches for better performing combinations of compiler optimizations. At any point in time, IODC employs the combination that yields the best possible performance among the combinations evaluated so far. We refer to the current best combination as the *production combination*, as it is the one currently being employed and producing output for the end user. At the same time, IODC evaluates other possible combinations in the background, hoping to identify a combination that yields even better performance. The strategy initiates with the default `-O3` optimization level as the current production combination, and evolves towards the best possible combination over time.

IODC's strategy uses a novel algorithm for managing costs and benefits from iterative optimization, much alike a 'savings account'. IODC starts off with a zero balance on the savings account, and for each record for which the selected combination of compiler optimizations performs better than the default compiler optimization, we consider that we achieve an execution time 'benefit', increasing our savings. A training run and recompilation 'spends' some of the earned benefits and decreases the balance on the savings account.

Figure 5 illustrates the general flow of IODC for MapReduce workloads. The master dispatches jobs to the workers, i.e., the master gets the workers to execute the Map and Reduce functions on a particular subset of the records. The master also controls iterative optimization, and keeps track of a performance database of previously evaluated combinations of compiler optimizations as well as the 'savings account' for managing iterative optimization overhead. We will describe IODC in more detail in the following paragraphs.

Sampling records for evaluating combinations. The master distributes records among the workers in a MapReduce workload. IODC will in addition direct the workers to randomly select a sample of its assigned records, and to use these as *evaluation records*. On all these evaluation records, the workers run the Map or Reduce functions, compiled with the default compiler optimization (i.e., `-O3`). In addition, the workers will also recompile the Map and Reduce functions and perform training runs using the evaluation records. The workers can then determine locally, among all the combinations evaluated, which one is the best. Then, they propagate this information back to the master for making a global decision on the best combination, see also Figure 5. The evaluation records are also used to detect program errors caused by compiler bugs during recompilation; we will discuss this further in Section 3.5.

Estimating the performance gain by a combination. The strategy spends only a fraction of the savings brought by good combinations, in order to achieve a net benefit at any time during the MapReduce run. This objective can only be met if the savings are properly evaluated. One way to accurately evaluate the performance benefit due to a combination is to execute each record twice, using the default compiler optimization and the other combination, which would introduce too high overhead. Instead, we estimate the average performance gain using the evaluation records only, not all records. For each of the evaluation records, the workers evaluate the speedup brought by the new combinations over the default compiler optimization, and send these results back to the master. The master uses this information and the knowledge on the total remaining number of records to estimate the new savings that could be achieved with the new anticipated production combination. This is done through linear extrapolation, referred to as the linear estimation model in Figure 5.

Based on the anticipated savings, the master decides how many combinations can be evaluated by the workers, and directs them to perform the corresponding number of evaluations. The principle is to 'invest' only a small fraction (P%) of the total savings in order to avoid recklessly spending the savings, we use P=20% in our setup. The evolution of savings is illustrated in Figure 6. Initially, with no savings, we invest only a small fraction of the total estimated workload execution time (i.e., 1% in our experiments) to do explorative evaluations (recompilations and training runs). Once better combinations are found, only P% of savings brought by these combinations are invested to initiate more evaluations for finding even better combinations. As a result, we keep most of the savings. Note that, in either case, as long as a program is repeatedly executed, explorative evaluations will continue. Better combinations will eventually be found even if they are rare in the optimization space as in the case of Figure 2(b). In the worst case,

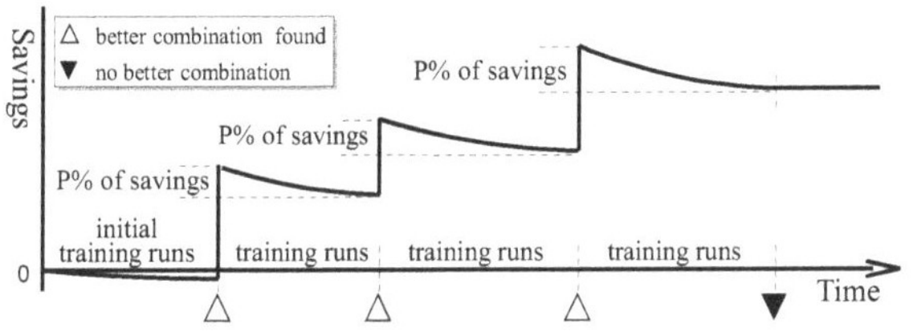

Figure 6. *Evolution of savings.*

i.e., if no better combinations are found, only a negligible loss is incurred.

Revisiting combinations vs. evaluating new combinations. As explained above and shown in Figure 5, the master will periodically allocate a certain amount of savings to workers for exploration purposes. The workers perform the explorative evaluations in parallel. Each worker evaluates one or a few combinations. The goal of the exploration is twofold: (i) to find new combinations that may perform better than the current best optimization, but also (ii) to revisit previous production combinations. The reason for both looking for new combinations and revisiting combinations, is to be able to continuously find the best possible optimization, even in the presence of time-varying inputs.

The master distributes to each worker a mix of new combinations and known combinations. As soon as the evaluations are performed, the workers send the speedup score of each evaluated combination to the master, see Figure 5 (top arrow from the workers to the master), which maintains a probability distribution characterizing the quality of each combination, based on the speedups recorded for that combination. The master selects the best combination known so far as the production combination, and propagates it to all the workers, see Figure 5 (bottom arrow from the master to the workers).

Within-run IODC vs. across-run IODC. IODC can be applied both within a single run and across runs. Within a MapReduce run, a large number of Map and Reduce operations are dispatched by the master to the workers, i.e., each worker operates on a set of assigned records. Once IODC finds a better combination than the current production combination, this better combination becomes the new current production combination, and it is immediately used to process the remaining records. This is referred to as within-run IODC. Well-performing production combinations can also be used across multiple runs of the same MapReduce workload (e.g., by different users), and IODC can continue to optimize the production combination across runs. Across-run IODC maintains optimization information across runs, which allows for continuously optimizing the production combination.

3.3 Extending IODC to any server application

While MapReduce is well suited for implementing iterative optimization because of the large number of records that need to be processed in parallel, the concept developed so far can be extended to any application running on a server. Contemporary throughput compute-intensive server applications (i.e., non-MapReduce batch-style workloads) do not typically run many instances of the same application at the same time, as is the case for MapReduce workloads. However, over a sufficiently long period of time, a similarly large number of runs are performed with different data sets for each run.

We therefore develop a modified iterative optimization strategy that does not rely on multiple simultaneous runs and a master/worker relationship, but which instead stores a *history* of combinations of compiler optimizations for each program. The strategy is implemented as a standalone script, running on one of the server nodes; the overhead of running the strategy script is factored in our evaluation, though it is actually negligible. As shown in Figure 7, the modifications to the strategy are the following.

Sample data sets. We maintain a pool of D randomly selected data sets, which we use the same way as the evaluation records for the MapReduce workloads: we use these evaluation data sets to evaluate the performance of alternative combinations of compiler optimizations. This pool is periodically refreshed as new data sets come in, in order to adapt to the possibly changing nature of data sets over time.

D has to be kept small, lest the overhead of the comparison is too high, i.e., $D = 3$ is the default value of the strategy in our setup. Because D is small, the comparison between the default and an alternative combination of compiler optimizations may be inaccurate so we check whether the mean execution times (over the D data sets) are statistically significant. For that purpose, we use the t-test with resampling [27]. If the comparison shows that the new combination would bring a performance improvement of at least 1% at a 95% confidence level, we replace the current production combination with the new combination.

Conservative and aggressive modes. Unlike in MapReduce, the strategy cannot estimate upfront the total savings brought by a better combination because the total number of runs of the program (over its entire lifetime on the server) is unknown. Therefore, exploration decisions have to be revisited after each run. The amount of exploration the strategy can afford to perform at any given time depends on the accumulated savings so far, and upon the rate at which better combinations are found. The latter criterion is the motivation for two modes: if better combinations are frequently found, future savings and the promise of even greater savings justify to quickly search for new combinations; otherwise, exploration must proceed more carefully.

The strategy toggles automatically between a 'conservative' and an 'aggressive' mode. The only distinction between these modes is the percentage P of savings that we are ready to spend. We use $P = 5\%$ in conservative mode, and $P = 50\%$ in aggressive mode. This percentage does not apply to all cumulated savings since the beginning of the task, but only to the cumulated savings since the last mode change. As a result, all savings accumulated till the end of a mode are definitely won.

Consider the example of Figure 8. Initially, the strategy starts in aggressive mode, speculatively investing future savings in order to quickly find better combinations. In this example, we assume that the exploration performed on the first data sets finds some better performing combination. The strategy will decide to stay in aggressive mode, postulating even better combinations can be found. After several more combinations being evaluated without showing an additional benefit, the strategy toggles back to conservative mode. No exploration will take place until the overhead of the last evaluations correspond to no more than 5% of the cumulated savings so far. When that happens, a few more combinations are explored. If that exploration is successful again, i.e., an even better combination is found, the strategy toggles back to aggressive mode, and so on.

3.4 Implementing IODC

We now discuss a number of IODC implementation issues which we find useful mentioning.

MapReduce. Implementing IODC in MapReduce requires that the worker nodes know where to find the Map and Reduce functions for recompilation. In our implementation, a new API was added so that the user can specify the location of the source code of the Map and Reduce functions for automatic recompilation. An alternative approach would be to use Unix environment variables for passing location information.

Capturing inputs and outputs. Iterative optimization uses recompilation and training runs to evaluate different combinations of compiler optimizations. In order to be transparent to the users, we need to automatically retain the inputs of evaluation runs and

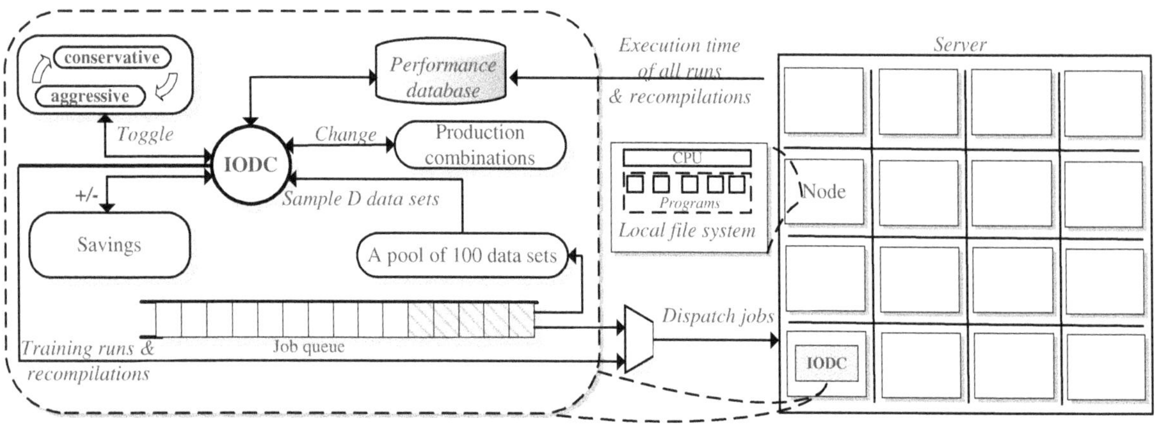

Figure 7. *IODC for throughput compute-intensive server applications.*

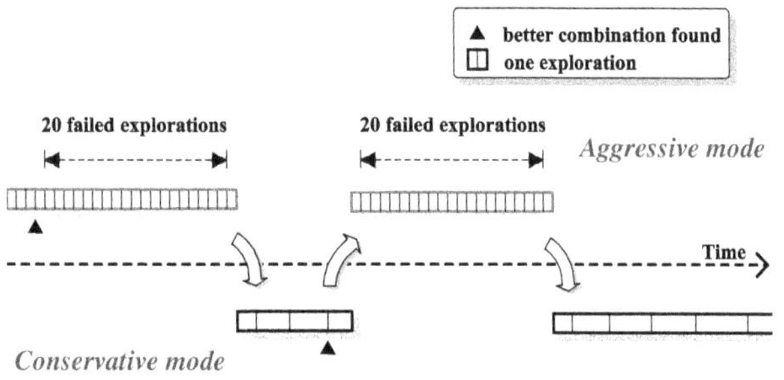

Figure 8. *Toggling between conservative and aggressive modes.*

capture their outputs. In the MapReduce framework, the runtime system is in charge of capturing, transferring and storing the input and output data of user-defined Map and Reduce functions, while the user only needs to specify the locations of input and output through a set of framework-specific API calls. In the runtime, we intercept messages between the master and the workers in order to know the input location and sample them for evaluation runs. To reduce disk seek time, we sample the input at the granularity of a group of consecutive records, not individual records. We also modified the runtime to not transfer nor store the outputs of Map and Reduce functions during evaluation.

Propagating recompiled code. Once the current best combination gets promoted as the next production combination, we need to propagate this information from the master to the workers. In the MapReduce implementation, only the combination itself is sent to the other workers, which perform recompilations locally. In the server implementation, IODC sends the recompiled code across the nodes. The time required for either propagation method is factored in our performance measurements.

IODC for server applications. For retaining the D data sets in IODC for server applications, we leverage the replay strategy which is commonly used in large-scale servers for fault-tolerant computing [2, 23]. Because the failure rate in servers is high, software infrastructures on servers embed a replay capability to rerun a data set if the previous run did not complete. That capability

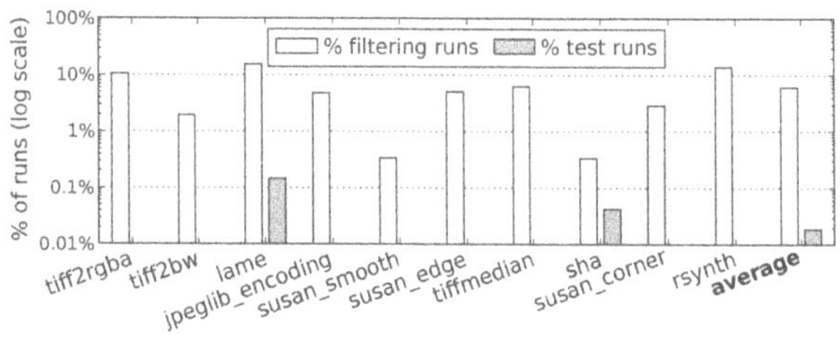

Figure 9. *Percentage of runs where a compiler bug was detected (1000 runs for each benchmark application).*

requires to temporarily retain the data set, which we leverage in IODC.

Heterogeneous servers. So far, we have assumed that all the machines in a cluster are the same, so that results gathered on one node can be factored in for other nodes. It is straightforward to extend the strategy to factor in heterogeneous nodes: the information on which combinations perform best must only be partitioned into classes, each class corresponding to a node type or configuration.

3.5 Compiler bugs

The interplay among different compiler optimizations is particularly complex, up to the point where it is difficult for compiler designers to ensure that any combination of compiler optimizations will always result in bug-free programs. Therefore, we need to add a safeguard mechanism to check the correctness of code recompiled with complex combinations of compiler optimizations.

For that purpose, we leverage our evaluation records again and the aforementioned facilities for capturing output. The output of the evaluation records, compiled with the default compiler optimization, are stored. Whenever a new combination is evaluated on one of these evaluation records, the outputs are compared. If there is any difference (or if the run crashes for that record), the combination is flagged as potentially buggy and not authorized for production runs.

In order to illustrate how frequent the problem is, and to assess the efficiency of our safeguard mechanism, we proceed as follows. We generate random combinations of compiler optimizations for the GNU C compiler, and we emulate the safeguard mechanism by running each combination on 5 randomly selected data sets for each of the benchmark applications; we repeat this process until we identify 300 fault-free combinations; the experimental framework is presented in more details in Section 4. The percentage of faulty runs is shown in Figure 9, see the '% filtering runs' bars. Any combination found to be faulty is no longer considered, it is deemed filtered by the safeguard. Then, in order to assess the efficiency of the safeguard, we run the remaining, filtered, 300 combinations on the 1000 data sets of our 10 benchmark applications, 3 million runs in total. The fraction of invalid runs is reported in Figure 9, see '% test runs'. While some compiler bugs were not captured by the filtering process, their occurrence is rare, 0.02% on average. We repeated the same experiment with a commercial compiler, Intel ICC, for which 3.3% of filtering runs were faulty, and for which we found no remaining compiler bugs after filtering.

4. Methodology

Before presenting the evaluation of IODC, we first describe our experimental setup.

4.1 Servers

We evaluate IODC on three different kinds of servers. The first one is a 7-node DELL cluster, with 3GHz Intel Xeon dual-core processors (E3110 family), 2GB RAM, 2x3MB L2 cache, running CentOS release 5.3 (Final). We refer to this cluster as the *Intel cluster* in the remainder of the paper. The second one contains 8 dual-core AMD Opteron processors (8218), 16GB RAM, 2x1MB L2 cache, running Red Hat Enterprise Linux 4.4. We refer to this cluster as the *AMD cluster*. The third one is a 32-node cluster with Loongson 2F processors [22], running Red Flag Linux 6.0; Loongson 2F is an 800MHz MIPS-compatible general-purpose CPU, with a 512KB L2 cache and 512MB RAM. We refer to this cluster as the *Loongson cluster*. In order to perform the very large number of runs described below in a reasonable amount of time, we partitioned our benchmarks across these three clusters as indicated in Table 1.

4.2 Benchmarks and data sets

We consider three groups of workloads for evaluating IODC, see also Table 1.

MapReduce applications. The first group of workloads is a set of five MapReduce applications: `minhash`, `ann`, `kmeans`, `knn`, and `pfsp`. `minhash` is a probabilistic clustering algorithm implemented as a MapReduce component in the Google News service [10]. `ann` is a back-propagation algorithm for training the weights of a three-layer artificial neural network [21]; `kmeans` and `knn` are MapReduce implementations of k-means clustering [28] and the k-nearest neighbor algorithm [17], respectively; `pfsp` relies upon a genetic algorithm and a NEH-based heuristic method [24] to solve the permutation flowshop scheduling problem, which is an important task in industrial engineering, aiming at finding a job sequence with minimal makespan [35].

The MapReduce implementation we use is Sector/Sphere [18], an open-source high-performance distributed file system and parallel data processing engine. We generated 1,550,000 to 310,000,000 inputs (records) for these tasks, either based on a uniform distribution, or a distribution extracted from real-world data, see also Table 1. We randomly grouped these records into 5 different data sets of the same size, for each of the applications. We will use these 5 data sets to evaluate within-run IODC versus across-run IODC.

Compute-intensive server applications. The second group of workloads contains six programs, five of which are extracted from the PARSEC benchmark suite [5]: `x264`, `ferret`, `freqmine`, `blackscholes`, and `canneal`; the sixth server application is `bzip2e`, the well-known file compression utility. These programs are similar to emerging compute-intensive server applications used in several popular web services. `x264` is an H264 video compression program, which is the kind of tasks run on YouTube servers, among others. `ferret` performs content-based similarity on images; Google Picasa and Flickr both rely on content-based similarity for identifying faces within images. `freqmine` is a typical data mining program aiming at finding frequent item sets; Amazon uses similar algorithms to recommend related books. `blackscholes` is an option-pricing prediction model, popular in financial institutions; it is used for instance by Morgan Stanley and Goldman Sachs. `canneal` is a chip routing application, similar to the place and route algorithms used by EDA companies (e.g., Xilinx). `bzip2e` is a compression algorithm, broadly used in file sharing web sites, such as the GNU FTP. For these six programs, we collect between 28,000 to 177,119 data sets, see Table 1, corresponding to a total storage of 9.54TB. In all experiments, we use each data set only *once*, thereby emulating distinct production runs.

Benchmark applications. The third group of benchmarks are a collection of ten relatively small applications, which are similar to tasks running in the backbone of popular web services. These benchmarks are taken from well-known open-source projects. We use these benchmark applications for fine-tuning IODC in a reasonable amount of time prior to running the more complex and long-running MapReduce and server applications.

We consider the following *benchmark applications*. `rsynth` performs text-to-speech conversion, as provided by the service `readthewords.com`; `susan_corner`, `susan_edge`, and `susan_smooth` (all from susan) perform standard and compute-intensive image processing steps of image recognition applications, as in `myheritage.com`; `jpeglib_encoding` (from jpeglib), `tiff2median`, `tiff2bw`, `tiff2rgba` perform image conversions, as provided by `converthub.com` or `go2convert .com`; `lame` is an mp3 encoder, as provided by `media.io`; `sha` is the SHA hashing algorithm, broadly used in servers [29].

Combinations of compiler optimizations. For all experiments, we use the GNU GCC v4.4 compiler, and the optimization level `-O3` as the baseline. We selected 127 compiler options of GCC that control inlining, unrolling, vectorization, scheduling, register allocation, constant propagation, among other optimizations known to have a potential impact on performance. We then create 300 randomly chosen combinations of these compiler optimizations. We explore these combinations in random order in the experiments. Note that other exploration methods [1, 6, 25], which may require extensive training and/or program feature extraction, can also be integrated into IODC.

4.3 Measurements

We measure end-to-end wall clock time, and we report speedups over the GCC `-O3` optimization level. The performance numbers reported in the paper include all sources of overhead, including the cost of recompilations, training runs, communication overhead between the master and the workers, etc. The total CPU time was 110 days for the MapReduce applications, 440 days for the server applications, and 18 days for the benchmark applications.

5. Performance Evaluation

We now evaluate IODC. This is done in a number of steps. We first evaluate IODC for MapReduce and server workloads. We subsequently evaluate IODC's impact on energy consumption, and we explore various optimizations of the IODC framework.

5.1 MapReduce

Figure 10 reports the speedup achieved by within-run IODC. Speedups range up to 1.91×, with an average speedup of 1.29×. There is a slight performance degradation for `kmeans` due to the initial 'investment' into the exploration of combinations which failed to find a better combination than GCC's default `-O3` optimization level, and which results in a 1.24% slowdown. Note though that we

Benchmark suite	Program (domain)	Data set number (total file size)	Data set description	Cluster
MapReduce applications	minhash (probabilistic clustering)	10830935 (6GB)	Generated data sets obeying distribution extracted from MovieLens[34]; each record represents a movie history seen by one user.	Loongson [22]
	ann (model training)	310000000 (222GB)	Generated data sets obeying uniform distribution; each record consists of input and output for the artificial neural network.	Loongson
	kmeans (distance-based clustering)	4294720 (320GB)	Generated data sets obeying uniform distribution; each record represents a multi-dimension point.	Loongson
	knn (query-based learning)	387500000 (580GB)	Generated data sets obeying uniform distribution; each record consists of an instance and its label.	Loongson
	pfsp (scheduling problem)	1550000 (591MB)	Generated data sets obeying uniform distribution; each record represents a job scheduling scheme.	Loongson
Server applications	bzip2e (compression)	28000 (438GB)	Uncompressed tar balls of source and binary packages of various Linux distributions.	Loongson
	ferret (image similarity search)	58430 (187GB)	Groups of query images constructed using 1,166,657 JPEG files downloaded from 130 different web sites.	Intel
	freqmine (data mining)	61655 (4.05TB)	Lists of transactions randomly generated using IBM Quest Market-Basket Synthetic Data Generator [3].	AMD
	x264 (video encoding)	67571 (2.28TB)	Yuv4mpeg videos converted from MKV and RMVB files downloaded from the Internet.	Loongson
	canneal (electronic design automation)	177119 (2.15TB)	Netlists randomly generated with an enhanced version of the input generator provided by PARSEC.	Intel
	black- scholes (financial analysis)	43354 (434GB)	Lists of options randomly generated based on the value ranges deduced from the 1000 inputs provided by PARSEC.	AMD
Benchmark applications	10 benchmark applications	1000 each (10GB)	1000 data sets per benchmark collected from various web sites [7].	Intel

Table 1. *Benchmarks, data sets and servers considered in this study.*

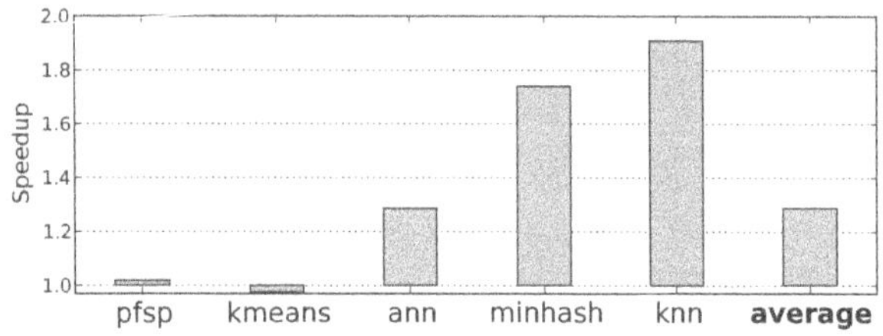

Figure 10. *Speedup for the MapReduce applications for within-run IODC.*

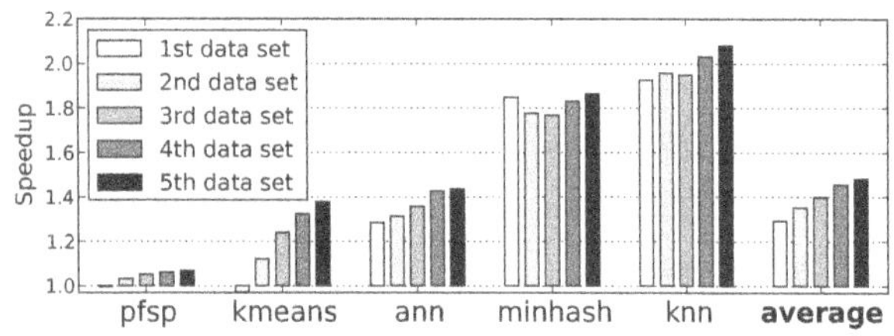

Figure 11. *Speedup for the MapReduce applications using both within-run IODC (1ste data set) and across-run IODC (2nd through 5th data set).*

perform within-run IODC only in this experiment, which explains the slowdown for `kmeans`.

To evaluate across-run IODC, we now consider five data sets to emulate five consecutive runs of the same MapReduce workload with different inputs, see Figure 11. On average, the speedup achieved across runs for the combined strategy is 1.48× after 5 data sets, versus 1.29× after 1 data set. The maximum speedup is 2.08×, achieved for `knn` after 5 data sets. Note that we now achieve a speedup of 1.38× after 5 data sets of across-run IODC for the `kmeans` which showed a 1.24% slowdown with within-run IODC.

5.2 Server applications

In Figure 12, we report the cumulated speedup for the server applications using unique data sets. The curves report how performance speedup improves over time. At any given point in time, the cumulated speedup is computed as the ratio of the wall clock time for all runs compiled with `-O3` versus all runs compiled with production combinations. The 'with overhead' curve accounts for all the overhead costs, whereas the 'no overhead' curve discounts any source of overhead; the delta between both curves quantifies the overhead.

We observe that, initially, when the strategy searches for good combinations, the cost of recompilations and training runs results in a slowdown. However, the corresponding slowdown is on the order of 1% on average. The initialization phase does not take that long; after a couple thousand runs (2670 runs on average), IODC yields a net performance benefit; the reason is that combinations that outperform the default `-O3` production combination can usually be found quickly. As shown in Figure 12, the proposed strategy achieves a cumulated speedup of 1.39× for `bzip2e`, 1.12× for `blackscholes` and `freqmine`, 1.10× for `x264`, 1.08× for `canneal`, 1.06× for `ferret`, with an average of 1.14×. We also find the overhead of IODC to be small, a few percent only.

Also note the thin marks at the bottom of each of the graphs in Figure 12. These marks indicate when the strategy searches for a new combination. Note that there is sometimes an inflection point after which a much better combination is found; the cumulated speedup stops increasing at a fast pace for a little while, and then after the inflection point, it starts increasing faster, see `ferret` for the most notable example. Right before the inflection point reflects the aggressive mode. Once a better combination is found, the strategy transitions back to conservative model, after which performance benefit increases again.

In the different graphs of Figure 12, performance plateaus after some time because we use a uniform random mix of data sets, so the strategy will eventually end up finding a program-optimal combination, i.e., a combination that performs well across many data sets. With a less uniform mix, the choice of the best combination has to be constantly revisited, which is described in Section 5.6.

Overall, these experiments show that, even under conditions with unique data sets and factoring in all the overhead costs, IODC improves the performance in a consistent way, i.e., without incurring performance degradation at any time except in the initial phase.

5.3 Energy reduction

We now quantify the energy implications of IODC. Given the importance of energy consumption on total cost of ownership (TCO), reduction in energy consumption immediately translates into proportional cost reductions. We use a simple linear model to estimate energy consumption based on CPU utilization, as proposed

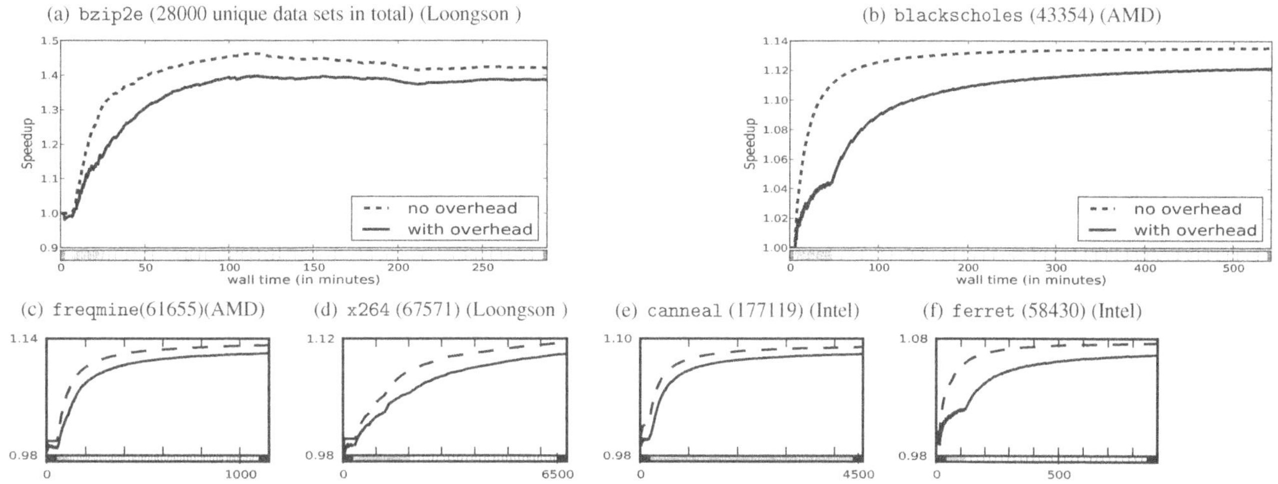

Figure 12. *Cumulated speedup profiles for* `bzip2e`*,* `blackscholes`*,* `freqmine`*,* `x264`*,* `canneal`*, and* `ferret`*.*

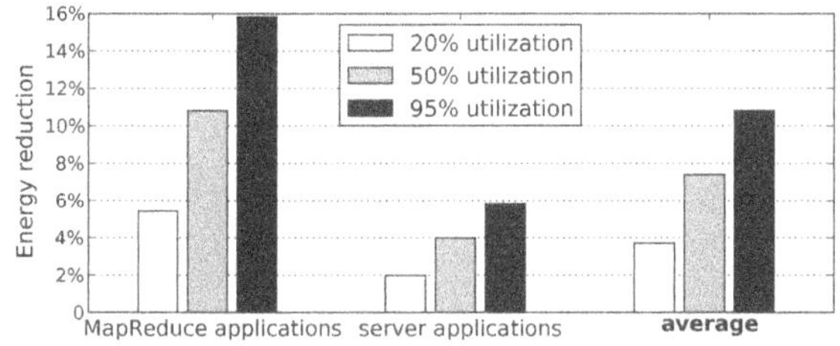

Figure 13. *Estimating energy saving through IODC at different system utilization levels.*

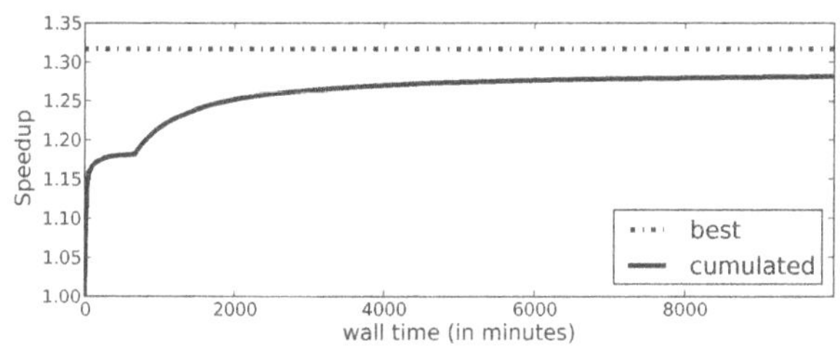

Figure 14. *Cumulated speedup profile averaged across the benchmark applications.*

by Fan [12]:

$$power = P_{idle} + (P_{busy} - P_{idle}) * u \quad (1)$$

where P_{busy} is the power of the server running the most power-intensive tasks; P_{idle} is the power consumption in idle state, and it is equal to half that of P_{busy} according to the results by Fan et al. [12]; u is CPU utilization. We consider three different utilizations: 20%, 50% and 95%. We report the results in Figure 13 and find that we can achieve energy gains ranging between 3.7% and 11% on average, depending on the level of utilization. The reason why energy savings increase with utilization level is that there are more energy saving opportunities for iterative optimization at high utilization levels, i.e., the more work done by the server, the more iterative optimization saves energy because it gets the work done faster.

5.4 Benchmark applications

We also evaluate IODC with the benchmark applications and its 1000 data sets, albeit we reuse the data sets in these experiments. As explained in Section 4, the motivation for these experiments is to address several questions which would have been too time-consuming to explore with the large number of unique data sets using the MapReduce and server applications. Relevant questions are: (1) How far is the strategy from the optimal performance of iterative optimization? (2) Is there value in a strategy that factors in the costs and benefits of multiple programs at the same time? (3) How does the strategy perform when data sets are non-uniformly mixed? Because we can apply all 300 combinations on all data sets, it is possible to address all these issues for these benchmark applications. In this section, we essentially want to validate that the convergence profiles of the benchmark applications are similar to the profiles of the MapReduce and server applications, suggesting they respond similarly to IODC. We address points (2) and (3) in the next two sections.

As reported in Figure 14, the cumulated speedup curves are similar for the benchmark applications as for the MapReduce and server applications, i.e., performance speedup improves over time. The 'best' curve in Figure 14 corresponds to the performance obtained if an oracle would choose the best combination for each data set of each program, with all overheads (recompilations and training runs) factored in, though. In other words, it is the maximum performance that can be achieved, in theory. We find that the plateau performance of IODC is within 98% of this best possible performance, in large part because IODC can keep the overhead of recompilations and training runs small enough.

5.5 Shared budget

IODC manages the costs/savings budget for each program separately. Since multiple programs are usually run simultaneously within servers, one could also consider a *shared-budget* IODC strategy in which programs share their costs and savings. For instance, if one program has many good combinations, it will quickly achieve significant savings, and most of its latter explorations will be useless. On the other hand, a program with few good combinations may require a lot of time to converge, delaying potential savings. If these two programs were to share costs and savings, the second program could use some of the savings of the first program to find good combinations faster, increasing overall benefits.

We have setup an experiment to evaluate the shared-budget idea. `rsynth` is a program that converges slowly, even though it can potentially achieve a significant speedup; `susan_corner` converges quickly. When the programs do not share their budget, the convergence profiles are as shown in Figure 15(a). After a little while, `susan_corner` converges to a speedup of 1.5, while `rsynth`

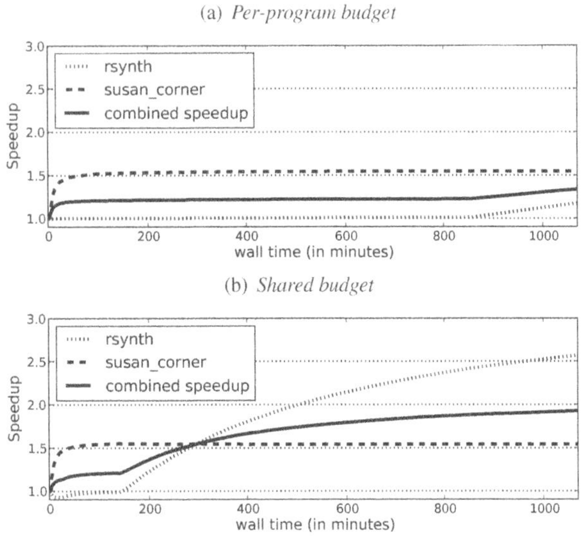

Figure 15. *Per-program vs. shared-budget IODC.*

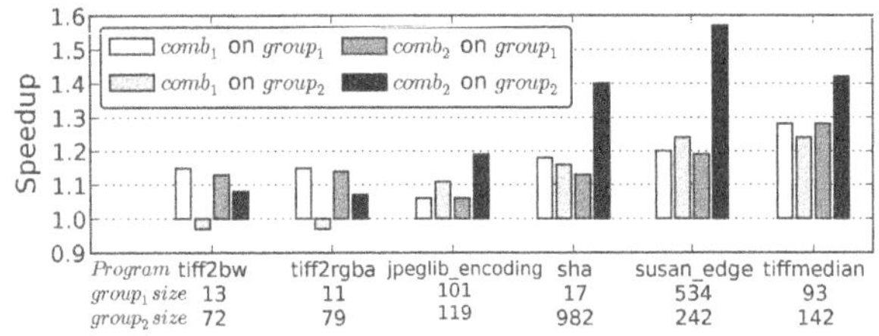

Figure 16. *Evaluating non-uniform data sets: Applying combinations, favored by one group of data sets, to another group of data sets.*

is still in the process of converging. The convergence profiles with a shared budget are shown in Figure 15(b): `rsynth` converges faster and achieves a higher speedup than with separate budgets in the same amount of time. `susan_corner`, which has contributed some of its savings to `rsynth`, performs only slightly worse than with separate budgets. Overall, the combined speedup is significantly higher within the same amount of time.

5.6 Non-uniform mix of data sets

In the experiments done so far, we have assumed the data set characteristics to be uniformly distributed over time. In the more likely case where each user runs data sets with certain common characteristics, data set characteristics are likely to be clustered over time. In this section, we emulate a scenario in which data set characteristics are clustered over time based on how they react to combinations. We cluster the data sets into two groups ($group_1$ and $group_2$) based on how they react to different combinations. We then find the best combination $comb_1$ based on the $group_1$ data sets (average performance across all $group_1$ data sets), and $comb_2$ only using $group_2$ data sets. While the spirit of this experiment is similar to the example of Section 2.4, here, we find $comb_1$ and $comb_2$ using a whole group of data sets, not just one, thereby emulating more closely the selection of combinations over multiple data sets, and the fact that data sets characteristics can be clustered over time.

In Figure 16, we present results for six programs. We apply $comb_1$ to $group_2$ and compare against the speedups obtained with $comb_2$ on $group_2$, and vice versa. For some benchmarks, $comb_1$ performs poorly for the $group_2$ data sets; similarly, $comb_2$ performs poorly for the $group_1$ data sets. This confirms the need for the continuous exploration of combinations of compiler optimizations, in case data set characteristics change over time. In Figures 17 and 18, we show that IODC can adapt to the changing data sets using `susan_edge` and `tiff2bw` as example benchmarks, respectively. The solid curves represent the default IODC strategy. The dotted curves show a variant in which the exploration stops after convergence. We start with data set $group_1$. After both strategies converged, we switch to data set $group_2$. As shown, with continuous exploration, IODC reacts quickly to the change, resulting in higher performance gains.

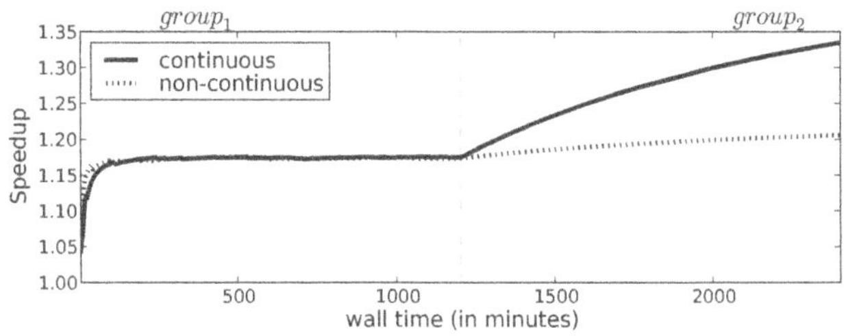

Figure 17. *Continuous vs. non-continuous exploration with non-uniform mix of data sets for* `susan_edge`.

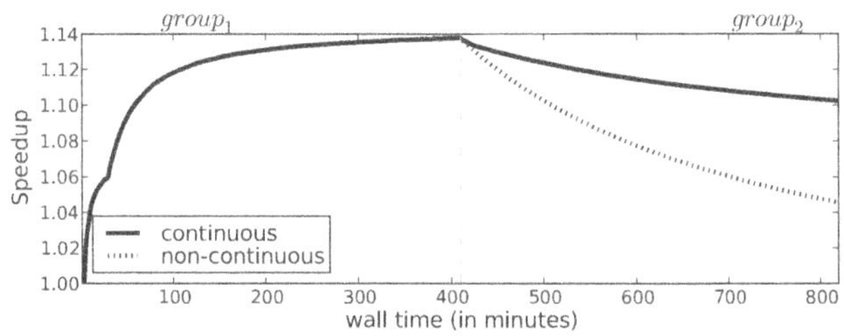

Figure 18. *Continuous vs. non-continuous exploration with non-uniform mix of data sets for* `tiff2bw`.

6. Related Work

MapReduce [11] has been applied to a broad set of algorithms since its introduction [10, 17, 21, 28, 35]. Aside from Google's proprietary implementation of MapReduce, other open-source implementations include Hadoop [33] and Sector/Sphere [18]. To the best of our knowledge, there is no prior work on applying iterative optimization to MapReduce, nor to the data center context at large.

However, there is a large body of research on iterative optimization. A large share of this research is dedicated to showing the performance potential of iterative optimization [1, 6, 8, 9, 13, 14, 25, 30]. A substantial number of studies aim at reducing the number of recompilations and training runs required to converge [1, 6, 8, 25, 30]. Some papers [15, 26] propose to improve the performance of iterative optimization by tuning at a finer granularity than the whole program. For most studies, the goal is to find the best possible combination, but not to find them in a cost-efficient manner that factors in the overhead of training, nor to adapt to the changing nature of data sets, i.e., it is assumed that iterative optimization can be done offline.

Most of the prior work in iterative optimization assumes a single or a limited number of data sets. A couple studies investigate input data set sensitivity. Berube and Amaral study the training input sensitivity of feedback-directed optimizations [4]. They collect 116 inputs in total for seven SPEC CPU benchmarks and study the impact of different training inputs on inlining decisions. Haneda et al. [19] investigate the input sensitivity of iterative optimization.

They perform iterative optimization using GCC and the `train` inputs on seven SPEC CPU benchmarks. The authors find that the best combination of optimizations found using the `train` input works well when applied to the `ref` input. Fursin et al. [14] proposed MiDataSets which includes 20 data sets in total per program. Only recently did Chen et al. [7] propose KDataSets, a suite of 1000 data sets per program, for evaluating iterative optimization with respect to data set sensitivity. They concluded that it is possible to find a program-optimal combination of compiler optimizations that performs well compared to the best possible combination for each specific data set. The program-optimal combination was chosen post-mortem though, with the assumption that all data sets are known, which we could not rely upon in the online system proposed in this paper.

A number of studies employ iterative optimization to optimize performance during run time. Voss et al. [36] propose ADAPT. They compile code sections into different versions and select the best performing ones during run-time in order to adapt to different architectures and inputs. Fursin et al. [16] use MiDataSets to understand how iterative optimization behaves in a more realistic setting where input data sets vary across executions. However, because of the limited number of input data sets, they have to reuse data sets, in contrast to this work. Their strategy is to generate a binary with two versions of the most time-consuming routines, each version optimized with a different combination. They then compare the performance of the two versions in a statistical way once enough calls to the two versions of the routines have been performed. They then pick the best performing version as the production combination. Stephenson [32] proposes a similar approach within a Java virtual machine. In contrast to this collection of prior work, IODC carefully manages the costs versus benefits, enabling online iterative optimization in the data center. In addition, IODC explores a larger combination space of compiler optimizations during run time.

7. Conclusion

Implementing iterative optimization in an efficient way so that it can be deployed in an online environment is non-trivial for a number of reasons: a potentially large number of recompilations and training runs may be needed to find a good combination of compiler optimizations; the process can be data set dependent; and the overhead of recompilations and training runs can easily wipe out the performance benefits from iterative optimization. In this paper, we proposed and explored Iterative Optimization for the Data Center (IODC), and we made the case that servers and data centers offer a context in which iterative optimization can be implemented as an online optimization technique. The key insight behind IODC is to carefully manage the number of recompilations and training runs so that they do not nullify the benefits from iterative optimization. We demonstrated that IODC can be applied to both MapReduce workloads as well as throughput compute-intensive server applications, and is completely transparent to the end user. We evaluated IODC using a very large number of data sets per benchmark, enough to use each data set (or record) only once. We report an average performance improvement of 1.48×, and up to 2.08×, for a set of MapReduce applications, and 1.14×, and up to 1.39×, for a set of contemporary throughput compute-intensive server applications.

Acknowledgments

We would like to thank the anonymous reviewers for their valuable feedback. We also thank Xiaguang Qi, Wenting He, Dongni Han for helping collect some of the data sets used in this paper. Lieven Eeckhout is supported through the FWO projects G.0232.06, G.0255.08, and G.0179.10, the UGent-BOF projects 01J14407 and 01Z04109, and the European Research Council under the European Community's Seventh Framework Programme (FP7/2007-2013) / ERC Grant agreement No. 259295. Olivier Temam is supported by HiPEAC-2 NoE under grant European FP7/ICT 217068 and INRIA YOUHUA associated team funding. The rest of the authors are supported by the National Natural Science Foundation of China under grants No. 60873057, 60921002 and 61033009; the National Basic Research Program of China under grant No. 2011CB302504; and the National Science and Technology Major Project of China under grants No. 2009ZX01036-001-002 and 2011ZX01028-001-002.

References

[1] F. Agakov, E. Bonilla, J. Cavazos, B. Franke, G. Fursin, M. F. P. O'Boyle, J. Thomson, M. Toussaint, and C. K. I. Williams. Using machine learning to focus iterative optimization. In *Proceedings of the International Symposium on Code Generation and Optimization (CGO)*, pages 295–305, March 2006.

[2] N. Aghdaie and Y. Tamir. Implementation and evaluation of transparent fault-tolerant web service with kernel-level support. In *Proceedings of 11th International Conference on Computer Communications and Networks (ICCCN)*, pages 63–68. IEEE, October 2002.

[3] R. Agrawal and R. Srikant. Fast algorithms for mining association rules in Large Databases. In *Proceedings of 20th International Conference on Very Large Data Bases (VLDB)*, pages 487–499, September 1994.

[4] P. Berube and J. Amaral. Aestimo: a feedback-directed optimization evaluation tool. In *Proceedings of the IEEE International Symposium on Performance Analysis of Systems and Software (ISPASS)*, pages 251–260, March 2006.

[5] C. Bienia, S. Kumar, J. P. Singh, and K. Li. The PARSEC benchmark suite: characterization and architectural implications. In *Proceedings of the 17th International Conference on Parallel Architectures and Compilation Techniques (PACT)*, pages 72–81, October 2008.

[6] J. Cavazos, G. Fursin, F. Agakov, E. Bonilla, M. F. P. O'Boyle, and O. Temam. Rapidly selecting good compiler optimizations using performance counters. In *Proceedings of the International Symposium on Code Generation and Optimization (CGO)*, pages 185–197, March 2007.

[7] Y. Chen, Y. Huang, L. Eeckhout, G. Fursin, L. Peng, O. Temam, and C. W. u. Evaluating iterative optimization across 1000 data sets. In *Proceedings of the ACM SIGPLAN 2010 Conference on Programming Language Design and Implementation (PLDI)*, pages 448–459, June 2010.

[8] K. Cooper, P. Schielke, and D. Subramanian. Optimizing for reduced code space using genetic algorithms. In *Proceedings of the Conference on Languages, Compilers, and Tools for Embedded Systems (LCTES)*, pages 1–9, July 1999.

[9] K. D. Cooper, A. Grosul, T. J. Harvey, S. Reeves, D. Subramanian, L. Torczon, and T. Waterman. ACME: adaptive compilation made efficient. In *Proceedings of the ACM SIGPLAN/SIGBED Conference on Languages, Compilers, and Tools for Embedded Systems (LCTES)*, pages 69–77, July 2005.

[10] A. S. Das, M. Datar, A. Garg, and S. Rajaram. Google news personalization: scalable online collaborative filtering. In *Proceedings of the 16th international conference on World Wide Web (WWW)*, pages 271–280, May 2007.

[11] J. Dean and S. Ghemawat. MapReduce: Simplified Data Processing on Large Clusters. In *Proceedings of the 6th Conference on Symposium on Operating Systems Design & Implementation (OSDI)*, pages 107–113, December 2004.

[12] X. Fan, W. Weber, and L. Barroso. Power provisioning for a warehouse-sized computer. In *Proceedings of the 34th annual international symposium on Computer architecture*, pages 13–23, 2007.

[13] B. Franke, M. O'Boyle, J. Thomson, and G. Fursin. Probabilistic source-level optimisation of embedded programs. In *Proceedings of the ACM SIGPLAN/SIGBED Conference on Languages, Compilers, and Tools for Embedded Systems (LCTES)*, pages 78–86, July 2005.

[14] G. Fursin, J. Cavazos, M. O'Boyle, and O. Temam. Midatasets: Creating the conditions for a more realistic evaluation of iterative optimization. In *Proceedings of the International Conference on High*

Performance Embedded Architectures & Compilers (HiPEAC), pages 245–260, January 2007.

[15] G. Fursin, A. Cohen, M. O'Boyle, and O. Temam. A practical method for quickly evaluating program optimizations. In *Proceedings of the 1st International Conference on High Performance Embedded Architectures & Compilers (HiPEAC)*, pages 29–46, November 2005.

[16] G. Fursin and O. Temam. Collective optimization. In *Proceedings of the International Conference on High Performance Embedded Architectures & Compilers (HiPEAC)*, pages 34–49, January 2009.

[17] D. Gillick, A. Faria, and J. DeNero. MapReduce: Distributed computing for machine learning. Technical report, UC Berkeley, December 2006.

[18] Y. Gu and R. L. Grossman. Sector and Sphere: The Design and Implementation of a High Performance Data Cloud. In *Theme Issue of the Philosophical Transactions of the Royal Society A: Crossing Boundaries: Computational Science, E-Science and Global E-Infrastructure*, June 2009.

[19] M. Haneda, P. Knijnenburg, and H. Wijshoff. On the impact of data input sets on statistical compiler tuning. In *Proceedings of the 20th IEEE International Parallel and Distributed Processing Symposium (IPDPS)*, pages 385–385, April 2006.

[20] P. Kulkarni, S. Hines, J. Hiser, D. Whalley, J. Davidson, and D. Jones. Fast searches for effective optimization phase sequences. In *Proceedings of the ACM SIGPLAN Conference on Programming Language Design and Implementation (PLDI)*, pages 171–182, June 2004.

[21] Z. Liu, H. Li, and G. Miao. MapReduce-based backpropagation neural network over large scale mobile data. In *Proceedings of the 6th International Conference on Natural Computation (ICNC)*, August 2010.

[22] Loongson 2F. `http://www.loongson.cn/`.

[23] M. Marwah, S. Mishra, and C. Fetzer. Enhanced server fault-tolerance for improved user experience. In *Proceedings of the IEEE International Conference on Dependable Systems and Networks With FTCS and DCC (DSN)*, pages 167–176, June 2008.

[24] M. Nawaz, E. E. Enscore Jr, and I. Ham. A heuristic algorithm for the m-machine, n-job flow-shop sequencing problem. *OMEGA: International Journal of Management Science*, pages 91–95, 1983.

[25] Z. Pan and R. Eigenmann. Fast and effective orchestration of compiler optimizations for automatic performance tuning. In *Proceedings of the International Symposium on Code Generation and Optimization (CGO)*, pages 319–332, March 2006.

[26] Z. Pan and R. Eigenmann. Fast automatic procedure-level performance tuning. In *Proceedings of the Conference on Parallel Architectures and Compilation Techniques (PACT)*, pages 173–181, September 2006.

[27] S. Patil and D. Lilja. Using Resampling Techniques to Compute Confidence Intervals for the Harmonic Mean of Rate-Based Performance Metrics. *Computer Architecture Letters*, pages 1–4, 2010.

[28] C. Ranger, R. Raghuraman, A. Penmetsa, G. Bradski, and C. Kozyrakis. Evaluating MapReduce for multi-core and multiprocessor systems. In *Proceedings of the 2007 IEEE 13th International Symposium on High Performance Computer Architecture (HPCA)*, pages 13–24, February 2007.

[29] B. Schneier. *Applied Cryptography*. John Wiley & Sons, 1996.

[30] M. Stephenson and S. Amarasinghe. Predicting unroll factors using supervised classification. In *Proceedings of the International Symposium on Code Generation and Optimization (CGO)*, pages 123–134, March 2005.

[31] M. Stephenson, M. Martin, and U. O'Reilly. Meta optimization: Improving compiler heuristics with machine learning. In *Proceedings of the ACM SIGPLAN Conference on Programming Language Design and Implementation (PLDI)*, pages 77–90, June 2003.

[32] M. W. Stephenson. *Automating the Construction of Compiler Heuristics Using Machine Learning*. PhD thesis, MIT, USA, January 2006.

[33] Apache Hadoop. http://hadoop.apache.org, 2010.

[34] MovieLens data sets. http://www.grouplens.org/node/73, 2010.

[35] A. Verma, X. Llora, D. E. Goldberg, and R. H. Campbell. Scaling genetic algorithms using mapreduce. In *Proceedings of the 9th International Conference on Intelligent Systems Design and Applications (ISDA)*, pages 13–18, November 2009.

[36] M. Voss and R. Eigenmann. ADAPT: Automated de-coupled adaptive program transformation. In *Proceedings of the International Conference on Parallel Processing (ICPP)*, pages 163–170, August 2000.

Tarazu: Optimizing MapReduce On Heterogeneous Clusters

Faraz Ahmad†, Srimat Chakradhar‡, Anand Raghunathan†, T. N. Vijaykumar†
†School of Electrical and Computer Engineering, Purdue University, IN, USA
‡NEC Laboratories America, Princeton, NJ, USA
{fahmad,raghunathan,vijay}@ecn.purdue.edu chak@nec-labs.com

Abstract

Data center-scale clusters are evolving towards heterogeneous hardware for power, cost, differentiated price-performance, and other reasons. MapReduce is a well-known programming model to process large amount of data on data center-scale clusters. Most MapReduce implementations have been designed and optimized for homogeneous clusters. Unfortunately, these implementations perform poorly on heterogeneous clusters (e.g., on a 90-node cluster that contains 10 Xeon-based servers and 80 Atom-based servers, Hadoop performs worse than on 10-node Xeon-only or 80-node Atom-only homogeneous sub-clusters for many of our benchmarks). This poor performance remains despite previously proposed optimizations related to management of straggler tasks.

In this paper, we address MapReduce's poor performance on heterogeneous clusters. Our first contribution is that the poor performance is due to two key factors: (1) the non-intuitive effect that MapReduce's built-in load balancing results in excessive and bursty network communication during the Map phase, and (2) the intuitive effect that the heterogeneity amplifies load imbalance in the Reduce computation. Our second contribution is *Tarazu*, a suite of optimizations to improve MapReduce performance on heterogeneous clusters. Tarazu consists of (1) *Communication-Aware Load Balancing of Map computation (CALB)* across the nodes, (2) *Communication-Aware Scheduling of Map computation (CAS)* to avoid bursty network traffic and (3) *Predictive Load Balancing of Reduce computation (PLB)* across the nodes. Using the above 90-node cluster, we show that Tarazu significantly improves performance over a baseline of Hadoop with straightforward tuning for hardware heterogeneity.

Categories and Subject Descriptors: D.1.3 [**Software**]: Programming Techniques - *Concurrent Programming*
General Terms: Design; Measurement; Performance
Keywords: Heterogeneous clusters, MapReduce, Shuffle, Load imbalance, Cluster Scheduling.

1 Introduction

Data centers are the compute platforms of choice for the emerging era of cloud computing. Data center-scale clusters are evolving toward heterogeneous hardware — a mix of high-performance and low-power nodes of disparate hardware architectures. Such heterogeneity stems from the diversity in the performance needs faced by the clusters, ranging from the most stringent of service-level requirements (e.g., on-line search and real-time computations) to more lenient requirements (e.g., data analysis, email or batch jobs). Exploiting this diversity to provide differentiated price-performance (e.g., EC2 [2]) and to optimize power [9], real-estate foot print, and cost often leads to a mix of nodes designed for different power-performance points (e.g., Xeons and Atoms). Even when heterogeneity is not introduced by design, the common practice of phased addition of nodes to the cluster over time implies that the nodes are often some hardware generations apart resulting in performance variation (e.g, adding nodes over 5-7 years implies 2-3 generations apart). While heterogeneity could also be due to other factors such as background load variation [37], or to the use of GPUs and other accelerators, we focus on heterogeneous, general-purpose CPU architectures.

MapReduce [10], a programming model for data-intensive applications, greatly improves programmability by providing automatic data management and transparent fault detection and recovery. MapReduce's programmability has led to quick adoption (e.g., Google [10], Yahoo [14], Microsoft [18,35] and Facebook [11]). To date, however, most MapReduce implementations have been designed and optimized for homogeneous clusters (e.g., Hadoop [14]). Unfortunately, these implementations perform poorly on heterogeneous clusters. For example, on a heterogeneous cluster of 10 Xeon-based servers and 80 Atom-based servers, Hadoop performs 20-75% worse than 10-node Xeon-only or 80-node Atom-only homogeneous sub-clusters for six out of our eleven benchmarks. This poor performance occurs despite Hadoop's built-in load-balancing scheduler and straightforward tuning for hardware heterogeneity (e.g., customizing the number of processes per node for each type of node and optimizing the memory buffer sizes).

LATE [37] is a significant effort to optimize MapReduce on heterogeneous clusters, and focuses specifically on straggler management. For fault tolerance, MapReduce identifies stragglers (i.e., tasks that are slow due to a presumed problem with their nodes) and speculatively runs backup copies for faster completion. LATE points out that straggler management results in excessive speculation in the presence of heterogeneity, and proposes techniques to improve straggler management. Unfortunately, LATE (or, in general, straggler management) alone is not sufficient to address hardware heterogeneity which raises other important issues, as described in this paper. As such, LATE is unable to improve MapReduce performance on our heterogeneous cluster.

In this paper, we explain the reasons behind MapReduce's poor performance on heterogeneous clusters and propose *Tarazu*[1], a

ASPLOS'12 March 3-7, 2012, London, England, UK.

1. An Urdu word that means balance.

suite of optimizations to exploit the full performance potential of such clusters.

Our first contribution is the key finding that the poor performance is due to two key factors: (1) the non-intuitive effect that MapReduce's built-in load balancing of Map computation results in excessive network communication and (2) the intuitive effect that the heterogeneity amplifies the load imbalance in Reduce computation. These factors extend beyond the issues of stragglers and speculative execution.

The Map-side effect has three components: First, the built-in load balancing of Map computation leads to faster high-performance nodes stealing[2] work from slower low-power nodes. The pronounced difference in the nodes' compute capabilities implies that a considerable amount of Map work is stolen. Unfortunately, input data for the stolen work remains at low-power nodes, resulting in numerous *remote* Map tasks at high-performance nodes and greatly increased network load. Note that the stolen tasks are simply the tasks that have not begun execution — not stragglers, which are slow-running tasks. Skewing the input data distribution towards high-performance nodes to convert remote tasks into local tasks incurs many problems, as explained in Section 2. This remote task problem does not exist in homogeneous clusters which are naturally load balanced, and hence, run only a few remote tasks. Second, the remote Map tasks compete with the Shuffle — the all-to-all communication from Map tasks to Reduce tasks — for the network bandwidth, severely worsening the bandwidth pressure. Finally, to reduce inter-node communication while load balancing in current MapReduce implementations, each node exhausts its local Map tasks (i.e., tasks whose input data is on local disk) before stealing tasks from another node (remote tasks). This strategy leads to execution of remote tasks only when necessary. Unfortunately, in heterogeneous clusters, this strategy temporally concentrates all remote Map tasks at the end of the Map phase, creating bursty network load.

The Reduce-side load imbalance stems from the fact that MapReduce implementations distribute the keys equally among Reduce tasks assuming homogeneous nodes. However, this equal distribution creates load imbalance among the heterogeneous nodes which have disparate compute capability. We crystallize the above insights using a simple analytical model.

Our second contribution is Tarazu, which consists of a set of three schemes to address the performance problems. First, we propose *Communication-Aware Load Balancing of Map computation (CALB)* based on the key observation that MapReduce implementations overlap Map computation and Shuffle, and either Shuffle or Map computation is in the critical path of execution depending upon MapReduction's Shuffle load and cluster hardware characteristics. When Shuffle is critical, CALB prevents all task stealing and increases the chances of tasks being performed locally, thereby eliminating remote Map task traffic and aggravation of the Shuffle — the first and second Map-side components above. While this prevention increases computation at low-power nodes, CALB hides extra work under the critical Shuffle. When Map computation is critical, CALB allows controlled task stealing to load-balance Map computation and hides resulting remote task traffic under low-power nodes' computation. Thus, CALB shortens the critical path in both cases — by not aggravating the Shuffle in the former case and by load-balancing Map computation in the latter. Second, to avoid bursty remote task communication in Map-critical MapReductions — the third Map-side component above, we propose *Communication-Aware Scheduling of Map computation (CAS)* which spreads out remote tasks throughout the Map phase. We propose heuristics based on online measurements to estimate the information needed by CALB and CAS for making application- and cluster-aware decisions. Third, we propose *Predictive Load Balancing of Reduce computation (PLB)* by skewing the key distribution among Reduce tasks based on the compute capabilities of nodes. To address the challenge that PLB's skew factors need to be known *before* the Reduce phase begins, we use measurements from the Map phase to predict the Reduce phase's skew factor.

In summary, the key contributions of this paper are:

- identifying the key reasons for MapReduce's poor performance on heterogeneous clusters;
- *Communication-Aware Load Balancing of Map computation (CALB)* across nodes;
- *Communication-Aware Scheduling of Map computation (CAS)* for spreading out remote Map task traffic over time;
- *Predictive Load Balancing of Reduce computation (PLB)* across nodes; and
- on-line measurement-based heuristics to estimate information needed for making application- and cluster-aware decisions.

We evaluate Tarazu using Hadoop running a suite of eleven typical MapReduce applications. Using a heterogeneous cluster of 10 Xeon-based servers and 80 Atom-based servers, we show that on average Tarazu achieves 40% speedup over a baseline of Hadoop that includes straightforward tuning for hardware heterogeneity.

The rest of the paper is organized as follows. We discuss MapReduce's issues with heterogeneity in Section 2 and describe Tarazu in Section 3. We present our experimental methodology in Section 4, and our results in Section 5. We discuss some related work in Section 6 and conclude in Section 7.

2 Issues with heterogeneity

We start with a brief background on MapReduce and then discuss the issues with MapReduce on heterogeneous clusters.

2.1 Background: MapReduce

In MapReduce's *programming model* [10], programmers specify a *Map* function that processes input data to generate intermediate data in the form of <*key, value*> tuples, and a *Reduce* function that merges the values associated with a key.

MapReduce's *execution model* has four phases [10]. In the first execution phase, *Map* computation produces <*key,value*> tuples. This phase is completely parallel and can be distributed easily over a cluster. The second phase performs an all-Map-to-all-Reduce personalized communication, called *Shuffle*, in which all tuples for a particular key are sent to a single Reduce task. Because there are usually many more keys than Reduce tasks, each Reduce task may process more than one key. The third phase *sorts* the tuples on the key field, essentially grouping all the tuples for the same key. This grouping does not occur naturally because the tuples for the differ-

2. While task stealing generally implies one thread running the tasks already assigned to another thread, we use the term to indicate a node processing data that is resident on the disk of another node to which the processing is likely to be assigned due to locality reasons.

ent keys meant for a Reduce task may be jumbled. Finally, the fourth phase of *Reduce* computation processes all the tuples for a key and produces the final output. Like Map tasks, Reduce tasks run in parallel.

A run-time system automatically partitions the input data, schedules the Map tasks across the nodes, orchestrates the Shuffle, and schedules the Reduce tasks. The run-time system also provides fault tolerance by re-executing computations when machines fail or become abnormally slow.

The growing interest in heterogeneous clusters comprising nodes designed for different performance-power points raises the question of how MapReduce implementations would perform on such clusters. Before we address this issue, we briefly describe the aspects of the MapReduce run-time framework that are most relevant to our context.

First, MapReduce frameworks employ a dynamic load-balancing scheduler, which tracks the execution status of nodes and assigns new tasks to free nodes. In doing so, the scheduler also considers locality. For example, the scheduler prefers tasks that process data resident on a node's local disk over tasks that require data from other nodes in the cluster (remote tasks). Second, in order to utilize maximum parallelism in both the Map and Reduce phases, Map and Reduce tasks occupy the entire cluster instead of space-sharing the cluster. Consequently, the all-Map-to-all-Reduce Shuffle amounts to all-nodes-to-all-nodes communication which stresses the scarce network bisection bandwidth [10, 32, 31, 36, 13]. While network switch bandwidth does scale with hardware technology, bisection bandwidth is a global resource which is hard to scale up with the number of nodes (e.g., around 50 Mbps per node for current clusters with thousands of nodes [10, 32, 31]). To alleviate this problem, the Shuffle is overlapped with Map computation where Reduce tasks "pull" intermediate data from earlier Map tasks while later Map tasks execute. To achieve this overlap, the scheduler creates and assigns Reduce tasks to nodes early during the Map phase (Map and Reduce tasks time-share the nodes, although Reduce computation does not start until Map and Shuffle phases have finished). Finally, in addition to these basic optimizations, MapReduce frameworks also have mechanisms for dealing with straggler tasks (tasks that take an unusually long time to execute and delay the completion of a phase [10]), by speculatively creating backup copies of tasks and terminating all outstanding copies when one copy finishes.

2.2 Reasons for poor performance on heterogeneous clusters

At first glance, it might appear that the dynamic load-balancing approach makes MapReduce frameworks inherently well-suited to heterogeneous clusters: slower (low-power) nodes would be assigned fewer tasks, while faster (high-performance) nodes would be assigned more tasks, leading to good load balance subject to the limits imposed by task granularity [10]. To test this hypothesis, we ran a suite of eleven MapReduce benchmarks on a 90-node, heterogeneous cluster comprising 10 Xeon-based nodes and 80 Atom-based nodes, using Hadoop [14] extended with suitable straggler optimizations [3,37]. We also tuned Hadoop for hardware heterogeneity by customizing the number of worker threads per node for each node type to account for nodes' differing core counts and optimizing memory buffer sizes to match nodes' memory capacities. We observed that the 90-node heterogeneous cluster was 20-75% slower than 10-node Xeon-only or 80-node Atom-only homogeneous sub-clusters for six out of eleven of our benchmarks. In other words, adding heterogeneous hardware resources actually degrades performance. This poor performance underscores the fact that MapReduce frameworks designed and optimized for homogeneous clusters do not directly scale to heterogeneous clusters.

Table 1: Map task distribution in homogeneous vs. heterogeneous clusters

	Homogeneous		Heterogeneous	
	Xeon-only	Atom-only	Xeons	Atoms
local	~100%	98%	45%	95%
remote	~0%	2%	55%	5%

The poor performance of MapReduce is due to two key factors, one non-intuitive and the other intuitive.

2.2.1 Factor 1 (non-intuitive): Interaction between load balancing and network traffic in Map

The MapReduce scheduler schedules remote Map tasks when a node no longer has any local data to process. In the context of a cluster with high-performance and low-power nodes, high-performance nodes finish their local Map tasks before low-power nodes, leading to the scheduling of many remote Map tasks that read input data from low-power nodes and incur greatly increased network load. Table 1 shows the break down of Map tasks into local and remote tasks for our above 90-node cluster. We see that because the homogeneous sub-clusters (Xeon-only and Atom-only) are well-balanced naturally, there are only a few remote Map tasks. In contrast, in the heterogeneous cluster, almost half of the Xeon-based nodes' Map tasks are remote (stolen from the Atom-based nodes). Because the Atom-based nodes are slower, they execute only a few remote tasks. We clarify that (1) the input data traffic for these Map tasks is distinct from the Shuffle which is the Map-to-Reduce communication, and (2) the remote tasks correspond to low-power nodes' tasks that have not begun execution — not stragglers which are slow-running tasks.

This network traffic problem is exacerbated in MapReductions with heavy Shuffle, where remote Map traffic must compete with the Shuffle for network bandwidth (recall that the Shuffle is overlapped with the Map phase). Figure 1 depicts the activities of high-performance and low-power nodes (Y axis) over time (X axis) during Map and Reduce phases. In the Map phase, the Shuffle is overlapped with Map tasks in the nodes. The high-performance nodes' remote Map traffic competes with the Shuffle. The local tasks at low-power nodes are slowed down due to the I/O processing required to service the high-performance nodes' remote tasks.

Furthermore, remote Map traffic is concentrated at the end of the Map phase because remote tasks are scheduled only after a node has finished processing its local data, as shown in Figure 1 for high-performance nodes. Figure 2 plots the remote Map traffic (Y axis) over Map phase execution time (X axis) showing the traffic burst at the Map phase end. Thus, despite being locality-aware (which in general reduces communication), the scheduler greatly increases network traffic in heterogeneous clusters.

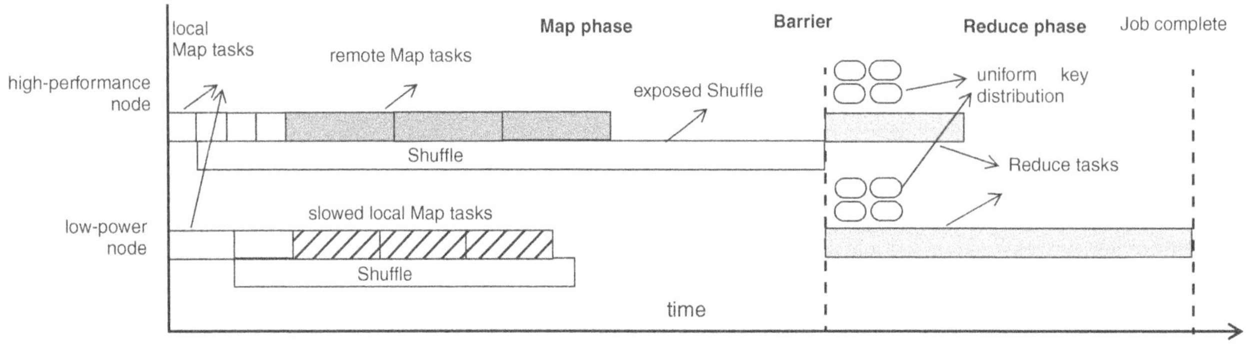

FIGURE 1: MapReduce performance issues on heterogeneous clusters

2.2.2 Factor 2 (intuitive): Reduce phase imbalance amplified by heterogeneity

The run-time system attempts to load balance the Reduce phase by assigning keys uniformly to each of the Reduce tasks, and scheduling tasks to the nodes in the cluster. The ability to dynamically load balance Reduce tasks is drastically limited by the fact that the number of Reduce tasks is typically only a small multiple of the number of nodes in the cluster in order to limit output fragmentation [10]. In the context of heterogeneous clusters, Reduce phase load imbalance is amplified due to the different processing speeds of different node types. Although the keys are distributed uniformly, low-power nodes take longer. The Reduce phase depicted in Figure 1 illustrates this issue. It is difficult for the scheduler to rectify this imbalance given the small number of Reduce tasks at each node. Treating Reduce tasks on low-power nodes as stragglers and running backup copies on high-performance nodes would effectively amount to not utilizing low power nodes in the Reduce phase. Furthermore, different Reduce tasks could process different amounts of data in both homogeneous and heterogeneous clusters, depending on the distribution of the values per key. However, addressing the value-per-key variability is harder than the variability due to heterogeneity, as discussed in Section 3.3.

2.3 A simple analytical model

To crystallize the above insights, we propose a simple performance model for MapReduce execution on a heterogeneous cluster. For ease of illustration, we describe our model for two types of nodes: high performance nodes (*hp*) and low-power nodes (*lp*). Our model assumes information such as the average execution times of Map and Reduce tasks on different types of nodes and total volume of

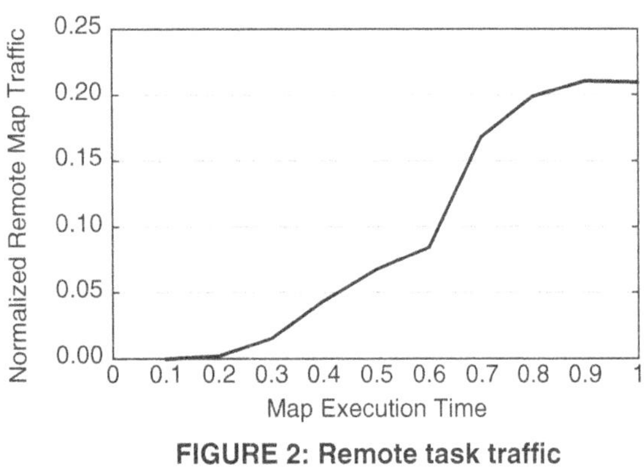

FIGURE 2: Remote task traffic

Shuffle data (e.g., collected through profiling). The model expresses a MapReduction's execution time as a function of various known parameters and key unknowns — the ratio in which Map tasks and Reduce tasks are partitioned among different node types. The inputs to the model are as follows:

- N_{hp} (N_{lp}) — number of high-performance (low-power) cores (not nodes) in the cluster;
- *ChunkSize* — size of one input data chunk in bytes;
- D_{hp} (D_{lp}) — number of input data chunks stored on high-performance (low-power) nodes, without counting replicas;
- $Tmap_{l,hp}$ ($Tmap_{r,hp}$) — average execution time of local (remote) Map task on a high-performance node;
- $Tmap_{l,lp}$ ($Tmap_{r,lp}$) — average execution time of local (remote) Map task on a low-power node;
- *Nkeys* — total number of keys processed by Reduce;
- $Tred_{hp}$ — average time taken to perform Reduce (including Sort) on a single key on a high performance node;
- $Tred_{lp}$ — average time taken to perform Reduce (including Sort) on a single key on a low power node;
- $BW_{bisection}$ — bisection bandwidth of the cluster in bytes/sec; and
- *ShuffleData* — total Shuffle traffic in bytes.

The unknowns (to be determined) are:

- $Nmap_{l,hp}$ ($Nmap_{r,hp}$) — number of local (remote) Map tasks executed on high-performance nodes;
- $Nmap_{l,lp}$ ($Nmap_{r,lp}$) — number of local (remote) Map tasks executed on low-power nodes; and
- $Nkeys_{hp}$ ($Nkeys_{lp}$) — number of keys processed by Reduce on high-performance (low-power) nodes.

Our model is described by the following linear equations for each of the Map, Shuffle and Reduce phases:

Map phase: Due to symmetry, we assume perfect load balance of Map tasks within high-performance and low-power nodes (but not across the two types of nodes). We intentionally ignore stragglers because it is not our intent to address them (previously proposed straggler management techniques may be used). Consequently, data chunks that reside on a high-performance node must be processed either by local Map tasks or by remote Map tasks on low-power nodes, and vice-versa for data chunks on a low-power node. Further, we assume that a chunk is located on a high-performance node if a single replica is available on a high-performance node. Hence,

$$Nmap_{l,hp} + Nmap_{r,lp} = D_{hp}$$
$$Nmap_{l,lp} + Nmap_{r,hp} = D_{lp}$$

Map Finish Time (MFT) can be computed as:

$$MFT_{hp} = (Nmap_{l,hp}*Tmap_{l,hp}+Nmap_{r,hp}*Tmap_{r,hp}) / N_{hp}$$

$$MFT_{lp} = (Nmap_{l,lp} * Tmap_{l,lp} + Nmap_{r,lp} * Tmap_{r,lp}) / N_{lp}$$

$$MFT = \max(MFT_{hp}, MFT_{lp}) \quad \text{(EQ 1)}$$

Shuffle phase: For simplicity, we assume that all of the remote Map reads and Shuffle data cross the cluster bisection, as given by:

$$D_{bisection} = (Nmap_{r,lp} + Nmap_{r,hp}) * ChunkSize + ShuffleData \quad \text{(EQ 2)}$$

To compute Shuffle Finish Time (SFT), we make simplifying assumptions that (1) the remote Map reads are spread out evenly throughout the Map phase while, in practice, the reads are concentrated at the Map phase end as discussed in Section 2.2.1 and (2) the Shuffle starts at the beginning of the Map phase (though in real implementations, the Shuffle starts a little later in the phase). Because the Map computation overlaps with the Shuffle and remote Map reads, SFT can be computed as:

$$SFT = \max(D_{bisection}/BW_{bisection}, MFT) \quad \text{(EQ 3)}$$

Because the remote Map reads are bursty, their overlap with the Map is imperfect causing SFT to be longer in practice. If the Shuffle is hidden completely under Map then $SFT = MFT$; otherwise, there is some exposed Shuffle and $SFT > MFT$.

Reduce phase: Reduce Finish Time (RFT) is given by:

$$RFT = SFT + \max(Nkeys_{lp}*Tred_{lp}/N_{lp}, Nkeys_{hp}* Tred_{hp}/N_{hp}) \quad \text{(EQ 4)}$$

We note that the model consists of linear equalities and inequalities in the unknown variables (max can be expressed as multiple linear inequalities). Therefore, the model can be solved exactly to minimize the total execution time (Reduce finish time, RFT), subject to the above constraints. Intuitively, this model captures the following trade-offs engendered by MapReduce execution on heterogeneous clusters:

- The ratio of input data stored on high-performance nodes to that on low-power nodes may be different from the ratio of the nodes' processing rates ($Tmap_{l,lp}/Tmap_{l,hp}$).
- The Map phase could be load balanced by executing remote Map tasks ($Nmap_{r,lp} > 0$ or $Nmap_{r,hp} > 0$), as is typical in current MapReduce frameworks, but doing do may increase the data crossing the cluster bisection due to remote Map reads ($D_{bisection}$), possibly delaying the Shuffle finish time (SFT).
- For Shuffle-light MapReductions, *ShuffleData* is small, and the Shuffle is hidden under the Map phase. For Shuffle-heavy MapReductions with large *ShuffleData*, the Shuffle is exposed.
- The Reduce phase can be load-balanced by assigning different number of keys to each type of nodes ($Nkeys_{hp}$, $Nkeys_{lp}$).

While the above model is useful to understand the trade-offs involved in MapReduce execution on heterogeneous clusters, the extensive information required (application and cluster characteristics, and task execution times) make it infeasible to use in practice. Requiring a priori application profiling on the target cluster greatly diminishes the agility and ease of use that is inherent to MapReduce. Therefore, we propose to use some heuristics based on online measurements to achieve the same goal in Tarazu.

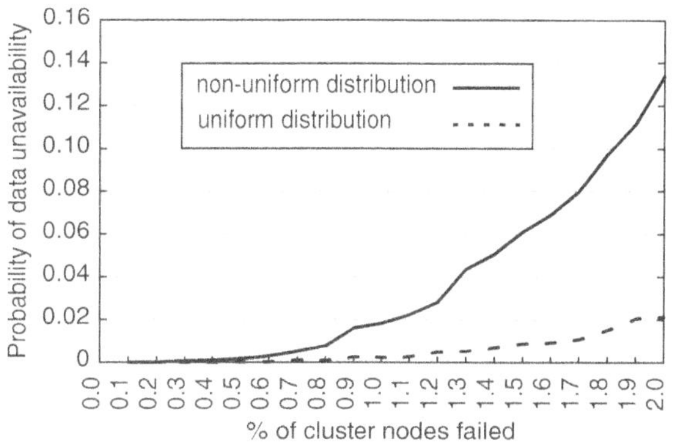

FIGURE 3: Probability of data unavailability with skewed distribution

2.4 Alternative approaches

One may argue that the aforementioned issues could be addressed using alternative approaches, including skewed data distribution, backup tasks, re-organization of the cluster hardware, and employing fine-grained Reduce tasks. We consider each of these in turn and argue their merits and de-merits in order to justify our approach.

Because node disk capacities are not directly correlated to compute capabilities (low-power nodes are available with similar disk capacities as high-performance nodes), it is natural to distribute data uniformly across the disks. However, one could skew Map input data distribution such that the amount of input data stored on each node is proportional to the node's processing capability. Doing so would imply that a high-performance node has more local Map data than a low-power node so that high-performance nodes do not exhaust local data much earlier than low-power nodes, resulting in far fewer remote Map tasks and far less network traffic. However, determining a good skew factor is hard in practice because the relative processing speeds of different types of nodes, and hence the skew factor, vary significantly from application to application. For example, in our suite of 11 MapReduce benchmarks, the ratio of Map task processing times on Atom-based to Xeon-based nodes vary from 1.5:1 to 4.5:1. Thus, despite skewing the data distribution, a significant number of remote tasks will remain, leading to the performance issue outlined above (see Section 5.5). Furthermore, skewing the data distribution incurs other significant problems: (i) Skewing would cause under-utilization of the cluster storage capacity because commodity disk capacities are unlikely to match our skew factors. In fact, Hadoop uses a "disk re-balancer" to prevent any unintentional skew to achieve good storage utilization [38]. (ii) Skewing would compromise fault tolerance achieved by data replication (nodes that store more data will have a much higher impact when they fail). Based on a Monte-Carlo simulation of node failures in a 1000-node cluster (100 high-performance nodes and 900 low-power nodes) with 3-way data replication of 640 GB, we determined that the probability of data becoming unavailable when 1% of the nodes fail is 0.0022 for uniform data distribution, and 0.0182 (an increase of 8.3X) when the distribution is skewed in the ratio of 1:4 between low-power and high-performance nodes. In Figure 3, we show the probability of data becoming unavailable (Y axis) when 0-2% of the nodes fail

(X axis) for the two data distribution schemes (higher node failure rates are unlikely). To avoid these reliability problems, we explore a solution that addresses the more realistic scenario where a significant number of remote tasks need to be executed, with or without skewed data distribution.

Backup tasks could be used to improve the load balancing capability of the scheduler in the presence of heterogeneity: upon completing all their local tasks, high-performance nodes can speculatively execute backup copies of tasks running on low-power nodes, reducing the chance of imbalance. Doing so, however, would imply that low-power nodes are under-utilized. In addition, the backup tasks may even hurt performance by creating additional load on the network.

Increasing the replication factor for data would increase the probability that data is local to a node and would reduce the number of remote tasks. This option, however, imposes a significant penalty on the cluster storage capacity.

Increasing the number of Reduce tasks (finer-grained Reduce tasks executed in multiple batches) could improve the Reduce phase's load balance because high-performance nodes would automatically execute more Reduce tasks. However, typical MapReduce jobs use a single batch of coarse-grained Reduce tasks due to two reasons. (1) With multiple batches, the Shuffle cannot hide under Map computation in later batches (Map completes before the first Reduce batch) and Reduce computation is usually too short to fully hide the Shuffle. The exposed Shuffle often makes multiple Reduce batches slower than one batch. (2) Unlike a MapReduction's input and final output, the intermediate Map output is not replicated for fault tolerance. To reduce the probability of loss of the intermediate data and subsequent re-run of Map tasks, the Reduce phase follows soon after Map in the single-batch case, whereas multiple batches often delay the Reduce phase.

In summary, MapReduce application developers expect their applications' performance to scale in proportion to the cluster's compute resources, irrespective of whether the hardware is homogeneous or heterogeneous. Based on the above insights, we propose a suite of optimizations called Tarazu.

3 Tarazu

Recall from above that (1) the Map-side built-in load balancing results in numerous remote Map tasks which increase the network load (i.e., $D_{bisection}$ in EQ 2 and EQ 3), compete with the Shuffle, and create bursty network load by being concentrated at the end of the Map phase, and (2) hardware heterogeneity amplifies the Reduce-side load imbalance across the nodes (i.e., increases the max term for RFT in EQ 4). To address these issues, we propose Tarazu, a suite of optimizations to improve MapReduce performance on heterogeneous clusters. As illustrated in Figure 4, Tarazu consists of three components:

- *Communication-Aware Load Balancing of Map computation (CALB),* which regulates the use of remote Map tasks based on whether Map or Shuffle is likely to be in the critical path (Section)
- *Communication-Aware Scheduling of Map computation (CAS)* to spread out remote Map tasks throughout the Map phase (Section 3.2), and
- *Predictive Load Balancing of Reduce computation (PLB)* across the heterogeneous nodes (Section 3.3).

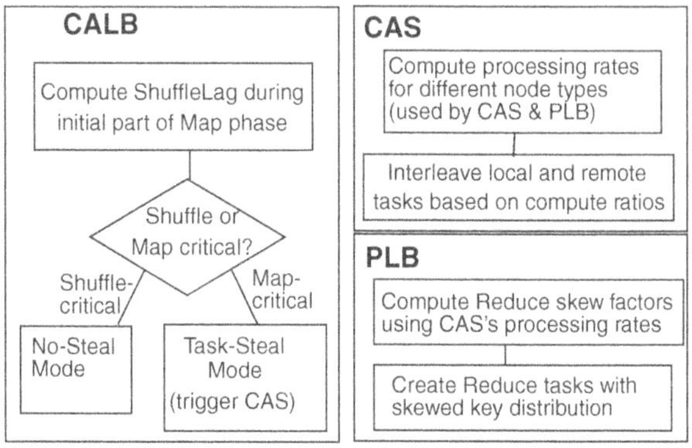

FIGURE 4: Overview of Tarazu

3.1 Communication-Aware Load Balancing of Map (CALB)

CALB is based on the key observation that due to the overlap between Map computation and Shuffle, either the Shuffle or the Map computation is in the critical path, depending upon the MapReduction's Shuffle load and the cluster hardware characteristics. As shown in Figure 4, CALB uses on-line measurements during the initial part of the Map phase to choose one of two operating modes, depending on whether Shuffle or Map is critical. In the initial part, all MapReductions start in the *task-steal* mode which allows controlled task stealing to load-balance the Map computation (i.e., lower MFT in EQ 1).

For MapReductions where the Shuffle is critical, CALB switches to *no-steal mode* where CALB prevents task stealing for most of the Map phase, preventing further aggravation of the Shuffle traffic (i.e., lower $D_{bisection}$ in EQ 2 and EQ 3) and increasing the chances of tasks being executed locally. When the Shuffle traffic falls below a threshold, called *shuffleEndThreshold*, (i.e., towards the end of the Map phase), CALB allows task stealing to load-balance any remaining tasks (naturally, faster nodes steal work from slower nodes). Figure 5 shows how the no-steal mode operates for the example of Figure 1. Like Figure 1, Figure 5 depicts the activities of high-performance and low-power nodes (Y axis) over time (X axis) during Map and Reduce phases. The Shuffle is critical in this example. For most of the Map phase, high-performance nodes do not steal tasks, allowing the low-power nodes to run the tasks locally. At the end of the Map phase when the Shuffle ends, high-performance nodes pick up a few remote tasks.

The *no-steal* mode has three benefits: (i) There are no remote Map tasks to compete with the Shuffle (Figure 5), (ii) Avoiding remote tasks also reduces the I/O processing overhead at senders and receivers. (iii) Because of no task stealing, slower nodes perform more work compared to the case with task stealing. Despite being slower, nodes' extra work is hidden under the critical Shuffle which exists irrespective of whether task-stealing occurs or not (Figure 5). By avoiding the contention due to remote tasks and their traffic, CALB enables the critical Shuffle to proceed faster, resulting in faster overall execution.

One may think that the residual task stealing at the end of the Map phase in the no-steal mode could create a burst of remote task traffic. However, this problem does not arise because (1) the number of remote tasks at this point is usually small (e.g., 1-2% of Map

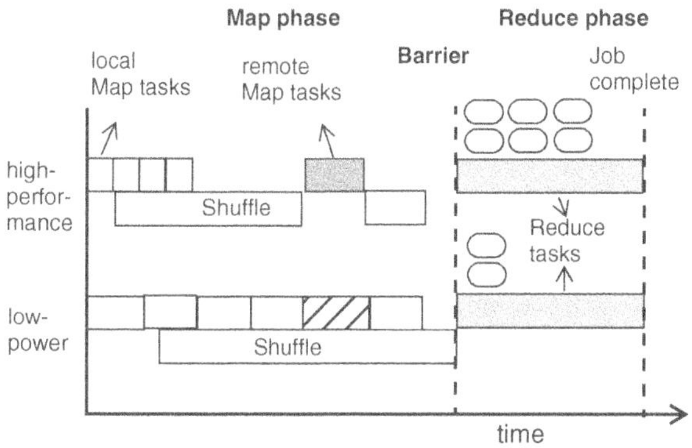

FIGURE 5: Communication-aware load balancing of Map (CALB) *no-steal* mode

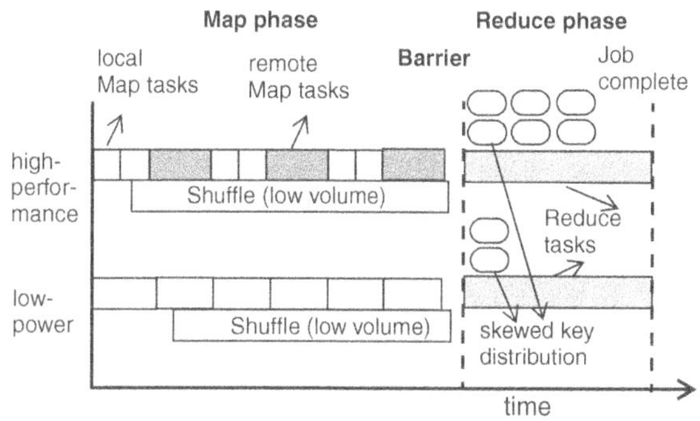

FIGURE 6: Communication-aware scheduling of Map (CAS) and Predictive Load Balancing of Reduce (PLB)

tasks) and (2) most of the Shuffle has finished by that time, so the remote traffic does not interfere with the Shuffle.

For MapReductions where the Map computation is critical, CALB continues in the task-steal mode. Note that the number of remote tasks needed and when to schedule them are the concern of CAS, which is discussed in the next sub-section. Figure 6 shows the task-steal mode for an example where Map computation is critical. As before, the Y axis shows the nodes' activities and the X axis shows time. In the Map phase, high-performance nodes steal tasks from low-power nodes. CALB hides the resultant high-performance nodes' remote task traffic under the low-power nodes' computation (Figure 6). By load-balancing Map computation, CALB shortens the critical path in this case.

The remaining issue is the detail of determining CALB's mode for a given application-cluster combination based on whether the Shuffle or the Map computation is critical. To this end, we observe that the Shuffle is critical when Map tasks complete their computation at a faster rate than their communication to Reduce tasks. Fortunately, MapReduce implementations already monitor, for fault tolerance purposes, the number of Map tasks that have completed their computation ($numComputed_i$) and the number that have completed their communication ($numCommunicated_i$) for each node i (these are sent at each heartbeat by worker nodes to the master node). We aggregate these numbers for the entire cluster and denote the aggregate values as $numComputed_{all}$ and $numCommunicated_{all}$. The difference between the two numbers, which we call *shuffleLag*, indicates the extent to which the Shuffle lags the Map computation. If *shuffleLag* increases over time, it implies that the Shuffle is likely to be critical.

We monitor the trend in *shuffleLag* over a time window between two points during the Map phase, denoted by *measureBegin* and *measureEnd*. Recall that the Shuffle communication starts only after Reduce tasks have been created, which occurs after some Map tasks are underway (Section 2). Consequently, we set *measureBegin* as the point where at least some Map tasks have completed their communication so that we obtain reliable readings for $numCommunicated_i$. *measureEnd* is constrained by the fact that the earlier the window ends, the fewer the samples whereas the later the window ends, the less time there is for taking the necessary action. We set *measureEnd* to achieve a good compromise between these opposing requirements. If the slope of the time series of *shuffleLag* measurements over the monitoring interval is positive, CALB enters no-steal mode; otherwise, it enters task-steal mode. CALB uses this simple approach to decide whether the Shuffle or the Map computation is critical for an application-cluster combination.

In no-steal mode, CALB detects the end of the Shuffle by continuing to monitor *shuffleLag* beyond *measureEnd*. The end is detected when *shuffleLag* as a fraction of $numComputed_{all}$ falls below *shuffleEndThreshold*.

It may seem that CALB may sub-optimally choose the task-steal mode for straddler MapReductions where the Map computation is only slightly more critical than the Shuffle. However, because all MapReductions start with task-steal mode in which they stay till *measureEnd*, our measurements ($numCommunicated_i$) include the effect of remote tasks due to task stealing on the network traffic in the measurement time window. CALB chooses task-steal mode only if the Map computation lags the Shuffle in the presence of the remote tasks. Therefore, CALB's choice of task-steal mode is not likely to be sub-optimal. Moreover, because Shuffle or Map criticality does not change within a MapReduction, deciding the source of criticality once is enough without the need for repeated, dynamic checks.

Although we have used two types of nodes — high-performance and low-power nodes — to illustrate our ideas, our description of CALB does not assume any specific number of types of nodes. As such, CALB is applicable to a heterogeneous cluster with any number of node types.

3.2 Communication-Aware Scheduling of Map (CAS)

While CALB decides whether or not allowing remote tasks would be beneficial for a given MapReduction, CAS determines how many remote tasks are needed and when to execute them in the task-steal mode (Figure 4). Recall from Section 2 that in current MapReduce implementations, task stealing occurs at the end of the Map phase, creating a surge of traffic. Also, as discussed in Section 2.3, this bursty traffic increases *SFT* (EQ 3). To avoid this problem, CAS spreads out the remote tasks (during initial part of the Map phase, and in CALB's task-steal mode) by interleaving them with local tasks. Figure 6 shows that high-performance nodes uniformly interleave their local and remote tasks. In addition to avoiding the bursty traffic, CAS has other benefits: (1) By interleaving remote tasks with local tasks in the Map phase, CAS achieves better overlap between remote task communication and local task computation on both sender and receiver sides (low-power and high-performance nodes, respectively, in Figure 6). (2) The remote tasks read input data faster by avoiding bursts. These benefits shorten Map computation, which is the critical path relevant for CAS.

In current MapReduce implementations, remote tasks are executed by a node only after it runs out of local tasks, and hence it is known for sure that remote tasks are required. In contrast, CAS requires task stealing to occur throughout the Map phase when the number of remote tasks is not known. To address this issue, we measure the average Map task execution times for each node type in the cluster and compute the ratios of the execution times for each pair of types ($mapComputeRatio_{i,j}$ defined as execution time of type j / execution time of type i). Because we need only one of $mapComputeRatio_{i,j}$ and $mapComputeRatio_{j,i}$, we choose numerator node type j to be the slower one. (In the simple case where there are only two node types, *mapComputeRatio* is a single number.) CAS uses these ratios to determine the number of remote tasks to be moved from one node to another. Because current MapReduce implementations already track the identity of the pair of source and destination nodes involved in task stealing, CAS can apply the specific pair's *mapComputeRatio*.

We continually monitor the execution times of local Map tasks that have completed their execution and calculate $mapComputeRatio_{i,j}$ for all i and j. As CAS triggers task stealing throughout the Map phase, each task stealing instance uses the ratio available at the time of the instance.

Unlike CALB which is naturally independent of the number of node types in the cluster, CAS needs per-pair ratios. However, because this number is likely to be small in real-world clusters, computing the ratios poses insignificant overhead.

Finally, CAS applies some more optimizations. First, to avoid overwhelming a node and causing thrashing, CAS limits the maximum number of remote tasks that can concurrently read input data from a node to *remoteServeThreshold*. Second, CAS prevents slower nodes from running local tasks whose input data is replicated at a faster node by using the replica locations of data (which is tracked by current MapReduce implementations for locality purposes). Third, CAS prevents task stealing from a node if the node has fewer remaining tasks than *localRemainingThreshold*. The rationale is that the node will likely execute the tasks faster than communicating the data for remote execution.

3.3 Predictive load balancing of Reduce (PLB)

While CALB and CAS optimize the Map phase, PLB achieves better load balance in the Reduce phase by skewing the intermediate key distribution among the Reduce tasks based on the type of the node on which a Reduce task runs (Figure 4). Such load balancing reduces the max term for *RFT* in EQ 4. While current implementations create as many bins per Map task as there are Reduce tasks, PLB creates more hash bins (by a factor of *binMultiplier*) as the number of Reduce tasks to achieve the skew (e.g., *binMultiplier* = 4). PLB uniformly distributes keys to the bins and then assigns as many bins to each Reduce task on node i as is dictated by the skew factor, $reduceSkewFactor_i$. For example, if a fast node is three times as fast as a slow node, then $reduceSkewFactor_i$ for the fast node is 3 and that for the slow node is 1. Therefore, a Reduce task on a fast node gets three times as many bins as a Reduce task on a slow node, as shown in the Reduce phase in Figure 6. To implement assigning multiple bins per Reduce task, we modify the MapReduce implementation to allow multiple sends from a Map task to a Reduce task (the baseline implementation assigns and sends only one bin from a Map task to a Reduce task). Note that although we create more hash bins per Map task than the baseline, we have the same number of Reduce tasks as the baseline and therefore do not incur any extra output fragmentation (Section 2.2.2).

Ideally, $reduceSkewFactor_i$ should be the ratio of the processing speeds of Reduce computation on the types of nodes in the cluster. However, because Reduce tasks are launched early in the Map phase to avoid delaying the Shuffle, the processing speeds are not available at the beginning of the Reduce phase. Moreover, starting with a default skew factor and changing it during the Reduce phase would incur the prohibitive cost of re-shuffling of data. Consequently, we use CAS's $mapComputeRatio_{i,j}$ for each pair of node types to compute $reduceSkewFactor_i$ and normalize this factor with respect to that of the slowest node. Thus, we use measurements from the Map phase to predict the Reduce phase's skew factor (we could use generic performance ratios of the node types but doing so would likely be no better than using the Map phase ratios).

While PLB skews the key distribution, the imbalance in the Reduce tasks may also come from the variability in the actual number of values per key. However, the requirement that the number of values per key has to be learnt early in the Map phase could make any estimates inaccurate. Therefore, we do not pursue this option.

Finally, PLB's skewed key distribution results in the Reduce output being skewed across nodes. However, the Reduce output is not uniform even in homogeneous clusters due to the variability in the number of values per key. In fact, MapReduce implementations provide a disk re-balancer to address this issue (Section 2).

3.4 Other issues

We discuss a few remaining issues related to Tarazu.

Because our schemes merely affect the creation and scheduling of the tasks, MapReduce's fault tolerance schemes and speculative execution of stragglers remain intact.

Although our implementation is based on Hadoop, our schemes are general and apply to other implementations [11,18,27]. Further, our schemes would default to Hadoop for homogeneous clusters. CALB's no-steal mode would amount to a few remote tasks at the end of the Map phase, similar to Hadoop. In CALB's task-steal mode, CAS would not kick in because a homogeneous cluster has only one type of nodes. Consequently, CALB's task-steal mode would also default to current Hadoop. PLB would not kick in due to the same reasons as CAS.

Our schemes are applicable to heterogeneous clusters with any number of types of nodes, and may be useful under different forms of hardware heterogeneity. For example, clusters where some nodes are GPU accelerated while others are not will also be subject to the issues that we address.

Despite the disadvantages of doing so, Map input data distribution may be skewed such that more data is placed on faster nodes to reduce remote Map tasks (Section 2). If the skewing is only moderate where faster nodes still finish before slower nodes, CALB would work as described. However, CAS's execution time ratios would have to be adjusted by the data skew factor (e.g., if CAS's *mapComputeRatio* ratio is 3:1 and faster nodes have twice as much data as slow nodes, then the new ratio would be 1.5:1). On

Table 2: Hadoop parameters

mapred.tasktracker.map.tasks.maximum	8 for Xeons, 2 for Atoms
mapred.tasktracker.reduce.tasks.maximum	2
io.sort.factor	5
mapred.inmem.merge.threshold	100
mapred.job.shuffle.merge.percent	0.50
DFS block size	64 MB
DFS replication factor	3
Maps to be completed before reduce creation	5%
Speculative execution enabled	Yes
Heartbeat interval	6 sec

the other hand, if faster nodes have so much data that they finish after slower nodes, then CALB's no-steal mode would proceed as before with a few remote tasks migrating from fast nodes to slow nodes at the end of the Map phase. In CALB's task-steal mode, CAS's adjusted ratios would flip directions and force the slower nodes to steal tasks from the faster nodes. Because skewing is only for the Map input data, PLB is not affected.

4 Experimental Methodology

We evaluate Tarazu by modifying Hadoop's public-domain MapReduce implementation (version 0.20.2) [14]. We use a heterogeneous cluster of 90 servers comprising 10 Xeon-based and 80 Atom-based server nodes.

4.1 MapReduce Implementations

Hadoop implements MapReduce as a run-time system linked with user-supplied Java classes for Map, Combiner (optional), and Reduce functionality. Hadoop uses a single master (JobTracker) for the whole cluster to create and schedule Map and Reduce tasks, monitor node health, and trigger backup tasks if needed.

We compare Tarazu against Hadoop as well as LATE [37]. For a fair comparison, we tune Hadoop for hardware heterogeneity by customizing the number of processes per node for each node type to account for the differences in core counts across node types and optimizing memory buffer sizes to match the memory sizes (e.g. our Xeon-based and Atom-based nodes have 8 cores with 48 GB DRAM per node and 2 cores with 4 GB DRAM per node, respectively, and Atom-based nodes thrash or run out of memory with default Hadoop settings). We list these and other parameters in Table 2. Further, for better performance, we replace Hadoop's synchronous write of the final Reduce output, which is replicated for fault tolerance, with asynchronous write in all cases (Hadoop, LATE, and Tarazu). We ensure that our measurements include the time for asynchronous writes in the background to finish.

We implement LATE and use the above tuned parameters. Further, we use the same values for *SpeculativeCap* and *SlowTaskThreshold*, as recommended in the paper. We tune *SlowNodeThreshold* so that LATE can correctly detect Xeon-based and Atom-based nodes as fast and slow nodes, respectively. We use the same heuristics to estimate the tasks' progress rates and finish times as in [37]. We ensure that LATE always schedules backup tasks on a Xeon-based node.

We run Tarazu with the parameters listed in Table 3. The master node samples $numComputed_i$ and $numCommunicated_i$ at every heartbeat for each node type in the time interval between *measureBegin* and *measureEnd* (Section), computes $mapComputeRatio_{i,j}$ for each pair of node types to determine the number of remote Map tasks (Section 3.2) and $reduceSkewFactor_i$ for each node type to skew the key distribution to Reduce tasks across the node types (Section 3.3). In PLB, we use the same heuristic as Hadoop to launch the Reduce tasks, with the additional requirement that at least one Map task on each node type is complete. This requirement ensures that we have valid $reduceSkewFactor_i$ for assigning hash bins to Reduce tasks.

4.2 Platform

We use a 90-node cluster comprising 10 Xeon-based and 80 Atom-based nodes. Each Xeon-based node is a dual-socket machine, where each socket has a quad-core Xeon E5620. Overall, each node has 8 cores running at 2.4 GHz, 12 MB L2, 48 GB of DDR3 RAM, and a 1-TB SATA hard disk. Each Atom-based node has an Intel Dual Core Atom D510 processor with each core at 1.66GHz, 2MB L2, 4 GB of DDR3 RAM, and a 500-GB SATA hard disk. All the systems run Ubuntu 10.04. Because of real system artifacts such as differences in disk seek times and OS scheduling variations, the execution time for the same job can vary across runs. However, we did not see any significant variations in our runs.

Our cluster uses two levels of non-blocking Gigabit Ethernet switches to connect the 90 nodes, which results in a per node bisection bandwidth (around 1 Gbps) that is much higher than that available in typical large-scale clusters (around 50 Mbps [10, 32, 31], as discussed in Section 2.1). While the Shuffle stresses the network bisection in typical large clusters [36, 13] especially in the case of Shuffle-heavy MapReductions, our cluster's high bandwidth unrealistically eliminates the impact of the Shuffle. For example, our Shuffle-heavy MapReductions running on a homogeneous Amazon EC2 cluster of 128 Xeon-based nodes spend about 20% of their total execution times in exposed Shuffle as compared to less than 5% on our homogeneous Xeon-node sub-cluster (the clusters use similar nodes and therefore the Map computation should hide the Shuffle to the same extent in the two clusters). To address this issue, we simulate realistic bisection bandwidth by dividing our cluster into nine sub-clusters of 10 nodes each (in some experiments, we use Xeon-only (10 nodes) and Atom-only (80 nodes) clusters where we divide the Xeon-only cluster into two five-node sub-clusters and the Atom-only cluster into eight 10-node sub-clusters). We use the network-utility tools *tc* and *iptables* to limit per-node bandwidths from one sub-cluster to another to 50 Mbps without limiting the bandwidths within each sub-cluster.

Table 3: Tarazu parameters

CALB *measureBegin*	0.4
CALB *measureEnd*	0.5
CALB *shuffleEndThreshold*	0.02
CAS *remoteServeThreshold*	1
CAS *localRemainingThreshold*	2
PLB *binMultiplier*	4

Table 4: Benchmark Characteristics

Benchmark	Input size (GB)	Input data	#Maps & #Reduces	Run time on Hadoop	Shuffle volume (GB)	mapCompute Ratio	Critical path
self-join	250	synthetic	3720 & 180	1929	246	1.76	Shuffle
tera-sort	300	synthetic, random	4500 & 180	2353	300	2.02	Shuffle
ranked-inverted-index	205	multi-wordcount output	3204 & 180	2322	219	2.50	Shuffle
kmeans	100	Netflix data, $k = 6$	1602 & 6	4608	106	4.43	compute
inverted-index	250	wikipedia	3764 & 180	1714	57	3.40	compute
term-vector	250	wikipedia	3764 & 180	1874	59	3.36	compute
word-count	250	wikipedia	3764 & 180	1035	49	3.17	compute
multi-word-count	250	wikipedia	3764 & 180	2703	248	4.40	compute
histogram-movies	215	Netflix data	3223 & 180	416	2×10^{-3}	1.44	compute
histogram-ratings	215	Netflix data	3223 & 180	685	1.2×10^{-3}	2.50	compute
grep	250	wikipedia	3764 & 180	459	1.3×10^{-3}	1.71	compute

4.3 Benchmarks

Because there are only three interesting MapReductions — *tera-sort*, *word-count*, and *grep* — in the Hadoop release, we add eight more MapReductions covering Shuffle-heavy and Shuffle-light categories.

4.3.1 Shuffle-heavy MapReductions

Our Shuffle-heavy MapReductions include *self-join, tera-sort, ranked-inverted-index, k-means, term-vector, inverted-index, word-count*, and *multi-word-count*. *Self-join* is similar to the candidate generation part of the *a priori* data mining algorithm to generate association among *k+1* fields given the set of *k*-field associations [1]. *Tera-sort* is based on NOWsort [6] for sorting 100-byte tuples with first 10 bytes of each record as the key and the remaining 90 bytes as the value. *Ranked-inverted-index* takes lists of words and their frequencies in a file, and generates lists of files containing the given words in decreasing order of frequency. *k-means* is a popular data-mining algorithm used to cluster input data into *k* clusters. *k-means* iterates to successively improve clustering [21]. *Inverted-index* takes a list of documents as input and generates word-to-document indexing. *Term-vector* determines the most frequent words in a host (above some cut-off) to aid analyses of the host's relevance to a search. *Word-count*, a well-known application, counts all unique words in a set of documents. *Multi-word-count* generates a count of all unique sets of three consecutive words in the set of documents.

We summarize input data sizes, dataset descriptions, run times of baseline Hadoop, and the Shuffle volume in Table 4. The Shuffle volume is high despite using Combiners. The table also shows *mapComputeRatio*, the ratio of local Map execution time on the Atom-based nodes to that on the Xeon-based nodes (Section 3.2). These ratios show the extent of our cluster's heterogeneity as seen by the MapReductions.

Although all MapReductions have large Shuffle volume, the critical path is not the same for all the MapReductions running on the baseline Hadoop. In *self-join*, *tera-sort*, and *ranked-inverted-index*, the Shuffle is exposed well past the Map computation in the Xeon-based nodes. Though the Shuffle is exposed less in the slower Atom-based nodes, the Shuffle remains the critical path in these MapReductions. On the other hand, the Map computation in both Xeon-based and Atom-based nodes completely hides the Shuffle for *k-means*, *inverted-index*, *term-vector*, *word-count*, and *multi-word-count*. Consequently, the Map computation is the critical path in these five MapReductions. The last column of Table 4 lists the critical path for each MapReduction (i.e., whether Map computation or Shuffle is critical).

4.3.2 Shuffle-light MapReductions

Our Shuffle-light MapReductions include *histogram-movies*, *histogram-ratings*, and *grep*. We classified movies based on their ratings using Netflix's data [26]. While *Histogram-movies* generates a histogram of movies based on their average ratings (Netflix data), *Histogram-ratings* generates a histogram of the ratings. *grep*, a well-known application, searches for an input string in a set of documents. These MapReductions are also summarized in Table 4. In all these MapReductions, the Map computation in both Xeon-based and Atom-based nodes completely hides the Shuffle. Consequently, the Map computation is the critical path in all of the Shuffle-light MapReductions.

5 Experimental Results

We start by comparing Tarazu against Hadoop and LATE, followed by isolating the impact of CALB, CAS and PLB. We then show the impact of Tarazu's sensitivity to the extent of hardware heterogeneity by varying the mix of Xeons and Atoms in our cluster. The above experiments use uniform Map input data distribution on the cluster which is default for Hadoop DFS. Finally, we show the impact of skewed input data distribution on Tarazu's speedups.

5.1 Performance

We compare Tarazu with Hadoop and LATE both of which include straight-forward tuning for hardware heterogeneity (Section 4.1). We also present results for Hadoop on each of the homogeneous sub-clusters of 10 Xeon-based nodes (*Xeon-only*) and of 80 Atom-based nodes (*Atom-only*).

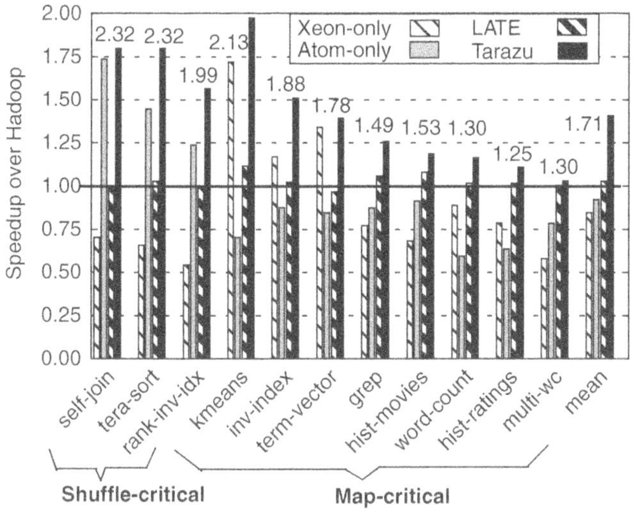

FIGURE 7: Performance comparison

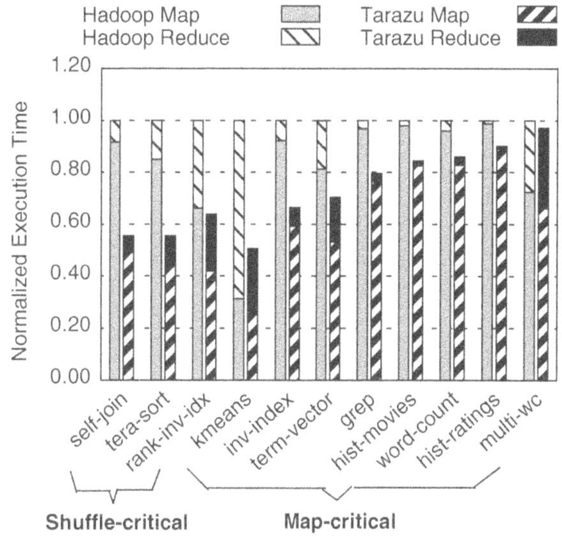

FIGURE 8: Impact of CALB, CAS, and PLB

In Figure 7, the Y-axis shows the speedups of Xeon-only, Atom-only, LATE, and Tarazu over Hadoop. The X-axis shows our benchmarks, of which the first three from the left are Shuffle-critical and the rest are Map-critical. The numbers above the bars show the speedups for an ideal case which (1) achieves perfect Map-Shuffle overlap for Shuffle-critical MapReductions and perfect load balance of the Map computation across Xeon-based and Atom-based nodes for Map-critical MapReductions and (2) achieves perfect load balance across Xeon-based and Atom-based nodes for the Reduce computation. We create the ideal case by post-processing Hadoop's execution logs. The ideal speedups range from 1.25 to 2.32, illustrating that there is significant scope for improvement over Hadoop. The high ideal speedups for Shuffle-critical MapReductions highlight the severity of the network bottleneck.

From the figure, we see that Hadoop on either of the homogeneous Xeon-only and Atom-only sub-clusters performs better than the baseline Hadoop on the heterogeneous cluster for the leftmost six out of eleven MapReductions. This result, one of the key motivations for this paper, shows that current MapReduce implementations do not perform well on heterogeneous clusters. LATE performs only slightly better than Hadoop by scheduling backup tasks on faster Xeon-based nodes for the stragglers running on slower Atom-based nodes. However, because remote Map task traffic and Reduce-side load imbalance are significant problems in heterogeneous clusters, regulating stragglers alone is insufficient to address hardware heterogeneity. On other hand, by addressing these problems, Tarazu achieves significant improvement with a mean speedup of 1.4, which includes high speedups for Shuffle-critical MapReductions (mean of 1.72, not shown) and good speedups for Map-critical MapReductions (mean of 1.3, not shown).

We also implemented and ran Mantri [3] which improves upon LATE's straggler identification. Though not intended for heterogeneous clusters, Mantri's accurate straggler identification may improve performance. However, for our cluster, we found that Mantri does not fare better than LATE for the same reasons stated above.

Finally, although Tarazu performs well, it still lags behind the ideal case due to two main reasons: (1) For Shuffle-critical MapReductions, CALB's on-line measurements for deciding the mode are performed only after some of the Map tasks have executed, by which time some unnecessary remote Map tasks may have been executed. (2) For Map-critical MapReductions, CAS's scheduling is not perfect and incurs some network contention among the remote tasks on different nodes.

In the following sections, we isolate the effects of CALB, CAS, and PLB, and show other data to explain Tarazu's speedups.

5.2 Effect of CALB and CAS

Figure 8 isolates the impact of CALB, CAS, and PLB. Because CAS is triggered only in CALB's task-steal mode (Section), we show the impact of CALB and CAS together. In Figure 8, the Y-axis shows Tarazu's execution times normalized to that of Hadoop. The execution times are broken up into two components, one for the Map phase including the Shuffle and the other for the Reduce phase. CALB and CAS target the Map phase and PLB targets the Reduce phase. Recall that on the Map side, the issues are remote Map traffic which competes with the Shuffle and is bursty, and on the Reduce side, the issue is load imbalance.

CALB predictions of whether each benchmark is Map- or Shuffle-critical agree perfectly with the characterization listed in Table 4. CALB's no-steal mode targets Shuffle-critical MapReductions (CAS is not triggered in this case). From the figure, we see that CALB significantly shortens the Map phase for these MapReductions, contributing to a large fraction of Tarazu's speedups. To

Table 5: Impact of CALB on remote tasks

Benchmark	Fraction of remote tasks on Xeons		Reduction in bisection traffic for Xeons
	Hadoop	Tarazu	
self-join	0.20	0.06	57%
rank-inv-idx	0.29	0.03	52%
tera-sort	0.24	0.08	50%

Table 6: Impact of CAS on remote tasks

Benchmark	Remote task execution times (s)		
	Hadoop	Tarazu	% speedup
kmeans	87.58	82.55	6%
inverted-index	58.59	43.12	36%
term-vector	57.71	43.04	34%
grep	56.00	37.47	49%
histogram-movies	49.31	43.17	14%
word-count	56.56	42.14	34%
histogram-ratings	54.93	45.46	21%
multi-word-count	99.95	94.50	6%

explain these improvements, Table 5 shows the fraction of remote tasks over all Map tasks on Xeon-based nodes in Hadoop and Tarazu, and Tarazu's reduction over Hadoop in the Xeon-based nodes' bisection traffic (Atom-based nodes run only a few remote tasks even in Hadoop).

We see that CALB significantly reduces the number of remote Map tasks and their traffic. By preventing remote tasks on the Xeon-based nodes, CALB allows Atom-based nodes to execute tasks locally hidden under the Shuffle. By avoiding the aggravation of the critical Shuffle due to remote traffic, CALB improves these MapReductions.

CALB's task-steal mode triggers CAS for Map-critical MapReductions. From Figure 8, we see that CAS significantly shortens the Map phase and is responsible for a large fraction of Tarazu's speedups for these MapReductions. To explain these speedups, we compare Hadoop and Tarazu in Figure 9 in terms of the distribution of remote Map traffic over Map execution time and in Table 6 in terms of the remote task execution times. We see that while Hadoop's traffic is bursty at the end of the Map phase, CAS evenly distributes the traffic. As a result, CAS achieves much faster remote task execution (Table 6) which translates to faster completion of the Map phase.

5.3 Effect of PLB

Figure 8 shows PLB's impact on the Reduce phase. In baseline Hadoop, the Reduce phase is much shorter than the Map phase for most of our MapReductions except *ranked-inverted-index, k-means, term-vector,* and *multi-word count*. Consequently, PLB's contributions to Tarazu's speedups are less than those of CALB

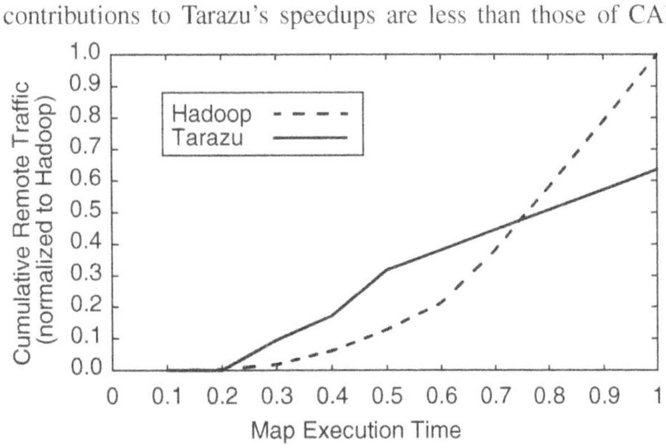

FIGURE 9: Impact of CAS on remote task traffic

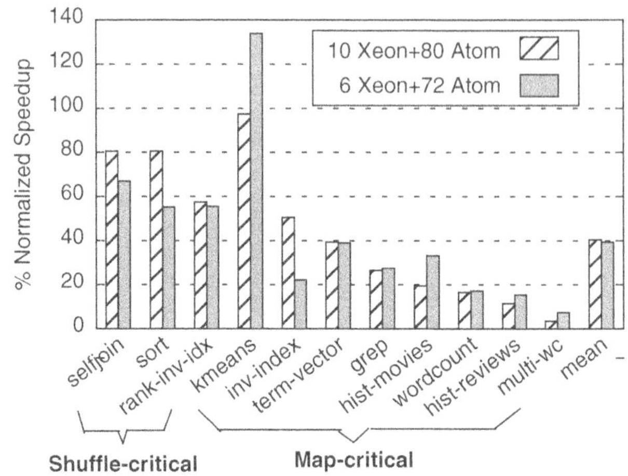

FIGURE 10: Sensitivity to heterogeneity mix

and CAS. PLB improves *k-means* significantly. *k-means* has only six Reduce tasks (number of centroids = 6, as shown in Table 4). Hadoop assigns Reduce tasks to nodes on a first-come-first-served basis where tasks have a high probability of being assigned to the slower Atom-based nodes which are more in number than the Xeon-based nodes (80 versus 10). In contrast, PLB assigns all Reduce tasks to the Xeon-based nodes. In *multi-word-count*, PLB slightly degrades performance because the ratio used for key distribution, $reduceSkewFactor_i$, which is predicted using measurements from the Map phase (Section 3.3), is inaccurate (the Xeon-based nodes are 4.4 times faster than the Atom-based nodes for *multi-word-count*'s Reduce tasks whereas the predicted skew is 1.5). For the other MapReductions, the prediction is reasonably accurate.

5.4 Sensitivity to extent of heterogeneity

We show Tarazu's sensitivity to the extent of heterogeneity by considering two different ratios of the number of Xeon-based nodes (8 cores/node) to that of Atom-based nodes (2 cores/node) — 10 to 80 (default) and 6 to 72. In first cluster, 33% of the cores are Xeons whereas in the second cluster this fraction is 25%. We note that extreme ratios where Xeons or Atoms are dominant make the clusters nearly homogeneous and hence are not interesting. Further, because Atoms are 3-4 times slower than Xeons, ratios with fewer Atom-based cores than Xeon-based cores also lead to Xeon-dominant clusters. Figure 10 shows Tarazu's speedups over Hadoop on these two clusters. We see that Tarazu works well on both the clusters.

5.5 Effect of skewed input data distribution

Recall from Section 2.4 that skewing the input data can reduce the number of remote Map tasks by placing more data on high-performance nodes than on low-power nodes. We show the effect of such skewed input data distribution on Tarazu in Figure 11. The input data is skewed on Xeon-based and Atom-based nodes in the ratio of 3:1 which is the mean $mapComputeRatio_{Xeon,\ Atom}$ for our benchmarks (Table 4). In the figure, the Y-axis shows Tarazu's speedups over Hadoop. From the figure, we see that Tarazu achieves a mean speedup of 1.22, highlighting the fact that a single skew ratio is not optimal for all the benchmarks and therefore skewing does not eliminate Tarazu's opportunity. As expected, this

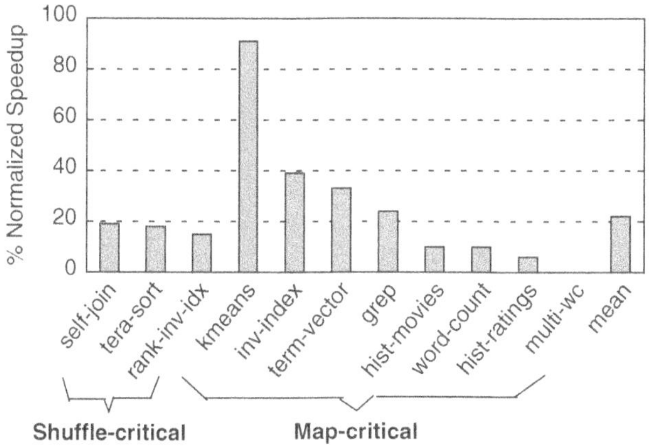

FIGURE 11: Impact of skewed input data distribution

mean speedup is lower than that in the non-skewed case (1.4 in Figure 7) due to fewer remote Map tasks in Hadoop. However, as mentioned in Section 2.4, skewing input data compromises reliability and hence may not be a viable approach. Tarazu achieves better performance than skewing without degrading reliability.

6 Related Work

The interest in heterogeneous clusters has been spurred by recent studies of servers designed with low-power processors [4,20,24]. A number of start up companies are developing servers using low-power processors, such as [7,30,17]. Hamilton [15] and Lang et al. [23] argue that not all workloads perform well on clusters built with low-power nodes, and [23] specifically demonstrates that enterprise databases do not. While these studies consider only homogeneous clusters constructed with low-power components, or "wimpy" nodes, Chun et al. [9] argue that hybrid data centers that mix nodes designed to a multitude of power/performance points, can handle diverse workloads in an energy-efficient manner. Towards this end, NapSAC, an energy-proportional web server cluster designed using three classes of servers based on Xeon, Atom, and ARM processors was proposed in [22], together with provisioning and load balancing algorithms for such a heterogeneous cluster. Further efforts along this direction were reported in [28]. Our work fundamentally differs from [22,28] in the nature of the workload targeted (interactive and highly time-varying versus batch), and therefore the challenges involved in efficiently utilizing a heterogeneous cluster are quite different.

Several implementations of MapReduce frameworks have been developed that support extensions such as relational data processing [14,11,34,35,27]. In addition, domain-specific libraries that implement various algorithms on top of MapReduce frameworks have been developed [5,33]. Due to the abundance of workloads and applications based on MapReduce, optimizing their performance on heterogeneous clusters is of great importance.

LATE [37] was the first work to point out and address the shortcomings of MapReduce in heterogeneous environments. They specifically focus on the observation that under heterogeneity, the mechanisms built in to MapReduce frameworks for identifying and managing straggler tasks break down, and propose better techniques for identifying, prioritizing, and scheduling backup copies for slow tasks. Techniques to improve the accuracy of progress estimation for tasks in MapReduce were reported in [8]. Mantri [3] explores various causes of outlier tasks in further depth, and develops cause- and resource-aware techniques to act on outliers more intelligently, and earlier in their lifetime.

As described in Section 2, our work addresses fundamentally different issues than [3,8,37]. We demonstrate that despite straggler optimizations, the performance of MapReduce frameworks on clusters with architectural heterogeneity remains poor, and we identify and address the causes of this poor performance. Therefore, we also report results comparing our techniques to baselines that already incorporate straggler optimizations. MapReduce frameworks have also been developed for other types of heterogeneous computing platforms such as multi-core processors and accelerators [16,29,25]. In addition to the fact that our work is complementary to these efforts, we note that the use of accelerators in a subset of the nodes of a cluster would also result in cluster-level heterogeneity, necessitating the use of our techniques (e.g., nodes with GPUs would process data at a faster rate than nodes without GPUs, leading to the performance issues that we outline).

Finally, many recent papers optimize multi-tenant MapReduce jobs on homogeneous clusters [19,12,36]. These papers propose schedulers which, in one way or another, prioritize local tasks over remote tasks across multiple jobs. In a heterogeneous cluster, however, high-performance nodes would run out of local tasks in all the jobs, incurring the remote task problem addressed by Tarazu.

7 Conclusion

Current MapReduce frameworks perform poorly on heterogeneous clusters. We analyzed the performance of MapReduce workloads on a heterogeneous cluster composed of high-performance and low-power nodes, and identified the key causes of poor performance as follows: (1) the load balancing used in MapReduce causes excessive and bursty network communication during the Map phase, which competes with the Shuffle for the scarce bisection bandwidth and (2) the heterogeneity amplifies the Reduce's load imbalance. Addressing these issues require judicious run-time decisions based on application and cluster characteristics (e.g., the decisions of whether, how much, and when to steal tasks depend upon whether Map or Shuffle is critical, and the relative rates of Map computation and communication).

We proposed Tarazu to perform these decisions via Communication-Aware Load Balancing of Map computations (CALB), Communication-Aware Scheduling of Map computations (CAS-CAS), and Predictive Load-Balancing of Reduce computations (PLB). Tarazu incorporates application and cluster characteristics through various heuristics driven by on-line measurements We implemented the proposed techniques in the Hadoop framework, and showed that, on a 90-node heterogeneous cluster and across a suite of 11 benchmarks, Tarazu achieves an average speedup of 40% over Hadoop.

Due to its effectiveness, Tarazu will be valuable in realizing the potential of heterogeneous clusters for the important class of large-scale data-intensive applications. The growing importance and prevalence of heterogeneous clusters suggest that Tarazu will be an important tool for these applications in the future.

References

[1] R. Agrawal and R. Srikant. Fast algorithms for mining association rules. *Proceedings of 20th Intl. Conference on Very Large Data Bases, VLDB*, 1994.

[2] Amazon EC2. http://aws.amazon.com/ec2.

[3] G. Ananthanarayanan, S. Kandula, A. Greenberg, I. Stoica, Y. Lu, B. Saha, and E. Harris. Reining in the outliers in Map-Reduce clusters using Mantri. In *Proceedings of the Usenix Symposium on Operating Systems Design and Implementation (OSDI)*, 2010.

[4] D. G. Andersen, J. Franklin, M. Kaminsky, A. Phanishayee, L. Tan, and V. Vasudevan. FAWN: A Fast Array of Wimpy Nodes. In *Proceedings of the ACM Symposium on Operating Systems Principles (SOSP)*, 2009.

[5] Apache Mahout: Scalable machine learning and data mining. http://mahout.apache.org.

[6] A. C. Arpaci-Dusseau, R. H. Arpaci-Dusseau, D. E. Culler, J. M. Hellerstein, and D. A. Patterson. High-performance sorting on networks of workstations. In *Proceedings of the SIGMOD International Conference on Management of Data*, pages 243–254, Tucson,Arizona, May 1997.

[7] Calxeda, Inc. http://www.calxeda.com.

[8] Q. Chen, D. Zhang, M. Guo, Q. Deng, and S. Guo. SAMR: A Self-adaptive MapReduce Scheduling Algorithm in Heterogeneous Environment. In *Proceedings of the International Conference on Computer and Information Technology (CIT)*, 2010.

[9] B.-G. Chun, G. Iannaccone, G. Iannaccone, R. Katz, G. Lee, and L. Niccolini. An Energy Case for Hybrid Datacenters. In *SOSP Workshop on Power Aware Computing and Systems (HotPower)*, 2009.

[10] J. Dean and S. Ghemawat. MapReduce: Simplified data processing on large clusters. *Commun. ACM*, pages 107–113, Jan. 2008.

[11] Facebook Hive. http://hadoop.apache.org/hive.

[12] A. Ghodsi, M. Zaharia, B. Hindman, A. Konwinski, S. Shenker, and I. Stoica. Dominant Resource Fairness: Fair allocation of multiple resource types. In *Proceedings of the 8th USENIX conference on Networked systems design and implementation(NSDI)*, 2011.

[13] A. Greenberg, J. R. Hamilton, N. Jain, S. Kandula, C. Kim, P. Lahiri, D. A. Maltz, P. Patel, and S. Sengupta. VL2: A scalable and flexible data center network. In *Proceedings of the SIGCOMM conference on Data Communication*, pages 51–62, 2009.

[14] Hadoop. http://lucene.apache.org/hadoop/.

[15] J. Hamilton. When Very Low-Power, Low-Cost Servers Don't Make Sense. In *http://perspectives.mvdirona.com/2010/05/18/WhenVeryLowPowerLowCostServersDontMakeSense.aspx*, 2010.

[16] B. He, W. Fang, Q. Luo, N. K. Govindaraju, and T. Wang. Mars: A MapReduce framework on graphics processors. In *Proceedings of the 17th international conference on Parallel Architectures and Compilation Techniques*, pages 260–269, 2008.

[17] HP Labs. Project Moonshot. In *http://www.hp.com/hpinfo/newsroom/press_kits/2011/MoonshotInfrastructure/index.html*, 2011.

[18] M. Isard, M. Budiu, Y. Yu, A. Birrell, and D. Fetterly. Dryad: Distributed data-parallel programs from sequential building blocks. In *EuroSys '07: Proceedings of the 2nd SIGOPS/EuroSys European Conference on Computer Systems*, 2007.

[19] M. Isard, V. Prabhakaran, J. Currey, U. Wieder, K. Talwar, and A. Goldberg. Quincy: Fair scheduling for distributed computing clusters. In *Proceedings of the 22nd symposium on Operating systems principles*, SOSP, pages 261–276, USA, 2009.

[20] V. Janapa Reddi, B. C. Lee, T. Chilimbi, and K. Vaid. Web search using mobile cores: Quantifying and mitigating the price of efficiency. In *Proceedings of the International Symposium on Computer Architecture (ISCA)*, 2010.

[21] J.Hartigan. *Clustering Algorithms. Wiley*, 1975.

[22] A. Krioukov, P. Mohan, S. Alspaugh, L. Keys, D. E. Culler, and R. H. Katz. NapSAC: Design and implementation of a power-proportional web cluster. *ACM Computer Communication Review*, 41(1), 2011.

[23] W. Lang, J. M. Patel, and S. Shankar. Wimpy node clusters: What about non-wimpy workloads? In *Proceedings of the International Workshop on Data Management on New Hardware (DaMoN)*, 2010.

[24] K. Lim, P. Ranganathan, J. Chang, C. Patel, T. Mudge, and S. Reinhardt. Understanding and Designing New Server Architectures for Emerging Warehouse-Computing Environments. In *Proceedings of the 35th Annual International Symposium on Computer Architecture* (ISCA), pages 315–326, 2008.

[25] M. D. Linderman, J. D. Collins, H. Wang, and T. H. Meng. Merge: A programming model for heterogeneous multi-core systems. In *Proceedings of the 13th international conference on Architectural Support for Programming Languages and Operating Systems (ASPLOS)*, 2008.

[26] Netflix movies data. *http://www.netflixprize.com/download.*

[27] C. Olston, B. Reed, U. Srivastava, R. Kumar, and A. Tomkins. Pig latin: a not-so-foreign language for data processing. In *Proceedings of the 2008 international conference on Management Of Data*, SIGMOD, pages 1099–1110, 2008.

[28] M. M. Rafique, N. Ravi, S. Cadambi, S. T. Chakradhar, and A. R. Butt. Power Management for Heterogeneous Clusters: An Experimental Study. In *Proceedings of the IEEE International Conference on Green Computing*, 2011.

[29] C. Ranger, R. Raghuraman, A. Penmetsa, G. Bradski, and C. Kozyrakis. Evaluating MapReduce for Multi-core and Multiprocessor Systems. In *13th International Symposium on High Performance Computer Architecture, HPCA*, pages 13–24, 2007.

[30] SeaMicro, Inc. http://www.seamicro.com.

[31] A. Vahdat, M. Al-Fares, N. Farrington, R. N. Mysore, G. Porter, and S. Radhakrishnan. Scale-Out Networking in the Data Center. *IEEE Micro*, 30:29–41, July 2010.

[32] D. Weld. Lecture notes on MapReduce (based on Jeff Dean's slides). *http://rakaposhi.eas.asu.edu/cse494/notes/s07-map-reduce.ppt*, 2007.

[33] X-RIME: Hadoop based large scale social network analysis. http://xrime.sourceforge.net/.

[34] H.-C. Yang, A. Dasdan, R.-L. Hsiao, and D. S. Parker. Map-reduce-merge: Simplified relational data processing on large clusters. In *Proceedings of the SIGMOD international conference on Management Of Data*, 2007.

[35] Y. Yu, M. Isard, D. Fetterly, M. Budiu, U. Erlingsson, P. K. Gunda, and J. Currey. DryadLINQ: A System for General-Purpose Distributed Data-Parallel Computing Using a High-Level Language. In *Proceedings of International Symposium on Operating System Design and Implementation (OSDI)*, 2008.

[36] M. Zaharia, D. Borthakur, J. Sen Sarma, K. Elmeleegy, S. Shenker, and I. Stoica. Delay Scheduling: A simple technique for achieving locality and fairness in cluster scheduling. In *Proceedings of the 5th European conference on Computer systems*, EuroSys '10, pages 265–278, 2010.

[37] M. Zaharia, A. Konwinski, A. Joseph, R. Katz, and I. Stoica. Improving MapReduce performance in heterogeneous environments. In *Proceedings of the Usenix Symposium on Operating Systems Design and Implementation (OSDI)*, 2008.

[38] Hadoop rebalancer. http://hadoop.apache.org/common/docs/r0.17.2/hdfs_user_guide.html#Rebalancer.

Leveraging Stored Energy for Handling Power Emergencies in Aggressively Provisioned Datacenters

Sriram Govindan
Datacenter Compute Infrastructure Team, Microsoft,
Redmond, WA, USA
srgovin@microsoft.com

Di Wang Anand Sivasubramaniam
Bhuvan Urgaonkar
Department of Computer Science and Engineering,
The Pennsylvania State University, PA 16802
{diw5108,anand,bhuvan}@cse.psu.edu

Abstract

Datacenters spend $10-25 per watt in provisioning their power infrastructure, regardless of the watts actually consumed. Since peak power needs arise rarely, provisioning power infrastructure for them can be expensive. One can, thus, aggressively under-provision infrastructure assuming that simultaneous peak draw across all equipment will happen rarely. The resulting non-zero probability of emergency events where power needs exceed provisioned capacity, however small, mandates graceful reaction mechanisms to cap the power draw instead of leaving it to disruptive circuit breakers/fuses. Existing strategies for power capping use temporal knobs local to a server that throttle the rate of execution (using power modes), and/or spatial knobs that redirect/migrate excess load to regions of the datacenter with more power headroom. We show these mechanisms to have performance degrading ramifications, and propose an entirely orthogonal solution that leverages existing UPS batteries to temporarily augment the utility supply during emergencies. We build an experimental prototype to demonstrate such power capping on a cluster of 8 servers, each with an individual battery, and implement several online heuristics in the context of different datacenter workloads to evaluate their effectiveness in handling power emergencies. We show that: (i) our battery-based solution can handle emergencies of short duration on its own, (ii) supplement existing reaction mechanisms to enhance their efficacy for longer emergencies, and (iii) battery even provide feasible options when other knobs do not suffice.

Categories and Subject Descriptors C.0 [*Computer Systems Organization*]: General

General Terms Design, Experimentation, Measurement, Performance

Keywords UPS, Batteries, Data center, Peak power, Stored energy, Provisioning, Cap-ex, Peak shaving

1. Introduction

Datacenters incur capital expenditure (cap-ex) of $10-25 per watt of provisioned power capacity, regardless of whether this watt is actually consumed [4, 23]. The power delivery infrastructure amounts to several million dollars in cap-ex [5], contributing over a third of the amortized monthly datacenter costs [4]. Although not all of this may go towards the power delivery for IT equipment, since there is other supporting infrastructure including HVACs, fans, etc., the IT-related power network is still a substantial component that warrants meticulous planning and provisioning. Provisioning for the theoretical peak (using face-plate ratings of equipment) that may never happen, or even the occasional peak (which requires all equipment to simultaneously exercise their maximum draw), can prove very expensive. A study of power consumption in a Google datacenter, depicted in Figure 1, reiterates this observation showing a very low probability of reaching close to the provisioned peak (probability of exceeding 90% of the potential peak is less than 1%), with a profile that is highly skewed around the average. Aggressive provisioning of power infrastructure can thus yield substantial cap-ex savings. The goal of this paper is to deal with the rare ("black swan") power emergencies (when the draw exceeds provisioned power) that arise in such aggressively provisioned datacenters in a seamless and graceful fashion.

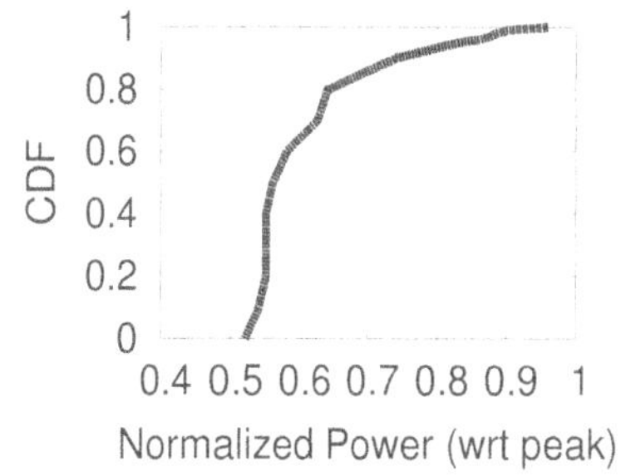

Figure 1. Rack Power profile of a Google datacenter [12].

The temporal and spatial load variations, and resulting power draw, in a datacenter offer a strong reason for leveraging statistical multiplexing to under-provision the power infrastructure. Circuit-breakers are used to ensure equipment safety and handle power spikes lasting several seconds [9], abruptly cutting off power supply upon an overdraw. *Can we employ alternate solutions that handle emergencies more gracefully by removing/easing such spikes, thereby reducing the probability of hitting these safety limits?* Circuit-breakers would continue to be used, but only as the last line of defense. Also, datacenters have power upgrade cycles to handle growing IT load. The probability of emergencies can increase as we get closer to the next upgrade, and such solutions can

ASPLOS'12, March 3–7, 2012, London, England, UK.

help relieve disruptions during these periods. Gracefully handling emergencies, while meeting performance SLAs, would allow more aggressive power provisioning [1].

Software mechanisms for power capping have been examined to some depth [12, 13, 16, 19, 25, 37, 38, 47]. Broadly, we can classify existing solutions into two categories. The first set of knobs are local to servers, where temporal load-shifting/demand-shaping is used to control the rate of workload execution (and thereby control power consumption which grows with utilization). Apart from scheduling the load (temporally spacing it out using CPU scheduling), hardware power mode control - clock throttling states (including server shutdown [7, 36]) and/or dynamic voltage-frequency modulation states (DVFS) - is also used to control the rate of workload execution (with different trade-offs between performance and power) [16, 47]. The second set of knobs exploits spatial non-uniformity in power profiles across (groups of) servers, and dynamically redirects/migrates load to regions of the datacenter with more headroom. While local knobs are agile and effective for handling short-lived emergencies, prolonged throttling can impact performance. While spatial migration is better for longer emergencies, there can be overheads during and after (load imbalance on some nodes, loss of locality, etc.) migration, in addition to the need for headroom elsewhere in the datacenter. The load may also not be "move-able" to other servers in some cases. Regardless, both these strategies can have substantial performance repercussions.

This problem is analogous to supply-demand mismatch issues on the electrical grid, and the solutions above are analogous to "demand-response" mechanisms in that context. However, one solution - energy storage - that is used in normal grids to amplify the efficacy of demand-response has been little explored in the datacenter context. Energy storage can be used to (i) deal with short/small power spikes without even requiring other reaction mechanisms (temporal/spatial) which have performance consequences, (ii) supplement existing mechanisms to improve their efficacy in meeting application SLAs, and (iii) offer remedial solutions, even if they are temporary, when other mechanisms may not find feasible options to meet application SLAs. Further, unlike in grids where energy storage may be a costly proposition, datacenters already have storage built-in in the form of UPS units to handle power disruptions - *can we tap into these for emergency handling without impinging on the availability mandates?*

There are different choices for UPS placement - from a centralized (usually redundant) configuration, to a distributed version at each server as in Google datacenters [18], as well as at intermediate levels (e.g., per-rack) similar to the ones in Microsoft [33] and Facebook [11] datacenters. Server-level UPS, when incorporated with the power supply, can help eliminate double-conversion needs and the associated energy losses. We assume a server-level UPS unit, although many of our ideas will also apply to other configurations . In general, UPS batteries help reduce/cap power draw at and above the level in the power hierarchy where they are placed. When using batteries beyond their original role, we must ensure that the datacenter's power availability (upon utility outages), as well as the batteries' normal lifetime (3-5 years for lead-acid) are not compromised. Since UPS units are mainly transitionary devices to temporarily handle load until diesel generators are started (which takes around 15-30 seconds), we are able to utilize them for a couple of minutes for our purposes while still leaving enough charge for availability purposes. To facilitate aggressive power provisioning, this paper makes the following contributions:

[1] As Taleb says in his book [42]: "Black Swans being unpredictable, we need to adjust to their existence rather than naively try to predict them." Even if the datacenter power profile may follow bell-curve behavior as in Figure 1, the extreme consequences of ignoring the "highly improbable" tail makes emergency handling a critical problem.

- We present an offline theoretical framework combining all knobs - batteries, power states, migration (both within and across datacenter clusters) - to find the performance optimal way of handling an emergency for a given level of power underprovisioning. This serves as a reference point for how well we can do and offers insights on what knobs/combinations work for given workload-emergency combinations.
- Since emergencies are inherently unpredictable (when? how severe? how long?), we develop several on-line heuristics employing existing temporal and spatial knobs, and combinations thereof. We also introduce battery-based emergency handling techniques, accommodating different drain rates (slow and fast), and combine them with existing knobs in interesting ways.
- We develop an experimental prototype of 8 servers with individual UPS units, and implement seven control heuristics. We examine emergencies in the context of several representative datacenter workloads with unique characteristics: (i) TPC-W [40] and Specjbb [41] server-based workloads with emergencies arising from load spikes (e.g., flash crowds), (ii) a MapReduce [22] application where the map phase introduces power spikes substantially higher than the reduce phase, (iii) a streaming media server where handling the power spike caused by a surge of new connections leads to jitters in existing streams, and (iv) a multi-programmed GPU + Virus scan application pair that is tied to a particular set of servers (migration is not an option) which when run together introduces a high power draw (requiring them to be temporally spaced out).
- We consider different degrees of under-provisioning, and show that battery by itself can sustain short emergencies (around 10-20 minutes on our prototype). Longer emergencies (30 minutes or higher), require migration since sustained local throttling hurts performance. On the other hand, performance overheads of migration makes it less attractive for shorter emergencies. Our battery solution, in conjunction with migration, provides a seamless bridge across the spectrum of these duration, and is able to reduce the performance impact of these intermediate duration. In most cases, battery-based heuristics, with these knobs, help us get within 10-20% of the theoretical bounds.

2. Related Work

Tighter Power Provisioning: Statistical multiplexing-based overbooking/underprovisioning of resources, a widely used yield management technique in different domains, including IT resources in datacenters [43, 46], is now being suggested for the power infrastructure. This ranges from components within servers [13, 25], to groups/ensembles of servers and other equipment [19, 26, 35, 39, 48]. The basic underlying idea is to exploit the low likelihood of simultaneous peak power needs of all components/servers [12, 13, 25]. Such provisioning requires agile reactive techniques to ensure the power consumption stays below capacity to allow safe operation with satisfactory workload performance. These techniques include device power state control [10, 14, 16, 32, 37, 38, 47, 49] and workload scheduling or migration within or even outside the datacenter [2, 17, 19, 30, 34, 45].

Battery-based power management: While battery management has been studied in the mobile/embedded domains [15, 50, 51] (e.g., drain rate adjustment for longevity), their use in datacenters has been limited to mere transition devices during utility failure. Recent work has looked at using UPS batteries to reduce electricity operational costs [20, 44], but their role in tighter provisioning for reducing cap-ex is entirely novel. To our knowledge, we are the first to explore the use of stored energy (UPS batteries) for tighter provisioning.

3. Problem Details and Solutions

3.1 The Problem

Underprovisioning of power (equipment) does not have to be restricted to the highest level in the hierarchy. As we aggressively push such underprovisioning to equipment at lower levels, there is scope for additional cap-ex savings. However, going deeper lessens the potential for exploiting statistical multiplexing of power demands across underlying servers. The higher burstiness (variance) at deeper levels can result in higher probability for emergencies/violations. A more rigorous cost-benefit analysis is necessary to find out how much to underprovision at each level of the hierarchy. We consider this beyond the scope of this paper, and focus here on the following consequent problem: given a level c aggressively underprovisioned at P_{budget} to accommodate N servers under it, how do we cap the net power draw of these servers to P_{budget} at all times? We will consider different values of P_{budget} relative to the maximum possible peak draw by the N servers, henceforth referred to as a *cluster* (c).

If $P_j(t)$ represents power draw of server j at time t, then underprovisioning power capacity exploits the statistical property $Probability(\sum_{j=1}^{N} P_j(t) > P_{budget}) \leq \epsilon, \forall t$. Just as in other domains where underprovisioning is used, there are consequences to be carefully traded-off against its benefits. Since ϵ is non-zero, despite being small, there would inevitably be situations when the aggregate power draw of the N servers cannot be safely accommodated by the infrastructure at level c. Since ϵ may not be identified precisely (Section 1), we need reactive mechanisms to deal with the power overdraw situations. Normally, during such an episode of power overdraw, circuit-breakers/fuses at level c would kick in to ensure safety from fire hazards and overdraw-induced equipment burnout. Such workload-oblivious reaction mechanisms are highly undesirable in the datacenter context since they can lead to lost computation and inconsistent states or even impact IT equipment reliability (e.g., hard disk failures [52]). Therefore, when underprovisioning, it is essential to additionally employ workload-aware reaction mechanisms to operate gracefully under such emergencies, while continuing to leave circuit-breakers/fuses as the last line of defense. Such mechanisms should also be agile to quickly control the power draw. Fortunately, existing work has shown that such agile power capping can be realized well within the time limits (typically sub-second to a few seconds) imposed by circuit-breakers [19, 25, 48].

3.2 Current Solution Strategies

We classify existing workload-aware reaction mechanisms into two broad categories: temporal and spatial. Temporal mechanisms adjust the rate of resource usage within a server. Since the rate of resource usage (particularly the CPU) affects power consumption, it can be used as a knob for demand response. Two common temporal mechanisms include (i) scheduling to defer some of the peak load to a non-emergency period, and (ii) employing power states - dynamic voltage and frequency scaling (DVFS), clock throttling, and even sleep/shutdown states.

Spatial mechanisms direct/migrate excess load to servers and/or regions of the datacenter that have headroom in their power budgets. Here again, we consider two broad strategies: (i) load redirection/migration/consolidation to one or more servers within the hierarchy at level c, allowing some servers in c to be shut/slowed down. (ii) load movement/migration to one or more servers elsewhere in the datacenter (outside c), with headroom for the increased load. Many existing techniques [3, 6, 27, 36] on load balancing/unbalancing for energy/power reduction fall into this category. Such load movement could be achieved by (a) request redirection as in many network-based services [36], (b) "fault-tolerant" applications that detect server unavailability and automatically rebalance themselves amongst the available servers [22], and (c) dynamic process/VM migration [8].

All these mechanisms can have performance consequences with different pros and cons in the options that they offer. Temporal mechanisms are local to a server, and do not require headroom elsewhere in the datacenter. These mechanisms are also quite agile, since power mode control and scheduling decisions can be performed at a fine time granularity with the effects materializing quickly. The downside to these mechanisms is their performance degrading effect, especially when the applications do not provide sufficient slack in their offered load and SLA specifications. Finally, since the load is not moved/migrated elsewhere, the duration of emergency is dictated by the application load, making these mechanisms less desirable for handling long duration emergencies. Temporal dampening mechanisms have to be continuously applied as long as the high load persists.

On the other hand, spatial techniques can work well with long periods of high load since they can move demands to regions of the datacenter with sufficient headroom. However, these techniques have their limitations: (i) they are less agile than temporal mechanisms, implying their inadequacy in handling emergencies on their own. Reacting to an emergency can take a long time, during which a temporal mechanism must be relied upon to cap the power draw, making them only suitable for long-duration emergencies; (ii) migration can be expensive, depending on the application state that needs to be migrated. This can not only impact performance during migration (which can take a few minutes) and after migration (due to loss of locality), but can also temporarily increase power draw of concerned servers; (iii) they require headroom elsewhere in the datacenter which may not always be available (and sometimes undesirable due to administrative boundaries); (iv) not all applications are amenable to migration, since they may require resources (a graphics application requiring a GPU card, virus scan requiring the local disk), on specific servers.

In general, a combination of these techniques can be used depending on the duration of emergency and SLAs of involved workloads. Further, these decisions may not necessarily be static (i.e., determined completely at the beginning of the emergency), with possibly an online algorithm that starts with a temporal mechanism which optimistically looks for a purely local solution, and then adaptively migrates load if needed. *Regardless, all such algorithms have performance degrading consequences either by throttling using power states/shutdown, and/or due to the overheads of load migration (during the movement, loss of locality after the movement, etc.).*

3.3 Our Proposal: Employing Batteries

We now present an entirely orthogonal and novel solution of using battery-based energy storage for handling emergencies that can avoid/reduce the performance consequences of existing techniques. Batteries are analogous to buffers that are used in networks to smoothen out spikes and alleviate mismatches between workload demand and capacity availability. Rather than additional batteries, we propose to use UPS batteries that are already present in datacenters for handling power outages. While most current datacenters employ centralized UPS, we consider a distributed server-level UPS, similar to that in Google datacenters [18]. Our ideas are also applicable to a shared cluster-level UPS (with N times the capacity of a server-level UPS), where we only need to enforce how much draw comes from utility versus from these UPSes. Evaluating such a configuration is part of our future work.

Battery Capacity: We denote by t_b the duration for which a UPS can sustain the associated server's peak power needs. Typically, provisioned UPS battery capacities are for t_b ranging up to a few minutes. There can also be redundancy in the UPS units to accommodate UPS failures, implying higher gross battery capacity. In addition to availability criteria, these capacities are also determined by the discrete units of capacities that different vendors provide. For instance, many APC battery offerings are in discrete capacities of 4, 8, 16, 24 minutes, all rated at a certain peak power draw. In our setup, we consider a UPS with $t_b = 4$ minutes, which is in line with (in fact, at the low-end of) existing capacities. There are cost-benefit trade-offs with investing in higher battery capacities for additional cap-ex savings achieved by aggressive power infrastructure underprovisioning. A preliminary study suggests that the costs of extra battery capacity is worthwhile (see section 7.6), though a detailed study of such economics is beyond the scope of this paper.

Sourcing Power: While a server could potentially draw current simultaneously from the UPS and the power line (one source for each of its dual power supplies), we do not consider this option since our experimental platform does not allow this. Consequently, at any time, a server either draws all of its current from its UPS or from the power line. It is possible to meet a power budget over an extended period of time (beyond what a single battery offers), since servers could take turns sourcing power from their batteries at different times. E.g., if reducing the power draw of 1 server using its UPS meets the overall power budget for 2 minutes, then a cluster of 8 servers can stay within the power budget for up to 16 minutes.

Battery Runtime: Batteries (including lead-acid used in most UPS units) are characterized by their runtime chart as approximated by Peukert's Law [28], which shows the time to drain a certain capacity for different power draws. Runtime of $t_b = 4$ minutes is at the maximum power draw of a server, and the duration of possible battery draw is much higher for lower power draws. For instance, a draw of 50% of the peak, allows the battery to last 11 minutes. We will exploit this property to force a lower draw for longer battery operation.

Availability and Lifetime Concerns: Since we are using UPS battery beyond its normal purpose (handling power outages), we need to ensure that we do not compromise on datacenter availability. In recent work [21], we have modeled datacenter availability as a function of UPS battery capacities for different placement strategies across the layers of the power delivery hierarchy. Across these strategies, we have shown that leaving a 2 minute residual capacity suffices to ensure a high availability of up to five nines. Consequently, in all our experiments in this paper, we always leave 2 minutes of reserve capacity (to operate at full load) in each UPS battery.

Another concern is the lifetime (reliability) of the battery itself: the normal lead-acid battery typically lasts for about 3-5 years [31]. Since charge-discharge cycles can reduce its effective lifetime, we have to ensure that our approach does not result in replacement of batteries sooner than its expected lifetime. We leverage of our recent work [20] to address this concern, where we have conducted an extensive analysis of the impact of battery discharges cycles on its lifetime. Using this analysis, we find that one can handle these relatively rare power emergencies well within the expected battery lifetime.

Efficiency and Additional Power of Batteries: Each charge-discharge cycle has energy loss, which we find experimentally to be 28% of the overall energy drawn in the worst case. Since such loss is restricted to "rare" emergencies, we do not expect it to significantly impact operational costs. However, battery charging itself adds to instantaneous power draw and this must be considered for adhering to the budget. There are different strategies for dealing with this issue - restricting charging to non-emergency periods, slow-charging so that the instantaneous draw is not significant, and/or compensating with aggressive spatio-temporal workload throttling mechanisms. In this work, we employ the first strategy.

4. Handling Emergencies: An Offline Theoretical Framework

Having discussed the pros and cons of various strategies, we now turn our attention to combining their best features.

Is migration (spatial) of one or more workloads on the N servers under c even an option? There are different situations where a spatial knob may not be applicable, even if workloads have sufficient slack in their SLAs. First, there must be headroom elsewhere in the datacenter to accommodate the migrated load, which may not happen if the entire datacenter is highly utilized. Second, certain workloads may not be amenable to migration: consider a workload that needs a resource only available locally, e.g., a graphics application requiring a GPU card.

Even if migration is an option, can local (temporal + battery) knobs alone handle the emergency while meeting application SLAs? If yes, there is no reason to look for headroom elsewhere in the datacenter and incur additional migration costs. The agility of temporal knobs makes them more attractive over spatial knobs in this case.

When local (temporal + battery) knobs do not suffice because of the emergency duration and stringency of application SLAs, which workloads should we migrate and at what time? These decisions should be determined based on what impacts the application SLAs the least while meeting the power budget. We develop a simple framework to conduct such decision-making. Let us denote the remaining time for an application to complete [2], at the beginning of an emergency, as t_f. Let t_m denote the time (from the emergency beginning) when the application is migrated, if at all. t_m would be a function of migration overhead: $t_m = 0$ implies immediate migration (for relatively stateless applications with little migration overhead), and a larger t_m implies local knobs will be employed as much as possible until they become infeasible and migration is necessary. If t_m is larger than emergency duration, then it implies that local knobs suffice to handle the emergency without requiring any migration. To determine t_m, we denote the relative speed at which the application runs on the destination server(s) with respect to the source server(s) as s_r (the slowdown). We assume that there is sufficient power capacity at the destination, and the slowdown can be approximated using a simple slowdown factor s_r. However, the application runs until time t_m locally before migration, and would have been subjected to local temporal knobs which would have also slowed it down. This slowdown, is dependent on t_m itself (i.e., local knobs affect execution time) and we denote it as $s_l(t_m)$. Since $t_f - t_m * s_l(t_m)$ is the remaining time for the application at migration time t_m, its remaining execution time on the remote server(s) needs to be scaled as $(t_f - t_m * s_l(t_m)) * s_r$. The resulting total execution time of the application with migration (as depicted in Figure 2), which needs to be minimized, can now be expressed as

$$\min_{t_m=0}^{t_m=t_f} (t_m + (t_f - t_m * s_l(t_m)) * s_r)$$

The relative impact of the slowdown with local (temporal + battery) and migration (spatial) knobs is captured by $s_l(t_m)$ and s_r (both lie between 0 and 1). Of these two, s_r is mainly application governed by its locality properties, since we assume the destination has enough headroom to run it without any power-related dampening. However, s_l is crucially dependent on t_m, and how the local

[2] Even for applications without an explicit notion of remaining time (e.g., a Web server running forever), an equivalent framework, say based on execution rate, can be developed.

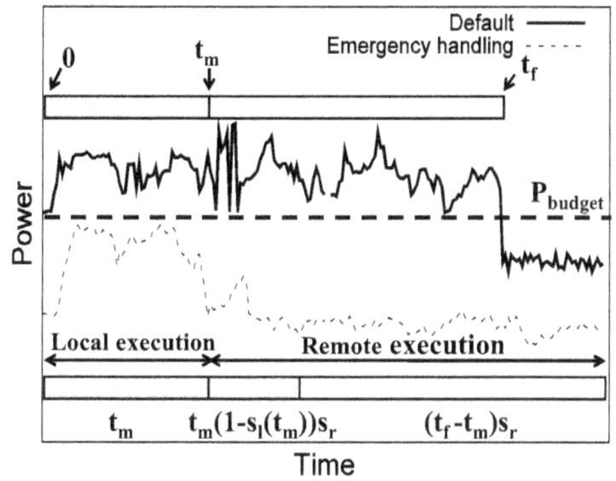

Figure 2. Timeline — above for default, and below for emergency handling with local and spatial knobs. Migration happens at t_m instantaneously in this illustration. Note the elongation in execution time due to s_l and s_r. Resulting lower power draw for the emergency between 0 and t_f, compared to default is also shown.

knobs were employed to meet the power budget over t_m. This, in turn, leads us to the following optimization problem: given a t_m, how should the local (battery + temporal) knobs be used to meet performance SLAs?

We use a generic metric R, whose minimization corresponds to meeting the application's SLA, to cast this optimization problem. R is general enough to capture a wide range of application metrics, e.g., response time (as in TPC-W used in our evaluation), reciprocal of throughput (in transaction-oriented applications such as Specjbb), time-to-finish (for long running applications such as Map-Reduce and virus scan), rate of playback discontinuities for a streaming media server, etc. We view the duration t_m as being divided into W equal-sized intervals. We use R_{ij} to denote average response time offered by server j in time interval i. We can now express the problem of minimizing R (i.e., minimizing $s_l(t_m)$) for a given t_m using purely local knobs (battery + power states)). This can then be iterated over different values of t_m between 0 to W to determine when to migrate.

Minimizing** R **Using Only Local Knobs: Let the battery on server j have upto B_j joules of energy that it can safely provide for this emergency, accounting for any residual energy that needs to be maintained for availability. Each server $j = 1, \ldots, N$, can operate during an interval within this emergency in a particular power mode (server off, DVFS and Clock throttling states), ordered as D_0 where the server is off, to D_d which is the highest power consuming state and best in performance. We denote the intensity of a workload during this emergency as L, discretized for the spectrum of intensities between the minimum and maximum for a given workload as $L_1, \ldots, L_l$. For instance, in Specjbb, the transaction rate specifies the intensity, and we can histogram this rate between a minimum and maximum into l buckets.

The response time $R_{ij}(L_{ij}, D_{ij})$ offered by server j during interval i depends on the load L_{ij} that is imposed on that server during i and its power mode D_{ij}, where $L_{ij} \in [L_1, \ldots, L_l]$ and $D_{ij} \in [D_0, D_1, \ldots, D_d]$. The power consumption of this server during i can be specified as $P_{ij}(L_{ij}, Dij)$, and this can also be calculated a priori and made available to the optimizer for different (L, D) combinations. We can then phrase our objective function of minimizing average response time over W by employing purely local (battery + power state) knobs as:

$$minimize \quad \sum_{i=1}^{W}\sum_{j=1}^{N} R_{ij}(L_{ij}, Dij).$$

Let b_{ij} denote whether server j sources its power needs in the i-th interval from its battery ($b_{ij} = 1$) or the power line ($b_{ij} = 0$). Since we cannot drain more than B_j for this peak, we have: $\Sigma_{i=1}^{W} b_{ij} * P_{ij}(L_{ij}, Dij) \leq B_j, \forall j$. The resulting total power draw on the line, which has to adhere to the specified budget P_{budget}, is given by: $\Sigma_{j=1}^{N} \overline{b_{ij}} * P_{ij}(L_{ij}, Dij) \leq P_{budget}, \forall i$.

5. Online Heuristics

Our theoretical framework is impossible to use in practice since it requires a priori knowledge of the emergency duration and intensity. Even if such knowledge were available, it may be computationally prohibitive. *However, we still use it as a baseline for comparison with the practical solutions we develop next.* We refer to the solution offered by our framework above as `Opt`, and the solution it offers solely using local knobs as `Opt-local`.

	Heuristics	Description
Local to server	Throt	Use only power states
	BattFast+Throt	Drain batt. first before throttling
	BattSlow+Throt	Drain batt. slowly while throttling
Local to cluster	cMig	Mig. within cluster and turnoff servers
	BattSlow+Throt+cMig	Delay cMig as far as possible
Across datacenter	dMig	Mig. to elsewhere in datacenter
	BattSlow+Throt+dMig	Delay dMig as far as possible

Table 1. Summary of our online heuristics

We consider seven online heuristics (Table 1) based on whether the knob of adhering to P_{budget} under c is (a) local to a server, (b) local to the cluster of servers under c, or (c) pertains to the entire datacenter. As before, we assume a priori knowledge of performance ($R_{ij}(l, d)$) and power ($P_{ij}(l, d)$) for different loads (l) and power states (d) of a server for the application. Further, even though the above theoretical framework allows a different power state (d) for each server at a given time, our heuristics only consider a restricted version that employs the same state across all N servers at any time. The resulting detrimental effects (if any), would materialize in our results.

Heuristics Local to a Server: One would like to preferably use knobs local to a server, namely battery, power state modulation, and/or temporal deferring of the load to deal with the emergency, because of their agility and less disruption in the datacenter. Our first set of 3 heuristics - `Throt`, `BattFast+Throt`, and `BattSlow+Throt` - employ only such local knobs. `Throt` employs only power state modulation (DVFS and/or clock throttling) and temporal scheduling, and is representative of the power throttling mechanisms available today. With knowledge of the power consumption in different states for the current load, this heuristic picks the least performance impacting power state for all N servers, ensuring adherence to P_{budget}. `BattFast+Throt` and `BattSlow+Throt` supplement temporal knobs with battery to reduce performance impact, and thereby sustain longer emergency handling. The two differ in battery drain rate. `BattFast+Throt` is relatively optimistic about the emergency duration, and drains the battery fully before resorting to power mode knobs, thereby not requiring the latter if the battery can sustain the entire load for short emergencies. `BattSlow+Throt` is conservative, and tries to prolong the battery usage. Recall that we are using the same power state d across all N servers at any time, and our experimental setup allows the drain rate from the battery at only server granularity (i.e., a single server cannot source partly from battery and partly from the power line, which is possible in dual power supply servers). Consequently, we require $(N-1) * P(l,d) \leq P_{budget}$, since the remaining server, by sourcing its power from battery, would help reduce the overall draw from power line to adhere to the budget. Hence, in `BattSlow+Throt`, a single server draws power from the battery at a power state d, while the other servers (also operating at state d) draw their power from the normal supply. d is the highest power state (i.e., least performance impacting) that obeys the above conditions. This scheme can thus sustain a longer duration of battery operation than `BattFast+Throt`, though the performance consequences can be felt even earlier (where the battery alone may have been sufficient to handle the emergency in `BattFast+Throt`).

Heuristics Local to Cluster c: With longer emergencies, local knobs may not suffice to meet application SLAs within the stipulated power budget. One option may be to migrate the load. It may sometimes be desirable to simply re-arrange load within c during an emergency, since (a) migration outside of c may not be possible (either there is no headroom or administrative reasons force the application to be tied to nodes within c), and/or (b) the locality of application needs (frequent communication, data stored locally, etc.) may get impacted when parts of the application are forced out of c. The downside to migrating (redistributing the load) within the cluster is that performance may be impacted if the existing load is already pushing individual servers to high resource utilization (which is usually what leads to the emergency). When migrating within c, we consider two heuristics: `cMig` and `BattSlow+Throt+cMig`. In `cMig`, the load is immediately migrated at the beginning of the emergency, from one or more servers and these servers are subsequently shut down. The number of servers from which the load is to be migrated depends on how many need to be taken down to get the total subsequent power consumption within P_{budget}. Since migration is typically intended to be the option of last resort, we do not consider local knobs (either battery or power modes) after the migration. Using the same rationale, `BattSlow+Throt+cMig` defers the migration point to a time using the above-mentioned `BattSlow+Throt` strategy until the battery capacity reaches residual capacity needed for availability (2 minutes), and then employs `cMig` within c. While there are numerous ways of performing load migration (see Section 3) we restrict our evaluations to virtual-machine based (live) migration [8], which is a convenient vehicle for performing this task at the infrastructure level without any application-level knowledge/mechanism. We can explore other strategies in future work.

Heuristics Across Clusters: Handling an extended emergency without substantial performance repercussions may need moving or migrating load outside of c to parts of the datacenter with sufficient headroom. In this paper, we do not consider the problem of where to move this load, and simply assume that it can be accommodated elsewhere. As explained above, the loss in locality (communication and storage) after migration can impact subsequent performance, and we again explore two strategies - `dMig`, which performs the migration right at the beginning of the emergency, and `BattSlow+Throt+dMig`, which delays the migration as much as possible.

6. Implementation and Experimental Setup

We use a scaled-down experimental prototype to evaluate our heuristics and compare them with `Opt-local` and `Opt`. Our prototype uses a cluster c (Figure 3) of N=8 DELL PowerEdge servers with two Intel Xeon 3.4GHz processors each, running RedHat Linux 5.5. The face-plate rating of these servers is 450W. Their idle power consumption is around 120W and the peak power that we can push the server to across our workloads is 320W. The dynamic power consumption can be modulated with 4 DVFS states (P-states: 3.4GHz, 3.2GHz, 3.0GHz, and 2.8GHz) and 8 clock throttling states (T-states: 12.5%, 25%, ..., 100%). To change power states, we write custom drivers using the $IA32\_PERF\_CTL$ and $IA32\_CLOCK\_MODULATION$ MSR registers. Each server is directly connected to a 1000W APC UPS [1] which, in turn, is connected to an outlet of a 30Amp Raritan PDU.

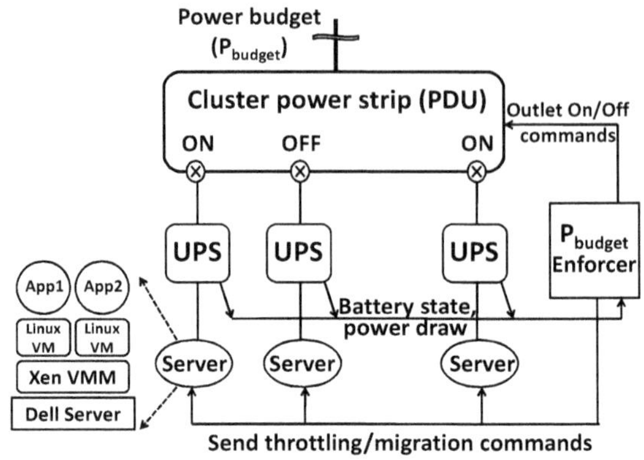

Figure 3. Experimental prototype.

Although we have a 1000W UPS unit connected to each server, for all our experiments we only assume a 330W UPS (close to the maximum power consumed by our server) and drain the UPS using a corresponding scaled-down runtime chart [3]. We consider a 4-minute battery per server which is relatively on the lower end, of which we leave a residual capacity of 2 minutes, required for availability guarantees. The UPS is capable of reporting its load, power draw and remaining battery runtime over an RS232 serial interface. The PDU is capable of dynamically switching ON/OFF the supply to individual UPS units with SNMP commands over Ethernet. By turning on/off individual outlets, we can selectively have a server source power from either the battery or the power line. We use a separate machine ("Power Budget Enforcer") to implement the heuristics - send throttling, migration and PDU turn on/off commands. Our cluster has a shared NAS box which is mounted as a NFS storage volume by all the servers. We use another cluster (not shown in the figure) of 8 servers as the destination for migrating workloads in `dMig` and `dMig+BattSlow+Throt`. All our applications are hosted as VMs under Xen on each server.

7. Evaluation

We use four case studies involving six different applications to evaluate the efficacy of our online heuristics. In each, we present (i) salient workload properties, (ii) emergencies lasting a range of durations and corresponding to degrees (as 10-30% of potential peak) of underprovisioning, (iii) the remedial actions corresponding to our heuristics, and (iv) a comparison of their efficacy in alleviating the emergency with respect to `Opt-local` and `Opt`. Note that we are only concerned with performance during an emergency in this work. The remedial actions for emergencies lasting several hours will typically mandate migration and there are no further insights to be gained by studying such long durations. As discussed earlier, we have profiled the performance ($R(l,d)$) and power ($P(l,d)$) of

[3] The minimum capacity of UPS units available from APC is 500W. Although UPS units are typically over-provisioned, we assume this conservative tight provisioning of 330W for our experiments.

each workload a priori. In general, enterprise/internet applications typically undergo extensive profiling for right-sizing of datacenter IT resources. Even for cloud-hosted third-party applications, resource usage can be determined via offline/online profiling. Such profiling, with readily available power meters [25] on those platforms, or in combination with well-understood power models [16] that are based on resource utilization, can be used to determine $R_{ij}(l,d)$ and $P_{ij}(l,d)$. Since, we already have plenty of ground to cover in this paper, for the purposes of this work we assume that R_{ij} and P_{ij} for a given workload, as a function of different power states is made available. A more detailed treatment of these issues can be considered in future work.

7.1 TPC-W and SPECjbb

We study two well-known server benchmarks: TPC-W [40] and SPECjbb [41]. TPC-W emulates a 3-tiered (Apache, Tomcat, and MySQL) transactional Web-based eCommerce bookstore. The Apache front-end runs on a dedicated server, while the other two tiers run on a set of servers whose size is chosen to accommodate the workload intensity. Apache employs a request distribution module to balance requests among replicas of Tomcat. We use the clustered MySQL database engine that provides a replicable, shared-nothing database tier. Each Tomcat and MySQL instance runs in its own Xen domain. TPC-W services a specified number of clients over persistent HTTP sessions. We use the average client response time during the emergency as the performance metric (R) for TPC-W. SPECjbb is a 3-tiered server-side Java warehouse management application. We use the average transactions/second (tps) as our performance metric (R) for SPECjbb.

Emergency Handling for TPC W: Applications like TPC-W are known to experience significant temporal variations in the load. Many such variations can be predicted (e.g., time-of-day behavior) to ensure that enough power capacity is provisioned. However, there are other variations not amenable to such prediction (e.g., flash crowds) which can cause emergencies when underprovisioning. Responding to the growing workload, the datacenter incrementally adds replicas of Tomcat and MySQL on new servers till all 8 servers are utilized. This can cause an emergency since the aggregate draw of these servers can exceed the power budget of the underprovisioned cluster. For instance, when the workload saturates all 8 servers, the aggregate power consumption hits 1630W. If the infrastructure is underprovisioned by 10%, 20% and 30%, then the corresponding P_{budget} limits are 1470 W, 1300 W, and 1140 W respectively. We inject load to introduce emergency durations of 2, 8, 15, 30, and 60 minutes, over these provisioned limits.

Figures 4(a) and (b) present the degradation in average response times of TPC-W with 10 and 30% underprovisioning. `Throt` chooses (2.8Ghz, 100%Clk) and (2.8Ghz, 25%Clk) for 10% and 30% underprovisioing, respectively, and severely degrades performance (going from 30% degradation to over 500% in the more underprovisioned case) in these high utilization regimes. On the other hand, `BattFast+Throt` is better, particularly for short to moderate emergency durations (upto 15 minutes). For such emergencies, it is able to completely source the excess power from batteries without throttling. For longer durations (30 minutes and more), the batteries run out, mandating throttling which degrades performance. The high sensitivity of performance to even small CPU rate modulation makes `BattSlow+Throt` mostly ineffectual: for short emergencies (upto 15 minutes), it unnecessarily throttles due to its conservative (slow) drain from batteries; for moderate durations (upto 30 minutes), it stretches the battery runtime, but the accompanying throttling hurts performance; for long durations (more than 30 minutes), batteries run out with subsequent consequences similar to `BattFast+Throt`.

Next we consider the cluster-level migration, `cMig`. `cMig` employs Xen's live migration facility [8] to seamlessly migrate a subset of (let us denote its size as n) Tomcat/MySQL replicas from their original servers and co-locates them with those on the remaining $8-n$ servers - which in turn become overloaded. These n unoccupied servers are now turned off. We find n to be 1 and 3 for underprovisioning degrees of 10% and 30%, respectively. For the 30% underprovisioning, all 5 active servers continue to operate at their highest power states. Since the TPC-W components were operating at their peak requirements, the components that are co-located experience significant resource shortage, causing response time to nearly double. In fact, `cMig` fares worse than the earlier two heuristics involving the battery. The idea behind `BattSlow+Throt+cMig` is to improve upon `cMig` by postponing migration as much as possible; it starts as `BattSlow+Throt` and switches to `cMig` when the batteries run out. For small/moderate emergencies, this defaults to `BattSlow+Throt` with the same pros and cons - essentially undesirable for TPC-W. It is worse for longer emergencies since it will end up switching to `cMig`, which we have already found to hurt TPC-W.

Finally, let us discuss the efficacy of `dMig`. We migrate 1 and 3 Tomcat/MySQL VM pairs for 10% and 30% underprovisioning respectively. Live migration can be carried out relatively quickly for TPC-W (about 2 minutes) [4]. Furthermore, loss of data locality suffered by migrated VMs is negligible in this case (i.e. small s_r), implying little performance consequence after the migration. Consequently, `dMig` turns out to be the most effective heuristic and is able to handle the entire range of emergencies with little performance consequence (though requiring the battery to temporarily handle the power spike during the act of migration). The only situations where `dMig` is an unwise choice is when the emergency lasts less than the migration duration of 2 minutes. `BattSlow+Throt+dMig` attempts to postpone the remote migration invocation and ends up offering worse performance than `dMig` due to TPC-W's sensitivity to even small degrees of throttling.

`BattFast+Throt` comes close to `Opt-local` for emergencies less than 15 minutes, while `BattSlow+Throt` is closer to `Opt-local` for longer emergencies. Incidentally, `Opt-local` never chooses `Throt` when we examine (post-mortem) decisions reached by the offline algorithm for durations less than 15 minutes, and in longer durations it chooses heterogeneous power states across the servers, while our battery based heuristics choose the same state across all servers at any time. Specifically, `Opt-local` uses a lower power state on servers that source from batteries, stretching the battery runtime. In this case study, `Opt` first drains the battery fully, and then immediately migrates the load to a remote node since there is little performance impact after migration.

Emergency Handling for SPECjbb: Emergency handling in SPECjbb is similar to TPC-W, with similar results. The 8 servers housing SPECjbb replicas end up operating close to saturation, and their aggregate power consumption is found to be 1875W. Figures 4(c) and (d) present the degradation in average tps during various emergencies.

Key Insights: (i) CPU throttling is undesirable for this class of applications, even for short or moderate durations. (ii) batteries are helpful for a wide range of emergencies (upto 30 minutes). (iii) batteries can offer lower power draws than even the deepest

[4] Incidentally, though we do not explicitly present those details, we wish to point out that migration itself does introduce a spike in power consumption (of 10%) for this workload, and the battery is still needed (in solutions such as `cMig` and `dMig`) to temporarily get the power draw under control during the act of migration.

Legends for Bar Charts: Note that the legend numbers are given above some of the bars for easier readability. Opt and Opt-local lines are also drawn as reference lower bounds.

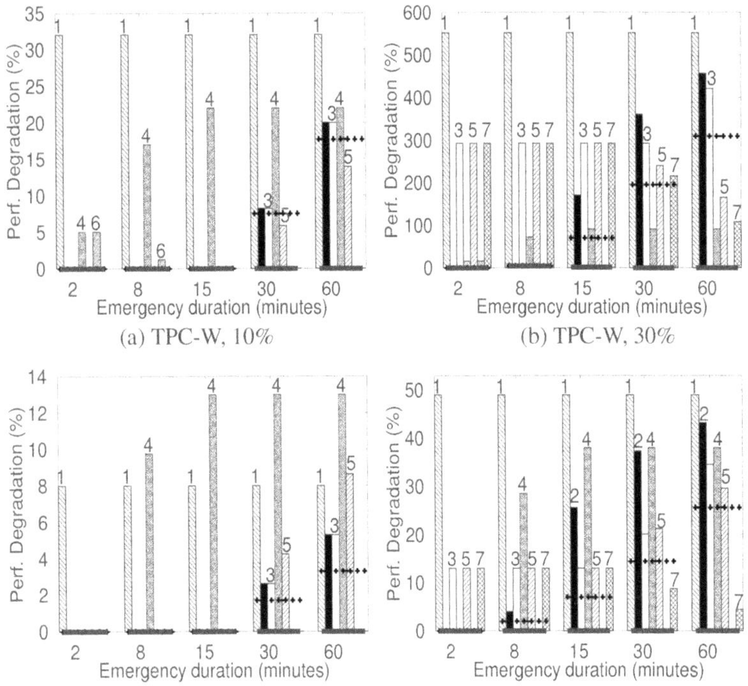

(a) TPC-W, 10% (b) TPC-W, 30%

(c) Specjbb, 10% (d) Specjbb, 30%

Figure 4. TPC-W and Specjbb results

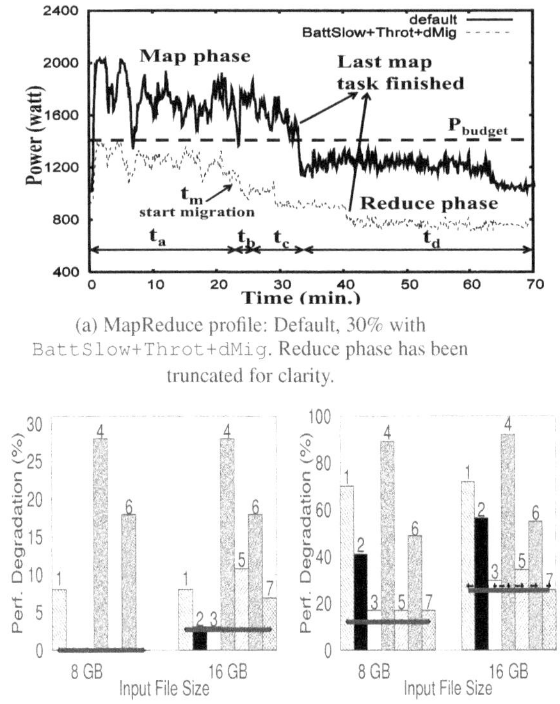

(a) MapReduce profile: Default, 30% with BattSlow+Throt+dMig. Reduce phase has been truncated for clarity.

(b) MapReduce, 10% (c) MapReduce, 30%

Figure 5. MapReduce results

power states. (iv) the low/zero slowdown after migration (s_r), favors dMig (coming close to Opt), though the battery is still needed to handle the initial power spike during migration (which takes 1-2 minutes). (v) Opt-local and Opt point towards the possibility of *heterogeneous* power state assignment to servers to achieve better power/performance trade-offs than offered by our heuristics.

7.2 MapReduce

This workload represents a growing and important class of parallel applications used in domains such as search engines. We run a word count application using Hadoop [22]. It schedules the mapper and reducer tasks across a set of specified servers and reports the application finish time as its performance metric. We consider 8 GB and 16 GB for input file sizes. MapReduce inherently uses distributed storage, placing computations closer to the data that it needs. If one considers a server's storage volume to be part of the VM, then cMig and dMig based on infrastructure-level VM migration would require moving all of this data to the destination node (which can be quite large), rather than just the data needed by subsequent computation. While one could consider this in future work, in this set of experiments, we assume storage to be decoupled from the VM image (by implementing the local storage as a NFS-mounted server), and only move the VM image for migration, with the subsequent computation making NFS calls to get the specific data that it needs from the source cluster c (where the data is replicated for availability even if servers go down).

Emergency Handling for MapReduce: Figure 5(a) shows evolution of the aggregated power of the 8 servers running MapReduce (labeled as *default*) with the 16GB input. We see high power variation over time, suggesting under-utilization if we provision for the peak. Specifically, the mapper phase (upto 30 min.) consumes significantly higher power that reaches up to 2020W. Consequently, a surge of mapper activities across the cluster can sometimes lead to emergencies in an aggressively underprovisioned system. Delaying the mappers and/or spreading them temporally/spatially can delay the application and possibly impact its locality.

Figures 5(b) and (c) compare the performance of our heuristics for underprovisioning of 10% and 30% (with respect to 2020W), respectively. For the 8GB input, we find battery-based techniques are able to handle the emergency with little/no performance consequences for 10% underprovisioning (comparable to Opt). The emergency duration for this input is roughly 15 minutes, which can be easily sustained by each of the 8 servers (only 1 server needs to not source from power line to meet power bounds) taking turns sourcing power from the battery for roughly 2.3 minutes each. In fact, the power state modulation and migration mechanisms do not even kick in when the battery is complemented with these knobs. However, for 30% underprovisioning, the other knobs are also employed, and the performance progressively degrades. Still, the battery-supplemented techniques do better than without this knob. Further, while BattFast+Throt does better than BattSlow+Throt in the 20% underprovisioning case (not shown in figure), the results are reversed in the 30% underprovisioning case (shown in Figure 5 (c)) where the emergency mandates a higher power shaving, causing the battery to run out faster if that is the first knob of choice. Sustaining a longer period of operation with the battery (a slow drain rate achieved with simultaneous power state control) is a better option in such cases of high under-provisioning.

The 16GB input extends the emergency duration to roughly 30 minutes, making it necessary to supplement battery with power state modulation and/or migration. This degrades performance even in the 10% underprovisioning case. In both 8GB and 16GB experiments, we find migration does relatively worse than using local knobs alone. This is because of migration overheads, where doing it locally (cMig) results in increasing the load on one or more slave nodes within the cluster, delaying the progress of the application. dMig for MapReduce, has a different problem - loss of data locality requiring considerable data movement across clusters - which tremendously impacts performance (though this is still better performing than cMig which overloads servers). MapReduce, thus, depicts a spectrum of workloads not as conducive to migration for emergency reaction (unlike the stateless applications in previous subsection) impacting performance not just during the migration but also subsequently. Like before, supplementing migration with local knobs helps defer t_m (to about 23 minutes in the 16GB experiment), to lessen the subsequent performance slowdown (s_r) after migration in both cMig and dMig cases. Migration is more competitive for longer emergency durations - for instance, consider the 16GB degradation results in 30% underprovisioning for cMig (92%) and dMig (55%) with respect to BattSlow+Throt (34%), and compare them with those for the 8GB degradation where BattSlow+Throt suffers only 16% degradation while cMig and dMig still suffer 89% and 49% degradation. The local knobs supplemented with migration can thus help bridge the emergency duration gap when migration becomes more competitive.

Figure 5(a) presents salient decisions made by our heuristic, BattSlow+Throt+dMig (the closest heuristic to Opt) during the emergency with 30% under-provisioning: (i) *Duration t_a:* one server at a time is sourced from its battery and all 8 servers are operated at 2.8GHz DVFS till $t = 23$ minutes; (ii) *Duration t_b:* migrating 3 mapper VMs to another cluster which takes 1-2 minutes; (iii) *Duration t_c:* 3 machines are shut down after migration, and the remaining 5 servers operate at the highest 3.4GHz DVFS state. (iv) *Duration t_d:* which is the "reduce" phase where there is no longer an emergency, though we do not consider the option of moving back the VMs to c in our experiments. Note that we adhere to the 1420W cap (30% underprovisioning) over the entire duration.

Performance degradation of Opt closely matches our heuristics that only use the server-local knobs for 10% underprovisioning where migration is less desirable (Opt does not choose migration in this case). We observe the same behavior for the 8GB input at 30% underprovisioning where Opt only uses local knobs for the entire emergency. One interesting observation is that for the 16GB input at 30% underprovisioning, Throt becomes very expensive - about 72% decrease in throughput. Opt resorts to dMig at $t_m = 24$ minutes in this case, which closely matches the decision by BattSlow+Throt+dMig where the battery runs out of charge at approximately the 23rd minute and migration is initiated. It is important to note that MapReduce is very sensitive to the value of t_m and migrating before or after 24 minutes results in poor performance.

Key Insights: (i) Longer emergencies may mandate migration, but this slows down the application either due to overload of some servers in the cluster (cMig) or poor data locality (dMig); (ii) BattSlow+Throt postpones migration, and allows it to become more competitive; (iii) when migration is expensive, Opt refrains from migration for short emergencies (BattFast+Throt comes close) and defers migration as long as possible for long emergencies (BattSlow+Throt+dMig comes close).

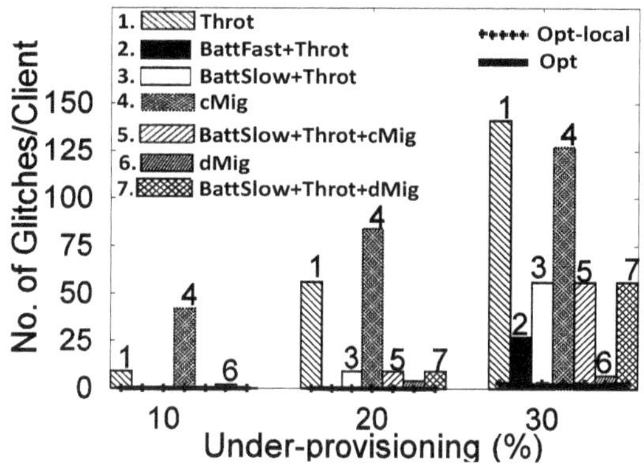

Figure 6. Media Server Results.

7.3 Streaming Media Server

Our third case study uses a multi threaded 1.5 Mbps streaming MPEG media server that services several Java clients. It spawns a separate thread for each client, which does password authentication before it starts streaming. A 4.5MB buffer is used at the client to smoothen traffic variations. There could still be playback discontinuities ("glitches") when the buffer becomes empty. The server runs on all 8 machines, streaming a 60-minute long video for a total of 2400 clients.

Emergency Handling: During the initial phase (say first 10 minutes), when the clients try to connect to the server, we observe a power spike of about 1700W, compared to the steady state draw of 1200W when there is only subsequent streaming. This initial connection/authorization phase can be viewed as the emergency duration and we evaluate our heuristics over this duration for 10%, 20% and 30% underprovisioning in Figure 7.2.

Throt degrades with aggressive underprovisioning (from 8 glitches per client for 10% underprovisioning to over 100 for 30%), since it is not able to sustain the streaming needs. Due to the short emergency (about 10 minutes), BattFast+Throt is able to handle it without throttling and hence performs much better than BattSlow+ Throt. In fact, BattFast+Throt performs very well even at 30% underprovisioning, incurring only one-fifth of the glitches compared to Throt. We note that cMig hurts performance even for small underprovisioning, since each server is already saturated. BattSlow+Throt+cMig is able to delay (actually avoids migration completely because the battery is able to fully sustain the emergency) this migration, defaulting to BattSlow+Throt. It is interesting that dMig, which had poor performance for MapReduce does very well since there is almost no performance impact after the migration (s_r is negligible). It takes only about 30 seconds for the media server VM to migrate and we find that the client buffer size is good enough to sustain the performance impact for most of this duration. While the battery serves as a buffer to allow temporary power spikes at the media servers (as in earlier case studies), a similar effect is achieved by the client buffer which allow the media servers to slowdown (either by power state transition or migration) temporarily - thus reducing their power draw. We also observe that unlike MapReduce, it does not make sense to delay migration (BattSlow+Throt+dMig) since migration overheads are low, and throttling has severe performance impact.

Opt chooses to use the battery alone for 10% and 20% underprovisioning, equivalent to BattFast+Throt and does not incur any degradation. For 30% underprovisioning, battery cannot fully sustain the peak and Opt uses datacenter-level migration which results in just 2 glitches per client. In this application, we find $t_m = 7$ minutes for Opt (unlike 23 minutes in MapReduce), since migration overhead is negligible. Interestingly, when our optimization (Opt-local) is run with just the local knobs where we see that for 30% underprovisioning it is comparable to Opt and achieves as few as 3 glitches per client compared to the best local knob heuristic - BattFast+Throt - which incurs 27 glitches/client. When we analyzed the Opt-local results, we noticed that it sources battery from 2 servers at any time and uses throttling to shave only the remaining 10%. This behavior is somewhere in-between our battery-aggressive, BattFast+Throt and battery-conservative, BattSlow+Throt heuristics which source from 3 servers and 1 server respectively from battery and shave the rest by throttling. This shows the importance of dynamically adjusting battery drain rate, which we plan to investigate in future work.

Key Insights: (i) Battery-based heuristics perform very well due to the smaller emergency duration. (ii) The battery and client buffer, in combination, provide a seamless strategy for offloading the work to elsewhere in the datacenter, and hide migration cost.

7.4 Graphics Application and Virus Scan

This case study involves two applications: a GPU application in CUDA implementing the Black-Scholes financial model using a NVIDIA card, and VirusScan (Linux AVG [29]) which needs to run on the local machine to scan its 40GB hard drive. Not all datacenter servers may offer the required graphics support (e.g., Amazon EC2 offers separate GPU cluster instances), and moving the VirusScan elsewhere is not an option. VirusScan is a strawman we use to illustrate applications, that (i) are tied to a specific server, (ii) are fairly flexible in their processing rate (low-priority), and (iii) have some kind of deadline (24 hours in this case). Other examples include back-ups, search-engine indexing, etc. Even though the deadlines are "soft" in these examples, we will use a *"hard" deadline for more general illustration*. We vary the rate at which GPU applications arrive which can, in turn impact the schedulability of VirusScan, and report throughput (GPU ops/sec) subject to the 24 hour deadline for VirusScan that needs to be met. In our servers, the GPU application running alone consumes 250W, the VirusScan at full-throttle runs at 208W taking 45 minutes to complete, and the two together at full-throttle hit 315W.

Emergency Handling: We define an emergency in this case as an out-of-the-ordinary day wherein the VirusScan does not get sufficient bandwidth (because of the power budget) to run until the last x minutes before the 24 hour deadline, and we vary x between 240 to 45 minutes (beyond 240 minutes there is sufficient bandwidth for our considered load). This setup is different from the earlier case studies, since we have multiple applications. We adapt Throt, BattFast+Throt and BattSlow+Throt for this scenario since migration is not an option. We do not explicitly discuss results for BattSlow+Throt whose behavior is not very different from BattFast+Throt. Throt does power state modulation continuously over the last x minutes for VirusScan to finish its remaining execution before the 24 hour deadline. CPU throttling states have little impact on the progress or power consumption of the GPU application (as it depends mainly on the GPU). Hence, if there is not enough slack at a given time to meet the VirusScan deadline, the GPU application is put on hold (suspended), and VirusScan is run at full-throttle until there is slack again. BattFast+Throt employs battery as long as possible from the beginning of the x minutes, until it is drained to residual capacity of 2 minutes (required for availability), with VirusScan running at full-throttle. Subsequently, Throt is employed.

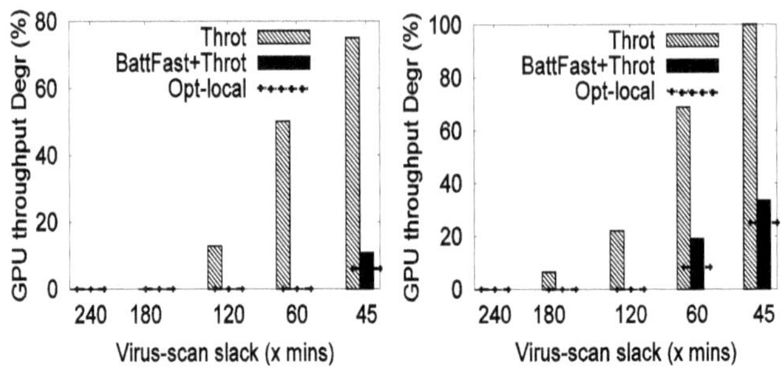

(a) 80% GPUapp (b) 100% GPUapp

Figure 7. Performance of GPU application during various emergencies caused by VirusScan's deadline. (10% underprovisioning)

A representative result for 10% power underprovisioning (with respect to the maximum possible draw of 2520W) is given in Figure 7. The emergency is captured by different values of x on the x-axis, and we present the percentage degradation in GPU ops on the y-axis. This degradation is shown for different imposed loads by GPU application, with intensities depicted as 80% and 100%, i.e. percentage of time that the GPU is active. Throt by itself suffices when there is sufficient notice ($x > 240$) given to run these algorithms. Getting closer to the deadline to react does not allow much room for Throt to run both applications without affecting the GPU application. There is 50-60% slowdown in GPU ops during the last hour with Throt. Higher GPU application intensity leaves even less room for Throt to allocate sufficient bandwidth for the two, thereby impacting throughput. The battery-based solution, on the other hand, is able to do much better across the entire spectrum, not suffering any loss for $x \geq 120$. It is only at very high GPU application intensities, and very little reaction time (in the last hour) that it results in performance loss, and even then does significantly better than Throt. Further, the battery based solution comes quite close to Opt, with the latter doing slightly better because of more leeway in what gets scheduled (GPU or VirusScan) at any time on different servers, and the possible heterogeneous power states assignment across the servers at a given time.

Key Insights: (i) Application intensity, slack in scheduling and reaction window, all impact throughput. (ii) Power state modulation alone is not able to handle high intensities when sufficient slack is absent. (iii) Battery provides substantial leeway in handling emergencies for scheduling workloads with both temporal (deadlines) and spatial (need to run on specific servers) constraints.

7.5 Summary of Observations

Table 2 summarizes the results from the six different application case-studies evaluated above, pointing out the efficacy of the knob(s) towards handling the different performance-power characteristics.

7.6 Invest in additional battery capacity?

Even though we have considered a conservative 4-minute battery capacity in our experiments, one may ask whether the cost of additional battery capacity can be justified by the potential reduction in datacenter power infrastructure costs that we can gain by underprovisioning. Let us denote the cost of procuring additional battery capacity to sustain e hours of emergency as $e \cdot c_{bat}$ \$/watt, and the cap-ex cost of the power infrastructure to under-provision by c_{cap} \$/watt. Lead-acid battery costs (c_{bat}) reported in literature (see DOE/Sandia data [24]) are in the 100-300 \$/kWh range, and we consider conservative values as high as 500 \$/kWh. Datacenter

Application characteristics	Emergency handling (knob selection)
Short peak widths	Batteries are self-sufficient in handling peaks up to 30 mins without requiring expensive throttling
Medium peak widths	Batteries supplement power state throttling to reduce performance overheads
Long peak widths	Immediate migration is benefitial, Batteries hide power spike during migration
Sensitive to data locality	Migration may impact performance, Batteries help postpone migration
Slack-based workloads	Shift peak temporally via flexible workload scheduling, Batteries help create more slack

Table 2. Summary of Results

Battery cost	Emergency duration	Assumed Cap-ex $/W for IT --> 1$/W	2$/W	5$/W	10$/W	15$/W
100 $/KWh	5 mins	39.0	79.0	199.0	399.0	599.0
	15 mins	12.3	25.7	65.7	132.3	199.0
	30 mins	5.7	12.3	32.3	65.7	99.0
	1 hour	2.3	5.7	15.7	32.3	49.0
	4 hours	-0.2	0.7	3.2	7.3	11.5
300 $/KWh	5 mins	12.3	25.7	65.7	132.3	199.0
	15 mins	3.4	7.9	21.2	43.4	65.7
	30 mins	1.2	3.4	10.1	21.2	32.3
	1 hour	0.1	1.2	4.6	10.1	15.7
	4 hours	-0.7	-0.4	0.4	1.8	3.2
500 $/KWh	5 mins	7.0	15.0	39.0	79.0	119.0
	15 mins	1.7	4.3	12.3	25.7	39.0
	30 mins	0.3	1.7	5.7	12.3	19.0
	1 hour	-0.3	0.3	2.3	5.7	9.0
	4 hours	-0.8	-0.7	-0.2	0.7	1.5

Figure 8. ROI with additional battery capacities. Positive values indicates investment is worthwhile (magnitude indicates higher returns) while negative values suggest not investing in higher capacities.

power infrastructure cap-ex is reported to grow by $10-25 for every provisioned watt [4, 23]. Since this includes costs for cooling, Diesel Generators, UPS, etc., it is non-trivial to isolate the $/W for the IT power infrastructure. Consequently, we study a wide range for c_{cap} starting from as low as 1 $/W going all the way to 15 $/W. We can then calculate the Return-On-Investment (ROI) for additional battery capacity as: $\frac{c_{cap} - e \cdot c_{bat}}{e \cdot c_{bat}}$ and show these in Figure 8 for emergency durations ranging from 5 minutes to 4 hours. In these calculations, we ensure that battery costs are amortized over 4 year lifetimes while infrastructure costs are amortized over 12 year lifetimes. We find a positive ROI (very high ROI in many cases) for most of the operating regions, despite considering pessimistic scenarios. This suggests that investing in additional battery capacity may be worthwhile, although a more in-depth economic analysis is warranted in future work.

8. Concluding Remarks

We have presented a framework for dealing with emergencies arising from aggressive underprovisioning of the power infrastructure. Rather than disruptive fuses/circuit-breakers, IT controlled techniques such as power state modulation, and workload migration can be supplemented with our new proposal of leveraging already existing UPS batteries to gracefully deal with emergencies. We demonstrate using an experimental prototype, with several interesting use cases, that the battery based approaches are (i) self-sufficient to deal with short duration emergencies, (ii) supplement existing solutions to enhance their efficacy over a wider range of operating conditions, and (iii) create opportunities where other options are infeasible. We have also presented an offline theoretical framework to find bounds on how well we can perform under these emergencies, and presented several online heuristics that can adapt themselves to work under these unpredictable black swan events (when? how severe? how long?). Since these emergencies are typically a consequence of load surges, existing solutions - power state throttling and migration - by themselves can have serious performance implications. Overall, we find that when migration/load-redirection overhead is low, a fast drain of the battery locally to control the power surge until migration is complete, works quite well. At the other extreme, when migration costs are high, delaying the migration with a combination of slow battery drain and power mode control is the better option. The battery is thus an agile and useful stand-alone and/or complementary solution to address both short and long duration emergencies.

Acknowledgments

This work was supported, in part, by NSF grants CNS-0720456, CNS-0615097, CAREER award 0953541, and research awards from Google and HP. We would like to thank Luiz Barroso from Google, who provided valuable inputs on motivating and shaping the work presented in this paper.

References

[1] 1 KW APC UPS - SURTA1500RMXL2U. http://www.apc.com/products/.

[2] F. Ahmad and T. N. Vijaykumar. Joint optimization of idle and cooling power in data centers while maintaining response time. In *Proceedings of the Architectural support for programming languages and operating systems (ASPLOS)*, 2010.

[3] H. Amur, J. Cipar, V. Gupta, G. R. Ganger, M. A. Kozuch, and K. Schwan. Robust and flexible power-proportional storage. In *Proceedings of the ACM Symposium On Cloud Computing (SOCC)*, 2010.

[4] L. A. Barroso and U. Holzle. *The Datacenter as a Computer: An Introduction to the Design of Warehouse-Scale Machines*. Morgan and Claypool Publishers, 2009.

[5] D. Bhandarkar. Watt Matters in Energy Efficiency, Server Design Summit, 2010.

[6] J. Chase, D. Anderson, P. Thakur, and A. Vahdat. Managing Energy and Server Resources in Hosting Centers. In *Proceedings of the Symposium on Operating Systems Principles (SOSP)*, 2001.

[7] Y. Chen, A. Das, W. Qin, A. Sivasubramaniam, Q. Wang, and N. Gautam. Managing Server Energy and Operational Costs in Hosting Centers. In *Proceedings of the Conference on Measurement and Modeling of Computer Systems (SIGMETRICS)*, 2005.

[8] C. Clark, K. Fraser, S. Hand, J. Hansen, E. Jul, C. Limpach, I. Pratt, and A. Warfield. Live migration of virtual machines. In *Proceedings of the Symposium on Networked Systems Design and Implementation (NSDI)*, 2005.

[9] Commercial circuit breakers, 2008. http://circuit-breakers.carlingtech.com/all_circuits.asp.

[10] Q. Deng, D. Meisner, L. Ramos, T. F. Wenisch, and R. Bianchini. Memscale: active low-power modes for main memory. In *Proceedings of Architectural Support for Programming Languages and Operating Systems (ASPLOS)*, 2011.

[11] Facebook Open Compute Project, 2011. http://opencompute.org.

[12] X. Fan, W.-D. Weber, and L. A. Barroso. Power provisioning for a warehouse-sized computer. In *Proceedings of the International Symposium on Computer Architecture (ISCA)*, 2007.

[13] W. Felter, K. Rajamani, C. Rusu, and T. Keller. A Performance-Conserving Approach for Reducing Peak Power Consumption in Server Systems. In *Proceedings of the International Conference on Supercomputing (ICS)*, 2005.

[14] M. E. Femal and V. W. Freeh. Safe overprovisioning: Using power limits to increase aggregate throughput. In *Workshop on Power-Aware Computer Systems (PACS)*, 2004.

[15] J. Flinn and M. Satyanarayanan. Managing battery lifetime with energy-aware adaptation. *Transaction On Computer Systems (TOCS)*, 2004.

[16] A. Gandhi, M. Harchol-Balter, R. Das, and C. Lefurgy. Optimal power allocation in server farms. In *Proceedings of the Conference on Measurement and Modeling of Computer Systems (SIGMETRICS)*, 2009.

[17] L. Ganesh, J. Liu, S. Nath, G. Reeves, and F. Zhao. Unleash Stranded Power in Data Centers with RackPacker. In *Workshop on Energy-Efficient Design (WEED)*, 2009.

[18] Google Server-level UPS for improved efficiency. `http://news.cnet.com/8301-1001_3-10209580-92.html`.

[19] S. Govindan, J. Choi, B. Urgaonkar, A. Sivasubramaniam, and A.Baldini. Statistical profiling-based techniques for effective power provisioning in data centers. In *Proceedings of the International European Conference on Computer Systems (EUROSYS)*, 2009.

[20] S. Govindan, A. Sivasubramaniam, and B. Urgaonkar. Benefits and Limitations of Tapping into Stored Energy For Datacenters. In *Proceedings of the International Symposium of Computer Architecture (ISCA)*, 2011.

[21] S. Govindan, D. Wang, L. Chen, A. Sivasubramaniam, and B. Urgaonkar. Towards Realizing a Low Cost and Highly Available Datacenter Power Infrastructure. In *Proceedings of the Workshop on Power Aware Computing and Systems (HotPower)*, 2011.

[22] Hadoop Map Reduce. `http://hadoop.apache.org/mapreduce/`.

[23] J. Hamilton. Internet-scale Service Infrastructure Efficiency, ISCA Keynote 2009.

[24] Lead-acid battery cost. `http://photovoltaics.sandia.gov/Pubs_2010/PV%20Website%20Publications%20Folder_09/Hanley_PVSC09%5B1%5D.pdf`.

[25] C. Lefurgy, X. Wang, and M. Ware. Server-Level Power Control. In *Proceedings of International Conference on Autonomic Computing (ICAC)*, 2007.

[26] H. Lim, A. Kansal, and J. Liu. Power budgeting for virtualized data centers. In *Proceedings of the 2011 USENIX conference on USENIX annual technical conference (USENIX)*, 2011.

[27] M. Lin, A. Wierman, L. L. H. Andrew, and E. Thereska. Dynamic right-sizing for power-proportional data centers. In *Proceedings of the IEEE International Conference on Computer Communications (INFOCOMM)*, 2011.

[28] D. Linden and T. B. Reddy. *Handbook of Batteries*. McGraw Hill Handbooks, 2002.

[29] Linux AVG Anti Virus. `http://free.avg.com/`.

[30] K. Ma, X. Li, M. Chen, and X. Wang. Scalable power control for many-core architectures running multi-threaded applications. In *Proceedings of the International Symposium on Computer Architecture (ISCA)*, 2011.

[31] S. McCluer. APC White paper 30 (Revision 11): Battery Technology for Data Centers and Network Rooms: Lead-acid Battery Options, 2005.

[32] D. Meisner, C. M. Sadler, L. A. Barroso, W. Weber, and T. F. Wenisch. Power management of online data-intensive services. In *Proceedings of the International Symposium on Computer Architecture (ISCA)*, 2011.

[33] Microsoft Reveals its Speciality Servers, Racks, 2011. `http://www.datacenterknowledge.com/archives/2011/04/25/microsoft-reveals-its-speciality-servers-racks/`.

[34] J. Moore, J. Chase, P. Ranganathan, and R. Sharma. Making scheduling cool: Temperature-aware workload placement in data centers. In *Proceedings of the Usenix Annual Technical Conference (USENIX)*, 2005.

[35] S. Pelley, D. Meisner, P. Zandevakili, T. F. Wenisch, and J. Underwood. Power Routing: Dynamic Power Provisioning in the Data Center. In *Proceedings of Architectural Support for Programming Languages and Operating Systems (ASPLOS)*, 2010.

[36] E. Pinheiro, R. Bianchini, E.Carrera, and T. Heath. Load Balancing and Unbalancing for Power and Performance in Cluster-Based Systems. In *Workshop on Compilers and Operating Systems for Low Power (COLP)*, 2001.

[37] R. Raghavendra, P. Ranganathan, V. Talwar, Z. Wang, and X. Zhu. No Power Struggles: Coordinated multi-level power management for the data center. In *Proceedings of Architectural Support for Programming Languages and Operating Systems (ASPLOS)*, 2008.

[38] L. Ramos and R. Bianchini. C-Oracle: Predictive thermal management for data centers. In *proceedings of the International Symposium on High-Performance Computer Architecture (HPCA)*, 2008.

[39] P. Ranganathan, P. Leech, D. Irwin, and J. Chase. Ensemble-level Power Management for Dense Blade Servers. In *Proceedings of International Symposium on Computer Architecture (ISCA)*, 2006.

[40] W. Smith. TPC-W: Benchmarking An Ecommerce Solution. `http://www.tpc.org/information/other/techarticles.asp`.

[41] SPEC JBB2005: Java Business Benchmark. `http://www.spec.org/jbb2005/`.

[42] N. N. Taleb. *The Black Swan: The Impact of the Highly Improbable*. Random House, 2007.

[43] B. Urgaonkar, P. Shenoy, and T. Roscoe. Resource Overbooking and Application Profiling in Shared Hosting Platforms. In *Proceedings of the Symposium on Operating Systems Design and Implementation (OSDI)*, 2002.

[44] R. Urgaonkar, B. Urgaonkar, M. J. Neely, and A. Sivasubramaniam. Optimal Power Cost Management Using Stored Energy in Data Centers. In *Proceedings of the Conference on Measurement and Modeling of Computer Systems (SIGMETRICS)*, 2011.

[45] A. Verma, P. De, V. Mann, T. Nayak, A. Purohit, G. Dasgupta, and R. Kothari. Brownmap: Enforcing power budget in shared data centers. In *Proceedings of the Conference on Middleware (MIDDLEWARE)*, 2010.

[46] C. Waldspurger. Memory Resource Management in VMWare ESX Server. In *Proceedings of the Symposium on Operating System Design and Implementation (OSDI)*, 2002.

[47] X. Wang and M. Chen. Cluster-level feedback power control for performance optimization. In *Proceedings of the International Symposium on High-Performance Computer Architecture (HPCA)*, 2008.

[48] X. Wang, M. Chen, and C. Lefurgy. How much power oversubscription is safe and allowed in data centers? In *Proceedings of the International Conference on Autonomic Computing (ICAC)*, 2011.

[49] A. Weisel and F. Bellosa. Process cruise control-event-driven clock scaling for dynamic power management. In *Proceedings of Compilers, Architecture and Synthesis for Embedded Systems (CASES)*, 2002.

[50] H. Zeng, X. Fan, C. Ellis, A. Lebeck, and A. Vahdat. ECOSystem: Managing Energy as a First Class Operating System Resource. In *Proceedings of the Conference on Architectural Support for Programming Languages and Operating Systems (ASPLOS)*, 2002.

[51] F. Zhang, Z. Shi, and W. Wolf. A dynamic battery model for co-design in cyber-physical systems. In *Proceedings of the International Conference on Distributed Computing Systems Workshops (ICDCSW)*, 2009.

[52] Q. Zhu, Z. Chen, L. Tan, Y. Zhou, K. Keeton, and J. Wilkes. Hibernator: helping disk arrays sleep through the winter. In *Proceedings of the Symposium on Operating Systems Principles (SOSP)*, 2005.

Understanding Modern Device Drivers

Asim Kadav and Michael M. Swift
Computer Sciences Department, University of Wisconsin-Madison
{kadav, swift} @cs.wisc.edu

Abstract

Device drivers are the single largest contributor to operating-system kernel code with over 5 million lines of code in the Linux kernel, and cause significant complexity, bugs and development costs. Recent years have seen a flurry of research aimed at improving the reliability and simplifying the development of drivers. However, little is known about what constitutes this huge body of code beyond the small set of drivers used for research.

In this paper, we study the source code of Linux drivers to understand what drivers actually do, how current research applies to them and what opportunities exist for future research. We determine whether assumptions made by driver research, such as that all drivers belong to a class, are indeed true. We also analyze driver code and abstractions to determine whether drivers can benefit from code re-organization or hardware trends. We develop a set of static-analysis tools to analyze driver code across various axes. Broadly, our study looks at three aspects of driver code (i) what are the characteristics of driver code functionality and how applicable is driver research to *all* drivers, (ii) how do drivers interact with the kernel, devices, and buses, and (iii) are there similarities that can be abstracted into libraries to reduce driver size and complexity?

We find that many assumptions made by driver research do not apply to all drivers. At least 44% of drivers have code that is not captured by a class definition, 28% of drivers support more than one device per driver, and 15% of drivers do significant computation over data. From the driver interactions study, we find that the USB bus offers an efficient bus interface with significant standardized code and coarse-grained access, ideal for executing drivers in isolation. We also find that drivers for different buses and classes have widely varying levels of device interaction, which indicates that the cost of isolation will vary by class. Finally, from our driver similarity study, we find 8% of all driver code is substantially similar to code elsewhere and may be removed with new abstractions or libraries.

Categories and Subject Descriptors D.4.7 [*Operating Systems*]: Organization and Design

General Terms Measurement, Design

Keywords Device Drivers, Measurement

ASPLOS'12, March 3–7, 2012, London, England, UK.

1. Introduction

Modern computer systems are communicating with an increasing number of devices, each of which requires a driver. For example, a modern desktop PC may have tens of devices, including keyboard, mouse, display, storage, and USB controllers. Device drivers constitute 70% of the Linux code base [32], and likely are a greater fraction of the code written for the Windows kernel, which supports many more devices. Several studies have shown that drivers are the dominant cause of OS crashes in desktop PCs [14, 28]. As a result, there has been a recent surge of interest in techniques to tolerate faults in drivers [12, 38, 39, 47], to improve the quality of driver code [20]; and in creating new driver architectures that improve reliability and security [4, 15, 21, 23, 24, 31, 44].

However, most research on device drivers focuses on a small subset of devices, typically a network card, sound card, and storage device, all using the PCI bus. These are but a small subset of all drivers, and results from these devices may not generalize to the full set of drivers. For example, many devices for consumer PCs are connected over USB. Similarly, the devices studied are fairly mature and have standardized interfaces, but many other devices may have significant functionality differences.

Thus, it is important to study all drivers to review how the driver research solutions being developed are applicable to all classes of drivers. In addition, a better understanding of driver code can lead to new abstractions and interfaces that can reduce driver complexity and improve reliability.

This paper presents a comprehensive study of all the drivers in the Linux kernel in order to broadly characterize their code. We focus on (i) what driver code does, including where driver development work is concentrated, (ii) the interaction of driver code with devices, buses, and the kernel, and (iii) new opportunities for abstracting driver functionality into common libraries or subsystems. We use two static analysis tools to analyze driver code. To understand properties of driver code, we developed DrMiner, which performs data-flow analyses to detect properties of drivers at the granularity of functions. We also developed the DrComp tool, which uses geometric shape analysis [3] to detect similar code across drivers. DrComp maps code to points in coordinate space based on the structure of individual driver functions, and similar functions are at nearby coordinates.

The contributions of this paper are as follows:

- First, we analyze what driver code does in order to verify common assumptions about driver code made by driver research. We show that while these assumptions hold for most drivers, there are a significant number of drivers that violate these assumptions. We also find that several rapidly growing driver classes are not being addressed by driver research.
- Second, we study driver *interactions* with the kernel and devices, to find how existing driver architecture can adapt to a world of multicore processors, devices with high-power processors and virtualized I/O. We find that drivers vary widely

by class, and that USB drivers are more efficient in supporting multiple chipsets than PCI drivers. Furthermore, we find that XenBus drivers may provide a path to executing drivers outside the kernel and potentially on the device itself.

- Third, we study driver code *contents* to find opportunities to reduce or simplify driver code. We develop new analysis tools for detecting similar code structures and their types that detect over 8% of Linux driver code is very similar to other driver code, and offer insights on how this code can be reduced.

In the remainder of this paper, we first discuss device driver background and develop a taxonomy of drivers. We then present the three broad classes of results on driver behavior in Sections 3 and 4. In Section 5 we present results showing the extent of repeated code in drivers. Section 6 discusses our findings.

2. Background

A device driver is a software component that provides an interface between the OS and a hardware device. The driver configures and manages the device, and converts requests from the kernel into requests to the hardware. Drivers rely on three interfaces: (i) the interface between the driver and the kernel, for communicating requests and accessing OS services; (ii) the interface between the driver and the device, for executing operations; and (iii) the interface between the driver and the bus, for managing communication with the device.

2.1 Driver/Device Taxonomy

The core operating system kernel interacts with device drivers through a set of interfaces that abstract the fundamental nature of the device. In Linux, the three categories of drivers are *character* drivers, which are byte-stream oriented; *block* drivers, which support random-access to blocks; and *network* drivers, which support streams of packets. Below these top-level interfaces, support libraries provide common interfaces for many other families of devices, such as keyboards and mice within character drivers.

In order to understand the kinds of drivers Linux supports, we begin by taxonomizing drivers according to their interfaces. We consider a single driver as a module of code that can be compiled independently of other code. Hence, a single driver can span multiple files. We consider all device drivers, bus drivers and virtual drivers that constitute the driver directories (`/sound` and `/drivers`) in the Linux 2.6.37.6 kernel, dated April, 2011. We perform our analyses on all drivers that compile on the x86 platform, using the kernel build option to compile all drivers. Overall, we consider 3,217 distinct drivers. While there are a significant number of Linux drivers that are distributed separately from the kernel, we do not consider them for this work.

We detect the class of a driver not by the location of its code, but by the interfaces it registers: *e.g.*, `register_netdev` indicates a driver is a network device. We further classify the classes into sub-categories to understand the range of actual device types supported by them through manual classification, using the device operations they register, the device behavior and their location. While Linux organizes related drivers in directories, this taxonomy is not the same as the Linux directory organization: network drivers are split under *drivers/net*, *drivers/atm* and other directories. However, block drivers are split by their interfaces under *drivers/scsi*, *drivers/ide* and other directories

Figure 1 shows the hierarchy of drivers in Linux according to their interfaces, starting from basic driver types i.e. char, block and net. We identify 72 unique classes of drivers. The majority (52%) of driver code is in character drivers, spread across 41 classes. Network drivers account 25% of driver code, but have only 6 classes. In contrast to the rich diversity of Figure 1, Table 1 lists the

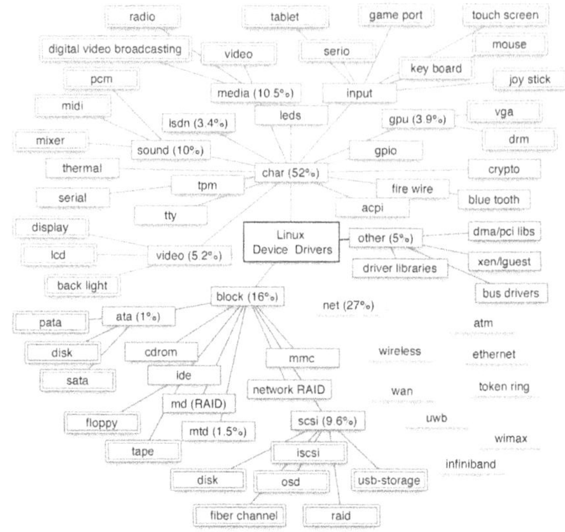

Figure 1. The Linux driver taxonomy in terms of basic driver classes. The size (in percentage of lines of code) is mentioned for 5 biggest classes. Not all driver classes are mentioned.

driver types used in research. Most driver research (static-analysis tools excepted) neglects the heavy tail of character devices. For example, video and GPU drivers contribute significantly towards driver code (almost 9%) due to complex devices with instruction sets that change each generation, but these devices are largely ignored by driver research due to their complexity.

We also looked at low-level buses, which provide connectivity to devices and discover the devices attached to a system. The majority of devices are either PCI (36% of all device identifiers) or USB (35%), while other buses support far fewer: I2C represents 4% of devices, PCMCIA is 3% and HID is 2.5% (mostly USB devices). The remaining devices were supported by less popular or legacy buses such as ISA or platform devices. We also found that 8% of devices perform low-level I/O without using a bus, interconnect, or support virtual devices. Higher-level protocols such as SCSI (8.5%) and IDE (2%) use one of these underlying low-level buses such as PCI and USB. While PCI drivers still constitute the greatest fraction of drivers, the number of devices supported by USB is similar to PCI. Hence, driver research should validate their performance and reliability claims on USB devices as well.

2.2 Driver Research Assumptions

Most research makes some simplifying assumptions about the problem being solved, and driver research is no different. For example, Shadow Drivers [38] assume that all drivers are members of a class and there are no unique interfaces to a driver. Similarly, the Termite driver-synthesis system assumes that drivers are state machines and perform no computations [33]. Table 2 lists the assumptions made by recent research into device drivers.

We separate these assumptions into two categories: (i) *interactions* refers to assumptions about how drivers interact with the kernel, and (ii) *architecture* refers assumptions about the role of the driver: is it a conduit for data, or does it provide more substantial processing or services? Interaction assumptions relate to how the kernel and driver interact. For example, systems that interpose on driver/device communication, such as Nooks [39], typically assume that communication occurs over procedure calls and not shared memory. Nooks' isolation mechanism will not work otherwise. Similarly, Shadow Drivers assume that the complete state of the device is available in the driver by capturing kernel/driver in-

Improvement type	System	Driver classes tested	Drivers tested
New functionality	Shadow driver migration [19]	net	1
	RevNIC [6]	net	4
Reliability (H/W Protection)	CuriOS [9]	serial port, NOR flash	2
	Nooks [39]	net, sound	6
	Palladium [7]	custom packet filter	1
	Xen [12]	net, sound	2
Reliability (Isolation)	BGI [5]	net, sound, serial, ramdisk, libs	16
	Shadow Drivers [38]	net, sound, IDE	13
	XFI [40]	ram disk, dummy	2
Specification	Devil [25]	scsi, video	2
	Dingo [32]	net	2
	Laddie [45]	net, UART, rtc	3
	Nexus [44]	net, sound, USB-mouse, USB-storage	4
	Termite [33]	net, mmc	2
Static analysis tools	Carburizer [18]	All/net	All/3
	Cocinelle [29]	Various	All
	SDV [2]	basic ports, storage, USB, 1394-interface, mouse, keyboard, PCI battery	126
Type safety	Decaf Drivers [31]	net, sound, USB controller, mouse	5
	Safedrive [47]	net, USB, sound, video	6
	Singularity [37]	Disk	1
User-level device drivers	Micro-drivers [15]	net, sound, USB controller	4
	SUD [4]	net, wireless, sound, USB controllers, USB	6/1
	User-level drivers [21]	net, disk (ata)	2

Table 1. Research projects on drivers, the improvement type, and the number and class of drivers used to support the claim end to end. Few projects test all driver interfaces thoroughly. Static analysis tools that do not require driver modifications are available to check many more drivers. Also, some solutions, like Carburizer [18], and SUD [4] support the performance claims on fewer drivers.

Driver interactions
Class membership: Drivers belong to common set of classes, and the class completely determines their behavior.
Procedure calls: Drivers always communicate with the kernel through procedure calls.
Driver state: The state of the device is completely captured by the driver.
Device state: Drivers may assume that devices are in the correct state.
Driver architecture
I/O: Driver code functionality is only dedicated to converting requests from the kernel to the device.
Chipsets: Drivers typically support one or a few device chipsets.
CPU Bound: Drivers do little processing and mostly act as a library for binding different interfaces together.
Event-driven: Drivers execute only in response to kernel and device requests, and to not have their own threads.

Table 2. Common assumptions made in device driver research.

teractions [38]. However, network cards that do TCP-offload may have significant protocol state that is only available in the device, and cannot be captured by monitoring the kernel/driver interface.

Several recent projects assume that drivers support a single chipset, such as efforts at synthesizing drivers from a formal specification [33]. However, many drivers support more than one chipset. Hence, synthesizing the replacement for a single driver may require many more drivers. Similarly, enforcing safety properties for specific devices [44] may be cumbersome if many chipsets must be supported for each driver. Other efforts at reverse engineering drivers [6] similarly may be complicated by the support of many chipsets with different hardware interfaces. Furthermore, these synthesis and verification systems assume that devices always behave correctly, and their drivers may fail unpredictably with faulty hardware.

Another assumption made by driver research is that drivers are largely a conduit for communicating data and for signaling the device, and that they perform little processing. Neither RevNIC [6]) nor Termite [33] support data processing with the driver, because it is too complex to model as a simple state machine.

While these assumptions all hold true for many drivers, this research seeks to quantify their real generality. If these assumptions are true for all drivers, then these research ideas have broad applicability. If not, then new research is needed to address the outliers.

3. What Do Drivers Do?

Device drivers are commonly assumed to primarily perform I/O. A standard undergraduate OS textbook states:

> A device driver can be thought of a translator. Its input consists of high-level commands such as "retrieve block 123." Its output consists of low-level, hardware-specific instructions that are used by the hardware controller, which interfaces the I/O device to the rest of the system."
>
> *Operating Systems Concepts* [36]

However, this passage describes the functions of only the small portion of driver code that which actually performs I/O. Past work revealed that the bulk of driver code is dedicated to initialization and configuration for a sample of network, SCSI and sound drivers [15].

We seek to develop a comprehensive understanding of what driver code does: what are the tasks drivers perform, what are the interfaces they use, and how much code does this all take. The goal of this study is to verify the driver assumptions described in the previous section, and to identify major driver functions that could benefit from additional research.

3.1 Methodology

To study the driver code, we developed the *DrMiner* static analysis tool using CIL [27] to detect code properties in individual drivers. DrMiner takes as input unmodified drivers and a list of driver data-structure types and driver entry points. As drivers only execute when invoked from the kernel, these entry points allow us to determine the purpose of particular driver functions. For example, we find the different devices and chipsets supported by analyzing the `device_id` structures registered (*e.g.*, `pci_device_id`, `acpi_device_id` etc.) with the kernel. We also identify the driver entry points from the driver structure registered (*e.g.*, `pci_driver`, `pnp_device`) and the device operations structure registered (*e.g.*, `net_device`). DrMiner analyzes the function pointers registered by the driver to determine the functionality of each driver. We then construct a control-flow graph of the driver that allows us to determine all the functions reachable through each entry point, including through function pointers.

We use a *tagging* approach to labeling driver code: DrMiner tags a function with the label of each entry point from which it is reachable. Thus, a function called only during initialization will be labeled initialization only, while code common to initialization and shutdown will receive both labels. In addition, DrMiner identifies specific code features, such as loops indicating computation.

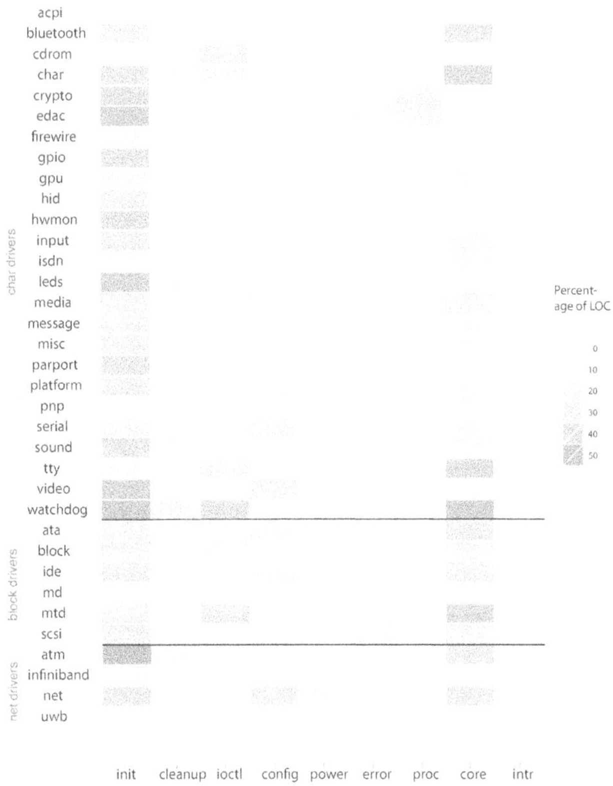

Figure 2. The percentage of driver code accessed during different driver activities across driver classes.

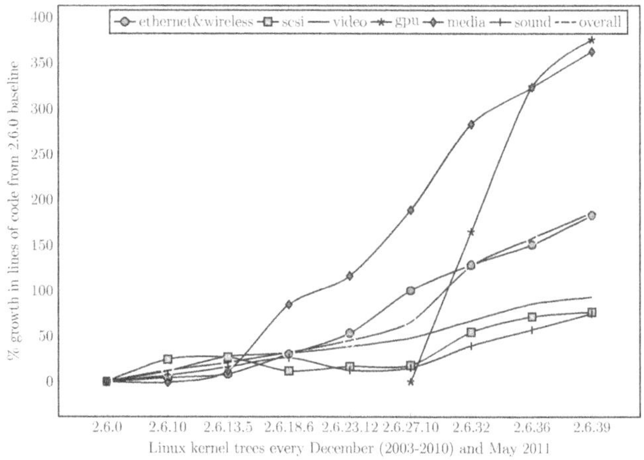

Figure 3. The change in driver code in terms of LOC across different driver classes between the Linux 2.6.0 and Linux 2.6.39 kernel.

We run these analyses over the entire Linux driver source and store the output in a SQL database. The database stores information about each driver as well as each function in the driver. The information about the driver consists of name, path, size, class, number of chipsets, module parameters, and interfaces registered with the kernel. The information about each driver function consists of function name, size, labels, resources allocated (memory, locks etc.), and how it interacts with the kernel and the device. From the database, determining the amount of code dedicated to any function is a simple query. In our results, we present data for about 25 classes with the most code.

3.2 What is the function breakdown of driver code?

Drivers vary widely in how much code they use for different purposes; a simple driver for a single chipset may devote most of its code to processing I/O requests and have a simple initialization routine. In contrast, a complex driver supporting dozens of chipsets may have more code devoted to initialization and error handling than to request handling.

Figure 2 shows the breakdown of driver code across driver classes. The figure shows the fraction of driver code invoked during driver initialization, cleanup, ioctl processing, configuration, power management, error handling, `/proc` and `/sys` handling, and most importantly, core I/O request handling (*e.g.*, sending packet for network devices, or playing audio for sound card) and interrupt handling across different driver classes.

The largest contributors to driver code are initialization and cleanup, comprising almost 36% of driver code on average, error handling (5%), configuration (15%), power management (7.4%) and ioctl handling (6.2%). On average, only 23.3% of the code in a driver is dedicated to request handling and interrupts.

Implications: These results indicate that efforts at reducing the complexity of drivers should not only focus on request handling, which accounts for only one fourth of the total code, but on better mechanisms for initialization and configuration. For example, as devices become increasingly virtualization aware, quick ways to initialize or reset are critical for important virtualization features such as re-assignment of devices and live migration [19]. Drivers contain significant configuration code (15%), specifically in network (31%) and video (27%) drivers. As devices continue to become more complex, driver and OS research should look at efficient and organized ways of managing device configuration [35].

3.3 Where is the driver code changing?

Over time, the focus of driver development shifts as new device classes become popular. We compared the breakdown of driver code between the 2.6.0 and 2.6.39 for new source lines of code added annually to different driver classes. We obtain the source lines of code across different classes in 9 intermediate revisions (every December since 2.6.0) using sloccount [43].

Figure 3 shows the growth in driver across successive years from the 2.6.0 baseline for 8 major driver classes. Overall, driver code has increased by 185% over the last eight years. We identify three specific trends in this growth. First, there is additional code for new hardware. This code includes wimax, GPU, media, input devices and virtualization drivers. Second, there is increasing support for certain class of devices, including network (driven by wireless), media, GPU and SCSI. From 2.6.13 to 2.6.18, the devices supported by a vendor (QLogic) increased significantly. Since, they were very large multi-file SCSI drivers, the drivers where coalesced to a single driver, reducing the size of SCSI drivers in the driver tree. In Section 5, we investigate whether there are opportunities to reduce driver code in the existing code base. Third, there is minor code refactoring. For example, periodically, driver code is moved away from the driver or bus library code into the respective classes where they belong. For example, drivers from the i2c bus directory were moved to misc directory.

Implications: While Ethernet and sound, the common driver classes for research, are important, research should look further into other rapidly changing drivers, such as media, GPU and wireless drivers.

```
drivers/ide/ide-cd.c:
static int cdrom_read_tocentry(...) {
  // Read table of contents data
  for (i = 0; i <= ntracks; i++) {
    if (drive->atapi_flags &
        IDE_AFLAG_TOCADDR_AS_BCD) {
      if (drive->atapi_flags &
          IDE_AFLAG_TOCTRACKS_AS_BCD)
        toc->ent[i].track =
          bcd2bin(toc->ent[i].track);
      msf_from_bcd(&toc->ent[i].addr.msf);}
    toc->ent[i].addr.lba =
      msf_to_lba(toc->ent[i].addr.msf.minute,
                 toc->ent[i].addr.msf.second,
                 toc->ent[i].addr.msf.frame);
  }
}
```

Figure 4. The IDE CD-ROM driver processes table-of-contents entries into a native format.

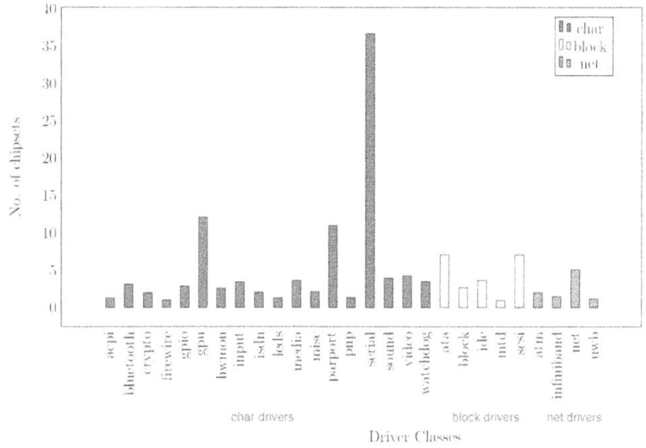

Figure 5. The average number of chipsets supported by drivers in each class.

3.4 Do drivers belong to classes?

Many driver research projects assume that drivers belong to a class. For example, Shadow Drivers [38] must be coded with the semantics of all calls into the driver so it can replay them during recovery. However, many drivers support proprietary extensions to the class interface. In Linux drivers, these manifest as private `ioctl` options, `/proc` or `/sys` entries, and as load-time parameters. If a driver has one of these features, it may have additional behaviors not captured by the class.

We use DrMiner to identify drivers that have behavior outside the class by looking for load-time parameters and code to register `/proc` or `/sys` entries. We do not identify unique `ioctl` options. Overall, we find that most driver classes have substantial amounts of device-specific functionality. Code supporting `/proc` and `/sys` is present in 16.3% of drivers. Also, 36% of drivers have load-time parameters to control their behavior and configure options not available through the class interface. Overall, 44% of drivers use atleast one of the two non-class features. Additionally, `ioctl` code comprises 6.2% of driver code, can also cause non-class behavior.

As an example of how these class extensions are used, the e1000 gigabit network driver has 15 load-time parameters that allow control over interrupt processing and transmit/receive ring sizing, and interrupt throttling rate. This feature is not part of any standard network device interface and is instead specific to this device. Similarly, the i915 DRM GPU driver supports load parameters for down-clocking the GPU, altering graphic responsibilities from X.org to the kernel, and power saving. These parameters change the code path of the driver during initialization as well as during regular driver operations. While the introduction of these parameters does not affect the isolation properties of the reliability solutions, as the interfaces for setting and retrieving these options are standard, it limits the ability to restart and restore the driver to a previous state since the semantics of these options are not standardized.

Implications: While most driver functionality falls into the class behavior, many drivers have significant extensions that do not. Attempts to recover driver state based solely on the class interface [38] or to synthesize drivers from common descriptions of the class [6, 33] may not work for a substantial number of drivers. Thus, future research should explicitly consider how to accommodate unique behaviors efficiently.

3.5 Do drivers do significant processing?

As devices become more powerful and feature processors of their own, it is often assumed that drivers perform little processing and simply shuttle data between the OS and the device. However, if drivers require substantial CPU processing, for example to compute parity for RAID, checksums for networking, or display data for video drivers, then processing power must be reserved. Furthermore, in a virtualized setting, heavy I/O from one guest VM could substantially reduce CPU availability for other guest VMs.

DrMiner detects processing in drivers by looking for loops that (i) do no I/O, (ii) do not interact with the kernel, and (iii) are on core data paths, such as sending/receiving packets or reading/writing data. This ensures that polling loops, common in many drivers, are not identified as performing processing.

We find that 15% of drivers have at least one function that performs processing, and that processing occurs in 1% of all driver functions. An even higher fraction (28%) of sound and network drivers do processing. Wireless drivers, such as ATH, perform processing to interpolate power levels of the device under different frequencies and other conditions. Many network drivers provide the option of computing checksums on the outgoing/incoming packets. Finally, even CD-ROM drivers, which largely read data off the device, do computation to analyze the table of content information for CD-ROMs, as shown in Figure 4.

Implications: A substantial fraction of drivers do some form of data processing. Thus, efforts to generate driver code automatically must include mechanisms for data processing, not just converting requests from the OS into requests to the device. Furthermore, virtualized systems should account for the CPU time spent processing data when this processing is performed on behalf of a guest VM. These results also point to new opportunities for driver and device design: given the low cost of embedded processors, can all the computation be offloaded to the device, and is there a performance or power benefit to doing so?

3.6 How many device chipsets does a single driver support?

Several driver research projects require or generate code for a specific device chipset. For example, Nexus requires a safety specification that is unique to each device interface [44]. If a driver supports only a single device, this requirement may not impose much burden. However, if a driver supports many devices, each with a different interface or behavior, then many specifications are needed to fully protect a driver.

We measure the number of chipsets or hardware packagings supported by each Linux driver by counting the number of PCI, USB or other bus device IDs (*i.e.*, i2c, ieee1394) that the driver recognizes. These structures are used across buses to identify (and match) different devices or packagings that are supported by the

```
static int __devinit cy_pci_probe(...)
{
 if (device_id == PCI_DEVICE_ID_CYCLOM_Y_Lo) {
   ...
 if (pci_resource_flags(pdev,2)&IORESOURCE_IO){
   ..
 if (device_id == PCI_DEVICE_ID_CYCLOM_Y_Lo ||
      device_id == PCI_DEVICE_ID_CYCLOM_Y_Hi) {
    ..
}else if (device_id==PCI_DEVICE_ID_CYCLOM_Z_Hi)
 ....
 if (device_id == PCI_DEVICE_ID_CYCLOM_Y_Lo ||
      device_id == PCI_DEVICE_ID_CYCLOM_Y_Hi) {
  switch (plx_ver) {
   case PLX_9050:
   ...
  default:     /* Old boards, use PLX_9060 */
   ...
}
```

Figure 6. The cyclades character drivers supports eight chipsets that behaves differently at each phase of execution. This makes driver code space efficient but extremely complex to understand.

driver. Figure 5 shows the average number of chipsets supported by each driver in each driver class. While most drivers support only a few different devices, serial drivers support almost 36 chipsets on average, and network drivers average 5. The Radeon DRM driver supports over 400 chipsets, although many of these may indicate different packagings of the same internal chipset. Generic USB drivers such as usb-storage and usb-audio support over 200 chipsets each, and the usb-serial driver supports more than 500 chipsets. While not every chipset requires different treatment by the driver, many do. For example, the `3c59x` 100-megabit Ethernet driver supports 37 chipsets, 17 sets of features that vary between chipsets, and two complete implementations of the core send/receive functionality. Overall, we find that 28% of drivers support more than one chipset and these drivers support 83% of the total devices.

In order to measure the effects of number of chipsets on driver code size, we measured the least-square correlation coefficient between the number of chipsets support by a driver and the amount of code in the driver and found them to be weakly correlated (0.25), indicating that drivers supporting more chipsets were on average larger than those that did not. However, this does not completely explain the amount of initialization code, as the correlation between the number of chipsets and the percentage of initialization code was 0.07, indicating that the additional chipsets increased the amount of code throughout the driver.

Implications: These results indicate that Linux drivers support multiple chipsets per driver and are relatively efficient, supporting 14,070 devices with 3,217 device and bus drivers, for an average of approximately 400 lines of code per device. Any system that generates unique drivers for every chipset or requires per-chipset manual specification may lead to a great expansion in driver code and complexity. Furthermore, there is substantial complexity in supporting multiple chipsets, as seen in Figure 6, so better programming methodologies, such as object-oriented programming [31] and automatic interface generation, similar to Devil [25], should be investigated.

3.7 Discussion

The results in this section indicate that while common assumptions about drivers are generally true, given the wide diversity of drivers, one cannot assume they always hold. Specifically, many drivers contain substantial amounts of code that make some of the existing research such as automatic generation of drivers difficult, due to

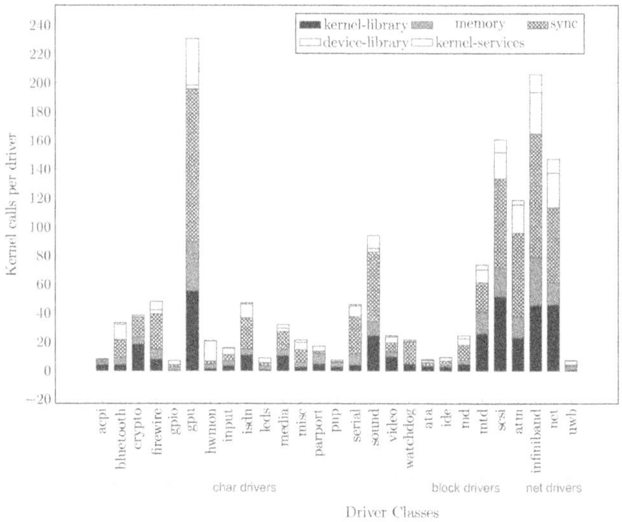

Figure 7. The average kernel library, memory, synchronization, kernel device library, and kernel services library calls per driver (bottom to top in figure) for all entry points.

code unique to that driver and not part of the class, code that processes data, and code for many chip sets.

4. Driver Interactions

The preceding section focused on the *function* of driver code, and here we turn to the *interactions* of driver code: how do drivers use the kernel, and how do drivers communicate with devices? We see three reasons to study these interactions. First, extra processing power on devices or extra cores on the host CPU provide an opportunity to redesign the driver architecture for improved reliability and performance. For example, it may be possible to move many driver functions out of the kernel and onto the device itself. Or, in virtualized systems, driver functionality may execute on a different core in a different virtual machine. Second, much of the difficulty in moving drivers between operating systems comes from the driver/kernel interface, so investigating what drivers request of the kernel can aid in designing more portable drivers. Third, the cost of isolation and reliability are proportional to the size of the interface and the frequency of interactions, so understanding the interface can lead to more efficient fault-tolerance mechanisms.

We examine the patterns of interaction between the driver, the kernel and the device, with a focus on (i) which kernel resources drivers consume, (ii) how and when drivers interact with devices, (iii) the differences in driver structure across different I/O buses, and (iv) the threading/synchronization model used by driver code.

4.1 Methodology

We apply the DrMiner tool from Section 3 to perform this analysis. However, rather than propagating labels down the call graph from entry points to leaf functions, here we start at the bottom with kernel and device interactions. Using a list of known kernel functions, bus functions, and I/O functions, we label driver functions according to the services or I/O they invoke. Additionally, we compute the number of invocations of bus, device and kernel invocations for each function in a driver. These call counts are also propagated to determine how many such static calls could be invoked when a particular driver entry point is invoked.

4.2 Driver/Kernel Interaction

Drivers vary widely in how they use kernel resources, such as memory, locks, and timers. Here, we investigate how drivers use these resources. We classify all kernel functions into one of five categories:

1. Kernel library (*e.g.*, generic support routines such as reporting functions,[1] timers, string manipulation, checksums, standard data structures)
2. Memory management (*e.g.*, allocation)
3. Synchronization (*e.g.*, locks)
4. Device library (*e.g.*, subsystem libraries supporting a class of device and other I/O related functions)
5. Kernel services (*e.g.*, access to other subsystems including files, memory, scheduling)

The first three are generic library routines that have little interaction with other kernel services, and could be re-implemented in other execution contexts. The fourth category, device library, provides I/O routines supporting the driver but does not rely other kernel services, and is very OS dependent. The final category provides access to other kernel subsystems, and is also OS dependent.

Figure 7 shows, for each class of drivers, the total number of function calls made by drivers in every class. The results demonstrate several interesting features of drivers. First, the majority of kernel invocations are for kernel library routines, memory management and synchronization. These functions are primarily *local* to a driver, in that they do not require interaction with other kernel services. Thus, a driver executing in a separate execution context, such as in user mode or a separate virtual machine, need not call into the kernel for these services. There are very few calls into kernel services, as drivers rarely interact with the rest of the kernel.

The number of calls into device-library code varies widely across different classes and illustrates the abstraction level of the devices: those with richer library support, such as network and SCSI drivers, have a substantial number of calls into device libraries, while drivers with less library support, such as GPU drivers, primarily invoke more generic kernel routines.

Finally, a number of drivers make very little use of kernel services, such as ATA, IDE, ACPI, and UWB drivers. This approach demonstrates another method for abstracting driver functionality when there is little variation across drivers: rather than having a driver that invokes support library routines, these drivers are themselves a small set of device-specific routines called from a much larger common driver. This design is termed a "miniport" driver in Windows. Thus, these drivers benefit from a common implementation of most driver functionality, and only the code differences are implemented in the device-specific code. These drivers are often quite small and have little code that is not device specific.

These results demonstrate a variety of interaction styles between drivers and the kernel: drivers with little supporting infrastructure demonstrate frequent interactions with the kernel for access to kernel services but few calls to device support code. Drivers with a high level of abstraction demonstrate few calls to the kernel over all. Drivers with a support library demonstrate frequent calls to kernel generic routines as well as calls to device support routines.

Implications: Drivers with few calls into device libraries may have low levels of abstraction, and thus are candidates for extracting common functionality. Similarly, drivers with many kernel interactions and device library interaction may benefit from converting to a layered on "miniport" architecture, where more driver functionality is extracted into a common library.

[1] We leave out `printk` to avoid skewing the numbers from calls to it.

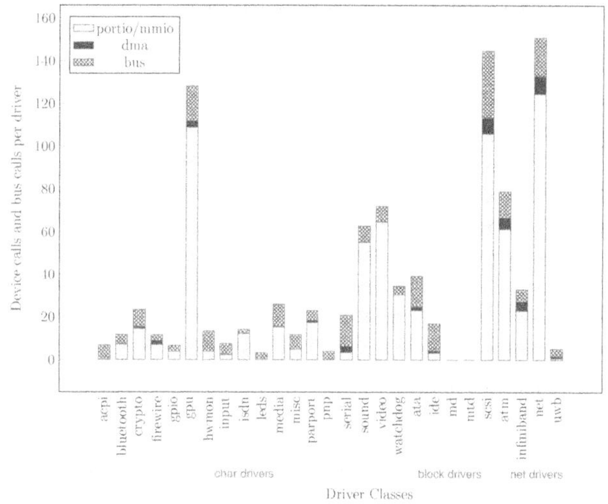

Figure 8. The device interaction pattern representing port I/O, memory mapped I/O, bus resources (bottom to top) invoked via all driver entry points.

Furthermore, a large fraction of driver/kernel interactions are for generic routines (memory, synchronization, libraries) that do not involve other kernel services. Thus, they could be implemented by a runtime environment local to the driver. For example, a driver executing in a separate virtual machine or on the device itself can make use of its local OS for these routines, and drivers in user space can similarly invoke user-space versions of these routines, such as the UML environment in SUD [4].

4.3 Driver/Device Interaction

We next look at interaction between the driver and the device. We analyzed all functions in all drivers, and if a function does I/O itself, or calls a function that results in an I/O, we label it as *perform I/O*. We categorize driver/device interactions around the type of interaction: access to memory-mapped I/O (MMIO) regions or x86 I/O ports (port IO) are labeled *mmio/portio*, *DMA* is DMA access, either initiated by the driver or enabled by the driver creating a DMA mapping for a memory region, and calls to a bus, such as USB or PCI (*bus*). We could not determine statically when a device initiates DMA, although we do count calls to map a page for future DMA (*e.g.*, `pci_map_single`) as a DMA action. Our analysis can detect memory mapped I/O through accessor routines such as `read/writeX` family, `ioread/iowrite` family of routines and port I/O using the `in/outX` family. DrMiner cannot identify direct dereferences of pointers into memory-mapped address ranges. However, direct dereference of I/O addresses is strongly discouraged and most non-conforming drivers have been converted to use accessor routines instead. We also note that all I/O routines on x86 eventually map down to either port or MMIO. Here, though, we focus on the I/O abstractions used by the driver.

Figure 8 shows, for each class of device, the number of device interactions in the entire driver. The results demonstrate that driver classes vary widely in their use of different I/O mechanisms. IDE and ATA drivers, both block devices, show very different patterns of interaction: IDE drivers do very little port or MMIO, because they rely on the PCI configuration space for accessing device registers. Hence, they show a greater proportion of bus operations. Additionally, virtual device classes such as md (RAID), do page-level writes by calling the block subsystem through routines like `submit_bio` rather than by accessing a device directly.

BUS	Kernel Interactions					Device Interactions			
	mem	*sync*	*dev lib.*	*kern lib.*	*kern services*	*port/mmio*	*dma*	*bus*	*avg devices/driver*
PCI	15.6	57.8	13.3	43.2	9.1	125.1	7.0	21.6	7.5
USB	9.6	25.5	5.6	9.9	3.0	0.0	2.2[2]	13.8	13.2
Xen	10.3	8.0	7.0	6.0	2.75	0.0	0.0	34.0	1/All

Table 3. Comparison of modern buses on drivers across all classes. Xen and USB drivers invoke the bus for the driver while PCI drivers invoke the device directly.

Second, these results demonstrate that the cost of isolating drivers can vary widely based on their interaction style. Direct interactions, such as through ports or MMIO, can use hardware protection, such as virtual memory. Thus, an isolated driver can be allowed to access the device directly. In contrast, calls to set up DMA or use bus routines rely on software isolation, and need to cross protection domains. Thus, drivers using higher-level buses, like USB, can be less efficient to isolate, as they can incur a protection-domain transition to access the device. However, as we show in the next section, access devices through a bus can often result in far fewer operations.

Implications: The number and type of device interactions vary widely across devices. Thus, the cost of isolating drivers, or verifying that their I/O requests are correct (as in Nexus [44]) can vary widely across drivers. Thus, any system that interposes or protects the driver/device interaction must consider the variety of interaction styles. Similarly, symbolic execution frameworks for drivers [20] must generate appropriate symbolic data for each interaction style.

4.4 Driver/Bus Interaction

The plurality of drivers in Linux are for devices that attach to some kind of PCI bus (*e.g.*, PCIe or PCI-X). However, several other buses are in common use: the USB bus for removable devices and XenBus for virtual devices [46]. Architecturally, USB and Xen drivers appear to have advantages, as they interact with devices over a message-passing interface. With USB 3.0 supporting speeds up to 5 Gbps [42] and Xen supporting 10 Gbps networks [30], it is possible that more devices will be accessed via USB or XenBus.

In this section, we study the structural properties of drivers for different buses to identify specific differences between the buses. We also look for indications that drivers for a bus may have better architectural characteristics, such as efficiency or support for isolation. We focus on two questions: (i) does the bus support a variety of devices efficiently, (ii) will it support new software architectures that move driver functionality out of the kernel onto a device or into a separate virtual machine? Higher efficiency of a bus interface results from supporting greater number of devices with standardized code. Greater isolation results from having less device/driver specific code in the kernel. If a bus only executes standardized code in the kernel, then it would be easier to isolate drivers away from kernel, and execute them inside a separate virtual machine or on the device itself such as on an embedded processor.

Table 3 compares complexity metrics across all device classes for PCI, USB, and XenBus. First, we look at the efficiency of supporting multiple devices by comparing the number of chipsets supporting by a driver. This indicates the complexity of supporting a new device, and the level of abstraction of drivers. A driver that supports many chipsets from different vendors indicates a standardized interface with a high level of common functionality. In contrast, drivers that support a single chipset indicate less efficiency, as each device requires a separate driver.

The efficiency of drivers varied widely across the three buses. PCI drivers support 7.5 chipsets per driver, almost always from the same vendor. In contrast, USB drivers average 13.2, often from many vendors. A large part of the difference is the effort at standardization of USB protocols, which does not exist for many PCI devices. For example, USB storage devices implement a standard interface [41]. Thus, the main USB storage driver code is largely common, but includes call-outs to device-specific code. This code includes device-specific initialization, suspend/resume (not provided by USB-storage and left as an additional feature requirement) and other routines that require device-specific code. While there are greater standardization efforts for USB drivers, it is still not complete

Unlike PCI and USB drivers, XenBus drivers do not access devices directly, but communicate with a back-end driver executing in a separate virtual machine that uses normal Linux kernel interfaces to talk to any driver in the class. Thus, a single XenBus driver logically supports *all* drivers in the class. in a separate domain so we report them as a single chipset. However, device-specific behavior, described above in Section 3.4, is not available over XenBus; these features must be accessed from the domain hosting the real driver. XenBus forms an interesting basis for comparison because it provides the minimum functionality to support a class of devices, with none of the details specific to the device. Thus, it represents a "best-case" driver.

We investigate the ability of a bus to support new driver architectures through its interaction with the kernel and device. A driver with few kernel interactions may run more easily in other execution environments, such as on the device itself. Similarly, a driver with few device or bus interactions may support accessing devices over other communication channels, such as network attached devices [26]. We find that PCI drivers interact heavily with the kernel unless kernel resources are provided by an additional higher-level virtual bus (*e.g.*, ATA). In contrast, Xen drivers have little kernel interaction, averaging only 34 call sites compared to 139 for PCI drivers. A large portion of the difference is that Xen drivers need little initialization or error handling, so they primarily consist of core I/O request handling.

The driver/device interactions also vary widely across buses: due to the fine granularity offered by PCI (individual bytes of memory), PCI drivers average more device interactions (154) than USB or XenBus devices (14-34). Thus, USB drivers are more economical in their interactions, as they batch many operations into a single request packet. XenBus drivers are even more economical, as they need fewer bus requests during initialization and as many operations as USB for I/O requests. Thus, USB and XenBus drivers may efficiently support architectures that access drivers over a network, because access is less frequent and coarse grained.

Implications: These results demonstrate that the flexibility and performance of PCI devices comes with a cost: increased driver complexity, and less interface standardization. Thus, for devices that can live within the performance limitations of USB or in a virtualized environment for XenBus, these buses offer real architectural advantages to the drivers. With USB, significant standardization enables less unique code per device, and coarse-grained access allows efficient remote access to devices [1, 10, 17].

[2] USB drivers invoke DMA via the bus.

XenBus drivers push standardization further by removing *all* device-specific code from the driver and executing it elsewhere. For example, it may be possible to use XenBus drivers to access a driver running on the device itself rather than in a separate virtual machine; this could in effect remove many drivers from the kernel and host processor.

The mechanism for supporting non-standard functionality also differs across these buses: for PCI, a vendor may write a new driver for the device to expose its unique features. For USB, a vendor can add functionality to the existing common drivers just for the features. For XenBus, the features must be accessed from the domain executing the driver and are not available to a guest OS.

4.5 Driver Concurrency

Another key requirement of drivers in all modern operating systems is the need to multiplex access to the device. For example, a disk controller driver must allow multiple applications to read and write data at the same time, even if these applications are not otherwise related. This requirement can complicate driver design, as it increases the need for synchronization among multiple independent threads. We investigate how drivers multiplex access across long-latency operations: do they tend towards threaded code, saving state on the stack and blocking for events, or toward event-driven code, registering callbacks either as completion routines for USB drivers or interrupt handlers and timers for PCI devices. If drivers are moved outside the kernel, the driver and kernel will communicate with each other using a communication channel and supporting event-driven concurrency may be more natural.

We determine that a driver entry point requires a threaded programming style if it makes blocking calls into the kernel, or busy-waits for a device response using `msleep()` which enables blocking. All other entry points are considered "event friendly", in that they do not suspend the calling thread. We did not detect specific routines that use event-based synchronization, as they often rely on the device to generate the callback via an interrupt rather than explicitly registering with the kernel for a callback .

The results, shown in Figure 9 in the bars labeled *event friendly* and *threaded*, show that the split of threaded and event-friendly code varies widely across driver classes. Overall, drivers extensively use both methods of synchronization for different purposes. Drivers use threaded primitives to synchronize driver and device operations while initializing the driver, and updating driver global data structures, while event-friendly code is used for core I/O requests. Interestingly, network drivers and block drivers, which are not invoked directly by user-level code, have a similar split of code to sound drivers, which are invoked directly from application threads. This arises because of the function of most driver code, as reported in Section 3.2: initialization and configuration. This code executes on threads, often blocking for long-latency initialization operations such as device self-test.

Implications: Threaded code is difficult to run outside the kernel, where the invoking thread is not available. For example, Microdrivers [16] executes all driver code in an event-like fashion, restricting invocation to a single request at a time. Converting drivers from threads to use event-based synchronization internally would simplify such code. Furthermore, events are a more natural fit when executing driver code either in separate virtual machine or on a device itself, as they naturally map to a stream of requests arising over a communication channel [34].

5. Driver Redundancy

Given that all the drivers for a class perform essentially the same task, one may ask why so much code is needed. In some cases, such as IDE devices, related devices share most of the code with

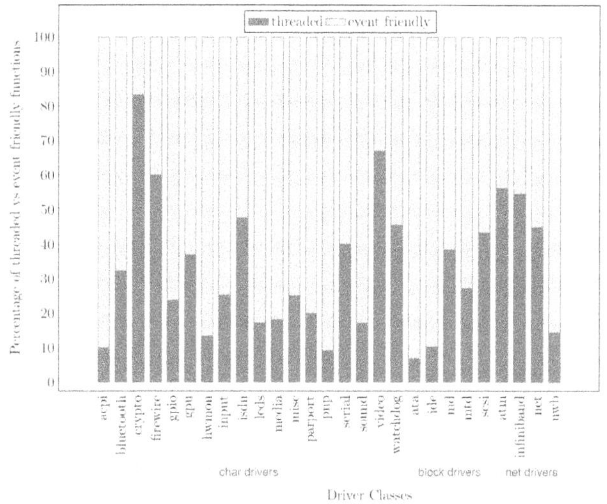

Figure 9. The percentage of driver entry points under coverage of threaded and event friendly synchronization primitives.

```
DrComp signature: 1.798865
static int hpt374_fn1_cable_detect(.....)
{
  struct pci_dev *pdev = to_pci_dev(...);

  unsigned int mcrbase = 0x50
             + 4 * ap->port_no;

  u16 mcr3;
  u8 ata66;

  /*Do the extra channel work */
  pci_read_config_word(pdev,
                 mcrbase+2,&mcr3);
  /*Set bit 15 of 0x52 to enable ..*/
  pci_write_config_word(pdev,
                 mcrbase + 2,..);
  pci_read_config_byte(pdev,
                 0x5A,&ata66);
  /*Reset TCBLID/FCBLID to output */
  pci_write_config_word(pdev,
                 mcrbase+2,mcr3);
  if (ata66 & (2 >> ap->port_no))
      return ATA_CBL_PATA40;
  else
      return ATA_CBL_PATA80;
}
```

```
DrComp signature: 1.8
static int hpt37x_cable_detect(...)
{
  struct pci_dev *pdev = to_pci_dev(...);

  u8 scr2, ata66;

  pci_read_config_byte(pdev,
                     0x5B, &scr2);
  pci_write_config_byte(pdev,
                     0x5B,...);

  udelay(10); /* debounce */

  /* Cable register now active */
  pci_read_config_byte(pdev,
                     0x5A,&ata66);
  /* Restore state */
  pci_write_config_byte(pdev,
                     0x5B,scr2);
  if (ata66 & (2 >> ap->port_no))
      return ATA_CBL_PATA40;
  else
      return ATA_CBL_PATA80;
}
```

Figure 10. Similar code between two different HPT ATA controller drivers essentially performing the same action. These are among the least-similar functions that DrComp is able to detect these functions as related. The boxes show differentiating statements in the two functions that account for the close signature values.

a small amount of per-device code. Most device classes, though, replicate functionality for every driver. The problem of writing repeated/redundant code is well documented. It causes maintainability issues in software development [13], and is also a significant cause of bugs in the Linux kernel [8, 22, 29]. Providing the right abstractions also helps in code standardization and integrating kernel services such as power management in a correct fashion across all drivers. Without a global view of drivers, it can be difficult to tell whether there are opportunities to share common code.

To address this question, we developed a scalable, code similarity tool for discovering similar code patterns across related drivers and applied it to Linux drivers. The goal of this work is to find driver functions with substantially similar code, indicating that the common code could be abstracted and removed from all drivers to reduce driver code size and complexity.

5.1 Methodology

We developed a new code-similarity tool to handle the number of Linux drivers to find similarities rather than exact copies. We

```
DrComp signature:1.594751
static int nv_pre_reset(......)
{
..struct pci_bits nv_enable_bits[] = {
    { 0x50, 1, 0x02, 0x02 },
    { 0x50, 1, 0x01, 0x01 }
};

struct ata_port *ap = link->ap;
struct pci_dev *pdev = to_pci_dev(...);
if (!pci_test_config_bits
   (pdev,&nv_enable_bits[ap->port_no]))
 return -ENOENT;
return ata_sff_prereset(..);
}
```

```
DrComp signature:1.594751
static int amd_pre_reset(...)
{
..struct pci_bits amd_enable_bits[] = {
    { 0x40, 1, 0x02, 0x02 },
    { 0x40, 1, 0x01, 0x01 }
};

struct ata_port *ap = link->ap;
struct pci_dev *pdev = to_pci_dev(...);
if (!pci_test_config_bits
   (pdev,&amd_enable_bits[ap->port_no]))
 return -ENOENT;
return ata_sff_prereset(..);
}
```

Figure 11. The above figure shows identical code that consumes different register values. Such code is present in drivers where multiple chipsets are supported as well as across drivers of different devices. The functions are copies except for the constants as shown in the boxes.

needed to parse through the entire driver source tree consisting of 5 million lines of code, with close to a million lines of code in large classes like network drivers. Most existing clone-detection tools develop a stream of tokens or tree/graphs and perform an n x n comparison of all code snippets to detect clones, which given the size of the driver classes, is not possible. In addition, we needed a *similarity* detector for finding code that that is closely related but not identical. With more control over how similar regions are detected using information from the semantics of drivers, we are able to detect more useful similar code. For example, while parsing function calls, we treat calls to the device and kernel differently, improving the accuracy of our similarity-detection tool.

Our similarity tool, *DrComp*, is based on *shape analysis*[3] [11]. This is a method to determine whether clusters of points have a similar shape and variants of these technique are often used to cluster data, to determine nature of data distribution, and to detect identical shapes in computer vision [3].

DrComp generates a set of multidimensional coordinates for every function in every driver. It then detects as similar two functions whose coordinate sets (*shape*) are similar. DrComp processes a driver function and adds a point to the function's shape for every statement or action in statement for loop, kernel interaction, conditionals, device interaction, variable assignment, break and return statements. The coordinates of the point are the offset into the function (line number) and the statement type. To improve accuracy, it is important that the generated shape of the code emphasizes the important characteristics of the function. Hence, we also reinforce the shape of the function by weighting statements that are important yet sparse, such as a function returns and calls to kernel functions. The shape of each driver function is a cloud of points on plane representing the structure of the program. While we consider only two dimensions of the code, the statement type and edit distance to generate the points, our tool can easily be extended to include additional dimensions based on code features (such as nesting depth) or driver features (such as interrupt frequency).

To eliminate complex comparison of two driver functions, we further reduce the shape of a driver down to a single *signature* value. We compute the signature as a function of Euclidean distance between all the points in the code cluster obtained above. The output of DrComp is a signature for every function in every driver. Thus, two functions with identical code will have identical signatures. Furthermore, code that is similar, in that it has a similar structure of loops and I/O operations, will have similar signatures.

Figure 10 shows an example of some of the *least similar* related code in drivers we found. These two functions have signatures within 0.05% of each other. DrComp only looks for the code structure from statement types (also distinguishing kernel and device invocations) and edit distance, so functions may use different arguments (register values), compare against different values or loop on different conditions, and still be grouped as similar code.

[3] We perform geometric shape analysis, not the program analysis technique of the same name.

5.2 Redundancy Results

DrComp detected that 8% of all driver code is very similar to other driver code. The results of our similarity study are shown in Table 4. For classes with many similarities, we show the number of fragment clusters (sets of similar code), as well as the total number of functions that are similar to another function. For the results in above table, we show results within individual driver classes and not across classes, as they are less likely to benefit from a shared abstraction.

Overall, we identified similarities within a single driver, across a subset of drivers in a class, and in some cases across most drivers in a class. Within a single driver, we found that the most common form of repeated code was wrappers around device I/O, driver library or kernel functions. These wrappers either convert data into the appropriate format or perform an associated support operation that is required before calling the routines but differ from one another because they lie on a different code path. These wrappers could be removed if the kernel interface supported the same data types as the device or if drivers provided appropriate abstractions to avoid such repeated code.

We also find swaths of similar functions across entire classes of drivers. The major difference between drivers for different chipsets of the same device are often constant values, such as device registers or flag values. For example, ATA disk drivers abstract most of the code into a core library, `libata`, and each driver implements a small set of a device-specific functionality. Commonly, these functions are short and perform one or two memory-mapped I/O reads or writes, but with different values for every driver. Figure 5 shows two functions from different ATA drivers with substantially similar code. This practice generates large bodies of very similar drivers with small differences. Further abstraction could additionally simplify these drivers, for example, replacing these routines with tables encoding the different constants. Similarly, a hardware specification language [25] may be able to abstract the differences between related devices into a machine-generated library.

Finally, we note similarities across subsets of drivers in a class. For example, another common class of similarities is wrappers around kernel functions and driver libraries for that class: the `release` method for frame buffers is virtually identical across many of the drivers, in that it checks a reference count and restores the VGA graphics mode. There are a few small differences, but refactoring this interface to pull common functionality into a library could again simplify these drivers.

Implications: Overall, these results demonstrate that there are many opportunities for reducing the volume of driver code by abstracting similar code into libraries or new abstractions. We visually inspected all function clusters to determine how a programmer could leverage the similarity by having a single version of the code. We see three methods for achieving this reduction: (i) procedural abstractions for driver sub-classes, (ii) better multiple chipset support and (iii) table driven programming.

The most useful approach is *procedural abstraction*, which means to move the shared code to a library and provide parameters covering the differences in implementation. There is significant code in single drivers or families of drivers with routines performing similar functions on different code paths. Creating driver-class or sub-class libraries will significantly reduce this code. Second, existing driver libraries can be enhanced with new abstractions that cover the similar behavior. There are many families of drivers that replicate code heavily, as pointed out in Table 4. Abstracting more code out these families by creating new driver abstractions that

Driver class	Driver subclass	Similar code fragments	Fragment clusters	Fragment size (Avg. LOC)	Redundancy results and action items to remove redundant code
char	acpi	64	32	15.1	Procedural abstraction for centralized access to kernel resources and passing get/set configuration information as arguments for large function pairs.
	gpu	234	108	16.9	Procedural abstractions for device access. Code replicated across drivers, like in DMA buffer code for savage, radeon, rage drivers, can be removed by supporting more devices per driver.
	isdn	277	118	21.0	Procedural abstraction for kernel wrappers. Driver abstraction/common library for ISDN cards in hisax directories.
	input	125	48	17.23	Procedural abstraction for kernel wrappers. Driver abstraction/common driver for all touchscreen drivers. Procedural abstraction in Aiptek tablet driver.
	media	1116	445	16.5	Class libraries for all Micron image sensor drivers. Procedural abstraction in saa 7164 A/V decoder driver and ALI 5602 webcam driver.
	video	201	88	20	Class libraries for ARK2000PV, S3Trio, VIA VT8623drivers in init/cleanup, power management and frame buffer operations. Procedural abstraction in VESA VGA drivers for all driver information functions.
	sound	1149	459	15.1	Single driver for ICE1712 and ICE1724 ALSA drivers. Procedural abstraction for invoking sound libraries, instead of repeated code with different flags. Procedural abstraction for AC97 driver and ALSA driver for RME HDSPM audio interface.
block	ata	68	29	13.3	Common power management library for ALI 15x3, CMD640 PCI, Highpoint ATA controllers, Ninja32, CIL 680, ARTOP 867X, HPT3x3, NS87415 PATA drivers and SIS ATA driver. Table driven programming for device access in these drivers.
	ide	18	9	15.3	Procedural abstraction for the few wrappers around power management routines.
	scsi	789	332	25.6	Shared library for kernel/scsi wrappers for Qlogic HBA drivers; pmc sierra and marvell mvsas drivers. Large redundant wrappers in mp2sas firmware, Brocade FC port access code.
net	Ethernet/ wireless	1906	807	25.1	Shared library for wireless drivers for talking to device/kernel and wireless routines. Lot of NICs share code for most routines like configuration, resource allocation and can be moved to a single driver with support for multiple chipsets. A driver sub-class library for all or vendor specific Ethernet drivers.
	infiniband	138	60	15.0	Procedural abstraction for Intel nes driver.

Table 4. The total number of similar code fragments and fragment clusters across driver classes and action items that can be taken to reduce them.

support multiple chipsets can simplify driver code significantly. Finally, functions that differ only by constant values can be replaced by table-driven code. This may also be applicable to drivers with larger differences but fundamentally similar structures, such as network drivers that use ring buffers to send and receive packets. By providing these abstractions, we believe there is an opportunity to reduce the amount of driver code, consequently reducing the incidence of bugs and improving the driver development process by producing concise drivers in the future.

6. Conclusions

The purpose of this study is to investigate the complete set of drivers in Linux, to avoid generalizing from the small set of drivers commonly used for research, and to form new generalizations.

Overall, we find several results that are significant to future research on drivers. First, a substantial number of assumptions about drivers, such as class behavior, lack of computation, are true for many drivers but by no means all drivers. For example, instead of request handling, the bulk of driver code is dedicated to initialization/cleanup and configuration, together accounting for 51% of driver code. A substantial fraction (44%) of drivers have behavior outside the class definition, and 15% perform significant computations over data. Thus, relying on a generic frontend network driver, as in Xen virtualization, conceals the unique features of different devices. Similarly, synthesizing driver code may be difficult, as this processing code may not be possible to synthesize. Tools for automatic synthesis of driver code should also consider driver support for multiple chipset as we find that Linux supports over 14,000 devices with just 3,217 bus and device drivers.

Second, our study of driver/device/kernel interactions showed wide variation in how drivers interact with devices and the kernel. At one end, miniport drivers contain almost exclusively device-specific code that talks to the device, leaving kernel interactions to a shared library. At the other end, some drivers make extensive calls to the kernel and very few into shared device libraries. This latter category may be a good candidate for investigation, as there may be shared functionality that can be removed. Overall, these results also show that the cost of isolating drivers may not be constant across all driver classes.

Third, our investigation of driver/device interaction showed that USB and XenBus drivers provide more efficient device access than PCI drivers, in that a smaller amount of driver code supports access to many more devices, and that coarse-grained access may support moving more driver functionality out of the kernel, even on the device itself. Furthermore, many drivers require very little access to hardware and instead interact almost exclusively with the bus. As a result, such drivers can effectively be run without privileges, as they need no special hardware access. We find that USB and Xenbus provide the opportunity to utilize the extra cycles on devices by executing drivers on them and can effectively be used to remove drivers from the kernel leaving only standardized bus code in the kernel.

Finally, we find strong evidence that there are substantial opportunities to reduce the amount of driver code. The similarity analysis shows that there are many instances of similar code patterns that could be replaced with better library abstractions, or in some cases with tables. Furthermore, the driver function breakdown in Section 3 shows that huge amounts of code are devoted to initialization; this code often detects the feature set of different chipsets. Again, this code is ripe for improvement through better abstractions, such as object-oriented programing technique and inheritance [31].

While this study was performed for Linux only, we believe many similar patterns, although for different classes of devices, will show in other operating systems. It may also be interesting to compare the differences in driver code across operating systems, which may demonstrate subtle differences in efficiency or complexity. Our study is orthogonal to most studies on bug detection. However, correlating bugs with different driver architectures can provide insight on the reliability of these architectures in real life.

Acknowledgements

This work is supported in part by National Science Foundation (NSF) grants CNS-0915363 and CNS-0745517 and a grant from Google. We also thank Matt Renzelmann and the anonymous reviewers for their invaluable feedback. Swift has a significant financial interest in Microsoft.

References

[1] J. Andrus, C. Dall, A. Vant Hof, O. Laadan, and J. Nieh. Cells: A virtual mobile smartphone architecture. In *SOSP*, 2011.

[2] T. Ball, E. Bounimova, B. Cook, V. Levin, J. Lichtenberg, C. McGarvey, B. Ondrusek, S. K. Rajamani, and A. Ustuner. Thorough static analysis of device drivers. In *Eurosys*, 2006.

[3] S. Belongie, J. Malik, and J. Puzicha. Shape matching and object recognition using shape contexts. *Transactions on Pattern Analysis and Machine Intelligence*, 2002.

[4] S. Boyd-Wickizer and N. Zeldovich. Tolerating malicious device drivers in linux. In *USENIX ATC*, 2010.

[5] M. Castro, M. Costa, J.-P. Martin, M. Peinado, P. Akritidis, A. Donnelly, P. Barham, and R. Black. Fast byte-granularity software fault isolation. In *SOSP*, 2009.

[6] V. Chipounov and G. Candea. Reverse engineering of binary device drivers with RevNIC. In *Eurosys*, Apr. 2010.

[7] T.-c. Chiueh, G. Venkitachalam, and P. Pradhan. Integrating segmentation and paging protection for safe, efficient and transparent software extensions. *Operating Systems Review*, 33, 1999.

[8] A. Chou, J. Yang, B. Chelf, S. Hallem, and D. Engler. An empirical study of operating system errors. In *SOSP*, 2001.

[9] F. M. David et al. CuriOS: Improving reliability through operating system structure. In *OSDI*, 2008.

[10] Digi International. AnywhereUSB. `http://www.digi.com/products/usb/anywhereusb.jsp`.

[11] I. Dryden and K. Mardia. *Statistical shape analysis*, volume 4. Wiley New York, 1998.

[12] K. Fraser et al. Safe hardware access with the Xen virtual machine monitor. In *OASIS Workhop*, 2004.

[13] M. Gabel, J. Yang, Y. Yu, M. Goldszmidt, and Z. Su. Scalable and systematic detection of buggy inconsistencies in source code. In *OOPSLA*, 2010.

[14] A. Ganapathi, V. Ganapathi, and D. A. Patterson. Windows xp kernel crash analysis. In *LISA*, 2006.

[15] V. Ganapathy, A. Balakrishnan, M. M. Swift, and S. Jha. Microdrivers: A new architecture for device drivers. In *HOTOS11*, 2007.

[16] V. Ganapathy, M. J. Renzelmann, A. Balakrishnan, M. M. Swift, and S. Jha. The design and implementation of microdrivers. In *ASPLOS*, Mar. 2008.

[17] A. Hari, M. Jaitly, Y.-J. Chang, and A. Francini. The swiss army smartphone: Cloud-based delivery of usb services. In *Mobiheld*, 2011.

[18] A. Kadav, M. J. Renzelmann, and M. M. Swift. Tolerating hardware device failures in software. In *SOSP*, 2009.

[19] A. Kadav and M. Swift. Live migration of direct-access devices. *Operating Systems Review*, 43(3):95–104, 2009.

[20] V. Kuznetsov, V. Chipounov, and G. Candea. Testing closed-source binary device drivers with DDT. In *USENIX ATC*, 2010.

[21] B. Leslie et al. User-level device drivers: Achieved performance. *Jour. Comp. Sci. and Tech.*, 2005.

[22] Z. Li, S. Lu, S. Myagmar, and Y. Zhou. CP-Miner: A tool for finding copy-paste and related bugs in operating system code. In *OSDI*, 2004.

[23] Y. Mao, H. Chen, D. Zhou, X. Wang, N. Zeldovich, and M. Kaashoek. Software fault isolation with api integrity and multi-principal modules. In *SOSP*, 2011.

[24] A. Menon, S. Schubert, and W. Zwaenepoel. Twindrivers: semi-automatic derivation of fast and safe hypervisor network drivers from guest os drivers. In *ASPLOS*, 2009.

[25] F. Mérillon, L. Réveillère, C. Consel, R. Marlet, and G. Muller. Devil: An IDL for hardware programming. In *OSDI*, 2000.

[26] Microsoft Corp. Web services on devices. `http://msdn.microsoft.com/en-us/library/aa826001%28v=vs.85%29.aspx`.

[27] G. C. Necula, S. Mcpeak, S. P. Rahul, and W. Weimer. CIL: Intermediate language and tools for analysis and transformation of C programs. In *Compiler Construction*, 2002.

[28] V. Orgovan and M. Tricker. An introduction to driver quality. Microsoft WinHec Presentation DDT301, 2003.

[29] Y. Padioleau, J. Lawall, R. R. Hansen, and G. Muller. Documenting and automating collateral evolutions in linux device drivers. In *Eurosys*, 2008.

[30] K. K. Ram, J. R. Santos, Y. Turner, A. L. Cox, and S. Rixner. Achieving 10 gb/s using safe and transparent network interface virtualization. In *VEE*, 2009.

[31] M. J. Renzelmann and M. M. Swift. Decaf: Moving device drivers to a modern language. In *USENIX ATC*, June 2009.

[32] L. Ryzhyk, P. Chubb, I. Kuz, and G. Heiser. Dingo: Taming device drivers. In *Eurosys*, 2009.

[33] L. Ryzhyk, P. Chubb, I. Kuz, E. Le Sueur, and G. Heiser. Automatic device driver synthesis with Termite. In *SOSP*, 2009.

[34] L. Ryzhyk, Y. Zhu, and G. Heiser. The case for active device drivers. In *APSys*, Aug. 2010.

[35] A. Schüpbach, A. Baumann, T. Roscoe, and S. Peter. A declarative language approach to device configuration. In *ASPLOS*, 2011.

[36] A. Silberschatz, P. B. Galvin, and G. Gagne. *Operating System Concepts*. John Wiley and Sons, eighth edition, 2009.

[37] M. Spear et al. Solving the starting problem: Device drivers as self-describing artifacts. In *Eurosys*, 2006.

[38] M. M. Swift, M. Annamalai, B. N. Bershad, and H. M. Levy. Recovering device drivers. In *OSDI*, 2004.

[39] M. M. Swift, B. N. Bershad, and H. M. Levy. Improving the reliability of commodity operating systems. *In TOCS*, 2005.

[40] Úlfar Erlingsson et al. Xfi: software guards for system address spaces. In *OSDI*, 2006.

[41] USB Implementors Forum. Universal serial bus mass storage class specification overview. `http://www.usb.org/developers/devclass_docs/usb_msc_overview_1.2.pdf`, 2003.

[42] USB Implementors Forum. Universal serial bus 3.0 specification. http://www.usb.org/developers/docs/usb_30_spec_071311.zip, 2011.

[43] D. A. Wheeler. Sloccount. `http://www.dwheeler.com/sloccount/`.

[44] D. Williams, P. Reynolds, K. Walsh, E. G. Sirer, and F. B. Schneider. Device driver safety through a reference validation mechanism. In *OSDI*, 2008.

[45] L. Wittie. Laddie: The language for automated device drivers (ver 1). Technical Report 08-2, Bucknell CS-TR, 2008.

[46] Xen.org. Writing xen drivers: Using xenbus and xenstore. `http://wiki.xensource.com/xenwiki/XenBus`, 2006.

[47] F. Zhou et al. SafeDrive: Safe and recoverable extensions using language-based techniques. In *OSDI*, 2006.

Chameleon: Operating System Support for Dynamic Processors

Sankaralingam Panneerselvam and Michael M. Swift
Computer Sciences Department, University of Wisconsin–Madison
{sankarp, swift}@cs.wisc.edu

Abstract

The rise of multi-core processors has shifted performance efforts towards parallel programs. However, single-threaded code, whether from legacy programs or ones difficult to parallelize, remains important. Proposed asymmetric multicore processors statically dedicate hardware to improve sequential performance, but at the cost of reduced parallel performance.

However, several proposed mechanisms provide the best-of-both-worlds by combining multiple cores into a single, more powerful processor for sequential code. For example, Core Fusion merges multiple cores to pool caches and functional units, and Intel's Turbo Boost raises the clock speed of a core if the other cores on a chip are powered down.

These reconfiguration mechanisms have two important properties. First the set of available cores and their capabilities can vary over short time scales. Current operating systems are not designed for rapidly changing hardware: the existing hotplug mechanisms for reconfiguring processors require global operations and hundreds of milliseconds to complete. Second, configurations may be mutually exclusive: using power to speed one core means it cannot be used to speed another. Current schedulers cannot manage this requirement.

We present Chameleon, an extension to Linux to support *dynamic processors* that can reconfigure their cores at runtime. Chameleon provides *processor proxies* to enable rapid reconfiguration, *execution objects* to abstract the processing capabilities of physical CPUs, and a *cluster scheduler* to balance the needs of sequential and parallel programs. In experiments that emulate a dynamic processor, we find that Chameleon can reconfigure processors 100,000 times faster than Linux and allows applications full access to hardware capabilities: sequential code runs at full speed on a powerful execution context, while parallel code runs on as many cores as possible.

Categories and Subject Descriptors D.4.7 [*Operating Systems*]: Organization and Design

General Terms Design, Performance

Keywords Dynamic Processors, Hotplug, Processor Proxy, Reconfiguration, Scheduling

ASPLOS '12 March 3–7, 2012, London, England, UK.

1. Introduction

Multicore processors require parallel code to achieve high performance. However, parallel programming is hard, and legacy code may never be rewritten to take advantage of extra processing cores. Asymmetric chip multi-processors (ACMP) provision a chip with a small number of powerful processors for sequential code and simpler processors for parallel code [18, 32]. These processors also improve power efficiency for code that sees little benefit from powerful processors. Commercial examples of the ACMP architecture include combined CPU/GPU chips such as AMD's Fusion processor [8], and the TI OMAP 5 [56]. However, high performance on sequential code sacrifices parallel performance: the chip area and power dedicated to powerful cores could provide many more simple cores for parallel execution.

Hardware techniques that combine multiple cores or hardware threads into a more powerful execution engine have the potential to provide high performance on both parallel and sequential code. On parallel code, the processor can be configured into a large set of less-powerful cores, providing performance through parallelism. On sequential code, such a processor can combine several of the cores to improve the performance of a single thread. Such a *dynamic processor* can provide high performance over a wide range of workloads by switching between parallel and sequential modes [22]. For example, Core Fusion [26] pools execution resources such as caches and functional units to improve performance. Speculative multi-threading [20, 31, 37] executes different portions of a single thread in parallel on different cores, and Intel's Turbo boost increases the speed of one core when others are disabled [9]. Such processors may be able to reconfigure between sequential and parallel modes in microseconds.

Current operating systems are ill equipped for processors that can be reconfigured at runtime. They must know at all times which processors are available for cross-processor communication and global operations, which occur tens to hundreds of times per second. Furthermore, they require expensive global operations to reconfigure when changes occur. For example, the hotplug mechanism in Linux can take more than 200ms to add a new processor, far longer than the projected reconfiguration time for dynamic processors. In addition, processors may have mutually exclusive configurations, such as borrowing resources from one core to improve performance of another, that existing schedulers do not support.

Chameleon is an operating system extension to Linux that supports dynamic processors with three new capabilities. First, *processor proxies* enable rapid reconfiguration by removing global operations. Instead, another processor takes the place of an offline processor in any communication or global operation. Second, *execution objects* abstract physical cores and hardware threads into logical objects against which threads are scheduled, so the scheduler need not be aware of physical hardware details. Third, Chameleon's *cluster scheduler* decides when and what to reconfigure and provides a *taxation* mechanism that allows a program or administrator to balance the benefit of faster sequential execution against reduced performance for other threads.

Chameleon focuses on the mechanisms needed to support reconfiguration but does not predict or measure the speedup a thread achieves in different configurations. Recent work on asymmetric processors addresses many issues that are also applicable to dynamic processors, such as identifying code that benefits from more powerful processors [48] or sequential bottlenecks in parallel programs [55]. These mechanisms are orthogonal to Chameleon's purpose, and could be incorporated to notify the system of when faster sequential performance is desirable or possible.

We evaluate Chameleon by emulating dynamic processors on conventional hardware and show that: (i) processor proxies reduce the latency of reconfiguration from 150ms to 2.5μs, (ii) Chameleon can leverage idle cores to achieve maximum performance for either parallel or sequential tasks via reconfiguration, (iii) fast reconfiguration allows productive use of a configuration for even a single scheduling quantum, and (iv) under contention, Chameleon's taxation allows flexible control over whether parallel or sequential code is favored. This can either allow high-priority sequential code to preempt other processors or prevent important parallel programs from having processors borrowed for sequential programs.

We begin by reviewing dynamic processor technology in Section 2. We follow with the design of Chameleon in Section 3 and implementation details in Section 4. We evaluate Chameleon in Section 5, and finish with related work and conclusions.

2. Dynamic Processors

While most computers have a static set of processors, hardware trends indicate that future computers may support a dynamically variable set of processors, either for performance, reliability, or power efficiency.

2.1 Hardware Mechanisms

We see at least four reasons why the number of execution contexts exposed to an operating system may vary at runtime.

Performance techniques. Many researchers have demonstrated single-thread performance increases by combining several cores into a single more powerful processing element. Core Fusion and TRIPS increase performance by combining resources, such as functional units, into a larger execution engine that can achieve higher ILP [26, 50]. Core Fusion, for example, claims nearly 80% speedup for some programs and requires only 400 cycles to reconfigure. Speculative multi-threading executes loop iterations or function calls in parallel [20, 31, 37, 44]. Sun's canceled Rock processor had SMT contexts that could switch to automatically prefetch data into the cache [10] for improved sequential performance.

Figure 1 shows an example of these architectures. Part (a) shows the native cores on a system, and part (b) shows how cores can be fused together to act as more powerful cores. This example is representative of Core Fusion and speculative multithreading.

A common feature of all these mechanisms is that the performance gain is less than linear in the number of cores: executing two threads on two cores accomplishes more work than executing a single thread on a fused core. Thus, a system must balance the need for sequential performance against other uses of the cores.

Power management. Processors may disable cores to save power or to transfer power to the remaining cores, as in Intel's Nehalem Turbo Boost feature [9]. In addition, processors may be *over provisioned*, in that they contain more processing elements than can be used simultaneously [15]. As a result, a system may switch between a single large, fast core and a smaller number of more efficient and slower cores when parallelism is available or better cores provide

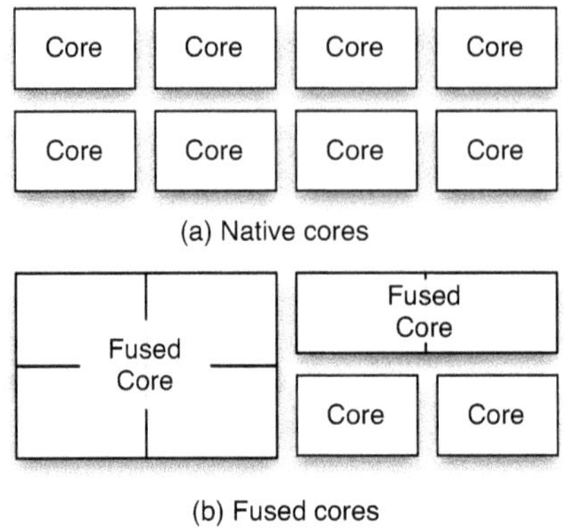

Figure 1. The native cores shown in (a) can be reconfigured, for example into a 4-core unit and a 2-core unit shown in (b).

little benefit [42]. This also enables a variety of specialized processors for specific tasks, such as encryption.

Reliability techniques. Processing cores may be combined to improve reliability. For example, redundant execution techniques run a thread simultaneously on multiple cores and automatically recover from failures when outputs differ [1, 47, 57]. When surplus cores are available, these techniques promise inexpensive error detection and fault tolerance.

Virtualization. When hosting a web site at a cloud provider, a VM can drop to a single processor when workloads are light and use more virtual processors when workloads are heavy.

2.2 Operating System Impact of Reconfiguration

These mechanisms all vary the set of processors available to the operating system. However, most OSes must know exactly which CPUs are available at all times. For example, interprocessor communication, whether through inter-processor interrupts or lightweight RPC [5], requires that the OS know if the destination processor is available. In addition, operating systems maintain *per-CPU data structures*, such as run-queues or packet receive queues, to avoid lock and memory contention. Finally, operating systems perform *all-processor operations* that require the cooperation of all processors, such as read-copy-update (RCU) operations on Linux [39]. Thus, the OS must reconfigure internal data structures whenever the set of available processors change.

We examined the Linux 2.6.31-4 kernel to discover the extent and frequency of these operations. We measure inter-processor communication running `pmake` to build the Linux kernel on a 24-CPU machine with 24 `pmake` processes.

- *Inter-processor interrupts.* Running `pmake` resulted in delivery of 40 IPIs/second/CPU for rescheduling and TLB shootdowns.
- *All-processor operations.* Global RCU callbacks were invoked 140 times per second per CPU when running `pmake`.
- *Per-CPU structures.* We found 446 separate variables in Linux that are defined as per-CPU. The *arch* subdirectory defines 294 variables, which mostly refer to hardware structures. If the set of processors change, these per-CPU data structures must be updated or initialized to reflect the change: 15 subsystems register 35 callbacks to update their per-CPU structures when the set of CPUs change.

Based on these observations, we find that the Linux kernel is intimately aware of the set of available processors. If this set were to change rapidly, numerous subsystems would have to be notified and many per-CPU structures updated. Furthermore, operations that require all processors can only execute when the set of CPUs is stable, either delaying these operations or blocking frequent reconfiguration. While virtual machines can implement reconfiguration, frequent cross-processor communication demonstrates that operating systems must know the set of available processors.

3. Design

Chameleon is an operating system extension to support dynamic processors. We have three design goals for Chameleon:

1. *Rapid adaptation* allows the use of a processor configuration for short periods with low overhead.
2. *Abstracted hardware* provides the operating system with a set of hardware configurations for scheduling threads.
3. *Flexible, intuitive scheduling* allows existing scheduling paradigms/controls, such as fairness and priority, to apply to dynamic processors.

We seek maximum flexibility in the use of dynamic processors, and thus want to minimize the overhead introduced by the OS when reconfiguring hardware. Low cost allows use of fine-grain reconfiguration, as often as every scheduling quantum. In addition, we want to maintain the operating system's abstract view of hardware so it need not be aware of the details of how a dynamic processor reconfigures, just that other configurations are available. Finally, we seek to extend existing thread schedulers to use dynamic processors, so that existing scheduling policies are naturally extended to cover reconfiguration.

We target Chameleon at dynamic processors with a single instruction set that offer increased performance by disabling some execution contexts and reusing the hardware or power from those contexts. The rapid adaptation targets processors that cannot receive interrupts at all cores in some configurations, such as Core Fusion. In contrast, with Intel's Turbo Boost disabled cores can still receive interrupts, and hence do not benefit from this mechanism.

Our design follows a best-effort approach: the system makes no real-time guarantees, but strives to execute programs as fast as possible. Furthermore, we designed Chameleon to improve performance rather than manage power: the same mechanisms should apply, but must be driven by different policies because fusing CPUs is likely to be less efficient than running on a native CPU. Finally, Chameleon does not address uses of dynamic processors for reliability [1, 57]. Such systems place mandatory requirements on the OS like certain threads must always run in a reliable configuration.

3.1 Rapid Adaptation

Future dynamic processors may be able to change the set of available processors rapidly. Operating systems currently use a *hotplug mechanism* or *power management* to adapt to the changes in the set of processors.

Hotplug. Processor hotplug mechanisms [33, 43, 53] allow an operating system to accommodate the addition, removal, or replacement of a processor. They are designed for two uses: maintenance, to remove a failing processor or dynamically add capacity; and virtualization, to change the allocation of processors to a virtual machine. These are both infrequent events, so hotplug implementations optimize for low overhead in the common (no reconfiguration) case, rather than for frequent changes. Reconfigurations that leave a processor able to receive interrupts, such as low-power states [2], can be done with power management rather than hotplug as we describe below.

We measured the performance of hotplug in Linux, and found that it takes 150ms to take a processor offline and 220ms to bring it online. In comparison, the hardware latency of starting a processor is only 10ms. Much of the software overhead in hotplug comes from constructing and distributing per-CPU data structures and quiescing the system with a global barrier so that the mask of available processors can change. The extra delay when bringing a processor online is largely due to initializing architecture-related registers.

Power management. Operating systems also support power management, which can take a processor offline for short periods to conserve energy. The latency of entering a sleep state is on the order of microseconds, of which very little is spent in software. However, in a sleep state the processor can still receive interrupts, so it is still available to the operating system when needed and global state updates are not necessary.

Thus, power management can only be used for reconfiguration if a processor can still receive interrupts. While this is possible for current architectures, such as Turbo Boost, it may not be possible for architectures that reconfigure hardware, such as Core Fusion.

Thus, we find that both hotplug and power management are inadequate for dynamic processors: hotplug is too slow for frequent reconfiguration, and power management places requirements on the hardware such as receiving interrupts.

Processor proxies. Chameleon provides rapid reconfiguration through *processor proxies*, which are agents running on a separate processor that act on behalf of an offline processor. The proxy can access the private per-CPU data structures of the unavailable CPU. When a physical CPU is temporarily offline due to reconfiguration, Chameleon creates a processor proxy for it on another CPU. The kernel moves its communication endpoints, such as interrupts, to that CPU. Operations that require the presence of a core, such as a TLB shootdown or a read-copy-update (RCU) operation, invoke the proxy and therefore can continue without waiting for the unavailable CPU.

Processor proxies are similar to multiplexing virtual CPUs on a single processor with a hypervisor. However, processor proxies only virtualize the external interface to a processor, such as interrupts and RCU operations. Thus, a processor proxy does not schedule or run threads. In contrast, a VCPU may run any code and forces the hypervisor to schedule or timeslice multiple CPUs on a single physical CPU.

3.2 Abstracted Hardware

Increasingly, operating systems must know the topology of the processor on which they run: whether two execution contexts are hyperthreads on the same core, whether they are cores that share a cache, and whether they share an interface to memory as in a NUMA configuration. The topology allows the operating system to make intelligent scheduling and memory-management decisions, such as to schedule threads from the same process on hyperthreads that share a core, and to allocate memory from a region attached to the thread's core. Asymmetric multiprocessors similarly require informing the OS of a core's increased (or decreased) capabilities.

With dynamic processors, this need for hardware information increases: in addition to the static configuration of hardware, the OS must know about possible dynamic configurations. In Figure 1, for example, the OS must know that the four cores on the left and the pair on the right can be fused into more powerful processors.

Execution objects. Chameleon abstracts the physical capabilities of the machine with an indirection layer called *execution objects*. We call the hardware state needed to run a thread (registers, program counter) an *execution context*, which may be a core, a hyperthread, or a fused set of cores. An execution object is a kernel structure that represents a possible execution context, and contains information about the capabilities of the context along with `activate` and `deactivate` methods for reconfiguring the hardware. The smallest native context (*i.e.*, no combining of processors) is a

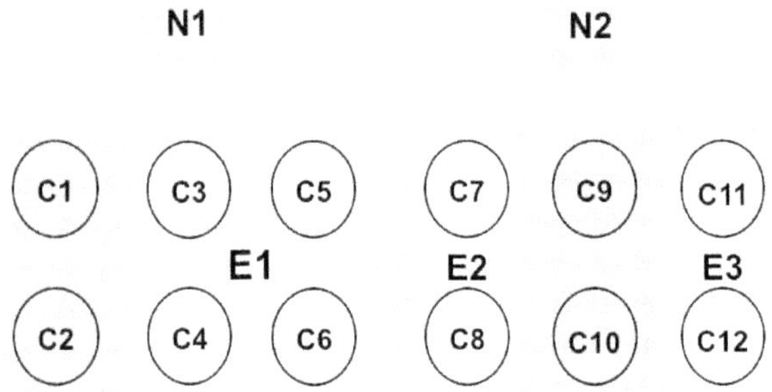

Figure 2. System with 12 CPUs (C1-12) managed through nodes.. E2 and E3 are execution objects with two CPUs and E1 with four CPUs.

CPU (also referred to as a thread context). A *fused execution object* (or fused object) represents an object that requires more than one native CPU. For example, in Figure 1(b), Chameleon creates a fused object for each fused core.

At any time, the current hardware configuration can be represented as a set of *active* execution objects. Chameleon creates an object when needed by a thread, and the OS invokes `activate` when dispatching a thread to the hardware configuration represented by the object. Each execution object identifies a *representative CPU*, which is the CPU to which interrupts must be delivered when the object is in use.

Execution objects expose *properties* to aid in scheduling decisions. A property is a characteristic of the underlying hardware, such as the relative performance of the configuration or whether additional features/instructions are available (*e.g.*, if only some configurations support SIMD or floating-point operations).

Nodes. Chameleon separates processors into *nodes*, which are groups of CPUs managed together. Each node has a *node manager*, which is responsible for selecting native CPUs within the node to merge into an execution object. The node manager knows the constraints of the hardware, such as which CPUs can be fused or which CPUs can shift power. In addition, it knows the properties of every execution object it can create. Figure 2 shows an example of 2 nodes.

When a thread requests an execution object with a property (described in Section 3.3), the scheduler selects a node and invokes its manager to request an execution object. The manager makes its best effort to assign the requested resources to the application from the CPUs it manages. As long as a thread is scheduled on an execution object, the node manager keeps the execution object alive. When the thread terminates or requests a different object, the resulting free CPUs can now be assigned to another execution object or left available. The manager prevents fragmentation, which can occur when idle cores are available but hardware constraints prevent them from being fused, by reshuffling the assignment of physical resources to execution objects.

The node manager assigns the CPUs comprising an execution object when creating the object, and does not choose from available CPUs when dispatching a thread. However, a rebalancing mechanism, described in Section 4 can relocate threads and create new execution objects if needed.

Node managers are similar to the system knowledge base (SKB) in Barrelfish [5] and Linux and Windows scheduling domains used for NUMA processors [40, 51]. Unlike the SKB, node managers have a restricted focus on processing. Compared to scheduling domains, nodes add constraints on which execution objects can be used simultaneously.

3.3 Scheduling

Chameleon extends the OS to schedule threads on execution objects in addition to physical CPUs. The major challenges Chameleon addresses are:

- *Which:* Finding the possible execution objects upon which to schedule a thread.
- *When:* Prioritizing threads relative to each other.
- *Where:* Moving threads to avoid conflicts and minimize reconfiguration overhead.

The Chameleon scheduler leaves scheduling queues attached to native CPUs. When a thread is ready to run, it decides whether to activate an execution object.

Property matching. A key challenge for any asymmetric processor is determining whether and how much a thread benefits from an enhanced execution context. Chameleon does not address this problem, but instead provides a general mechanism to match threads to execution objects. As previously noted, node managers associate properties with a fused object that describe its capabilities, and implement logic to match a request for specific processing features against the properties of different configurations. For example, an execution object providing high instruction-level parallelism for fast sequential execution could have the property `sequential`.

Currently, Chameleon requires that threads specify their desired properties. This could be done explicitly, through a system call, or implicitly by a separate profiling mechanism as in ACMP schedulers (*e.g.*, CAMP [48]). However, Chameleon should work with any mechanism that assigns properties to threads. In the case of a single threaded program, the property might be `sequential`, indicating that the program wants fast execution and does not depend on other threads.

When placing threads in a run queue, the Chameleon scheduler selects a node and invokes its manager to match the desired properties of a thread with the properties offered by the node's execution objects. If there is a match, the node manager creates the object, and Chameleon adds the thread to the run queue of the object's representative CPU and attaches the execution object to the thread; otherwise, it relies on the native OS scheduler to place the thread. This is similar to the matchmaking process of the Condor cluster system [46], but with a restricted set of properties.

Cluster scheduling. Chameleon schedules a thread on an execution object as if it is gang scheduling a group of threads on the constituent native CPUs: when all the CPUs are available, the thread will activate the execution object to fuse them. However, Chameleon's scheduler can also elect not to use all the CPUs and instead execute the thread on a single native CPU. Thus, when a thread becomes the next to run, the scheduler determines whether to activate an execution object. We term this *cluster scheduling*.

Chameleon decides when to fuse CPUs together and when to let them run their own threads. Each native CPU in an execution object has its own run queue with threads to execute. When a thread using an execution object becomes ready (*i.e.*, runnable), Chameleon adds it to the run queue for the execution object's representative CPU, and creates *virtual threads* that represent it in the run queues of the CPUs it will borrow. For example, in Figure 2, a thread desiring to run on fused context E2 would be placed in its representative, CPU C7, and would have a virtual thread representing it on CPU C8.

Virtual threads represent a thread's ability to borrow CPUs to form a fused object: if a virtual thread has the priority to be dispatched, then its thread can borrow the CPU. Until then, the CPU is available for its own threads. When the scheduler dispatches a thread using an execution object, it checks whether it can activate

Component	Lines
Processor Proxies	600
Execution Objects	850
Cluster Scheduling	550

Table 1. Implementation Complexity

the execution object. For example, when the scheduler dispatches a sequential thread on C7, it checks to see whether the virtual thread would have been dispatched on the other CPU C8. If so, it preempts any thread on C8, activates the execution object E2, and then dispatches the thread. If not, the thread is directly dispatched on C7.

Cross-CPU contention. Standard CPU scheduling assumes a many-to-one relationship between threads and CPUs, in that many threads share a single CPU and no thread uses more than one CPU. As a result, traditional notions of priority and fair share for threads apply only to a single CPU. However, dynamic processors introduce a new possibility: a thread can preempt multiple CPUs. Thus, threads must have a separate priority or a share for CPUs they borrow. Simply assigning a thread a global share across several CPUs, as in Linux group scheduling [12] is insufficient because it does not reflect the inefficiency of fused objects: under contention, a thread does better on a single CPU than it does running half as long on two CPUs, because speedups are less than linear. With a Linux process group, both configurations would be treated as equivalent.

Chameleon extends the existing notion of priority and share by allowing a thread to have different priorities on its representative CPU and on the CPUs it wants to borrow. We term this mechanism *taxation*: a thread is charged for its use of other CPUs adjusted by a tax rate. Effectively, this means that virtual threads may have different priorities than the thread on the representative CPU. If the tax rate is high, then a thread is charged more for borrowing a CPU than the threads that live on that CPU; thus, its priority is effectively lower and it will not be able to preempt those threads. If the tax rate is low, then it will be able to use other CPUs more cheaply than the threads on those CPUs, and it will be able to preempt them.

4. Implementation

Chameleon is implemented as an extension to the Linux 2.6.31-4 kernel. The code changes required by Chameleon were largely concentrated in two Linux subsystems: inter-processor interrupts, to implement proxies; and scheduling, to call into Chameleon during a context switch when activating execution objects. Table 1 shows the amount of code comprising Chameleon's major components.

4.1 Processor Proxies

Processor proxies speed reconfiguration because they remove much of the work to change the set of processors. Proxies consist of two elements: (i) methods to create and destroy proxies, (ii) a new execution context for executing interrupts and bottom halves on behalf of the disabled context. The CPU going offline is the *proxied CPU*, and the one that will act as its proxy is the *proxying CPU*.

Proxy creation. The activation of an execution object launches the creation of a proxy by sending a notification to the proxied CPU. The CPU that sends this request will be the proxy. The receiving CPU prepares to go offline by switching to the idle thread, which removes the need to participate in RCU operations, and by ensuring interrupts for the CPU will be delivered to its proxy. These interrupts fall into two categories: device interrupts, which can be redistributed to any online CPUs, and IPIs, which must be sent to the proxying CPU. Each is handled by a separate mechanism.

For device interrupts, the IOAPIC maintains a redirection table indicating the core to which external interrupts should be sent [24]. However, reprogramming the IOAPIC is slow, as we show in Section 5. Instead, Chameleon leverages APIC *logical addressing* when possible: device interrupts are broadcast to a logical address and each CPU ANDs a local mask against the interrupt's address and delivers the interrupt if any common bits are set. Chameleon therefore does logical-address renaming by adding the proxied CPU's identifier to the mask for the proxying CPU and resetting the identifier for the proxied CPU. This causes interrupts, both external and inter-processor, destined for the proxied CPU to be delivered to the proxying CPU automatically.

However, logical address renaming may not be available on all systems because the number of bits representing different CPUs is limited. Thus, we implemented a separate software mechanism to redirect IPIs to the proxying CPU. When creating a proxy, Chameleon records in a *redirection table* that the proxied CPU is being proxied. When a CPU sends an IPI, it consults the redirection table to learn where the IPI should be sent. In this case, Chameleon reprograms the IOAPIC to redirect device interrupts.

When using logical address renaming, redirecting interrupts can cause an IPI to be delivered to two CPUs or not delivered at all, based on the order in which the mask of proxying CPU and proxied CPU are changed. Since IPI handlers in Linux are idempotent and may be called multiple times without harm, Chameleon always updates the local mask of proxying CPU to include proxied CPU's identifier before resetting the mask of proxied CPU. Reversing this order could result in loss of IPIs. Furthermore, when tearing down a proxy, Chameleon invokes IPI handlers on the proxied CPU before invoking the scheduler in case an IPI was lost. These issues do not arise with device interrupts because the hardware ensures they are delivered to only one CPU even if the logical address matches multiple CPUs.

Proxy context. We add a new execution context to the OS, in addition to process context and interrupt context, termed a *proxy context*. A separate proxy context exists on a CPU for each of the processors it proxies and executes only when the proxying CPU receives inter-processor interrupts (IPIs) on behalf of the proxied CPU. We augmented the per-CPU structures with two variables to track proxies: `proxied_by` for a CPU that is being proxied, and `proxying_for` on a CPU that is acting as a proxy.

On receiving any IPIs, the proxying CPU invokes the corresponding IPI handler natively for the proxying CPU in the proxied CPU's context. Handling IPIs requires access to per-CPU variables, which are normally accessed through the x86 segment registers. When entering proxy context, Chameleon sets the FS register to point to the per-CPU data of the proxied CPU, and resets the register when leaving proxy context. In addition, we modified the `thread_info` macro, which normally uses the stack pointer to find the CPU state of the running task. In proxy context, the macro directs accesses to the data for the proxied CPU.

With proxies, Chameleon ensures that kernel operations requiring the involvement of an offline CPU can proceed, as the role of that CPU is handled by its proxy. This includes inter-processor interrupts for scheduling, read-copy-update operations, and TLB shootdowns, which are dropped because the proxy code flushes the TLB when resuming normal operation.

In some architectures processor proxies may not always be needed: if CPUs can continue to receive interrupts when disabled, the object does not create a proxy but instead halts the CPUs. This occurs when using Chameleon with hyperthreads: the execution object schedules the idle thread on the other hyperthread. Similarly, with Intel's Turbo Boost feature other cores enter a sleep state but can still receive interrupts.

4.2 Execution Objects and Node Managers

Chameleon assigns all the CPUs on a socket to a node and instantiates a node manager for each node. The node manager is a kernel component that tracks the execution objects and CPUs on a node. For now, Chameleon uses the existing topology information provided by platform drivers (*e.g.*, ACPI). We emulate a dynamic processor by informing node managers that they may construct fused execution objects for pairs of hyperthreads on a core and pairs of adjacent cores.

The only property we have implemented is `sequential` with a level, which is the $\log_2$ of the number of hyperthreads in the object. Threads can request a sequential object of a specified level. Property matching compares the desired level of a thread against available execution objects to find one with the same level. The `activate` method on an execution object configures the hardware to create the desired execution context, and must be called from the object's representative CPU (the lowest numbered CPU in the set). It also creates proxies for the native CPUs borrowed by the object, and then directs the hardware to reconfigure. The `deactivate` method does the reverse of `activate`; it directs the hardware to enable native CPUs and removes proxies for all the CPUs involved.

A thread invokes the node manager to request an execution object. The node manager creates an execution object and assigns unallocated CPUs that fit the object's constraints (contiguous IDs for our emulation) to the execution object. A CPU can only belong to one non-nested execution objects. Thus, in Figure 2, CPU C10 could not be part of objects E2 and E3. This constraint may be mandatory for processors that share physical resources, such as Core Fusion, but could be relaxed for systems with more flexible resource sharing.

Any request for change in the type of execution object for a thread also invokes the node manager. If the set of available native CPUs changes, such as when a thread terminates or changes its request for an execution object, the node manager can reassign CPUs between objects to avoid fragmentation that arises when enough idle CPUs are available to create a fused object, but hardware constraints prevent its creation.

4.3 Cluster Scheduling

Chameleon's cluster scheduler is built on top of the native Linux scheduler, the Completely Fair Scheduler (CFS) [28]. CFS is similar to Borrowed Virtual Time scheduling [14], and schedules tasks according to the CPU time they have used recently rather than priority. The tasks within a runqueue are ordered by a *virtual runtime* value (`vruntime` in the task structure), which is a measure of how long the task has run. The task with the lowest virtual runtime value (*i.e.*, is the furthest behind) is selected to run next. The virtual runtime value increases in proportion to the time spent executing.

Chameleon schedules all tasks in native Linux run queues. For threads requesting an execution object, Chameleon adds the thread to the run queue of the object's representative CPU. However, virtual threads, used to track a thread's priority on the borrowed CPUs, are *not* added to run queues. Instead, Chameleon leverages the CFS scheduler design: it records the virtual runtime value a thread *would receive* on another CPU had it been scheduled. This value is set when a thread is added to the queue and does not change, making it fast to record. When seeking to activate an object for a thread, the cluster scheduler is allowed to borrow a CPU, say C, if the thread's recorded virtual runtime value for CPU C is below the virtual runtime value of the thread currently running on CPU C. This indicates that, had it been a real thread, it would have been dispatched already. We describe below how this comparison is performed efficiently.

4.3.1 Activating execution objects

When a thread reaches the head of the run queue, Chameleon consults the thread's task structure to see whether the thread requested an execution object. If so, it checks whether it can activate the object. To make this efficient, Chameleon extends the Linux task structure with a `vruntimes[]` array containing an element for each CPU comprising an execution object. When adding a thread to a run queue, the cluster scheduler updates `vruntimes[]` for the CPUs in the execution object. In addition, each CFS runqueue stores the `vruntime` value a new thread would receive in its `min_vruntime` variable, and Chameleon copies this into the thread when initializing `vruntimes[]`.

When a thread finally becomes the next to run, the cluster scheduler compares the thread's `vruntimes[CPU]` with the virtual runtime value of the active thread for each CPU it needs to borrow. It only preempts the neighboring CPUs if the thread's `vruntime` is lower on *all* the needed CPUs. This requires preempting other threads, so we enable kernel preemption.

If the scheduler cannot form the execution object desired by a thread, it will try to instantiate an object with just the available CPUs, if one has the thread's requested properties (*e.g.*, sequential). For example, in Figure 2, if a thread wants object E1 but either CPU C5 or C6 is unavailable, the scheduler will see if it can form an object from CPUs C3 and C4. If so, it activates the execution object with just the available CPUs.

4.3.2 Preempting Execution Objects

While a thread executes on a fused object, threads scheduled on its borrowed CPUs may wake up and become runnable at higher priority. In addition, as a thread on a fused object executes, its `vruntime` increases so that it may no longer be the highest priority thread on all the borrowed CPUs.

Chameleon tracks how long a thread on a fused object can run by calculating when the next thread on every borrowed CPU is allowed to run, based on `vruntime` values of the threads it preempted and the running thread's `vruntimes[]` values. During every timer tick, the cluster scheduler checks whether any of the threads on a fused object's constituent CPUs are allowed to run, and if so deactivates the object and reschedules the running thread.

Reconfiguration takes time, so care must be taken to avoid reconfiguring too often. As we show in Section 5, fusing an execution object can take up to 8 μs. Chameleon relies on the existing `sysctl_sched_min_granularity` variable from CFS to set how long a thread can run before being preempted when it is no longer the highest priority thread.

4.3.3 Taxation

Taxation controls the relative priority of threads executing natively and threads that want to borrow a CPU for an execution object. CFS already adjusts the rate at which virtual runtime accrues based on priority: lower-priority tasks accumulate virtual runtime faster, so they must wait longer to execute again, while high priority tasks accumulate it more slowly, letting them run sooner. Taxation further adjusts that rate. Much as priority adjusts both scheduling latency and CPU share, taxation can act as a share, so that unimportant tasks only use idle CPUs for fused objects, or as a mechanism to reward threads that achieve high speedups with a fused object.

Chameleon adds an `eo_tax_percent` field to every task structure. When a thread runs on an execution object, the scheduler calculates the delta to its `vruntime` for the representative CPU and all borrowed CPUs, weighted by its priority. For borrowed CPUs, the scheduler multiplies the delta by the tax rate before adding to the `vruntimes[]` array.

Figure 3 shows the impact of changing the tax rate when running two CPU-bound tasks on neighboring CPUs. Task A requests an execution object, while B runs on one of the CPUs assigned to the execution object. If the tax rate is high (>> 1), then task A is charged more than task B for using its CPU and thus it sticks with native execution. If the tax rate is 1, then task A receives all of its

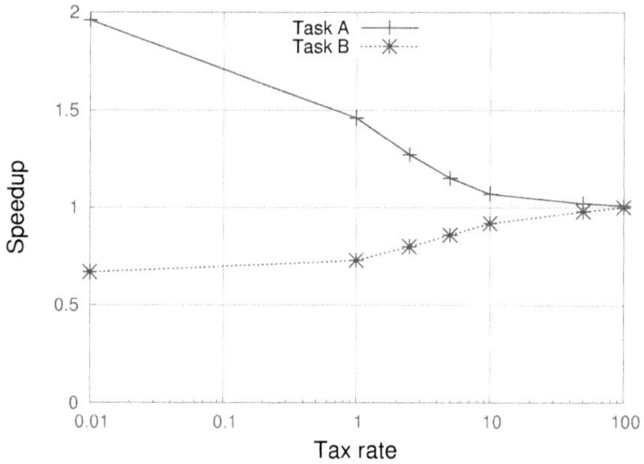

Figure 3. The effect of taxation on two identical tasks. Execution time is relative to the thread executing alone on a single native CPU.

CPU plus half of task B's CPU. If the tax rate is low (<< 1), then task A can preempt task B much of the time because it is charged less than B for using the CPU. Thus, taxation implements a cross-CPU priority mechanism.

Tax rates can be set automatically from the speedup a thread receives on a fused context. We observe that a thread that shows a good speedup deserves more access to a fused object. If progress rates metrics, such as hardware performance counters or application-specific heartbeats [23] are available, a thread's taxation rate can be set according to its speedup. Threads with good speedups deserve lower tax rates, allowing them to borrow neighboring CPUs aggressively, while threads with low speedups should only borrow idle CPUs and deserve high tax rates.

4.3.4 Property Matching

A thread declares its properties of interest by providing the identity of the property (an integer identifier), and a weight indicating the importance of the property. The node manager matches properties by comparing a thread's requested properties against the properties of all possible fused objects in the node. The matching process produces a list of possible execution objects. Currently, all properties are optional, so a thread will still be scheduled on any available CPU if an object with its requested properties is not available.

The current Chameleon implementation relies on a programmer or external agent to specify the properties a thread desires. To prioritize threads that benefit more from a fused object, the node manager uses the weight provided by a thread to identify which thread receives more benefit from a fused object when there is contention. Existing ACMP scheduling mechanisms or static profiling could provide information about the speedup of fused objects [49].

4.3.5 Rebalancing

The node manager spreads out threads requiring a fused object within a node so they can run concurrently, and to shift resources to threads that benefit from them more. When an execution object is freed, the CPUs it used are given to the active execution objects if they need them, such as an execution object that requested 4 CPUs but received only 2 CPUs. This assignment is prioritized based on the weight assigned to threads' properties.

When the node manager is not able to assign the requested number of native CPUs to an execution object, it tries to reclaim CPUs from low-priority threads and reassign these CPUs to a new fused object. If this is not possible, the node manager breaks the largest execution object and assign half the CPUs to a new execution object. This ensures that native CPUs are not reserved for a single thread when multiple threads request fused objects.

In addition, the node manager defragments execution objects. If the requested number of CPUs for an execution object are available within a node, but physical constraints prevent them from being fused (*e.g.*, they are not physically contiguous), the node manager detects fragmentation. It will then migrate threads to create a contiguous block of CPUs that can be used to satisfy future requests. Whenever the node manager makes any change to the physical resource assignment to the execution object, it notifies the execution object, which also updates the `vruntimes[]` for any threads scheduled on the object.

5. Evaluation

We evaluate Chameleon through emulation to answer these questions:

1. *Cost:* What is the latency of reconfiguring with processor proxies, and the added costs of scheduling with execution objects?
2. *Benefit:* Does Chameleon enable threads needing higher sequential performance to receive it, while allowing parallel programs full use of the CPUs in a system?
3. *Contention:* Does Chameleon behave reasonably and predictably when there are many threads contending for resources?

As dynamic processing hardware is not yet available, we evaluate Chameleon through emulation.

5.1 Experimental Platform

We emulate dynamic processors and ACMPs on a standard multicore system by varying the performance of the different CPUs. We performed our experiments on 32-bit Linux kernel version 2.6.31-4 running on a system with 12 GB RAM and two Intel Xeon X5650 chips, each chip containing six cores and each core with two hyperthreads. We refer hyperthreads as CPUs in this section. We instructed Chameleon to create two nodes of 6 cores (12 CPUs) each, and allow each node to create execution objects with 2 or 4 CPUs. We disabled TurboBoost because it varied the frequency when the system entered the P0 state, leading to widely fluctuating results. We leave the minimum scheduling granularity at the default value, 16ms.

We could not use DVFS to emulate asymmetric performance, as on our platform it applies to an entire socket rather than a single CPU. Instead, we use Intel's *clock-modulation* feature [25, 58] similar to past research on dynamic processors [3]. This mechanism is used for thermal throttling and controls the processor duty cycle by stopping the clock for short periods (less than 3μs) at regular intervals. There are eight levels available through the `IA32_CLOCK_MODULATION` model specific register (MSR). These levels reduce performance from 100% down to 12.5% of full performance in steps of 12.5%. For emulation, the `activate` method on an execution object creates the processor proxy and raises the duty cycle. Unlike real ACMPs or dynamic processors, the performance impact of clock modulation is independent of the code execution. Thus, a program sees a performance drop of 50% if the duty cycle is cut in half.

Table 2 lists the configurations we use in experiments. In all cases, we assume the baseline performance is 50% of maximum, and we emulate a faster CPU or fused object by increasing the duty cycle. For a symmetric CMP, we set all 24 CPUs to the baseline speed. For other models, we try to keep the approximate chip complexity similar. The emulated asymmetric CMP systems have either 3 or 6 fast CPUs with 75% or 100% of native performance. We use the native Linux scheduler in ACMP configuration but pin specific threads to the more powerful CPUs. As different programs see different speedups on asymmetric processors, we assign sequen-

Architecture Model	CPUs slow, fast	Speedup in Duty Cycle percent low	med	high
CMP	24, -	50	50	50
ACMP-3	12, 3	75	87.5	100
ACMP-6	12, 6	62.5	75	75
Dynamic	Fuse 2 threads	62.5	75	75
	Fuse 4 threads	75	87.5	100

Table 2. CMP, ACMP, and Dynamic configurations

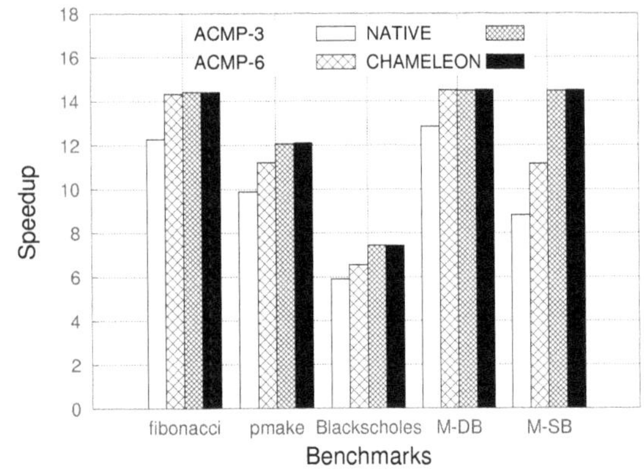

Figure 4. Performance of parallel programs.

tial programs to three performance categories (low, medium, high), with different speedups on the fast CPUs.

For dynamic processors, we follow past work [22] and set the maximum performance of fusing 2 threads to 75% (a 50% improvement over the base CPU's performance), and of 4 threads to 100%, doubling the performance of a base CPU. Again, we set different speedups for each sequential performance category to mirror the ACMP speedups. Achieving the same speedups with ACMP and dynamic processors may be optimistic, but it helps illustrate the benefit of being able to reconfigure.

We do not add additional delay to emulate the hardware cost of reconfiguring. Core Fusion estimates the delay at 400 cycles plus a pipeline flush [26], and other systems do not give any latencies. However, processor proxies flush the TLB when they are torn down, so the flush plus cost of subsequent TLB misses is included in our results.

5.2 Workloads

Past work has shown that I/O and memory-bound workloads receive little benefit from faster cores [4], so we largely evaluate with CPU-bound programs. Table 3 lists the workloads we use to evaluate Chameleon. As we do not have real hardware, variations in how a program performs on specific hardware cannot be evaluated. Thus, we instead evaluate on programs with different styles of a parallelism: task parallel threads on Intel's Thread Building Blocks (Fibonacci), task parallel processes (pmake); data-parallel threads (Blackscholes), OpenMP with a static binding of tasks to threads (Mandelbrot-SB); and OpenMP with a dynamic binding of tasks to threads (Mandelbrot-DB), which can execute more tasks given a more powerful CPU. We ran a variety of SpecCPU benchmarks on our emulator, and found they performed similarly to simple kernel benchmarks, so we also use a simple N-Queen program for sequential programs. We repeat experiments at least three times and report the average results. As there is little variance in the measurements, we do not include error bars.

5.3 Baseline Results

We evaluate Chameleon on single workloads to validate the emulator and to evaluate how close Chameleon gets to ideal performance.

Program	Description
Fibonacci	Task-parallel threads
pmake	Task-parallel processes
Blackscholes [7]	Data-parallel threads
Mandelbrot-DB (M-DB)	OpenMP kernel, dyn. binding
Mandelbrot-SB (M-SB)	OpenMP kernel, static binding
gcc [21]	Low-CPU single thread
astar [21]	Low-CPU single thread
dealII [21]	Medium-CPU single thread
lbm [21]	Medium-CPU single thread
sjeng [21]	High-CPU single thread
N-Queen [34]	High-CPU single thread
h264ref [21]	High-CPU single thread

Table 3. Workloads

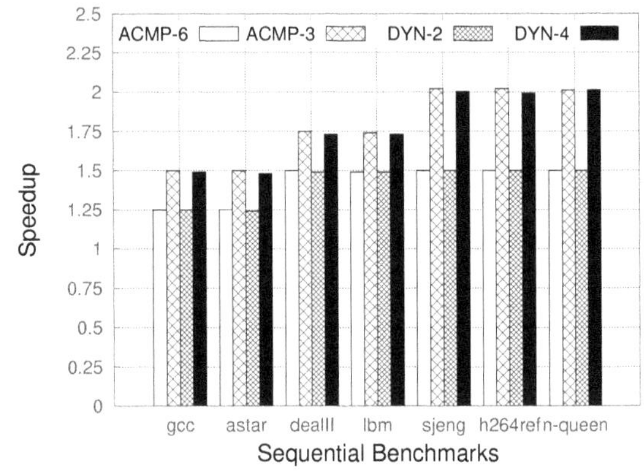

Figure 5. Performance of sequential programs.

Parallel performance. Figure 4 shows the performance of parallel workloads on four configurations: the CMP, the two ACMP models, and Chameleon. For all the parallel workloads, the best performance comes from the CMP configuration, which provides 24 CPUs. In the ACMP models, the lost parallelism outweighs the powerful CPUs present in the system except for Fibonacci and Mandelbrot with dynamic scheduling. Programs with static thread scheduling, such as Blackscholes, suffer from load imbalance when the threads on the fast CPUs wait for the threads on slow ones to finish. Chameleon uses all CPUs to achieve performance similar identical to the CMP.

Sequential performance. Figure 5 shows the performance of single-threaded workloads with varying benefit from faster CPUs. We execute each program on a single hyperthread, with the rest of the system idle. On ACMP systems we pin the program to a powerful core. For Chameleon, we evaluate both fusing two and four CPUs (DYN-2 and DYN-4). For these workloads, Chameleon is able to achieve the same performance as the asymmetric systems, despite using processor proxies. These results demonstrate that proxying introduces very little overhead and allow programs full access to the hardware's performance. In addition, they demonstrate that our emulation mechanism provides identical speedups across different programs.

Overhead. The overhead of Chameleon arises in two places: reconfiguration and scheduling. The latency of fusing and splitting CPUs is shown in Table 4. We present two versions of Chameleon's split and fuse operations: **Proxy - APIC** reprograms the IOAPIC to deliver interrupts to the proxying CPU during a fuse, and **Proxy - Logical** uses the logical addressing technique described in Section 4.1. When reprogramming the IOAPIC, proxy creation takes between 250-375μs. Logical addressing does not communicate with the slow IOAPIC and is 50-100 times faster. Compared to the native Linux hotplug mechanism, Chameleon is up to 75,000 times

Operation	Hotplug	Proxy - APIC	Proxy - Logical
Fuse 2 CPUs	150ms	250μs	2μs
Fuse 4 CPUs	430ms	375μs	8μs
Split 2 CPUs	220ms	20μs	1.5μs
Split 4 CPUs	640ms	60μs	4.2μs

Table 4. Latency of reconfiguration

faster at fusing (hot *un*plugging a CPU) and 160,000 times faster at splitting an execution object of two CPUs (hot plugging a CPU).

The number of processors that can be addressed with logical addresses may be limited in some systems, and in such cases IOAPIC reprogramming is needed. The fuse case for **Proxy - APIC** is more expensive than splitting because Chameleon reprograms the IOAPIC to remove the proxied CPU. When splitting a proxy, it does not reprogram the IOAPIC to include the proxied CPU (this is the same behavior as Linux hotplug). Fusing and splitting four CPUs is costlier since the proxy creation and destruction phases are carried out sequentially. The major savings compared to hotplug come from avoiding the notification of subsystems that the set of CPUs has changed. The remainder of our experiments uses the IOAPIC reprogramming method, as logical addressing does not currently support 24 CPUs.

We measured the added scheduling work during context switches, and there was no difference between context switching native threads on Chameleon and native Linux: both took between 2.5μs - 3μs. These results demonstrate that the added latency of Chameleon's scheduling techniques is low.

IPIs handled by proxy. We ran the pmake workload alongside a sequential application making use of an execution object with 4 CPUs. The proxy created during the activation of the execution object is responsible for handling the IPIs destined to the CPUs of the execution object and in this case was proxying for 3 CPUs. The proxy handled 10 IPIs per second, mostly TLB shootdowns. This is lower than the 40 IPIs/second reported in Section 2 because the offline CPUs switch to the idle thread, which avoids rescheduling IPIs. However, the proxy still receives TLB shootdowns because the idle thread leaves the previous user-mode address space from `pmake` on the processor.

5.4 Scheduling Mixed Workloads

We evaluate Chameleon with a mix of workloads under two situations: *over-provisioned*, when there are more CPUs than threads; and *under-provisioned*, where there are not enough CPUs. In each case, we start a mix of parallel and sequential programs at the same time and measure their completion time. If one program finishes early, the other program can make use of its CPUs. We use the Mandelbrot and N-Queen kernels because they are purely CPU bound and their performance reflects only the added effect of scheduling decisions by Chameleon, as shown in Figure 5.

Ideally, when there are idle CPUs, Chameleon will opportunistically use them to execute sequential tasks. When there is contention, Chameleon should only use them if the tax rate allows sequential threads to preempt threads on neighboring CPUs.

Over-provisioned performance. We measure the performance of executing a parallel program requiring 16 CPUs and 2-4 sequential programs simultaneously. The results in Figure 6 show that for two sequential programs, Chameleon creates a 4-CPU fused object for each task that achieves almost double the baseline performance. The four sequential threads are scheduled on 2-CPU fused objects, and achieve 50% speedup over baseline. The case of 3 sequential threads is explained more in the following paragraph. Thus, Chameleon is able to effectively place sequential threads when there are idle CPUs, and can balance them to achieve maximum performance.

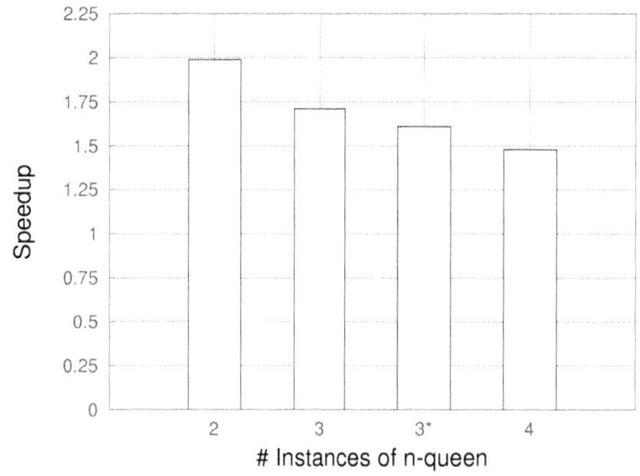

Figure 6. Over-provisioned performance of 2-4 sequential programs and a parallel program. The column marked by 3* was run without the node manager notification mechanism.

This experiment also demonstrates Chameleon's load balancing capability. With three sequential threads and eight available CPUs, one of the threads can run on a 4-CPU fused object, while the others run on 2-CPU fused objects. When the faster thread completes, the node manager distributes the physical resource used by the just finished thread to currently active threads, allowing both remaining threads to use 4-CPU fused objects. The column labeled 3* shows the benefit of notifying the node manager when a task completes. When we disable notification, which redistributes idle CPUs, performance suffers because only one thread uses a 4-CPU fused object even when idle CPUs are available.

Under-provisioned performance. We perform a similar test using three sequential programs and a parallel program with 24 threads. As there are no idle CPUs, Chameleon must decide whether to timeshare CPUs between the two programs. For these experiments, we test with both static and dynamic binding of the parallel threads, and vary the tax rate between 0.01, 1, and 100. We also present the result for the ACMP-3 configuration. In the ACMP configuration, the sequential programs were pinned to the fast CPUs while letting Linux schedule 15 parallel threads.

Figure 7 shows the speedup for the sequential and parallel programs relative to running on a single baseline CPU. As this is a single hyperthread, the speedup from using more CPUs is less than linear in the number of CPUs available. With a low tax rate, the sequential program is able to borrow the neighboring CPUs most of the time for a speedup of 97% over baseline (the speedup is less than 100% because the parallel thread occasionally uses the CPU). With a tax rate of 1, the sequential program borrows CPUs approximately half the time. But since the parallel threads also use the CPU the observed speedup is less than 50%. With a high tax rate, the sequential workloads were not able to preempt the parallel threads. As a result they complete at baseline speedup.

The parallel program shows similar variation: for dynamic scheduling where threads can have varying amounts of work, performance drops in direct proportion to the time N-Queen borrows a CPU: with the high tax rate, it gets a 11.4x speedup over baseline, while with a low tax that drops to 10x. With a low tax, N-Queen finishes quickly and the parallel program then uses all 24 CPUs. With static scheduling, where every thread must perform the same amount of work, performance varies from 11.4x speedup with the high tax rate to 8.8x speedup with a low tax rate, because of load imbalance while the N-Queen is running. Thus, the use of tax must consider both the benefit to sequential programs and the cost to the parallel programs that are preempted. The N-Queen program's use of the CPU is similar when run with both the static and dynamic parallel programs, so its performance does not change.

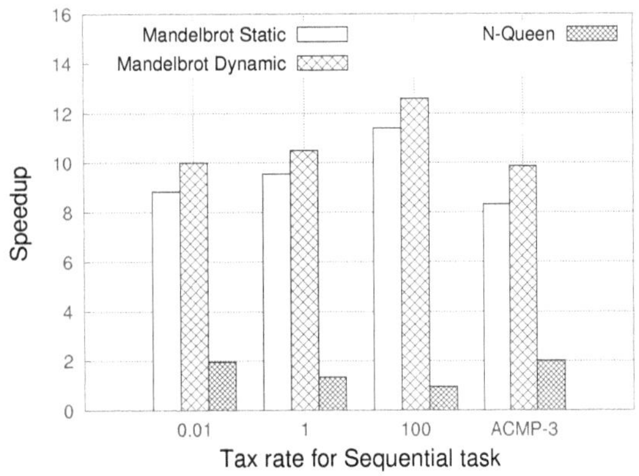

Figure 7. Under-provisioned performance of 3 instances of N-Queen program and a parallel program with varying taxation rates.

Compared to the ACMP, Chameleon achieves the same sequential performance and parallel performance on the dynamic parallel program with a low tax rate because it has more CPUs. The higher tax rates trade lower sequential performance for parallel performance exceeding the ACMP. These results show how taxation adjusts the priority of sequential and parallel programs. Its benefit may depend on how well parallel programs react to losing a CPU.

Mixed sequential workloads. This experiment demonstrates Chameleon's ability to prioritize the use of CPUs based on the speedup a thread achieves. In this experiment we ran a mix of sequential workloads of different classes: one high CPU (sjeng), one medium CPU (lbm) and two low-CPU workloads (astar) with staggered start times. We annotated each program's thread with its speedup as the weight on its sequential property, similar to what might be provided by an ACMP scheduler. We constrained all the programs to a single node with a total of 10 CPUs.

Ideally, the rebalancer will spread the available CPUs across the sequential programs and prioritize remaining CPUs to the programs with the best speedup. Figure 8 shows the results of this experiment. The two low CPU (astar) workloads were started first and were each given a 4-CPU fused object by the node manager. When lbm – a medium speedup application – was started subsequently, the manager borrowed 2 CPUs from one of the low-speedup astar applications and gave them to lbm at event ⓐ. Similarly, when sjeng – a high speedup application – started, it borrowed 2 CPUs, one each from lbm the other astar, at event ⓑ.

In short, when the remaining two workloads started, the node manager noted that the demand for sequential performance (a total of 16 CPUs forming 4 fused objects) exceeded the supply (10 CPUs), and split the objects in use by the astar instances so the two remaining programs could each receive a fused object. As described in Section 4.3.5, the node manager uses the speedups of the programs to allocate the remaining CPUs to the program receiving the most benefit, sjeng, which then runs on a 4-CPU fused object. The other three programs all used a 2-CPU fused object. Upon exit of any workload, the node manager distributes the released CPUs to the active workloads based on their speedup. In this case lbm completes first at event ⓒ and its resources are given to one astar instance. After sjeng exits at event ⓓ, its resources are given to the second astar.

Thus, Chameleon's node manager and rebalancer are able to allocate CPUs across a set of workloads with different speedups, when notified of those speedups.

5.5 Chameleon on Real Hardware

The previous results show that Chameleon can exploit the flexibility of dynamic processors to achieve improved performance.

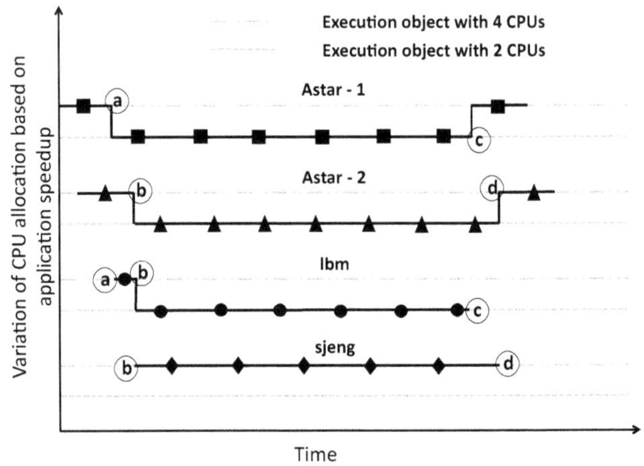

Figure 8. CPU allocation to execution object in a workload mix of sequential programs with different speedups.

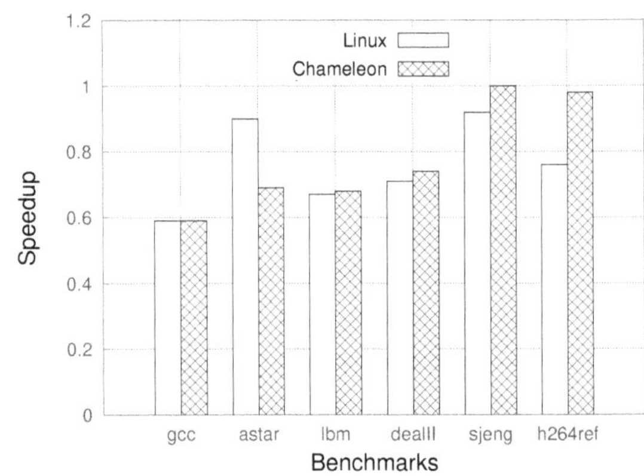

Figure 9. Chameleon on SMT.

Chameleon can also prioritize threads on existing hyperthreaded processors. Since hyperthreads share the cache and processor pipeline, running two hyperthreads on a core may reduce the performance when compared to running a single thread. As a result, the Linux scheduler tries to schedule threads on separate cores before using two hyperthreads on a single core. However, when there are more threads than cores, it is possible that a thread that benefits from running alone on a core may get scheduled on a shared CPU.

We apply Chameleon's cluster scheduler to this problem by treating each core as a fused execution object, which when activated forces one of the hyperthreads to idle. We ran one instance of six SPEC application annotated by their corresponding speedup values as listed in Table 3 over 4 physical CPUs (8 hyperthreads) with the native Linux scheduler and Chameleon. The baseline is the application running on a non-shared CPU. Figure 9 compares the speedup achieved on the two systems. Linux has no knowledge each application's speedup and thus any application may be scheduled on a non-shared core. In this case, astar and sjeng achieve a good speedup. Chameleon therefore prioritizes these two programs and schedules them on non-shared cores. Thus, Chameleon is able to prioritize resources for threads that benefit more from running alone, while Linux treats all threads equally.

6. Related Work

Asymmetric Scheduling. Several recent works investigate scheduling parallel and multiprogrammed workloads on asymmetric or heterogeneous processors [19, 30, 35, 48, 49]. However, many of these systems focus on power efficiency, so they seek to identify which threads gain the most efficiency. Chameleon could use these techniques to identify which threads would perform best on a powerful execution object. Mogul et al. investigate the use of ACMPs for operating systems [42], but focus on static assignment of OS threads to simple cores; Chameleon could implement this policy using its property mechanism. Most similar to Chameleon is Luo et al.'s work on the use of helper threads and cache resizing on an ACMP [38]. Similar to Chameleon, this work determines when to allocate resources to speed sequential threads, but focuses again on identifying which threads gain the most benefit. ACS accelerates critical sections on an ACMP [55]. However, the latency of Chameleon's reconfiguration is still too long to help individual critical sections.

Gang scheduling. Chameleon's cluster scheduling is similar to gang scheduling in that it will try to schedule multiple CPUs simultaneously. Past work on gang scheduling [45, 27, 16, 6] focuses primarily on time-sharing gangs of threads. While Chameleon can do this, there is little benefit because performance improves by running time-sliced threads in parallel on separate cores. Thus, Chameleon is most effective when there are idle threads to be used opportunistically, or when a sequential thread has higher priority than competing workloads.

Tesselation uses a form of gang scheduling to provide a *cell* of processors to an application, which is similar to Chameleon's execution objects [11]. However, it provides cores for software process to use, while Chameleon provides cores to hardware for an enhanced CPU.

Support for reconfigurable hardware. Recent work on scheduling for reconfigurable hardware has largely focused on embedded and real-time systems [52, 29, 17]. In these environments, precise models of the transition costs and the execution time of code on different hardware are needed. These systems also place mandatory requirements on scheduling, so flexible tradeoffs like Chameleon's taxation are not used. In contrast, Chameleon focuses largely on best-effort workloads and must rely on admission control to meet performance goals.

Several projects discuss OS support for introducing reconfigurable logic onto a processor [13, 36, 54]. However, OS support for these systems focuses on efficiently allocating the reconfigurable logic to specific functions rather than on thread scheduling.

Windows 7's support for core parking [41], which coalesces threads onto a single core to disable the remaining cores, is similar to Chameleon's scheduling of threads on the execution object. It is also used to balance threads between hyperthreads. However, core parking targets all threads at a specific subset of CPUs, rather than context switching between configurations.

7. Conclusions

Dynamic processors will lead to new opportunities for improving performance, reliability, and power consumption by reconfiguring the set of running processors. Existing operating systems cannot react to changes fast enough to fully utilize reconfiguration, and do not have scheduling mechanisms to take advantage of them. Chameleon extends Linux to enable rapid reconfiguration through processors proxies, allowing use of reconfiguration even for short periods. It abstracts the reconfiguration abilities of the hardware with execution objects and nodes, which expose the new capabilities of the hardware to programmers and the scheduler. Chameleon's cluster scheduling with taxation allows sequential code to use idle cores and provides a flexible tradeoff between single-thread performance and parallel performance.

We plan to extend Chameleon for other uses of dynamic processors. Chameleon focuses on performance benefits of dynamic processors, but they should also promise power efficiency and reliability, which demand different scheduling policies. In addition, we plan to investigate other forms of dynamic processors that may not fit Chameleon's model. For example, processors with dark silicon accelerators cannot be used unless other cores are powered off.

Acknowledgements

This work is supported in part by National Science Foundation (NSF) grant CNS-0834473. We would like to thank our shepherd, Angela Demke Brown, and the anonymous reviewers for their invaluable feedback. Swift has a significant financial interest in Microsoft.

References

[1] N. Aggarwal, P. Ranganathan, N. P. Jouppi, and J. E. Smith. Configurable isolation: Building high availability systems with commodity multi-core processors. In *Proc. of the 34th ISCA*, June 2007.

[2] J. Allarey, V. George, and S. Jahagirdar. Power management enhancements in the 45nm intel core microarchitecture. *Intel Technical Journal*, 12(3):169–178, oct 2008.

[3] M. Annavaram, E. Grochowski, and J. Shen. Mitigating amdahl's law through epi throttling. In *Proc. of the 32nd ISCA*, pages 298 – 309, June 2005.

[4] L. A. Barroso, K. Gharachorloo, R. McNamara, A. Nowatzyk, S. Qadeer, B. Sano, S. Smith, R. Stets, and B. Verghese. Piranha: A scalable architecture based on single-chip multiprocessing. In *Proc. of the 27th ISCA*, pages 282–293, June 2000.

[5] A. Baumann, P. barham, P.-E. Dagand, T. Harris, R. Isaacs, S. Peter, T. Roscoe, A. Schupbach, and A. Singhania. The multikernel: A new os architecture for scalable multicore systems. In *Proc. 22nd SOSP*, Oct 2009.

[6] M. Bhadauria and S. A. McKee. An approach to resource-aware co-scheduling for cmps. In *Proc. of the 24th ICS*, pages 189–199, 2010.

[7] C. Bienia and K. Li. PARSEC 2.0: A new benchmark suite for chip-multiprocessors. In *Proc. 5th Workshop on Modeling, Benchmarking and Simulation*, June 2009.

[8] N. Brookwood. Amd fusion. family of apus: Enabling a superior, immersive pc experience. `http://sites.amd.com/us/Documents/48423B_fusion_whitepaper_WEB.pdf`, Mar 2010.

[9] J. Charles, P. Jassi, A. N. S, A. Sadat, and A. Fedorova. Evaluation of the Intel Core i7 Turbo Boost feature. In *Proc. International Symposium on Workload Characterization*, Oct. 2009.

[10] S. Chaudhry, R. Cypher, M. Ekman, M. Karlsson, A. Landin, S. Yip, H. Zeffer, and M. Tremblay. Simultaneous speculative threading: A novel pipeline architecture implemented in sun's rock processor. In *Proc. of the 36th ISCA*, June 2009.

[11] J. A. Colmenares, S. Bird, H. Cook, P. Pearce, D. Zhu, J. Shalf, S. Hofmeyr, K. Asanovic, and J. Kubiatowicz. Resource management in the tessellation manycore os. In *HotPAR*, 2010.

[12] J. Corbet. CFS group scheduling. `http://lwn.net/Articles/240474/`, 2007.

[13] M. Dales. Managing a reconfigurable processor in a general purpose workstation environment. In *Proc. Design, Automation and Test in Europe*, 2003.

[14] K. J. Duda and D. R. Cheriton. Borrowed-virtual-time (bvt) scheduling: supporting latency-sensitive threads in a general-purpose scheduler. In *Proc. 17th SOSP*, 1999.

[15] H. Esmaeilzadeh, E. Blem, R. S. Amant, K. Sankaralingam, and D. Burger. Dark silicon and the end of multicore scaling. In *Proc. of the 38th ISCA*, June 2011.

[16] D. G. Feitelson and L. Rudolph. Gang scheduling performance benefits for fine-grain synchronization. *JPDC*, 16(4):306 – 318, 1992.

[17] W. Fu and K. Compton. Scheduling intervals for reconfigurable computing. In *Proc. 16th FCCM*, Apr. 2008.

[18] R. Grant and A. Afsahi. Power-performance efficiency of asymmetric multiprocessors for multi-threaded scientific applications. In *Proc. 20th IPDPS*, Apr. 2006.

[19] B. Hamidzadeh, Y. Atif, and D. J. Lilja. Dynamic scheduling techniques for heterogeneous computing systems. *Concurrency: Practice and Experience*, 7(7):633–652, 1995.

[20] L. Hammond, B. Hubbert, M. Siu, M. Prabhu, M. Chen, and K. Olukotun. The stanford hydra cmp. *IEEE Micro*, pages 71–84, March-April 2000.

[21] J. L. Henning. Spec cpu2006 benchmark descriptions. *Computer Architecture News*, 34(4):1–17, 2006.

[22] M. D. Hill and M. R. Marty. Amdahl's law in the multicore era. *IEEE Computer*, pages 33–38, July 2008.

[23] H. Hoffmann, J. Eastep, M. D. Santambrogio, J. E., Miller, and A. Agarwal. Application heartbeats: A generic interface for specifying program performance and goals in autonomous computing environments. In *Proc. 7th ICAC*, 2010.

[24] Intel Corp. 82093AA I/O ADVANCED PROGRAMMABLE INTERRUPT CONTROLLER (IOAPIC). http://www.intel.com/design/chipsets/datashts/29056601.pdf, 1996.

[25] Intel Corp. Thermal protection and monitoring features: A software perspective. http://www.intel.com/cd/ids/developer/asmo-na/eng/downloads/54118.htm, 2005.

[26] E. Ipek, M. Kirman, N. Kirman, and J. F. Martinez. Core fusion: Accomodating software diversity in chip multiprocessors. In *Proc. of the 34th ISCA*, June 2007.

[27] Y. Jiang, X. Shen, J. Chen, and R. Tripathi. Analysis and approximation of optimal co-scheduling on chip multiprocessors. In *Proc. of the 17th PACT*, 2008.

[28] M. T. Jones. Inside the linux 2.6 completely fair scheduler, Dec 2009. http://www.ibm.com/developerworks/linux/library/l-completely-fair-scheduler/.

[29] H. Kooti, E. Bozorgzadeh, S. Liao, and L. Bao. Transition-aware real-time task scheduling for reconfigurable embedded systems. In *Proc. Design, Automation and Test in Europe*, Mar. 2010.

[30] D. Koufaty, D. Reddy, and S. Hahn. Bias scheduling in heterogeneous multi-core architectures. In *Proc. EuroSys*, 2010.

[31] V. Krishnan and J. Torrellas. Hardware and software support for speculative execution of sequential binaries on a chip-multiprocessor. In *Proc. ICS*, pages 85–92, July 1998.

[32] R. Kumar, K. I. Farkas, N. P. Jouppi, P. Ranganathan, and D. M. Tullsen. Single-isa heterogeneous multi-core architectures: The potential for processor power reduction. In *Proc. of the 36th MICRO*, Dec. 2003.

[33] M. Laux. Solaris processor sets made easy. http://developers.sun.com/solaris/articles/solaris_processor.html, 2001.

[34] C. Letavec and J. Ruggiero. The n-queens problem. *INFORMS Transactions on Education*, 2(3), 2002.

[35] T. Li, D. Baumberger, D. A. Koufaty, and S. Hahn. Efficient operating system scheduling for performance-asymmetric multi-core architectures. In *Proc. of SC2007*, Nov. 2007.

[36] E. Lübbers and M. Platzner. Reconos: Multithreaded programming for reconfigurable computers. *ACM Trans. Embed. Comput. Syst.*, 9, October 2009.

[37] P. Marcuello, A. Gonzalez, and J. Tubella. Speculative multithreaded processors. In *Proc. of the 1998 ICS*, pages 77–84, July 1998.

[38] Y. Luo, V. Packirisamy, W.-C. Hsu, and A. Zhai. Energy efficient speculative threads: dynamic thread allocation in same-isa heterogeneous multicore systems. In *Proc. 19th PACT*, pages 453–464, 2010.

[39] P. E. McKenney, J. Appavoo, A. Kleen, O. Krieger, , R. Russell, D. Sarma, and M. Soni. Read-copy update. In *Proc. of the Ottawa Linux Symposium*, July 2001.

[40] Microsoft Corp. New NUMA Support with Windows Server 2008 R2 and Windows 7. http://archive.msdn.microsoft.com/64plusLP, 2008.

[41] Microsoft Corp. Processor power management in windows 7 windows server 2008 r2. http://download.microsoft.com/download/3/0/2/3027D574-C433-412A-A8B6-5E0A75D5B237/ProcPowerMgmtWin7.docx, Jan. 2010.

[42] J. C. Mogul, J. Mudigonda, N. L. Binkert, P. Ranganathan, and V. Talwar. Using asymmetric single-isa cmps to save energy on operating systems. *IEEE Micro*, 28(3):26–41, 2008.

[43] Z. Mwaikambo, R. Russell, A. Raj, and J. Schopp. Linux kernel hotplug CPU support. In *Proc. of the Ottawa Linux Symposium*, pages 181–194, 2004.

[44] J. T. Oplinger, D. L. Heine, and M. S. Lam. In search of speculative thread-level parallelism. In *Proc. 8th PACT*, Oct. 1999.

[45] J. Ousterhout. Scheduling techniques for concurrent systems. In *Proc. of the 3rd ICDCS*, pages 22–30, 1982.

[46] R. Raman, M. Livny, and M. Solomon. Matchmaking: distributed resource management for high throughput computing. In *Proc. HPDC*, pages 140 –146, July 1998.

[47] S. K. Reinhardt and S. S. Mukherjee. Transient fault detection via simultaneous multithreading. In *Proc. of the 27th ISCA*, pages 25–36, June 2000.

[48] J. C. Saez, M. Prieto, A. Fedorova, and S. Blagodurov. A comprehensive scheduler for asymmetric multicore systems. In *Proc. EuroSys*, 2010.

[49] J. C. Saez, D. Shelepov, A. Fedorova, and M. Prieto. Leveraging workload diversity through os scheduling to maximize performance on single-isa heterogeneous multicore systems. *J. Parallel Distrib. Comput.*, 71:114–131, January 2011.

[50] K. Sankaralingam, R. Nagarajan, H. Liu, C. Kim, J. Huh, D. Burger, S. W. Keckler, and C. Moore. Exploiting ilp, tlp, and dlp with the polymorphous trips architecture. In *Proc. of the 30th ISCA*, pages 422–433, June 2003.

[51] S. Siddha and V. Pallipadi. Chip multi processing aware Linux kernel scheduler. In *Proc. of the Ottawa Linux Symposium*, pages 337–348, 2006.

[52] S. P. Smith. Dynamic scheduling and resource management in heterogeneous computing environments with reconfigurable hardware. In *International Conference on Computer Design*, 2006.

[53] W. Stanek. Windows Server 2008 R2: A primer. http://technet.microsoft.com/en-us/magazine/ee677582.aspx, Nov. 2009.

[54] C. Steiger, H. Walder, and M. Platzner. Operating systems for reconfigurable embedded platforms: online scheduling of real-time tasks. *IEEE Trans. Computers*, 53(11), Nov. 2004.

[55] M. A. Suleman, O. Mutlu, M. K. Qureshi, and Y. N. Patt. Accelerating critical section execution with asymmetric multi-core architectures. In *Proc. 14th ASPLOS*, 2009.

[56] Texas Instruments. OMAP 5 platform. http://www.ti.com/ww/en/omap/omap5/omap5-OMAP5430.html, 2011.

[57] P. Wells, K. Chakraborty, and G. Sohi. Mixed-mode multicore reliability. In *Proc. of the 14th ASPLOS*, Mar. 2009.

[58] X. Zhang, S. Dwarkadas, and K. Shen. Hardware execution throttling for multi-core resource management. In *Proc. USENIX ATC*, 2009.

Cosmic Rays Don't Strike Twice: Understanding the Nature of DRAM Errors and the Implications for System Design

Andy A. Hwang Ioan Stefanovici Bianca Schroeder
Department of Computer Science, University of Toronto
{hwang, ioan, bianca}@cs.toronto.edu

Abstract

Main memory is one of the leading hardware causes for machine crashes in today's datacenters. Designing, evaluating and modeling systems that are resilient against memory errors requires a good understanding of the underlying characteristics of errors in DRAM in the field. While there have recently been a few first studies on DRAM errors in production systems, these have been too limited in either the size of the data set or the granularity of the data to conclusively answer many of the open questions on DRAM errors. Such questions include, for example, the prevalence of soft errors compared to hard errors, or the analysis of typical patterns of hard errors.

In this paper, we study data on DRAM errors collected on a diverse range of production systems in total covering nearly 300 terabyte-years of main memory. As a first contribution, we provide a detailed analytical study of DRAM error characteristics, including both hard and soft errors. We find that a large fraction of DRAM errors in the field can be attributed to hard errors and we provide a detailed analytical study of their characteristics. As a second contribution, the paper uses the results from the measurement study to identify a number of promising directions for designing more resilient systems and evaluates the potential of different protection mechanisms in the light of realistic error patterns. One of our findings is that simple page retirement policies might be able to mask a large number of DRAM errors in production systems, while sacrificing only a negligible fraction of the total DRAM in the system.

Categories and Subject Descriptors B.8.0 [*Hardware*]: Performance and Reliability

General Terms Reliability, Measurement

1. Introduction

Recent studies point to main memory as one of the leading hardware causes for machine crashes and component replacements in today's datacenters [13, 18, 20]. As the amount of DRAM in servers keeps growing and chip densities increase, DRAM errors might pose an even larger threat to the reliability of future generations of systems.

ASPLOS'12, March 3–7, 2012, London, England, UK.

As a testament to the importance of the problem, most server systems provide some form of protection against memory errors. Most commonly this is done at the hardware level through the use of DIMMs with error correcting codes (ECC). ECC DIMMs either provide single-bit error correction and double-bit error detection (SEC-DED); or use more complex codes in the chipkill family [4] that allow a system to tolerate an entire chip failure at the cost of somewhat reduced performance and increased energy usage. In addition, some systems employ protection mechanisms at the operating system level. For example, Solaris tries to identify and then retire pages with hard errors [3, 20]. Researchers have also explored other avenues, such as virtualized and flexible ECC at the software level [24].

The effectiveness of different approaches for protecting against memory errors and the most promising directions for designing future systems that are resilient in the face of increased DRAM error rates depend greatly on the nature of memory errors. For example, SEC-DED based ECC is most effective for protecting against transient random errors, such as soft errors caused by alpha particles or cosmic rays. On the other hand, mechanisms based on page retirement have potential only for protecting against hard errors, which are due to device defects and hence tend to be repeatable. In general, any realistic evaluation of system reliability relies on accurate assumptions about the underlying error process, including the relative frequency of hard versus soft errors, and the typical modes of hard errors (e.g. device defects affecting individual cells, whole rows, columns, or an entire chip).

While there exists a large body of work on protecting systems against DRAM errors, the nature of DRAM errors is not very well understood. Most existing work focuses solely on soft errors [1, 6, 9, 12, 14, 15, 21, 22, 25, 27] as soft error rates are often assumed to be orders of magnitudes greater than typical hard-error rates [5]. However, there are no large-scale field studies backing up this assumption. Existing studies on DRAM errors are quite old and rely on controlled lab experiments, rather than production machines [15, 25, 26, 28], and focus on soft errors only [10]. A notable exception is a recent study by Li et al. [11], which analyzes field data collected on 200 production machines and finds evidence that the rate of hard errors might be higher than commonly assumed. However, the limited size of their data set, which includes only a total of 12 machines with errors, makes it hard to draw statistically significant conclusions on the rate of hard versus soft errors or common modes of hard errors. Another recent field study [19] speculates that the rate of hard errors might be significant based on correlations they observe in error counts over time, but lacks more fine-grained data, in the form of information on the location of errors, to validate their hypothesis.

System	Time (days)	Nodes	# DIMMs	DRAM in system (TB)	TByte years	Nodes with errors	Nodes w/ chipkill errs	Total # Errors	FIT
BG/L	214	32,768	N/A	49	28	1,742 (5.32%)	N/A	$227 \cdot 10^6$	97,614
BG/P	583	40,960	N/A	80	127	1,455 (3.55%)	1.34%	$1.96 \cdot 10^9$	167,066
SciNet	211	3,863	31,000	62	35	97 (2.51%)	N/A	$49.3 \cdot 10^6$	18,825
Google	155	20,000	~ 130,000	220	93	20,000	N/A	$27.27 \cdot 10^9$	N/A

Table 1. Summary of system configurations and high-level error statistics recorded in different systems

The goal of this paper is two-fold. First, we strive to fill the gaps in our understanding of DRAM error characteristics, in particular the rate of hard errors and their patterns. Towards this end we provide a large-scale field study based on a diverse range of production systems, covering nearly 300 terabyte-years of main memory. The data includes detailed information on the location of errors, which allows us to statistically conclusively answer several important open questions about DRAM error characteristics. In particular, we find that a large fraction of DRAM errors in the field can be attributed to hard errors and we provide a detailed analytical study of their characteristics.

As a second contribution, the paper uses the results from the measurement study to identify a number of promising directions for designing more resilient systems and evaluates the potential of different protection mechanism in the light of realistic error patterns. One of our findings is that simple page retirement policies, which are currently not widely used in practice, might be able to mask a large number of DRAM errors in production systems, while sacrificing only a negligible fraction of the total system's DRAM.

2. Background

2.1 Overview of data and systems

Our study is based on data from four different environments: the IBM Blue Gene/L (BG/L) supercomputer at Lawrence Livermore National Laboratory, the Blue Gene/P (BG/P) from the Argonne National Laboratory, a high-performance computing cluster at the SciNet High Performance Computing Consortium, and 20,000 machines randomly selected from Google's data centers. Below we provide a brief description of each of the systems and the data we obtained.

BG/L: Our first dataset is from the Lawrence Livermore National Laboratory's IBM Blue Gene/L (BG/L) supercomputer. The system consists of 64 racks, each containing 32 node cards. Each node card is made up of 16 compute cards, which are the smallest replaceable hardware component for the system; we refer to the compute cards as "nodes". Each compute card itself contains two PowerPC 440 cores, each with their own associated DRAM chips, which are soldered onto the card; there is no notion of a "DIMM" (see [7] for more details).

We obtained BG/L logs containing data generated by the system's RAS infrastructure, including count and location messages pertaining to correctable memory errors that occur during a job and are reported upon job completion.

The BG/L memory port contains a 128-bit data part that's divided divided into 32 symbols, where the ECC is able to correct any error pattern within a single symbol, assuming no errors occur in any other symbols. However, the system can still function in the event of two symbols with errors by remapping one of the symbols to a spare symbol, and correcting the other with ECC [16].

Due to limitations in the types of messages that the BG/L log contains, we are only able to report on multi-bit errors that were detected (and corrected) within a single symbol. As such, we refer to these as MBEs (multi-bit errors) for the BG/L system throughout the paper. However it's worth noting that 350 compute cards (20% of all compute cards with errors in the system) reported activating symbol steering to the spare symbol. This is indicative of more severe errors that required more advanced ECC technologies (like bit-sparing) to correct. In addition, a cap was imposed on the total count of correctable errors accumulated during a job for part of the dataset, making our results for both multi-bit errors and total correctable error counts very conservative compared to the actual state of the system.

BG/P: The second system we studied is the Blue Gene/P (BG/P) from the Argonne National Laboratory. The system has 40 racks containing a total of 40,960 compute cards (nodes). Each node in BG/P has four PowerPC 450 cores and 40 DRAM chips totalling 2GB of addressable memory. As the successor to BG/L, BG/P has stronger ECC capabilities and can correct single and double-symbol errors. The system is also capable of chipkill error correction, which tolerates failure of one whole DRAM chip [8].

We obtained RAS logs from BG/P reporting correctable error samples. Only the first error sample on an address during the execution of a job is reported, and total occurrences for each error type summarized at the end. Due to the sampling and counter size, the amount of correctable errors are once again very conservative. However, the correctable samples provide location information which allows us to study the patterns and physical distribution of errors.

Unlike BG/L, there is no bit position information for single-symbol errors. There is no way to determine the number of bits that failed within one symbol. Therefore, we report single-symbol errors as single-bit errors and double-symbol errors as multi-bit errors, and refer to the latter as MBEs for the BG/P system. A double-symbol error is guaranteed to have at least two error bits that originate from the pair of error symbols. This is once again an under-estimation of the total number of multi-bit errors.

SciNet: Our third data source comes from the General Purpose Cluster (GPC) at the SciNet High Performance Computing Consortium. The GPC at SciNet is currently the largest supercomputer in Canada. It consists of 3,863 IBM iDataPlex nodes, each with 8 Intel Xeon E5540 cores and 16GB of addressable memory that uses basic SEC-DED ECC. The logs we collected consist of hourly-dumps of the entire PCI configuration space, which expose the onboard memory controller registers containing counts (with no physical location information) of memory error events in the system.

Google: Our fourth data source comes from Google's datacenters and consists of a random sample of 20,000 machines that have experienced memory errors. Each machine comprises a motherboard with some processors and memory DIMMs. The machines in our sample come from 5 different hardware platforms, where a platform is defined by the motherboard and memory generation. The memory in these systems covers a wide variety of the most

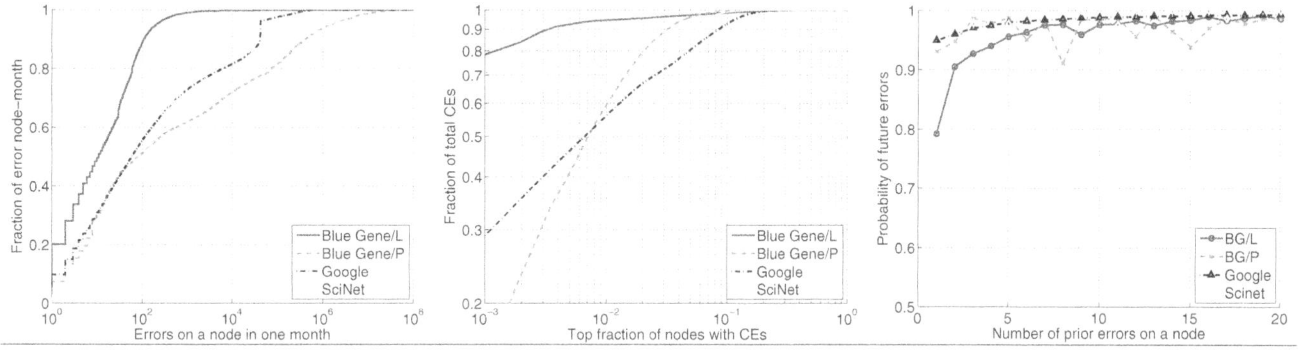

Figure 1. The left graph shows the CDF for the number of errors per month per machine. The middle graph shows the fraction y of all errors that is concentrated in the top x fraction of nodes with the most errors. The right graph shows the probability of a node developing future errors as a function of the number of prior errors.

commonly used types of DRAM. The DIMMs come from multiple manufacturers and models, with three different capacities (1GB, 2GB, 4GB), and cover the three most common DRAM technologies: Double Data Rate (DDR1), Double Data Rate 2 (DDR2) and Fully-Buffered (FBDIMM). We rely on error reports provided by the chipset. Those reports include accurate accounts of the total number of errors that occurred, but due to the limited number of registers available for storing addresses affected by errors only provides samples for the addresses of errors. For this reason, the number of repeat errors we observe and the probability of errors repeating are very conservative estimates, since there might be repeat errors that we missed because they were not sampled.

2.2 Methodology

A memory error only manifests itself upon an access to the affected location. As such, some systems employ a *memory scrubber* (a background processes that periodically scans through all of memory) to proactively detect errors before they are encountered by an application. However, except for some of the Google systems, all the systems we study rely solely on application-level memory accesses without the use of a scrubber.

Categorizing errors observed in the field as either hard or soft is difficult as it requires knowing their root cause. Obtaining a definite answer to the question of whether an observed error is hard and what type of hard error it is (e.g. a stuck bit or a bad column) would require some offline testing of the device in a lab or at least performing some active probing on the system, e.g. by running a memory test after each error occurrence to determine whether the error is repeatable. Instead we have to rely on observational data, which means we will have to make some assumptions in order to classify errors. Matters are complicated further by the fact that many hard errors start out as intermittent errors and only develop into permanent errors over time.

The key assumption that we rely on in our study is that repeat errors at the same location are likely due to hard errors since it would be statistically extremely unlikely that the same location would be hit twice within our measurement period by cosmic rays or other external sources of noise. We therefore view such repeat errors as likely being caused by hard errors. Note however that in practice, hard errors manifest themselves as intermittent rather than on every access to a particular memory location.

We consider different granularities for locations at which errors can repeat. We start by looking at repeats across nodes, but then mainly focus at locations identified by lower-levels in the hardware. Recall that a DIMM comprises multiple DRAM chips, and each DRAM chip is organized into multiple banks, typically 8 in today's systems. A bank consists of a number of two-dimensional arrays of DRAM cells. A DRAM cell is the most basic unit of storage, essentially a simple capacitor representing one bit. The two dimensions of an array are also referred to as rows and columns. We look at repeats of errors at the level of physical addresses, but also with respect to bank, rows and columns at the chip level.

3. Study of error characteristics

3.1 High-level characteristics

We begin with a summary of the high-level characteristics of memory errors at the node level. The right half of Table 1 summarizes the prevalence of memory errors in the four different systems. We observe that memory errors happen at a significant rate in all four systems with 2.5-5.5% of nodes affected per system. For each system, our data covers at least tens of millions of errors over a combined period of nearly 300 Terabyte years. In addition to correctable errors (CEs), we also observe a non-negligible rate of "non-trivial" errors, which required more than simple SEC-DED strategies for correction: 1.34% of the nodes in the BG/P system saw at least one error that required chipkill to correct it.

Figure 1 (left) and Figure 1 (middle) provide a more detailed view of how errors affect the nodes in a system. Figure 1 (left) shows the cumulative distribution function (CDF) of the number of errors per node for those nodes that experience at least one error. We see that only a minority (2-20%) of those nodes experience just a single error occurrence. The majority experiences a larger number of errors, with half of the nodes seeing more than 100 errors and the top 5% of nodes each seeing more than a million errors. Figure 1 (middle) illustrates how errors are distributed across the nodes within each system. The graph shows for each system the fraction of all errors in the system (X-axis) that is concentrated on just the y% of nodes in the system with the largest number of errors (Y-axis). In all cases we see a very skewed distribution with the top 5% of error nodes accounting for more than 95 % of all errors.

Figure 1 (left) and (middle) indicate that errors happen in a correlated fashion, rather than independently. This observation is validated in Figure 1 (right), which shows the probability of a node experiencing future errors as a function of the number of past errors. We see that even a single error on a node raises the probability of future errors to more than 80%, and after seeing just a handful of errors this probability increases to more than 95%.

The correlations we observe above provide strong evidence for hardware errors as a dominant error mechanisms, since one would not expect soft errors to be correlated in space or time. Our observations agree with similar findings reported in [11, 19]. However, the results in [11] were based on a small number of machines (12 machines with errors) and the analysis in [19] was limited to a relatively homogeneous set of systems; all machines in the study were located in Google's datacenters. Our results show that these trends generalize to other systems as well and add statistical significance.

In addition to error counts, the BG systems also record information on the mechanisms that were used to correct errors, which we can use as additional clues regarding the nature of errors. In particular, both BG/P and BG/L provide separate log messages that allow us to distinguish multi-bit errors, and BG/P also records information on chipkill errors (i.e. errors that required chipkill to correct them). We observe that a significant fraction of BG/P and BG/L nodes experiences multi-bit errors (22.08% and 2.07%, respectively) and that these errors account for 12.96% and 2.37% of all observed errors, respectively. The fraction of nodes with chipkill errors on BG/P only is smaller, with 1.34% of nodes affected, but still significant. Interestingly, while seen only on a small number of nodes, chipkill errors make up a large fraction of all observed errors: 17% of all errors observed on BG/P were not correctable with simple SEC-DED, and required the use of chipkill ECC to be corrected.

We summarize our main points in the following three observations which motivate us to take a closer look at hard errors and their patterns in the remainder of this paper.

Observation 1: There are strong correlations between errors in space and time. These correlations are highly unlikely if soft errors were the dominating error mode, pointing to hard errors as the leading cause of memory errors.

Observation 2: The significant frequency of multi-bit and chipkill errors is another pointer towards hard errors as an important error mode, as these types of errors are unlikely to arise from soft errors.

Observation 3: A significant number of nodes with correctable errors activated more advanced ECC mechanisms; 20%-45% activated redundant bit-steering, and 15% activated Chipkill.

3.2 Error patterns

In this section, we attempt to categorize all banks with errors in our datasets into known error patterns related to hardware defects: single (transient) events, bad cells, bad rows, bad columns, and a whole chip error. A definite answer to the question which category a device with an error falls into would require offline testing of the device in a lab setting. Instead we have to rely on observational data, which means we will have to make a few assumptions when classifying devices. We group all banks that have at least one error into one of the following categories:

repeat address: The bank has at least one error that repeats, i.e. there is at least one address on this bank that is reported twice.
repeat row: The bank has at least one row that has experienced errors at two different locations, i.e. two different addresses on the row.
repeat column: The bank has at least one column that has experienced errors at two different locations, i.e. two different addresses on the column.
corrupt row: The bank has at least one row that has experienced errors at two different addresses on the row and one of these is a repeat address.
corrupt column: The bank has at least one column that has experienced errors at two different addresses on the column and one of these is a repeat address.

Error mode	BG/L Banks	BG/P Banks	Google Banks
repeat address	80.9%	59.4%	58.7%
repeat address w/o row/cols	72.2%	30.0%	46.1%
repeat row	4.7%	31.8%	7.4%
repeat column	8.8%	22.7%	14.5%
corrupt row	3.0%	21.6%	4.2%
corrupt column	5.9%	14.4%	8.3%
whole chip	0.53%	3.20%	2.02%
single event	17.6%	29.2%	34.9%

Table 2. Frequency of different error patterns

single event: These are banks that have only single events, i.e. they have no repeat errors on any of their addresses, rows or columns.
whole chip: These are banks that have a large number of errors ($>$ 100 unique locations) distributed over more than 50 different rows and columns.

Table 2 groups each error bank in our dataset into one of the above categories and reports for each system the fraction of banks that falls into each of these categories. Note, that the repeat-address category overlaps with the corrupt row and corrupt column categories. We therefore created an additional entry that reports banks with repeat addresses that do not exhibit corrupt rows or columns.

We make a number of interesting observations. The vast majority (65-82%, depending on the system) of all banks experiences some form of error pattern that points towards hard errors, i.e. an error pattern other than single events. This observation agrees with the findings in [11], however the conclusions on the frequency of different patterns in [11] are limited due to their small dataset (12 machines with errors). We find that among all error patterns the single most common one are repeat addresses. Consistently for all systems, more than 50% of all banks with errors are classified as repeat addresses. For all systems, corrupt rows and corrupt columns happen at a significant rate. We note that each system has a clear tendency to develop one type over the other, where the more common type is approximately twice as often observed as the other one. For example, in the case of BG/L and Google, corrupt columns are twice as likely as corrupt rows, while for BG/P it is the other way around. This is likely due to the fact that there are twice as many rows in BG/P banks than in BG/L banks.

Note that the above numbers on hard error patterns are conservative, and in practice likely higher. Since our observation period for each of the systems is limited and we depend on accesses to memory cells to detect errors, many of the non-repeat errors in our study might eventually have turned out to be repeat errors, but the repeat did not fall into our measurement period. We observe for example that for the systems with shorter observation time (BG/L and Google), the fraction of banks with only repeat addresses, but no bad rows/columns, is higher than in the BG/P system whose data spans a longer observation period. Most likely, the longer observation time increased the chances that a repeat error will manifest and move a repeat row/column to the corrupt row/column category. That indicates that a large fraction of errors we categorize conservatively as repeat rows/columns might actually be true broken rows/columns.

Observation 4: The error patterns on the majority of the banks (more than two thirds) in our study can clearly be attributed to patterns linked to hard errors. Among those patterns the most common one is a repeat address, although row and column patterns do also happen at a significant rate.

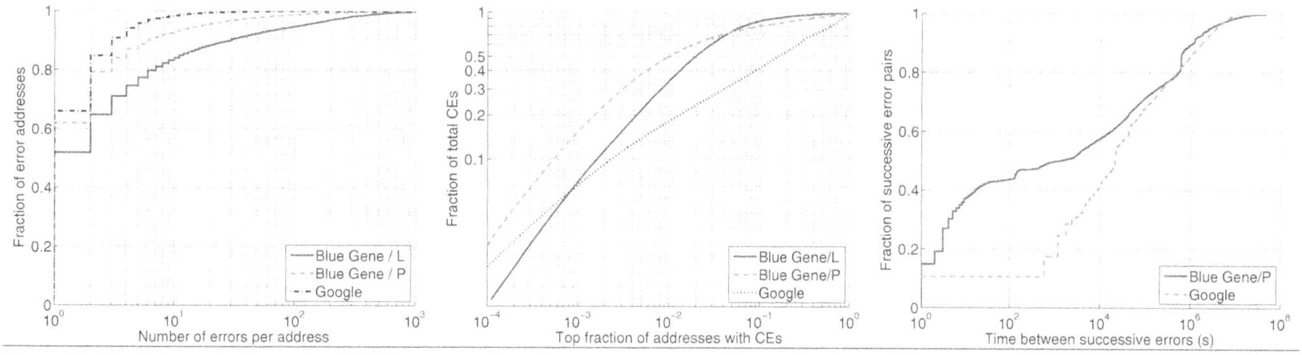

Figure 2. The left graph shows the CDF for the number of repeat errors per address (for those addresses with at least on repeat). The middle graph shows the fraction y of all errors that is concentrated in the top x fraction of addresses with the most errors. The right graph shows the CDF of the time between successive errors on an address.

3.3 Repeat errors on addresses

The previous section identified repeat addresses as the dominant error pattern, but did not provide any details on their characteristics. The only prior work that hints at repeat addresses as a common error pattern in the field is based on a data set (a dozen machines with errors) that is too small for a detailed study of repeat error characteristics [11]. We therefore study this question in more detail in this subsection.

	BG/L	BG/P	Google
# of error samples	201,206	308,170	1,091,777
# of unique addresses	9,076	44,624	556,161
% unique	4.5	14.5	50.9
% of addresses with repeats	48.2	30.6	32.6
Avg. # of errors / address	44.9	20.3	4.0

Table 3. Statistics on repeat addresses

We begin by providing some statistics on the frequency of repeat errors on addresses in Table 3 above. We observe that a high fraction of addresses with errors experience later repeat errors on the same address: a third (for Google) to nearly a half (for BG/L). The average number of repeat errors per address ranges from 4 for Google to as many as 44 for BG/L. For a more detailed view, Figure 2 (left) shows the cumulative distribution function (CDF) for the number of repeats per address. Most addresses with repeats (50-60%) see only a single repeat and another 20% see only two repeats. However, the distribution is very skewed with a long tail, where a small fraction of addresses at the end of the tail experiences a huge number of repeats. Figure 2 (middle) illustrates the skew in the distribution by plotting the fraction of errors that is made up by the top x% of addresses with the highest error count. It shows that 10% of all addresses with errors account for more than 90% of all observed errors.

When trying to protect against repeat errors it is useful to understand the temporal characteristics of errors. For example, a system using page retirement for pages with hard errors might want to wait before retiring a page that experiences an error until a repeat error occurs, providing some confidence that the problem is indeed due to a hard error. An interesting question is therefore how long it will take before a repeat error happens and an error can confidently be classified as hard. To help answer this question, Figure 2 (right) plots the CDF of the time between repeat errors on the same address. The graph shows that, if there is a repeat error it typically happens shortly after the first error occurrence. In BG/P more than half of repeats happen within less than a couple of minutes after the first occurrence. The timing information in the Google data is at a much coarser granularity (recall Section 2) and due to sampling we might not see all repeats, which leads to generally longer times until a repeat error shows up. However, we can conclude that more than half of the repeats happen within less than 6 hours. Interestingly, for larger timescales, e.g. on the order of days, where the timing granularity of the Google data should have less of an effect the trends for both systems start to look very similar. In both systems, 90% of all repeat errors are detected within less than 2 weeks.

When interpreting data regarding repeat of errors, it is important to recall that repeat errors (or any errors) are not detected until either the application or a hardware scrubber accesses the affected cell. For the Blue Gene systems, we know that hardware scrubbers are implemented as a feature, but we were not able to determine whether this feature was actually enabled in our systems under study. On the other hand, for the Google machines we know that a subset of them does employ a hardware scrubber that periodically in the background reads through main memory to check for errors. This scrubber reads memory at a rate of 1GB per hour, which means that each memory cell should be touched at least once every day.

To determine how much earlier repeat errors could be detected if a memory scrubber is used we compared the time until a repeat error is detected for those systems with and without the hardware scrubber separately. Interestingly, we find that the use of a scrubber does not significantly reduce the time until a repeat error is detected. Even in the tail of the distribution, where it takes a relatively long time (e.g. several days or more) to identify a repeat error, there is not much difference between systems with and without a scrubber. One possible explanation is that repeat errors might not always be due to stuck bits, where a cell is permanently stuck at a particular value. Instead, they might be due to weaknesses in the hardware that get exposed only under certain access patterns.

The three points below summarize our main observations.

Observation 5: A large fraction of addresses with errors (30-50%) experience a later repeat error on the same address. This points to hard errors as a dominant error mode.

Observation 6: If an address experiences multiple errors (indicating a hard error), then 90% of all repeat errors show up within less than 2 weeks after the first error.

Observation 7: The use of a background scrubber does not significantly shorten the amount of time until a repeat error is detected. This indicates that a significant fraction of errors are intermittent and only manifest themselves under certain access patterns.

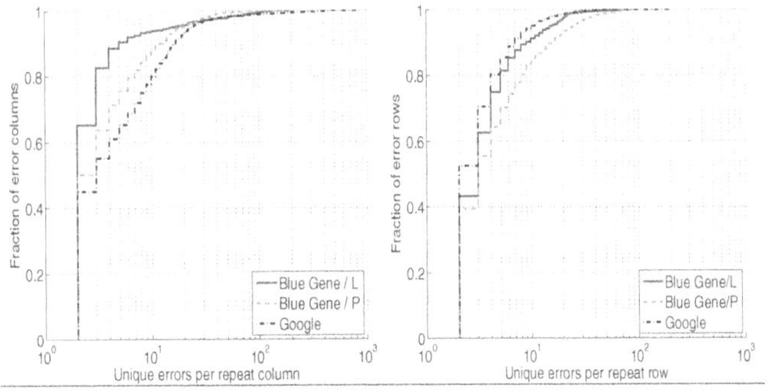

Figure 3. Number of errors per repeat row/column

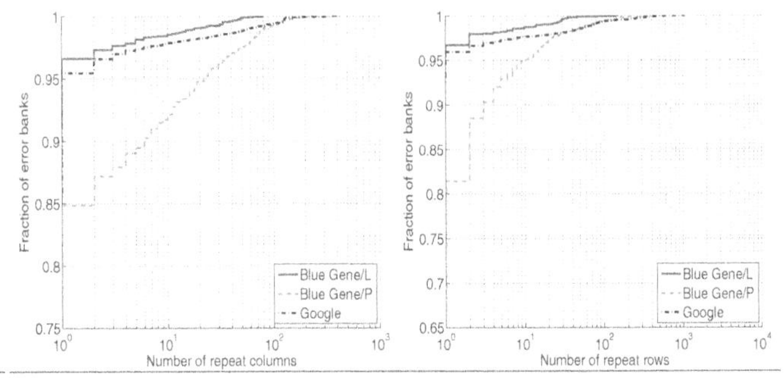

Figure 4. Number of repeat rows/columns per bank

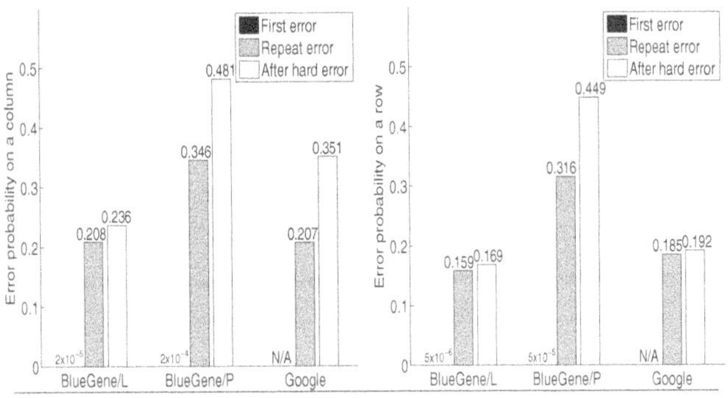

Figure 5. The two graphs show the probability that a column (left graph) and a row (right graph) will have an additional error after having one error (middle bar of each group of bars) and the probability that it will have an additional unique error (right bar of each group of bars), i.e. an additional error at an address different from the first.

3.4 Repeat errors within a row/column

Memory errors that are due to hardware problems don't only manifest themselves in the form of repeat errors on the same cell. Section 3.2 pointed to repeating errors on different locations within the same row or the same column as another common error mode (recall Table 2). This subsection takes a closer look at the characteristics of repeat rows and repeat columns.

We begin by looking at the probability that an error at an individual address will develop into a row or column error. Understanding those probabilities might help predict impending row/column errors, allowing a system to take proactive measures. The three groups of bars in Figure 5 (left) summarize our results for columns and Figure 5 (right) shows the corresponding results for rows. The gray center bar in each group of bars shows the probability that after an error occurs on an address another error will later develop at a different address along the same column (Figure 5 left) and row (Figure 5 right), respectively (turning the error from a single event error into a repeat column/row). We observe that in all three cases these probabilities are significant for all systems, with probabilities in the 15% to 30% range.

To put the above repeat probabilities in perspective, we compare them with the unconditional probability of a random bank/row/column developing an error, shown in the black (left-most) bar (the bar is barely visible due to its small magnitude). We see that the unconditional probabilities are orders of magnitude smaller.

We also study the probability that a repeat error on an address (rather than a single event error) will turn into a row/column error, i.e. the probability that after a repeat error on an address another address along the same row/column experiences an error. Those probabilities are shown in the white right-most bar in each group of bars in Figure 5. In all systems, the presence of a repeat address on a row/column further increases the probability of future errors on this bar/column. In some cases this increase is quite large. For example, for BlueGene/P after observing a repeat error on an address the probability of observing an additional error on another location on the same row/column increases to more than 40%. Again, recall that BG/P is the system with the longest observation period among our datasets, so the probabilities of repeat errors developing into row/column errors effect might be equally strong in the other systems and we might just not observe it due to the shorter timespan of the data.

While we have provided information on the probabilities of rows/columns developing multiple errors, another question is how many errors repeat rows and columns typically experience. Figure 3 (left) and (right) provide the CDF for the number of unique locations per row/column that experience errors. We see that most rows/columns with multiple errors (40-60%) don't develop more errors beyond the initial 2 errors. However, the top 10-20% of rows/columns develop errors on dozens of unique locations.

Section 3.2 showed that a significant number of error banks exhibit row/column errors, but does not quantify the number of repeat rows/columns. We find that the most common case are banks with only a single repeat row/column. Depending on the system, 80-95% of all banks with repeat rows/columns have only a single one (see Figure 4). Around 3-8% of banks develop more than 10 repeat columns and 2-5% develop more than 10 repeat rows.

Interestingly, we observe that a significant number of all banks (3.4%, 17.4%, and 4.4%, for BG/L, BG/P and Google, respectively) experience both repeat rows and repeat columns. To better understand the relationship between the number of repeat rows and columns on a bank, the scatter plot in Figure 6 shows for banks with at least one repeat row or column the number of repeat rows and columns. The marker at coordinates (x,y) reflects the fraction of banks that have x repeat columns and y repeat rows. The size of the marker in the scatter plot indicates the fraction of error banks that fall into each of the categories and is chosen to be proportional to the logarithm of the probabilities. For all three systems we observe that banks that have a larger number of repeat rows tend to also have a larger number of repeat columns, and vice versa.

Below we summarize the main observations regarding repeat rows and columns.

Observation 8: The probability of seeing an error on an address on a particular row or column increases by orders of magnitude once we have seen an error on another location on the same row or column. 15-30% of errors turn into repeat rows/columns, and up to 40% of repeat errors turn into repeat rows/columns.

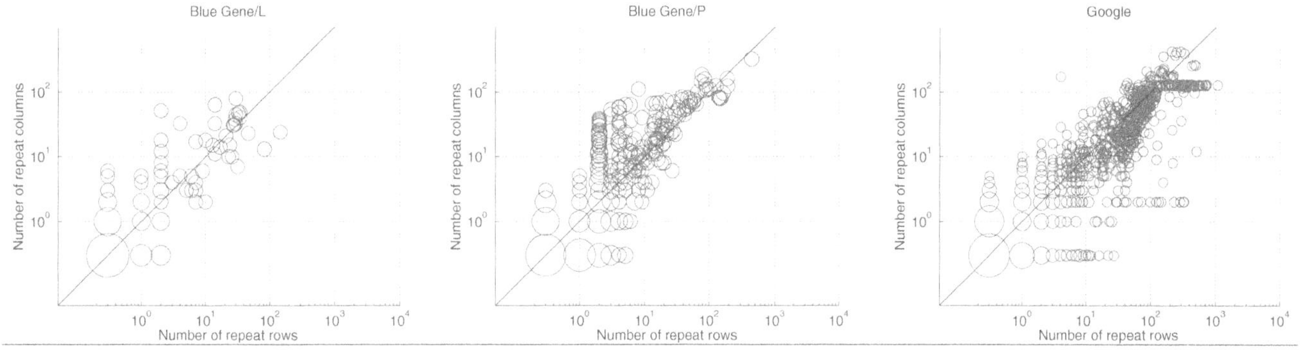

Figure 6. The distribution of the number of repeat rows and repeat columns per bank

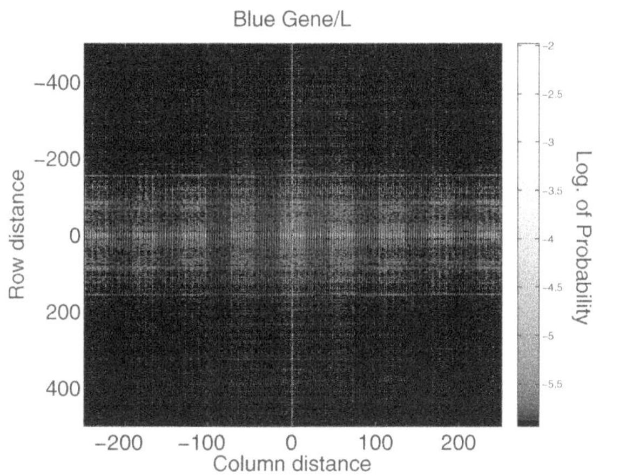

Figure 7. A visualization of correlations between errors as a function of their distances in row/column space

Observation 9: Among error banks that have both repeat rows and repeat columns, those banks that have a large number of repeat rows often also have a large number of repeat columns, and vice versa.

3.5 Correlations across rows/columns

While the previous subsection demonstrated that an error on a row or column increases the probability of follow-up errors on the same row/column, it does not tell us anything about correlations between nearby rows/columns, e.g. do multiple errors on a row make it more likely that also some nearby rows will have errors. In this subsection we answer the more general question of how the error probabilities between cells are correlated depending on the physical distance in row and column space between those cells.

The heatmap in Figure 7 is an attempt to visualize those correlations. The pixel at the center of the plot at coordinates (0,0) represents a cell with an error. The pixel at coordinates (x,y) represents the probability that the cell that is x columns and y rows away from the original error cell (i.e. at row/column coordinates (a+x, b+y) where (a,b) are the row/column coordinates of the original error) has an error as well. Lighter colors represent higher probabilities.

Not surprisingly, we observe that cells along the same row or column as the original error cell have increased error probabilities, as indicated by the bright vertical and horizontal line crossing through (0,0). This agrees with our previous observations that errors have a high probability of turning into repeat rows/columns. But we also observe that the error probabilities are increased within a wide band of neighboring rows and columns. For example, a closer study of the error probabilities as a function of row/column distance shows that rows and columns that are within a distance of 10 of the original error have an error probability of 2-5%. While this probability is clearly smaller than that of developing errors on the same row/column, it is significantly larger than that of an average row/column. We also find that the error probabilities show a roughly exponential drop-off as a function of the row/column distance, and that the probabilities are still significantly increased within a range of up to 50-100 rows/columns, compared to an average row/column.

Our study of error probabilities as a function of distance from another error also shows evidence for other patterns, beyond just proximity. In particular, we observe for some systems that cells whose column or row distance from the original error is a multiple of certain powers of two have increased likelihood of errors. Evidence for these regular patterns show up in the heatmap in the form of a grid-like background pattern. By studying the CDF of the pairwise distances between errors, we find for example that for all systems (BG/P, BG/L, Google), cells with distances in row space that are multiples of 4 have noticeably increased error probabilities. Some systems also exhibit other patterns. For example, BG/P also shows clearly increased probabilities at row distances that are multiples of 128.

Observation 10: Errors do not only tend to cluster along the same row or column. The probability of errors is also significantly increased along all cells in the band of nearby rows and columns.

3.6 Error density in different areas of a chip

In this subsection we look at the correlation between errors and their physical location on a chip, i.e. we are asking the question of whether some areas of a chip are more likely than others to experience errors. As before, we use bank, row and column information to distinguish different locations on a chip. We first divide the row/column space of each bank into equal sized square areas of 128x128 rows/columns, i.e. chunks of size 16KB. We then determine for each of these square areas the probability of observing an error in this area, i.e. the fraction of all unique banks in the system (across all nodes) that have at least one error in this area. Figure 8 shows a graphical representation of the results. For this analysis, we report results separately for BG/P and BG/L and for the four different hardware platforms that the Google data covers. Each graph represents the row/column space for one of the systems, each divided into the 128x128 sized squares as described above. Each square is colored according to the observed probability of errors in this area, where darker colors correspond to higher probabilities.

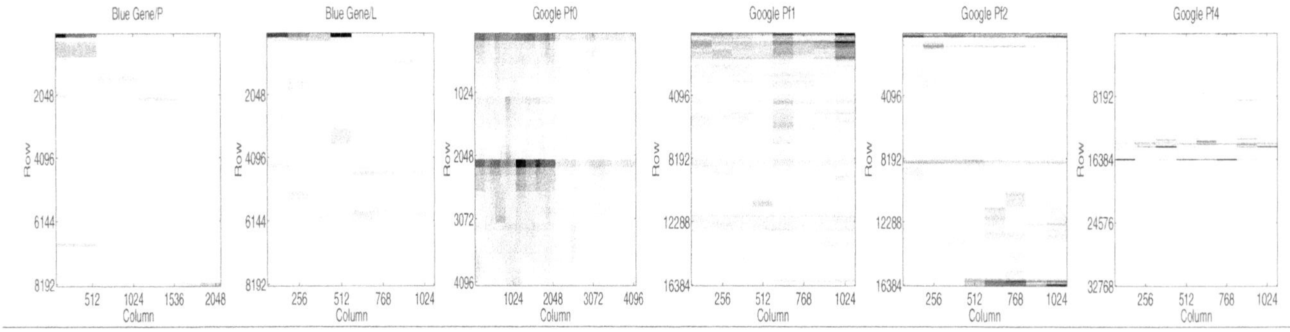

Figure 8. The error probabilities for different areas in the row/column space of a bank.

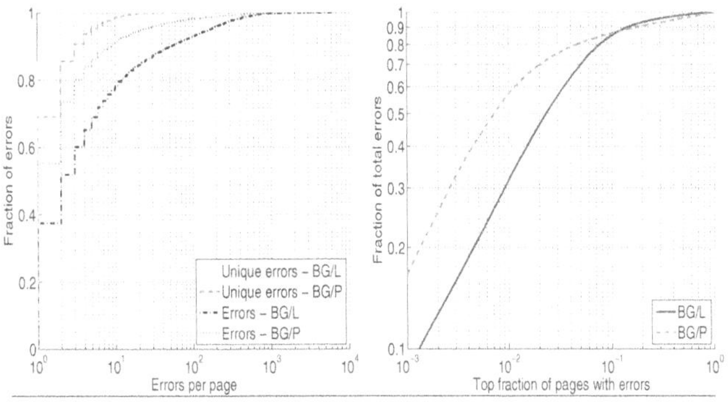

Figure 9. Error distribution over pages.

Figure 8 shows several interesting trends that are consistent across systems. Focusing on the dark areas in each graph, which present concentrations of errors, we first see that for all systems consistently the top left area shows increased error density. This area tends to span at least the first 512 columns and the first 512 rows. For several of the systems, a whole band along the very top of the row space, across all columns, shows increased error rates. For two of the six systems we observe similar concentrations of errors at the end of the row/column space, i.e. in the bottom right of the graphs at the highest numbered rows and columns. Secondly, we find that for three of the systems the entire rows in the center of the row space exhibit increased error probabilities.

Observation 11: Not all areas on a chip are equally likely to be affected by errors. In particular, the top and the bottom of the row/column space on a bank seem to be more likely to experience errors. Additionally, the upper-left corner corresponds to memory used by the OS, which may play a role in the increased error probabilities.

3.7 Hard errors from the OS's point of view

Throughout this section we have observed different ways in which DRAM errors tend to cluster in space. We have seen that errors tend to repeat on the same address, along the addresses of a row/column and on certain areas of a chip. All these measures for spatial clustering were very hardware oriented. In order to explore protection mechanisms at the OS level, an important question is how the clustering of errors translates to the operating system level. For example, retiring pages with errors would work most efficiently and effectively if most of the errors tended to cluster on a small number of pages. Unfortunately, error clusters at the hardware level do not directly translate to clusters on pages. For example, errors along the same row or column do not necessarily lie on the same page.

To shed some light on how errors are distributed across pages, Figure 9 (left) shows the CDF for the number of errors per page and the number of unique locations with errors per page for those systems for which the information is available (BG/L and BG/P). The number of unique locations with errors per page is low (on average 1.4 and 1.8 for BG/L and BG/P, respectively) and around 90% of all pages have only a single one. However the total number of errors observed per page is still quite large, most likely due to repeat addresses. More than 60% of the pages experience more than one error, and the average number of errors per page is 31 and 12, for BG/L and BG/P respectively. More importantly, the distribution of errors across pages is very skewed, maybe not surprisingly given the frequency of repeat addresses that we observed earlier. Figure 9 (right) shows the fraction of all errors that is contributed by the fraction of the top x% of pages with the most errors. 1% of all pages with errors account for 30-60% of all errors, depending on the system, and the top 10% of all pages with errors account for more than 90% of all errors for both BG/L and BG/P. This skew in the number of errors page is good news for techniques relying on page retirement, as it means that by retiring a small fraction of pages a large number of errors can be prevented.

Observation 12: More than 60% of pages that experience an error, experience at least on follow-up error. The distribution of the number of errors per page is highly skewed, with some pages accounting for a large fraction of errors.

Observation 13: An operating system that could identify and retire those pages that are likely to develop a large number of errors, would avoid a large fraction of errors (90%) by retiring only a small fraction (10%) of pages with errors.

This observation motivates us to study the possible effectiveness of different page retirement policies in Section 4.

3.8 Hard errors and multi-bit / chipkill errors

From a systems point of view the most worrisome type of errors are multi-bit and chipkill errors, as these are the errors that in the absence of sufficiently powerful hardware ECC turn into uncorrectable errors leading to a machine crash (or if undetected to the use of corrupted data). Given the correlations we observed between errors in the previous subsections, an interesting question is whether it is possible to predict an increased likelihood of future multi-bit or chipkill errors based on the previous error behavior in the system. In particular, one might speculate that prior repeat errors, which likely indicate hard errors, will increase the probability of later multi-bit or chipkill errors. Knowledge about the increased likelihood of future multi-bit or chipkill errors could be used by an adaptive system to take proactive measures to protect against errors.

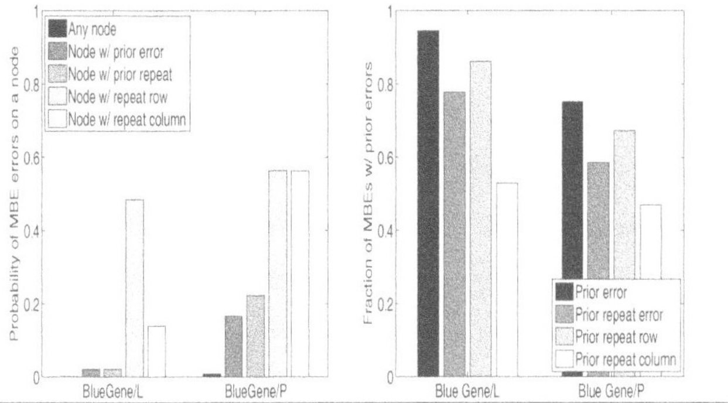

Figure 10. The relationship between multi-bit errors and prior errors.

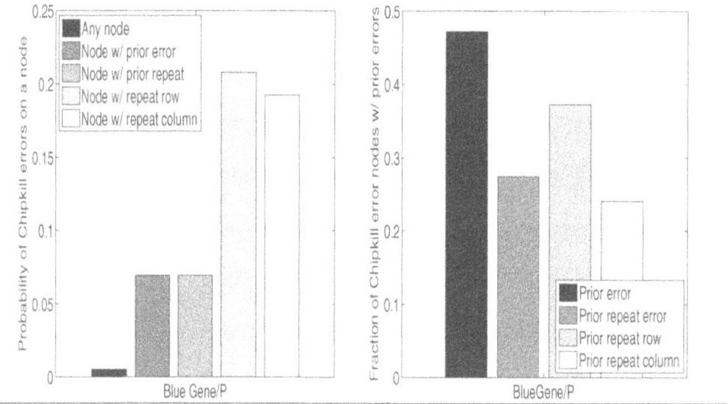

Figure 11. The relationship between chipkill errors and prior errors.

To shed some light on this question, we plot in Figure 10 (left) the probability that a node develops a multi-bit error after seeing previous errors of different types for BG/L and BG/P. More precisely, each set of 5 bars in the graph shows the following 5 probabilities: The first bar in each group of five bars represents the baseline probability of a random node seeing a multi-bit error. (Note, that this probability is so small that it is barely visible in the graph.) The second bar represents the probability that a node that has seen a prior error (of any type) will later experience a multi-bit error. The other three bars show the probability that a node will experience a later multi-bit error after experiencing a repeat address, a repeat row or a repeat column, respectively. The figure clearly indicates that for both systems the probability of a multi-bit error increases, after seeing previous errors. It also shows that the probability increases dramatically if a previous error was a repeat error.

Figure 10 (left) tells us only that the probability of multi-bit errors increases after other errors have been observed. It does not tell us whether most multi-bit errors were in fact preceded by prior errors (which a system could use as an early warning sign of impending multi-bit errors). In order to look at this side of the story, Figure 10 (right) plots the fraction of multi-bit errors that were preceded be the four types of errors we considered previously (any error, repeat address, repeat row, repeat column). The graph shows that multi-bit errors don't happen without prior warning: 60-80% of multi-bit errors were preceded by repeat addresses, 70-85% of multi-bit errors were preceded by a repeat row and 40-50% of multi-bit errors were preceded by a repeat column.

Figure 11 repeats the same analysis for chipkill errors, rather than multi-bit errors (for BG/P only, as chipkill errors do not apply to BG/L). While the overall probabilities are smaller (due to the lower rate of chipkill errors), we observe the same trends. Prior errors greatly increase the probability of a later chipkill error. Among nodes with prior error the probability increases to 7%. If there is a repeat row or repeat column present in the system, the likelihood of a later chipkill error increases to around 20%.

Observation 14: The incidence of errors in the system, in particular repeat errors, increases the likelihood of later multi-bit and chipkill errors by more than an order of magnitude. A large fraction (more than half) of multi-bit and chipkill errors are preceded by early warning signs in the form of repeat errors.

4. Implications for system design

An underlying theme throughout the previous section has been the study of hard errors as the dominating error mode among DRAM errors in the field. Compared to soft errors, hard errors have a greater potential to increase error rates, due to their repetitive nature, and to increase the chance of future uncorrectable errors. On the positive side, the repeating nature of hard errors makes them also more predictable than soft errors creating a potential for taking proactive measures against them. In this section, we discuss various implications on resilient system that follow from the insights derived from our measurement study.

4.1 Page retirement

While error protection at the hardware level in the form of ECC is effective, it is not always the most desirable option. In addition to the cost factor, another concern, in particular for the more powerful ECC codes, is the increase in energy consumption and the possible impact on performance.

As an alternative or extra level of protection in addition to the use of ECC DIMMs, one could consider the retirement of pages that have experienced previous (hard) errors. Page retirement can be accomplished by having the OS isolate pages containing errors and prevent them from being allocated in the future. While this technique is not widely used in today's data centers, some operating systems, such as Solaris [3, 20], offer build-in support for page retirement. For the standard Linux kernel there exists a patch that allows one to retire bad pages [17]. However, there is no rigorous study on the possible effectiveness of page retirement for realistic error patterns and there is no published work comparing different policies for deciding on when to retire a page.

The main trade-off in retiring pages is the amount of memory lost due to retired pages versus the number of future errors prevented. An ideal retirement policy detects as early as possible pages that are likely to develop a large number of errors in the future and retires only those pages. We have observed several indicators that lend themselves well for such predictions. Below are a few simple policies that were directly derived from the findings in Section 3.

repeat-on-address: Once an address experiences a repeat error the corresponding page is retired.

1-error-on-page: Since a large fraction of addresses with errors experiences a repeat, this policy pessimistically assumes after the first occurrence of an error on a page that it will turn into a hard error and retire the page.

2-errors-on-page: This policy retires a page once two errors have been observed on this page (either on the same address or on two different addresses on the page).

repeat-on-row: Since a row with 2 unique addresses has high chances of developing additional errors, this policy retires all the pages on a row after two errors have been observed.

repeat-on-column: Equivalent to repeat-on-row, but for columns.

We simulate all of the above policies on our trace data for BG/L and BG/P and report the results in Table 4. For each policy

		All nodes with errors					Nodes w/ multi-bit/ chipkill error	
System	Policy	Pages retired	95%ile pages retired	Errors avoided (%)	MBEs avoided (%)	Chipkill avoided (%)	Pages retired	95%ile pages retired
BG/L	repeat on address	2.2	2	94.2	88.1	N/A	15.8	103.25
	any 1 error on page	3.8	4	96.8	96.7	N/A	42.4	319
	any 2 errors on page	2.4	3	94.9	94.8	N/A	24.6	123.8
	repeat on row	33.9	32	95.6	97.3	N/A	245.5	1620
	repeat on column	14,336	16,384	96.5	90.6	N/A	257,930	1,212,416
BG/P	repeat on address	4.8	18	86.3	86.4	61.8	4.8	18
	any 1 error on page	17.6	62.7	91.4	91.5	71.0	17.7	62.7
	any 2 errors on page	6.9	25.6	88.1	88.1	64.7	6.9	25.6
	repeat on row	158.0	576	92.6	92.7	77.0	158	576
	repeat on column	49,989	266,650	91.9	92	67.3	49,972	266,650

Table 4. Effectiveness of page retirement

we include the average number of pages it retires per machine with errors, the 95th percentile of the number of pages retired per machine, the percentage of all errors in the system that would have been prevented by this policy (because they fall on previously retired pages) and the percentage of all multi-bit and chipkill errors that could have been prevented.

We find that even the simple policies we are considering are quite effective at reducing the number of errors a system would observe: All policies are able to prevent nearly 90% of all errors. The most aggressive policies (retiring a page immediately after just one error, or retiring whole rows and columns) are able to avoid up to 96% of all errors. The main difference between policies lies in the cost involved in achieving this performance. The number of pages retired per machine averages at only 2.2 - 4.8 for the repeat-on-address policy, which is a small price to pay for a large gain in the number of avoided errors. For policies that retire entire rows or columns this number can grow into hundreds or thousands of pages retired per machine. Retiring entire columns is particularly expensive, due to the large number of pages that a column spans, and is prohibitive, at least in the form of the very simple policies that we have experimented with.

Another interesting finding from our simulation study is the effectiveness of page retirements in avoiding multi-bit and chipkill errors. All policies are able to avoid around two thirds of all chipkill errors and nearly 90% of all multi-bit errors. While a system with chipkill ECC would have been able to mask all of these errors, the high reduction of errors under page retirement is still interesting as it does not come with an increase in hardware cost or energy consumption. The only price to pay is the reduced amount of memory available, due to retired pages.

While the average number of pages retired per machine averaged across all machines with errors is low when the right policy is chosen, this number might be higher for machines that experience multi-bit or chipkill errors (or more precisely would have experienced multi-bit or chipkill errors in the absence of page retirement). We therefore also computed the statistics for the number of pages retired per machine for only those machines in our dataset that experienced multi-bit and chipkill errors and report the results in the right half of the above table. We find that both the average number of pages retired and the 95th percentile of the number of pages retired is still very small, compared to the total amount of memory in modern server systems. For example, under the repeat-on-address policy 5-16 pages are retired for an average machine with errors. A machines in the 95th percentile of number of retires pages, still sacrifices only 18-104 pages, i.e. less than half a MByte of total DRAM space. Even the for the more aggressive 1-error-on-a-page policy the number of retired pages is still in the same order of magnitude. More elaborate techniques based on statistical modeling or machine learning might be able to further improve on the cost-efficiency trade-off of page retirement policies.

4.2 Selective error protection

Several of our findings indicate that errors are not uniformly distributed in space. For example, we saw evidence that some parts of a chip and of the physical address space experience higher error rates than others. This implies that selective error protection mechanisms might be an interesting avenue for future work. For example, approaches along the lines of the recent work on virtualized and flexible ECC [24] might provide effective solutions that exploit the differences in error rates in different parts of the system.

4.3 Proactive error detection and monitoring

The two previous subsections provide examples for techniques that operating systems can use to exploit the characteristics of hard errors in order to reduce the negative impact of DRAM errors on system availability. However, such techniques require that the operating system has full knowledge of all errors happening at the underlying hardware level, including error counts, as well as more detailed information, such as the addresses that were affected. ECC protection used in most server systems masks the presence of errors and it is typically not trivial to obtain location information on errors. Our findings about the nature of DRAM errors provide strong encouragement to improve error tracking and reporting to the operating systems.

The second factor limiting the amount of knowledge about the underlying error process stems from the fact that DRAM errors are latent, i.e. they will not be detected until the affected cell is accessed. The chances that an error will eventually lead to an uncorrectable error, causing system downtime, increases the longer it is left latent. While hardware scrubbers provide an attempt to proactively detect errors and hence reduce this time, we observed in Section 3.3 that their effectiveness might be limited. We speculate that this is likely due to the passive monitoring approach that they are taking, rather than actively attempting to expose errors. Given the large amount of idle time that typical servers in data centers experience [2], it might be worthwhile to invest a small fraction of this idle time to periodically run a memory test, similar in functionality to memtest86, that actively probes the DRAM for memory errors. Memory tests have a much higher potential for detecting hard errors than a scrubber, since they can create access patterns that stress the memory, and because they actively write to memory cells, rather than just checking the validity of currently written values. Such tests could either be done periodically on all machines, or they could be used selectively in cases where there is a suspected hard error, e.g. after observing an earlier error in the system (that has not yet repeated).

4.4 Effectiveness of hardware mechanisms

While this was not the original focus of our study, our analysis lets us also draw conclusions about the practical value of hardware mechanisms, such as chipkill ECC, in reducing the rate of machine crashes due to uncorrectable errors. In the presence of only soft errors, the occurrence of error patterns requiring chipkill ECC would be extremely unlikely. Our observation that a large number of errors observed in the field is likely due to hard errors provides firmer grounding for using these techniques in practice, despite their added cost and energy overheads.

Only one earlier study [19] that is based on large-scale field data comments on the effectiveness of chipkill, however they only observe that in their systems under study hardware platforms with chipkill show lower rates of uncorrectable errors than hardware platforms without chipkill. They are not able to quantify how much of this difference in error rates is due to the use of chipkill versus other hardware differences between the platforms.

Our fine-grained data allowed us to quantify exactly the number of errors that required chipkill to be corrected and that would have led to a machine crash in the absence of chipkill. We find that a significant fraction of machines experienced chipkill errors, i.e. errors whose correction was only possible with the use of chipkill techniques. In fact, among the errors in our study, a large fraction (17%) of them required the use of chipkill for correction providing some tangible benefits of the use of chipkill. We can therefore conclude that for systems with stringent availability requirements the reduction in machine crashes due to uncorrectable errors might make chipkill well worth the price.

4.5 System evaluation

Any evaluation of the impact of DRAM errors on system reliability or the effectiveness of mechanisms protecting against them relies on realistic assumptions about the characteristics of the underlying error process. In the absence of field data (or realistic models built based on field data), both analytical and experimental work typically rely on very simplistic assumptions about errors. For example, analytical models often assume that errors follow a Markov process and experimental work often relies on injecting errors at uniformly randomly generated locations. Given the high occurrence rate of hard errors, these simple approaches are likely to give misleading results (or results that represent only the less relevant scenario of a system experiencing only soft errors), as they do not capture any of the correlations and patterns present in hard errors.

While we are hoping that the findings we report here will help researchers and practitioners to base their work on more realistic assumptions on DRAM errors, we believe that more work in this direction is necessary. Towards this end, we are currently working on developing statistical models capturing the various properties of DRAM error process that can be used to generate realistic patterns in simulation or for error injection. More importantly, it seems that the current lack of publicly available field data that researchers can use to drive their experiments is a major roadblock. Li et al. have graciously made the data collected for their study on DRAM errors [11] publicly available. While we were unfortunately not able to obtain permission to share the Google data used in this study, we are currently preparing a public database of all error patterns that we have extracted from the data for the Blue Gene systems. This database and the raw logs for the Blue Gene systems will be made publicly available as part of the Usenix Failure Data Repository [23].

5. Conclusions

While a large body of work has been dedicated to studying the characteristics of DRAM errors and how to best protect against them, the large majority of this work has focused on soft errors in DRAM. Our work presents the first study based on data from a large number of production systems that shows that a large fraction of errors observed in the field can be traced back to hard errors. For all systems we studied, more than a third of all memory banks that experienced errors show signs of hard errors, most commonly in the form of repeating errors on the same physical address within less than 2 weeks. Repeating errors on the same row/column are also common error modes. For some systems, as many as 95% of all observed errors can be attributed to hard errors. We also provide a detailed study of the statistical characteristics of hard errors. Some of these provide direct insights useful for protecting against errors. For example, we observe that not all areas in memory are equally likely to be affected by errors; specific regions such as low rows/columns have higher error probabilities. We speculate that this might be due to different usage patterns in different memory areas, as we observe for example that those areas used by the OS tend to see larger error counts. Furthermore, from the perspective of the OS, a large fraction of the errors observed in a system is usually concentrated on a small set of pages providing some motivation for proactively retiring pages after they experience errors. We also observed that errors that have the highest potential to be uncorrectable, such as multi-bit errors and errors that require chipkill for correction, are usually preceded by more benign early warning signs, such as repeating errors on individual addresses, rows or columns. Finally, we observe that a significant number of errors is complex enough to require more than simple SEC-DED error correction to be corrected. A significant number of nodes with correctable errors in our study activated more advanced ECC mechanisms (20%-45% activated redundant bit-steering, and 15% activated Chipkill) and a large fraction (17%) of all errors required the use of chipkill for error correction.

As a second contribution, we identify various implications on resilient system design that follow from the insights derived from our measurement study. One of our findings is that simple page retirement policies can potentially mask a large number of errors with only a small sacrifice in the amount of available DRAM. For example, a simple policy that retires a page after the first repeat error on an address on this page can mask up to 95% of all errors and up to 60% of errors that would require chipkill for correction, while giving up only a few dozen pages of main memory. This is an interesting finding, since based on discussions with administrators of large datacenters, the use of page retirement is not widely spread in practice, although it has been implemented in some systems in the past [3]. On the other hand, we find that a commonly used technique for proactively detecting memory errors, the use of background memory scrubbers, might not be as effective as one might think. We hypothesize that this is because a large fraction of errors are intermittent, i.e. they manifest only under certain access patterns. This observation, together with the observed high frequency of hard (and hence repeatable) errors, might make it worthwhile to use the idle time that most servers in datacenters experience to periodically run a memory test to actively probe for errors, in particular after observing prior errors on a node. Finally, the fact that different areas of memory experience different error rates and that usage likely plays a role in error frequencies suggests an interesting avenue for future work might be selective error protection mechanisms, where different protection mechanisms are used for different areas of memory.

Acknowledgments

We would like to thank Thomas Gooding, Mark Megerian, and Rob Wisniewski from IBM for helping us acquire very detailed information about the BlueGene systems. We would also like to thank Pete Beckman, Rinku Gupta, Rob Ross and everybody else at Argonne National Laboratory who was involved in collecting and making available the BG/P data and helped us interpret the data. The third author thanks Google for hosting her as a visiting faculty during the summer of 2009, where part of this work started. In particular, she would like to thank John Hawley, Xin Li, Eduardo Pinheiro, Nick Sanders, and Wolf-Dietrich Weber for their help in accessing the data and answering questions about the data and systems at Google. We thank Adam Oliner, Jon Stearley and Sandia National Laboratories for making the BG/L data available. Finally, we would like to thank the members of SciNet, in partiular Chris Loken and Ching-Hsing Yu, for providing us with the data from their GPC system. This work has been funded by an NSERC discovery grant.

References

[1] Soft errors in electronic memory – a white paper. *Tezzaron Semiconductor*. URL `http://tezzaron.com/about/papes/soft_errors_1_1_secture.pdf`.

[2] L. A. Barroso and U. Hölzle. The case for energy-proportional computing. *IEEE Computer*, 40(12), 2007.

[3] T. M. Chalfant. Solaris operating system availability features. In *SunBluePrints Online*, 2004.

[4] T. J. Dell. A white paper on the benefits of chipkill-correct ECC for PC server main memory. *IBM Microelectronics*, 1997.

[5] T. J. Dell. System RAS implications of DRAM soft errors. *IBM J. Res. Dev.*, 52(3), 2008.

[6] P. E. Dodd. Device simulation of charge collection and single-event upset. *IEEE Nuclear Science*, 43:561–575, 1996.

[7] A. Gara. Overview of the Blue Gene/L system architecture. *IBM J. Res. Dev.*, 49:195–212, March 2005.

[8] IBM journal of Research and Development staff. Overview of the IBM Blue Gene/P project. *IBM J. Res. Dev.*, 52(1/2):199–220, January 2008.

[9] H. Kobayashi, K. Shiraishi, H. Tsuchiya, H. Usuki, Y. Nagai, and K. Takahisa. Evaluation of lsi soft errors induced by terrestrial cosmic rays and alpha particles. Technical report, Sony corporation and RCNP Osaka University, 2001.

[10] X. Li, K. Shen, M. Huang, and L. Chu. A memory soft error measurement on production systems. In *Proc. USENIX Annual Technical Conference (ATC '07)*, pages 21:1–21:6, 2007.

[11] X. Li, M. C. Huang, K. Shen, and L. Chu. A realistic evaluation of memory hardware errors and software system susceptibility. In *Proc. USENIX Annual Technical Conference (ATC '10)*, pages 75–88, 2010.

[12] T. C. May and M. H. Woods. Alpha-particle-induced soft errors in dynamic memories. *IEEE Transactions on Electron Devices*, 26(1), 1979.

[13] B. Murphy. Automating software failure reporting. *ACM Queue*, 2, 2004.

[14] E. Normand. Single event upset at ground level. *IEEE Transaction on Nuclear Sciences*, 6(43):2742–2750, 1996.

[15] T. J. O'Gorman, J. M. Ross, A. H. Taber, J. F. Ziegler, H. P. Muhlfeld, C. J. Montrose, H. W. Curtis, and J. L. Walsh. Field testing for cosmic ray soft errors in semiconductor memories. *IBM J. Res. Dev.*, 40(1), 1996.

[16] M. Ohmacht. Blue Gene/L compute chip: memory and Ethernet subsystem. *IBM J. Res. Dev.*, 49:255–264, March 2005.

[17] R. V. Rein. BadRAM: Linux kernel support for broken RAM modules. URL `http://rick.vanrein.org/linux/badram/`.

[18] B. Schroeder and G. A. Gibson. A large scale study of failures in high-performance-computing systems. In *Proc. Int'l Conf. Dependable Systems and Networks (DSN 2006)*, pages 249–258, 2006.

[19] B. Schroeder, E. Pinheiro, and W.-D. Weber. DRAM errors in the wild: a large-scale field study. In *Proc. 11th Int'l Joint Conf. Measurement and Modeling of Computer Systems (SIGMETRICS '09)*, pages 193–204, 2009.

[20] D. Tang, P. Carruthers, Z. Totari, and M. W. Shapiro. Assessment of the effect of memory page retirement on system RAS against hardware faults. In *Proc. Int'l Conf. Dependable Systems and Networks (DSN 2006)*, pages 365–370, 2006.

[21] H. H. Tang. Semm-2: a new generation of single-event-effect modeling tools. *IBM J. Res. Dev.*, 52:233–244, May 2008.

[22] H. H. K. Tang, C. E. Murray, G. Fiorenza, K. P. Rodbell, M. S. Gordon, and D. F. Heidel. New simulation methodology for effects of radiation in semiconductor chip structures. *IBM J. Res. Dev.*, 52:245–253, May 2008.

[23] USENIX. The computer failure data repository (CFDR). URL `http://cfdr.usenix.org/`.

[24] D. H. Yoon and M. Erez. Virtualized and flexible ECC for main memory. In *Proc. 15th Int'l Conf. Architectural Support for Programming Languages and Operating Systems (ASPLOS '10)*, pages 397–408, 2010.

[25] J. Ziegler. IBM experiments in soft fails in computer electronics. *Political Analysis*, 40(1):3–18, 1996.

[26] J. F. Ziegler. Terrestrial cosmic rays. *IBM J. Res. Dev.*, 40:19–39, January 1996.

[27] J. F. Ziegler and W. A. Lanford. Effect of Cosmic Rays on Computer Memories. *Science*, 206:776–788, 1979.

[28] J. F. Ziegler, M. E. Nelson, J. D. Shell, R. J. Peterson, C. J. Gelderloos, H. P. Muhlfeld, and C. J. Montrose. Cosmic ray soft error rates of 16-Mb DRAM memory chips. *IEEE J. Solid-state Circuits*, 33:246–252, 1998.

Relyzer: Exploiting Application-Level Fault Equivalence to Analyze Application Resiliency to Transient Faults *

Siva Kumar Sastry Hari,[1] Sarita V. Adve,[1] Helia Naeimi,[2] and Pradeep Ramachandran[3]

[1]Department of Computer Science, University of Illinois at Urbana-Champaign, USA
[2]Intel Labs, Intel Corporation, Santa Clara, CA, USA
[3]Intel Corporation, India
{shari2,sadve}@illinois.edu, {helia.naeimi,pradeep.ramachandran}@intel.com

Abstract

Future microprocessors need low-cost solutions for reliable operation in the presence of failure-prone devices. A promising approach is to detect hardware faults by deploying low-cost monitors of software-level symptoms of such faults. Recently, researchers have shown these mechanisms work well, but there remains a non-negligible risk that several faults may escape the symptom detectors and result in silent data corruptions (SDCs).

Most prior evaluations of symptom-based detectors perform fault injection campaigns on application benchmarks, where each run simulates the impact of a fault injected at a hardware site at a certain point in the application's execution (application fault site). Since the total number of application fault sites is very large (trillions for standard benchmark suites), it is not feasible to study all possible faults. Previous work therefore typically studies a randomly selected sample of faults. Such studies do not provide any feedback on the portions of the application where faults were not injected. Some of those instructions may be vulnerable to SDCs, and identifying them could allow protecting them through other means if needed.

This paper presents Relyzer, an approach that systematically analyzes all application fault sites and carefully picks a small subset to perform selective fault injections for transient faults. Relyzer employs novel fault pruning techniques that prune faults that need detailed study by either predicting their outcomes or showing them equivalent to other faults. We find that Relyzer prunes about 99.78% of the total faults across twelve applications studied here, reducing the faults that require detailed simulation by 3 to 5 orders of magnitude for most of the applications. Fault injection simulations on the remaining faults can identify SDC causing faults in the entire application. Some of Relyzer's techniques rely on heuristics to determine fault equivalence. Our validation efforts show that Relyzer determines fault outcomes with 96% accuracy, averaged across all the applications studied here.

Categories and Subject Descriptors B.8.1 [*Hardware*]: Performance and Reliability—Reliability, Testing, and Fault-Tolerance

General Terms Design, Experimentation, Measurement, Reliability

Keywords Low-Cost Hardware Resiliency, Hardware Reliability Evaluation, Silent Data Corruption, Transient Faults, Architecture

1. Introduction

As process technology scales, the increasingly smaller devices become susceptible to a variety of in-field hardware failure sources; e.g., high-energy particle strikes (soft-errors), voltage droops, wear-out, and design bugs [4]. This increases the likelihood of a hardware failure in the field. Future systems must therefore handle such failures through in-field fault detection, diagnosis, repair, and recovery mechanisms to guarantee continuous error-free operation.

Hardware fault detection mechanisms form a crucial part in devising such reliability solutions. Traditional solutions use heavy amounts of redundancy (in space or time) to detect hardware faults. Owing to their prohibitive costs, such detection mechanisms are increasingly unacceptable for modern commodity systems. Instead, there is a growing recognition that a wide spectrum of the commodity space will accept only much lower cost solutions (in area, power, and performance), perhaps at the cost of tolerating very occassional failures.

Recently, there has been a surge of research in software-level symptom based fault detection techniques [5, 7, 13, 14, 16, 19, 20, 25] that provide promising such low-cost alternatives. These techniques detect only those hardware faults that corrupt software execution by monitoring for anomalous software behavior using simple, low-cost monitors. Despite the simplicity of their detectors, these techniques have demonstrated impressively high detection rates. Unfortunately, some fraction of faults do escape the detection mechanism and silently impact the correctness of the program output. Such faults are called silent data corruptions or SDCs. As an example, SWAT (SoftWare Anomaly Treatment) [8, 12, 22], a state-of-the-art reliability solution, reports an SDC rate of <0.5% across several (compute-intensive, media, and distributed client-server) workloads for both permanent and transient faults in all hardware units studied except the data-centric FPU.

By their nature, the effectiveness of symptom-based detection solutions depends on the application running on the system and when the fault manifests during the application's execution. Comprehensive evaluation of the effectiveness for a given application

* This work is supported in part by the Gigascale Systems Research Center (funded under FCRP, an SRC program) and the National Science Foundation under Grant CCF 0811693. Pradeep Ramachandran was supported by an Intel PhD fellowship and an IBM PhD scholarship. This work was done when Pradeep Ramachandran was a graduate student at the University of Illinois at Urbana-Champaign.

ASPLOS'12, March 3–7, 2012, London, England, UK.

requires studying the impact of all faults of interest injected at each cycle of the application's execution (one at a time). Below, when we refer to a *fault*, we include both the hardware site *where* a fault is injected as well as *when* it is injected in an application's execution (the application site). After injecting a fault (at a given cycle), the application must be allowed to run potentially to completion to determine if the fault is masked, results in SDC, or is detected (in the latter case, the execution may be stopped on detection). For application benchmarks with billions of instructions, this translates (conservatively) into trillions of fault injection runs for most benchmark suites and fault models of interest. Such a comprehensive fault injection campaign is clearly infeasible.

While most symptom-based detection techniques have been evaluated through fault injection campaigns [13, 14, 16], these studies bound the experiment time by studying a randomly selected sample of faults (typically of the order of thousands of faults per application) out of all the faults possible (more than a trillion faults for this study). While these methods may provide statistical guarantees SDC rates, certain faults that may be important to the application may be sampled out. Equally important, such statistical sampling provides virtually no feedback on which parts of the application remain vulnerable (other than the few instructions where faults were injected) and might need protection in other ways to reduce the SDC rate. With the ever-increasing constraints on power, performance, and area, such application-specific customization of resiliency solutions is desirable. Thus, for symptom-based detectors to become comercially adopted, it is important to provide firmer guarantees on SDC rates and to better identify the remaining vulnerable portions of the program to reduce the SDC rate.

This paper focuses on transient faults and seeks to dramatically reduce the number of faults to simulate while still preserving the ability to accurately determine the SDC rate and SDC vulnerable portions of the application. As mentioned above, the number of faults is large both due to the large number of hardware sites (*where*) and application execution sites (*when*) that a fault could be injected. There has been significant work in the literature to explore the impact of where in the hardware faults are injected, including understanding tradeoffs in injecting faults at the gate, microarchitectural, and architectural levels [10, 11, 17] and extensive work on notions of fault equivalence in the testing literature [1]. However, there is limited work on when in the application execution should faults be injected.

This paper presents *Relyzer*, a resiliency analyzer that systematically analyzes all (dynamic) application sites to determine a minimal set for when faults need to be injected.[1] Since our focus is not on the hardware sites, we choose two examples: transient single-bit flip faults in (architectural) integer registers and in output latches of address generation units.

Relyzer first lists all application sites that can be directly affected by our chosen transient faults. For some of these faults, Relyzer can directly predict their outcome (detection, masking, or SDC) through simple static analysis and dynamic profiling of the fault-free execution. These faults do not need detailed fault injection experiments. For the remaining faults, Relyzer primarily uses the insight that faults propagating "similarly" through the program are likely to result in similar outcomes. We propose novel heuristics based on static and dynamic control flow and data flow to capture the notion of "similar" for faults in different types of instructions. Using these heuristics, we categorize application fault sites into equivalence classes. We then select a representative from each equivalence class and thoroughly study it through a detailed fault injection experiment.

[1] We only consider single-threaded applications in this work and leave the exploration of multithreaded applications to future work.

Our results show that Relyzer significantly reduces the number of faults that require detailed fault injection experiments. Relyzer pruned about 99.78% of the total faults in the twelve applications studied here (three to five orders of magnitude reduction for all but one application). We validated the pruning techniques that use heuristics by matching the fault injection outcomes of the representative faults against outcomes of a sample of faults they each represent. Each pruning technique and fault model combination individually gave an accuracy of >92%, averaged across all studied applications. Overall, with the combination of all pruning techniques, Relyzer was able to correctly determine the outcomes of 96% of all faults, averaged across all twelve applications studied.

Overall, Relyzer significantly reduces the number of application fault sites that require thorough fault injection experiments, bringing them to a point where studying virtually all of them becomes practically viable. Further, it does so in a way that allows identifying the application sites vulnerable to SDCs (the equivalence classes whose representatives result in SDCs). To our knowledge, Relyzer is the first work to develop such a notion of fault equivalence for application fault sites (analogous to that of hardware fault equivalence). Section 5 describes the relationship with other work that has similar, but not identical, goals [2, 6, 18, 23].

2. Fault Pruning Techniques

Relyzer systematically analyzes all application fault sites and carefully selects a small subset for thorough fault injection experiments such that it can still estimate the outcomes of all the faults in the application. To achieve this goal, Relyzer applies a set of pruning techniques that are classified as *known-outcome* and *equivalence-based* pruning techniques. The known-outcome techniques largely use static (and some dynamic) program analyses to predict the outcome of a fault. The equivalence-based techniques prune faults by showing them equivalent to others using static and dynamic analyses and/or heurstics.

Relyzer first enumerates all the faults that can impact the application. We require a fault-free execution trace for a given application (and input) for this step. Each dynamic instruction instance in the trace forms a potential application fault site. At this site, we consider injecting faults in the hardware units that would be exercised by this instruction (one fault at a time). Since our focus is on the choice of application fault sites and not on exhaustively studying all hardware faults, we choose to study transient faults (single bit flips) in architectural integer registers and in output latches of address generation units. As an example, consider an add instruction with register operands g1, g2, and l1 as an instruction appearing in the dynamic instruction trace. We consider injecting single-bit-flips in the integer registers g1, g2, and l1 that are accessed by this instruction (one at a time, in different bits). Faults in the address generation unit will be considered only when it is exercised; i.e., in load and store instructions.

While enumerating the list of all application fault sites, Relyzer stores all the fault related information in a data structure called the fault database, shown in figure 1. In particular, it stores the identity of the static instruction (program counter), the hardware fault sites that can affect the instruction (e.g., names of registers), and the number of dynamic instances of the instruction. The rest of the fields in figure 1 apply to specific pruning techniques and are described with those techniques.

Relyzer next applies the fault pruning techniques on this initial set of faults. While the fault pruning is being performed, all the required information for successful computation of overall SDC rate and the SDC rate for each static instruction is logged in the fault database (figure 1). Additionally, some dynamic information to assist the later development of low-cost detectors can also be logged,

Fault Site			For known-outcome pruning techniques			For precise equivalence-based pruning techniques		For store- and control-equivalence pruning
Static Instruction (PC)	Faulty unit ID	Number of dynamic instances	Bit min	Bit max	Expected outcome	Equivalent instruction (PC)	Faulty unit ID	List of pilots

Pilot ID	Faulty unit ID and bit location	Population	Outcome	Extra information

Figure 1. Fault database. The first three fields in the first table store basic information regarding a fault site and the static instruction. The bit min and bit max fields indicate the amount of pruning performed by the known-outcome pruning techniques – faults in the bits between bit min and bit max are pruned and their predicted outcome is recorded in the expected outcome field. The equivalent instruction and the faulty unit ID fields store information for the precise equivalence-based pruning techniques. The information regarding pilots that are obtained by the store- and control-equivalence based pruning techniques is stored in a separate table. It also stores some extra information that can aid the development of low-cost detectors.

but we leave the exploration of such information and detectors to future work.

2.1 Known-outcome pruning technique

Bounding addresses: Transient hardware faults can make applications access memory locations that fall out of the range of the allocated address space. Such accesses are likely to result in detectable symptoms (e.g., fatal traps, segmentation faults, application aborts, and kernel panic). SWAT employs detectors specifically to detect such scenarios within recoverable latencies (e.g., out-of-bounds detectors [21]). We do not need injection experiments to identify the outcome of most such faults and can directly prune them as follows.

We determine the range of valid addresses, for both the stack and the heap, by studying the dynamic memory profile of the application. To keep our implementation simple, we monitor global and heap addresses together. This also eliminates the problem of distinguishing them from each other while profiling. This approximation only makes our technique conservative if we assume that the out-of-bounds detector can also detect faults in addresses that make accesses cross the global-heap boundary.

Once we identify the range of the valid addresses, we prune faults that would allow a memory instruction to access an invalid address (e.g., faults in high order bits of the address when the fault-free trace shows valid addresses are within lower order bits). This technique is applicable to memory instructions (both loads and stores).

Information for fault database: The known-outcome technique prunes faults by declaring them as detected. Hence, very little information is needed to be recorded in the fault database. We record the range of the bits that are pruned in the bit min and bit max field along with the estimated outcome (detected) in the expected outcome field of the fault database (figure 1).

2.2 Equivalence-based pruning techniques

This class of pruning techniques eliminates faults that are equivalent to each other from the initial set of faults and retains only the representative faults for thorough fault injection experiments. We further categorize pruning techniques in this section as *precise* and *heuristics-based*, based on whether they use accurate analyses or heuristics to form the equivalence classes.

2.2.1 Precise equivalence

Def-use analysis: A register definition is created whenever a register is used as a destination operand in an instruction. Faults in the definition of a register have similar behavior to that of faults in the first use of this definition. Therefore, we prune out faults in the definition and retain faults in the first use. Note that this technique prunes faults only in the definition and not in the uses. There can be multiple uses of a definition, and faults in different uses may have different fault propagation. Whenever a definition is pruned, we record the information of the first use at the definition. This allows relating the outcomes of the faults in the first use to those that of the definition's at a later stage.

Ideally, the destination register operands of all the instructions should be pruned by this technique. In our experiments, however, we prune faults in only those destination registers that have a first use within the same basic-block. Since we implemented this technique as a static program pass, accounting for this equalization in the fault database (i.e., associating faults in the first use to that of the definition's) was non-trivial for the cases where the def to first-use chains spanned across multiple basic blocks. Moreover, in the presence of conditional move operations, it was unclear whether a static pass can still prune faults without compromising on the precise association of a definition with the first-use. Hence, we limited ourselves to a conservative but precise implementation.

Information for fault database: The entries of the fault sites that are pruned by this technique record the information of the fault sites that represent them. In other words, the definition records the identity of the first use (the program counter of the instruction and the faulty unit id, as in figure 1).

2.2.2 Heuristics-based equivalence

Control-equivalence: This heuristic pruning technique uses the observation that faults propagating through similar code sequences are likely to behave similarly. It also uses the observation that a majority of the faults appear in code sequences that are executed many times. Consider a static instruction I with many dynamic instances in the fault-free execution under consideration. The pruning technique attempts to partition all these dynamic instances of I into equivalence classes, based on the control flow path followed after the dynamic instance.

It is convenient to describe and implement the algorithm at the basic block level. The technique uses the fault-free application execution to enumerate all possible control flow paths up to a depth n starting at the basic block that contains the instruction of interest. Depth is defined as the number of branch or jump instructions encountered. For the paths that were exercised multiple times in the execution, it randomly selects one dynamic occurrence, a pilot. It prunes all other unselected executions of such paths (population) and assumes that faults in those dynamic executions are represented by the selected ones (pilots). More precisely, a dynamic instruction instance on a pilot path serves as a pilot for other instances with the same PC on the other paths in its population.

Figure 2 explains through an example how this pruning technique selects pilots. The figure presents a control flow graph of a small program, with the basic blocks represented by the black and grey circles with numbers on their sides. Assume the grey basic block is not exercised by the dynamic execution of interest. Assume $n = 5$ (depth until which control flow is tracked). Suppose we are interested in finding the representative pilots for an instruction in basic block 1. We enumerate all control flow paths starting at basic block 1 up to a depth of 5 that are executed in the dynamic

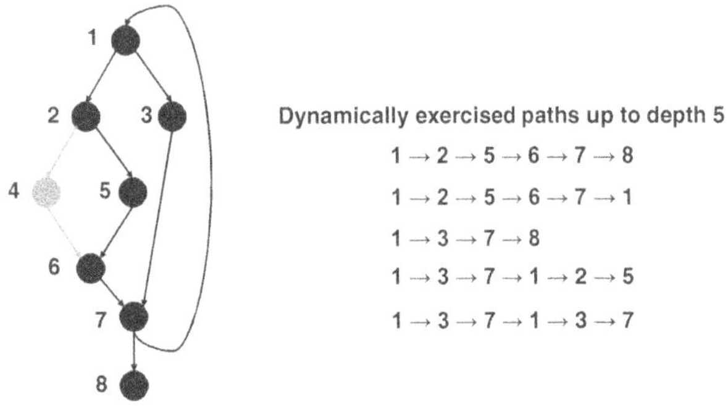

Figure 2. Control-equivalence. The figure shows a CFG for a small program starting at basic block 1 and ending at basic block 8. We enumerate all dynamically exercised control paths up to a depth, say 5. Here basic block 4 (showed in grey) never gets exercised. Therefore control flow paths through this node do not appear on the list of dynamically exercised paths. The executions along each of these paths form the equivalence classes for similar fault outcomes.

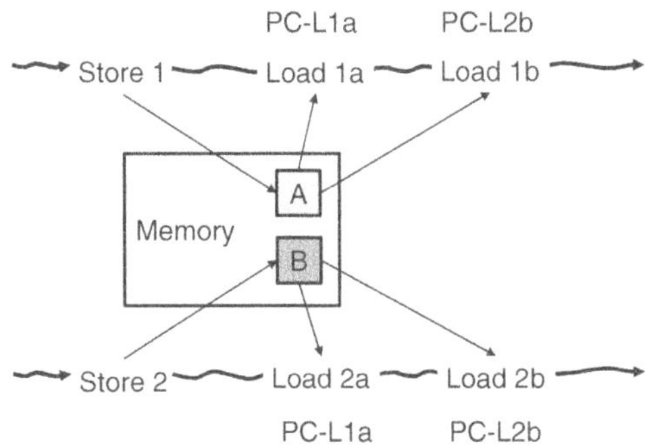

Figure 3. Store-equivalence. Store 1 and Store 2 are two store instructions from the same static instruction writing to addresses A and B respectively. Load 1a with program counter PC-L1a and Load 1b with program counter PC-L1b are two load instructions reading the value from address A. Similarly, Load 2a and Load 2b are two loads from address B with program counters PC-L2a and PC-L2b respectively. The store-equivalence heuristic requires that PC-L1a equal PC-L2a and PC-L1b equal PC-L2b.

fault-free execution of interest. Basic block 4 is never executed and hence it does not appear in the list of dynamically exercised paths. We identify each path as forming a new equivalence class. There will be potentially many instances of such paths in the dynamic execution trace. We randomly select one dynamic execution sequence for each equivalence class and name it as the pilot for that class. As mentioned before, a dynamic instruction instance on a pilot path serves as a pilot for other instances with the same PC on the other paths in its population.

We apply this technique to prune faults in all instructions other than stores and those that affect stores within a basic block. This is because the propagation of a fault in a store also depends on the addresses of the loads in the control flow path taken (only loads to the same address as the store will propagate the fault). The next technique described deals with this distinction. Exceptions to the above are a few SPARC specific instructions; namely, *save*, *restore*, *call*, *return*, and *read state register*. In this study, we do not inject faults in these instructions and therefore do not consider them any further. We also do not inject faults in dead instructions and do not consider those any further either.

Overall, control-equivalence has the potential of pruning a large fraction of the faults by softening the constraint on evaluating all dynamic occurrences from a specific code section.

Store-equivalence: A fault in a store instruction propagates through the loads that read the faulty values. Load addresses are not entirely captured by the control flow path taken after the store. We therefore developed an alternate heuristic, called store-equivalence, for faults in store instructions or in instructions that a store depends on within the same basic block. This heuristic captures the fault propagation behavior by observing the addresses that a store writes in a fault-free execution and recording all read accesses to this address. It treats the faults in stores differently whenever a different permutation of load instructions read the stored value.

Figure 3 illustrates our heuristic with an example. Consider Store 1 and Store 2 as two dynamic store instruction instances from the same static instruction. To determine if the faults in these two store instructions will have the same outcomes, we examine all the loads that return the values written by these stores in the fault-free execution, i.e., Load 1a and Load 1b for Store 1 and Load 2a and Load 2b for Store 2 from the figure. We first check whether the number of such loads is the same (two for each store in the figure). If this is the case, then we check whether the static instructions (program counters) of the corresponding loads are the same; e.g., if the program counters of Load L1a and Load L2a are the same and if those of Load L1b and Load L2b are the same in the figure. If these match, then we conclude that the two dynamic store instructions are very likely to have similar fault outcomes and we place them both in the same equivalence class.

Information for fault database: We record the information regarding the pilots in the fault database (figure 1). In particular, we record the unique pilot id and the size of the population it represents. We can also record additional information such as the control path (sequence of instructions) this pilot represents for control-equivalence or the usage pattern of the stored value (e.g., number of loads and their program counters) for store-equivalence in the extra information field. This information may be helpful for the applications of Relyzer (e.g., understanding and protecting SDC causing fault sites).

2.3 Other pruning techniques

We considered several other pruning techniques, but they provided limited benefit. We include them here for completeness.

Bounding branch targets (known-outcome category): Analogous to the bounding addresses case (known-outcome pruning technique), a fault that causes a control instruction to jump to a location that is not in the application instruction space is likely to result in a detectable symptom (e.g., SWAT's fatal trap and app-abort detectors or an out-of-bounds detector analogous to that for data addresses can detect such faults).

The address range that contains all possible targets can be obtained by noting the start and the end of the text section of an application. Typically, the text section is small (for applications with under million instructions; i.e., under 32 bits) and hence a large fraction (over 50% on 64-bit machines) of faults in branch targets can be predicted as detected and pruned by this technique. This bounding technique may not be directly applicable to jumps to shared libraries because the registers used by these operations may already contain addresses that are out of the text section.

We performed an optimistic experiment on the studied fault models and applications and found that it only provides a pruning of 0.5%. Hence, we do not include the bounding branch targets technique in our study here. However, this technique may be effective for other faults models; e.g., faults in immediate operands. Many branch instructions specify PC-relative displacements as immediate operands, and could benefit from this technique.

Constant-based bit masking (known-outcome category): In some logical operations, only a subset of the bit locations in the source operands are used to produce the destination register value. Hence, faults in the source operand's bit locations that are usually discarded will be masked. Currently we apply this technique only on logical shift operations, where the shift count is a constant. We prune faults in the source register's bit locations that are not used to produce the destination register value and treat them as masked.

This technique provides a modest benefit for the unoptimized version of our applications. We, however, do not report it for the optimized version of our applications because preliminary experiments showed that it provides insignificant benefits.

Several other instruction-specific pruning techniques (similar to the one above) have a potential of providing added pruning. This is a part of our future work.

Constant-based equivalence (precise-equivalence category): We applied the principal of constant propagation to prune faults from operands of instructions that use constants. For such instructions, the effect of a fault in the source register (non-constant) operand can often be studied directly in the destination operand; therefore, we can prune faults from such source operands. In our implementation, this pruning technique is currently limited to only those logical operations where a single-bit fault in the source operand propagates as a single-bit fault in the destination (e.g., logical `xor`). This technique also provides negligible benefit for the optimized applications. Hence we report it only for the unoptimized applications.

Information for fault database: The first two techniques above qualify as known-outcome based because they prune faults by declaring them as detected or masked. Hence, similar to the bounding addresses case, we record the range of the bits that are pruned in the bit min and bit max field along with the estimated outcome in the expected outcome field of the fault database (figure 1).

The third technique above is similar to def-use analysis. Consequently, the fault database is updated with the information about the fault equalization, i.e., the information of the destination operand (program counter of the instruction and the faulty unit id in figure 1) is recorded at the source operand.

2.4 Implementation

Relyzer implements the pruning techniques using static and dynamic program analyses. For example, the def-use and known-outcome pruning techniques are implemented largely as a static program pass (they use some basic information from the dynamic fault-free execution profile). Store- and control-equivalence techniques, on the other hand, largely use the dynamic information.

As a first step, Relyzer initializes the fault database and computes the initial set of faults. The information about the number of dynamic instances of each static instruction is required to compute the size of the initial set of faults and is obtained through a dynamic profile of the application. Relyzer then applies the first pruning technique – known-outcome address bounding, which is implemented as a static program pass. This technique requires the knowledge about the boundaries of stack and heap addresses accessed during the entire course of the program and this information is obtained through dynamic profiling. Relyzer next performs the def-use analysis (the precise equivalence based pruning technique), which is also implemented as a static program pass. For applications with unoptimized codes, it also applies the two constant-based pruning techniques at this step.

Once these static techniques are applied, Relyzer prepares the application codes for dynamic analysis for the heuristics-based equivalence pruning techniques (control- and store-equivalence). It first labels all static instructions to indicate which (if any) of the heuristics-based pruning techniques will be applicable to them. For instructions within a given basic block, all stores and the instructions that any store is dependent on are labeled to be pruned by store-equivalence. Since the dynamic store-equivalence based analysis is performed only on store instructions, the identity of the store instruction is recorded with the instructions that affect this store (in other words, the instructions that any store depends on also record the identity of the store instruction). Once the instructions for store-equivalence labeled, all other remaining instructions (with the earlier mentioned exceptions) are marked to be pruned by control-equivalence.

Relyzer then profiles the instructions and memory in more detail to obtain dynamic control- and store-equivalence classes as discussed in Section 2.2. It next uses the store-equivalence classes (for store instructions) and associates them with the instructions that recorded the identity of these stores (as mentioned above) to obtains the respective classes for all instructions that stores depend on. As a last step, Relyzer computes the remaining number of pruned faults by analyzing the updated fault database.

2.5 Computing SDC rates

Once all the pruning techniques are applied, the fault injection experiments on the remaining fault locations are performed. The SDC rate of the application can now be computed by using the information stored in the fault database (figure 1) as follows.

We start by computing the SDC rate for a static instruction, examining each faulty unit affecting the instruction. If a heuristics-based equivalence technique is employed for the unit, then we examine the outcomes of the instruction's pilots for each bit of the faulty unit not already pruned by the known-outcome techniques.[2] For each pilot and faulty bit combination that produces an SDC, we use the pilot's total population to increment a count of the total SDCs attributed to the faulty unit for this instruction.

For a faulty unit on which a precise-equivalence pruning technique is applied, we use the SDC count computed for the static instruction and faulty unit combination that was determined to be equivalent to the fault being examined (e.g., first use of a definition).

The total SDC count for a static instruction is the sum of the SDC counts for all its faulty units as obtained above. The SDC rate for a static instruction is its SDC count divided by the total number of initial faults attributed to this instruction. The SDC rate of an application is now simply the total SDC count of all the static instructions divided by the total number of initial faults in the application.

3. Methodology

3.1 Workloads

We implemented the pruning techniques described in Section 2 for single-threaded applications compiled for the SPARC V9 [26] architecture, assuming the hardware fault models previously described. We selected twelve applications – four each (randomly selected) from the SPLASH-2 [27], PARSEC [3], and SPEC CPU2006 [9] benchmark suites. Table 1 provides a brief description of these applications, including the inputs used, the dynamic instruction count, and the number of faults prior to applying any

[2] We assume the known-outcome techniques do not determine SDCs. The SDC count from faults pruned by future such techniques can be easily incorporated.

pruning. We do not include the initialization and the output phases of the applications in our study – these phases are usually dominated by file reads and writes, memory allocation and deallocation, etc. We found that the effectiveness of the developed pruning techniques varies significantly depending on whether the applications are optimized. We focus our results primarily on the optimized versions of the applications. Section 4.1, however, briefly summarizes the impact of optimizations for a subset of the above applications. The dynamic instruction counts and the number of faults in table 1 pertain to the optimized version of the applications.

3.2 Fault injection framework

As previously mentioned, the fault models we study are single bit flips in architectural integer registers and in the output latches of the address generation units (for loads and stores). Our fault injection simulation infrastructure uses a full system simulation environment comprising of Wind River Simics [24] and the GEMS microarchitectural and memory timing simulator [15], running our applications on the OpenSolaris operating system and compiled to the SPARC V9 ISA. This framework is similar to that used in the previous work on SWAT (e.g., [13]) with some modifications.

Our framework allows us to inject faults at any point in the application execution. This is the chosen application fault site, as represented by a dynamic instruction in the fault-free execution. To inject a fault, we start the application and execute it in functional mode (Simics-only) up to 500 cycles before the chosen application fault site. Then we start detailed timing simulation (Simics+GEMS) and inject the fault when the application fault site is reached. Thus, for address generation unit faults, we flip the specified bit in the unit's output latch when it generates the address for the specified dynamic instruction. For integer register faults, we flip the specified bit in the specified register when the specified dynamic instruction reads the register (for a source) or writes the register (for a destination). The flipped bit retains its state until the latch or register is overwritten. We then simulate the application for another 500 instructions in the detailed mode before switching to the functional mode and running it to completion.

We check for all SWAT symptoms [21] (fatal traps, application aborts, and kernel panics) in the detailed mode and a reduced set of symptoms (fatal traps, kernel panics, and system error messages) in the functional simulation phase. If a symptom is detected or a timeout condition is met (the application executes more than twice its expected runtime before producing the output), then we terminate the simulation and the outcome is recorded as detected. Otherwise, the output of the application is collected and compared with the fault-free output. We record the outcome as masked or an SDC depending on whether the two outputs are or are not the same respectively.

Note that when we inject a fault, there is always an instruction that consumes a faulty value or uses a faulty address. Thus, compared to pure microarchitecture-level injection simulations, we see no microarchitectural masking and very limited architectural masking. This is by design since we wish to maximize the injections that might lead to SDCs.

3.3 Pruning techniques

The pruning techniques require both static and dynamic analyses of the application. The static analyses study the binary and extract several properties that are either directly applied towards fault pruning or are later used by the dynamic technique. Since our fault injection infrastructure is developed for the SPARC V9 ISA model, we restrict our study to SPARC V9 binaries. We could not find any publicly available tools to analyze SPARC binaries, so we developed our own static binary analyzer that performs basic control flow and data flow analyses.[3] Using this static infrastructure, we traverse the application and create the set of all transient fault sites. We then apply the static pruning techniques, compute the pruned fault set, and collect information for dynamic analyses. The dynamic analyzer profiles the branches, the memory access patterns (for store-equivalence technique), instruction control flow patterns (for control-equivalence technique), etc. We use Wind River Simics [24] to implement these dynamic profilers. Finally, we use the information from both the static and dynamic analyses to generate the final pruned fault set.

For store-equivalence pruning, we dynamically observe every store instruction, the addresses they write to, and record all loads that read the stored value (as explained in Section 2.2). For mcf, however, we record only the first ten loads instead of all loads for forming the store-equivalence classes such that our store-equivalence algorithm finishes in a reasonable time of <10 hours.

To quantify the impact of the pruning techniques, we report the percentage of total faults that are pruned (in total and by the individual techniques) and the absolute number of remaining faults (pilots) that must be simulated to determine the resiliency of an application.

3.4 Validating pruning techniques

The control- and store-equivalence based fault pruning techniques use heuristics and require validation. Each of these pruning techniques chooses a dynamic instruction (*pilot*) to represent the outcome of several other dynamic instructions (the *population*). We quantify the validity of these techniques by quantifying the extent to which the pilots correctly represent the population. For example, suppose the injection of a fault in a pilot results in masking the fault. Suppose the injection of an analogous (hardware) fault in all members of the population results in 98% of the outcomes being masked and 2% detected or SDC. Then we say that the prediction rate of the pilot is 98%. The overall prediction rate for the pruning techniques is the weighted average of the prediction rate for all the pilots for that technique, weighted by the fault populations represented by the pilots.

To find the exact misprediction rate, ideally, we would run fault injections for all the pilots and all their associated populations. Simulating this combination is clearly prohibitive in simulation time. To reduce this time, we first restrict our validations only to the optimized applications. Further, for a given pilot, we randomly sample its population to determine the prediction rate. We select the sample size such that the 99% confidence interval for prediction is within 5% of the actual prediction rate.[4] We then inject transient faults in the pilot and the selected samples to obtain the prediction rate. Ideally, we would inject faults in all bit locations in the appropriate faulty units for the pilot, but the simulation time would be prohibitive. We instead injected faults in every 8th bit (bits 0, 8, 16, 24, 32, 40, 48, and 56 for a 64-bit register or the output latch of the address generation unit) that was not already pruned by the known-outcome pruning technique (e.g., if the known-outcome pruning technique prunes higher-order 32 bits, then we inject faults only in bits 0, 8, 16, and 24).

Sampling the population for a given pilot still leaves the problem that there are many pilots, each of which would require a

[3] We use the dynamic branch profile to create a correctly connected control flow graph because jump and link instructions create broken edges in the graph that may not be completed through static information alone.

[4] The pilot requires only one fault injection experiment to obtain the outcome A. We can formulate the fault injection experiments for the population as a Bernoulli trial with outcomes being either A or not A. Assuming all the experiments are independent, we can apply the principals of confidence intervals used for normal distributions.

Benchmark Suite	Application	Description	Input	Num. Dynamic Instructions	Num. Faults
Parsec 2.1	Blackscholes	Calculates prices of options with Black-Scholes partial differential equation	sim-large	22.3 Million	1.9 Billion
	Fluidanimate	Simulates an incompressible fluid for interactive animation purposes	sim-small	611.4 Million	102.5 Billion
	Streamcluster	Solves the online clustering problem	sim-small	1.44 Billion	106 Billion
	Swaptions	Computes prices of a portfolio of swaptions using Monte Carlo simulations	sim-small	922.2 Million	97.3 Billion
Splash-2	FFT	1D Fast Fourier Transform	64K points	548 Million	48.7 Billion
	LU	Factors a matrix into the product of a lower & upper triangular matrix	512×512 matrix 16×16 blocks	402.8 Million	33.2 Billion
	Ocean	Simulates large-scale ocean movements based on eddy and boundary currents	258×258 ocean	358 Million	21.7 Billion
	Water	Evaluates forces and potentials that occur over time in a system of water molecules	512 molecules	504.3 Million	36.6 Billion
SPEC-Int 2006	Gcc	Based on gcc Version 3.2, generates code for Opteron	test	3.8 Billion	500.4 Billion
	Libquantum	Simulates a quantum computer running Shor's polynomial time factorization algorithm	test	235.4 Million	27.4 Billion
	Mcf	Vehicle scheduling using a network simplex algorithm	test	4.57 Billion	485.4 Billion
	Omnet++	Uses the OMNet++ discrete event simulator to model a large ethernet campus network	test	1.35 Billion	146 Billion

Table 1. Applications studied. The number of dynamic instructions and faults pertains to the optimized versions of the applications.

large number of simulations for validation. We therefore restricted the number of pilots such that it was feasible to simulate all of them (and their sampled populations) in the available time. We selected enough pilots such that the total number of fault injections we had to perform for validation (for pilots and the population) was over one million for each of control- and store-equivalence (1,378,000 for control and 1,093,000 for store) across all fault models. In particular, for validating control-equivalence, we performed approximately 1,092,000 and 286,000 injections for integer register and address generation unit fault models respectively. For store-equivalence, he corresponding number of injections are 835,000 and 258,000. Further, each selected pilot represented a population of at least 1,000. For the 99% confidence interval, our average validation results for control-equivalence pruning have error bars of 1.84% and 3.67% for the integer register and address generation unit fault models respectively. For store-equivalence pruning, the corresponding error bars are 2.85% and 4.61%.

4. Results

4.1 Effectiveness of pruning techniques

4.1.1 Overall pruning effectiveness

Tables 2(a) and (b) show the overall effectiveness of Relyzer's pruning techniques by presenting the percentage of total faults pruned for the optimized and unoptimized applications respectively. The tables also show the absolute number of total faults and the faults remaining after pruning. The applications are ordered according to the total number of original faults.

For optimized applications, we find that Relyzer prunes an aggregate of 99.78% of all the studied faults across all applications. The total number of faults that need to be simulated reduces from 1.6 trillion to 3.52 billion, a three to five orders of magnitude reduction for all applications except mcf. The lowest pruning rate for a single application was 99.43% (for mcf) while most applications saw a pruning rate of 99.99%. For mcf,[5] two stores observed a pruning of 20%, bringing down mcf's overall pruning rate. The number of remaining faults in these two stores and the instructions that these stores depend on alone accounted for 83% of the total remaining faults for mcf.

4.1.2 Pruning effectiveness of individual techniques

Figures 4(a) and (b) show the effectiveness of Relyzer's individual pruning techniques for the optimized and unoptimized applications respectively. The stacks in each bar show the contributions of the individual pruning techniques when applied in the order shown (bottom to top) for all the faults in the application. There is no stack for constant-based pruning techniques in part (a) because our preliminary experiments showed these techniques provide limited benefit for those applications.

Focusing on the optimized applications, we found that the known-outcome pruning technique pruned an average of approximately 27% of all the faults. Def-use analysis prunes 15% of all the faults on average. Thus, the above mostly static techniques alone provided approximately 42% of pruning across our applications. Control-equivalence is overall the most effective individual technique for these applications, providing 48% of the pruning on average. Finally, store-equivalence technique pruned about 10% of all the faults.

The unoptimized applications show slightly different behavior. First, store-equivalence provides notably more pruning than in the optimized applications. A likely reason is that there are more memory operations in unoptimized codes since they use the stack heavily and the registers poorly. Moreover, these store operations are often represented by a small number of pilots because they observe few permutations of loads during store-equivalence pruning. Second, the constant-based techniques provide significantly

[5] For forming the store-equivalence classes for mcf, we accounted for the first ten loads instead of all loads so that our algorithm finished in a reasonable time of <10 hours.

Application	Initial faults (in billions)	Total pruning	Remaining faults (in millions)
Blackscholes	1.9	99.99%	0.07
Ocean	21.7	99.99%	2.9
Libquantum	27.4	99.98%	4.1
LU	33.2	99.99%	1.1
Water	36.6	99.99%	2.1
FFT	48.7	99.99%	0.3
Swaptions	97.3	99.99%	0.6
Fluidanimate	102.5	99.91%	92
Streamcluster	106	99.99%	8.6
Omnet++	146	99.99%	2.2
Mcf	485.4	99.43%	2,781
Gcc	500.4	99.88%	627.5

(a) Optimized applications.

Application	Initial faults (in billions)	Total pruning	Remaining faults (in millions)
Blackscholes	4.01	99.99%	0.03
FFT	61.18	99.99%	0.16
Libquantum	127.03	99.93%	3.40
LU	175.36	99.99%	0.80
Swaptions	318.66	99.99%	0.08

(b) Unoptimized applications.

Table 2. Effectiveness of Relyzer's pruning on (a) optimized and (b) unoptimized applications. The applications are in increasing order of total number of original faults.

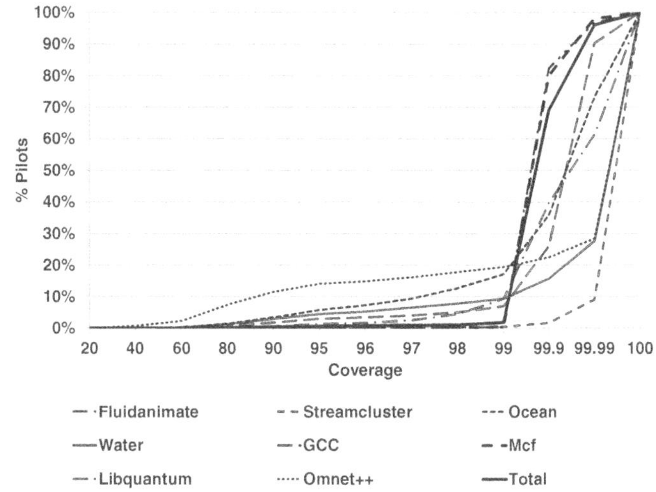

Figure 5. The percentage of pilots (y-axis) required to provide a desired amount of fault coverage (x-axis) for optimized applications. The x-axis shows the percentage of the total initial number of faults that are covered by the corresponding percentage of pilots. This includes the faults from the known-outcome category which are always considered covered. Note that the scale on the x-axis is not linear. Only individual applications that have more than 1 million remaining (not pruned) faults are shown, along with a curve for the aggregate faults across all applications.

more pruning for the unoptimized applications (about 6.5% of total faults). We observed that the number of remaining faults increases significantly (by about 100%) when this technique was excluded for the unoptimized applications. However, it had negligible impact on optimized applications. Overall, figure 4 shows significant differences in the relative effectiveness of the pruning techniques between the optimized and unoptimized codes, showing that compiler optimizations do impact the behavior of fault propagation.

4.1.3 Trading off simulation time with coverage

Although Relyzer is able to prune faults effectively, there are still a relatively large number of remaining faults that need to be simulated, especially for the longer applications. Relyzer allows a systematic method to trade off simulation time with coverage, revealing sweet spots that dramatically reduce simulation time with modest reduction in coverage.

Figure 5 shows the percentage of pilots (y-axis) needed to provide a desired coverage of the faults across the entire application (x-axis) after applying all pruning techniques for the optimized applications. These pruning techniques include the known-outcome class, which is considered to be always covered. For readability, we plot only the individual applications that had more than 1 million remaining faults that need simulation. For the full picture, we also plot the data for the total number of faults.

It is evident from the figure that only a small fraction of the pilots cover most of the faults. For example, 99% of all the faults across all the studied applications can be covered by 1.81% of the pilots. This corresponds to approximately 32 million faults. We can reduce this set further by compromising on the bit locations; e.g., injecting a fault in only every eighth bit of a given dynamic instruction, as in our validation experiments. With our existing simulation speeds, this set of faults can be simulated in approximately 11 days on a cluster of 200 cores.

We observed similar results for unoptimized codes as well, but do not present them here because most of the unoptimized applications we studied have under 1 million remaining faults.

4.2 Validation of heuristics-based pruning techniques

4.2.1 Prediction rate for control- and store-equivalence

We validated the heuristics-based pruning techniques, namely control- and store-equivalence, for the optimized applications as described in Section 3.4. Figure 6 shows the prediction rate of the pilots for all twelve applications and both the studied hardware fault models (integer register or *reg* and output latch of address generation unit or *agen*). The combined bar for each application shows the observed prediction rate across all studied fault models after applying all pruning techniques. For each application, the combined bar is the average of the prediction rate of each pruning technique and fault model combination, weighted by the fraction of faults pruned by that combination. Specifically, in addition to accounting for control- and store-equivalence, this bar also accounts for faults pruned by def-use pruning (by associating a def-use pruned fault's prediction rate with that of its representative faults' rate). It also accounts for known-outcome based pruning, assuming a 100% prediction rate for that technique.

Figure 6 shows that the pilots selected through control-equivalence predict the outcome of their populations with an average (across all applications) accuracy of 95.7% for reg faults and 94.5% for agen faults. The pilots selected by store-equivalence predict their population's outcomes with an average accuracy of 95.4% for reg faults and 92.6% for agen faults. The figure also shows that for each individual application, Relyzer predicts the outcome across all fault models and pruning techniques with an accuracy of >91% (shown by the *combined* bar). This prediction rate averaged across all applications is 96%.

Integer register faults observe a prediction accuracy of approximately 90% or higher for all applications except Ocean. On the

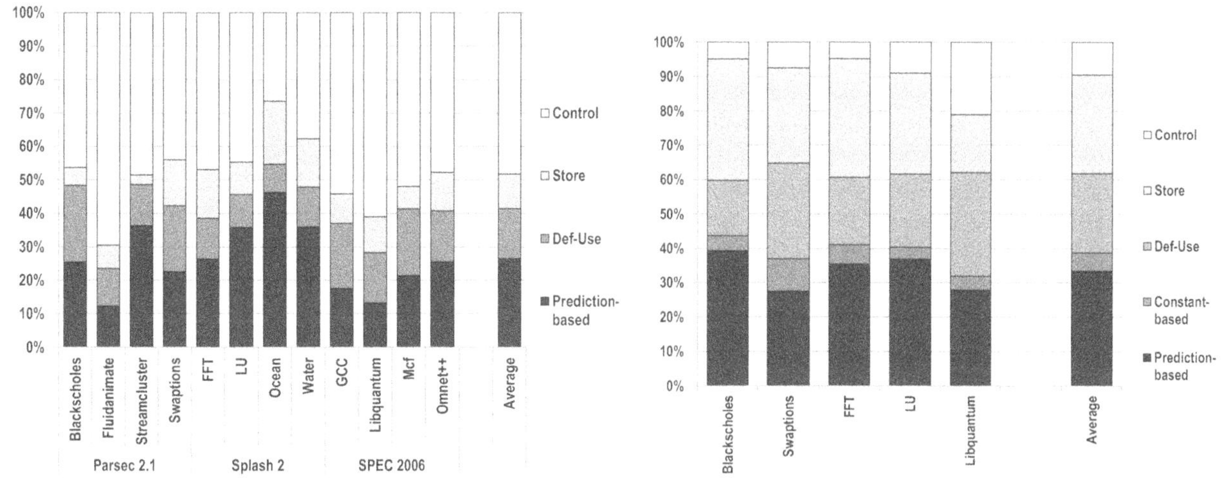

(a) Optimized applications

(b) Unoptimized applications

Figure 4. Effectiveness of the individual pruning techniques for (a) optimized and (b) unoptimized applications.

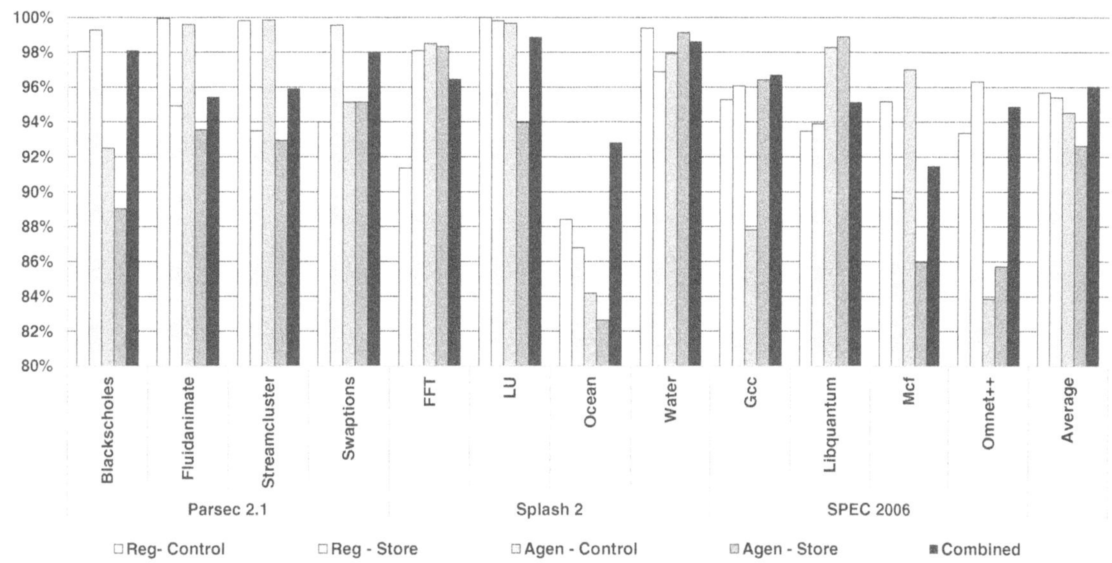

Figure 6. Validation of control- and store- equivalence for integer register (reg) and output latch of address generation unit (agen) faults for optimized applications. The *combined* bars for each application show the prediction rate across all fault models and pruning techniques.

other hand, agen faults showed $< 90\%$ (the lowest is about 82%) for some cases for five applications – Blackscholes, Ocean, Gcc, Mcf, and Omnet++. We examined a few of these cases to understand why the prediction rate was not higher, and believe many of these can be eliminated by refining our heuristics.

For example, for Omnet++, a notable contributor to the mispredictions with control-equivalence for agen faults was a load instruction that should have been labeled for store-equivalence pruning. The instruction directly affected a store (and nothing else), but in the next basic block. Since our analysis looks only within the basic block for such data dependences to select instructions for store-equivalence pruning, it could not find this dependency. We plan to extend our static techniques in the future to enable correct labels in such cases.

As another example, we examined Blackscholes for store-equivalence pruning for agen faults. The major contributor to the misprediction rate was a load instruction loading values from faulty addresses. In several cases, it so happened that the faulty and correct address had the same value; therefore, the fault was masked rightaway. On the other hand, sometimes this was not the case, and the fault led to an SDC. A common pilot represented both classes of cases, leading to mispredictions. The fundamental issue is that our heuristics do not examine the faulty value. For Blackscholes, we could easily modify our implementation so that during our profiling step (fault-free execution), for every potential fault in a load address, we check the faulty address to determine if the value is different. This leads to a known-outcome based technique that can immediately determine if such a fault would be masked.

Examining the mispredicted cases in Ocean for agen faults pruned by store-equivalence exposed a more difficult limitation of Relyzer. A store instruction with a faulty address was one of the major sources of the high misprediction rate in Ocean. Such a store corrupts the intended address by not writing the value from the source register and also the faulty address by writing an unintended value. We found the root cause of the misprediction to be the writing of the source register value in the faulty address. Since Relyzer cannot examine fault propagation through faulty addresses, this becomes a fundamental limitation and overcoming it is an interesting future direction.

4.2.2 SDC vs. non-SDC prediction rate

A key application of Relyzer is identifying SDC causing fault sites; therefore, we would like to ensure that Relyzer's prediction rate for SDC causing faults is also high. The data in figure 6 showed the prediction accuracy for masked and detected faults as well. Here, we distinguish only between SDC and non-SDC outcomes, treating the masked and detected outcomes the same. With just the SDC and non-SDC categories in mind, we revisited the validation results in figure 6. We observed that the average (across all applications) prediction rate for control-equivalence for reg and agen faults is 96.6% and 96.2% respectively, slightly higher than the overall prediction rate which also distinguished between the two non-SDC outcomes. Similarly, the average prediction rate for store-equivalence for reg and agen faults is also a higher 95.9% and 94.9% respectively.

4.2.3 Outcomes for fault injections in pilots

We next show that our choice of pilots is not biased towards any specific fault outcome. We plotted the outcomes from the fault injection experiments of the pilots that were selected for validation (described in Section 3.4). Figure 7 shows the distribution of the outcomes for reg faults in part (a) and agen faults in part (b). These two figures represent just 3,298 fault injection experiments. Each bar in figure 7 has between 129 and 320 injections for part (a) and between 27 and 102 for part (b). Even with such small sample sizes, the fault outcomes have a significant fraction of SDCs. In aggregate, about 23% of the pilots result in SDCs for both reg and agen faults. This result indicates that Relyzer can be effective in finding SDC causing fault sites.

4.2.4 Need for multiple pilots per static instruction

Our control- and store-equivalence heuristics partition the dynamic instances of a static instruction into multiple equivalence classes. Here we provide evidence for the need for such partitioning. In other words, we show that a naive algorithm that chooses just one pilot for each static instruction may be insufficient. Figure 8 shows the fraction of static instructions that are represented by different numbers of pilots. It shows that across all applications, at least 47% of the static instructions that are marked to be pruned by either store- or control-equivalence are represented by at least two pilots.

To provide further evidence for the need for such categorization, we examined one of the static instructions in LU that had multiple pilots representing it (12 in this case). We found that 8 of them resulted in SDCs (together representing 70% of the dynamic instances of that instruction) and 4 in Masking (all these pilots showed very high prediction rates).

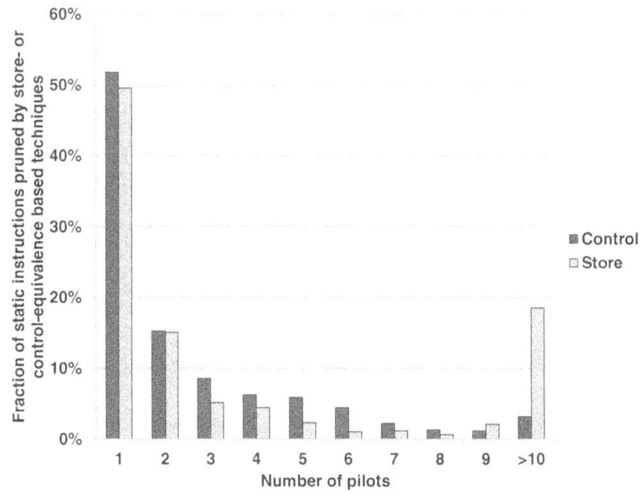

Figure 8. Pilots per static instruction. The figure shows the fraction of static instructions (averaged across all the optimized applications, pruned either by store- or control-equivalence) that are represented by a specified number of pilots. For example, 15% of the static instructions that are pruned by store-equivalence are represented by 2 pilots.

5. Related Work

There has been much work in the area of symptom-based fault detection that uses inexpensive monitors for anomalous software behavior to detect hardware faults [5, 7, 13, 14, 16, 19, 20, 25]. Much of this work is evaluated using fault injection campaigns on architecture-, microarchitecture-, or gate-level simulators or FPGA emulators running various benchmark applications. The hardware and software locations are typically randomly selected to achieve some statistical confidence. To our knowledge, these sampling mechanisms, particularly for application injection sites, have not been validated. Further, the fault injection results do not provide any insight on the parts of the application that remain vulnerable to SDCs (other than for the relatively few application sites where faults were actually injected and simulated). Relyzer selects sample application injection points derived from static and dynamic properties of the program. Each sample identifies a population of fault injection sites that are expected to have the same behavior, and all the populations together represent the entire execution. Further, Relyzer also exposes the execution trace responsible for an SDC so that alternate, customizable protection mechanisms can be designed.

Although we are not aware of other techniques that provide *all* of the above benefits of Relyzer, there are several studies that have related goals and, in some cases, are complementary to Relyzer.

SimPLFIED [18] shares Relyzer's high-level goal of finding all faults that escape detection and lead to SDCs. It uses a powerful symbolic execution method to abstract the state of erroneous values in the program. It injects such a symbolic error at all possible application sites (one at a time) and uses model checking with the abstract execution technique to explore all possible paths with the symbolic error and determines the outcomes of such paths (masking, detection, or SDC). The focus of SimPLFIED is to reduce the number of fault values per application site that need to be injected (hence the symbolic fault), which is orthogonal to our work. Our focus is to reduce the number of application sites where the fault is injected (we restrict the values by simply restricting our hardware fault models since that is not the focus of our work). It would be interesting to combine SimPLFIED with Relyzer. However, it is unclear if the model checking techniques used in SimPLFIED can scale to large applications; so far, it has been applied to only a few small benchmarks (e.g., a Siemens benchmark).

Shoestring [6] is a purely static technique that shares our goal of finding application sites where a fault may escape detection using symptom-based detectors. Shoestring provides a static analysis that identifies static instructions where faults are likely to be detected quickly enough; e.g., there is a short-enough path in the dataflow graph from such a fault to enough potentially symptom-

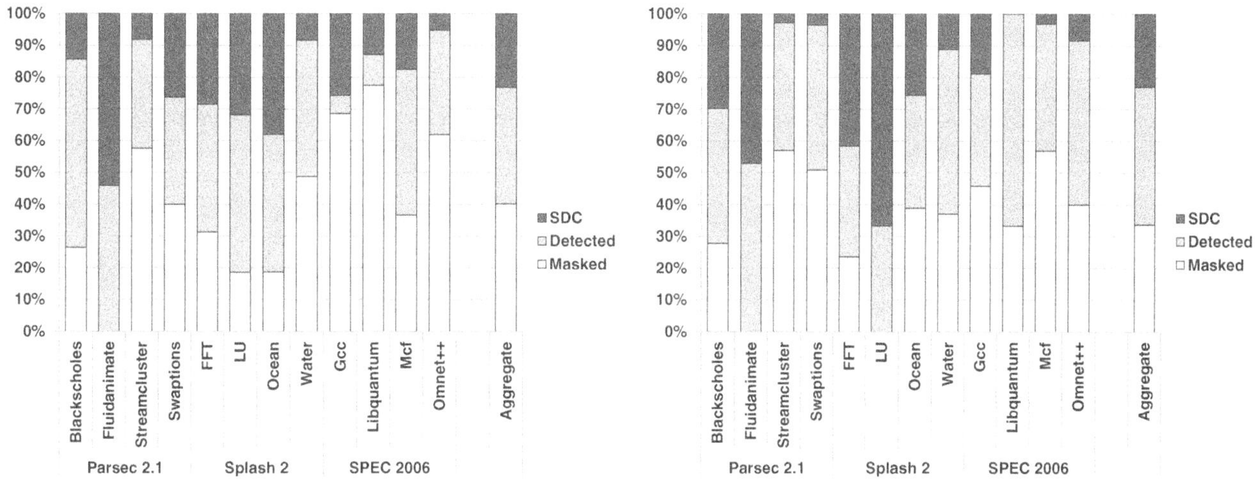

(a) Reg faults

(b) Agen fault

Figure 7. Breakdown of outcomes obtained from fault injections in the sampled pilots.

generating instructions. The rest of the faults are considered vulnerable and the important ones among these (currently, stores) are protected by duplicating any instructions that produce data that feeds into them. Shoestring succeeds in its goal of reducing the SDC rate by about 34% to 1.6%. However, this improvement comes at the cost of 15.8% performance overhead, which is prohibitive for the systems we target. One shortcoming of Shoestring is that it only employs static analysis to identify vulnerable instructions. Relyzer, on the contrary, applies a set of dynamic analyses that can distinguish between different instances of a static instruction and also exploit information known only at execution time (e.g., store and load addresses). It uses a combination of static and dynamic analyses to bin application fault locations into equivalence classes and then performs accurate fault simulation of the representative fault to identify the outcome. This allows Relyzer to account for masking of a fault, quantify a program's SDC rate, and enumerate the dynamic conditions that make code sections SDC prone. Shoestring's static analysis cannot achieve any of these. It would be interesting to combine the analyses of Shoestring and Relyzer in future work.

Benso et al. [2] proposed a solution that performs runtime analysis of the application variables to obtain the criticality behavior of every variable. That work developed an analytical model for this purpose that considers three variables – lifetime of the application variable, number of reads to it, and whether it is a pointer or not. The work proposes that the contribution of each of these variables is application independent and once the parameters of the model are set they remain fixed for all other applications. The results show that this solution observes low inaccuracies in predicting the criticality of variables. However, the results were shown on small applications with few variables. Relyzer, on the other hand, captures the fault propagation behavior from the fault-free execution of the application and uses it to categorize faults into different equivalence classes. It, however, relies on fault injection experiments on the pilots to estimate the outcome of the population (as opposed to estimating the outcomes based on static application-independent parameters).

Sridharan et al. [23] quantify the reliability behavior of an application using a metric called Program Vulnerability Factor (PVF). PVF is a microarchitecture-independent method to quantify architectural fault masking inherent to a program. PVF focuses on identifying only those faults that are masked by the application. It does not attempt to distinguish faults that lead to SDCs from the ones that result in detection, but this distinction becomes crucial with symptom-based detection in place. Hence, Relyzer focuses on distinguishing SDCs from detections. It is unclear whether PVF can make this distinction.

6. Conclusions and Future Work

Hardware reliability has become a major challenge, requiring low-cost and effective fault detection mechanisms. This paper concerns a promising approach, namely symptom-based detection, where low-cost monitors are deployed to monitor for anomalous software behavior as symptoms of hardware faults. There has been much recent work on such techniques, showing they provide high fault coverage at very low cost. However, for some cases, the SDC rate is still non-negligible, the evaluation techniques typically based on randomly selected fault injection campaigns are not validated, and the random injections do not provide insight on the vulnerable portions in the rest of the application that might need protection.

This paper presents Relyzer, a technique to systematically analyze all fault injection sites in an application for transient faults. Relyzer seeks to identify all SDC causing instruction instances, both to enable quantifying the application's true SDC vulnerability and to motivate low-cost application-specific protection mechanisms for the desired SDC-vulnerable cases.

Relyzer employs a set of novel fault pruning techniques that dramatically reduce the number of faults (application sites) that require thorough fault simulations. Relyzer predicts the outcome of several faults, eliminating the need for thorough fault injection experiments for them. It then exploits the fact that several application fault sites are impacted in a similar way by certain hardware faults, and develops heuristics to identify such application-level fault equivalence. Relyzer employs a series of static and dynamic techniques to categorize equivalence classes of faults, such that only one pilot fault from an equivalence class needs to be thoroughly studied through fault injection experiments. Through these techniques, we show that Relyzer prunes the set of faults by 99.78% across the twelve studied applications.

We also validated the heuristics-based fault pruning techniques by matching the results from fault simulations for the pilots with results from fault simulations with samples of the represented fault populations. Each pruning technique and fault model combination individually gave an accuracy of >92%, averaged across all studied applications. Aggregating all the pruning techniques (heuristics- and analysis-based) and faults, Relyzer correctly determined the outcomes of 96% of the faults, averaged across all applications. Overall, Relyzer significantly reduced the application-level fault sites that require time-consuming simulations, making it feasible to study a complete application through a relatively small number of fault injection experiments.

For our future work, we plan to perform a sensitivity analysis of the control- and store-equivalence based techniques on the parameters such as the depth of the control flow (used to identify the control-equivalence classes) and limiting the number of tracked loads (used for finding store-equivalence classes). Our current solution prunes faults in instructions that affect a store through store-equivalence. However, the outcome of this fault may also be dependent on the control sequence of the instructions that produce the store value and accounting for this information may further improve the prediction rate. Hence it will be interesting to combine both control- and store-equivalence based pruning techniques into a unified technique. For microarchitectural fault models, applying value perturbation based refinement to the existing pruning techniques is an attractive future work because it can potentially improve the existing prediction rate (especially for Blackscholes).

In the future, we also plan to extend our study to more fault models, which might involve the development of new pruning techniques. It will be interesting to understand how this approach can be applied to permanent faults. Relyzer has been concerned, so far, about the accurate evaluation of the fault outcomes. However, evaluating the fault detection latency with high accuracy is also important. We plan to extend Relyzer in this direction as well. Since a thorough evaluation of a fault through fault simulation is expensive in time, Relyzer focused on reducing the number of fault sites requiring thorough fault injection experiments. However, techniques that directly reduce the time for each fault injection experiment are in need as well. We plan to incorporate in Relyzer an analysis that can significantly reduce the time for each fault simulation as well.

Utilizing Relyzer for evaluating an application's resiliency and identifying the SDC causing fault sites is one of our core future directions. In this work, we also plan to exploit Relyzer's ability to provide added information about the fault site and the path to the SDC in understanding the characteristics of SDC causing fault sites and developing low-cost detectors for them.

References

[1] M. Abramovici, M. A. Breuer, and A. D. Friedman. *Digital Systems Testing and Testable Design*. 1993.

[2] A. Benso, S. Di Carlo, G. Di Natale, P. Prinetto, and L. Taghaferri. Data Criticality Estimation in Software Applications. In *International Test Conference*, 2003.

[3] C. Bienia and K. Li. PARSEC 2.0: A New Benchmark Suite for Chip-Multiprocessors. In *Proc. of 5th Workshop on Modeling, Benchmarking and Simulation*, 2009.

[4] S. Borkar. Designing Reliable Systems from Unreliable Components: The Challenges of Transistor Variability and Degradation. *IEEE Micro*, 25(6), 2005.

[5] M. Dimitrov and H. Zhou. Unified Architectural Support for Soft-Error Protection or Software Bug Detection. In *International Conference on Parallel Archtectures and Compilation Techniques*, 2007.

[6] S. Feng, S. Gupta, A. Ansari, and S. Mahlke. Shoestring: Probabilistic Soft Error Reliability on the Cheap. In *International Conference on Architectural Support for Programming Languages and Operating Systems*, 2010.

[7] O. Goloubeva, M. Rebaudengo, M. S. Reorda, and M. Violante. Soft-Error Detection Using Control Flow Assertions. In *International Symposium on Defect and Fault Tolerance in VLSI Systems*, 2003.

[8] S. K. S. Hari, M.-L. Li, P. Ramachandran, B. Choi, and S. V. Adve. Low-cost Hardware Fault Detection and Diagnosis for Multicore Systems. In *International Symposium on Microarchitecture*, 2009.

[9] J. L. Henning. SPEC CPU2006 benchmark descriptions. *SIGARCH Comput. Archit. News*, 34:1–17, September 2006.

[10] Z. Kalbarczyk, R. Iyer, G. Ries, J. Patel, M. Lee, and Y. Xiao. Hierarchical Simulation Approach to Accurate Fault Modeling for System Dependability Evaluation. *Software Engineering, IEEE Transactions on*, 25(5):619 –632, sep/oct 1999.

[11] M.-L. Li, P. Ramachandran, R. U. Karpuzcu, S. K. S. Hari, and S. V. Adve. Accurate Microarchitecture-Level Fault Modeling for Studying Hardware Faults. In *International Symposium on High Performance Computer Architecture*, 2009.

[12] M.-L. Li, P. Ramachandran, S. Sahoo, S. V. Adve, V. Adve, and Y. Zhou. Trace-Based Microarchitecture-Level Diagnosis of Permanent Hardware Faults. In *International Conference on Dependable Systems and Networks*, 2008.

[13] M.-L. Li, P. Ramachandran, S. Sahoo, S. V. Adve, V. Adve, and Y. Zhou. Understanding the Propagation of Hard Errors to Software and Implications for Resilient Systems Design. In *International Conference on Architectural Support for Programming Languages and Operating Systems*, 2008.

[14] G. Lyle, S. Cheny, K. Pattabiraman, Z. Kalbarczyk, and R. Iyer. An End-to-end Approach for the Automatic Derivation of Application-Aware Error Detectors. In *International Conference on Dependable Systems and Networks*, 2009.

[15] M. Martin et al. Multifacet's General Execution-Driven Multiprocessor Simulator (GEMS) Toolset. *SIGARCH Computer Architecture News*, 33(4), 2005.

[16] A. Meixner, M. E. Bauer, and D. J. Sorin. Argus: Low-Cost, Comprehensive Error Detection in Simple Cores. In *International Symposium on Microarchitecture*, 2007.

[17] S. Mirkhani, M. Lavasani, and Z. Navabi. Hierarchical Fault Simulation using Behavioral and Gate Level Hardware Models. In *Asian Test Symposium (ATS)*, pages 374 – 379, Nov. 2002.

[18] K. Pattabiraman, N. Nakka, Z. Kalbarczyk, and R. Iyer. Symplfied: Symbolic Program-level Fault Injection and Error Detection Framework. In *International Conference on Dependable Systems and Networks*, 2008.

[19] K. Pattabiraman, G. P. Saggese, D. Chen, Z. Kalbarczyk, and R. K. Iyer. Dynamic Derivation of Application-Specific Error Detectors and their Implementation in Hardware. In *European Dependable Computing Conference*, 2006.

[20] P. Racunas, K. Constantinides, S. Manne, and S. S. Mukherjee. Perturbation-based Fault Screening. In *International Symposium on High Performance Computer Architecture*, 2007.

[21] P. Ramachandran. *Detecting and Recovering from In-Core Hardware Faults Through Software Anomaly Treatment*. PhD thesis, University of Illinois, Urbana Champaign, 2011.

[22] S. Sahoo, M.-L. Li, P. Ramchandran, S. Adve, V. Adve, and Y. Zhou. Using Likely Program Invariants to Detect Hardware Errors. In *International Conference on Dependable Systems and Networks*, 2008.

[23] V. Sridharan and D. R. Kaeli. Eliminating Microarchitectural Dependency from Architectural Vulnerability. In *International Symposium on High Performance Computer Architecture*, 2009.

[24] Virtutech. Simics Full System Simulator. Website, 2006. `http://www.simics.net`.

[25] N. Wang and S. Patel. ReStore: Symptom-Based Soft Error Detection in Microprocessors. *IEEE Transactions on Dependable and Secure Computing*, 3(3), July-Sept 2006.

[26] D. L. Weaver and T. Germond, editors. *The SPARC Arch. Manual*. Prentice Hall, 1994. Version 9.

[27] S. C. Woo, M. Ohara, E. Torrie, J. P. Singh, and A. Gupta. The SPLASH-2 Programs: Characterization and Methodological Considerations. In *International Symposium on Computer Architecture*, 1995.

Comprehensive Kernel Instrumentation via Dynamic Binary Translation

Peter Feiner Angela Demke Brown Ashvin Goel
University of Toronto
{peter,demke}@cs.toronto.edu, ashvin@eecg.toronto.edu

Abstract

Dynamic binary translation (DBT) is a powerful technique that enables fine-grained monitoring and manipulation of an existing program binary. At the user level, it has been employed extensively to develop various analysis, bug-finding, and security tools. Such tools are currently not available for operating system (OS) binaries since no comprehensive DBT framework exists for the OS kernel. To address this problem, we have developed a DBT framework that runs as a Linux kernel module, based on the user-level DynamoRIO framework. Our approach is unique in that it controls all kernel execution, including interrupt and exception handlers and device drivers, enabling comprehensive instrumentation of the OS without imposing any overhead on user-level code. In this paper, we discuss the key challenges in designing and building an in-kernel DBT framework and how the design differs from user-space.

We use our framework to build several sample instrumentations, including simple instruction counting as well as an implementation of shadow memory for the kernel. Using the shadow memory, we build a kernel stack overflow protection tool and a memory addressability checking tool. Qualitatively, the system is fast enough and stable enough to run the normal desktop workload of one of the authors for several weeks.

Categories and Subject Descriptors D.3.4 [*Programming Languages*]: Processors—Code generation, Run-time environments, Incremental compilers; D.2.5 [*Software Engineering*]: Testing and Debugging—Debugging aids, Monitors; D.4.m [*Operating Systems*]: Miscellaneous

General Terms Design, Performance

Keywords Dynamic binary translation, operating system instrumentation, Linux, interrupts

1. Introduction

Dynamic binary translation (DBT) entails monitoring and potentially manipulating every instruction in an existing binary before its execution. Several popular frameworks, such as DynamoRIO [5], Pin [16], and Valgrind [17] support the development of powerful tools for program analysis, debugging, and security. For example, DBT is used by Valgrind's Memcheck tool to detect memory referencing errors [22], by DynamoRIO's Program Shepherding to improve security [13], and by vx32 to enforce modularity [12]. Currently, these tools cannot be applied to operating system binaries, since there is no comprehensive DBT framework for the kernel. Motivated by the ever-growing size and complexity of kernel code, the importance of its correctness for overall robustness and security, and the continued prevalence of kernel bugs despite advances in static bug-detection tools, we have developed an in-kernel DBT framework.

The main contribution of our work is showing how to make DBT work for arbitrary devices and their drivers. Previous attempts recognized the value of DBT for kernel code, however they did not instrument important parts of the kernel or are limited to certain device drivers. For example, JIFL [19] only instruments code executed during system call handling; it does not cover interrupt handlers or kernel threads such as the Linux *flusher threads* that write dirty pages back to disk. PinOS [8] instruments all kernel code (including kernel threads and interrupt handlers) and user code running in a virtual machine. However, PinOS is incapable of instrumenting code that cannot run in a virtual machine, in particular, drivers for devices that the virtual machine monitor (VMM) does not support. Because VMMs support a small selection of devices by emulating hardware, most driver code cannot be debugged or secured with PinOS – an unfortunate limitation because drivers comprise a significant fraction of the code and the bugs in operating systems [11, 20]. A similar limitation exists with other VMMs [1] and emulators [23] that use DBT.

We identified four primary goals for a kernel DBT framework:

1. Provide full coverage of kernel code, including kernel threads, interrupt and exception handlers, and all native device drivers. This is essential to support existing techniques such as Program Shepherding and Memcheck.
2. Impose no direct overhead for user code. While whole-system instrumentation has its uses, it also has high overheads as demonstrated by PinOS. Since many applications spend little time executing in the kernel, the usability of the system will be greatly enhanced if user code is not impacted.
3. Preserve original concurrency and execution interleaving. To detect the full range of concurrency-related bugs that can arise during native execution, we must interfere minimally with thread scheduling or the points where interrupts can occur. We must be able to use all native CPU cores that are present, and be able to support kernel preemption.
4. Be transparent. Original kernel code may behave differently or break if it observes the state of the instrumented system, rather than the expected native state. This concern is common to all DBT frameworks, and is explained in more detail in the following section.

ASPLOS'12, March 3–7, 2012, London, England, UK.

Each of these goals presents its own challenges, but the key difficulty is in achieving all of them simultaneously, as we will discuss in Section 3. For example, the first goal requires our framework to maintain full control during all kernel execution, while the second one requires us to relinquish control when execution leaves the kernel. Naturally, this means that we must detect all kernel entry and exit points, and attach and detach our DBT framework correspondingly. User-space frameworks also support this ability to attach and detach during execution, however it is expected to be a rare event. In contrast, we expect frequent entries and exits, relative to the amount of time running in the kernel. A similar tension arises between providing full coverage while preserving the original execution interleavings. Typically, DBT frameworks control the points where signals (the user-space analog of interrupts) can occur because it simplifies many aspects of the implementation. It is tempting to take the same approach in the kernel, but as we will show, interrupt delivery cannot be controlled in the same way when we have full coverage of the interrupt handlers and all native device drivers.

Our approach has been to start with the user-level DynamoRIO DBT framework and transform it to run as a Linux kernel module; we call this module DRK. We chose to start with DynamoRIO because it is available as an open source project, and is full-featured, robust and high-performing. No other existing DBT framework that we are aware of meets these requirements. We do not require any kernel modifications, so DRK can instrument any Linux kernel and can handle binary-only device drivers. The DRK module can be run on either native operating systems (i.e. those that run on bare metal) or in a virtualized environment, since we do not make use of any hardware virtualization features. Thus, DRK can be deployed to instrument systems running in the cloud, an increasingly common scenario.

To help understand our work, we begin with some background on DynamoRIO in Section 2. Once initialized, DRK redirects all kernel entry points to itself, giving it full control over kernel execution. Wherever possible, we have chosen to port the existing DynamoRIO code to the kernel environment in the interests of getting experience with a working framework to guide future enhancements. Some key aspects, however, required different techniques to work in the kernel. Section 3 describes the design decisions we made, highlighting the differences of DRK over DynamoRIO. The "devil in the details" of the implementation can be found in Section 4. We evaluate the overhead of the framework and simple instrumentation clients in Section 5. We have only recently started to explore tools that are enabled by DRK. We describe a number of these in Section 6, ranging from simple ones (i.e., instruction and basic block profiling) to more sophisticated ones (i.e. an addressability checker and a stack overflow checker) that make use of a new shadow memory implementation for the kernel. We discuss related work in Section 7, and conclude in Section 8.

2. DBT Background

In this section, we give a brief overview of dynamic binary translation in general, and DynamoRIO in particular. Figure 1 illustrates the basic operation of a DBT framework. Two primary requirements govern the operation of any DBT system. First, all execution must be controlled by the DBT system. If native code is ever allowed to execute without first being translated by the DBT, it could perform arbitrary memory accesses and branches, defeating any analysis, security or debugging tools and making it impossible for the DBT framework to regain control. Second, the presence of the DBT framework must be transparent to the instrumented code, meaning that the behavior of the instrumented code must be the same as would have occurred on the native system. Existing DBT frameworks have varying degrees of transparency. For example, some will store their own state on the same stack used by the instrumented code to increase performance. On the other hand, DynamoRIO makes great efforts to be transparent; the authors of that system found this feature to be essential for instrumenting more complex Windows applications.

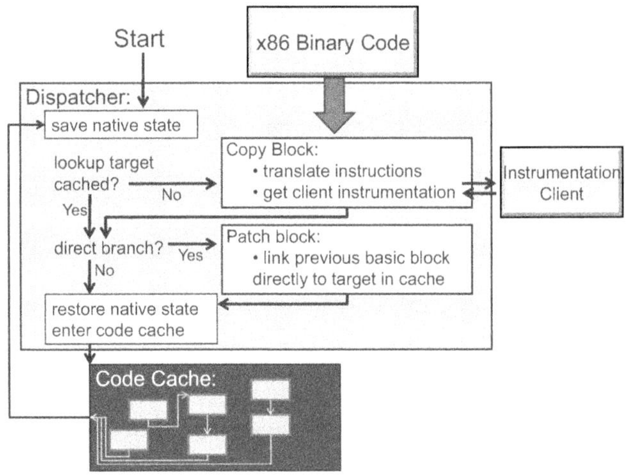

Figure 1. Basic operation of DBT framework.

Dynamic binary translators achieve reasonable performance by caching translated blocks of *native code* (i.e. the binary x86 instructions that the program counter normally points to) and re-executing them from a *code cache*. This allows the overhead of decoding the binary instructions and performing analysis and instrumentation to be amortized over a large number of uses of the cached block. Blocks typically begin at the target of some control transfer instruction (e.g., branch, call, return) and end at the next control transfer instruction (CTI) in the sequence. Thus, these units of cached code are sometimes referred to as *dynamic basic blocks* or simply *basic blocks*. Unlike conventional basic blocks, however, code within a dynamic basic block may be the target of a control transfer instruction. In this case, a new basic block is started when execution branches to the target, and the code between the newly-discovered target and the end of the basic block is duplicated in the code cache. These *replicated tails* increase the size of the cached code relative to the native code being translated.

To ensure that native code never executes, the CTIs that terminate basic blocks are manipulated to return control to the *dispatcher* component of the DBT framework. If the native CTI's target has already been copied into the cache, the dispatcher transfers control to the target's copy. Otherwise, the dispatcher interprets the target's code, which involves finding the extent of the basic block starting at the target's address, translating it, and copying the new basic block into the code cache. Finally, the dispatcher transfers control to the newly admitted block. Control transfers between the code cache and the framework are costly, because the state of the native code must be saved and restored to preserve transparency. To reduce the frequency of these *context switches*, DynamoRIO and other DBT frameworks perform additional optimizations. When the dispatcher is entered from the code cache, it checks if (a) the previous basic block ended with a direct branch and (b) the target is already in the code cache. If so, the code cache copy of the previous basic block is patched to jump directly to the target in the code cache, thereby eliminating any future exits to the dispatcher between these two basic blocks.

Indirect control transfers (e.g. indirect branches and function returns) cannot be linked directly to the target in the code cache, because they can have multiple targets. In the original program, these targets would be stored in memory that is read and written by the native code (e.g. the return address of a function call is pushed on the stack and popped upon return). To maintain transparency, the DBT framework must ensure that the native code sees the original values in its memory when it executes. For example, the original code may include checks on the values of function pointers, to ensure that they point to expected functions. If the checking code were to read the code cache addresses of the translated functions instead, it might conclude that the function pointers had been corrupted and execute some recovery path that should not actually be taken. Instead, the native addresses of indirect branch targets must be translated to their corresponding code cache address by the dispatcher. DynamoRIO uses a fast hash table lookup in this case.

A further optimization links sequences of basic blocks that are frequently executed together into *traces*. Several heuristics for trace selection have been explored, but DynamoRIO uses the *Next Executing Tail (NET)* heuristic pioneered by the HP Dynamo project [3]. DynamoRIO also maintains separate caches for basic blocks and for traces, but refers to units of code in either one as *fragments*. We do not cover traces in more detail because we have not yet applied this optimization to our kernel DBT implementation (DRK). Finally, DynamoRIO was designed as a framework upon which to build dynamic instrumentation or optimization tools. As such, it exports an API for use by *clients*, which specify the transformations to be applied to blocks of code during translation. The client API includes callbacks to be invoked when the main framework encounters events of interest, such as the creation of a new basic block to be added to the code cache. The framework also invokes a client callback to handle any synchronous exceptions that occur during the execution of client-added instrumentation from the code cache.

3. Architecture/Design

In this section we describe how DRK meets the goals laid out in Section 1. To do so, we discuss several challenges, mention some alternatives, and explain the solutions that we chose. We start with the simpler issues, before addressing the most challenging one, namely interrupts.

3.1 Detecting Kernel Execution

Our first goal of comprehensive coverage, needed for various security and memory checking tools, requires interposing on all code running in the kernel. Together with our second goal of no direct overhead for user-level code, this requires us to detect and interpose on all kernel entry points and relinquish control at all kernel exits.

Interposing on all kernel execution requires each kernel entry point to be replaced with a call to the dispatcher (see Figure 2). Normally, these entry points are stored in *descriptor tables* in memory, with the address of each table stored in a dedicated hardware register. To execute the dispatcher on kernel entry points, instead of executing the original entry point code directly, we maintain a *shadow descriptor table* for each descriptor table maintained by the kernel; we point the descriptor table registers to these shadow tables. In the shadow tables, each entry effectively calls dispatch on the corresponding entry point stored in the original descriptor table. Section 4.1.2 gives details on how we take control of kernel entry points.

In our current implementation, we have chosen to relax transparency in this case. That is, native code executing from the code cache that reads the hardware table descriptor registers would be able to observe that they point to DRK memory locations, rather than the original tables. To maintain transparency, native code instructions that read the descriptor table registers should be replaced with code cache instructions that load the original tables' addresses, which are stored in memory. The original tables should be write-protected so that changes can be detected and propagated to the

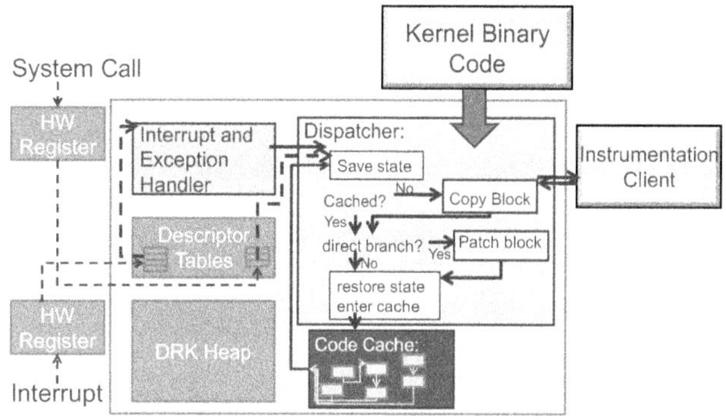

Figure 2. Schematic of DRK design. Dashed arrows indicate control flow that is triggered by hardware events such as system calls or interrupts.

shadow tables. Finally, translated code that changes the table descriptor registers in the code cache should be replaced with instructions that update the shadow registers in memory. In the Linux kernel, these tables are all initialized at boot time and not modified thereafter. As a result, we have not found any cases where this loss of transparency creates a problem in the Linux kernel.

Kernel exits are identified during fragment creation, since they are caused by the execution of specific instructions (e.g., `sysexit, sysret, iret`). Section 4.2.1 explains how we detach and resume native execution in user mode.

Compared to whole-system instrumentation, our design imposes no direct overhead on code executing in user mode. However, running kernel code under control of DRK may impose indirect costs due to potentially increasing cache and TLB misses.

3.2 Reentrancy

The problem of reentrancy arises for a DBT framework when its own interpretation code uses native code that it is in the middle of interpreting, for example, to perform heap allocation or I/O.

DBT frameworks avoid this problem by only using code that they do not interpret, i.e., their own code and the systems beneath them. Because the user-space frameworks do not interpret kernel code, they can safely make system calls. A VMM-based approach, such as PinOS, can make use of the VMM itself and virtual machines other than the one being instrumented (e.g., PinOS performs all I/O through Xen's Domain 0 guest). This approach is not available to us since there is no lower-level uninstrumented code that we can invoke. JIFL addressed the reentrancy problem by implementing its own heap management routines, and by detaching itself before calling the original I/O functions of the kernel. Detaching during I/O is not an acceptable option for DRK, since we aim to be comprehensive.

In our design, we avoid problems with reentrancy by making the dispatcher self-contained. Like JIFL, we allocate a large chunk of memory during initialization and implement our own heap allocator to manage this memory while DRK is running. The I/O problem is harder, since we cannot easily "push" data out of DRK without invoking functions that we are instrumenting. We solve this by adopting a "pull" model for I/O instead. We provide DRK functions that can be invoked by instrumented code (and are themselves instrumented). These functions simply copy data from DRK into a buffer supplied by the caller. In this way, user-level programs can be written to pull data out of DRK, and then use any of the normal I/O facilities (which will all be instrumented in the kernel) to display the data on screen, save it to a file, or send it out over the network. We explain how this works with standard Linux facilities in Section 4.1.1.

3.3 Preserving concurrency

To handle multithreaded code correctly, DBT frameworks must ensure that the dispatcher and execution in the code cache behave in a thread-safe manner. Concurrency problems arise in the dispatcher when it is used by multiple threads. For example, updates to shared data structures, such as the map of native-code addresses to code-cache addresses, cannot conflict. Concurrency problems arise during code cache execution because the translated code in the cache contains accesses to data structures that are shared with the dispatcher (e.g., to spill native register values when registers are used by instrumentation code, and to restore them when they are needed by the native code).

In user-space frameworks, two approaches are generally taken to managing concurrency: locking accesses to shared data or using thread-private data[1]. Although shared code caches and data structures use less memory and avoid redundant interpretation and copying, the overhead of locking and the mutual exclusion that it enforces can seriously perturb the original thread interleaving. In the thread-private data approach, each thread has its own private code cache and auxiliary data structures. Thus, threads are not forced to synchronize in ways other than in the original code. In practice, use of thread-private data is only suitable for programs with a small number of threads or programs in which threads access disparate code, such as desktop applications [6]. Because many threads run inside the kernel (i.e., all user and kernel threads), using thread-private data would have prohibitive memory and interpretation overheads.

A kernel DBT framework like DRK has another concurrency management technique at its disposal: CPU-private data (without control over preemption points, user-space frameworks cannot reliably use CPU-private data). Each CPU has its own private code cache and auxiliary data structures. This approach avoids locking while bounding redundant interpretation and copying. We adopt the CPU-private approach.

To support kernel preemption when using CPU-private data, care must be taken to ensure that no CPU-private state is saved in non-CPU-private locations when the preempted task context switches. Otherwise, if the preempted task later resumes on another CPU, it will use the wrong CPU's private data. Two scenarios can cause CPU-private state to be exposed. First, interrupt handlers can inspect the register state that was saved when the interrupt occurred. Thus, a register that temporarily holds CPU-private data may be exposed to the native interrupt handler. We avoid this problem by restoring native machine state before delivering interrupts and exceptions. Second, a DBT system may store CPU-private code cache addresses on the native stack to improve performance. We avoid this problem by always storing native code addresses, and not code cache addresses, on the native stack: we emulate `call` and `ret` by pushing and popping native addresses and calling the dispatcher. We further ensure that the interrupt stack contains native addresses when the native handler executes. Although JIFL also used CPU-private data and code caches, it did not work with preemptible kernels because it did not interpose on interrupt handlers, and therefore allowed CPU-private data to be exposed.

3.4 Interrupts and Exceptions

The way we handle interrupts and exceptions has an impact on most of our goals for DRK[2]. Comprehensiveness requires instrumenting exception and interrupt handlers. Using CPU-private data to manage multicore systems requires extra care to avoid exposing CPU-private data to another CPU following interrupts, as we discussed in the previous subsection. In addition, preserving concurrency means that we should allow interrupts to be delivered at all the points where they would normally occur in the native code. Finally, to be transparent, we must ensure that native interrupt and exception handlers observe machine state that could have occurred natively, rather than the DRK state.

We define *interrupts* to be asynchronous events, not caused by any particular instruction, that redirect execution to their handlers. We define *exceptions* to be synchronous events, triggered by instruction execution, that immediately invoke their handlers. The key distinction between the two is that interrupts can technically be handled at any time whereas exceptions must be handled before the triggering instruction can proceed. For example, an instruction that accesses memory and triggers a page fault exception cannot complete until the page fault is handled. In either case, we interpose on the native handlers by pointing the appropriate hardware registers at our own descriptor tables, as illustrated in Figure 2.

Because handlers can inspect machine state that was saved before their invocation (generally stack memory and registers), DBT frameworks must take care to present plausible machine state – i.e., machine state that could have been observed during native execution. This precaution is essential for correct execution. For example, Linux's page fault handler intentionally panics if a page fault exception arises in the kernel unless the triggering instruction has a pre-allowed address [4]. Under the control of a DBT framework, the pre-allowed instruction never executes – only its copy in the code cache. Hence, to avoid causing a kernel panic, the interposing handler has to translate the code cache address of the faulting instruction to the native instruction's address before invoking the kernel's page fault handler.

Presenting plausible machine state is tricky, particularly if an interrupt or exception arises during the execution of instrumentation code or the dispatcher. In this case, the interrupted instruction has no corresponding native code, thus translation to the native code address is impossible. Below, we describe how DRK handles exceptions and interrupts that occur during instrumentation code and dispatcher execution.

Exceptions triggered by instrumentation code are handled by restoring native machine state – analogous to how x86 hardware delivers precise exceptions [2] – and invoking the instrumented copy of the original handler. DynamoRIO requires framework clients to implement callback functions that translate machine state when exceptions arise during instrumentation code. These callback functions restore registers used by the instrumentation code and provide a native code address for the faulting instruction. We impose the same requirement on instrumentation writers in DRK.

Like other DBT frameworks, we only expect exceptions in the dispatcher while interpreting code. In this case, the dispatcher admits a copy of the code up to the exceptional instruction into the code cache and executes that copy before invoking the instrumented exception handler. To prevent page fault exceptions while fetching dispatcher and code cache instructions, the dispatcher and code cache are stored in page frames that are always present in all processes' page tables.

Asynchronous interrupts are harder to deal with. Because they can arise at any point, writing instrumentation callbacks to restore native machine state is intractable in general. Imposing this requirement would make it impossible to write many interesting instrumentation tools. To circumvent this problem, user-space DBT frameworks queue signals (the user-level analog of asynchronous interrupts) and deliver them at the next code cache exit, when the native state is known.

Imposing such a delay is contrary to our goal of preserving the original execution interleaving. However, even if we were willing to compromise on this goal, there is a more fundamental problem. When executing instrumented native kernel code, some of the in-

[1] Valgrind simply serializes all thread execution.

[2] Our goal of not instrumenting user code is the exception to this.

structions running from the code cache may observe or modify the hardware interrupt delivery state (e.g. by executing certain instructions such as `CLI` or `POPF` or by reading or writing device registers using memory mapped I/O). This can cause the hardware state to appear inconsistent to the instrumented code, since interrupts are being queued by DRK and have not yet been seen by the native handlers. In addition, by the time we reach the next code cache exit, the deliverability of the interrupt may have changed from the time when it was queued (e.g., the OS has disabled interrupts and thus expects that they will not be delivered).

Since we want to handle the full diversity of native hardware devices and drivers, trapping and emulating all instructions that might affect interrupt delivery becomes enormously complex. The difficulty is exacerbated by the need to do checks atomically with respect to other interrupt delivery, and to ensure that queued interrupts are delivered in the right order (respecting their priority levels). A VMM-based solution, like PinOS, has the advantage of only needing to manage the virtualized devices provided by the underlying hypervisor. Indeed, PinOS takes the approach of queuing interrupts, just like the user-space Pin framework. This, however, precludes instrumenting the native device drivers.

We chart a middle course instead of always delaying interrupts or always delivering them immediately. While executing from the code cache, we delay the delivery of interrupts only until the next native instruction boundary. This delay allows us to emulate the behavior expected of precise interrupts (i.e. the interrupted instruction is either committed or removed, but is not seen to have partially executed), thus preserving transparency. Since no native instruction executes between the arrival of the interrupt and the dispatch of the native handler, we ensure that there is no inconsistency between the native software and hardware state. Furthermore, we delay interrupts over any instrumentation, thus side stepping the problem of rolling back arbitrary instrumentation instructions. Upon return from the native interrupt handler, we invoke the dispatcher on the address of the interrupted native instruction. This dispatch can cause a new basic block to be emitted into the code cache, beginning with the interrupted instruction and replicating the remaining instructions in the original basic block. These *interrupt tails* have the potential to cause bloat in the code cache, but in practice we have not observed it to be a serious problem.

We disable interrupts while executing in the dispatcher, both because there is no corresponding native state and because the dispatcher is not itself reentrant. Before entering the code cache, we restore the native interruptability state. Because handling interrupts correctly involves many tricky corner cases, we explain our strategy in detail in Section 4.2.2

3.5 Code Cache Consistency

To faithfully emulate the native execution of the code being instrumented, a DBT framework must ensure that the code cache is kept consistent with native code. If some native code is modified after it has been copied into the cache, then the cached code is no longer valid. Likewise, if some native code becomes non-executable, then any cached blocks derived from it are no longer valid. Reliably detecting when native code and permissions change is a complex matter. Consequently, different frameworks maintain code cache consistency to various degrees (DynamoRIO, Valgrind, PinOS) or have no details published (JIFL, Pin, vx32).

We do not maintain code cache consistency in our current implementation. The various problems that can arise with inconsistent caches are fundamentally of two types. The first is problems due to code changes. The second is problems due to page mapping changes. Both can be addressed using shadow page tables, which we have not yet implemented. Despite this limitation, the Linux kernel runs stably when instrumented by DRK, because runtime code modification and page mapping changes for kernel code are rare events in Linux. Runtime code modification happens mainly during system boot and is already complete by the time our module loads. Other runtime modifications happen when the number of CPUs is dynamically reduced to a single CPU (to remove locking costs that are no longer needed), but we expect this is also a rare occurrence. The other problematic case occurs with module unloading, since cached copies of the unloaded module code should also be invalidated. These specific problems could be handled without shadow page tables, by detecting the relevant module unload or CPU change events, and flushing the code cache. This heavyweight solution would be acceptable for events that occur rarely.

3.6 Transparency Limitations in DRK

DRK is not fully transparent. However, it is transparent in places that matter to the native kernel code that we are instrumenting. As noted previously, native code could observe the addresses of DRK's shadow descriptor tables by reading the hardware registers that point to them. Also, DRK's lack of code cache consistency is essentially a transparency issue. In addition, since we do not have shadow page tables, native code could observe some inconsistencies in its page tables. For example, suppose some thread executes code from a newly-loaded module, causing it to be loaded into the code cache. Another thread running later on the same CPU will be able to execute the cached copies of those pages, even though its own top-level page table may be missing a mapping for the native module code address. We have not encountered any native Linux code that is affected by this inconsistency. With additional implementation effort, all of these issues could be addressed, but it has not been necessary to do so at this point.

4. Implementation of Framework

As we described in Section 3, DRK operates as a loadable kernel module which hijacks all kernel entry points to redirect execution to itself. We now describe the details of how this works in the Linux kernel, beginning with the initialization steps, and normal operation. We then take a detailed look at how we handle exceptional control flow, namely interrupts and exceptions.

4.1 Initialization

The module's initialization is divided into two phases: kernel and CPU initialization. During kernel initialization, the module directly invokes Linux code to make kernel requests; this is the only time the module uses possibly non-reentrant Linux code. These requests include memory allocation for DRK's heap and creating `ioctl` interfaces and `sysfs` entries for I/O with user space. The module's final request is for the kernel to begin the CPU initialization phase by calling a function on each processor via an inter-processor interrupt.

4.1.1 Kernel Initialization

DRK allocates memory for its heap using Linux's `vmalloc` memory allocator. When `vmalloc` returns, Linux ensures that physical pages for the memory request are allocated and mapped into the current process's page table and all newly created processes' page tables, but it does not ensure that all of these pages are mapped into other existing processes' page tables. In normal execution, Linux handles `vmalloc` page faults transparently by mapping in the missing page and resuming execution. However, DRK cannot use Linux's page fault handler because of reentrance and comprehensiveness. So, after getting the memory from Linux, DRK iterates through all of the existing processes and to check that its memory is mapped in all of them. In our current system, this check always succeeds, so we have not yet implemented code to install any missing mappings during initialization.

DynamoRIO requires its heap to be located within 2GB of its text and data segments so that generated code can refer to DynamoRIO symbols using PC-relative addresses (i.e., specified by a signed 32-bit offset from the PC). However, normally on x86-64, Linux allocates virtual addresses for `vmalloc`'d memory some 55TB away from the virtual addresses used to allocate module memory (i.e. module text and data). Thus, DRK cannot obtain memory directly from `vmalloc` while still meeting the requirements of DynamoRIO. Instead, DRK uses the special `module_alloc` interface, which returns `vmalloc`'d memory that is close enough to its text and data.

I/O is accomplished asynchronously by copying memory. During initialization, the DRK module and its instrumentation clients create `sysfs` entries for their outputs. A `sysfs` file provides usermode programs with a standard file interface that they can read from and write to. When a user program reads from a `sysfs` file, Linux calls the file's registered callback function with a buffer for the output. The DRK callback functions simply copy the requested output from DRK's memory. For example, the instrcount instrumentation (described later in Section 5.1) keeps a CPU-private dynamic instruction count. When a user call reads from `/sys/module/instrcount/dynamic/cpu0`, cpu0's instruction count is copied into the supplied buffer.

4.1.2 CPU Initialization

One CPU is arbitrarily designated as the main CPU. The main CPU executes DynamoRIO's main initialization routine, which sets up global resources like the heap, and waits to continue. After the main CPU has initialized the global resources, the other CPUs call DynamoRIO's thread initialization routine, which creates thread-specific resources like per-CPU code caches.

As a part of each CPU's initialization, the kernel entry points are replaced with calls to the DRK module. The 64-bit x86 architecture permits entry into the kernel via interrupts, system call instructions (`syscall` and `sysenter`), and certain far `call` and `jmp` instructions [2] (see [21] for a more concise explanation than [2]). However, the Linux kernel only enables entry via system calls and interrupts.

For `syscall` and `sysenter`, the entry point is stored in a model-specific register (MSR). DRK can optimize these entry points because execution must have been in userspace prior to a system call entry (i.e. not already in the kernel). During initialization, DRK overwrites the system call MSRs with the addresses of fragments that are created from their native contents.

For interrupts, the entry point for each interrupt vector is stored in the interrupt descriptor table, which is pointed to by the interrupt descriptor table register (IDTR). To redirect execution to the DRK module on interrupts, DRK replaces the native IDTR with a pointer to its own table of DRK interrupt entry points. Unlike the system call entry points, DRK cannot simply redirect interrupt entry points to fragments built from the corresponding native interrupt entry points. As described in Section 3, either the dispatching of interrupt handlers has to be delayed or the machine state has to be manipulated, or both, in some cases. To handle this requirement, the DRK interrupt descriptor table redirects all interrupt entry points to the same routine, which is described by the algorithm HANDLE-INTERRUPT in Figure 3. Section 4.2.2 describes the algorithm in detail, but first we show how DRK operates during normal control flow.

4.2 Running

4.2.1 Normal Operation

When execution enters the kernel, DRK operates like userspace DBT frameworks, as described in Section 2. The dispatcher determines the extent of the next basic block of native code, creates a fragment from a copy of that code with client-added instrumentation, emits the fragment into the code cache, and enters the code cache by context switching to the beginning of the fragment. When execution reaches the end of a fragment, the target of the native control transfer instruction that terminated the block of native code determines the next address to dispatch on. DRK applies standard optimizations to avoid context switches: fragments ending in direct branches are directly linked to their target fragments and fragments ending in indirect branches are indirectly linked to their targets via a fast hash table lookup.

When execution reaches a kernel exit point, DRK executes the exit instruction from a native context, thus returning to native usermode execution. When creating fragments, DRK recognizes instructions that might cause exits. Instructions that always exit the kernel (i.e., the system call return instructions `sysret` and `sysexit`) are simply copied into the code cache; when execution arrives at the end of the fragment with a system call return, the CPU will already be in a native context. Instructions that conditionally exit the kernel (i.e., the interrupt return instruction `iret`) are translated to return control to the dispatcher. In the dispatcher, DRK determines if the interrupt return is going to the kernel or to usermode based on the privilege level of the interrupted context stored on the interrupt stack frame. If the kernel was interrupted, then DRK treats an interrupt return like any other indirect control transfer: the interrupt stack frame is popped off of the stack and the interrupted instruction address is dispatched on. If usermode was interrupted, then DRK context switches and executes the interrupt return instruction natively.

4.2.2 Exceptional Control Flow

When an interrupt or exception arrives, DRK needs to arrange for its native handler to be run through the dispatcher. In this discussion we use the term "interrupt" to refer to both asynchronous interrupts and exceptions; we use the more precise term when a distinction needs to be made between them. DRK must ensure that the native handler runs while the computer is in a state that could be observed natively. As explained in Section 3, the pertinent observable native state comprises registers, relevant memory (such as return addresses stored on the stack), and the state of interrupt-generating hardware.

Natively, x86 guarantees precise interrupt delivery: an interrupt will arrive only on instruction boundaries; all instructions have either executed entirely or not at all before the handler is invoked. However, because native instructions may be translated into multiple code cache instructions to emulate their operation, interrupts will sometimes arrive when native instructions have been partially emulated. To emulate precise interrupt delivery, DRK simulates delivering interrupts on native instruction boundaries by either recreating native state at a native instruction boundary or delaying the interrupt until the end of the partially executed translation. Although most translations simply copy the native instruction, others are complex, namely the translations of native control transfer instructions, which involve the dispatcher. DRK's interrupt handler determines what translation was interrupted and the appropriate action to take.

Because correct interrupt emulation is extremely tricky, we describe the different cases in detail. The algorithm for handling interrupts is presented in Figure 3. When an interrupt arrives, the hardware disables asynchronous interrupts, pushes an interrupt stack frame, and redirects execution to DRK's interrupt handler. The interrupt stack frame contains information about how to return to the interrupted instruction, in particular, the interrupted instruction's address and a flag indicating whether or not the CPU had asyn-

```
HANDLE-INTERRUPT(ISF, REGS, vector)
 1  Hardware pushes interrupt stack frame ISF
 2  Switch stacks and save pre-interrupt registers REGS
 3  Interrupts-Were-Enabled = ISF.interrupts_enabled
 4  Invoke client's interrupt instrumentation
 5  if Client handled interrupt
 6      goto 35
 7  elseif Interrupted in user space
 8      DISPATCH(NATIVE-HANDLERS[vector], REGS)
 9  elseif Interrupted in fragment F on instruction I
10      Determine source S of I
11      if Interrupt is an exception
12          Recreate native register state REGS
13          goto 31
14      elseif S is a control transfer instruction
15          Unlink F
16          goto 33
17      elseif S is a native instruction
18          goto 12
19      elseif S is an instrumentation instruction
20          Determine next instruction N following S
            with a native source
21          Patch start of translation for N to return to dispatcher
22          goto 33
23  elseif Interrupted during indirect branch lookup
24      Patch last instruction of lookup routine
        to return to dispatcher
25      goto 33
26  elseif Interrupted while exiting code cache
27      goto 33
28  elseif Interrupted while entering code cache
29      REGS = registers saved during last
        code cache exit
30      goto 31
31  Pending-Vector = vector
32  DISPATCH(NATIVE-HANDLERS[vector], REGS)
    N.B. DISPATCH does not return.
33  Pending-Vector = vector
34  Disable interrupts on ISF
35  Switch stacks and restore registers REGS
36  Pop ISF
37  Return to interrupted code cache instruction

DISPATCH(TARGET, REGS)
1  if Pending-Vector ≠ NULL
2      Relink fragment or unpatch code if necessary
3      Push interrupt stack frame ISF for TARGET and REGS
4      ISF.interrupts_enabled = Interrupts-Were-Enabled
5      TARGET = NATIVE-HANDLERS[Pending-Vector]
6      Pending-Vector = NULL
7  Enter code cache at fragment for TARGET and restore REGS
```

Figure 3. Interrupt handling algorithm. HANDLE-INTERRUPT shows DRK's interrupt handler and DISPATCH shows the relevant parts of the dispatcher.

chronous interrupts enabled prior to interruption[3]. The register state prior to interruption is also available, which DRK saves to its own stack upon entry to its interrupt handler. Lines 1–3 of HANDLE-INTERRUPT show these state-saving steps, which are common to all interrupt handling cases. Next, DRK gives the instrumentation client (if one exists) a chance to handle the interrupt (lines 4–6). If the client has not fully handled the interrupt, DRK then decides to either compute native state and immediately dispatch or delay the interrupt.

[3] Recall that exceptions and non-maskable interrupts may occur even if the CPU had asynchronous interrupts disabled.

When DRK recreates native state, it records the pending interrupt vector and transfers control to the dispatcher immediately (lines 31–32 of HANDLE-INTERRUPT).

To delay an interrupt, DRK records the pending interrupt, arranges for execution to return to the dispatcher at the boundary between the current translation and the translation for the next native instruction, and returns to the interrupted instruction with interrupts disabled (lines 33–37 of HANDLE-INTERRUPT). Interrupts are disabled so that another interrupt doesn't arrive before the pending interrupt is delivered, leaving hardware to implicitly queue subsequent device interrupts. Letting hardware queue interrupts avoids the problem of queueing interrupts in software (which, in itself is challenging for general hardware because emptying the queue requires an understanding of hardware interrupt routing). When execution reaches the dispatcher after the delayed interrupt, the arrival of the pending interrupt is emulated (lines 1–6 of DISPATCH). Because interrupts were artificially disabled before returning to the dispatcher, the wrong interruptibility state will have been saved during the last context switch. However, since *Pending-Vector* is not NULL, the last code cache exit must have been caused by a pending asynchronous interrupt, therefore the dispatcher modifies the emulated interrupt stack frame to indicate the native state of the interrupt flag (line 4 of DISPATCH). Then the dispatcher enters the code cache at the fragment for the delayed interrupt's handler.

The remainder of this section describes why DRK delays interrupts or immediately transfers to the dispatcher when an interrupt arrives. The decision to delay or not depends on where the CPU is interrupted.

Case 1: Interrupt in user mode. Because usermode execution is not instrumented, the interrupted instruction will always be on a native instruction boundary, hence no undoing or delaying is necessary. In this case, DRK simply calls dispatch on the native interrupt handler (lines 7–8 of HANDLE-INTERRUPT).

Case 2: Interrupted in a code cache fragment. To handle interrupts in code cache fragments, DRK first determines what kind of translation the interrupted instruction came from (line 10). To determine the translation, DRK makes use of DynamoRIO's state recreation code for synchronous userspace signals.

Case 2A: Exception in fragment. Exceptions are synchronous interrupts triggered by an instruction, such as a page fault. Natively, the exception is delivered with the state of the CPU before the exceptional instruction executed. DRK is therefore forced to determine native state at the exceptional instruction (line 12) and dispatch on the exception handler (line 13). DRK uses DynamoRIO's state recreation code to determine native state. This code scans from the beginning of the interrupted fragment to the interrupted instruction address; it keeps track of outstanding register spills and adjustments to the stack pointer made by DynamoRIO's translations and reverts them. Because it is impossible to undo arbitrary translations, DRK (like DynamoRIO) requires clients to handle any exceptions that their instrumentation code generates (line 5).

Case 2B: Interrupted during the translation of a control transfer instruction. Interrupts are delayed until the target of the control transfer instruction. This approach avoids creating a redundant fragment tail because the target of the control transfer instruction would be the beginning of a new fragment in spite of interruption. This is accomplished by unlinking the last instruction in the fragment's control transfer translation, via patching, to return to the dispatcher (line 15 of HANDLE-INTERRUPT). After the fragment is unlinked, execution returns to the interrupted translation with interrupts disabled (lines 33–37). When the CPU executes the dispatcher next, it sees the pending interrupt and emulates its arrival. Translations for control transfer instructions involve emulation in some cases. For instance, a return instruction's translation involves spilling a register, popping the return address off of the stack into the spilled register, jumping to the indirect branch lookup routine, and returning to the dispatcher if the lookup fails to find the fragment for the return address. Interrupts during the first three steps (spilling, popping, and jumping), take place in the fragment and are thus handled by Case 2B. Interrupts during the last two steps are handled by Case 3 and Case 4.

Case 2C: Interrupted during a native instruction translation. Native state is recreated and the dispatcher is invoked immediately. The interrupt cannot be delayed because subsequent native instructions might affect interrupt delivery.

Case 2D: Interrupted during instrumentation. Undoing in this case is unfeasible because instrumentation is arbitrary code. So the interrupt is delayed until the end of the instrumentation (line 20). The translation following the interrupted instrumentation is patched with a control transfer to the dispatcher (line 21). Because DRK uses CPU-private code caches, this patch will not affect other CPUs. However, a shared code cache could be patched atomically if instructions following instrumentation code were padded to the proper alignment.

Case 3: Interrupted during indirect branch lookup routine. On the hit path of the indirect branch lookup routine, there is a final jump instruction that transfers control to the fragment. To delay interrupts in this case, this final jump is patched to return to the dispatcher (line 24), effectively delaying the interrupt. DRK uses CPU-private indirect branch lookup routines to make patching simple and efficient. However, the patch could be done atomically for shared caches at the performance cost of spurious code cache exits on other CPUs.

Case 4: Interrupted while exiting the code cache. DynamoRIO saves the kernel's native state when control exits the code cache and enters the dispatcher. If interrupted during a context switch, DRK needs to delay the interrupt until the context switch finishes to allowing the remaining native state to be saved. To delay interrupts in this case, DRK simply makes note of the pending interrupt and returns to the interrupted context switch (line 27 of HANDLE-INTERRUPT).

Case 5: Interrupted while entering the code cache. DRK has nothing to undo because the native state was recorded during the last code cache exit. DRK makes note of the pending interrupt and calls DISPATCH with the registers saved during the last code cache exit (line 29 of HANDLE-INTERRUPT).

5. Framework Evaluation

Before examining applications that are enabled by DRK, we evaluate the overhead of the framework alone and with a simple instrumentation client. For these experiments, we operate with a large enough maximum code cache size so that flushes do not occur. We perform a number of stress tests with a high level of kernel activity, to show the robustness of DRK and to illustrate worst-case behavior. As noted in Section 2, we have not yet ported certain DynamoRIO optimizations, such as traces, to DRK. The current results are therefore conservative.

	nthreads	data size
fileserver	50	1.25 GB
webserver	100	15.6 MB
webproxy	100	15.6 MB
varmail	16	15.6 MB

Table 1. Filebench parameters

5.1 Simple Tools

We implemented two simple instrumentation clients to illustrate the overhead of the DRK framework. *Null Client* does nothing. This client illustrates DRK's bare performance. *Instruction Count* keeps a per-CPU tally of the number of instructions that have executed. *Instruction Count* instruments every basic block to increment the CPU's counter by the number of instructions in the basic block. Our implementation of this client uses a standard optimization that avoids spilling and restoring the CPU's arithmetic flags if they are dead. Note that if an interrupt arrives after the *Instruction Count* instrumentation clobbers the flags, but before the native instruction kills the flags, then the interrupt handler will see the non-native flag state. During our experiments, we have not seen this affect the correctness of the kernel execution.

5.2 Experimental Results

Our test system is a Dell Optiplex 980 with 8 GB of RAM and 4 64-bit Intel Core i7 CPUs operating at 2.8GHz. We disabled hyperthreading in the BIOS for our performance experiments, but note that DRK runs stably with all 8 cores that are available when hyperthreading is enabled. We use lmbench version 3.0 to get a fine-grained view of the performance during a variety of system activities[4]. We then present server and desktop benchmarks. All results are an average of five warm runs.

Figure 4 shows the lmbench results. We have grouped tests with similar original native performance into subfigures to better show the performance. For simple system calls, our slowdown with the *Null client* ranges from 1.4 (for the null system call) to 2.7 for open+close. Other "fast" kernel operations have higher overheads, with a worst-case slowdown of 4.9 during protection faults. Signal delivery and page faults on file pages are more like system calls, with slowdowns of 2.8 and 2.1 respectively. The results for the other system calls are similar. The slowdowns on select and pipe range from 1.9 to 2.5, although sock is worse. The slowdowns for the fork calls are also similar, ranging from 2.2 up to 2.7. The *Instruction Count* client adds significant additional overhead for these simple microbenchmark tests, although as the complexity of the operation increases, the additional overhead of *Instruction Count* is less significant, as can be seen for the fork operations.

We observe that the overheads are lower for simple system calls than for protection faults because DRK points system call entries directly to their fragments in the code cache (as described in Section 4.1.2), while other entry points to the kernel are more costly. Based on these results, we are investigating optimizations for other entry points, especially page fault exceptions.

We use the Linux port of Filebench version 1.4.9, with four of the standard workload personalities, using the default settings for each[5]. The relevant parameters for the workloads are in Table 1. With the default parameters, the datasets easily fit in memory on our test machine, so the workloads are not limited by the performance of I/O operations. The filebench workloads use a specified number of threads to perform file system operations. These threads

[4] We present the most interesting lmbench results here. The raw data for all experiments is available from our website at http://csng.cs.toronto.edu/projects/23

[5] The oltp workload hung our native system regularly.

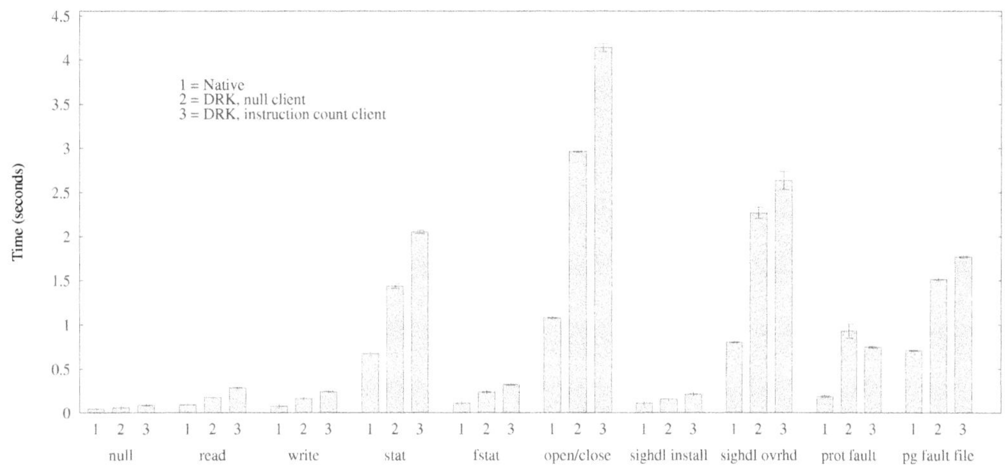

(a) Fast operations

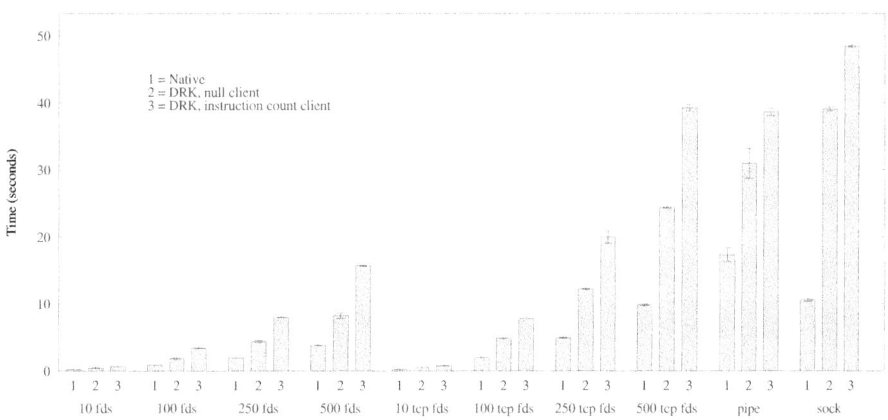

(b) Communication related (select on varying numbers of fds, pipe, sock) operations

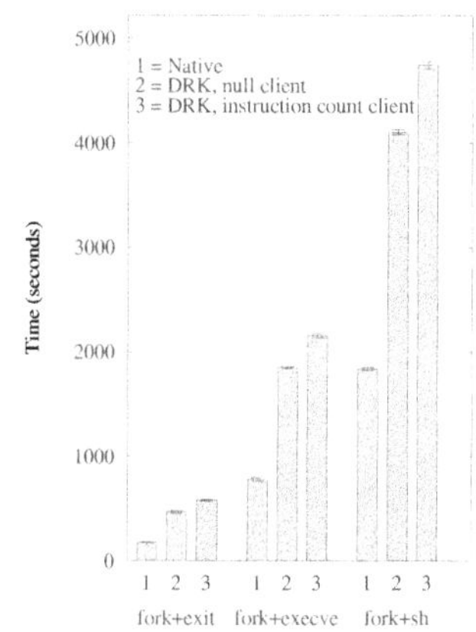

(c) Fork operations

Figure 4. Microbenchmark results from lmbench

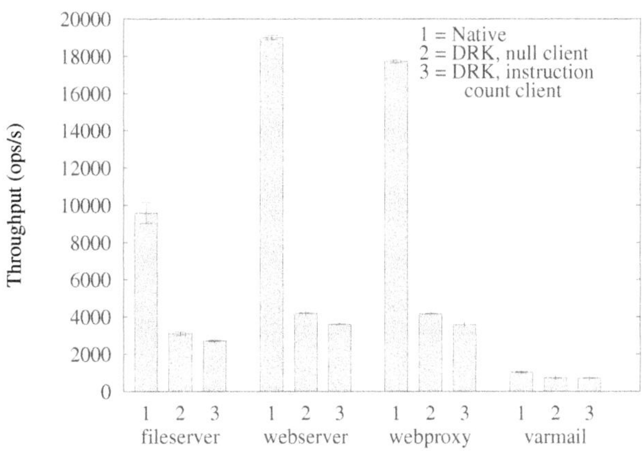

(a) Filebench throughput

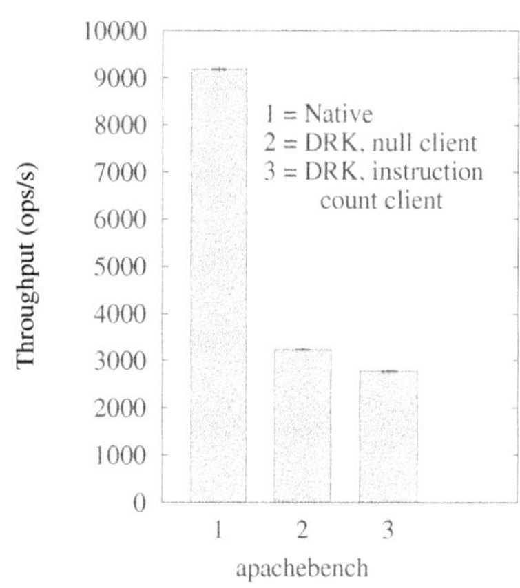

(b) Apachebench throughput

Figure 5. Throughput results on server benchmarks

	User time (s)	System time (s)	Page faults (major + minor)	context switches (vol + invol)
native	853.5	90.4	0.0 maj + 44330667.2 min	381416.2 vol + 318502.4 invol
null client	1008.6	219.8	0.0 maj + 44330627.8 min	411537.6 vol + 367363.6 invol
instruction count client	1044.3	262.9	0.0 maj + 44331392.0 min	416782.2 vol + 377980.2 invol

Table 2. Kernel compile statistics (make -j4)

use shared memory and synchronization primitives to communicate with each other. This means we are really testing the performance of a varying number of threads that exercise IPC and kernel operations heavily, rather than file system performance. The exception is varmail, which has some I/O activity due to issuing sync calls.

The throughput of the Filebench workloads, in file system operations per second, is shown in Figure 5(a). *Null Client* reduces throughput by 3X for fileserver, and by 4.5X and 4.2X for webserver and webproxy, respectively. There is only a small additional reduction in throughput with *Instruction Count*. We can see that the drop in throughput is correlated with the number of threads used in the workload, with webserver and webproxy both using 100 threads. The overhead for varmail, which syncs its data to disk frequently, is much lower, with only a 1.4X drop in throughput.

To get a better sense of the impact on server workloads, we set up an apache web server (using default settings) on our instrumented system and ran apachebench from a separate client machine connected via gigabit ethernet. We used 500K requests and a concurrency level of 200. We found that our client was unable to generate enough load to saturate the CPUs on the 4-core test system. In this configuration, there was effectively no loss in throughput as measured at the client, since the server CPU (which is affected by the overhead of DRK) was not the bottleneck. We therefore configured our test system to boot with a single CPU and verified that the client running apachebench was able to saturate the CPU on the server running natively. With this setup, we observed roughly 28% of the CPU time was spent in system mode, with another 38% of the CPU time spent in interrupt handling. Figure 5(b) shows the throughput measured at the client. As with the CPU-bound Filebench workloads, there is a 3X drop in throughput. This is not surprising given the high proportion of time spent handling interrupts, and the costs of recreating native state to handle interrupt delivery, as detailed in Section 4.2.2.

To assess the impact on desktop workloads, we timed a compile of the Linux kernel tree, using "make -j4" on the 4-core system. Table 2 shows the relevant statistics. We show the user and kernel time accumulated by all sub-processes of make. Here, we can see the indirect impact of DRK on the user-time, as well as the much higher kernel overheads. The overall CPU time (user+kernel) to complete the compile with *Null Client* increased by about 30%. *Instruction Count* adds an additional 8% overhead to the CPU time. We also tested kernel compile with the 1-CPU system and obtained essentially the same results.

We also tested browser javascript performance using the Mozilla Kraken benchmark. In this case, the total time to run the benchmark increased by only 3% over native when running with DRK (the Null client and Instruction Count client were essentially the same). This result is expected since javascript execution has little kernel interaction, and is largely unaffected by DRK. Small, but noticeable, overheads occur primarily in the tests that use a large amount of memory (and hence have many page faults).

6. Applications

This section describes more sophisticated DBT applications we have built using DRK. Before introducing these applications, we describe our shadow memory implementation. Then, we give examples of two non-trivial debugging tools built using DRK.

`0000000000000000-00007fffffffffff`	user space
`0008000000000000-ffff7fffffffffff`	sign extension
`ffff800000000000-ffff80ffffffffff`	guard hole
`ffff880000000000-ffffc7ffffffffff`	physical direct map
`ffffc80000000000-ffffc8ffffffffff`	**unused (1TB)**
`ffffc90000000000-ffffe8ffffffffff`	vmalloc
`ffffe90000000000-ffffe9ffffffffff`	**unused (1TB)**
`ffffea0000000000-ffffeaffffffffff`	virtual memory map
`ffffeb0000000000-ffffffff7fffffff`	**unused ($\approx$ 21TB)**
`ffffffff80000000-ffffffffa0000000`	kernel text
`ffffffffa0000000-ffffffffff00000`	modules
`fffffffffff00001-ffffffffffffffff`	**unused ($\approx$ 1GB)**

Figure 6. Map of 64-bit x86 Linux kernel memory, adapted from [14]. The kernel's valid virtual addresses are in the range shown between two horizontal lines, which is 120TB in size. 24TB of the address space is unused.

6.1 Shadow Memory

Shadow memory is a technique for storing metadata about every byte of memory that a program uses. Some of the most popular userspace applications of DBT rely on shadow memory. For example, Memcheck [22] keeps track of the addressability of memory with byte-level granularity and tracks definedness with bit-level granularity.

The main challenge in implementing shadow memory is implementing an efficient mapping between application memory and shadow memory. The simplest scheme directly maps addresses to shadow addresses by a constant offset. However, this simple scheme requires a region of address space as large as the range of addresses being shadowed. If such a region does not exist, then an indirect mapping scheme is required. Indirect mapping associates chunks of application addresses with chunks of shadow addresses.

For the 64-bit x86 Linux kernel, direct shadow mapping is inapplicable. As Figure 6 shows, the kernel addresses 120TB of memory with only 1GB to spare. Note that the lower half of the virtual address space where user mappings reside cannot be used to map shadow memory because user mappings are changed arbitrarily by the kernel. So kernel shadow memory requires an indirect mapping.

We decided to port the userspace Umbra shadow memory framework [25] for 64-bit x86 to the Linux kernel. Umbra is implemented using DynamoRIO, making it a DynamoRIO client. However it is a general framework for use by tools that require shadow memory – such tools are in turn referred to as Umbra clients. Umbra implements a simple indirect mapping. It divides the virtual address space into 4GB-aligned ranges called *application units*. When an application unit is in use, shadow memory is allocated. Umbra keeps a list of application units and the offset to their shadows. On every memory access, Umbra's instrumentation searches the list of application units to find the offset for the unit being accessed. To avoid searching in most cases, Umbra caches the last application unit and offset for each instruction.

Our port of Umbra allocates virtual address for shadow units when a kernel memory 'application unit' is first accessed. Shadow virtual address is allocated by stealing unused page table entries from the unused ranges in Linux's virtual memory map (Figure 6). Initially, all pages in a shadow unit are mapped copy-on-write to a single default physical page initially populated with client-specified data. Pages for the shadow are taken from the kernel when the module loads and kept in a *shadow page pool* to satisfy copy-on-write faults on the default shared shadow page.

DRK shadow memory is a heavyweight instrumentation that results in roughly 10X overhead compared to native performance.

6.2 KAddrcheck

We implemented an addressability checking tool, called *KAddrcheck*, for Linux's slab allocator using our kernel version of Umbra. The slab allocator is a general purpose memory allocator used by virtually every part of the kernel; Linux's analog to `malloc`, called `kmalloc`, is implemented using the slab allocator. KAddrcheck checks, at byte granularity, if memory on pages allocated by Linux's slab allocator is addressable.

The slab allocator maintains lists of free objects of various sizes. To satisfy an allocation request of a certain size, the slab allocator returns the next free object from the list of the requested size. If the list is empty, then the slab allocator extends the list using pages allocated by Linux's lower-level *page allocator*. To free an object, the slab allocator adds it back to the freelist of the page from whence it came. When a page contains only free objects, the slab allocator may return the page to the page allocator.

KAddrcheck maintains the addressability state for every byte of kernel memory using our Umbra port. Memory on slab freelists, allocated objects' metadata, and wasted bytes due to alignment are considered *unaddressable*. Accessing (i.e., reading or writing) unaddressable memory is an error. Memory on a slab page that is part of an allocated object is considered *addressable*. Memory that is not on a slab page is also considered addressable because we do not keep track of it.

The KAddrcheck client marks all bytes on the default read-only shadow page as addressable, effectively setting the state for all memory to addressable. During initialization, KAddrcheck scans the slab allocator's data structures to locate all of its pages and their freelists. Shadow bytes for objects on freelists are marked as unaddressable; these initial writes to the shadow memory cause copy-on-write faults for each page, which are handled by allocating a new page from the shadow page pool and updating the mapping.

KAddrcheck wraps calls to the slab allocator's interfaces to track changes to slab memory. To wrap a slab allocator interface, KAddrcheck instruments its entry point to execute the pre-interface wrapper and pushes a stack frame for the post-wrapper. When slab objects are allocated and freed, KAddrcheck's wrappers mark them as addressable and unaddressable respectively. When the slab allocator acquires a page, it is marked as unaddressable because nothing has been allocated from the page yet. When a page is released, KAddrcheck marks the entire page as addressable because it no longer tracks it.

On every memory access, KAddrcheck's instrumentation checks if the shadow memory is marked as unaddressable, and if so, reports an error. Errors are suppressed if the unaddressable access happens while a wrapped slab function is on the call stack.

We tested the KAddrcheck tool on our own code in which we deliberately inserted various memory addressing errors. These bugs were reported by KAddrcheck, confirming that it operates as expected. We have also run KAddrcheck on the Linux kernel during our performance tests. Since we are using a stable kernel version, it is not surprising that no errors were reported during these tests. A heavyweight instrumentation tool like this is most suited for use on code that is still under development, where memory referencing bugs are more likely.

6.3 Stackcheck

Natively, when the Linux kernel crashes fatally, it does a post-mortem check on the current thread's stack. Linux checks to see if the last 4 bytes of the stack match a magic number written when the stack was created.

The Stackcheck tool proactively guards against stack overflow. Stackcheck marks the shadow for the last 4 bytes of all kernel stacks as unaddressable. If an addressability error occurs on a write to the unaddressable stack bytes, then Stackcheck redirects execution to Linux's `oops` function, which kills the calling thread and continues running. Unlike Linux's native stack magic check, Stackcheck can detect an overflow early enough to keep the rest of the system running.

The Stackcheck tool is a modified version of KAddrcheck. In addition to monitoring for accesses to unaddressable slab memory, Stackcheck checks for overflow of kernel stacks. To guard against overflow, Stackcheck marks the shadow for the last 4 bytes of all kernel stacks as unaddressable. Stackcheck wraps kernel stack allocation and deallocation functions to know when to protect and unprotect stack memory.

7. Related Work

There are several widely-used userspace DBT instrumentation frameworks, including DynamoRIO [5], Pin [16], and Valgrind [17], all of which aim to offer comprehensive instrumentation for the user space, and export instruction inspection and manipulation APIs. Analogous to DRK's handling of hardware-generated interrupts, these frameworks interpose on signal delivery. However, all of them delay asynchronous signals until code cache exits, which happens in some pathological cases after an unbounded amount of time. Worse, pending signals might be dropped if too many signals are queued. DRK avoids these problems by dispatching on interrupt handlers as soon as possible.

JIFL [19] instruments native operating systems using DBT by providing an API for instrumenting system calls. Unlike DRK, JIFL does not aim to be comprehensive as JIFL does not instrument interrupt handlers or kernel threads, precluding many kinds of instrumentation. Furthermore, unlike DRK, JIFL is incompatible with preemptible kernels.

PinOS is a whole-system instrumentation framework based on Pin and the paravirtualized Xen hypervisor [8]. PinOS captures all virtual machine execution, including booting and usermode execution, unlike DRK which is attached after startup and only instruments the kernel. PinOS's increased coverage comes at the cost of overhead, which is 50x higher than DRK in the case of ApacheBench. Because paravirtualized Xen emulates all of its interrupt-generating hardware, it is feasible for PinOS to delay interrupts until code cache exits, similar to the userspace frameworks. This convenience comes at the cost of not being able to instrument native device drivers.

VMWare's virtual machine monitor implements virtualization using DBT (i.e., as an alternative to using hardware virtualization) [1]. Although VMWare is not intended as an instrumentation platform, it could presumably be adapted to expose an instrumentation API. However, like PinOS, VMWare emulates devices, precluding instrumentation of the native devices drivers.

Note that both Xen and VMWare support device passthrough, which enables VMs to interact with native devices directly [9]. Although this approach puts native device drivers back in the VM, it also removes device emulation from the VMM. Without the convenience of emulated devices, delaying interrupts until code cache exits becomes intractable. So DBT that used device passthrough would have essentially the same interrupt delivery problem that we have solved with DRK.

Kprobes [15], KernInst [24], and DTrace [10] are dynamic kernel instrumentation frameworks, designed for debugging and profiling. These frameworks work by patching entry points of functions with trampolines to instrumentation routines. However, the overhead of trampolines and context switching to instrumentation routines is prohibitive for fine-grained instrumentation as simple as instruction counting [19]. DRK avoids this overhead by providing an API for inline instrumentation.

Memcheck [22] and Dr. Memory [7] are full-featured memory checking tools for userspace built using shadow memory on top of Valgrind and DynamoRIO respectively. Like our KAddrcheck tool, Memcheck and Dr. Memory wrap heap functions and check for addressability of accesses. In addition, Memcheck and Dr. Memory propagate definedness through registers and memory. These tools raise errors for undefined accesses of consequence (e.g., dereferencing an undefined pointer). We plan on adding definedness checking and propagation to KAddrcheck in the future.

Included with the Linux kernel, kmemcheck [18] uses page protection and single stepping to implement addressability checking and limited definedness checking for slab memory. We plan to compare our approach with kmemcheck once propagation tracking is implemented in Kaddrcheck.

8. Conclusions and Future Work

We have presented the design and implementation of DRK, a dynamic binary translation-based kernel instrumentation framework. DRK provides complete control over all kernel execution, including interrupt and exception handlers and device drivers, enabling comprehensive instrumentation of the OS without imposing any direct overhead on user-level code. We found that the most challenging aspect of our design involved handling interrupts without relying on emulated interrupt-generating hardware, while meeting our goals of preserving execution interleaving and execution transparency.

Our results show that DRK's performance equals or far exceeds existing fine-grained kernel instrumentation frameworks. We also demonstrated the utility of DBT-based kernel instrumentation by implementing two useful debugging tools, KAddrcheck and Stackcheck. As future work, we plan on enhancing KAddrcheck to match the features provided by Dr. Memory and Memcheck.

9. Acknowledgements

We thank Derek Bruening and Qin Zhao for answering questions about DynamoRIO and giving early feedback on our plan to port DynamoRIO to the Linux kernel. We also thank the anonymous reviewers for their insightful comments. This research was supported by NSERC through a Canada Graduate Scholarship for Peter Feiner and the Discovery Grants program.

References

[1] Keith Adams and Ole Agesen. A comparison of software and hardware techniques for x86 virtualization. In *ASPLOS*, pages 2–13, San Jose, CA, 2006. ACM.

[2] Advanced Micro Devices. *AMD64 Architecture Programmer's Manual Volume 2: System Programming*. 3.15 edition, 2009.

[3] Vasanth Bala, Evelyn Duesterwald, and Sanjeev Banerjia. Dynamo: A Transparent Dynamic Optimization System. *PLDI*, pages 1–12, 2000.

[4] Daniel P. Bovet and Marco Cesati. *Understanding the Linux Kernel*. O'Reilly, Sebastopol, CA, 3rd edition, 2005.

[5] Derek Bruening. *Efficient, Transparent, and Comprehensive Runtime Code Manipulation*. Ph.d. thesis, Massachusetts Institute of Technology, 2004.

[6] Derek Bruening, Vladimir Kiriansky, Timothy Garnett, and Sanjeev Banerji. Thread-shared software code caches. In *CGO*, New York, NY, 2006. ACM.

[7] Derek. Bruening and Qin Zhao. Practical memory checking with dr. memory. In *CGO*, pages 213–223, april 2011.

[8] P. P. Bungale and C. K. Luk. PinOS: A programmable framework for whole-system dynamic instrumentation. In *VEE*, pages 137–147, San Diego, CA, 2007. ACM.

[9] T. W. Burger. Intel Virtualization Technology for Directed I/O (VT-d): Enhancing Intel platforms for efficient virtualization of I/O devices. http://software.intel.com/en-us/articles/intel-virtualization-technology-for-directed-io-vt-d-enhancing-intel-platforms-for-efficient-virtualization-of-io-devices/. Last accessed July 25, 2011. 2009.

[10] Bryan M. Cantrill, Michael W. Shapiro, Adam H. Leventhal, and Sun Microsystems. Dynamic instrumentation of production systems. In *USENIX ATC*, pages 15–28. USENIX Association, 2004.

[11] Andy Chou, Junfeng Yang, Benjamin Chelf, Seth Hallem, and Dawson Engler. An empirical study of operating systems errors. In *SOSP*, pages 73–88, Banff, Canada, 2001. ACM.

[12] Bryan Ford and Russ Cox. Vx32: Lightweight user-level sandboxing on the x86. In *USENIX ATC*, Boston, MA, 2008. USENIX Association.

[13] Vladimir Kiriansky, Derek Bruening, and Saman P. Amarasinghe. Secure Execution via Program Shepherding. In *USENIX Security*, pages 191–206, San Francisco, CA, 2002. USENIX Association.

[14] Andi Kleen. Linux Kernel Documentation: Virtual memory map with 4 level page tables. http://www.kernel.org/doc/Documentation/x86/x86_64/mm.txt. Last accessed July 24th, 2011. 2004.

[15] Linux Technology Center. KProbes. http://sourceware.org/systemtap/kprobes/. Last accessed May 2nd, 2010.

[16] C. K. Luk, Robert Cohn, Robert Muth, Harish Patil, Artur Klauser, Geoff Lowney, Steven Wallace, V. J. Reddi, and K. Hazelwood. Pin: building customized program analysis tools with dynamic instrumentation. In *PLDI*, pages 190–200, Chicago, IL, 2005. ACM.

[17] Nicholas Nethercote and Julian Seward. Valgrind: a framework for heavyweight dynamic binary instrumentation. In *PLDI*, pages 89–100, San Diego, CA, 2007. ACM.

[18] Vegard Nossum. kmemcheck: trap uses of uninitialized memory. http://lwn.net/Articles/259974/. Last accessed July 25th, 2011. 2007.

[19] Marek Olszewski, Keir Mierle, Adam Czajkowski, and Angela Demke Brown. JIT Instrumentation: a Novel Approach to Dynamically Instrument Operating Systems. In *EUROSYS*, pages 3–16, Lisbon, Portugal, 2007. ACM.

[20] Nicolas Palix, Gaël Thomas, Suman Saha, Christophe Calvès, Julia Lawall, and Gilles Muller. Faults in linux: ten years later. In *ASPLOS*, ASPLOS '11, pages 305–318, New York, NY, USA, 2011. ACM.

[21] Arvind Seshadri, Mark Luk, Ning Qu, and Adrian Perrig. SecVisor : A Tiny Hypervisor to Provide Lifetime Kernel Code Integrity for Commodity OSes. In *SOSP*, pages 335–350, Stevenson, WA, 2007. ACM.

[22] Julian Seward and Nicholas Nethercote. Using Valgrind to Detect Undefined Value Errors with Bit-Precision. In *USENIX ATC*, pages 17–30, Anaheim, CA, 2005. USENIX Association.

[23] Dawn Song, David Brumley, Heng Yin, Juean Caballero, Ivan Jager, Min Gyung Kang, Zhenkai Liang, James Newsome, Pongsin Poosankam, and Prateek Saxena. BitBlaze: A New Approach to Computer Security via Binary Analysis. In *ISS. Keynote invited paper*, Hyderabad, India, 2008.

[24] Ariel Tamches and Barton P. Miller. Fine-grained dynamic instrumentation of commodity operating system kernels. In *OSDI*, pages 117–130, Berkeley, CA, USA, 1999. USENIX Association.

[25] Qin Zhao, Derek Bruening, and Saman Amarasinghe. Umbra: Efficient and Scalable Memory Shadowing. In *ASPLOS*, Toronto, Canada, 2010. ACM.

Continuous Object Access Profiling and Optimizations to Overcome the Memory Wall and Bloat

Rei Odaira, Toshio Nakatani

IBM Research – Tokyo

1623-14 Shimotsuruma, Yamato-shi, Kanagawa-ken, 242-8502, Japan

{ odaira, nakatani } @jp.ibm.com

Abstract

Future microprocessors will have more serious memory wall problems since they will include more cores and threads in each chip. Similarly, future applications will have more serious memory bloat problems since they are more often written using object-oriented languages and reusable frameworks. To overcome such problems, the language runtime environments must accurately and efficiently profile how programs access objects.

We propose Barrier Profiler, a low-overhead object access profiler using a memory-protection-based approach called *pointer barrierization* and adaptive overhead reduction techniques. Unlike previous memory-protection-based techniques, pointer barrierization offers per-object protection by converting all of the pointers to a given object to corresponding barrier pointers that point to protected pages. Barrier Profiler achieves low overhead by not causing signals at object accesses that are unrelated to the needed profiles, based on profile feedback and a compiler analysis. Our experimental results showed Barrier Profiler provided sufficiently accurate profiles with 1.3% on average and at most 3.4% performance overhead for allocation-intensive benchmarks, while previous code-instrumentation-based techniques suffered from 9.2% on average and at most 12.6% overhead. The low overhead allows Barrier Profiler to be run continuously on production systems. Using Barrier Profiler, we implemented two new online optimizations to compress write-only character arrays and to adjust the initial sizes of mostly non-accessed arrays. They resulted in speed-ups of up to 8.6% and 36%, respectively.

Categories and Subject Descriptors D.3.4 [**Programming Languages**]: Processors – optimization

General Terms Algorithms, Performance, Experimentation.

Keywords Memory protection; memory management; profiling

1. Introduction

Increasing numbers of cores and threads on each chip have reduced the per-core and per-thread caches and memory bandwidth. This trend results in the problem called *memory wall*, a long latency for programs to access data in memory. Typical programs written in object-oriented languages such as Java exacerbate the memory wall because they allocate and access a large number of objects [31]. Such programs are called *allocation-intensive* programs. Allocating many objects also causes frequent GC invocations and increases the GC overhead.

Recent research [14,29] has shown that a large fraction of those object allocations are wasted, since they do not involve any data that actually contribute to the output of the program. This problem is often called *memory bloat*. Memory bloat happens because more programs are written using reusable libraries and frameworks. Such libraries and frameworks can allocate large data structures for generic usage but are not optimal for particular use cases. Memory bloat not only interferes with the efficient use of memory, but also makes the memory wall even higher since more of the actually useful data is evicted from CPU caches.

To reduce the effects of the memory wall and memory bloat, language execution environments such as Java VMs need to profile the program accesses of objects and then to optimize those objects. Object access profiles include properties such as write-only objects, immutable objects, and non-accessed bytes based on the information about which program instructions access which fields of which objects. Object access profiling is crucial for many object optimizations, including object compression [5,12,21], lazy allocation [5,24], field reordering [6], and object merging [12]. For example, if certain objects are unlikely to be accessed after initialization, they should be compressed.

There are two requirements for an object access profiler. First, it must be lightweight so that it can be used online. Although the object optimizations can be done offline by hand or by a compiler, offline optimizations cannot capture the dynamic behavior of programs. Thus language execution environments should profile and optimize object accesses online. Second, it must be accurate for maximum performance, especially when using speculative object optimizations. Because many object optimizations are speculative, inaccurate profiles can result in speculation failures. To obtain accurate object access profiles, the profiler must track the entire lifetimes of objects, not small portions. For example, to determine immutability the profiler must confirm that all reads come after all writes to an object. Thus it must be able to detect all of the accesses to the object, or at least all of the accesses that affect the accuracy of the access profiles.

In this paper, we propose *Barrier Profiler*, an accurate object access profiler with low performance overhead. It is based on per-object memory protection combined with profile-directed adaptive techniques for overhead reduction. Barrier Profiler uses *pointer barrierization*, which reserves a protected region outside of the heap region, instead of protecting the pages containing the profiled objects. At object allocation time, pointer barrierization converts all of the pointers to a given object to corresponding

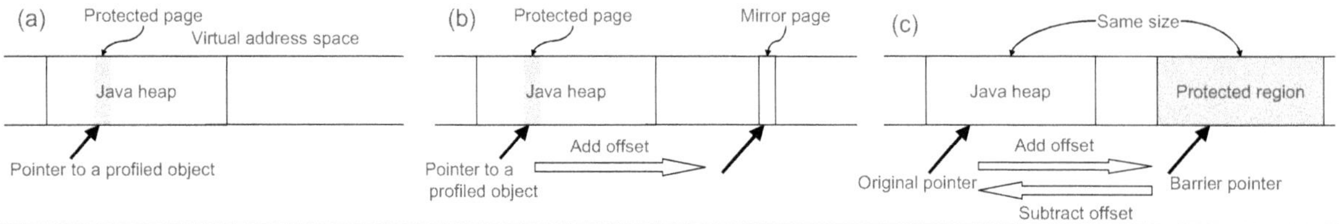

Figure 1. (a) Basic memory protection causes a race condition. (b) Mirror pages still suffer from coarse-grain page-level protection. (c) Pointer barrierization provides per-object protection.

barrier pointers that point to the protected region. All of the accesses via the barrier pointers cause hardware exceptions, allowing the profiler in the exception handler to track the lifetime of the object. Since hardware exceptions occur only via the barrier pointers, the protection granularity is not per page but per object.

Using pointer barrierization as a substrate, Barrier Profiler profiles frequently-allocated short-lived objects, because such objects affect the performance by polluting CPU caches and squandering memory bandwidth, especially in multi-core systems [31]. To reduce the profiling overhead, Barrier Profiler samples only a small number of objects at each allocation site and profiles the accesses to the sampled objects. Barrier Profiler further reduces the overhead by profile-directed adaptive object sampling and *unbarrierization*. If the target of an object access optimization is an immutable object, for example, what is crucial is not the accurate numbers of accesses but the object accesses that affect the immutability. Thus Barrier Profiler can skip sampling the objects that are unlikely to be immutable and profiling the objects that are no longer immutable. Our experiments showed that these techniques provided sufficiently accurate profiles with low overhead. Thus Barrier Profiler can run continuously in production systems.

We implemented two new online object-access optimizations to demonstrate the usefulness of Barrier Profiler. One is an online speculative compression of character arrays. Based on the online feedback from Barrier Profiler, the arrays that are unlikely to be accessed after their initialization are compressed if they contain only ISO-8859 characters. The other optimization is dynamic adjustment of the initial sizes of container arrays. Programmers often over-allocate large arrays as buffers, but access only the first few elements. Barrier Profiler successfully identified optimal sizes based on the non-accessed-byte profiles and dynamically performed recompilation to inline the allocation contexts and to embed the optimal sizes as compile-time constants.

In summary, our contributions are:

- We propose Barrier Profiler, an accurate object access profiler with low performance overhead, which is suitable for continuous profiling in the field. Per-object accurate profiling is enabled by pointer barrierization (Section 3). Barrier Profiler is lightweight because of its profile-directed adaptive object sampling and unbarrierization (Section 4).
- We implemented Barrier Profiler in the IBM J9/TR [7], a production-quality Java VM with a just-in-time (JIT) compiler. We conducted experiments on its accuracy and overhead (Section 5), using the industry standard SPECjvm2008, SPECjbb2005, and DaCapo benchmarks.
- We quantitatively compared Barrier Profiler with existing code-instrumentation-based techniques including Bursty Tracing [1,8] (Section 5).
- We implemented and evaluated two new online object-access optimizations to demonstrate the usefulness of Barrier Profiler (Section 6). Both of them are feasible for the first time by using the lightweight object access profiler.

2. Related Work

Code instrumentation [2,4,5,12,24,30] has been a standard technique for object access profiling. However, executing additional code at every heap access results in prohibitive overhead. Both memory and performance overheads were reportedly increased by more than a factor of 10 [12]. One way to mitigate the overhead is access sampling like Bursty Tracing [1,8], which enables the instrumentation only during a profiling phase. However, our experiments showed excessive overhead even at low sampling frequencies.

In addition, the access sampling approaches are inaccurate because they can only sample some fraction of the accesses to arbitrary objects. They cannot track the life of an object, for example to detect immutable fields [26] or to find last access points [22]. What is needed is a lightweight profiler that samples objects and detects *all* of the accesses to the sampled objects, or at least all of the accesses that affect the accuracy of the access profiles.

To detect the accesses to the objects without the code instrumentation overhead, memory protection with signal handling has been used in many systems [15,16,19,25,27,30]. Hound [16] and pointer swizzling [27] simply protect the pages that contain the target objects, as shown in Figure 1(a). However, this basic protection does not work for object access profiling because of race conditions. For example, Hound uses the basic protection to confirm the staleness of the objects that are segregated at allocation time. Once the application accesses a protected page, all of the objects in that page become fresh and the page is unprotected. In contrast, for more general object access profiles such as write-only objects, immutable objects, and non-accessed bytes, the page cannot be unprotected after just one access to an object being profiled. However, when a thread accesses a protected object, it must temporarily disable the protection to access its content. In the meantime, race conditions can occur because other threads might access that object or other objects contained in the same page without causing hardware exceptions.

To avoid the race conditions, Memalyze [25], Archipelago [15], and other systems [19,30] use mirror pages that map the physical pages of the protected virtual pages to other virtual addresses, as shown in Figure 1(b), allowing the signal handler to access the data of the protected object without unprotecting the page that contains it. However, these techniques still suffer from too much performance overhead to use online. First, the signal handling by an OS can result in more than a 50% performance overhead in allocation-intensive programs [16]. It is important to reduce the number of hardware exceptions without compromising the profile accuracy. Second, the page-level protection is too coarse-grained. Accesses to objects that are not being profiled but that reside in the protected page suffer from hardware exceptions. The granularity problem can be mitigated by segregating the profiled objects into the protected pages [16,30]. However, this requires a new memory allocator specialized for those protected pages, complicating the system design.

Pointer barrierization enables per-object protection by enhancing the mirror page approach. It does not protect the pages containing the profiled objects but instead reserves a protected region outside of the heap region, as shown in Figure 1(c). Chen et al. [5] presented a very basic form of pointer barrierization to detect accesses to compressed objects. After compressing objects during GC, their approach sets the highest order bit of each pointer to 1 for each compressed object, based on the assumption that an embedded system will not use a virtual address space larger than 2GB. Their original technique uses code instrumentation, and as an enhancement, they described a technique to use hardware memory protection. However, they did not explain the details of their algorithm. Li et al. [11] used a similar technique to detect accesses to aliased stack slots. In fact, pointer barrierization will not work correctly on objects in the heap if internal pointers and atomic instructions are ignored. These details are addressed for the first time in our work. Also, we show that pointer barrierization is useful for object access profiling when combined with the overhead reduction techniques.

QVM [2] detects defects in production systems using techniques similar to Barrier Profiler. It continuously monitors accesses and method invocations on the objects that are sampled adaptively. However, because it uses code instrumentation, users of QVM need to specify which program points to instrument to avoid the large overhead of instrumenting every point. Also, its adaptive object sampling is based only on system overhead, while ours is profile-directed and thus is more suitable for insuring the accuracy of the collected object access profiles.

There have been many other research proposals to overcome memory bloat. Xu et al. proposed a static analysis [28] and a profiling method [29] to reduce memory bloat in Java. However, they were designed for offline code rewriting. The runtime slowdown by the profiling was more than 10-fold. Sartor et al. [21] estimated potential space savings by various existing object compression algorithms, but they did not focus on how to implement them online. In contrast, Barrier Profiler is a novel infrastructure for online reduction of memory bloat. Discontiguous arrays with lazy allocation [5,20] can dynamically reduce memory bloat in large arrays. However, even when using highly optimized z-rays [20], performance degradation was more than 10% on average. Our dynamic adjustment of initial array sizes using Barrier Profiler has the same effect as using discontiguous arrays for certain array usage patterns, but has much lower overhead than z-rays. Chameleon [23] can also find similar opportunities through code instrumentation, but its performance overhead is 6 times at maximum.

3. Pointer Barrierization

In this section, we describe a pointer barrierization algorithm and what needs to be considered in code generation and GC. Pointer barrierization enables per-object access detection and is compatible with all types of memory allocator. Throughout this paper, we assume Java is our target environment, but pointer barrierization and Barrier Profiler could be adapted to the environments of other languages and be effective on both 32-bit and 64-bit architectures.

3.1 Basic pointer barrierization

The easiest pointer barrierization is to add to a pointer the offset between the Java heap region and a read-write-protected region whose size matches the heap region. Figure 1(c) shows a memory layout. Note that the protected region does not require the assignment of real memory.

Pointer barrierization can be performed at allocation or GC time. For pointer barrierization to work correctly, it is important to barrierize all of the pointers that point to a target object. Since only one pointer in a register points to an allocated object immediately after allocation, it suffices to barrierize that register in the generated JIT code or in a modified interpreter. GC can do pointer barrierization when traversing all of the pointers to the object.

3.2 Virtual-memory-efficient pointer barrierization

The basic pointer barrierization requires a protected region whose size is not smaller than the Java heap region. In a 32-bit environment, however, the virtual address space is a limited resource. It is best to make the protected region as small as possible.

For a smaller protected region, Java VM can take advantage of the fact that all Java objects are aligned on a 4- or 8-byte boundary. This is true for production-quality Java VMs [7][17]. Since the last 2 or 3 bits of each object pointer are zero, it can be shifted right by 2 or 3 bits without losing any information. Thus the size of the protected region can be 1/4 or 1/8 that of the Java heap region. A difficulty in this approach is that an access through a barrier pointer can point outside of the protected region. Thus when barrierizing the pointers to an object, the sum of the barrier pointer and the object size must not exceed the top address of the protected region. If this condition fails, barrierization cannot be used, but this is a rare case.

In some CPU architectures, unaligned accesses via a pointer whose last bits are set cause a bus error. However, pointer barrierization cannot take advantage of this mechanism in general, because byte accesses through such a pointer do not cause the error.

To further reduce the size of the protected region, a Java VM can use an OS-protected region. For example, by default the Linux and Windows OS [13] occupies the highest 1/4 or 1/2 of a virtual address space, and cannot be accessed by users. In this case, pointer barrierization can shift a pointer right by at least 2 bits and set the topmost 2 bits. The Java VM does not need to reserve any protected region in the user space.

3.3 Signal handling

Accesses through barrier pointers always cause hardware memory exceptions, which are converted to signals by the OS. Figure 2 shows the signal-handling algorithm implemented in a Java VM.

Restoring a header pointer

The handler first checks whether the excepting data address is within the protected region by address comparison (Line 2). If so, the handler must restore the pointer to the head of the accessed object, which we call a *header pointer*. A pointer to the middle of the object, which we call an *internal pointer*, is not sufficient because an object access profiler must identify which object is being accessed to detect, for example, the immutability of the object (Line 11). Generally, unbarrierizing the excepting data address only produces an internal pointer.

We propose two approaches to restore the header pointer. One is to use an ordered set, normally a balanced tree. At pointer barrierization time, the barrier pointer, which corresponds to a header pointer to an object, is stored in the ordered set. To restore the header pointer, the highest barrier pointer that is lower than the excepting data address is looked up in the ordered set (Line 5). This search requires synchronized tree traversal and can result in a bottleneck in multithreaded execution.

The other approach is to restrict the format of the instructions that access objects. This means one of the register arguments of a memory reference must be a header pointer. For example, in a memory reference of the form `[base_reg, offset_reg/immediate]`, `base_reg` must be a header pointer.

```
01: handle_signal(code_addr, data_addr, context) {
02:   if (is_in_protected_region(data_addr)) {
03:     base_reg_num = decode_instruction(code_addr);
04:     base_reg = get_reg_contents(base_reg_num, context);
    #if USE_ORDERED_SET
05:     bar_object_head = search_ordered_set(data_addr);
    #else
06:     if (is_internal_pointer_access(code_addr))
07:       bar_object_head = get_array_head(code_addr);
08:     else
09:       bar_object_head = base_reg;
    #endif
10:     orig_object_head = unbarrierize(bar_object_head);
11:     record_access(code_addr, orig_object_head);
12:     if (is_LL(code_addr) ||
13:         is_uninteresting(orig_object_head) &&
14:           safe_to_unbarrierize_at(code_addr)) {
15:       write_to_context(context, base_reg_num,
            base_reg + orig_object_head - bar_object_head);
16:       return_to(code_addr);
17:     }
18:     do_load_or_store(code_addr, orig_object_head, context);
19:     return_to_next_instruction(code_addr);
20:   }
21:   ...
```

Figure 2. Signal handling algorithm.

Then the barrierized header pointer can be obtained by decoding the instruction and loading the content of `base_reg` from the signal context (Lines 3-4). We believe that these restrictions are usually satisfied in existing Java VMs and JIT compilers.

However, the restrictions may be violated when accessing large objects, especially arrays, due to the results of loop induction variable optimization. For those instructions that use internal pointers, JIT-generated code maintains a header pointer in a register or in a stack slot of the method. Many JIT compilers already support this function to help the GC mark or move the objects pointed to by internal pointers. In addition, the JIT compiler maintains a hash table to associate each instruction that uses an internal pointer with a register number or a stack offset that holds the header pointer. This allows the signal handler to obtain the header pointer from the excepting code address (Lines 6-7). Since most of the object access instructions do not use internal pointers, the data structure for the association will not grow excessively.

The second approach is more lightweight in general, but we used the first approach because our preliminary experiments showed that its overhead was small enough, thanks to the low object sampling frequency of our Barrier Profiler.

Handling atomic instructions

After unbarrierizing the header pointer (Line 10), the handler records the access (Line 11) and emulates the execution of the excepting instruction (Line 18). For example, emulating a load means executing a load on behalf of the excepting load instruction and then writing the loaded value to the target register in the signal context. Note that the handler is not allowed in general to write the unbarrierized pointer to the base register and return to the excepting instruction to execute it again. This approach could change the semantics of a program because the same object is represented by two different pointer values, causing a pointer equality operation to return false even when the two pointers do refer to the same object. After the emulation, the handler returns to the next instruction (Line 19).

There is a subtle problem in handling atomic instructions (Lines 12, 15-16). The signal handler can correctly emulate a compare-and-swap (CAS) instruction. However, for a load-linked (LL) instruction, even if the handler executes an LL, that reservation is likely be lost before the execution reaches a corresponding store-conditional (SC) instruction. This is because the OS can execute another LL/SC pair after the signal handler and before the

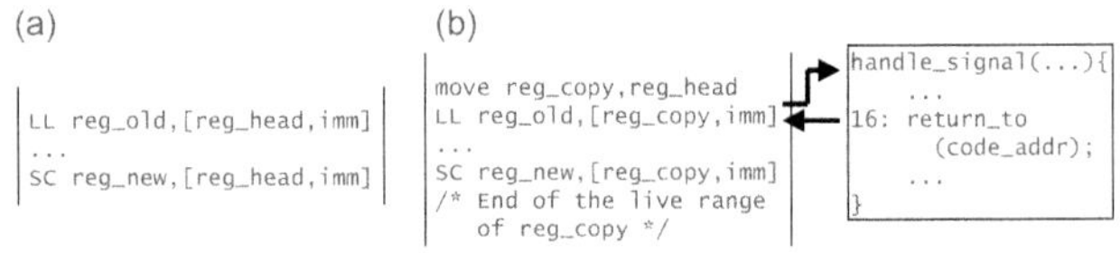

Figure 3. (a) Original code sequence for LL/SC in JIT or interpreter code. (b) With barrier pointers, a base register is copied to another register (`reg_copy`), and LL/SC use that register. If the LL causes an exception, the signal handler modifies `reg_copy` to an unbarrierized pointer, and the LL is executed again.

SC. We solve this problem by executing the LL again with an unbarrierized register, as shown in Figure 3. To avoid the problem of incorrect pointer equality, the base register is copied to another register immediately before the LL, and the LL uses that register. Thus the original base register still contains a barrier pointer. In addition, the following SC must also use the copied register. Otherwise, another hardware exception would occur at the SC, and the reservation might be lost. In Java, LL/SC pairs can be performed on objects only for monitor entrances and exits, so it is easy to modify a JIT compiler or Java VM to use LL/SC in the required way. The conditions in Lines 13 and 14 reduce the overhead and are explained in Section 4.2.

3.4 GC

With pointer barrierization, most GC implementations need only minor changes to run correctly. An efficient marking GC uses a marking table outside of the Java heap region. It finds the corresponding mark bit of an object by bit-operations on the pointer to the object. Thus, before marking, the GC must check whether or not the pointer is a barrier pointer. If so, it must obtain the original pointer by unbarrierization. The same operation is needed for marking a card table for generational or concurrent GC.

In the GC algorithms that move objects, each pointer field is modified so that it points to the new location of the pointed-to object. If the original pointer is a barrier pointer, the new pointer must be one, too. Thus GC needs a check at each pointer traversal, and it must perform unbarrierization and barrierization as needed.

4. Barrier Profiler

Barrier Profiler is a lightweight object-access profiler using pointer barrierization. It is focused on frequently allocated short-lived objects, because such objects often affect the performance in multi-core systems [31]. Pointer barrierization could also be used for profiling long-lived objects. This is left for future work.

4.1 Basic algorithm

To profile the frequently allocated objects, the interpreter and JIT compiler were modified to use pointer barrierization at all allocation sites. To reduce the profiling overhead, Barrier Profiler applies pointer barrierization to only a small fraction of the objects at each allocation site. This object sampling should be based not on the allocated number of objects but on the allocated bytes, because cache pressure, memory bandwidth usage, GC frequency, and memory bloat are all related to the allocated bytes.

Figure 4 shows the pseudocode at an allocation site. After allocating an object (Line 1), the addresses of the head and tail of the object are XORed and ANDed with a mask to check whether the object is allocated across an aligned boundary (Line 3). The

```
1: object = allocate_object(class);
2: object_tail = object + object_size;
3: if (((object ^ object_tail) & mask[site_id]) != 0) {
4:   record_allocation(site_id, object);
5:   object = barrierize(object);
6:   mask[site_id] = get_next_mask(site_id);
7: }
```

Figure 4. Code at an allocation site in Barrier Profiler.

per-allocation-site mask is of the form 11…100…0. For example, if the number of zeros is 20, Barrier Profiler samples the objects that extend across 1-MB-aligned boundaries at this allocation site. More zeros in the mask mean lower overhead but larger errors in the profiles. If the masked results are not all zero, then the allocation is recorded (Line 4) and the pointer is barrierized (Line 5). The mask can be updated as needed (Line 6).

Barrier Profiler records the per-object access profiles in object information structures. One object information structure corresponds to one sampled object. It is created outside of the Java heap at the allocation time of the sampled object (Line 4) and contains the ID of the allocation site. In addition, the allocation context is obtained by stack walking, and the ID assigned to the context is stored in the information structure. When a sampled object is accessed (Line 11 of Figure 2), the corresponding information structure is fetched via a hash table using the object head address as a key. Alternatively, if the ordered set is used to restore a header pointer, the set can also be used as a map to store and to fetch the information structures in addition to header pointers. Per-object access profiles such as the number of reads and writes, whether the object is write-only or not, etc. are recorded in the object information structure. At the end of each GC, every object information structure is visited to check whether or not its corresponding object is dead. If it is dead, the per-object access profiles are accumulated into the per-allocation-site and per-allocation-context information structures that correspond to the allocation site and context, respectively, of the dead object. The object information structure is then reclaimed.

4.2 Performance overhead reduction

We devised six techniques to reduce the performance overhead of Barrier Profiler by decreasing the number of hardware exceptions: three that lower the frequency of object sampling and three that unbarrierize some of the objects being profiled. A key constraint is to avoid compromising the accuracy of the profiles.

Adaptive object sampling

There are three cases where the sampling frequency can be decreased without increasing the profile errors too much. First, Barrier Profiler can reduce the sampling frequency at uninteresting allocation sites based on the object access optimizations. For example, if a target optimization is to lazily allocate non-accessed objects, the objects allocated at a site that has allocated some or many non-accessed objects should be sampled frequently to carefully assess whether or not it is worth delaying object creation at this site. In contrast, the objects allocated at a site that has always allocated accessed objects can be sampled less frequently, although the sampling should not be completely disabled to adapt to dynamic behavior changes. Based on the feedback from the per-allocation-site profiles, our implementation lowers the sampling frequency at the allocation sites whose ratios in bytes of write-only objects, immutable objects, and non-accessed bytes to all of the objects sampled at the sites are all less than 1%.

Second, we found a few small objects received quite a large number of accesses in some benchmark programs. Such a small number of small objects have little effect on the memory wall or bloat problems. If they happen to be sampled, however, performance degradation is significant. Based on the per-allocation-site profile, Barrier Profiler decreases the sampling frequency at the allocation sites (1) whose sampled objects account for only a small portion (less than 0.5% in bytes, in our implementation) of all sampled objects, and (2) that have ever allocated an object whose ratio of the number of accesses to its size exceeded a threshold (50, in our implementation).

Finally, Barrier Profiler should sample large objects less frequently than small ones because the algorithm in Figure 4 can sample too many large objects, especially in scientific applications. Preliminary experiments show that we should treat objects from 1 KB and up as large objects.

Adaptive unbarrierization

Barrier Profiler stops profiling particular objects in three cases: two at GC time and one during the execution of the program. To disable the profiling of an object, all of the barrier pointers to the object must be unbarrierized. Otherwise, partial unbarrierization could cause incorrect pointer equality as described in Section 3.3.

First, if an object being profiled no longer satisfies the property of the profiles being collected, such as immutability, profiling of accesses to the object can be stopped. After Barrier Profiler records an access to an object, it checks whether the object is still worth profiling. If not, it sets a flag in the corresponding object information structure, indicating the object is no longer interesting. Barrier Profiler performs the unbarrierization of the uninteresting object during stop-the-world GC, when all of the pointers to the object are traversed.

Second, Barrier Profiler also does temporary unbarrierization during the execution of the program, so that the uninteresting object does not continue to be profiled until the next GC. In the signal handler, a barrier pointer in the base register can be unbarrierized and written back, as shown in Line 15 of Figure 2. As a result, the following accesses using this base register do not cause hardware exceptions. To avoid the problem of incorrect pointer equality, a compiler analysis insures that this base register will not be used as an operand of any pointer comparison instructions. Because our implementation does not use alias or inter-method analysis, the base register also must not be used as an argument of method invocations, a method return value, or for data to be stored in the heap. If the base register satisfies these conditions, the address of the instruction is registered in a global hash table. In the signal handler, if the object is uninteresting and the excepting address is registered in the table (Lines 13-14 of Figure 2), the base register is unbarrierized.

Finally, many long-lived objects receive a large number of accesses without changing their object access properties such as immutability. Thus Barrier Profiler stops profiling long-lived objects based on how many times they survive GC. Each time an object survives GC, its age is incremented in its object information structure. After its age exceeds a predefined threshold (8, in our implementation), it is unbarrierized at the next GC.

Discussion

Some of the overhead reduction techniques cannot be used when collecting certain types of object access profiles. For example, profiling the last access points of objects is useful for inserting cache-flush instructions. However, there is no known time when an object becomes "uninteresting" in terms of its last access point. Thus sampled objects should not be unbarrierized.

5. Experimental Results

This section describes our implementation of Barrier Profiler. Then our experimental results are presented to assess the accuracy and overhead of Barrier Profiler.

5.1 Implementation

We implemented Barrier Profiler in a development version of the 32-bit IBM J9/TR [7] 1.6.0 SR6 for the Power architecture [18]. We used the basic pointer barrierization described in Section 3.1. We allocated 1 GB for the Java heap and also reserved 1 GB for the protected region. We used mark-and-sweep GC that invoked occasional compaction when the fragmentation became excessive. We measured the effects of the six overhead reduction techniques described in Section 4.2 by enabling and disabling all of them, which we call Opt and NoOpt, respectively.

We modified the interpreter to execute the pointer barrierization code in Figure 4 and the JIT compiler to insert the code into all of the allocation sites in the JIT-compiled methods. J9/TR first executes Java methods with the interpreter, and if a method is frequently invoked, then it is JIT-compiled. We inserted the pointer barrierization code immediately after the initialization of the object header fields and the zero-clearing of the non-header fields. This means these initialization-related writes did not appear in the collected profiles.

For the mask value in Figure 4, we used a fixed value during each run of a benchmark, except for the optimizations in the Opt configuration. We tried five mask values, with 17, 20, 23, 26, and 29 zeros. This corresponds to sampling one object per each allocated 128 KB up to each 512 MB. In this section, we use these numbers of sampling intervals to denote each configuration. In the JIT-compiled code, the mask is embedded as an immediate value in the AND instruction at Line 3 of Figure 4. The mask value can be updated by code patching. In the Opt configuration, we increased the number of masking zeros by three when decreasing the sampling frequency. For object allocation in the interpreter, our implementation uses a global fixed mask value.

The total real memory requirement of Barrier Profile was less than 8 MB even at the most frequent sampling interval of 128 KB. More than 90% of the memory was for the information structures described in Section 4.1. Note that these data structures are not Barrier-Profiler-specific. They are needed for code-instrumentation-based object access profilers too.

5.2 Code instrumentation techniques

We implemented two code instrumentation techniques in J9/TR for comparison. The first one is full instrumentation to simulate Bursty Tracing [8]. Bursty Tracing is based on the Arnold-Ryder framework [1] and aims for temporal profiling similar to Barrier Profiler. It duplicates the JIT-compiled code for every method. One is a checking version and the other is an instrumented version. Most of the time, the checking version is executed, but the execution occasionally switches to the instrumented version. The checking version contains only checks at method entries and loop back-edges that decrement a counter and jump to the instrumented version if it reaches zero. The instrumented version also contains the same checking code for the other counter to jump back to the checking version. Although we did not implement all of the parts of Bursty Tracing, we can estimate its overhead by the sampling rate and by the overhead of the instrumented code, as explained in [8]. To that end, we implemented full instrumentation that inserts profiling code at every heap access.

We also implemented another code instrumentation technique based on the idea of Barrier Profiler. We call it *Instrumented Barrier Profiler*. It performs pointer barrierization at allocation sites as in Barrier Profiler, but instead of relying on hardware exceptions, it inserts check instructions at every heap access. It uses the basic pointer barrierization in Section 3.1, although we did not need to actually reserve the protected region. To make the check simple, we guaranteed that the lower 16 bits of the bottom address of the protected region were all zero. The check consists of three instructions: The first instruction logically shifts a pointer right by 16 bits. The second instruction uses a 16-bit immediate comparison instruction to compare the shifted value with the constant that is the higher 16 bits of the bottom address of the protected region. The third instruction is a branch instruction based on the result of the comparison. If the pointer is equal to or larger than the bottom address, the execution jumps to a profiling snippet, which is basically the same as the signal handler in Figure 2. We also implemented a compiler optimization to merge instrumentations for the same object within a basic block, combined with temporary un-barrierization in the snippet. Instrumented Barrier Profiler can also benefit from the optimizations in Section 4.2. To obtain the same profiling accuracy as Barrier Profiler, Instrumented Barrier Profiler must always be enabled.

5.3 Benchmarks and evaluation environment

To evaluate the accuracy and overhead of Barrier Profiler, we used SPECjvm2008, the DaCapo Benchmarks 9.12, and SPECjbb2005. We ran the benchmarks six times, restarting the JVM each time, and took the averages during the steady state. We ran the benchmarks on a 4-core 2-way-SMT 4.0-GHz POWER6 [10] machine with 32 GB of main memory running Linux 2.6.18. For SPECjvm2008, we ran a 2-minute warm-up and a 4-minute measurement iteration. We used small data sets for the "scimark" benchmarks in SPECjvm2008. For DaCapo, we used the largest data sets for each benchmark. We ran each benchmark for 6 minutes and used the last 4 minutes as a measurement period. We excluded eclipse, tradebeans, and tradesoap from DaCapo, because they did not run correctly on the development version of the JVM we used, even without Barrier Profiler. For SPECjbb2005, we used a single JVM, which ran a 3.5-minute warm-up and a 4-minute measurement run with 8 warehouses.

The main targets of Barrier Profiler are allocation-intensive programs that allocate and use large numbers of objects, causing memory wall and memory bloat problems. Zhao et al. [31] categorized the SPECjvm2008 programs into allocation-intensive and non-allocation-intensive programs and pointed out that the allocation-intensive ones suffered from serious scalability issues on multi-core systems. Table 1 shows the per-hardware-thread allocation rates of the benchmarks we used. The rates are normalized to scimark.montecarlo as 1. The left side is allocation-intensive, while the right side is non-allocation-intensive. In SPECjvm2008, compiler.compiler, derby, serial, sunflow, xml.transform, xml.validation, and compiler.sunflow are allocation-intensive. These results match Zhao et al.'s categorization.

5.4 Collected object access profiles

Using Barrier Profiler, we collected three kinds of object access profiles: write-only objects, immutable objects, and non-accessed bytes. In our experiments, we collected all of the three profiles at the same time. Write-only objects are those objects for which none of the non-header fields are read. These objects are useless for the executed paths of the benchmarks, making them candidates for object optimizations such as allocation-time compression or lazy allocation [5,24]. Barrier Profiler can estimate how frequently each allocation site allocates write-only objects. If an allocation site always or mostly allocates write-only objects, then that site should be a target for the object optimizations.

The second object access profile we collected is for immutable objects. These are the objects for which all of the writes to their non-header fields precede all of the reads from their non-header fields. They can be considered as runtime constant objects, and thus they can be exploited for lazy allocation, or more specifically, for copy-on-write. Note that this kind of object access profiling cannot be collected by using access-sampling-based methods, because such methods cannot track the entire life of a particular object. In our definition, all of the write-only objects are also immutable objects.

The last object access profile is the non-accessed-byte profile. A non-accessed byte in an object is a non-header byte for which there is no read or write after the header initialization and zero-filling. Such a byte only wastes space and should be eliminated. Note that this is a per-byte property, while the previous two profiles are per-object properties.

5.5 Accuracy of profiling

To evaluate the accuracy of object access profiling, we need to have perfect reference profiles, which we also obtained with a modified form of Barrier Profiler. We added to Barrier Profiler a mechanism to enable or disable the profiling. Pointer barrierization code at allocation sites was skipped by branch instructions during start-up. After the program reached a steady state, the profiling was enabled by patching the branch instructions to no-ops. This profiling was different from that in Figure 4 in that it sampled *all* of the allocated objects. After the patching, the program continued execution to the end, profiling all of the accesses to the objects. We call these results the "full trace". For evaluation, we also counted how many bytes of the objects were actually allocated at each allocation site in the steady state. We call this the actual allocated bytes of the allocation site.

Here is how we evaluated the accuracy of object access profiles such as for the write-only objects. For each allocation site, we computed an estimated write-only ratio by dividing the total bytes of the sampled write-only objects allocated at the site by the total bytes of all of the sampled objects allocated at the site. If no object was sampled at an allocation site, we assumed the estimated write-only ratio of the site to be zero. We also calculated an actual write-only ratio for each allocation site, using the full trace results. The estimation error in the allocated bytes of write-only objects is the total of the actual allocated bytes of each allocation site multiplied by the absolute difference between its estimated and actual write-only ratios. In other words, the estimation error is the average of the absolute differences weighted by the actual allocated bytes. We computed estimation errors for immutable objects and non-accessed bytes in the same way.

Since Barrier Profiler is sampling-based, long-term profiling will eventually reach the correct values. However, it should return the correct values even from short-term profiling, so that it can react quickly to dynamic behavior changes. Thus for the experiments in Section 5.5 and 5.7, we report the profiling results obtained during the measurement period of each benchmark, as described in Section 5.3. The profiling is always enabled, but all of the profiles collected during the warm-up period are discarded before the measurement period. Investigating the sensitivity of the accuracy to the profiling length is left for future work.

Figure 5 shows the estimation errors for write-only objects, relative to the total actual allocated bytes in compiler.compiler, derby, xml.transform, and xml.validation. Here we show only the

Allocation-intensive benchmarks	Norm. allocation rate	Non-allocation-intensive benchmarks	Norm. allocation rate
compiler.compiler	15.8	compress	1.3
derby	39.3	crypto.aes	11.7
serial	20.5	crypto.rsa	1.3
sunflow	16.4	crypto.signverify	3.7
xml.transform	21.5	mpegaudio	2.1
xml.validation	24.8	scimark.fft	4.2
compiler.sunflow	15.4	scimark.lu	6.4
fop	33.2	scimark.sor	6.5
jython	40.7	scimark.sparse	1.0
lusearch	850.3	scimark.montecarlo	1.0
pmd	27.8	avrora	1.3
sunflow (DaCapo)	119.8	batik	5.0
tomcat	71.6	h2	6.1
xalan	128.1	luindex	3.6
SPECjbb2005	16.8		

Table 1. Normalized per-hardware-thread allocation rates of the benchmarks (bytes/second). The rates are normalized to scimark.motecarlo as 1. The targets of Barrier Profiler are the allocation-intensive benchmarks on the left side.

results of the 4 representative allocation-intensive benchmarks, and we omit the results for immutable objects and non-accessed bytes. The estimation error ratios mostly decreased as the sampling interval was reduced except in derby, where the error ratios were always less than 2%. At 8-MB/Opt, the estimation error ratios in the allocation-intensive benchmarks were within 10%, 16%, and 6% for the write-only objects, immutable objects, and non-accessed bytes, respectively. The estimation error ratios of immutable objects were larger than those of write-only objects and non-accessed bytes, because the immutable objects accounted for more than 50% of the total actual allocated bytes in most benchmarks, while the write-only objects and non-accessed bytes rarely exceeded 20%.

When comparing Opt with NoOpt, the estimation error ratios were almost always worse, but within 5% difference. Further investigation revealed that most of the inaccuracy in Opt resulted from lowered sampling frequencies at uninteresting allocation sites. Surprisingly, Opt sometimes resulted in smaller estimation error ratios than NoOpt, as shown in compiler.compiler and xml.validation of Figure 5. This was because NoOpt was so slow that it could not sample enough number of objects during the measurement period.

5.6 Performance overhead of profiling

How accurate object access profiling should be depends on how much overhead the profiling incurs and how sensitive an object access optimization is to the errors in the profiles. Figure 6 presents the relative performance overheads of all of the Barrier Profiler configurations in the 4 representative allocation-intensive benchmarks, compared with the baseline without Barrier Profiler. The sampling intervals of 1 MB or less suffered from significant overhead. For example, in compiler.compiler, 512MB/Opt caused $1.5 * 10^4$ profiled accesses per minute, 8MB/Opt did $1.5 * 10^6$, and 128KB/Opt did $2.2 * 10^7$. Based on these results, we chose 8-MB as the best to balance accuracy with overhead.

When comparing Opt with NoOpt, their differences were statistically significant at the 8-MB-or-shorter intervals in most benchmarks. At the 8-MB interval, the adaptive object sampling contributed to most of the overhead reduction. The GC-time unbarrierization rarely occurred at the 8MB-or-longer intervals. As

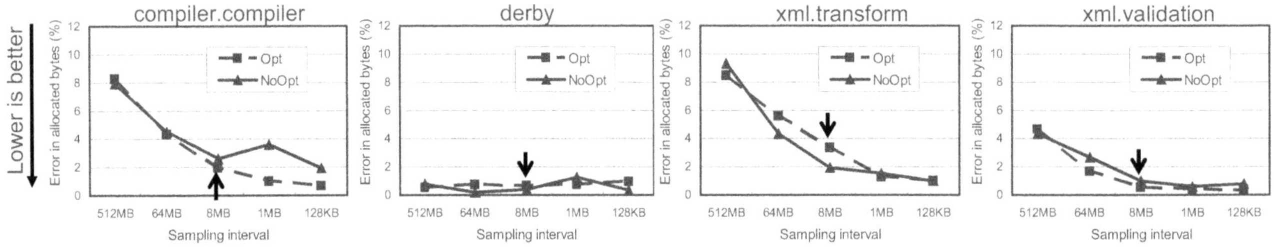

Figure 5. Accuracy: estimation error ratios in the allocated bytes of write-only objects for 4 representative allocation-intensive benchmarks, comparing the 10 combinations of 512-MB/64-MB/8-MB/1-MB/128-KB and Opt/NoOpt (= with/without the overhead reduction techniques in Section 4.2). Black arrows point to 8-MB/Opt, which we chose as the best configuration to balance accuracy with overhead.

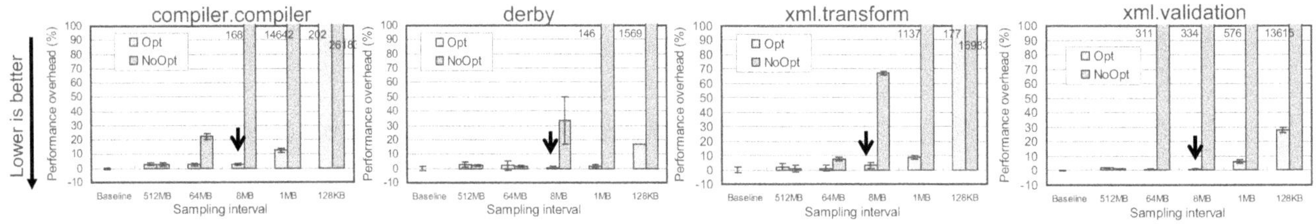

Figure 6. Performance overhead: relative overheads in the 4 benchmarks with 90% confidence intervals, comparing the 10 configurations. Black arrows point to 8-MB/Opt, which was the best configuration to balance accuracy with overhead.

the interval became shorter, the adaptive unbarrierization had larger effect on the performance.

With the 8-MB/Opt configuration, an object access optimization needs to tolerate at most 10% errors in the write-only ratios at each allocation site, as described in Section 5.5. Suppose we use a speculative optimization that compresses the objects allocated at sites whose sampled objects have been 100% write-only. In the xml.transform benchmark, for example, the estimation error ratio of 8-MB/Opt is 3.3% for write-only objects, as shown in Figure 5. Therefore, that speculative optimization should provide a benefit even when 3.3% of the objects allocated at the sites are actually not write-only.

5.7 Comparison with previous techniques

Figure 7 is for the comparison between simulated Bursty Tracing, Instrumented Barrier Profiler (8-MB/Opt), Barrier Profiler (8-MB/NoOpt), and Barrier Profiler (8-MB/Opt) for the estimation error ratios of write-only objects. The geometric means for the profiles of immutable objects and non-accessed bytes are shown on the right side. The upper graph presents the results of the allocation-intensive benchmarks, and the lower graph is the non-allocation intensive benchmarks.

It is difficult to precisely measure the estimation errors of Bursty Tracing without fully implementing it. We took advantage of the mechanism to collect the full traces described in Section 5.5. We still sampled all of the allocated objects, but instead of always profiling all of the accesses to the sampled objects, we collected the profiles only during the instrumented period. Moreover, we only profiled the accesses to the objects sampled during the instrumented period. Instead of counting method entries and loop back-edges as the original Bursty Tracing does, we counted the number of accesses to any of the sampled objects. We assumed a sampling rate of 1/201, which is the least frequent rate tested in [8]. We tried 20000:100, 200000:1000, 2000000:10000, and 20000000:100000 as the ratios between the checking and instrumented period, and found 2000000:10000 to be the most accurate.

The accuracy of Instrumented Barrier Profiler is the same as that of Barrier Profiler if their sampling intervals and Opt/NoOpt choices are the same. To fairly compare their performance overheads, we used 8-MB/Opt for Instrumented Barrier Profiler too.

As shown in Figure 7, Bursty Tracing is not useful as an object access profiler. The large errors were due to profiling only a subset of the accesses to a sampled object. Increasing the instrumented period did not necessarily mean reducing the errors, because it also increased the checking period and failed in sampling at important allocation sites. Barrier Profiler (8-MB/Opt) was close to Barrier Profiler (8-MB/NoOpt). Its estimation error ratios were worse by 0.1%, 0.6%, and 0.3% in write-only objects, immutable objects, and non-accessed bytes, respectively, on the average of the allocation-intensive benchmarks. We believe these levels of errors are acceptable for object access optimizations. In some non-allocation-intensive benchmarks, the error ratios were almost zero, because they allocated few write-only objects.

Figure 8 compares the relative overheads of simulated Bursty Tracing, Instrumented Barrier Profiler (8-MB/Opt), and Barrier Profiler (8-MB/NoOpt and 8-MB/Opt). To estimate the overhead of Bursty Tracing, as explained in Section 5.2, we measured the overhead of the full instrumentation that inserted profiling code at every heap access. The full instrumentation was 6-10 times slower than the baseline. We assumed a sampling rate of 1/201 and the basic checking overhead of 4.9% reported in [1], and calculated the overhead of Bursty Tracing using Equation 4 in [8].

As shown in Figure 8, Barrier Profiler with 8-MB/Opt incurred at most 3.4% runtime overhead in compiler.sunflow among the allocation-intensive benchmarks. Compiler.sunflow caused the largest number of profiled accesses, which resulted in the largest runtime overhead. The average performance overhead of 8-MB/Opt was 1.3% in the allocation-intensive benchmarks, while that of 8-MB/NoOpt was 75.2%. The large performance differences in SPECjvm2008 and some non-allocation-intensive benchmarks were due to decreasing the sampling frequency for large objects. These results show the effectiveness of the overhead reduction techniques.

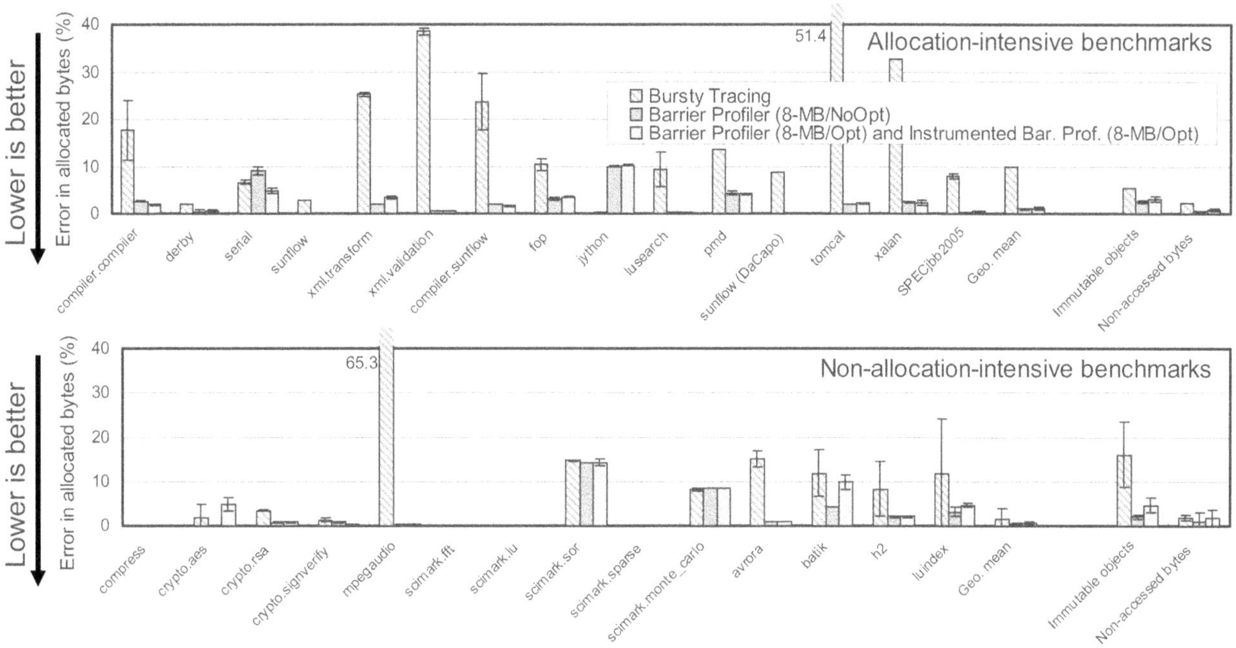

Figure 7. Accuracy: estimation error ratios in the allocated bytes of write-only objects for Bursty Tracing, Instrumented Barrier Profiler (8-MB/Opt), and Barrier Profiler (8-MB/NoOpt and 8-MB/Opt), with 90% confidence intervals. Note that Barrier Profiler (8-MB/Opt) and Instrumented Barrier Profiler (8-MB/Opt) are the same in terms of the accuracy of the profiles.

The overhead of the code instrumentation techniques was larger than that of Barrier Profiler (8-MB/Opt). Bursty Tracing suffered from at most 12.6% and on average 9.2% performance overhead in the allocation-intensive benchmarks, which matches the results in [1]. Even with the Opt configuration, the overhead of Instrumented Barrier Profiler (8-MB/Opt) was 12.4% on average and up to 22.6%. This is 6-9% larger than the instrumentation overhead presented in [3,4], and even larger than that reported in [5]. This is because the instrumentation in [3,4] is inserted only at reference loads. One reason for the difference between [5] and our results may be that the implementation in [5] was done in an embedded JVM, which performs less aggressive JIT optimizations than J9/TR. By removing unnecessary computations, the overhead of the instrumentation is more visible. Another reason appears to be that the instrumentation in [5] was to detect accesses to compressed objects and to decompress them. If one instrumentation dominates the other instrumentation code for the same object in the control flow, then that code can be eliminated. However, for accurate object access profiling, the instrumentation code can only be merged within a basic block.

In the non-allocation-intensive benchmarks, all of the profiling methods suffered from lager runtime overheads than in the allocation-intensive benchmarks because of frequent array accesses. On average, the runtime overhead was 14%, 36%, 666%, and 14% with simulated Bursty Tracing, Instrumented Barrier Profiler (8-MB/Opt), and Barrier Profiler (8-MB/NoOpt and 8-MB/Opt), respectively. Although the 14% overhead is excessive for online profiling, Barrier Profiler is still useful as one of the lowest overhead offline profilers.

In summary, Barrier Profiler achieved sufficiently accurate profiling with low overhead for the allocation-intensive programs, which allows it to be used continuously in the field.

5.8 Results of profiling

So far, we have discussed the accuracy of the profiling, but the profiling results themselves revealed interesting characteristics in the Java benchmarks. First, quite a large number of objects were write-only in some programs. In SPECjbb2005, 99% of the write-only objects were String objects and their associated character arrays. These objects were created for logging, which actually was not enabled during the benchmark run. They are good candidates for removal or compression.

Second, except for xml.validation, more than half of the allocated bytes were immutable objects in the allocation-intensive benchmarks. This matches the report in [26] that many fields in Java object can be considered `final`. Not all of the immutable objects were instances of the classes that are defined as immutable in Java, such as `String`. For 90% of the immutable objects in compiler.compiler and 42% in xml.transform, they were not instances of those known immutable classes. Since the immutable objects cannot be modified, a program should not copy the values of such objects to other objects. Instead, the objects should be shared with a copy-on-write mechanism.

Third, among the allocation-intensive benchmarks more than 20% of the total allocated bytes were never accessed in serial, xml.transform, xml.validation, lusearch, tomcat, and xalan. More than half of the non-accessed bytes were in arrays. Those arrays were buffers allocated with large initial sizes, but only small portions were actually used. Barrier Profiler is useful for tuning the initial sizes to avoid such memory bloat.

6. Online Object Access Optimizations

We demonstrated the usefulness of Barrier Profiler by implementing two new online object access optimizations. One is speculative compression of character arrays, which also uses pointer barrierization as a recovery mechanism, and the other is dynamic adjustment of initial array sizes.

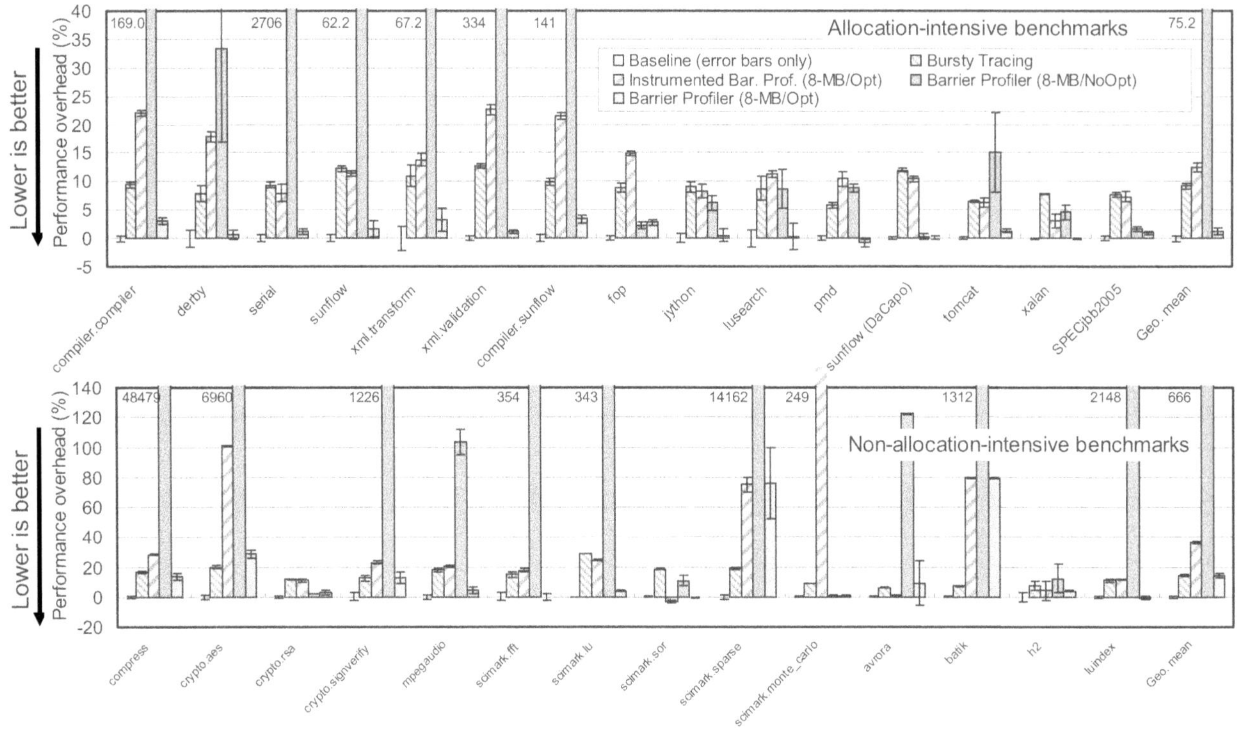

Figure 8. Performance overhead: relative overheads of Bursty Tracing, Instrumented Barrier Profiler(8-MB/Opt), and Barrier Profiler (8-MB/NoOpt and 8-MB/Opt), with 90% confidence intervals. The leftmost error bar of each benchmark is for the baseline.

6.1 Speculative online compression of character arrays

As shown in Section 5, many objects were found to be write-only by Barrier Profiler. In SPECjbb2005, character arrays associated with String objects account for most of the write-only objects. These arrays are created by a String constructor `java/lang/String.<init>([C)V`, which allocates a new character array and copies the contents of its parameter array into the new array. Barrier Profiler revealed that there was no write or read to the character arrays outside of the constructor. Therefore, these arrays are good candidates for initialization-time compression.

A 16-bit Unicode character in Java can be compressed by half if it contains an 8-bit ISO-8859 character. A previous compression algorithm [32] that takes advantage of this fact allows direct read and write accesses to a compressed character array by halving the access indices. However, this approach comes at a cost of restricting the format of the compressed character array, so that it can be directly accessed with low overhead. In contrast, since we now expect that the character array will rarely be accessed, the compressed format can be more flexible.

Figure 9 shows the compression algorithm. Figure 9(a) is a simplified version of the original `java/lang/String.<init>([C)V`. We modified the JIT compiler to generate the code in Figure 9(b) for particular allocation sites that always allocate write-only character arrays according to the online feedback from Barrier Profiler. When allocating a character array at Line 1, the JIT code allocates only a half-sized array. A particular bit in the header of the array is set to indicate that it is a compressed character array. The JIT code stores a barrier pointer to the String object (Lines 2 and 3) to protect accesses to the compressed array. It then copies the array contents with compression (Line 4). If the compression fails due to a non-ISO-8859 character, it uses the original code (Lines 5-9). Figure 9(c) illustrates the copying-with-compression algorithm. Each gray box represents a byte, and a pair denotes a Unicode character. Taking advantage of 8-byte load and store instructions, the algorithm handles 8 characters at a time. The first 8 bytes of `data[]` are shifted left by 1 byte, ORed with the second 8 bytes, and stored into `array[]`. At the same time, these two 8 bytes are ORed and masked to check their high order bytes. When an access to the compressed array is detected by a hardware memory exception, the signal handler decompresses the array in the same way as in previous work [5][32]. That is done by allocating another character array of the original size, decompressing the characters into the new array, and storing a forward pointer in the header of the old array.

We implemented the initialization-time compression of character arrays on top of the pointer barrierization framework described in Section 5.1. We observed an 8.6% speed-up in SPECjbb2005. Since the target character arrays are never accessed, we incurred no overhead due to the signal handling. We found that reduced GC time contributed to about 4.5% improvement. The memory allocation rate was reduced by 17%. The other benchmark programs were not improved, but the overhead was not larger than that of Barrier Profiler in Figure 8.

6.2 Dynamic adjustment of initial array sizes

Programmers often over-allocate large arrays as buffers [20,23]. An example is `BufferedReader` in the Java standard library. It allocates an 8-K-element character array in the constructor, but a short input stream will use only the first few dozen elements. Another example is `StringBuilder`, which initially allocates a short fixed-length array and extends it as needed. However, even

(a)

```
public String(char[] data) {
  array = new char[data.length];
  this.value = array;
  System.arraycopy(data, 0, array, 0, data.length);
}
```

(b)

```
public String(char[] data) {
  array = new compressed_char[data.length / 2];
  bar_array = barrierize(array);
  this.value = bar_array;
  if (arraycopy_compress(data, 0, array, 0, data.length)
      == FAILURE) {
    array = new char[data.length];
    this.value = array;
    System.arraycopy(data, 0, array, 0, data.length);
  }
}
```

(c)

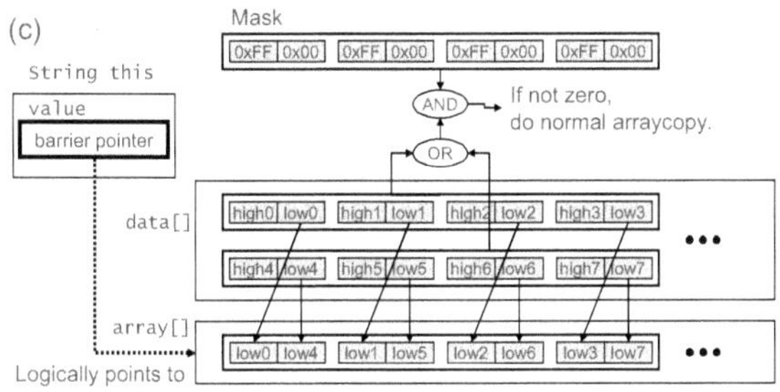

Figure 9. Initialization-time compression of a character array. (a) Original `java/lang/String.<init>([C)V` . (b) Code generated by our JIT compiler. (c) Word-by-word copying with compression.

the initial short length can be too long for very small input, and to make matters worse, some programs allocate millions of such wasteful container objects. Those objects are all short-lived, and thus the GC-time truncation of trailing zeros [5] cannot be used. These programming patterns prevail not only in the standard library but also in user-written programs.

Note that it is always safe to specify shorter initial sizes in these programming patterns, though it could be inefficient. Even if the initial sizes are too short, `BufferedReader` just needs to read from its underlying input stream more often, and `StringBuilder` just needs to extend the arrays more times. Although all of the example classes provide programmers with constructors to specify the initial sizes, such interfaces are often not used to simplify the programming. In addition, it is difficult to estimate the best initial sizes statically, because they depend on the input data and the calling contexts of the constructors. To the best of our knowledge, no system has ever efficiently offered dynamic adjustment of the initial array sizes, probably because of a lack of the key technology, a lightweight object access profiler.

We are proposing a new system that combines Barrier Profiler with a new API and a JIT compiler. Rather than using a complex compiler analysis to find the programming patterns in programs, we will provide programmers with a new API to specify the allocation sites of the arrays whose sizes are to be adjusted. The new API will have a set of static methods added to a standard class, in our prototype, `java.lang.System`. Each method receives a default size as a parameter and returns an array of the default size or an adjusted size. For all of the primitive array types such as `byte[]`, `char[]`, ..., and `Object[]`, corresponding methods are provided. Figure 10 shows a new method for character arrays, `getCharArrayOfBestSize()`, and its usage in `BufferedReader`. The only change required is to wrap the allocation of the character array with the new API (Line 7). The users of `BufferedReader` do not need to change their code.

The default implementation of the new API is just to return an array of the requested size (Lines 1-3), but this implementation is

```
   public final class System {
1: public static char[] getCharArrayOfBestSize(int defaultSize) {
2:   return new char[defaultSize];
3: }
   ...
   }
   public class BufferedReader {
4: public BufferedReader(Reader in) {
5:   this.in = in;
6:   //this.cb = new char[8192];  // Original implementation
7:   this.cb = System.getCharArrayOfBestSize(8192);
8:   this.length = this.cb.length;
9: }
   ...
   }
```

Figure 10. A new API for the dynamic adjustment of initial array sizes and its usage in `BufferedReader`.

Allocation-intensive benchmarks	Reduction in alloc. rate (%)	Speed-up with 2x the min heap (%)	Speed-up with 1-GB heap (%)
compiler.compiler	-1.2	-5.9	-2.9
derby	5.9	-3.8	-2.0
serial	9.0	-1.8	-1.3
sunflow	-2.1	-3.2	-2.2
xml.transform	-0.3	-6.2	-1.7
xml.validation	-0.7	-3.3	-2.1
compiler.sunflow	-1.8	-7.4	-2.8
fop	-1.2	-3.0	-1.5
jython	5.5	-2.7	-1.4
lusearch	90.6	298.2	36.3
pmd	3.9	-3.4	1.4
sunflow (DaCapo)	-0.8	-3.5	-0.4
tomcat	6.4	-1.0	-0.5
xalan	27.2	17.3	5.9
SPECjbb2005	2.6	-0.3	-0.3
Geo. mean	17.8	7.4	1.3

Table 2. Effectiveness of the dynamic adjustment of initial array sizes. It sped up lusearch and xalan. Overheads in other benchmarks were due to Barrier Profiler.

hidden from the programmers and cannot be relied on. Using the non-accessed-byte profile, Barrier Profiler records the offsets of the last accessed bytes of the sampled arrays allocated in the new API. The records are summarized on a per-allocation-context basis. When a context records a sufficient number (10, in our prototype) of samples and the maximum recorded offset is smaller than the default size, the JIT compiler is invoked to inline the allocation context and to embed the maximum offset as a constant in the allocation site, instead of the default size.

We modified `BufferedReader` and `StringBuilder`, and two classes in lusearch and three in xalan to use our new API. All of the modified classes in lusearch and xalan have the same programming pattern as `StringBuilder`. The second column in Table 2 summarizes the reductions in allocation rates for the allocation-intensive benchmarks. The third column shows the performance improvements when running with twice the minimum Java heap that can run each benchmark. The fourth column is for a 1-GB Java heap, which is used by the experiments in Section 5. The maximum improvement was in lusearch: 36.3% with the 1-GB heap, since it allocates many character arrays of 16-K elements, but never uses more than the first 100 elements. Xalan was also improved, especially in the memory-constrained environment. The performance improvement was mainly because of the reduction in GC frequency. We did not observe performance degradation except for the overhead of Barrier Profiler itself, showing the accuracy of profiling by Barrier Profiler.

7. Conclusion and Future Work

In this paper, we propose a novel low-overhead object access profiler called *Barrier Profiler*, which uses *pointer barrierization* and adaptive overhead reduction techniques. Pointer barrierization converts all of the pointers to certain objects to corresponding *barrier pointers* that point to read-write-protected pages. Unlike previous memory-protection-based profilers, it enables per-object profiling. Barrier Profiler samples objects at allocation sites, performs pointer barrierization, and detects accesses to the sampled objects. It reduces the number of heavy hardware exceptions by using profile-directed adaptive sampling and unbarrierization. Our experimental results showed that in allocation-intensive benchmarks Barrier Profiler provided sufficiently accurate profiles of write-only, immutable, and non-accessed data with 1.3% on average and at most 3.4% runtime overhead. In contrast, code-instrumentation-based approaches suffered from overhead of 9.2% up to 12.6%. Barrier Profiler is the first low-overhead object access profiler that can be run continuously on production systems. Using Barrier Profiler, we implemented two new online optimizations to compress write-only character arrays and to adjust the initial sizes of mostly non-accessed arrays. Both of them are feasible for the first time by using lightweight Barrier Profiler. They resulted in speed-ups of up to 8.6% and 36%, respectively.

In the future, we plan to use Barrier Profiler for detecting last access points and dead stores. We are also interested in investigating the effectiveness of Barrier Profiler on large-scale server-side applications.

Acknowledgments

We would like to thank Peter F. Sweeney and other members in IBM Research – Tokyo and Watson Research Center for helpful discussions. We are also grateful to anonymous reviewers for providing us with helpful comments.

References

[1] Arnold, M. and Ryder, B. G. A framework for reducing the cost of instrumented code. In *PLDI*, pp. 168-179, 2001.

[2] Arnold, M., Vechev, M., and Yahav, E. QVM: An efficient runtime for detecting defects in deployed systems. In *OOPSLA*, pp. 143-162, 2008.

[3] Blackburn, S. M. and Hosking, A. L. Barriers: friend or foe? In *ISMM*, pp. 143-151, 2004.

[4] Bond, M. D. and McKinley, K. S. Leak pruning. In *ASPLOS*, pp. 277-288, 2009.

[5] Chen, G., Kandemir, M., Vijaykrishnan, N., Irwin, M. J., Mathiske, B., and Wolczko, M. Heap compression for memory-constrained Java environments. In *OOPSLA*, pp. 282-301, 2003.

[6] Chilimbi, T. M., Davidson, B., and Larus, J. R. Cache-conscious structure definition. In *PLDI*, pp. 13-24, 1999.

[7] Grcevski, N., Kilstra, A., Stoodley, K., Stoodley, M., and Sundaresan, V. Java just-in-time compiler and virtual machine improvements for server and middleware applications. In *Proceedings of the 3rd Virtual Machine Research and Technology Symposium*, pp. 151-162, 2004.

[8] Hirzel, M. and Chilimbi, T. M. Bursty tracing: a framework for low-overhead temporal profiling. In *Proceedings of the 4th Workshop on Feedback-Directed and Dynamic Optimization*, pp. 117-126, 2001.

[9] Java SE 6 API Specification. http://java.sun.com/ javase/6/docs/api/ .

[10] Le, H. Q., Starke, W. J., Fields, J. S., O'Connell, F. P., Nguyen, D. Q., Ronchetti, B. J., Sauer, W. M., Schwarz, E. M., and Vaden, M. T. IBM POWER6 microarchitecture, *IBM Journal of Research and Development*, Vol. 51 (6), pp. 639–662, 2007.

[11] Li, J, Wu, C., and Hsu W. Dynamic register promotion of stack variables. In *CGO*, pp. 21-31, 2011.

[12] Marinov, D. and O'Callahan, R. Object equality profiling. In *OOPSLA*, pp. 313-325, 2003.

[13] Microsoft. Process Address Space. http://technet.microsoft.com/en-us/library/ms189334.aspx .

[14] Mitchell, N. and Sevitsky, G. The causes of bloat, the limits of health. In *OOPSLA*, pp. 245-260, 2007.

[15] Novark, G. Hardening software against memory errors and attacks. Dissertation. University of Massachusetts - Amherst, 2011.

[16] Novark, G., Berger, E. D., and Zorn, B. G. Efficiently and precisely locating memory leaks and bloat. In *PLDI*, pp. 397-407, 2009.

[17] Oracle. HotSpot VM. http://www.oracle.com/technetwork/ java/javase/overview/index.html .

[18] Power.org. http://www.power.org/ .

[19] Rehr, M. and Vinter, B. The user-level remote swap library. In *Proceedings of the 2010 IEEE 12th International Conference on High Performance Computing and Communications*, pp. 164-171, 2010.

[20] Sartor, J. B., Blackburn, S. M., Frampton, D., Hirzel, M., and McKinley, K. S. Z-rays: divide arrays and conquer speed and flexibility. In *PLDI* , pp. 471-482, 2010.

[21] Sartor, J. B., Hirzel, M., and McKinley, K. S. No bit left behind: the limits of heap data compression. In *ISMM*, pp. 111-120, 2008.

[22] Sartor, J. B., Venkiteswaran, S., McKinley, K. S. and Wang, Z. Co-operative caching with Keep-Me and Evict-Me. In *Proceedings of the 9th Annual Workshop on Interaction between Compilers and Computer Architectures*, pp. 45-57, 2005.

[23] Shacham, O., Vechev, M., and Yahav, E. Chameleon: adaptive selection of collections. In *PLDI*, pp. 408-418, 2009.

[24] Shaham, R., Kolodner, E. K., and Sagiv, M. Heap profiling for space-efficient Java. In *PLDI*, pp. 104-113, 2001.

[25] Skape. Memalyze: Dynamic analysis of memory access behavior in software. *Uninformed Journal*, Vol. 7, http://uninformed.org/?v=7, 2007.

[26] Unkel, C. and Lam, M. S. Automatic inference of stationary fields: a generalization of java's final fields. In *POPL*, pp. 183–195, 2008.

[27] Wilson P. R. Pointer swizzling at page fault time: efficiently supporting huge address spaces on standard hardware. *University of Illinois at Chicago Technical Report* UIC-EECS-90-6, 1990.

[28] Xu, G. and Rountev, A. Detecting inefficiently-used containers to avoid bloat. In *PLDI*, pp. 160-173, 2010.

[29] Xu, G., Arnold, M., Mitchell, N., Rountev, A., and Sevitsky, G. Go with the flow: profiling copies to find runtime bloat. In *PLDI*, pp. 419-430, 2009.

[30] Zhao, Q., Rabbah, R. M., Amarasinghe, S. P., Rudolph, L., and Wong, W. How to do a million watchpoints: efficient debugging using dynamic instrumentation. In *Proceedings of the 17th International Conference on Compiler Construction*, pp. 147-162, 2008.

[31] Zhao, Y., Shi, J., Zheng, K., Wang, H., Lin, H., and Shao, L. Allocation wall: a limiting factor of Java applications on emerging multi-core platforms. In *OOPSLA*, pp. 361-376, 2009.

[32] Zilles, C. Accordion arrays: selective compression of Unicode arrays in Java. In *ISMM*, pp. 55-66, 2007.

A Case for Unlimited Watchpoints

Joseph L. Greathouse[†] Hongyi Xin[‡ *] Yixin Luo[†§] Todd Austin[†]
jlgreath@umich.edu hxin@cs.cmu.edu luoyixin@umich.edu austin@umich.edu

[†]Advanced Computer Architecture Laboratory
University of Michigan
Ann Arbor, MI, USA

[‡]SAFARI Research Group
Carnegie Mellon University
Pittsburgh, PA, USA

[§]UM-SJTU Joint Institute
Shanghai Jiao Tong University
Shanghai, China

Abstract

Numerous tools have been proposed to help developers fix software errors and inefficiencies. Widely-used techniques such as memory checking suffer from overheads that limit their use to pre-deployment testing, while more advanced systems have such severe performance impacts that they may require special-purpose hardware. Previous works have described hardware that can accelerate individual analyses, but such specialization stymies adoption; generalized mechanisms are more likely to be added to commercial processors.

This paper demonstrates that the ability to set an unlimited number of fine-grain data watchpoints can reduce the runtime overheads of numerous dynamic software analysis techniques. We detail the watchpoint capabilities required to accelerate these analyses while remaining general enough to be useful in the future. We describe a hardware design that stores watchpoints in main memory and utilizes two different on-chip caches to accelerate performance. The first is a bitmap lookaside buffer that stores fine-grained watchpoints, while the second is a range cache that can efficiently hold large contiguous regions of watchpoints. As an example of the power of such a system, it is possible to use watchpoints to accelerate read/write set checks in a software data race detector by nearly 9×.

Categories and Subject Descriptors B.3.2 [*Memory Structures*]: Design Styles—cache memories; C.0 [*General*]: hardware/software interfaces; D.2.0 [*Software Engineering*]: General—protection mechanisms; D.2.5 [*Software Engineering*]: Testing and Debugging—debugging aids, testing tools

General Terms Design, Performance

Keywords Watchpoints, Data Race Detection, Deterministic Concurrent Execution, Taint Analysis, Demand-Driven Analysis

1. Introduction

Billions of dollars and millions of man-hours are spent each year attempting to build correct programs. As Bessey *et al.* stated, "Assuming you have a reasonable [software analysis] tool, if you run it over a large, previously unchecked system, you will always find bugs" [7]. The fact that developers looking to increase performance on multiprocessors must explicitly utilize concurrency only adds to this problem.

Numerous tools exist to help developers make more robust software. Valgrind's MemCheck, for instance, checks dynamic memory operations for errors such as memory leaks [37]. While such dynamic tools are powerful, they suffer from large computational overheads that limit their adoption to small groups of developers and dedicated testers. MemCheck can cause the original program to run 30× slower, while more heavyweight tools, such as Larson and Austin's symbolic execution engine, see slowdowns of over 200× [24]. More insidiously, because dynamic analyses can only observe bugs on executed paths, the power of these tools is further limited by slowdowns that reduce the number of situations observable in a reasonable amount of time.

Application-specific hardware is one way of solving this problem. Such mechanisms are custom-designed to accelerate individual analyses, but none offers a comprehensive way of accelerating many tools. As such, they are unlikely to meet the stringent requirements needed to be integrated into a modern commercial microprocessor; their benefits are too narrowly defined compared to their high area, design, and verification costs.

Commercial processors tend to favor generic solutions, where costs can be amortized across multiple uses. As an example, the performance counters available on modern microprocessors are used to find performance-degrading hotspots in software [39], but they are also used during hardware bring-up to identify correctness issues [48]. Similarly, while Sun added hardware into their prototype Rock processor in order to support transactional memory [10], the same mechanisms were also used to support runahead execution and speculative execution [11].

1.1 Contributions of This Paper

We theorize that a general acceleration mechanism should alert programmers when specified locations in memory are being accessed. In other words, having the ability to set a large number of data watchpoints (WPs) would benefit a wide range of analyses.

As the original program executes, many runtime analysis systems also perform actions on shadow values. In taint analysis, for example, each location in memory has a shadow value that marks it as trusted or untrusted. Checking this meta-data, in order to decide if analyses should occur, is slow. As an example, we previously demonstrated that checking read/write sets using software routines was 3-10× slower than using hardware to do the same [19].

* Author was at the University of Michigan and Shanghai Jiao Tong University while working on this project.

ASPLOS'12, March 3–7, 2012, London, England, UK.

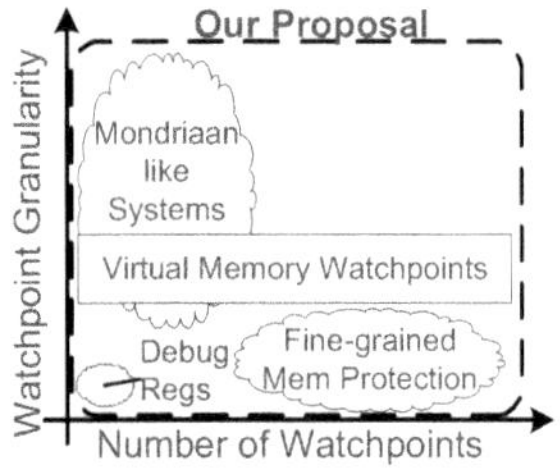

Figure 1: Existing Watchpoint Systems Are Inadequate. WP registers are too few in number. VM's granularity is too coarse. Mondriaan-like systems cannot quickly change many WPs, and other systems are often only useful for small regions.

This paper makes a case for the hardware-supported ability to set a virtually unlimited number of fine-grained data watchpoints. We will show that this mechanism can accelerate numerous software tools and is more general than the application-specific hardware often touted in the literature.

This is an improvement over existing memory-watching mechanisms, as qualitatively illustrated in Figure 1. Hardware watchpoint registers are too limited in number for the advanced systems we wish to accelerate. Virtual memory watchpoints, which are not constrained by hardware resources, are limited by the coarse granularity of pages. Finally, a number of proposals for fine-grained hardware memory protection and tagged memory systems exist in the literature, but they too are not general enough.

We present a mechanism that avoids these limitations. Our hardware/software hybrid watchpoint system stores per-thread virtual address watchpoints in main memory, avoiding hardware limitations on the total number of watchpoints. It makes use of two on-chip caches to hold these watchpoints closer to the pipeline. The first is a modified version of the range cache proposed by Tiwari *et al.* [40], which efficiently encodes continuous regions of watched memory. The second is a bitmapped lookaside cache, which increases the number of cached WP ranges when they are small.

By combining these mechanisms with the abilities to take fast WP faults and set WPs with user-level instructions, we can greatly accelerate tools that work on shadow data while remaining general enough to be useful for other memory-watching tasks. Our simulated results show, for instance, that a data race detector built using our technique can check read/write sets up to 9× faster than one built entirely with binary instrumentation and 3× faster than one using other fine-grained memory protection systems.

This paper presents the following novel contributions:

- We design hardware that allows software to set a *virtually unlimited number of byte-accurate watchpoints.*
- We study numerous dynamic software analysis tools and show how they can utilize watchpoints to *run more accurately and much faster.*
- We demonstrate that this design performs better on a wide range of tools and applications than other state-of-the-art memory monitoring technologies.

We detail the design of our watchpoint hardware in Section 2 and discuss software systems that could be built with it in Section 3. We compare our system to previous fine-grain memory protection works while running a variety of software analysis tasks in Section 4. Finally, we review other related works in Section 5 and conclude in Section 6.

Table 1: Hardware Watchpoint Support in Modern ISAs. Most ISAs support a small number of hardware-assisted watchpoints. While they reduce debugger overheads, their small numbers and reach are usually inadequate for more complex tools.

ISA	#	Known As	Possible Size
x86 [-64]	4	Debug Register	1, 2, 4, [8] bytes
ARMv7	16	Debug Register	1-8 bytes or up to 2GB using low-order masking
ePOWER	2	Data Address Compare	1 byte or 64-bit address with any bit masked or range up to 2^{64} bytes
Itanium	4	Data Breakpoint Register	1 byte to 64PB using low-order masking
MIPS	8	WatchLo/Hi	8 bytes, naturally aligned
POWER	1	DABR	1-8 bytes
SPARC	2	Watchpoint Reg.	1-8 bytes
z/Arch	1	PER	RO Range up to 2^{64} bytes

2. Fast Unlimited Watchpoints

This section describes a system that allows software to set a virtually unlimited number of byte-accurate watchpoints. We first review existing WP hardware and list what properties are needed to effectively accelerate a variety of software. We then present a design that meets these needs.

2.1 Existing HW Watchpoint Support

Watchpoints, also known as data breakpoints, are debugging mechanisms that allow a developer to demarcate memory regions and take interrupts whenever they are accessed [22, 27]. Using software to check each memory access can cause slowdowns, so most processors include some form of hardware support for watchpoints.

As Wahbe discussed, existing support can be broken down into specialized hardware watchpoint mechanisms and virtual memory [43]. The first commonly takes the form of watchpoint registers that hold individual addresses and raise exceptions when these addresses are touched. Unfortunately, as Table 1 shows, no modern ISA offers more than a small handful of these registers. This makes them difficult (if not impossible) to use for many analyses [14].

The second method marks pages containing watched data as unavailable or read-only in the virtual memory system. The kernel then checks the offending address against a list of watchpoints during each page fault. Though this system has been implemented on existing processors [4, 36], it has a number of restrictions that limit its usefulness.

Individual threads within a process cannot easily have different VM watchpoints. Additionally, the large size of pages reduces their effectiveness. Faults taken when accessing unwatched data on pages that also contain watched data can result in unacceptable performance overheads; we measured pathological cases on x86 Solaris that showed slowdowns of over 10,000×. Ho *et al.* also observed this problem and claimed that they "anticipate that using [finer-granularity] techniques would greatly improve performance" [21].

ECC memory can be used to set watchpoints at a finer granularity [32, 34]. By setting a value in memory with ECC enabled, then disabling ECC, writing a scrambled version of the data into the same location, and finally re-enabling error correction, it is possible to take a fault whenever a watched memory line is accessed. However, changing watchpoints, as well as taking watchpoint faults, is extremely slow in such a system. We do not explore this further.

In all, existing hardware is inadequate to support the varied needs of the wide range of dynamic analysis tools.

2.2 Unlimited Watchpoint Requirements

While this tells us what current systems do *not* offer, we must still answer the question of what a WP system *should* offer. Section 3 will detail watchpoint-based algorithms for numerous dynamic analysis systems, but in the vein of Appel and Li's paper on virtual memory primitives [2], we first list the properties which should be made available:

- **Large number**: Some systems watch gigabytes of data to observe program behavior.
- **Byte/word granularity**: Many tools use watchpoints at a very fine granularity to reduce false faults.
- **Fast fault handler**: Some applications take many faults, so this would greatly increase their performance.
- **Fast watchpoint changes**: Numerous tools frequently change WPs in response to the program's actions.
- **Per-thread**: Separate watchpoints on threads within a single process would allow tools to use watchpoints in parallel programs without taking false faults.
- **Set ranges**: Many tools require the ability to watch large ranges of addresses without needing to mark every component byte individually.
- **Break ranges**: It is also important to be able to quickly remove sections in the middle of ranges without rewriting every byte's WP. This is often used to carve out a working set of unwatched data.

2.3 Efficient Watchpoint Hardware

This section describes a hardware mechanism that operates in parallel with the virtual memory system in order to deliver on these requirements. Each watchpoint is defined by two bits that indicate whether it is read- and/or write-watched. To allow a ***large number*** of these watchpoints, the full list of watched addresses is stored in main memory. Accessing memory for each check would be prohibitively slow, so virtual addresses are first sent from the address generation unit (AGU) to an on-chip WP cache that is accessed in parallel to the data translation lookaside buffer (DTLB), as shown in Figure 2.

To deliver these watchpoints at ***byte granularity***, the cache compares each virtual address that the instruction touches and outputs a logical OR of their watched statuses. This check need not complete until the instruction attempts to commit, and so it may be pipelined.

If the WP unit indicates a fault, a precise exception is raised upon attempting to commit the offending instruction. This could either be a user-level fault, which is treated as a mispredicted branch, or a kernel fault. We assume the former in order provide a ***fast fault handler***. Using such handlers for kernel-controlled watchpoints, or cross-process watchpoints, is beyond the scope of this paper.

In order to yield ***fast watchpoint changes***, it is important that the on-chip caches be able to hold dirty data and only write back to main memory on dirty evictions. This, and the fact that the watchpoints are stored as virtual addresses, means that watchpoints can be changed with simple user-level instructions instead of system calls.

In order to support ***per-thread*** (rather than per-core) watchpoints, any dirty state in the WP cache will necessarily be part of process state. This can be switched lazily, only being saved if another process utilizing watchpoints is loaded, to increase performance. Additionally, each core will require a thread ID register so that individual threads can be targeted with watchpoint changes.

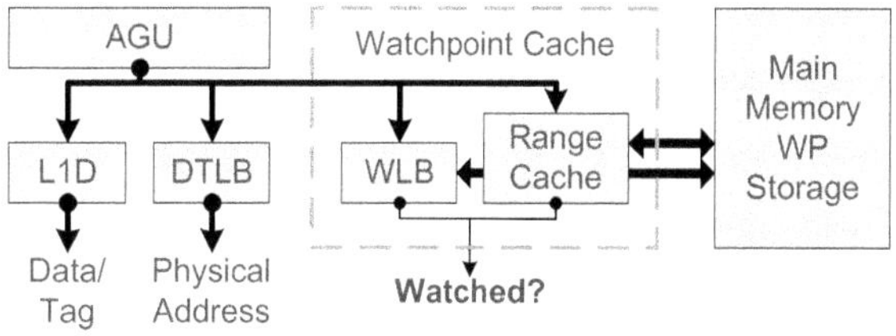

Figure 2: Watchpoint Unit in the Pipeline. Because watchpoints are set on virtual addresses, the WP system is accessed in parallel with the DTLB. This also allows WPs to be set with user-level instructions while not affecting the CPU's critical path.

Watchpoints are stored on-chip in three different forms. They are first stored in a range cache (RC), which holds the start and end addresses of each cached watchpoint and status values that hold each range's 2-bit watchpoint. This system, which is further explained in Section 2.3.1, helps support ***setting and breaking ranges***.

Small ranges can negatively impact the reach, or the number of addresses covered by all entries, of the RC. In this case, the WPs within a contiguous region of memory can be held in a single bitmap stored in main memory, rather than as multiple small ranges. The RC then stores the boundary addresses for the entire bitmapped region, and the status bits associated with that entry will point to the base of the bitmap. Accessing this bitmap would normally require a load from main memory, so we also include a Watchpoint Lookaside Buffer (WLB) that is searched in parallel with the RC. This is detailed further in Section 2.3.2.

Finally, because creating bitmaps can be slow (requiring kilobytes of data to be written to main memory), it can be useful to store small bitmaps directly on chip. By using the storage that normally holds a pointer to a bitmap, it is possible to also make an On-Chip Bitmap (OCBM) that stores the watchpoints for a region of memory that is larger than a single byte but smaller than a main memory bitmap. This is described in Section 2.3.3.

2.3.1 Range Cache

The first mechanism for storing watchpoints within the core is a modified version of the range cache proposed by Tiwari *et al.* [40]. They made the observation that "many dataflow tracking applications exhibit very significant range locality, where long blocks of memory addresses all store the same tag value," and we have found this statement even more accurate when dealing with 2-bit watchpoints rather than many-bit tags. This cache, shown as part of Figure 3, stores the boundary addresses for numerous ranges within the virtual memory space of a thread as well as the 2-bit watchpoint status associated with each of these regions.

Virtual addresses are sent to the RC in parallel with DTLB lookups, and the boundary addresses of each access are compared with those of the cached ranges. When any address that a memory instruction is attempting to access overlaps with a range stored in the RC, the hardware checks that range's watchpoint bits. If an overlapping range is marked as watched for this type of access, the instruction is set to cause a watchpoint fault when it commits. This will cause execution to jump to a software fault handler.

If there are no watchpoints set on a region of memory, the RC will hold a region with R- and W-watched bits both '0'. This means that if the range cache *misses* on any lookup, it should attempt to retrieve that range from main memory.

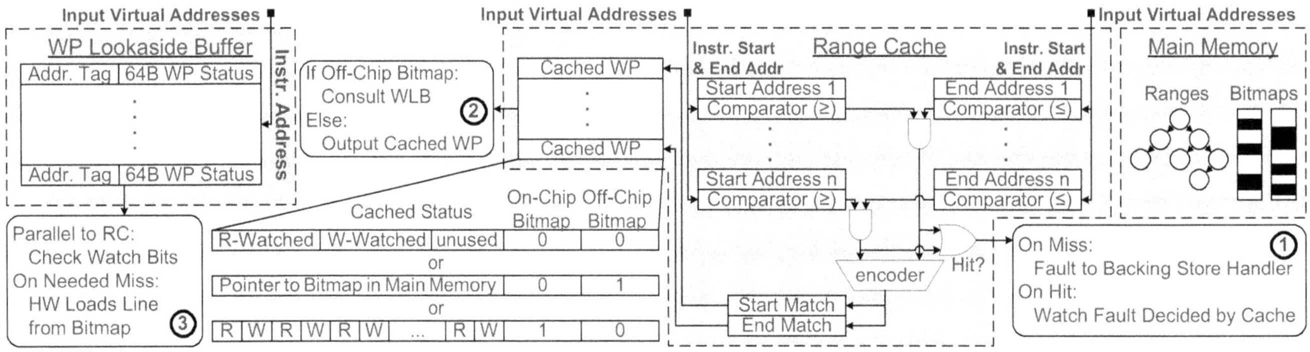

Figure 3: Unlimited Watchpoint Architecture. This system uses a combination of a range cache, center, with bitmaps and a lookaside buffer, left, to accelerate accesses to watchpoints that are stored into main memory, right. **(1)** On a RC access miss, a software handler loads new ranges from main memory. A hit causes the watchpoint system to check the associated status entry. **(2)** This range could be a uniform watchpoint, an off-chip bitmap, or an on-chip bitmap. In the case of an off-chip bitmap, the output of the lookaside buffer, which is accessed in parallel to the RC, is consulted. **(3)** If the WLB misses, the pointer from the RC status entry is used by the hardware to load a line in from the main memory bitmap.

The original RC design brought in 64 byte chunks from a two-level trie whenever it missed. We found this method inefficient for our tools, as it required a large number of writes to save non-aligned ranges. Instead, our RC causes a fault to a software handler on a miss. This handler loads an entire range from the storage system in main memory. We implemented a backing store handler that keeps a balanced tree of non-overlapping ranges, which was modeled after the watchpoint data structure in the OpenSolaris kernel.

Programs set watchpoints on their own memory space using range-based instructions, which are described in Section 2.3.4. These instructions can set or remove ranges by directly inserting the new watchpoint tag into the range cache, which uses a dirty-bit write-back policy to avoid taking a fault on every WP change. The RC employs a pseudo-LRU replacement policy, which keeps track of the most-likely candidate for eviction. If the range cache overflows and the LRU entry is dirty, the cache will cause a user-level fault that reroutes execution to the software backing store handler.

Updating a watchpoint range is more complicated than setting or removing, as it may require loading in ranges from the backing store to find the value that is to be modified.

2.3.2 Bitmap and Watchpoint Lookaside Buffer

The RC is designed to quickly handle large ranges of watchpoints, and its write-back policy reduces the number of writes to main memory. However, its reach can be limited if it contains many short ranges. In the worst case, a 128-entry RC, which takes up an area roughly equal to 4KB of L1D, may only have a reach of 128 bytes. We utilize a second hardware structure to handle these cases.

Bitmaps are a compact way of storing small watchpoint regions, because they only take 2 bits per byte within the region, as demonstrated in Figure 4. Instead of storing the start and end address for each small range, we therefore choose to sometimes store into the range cache the first and last address of a large region whose small watchpoints are contained in a bitmap in memory. This increases the required amount of status storage in the range cache, which originally only held the read-watched and write-watched bits. It instead requires 32 or 64 bits of storage to hold the pointer to the bitmap and one bit to denote whether an entry is a bitmap pointer or a range. The two watched bits can be mapped onto the pointer bits to save space.

We found it difficult to design a hardware-based algorithm to decide when to change a collection of ranges into a bitmap. Doing so in an intelligent manner requires knowing how many watchpoints are contained within a particular area of memory. This knowledge may best be gathered by the backing store software, as it can see the entire state of a process's watchpoints. We therefore leave it to the range cache miss handler to decide when to toggle a region of memory between a bitmap and ranges. The algorithm modeled in this paper moves a naturally aligned 4KB region from a range to a bitmap if the number of internal ranges exceeds an upper threshold of 16. The dirty eviction handler changes a bitmap back to ranges if this number falls below 4. This is illustrated in Figure 5.

While this mechanism increases the reach of the range cache, it could adversely affect performance if every access to a bitmapped range required checking main memory. This is especially true because WPs are set on virtual addresses, meaning that each access to the bitmap would wait on the TLB. In order to accelerate this process, our system includes a Watchpoint Lookaside Buffer (WLB). This cache is accessed in parallel to the RC, and any watchpoint status it returns is consulted if the RC indicates that this location is stored in a bitmap. On a miss in the WLB, a 64-byte line of WP bits is loaded by a hardware engine from the bitmap pointed to by the RC entry. Changes to the watchpoints in a bitmapped region cause a WLB eviction.

This WLB could be replaced with extended cache line bits, such as iWatcher uses to store its bitmapped watchpoints [50]. Sentry's power-saving method of only storing unwatched lines in the L1 (and thus only checking the WLB on cache misses) may also be useful [38]. We leave a more in-depth analysis of these tradeoffs for future work, and focus on a system with a separate watchpoint cache, much like MemTracker uses [42].

If a bitmapped range is evicted from the RC to main memory, the modeled software handler stores the entire range as a single entry in the balanced tree, along with the pointer. It then brings the entire bitmap range back into the range cache on the next miss, though it may also need to update the bitmap to handle changes that occurred in the range cache but have not yet been evicted.

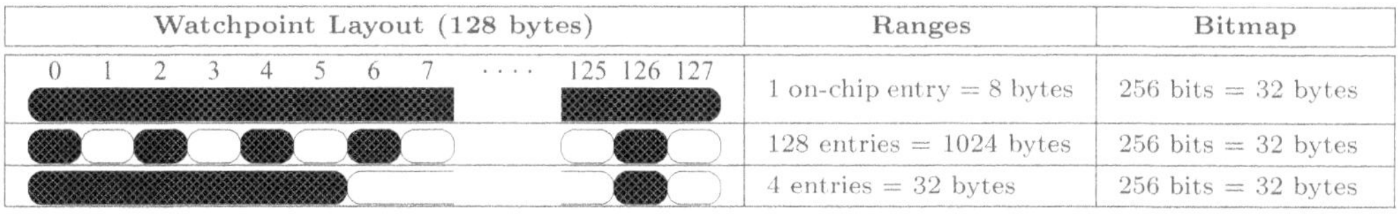

Figure 4: Different Watchpoint Storage Methods. This shows three examples of watched ranges. In the first, a range cache can hold the entire region in a single on-chip entry. The second, however, would take 1KB of on-chip storage if it were held in a range cache, while a bitmap method would only take 32 bytes. The final entry shows a break-even point between the two methods.

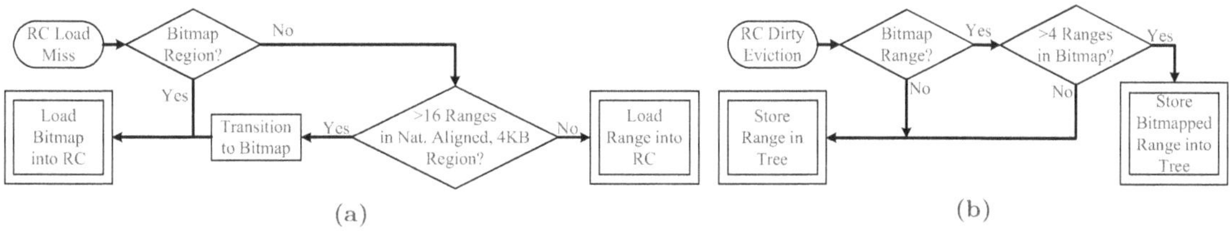

Figure 5: Software Algorithm for Bitmapped Ranges. Because hardware has a myopic view of the global status of watchpoints, we rely on the software fault handlers to choose when a region of watchpoints should toggle between bitmap and range.

2.3.3 On-Chip Bitmap

There are also situations where a collection of small ranges within a large region prematurely displace useful data from the range cache. Though the backing store handler may later fix this by changing the region to a bitmapped one, we also devised a mechanism to better utilize the pointer bits in a range cache entry when it is not bitmapped. It is possible to store a small bitmap for a region $\leq$16 bytes (on a 32-bit machine) within these bits, allowing the RC to slightly increase its reach. This on-chip bitmap (OCBM) range is stored much like a normal range, with an arbitrary start and end address. However, unlike a uniformly tagged range, the watchpoint statuses of OCBM entries are stored as a bitmap in the range cache's status tag bits, which normally hold either a pointer to a main memory bitmap or the 2-bit tag of a range. The low-order bits of the address are used to index into this bitmap, allowing a single range cache entry to hold up to 16 consecutive small ranges.

Unlike the bitmaps stored in main memory, the transition to OCBM requires little knowledge. Simply put, if a range becomes small enough to be held in a single OCBM entry, it is converted to one by the hardware. Returning to a uniform range will occur when the hardware detects that all of the watchpoints within the OCBM are equal. If an OCBM is chosen to be written back to memory, our backing store handler will store it as individual ranges. If two OCBMs cover adjacent ranges, the hardware will merge them only if their total size would still result in an OCBM.

2.3.4 ISA Changes

Interfacing with this watchpoint system requires modifications to the ISA. For instance, we must add instructions that can set or remove ranges from the RC, as well as instructions that allow the backing store handler to directly talk to the RC hardware. Table 2 lists the instructions that must be added and describes what each does.

The most complicated instruction semantics relate to modifying watchpoints in multi-threaded programs. The WLB, for example, must be able to respond to shootdown requests in order to remain synchronized across multiple threads. Most importantly, instructions must exist to add, remove, and update ranges of watchpoints for sibling processors. To do this quickly, our system must send these requests without going through the OS. One method of doing this involves broadcasting to all cores a process ID (e.g., the CR3 register in x86) and thread ID along with the request to perform a global update. Each core can then update its own cache entry if it matches the target process and thread ID. This instruction must be a memory fence, however, to maintain consistency between watchpoints and normal requests to watched memory locations. After the remote threads update their watchpoint cache, they must also send back acknowledgments. If any target thread ID does not return an acknowledgment within some timeout period, it may not be running, and its watchpoints may be saved in memory. The source processor must then raise an interrupt and allow the OS to update the unscheduled process's watchpoints.

3. Watchpoint Applications

This section analyzes potential applications for this watchpoint system. We detail how each requires some subset of the requirements listed in Section 2.1 and then develop watchpoint-based algorithms that can accelerate each analysis. Space limitations prevent us from detailing more than what we tested in our experiments, but Table 3 covers other tools, which are also briefly discussed in Section 5.

3.1 Dynamic Dataflow Analysis

Dynamic dataflow analyses associate shadow values with program data, propagate them alongside the execution of the program, and perform a variety of checks on them to find errors. This meta-data can represent myriad details about the associated memory location such as trustworthiness [12], symbolic limits [24], or identification tags [29]. Unfortunately, these systems suffer from high runtime overheads, as every memory access must first check its associated meta-data before calculating any propagation logic.

Ho *et al.* described a method for dynamically disabling a taint analysis tool when it is not operating on tainted variables, allowing the majority of memory operations to proceed without any analysis overheads [21]. Pages that contain any tainted data are marked unavailable in the virtual memory system. Programs will execute unencumbered when operating on untainted data, but will cause a page fault if they access data on a tainted page. At this point, the program can be moved into the slow analysis tool.

Table 2: ISA Additions for Unlimited Watchpoints. Watchpoint modifications must be memory fences, and instructions working on remote cores cause a shootdown in the remote WLB. Instructions used by the backing store handler can set all bits in a RC entry, and are also used during task switching.

Watchpoint Modifications	
`set_local_wp` *start, end,* {*r,w,rw,0*}	Adds a R/W/RW/not-watched range into this CPU's RC. Overwrites any overlapping ranges.
`add/rm_local_wp` *start, end,* {*r,w*}	Updates an entry in the RC of this CPU. If anything between *start* and *end* is not in the RC, it must be read from the backing store to properly update it.
`set_remote_wp` *start, end, tid,* {*r,w,rw,0*}	Adds an entry into the RC of the CPU with TID register *tid*.
`add/rm_remote_wp` *start, end, tid,* {*r,w*}	Updates an entry in the RC of the CPU with TID register *tid*.
Backing Store Handler	
`read_rc_entry` *n*	Reads the nth entry of the RC (LRU order). This allows the oldest entries to be sent to the backing store. A bulk-read instruction could be used for task-switching.
`store_rc_entry` *start, end, status_bits*	Allows writing an entire range (including bitmap and OCBM status bits) into a range cache entry. Used for reading in a watchpoint on a RC miss.
Watchpoint System Interface	
`enable/disable_wp`	Enable or disable the watchpoint system on this core. Kernel-level instruction.
`set_cpu_tid` *tid*	Set the TID register on this CPU at thread switch time.
`enable/disable_wp_thread` *tid*	Toggle WP operation for any core with the same PID as this core's and TID equal to *tid*.
`set_handler_addr` *addr*	Set the address to jump to when a watchpoint-related fault occurs. If faults are user-level, then this instruction is user-level.
`get_cpu_tid`	Find the value in this processor's TID register.

Ho *et al.* discussed the problem of *false tainting*, where the relatively coarse granularity of pages causes unnecessary page faults when touching untainted data. Ideally, such a demand-driven taint analysis tool would utilize byte-accurate watchpoints. Additionally, although they partially mitigated the slowdowns caused by the lack of a fast fault handler by remaining inside their analysis tool for long periods of time, this can limit performance. Their tool conservatively remains enabled while performing no useful analysis.

A WP-based algorithm for this type of system can be summarized as setting RW watchpoints on any data that is tainted and running until a WP fault occurs. The fault indicates that a tainted value is either being written over or read from, and the propagation logic or instrumented code should be called from the WP handler. The tool should also remain enabled while tainted data exists in registers, as those values cannot be covered by watchpoints.

3.2 Deterministic Concurrent Execution

Deterministic concurrent execution systems attempt to make more robust parallel programs by guaranteeing that the outputs of concurrent regions are the same each time a program is run with a particular input [5]. This can be accomplished by allowing parallel threads to run unhindered when they are not communicating, but only committing their memory speculatively. If one thread concurrently modifies the data being used by another, they must be serialized in some manner.

Grace, one example of this type of system, splits fork/join parallel programs into multiple processes and marks potentially shared heap regions as watched in the virtual memory system [6]. Any time the program reads or writes a new heap page, a watchpoint fault is taken, whereupon the page is put into that process's read or write set and marked as read-only or available, respectively. As the processes merge while joining, any conflicting write updates cause one of the threads to roll back and reexecute.

While Berger *et al.* demonstrated the effectiveness of this system for a collection of fork/join parallel programs, using virtual memory watchpoints in such a way limits the applicability of their system. First, it only works on programs that can easily be split into multiple processes, which can lead to performance and portability problems in some operating systems. Additionally, it can only look for conflicting accesses at the page granularity. While many developers work to limit false cache line sharing between threads, it is much less likely that they care to limit false sharing at the page granularity. Such a mismatch can lead to many unnecessary rollbacks, again reducing performance.

Our watchpoint-based deterministic execution algorithm is similar to Grace, except that it works on a per-thread basis and sets watchpoints at a 64B cache line granularity. This could also be done at the byte granularity, but with higher overheads.

3.3 Data Race Detection

Unordered accesses to shared memory locations by multiple threads, or data races, can allow variables to be changed in undesired orders, potentially causing data corruption and crashes [31]. Dynamic data race detectors can help programmers build parallel programs by informing them whenever shared memory is accessed in a racy way [35].

We previously showed a data race detection mechanism that operated on similar principles to demand-driven taint analysis, though it required the careful usage of performance monitoring hardware to observe cache events [19]. That system could run into performance problems due to false sharing and may miss some races due to cache size limitations, among other issues.

It is possible to build such a demand-driven analysis system using per-thread watchpoints. Similar to how Grace operates, all regions of shared memory are initially watched for each thread. As a thread executes, it will take a number of watchpoint faults in order to fill its read and write sets in a byte-accurate manner. In our implementation, reads that take a watchpoint fault remove the local read watchpoint and set a write watchpoint on all other threads (in order to catch WAR sharing), while writes completely remove the local watchpoint and set RW watchpoints on all other cores (to catch RAW and WAW sharing). Any time an instruction takes a WP fault, the software race detector can assume that it was caused by inter-thread data sharing, and should

Table 3: Applications of Watchpoints. This is a sample of software systems that could utilize hardware-supported watchpoints to perform more efficiently and accurately. High-level algorithms that focus on how such systems would interact with the watchpoint hardware are given for each, as well as an overview of the watchpoint capabilities that would be useful or needed for each algorithm.

Software System	High Level Algorithm	Large Number	Byte Granular	Fast Handler	Fast Changes	Per Thread	Set Ranges	Break Ranges
Demand-Driven Dataflow Analysis	`Set shadowed values as RW watched.` `Enable analysis tool only on watchpoint faults.`	X	X	X	X			

Deterministic Execution	`Start with shared memory RW watched in all threads.`
	`On local access fault:`
	    `Check for write conflict between threads. If so, serialize.`
	    `Unwatch (R or RW, depending on access) cache line locally.`
	    `Rewatch cache lines on other threads after serialization.`
		X				X	X	X

Demand-Driven Data Race Detection	`Start with shared memory RW watched in all threads.`
	`On local access fault:`
	    `Run software race detector on this access.`
	    `Unwatch (R or RW, depending on access) address locally.`
	    `Rewatch address on other threads.`
		X	X	X	X	X	X	X

Bounds Checking	`Set W-watchpoints on canaries, return addresses, and heap meta-data.`	X	X					

Speculative Program Optimization	`Mark data regions as W watched in speculative and normal threads.`
	`On faults:`
	    `Save list of modified regions (perhaps larger than pages).`
	    `Mark page available in this thread.`
	`Compare values in modified regions when verifying speculation.`
		X				X	X	X

Hybrid Transactional Memory	`At start of transaction, set local memory as RW watched.`
	`On local access fault:`
	    `Save original value for rollback.`
	    `Check for conflicts with other transactions.`
	    `Unwatch (R or RW, depending on access) address locally`
	`Unwatch memory for this thread on transaction commit.`
		X		X	X	X	X	X

Semi-space Garbage Collection	`During from-space/to-space switch:`
	    `Mark all memory in from-space as RW watched to executing threads.`
	    `Update dereferenced pointer to be consistent on faults.`
		X				X	X	

send the access through its slow race detection algorithm. A similar WP-based race detection method was recently demonstrated in DataCollider, though they are only able to concurrently watch four variables due to WP register limitations [16].

This tool is a prime example of the need to break large ranges, as the program initially starts by watching large ranges and slowly splits them to form a local working set.

4. Experiments

Any slowdowns caused by issues such as WP cache misses should not outweigh the performance gains a WP system offers software tools. To that end, this section presents experiments that evaluate the performance of our system and a collection of other fine-grained memory protection systems when they are used to accelerate dynamic analysis tools.

4.1 Experimental Setup

We implemented a high-level simulation environment using Pin [25] running on x86-64 Linux hosts. The software analysis tools were implemented as pintools and were used to analyze 32-bit x86 benchmark applications. These pintools communicated with a simulator that modeled the watchpoint hardware. It also kept track of events that would cause slowdowns. The overheads of events that were fully exposed to the pipeline (e.g. faults to the kernel) were calculated by multiplying the event count by values derived from running lmbench [28] on a collection of x86 Linux systems. These values are listed in Table 4.

Events that are not fully exposed, such as the work done by software handlers, were logged and run through a trace-based timing tool on a 2.4GHz Intel Core 2 processor running Red Hat Enterprise Linux 6.1. These actions are listed in Table 5. The runtime of the timing tool is recorded and used to derive the cycle overhead of such events.

While this setup is likely to have inaccuracies (due to, for instance, caches and branch predictors being in different states), it is still useful in giving rough estimates of the performance of numerous different systems across a multitude of tools and benchmarks. It's worth nothing that even "cycle-accurate" simulators have inaccuracies compared to real hardware [47]. The larger testing space available to our fast simulation can still lead to useful design decisions.

4.1.1 Hardware Designs Modeled

To compare our design to previous works that could also offer watchpoints, we built models for a number of other hardware memory protection mechanisms. We assume that every system except virtual memory has user-level faults so as not to bias our results away from other hardware designs.

Virtual Memory – This models the traditional way of offering large numbers of watchpoints [2]. Touching a page with watched data causes a page fault, whereupon the kernel looks through a list of byte-accurate watchpoints to decide if this was a true watchpoint fault. If so, a signal is sent to the user code. If not, the page is marked available, the next instruction single-stepped, and the page is then marked unavailable again after the subsequent return to the kernel. The overheads of this system can be estimated as: (# true faults $\times$ $(T_{kernel} + T_{signal})$) + (# false faults $\times$ $T_{kernel} \times 2$) + (# WP changes $\times$ $T_{syscall}$) + $T_{SWcheck} + T_{SWset} + T_{VM}$.

MemTracker – This implements a design that has a lookaside buffer that is separate from the L1D cache (called

Table 4: Exposed Latency Values. These events are counted in our simulator, and each event is estimated to take the listed number of cycles, on average.

Event	Added Cycles	Symbol
Kernel fault	700	T_{kernel}
Syscall entry	400	$T_{syscall}$
Signal from kernel	3000	T_{signal}
User-level fault time	20	T_{user}

the "Taint L1" in FlexiTaint [41] and "State L1" in MemTracker [42]). In these tests, the State L1 (SL1) was a 4KB, 4-way set associative cache with 64-byte lines. The original MemTracker did not have user-level faults, so their backing store was a bitmap in main memory. Our initial tests showed that the vast majority of time was spent writing data to this bitmap, so we changed the system to use a software-controlled backing store handler similar to our design. The overheads of this system can be estimated as: ((# of faults + # SL1 misses) × T_{user}) + $T_{SWcheck}$ + T_{SWset}.

Mondriaan Memory Protection – MMP utilizes a trie in main memory to store the watchpoints for individual bytes [46]. Upper levels of the table can be set to mark large, aligned regions as watched in one action. The protection lookaside buffer (PLB) is 256 entries and can hold these higher-level entries (using low order don't-care bits). We did not utilize the mini-SST optimization because Witchel later described how such entries can yield significant slowdowns if permission changes are frequent [45]. The overheads for this system are: (# of faults + T_{user}) + $T_{HWcheck}$ + T_{MLPT}

Range Cache – This system is a 128-entry range cache, where each entry holds 2 bits of WP data. Tiwari *et al.* estimated that a 128-entry range cache with 32-bit entries would take up nearly the same amount of space as 4KB of data cache [40]. The OH is: ((# of faults + # RC misses + # write-backs) × T_{user}) + (complex range updates × 64 cycles) + $T_{SWcheck}$ + T_{SWset}.

RC + Bitmap – Our technique adds bitmapped ranges, OCBMs, and a 2-way set-associative, 2KB WLB to the range cache design. The size of the RC is reduced to 64 entries because of the extra area needed for these features. This system can have further overhead-causing events besides those of the range cache: ($T_{HWcheck}$ on WLB miss) + (time to decide to switch to/from bitmap ranges) + T_{bitmap}.

4.1.2 Software Test Clients

The software analyses discussed in Section 3 are utilized as clients for the simulated hardware watchpoint system. The overheads caused by the tools themselves are common amongst all watchpoint designs and are not modeled. In other words, the reported performance differences are relative to the meta-data checks only, not the shadow propagation, serialization algorithms, or race detection logic.

Demand-Driven Taint Analysis – This tool performs taint analysis on target applications, marking data read from disk and the network as tainted. As a baseline, we compare against two state-of-the-art analysis systems. The first, MINEMU 0.3, is an extremely fast taint analysis tool that utilizes multiple non-portable techniques (such as using SSE registers to hold taint bits) in order to run as fast as possible [9]. Because this system is a full taint analysis tool, its measured overheads *do* include taint propagation and checks. The second baseline system is Umbra, a more general shadow memory system built on top of DynamoRio [49]. Its overheads come from calculating shadow value locations and accessing them on each memory operation. Similar to the tests done by Tiwari *et al.* [40], we test these systems using the SPEC CPU2000 integer benchmarks.

Table 5: Pipelined Events. These are pipelined events that cause overlapping slowdowns. They are logged and their overheads estimated using a trace-based timing simulator.

Event	Symbol
Load watchpoints using SW handler.	$T_{SWcheck}$
Store watchpoints using SW handler.	T_{SWset}
Load watchpoints using hardware	$T_{HWcheck}$
Change page table protection bits.	T_{VM}
Create MLPT entries in MMP.	T_{MLPT}
Write data into bitmaps.	T_{bitmap}

Deterministic Concurrent Execution – We test the deterministic execution tool in a similar manner to Grace by using the benchmark tests included in the Phoenix shared-memory MapReduce suite [33]. We also tested the SPEC OMP2001 benchmarks, another set of programs with the fork-join parallelism that Grace is designed to support.

Demand-Driven Data Race Detection – The default tool we compare against is a commercial data race detector that performs this sharing analysis in software. We test this system in a similar manner to our previous work [19] by running the Phoenix [33] and PARSEC [8] suites.

4.2 Results for Taint Analysis

Figure 6 details the average number of memory operations between each WP cache miss for all of the systems that use some cache mechanism (*i.e.*, not virtual memory). Because these programs have large regions of unwatched data, this tool shows the power of the range cache to cover nearly the entire working set of a program. Similarly, because the MMP PLB can hold aligned ranges, it has a larger reach than MemTracker's cache, which can only hold small sections of per-byte bitmaps. Nonetheless, Figure 7 shows that MMP has worse performance, on average, than MT. This is primarily because some benchmarks cause MMP to spend a great deal of time deciding whether to set or remove upper levels of the trie, in order to best utilize ranges in its PLB.

The taint analysis tool rarely causes our hybrid system to transition from using normal to bitmapped ranges. Because the size of the RC is reduced from 128 to 64 entries, its miss rate is slightly higher than the RC-only system's. The only counterexample is *255.vortex*, which taints a large number of small regions. However, when WLB misses are taken into account (the line "RC+Bitmap" only accounts for range cache misses), the total hit rate drops precipitously. This is because the benchmark has a large number of WP changes, and each change into a bitmapped region causes a WLB eviction.

Figure 7 compares the performance of the HW-assisted watchpoint systems against the two software-based shadow value analysis tools. The lower hit rate in the hybrid system means that it is about 7% slower than one with a larger RC. Nonetheless, the high hit rates of both systems mean that nearly every instruction that is not tainted suffers no slowdown, yielding large speedups over the software analysis tools. It is important to note, however, that MINEMU is also performing taint propagation, overheads which we do not analyze for our hardware systems. Nonetheless, using hardware-supported watchpoints can still result in large performance gains over an always-on tool like Umbra.

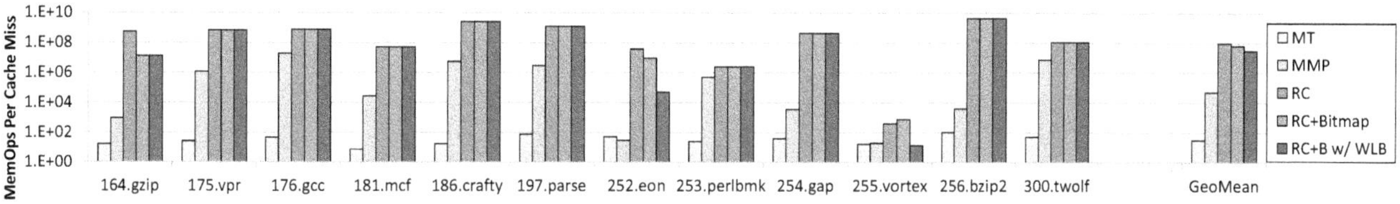

Figure 6: Memory Operations per Watchpoint Cache Miss for Taint Analysis. Most programs store a relatively small number of tainted regions, leading the range cache to have a very high hit rate (some of the benchmarks never miss). "RC+B w/ WLB" counts both range cache misses and the WLB misses, though the latter are filled much more quickly than the former.

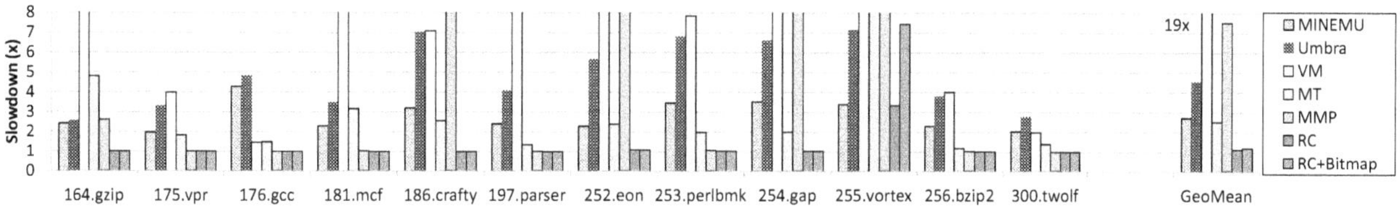

Figure 7: Performance of Demand-Driven Taint Analysis. The patterned are binary instrumentation systems that perform full taint analysis and shadow value lookup, respectively. The maximum slowdowns of the VM system are not shown, as they can go as high as 1400×. The RC + Bitmap solution performs poorly on 255.vortex because each WP change to a bitmapped region causes an eviction from the WLB, and these are quite frequent. Nonetheless, this system easily outperforms manual shadow value lookups.

This performance benefit is dampened in *255.vortex* by its extremely low cache hit rates. All of the demand-driven analysis systems performed poorly for this benchmark, and would probably continue to do so even with high cache hit rates, since the software analysis tool would rarely be disabled – almost 10% of the memory operations in *255.vortex* operate on tainted values. Demand-driven tools are poor at accelerating applications such as this, and would need mechanisms such as sampling to run faster [18].

4.3 Results for Deterministic Execution

Figures 8 and 9 show the cache miss rates and performance, respectively, of the WP-based deterministic execution system. The performance graph is normalized to a Grace-like system that removes watchpoints one page, rather than one cache line, at a time. The normalized performance of the more fine-grained mechanisms will be lower than 1.

Because this system operates on more watchpoints than the taint analysis tool, the cache hit rates are lower. Very few of the watchpoints used in this tool can be held in higher levels of the trie, so MMP's PLB has a much worse hit rate. On average, MemTracker's hit rate is higher than MMP's due to its larger cache. Despite the increased number of watchpoints, the range cache maintains a high hit rate. This can partially be attributed to the tool using watchpoints of 64 bytes in length at minimum, which increases the reach of the range cache in highly fragmented cases.

As Figure 9 illustrates, attempting to use finer-grained watchpoints in the virtual memory system reduces performance significantly (it averages out to 670× slower than using 4KB watchpoints). All of the systems designed for fine-grained watchpoints handle this change much better. The systems that utilize ranges execute at about 90% of the speed of the VM-based system that uses 4KB watchpoints, with the bitmapped range system edging slightly higher. Because this tool primarily works on ranges of data, both range-based systems perform better than the other hardware systems that operate solely on bitmaps.

4.4 Results for Data Race Detection

The cache miss rate for a demand-driven data race detector is shown in Figures 10. This tool deals with a much greater number of watchpoints, as it slowly unwatches data touched by individual threads at a byte granularity. The effect this has on the range cache can be easily observed in the Phoenix suite, as it falls from 100,000 memory operations between each range cache miss (in Grace) to 10,000 in this tool. The PARSEC benchmark *canneal* is particularly egregious, as none of the hardware caches go more than an average of 100 memory operations before missing. Because most of these benchmarks have a large number of relatively small ranges, however, this suite shows the benefit of the bitmapped ranges. In PARSEC, the geometric mean of the range cache hit rate is 5× higher when small ranges can be stored as bitmaps, even though the RC itself is half the size.

The performance of the hardware-assisted sharing detectors, shown in Figure 11, is almost always higher than when using software. In particular, the range based systems, even with low hit rates, can still outperform a software system that must check every memory access. The exception in *canneal*, where range-based hardware systems suffer high overheads from the backing store fault handler. In total, however, our hybrid system is able to demonstrate a 9× performance improvement, on average.

4.5 Experimental Takeaways

On the whole, the benefits of the range cache are pronounced. Its hit rate is significantly higher than caches that only store WP bitmaps. Perhaps even more importantly, it acts as a write filter. Many of the slowdowns seen by MemTracker are due to writing to the backing store repeatedly. In a similar vein, the algorithm for filling out the trie in MMP can take up a great deal of time when there are many WP changes, and breaking ranges apart can cause a large amount of memory traffic.

Nonetheless, we've found that the addition of a bitmap system to the range cache is beneficial when the watchpoints are small. There are numerous applications that create a large number of small ranges. *dedup* within a race detector, for instance, is significantly helped by the increased reach of the RC when using bitmapped ranges. We found, however, that the WLB miss rate was quite high in many cases. This is partially because writes to bitmapped regions currently evict matching entries from the WLB. It is also the case that

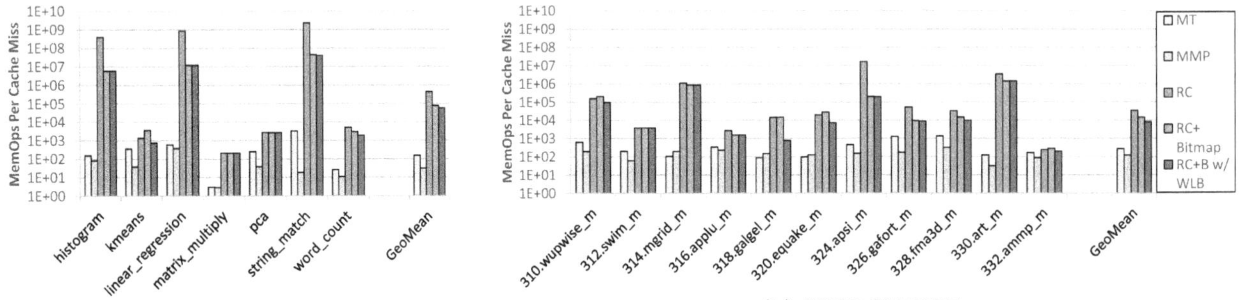

(a) Phoenix Suite (b) SPEC OMP2001

Figure 8: Memory Operations per WP Cache Miss for Deterministic Execution. The increased number of WPs causes the RC to have lower hit rates than it had for taint analysis. Because watchpoints are set and removed on cache line sized regions, the addition of a bitmap is only somewhat useful. It does not, however, increase the reach of the system as a whole since the size of the RC is reduced. Nonetheless, both systems take many fewer misses than other watchpoint hardware systems.

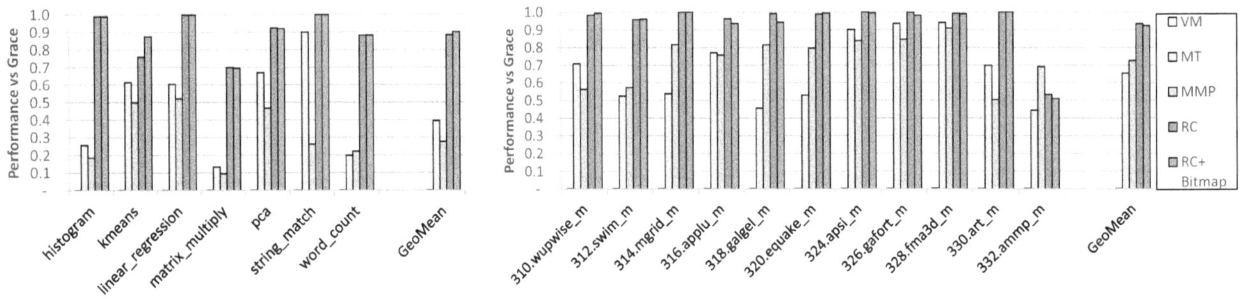

(a) Phoenix Suite (b) SPEC OMP2001

Figure 9: Deterministic Execution Performance: Cache Line vs. Page Granularity Watchpoints. The baseline system sets and removes watchpoints at the 4KB page granularity, while these systems operate on 64 byte lines. On average, both range-based systems operate at 90% of the baseline speed while maintaining more accurate checks.s

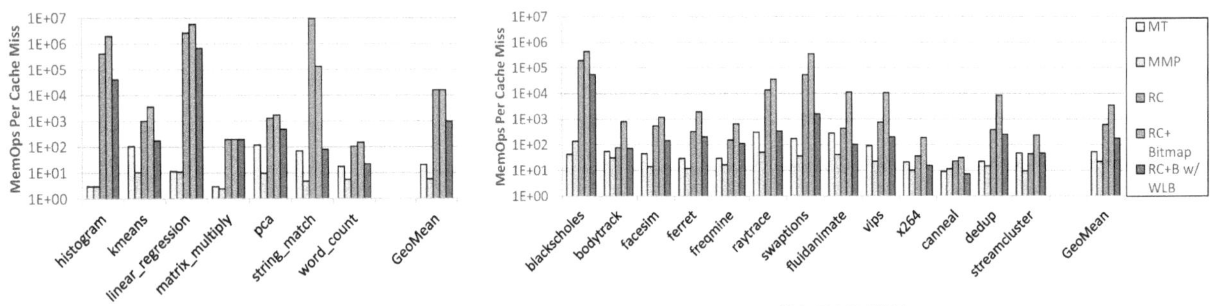

(a) Phoenix Suite (b) PARSEC

Figure 10: Memory Operations per WP Cache Miss for Data Race Detection. This system sets a large number of fine-grained watchpoints, making the bitmap addition especially useful. It increases the number of instructions between each RC miss by over 5× in PARSEC. The total miss rate with WLB included is higher, but those are filled much faster than RC misses.

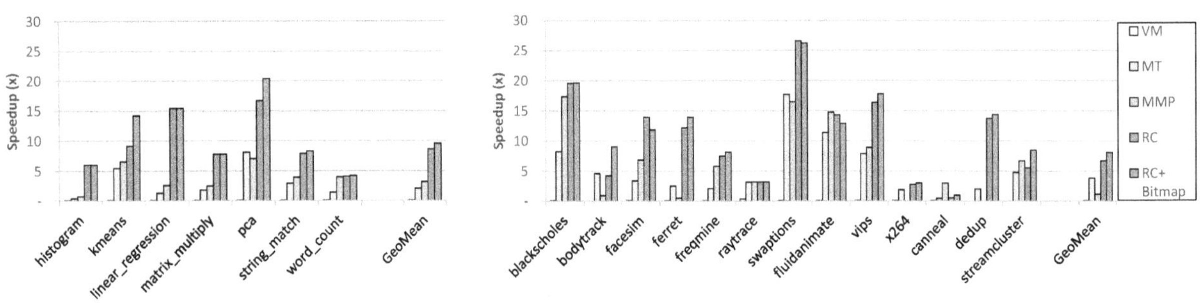

(a) Phoenix Suite (b) PARSEC

Figure 11: Performance of Demand-Driven Data Race Detection vs. Binary Instrumentation. Because the binary instrumentation tool is slow, most of the systems see significant speedups. The WLB miss handler is much faster than RC miss handler, so the bitmapped range system is noticeably faster than the RC system, even though it takes many WLB misses.

that bitmapped ranges are often enabled in sections of code that are difficult to cache. This warrants future research to perhaps find a better way to store these bitmapped ranges.

Though we did not illustrate the tests we did on the OCBM, we found that it was a net benefit, on average. However, its benefit was generally measured in single-digit percentages, rather than the larger gains we often saw with the full bitmap system.

Perhaps the most important area that could be improved in our system is the backing store handler. Range cache misses or overflows required hundreds to thousands of extra cycles to handle (depending on the size of backing store tree and the complexity of the insertion). With overheads this high, the range cache needs a particularly good hit rate to maintain high performance. One of the benefits we found with the bitmapped ranges was that the WLB miss handler was simpler and faster. It is probably possible to build more efficient backing store algorithms, such that they would switch between storage methods depending on the miss rate, eviction rate, and number of watchpoints in the system.

In summary, the hardware-assisted watchpoint systems allowed sizable performance improvements in demand-driven tools. For the deterministic execution system, the finer-grained watchpoints resulted in minor slowdowns, but allowed more accurate sharing analyses than can currently be performed at such a speed. This is the crux of the argument that hardware-assisted watchpoints are a generalized mechanism to improve software tools.

5. Related Works

This section explores works related to watchpoints and their uses. We first discuss hardware proposals that *could* be used to provide unlimited watchpoints, but which have limitations that keep them from being as general as we would like. We then list other applications that could potentially utilize an unlimited watchpoint system.

5.1 Memory Protection Systems

There have been numerous proposals for hardware that provides watchpoint-like mechanisms. Capabilities, for instance, can be used to control software's access to particular regions in memory [15]. Few capability-based systems were built, and even fewer still exist. Most recent publications focus instead on fine-grain memory protection.

One of the most widely cited works in this area is Mondriaan (also spelled Mondrian) Memory Protection [46]. MMP was designed with fine-grained inter-process protection mechanisms in mind, and is optimized for applications that do not perform frequent updates. The protection information is stored in main memory and is cached in a protection lookaside buffer (PLB). MMP utilized a ternary CAM for this cache, allowing naturally aligned ranges to be compactly stored. The first method Witchel proposed for storing protection regions in memory was a sorted segment table (SST), a list sorted by starting address. Though this allows $O(ln\ n)$ lookups and can efficiently store ranges, it is unsuitable for frequent updates. The second, a multi-level permission table (MLPT), is a trie that holds a bitmap of word-accurate permissions in its lowest level. It is beneficial to use upper levels of this table whenever possible in order to increase the PLB's reach. Checking ranges of permissions in order to "promote" a region can cause significant update slowdowns, however. In general, MMP is designed to work with tools that, while needing memory protection, do not perform frequent updates.

One common method of storing protection data is to put it alongside cache lines [30, 32, 50]. iWatcher, for example, stores per-word watchpoints alongside the cache lines that contain the watched data [50]. These bits are initially set by hardware and are temporarily stored into a victim table on cache evictions. The hardware falls back to virtual memory watchpoints if this table overflows. iWatcher can watch a small number of ranges, which must be pinned in physical memory. If this range hardware overflows, the system falls back to setting a large number of per-word watchpoints. In general, this system is inadequate for tools that require more than a small number of large ranges. Of note, Zhou *et al.* correctly state the usefulness of user-level faults in handling frequently-touched watchpoints. UFO, a similar system, used watchpoints to accelerate speculative software optimization [30]. Unfortunately, because it stores watchpoints in memory by updating the ECC bits of individual lines, it does not allow large ranges to be quickly set or removed. SafeMem uses a similar scheme [32].

MemTracker holds analysis meta-data (which is analogous to watchpoints) in a separate L1 cache, similar to our WLB. It also offers the option of using a hardware state machine to perform meta-data propagation [42]. This means that it can have even less overhead for some types of analyses than a system with a user-level fault handler. However, because its meta-data is stored as a packed array in main memory, it is time-consuming to set or remove watchpoints on large ranges. FlexiTaint, a follow-on work to MemTracker, has the same issues [41].

In order to reduce the number of accesses to the memory protection hardware, Sentry stores its protection data at the cache line granularity [38]. Every line in L1 is unwatched, and the on-chip protection structure is only checked on L1D misses. Their paper gives an excellent analysis of the type of hardware needed to perform watchpoints. However, their system has large overheads when performing frequent updates because it must go to a software handler on every change and evict cache lines accordingly.

5.2 Other Uses for Watchpoints

Watchpoints can also be used to accelerate software systems beyond the three examined in the experiments. Table 3 lists algorithms for the tools discussed in this section.

Hill *et al.* previously made an argument for deconstructed hardware transactional memory (TM) systems [20]. They pushed for HTM additions that could be used for other things, like watchpoints; we instead argue that watchpoints can be used to make (among other things) faster TM systems. A WP-based algorithm to accelerate software TM, as described by Baugh *et al.*, sets WPs on data touched by transactional code; any time another thread touches this data, a conflict will be caught [3]. If transactions are particularly long, forcibly setting watchpoints after every memory access may be slow. In this case, carving working sets out of large watched regions (as we demonstrated for deterministic execution and data race detection) may be faster, as the initial fault times are amortized across multiple memory operations.

Beyond correctness and debugging analyses, speculative parallelization systems allow some pieces of sequential code to run concurrently, and only later check if the result was indeed correct. In essence, watchpoints can be set on values created by the speculative code so that they are verified before being used elsewhere in the program. Fast Track performs these checks in software using virtual memory watchpoints [23].

Because they allow write faults to be taken on specified read-only regions of memory, watchpoints also enable security systems both as common as bounds checking [14] and as esoteric as kernel rootkit protection [44]. The latter requires little explanation, but it is useful to note that the authors lamented the "protection granularity gap," or the inability to set fine-grained watchpoints.

Watchpoints can even be used, in a fashion, for garbage collection. A semi-space collector will move all reachable objects from one memory space to another at collection time [13, 17]. To implement this efficiently, the program will continue to execute while data is moved, pausing if the program attempts to access data that has not yet been appropriately moved. Appel *et al.* did this by setting virtual memory watchpoints on each memory location that is to be moved [1]. This is similar to the mechanism that Lyu *et al.* use to perform online software updates [26].

6. Conclusion and Future Work

In this paper we presented a hardware design that allows software to utilize a virtually unlimited number of low-overhead watchpoints. By combining the ability of a range cache to store long watched regions with a bitmap's fast access and succinct encoding for small watchpoints, we were able to demonstrate an effective system for a collection of software tools. We used this system to demonstrate that the software community can benefit from generic primitives provided by hardware.

Though our results show that a design of this nature is promising, a number of avenues for future research remain open. Our range cache's software-controlled miss and eviction handler would be unusable without fast fault support. It may therefore be advantageous to look into hardware designs for operating on the backing store. There are also open questions as to the best algorithms for moving from ranges to bitmaps (and vice-versa). We presented a simple algorithm that showed decent results, but it is probably not optimal either in its runtime or its decisions.

Finally, there are potentially promising research results into new types of software tools that could be built on top of watchpoint systems. Software developers and researchers have been valiantly extending the uses of the virtual memory system for decades. This ingenuity may very well yield novel uses for a byte-granularity watchpoint system in the future.

Acknowledgments

We wish to thank Debapriya Chatterjee, Andrea Pellegrini, and the anonymous reviewers, whose suggestions greatly improved this work, as well as Evelyn Duesterwald from IBM Research, for assistance in the final revision. Thanks also to Qin Zhao for providing the Umbra code used in our experiments. The authors acknowledge the support of the Gigascale Systems Research Center, one of five research centers funded under the Focus Center Research Program, a Semiconductor Research Corporation program.

References

[1] A. W. Appel, J. R. Ellis, and K. Li. Real-time Concurrent Collection on Stock Multiprocessors. In *the Proc. of the Conference on Programming Language Design and Implementation (PLDI)*, 1988.

[2] A. W. Appel and K. Li. Virtual Memory Primitives for User Programs. In *the Proc. of the International Conference on Architectural Support for Programming Languages and Operating Systems (ASPLOS)*, 1991.

[3] L. Baugh, N. Neelakantam, and C. Zilles. Using Hardware Memory Protection to Build a High-Performance, Strongly-Atomic Hybrid Transactional Memory. In *the Proc. of the International Symposium on Computer Architecture (ISCA)*, 2008.

[4] B. Beander. VAX DEBUG: An Interactive, Symbolic, Multilingual Debugger. In *the Proc. of the Software Engineering Symposium on High-level Debugging*, 1983.

[5] T. Bergan, J. Devietti, N. Hunt, and L. Ceze. The Deterministic Execution Hammer: How Well Does it Actually Pound Nails? In *the Workshop on Determinism and Correctness in Parallel Programming (WoDet)*, 2011.

[6] E. D. Berger, T. Yang, T. Liu, and G. Novark. Grace: Safe Multithreaded Programming for C/C++. In *the Proc. of the International Conference on Object-Oriented Programming, Systems, Languages, and Applications (OOPSLA)*, 2009.

[7] A. Bessey, K. Block, B. Chelf, A. Chou, B. Fulton, S. Hallem, C. Henri-Gros, A. Kamsky, S. McPeak, and D. Engler. A Few Billion Lines of Code Later: Using Static Analysis to Find Bugs in the Real World. *Communications of the ACM*, 53(2):66–75, February 2010.

[8] C. Bienia, S. Kumar, J. P. Singh, and K. Li. The PARSEC Benchmark Suite: Characterization and Architectural Implications. In *the Proc. of the International Conference on Parallel Architectures and Compilation Techniques (PACT)*, 2008.

[9] E. Bosman, A. Slowinska, and H. Bos. Minemu: The World's Fastest Taint Tracker. In *the Proc. of the International Symposium on Recent Advances in Intrusion Detection (RAID)*, 2011.

[10] S. Chaudhry, R. Cypher, M. Ekman, M. Karlsson, A. Landin, S. Yip, H. Zeffer, and M. Tremblay. Rock: A High-Performance Sparc CMT Processor. *IEEE Micro*, 29(2):6–16, 2009.

[11] S. Chaudhry, R. Cypher, M. Ekman, M. Karlsson, A. Landin, S. Yip, H. Zeffer, and M. Tremblay. Simultaneous Speculative Threading: A Novel Pipeline Architecture Implemented in Sun's ROCK Processor. In *the Proc. of the International Symposium on Computer Architecture (ISCA)*, 2009.

[12] S. Chen, J. Xu, N. Nakka, Z. Kalbarczyk, and R. K. Iyer. Defeating Memory Corruption Attacks via Pointer Taintedness Detection. In *the Proc. of the International Conference on Dependable Systems and Networks (DSN)*, 2005.

[13] C. J. Cheney. A Nonrecursive List Compacting Algorithm. *Communications of the ACM*, 13(11):677–678, November 1970.

[14] T. Chiueh. Fast Bounds Checking Using Debug Registers. In *the Proc. of the International Conference on High Performance Embedded Architectures & Compilers (HiPEAC)*, 2008.

[15] D. R. Ditzel. Architectural Support for Programming Languages in the X-Tree Processor. In *Spring COMPCON*, 1980.

[16] J. Erickson, M. Musuvathi, S. Burckhardt, and K. Olynyk. Effective Data-Race Detection for the Kernel. In *the Proc. of the Symposium on Operating Systems Design and Implementation (OSDI)*, 2010.

[17] R. R. Fenichel and J. C. Yochelson. A LISP Garbage-Collector for Virtual-Memory Computer Systems. *Communications of the ACM*, 12(11):611–612, November 1969.

[18] J. L. Greathouse, C. LeBlanc, T. Austin, and V. Bertacco. Highly Scalable Distributed Dataflow Analysis. In *the Proc.*

of the Symposium on Code Generation and Optimization (CGO)*, 2011.

[19] J. L. Greathouse, Z. Ma, M. I. Frank, R. Peri, and T. Austin. Demand-Driven Software Race Detection using Hardware Performance Counters. In *the Proc. of the International Symposium on Computer Architecture (ISCA)*, 2011.

[20] M. D. Hill, D. Hower, K. E. Moore, M. M. Swift, H. Volos, and D. A. Wood. A Case for Deconstructing Hardware Transactional Memory Systems. Technical report, University of Wisconsin-Madison, 2007.

[21] A. Ho, M. Fetterman, C. Clark, A. Warfield, and S. Hand. Practical Taint-Based Protection using Demand Emulation. In *the Proc. of the European Conference on Computer Systems (EuroSys)*, 2006.

[22] M. S. Johnson. Some Requirements for Architectural Support of Software Debugging. In *the Proc. of the International Conference on Architectural Support for Programming Languages and Operating Systems (ASPLOS)*, 1982.

[23] K. Kelsey, T. Bai, C. Ding, and C. Zhang. Fast Track: A Software System for Speculative Program Optimization. In *the Proc. of the Symposium on Code Generation and Optimization (CGO)*, 2009.

[24] E. Larson and T. Austin. High Coverage Detection of Input-Related Security Faults. In *the Proc. of the USENIX Security Symposium*, 2003.

[25] C.-K. Luk, R. Cohn, R. Muth, H. Patil, A. Klauser, G. Lowney, S. Wallace, V. J. Reddi, and K. Hazelwood. Pin: Building Customized Program Analysis Tools with Dynamic Instrumentation. In *the Proc. of the Conference on Programming Language Design and Implementation (PLDI)*, 2005.

[26] J. Lyu, Y. Kim, Y. Kim, and I. Lee. A Procedure-Based Dynamic Software Update. In *the Proc. of the International Conference on Dependable Systems and Networks (DSN)*, 2001.

[27] R. E. McLear, D. M. Scheibelhut, and E. Tammaru. Guidelines for Creating a Debuggable Processor. In *the Proc. of the International Conference on Architectural Support for Programming Languages and Operating Systems (ASPLOS)*, 1982.

[28] L. McVoy and C. Staelin. lmbench: Portable Tools for Performance Analysis. In *the Proc. of the USENIX Annual Technical Conference*, 1996.

[29] S. Mysore, B. Mazloom, B. Agrawal, and T. Sherwood. Understanding and Visualizing Full Systems with Data Flow Tomography. In *the Proc. of the International Conference on Architectural Support for Programming Languages and Operating Systems (ASPLOS)*, 2008.

[30] N. Neelakantam and C. Zilles. UFO: A General-Purpose User-Mode Memory Protection Technique for Application Use. Technical report, University of Illinois at Urbana-Champaign, 2007.

[31] R. H. B. Netzer and B. P. Miller. What Are Race Conditions? Some Issues and Formalizations. *ACM Letters on Programming Languages and Systems*, 1(1):74–88, March 1992.

[32] F. Qin, S. Lu, and Y. Zhou. SafeMem: Exploiting ECC-Memory for Detecting Memory Leaks and Memory Corruption During Produciton Runs. In *the Proc. of the International Symposium on High-Performance Computer Architecture (HPCA)*, 2005.

[33] C. Ranger, R. Raghuraman, A. Penmetsa, G. Bradski, and C. Kozyrakis. Evaluating MapReduce for Multi-core and Multiprocessor Systems. In *the Proc. of the International Symposium on High-Performance Computer Architecture (HPCA)*, 2007.

[34] I. Schoinas, B. Falsafi, A. R. Lebeck, S. K. Reinhardt, J. R. Larus, and D. A. Wood. Fine-grain Access Control for Distributed Shared Memory. In *the Proc. of the International Conference on Architectural Support for Programming Languages and Operating Systems (ASPLOS)*, 1994.

[35] E. Schonberg. On-The-Fly Detection of Access Anomalies. In *the Proc. of the Conference on Programming Language Design and Implementation (PLDI)*, 1989.

[36] E. Schrock. Watchpoints 101. `http://blogs.oracle.com/eschrock/entry/watchpoints_101`, July 2004.

[37] J. Seward and N. Nethercote. Using Valgrind to Detect Undefined Value Errors with Bit-precision. In *the Proc. of the USENIX Annual Technical Conference*, 2005.

[38] A. Shriraman and S. Dwarkadas. Sentry: Light-Weight Auxiliary Memory Access Control. In *the Proc. of the International Symposium on Computer Architecture (ISCA)*, 2010.

[39] B. Sprunt. The Basics of Performance-Monitoring Hardware. *IEEE Micro*, 22(4):64–71, 2002.

[40] M. Tiwari, B. Agrawal, S. Mysore, J. Valamehr, and T. Sherwood. A Small Cache of Large Ranges: Hardware Methods for Efficiently Searching, Storing, and Updating Big Dataflow Tags. In *the Proc. of the International Symposium on Microarchitecture (MICRO)*, 2008.

[41] G. Venkataramani, I. Doudalis, Y. Solihin, and M. Prvulovic. FlexiTaint: A Programmable Accelerator for Dynamic Taint Propagation. In *the Proc. of the International Symposium on High-Performance Computer Architecture (HPCA)*, 2008.

[42] G. Venkataramani, B. Roemer, Y. Solihin, and M. Prvulovic. MemTracker: Efficient and Programmable Support for Memory Access Monitoring and Debugging. In *the Proc. of the International Symposium on High-Performance Computer Architecture (HPCA)*, 2007.

[43] R. Wahbe. Efficient Data Breakpoints. In *the Proc. of the International Conference on Architectural Support for Programming Languages and Operating Systems (ASPLOS)*, 1992.

[44] Z. Wang, X. Jiang, W. Cui, and P. Ning. Countering Kernel Rootkits with Lightweight Hook Protection. In *the Proc. of the Conference on Computer and Communications Security (CCS)*, 2009.

[45] E. Witchel. Considerations for Mondriaan-like Systems. In *the Workshop on Duplicating, Deconstructing, and Debunking (WDDD)*, 2009.

[46] E. Witchel, J. Cates, and K. Asanovic. Mondrian Memory Protection. In *the Proc. of the International Conference on Architectural Support for Programming Languages and Operating Systems (ASPLOS)*, 2002.

[47] M. T. Yourst. PTLsim: A Cycle Accurate Full System x86-64 Microarchitectural Simulator. In *the Proc. of the International Symposium on Performance Analysis of Systems and Software (ISPASS)*, 2007.

[48] M. Zagha, B. Larson, S. Turner, and M. Itzkowitz. Performance Analysis Using the MIPS R10000 Performance Counters. In *the Proc. of the ACM/IEEE Conference on Supercomputing*, 1996.

[49] Q. Zhao, D. Bruening, and S. Amarasinghe. Umbra: Efficient and Scalable Memory Shadowing. In *the Proc. of the Symposium on Code Generation and Optimization (CGO)*, 2010.

[50] P. Zhou, F. Qin, W. Liu, Y. Zhou, and J. Torrellas. iWatcher: Efficient Architectural Support for Software Debugging. In *the Proc. of the International Symposium on Computer Architecture (ISCA)*, 2004.

Aikido: Accelerating Shared Data Dynamic Analyses

Marek Olszewski Qin Zhao David Koh Jason Ansel Saman Amarasinghe

Computer Science and Artificial Intelligence Laboratory
Massachusetts Institute of Technology
{mareko, jansel, qin_zhao, dkoh, saman}@csail.mit.edu

Abstract

Despite a burgeoning demand for parallel programs, the tools available to developers working on shared-memory multicore processors have lagged behind. One reason for this is the lack of hardware support for inspecting the complex behavior of these parallel programs. Inter-thread communication, which must be instrumented for many types of analyses, may occur with any memory operation. To detect such thread communication in software, many existing tools require the instrumentation of all memory operations, which leads to significant performance overheads. To reduce this overhead, some existing tools resort to random sampling of memory operations, which introduces false negatives. Unfortunately, neither of these approaches provide the speed and accuracy programmers have traditionally expected from their tools.

In this work, we present Aikido, a new system and framework that enables the development of efficient and transparent analyses that operate on shared data. Aikido uses a hybrid of existing hardware features and dynamic binary rewriting to detect thread communication with low overhead. Aikido runs a custom hypervisor below the operating system, which exposes per-thread hardware protection mechanisms not available in any widely used operating system. This hybrid approach allows us to benefit from the low cost of detecting memory accesses with hardware, while maintaining the word-level accuracy of a software-only approach. To evaluate our framework, we have implemented an Aikido-enabled vector clock race detector. Our results show that the Aikido enabled race-detector outperforms existing techniques that provide similar accuracy by up to 6.0x, and 76% on average, on the PARSEC benchmark suite.

Categories and Subject Descriptors D.1.3 [*Programming Techniques*]: Concurrent Programming – Parallel Programming; D.2.5 [*Software Engineering*]: Testing and Debugging – Debugging Aids; D.4.0 [*Operating Systems*]: General

General Terms Design, Reliability, Performance

Keywords Data Race Detection, Debugging, Multicore

ASPLOS'12, March 3–7, 2012, London, England, UK.

1. Introduction

Despite recent significant efforts to simplify parallel programming, developing parallel applications remains a daunting task. To facilitate parallel software development, a number of tools, such as data-race detectors [28, 31, 30, 19, 27, 7, 16] and atomicity checkers [18, 32, 26, 20] have been proposed. While these tools can provide valuable insights into thread interaction and ultimately help developers discover both correctness and performance bugs, they have not seen widespread use. One reason behind this lack of adoption stems from the fact that for many use cases, they incur either large overheads or do not provide enough accuracy.

Performance issues are endemic to parallel debugging tools that rely on dynamic analyses to monitor access to shared data. These types of analyses, which we call *shared data analyses*, often require instrumentation of all memory operations that read or write to thread private data. Unfortunately, for most programming languages, it is impossible to statically determine which operations access shared memory or what data is shared. As a consequence, many shared data analyses will conservatively instrument all memory accesses and incur large overheads. For example, FastTrack [19], a vector clock based race detector for Java applications, incurs slowdowns of around 8.5x. Tools that operate directly on binaries, such as the Intel Thread Check race detector, incur even larger overheads that are on the order of 200x [30].

To deal with these performance problems, recent work has explored methods for improving race detector performance by trading false negatives for performance using either filtering or sampling techniques [30, 27, 7, 16]. These methods reduce the number of instructions that need to be instrumented in a manner that enables them to detect a subset of errors, typically without introducing false positives. While useful in discovering new bugs during testing, tools built around such techniques offer few benefits to developers that need assistance with debugging a specific bug they are already aware of.

In addition, because they introduction false negatives, such filtering methods are generally not applicable for accelerating existing tools used to verify correctness properties of a parallel program. For example, the Nondeterminator race detector [17] can guarantee that a lock-free Cilk [21] program will execute race free (on all runs for a particular input) provided that it has no false negatives. Likewise, detecting the absence of data races is a useful method of ensuring that an application executing with deterministically ordered synchronization operations (e.g. under a Weak/SyncOrder Deterministic system [29, 13, 25]) will execute deterministically for a given input. Such a guarantee can only be offered with a race detector that has no false negatives.

1.1 Aikido

This paper presents and evaluates Aikido, a new system and framework for developing efficient and transparent shared data analyses. Rather than instrumenting all memory accesses or a statistical subset, Aikido uses a hybrid of hardware and dynamic binary rewriting techniques to detect shared data at a coarse granularity and the instructions that operate on it. By limiting analysis to just this data, shared data analyses can be accelerated with almost no loss in accuracy. Our prototype system uses the following techniques to enable efficient and transparent shared data analyses:

- **Transparent Per-Thread Page Protection:** To avoid instrumenting all memory accesses, Aikido relies on a novel algorithm for efficiently detecting shared pages using per-thread page protection. Gaining access to per-thread page protection is difficult due to the lack of operating system support (which use a single page table per process). To overcome this challenge, researchers have turned to either modifying the Linux kernel [3], or creating custom compilers that construct multithreaded applications out of multiple processes [4, 24]. Unfortunately, these solutions require either changes to developer tool chains or to the underlying operating system. In contrast, Aikido employs a novel approach that provides per-thread page protection through a hypervisor (AikidoVM) without any modifications. The hypervisor exposes a hypercall-based API that enables user applications to perform per-thread protection requests. Using this approach, Aikido supports tools written to operate on native applications under native operating systems, allowing Aikido to be used today with almost no changes to the development infrastructure.
- **Shared Page Access Detection:** Aikido uses per-thread page protection to dynamically determine which pages each thread is accessing, as well as which instructions are accessing those pages. Pages accessed by more than one thread are deemed shared, and any instructions that access these pages are presented to the shared data analysis for instrumentation. However, because Aikido must detect all instructions that access a shared page, Aikido cannot unprotect a page once it has been found to be shared. Consequently, Aikido uses a novel dynamic rewriting technique to dynamically modify instructions that access shared pages to perform the accesses via a specially mapped *mirror* page. Mirror pages point to the same physical memory as the pages they are mirroring, but are not protected.

We have implemented Aikido as an extension to the Umbra project [34], an efficient framework for writing *shadow value tools* (tools that require per-address metadata) in the DynamoRIO [9] binary instrumentation system.

1.2 Experimental Results

We evaluate Aikido on applications from the PARSEC benchmark suite [6], using a dynamic race detector analysis that implements the FastTrack algorithm [19]. Our results show that Aikido improves the performance of a shared data analysis by 76% on average, and by up to 6.0x when running on applications that exhibit little data sharing.

1.3 Contributions

This paper makes the following contributions:

- **Accelerating Shared Data Analyses:** It presents a new system for accelerating shared data dynamic analyses and evaluates the performance of such a system.
- **Transparent Per-thread Page Protection:** It presents a new mechanism for providing per-thread page protection support to unmodified applications running under unmodified operating systems using a hypervisor.
- **AikidoVM:** It presents AikidoVM, a hypervisor that enables user applications to transparently perform per-thread protection requests.
- **Efficient Shared Page Detection:** It presents a new method of using per-thread page protection to dynamically and efficiently detect shared pages of memory.
- **Experimental Results:** It presents experimental results demonstrating Aikido's ability to enable efficient and transparent shared data analysis tools.

2. Background

In this section, we provide background on DynamoRIO and the Umbra shadow memory framework. Aikido uses these systems to perform dynamic instrumentation and as a basis for providing mirror-pages, which will be described in Section 3.

2.1 DynamoRIO

DynamoRIO [9, 10] is a dynamic instrumentation and optimization framework that supports both 32 and 64 Windows and Linux platforms. DynamoRIO allows programs to be dynamically instrumented both transparently and efficiently. Rather than executing a program directly, DynamoRIO runs application instructions through a *code cache* that is dynamically filled one basic block at a time. As basic blocks are copied into the code cache they are modified both by the DynamoRIO and by *tools* in the DynamoRIO system that are responsible for performing instrumentation and optimization. Blocks in the code cache are linked together via direct jumps or fast lookup tables so as to reduce the number of context switches to the DynamoRIO runtime system. In addition, DynamoRIO stitches sequences of hot code together to create single-entry multiple-exit traces that are stored in a separate trace cache for further optimization. DynamoRIO allows users to build DynamoRIO tools using the APIs provided. These tools can manipulate the application code by supplying callback functions which are called by DynamoRIO before the code is placed in either code caches.

2.2 Umbra

Umbra [33, 34] is an extension to the DynamoRIO binary instrumentation system that allows building efficient *shadow value tools* [8]. Shadow memory tools store information about every piece of application data, both dynamically and statically allocated. This information is called *shadow metadata*. Umbra supports arbitrary mappings from configurable number of bytes of application data to a configurable number of bytes of shadow metadata. This shadow metadata can be updated by DynamoRIO tools at the granularity of individual instructions as the application executes. Shadow value tools have been created for a wide variety of purposes, including finding memory usage errors, tracking tainted data, detecting race conditions, and many others. Like many software-based shadow value tools, Umbra dynamically inserts (using DynamoRIO) additional instructions into the target application to be executed along with the target code. This inserted instrumentation allows a shadow value tool to update shadow metadata during program execution.

The inserted instrumentation code performs three tasks: mapping an application data location to the corresponding shadow metadata location, updating metadata, and performing checks. These tasks represent the major source of runtime overhead in Umbra tools.

Umbra uses a translation scheme that incurs modest metadata mapping overhead. Umbra leverages the fact that application memory is typically sparsely populated, with only a small number of regions in memory that contain densely laid out memory allocations (such as the stack, heap, data and code segments). This observation allows Umbra to use a simple yet efficient shadow memory mapping scheme that uses such densely populated regions as a mapping unit: for each densely populated region of memory, the Shadow Metadata Manger allocates a shadow memory region and associates it with the application memory region. Umbra associates each region with one shadow memory region and maintains a table of offsets to convert an application address in a region to an address in the corresponding shadow memory region. By focusing on densely populated regions of memory rather than on the entire address space, Umbra is able to scale to large 64-bit address spaces without requiring multiple translation steps or extremely large tables.

Much of the performance of Umbra comes from many layers of caching for offsets from application data to shadow memory regions. In the common case, a lookup of shadow data will occur in an inlined memoization cache that is inserted directly into the application code. In the less common case, lookups will occur in one of three levels of thread-local caches that are checked in a *lean procedure* that executes without a stack and requires only a partial context switch away from user code. In rare cases, lookups need to be performed in a more expensive function that requires a full context switch to invoke.

3. Design and Implementation

This section describes the design and implementation of the complete Aikido system, which can be used to accelerate DynamoRIO tools that perform shared data analysis.

3.1 Overview

Figure 1 displays an overview of the Aikido system. The system is comprised of a hypervisor, a modified version of the DynamoRIO system, a sharing detector, and a user specified instrumentation tool that performs a shared data analysis.

At the base of the system is the *AikidoVM* hypervisor which transparently provides the per-thread page protection mechanism to any userspace application running under the guest operating system. AikidoVM exposes this new feature through the userspace *AikidoLib*, which communicates with the hypervisor using *hypercalls* that bypass the guest operating system. This library can be used by any userspace application wishing to use per-thread page protections. In Aikido, this library is linked with a version of DynamoRIO that is modified to support tools that wish to set per-thread page protection on any portion of a target application's address space. Using this mechanism, the Aikido sharing detector, or

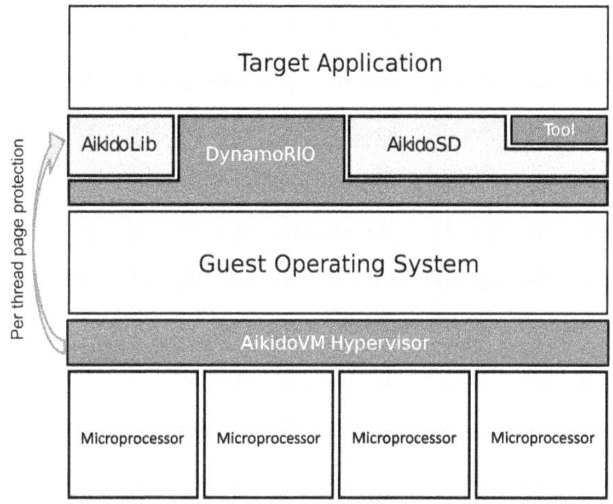

Figure 1. An overview of the Aikido system

AikidoSD, efficiently constructs a dynamic mapping of instructions to pages, which can be used to determine which pages of memory are shared within the target application, and which instructions access those pages. Once a page is discovered to be shared, AikidoSD presents all instructions that access it to the DynamoRIO tool for instrumentation. In this way, a DynamoRIO tool running under the Aikido system will only be presented with instructions that are guaranteed to access shared pages of memory.

3.2 AikidoVM

In this section, we discuss the design and implementation of the AikidoVM hypervisor. We first begin with an overview of the system. Next, we provide some background on memory virtualization and conclude with a description of our implementation.

3.2.1 Overview

AikidoVM is based on the Linux KVM virtual machine, a robust and lightweight virtual machine manager that supports a number of operating systems. AikidoVM extends KVM to transparently add support for per-thread page protection for user space applications executing in the guest operating system. AikidoVM targets Intel x86-64 processors and uses Intel's VMX virtualization extensions to virtualize privileged operations.

3.2.2 Traditional Memory Virtualization

Most operating systems today use page tables to translate virtual addresses to physical addresses. Each process is assigned its own page table, giving it a virtual address space that is isolated from other processes. To construct a shared address space for multiple threads executing in a single process, modern operating systems share the process's page table with all threads within the process. In addition to mapping virtual to physical addresses, page tables also store a protection level for each virtual page that is enforced by the machine hardware. Protection levels are specified by three bits that control whether a page is present (i.e. readable), writable, and userspace accessible. Because all threads within a process share a single page table, all threads running in the same address space must observe the same protection on all pages mapped in the address space.

In a typical hypervisor, a guest virtual machine is given the illusion of executing in a private physical machine that is isolated from all other virtual machines on the system. To guarantee memory isolation, hypervisors present each virtual machine with a *guest physical* address space by adding an extra level of indirection to the address translation. This translation maps *guest physical addresses*, which provide a software abstraction for the zero-based physical address space that the guest operating system expects, to *machine addresses*, which refer to actual memory in the physical machine, Subsequently, the guest operating system maintains a mapping of *guest virtual addresses* to *guest physical addresses* for each process, to complete the translation.

To perform this translation, today's hypervisors will either maintain *shadow page tables* in a software MMU which directly maps guest virtual addresses to machine addresses, or on newer hardware with support for *nested paging* (e.g. using Intel's VMX EPT and AMD-V extensions), maintain a page table that maps guest physical to machine addresses, and uses the hardware MMU to perform the complete address translation by walking both the guest OS and the hypervisor's page tables. In this work, we refer only to the former shadow paging strategy, though we believe that our techniques are generally applicable to hardware MMU virtualization systems based on nested paging as well.

In a software MMU, shadow page tables provide an efficient way of mapping guest virtual addresses directly to machine addresses. The processor uses these shadow page tables during execution instead of the guest page tables, caching the translations in the TLB allowing most memory accesses to avoid virtualization overhead. The shadow page tables must be kept in sync with the guest operating system's page tables by monitoring the guest's changes to these page tables. This is typically done by write-protecting the pages that comprise the guest page tables, allowing the hypervisor to intercept any changes made to them. Once a write is detected, the hypervisor will emulate the write on behalf of the guest and update the shadow page table accordingly. The hypervisor also intercepts all context switches performed by the guest OS by trapping on updates to the control register (CR3 on x86) that points to the root of the page table. On x86, this can be done using Intel VMX virtualization extensions to request an exit from the virtual machine on any write to the CR3 register. This allows the hypervisor to switch shadow page tables to correspond with the guest page tables on context switches.

3.2.3 Memory Virtualization in AikidoVM

Rather than maintaining a single shadow page for every page in the guest operating system, AikidoVM maintains multiple shadow pages, one for each thread in an Aikido enabled guest process. Each copy of a shadow page table performs the same mapping from virtual to physical memory, so each thread executing in the guest process will share the exact same view of memory. As with a traditional hypervisor, AikidoVM write protects the guest operating system's page table pages to detect updates to them. If a change is detected, AikidoVM updates each of the shadow page tables for each of the threads.

Additionally, AikidoVM must intercept all context switches between threads within the same address space so that it is able to switch shadow page tables. Unfortunately, modern operating systems do not write to the CR3 register on such context switches because such switches do not require a change in address space. Therefore, it is not possible to use traditional mechanisms for requesting an exit from the virtual machine during such context switches. As a result, we currently insert a hypercall into the context switch procedure of the guest operating system to inform AikidoVM of the context switch. However, to support truly unmodified operating systems, we are in the process of updating our system to request virtual machine exits on writes to the GS and FS segment registers. These registers are used in modern operating systems to specify thread local storage for each thread on x86 systems, and are updated on all context switches, including context switches between threads in the same process. Alternatively, a hypercall can be inserted into an unmodified guest operating system at runtime by inserting a trampoline-based probe [11] into the context switch function.

3.2.4 Per-Thread Page Protection

By maintaining multiple shadow page tables, AikidoVM is able to set different page protections for each thread in the Aikido-enabled guest userspace process. AikidoVM maintains a per-thread protection table that is queried and used to determine the protection bits on any new page table entry in a thread's shadow page table (see Figure 2). When a page fault occurs, AikidoVM first checks the current thread's protection table before checking the guest operating system's page table to determine whether the page fault was caused by an Aikdio initiated protection, or by regular behavior of the guest application and operating system. Being able to differentiate between the two types of page faults has proven to be extremely useful for our system, as it has greatly simplified the number of changes required to support Aikido in DynamoRIO.

When a guest operating system makes a change to its page tables, AikidoVM will trap and apply the changes to each of the thread's shadow page tables, updating the page protection bits according to the contents of the per-thread protection table. In order to do so, it must maintain two reverse mapping tables that map guest physical addresses to the per-thread shadow pages and to Aikido's per thread protection table.

3.2.5 Delivering Page Faults

For non-Aikido caused page faults, AikidoVM delivers the page fault to the guest operating system, allowing the guest operating system to handle it as it would normally. For Aikido related page faults, AikidoVM reuses the guest's signal delivery mechanisms by injecting a fake page fault at a special address predetermined with the Aikido library. To prevent the guest operating system from ignoring this page fault, Aikido requires that this predetermined address is mapped in the guest userspace application's address space and has the same page protection as the faulting location. This is achieved in the Aikido library by allocating a page with no write access and one with no read access and reporting both page addresses to the AikidoVM on initialization. To report the true faulting address, AikidoVM records the address at a memory location that is registered with the Aikido library. Subsequently, the signal handler that is handling the fault can both check whether a fault is Aikido related, and obtain the faulting address using the `aikido_is_aikido_pagefault()` function in the Aikido library.

3.2.6 Handling Guest Operating System Faults

Because the guest operating system is unaware of any additional page protection set by the guest userspace application through AikidoVM, it may cause a page fault when accessing a page in the application's address space, which it will not be able to handle. As a

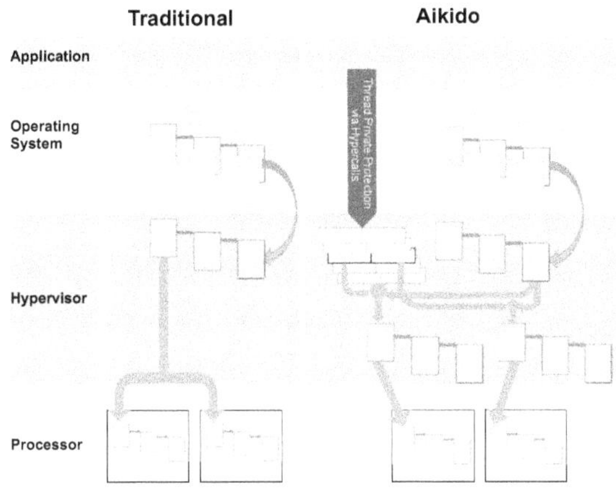

Figure 2. Compares the shadow page tables maintained by a traditional hypervisor to that of AikidoVM. A traditional hypervisor maintains one shadow page table for every page table in the guest operating system, while the AikidoVM maintains multiple shadow pages (one for each thread sharing the guest page table) for each guest page table, and multiple per-thread page protection tables that store the desired page protection.

result, AikidoVM detects such page faults and emulates the instruction in the guest operating system that caused the page fault. To prevent subsequent page faults (and further emulation) to the same page, AikidoVM will also temporarily unprotect the page. Unfortunately, because Intel's VMX extensions cannot be used to request VM exits when the guest operating system returns execution to the guest userspace application, AikidoVM has no way of reprotecting these pages before the guest userspace application resumes. Therefore, when temporarily unprotecting a page, AikidoVM ensures that it is not userspace accessible (i.e.: USER bit is not set). Thus, a page fault will be triggered when the userspace application attempts to access a temporarily unprotected page, at which point AikidoVM will restore the original protections to all pages accessed by the guest operating system.

3.3 AikidoSD

In this section, we describe the Aikido sharing detector (AikidoSD), the component that is responsible for instrumenting and tracking the target application's accesses to memory to determine which pages are shared. Once AikidoSD finds a shared page, it presents all instructions that access the page to a user supplied DynamoRIO tool for instrumentation.

3.3.1 Overview

AikidoSD is built on top of a version of the Umbra shadow memory framework that has been modified to map application addresses to *two* shadow addresses (instead of just one). The first of these two shadow memories is used to store metadata for the shared data analysis tool and to track the shared state of each page by the Aikido sharing detector. The second shadow memory is used to construct *mirror* pages. Mirror pages duplicate the content of the target application's address space without any additional protections added by AikidoSD. This provides AikidoSD a mechanism for accessing application data while the original location is protected.

3.3.2 Detecting Sharing

The Aikido sharing detector is designed with the key goal of ensuring that instructions that access only private data incur close to no overheads. With this goal in mind, the sharing detector relies on thread-private page protection to page protect each module of memory mapped by the target application. When the target application begins execution, AikidoSD will page protect all mapped pages in the target application's address space. When a thread accesses a page for the first time (first scenario in Figure 3), AikidoSD catches the segmentation fault delivered by AikidoVM, unprotects the page, sets the page's status to private and finally resumes execution. All subsequent accesses to the page by the thread will continue without additional page faults or overhead (second scenario in Figure 3). In this way, the Aikido sharing detector requires just one page fault per thread for each page that will remain private to a single thread throughout the execution of the target application.

If another thread accesses a page that has been previously marked private (third scenario in Figure 3), AikidoSD will catch the resulting segmentation fault and atomically set the state of the page to shared and globally protect the page so that it is not accessible by any thread. Once the page is globally inaccessible (last scenario in Figure 3), AikidoSD will receive a segmentation fault every time a new instruction attempts to access a shared page. At this point, any instruction that causes a page fault is known to be accessing shared data and can be instrumented by the DynamoRIO tool. This is accomplished by deleting all cached basic blocks that contain the faulting instruction and re-JITing them to include any desired instrumentation by the tool. Additionally, since the page being accessed by the faulting instruction is no longer accessible, AikidoSD must update the code in the basic block such that the instruction accesses all memory via mirror pages. This is achieved by either modifying the immediate effective address in direct memory instructions, or for indirect memory instructions, inserting a sequence of instruction that translate the base address of the instruction. AikidoSD uses the same efficient sequence of instructions used by Umbra to perform the translation. Finally, for indirect memory instructions only, which may continue to access shared or private data, AikidoSD will also emit a branch that checks whether the instruction is accessing a shared or private page on subsequent invocations. This check allows AikidoSD to jump over the instrumentation and memory address redirection code when the instruction accesses a private page. Figure 4 outlines the code sequence emitted by AikidoSD when instrumenting an instruction.

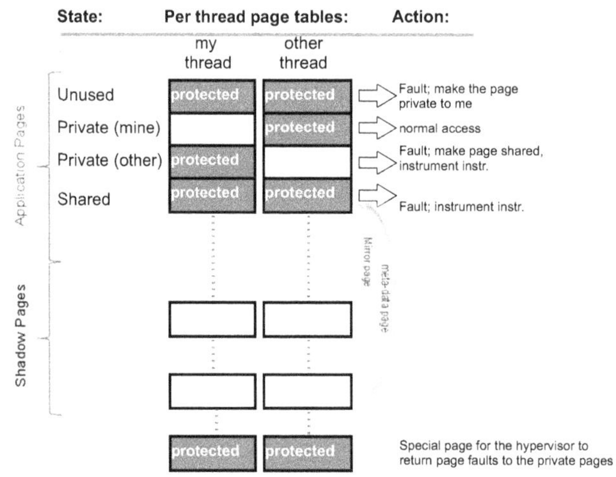

Figure 3. An example page protection state and the corresponding actions that will occur on a memory access to each page.

```
// Translate address from application to shadow
shd_addr = app_to_shd(app_addr);
if (page_status(shd_addr) == SHARED) {
  // Execute instrumentation emitted by the tool
  // (e.g. race detection instrumentation)
  tool_instrumentation_code(shd_addr);
  // Translate address from app to mirror
  mirror_addr = app_to_mirror(app_addr);
  // Redirect memory access to mirror page
  redirect(APP_INSTR, mirror_addr);
} else {
  // Execute the original application instr
  APP_INSTR;
}
```

Figure 4. Pseudocode of the instrumentation inserted at an instruction that has accessed a shared page

3.3.3 Mirror Pages

AikidoSD starts by mirroring all allocated pages within the target application's address space at program start. This is done by creating a new backing file for every segment of memory, copying the contents of memory to that file, and finally mmapping the file both over the originally allocated segment, and into the mirrored memory region for that segment.

After the application begins to execute, AikidoSD will intercept all `mmap` and `brk` system calls to ensure that all new memory allocations are correctly mirrored. For non-anonymous shared mmaps, AikidoSD simply performs the same mmap into the mirrored pages. For private (copy-on-write) mappings (including anonymous mappings), AikidoSD creates a new backing file, copies the contents of the original file and mmaps the new backing file twice using shared mappings. The new backing file is required so that its contents can be shared without affecting any other mappings of the original file. To handle extensions to the heap, AikidoSD intercepts all `brk` system calls and emulates their behaviour using mmaped files, which are again mapped twice in the address space.

3.4 Changes to DynamoRIO

DynamoRIO often needs access to the entire contents of the target application's address space. Furthermore, DynamoRIO will write-protect certain pages in the application's address space (to detect self-modifying code) and can get confused when it discovers unexpected page protections. As a result, we made a number of changes to DynamoRIO to have it support tools that use Aikido's per-thread page protections.

Most significantly, we updated the master signal handler to differentiate between Aikdio and non-Aikido page faults. When an Aikido page fault is discovered, DynamoRIO will check the location of the faulting instruction. If the page fault was triggered by the target application, DynamoRIO will forward the signal to the Aikido sharing detector for further examination. If it occurred within DynamoRIO or within a DynamoRIO tool, DynamoRIO will unprotect the page for that thread, and will add the page address to a list of unprotected pages. When returning control back to the target application, DynamoRIO will iterate through this list and reprotect all the pages that needed uprotecting.

3.5 Portability

While our implementation has been in the context of a Linux guest operating system, we believe that the approach we have taken can be easily applied to other operating systems, such as Microsoft Windows or Mac OS X. Indeed, great care was taken to ensure that the implementation is as portable as possible. Because of this, we expect that our system will operate almost out of the box when running on the Windows version of DynamoRIO.

4. Aikido Race Detector

To demonstrate the efficacy of Aikido in accelerating shared data analyses, we implemented a race detector that takes advantage of the sharing detection in Aikido to only check for races that occur in shared data. Our race detector implements the FastTrack [19] algorithm, an efficient *happens-before* race detector. We first provide background on the FastTrack algorithm and then present details of how we incorporated it into Aikido.

4.1 FastTrack Algorithm Background

FastTrack operates by computing a *happens-before* relation on the memory and synchronization operations in a program execution. A happens-before relation is a partial ordering on the instructions in the program trace that can be used to identify races. A race occurs when two instructions are not ordered by this happens-before relation, they read or write to the same variable, and one instruction is a write. FastTrack computes the happens-before relation by keeping track of a vector clock for each thread. Each thread is given a logical clock that is incremented each time a synchronization event occurs. Each thread's vector clock records the clock of every thread in the system. Entries for other threads in a vector clock are updated as synchronization occurs.

To update the thread vector clocks, each lock also maintains a vector clock, which serves as a checkpoint of how far along each thread was when it last accessed the lock. When a thread performs a lock acquire, the lock's vector clock is used to update the thread's vector clock, thus passing on information about happens-before invariants originating from past holders of the lock. Upon lock release, the lock's vector clock is updated using the thread's vector clock to record the event. Finally, after the lock is released, the thread increments its own clock.

Each variable in the program has two vector clocks, one for reads and one for writes. To detect races during program execution, FastTrack compares the clocks of each variable to the clock of the accessing thread. This check ensures that a read must occur after the last write from any other thread to that variable, and a write must occur after any read or write from any other thread. Upon a read or write, the entry corresponding to the thread performing the access in the variable's read vector clock or write vector clock is updated to contain the thread's clock.

FastTrack uses a novel optimization of this algorithm revolving around the concept of *epochs*, which reduces the metadata for variables by only recording information about the last access when a totally ordered sequence of accesses occurs. Like other *happens-before* race-detectors, FastTrack does not report false positives and can only find races that could manifest for a particular tested execution schedule for a given input.

4.2 Aikido Race Detector

There were a number of challenges in implementing FastTrack in DynamoRIO and Aikido. The largest issue resulted from operating on unmodified x86 binaries. While FastTrack operates on variables in Java, x86 binaries contain instructions that operate directly on memory and may contain overlapping accesses to data. To simplify the design, we divided the address space into fixed size (currently 8-byte) blocks that we considered "variables" for the FastTrack algorithm. This has the downside of possibly introducing false positives for tightly packed data, but simplifies the allocation of shadow memory to keep track of the metadata required by FastTrack. To store metadata we use thread-local storage for thread metadata, a hash-table for per-lock metadata, and shadow memory for storing metadata about each block of memory. The mechanism for providing shadow memory is summarized in Section 2.2. We use DynamoRIO to insert the instrumentation needed to perform metadata updates and checks for races.

Additionally, to simplify clock inheritance and metadata updates on thread creation, we serialize all thread creation using locking. We also added special handling to avoid reporting spurious races from the C/C++ libraries, the pthread library, and the loader.

When running under AikidoVM, our race detector only instruments instructions that access shared data and only maintains the epoch metadata for shared data. Initially, instructions are not instrumented and metadata is not maintained for memory. When Aikido finds shared data, the instructions accessing that data are instrumented and the metadata for the shared data is initialized. This achieves our performance improvements, but may prevents us from instrumenting instructions before they perform their *first* access to shared data (i.e. before we detected that the data was shared). This can potentially introduce a false negative if a race occurs between two instructions that are each the first instruction in their respective threads to access the same page.

5. Evaluation

In this section we evaluate the performance of Aikido on the race detector described in Section 4.

5.1 Experimental Setup

We tested Aikido on a quad-socket Xeon X7550 system running Debian 5.0 using 8 threads. We ran our race detector on 10 benchmarks from the PARSEC 2.1 benchmark suite [5, 6] using the simsmall input set.

5.2 Results and Analysis

Figure 5 compares the performance of our Aikido-FastTrack race detector versus the regular FastTrack tool. Both numbers are normalized to the native execution time, resulting in a slowdown number where lower is better. Aikido is able to improve the performance of 6 of the 10 benchmarks. In the remaining 4 benchmarks it exhibits little change for 3 benchmarks, and a 3% increase in overhead for fluidanimate. On average, Aikido is able to speed up the FastTrack race detector by 76%, and up to 6.0x for the raytrace benchmark.

Figure 6 shows the percentage of accesses in each benchmark that target shared pages. We see that the three top performing benchmarks: raytrace, swaptions, and blackscholes, all exhibit low levels of sharing between threads, which permits the up to 6.0x improvement in performance when run with Aikido. Likewise, Aikido's poor performance on fluidanimate can be explained in part by the large amount of sharing in the benchmark.

Table 1 shows how the overheads for our two worst performing benchmarks (fluidanimate and vips) change at different thread counts. For both benchmarks, the overheads are significantly lower at two threads than at 8 threads. Additionally, at thread counts of both two and four, Aikido-FastTrack always outperforms FastTrack for both of the two benchmarks. At two threads, Aikido-FastTrack is up to 45% faster than the FastTrack algorithm for vips.

Table 2 outlines a number of other statistics for each of the PARSEC benchmarks recorded while running the Aikido-FastTrack tool. The first column lists the number of memory accessing instructions executed by each of the benchmarks. This represents the number of instructions that would typically need to be instrumented by a race detector to conservatively instrument all accesses to shared memory. The second column displays the dynamic execution count of all instructions that were found to access shared pages, while the third column lists the number of times these instructions accessed a shared page, which indicates the number of times the Aikido-FastTrack instrumentation was executed. Lastly, the fourth column displays the number of segmentation faults delivered by the AikidoVM hypervisor. This number also represents

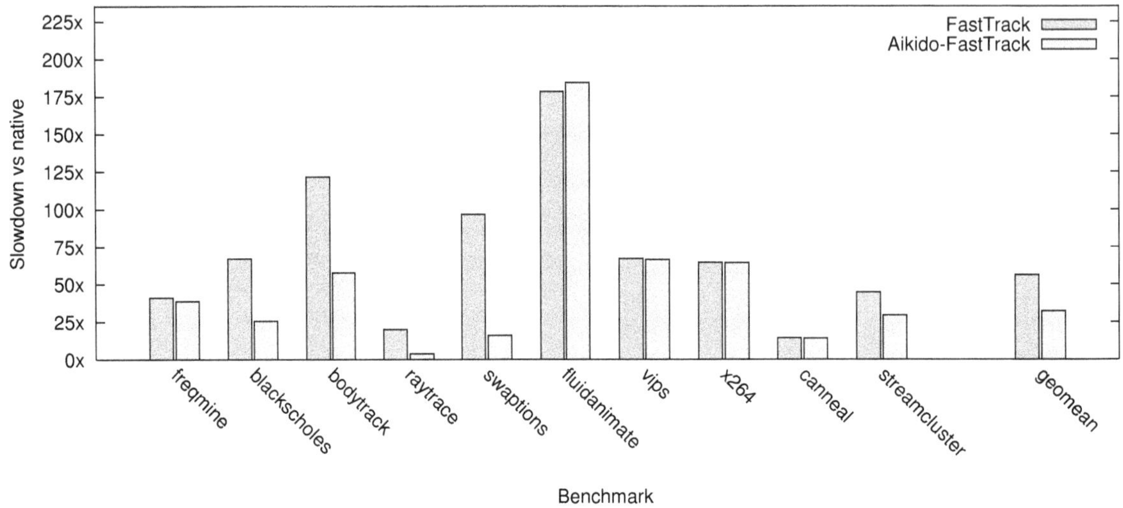

Figure 5. Performance of the FastTrack race detector algorithm when running both with and without the Aikido. Both numbers are normalized to the native execution time running without race detection (lower is better).

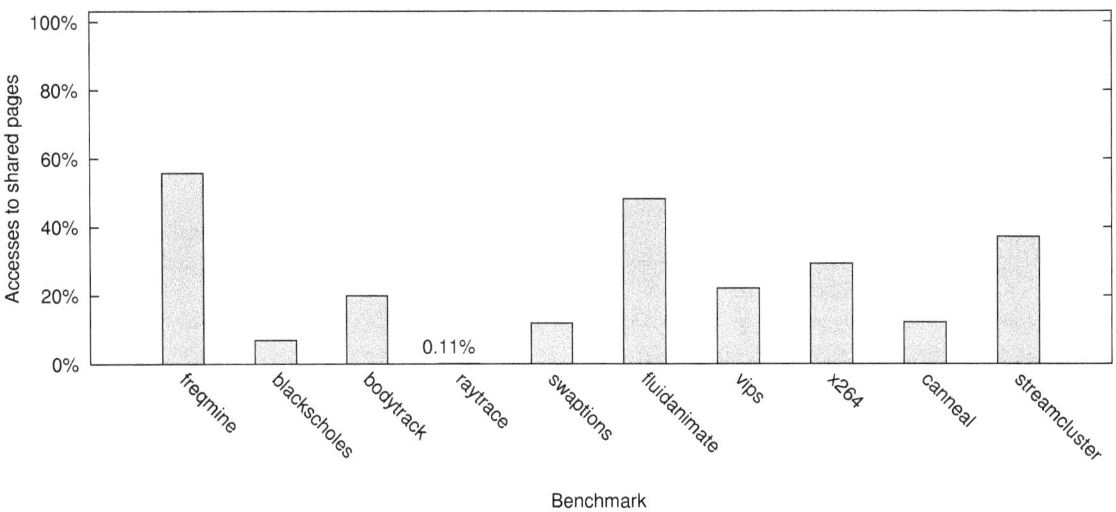

Figure 6. Percentage of accesses that target shared page for each benchmark.

the number of times DynamoRIO needed to rebuild a basic block (and potentially a trace).

By comparing the first two columns, it is possible to determine an upper bound, for each benchmark, on the amount of instrumentation that can be avoided using our approach when running with 8 threads. Across all of the benchmarks, our technique yields a geometric mean reduction of 6.75x in the number of memory accessing instructions that need to be instrumented.

5.3 Detected Races

We compared the outputs between both the FastTrack and Aikido-FastTrack tools to check that both tools were detecting the same races. In both tools, we found a number races in the PARSEC benchmark suite. We believe most of the races found were considered benign and the result of custom synchronization in libraries or "racy reads" where outdated results are acceptable to the programmer.

An example race we found was in the random number generator (based on Mersenne Twister) in the canneal benchmark. This might be considered a benign race, since there is no correct result of a random number generator. However, it is not clear that the known statistical properties of the Mersenne Twister function hold in a runtime with data races.

6. Discussion

AikidoSD determines whether a page is shared by waiting until two threads have accessed the same page, triggering two segmentation faults. Because of this, any tool built on top of Aikido may not instrument the first two instructions that access a particular piece of shared data. This fact introduces a small number of false negatives to such tools. While any degree of false negatives can be unde-

	2 Threads	4 Threads	8 Threads
fluidanimate (FastTrack)	55.79x	127.62x	178.60x
fluidanimate (Aikido-FastTrack)	48.11x	110.65x	184.33x
vips (FastTrack)	45.52x	53.34x	67.24x
vips (Aikido-FastTrack)	31.5x	35.96x	66.37x

Table 1. Performance overheads over native execution for the FastTrack and Aikido-FastTrack race detectors on the fluidanimate and vips benchmarks at different thread counts.

Benchmark	Instrs. Referencing Memory	Instrumented Instrs.	Shared Page Accesses	Segmentation Faults
freqmine	1,167,712,401	742,195,956	651,009,521	24,880
blackscholes	105,944,404	7,395,315	7,340,038	889
bodytrack	384,925,938	83,514,877	77,116,382	8,993
raytrace	13,186,394,771	16,920,360	14,419,167	23,350
swaptions	350,009,582	58,348,333	4,160,2078	1,778
fluidanimate	556,317,760	356,317,897	267,758,255	11,054
vips	1,044,161,383	253,794,130	231,533,572	10,227
x264	241,456,020	82,561,137	70,813,420	32,616
canneal	560,635,087	69,108,663	68,153,896	23,049
streamcluster	1,067,233,548	403,953,097	396,265,668	5,918

Table 2. Instrumentation statistics recorded while running the Aikido-FastTrack tool.

sirable, we were careful to design Aikido such that it introduces false negatives in a well-defined and targeted manner. We believe that our approach represents a point in the performance/soundness trade-off space is desirable. By limiting our false negatives to well defined application behaviors, false negatives can be handled separately in cases where they present a problem.

For example, in the context of Weak/SyncOrder Deterministic systems [29, 13, 25]), which will execute an application deterministically for a given input only if the program is guaranteed to be race free for that input, Aikido-FastTrack cannot provide a guarantee on the required race freedom. However, it can still be used to provide a guarantee on determinism if the underlying deterministic multithreading system also ensures that the first two memory accesses to any memory location are ordered deterministically. We believe that ordering such accesses can be achieved cheaply using off-the-shelf process-wide (i.e. non per-thread) page protection available in today's operating systems. We hope that similar workarounds can be applied for other scenarios where sound shared data analyses are currently required.

7. Related Work

We divide the discussion of related work into three areas. First, we cover related systems to AikidoVM's technique for providing per-thread page protection. Next, we discuss systems that also use mirror-pages, and finally we cover systems related to the race detector we implemented in Aikido.

7.1 Private Page Protections

Overshadow [12] is a hypervisor that isolates application memory from the operating system by encrypting any application memory that the operating system must be able to access. This provides a layer of security in case the operating system becomes compromised. Overshadow does not provide per-thread page protection, but uses a technique similar to AikidoVM's to present its encrypted and plain text views of memory to the system. Overshadow maintains multiple shadow page tables and encrypts (or decrypts) pages depending on which part of the system is attempting to read or write to a page.

The Grace [4] and DTHREADS [24] projects use per-thread page tables for the purpose of implementing language features and for deterministic multithreading [29, 14], in contrast to the shared data analyses targeted by Aikido. These systems achieve per-thread page tables by converting all threads into separate processes and taking steps to create the illusion of a single process and address space. While it does not require a custom hypervisor, this technique is operating system specific and may find it difficult to maintain the illusion of a single process for more complex applications. For example, without special care, file descriptors created in one process after all processes are forked, will not be visible in the other processes.

The dOS [3] project uses per-thread page tables to track ownership of pages in order to enforce deterministic ordering of memory operations. dOS implements per-thread page tables through extensive modifications to the 2.6.24 Linux kernel.

Finally, SMP-ReVirt [15] uses per-processor private page mappings within a modified Xen Hypervisor for efficient full-system record/replay that runs on commodity hardware. SMP-ReVirt implements the CREW [23] protocol at a page-level granularity to track and later replay page-ownership transitions. Like Aikido, SMP-ReVirt uses shadow page tables within the hypervisor to achieve the private page mappings. However, unlike Aikido, these mappings are per processor rather than per (guest) thread. While Aikido must determine whether each thread has accessed a particular page, the thread abstraction is irrelevant for STMP-ReVirt to replay the execution of an entire operating system, allowing it to track page ownership changes on (guest) physical pages.

7.2 Address Space Mirroring

Abadi et. al present a Software Transactional Memory (STM) system [1] that uses off-the-shelf page-level memory protection to lower the cost of providing strong atomicity guarantees for C# applications. Under this system, the C# application heap is mapped twice in virtual memory. One mapping is used by code executing within a transaction while the other mapping is used during non-transactional execution. Pages in the latter mapping are then dynamically page protected before every access to the heap within a transaction to ensure that all potentially conflicting non-transactional accesses trigger a segmentation fault. This allows the STM system to detect conflicting accesses to memory that occur between concurrently executing transactional and non-transactional code. Because such conflicts tend to be rare, the strategy achieves low overheads. Furthermore, in cases where a large amount of conflicts do occur, the system can patch instructions that frequently cause segmentation faults to jump to code that performs the same operation but within a transaction.

Aikido differs from this work in the following ways. First, Aikido maintains different page protections for each thread for the main (non-mirrored) pages of memory. This addition is very important to be able to efficiently determine which pages of memory are shared, as it enables accesses to private data to execute without redirection. Additionally, because Aikido must redirect all memory accesses that access shared memory (rather than just accesses that frequently conflict with transactions), it must dynamically rewrite all accesses to protected pages instead of just a small number of frequently occurring ones. Doing so efficiently is a significant challenge. Finally, Aikido's use of a hypervisor and binary rewriting transparently bring some of the benefits of mirror pages to a large number of applications (e.g. binary applications) and potential shared data analyses.

7.3 Race Detectors

Foremost in relevance to Aikido's race detector is the FastTrack [19] algorithm on which our race detector is based. We differ from FastTrack in that we operate directly on x86 binaries, as opposed to on Java variables, and that we only instrument accesses to shared data as opposed to all variables.

FastTrack (and our system) computes its happens-before [22] relation using a vector-clocks [28] based approach. This strategy has the advantage that it is precise, and does not introduce false positives. Alternate approaches, such as Eraser's LockSet algorithm [31], that try to associate locks with data protected by them, can report false positives. Other techniques in this area use a hybrid of these two approaches or explore the trade-offs between performance and precision by using sampling or heuristics to decide what to instrument [30, 27, 7, 16].

In each of these systems, the race detector's ability to detect races is often tied to the particular execution schedule seen by the application during execution, which may not be deterministic. This is in contrast to special purpose race detectors such as Nondeterminator and CilkScreen [17, 2] which are schedule independent and can have no false negatives for a subset of legal Cilk and Cilk++ code [21].

8. Conclusions

We have presented Aikido, a novel framework that enables the development of efficient and transparent shared data analysis tools. Aikido achieves transparency through the use of a custom hypervisor that exposes per-thread hardware protection mechanisms. This enables Aikido to use a hybrid hardware and dynamic binary instrumentation approach to dynamically detect shared data in parallel programs. Our results demonstrate that Aikido can be used to speed up shared data analyses. In particular, we have shown that it is possible to speed up existing race detectors by focusing attention to data races caused by instructions that access shared pages. The resulting race detector offers significant performance improvements over existing techniques that provide similar accuracy.

Enabling faster and more transparent shared data analysis can enable new, practical, analysis techniques. The end goal is to enable a new set of tools that helps developers write, understand, debug and optimize parallel programs.

Acknowledgments

We would like to thank the anonymous reviewers for their valuable and insightful comments. We also thank Stelios Sidiroglou for providing invaluable feedback on the manuscript and for numerous helpful discussions. This work was supported in part by NSF grant CCF-0832997, DOE SC0005288, and DARPA HR0011-10-9-0009.

References

[1] Martín Abadi, Tim Harris, and Mojtaba Mehrara. Transactional Memory with Strong Atomicity Using Off-the-Shelf Memory Protection Hardware. In *Proceedings of the 14th ACM SIGPLAN symposium on Principles and practice of parallel programming*, PPoPP '09, pages 185–196, New York, NY, USA, 2009. ACM.

[2] Michael A. Bender, Jeremy T. Fineman, Seth Gilbert, and Charles E. Leiserson. On-the-Fly Maintenance of Series-Parallel Relationships in Fork-Join Multithreaded Programs. In *Proceedings of the sixteenth annual ACM symposium on Parallelism in algorithms and architectures*, SPAA '04, pages 133–144, New York, NY, USA, 2004. ACM.

[3] Tom Bergan, Nicholas Hunt, Luis Ceze, and Steven D. Gribble. Deterministic Process Groups in dOS. In *Proceedings of the 9th USENIX conference on Operating systems design and implementation*, OSDI'10, pages 1–16, 2010.

[4] Emery D. Berger, Ting Yang, Tongping Liu, and Gene Novark. Grace: Safe Multithreaded Programming for C/C++. In *ACM SIGPLAN Conference On Object Oriented Programming Systems Languages and Applications*, OOPSLA '09, pages 81–96, New York, NY, USA, 2009. ACM.

[5] Christian Bienia. *Benchmarking Modern Multiprocessors.* PhD thesis, Princeton University, January 2011.

[6] Christian Bienia and Kai Li. PARSEC 2.0: A New Benchmark Suite for Chip-Multiprocessors. In *Proceedings of the 5th Annual Workshop on Modeling, Benchmarking and Simulation*, June 2009.

[7] Michael D. Bond, Katherine E. Coons, and Kathryn S. McKinley. PACER: Proportional Detection of Data Races. In *Proceedings of the 2010 ACM SIGPLAN conference on Programming language design and implementation*, PLDI '10, pages 255–268, New York, NY, USA, 2010. ACM.

[8] D. Bruening and Qin Zhao. Practical Memory Checking with Dr. Memory. In *Code Generation and Optimization (CGO), 2011 9th Annual IEEE/ACM International Symposium on*, pages 213 –223, april 2011.

[9] Derek Bruening, Timothy Garnett, and Saman Amarasinghe. An Infrastructure for Adaptive Dynamic Optimization. In *International Symposium on Code Generation and Optimization*, San Francisco, Mar 2003.

[10] Derek Bruening, Vladimir Kiriansky, Timothy Garnett, and Sanjeev Banerji. Thread-Shared Software Code Caches. In *Proceedings of the International Symposium on Code Generation and Optimization*, CGO '06, pages 28–38, Washington, DC, USA, 2006. IEEE Computer Society.

[11] Bryan M. Cantrill, Michael W. Shapiro, and Adam H. Leventhal. Dynamic Instrumentation of Production Systems. In *Proceedings of the annual conference on USENIX Annual Technical Conference*, ATEC '04, pages 2–2, Berkeley, CA, USA, 2004. USENIX Association.

[12] Xiaoxin Chen, Tal Garfinkel, E. Christopher Lewis, Pratap Subrahmanyam, Carl A. Waldspurger, Dan Boneh, Jeffrey Dwoskin, and Dan R.K. Ports. Overshadow: A Virtualization-Based Approach to Retrofitting Protection in Commodity Operating Systems. In *International conference on Architectural support for programming languages and operating systems*, ASPLOS XIII, pages 2–13, New York, NY, USA, 2008. ACM.

[13] Heming Cui, Jingyue Wu, Chia-Che Tsai, and Junfeng Yang. Stable Deterministic Multithreading Through Schedule Memoization. In *Proceedings of the 9th USENIX conference on Operating systems design and implementation*, OSDI'10, pages 1–13, 2010.

[14] Joseph Devietti, Brandon Lucia, Luis Ceze, and Mark Oskin. DMP: Deterministic Shared Memory Multiprocessing. In *Proceeding of the 14th international conference on Architectural support for programming languages and operating systems*, ASPLOS '09, pages 85–96, 2009.

[15] George W. Dunlap, Dominic G. Lucchetti, Michael A. Fetterman, and Peter M. Chen. Execution Replay of Multiprocessor Virtual Machines. In *VEE '08: Proceedings of the fourth ACM SIGPLAN/SIGOPS international conference on Virtual execution environments*, pages 121–130, New York, NY, USA, 2008. ACM.

[16] John Erickson, Madanlal Musuvathi, Sebastian Burckhardt, and Kirk Olynyk. Effective Data-Race Detection for the Kernel. In *Proceedings of the 9th USENIX conference on Operating systems design and implementation*, OSDI'10, pages 1–16, Berkeley, CA, USA, 2010. USENIX Association.

[17] Mingdong Feng and Charles E. Leiserson. Efficient Detection of Determinacy Races in Cilk Programs. In *Proceedings of the Ninth Annual ACM Symposium on Parallel Algorithms and Architectures (SPAA)*, pages 1–11, Newport, Rhode Island, June22–25 1997.

[18] Cormac Flanagan and Stephen N Freund. Atomizer: A Dynamic Atomicity Checker for Multithreaded Programs. In *Proceedings of the 31st ACM SIGPLAN-SIGACT symposium on Principles of programming languages*, POPL '04, pages 256–267, New York, NY, USA, 2004. ACM.

[19] Cormac Flanagan and Stephen N. Freund. FastTrack: Efficient and Precise Dynamic Race Detection. In *Proceedings of the 2009 ACM SIGPLAN conference on Programming language design and implementation*, PLDI '09, pages 121–133, New York, NY, USA, 2009. ACM.

[20] Cormac Flanagan, Stephen N. Freund, and Jaeheon Yi. Velodrome: A Sound and Complete Dynamic Atomicity Checker for Multithreaded Programs. In *Proceedings of the 2008 ACM SIGPLAN conference on Programming language design and implementation*, PLDI '08, pages 293–303, New York, NY, USA, 2008. ACM.

[21] Matteo Frigo, Charles E. Leiserson, and Keith H. Randall. The Implementation of the Cilk-5 Multithreaded Language. In *Proceedings of the ACM SIGPLAN '98 Conference on Programming Language Design and Implementation*, pages 212–223, Montreal, Quebec, Canada, June 1998.

[22] Leslie Lamport. Time, clocks, and the ordering of events in a distributed system. *Commun. ACM*, 21(7):558–565, 1978.

[23] T. J. LeBlanc and J. M. Mellor-Crummey. Debugging Parallel Programs with Instant Replay. *IEEE Trans. Comput.*, 36(4):471–482, 1987.

[24] Tongping Liu, Charlie Curtsinger, and Emery D. Berger. Dthreads: Efficient Deterministic Multithreading. In *Proceedings of the ACM SIGOPS 23rd symposium on Operating systems principles*, SOSP '11, New York, NY, USA, 2011. ACM.

[25] Li Lu and Michael L. Scott. Toward a Formal Semantic Framework for Deterministic Parallel Programming. In *Proceedings of the 25th International Symposium on Distributed Computing*.

[26] Shan Lu, Joseph Tucek, Feng Qin, and Yuanyuan Zhou. AVIO: Detecting Atomicity Violations via Access Interleaving Invariants. In *Proceedings of the 12th international conference on Architectural support for programming languages and operating systems*, ASPLOS-XII, pages 37–48, New York, NY, USA, 2006. ACM.

[27] Daniel Marino, Madanlal Musuvathi, and Satish Narayanasamy. LiteRace: Effective Sampling for Lightweight Data-Race Detection. In *Proceedings of the 2009 ACM SIGPLAN conference on Programming language design and implementation*, PLDI '09, pages 134–143, New York, NY, USA, 2009. ACM.

[28] Friedemann Mattern. Virtual Time and Global States of Distributed Systems. In *Parallel and Distributed Algorithms*, pages 215–226. North-Holland, 1989.

[29] Marek Olszewski, Jason Ansel, and Saman Amarasinghe. Kendo: Efficient Deterministic Multithreading in Software. In *The International Conference on Architectural Support for Programming Languages and Operating Systems*, Washington, DC, Mar 2009.

[30] Paul Sack, Brian E. Bliss, Zhiqiang Ma, Paul Petersen, and Josep Torrellas. Accurate and Efficient Filtering for the Intel Thread Checker Race Detector. In *Proceedings of the 1st workshop on Architectural and system support for improving software dependability*, ASID '06, pages 34–41, New York, NY, USA, 2006. ACM.

[31] Stefan Savage, Michael Burrows, Greg Nelson, Patrick Sobalvarro, and Thomas Anderson. Eraser: A Dynamic Data Race Detector for Multithreaded Programs. *ACM Trans. Comput. Syst.*, 15:391–411, November 1997.

[32] Min Xu, Rastislav Bodík, and Mark D. Hill. A Serializability Violation Detector for Shared-Memory Server Programs. In *Proceedings of the 2005 ACM SIGPLAN conference on Programming language design and implementation*, PLDI '05, pages 1–14, New York, NY, USA, 2005. ACM.

[33] Qin Zhao, Derek Bruening, and Saman Amarasinghe. Efficient Memory Shadowing for 64-bit Architectures. In *Proceedings of the 2010 international symposium on Memory management*, ISMM '10, pages 93–102, New York, NY, USA, 2010. ACM.

[34] Qin Zhao, Derek Bruening, and Saman Amarasinghe. Umbra: Efficient and Scalable Memory Shadowing. In *Proceedings of the 8th annual IEEE/ACM international symposium on Code generation and optimization*, CGO '10, pages 22–31, New York, NY, USA, 2010. ACM.

Data Races vs. Data Race Bugs: Telling the Difference with Portend

Baris Kasikci, Cristian Zamfir, and George Candea
School of Computer and Communication Sciences
École Polytechnique Fédérale de Lausanne (EPFL), Switzerland
{baris.kasikci,cristian.zamfir,george.candea}@epfl.ch

Abstract

Even though most data races are harmless, the harmful ones are at the heart of some of the worst concurrency bugs. Alas, spotting just the harmful data races in programs is like finding a needle in a haystack: 76%-90% of the true data races reported by state-of-the-art race detectors turn out to be harmless [45].

We present Portend, a tool that not only detects races but also automatically classifies them based on their potential consequences: Could they lead to crashes or hangs? Could their effects be visible outside the program? Are they harmless? Our proposed technique achieves high accuracy by efficiently analyzing multiple paths and multiple thread schedules in combination, and by performing symbolic comparison between program outputs.

We ran Portend on 7 real-world applications: it detected 93 true data races and correctly classified 92 of them, with no human effort. 6 of them are harmful races. Portend's classification accuracy is up to 89% higher than that of existing tools, and it produces easy-to-understand evidence of the consequences of harmful races, thus both proving their harmfulness and making debugging easier. We envision Portend being used for testing and debugging, as well as for automatically triaging bug reports.

Categories and Subject Descriptors D.2.5 [*Software Engineering*]: Testing and Debugging—Diagnostics

General Terms Reliability, Verification, Performance, Security

Keywords Data races, Concurrency, Triage, Testing

1. Introduction

A data race occurs when two threads access a shared memory location, at least one of the two accesses is a write, and the relative ordering of the two accesses is not enforced using synchronization primitives, like mutexes. Thus, the racing memory accesses may occur in any order or even simultaneously on a multi-processor. Data races are some of the worst concurrency bugs, even leading to the loss of human lives [35] and causing massive material losses [54]. As programs become increasingly parallel, we expect the number of data races they contain to increase; as hardware becomes increasingly parallel, we expect an increased probability that both orderings of any given race get exercised during normal executions.

Yet, eliminating all data races still appears impractical. First, synchronizing all racing memory accesses would introduce performance overheads that may be considered unacceptable. For example, for the last year, developers have not fixed a race in memcached that can lead to lost updates—ultimately finding an alternate solution—because it leads to a 7% drop in throughput [41]. Performance implications led to 23 data races in Internet Explorer and Windows Vista being purposely left unfixed [45]. Similarly, several races have been left unfixed in the Windows kernel, because fixing those races did not justify the associated costs [29].

Another reason why data races go unfixed is that 76%–90% of data races are actually harmless [15, 29, 45, 58]—*harmless races* do not affect program correctness, either fortuitously or by design, while *harmful races* lead to crashes, hangs, resource leaks, even memory corruption or silent data loss. Deciding whether a race is harmful or not involves a lot of human labor (with industrial practitioners reporting that it can take days, even weeks [23]), so time-pressed developers may not even attempt this high-investment/low-return activity. On top of all this, static race detectors can have high false positive rates (e.g., 84% of races reported by [58] were not true races), further disincentivizing developers. Alas, automated classifiers [27, 29, 45, 55] are often inaccurate (e.g., [45] reports a 74% false positive rate in classifying harmful races).

Given the large number of data race reports (e.g., Google's Thread Sanitizer [30] reports over 1,000 unique data races in Firefox when the browser starts up and loads http://bbc.co.uk), we argue that data race detectors should also triage reported data races based on the consequences they could have in future executions. This way, developers are better informed and can fix the critical bugs first. A race detector should be capable of inferring the possible consequences of a reported race: is it a false positive, a harmful race, or a harmless race left in the code perhaps for performance reasons? To our knowledge, no data race detector can do this soundly.

We propose Portend, a technique and tool that detects data races and, based on an analysis of the code, infers the races' potential consequences and automatically classifies them into four categories: "specification violated", "single ordering", "output differs", and "k-witness harmless". For harmful races, it produces a replayable trace that demonstrates the harmful effect, making it easy on the developer to fix the bug.

Portend operates on binaries, not on source code (more specifically on LLVM [33] bitcode obtained from a compiler or from an x86-to-LLVM translator like RevGen [11]). Therefore it can effectively classify both source-code-level races and assembly-level races that are not forbidden by any language-specific memory model (e.g., C [26] and C++ [25]).

ASPLOS'12, March 3–7, 2012, London, England, UK.

We applied Portend to 93 data race reports from 7 real-world applications—it classified 99% of the detected data races accurately in less than 5 minutes per race on average. Compared to state-of-the-art race classifiers, Portend is up to 89% more accurate in predicting the consequences of data races. This improvement comes from Portend's ability to perform multi-path and multi-thread schedule analysis, as well as Portend's fine grained classification scheme. We found not only that multi-path multi-schedule analysis is critical for high accuracy, but also that the "post-race state comparison" approach used in state-of-the-art classifiers does not work well on our real-world programs, despite being perfect on simple microbenchmarks (§5.2).

This paper makes three contributions:

- A ***technique for predicting the consequences of data races*** that combines multi-path and multi-schedule analysis with symbolic program-output comparison to achieve high accuracy in consequence prediction, and thus classification of data races according to their severity;
- A four-category ***taxonomy of data races*** that is finer grain, more precise and, we believe, more useful than what has been employed by the state of the art;
- Portend, a ***practical dynamic data race detector and classifier*** that implements this technique and taxonomy, and a demonstration that it works well for C and C++ software.

Portend presents two main benefits: First, it can triage data race reports automatically and prioritize them based on their likely severity, allowing developers to focus on the most important races first. Second, Portend's automated consequence prediction can be used to double check developers' manual assessment of data races; e.g., Portend may prove that a race that was deemed harmless and left in the code for performance reasons is actually harmful. Portend does not encourage sloppy or fragile code by entitling developers to ignore seemingly benign races, but rather it improves programmers' productivity so they can correctly fix as many important data race bugs as possible.

In the rest of the paper, we describe our proposed classification scheme (§2), Portend's design (§3) and implementation (§4), an evaluation on real-world applications and benchmarks (§5), discuss limitations (§6), related work (§7), and then we conclude (§8).

2. Data Race Classification

We now describe the key existing approaches to race classification (§2.1) and the challenges they face, the idea behind Portend (§2.2), and our proposed classification scheme (§2.3).

2.1 Background and Challenges

We are aware of three main approaches for classifying data races into harmful vs. harmless: heuristic classification, replay and compare, and ad-hoc synchronization identification.

Heuristic classification relies on recognizing specific patterns that correspond to harmless races. For instance, DataCollider [29] prunes data race reports that appear to correspond to updates of statistics counters, read-write conflicts involving different bits of the same memory word, or that involve variables known to developers to have intentional races (e.g., a "current time" variable is read by many threads while being updated by the timer interrupt). Like any heuristic approach, such pruning can lead to both false positives and false negatives, depending on how well suited the heuristics are for the target system's code base. For instance, updates on a statistics counter might be harmless for the cases investigated by DataCollider, but if a counter gathers critical statistics related to resource consumption in a language runtime, classifying a race on such a counter as benign may not be correct.

Replay-based classification [45] starts from an execution that experienced one ordering of the racing accesses ("primary") and re-runs it while enforcing the other ordering ("alternate"). This approach compares the state of registers and memory immediately after the race in the primary and alternate interleavings. If differences are found, the race is deemed likely to be harmful, otherwise likely to be harmless.

This approach faces three challenges: First, differences in the memory and/or register state of the primary vs. alternate executions may not necessarily lead to a violation of the program specification (e.g., otherwise-identical objects may be merely residing at different addresses in the heap). Second, the absence of a state difference may be merely an artifact of the inputs provided to the program, and for some other inputs the states might actually differ. Third, it may be impossible to pursue the alternate interleaving, e.g., because ad-hoc synchronization enforces a specific ordering: instead of employing synchronization primitives like `mutex_lock` or `cond_wait`, ad-hoc synchronization uses programmer-defined synchronization constructs that often rely on loops to synchronize threads via a shared variable [60]. In this case, replay-based classification [45] conservatively classifies the race as likely to be harmful. These three challenges cause replay based classification to have a 74% false positive rate in classifying harmful races [45].

Identification of ad-hoc synchronization helps improve accuracy of race classification [27, 55]. If a shared memory access is found to be protected via ad-hoc synchronization, then it is classified as harmless, because its accesses can occur in only one order. Existing approaches use heuristics or dynamic instrumentation to detect such cases with misclassification rates as high as 50% [27]. Pruning race reports due to ad-hoc synchronization is effective in reducing the reported harmless races, but it is still insufficient to correctly classify all races, as there are many other kinds of harmless races [29, 45].

2.2 Portend's Approach

Portend addresses two challenges left unsolved by prior work: (1) how to accurately distinguish harmful state differences from harmless ones, and (2) how to identify harmful races even when the state of the primary and alternate executions do not immediately differ. We observe that it is not enough to reason about one primary and one alternate interleaving, but we must also reason about the *different paths* that could be followed before/after the race in the program in each interleaving, as well as about the *different schedules* the threads may experience before/after the race in the different interleavings. This is because a seemingly harmless race along one path might end up being harmful along another. To extrapolate program state comparisons to other possible inputs, it is not enough to look at the explicit state—what we must compare are the *constraints placed on that state* by the primary and alternate executions. These observations motivate Portend's combination of multi-path and multi-schedule analysis with symbolic output comparison (§3). Thus, instead of employing heuristic-based classification as in previous work [27, 29, 55], Portend symbolically executes the program to reason precisely about the possible consequences of races.

2.3 A New Classification Scheme

A simple harmless vs. harmful classification scheme is undecidable in general (as will be explained below), so prior work typically resorts to "likely harmless" and/or "likely harmful." Alas, we find that, in practice, this is less helpful than it seems (§5). We therefore propose a new scheme that is more precise.

Note that there is a distinction between false positives and harmless races: when a purported race is not a true race, we say it is a *false positive*. Static [15], lockset [49], and hybrid [47] data race detectors typically report false positives. Detectors based on happens-before relationship [50] do not report false positives unless applications employ unrecognized happens-before relationships, such as ad-hoc synchronization. A false positive is clearly harmless (since it is not a race to begin with), but not the other way around.

Our proposed scheme classifies the true races into four categories: "spec violated", "output differs", "k-witness harmless", and "single ordering". We illustrate this taxonomy in Fig. 1.

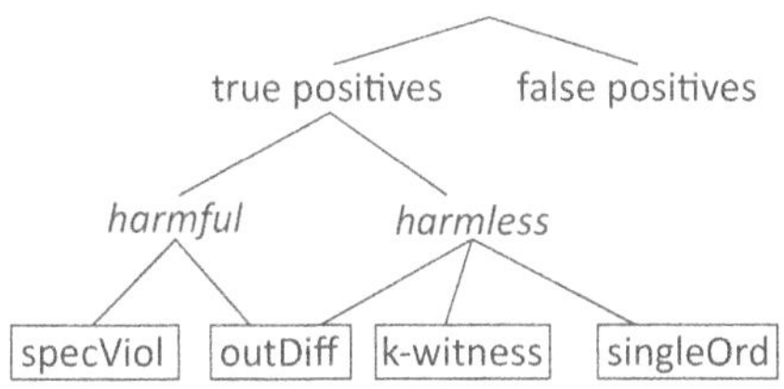

Figure 1. Portend taxonomy of data races.

"Spec violated" corresponds to races for which at least one ordering of the racing accesses leads to a violation of the program's specification. These are, by definition, harmful. For example, races that lead to crashes or deadlocks are generally accepted to violate the specification of any program; we refer to these as "basic" specification violations. Higher level program semantics could also be violated, such as the number of objects in a heap exceeding some bound, or a checksum being inconsistent with the checksummed data. Such semantic properties must be provided as explicit predicates to Portend, or be embedded as assert statements in the code.

"Output differs" is the set of races for which the two orderings of the racing accesses can lead to the program generating different outputs, thus making the output depend on scheduling. Such races are often considered harmful: one of those outputs is likely "the incorrect" one. However, "output differs" races can also be harmless, whether intentional or not. For example, a debug statement that prints the ordering of the racing memory accesses is intentionally order-dependent, thus an intentional harmless race. An example of an unintentional harmless race is one in which one ordering of the accesses may result in a duplicated syslog entry—while technically a violation of any reasonable logging specification, a developer may decide that such a benign consequence makes the race not worth fixing, especially if she faces the risk of introducing new bugs or degrading performance when fixing the bug.

As with all high level program semantics, automated tools *cannot* decide on their own whether an output difference violates some non-explicit specification or not. Moreover, it might even be subjective, depending on which developer is asked. It is for this reason that we created the "output differs" class of races. The key is to provide developers a clear characterization of the output difference, so they can easily decide whether that difference matters.

"K-witness harmless" are races for which the harmless classification is performed with some quantitative level of confidence: the higher the k, the higher the confidence. Such races are guaranteed to be harmless for at least k combinations of paths and schedules; this guarantee can be as strong as covering a virtually infinite input space (e.g., a developer may be interested in whether the race is harmless for all positive inputs, not caring about what happens for zero or negative inputs). Portend achieves this using a symbolic execution engine [6, 9] to analyze entire equivalence classes of inputs (e.g., all positive integer inputs for which the program executes along the same path). Depending on the time and resources available, developers can choose k according to their needs—in our experiments we found $k = 5$ to be sufficient to achieve 99% accuracy for all the tested programs. The value of this category will become obvious after reading §3.

"Single ordering" are races for which only a single ordering of the accesses is possible, typically enforced via ad-hoc synchronization [60]. In such cases, although no explicit synchronization primitives are used, the shared memory could be protected using busy-wait loops that synchronize on a flag. We consider this a race because the ordering of the accesses is not enforced using synchronization primitives (§1), even though it is not actually possible to exercise both interleavings of the memory accesses (hence the name of the category). Such ad-hoc synchronization, even if bad practice, is frequent in real-world software [60]. Previous data race detectors generally cannot tell that only a single order is possible for the memory accesses, and thus report this as a race; such cases turn out to be a major source of harmless data races [27, 55].

3. Design

Portend feeds the target program through its own race detector (or even a third party one, if preferred), analyzes the program and the report automatically, and determines the potential consequences of the reported data race. The report is then classified, based on these predicted consequences, into one of the four categories in Fig. 1. To achieve the classification, Portend performs targeted analysis of multiple schedules of interest, while at the same time using symbolic execution [9] to simultaneously explore multiple paths through the program; we call this technique *multi-path multi-schedule data race analysis*. Portend can thus reason about the consequences of the two orderings of racing memory accesses in a richer execution context than prior work. When comparing program states or program outputs, Portend employs *symbolic output comparison*, meaning it compares constraints on program output, instead of the concrete values of the output, in order to generalize the comparison to more possible inputs that would bring the program to the specific race condition. Unlike prior work, Portend can accurately classify even races that, given a fixed ordering of the original racing accesses, are harmless along some execution paths, yet harmful along others. In §3.1 we go over one such race (Fig. 4) and explain how Portend handles it. Fig. 2 illustrates Portend's architecture. Portend is based on Cloud9 [6], a parallel symbolic execution engine that supports running multi-threaded C/C++ programs.

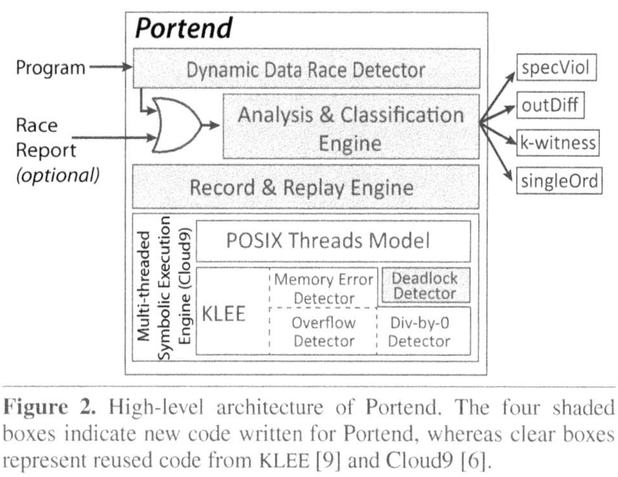

Figure 2. High-level architecture of Portend. The four shaded boxes indicate new code written for Portend, whereas clear boxes represent reused code from KLEE [9] and Cloud9 [6].

When Portend determines that a race is of "spec violated" kind, it provides the corresponding evidence in the form of program inputs (including system call return values) and thread schedule that reproduce the harmful consequences deterministically. Developers can replay this "evidence" in a debugger, to fix the race.

In the rest of this section, we give an overview of our approach and illustrate it with an example (§3.1), describe the first step, single-path/single-schedule analysis (§3.2), followed by the second step, multi-path analysis and symbolic output comparison (§3.3) augmented with multi-schedule analysis (§3.4). We describe Portend's race classification (§3.5) and the generated report that helps developers debug the race (§3.6).

3.1 Overview and Example

Portend's race analysis starts by executing the target program and dynamically detecting data races (e.g., developers could run their existing test suites under Portend). Portend detects races using a dynamic happens-before algorithm [31]. Alternatively, if a third party detector is used, Portend can start from an existing execution trace; this trace must contain the thread schedule and an indication of where in the trace the suspected race occurred. We developed a plugin for Thread Sanitizer [30] to create a Portend-compatible trace; we believe such plugins can be easily developed for other dynamic race detectors [24].

Portend has a record/replay infrastructure for orchestrating the execution of a multi-threaded program; it can preempt and schedule threads before/after synchronization operations and/or racing accesses. Portend uses Cloud9 to enumerate program paths and to collect symbolic constraints.

A trace consists of a schedule trace and a log of system call inputs. The schedule trace contains the thread id and the program counter at each preemption point. Portend treats all POSIX threads synchronization primitives as possible preemption points and uses a single-processor cooperative thread scheduler (see §6 for a discussion of the resulting advantages and limitations). Portend can also preempt threads before and after any racing memory access. We use the following notation for the trace: $(T_0 : pc_0) \to (T_1 \to RaceyAccess_{T_1} : pc_1) \to (T_2 \to RaceyAccess_{T_2} : pc_2)$ means that thread T_0 is preempted after it performs a synchronization call at program counter pc_0; then thread T_1 is scheduled and performs a memory access at program counter pc_1, after which thread T_2 is scheduled and performs a memory access at pc_2 that is racing with the previous memory access of T_1. The schedule trace also contains the absolute count of instructions executed by the program up to each preemption point. This is needed in order to perform precise replays when an instruction executes multiple times (e.g., a loop) before being involved in a race; this is not shown as part of the schedule trace, for brevity. The log of system call inputs contains the non-deterministic program inputs (e.g., *gettimeofday*).

In a first analysis step (illustrated in Fig. 3a), Portend replays the schedule in the trace up to the point where the race occurs. Then it explores two different executions: one in which the original schedule is followed (the *primary*) and one in which the alternate ordering of the racing accesses is enforced (the *alternate*). As described in §2.1, some classifiers compare the primary and alternate program state immediately after the race, and, if different, flag the race as potentially harmful. Even if program outputs are compared rather than states, "single-pre/single-post" analysis (Fig. 3a) may not be accurate, as we will show below. Portend uses "single-pre/single-post" analysis mainly to determine whether the alternate schedule is possible at all. In other words, this stage identifies any ad-hoc synchronization that might prevent the alternate schedule from occurring.

If there is a difference between the primary and alternate post-race states, we do not consider the race as necessarily harmful. Instead, we allow the primary and alternate executions to run, independently of each other, and we observe the consequences. If, for instance, the alternate execution crashes, the race is harmful. Of course, even if the primary and alternate executions behave identically, it is still not certain that the race is harmless: there may be

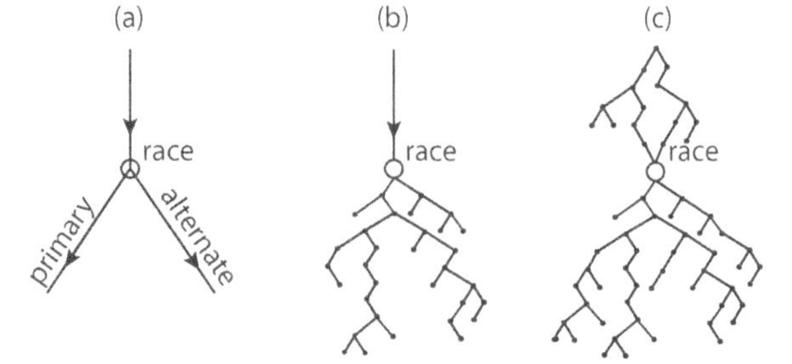

Figure 3. Increasing levels of completeness in terms of paths and schedules: [a. single-pre/single-post] $\ll$ [b. single-pre/multi-post] $\ll$ [c. multi-pre/multi-post].

some unexplored pair of primary and alternate paths with the same pre-race prefix as the analyzed pair, but which does not behave the same. This is why single-pre/single-post analysis is insufficient, and we need to explore *multiple* post-race paths. This motivates "single-pre/multi-post" analysis (Fig. 3b), in which multiple post-race execution possibilities are explored—if any primary/alternate mismatch is found, the developer must be notified.

Even if all feasible post-race paths are explored exhaustively and no mismatch is found, one still cannot conclude that the race is harmless: it is possible that the absence of a mismatch is an artifact of the specific pre-race execution prefix, and that some different prefix would lead to a mismatch. Therefore, to achieve higher confidence in the classification, Portend explores multiple feasible paths even in the pre-race stage, not just the one path witnessed by the race detector. This is illustrated as "multi-pre/multi-post" analysis in Fig. 3c. The advantage of doing this vs. considering these as different races is the ability to systematically explore these paths.

Finally, we combine multi-path analysis with *multi-schedule* analysis, since the same path through a program may generate different outputs depending on how its execution segments from different threads are interleaved. The branches of the execution tree in the post-race execution in Fig. 3c correspond to different paths that stem from both multiple inputs and schedules, as we detail in §3.4.

Of course, exploring all possible paths and schedules that experience the race is impractical, because their number typically grows exponentially with the number of threads, branches, and preemption points in the program. Instead, we provide developers a "dial" to control the number k of path/schedule alternatives explored during analysis, allowing them to control the "volume" of paths and schedules in Fig. 3. If Portend classifies a race as "k-witness harmless", then a higher value of k offers higher confidence that the race is harmless for *all* executions (i.e., including the unexplored ones), but it entails longer analysis time. We found $k = 5$ to be sufficient for achieving 99% accuracy in our experiments in less than 5 minutes per race on average.

To illustrate the benefit of multi-path multi-schedule analysis over "single-pre/single-post" analysis, consider the code snippet in Fig. 4, adapted from a real data race bug. This code has racing accesses to the global variable *id*. Thread T_0 spawns threads T_1 and T_2; thread T_1 updates *id* (line 15) in a loop and acquires a lock each time. However, thread T_2, which maintains statistics, reads *id* without acquiring the lock—this is because acquiring a lock at this location would hurt performance, and statistics need not be precise. Depending on program input, T_2 can update the statistics using either the *update1* or *update2* functions (lines 20-23).

Say the program runs in Portend with input *–use-hash-table*, which makes *useHashTable=true*. Portend records the primary trace $(T_0 : pc_9) \to ... (T_1 \to RaceyAccess_{T_1} : pc_{15}) \to (T_2 \to$

```
                    Thread T0
 1: int id = 0, MAX_SIZE = 32;
 2: int stats_array[MAX_SIZE];
 2: bool useHashTable;
 4:
 5: int main(int argc, char *argv[])){
 6:   pthread_t t1, t2;
 7:   useHashTable = getOption(argc, argv);
 8:   pthread_create (&t1, 0, reqHandler, 0);
 9:   pthread_create (&t2, 0, updateStats, 0);
10:   ...
                    Thread T1
11: void * reqHandler(void *arg){
12:   while(1){
13:     ...
14:     lock(l);
15:     id++;
16:     unlock(l);
17:     ...
                    Thread T2
18: void * updateStats(void* arg){
19:   if(useHashTable){
20:     update1();
21:     printf(..., hash_table[id]);
22:   } else {
23:     update2();
24:     ...

25:   void update1(){
26:     int tmp = id;
27:     if (hash_table.contains(tmp))
28:       hash_table[tmp] = getStats();

29:   void update2(){
30:     if (id < MAX_SIZE)
31:       stats_array[id] = getStats();
```

Figure 4. Simplified example of a harmful race from Ctrace [39] that would be classified as harmless by classic race classifiers.

$RaceyAccess_{T_2} : pc_{26}) \rightarrow ...\ T_0$. This trace is fed to the first analysis step, which replays the trace with the same program input, except it enforces the alternate schedule $(T_0 : pc_9) \rightarrow ...(T_2 \rightarrow RaceyAccess_{T_2} : pc_{26}) \rightarrow (T_1 \rightarrow RaceyAccess_{T_1} : pc_{15}) \rightarrow ...\ T_0$. Since the printed value of *hash_table[id]* at line 21 would be the same for the primary and alternate schedules, a "single-pre/single-post" classifier would deem the race harmless.

However, in the multi-path multi-schedule step, Portend explores additional paths through the code by marking program input as symbolic, i.e., allowing it to take on any permitted value. When the trace is replayed and Portend reaches line 19 in T_2 in the alternate schedule, *useHashTable* could be both true and false, so Portend splits into two executions, one in which *useHashTable* is set to *true* and one in which it is *false*. Assume, for example, that *id* = 31 when checking the if condition at line 30. Due to the data race, *id* is incremented by T_1 to 32, which overflows the statically allocated buffer (line 31). Note that in this alternate path, there are two racing accesses on *id*, and we are referring to the access at line 31.

Portend detects the overflow (via Cloud9), which leads to a crashed execution, flags the race as "spec violated", and provides the developer the execution trace in which the input is *–no-hash-table*, and the schedule is $(T_0 : pc_9) \rightarrow ...(T_2 \rightarrow RaceyAccess_{T_2} : pc_{30}) \rightarrow (T_1 \rightarrow RaceyAccess_{T_1} : pc_{15}) \rightarrow (T_2 : pc_{31})$. The developer can replay this trace in a debugger and fix the race.

Note that this data race is harmful only if the program input is *–no-hash-table*, the given thread schedule occurs, and the value of *id* is 31; therefore the crash is likely to be missed by a traditional single-path/single-schedule data race detector.

We now describe Portend's race analysis in detail: §3.2–§3.4 focus on the *exploration* part of the analysis, in which Portend looks for paths and schedules that reveal the nature of the race, and §3.5 focuses on the *classification* part.

Algorithm 1: Single-Pre/Single-Post Analysis (singleClassify)

```
   Input: Primary execution trace primary
   Output: Classification result ∈ {specViol, outDiff, outSame,
           singleOrd}
 1 current ← execUntilFirstThreadRacyAccess(primary)
 2 preRaceCkpt ← checkpoint(current)
 3 execUntilSecondThreadRacyAccess(current)
 4 postRaceCkpt ← checkpoint(current)
 5 current ← preRaceCkpt
 6 preemptCurrentThread(current)
 7 alternate ← execWithTimeout(current)
 8 if alternate.timedOut then
 9     if detectInfiniteLoop(alternate) then
10         return specViol
11     else
12         return singleOrd
13 else
14     if detectDeadlock(alternate) then
15         return specViol
16 primary ← exec(postRaceCkpt)
17 if detectSpecViol(primary) ∨ detectSpecViol(alternate)
   then
18     return specViol
19 if primary.output ≠ alternate.output then
20     return outDiff
21 else
22     return outSame
```

3.2 Single-Pre/Single-Post Analysis

The goal of this first analysis step is to identify cases in which the alternate schedule of a race cannot be pursued, and to make a first classification attempt based on a single alternate execution. Algorithm 1 describes the approach.

Portend starts from a trace of an execution of the target program, containing one or more races, along with the program inputs that generated the trace. For example, in the case of the Pbzip2 file compressor used in our evaluation, Portend needs a file to compress and a trace of the thread schedule. As mentioned earlier, such traces are obtained from running, for instance, the developers' test suites (as done in CHESS [44]) with a dynamic race detector enabled.

Portend takes the primary trace and plays it back (line 1). Note that *current* represents the system state of the current execution. Just before the first racing access, Portend takes a checkpoint of system state; we call this the *pre-race checkpoint* (line 2). The replay is then allowed to continue until immediately after the second racing access of the race we are interested in (line 3), and the primary execution is suspended in this post-race state (line 4).

Portend then primes a new execution with the pre-race checkpoint (line 5) and attempts to enforce the alternate ordering of the racing accesses. To enforce this alternate order, Portend preempts the thread that did the first racing access (T_i) in the primary execution and allows the other thread (T_j) involved in the race to be scheduled (line 6). In other words, an execution with the trace $...(T_i \rightarrow RaceyAccess_{T_i} : pc_1) \rightarrow (T_j \rightarrow RaceyAccess_{T_j} : pc_2)...$ is steered toward the execution $...(T_j \rightarrow RaceyAccess_{T_j} : pc_2) \rightarrow (T_i \rightarrow RaceyAccess_{T_i} : pc_1)...$

This attempt could fail for one of two reasons: (a) T_j gets scheduled, but T_i cannot be scheduled again; or (b) T_j cannot be scheduled, because it is blocked by T_i. Case (a) is detected by Portend via a timeout (line 8) and is classified either as "spec violated", corresponding to an infinite loop (i.e., a loop with a loop-invariant exit condition) in line 10 or as ad-hoc synchronization in line 12. Case (b) can correspond to a deadlock (line 15) and is detected by Portend by keeping track of the lock graph. Both the infinite loop and the deadlock case cause the race to be classified as "spec violated", while the ad-hoc synchronization case classifies the race as "single ordering" (more details in §3.5). While it may make sense to not stop if the alternate execution cannot be enforced, under the expectation that other paths with other inputs might permit the alternate ordering, our evaluation suggests that continuing adds little value.

If the alternate schedule succeeds, Portend executes it until it completes, and then records its outputs. Then, Portend allows the primary to continue (while replaying the input trace) and also records its outputs. During this process, Portend watches for "basic" specification violations (crashes, deadlocks, memory errors, etc.) as well as "high level" properties given to Portend as predicates—if any of these properties are violated, Portend immediately classifies (line 18) the race as "spec violated". If the alternate execution completes with no specification violation, Portend compares the outputs of the primary and the alternate; if they differ, the race is classified as "output differs" (line 20), otherwise the analysis moves to the next step. This is in contrast to replay-based classification [45], which compares the program state immediately after the race in the primary and alternate interleavings.

3.3 Multi-Path Data Race Analysis

The goal of this step is to explore variations of the single paths found in the previous step (i.e., the primary and the alternate) in order to expose Portend to a wider range of execution alternatives.

First, Portend finds multiple primary paths that satisfy the input trace, i.e., they (a) all experience the same thread schedule (up to the data race) as the input trace, and (b) all experience the target race condition. These paths correspond to *different* inputs from the ones in the initial race report. Second, Portend uses Cloud9 to record the "symbolic" outputs of these paths—that is, the constraints on the output, rather than the concrete output values themselves—and compares them to the outputs of the corresponding alternate paths; we explain this below. Algorithm 2 describes the functions invoked by Portend during this analysis in the following order: 1) on initialization, 2) when encountering a thread preemption, 3) on a branch that depends on symbolic data, and 4) on finishing an execution.

Unlike in the single-pre/single-post step, Portend now executes the primary *symbolically*. This means that the target program is given symbolic inputs instead of regular concrete inputs. Cloud9 relies in large part on KLEE [9] to interpret the program and propagate these symbolic values to other variables, corresponding to how they are read and operated upon. When an expression with symbolic content is involved in the condition of a branch, *both* options of the branch are explored, if they are feasible. The resulting path(s) are annotated with a constraint indicating that the branch condition holds true (respectively false). Thus, instead of a regular single-path execution, we get a tree of execution paths, similar to the one in Fig. 5. Conceptually, at each such branch, program state is duplicated and constraints on the symbolic parameters are updated to reflect the decision taken at that branch (line 11). Describing the various techniques for performing symbolic execution efficiently [6, 9] is beyond the scope of this paper.

An important concern in symbolic execution is "path explosion," i.e., that the number of possible paths is large. Portend offers two parameters to control this growth: (a) an upper bound M_p on the number of primary paths explored; and (b) the number and size of symbolic inputs. These two parameters allow developers to trade performance vs. classification confidence. For parameter (b), the fewer inputs are symbolic, the fewer branches will depend on symbolic input, so less branching will occur in the execution tree.

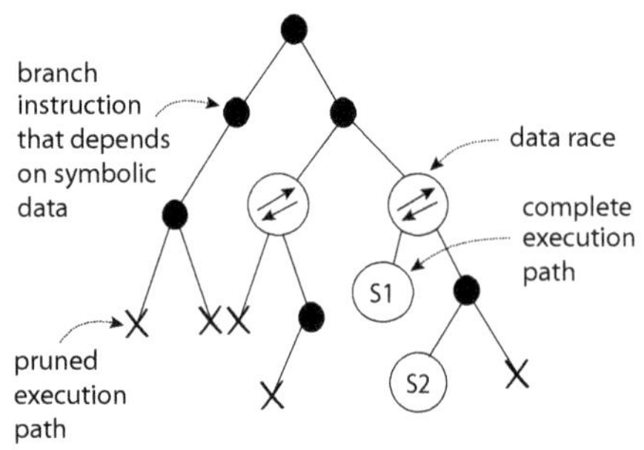

Figure 5. Portend prunes paths during symbolic execution.

Determining the optimal values for these parameters may require knowledge of the target system as well as a good sense of how much confidence is required by the system's users. Reasonable (i.e., good but not necessarily optimal) values can be found through trial and error relatively easily—we expect development teams using Portend to converge onto values that are a good fit for their code and user community, and then make these values the defaults for their testing and triage processes. We empirically study in §5 the impact of these parameters on classification accuracy on a diverse set of programs and find that relatively small values achieve high accuracy for a broad range of programs.

During symbolic execution, Portend prunes (Fig. 5) the paths that do not obey the thread schedule in the trace (line 8), thus excluding the (many) paths that do not enable the target race. Moreover, Portend attempts to follow the original trace only until the second racing access is encountered; afterward, it allows execution to diverge from the original schedule trace. This enables Portend to find more executions that partially match the original schedule trace (e.g., cases in which the second racing access occurs at a different program counter, as in Fig. 4). Tolerating these divergences significantly increases Portend's accuracy over the state of the art [45], as will be explained in §5.4.

Once the desired paths are obtained (at most M_p, line 14), the conjunction of branch constraints accumulated along each path is solved by KLEE using an SMT solver [19] in order to find concrete inputs that drive the program down the corresponding path. For example, in the case of Fig. 5, two successful leaf states S_1 and S_2 are reached, and the solver provides the inputs corresponding to the path from the root of the tree to S_1, respectively S_2. Thus, we now have $M_p = 2$ different primary executions that experience the data race.

3.3.1 Symbolic Output Comparison

Portend now records the output of each of the M_p executions, like in the single-pre/single-post case. However, this time it propagates the constraints on symbolic state all the way to the outputs, i.e., the outputs of each primary execution contain a mix of concrete values and symbolic constraints (i.e., symbolic formulae). Note that by output we mean all arguments passed to output system calls.

Next, for each of the M_p executions, Portend produces a corresponding alternate (analogously to the single-pre/single-post case) and records its outputs (lines 19-21). The function *singleClassify* in Algorithm 2 performs the analysis described in Algorithm 1. Portend then checks whether the outputs of each alternate satisfy the constraints of the corresponding primary's outputs, i.e., verifies equivalence between the (partly symbolic) outputs of the primary and those of the alternate. This is what we refer to as *symbolic output comparison* (line 22).

Algorithm 2: Multi-path Data Race Analysis (Simplified)

```
Input: Schedule trace trace, initial program state S_0, set of states
       S = ∅, upper bound M_p on the number of primary paths
Output: Classification result ∈ {specViol, outDiff, singleOrd
        k-witness}
function init ()
  S ← S ∪ S_0
  current ← S.head()
  pathsExplored ← 0
function onPreemption ()
  t_i ← scheduleNextThread(current)
  if t_i ≠ nextThreadInTrace(trace, current) then
    S ← S.remove(current)
    current ← S.head()
function onSymbolicBranch ()
  S ← S ∪ current.fork()
function onFinish ()
  classification ← classification ∪ classify(current)
  if pathsExplored < M_p then
    pathsExplored ← pathsExplored + 1
  else
    return classification
function classify (primary)
  result ← singleClassify(primary)
  if result = outSame then
    alternate ← getAlternate(primary)
    if symbolicMatch(primary.symOutput,
       alternate.output) then
      return k-witness
    else
      return outDiff
  else
    return result
```

When executing the primaries and recording their outputs, Portend relies on Cloud9 to track all symbolic constraints on variables, and Portend records these constraints as symbolic output. For example, when Portend runs the primary execution of "*i=getInput(); if(i ≥ 0) output(i);* " on input 10, it records the output as $i \geq 0$, not merely value $i = 10$. Thus, the outputs of primary executions are recorded as sequences of symbolic formulae.

The alternate executions are fully concrete, and Portend records their concrete outputs. When comparing outputs, Portend first checks that the number of output operations match in the two executions. If yes, then, for each output operation, it checks that the concrete output (from the alternate) is in the set of values allowed by the constraints of the symbolic output (from the primary). For the example above, any positive value output by the alternate will satisfy the primary's $i \geq 0$ output. This symbolic comparison enables Portend's analysis to extend over more possible primary executions for which i is a positive integer. This comes at the price of potential false negatives; despite this theoretical shortcoming, we have not encountered such a case in practice, but we plan to investigate further in future work. Of course, determining semantic equivalence of output is undecidable, and our comparison may still wrongly classify as "output differs" a sequence of outputs that are equivalent at some level (e.g., *<print ab; print c>* vs. *<print abc>*).

To determine if the concrete outputs satisfy the symbolic ones, Portend directly employs an SMT solver [19]. As will be seen in §5.2, using symbolic comparison leads to substantial improvements in classification accuracy.

We do not detail here the case when the program reads input *after* the race—it is a natural extension of the algorithm above.

3.4 Multi-Schedule Data Race Analysis

The goal of multi-schedule analysis is to further augment the set of analyzed executions by diversifying the thread schedule.

We mentioned earlier that, for each of the M_p primary executions, Portend obtains an alternate execution. Once the alternate ordering of the racing accesses is enforced, Portend randomizes the schedule of the *post-race* alternate execution: at every preemption point in the alternate, Portend randomly decides which of the runnable threads to schedule next. This means that every alternate execution will most likely have a different schedule from the original input trace (and thus from the primary).

Consequently, for every primary execution P_i, we obtain *multiple* alternate executions $A_i^1, A_i^2, ...$ by running up to M_a multiple instances of the alternate execution. Since the scheduler is random, we expect practically every alternate execution to have a schedule that differs from all others. Recently proposed techniques [43] can be used to quantify the probability of these alternate schedules discovering the harmful effects of a data race.

Portend then uses the same symbolic comparison technique as in §3.3.1 to establish equivalence between the concrete outputs of $A_i^1, A_i^2, ...A_i^{M_a}$ and the symbolic outputs of P_i.

Schedule randomization can be employed also in the pre-race stage of the alternate-execution generation as well as in the generation of the primary executions. We did not implement these options, because the level of multiplicity we obtain with the current design appears to be sufficient in practice to achieve high accuracy. Note however that, as we show in §5.2, multi-path multi-schedule analysis is indeed crucial to attaining high classification accuracy.

In summary, multi-path multi-schedule analysis explores M_p primary executions and, for each such execution, M_a alternate executions with different schedules, for a total of $M_p \times M_a$ path-schedule combinations. For races that end up being classified as "k-witness harmless", we say that $k = M_p \times M_a$ is the lower bound on the number of concrete path-schedule combinations under which this race is harmless.

Note that the k executions can be simultaneously explored in parallel: if a developer has p machines with q cores each, she could explore $p \times q$ parallel executions in the same amount of time as a single execution. Given that Portend is "embarrassingly parallel," it is appealing for cluster-based automated bug triage systems.

3.5 Data Race Classification

We showed how Portend explores paths and schedules to give the classifier an opportunity to observe the effects of a data race. We now provide details on how the classifier makes its decisions.

"Spec violated" races cause a program's explicit specification to be violated; they are guaranteed to be harmful and thus should have highest priority for developers. To detect violations, Portend watches for them during exploration.

First, Portend watches for "basic" properties that can be safely assumed to violate any program's specification: crashes, deadlocks, infinite loops, and memory errors. Since Portend already controls the program's schedule, it also keeps track of all uses of synchronization primitives (i.e., POSIX threads calls); based on this, it determines when threads are deadlocked. Infinite loops are diagnosed as in [60], by detecting loops for which the exit condition cannot be modified. For memory errors, Portend relies on the mechanism already provided by KLEE inside Cloud9. Even when Portend runs the program concretely, it still interprets it in Cloud9.

Second, Portend watches for "semantic" properties, which are provided to Portend by developers in the form of assert-like predicates. Developers can also place these assertions inside the code.

Whenever an alternate execution violates a basic or a semantic property (even though the primary may not), Portend classifies the corresponding race as "spec violated".

"Output differs" races cause a program's output to depend on the ordering of the racing accesses. As explained in §2.1, a difference between the post-race memory or register states of the primary and the alternate is not necessarily indicative of a harmful race (e.g., the difference may just be due to dynamic memory allocation). Instead, Portend compares the outputs of the primary and the alternate, and it does so symbolically, as described earlier. In case of a mismatch, Portend classifies the race as "output differs" and gives the developer detailed information to decide whether the difference is harmful or not.

"K-witness harmless" races: If, for every primary execution P_i, the outputs of alternate executions $A_i^1, A_i^2, ...A_i^{M_a}$ satisfy P_i's output constraints, then Portend classifies the race as "k-witness harmless", where $k = M_p \times M_a$, because there exist k executions witnessing the conjectured harmlessness. The value of k is often an underestimate of the number of different executions for which the race is guaranteed to be harmless; as suggested earlier in §2.3, symbolic execution can even reason about a virtually infinite number of executions.

Theoretical insights into how k relates to the confidence a developer can have that a "k-witness harmless" race will not cause harm in practice are beyond the scope of this paper. One can think of k in ways similar to code coverage in testing: 80% coverage is better than 60%, but does not exactly predict the likelihood of bugs not being present. For all our experiments, $k = 5$ was shown to be sufficient for achieving 99% accuracy. We consider "k-witness harmless" analyses to be an intriguing topic for future work, in a line of research akin to [43]. Note that Portend explores many more executions before finding the required k path-schedule combinations that match the trace, but the paths that do not match the trace are pruned early during the analysis.

"Single ordering" races are harmless races, because only one ordering of the racing accesses is possible. One might even argue they are not races at all. Yet, dynamic data race detectors are not aware of the implicit happens-before relationship and do report a race.

When Portend cannot enforce an alternate interleaving in the single-pre/single-post phase, this can either be due to ad-hoc synchronization that prevents the alternate ordering, or other thread in question cannot make progress due to a deadlock or an infinite loop. If none of the previously described infinite-loop and deadlock detection mechanisms trigger, Portend simply waits for a configurable amount of time and, upon timeout, classifies the race as "single ordering." Note that it is possible to improve this design with a heuristic-based static analysis that directly identifies ad-hoc synchronization [55, 60].

3.6 Portend's Debugging Aid Output

To help developers decide what to do about an "output differs" race, Portend dumps the output values and the program locations where the output differs. Portend also aims to help in fixing harmful races by providing for each race two items: a textual report and a pair of execution traces that evidence the effects of the race and can be played back in a debugger, using Portend's runtime replay environment. A simplified report is shown in Fig. 6.

In the case of an "output differs" race, Portend reports the stack traces of system calls where the program produced different output, as well as the differing outputs. This simplifies the debugging effort (e.g., if the difference occurs while printing a debug message, the race could be classified as benign with no further analysis).

```
Data Race during access to: 0x2860b30
current thread id: 3: READ
racing thread id: 0: WRITE
Current thread at:
  /home/eval/pbzip/pbzip2.cpp:702
Previous at:
  /home/eval/pbzip/pbzip2.cpp:389
size of the accessed field: 4 offset: 0
```

Figure 6. Example debugging aid report for Portend.

4. Implementation

The current Portend prototype consists of approximately 8 KLOC of C++ code, incorporating the various analyses described earlier and modifications to the underlying symbolic execution engine. The four shaded components in Fig. 2 were developed from scratch as part of Portend: the dynamic data race detector, the analysis and classification engine, the record-replay engine, and the deadlock detector.

Portend works on programs compiled to LLVM [33] bitcode and can run C/C++ programs for which there exists a sufficiently complete symbolic POSIX environment [6]. We have tested it on C programs as well as C++ programs that do not link to libstdc++; this latter limitation results from the fact that an implementation of a standard C++ library for LLVM is in progress, but not yet available [12]. Portend uses Cloud9 [6] to interpret and symbolically execute LLVM bitcode; we suspect any path exploration tool will do (e.g., CUTE [52], SAGE [22]), as long as it supports multi-threaded programs.

Portend intercepts various system calls, such as *write*, under the assumption that they are the primary means by which a program communicates changes in its state to the environment. A separate Portend module is responsible for keeping track of symbolic outputs in the form of constraints, as well as of concrete outputs. Portend hashes program outputs (when they are concrete) and can either maintain hashes of all concrete outputs or compute a hash chain of all outputs to derive a single hash code per execution. This way, Portend can deal with programs that have a large amount of output.

Portend clusters the data races it detects, in order to filter out similar races; the clustering criterion is whether the racing accesses are made to the same shared memory location by the same threads, and the stack traces of the accesses are the same. Portend provides developers with a single representative data race from each cluster.

The timeout used in discovering ad-hoc synchronization is conservatively defined as 5 times what it took Portend to replay the primary execution, assuming that reversing the access sequence of the racing accesses should not cause the program to run for longer than that.

In order to run multi-threaded programs in Portend, we extended the POSIX threads support found in Cloud9 to cover almost the entire POSIX threads API, including barriers, mutexes and condition variables, as well as thread-local storage. Portend intercepts calls into the POSIX threads library to maintain the necessary internal data structures (e.g., to detect data races and deadlocks) and to control thread scheduling.

5. Evaluation

In this section, we answer the following questions: Is Portend effective in telling developers which races are true bugs and in helping them fix buggy races (§5.1)? How accurately does it classify race reports into the four categories of races (§5.2)? How long does classification take, and how does it scale (§5.3)? How does Portend compare to the state of the art in race classification (§5.4)?

To answer these questions, we apply Portend to 7 applications: SQLite, an embedded database engine (used, for example, by Firefox, iOS, Chrome, and Android), that is considered highly reliable, with 100% branch coverage [53]; Pbzip2, a parallel implementation of the widely used bzip2 file compressor [20]; Memcached [16], a distributed memory object cache system (used, for example, by services such as Flickr, Twitter and Craigslist); Ctrace [39], a multi-threaded debug library; Bbuf [61], a shared buffer implementation with a configurable number of producers and consumers; Fmm, an n-body simulator from the popular SPLASH2 benchmark suite [59]; and Ocean, a simulator of eddy currents in oceans, from SPLASH2.

Portend classifies with 99% accuracy the 93 known data races we found in these programs, with no human intervention, in under 5 minutes per race on average. It took us one person-month to manually confirm that the races deemed harmless by Portend were indeed harmless—this is typical of how long it takes to classify races in the absence of an automated tool [23] and illustrates the benefits of Portend-style automation. For the deemed-harmful races, we confirmed classification accuracy in a few minutes by using the replayable debug information provided by Portend.

We additionally evaluate Portend on homegrown micro-benchmarks that capture most classes of harmless races [30, 45]: "redundant writes" (RW), where racing threads write the same value to a shared variable, "disjoint bit manipulation" (DBM), where disjoint bits of a bit-field are modified by racing threads, "all values valid" (AVV), where the racing threads write different values that are nevertheless all valid, and "double checked locking" (DCL), a method used to reduce the locking overhead by first testing the locking criterion without actually acquiring a lock. Table 1 summarizes the properties of our 11 experimental targets.

Program	Size (LOC)	Language	# Forked threads
SQLite 3.3.0	113,326	C	2
ocean 2.0	11,665	C	2
fmm 2.0	11,545	C	3
memcached 1.4.5	8,300	C	8
pbzip2 2.1.1	6,686	C++	4
ctrace 1.2	886	C	3
bbuf 1.0	261	C	8
AVV	49	C++	3
DCL	45	C++	5
DBM	45	C++	3
RW	42	C++	3

Table 1. Programs analyzed with Portend. Source lines of code are measured with the `cloc` utility.

We ran Portend on several other systems (e.g., HawkNL, pfscan, swarm, fft), but no races were found in those programs with the test cases we ran, so we do not include them here. For all experiments, the Portend parameters were set to $M_p = 5$, $M_a = 2$, and the number of symbolic inputs to 2. We found these numbers to be sufficient to achieve high accuracy in a reasonable amount of time. To validate Portend's results, we used manual investigation, analyzed developer change logs, and consulted with the applications' developers when possible. All experiments were run on a 2.4 GHz Intel Core 2 Duo E6600 CPU with 4 GB of RAM running Ubuntu Linux 10.04 with kernel version 2.6.33. The reported numbers are averages over 10 experiments.

5.1 Effectiveness

Of the 93 distinct races detected in 7 real-world applications, Portend classified 5 as definitely harmful by watching for "basic" properties (Table 2): one hangs the program and four crash it.

Program	Total # of races	# of "Spec violated" races		
		Deadlock	Crash	Semantic
SQLite	1	1	0	0
pbzip2	31	0	3	0
ctrace	15	0	1	0
fmm	13	0	0	1
memcached	18	0	1	0

Table 2. "Spec violated" races and their consequences.

To illustrate the checking for "high level" semantic properties, we instructed Portend to verify that all timestamps used in fmm are positive. This caused it to identify the 6th "harmful" race in Table 2; without this semantic check, this race turns out to be harmless, as the negative timestamp is eventually overwritten.

To illustrate a "what-if analysis" scenario, we turned an arbitrary synchronization operation in the memcached binary into a no-op, and then used Portend to explore the question of whether it is safe to remove that particular synchronization point (e.g., we may be interested in reducing lock contention). Removing this synchronization induces a race in memcached; Portend determined that the race could lead to a crash of the server for a particular interleaving, so it classified it as "spec violated".

Portend's main contribution is the classification of races. If one wanted to eliminate all harmful races from their code, they could use a static race detector (one that is complete, and, by necessity, prone to false positives) and then use Portend to classify these reports.

For every harmful race, Portend's comprehensive report and replayable traces (i.e., inputs and thread schedule) allowed us to confirm the harmfulness of the races within minutes. Portend's report includes the stack traces of the racing threads along with the address and size of the accessed memory field; in the case of a segmentation fault, the stack trace of the faulting instruction is provided as well—this information can help in automated bug clustering. According to developers' change logs and our own manual analysis, the races in Table 2 are the only known harmful races in these applications.

5.2 Accuracy and Precision

To evaluate Portend's accuracy and precision, we had it classify all 93 races in our target applications and micro-benchmarks. Table 3 summarizes the results. The first two columns show the number of distinct races and the number of respective instances, i.e., the number of times those races manifested during race detection. The "spec violated" column includes all races from Table 2 minus the semantic race in fmm and the race we introduced in memcached. In the "k-witness harmless" column we show for which races the post-race states differed vs. not.

By accuracy, we refer to the correctness of classification: the higher the accuracy, the higher the ratio of correct classification. Precision on the other hand, refers to the reproducibility of experimental results: the higher the precision, the higher the ratio with which experiments are repeated with the same results.

To determine accuracy, we manually classified each race and found that Portend had correctly classified 92 of the 93 races (99%) in our target applications: all except one of the races classified "k-witness harmless" by Portend are indeed harmless in an absolute sense, and all "single ordering" races indeed involve ad-hoc synchronization.

To measure precision, we ran 10 times the classification for each race. Portend consistently reported the same data set shown in Table 3, which indicates that, for these races and applications, it achieves full precision.

Program	Number of data races						
	Distinct races	Race instances	Spec violated	Output differs	K-witness harmless		Single ordering
					states same	*states differ*	
SQLite	1	1	1	0	0	0	0
ocean	5	14	0	0	0	1	4
fmm	13	517	0	0	0	1	12
memcached	18	104	0	2	0	0	16
pbzip2	31	97	3	3	0	0	25
ctrace	15	19	1	10	0	4	0
bbuf	6	6	0	6	0	0	0
AVV	1	1	0	0	1	0	0
DCL	1	1	0	0	1	0	0
DBM	1	1	0	0	1	0	0
RW	1	1	0	0	1	0	0

Table 3. Summary of Portend's classification results. We consider two races to be distinct if they involve different accesses to shared variables; the same race may be encountered multiple times during an execution—these two different aspects are captured by the *Distinct races* and *Race instances* columns, respectively. The last 5 columns classify the distinct races. The *states same/differ* columns show for how many races the primary and alternate states were different after the race, as computed by the Record/Replay Analyzer [45].

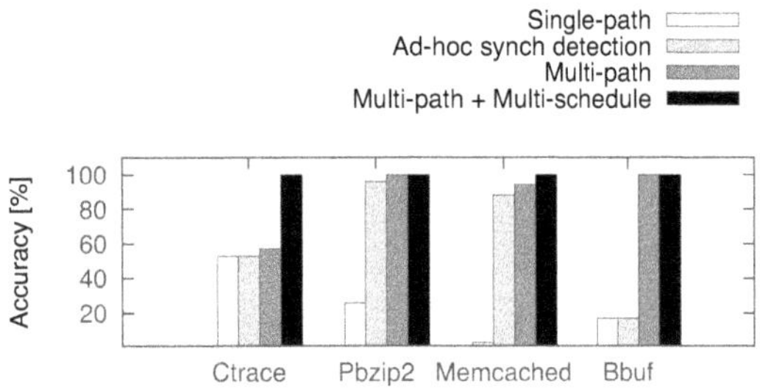

Figure 7. Breakdown of the contribution of each technique toward Portend's accuracy. We start from single-path analysis and enable one by one the other techniques: ad-hoc synchronization detection, multi-path analysis, and finally multi-schedule analysis.

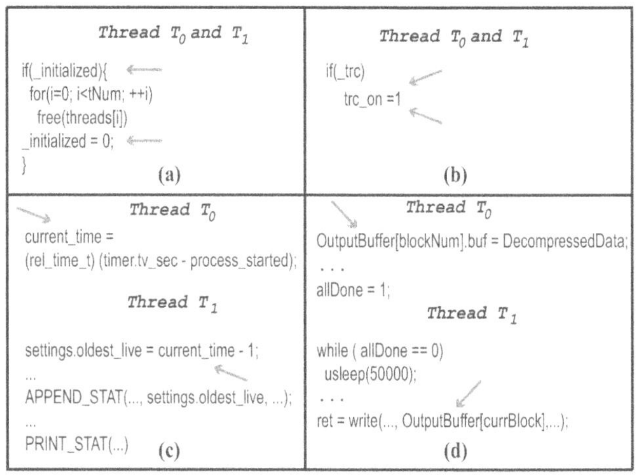

Figure 8. Simplified examples for each race class from real systems. (a) and (b) are from ctrace, (c) is from memcached and (d) is from pbzip2. The arrows indicate the pair of racing accesses.

As can be seen in the "k-witness harmless" column, for each and every one of the 7 real-world applications, a state difference (as used in [45]) does not correctly predict harmfulness, while our "k-witness harmless" analysis correctly predicts that the races are harmless with one exception.

This suggests that differencing of concrete state is a poor classification criterion for races in real-world applications with large memory states, but may be acceptable for simple benchmarks. This also supports our choice of using symbolic output comparison.

Multi-path multi-schedule exploration proved to be crucial for Portend's accuracy. Fig. 7 shows the breakdown of the contribution of each technique used in Portend: ad-hoc synchronization detection, multi-path analysis, and multi-schedule analysis. In particular, for 16 out of 21 "output differs" races (6 in bbuf, 9 in ctrace, 1 in pbzip2) and for 1 "spec violated" race (in ctrace), single-path analysis revealed no difference in output; it was only multi-path multi-schedule exploration that revealed an output difference (9 races required multi-path analysis for classification, and 8 races required also multi-schedule analysis). Without multi-path multi-schedule analysis, it would have been impossible for Portend to accurately classify those races by just using the available test cases. Moreover, there is a high variance in the contribution of each technique for different programs, which means that none of these techniques alone would have achieved high accuracy for a broad range of programs.

We also wanted to evaluate Portend's ability to deal with false positives, i.e., false race reports. Race detectors, especially static ones, may report false positives for a variety of reasons, depending on which technique they employ. To simulate an imperfect detector for our applications, we deliberately removed from Portend's race detector its awareness of mutex synchronizations. We then eliminated the races in our micro-benchmarks by introducing mutex synchronizations. When we re-ran Portend with the erroneous data race detector on the micro-benchmarks, all four were falsely reported as races by the detector, but Portend ultimately classified all of them as "single ordering". This suggests Portend is capable of properly handling false positives.

Fig. 8 shows examples of real races for each category: (a) a "spec violated" race in which resources are freed twice, (b) a "k-witness harmless" race due to redundant writes, (c) an "output differs" race in which the schedule-sensitive value of the shared variable influences the output, and (d) a "single ordering" race showing ad-hoc synchronization implemented via busy wait.

5.3 Performance (Time to Classify)

We evaluate the performance of Portend in terms of efficiency and scalability. Portend's performance is mostly relevant if it is to be used interactively, as a developer tool, and also if used for a

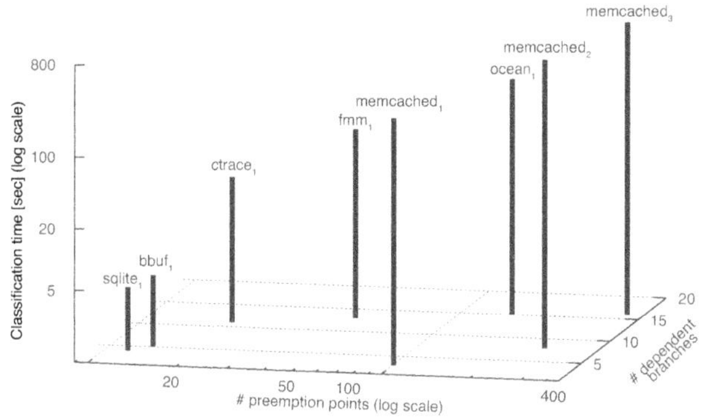

Figure 9. Change in classification time with respect to number of preemptions and number of dependent branches for some of the races in Table 3. Each sample point is labeled with race id.

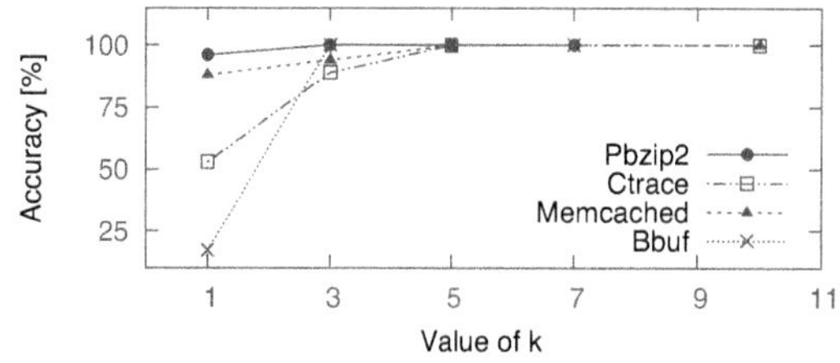

Figure 10. Portend's accuracy with increasing values of k.

large scale bug triage tool, such as in Microsoft's Windows Error Reporting system [21].

We measure the time it takes Portend to classify the 93 races; Table 4 summarizes the results. We find that Portend classifies all detected data races in a reasonable amount of time, the longest taking less than 11 minutes. For bbuf, ctrace, ocean and fmm, the slowest classification time is due to a race from the "k-witness harmless" category, since classification into this category requires multi-path multi-schedule analysis.

The second column reports the time it took Cloud9 to interpret the programs with concrete inputs. This provides a sense of the overhead incurred by Portend compared to regular LLVM interpretation in Cloud9. Both data race detection and classification are disabled when measuring baseline interpretation time. In summary, the overhead introduced by classification ranges from 1.1× to 49.9× over Cloud9.

In order to get a sense of how classification time scales with program characteristics, we measured it as a function of program size, number of preemption points, number of branches that depend (directly or indirectly) on symbolic inputs, and number of threads. We found that program size plays almost no role in classification time. Instead, the other three characteristics play an important role. We show in Fig. 9 how classification time varies with the number of dependent branches and the number of preemptions in the schedule (which is roughly proportional to the number of preemption points and the number of threads). Each vertical bar corresponds to the classification time for the indicated data race. We see that, as the number of preemptions and branches increase, so does classification time.

Program	Cloud9 running time (sec)	Portend classification time (sec)		
		Avg	*Min*	*Max*
SQLite	3.10	4.20	4.09	4.25
ocean	19.64	60.02	19.90	207.14
fmm	24.87	64.45	65.29	72.83
memcached	73.87	645.99	619.32	730.37
pbzip2	15.30	360.72	61.36	763.43
ctrace	3.67	24.29	5.54	41.08
bbuf	1.81	4.47	4.77	5.82
AVV	0.72	0.83	0.78	1.02
DCL	0.74	0.85	0.83	0.89
DBM	0.72	0.81	0.79	0.83
RW	0.74	0.81	0.81	0.82

Table 4. Portend's classification time for the 93 races in Table 3.

We analyzed Portend's accuracy with increasing values of k and found that $k = 5$ is sufficient to achieve overall 99% accuracy for all the programs in our evaluation. Fig. 10 shows the results for Ctrace, Pbzip2, Memcached, and Bbuf. We therefore conclude that it is possible to achieve high classification accuracy with relatively small values of k.

5.4 Comparison to State of the Art

We compare Portend to the Record/Replay-Analyzer technique [45], Helgrind$^+$'s technique [27], and Ad-Hoc-Detector [55] in terms of the accuracy with which races are classified. We implemented the Record/Replay-Analyzer technique in Portend and compared accuracy empirically. For the ad-hoc synchronization detection techniques, since we do not have access to the implementations, we analytically derive the expected classification based on the published algorithms. We do not compare to RaceFuzzer [51], because it is primarily a bug finding tool looking for harmful races that occur due to exceptions and memory errors; it therefore does not provide a fine-grain classification of races. Similarly, no comparison is provided to DataCollider [29], since race classification in this tool is based on heuristics that pertain to races that we rarely encountered in our evaluation.

In Table 5 we show the accuracy, relying on manual inspection as "ground truth". Record/Replay-Analyzer does not tolerate replay failures and classifies races that exhibit a post-race state mismatch as harmful (shown as specViol), causing it to have low accuracy (10%) for that class. When comparing to Helgrind$^+$ and Ad-Hoc-Detector, we conservatively assume that these tools incur no false positives when ad-hoc synchronization is present, even though this is unlikely, given that both tools rely on heuristics. This notwithstanding, both tools are focused on weeding out races due to ad-hoc synchronization, so they cannot properly classify the other races (36 out of 93). In contrast, Portend classifies a wider range of races with high accuracy.

	specViol	k-witness	outDiff	singleOrd
Ground Truth	100%	100%	100%	100%
Record/Replay Analyzer	10%	95%	0% (not-classified)	
Ad-Hoc-Detector, Helgrind$^+$	0% (not-classified)			100%
Portend	100%	99%	99%	100%

Table 5. Accuracy for each approach and each classification category, applied to the 93 races in Table 3. "Not-classified" means that an approach cannot perform classification for a particular class.

The main advantage of Portend over Record/Replay-Analyzer is that it is immune to replay failures. In particular, for all the races classified by Portend as "single ordering", there was a replay divergence (that caused replay failures in Record/Replay-Analyzer), which would cause Record/Replay-Analyzer to classify the corresponding races as harmful despite them being harmless; this accounts for 57 of the 84 misclassifications. Note that even if

Record/Replay-Analyzer were augmented with a phase that pruned "single ordering" races (57/93), it would still diverge on 32 of the remaining 36 races and classify them as "spec violated", whereas only 5 are actually "spec violated". Portend, on the other hand, correctly classifies 35/36 of those remaining races. Another advantage is that Portend classifies based on symbolic output comparison, not concrete state comparison.

We manually verified and, when possible, checked with developers that the races in the "k-witness harmless" category are indeed harmless. Except for one race, we concluded that developers intentionally left these races in their programs because they considered them harmless. These races match known patterns [29, 45], such as redundant writes to shared variables (e.g., we found such patterns in Ctrace). However, for one race in Ocean, we confirmed that Portend did not figure out that the race belongs in the "output differs" category (the race can produce different output if a certain path in the code is followed, which depends indirectly on program input). Portend was not able to find this path even with $k = 10$ after one hour. Manual investigation revealed that this path is hard to find because it requires a very specific and complex combination of inputs.

In summary, Portend is able to classify with 99% accuracy and full precision all the 93 races into four data race classes defined in §2.3 in under 5 minutes per race on average. Furthermore, Portend correctly identifies 6 serious harmful races. Compared to previously published race classification methods, Portend performs more accurate classification and is able to correctly classify up to 89% (83 out of 93) more data races than existing replay-based tools. Portend also correctly handles false positive race reports.

6. Discussion

In this section, we discuss Portend's usage model and limitations.

Data Race Detection. Portend currently only handles data races with respect to the POSIX threads synchronization primitives thus not detecting data races that may occur inside synchronization primitives (as in [29]). Detection is done on the LLVM bitcode, not x86 assembly; analyzing the program at this level shields Portend from the peculiarities of a specific CPU's ISA and memory consistency model, while at the same time being ignorant of features that may make code be correctly synchronized on a specific platform despite not using POSIX primitives.

Multi-processors and Memory Consistency. Portend works for multi-processors, however it can simulate only serializable schedules that assume sequential memory consistency [32]. In order to augment Portend with the capability to reason about weaker memory consistency models, two key aspects of such models need to be handled, namely the relaxation of write atomicity and program order modification [1]. In order to model the relaxation of the write atomicity requirement, it is possible to break non-atomic instructions into multiple LLVM instructions. Then, Portend would be able to generate currently missing schedules that stem from non-atomic operations. Modeling the modification of program order can be achieved using a technique similar to adversarial memory [17]. Adversarial memory maintains a history buffer of writes per shared memory location and, upon a read from that memory location, computes a subset of values that can be validly read under the constraints of a particular relaxed consistency model. Portend can use those different read values to explore more paths during multi-path multi-schedule analysis.

Language Memory Models. Several language specifications, such as Ada 83 [34] and the new C [26] and C++ [25] specifications, do not guarantee any semantics for programs that contain data races at the source level, essentially considering all such races to be harmful. In other words, the corresponding compilers are allowed to perform optimizations that break racy programs in arbitrary ways [4]. Nonetheless, races at assembly level are not disallowed by any specification (typically synchronization primitives are implemented with racy assembly code), and, more importantly, there is a plethora of software written with races at the source level. Since Portend operates on LLVM bitcode, it can classify both source-code-level races and LLVM bitcode-level races. Moreover, Portend can also correctly classify not-buggy-in-source races that the compiler (legitimately) turned into LLVM level buggy ones [4].

Single-Processor Scheduler. Most data race detectors use a single processor thread scheduler and Portend does too. Such a scheduler has the advantage that it simplifies the record/replay component and improves its performance: for example, Portend does not have to record the ordering of memory reads and writes in different threads, since they are naturally ordered by scheduling (a single thread at a time). The scheduler does not impact Portend's ability to detect races, but it may decrease the probability of exploring some atomicity violations [36] or thread interleavings that would occur on a multi-processor (and are specific to its memory model). This loss of coverage is compensated by the fact that, if, during the analysis, Portend detects a racing access, it will consider it as a possible preemption point. Moreover, Portend's multi-schedule analysis is more likely to uncover more interleavings than "single-pre/single-post" analysis, thus increasing the thread schedule coverage.

Scalability of Symbolic Execution. Advances in improving the scalability of symbolic execution would help Portend explore more executions in the same amount of time, improving triaging accuracy. Since Portend is "embarrassingly parallel", performance could also be improved by running Portend in a cluster.

K-witness Harmless Races. It is theoretically undecidable to say if a race classified as "k-witness harmless" by Portend is indeed harmless unless *all* thread interleavings and *all* possible inputs were analyzed. However, as we found in our evaluation, in most cases, Portend produces highly accurate (but not perfect) verdicts in a reasonable amount of time.

We envision integrating Portend with an IDE to perform race classification in the background while the developer is modifying the code, in the spirit of automated software reliability services [10]. Portend would perform race classification and warn the developer that a race on the variable in question can have harmful effects, and should be protected. Test cases that are generated by Portend in the background can be integrated into a test suite for developers to validate their applications as part of regression tests.

Portend could also use reports from static race detectors [15] by feeding them to an execution synthesis tool like ESD [63], which can try to obtain the desired trace and then classify it with Portend. If ESD finds such an execution, it effectively confirms that the race is not a false positive, and Portend can automatically predict its consequences.

While analyzing a specific data race, Portend may also detect other unrelated races. This is a side effect of exploring various different thread schedules during classification. Portend automatically detects these new races, records their execution trace, and analyzes them subsequently, one after the other.

7. Related Work

Data race detection techniques can be broadly classified into two major categories: static data race detection [15, 58] and dynamic data race detection [49, 50, 62]. Static data race detection attempts to detect races by reasoning about source code, and dynamic race detection discovers races by monitoring particular execution of a program. Dynamic data race detection can further be classified into three categories: (1) detection using the happens-before relationship [5, 31, 40, 42, 46, 48, 50], (2) detection based on the lockset algorithm [49, 62], and (3) hybrid algorithms that combine these two techniques [30, 47, 62]. Portend uses a happens-before algorithm.

Portend's race detector can benefit from various optimizations, such as hardware support [42, 48] that speeds up race detection, or sampling methods [5, 38] that reduce detection overhead.

Prior work on data race classification employs record/replay analysis [45], heuristics [29], detection of ad-hoc synchronization patterns [27, 55] or simulation of the memory model [17].

Record/replay analysis [45] records a program execution and tries to enforce a thread schedule in which the racing threads access a memory location in the reverse order of the original race. Then, it compares the contents of memory and registers, and uses a difference as and indication of potential harmfulness. Portend does not attempt an exact comparison, rather it symbolically compares outputs and explores multiple paths and schedules, all of which increase classification accuracy over replay-based analysis.

DataCollider [29] uses heuristics to prune predefined classes of likely-to-be harmless data races, thus reporting fewer harmless races overall. Portend does not employ heuristics to classify races, but instead employs precise analysis of the possible consequences of the data race.

Helgrind$^+$ [27] and Ad-Hoc Detector [55] eliminate race reports due to ad-hoc synchronization; Portend classifies such races as "single ordering". Detecting ad-hoc synchronizations or happens-before relationships that are generally not recognized by race detectors can help further prune harmless race reports, as demonstrated recently by ATDetector [28].

Adversarial memory [17] finds races that occur in systems with memory consistency models that are more relaxed than sequential consistency, such as the Java memory model [37]. This approach uses a memory that returns stale yet valid values for memory reads, in an attempt to crash target programs. This approach is useful for a race like DCL, which is harmless on x86 but can be harmful under weaker memory models. On the other hand, systems like Sober [7] and Relaxer [8] detect executions that do not obey sequential consistency under relaxed memory models while only exploring sequentially consistent executions. Either of these approaches can be used to enable Portend to reason about weaker memory consistency models.

RACEFUZZER [51] generates random schedules from a pair of racing accesses to determine whether the race is harmful. Therefore, RACEFUZZER performs multi-schedule analysis but not multi-path, and does so only with the goal of finding bugs, not classifying races. Portend uses multi-path analysis in addition to multi-schedule analysis to improve triage accuracy.

Output comparison was used by Pike to find concurrency bugs while fuzzing thread schedules [18]. Pike users can also write state summaries to expose latent semantic bugs that may not always manifest in the program output. If available, such state summaries could also be used in Portend.

Frost [57] follows a similar approach to Record/Replay Analyzer and Pike in that it explores complementary schedules (similar to primary and alternate schedules in Portend) and detects and avoids potentially harmful races comparing the program states after following these schedules. This detection is based on state comparison and therefore is prone to false positives as shown in §5.4. If used in conjunction with Portend, Frost could avoid provably harmful races.

Deterministic execution systems have recently gained popularity in academia [2, 3, 13, 14]. Deterministic execution requires making the program merely a function of its inputs [56]. In order to achieve this in the general case, races must be eliminated from programs, which leads to high overhead. Combined with Portend, it may be possible to relax determinism guarantees and eliminate races that really matter from the point of view of a developer or user, and make deterministic execution more practical.

8. Conclusion

This paper presents the first technique for triaging data races based on their potential consequences through an analysis that is both multi-path and multi-schedule. Triaging is done based on a new four-category data race classification scheme. Portend, an embodiment of our proposed technique, detected and classified 93 different data races in 7 real-world applications with 99% accuracy and full precision, with no human effort.

Acknowledgments

We thank the anonymous reviewers for providing insightful feedback and suggesting paths for future research. We thank Katerina Argyraki, Ryan Johnson, Olivier Crameri, Christopher Ming-Yee Iu, Sotiria Fytraki, and all our DSLAB colleagues for helping us improve this paper. We thank Microsoft for supporting Cristian Zamfir through an ICES grant.

References

[1] S. V. Adve and K. Gharachorloo. Shared memory consistency models: A tutorial. *IEEE Computer*, 1996.

[2] A. Aviram, S.-C. Weng, S. Hu, and B. Ford. Efficient system-enforced deterministic parallelism. In *Symp. on Operating Sys. Design and Implem.*, 2010.

[3] T. Bergan, O. Anderson, J. Devietti, L. Ceze, and D. Grossman. CoreDet: a compiler and runtime system for deterministic multithreaded execution. In *Intl. Conf. on Architectural Support for Programming Languages and Operating Systems*, 2010.

[4] H.-J. Boehm. How to miscompile programs with "benign" data races. In *USENIX Workshop on Hot Topics in Parallelism*, 2011.

[5] M. D. Bond, K. E. Coons, and K. S. McKinley. PACER: proportional detection of data races. In *Conf. on Programming Language Design and Implem.*, 2010.

[6] S. Bucur, V. Ureche, C. Zamfir, and G. Candea. Parallel symbolic execution for automated real-world software testing. In *ACM EuroSys European Conf. on Computer Systems*, 2011.

[7] S. Burckhardt and M. Musuvathi. Effective program verification for relaxed memory models. In *Intl. Conf. on Computer Aided Verification*, 2008.

[8] J. Burnim, K. Sen, and C. Stergiou. Testing concurrent programs on relaxed memory models. In *Intl. Symp. on Software Testing and Analysis*, 2011.

[9] C. Cadar, D. Dunbar, and D. R. Engler. KLEE: Unassisted and automatic generation of high-coverage tests for complex systems programs. In *Symp. on Operating Sys. Design and Implem.*, 2008.

[10] G. Candea, S. Bucur, V. Chipounov, V. Kuznetsov, and C. Zamfir. Automated software reliability services: Using reliability tools should be as easy as webmail. Symp. on Operating Sys. Design and Implem., 2010. Research Vision Session.

[11] V. Chipounov and G. Candea. Enabling sophisticated analyses of x86 binaries with RevGen. In *Intl. Conf. on Dependable Systems and Networks*, 2011.

[12] Chris Lattner. libc++. http://libcxx.llvm.org/ .

[13] H. Cui, J. Wu, C. che Tsai, and J. Yang. Stable deterministic multithreading through schedule memoization. In *Symp. on Operating Sys. Design and Implem.*, 2010.

[14] J. Devietti, B. Lucia, L. Ceze, and M. Oskin. DMP: deterministic shared memory multiprocessing. In *Intl. Conf. on Architectural Support for Programming Languages and Operating Systems*, 2009.

[15] D. Engler and K. Ashcraft. RacerX: Effective, static detection of race conditions and deadlocks. In *Symp. on Operating Systems Principles*, 2003.

[16] B. Fitzpatrick. memcached. http://memcached.org/ .

[17] C. Flanagan and S. N. Freund. Adversarial memory for detecting destructive races. In *Conf. on Programming Language Design and Implem.*, 2010.

[18] P. Fonseca, C. Li, and R. Rodrigues. Finding complex concurrency bugs in large multi-threaded applications. In *ACM EuroSys European Conf. on Computer Systems*, 2011.

[19] V. Ganesh and D. L. Dill. A decision procedure for bit-vectors and arrays. In *Intl. Conf. on Computer Aided Verification*, 2007.

[20] J. Gilchrist. Parallel BZIP2. http://compression.ca/pbzip2 .

[21] K. Glerum, K. Kinshumann, S. Greenberg, G. Aul, V. Orgovan, G. Nichols, D. Grant, G. Loihle, and G. Hunt. Debugging in the (very) large: ten years of implementation and experience. In *Symp. on Operating Systems Principles*, 2009.

[22] P. Godefroid, M. Y. Levin, and D. Molnar. Automated whitebox fuzz testing. In *Network and Distributed System Security Symp.*, 2008.

[23] P. Godefroid and N. Nagappan. Concurrency at Microsoft – An exploratory survey. In *CAV Workshop on Exploiting Concurrency Efficiently and Correctly*, 2008.

[24] Helgrind. http://valgrind.org/docs/manual/hg-manual.html .

[25] ISO/IEC 14882:2011: Information technology – programming languages – C++. International Organization for Standardization, 2011.

[26] ISO/IEC 9899:2011: Information technology – programming languages – C. International Organization for Standardization, 2011.

[27] A. Jannesari and W. F. Tichy. Identifying ad-hoc synchronization for enhanced race detection. In *Intl. Parallel and Distributed Processing Symp.*, 2010.

[28] Y. L. Jiaqi Zhang, Weiwei Xiong, S. Park, Y. Zhou, and Z. Ma. ATDetector: Improving the accuracy of a commercial data race detector by identifying address transfer. In *IEEE/ACM International Symposium on Microarchitecture*, 2011.

[29] S. B. John Erickson, Madanlal Musuvathi and K. Olynyk. Effective data-race detection for the kernel. In *Symp. on Operating Sys. Design and Implem.*, 2010.

[30] T. I. Konstantin Serebryany. ThreadSanitizer - data race detection in practice. In *Workshop on Binary Instrumentation and Applications*, 2009.

[31] L. Lamport. Time, clocks, and the ordering of events in a distributed system. *Communications of the ACM*, 21(7), 1978.

[32] L. Lamport. How to make a multiprocessor computer that correctly executes multiprocess programs. *IEEE Transactions on Computers*, 28(9):690–691, Sep 1979.

[33] C. Lattner and V. Adve. LLVM: A compilation framework for lifelong program analysis and transformation. In *Intl. Symp. on Code Generation and Optimization*, 2004.

[34] H. Ledgard. *Reference Manual for the ADA Programming Language*. Springer-Verlag New York, Inc., 1983.

[35] N. G. Leveson and C. S. Turner. An investigation of the Therac-25 accidents. *IEEE Computer*, July 1993.

[36] S. Lu, J. Tucek, F. Qin, and Y. Zhou. AVIO: Detecting atomicity violations via access interleaving invariants. In *Intl. Conf. on Architectural Support for Programming Languages and Operating Systems*, 2006.

[37] J. Manson, W. Pugh, and S. V. Adve. The Java memory model. In *Symp. on Principles of Programming Languages*, 2005.

[38] D. Marino, M. Musuvathi, and S. Narayanasamy. LiteRace: effective sampling for lightweight data-race detection. In *Conf. on Programming Language Design and Implem.*, 2009.

[39] C. McPherson. Ctrace. http://ctrace.sourceforge.net .

[40] J. Mellor-Crummey. On-the-fly detection of data races for programs with nested fork-join parallelism. In *Supercomputing*, 1991.

[41] Memcached issue 127. http://code.google.com/p/memcached/issues/detail?id=127 .

[42] S. L. Min and J.-D. Choi. An efficient cache-based access anomaly detection scheme. In *Intl. Conf. on Architectural Support for Programming Languages and Operating Systems*, 1991.

[43] M. Musuvathi, S. Burckhardt, P. Kothari, and S. Nagarakatte. A randomized scheduler with probabilistic guarantees of finding bugs. In *Intl. Conf. on Architectural Support for Programming Languages and Operating Systems*, 2010.

[44] M. Musuvathi, S. Qadeer, T. Ball, G. Basler, P. A. Nainar, and I. Neamtiu. Finding and reproducing Heisenbugs in concurrent programs. In *Symp. on Operating Sys. Design and Implem.*, 2008.

[45] S. Narayanasamy, Z. Wang, J. Tigani, A. Edwards, and B. Calder. Automatically classifying benign and harmful data races using replay analysis. *Conf. on Programming Language Design and Implem.*, 2007.

[46] A. Nistor, D. Marinov, and J. Torrellas. Light64: Lightweight hardware support for data race detection during systematic testing of parallel programs. In *IEEE/ACM International Symposium on Microarchitecture*, 2009.

[47] R. O'Callahan and J.-D. Choi. Hybrid dynamic data race detection. In *Symp. on Principles and Practice of Paralle Computing*, 2003.

[48] M. Prvulovic and J. Torrellas. ReEnact: using thread-level speculation mechanisms to debug data races in multithreaded codes. In *Intl. Symp. on Computer Architecture*, 2003.

[49] S. Savage, M. Burrows, G. Nelson, P. Sobalvarro, and T. Anderson. Eraser: a dynamic data race detector for multithreaded programs. *ACM Transactions on Computer Systems*, 15(4), 1997.

[50] E. Schonberg. On-the-fly detection of access anomalies (with retrospective). *SIGPLAN Notices*, 39(4), 2004.

[51] K. Sen. Race directed random testing of concurrent programs. *Conf. on Programming Language Design and Implem.*, 2008.

[52] K. Sen, D. Marinov, and G. Agha. CUTE: a concolic unit testing engine for C. In *Symp. on the Foundations of Software Eng.*, 2005.

[53] SQLite. http://www.sqlite.org/ , 2010.

[54] The Associated Press. General Electric acknowledges Northeastern blackout bug. http://www.securityfocus.com/news/8032 .

[55] C. Tian, V. Nagarajan, R. Gupta, and S. Tallam. Dynamic recognition of synchronization operations for improved data race detection. In *Intl. Symp. on Software Testing and Analysis*, 2008.

[56] N. H. Tom Bergan, Joseph Devietti and L. Ceze. The deterministic execution hammer: How well does it actually pound nails? In *Workshop on Determinism and Correctness in Parallel Programming*, 2011.

[57] K. Veeraraghavan, P. M. Chen, J. Flinn, and S. Narayanasamy. Detecting and surviving data races using complementary schedules. In *Symp. on Operating Systems Principles*, 2011.

[58] J. W. Voung, R. Jhala, and S. Lerner. RELAY: Static race detection on millions of lines of code. In *Symp. on the Foundations of Software Eng.*, 2007.

[59] S. C. Woo, M. Ohara, E. Torrie, J. P. Singh, and A. Gupta. The SPLASH-2 programs: characterization and methodological considerations. *Intl. Symp. on Computer Architecture*, 1995.

[60] W. Xiong, S. Park, J. Zhang, Y. Zhou, and Z. Ma. Ad-hoc synchronization considered harmful. In *Symp. on Operating Sys. Design and Implem.*, 2010.

[61] Y. Yang, X. Chen, G. Gopalakrishnan, and R. M. Kirby. Distributed dynamic partial order reduction based verification of threaded software. In *Intl. SPIN Workshop*, 2007.

[62] Y. Yu, T. Rodeheffer, and W. Chen. Racetrack: Efficient detection of data race conditions via adaptive tracking. In *Symp. on Operating Systems Principles*, 2005.

[63] C. Zamfir and G. Candea. Execution synthesis: A technique for automated debugging. In *ACM EuroSys European Conf. on Computer Systems*, 2010.

Scalable Address Spaces Using RCU Balanced Trees

Austin T. Clements M. Frans Kaashoek Nickolai Zeldovich
MIT CSAIL
{aclements,kaashoek,nickolai}@csail.mit.edu

Abstract

Software developers commonly exploit multicore processors by building multithreaded software in which all threads of an application share a single address space. This shared address space has a cost: kernel virtual memory operations such as handling soft page faults, growing the address space, mapping files, etc. can limit the scalability of these applications. In widely-used operating systems, all of these operations are synchronized by a single per-process lock. This paper contributes a new design for increasing the concurrency of kernel operations on a shared address space by exploiting read-copy-update (RCU) so that soft page faults can both run in parallel with operations that mutate the same address space and avoid contending with other page faults on shared cache lines. To enable such parallelism, this paper also introduces an RCU-based binary balanced tree for storing memory mappings. An experimental evaluation using three multithreaded applications shows performance improvements on 80 cores ranging from 1.7× to 3.4× for an implementation of this design in the Linux 2.6.37 kernel. The RCU-based binary tree enables soft page faults to run at a constant cost with an increasing number of cores, suggesting that the design will scale well beyond 80 cores.

Categories and Subject Descriptors D.4.1 [*Operating Systems*]: Process Management; E.1 [*Data Structures*]: Trees; D.1.3 [*Programming Techniques*]: Concurrent Programming—Parallel programming

General Terms Algorithms, Design, Performance

Keywords RCU, Virtual memory, Multicore, Lock-free algorithms, Concurrent balanced trees, Scalability

1. Introduction

A common parallel programming model is shared-memory multithreading, where all threads of an application share a single address space. Such shared address spaces require the kernel virtual memory (VM) system to be likewise concurrent, and the kernel's approach to concurrent address space operations can severely affect the concurrency of a multithreaded VM-intensive application as a whole. In fact, it is not uncommon for applications to use processes instead of threads to avoid a single, shared address space, but this complicates sharing. Applications can also unknowingly make intensive use of VM: libc may call mmap or munmap internally to grow the address space or memory-map files, and even a seemingly innocent memory access can result in a soft page fault that modifies the application's shared page tables. The overall goal of this paper is to make such multithreaded applications that use virtual memory intensively (knowingly or unknowingly) scale well.

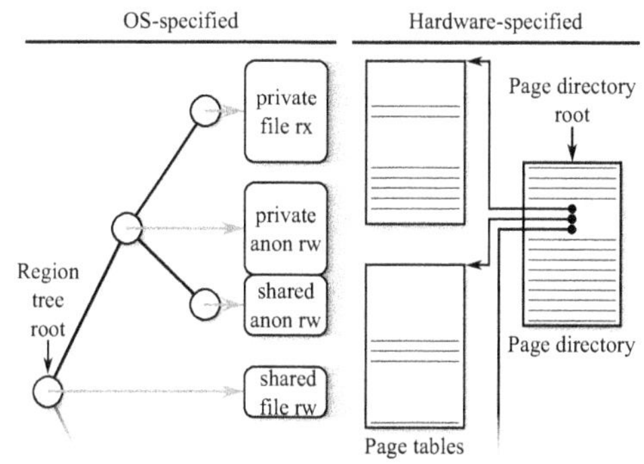

Figure 1. An address space with four mapped regions. Crossed-out page table entries do not map pages. Some pages have not been soft faulted yet, and thus do not map pages, despite being in a mapped region.

In most widely-used operating systems, an address space consists principally of a set of memory mapping regions and a page table tree, as shown in Figure 1. Each memory mapping region describes a range of virtual addresses and stores information about the mapping such as protection bits and backing files. Most widely-used operating systems use a tree to store the memory regions because applications often have thousands of memory regions (e.g., due to dynamic linking) and a tree enables the operating system to find the region containing a particular virtual address quickly. The page tables record the architecture-specific mapping from virtual pages to physical pages and, unlike the region tree, their structure is dictated by the hardware. This paper assumes x86-64 four-level page tables for concreteness, but the ideas are not specific to the x86.

Operating systems provide three address space operations of particular interest: the mmap and munmap system calls (collectively referred to as "memory mapping operations"), and page faults, which happen when the hardware cannot map a virtual address to a physical address. mmap creates memory mapping regions and adds them to the region tree. munmap removes regions from the tree and invalidates entries in the hardware page table structures. Page faults look up the faulting virtual address in the region tree and, if the virtual address is mapped, install an entry in the hardware page table and resume the application. We specifically focus on "soft" page faults, which may allocate new pages and new page tables or map pages already present in memory, but which do not page in data from an external drive.

The region tree and hardware page tables are shared by all threads in a process. To ensure correct behavior when several cores

ASPLOS'12, March 3–7, 2012, London, England, UK.

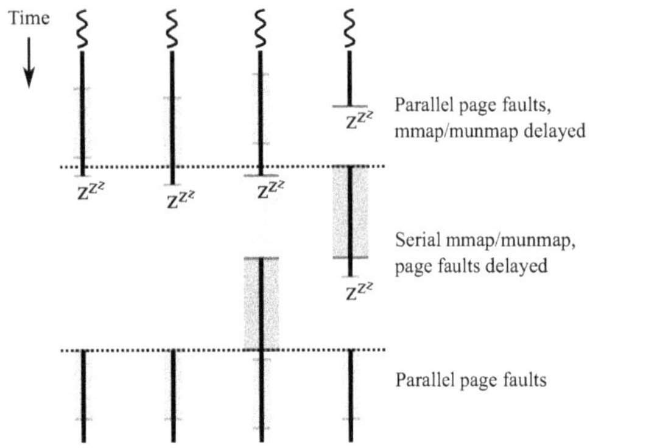

Figure 2. Linux address space concurrency with four threads. Page faults (skinny blue rectangles) and memory mapping operations (wide red rectangles) delay each other. Threads are sleeping in regions marked Z^{Z^Z}.

perform mmap, munmap, and page faults, most operating systems use several locks. Widely-used systems such as Solaris and Linux use a single read/write lock per process, which serializes page faults and memory mapping operations as shown in Figure 2, limiting the scalability of multithreaded VM-intensive applications. In these operating systems, a process can perform only one memory mapping operation at a time, and these operations also delay page faults. Page faults for different virtual addresses run concurrently, but block other threads from performing memory mapping operations.

Our goal is to make page faults scale to large numbers of cores. This requires addressing two basic forms of serialization. First, we must allow soft page faults to run concurrently with mmap and munmap operations to eliminate serialization on the per-process read/write lock. This is difficult because all three operations modify the address space data structures (the region tree, the page tables, or both). More subtly, we must also make page faults run without modifying shared cache lines to eliminate serialization caused by processor caches acquiring the cache line in an exclusive state. This is difficult because locks, even in read mode, require modifying shared cache lines.

To achieve our goal, this paper presents a new concurrent address space design that eliminates the above sources of contention by applying read-copy-update (RCU) [15] to the VM system and by introducing the BONSAI tree, an RCU-based concurrent balanced tree used as part of the design. While RCU is widely adopted in the Linux kernel, it has not been applied to the kernel's address space structures because of two significant challenges: the address space structures obey complex invariants that make RCU's restrictions on readers and writers onerous, and fully applying RCU to the address space structures requires an RCU-compatible concurrent balanced tree, for which no simple, applicable solutions exist.

To evaluate our approach, we implemented our concurrent address space design in Linux 2.6.37. This design leverages the BONSAI tree to apply RCU pervasively to both page table and tree operations, which allows page faults on distinct virtual addresses to proceed with no contention due to either locks or exclusive cache line accesses. For three VM-intensive workloads—Metis and Psearchy, from MOSBENCH [4], and Dedup from Parsec [2]—our design improves throughput on 80 cores by 3.4×, 1.8×, and 1.7× respectively, relative to stock Linux. Further, a microbenchmark demonstrates that the cost of handling a page fault in our design is nearly constant, independent of concurrent page faults or memory mapping operations, while this same cost grows rapidly in stock Linux as page fault and memory mapping load increases.

This paper contributes a novel design for an RCU-compatible balanced tree (BONSAI), a new address space design that uses BONSAI to achieve highly-scalable page fault handling, an implementation of that design in Linux, and an experimental evaluation using applications and microbenchmarks on an 80 core machine. Although our implementation is for Linux, we believe that our design could also be applied to other operating systems; while the details of address space management differ between kernels, most shared-memory kernels have similar address space representations.

The rest of the paper is organized as follows. Section 2 relates our contributions to previous work. Section 3 describes the design of the BONSAI tree. Section 4 covers existing address space designs in depth, using Linux as a case study. Section 5 describes our design for concurrent address space operations and section 6 summarizes its implementation in Linux. Section 7 reports on the experimental evaluation of our design and how it compares to the stock Linux approach and section 8 provides a brief discussion of our findings. Finally, section 9 summarizes our conclusions.

2. Background and related work

Address spaces in modern operating systems. Address spaces can consist of a large number of virtual address regions. As one example, on a typical Linux desktop, GNOME applications and web browsers such as Firefox and Chrome use nearly 1,000 distinct memory regions in each process. To manage this large number of regions, most modern operating systems use structures like the ones in Figure 1 to represent an address space. Linux uses a red-black tree for the regions, FreeBSD uses a splay tree, and Solaris and Windows (prior to Windows 7) use AVL trees [18, 24]. Linux and Solaris use a single read/write lock per address space. FreeBSD is more fine-grained: it uses a lock per region and a single write lock for mutating operations on an address space, serializing soft page faults with address space changes. Prior to Windows 7, Windows used a system-wide *PFN lock* [18]. Windows 7 uses fine-grained locking with better reported scaling results [24], but exact details are not public.

Since soft page faults must still modify address space structures (e.g., an entry in a page table), fine-grained locks are typically used in conjunction with per-process read locks to protect simultaneous page faults to nearby virtual addresses. The design proposed in this paper eliminates the read locks for page faults, but maintains the fine-grained locks for updates to page table entries. In many applications, including the three applications we study in this paper, these fine-grained locks are uncontended and typically stay in a core's cache, thus incurring negligible overhead.

Workarounds. It is not uncommon for system programmers to change their applications to use processes instead of threads to avoid contention caused by shared address space locking. For example, Psearchy, from MOSBENCH [4], was modified to use processes instead of threads. However, it is difficult to migrate an application from a shared address space to processes because sharing is less straightforward, and the added complexity makes it harder to maintain and evolve the application. Furthermore, using processes instead of threads can incur a performance penalty, since every process must fault on every shared page, rather than the entire application taking at most one fault per page [3].

Super pages can also increase scalability. On x86-64, this reduces the number of page faults by a factor of 512 (other platforms are similar), substantially reducing contention on the address space lock. However, applications that map many small regions (files or anonymous memory) cannot benefit from this solution. Furthermore, as memory demands and core counts grow, super pages will encounter the same scalability problems that regular pages currently contend with.

This paper presents a design that makes shared address space operations scalable, so that multithreaded applications can scale naturally to large numbers of cores, without the need to work around kernel limitations.

RCU. Our approach to increasing concurrency for address-space operations exploits the two key ideas of RCU [13]: allowing read operations to proceed without read locks, and delayed freeing of data structures to avoid races where a writer frees data while a reader is still using it. The benefit of avoiding read locks is twofold: not only does it allow read operations to proceed during write operations, but it eliminates the overhead of acquiring a read lock even when there are no writers. Even in read mode, acquiring a lock requires fetching the lock's cache line from the core that last updated the lock status; on today's multicore processors a contended cache line can take hundreds of cycles to fetch from a remote core, and RCU avoids this cost entirely.

Write operations, which coordinate using an exclusive lock, may change a data structure and remove entries from it while read operations are still using the removed entries. To ensure that these concurrent read operations do not observe invalid data, RCU delays freeing memory until it is guaranteed that all read operations that started before the data structure update have finished, at which point no further operations can observe the old data. Various schemes have been proposed to do the garbage collection of these delay-freed items, and the Linux kernel provides implementations ranging from a classic scheme that uses the scheduler to detect quiescence [17] to an epoch-based "sleepable" RCU implementation [14].

RCU data structures. The Linux kernel has increasingly adopted RCU for kernel data structures to improve scalability [16], but applying RCU is often not straightforward: RCU requires that mutating operations update only *one* pointer and that readers read each pointer at most once. This makes the update appear atomic: a reader will appear to execute either entirely before a concurrent update or entirely after, depending on when it reads the one updated pointer. More complex data structures such as balanced trees where mutation operations require multiple updates do not obviously fit with RCU, and none of the balanced trees in the Linux kernel use RCU. The BONSAI tree introduced by this paper is one solution to applying RCU to complicated data structures.

Trees with lock-free lookup. Fraser [6, 7] introduced a clever design for a red-black tree that allows read operations to proceed without locks, and write operations on different parts of the tree to proceed in parallel using fine-grained locks. To balance a tree, Fraser's design uses five fine-grained locks, one for each node involved in the balancing operation. Several other data structures, such as concurrent skip lists [20] and concurrent B-trees [10] also provide lock-free lookups with fine-grained write parallelism. However, such fine-grained parallelism is a poor match for address space concurrency because memory mapping operations must maintain invariants across *multiple* tree operations; maintaining internal tree consistency is not enough. The BONSAI tree takes advantage of the existing address space write-locking, and targets a simpler point in the design space that avoids the need for fine-grained locks.

Howard and Walpole [9] propose a relativistic red-black tree that supports lock-free lookups. By starting with a traditional lock-based tree, their design must explicitly handle tree rotations by considering several special cases. In contrast, BONSAI's design is based on an intuitively-correct tree design from functional languages, which achieves high performance with one key optimization to avoid path copying (described in §3.3). BONSAI's design is conceptually similar to Herlihy's approach for implementing concurrent data objects [8], but BONSAI derives additional simplicity by not handling concurrent modifications, which requires significant complexity in Herlihy's approach. All of the code for BONSAI, except for delete, is included in this paper, and the complete implementation is only 180 lines of code.

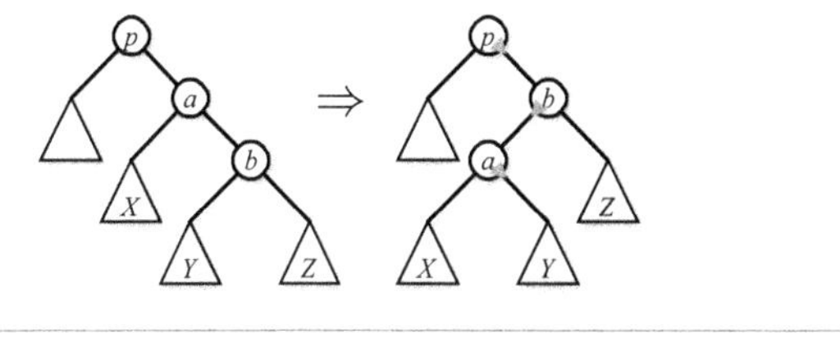

Figure 3. Single left rotation at a. Circles represent tree nodes, and triangles represent subtrees. The three updated pointers, at nodes p, a, and b are marked with red triangles.

3. An RCU-friendly balanced tree

This section describes the BONSAI tree, an RCU-compatible balanced binary tree based on the principle of non-destructive updates. As an RCU-compatible data structure, the BONSAI tree is designed to allow read operations such as lookup to proceed without locks in parallel with mutation operations such as insert and delete. Beyond the immediate concurrency implications of allowing read operations to proceed in parallel with writes, on large multicore machines, there are benefits to avoiding the cache coherence traffic caused by read locks. If the working set is in the local core's cache, read operations can proceed without any remote fetches. A single write lock is still used to coordinate mutation operations, but in many practical situations, including the Linux virtual memory system, the user of the tree must also ensure higher-level invariants across multiple tree operations and thus requires exclusive locks regardless.

The challenge to designing an RCU-compatible binary tree is keeping the tree balanced without introducing races with lock-free read operations, so that tree operations run in $O(\log n)$ time in the size of the tree. Maintaining balance requires mutation operations to perform tree *rotations*, which update multiple pointers across multiple tree nodes. If these updates are performed non-atomically, a concurrent, lock-free lookup may encounter a race condition where it observes only some of the pointer updates and returns an incorrect result.

For example, consider a single left rotation performed by an insert in order to rebalance a subtree—like the one pictured in Figure 3—and a concurrent lookup destined for a value in subtree Z. If the lookup reaches node a and then the rotation happens, it will proceed into subtree Y instead of subtree Z and miss the value it is searching for. The BONSAI tree avoids such races by design.

3.1 Approach

The design of the BONSAI tree is inspired by persistent data structures from functional programming. Such data structures are never modified in place; rather, the functional equivalent of a mutation operation leaves the existing data structure intact and returns a new instance of the data structure that reflects the change. This is kept efficient by sharing as much of the structure as possible between the original and "modified" instances.

Functional binary trees are an excellent example of this concept. Inserting into a functional binary tree constructs a new tree containing the original tree's elements, plus the newly inserted element. The two trees share all nodes except for those along the path from the newly inserted element to the root. Hence, like their in-place counterparts, insert into a functional tree requires time proportional to the height of the tree: it must traverse down the tree to find the insertion location, and then it must traverse back up the tree to construct the new path to the root and, ultimately, the new root node. Balanced trees are implemented by performing tree rotations as

```
typedef struct node
{
  struct node *left, *right;
  unsigned int size;
  int value;
} node_t;
```

Figure 4. Node structure

```
void
insert(node_t **root, int value)
{
  *root = doInsert(*root, value);
}

static node_t *
doInsert(node_t *node, int value)
{
  if (!node) return mkNode(NULL, NULL, value);

  if (value < node→value)
    return mkBalanced(node,
                  doInsert(node→left, value), node→right);
  if (value > node→value)
    return mkBalanced(node,
                  node→left, doInsert(node→right, value));
  return node;
}
```

Figure 5. Inserting into a tree

the tree is reconstructed from the bottom up, but, again, rotation is implemented by constructing a new, rotated subtree, rather than rotating a subtree in place.

Following this approach allows the BONSAI tree to be "correct by construction" in an RCU environment. In their simplest form, BONSAI operations construct a new tree non-destructively and then expose the modification in a single atomic step by updating a pointer to the tree's root node. If a lock-free reader reads the root node pointer before an update, it will operate entirely on the old tree; if it reads the root node pointer after an update, it will operate entirely on the new tree.

Steven Adams presents an elegant design for a functional sequential *bounded-balance tree* [1], and our tree derives from his design. Bounded-balance trees [19] exchange a certain degree of imbalance—controlled by a *weight* parameter—for fewer rotations than a strictly balanced tree. Combined with an optimization we describe in §3.3, this allows the BONSAI tree to produce fewer garbage nodes than a more conventional balanced tree, reducing stress on the memory allocator and CPU caches.

3.2 Algorithm

Figures 4 through 9 show the most important parts of an RCU-compatible bounded-balance tree, implemented in C but executing in a functional style. Each node has four fields (see Figure 4): a pointer to the left child, a pointer to the right child, the node's value, and a size field that records the number of nodes in the subtree rooted at that node.

doInsert, the core of insert, first recurses down the tree starting at the root until it falls off the edge of the tree. The recursive base case is easy: inserting a value into an empty tree simply creates a new node with no children. The actual work happens as doInsert unwinds its call stack, reconstructing the tree from the newly created node up to the root, ultimately returning a new tree that shares the majority of its structure with the original tree, but contains the

```
static node_t *
mkBalanced(node_t *cur, node_t *left, node_t *right)
{
  int ln = nodeSize(left);
  int rn = nodeSize(right);
  int value = cur→value;
  node_t *out;

  if (ln && rn && rn > WEIGHT * ln)
    out = mkBalancedL(left, right, value);
  else if (ln && rn && ln > WEIGHT * rn)
    out = mkBalancedR(left, right, value);
  else if (!UPDATE_IN_PLACE)
    out = mkNode(left, right, value);
  else
    goto updateInPlace;
  rcu_free(cur);
  return out;

updateInPlace:
  cur→left = left;
  cur→right = right;
  cur→size = 1 + ln + rn;
  return cur;
}
```

Figure 6. Balancing a subtree

inserted value. Finally, insert makes this entire updated tree visible to readers atomically by updating the pointer to the tree's root.

doInsert rebuilds each subtree using mkBalanced, shown in Figure 6. In its simplest form, mkBalanced takes a left subtree, left, and a right subtree, right, and returns a new node with value value conjoining the left and right subtrees. The reader can assume for now that UPDATE_IN_PLACE is false, as this enables an optimization which is described later.

If left and right subtrees are in balance (i.e., neither subtree contains more than a small multiple of the number of nodes in the other subtree), mkBalanced returns a new node with the given value and left and right children. If the new subtree would be out of balance, mkBalanced defers to either mkBalancedL or mkBalancedR, depending on which subtree is the smallest.

After constructing the new node, mkBalanced frees the original node being replaced, but does so in an RCU-delayed manner. Thus, the old node (and, in turn, the entire old tree) remains valid until every concurrent lookup that may be using the old tree completes.

mkBalancedL, shown in Figure 7, performs either single or double left rotation using singleL or doubleL, depending on the balance of the subtrees, returning the newly created, balanced subtree. singleL implements the single rotation of Figure 3, but does so without any in-place pointer updates, resulting in a new rotated subtree, like shown in Figure 8(a), where we see the two new nodes created by singleL, a' and b', as well as the new nodes created from p' up to the root by mkBalanced as doInsert unwinds its call stack. mkBalancedR, not shown, performs the equivalent right rotations.

lookup, shown in Figure 9, is identical to an ordinary, sequential tree look-up except for the enclosing calls to mark it as an RCU reader (which are no-ops in a non-preemptible Linux kernel). Because the BONSAI tree performs non-destructive updates and delay-frees all nodes, lookup does not require any locks, nor does it need any form of synchronization or atomic instructions on an x86 system.[1]

[1] Memory fence instructions are required on some non-x86 architectures, like the Alpha, for reading RCU-managed pointers between rcu_read_begin and rcu_read_end.

```
static node_t *
mkBalancedL(node_t *left, node_t *right, int value)
{
  if (nodeSize(right→left) < nodeSize(right→right))
    return singleL(left, right, value);
  return doubleL(left, right, value);
}

static node_t *
singleL(node_t *left, node_t *right, int value)
{
  node_t *out = mkNode(mkNode(left, right→left, value),
                       right→right,
                       right→value);
  rcu_free(right);
  return out;
}

static node_t *
doubleL(node_t *left, node_t *right, int value)
{
  node_t *out =
    mkNode(mkNode(left, right→left→left, value),
           mkNode(right→left→right, right→right,
                  right→value),
           right→left→value);
  rcu_free(right→left);
  rcu_free(right);
  return out;
}
```

Figure 7. Single and double left rotations

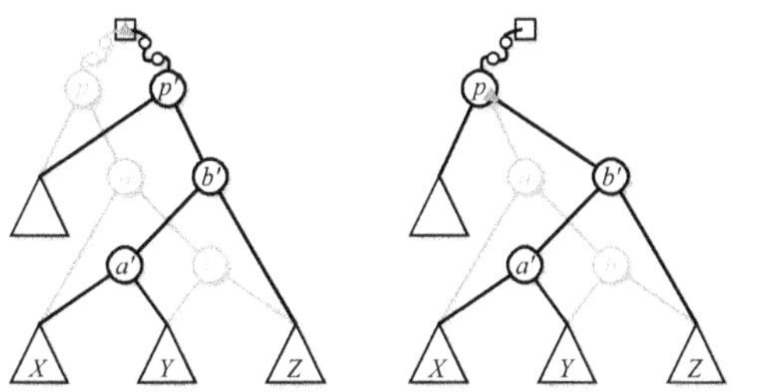

(a) Without optimization; O(log n) new nodes.

(b) With optimization; 2 new nodes.

Figure 8. Single left rotation at a, in functional style. The box represents the root node pointer. Garbage nodes are shown faded, new nodes are highlighted in green, and red triangles mark updated pointers.

```
bool
lookup(node_t **root, int value)
{
  rcu_read_begin();
  node_t *node = *root;
  while (node && node→value != value) {
    if (node→value > value)
      node = node→left;
    else
      node = node→right;
  }
  rcu_read_end();
  return node != NULL;
}
```

Figure 9. The lookup function

delete, not shown, has two cases. If the node to delete is a leaf, delete merely omits the node from the tree and rebuilds the path to the root using mkBalanced. If the node is an interior node, delete removes the node's successor from the tree (which must be a leaf and a descendant of the node being deleted) and substitutes it for the node being replaced, rebuilding from the successor up to the root.

3.3 Optimization

The implementation described so far allocates and frees $O(\log n)$ nodes for each insert. This is unavoidable in a true functional setting, where every version of the data structure must remain intact, but Bonsai has no such requirement. As presented, Bonsai delays the commit point—the time at which the inserted value becomes visible—until the final root pointer update. This is unnecessarily strict. For example, once a rotated subtree has been constructed, the remaining work is simply path copying to the root (assuming no additional rotations), but since this newly constructed path is structurally equivalent to the original path modulo the one pointer to the rotated subtree, we can atomically update this one pointer directly, rather than waiting to update the root pointer after reconstructing the entire path. The key to the resulting optimization is shown in Figure 8(b): once mkBalanced performs a non-destructive rotate, we can make that rotation visible immediately by updating a single pointer in p and avoid path copying. Furthermore, this optimization is safe under multiple rotations: since the contents of the tree are identical before and after a rotation, committing a rotation to the tree will have no affect on the results returned by a concurrent lookup.

By eliminating path copying, this optimization reduces the number of garbage nodes produced by insertion from $O(\log n)$ to $O(1)$ expected, which translates directly into less pressure on the memory allocator and the CPU cache, especially when combined with RCU delayed freeing. In practice, using a weight of 4, insertion performs only $\sim$0.35 rotations on average; with this optimization, this results in about 2 allocations and 1 free per insert on average, regardless of tree size.

The implementation of this optimization lies entirely in mkBalanced and does not affect the bottom-up insertion approach. If mkBalanced does not have to create a new node for rebalancing, it simply updates the current node in place. Typically, this will be a no-op, but if either left or right is the result of a rotation deeper in the tree, this will commit that rotation to the tree. mkBalanced also updates the size field in place; this need not be done atomically with the child pointer update because the size field is only accessed by writers.

Deletion can be optimized similarly, with one caveat. Since deleting an interior node requires two operations—removing the deleted node's successor and substituting it for the deleted node—delete must perform path copying from the successor up to the deleted node. By restricting itself to in-place updates only above the deleted node, delete accomplishes these two steps atomically.

This optimization is similar in effect to what Howard's relativistic red-black trees achieve [9], but its correctness is more readily apparent in Bonsai. Furthermore, it is generally applicable to other concurrent data structures derived from functional structures.

4. Address spaces in an operating system

Figure 1 in §1 briefly summarized the overall structure of an address space common to several kernels. An address space consists of a collection of non-overlapping memory regions or *virtual memory areas* (VMAs), where each area spans some set of pages in the virtual address space. On UNIX-like operating systems, these regions are manipulated by calls to memory mapping operations like mmap and munmap, though the regions may not correspond directly to the arguments to these calls. For example, an mmap adjacent to an existing VMA may simply extend that VMA, and an munmap in the middle of a VMA may split that VMA into two VMAs.

Each address space also maintains hardware page tables that map virtual addresses to physical addresses (on the x86, this consists of a tree of page directories and page tables, rooted at a root page directory). These hardware page tables are filled in lazily: creating a virtual memory area does *not* allocate pages or mark them present in the page tables. When an application tries to access a page of memory in a region spanned by some VMA for the first time, the hardware will generate a page fault, which the kernel will trap. The page fault handler looks for a VMA containing the faulting virtual address and, if one exists, only then will the kernel allocate a page and fill in the corresponding page table entry. Typically, the VMAs in an address space are kept in a balanced tree to facilitate efficiently looking up the VMA containing a faulting virtual address.

Multithreaded applications share an address space between threads, which, in most operating systems, means they share the set of VMAs as well as the hardware page tables. Memory mapping operations and page faults both access and modify these shared structures, and this concurrency must be addressed. Such address space designs suffer from four general classes of concurrency hazards, each mirroring some component of the address space structure: races involving the VMA tree, races involving VMA bound adjustment, races involving page table allocation and freeing, and races involving page allocation and freeing. These races are not simple coding errors, but design races that violate the semantics and invariants of address space operations. For example, in a naive solution, a race between an unmap operation and a page fault could result in a page being mapped in an otherwise unmapped region of memory.

The rest of this section uses the Linux kernel as a case study to illustrate how existing operating systems handle concurrent address space operations in multithreaded applications.

4.1 Linux case study: address space read/write locking

Linux, like many operating systems, protects address space structures using a per-process read/write lock, known as the mmap_sem read/write semaphore in Linux. This allows memory mapping operations like mmap and munmap, which acquire the lock in write mode, to perform complex operations atomically, while permitting page faults, which acquire the lock in read mode, to proceed in parallel with each other, as shown in Figure 2.

Running page faults concurrently is not straightforward, because page faults also modify the address space, and these modifications must be protected from concurrent page faults. At a minimum, a page fault must fill a page table entry, and it may have to allocate page tables or fill kernel-specific data structures. For this, Linux uses various fine-grained spinlocks, the two most notable of which are the page directory lock, which protects the insertion of new page directories and page tables into existing page directories, and the page table entry (PTE) lock, which protects the insertion of pages into page tables. Memory mapping operations generally do *not* acquire these fine-grained locks because they already acquire the mmap_sem in write mode, which prevents memory mapping operations and page faults from executing simultaneously. One exception is that munmap acquires PTE locks as it clears page tables. These locks are summarized below.

Lock	Type	Protects
mmap_sem	read/write per process	Address space
Page dir. lock	spinlock per process	Page dir. entries
PTE lock	spinlock per page table	Page table entries

Linux employs double-check locking to reduce both how frequently it must acquire these fine-grained locks and the duration they must be held for. For example, the page fault handler acquires the page directory lock only after observing a non-present page directory entry, and even then it acquires the lock only after optimistically allocating memory for the new page table. If a concurrent page fault has filled in the page directory entry in the meantime, it simply discards the optimistically allocated page table. Because of double-check locking, typically the only fine-grained lock the page fault handler acquires is the PTE lock. Indeed, recent versions of Linux have a separate PTE lock per page table to eliminate lock contention for all but nearby page faults (virtual addresses within 2 MB of each other on x86-64).

The write lock protects structures accessed and modified by memory mapping operations and the combination of the read lock and these fine-grained locks protects structures accessed and modified by the page fault handler, while still generally allowing page fault handlers to execute in parallel. Despite the scheme's sophistication, this locking has a concurrency cost: if any application thread is modifying the address space, no other thread can be taking page faults and if any thread is taking a page fault, no other thread can modify the address space. Furthermore, even in the absence of memory mapping operations, concurrent soft page faults still contend for the cache line that stores the state of the read/write lock. Under a heavy page fault load, the cost of this coherency traffic alone can affect application-level benchmark throughput.

5. Concurrent address spaces

In this section, we describe our concurrent address space design by introducing three increasingly-concurrent refinements of the baseline read/write locking employed by Linux. The first refinement, called fault locking, reduces the amount of time that memory mapping operations hold the mmap_sem read/write lock in write mode, allowing soft page faults to execute concurrently with the read-only parts of a memory mapping operation. The second refinement, called hybrid locking/RCU, eliminates the need for soft page faults to acquire the mmap_sem lock at all by applying RCU to the hardware page table structures and individual VMA entries, while protecting the VMA tree with a new read/write lock. The third refinement, called pure RCU, uses the RCU-based BONSAI tree to eliminate the read/write lock protecting the tree, eliminating any contended cache lines that must be modified by every soft page fault.

5.1 Fault locking

In this first refinement, we observe that memory mapping operations begin with a read-only phase in which they plan how to modify the address space before performing any data structure updates. In principle, page faults can safely proceed in parallel with the memory mapping operation during this time, hence permitting greater address space concurrency.

To take advantage of this observation, we add a *fault lock* to each address space and modify the page fault handler to acquire this lock in read mode, rather than the coarser mmap_sem. Memory mapping operations still acquire the mmap_sem in write mode and thus preclude races between each other, but before doing anything that could conflict with the page fault handler, they acquire the fault lock in write mode. The fault lock is released only when the mmap_sem is released, which, much like two-phase locking, keeps existing atomicity properties intact.

While memory mapping operations must acquire the fault lock before making any modifications, even before this, if they read anything that might be modified by a concurrent page fault, they must acquire the fault lock then to serialize the page fault. This complication will arise again in the RCU-based refinements, where it will require a more nuanced solution.

This refinement introduces no race conditions compared to stock Linux locking, but it only partially addresses the serialization between memory mapping operations and page fault handling, because it allows only marginally more concurrency between fault handlers and memory mapping operations.

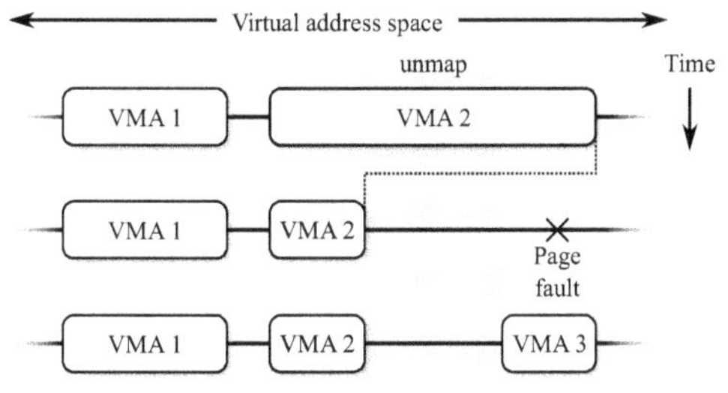

Figure 10. When splitting VMA 2 into two regions, the range originally covered by the top of VMA 2 can appear unmapped after VMA 2 is adjusted and before VMA 3 is created.

5.2 Hybrid locking/RCU

Our ultimate goal is to allow the page fault handler to run concurrently with both other page faults and memory mapping operations. Our solution to the problems that arise after eliminating the read lock around the page fault handler is twofold. Wherever possible, we apply RCU to eliminate the need for read locking. Then, in cases where a rare, non-benign race might arise, we detect inconsistencies and restart the page fault handler, this time with the mmap_sem held to ensure progress (similarly, we retry with locking in occasional "hard" cases).

The hybrid locking/RCU refinement approaches this goal without any structural changes to the address space. Other than the VMA tree, all of the data structures involved in the address space can be modified one step at a time without violating any invariants. This is not the case for the VMA tree, so this refinement still serializes access to the VMA tree using a read/write lock, which both the page fault handler and memory mapping operations acquire around tree operations. The pure RCU refinement, covered in the next section, tackles this last need for locking.

Removing the read lock around the page fault handler unleashes a number of races. We describe those that follow from the general address space design here and dive in to a few Linux-specific races in §6.

VMA split race. If no VMA contains the faulting address, the page fault could be a "segfault," or there may be a stack region that should be expanded to cover the faulting address, or we may be in the midst of a VMA split. The first two situations occur in stock Linux and we have to acquire the mmap_sem to handle them. The third situation is new and occurs because during a split, a region of memory can transiently appear unmapped, as shown in Figure 10. The munmap operation splits a VMA into two VMAs in two steps: it adjusts the bound of the existing VMA at time 2 and at time 3 it inserts the new VMA for the top part. Concurrently at time 2, a page fault handler may run that looks up an address in the top part of the VMA, which is momentarily not present. Since this race is unlikely, our approach is to simply retry the page fault with the mmap_sem held, which guarantees progress by preventing further races.

Page table deallocation race. Much like how pages are allocated on demand by soft page faults, page directories and tables are only allocated when a page fault encounters an empty page directory entry while installing mappings for a VMA that was faulted in. Conversely, unmapping a region recursively scans the page table tree, as illustrated in Figure 11, freeing not only the pages in that region, but also any page directories and tables that are no longer needed, clearing page directory entries that point to these. In the read/write locking refinement, the mmap_sem prevents a concurrent unmap and page fault within the same VMA. Without the mmap_sem, two problems arise from the race between page faults and the unmap scan. The first is classic RCU: the unmap may free VMAs, page

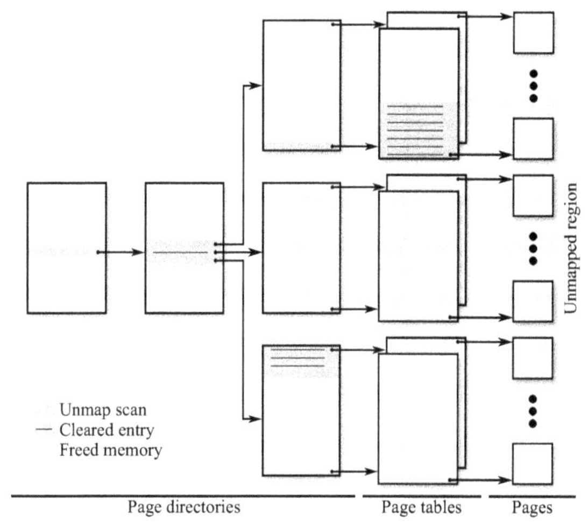

Figure 11. Unmapping a region of an x86-64 four-level page table tree. Unmapping recursively scans the page table tree to free unused page directories and page tables, in addition to freeing pages. Our design RCU-delays these frees. Unmapping must also clear page directory and page table entries that point to structures freed by the unmap, which introduces write-write races with page faults that fill these entries.

tables, or page directories that are being used by a concurrent page fault. To address this, we simply RCU-delay freeing these structures. The second is described next.

Page table fill race. A subtler race arises because both page faults and unmapping operations modify page directory and page table entries: page faults fill pointers to newly allocated pages and page tables, and unmapping operations clear pointers to freed page tables and pages. In both stock Linux and hybrid locking/RCU, fine-grained locking prevents simultaneous page fault handlers from filling the same page directory entry. However, this does not address the race between page faults and unmapping.

Consider a concurrent page fault and munmap on the same VMA, where the munmap has already surpassed the faulting address, delay freed the page table containing the faulting address, and cleared the corresponding page directory entry. The concurrent page fault will observe the blank page directory entry and could naively conclude that it needs to allocate a new page table and ultimately a new page. At best, these will never be freed; at worst, they could wreak havoc with a later mapping of the same region of memory. Luckily, this race is easy to detect: after acquiring the fine-grained PTE lock protecting the page table entry to be filled, but before actually filling it, the page fault handler double-checks that the VMA has not been marked as deleted and that the faulting address still falls within the VMA's bounds. In the unlikely event that the mapping of the faulting address has changed since the page fault's VMA lookup, this test will fail and the page fault handler will retry with the mmap_sem held. Curiously, this race check itself has a race: the mapping could still change after the check and before filling the page table entry, since mapping operations do not hold any fine-grained locks when manipulating VMAs. However, for numerous reasons, munmap does acquire PTE locks as it clears page tables, which is enough to ensure that, if the mapping does change, either the page fault handler's race check will observe the modified VMA, or munmap will observe and free pages allocated by the racing page fault.

While the solution to this race does not directly involve RCU, because of RCU, it is safe to *follow* page table pointers without any

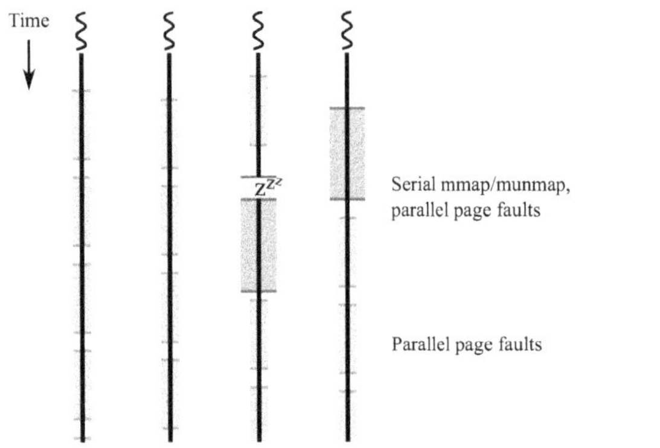

Figure 12. Pure RCU design concurrency with four threads. Page faults (skinny blue) neither delay memory mapping operations (wide red), nor are delayed by memory mapping operations, which benefits both page faults and memory mapping operations.

fine-grained locks. As a result, contention on the page directory lock and the PTE locks is virtually nonexistent.

Together, these three solutions address races involving bound adjustment and deletion of VMAs, allocation and freeing of page directories and page tables, and allocation and freeing of pages, three of the four major components of the address space. To address the fourth and final major component, the VMA tree, this refinement falls back on locking, which we remedy in our fourth concurrency refinement.

5.3 Pure RCU

Operating systems typically store the set of virtual memory areas in a balanced tree, such as a red-black or AVL tree, to facilitate fast lookup. However, these trees are not RCU-safe: as described in §3, a lock-less lookup during a concurrent insert or delete can result in the lookup failing, even if the element being looked-up is unrelated to the element being inserted or deleted.

Hence, to fully eliminate coarse-grained locking from the page fault handler, pure RCU further refines hybrid locking/RCU by replacing the locked red-black tree with the RCU-compatible BONSAI tree. This addresses races in all components of the address space, while BONSAI's lock-free lookups allow page faults to proceed fully in parallel both with each other and with memory mapping operations.

In contrast with the limited concurrency permitted by stock Linux's read/write locking, as shown in Figure 2, Figure 12 demonstrates the concurrency permitted by pure RCU page fault handling. In Figure 12, page fault handlers run concurrently with everything. As a result, the kernel can process page faults at a much higher rate and, furthermore, eliminating interference between page faults and memory mapping operations also improves memory mapping performance.

6. Implementation

We implemented the three new address space concurrency designs in the Linux 2.6.37 kernel. The implementation passes the Linux Test Project [11], as well as our own stress tests, and is further validated by a lock protection analysis we performed in the process of modifying the Linux virtual memory system and exhaustive schedule checking of a model of the VM system designed to capture key races. Our implementation consists of ~2,600 lines of code, and the core BONSAI tree implementation is 180 lines of code.

The current implementation handles regular soft page faults in anonymous memory mappings. For memory-mapped files and copy-on-write faults, the implementation retries the page fault with the lock held. Fortunately, retrying is fast, so this decision poses little overhead: almost always, the VMA found on the first try will still be applicable on the second try (which can be checked easily), thus avoiding the entire VMA lookup, and the page directory walk will still be hot in the CPU cache.

The implementation was guided by a lock protection analysis we performed using a version of QEMU [21] modified to trace every memory access and provide a hypercall interface for recording memory allocations and reachability, lock acquisitions, and lock releases. Using type information from memory allocations, this analysis tool inspected how frequently different variables and structure fields were accessed with and without certain locks, thus inferring what data was likely to be protected by what locks and where in the source code those variables and fields were read and written. While this analysis was far from perfect, it was a valuable tool for understanding the Linux virtual memory system and finding potential concurrency hazards and races.

Several advanced features of the Linux virtual memory system complicated the RCU-based implementations and introduced additional potential races. Several of these races relate to Linux's *reverse map*, which tracks all virtual mappings of each physical page to facilitate operations such as swapping. For example, the page fault handler is responsible for associating an "anon_vma" with each anonymous memory VMA for tracking reverse mappings in that VMA. Luckily, this operation occurs infrequently, so the implementation simply retries the page fault in such cases. Likewise, the implementation handles various other uncommon operations—such as Linux's stack guard reservations—using the same retry-with-locking mechanism used when races are detected.

The mmap_cache, a seemingly innocent feature of the Linux page fault handler, causes surprising trouble. This caches the most recent VMA tree lookup in each address space. Any VMA lookup first checks if the cached VMA satisfies the request; if so, it can return immediately; if not, it looks up the VMA and stores the result in the cache. Maintaining this cache in an RCU environment, where a VMA can be doomed to deletion by the time it is looked up, is possible (albeit difficult), but with many threads faulting on different VMAs, it does more harm than good: the hit rate will be low (below 1% in our benchmarks), so every page fault will update it, which can result in significant cache coherence traffic. Thus, for the two RCU-based designs, we simply disable the mmap_cache because it harms overall performance. A more complete solution might dynamically disable the mmap_cache for multithreaded processes.

7. Evaluation

This section evaluates the following hypotheses:

- Can application scalability be limited by bottlenecks in the implementation of address spaces?
- Do the techniques proposed in this paper eliminate those bottlenecks?
- Is a simple fine-grained locking approach sufficient to remove the bottlenecks or is RCU necessary?
- Are short-duration read-locks acceptable in the soft page fault handler, or is the complete application of RCU necessary for scalability?
- Are application workarounds still necessary to achieve peak scalability?

7.1 Evaluation method

Only VM-intensive applications benefit from the designs described in this paper, so we selected three VM-intensive benchmarks: Metis [12], a single-server multicore implementation of MapReduce from the MOSBENCH suite [4], used to compute a word position index from a 2 GB in-memory text file; Psearchy, a parallel text indexer based on searchy [23] (also from MOSBENCH), applied to the Linux 2.6.35-rc5 source tree; and Dedup, a deduplication-based file compressor from the Parsec benchmark suite [2], used to compress a 5.3 GB ISO image.

We selected these three benchmarks because they are multi-threaded (the other MOSBENCH applications are multi-process) and exhibit high page fault rates (the other Parsec applications do not), qualities we expect to see in more applications given trends towards higher core counts and larger data sets. Furthermore, the two MOSBENCH applications have alternate implementations that allow us to compare our general solutions with application-specific workarounds for address space scalability issues. The performance of other applications from the MOSBENCH and Parsec benchmark suites, which are not VM-intensive, is not affected by the three concurrent address space designs proposed in this paper.

We test the three benchmarks on Linux 2.6.37 with stock Linux as well as the three refinements described in §5. We also use microbenchmarks to evaluate the scalability and performance of just the page fault handler.

All experiments are performed on an 80 core machine with eight 2.4 GHz 10 core Intel E7-8870 chips and 256 GB of RAM on a Supermicro X8OBN base board. For both application benchmarks and microbenchmarks, we take the best of three runs to mitigate unrelated system activity. For application benchmarks, we spread enabled cores across sockets in order to maximizes the total cache and memory resources available to the application. The microbenchmarks are sensitive to cache size, so for these we group enabled cores on as few sockets as possible so that the per-core resources remain roughly constant across each experiment.

7.2 Application results

In all three applications, the greater address space concurrency of the pure RCU design results in significantly higher application throughput at large core counts; indeed, Metis and Dedup achieve near-perfect speed-up to 80 cores under the pure RCU design, while stock Linux read/write locking achieves 45× speed-up over single-core performance at best. Furthermore, as the number of cores increases, the gap between the pure RCU design and the three less-concurrent designs widens, suggesting that, as hardware becomes increasingly parallel, sophisticated concurrency schemes such as RCU and lock-free operation will become increasingly important.

Metis. Metis, shown in Figure 13, runs one worker thread per core, which together mmap and soft fault approximately 12 GB of anonymous memory as they generate intermediate tables between the map, reduce, and merge phases. As in the original MOSBENCH configuration, we use Metis with Streamflow [22], a scalable memory allocator, which mmaps allocation pools in 8 MB "segments," resulting in relatively few memory mapping operations compared to a more conservative allocator like glibc's malloc.

For Metis, the pure RCU design achieves near-perfect 75× speed-up at 80 cores and outperforms read/write locking by 3.4×. On the other hand, read/write locking's performance degrades with more cores because of both lock contention and cache contention for the mmap_sem. While the pure RCU design has less then 1% idle time at 80 cores, read/write locking has 12% idle time, waiting to acquire mmap_sem, and further spends 9.6% of its time contending for the mmap_sem's wait queue spinlock when it fails to acquire the lock. At the same time, it spends 31% of its time manipulating the mmap_sem cache line to acquire and release the lock. Finally, the increased contention in the kernel indirectly causes a 44% increase in the user time required to complete a job (e.g., due to increased cache pressure and interconnect traffic). Together, these factors account for the difference between the performance of read/write locking and

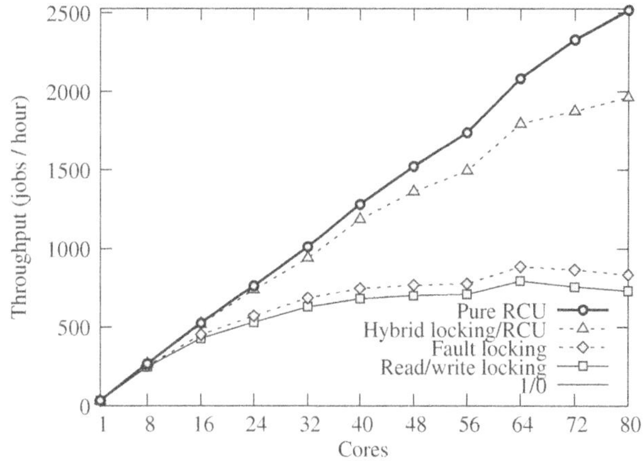

Figure 13. Metis throughput for each page fault concurrency design.

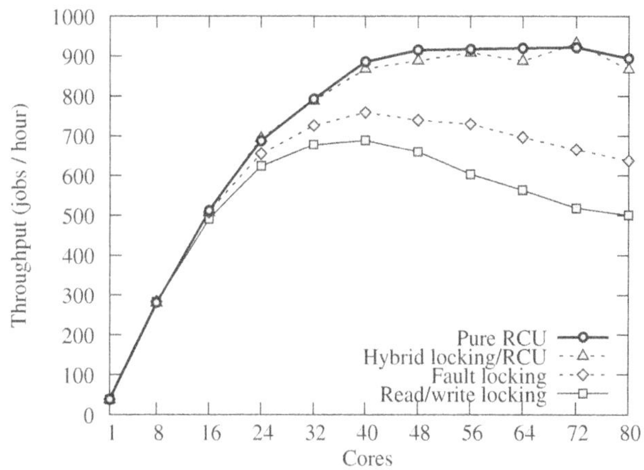

Figure 14. Psearchy throughput for each page fault concurrency design.

pure RCU at 80 cores. Fault locking shows little improvement over read/write locking. Hybrid locking/RCU outperforms read/write locking by 2.7×, but only achieves 59× speed-up because of the remaining contention on the lock protecting the VMA tree.

Psearchy. Psearchy is more heterogeneous than Metis, stressing both large and small memory regions. During initialization, Psearchy starts one worker thread per core, all of which simultaneously malloc and zero a 128 MB per-thread hash table; during main execution, these threads use libc's stdio library to read files, which internally calls mmap and munmap to manage memory for stream buffers, resulting in ~30,000 small anonymous mmap/munmap pairs. As in the original MOSBENCH configuration, we index the Linux 2.6.35-rc5 source tree, consisting of 368 MB of text across 33,312 source files. To avoid IO bottlenecks, all input files are in the buffer cache and all output files are written to tmpfs.

The results for Psearchy are shown in Figure 14. Psearchy performs 13× more memory mapping operations per second than Metis, and, as a result of this high rate, the serialization of mmap and munmap ultimately bottlenecks Psearchy's performance in all four concurrency designs. With read/write locking, this base lock contention is further aggravated by page faults acquiring the mmap_sem in read mode; indeed, performance decays beyond the peak at 32 cores owing to the non-scalability of Linux's read/

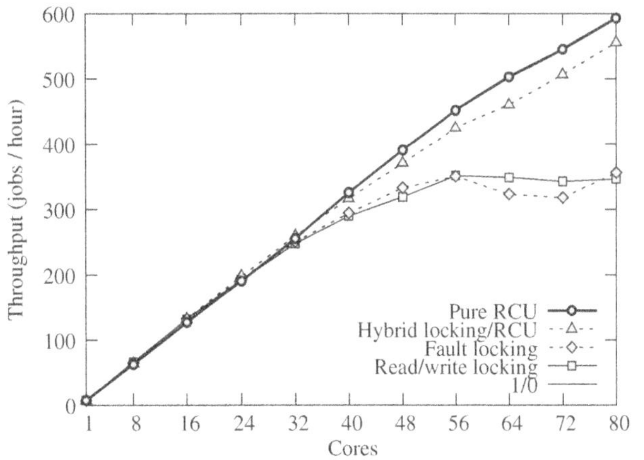

Figure 15. Dedup throughput for each page fault concurrency design.

Metis	user	sys	idle
Read/write locking	150 s	196 s	45 s
Fault locking	139 s	155 s	49 s
Hybrid locking/RCU	107 s	35 s	4 s
Pure RCU	102 s	11 s	1 s
Psearchy	user	sys	idle
Read/write locking	114 s	177 s	283 s
Fault locking	107 s	124 s	220 s
Hybrid locking/RCU	107 s	47 s	176 s
Pure RCU	107 s	12 s	201 s
Dedup	user	sys	idle
Read/write locking	465 s	146 s	248 s
Fault locking	567 s	35 s	239 s
Hybrid locking/RCU	426 s	18 s	93 s
Pure RCU	430 s	17 s	57 s

Table 1. Comparison of user, system, and idle time at 80 cores for a single "job" in each concurrency design.

write lock implementation. The other three designs perform better because they do not acquire the mmap_sem in the page fault handler, leaving only mmap and munmap to contend on that lock. Fault locking performs 27% better at 80 cores because it reduces this window of contention between memory mapping operations and page faults, even though it still acquires long-duration locks. Hybrid locking/RCU performs 1.7× better than stock because it nearly eliminates lock contention between memory mapping operations and page faults; its performance decays at high core counts because of contention for the cache line storing the lock that protects the VMA tree. Finally, the pure RCU design eliminates both lock and cache contention in the page fault handler, outperforming read/write locking by 1.8× and hybrid locking/RCU by 3.1%.

Metis and Psearchy provide alternate implementations specifically designed to work around address space scalability limits at the cost of increased application complexity. Metis can use 2 MB superpages, reducing the number of page faults by a factor of 512. Despite this optimization, unmodified Metis using the pure RCU design outperforms the optimized Metis using read/write locking; the former achieves 76× speed-up at 80 cores while the latter only 63× speed-up. Hence, for Metis, it is better to address the root problem in the kernel, rather than work around it in the application.

Psearchy requires relatively little shared state, so it can run in a multi-process configuration, avoiding shared address spaces altogether. Unlike Metis, Psearchy is ultimately limited both by lock contention between mapping operations and by lock contention within glibc itself, neither of which we address. Thus, while multi-threaded Psearchy using the pure RCU design significantly outperforms multi-threaded Psearchy using read/write locking, switching to a multi-process configuration proves even more effective, achieving 49× speed-up at 80 cores, versus 25× for multi-threaded Psearchy. Concurrent mapping operations would narrow this gap, but obviating this workaround requires improvements in user-space libraries as well as the kernel.

Dedup. Dedup, shown in Figure 15, deduplicates and compresses the blocks of an input file using a pipeline of communicating thread pools. We use a slightly modified version of Dedup that fixes one internal scalability bottleneck and substitutes jemalloc [5] for glibc's malloc because, in our experiments, jemalloc consistently outperformed and out-scaled glibc's malloc. Dedup's allocation pattern is similar to Metis: frequent heap allocation causes Dedup to mmap thousands of 4 MB–8 MB chunks and ultimately soft fault 13 GB of memory. As a result, the lock contention for the mmap_sem is comparatively low. For read/write locking and fault locking, the additional lock contention from page faults limits the overall scalability, but the two RCU-based designs scale much better: hybrid locking/RCU and pure RCU outperform read/write locking by 60% and 70%, respectively.

In all three benchmarks, system time on 80 cores drops precipitously with each increasingly concurrent address space design, as shown in Table 1. With read/write locking, system time represents a significant portion of each benchmark's running time. Pure RCU demonstrates between 88% and 94% less system time because of a combination of reduced cache contention, less time manipulating lock wait queues, and less time handling sleeps and wakeups.

7.3 Isolated VM performance

All three application benchmarks spend a substantial fraction of their time performing computation in user space, making it difficult to precisely quantify the performance gains in the virtual memory system. We employ a microbenchmark to isolate the performance of the VM system and closely analyze the costs and scalability of page fault handling. Our microbenchmark uses one core to perform mmap/munmap operations for a given fraction of time (to control how often the mmap_sem is held in write mode), while the remaining cores continuously take soft page faults. This microbenchmark also allows us to drive the VM system much harder than the application benchmarks do, giving a glimpse at how applications may perform at even higher core counts.

Figure 16 shows the base throughput of the microbenchmark without any mmap or munmap operations. In effect, this amplifies the behavior exhibited by Metis and Dedup. Because no locks are acquired in write mode, all non-scalability in this case is the result of cache contention for the cache line holding the mmap_sem. Figure 17 shows the corresponding average cost of a page fault. At 10 cores, page faults take approximately 7,400 cycles in all four designs. By 80 cores, page faults in the three lock-based designs are more than an order of magnitude more expensive. At 80 cores, read/write locking spends 84% of its cycles simply acquiring and releasing the mmap_sem in read mode. The pure RCU design, however, virtually eliminates cache contention; at 80 cores, the page faults take 8,869 cycles, demonstrating near-perfect scalability even at 20 million page faults per second. The few additional cycles are the result of slight non-scalability in the Linux page allocator.

Of course, any real application will also perform memory mapping operations. We simulate this by adjusting how frequently the microbenchmark calls mmap/munmap. For each design, we use enough page faulting cores to drive the design at its peak page

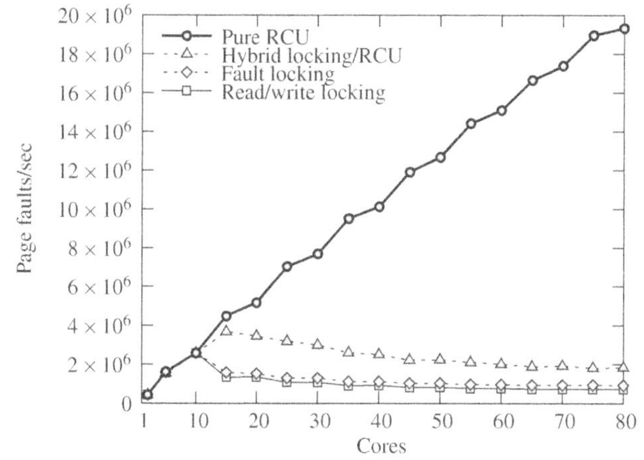

Figure 16. Microbenchmark throughput with no lock contention.

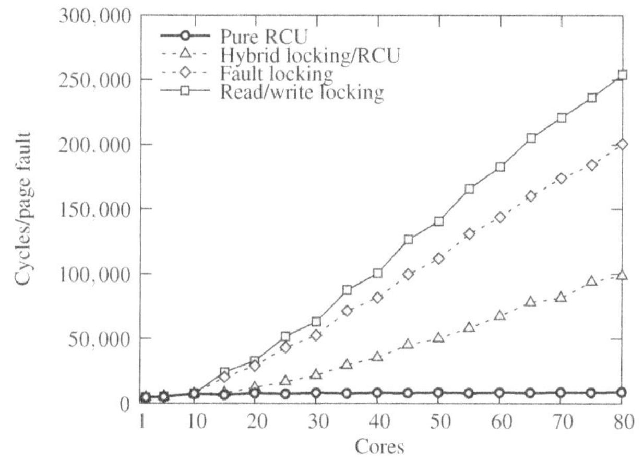

Figure 17. Microbenchmark page fault cost with no lock contention.

fault rate, both to focus on lock contention costs (excluding cache contention costs), and to maximally stress the page fault handler. Figure 18 shows the cost of the page fault handler as we increase the time spent in mmap and munmap. Since each design uses a different number of page fault cores, the base page fault cost—when no time is spent in mmap or munmap—differs slightly, hence we normalize to this base cost. Both read/write locking and fault locking exhibit exponential growth as the probability of lock conflicts increases, ultimately reaching 29× and 21× their base page fault costs, respectively. Hybrid locking/RCU behaves more modestly, as the window for conflicts between memory mapping operations and page faults is restricted to the time the tree lock is held, which is limited to a small fraction of the time that the mmap_sem is held. The pure RCU design again demonstrates near-constant cost, suggesting that the design will continue scaling well on systems that have more than 80 cores.

8. Discussion

We believe the Metis, Psearchy, and Dedup benchmarks highlight the address space concurrency issues faced by the increasingly important class of highly-threaded, VM-intensive applications. The pure RCU design makes Metis and Dedup scale well to 80 cores, but Psearchy suggests the importance of future research to improve write-side parallelism for address spaces. Applications must map memory in order to soft fault it, and, ultimately, the serialization of

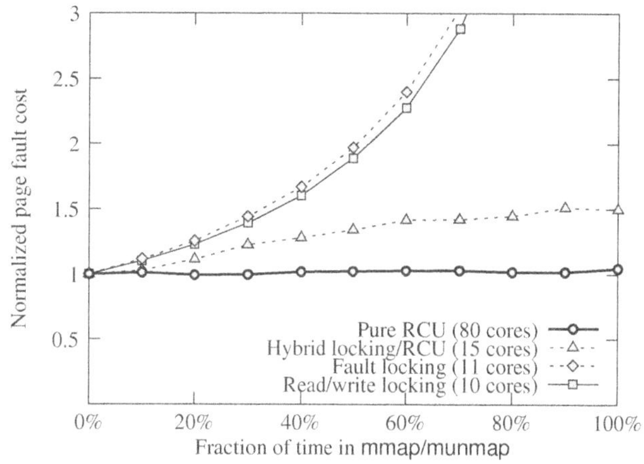

Figure 18. Microbenchmark page fault cost with varying time spent in mmap and munmap, shown relative to the cost with no concurrent memory mapping operations.

memory mapping operations will dominate any parallel component of the virtual memory system.

As the results show, the BONSAI tree allows the pure RCU design to scale at constant cost and, under highly parallel loads, achieve substantially better performance than its locked counterparts. While the BONSAI tree is well suited to storing memory mappings, its design is generic and could benefit other parallel components of the kernel as well as parallel applications. Furthermore, the derivation of the BONSAI tree from a sequential functional data structure and its path-copying optimization are equally applicable to other functional data structures and may yield RCU-compatible versions of other data structures typically protected by locks.

Likewise, little of the pure RCU design is specific to Linux. We believe that the pure RCU approach should apply equally well to other operating systems, and will result in similar scalability benefits.

9. Conclusion

As core counts increase, multithreaded VM-intensive applications can become bottlenecked by kernel operations on their shared address space. To avoid this bottleneck, this paper has introduced an address space design that uses RCU to manage VMAs, page directories, and page tables and uses a new RCU-based balanced tree, BONSAI, to manage the VMA set. Measurements on an 80 core Linux computer show that this design scales better than stock Linux and two other simpler but less-concurrent designs; its use of BONSAI allows the page fault handler to run at a constant cost, independent of the number of cores and of the memory mapping load. As this design applies to any VM system that tracks pages using a balanced tree, it should be applicable to many of the popular shared-memory operating systems.

The source code for our modified Linux kernel is available at `http://pdos.csail.mit.edu/mosbench`.

Acknowledgments

We thank Eddie Kohler, Paul McKenney, and Robert Morris for their feedback. Thanks to Alex Pesterev for getting the 80 core system used in our experiments to work. This work was partially supported by Quanta Computer and by NSF awards 0834415 and 0915164.

References

[1] S. Adams. Implementing sets efficiently in a functional language. Technical Report CSTR 92-10, University of Southampton, 1992.

[2] C. Bienia. *Benchmarking Modern Multiprocessors*. PhD thesis, Princeton University, January 2011.

[3] S. Boyd-Wickizer, H. Chen, R. Chen, Y. Mao, F. Kaashoek, R. Morris, A. Pesterev, L. Stein, M. Wu, Y. D. Y. Zhang, and Z. Zhang. Corey: An operating system for many cores. In *Proc. of the 8th OSDI*, December 2008.

[4] S. Boyd-Wickizer, A. Clements, Y. Mao, A. Pesterev, M. F. Kaashoek, R. Morris, and N. Zeldovich. An analysis of Linux scalability to many cores. In *Proc. of the 9th OSDI*, Vancouver, Canada, October 2010.

[5] J. Evans. A scalable concurrent malloc (3) implementation for FreeBSD. In *Proc. of the BSDCan Conference*, Ottawa, Canada, April 2006.

[6] K. Fraser. Practical lock freedom. Technical Report UCAM-CL-TR-579, Cambridge University, 2003.

[7] K. Fraser and T. Harris. Concurrent programming without locks. *ACM Transactions on Computer Systems*, 25(2), May 2007.

[8] M. Herlihy. A methodology for implementing highly concurrent data objects. Technical Report CRL 91/10, Digital Equipment Corporation, October 1991.

[9] P. W. Howard and J. Walpole. Relativistic red-black trees. Technical Report 10-06, Portland State University, Computer Science Department, 2010.

[10] P. L. Lehman and S. B. Yao. Efficient locking for concurrent operations on B-trees. *ACM Transactions on Database Systems*, 6:650–670, December 1981.

[11] Linux Test Project. `http://ltp.sourceforge.net/`.

[12] Y. Mao, R. Morris, and F. Kaashoek. Optimizing MapReduce for multicore architectures. Technical Report MIT-CSAIL-TR-2010-020, MIT CSAIL, May 2010.

[13] P. E. McKenney. *Exploiting Deferred Destruction: An Analysis of Read-Copy-Update Techniques in Operating System Kernels*. PhD thesis, OGI School of Science and Engineering at Oregon Health and Sciences University, 2004. Available: `http://www.rdrop.com/users/paulmck/RCU/RCUdissertation.2004.07.14e1.pdf`.

[14] P. E. McKenney. Sleepable RCU. Available: `http://lwn.net/Articles/202847/` Revised: `http://www.rdrop.com/users/paulmck/RCU/srcu.2007.01.14a.pdf`, October 2006.

[15] P. E. McKenney and J. D. Slingwine. Read-copy update: Using execution history to solve concurrency problems. In *Proc. of the 10th IASTED International Conference on Parallel and Distributed Computing and Systems*, pages 509–518, Las Vegas, NV, October 1998.

[16] P. E. McKenney and J. Walpole. Introducing technology into the Linux kernel: a case study. *SIGOPS Operating Systems Review*, 42(5):4–17, July 2008.

[17] P. E. McKenney, J. Appavoo, A. Kleen, O. Krieger, R. Russell, D. Sarma, and M. Soni. Read-copy update. In *Proc. of the Ottawa Linux Symposium*, pages 338–367, July 2001.

[18] Microsoft Corp. Windows research kernel. `http://www.microsoft.com/resources/sharedsource/windowsacademic/researchkernelkit.mspx`.

[19] J. Nievergelt and E. M. Reingold. Binary search trees of bounded balance. In *Proc. of the 4th STOC*, pages 137–142, Denver, CO, 1972.

[20] W. Pugh. Concurrent maintenance of skip lists. Technical Report CS-TR-2222, Dept. of Computer Science, University of Maryland, College Park, 1990.

[21] QEMU. `http://www.qemu.org/`.

[22] S. Schneider, C. D. Antonopoulos, and D. S. Nikolopoulos. Scalable locality-conscious multithreaded memory allocation. In *Proc. of the 2006 ACM SIGPLAN International Symposium on Memory Management*, Ottawa, Canada, June 2006.

[23] J. Stribling, J. Li, I. G. Councill, M. F. Kaashoek, and R. Morris. Overcite: A distributed, cooperative CiteSeer. In *Proc. of the 3rd NSDI*, San Jose, CA, May 2006.

[24] L. Wang. Windows 7 memory management, November 2009. `http://download.microsoft.com/download/7/E/7/7E7662CF-CBEA-470B-A97E-CE7CE0D98DC2/mmwin7.pptx`.

Applying Transactional Memory to Concurrency Bugs

Haris Volos[1], Andres Jaan Tack[2] *, Michael M. Swift[1], Shan Lu[1]

[1] Computer Sciences Department, University of Wisconsin–Madison
[2] Skype Limited
[1] {hvolos, swift, shanlu}@cs.wisc.edu, [2] andres.jaan.tack@skype.net

Abstract

Multithreaded programs often suffer from synchronization bugs such as atomicity violations and deadlocks. These bugs arise from complicated locking strategies and ad hoc synchronization methods to avoid the use of locks. A survey of the bug databases of major open-source applications shows that concurrency bugs often take multiple fix attempts, and that fixes often introduce yet more concurrency bugs. Transactional memory (TM) enables programmers to declare regions of code atomic without specifying a lock and has the potential to avoid these bugs.

Where most previous studies have focused on using TM to write new programs from scratch, we consider its utility in fixing existing programs with concurrency bugs. We therefore investigate four methods of using TM on three concurrent programs. Overall, we find that 29% of the bugs are not fixable by transactional memory, showing that TM does not address many important types of concurrency bugs. In particular, TM works poorly with extremely long critical sections and with deadlocks involving both condition variables and I/O. Conversely, we find that for 56% of the bugs, transactional memory offers demonstrable value by simplifying the reasoning behind a fix or the effort to implement a fix, and using transactions in the first place would have avoided 71% of the bugs examined. We also find that ad hoc synchronization put in place to avoid the overhead of locking can be greatly simplified with TM, but requires hardware support to perform well.

Categories and Subject Descriptors D.1.3 [*Programming Techniques*]: Concurrent Programming; D.2.5 [*Software Engineering*]: Testing and Debugging

General Terms Languages, Reliability

Keywords Transactional memory, concurrent program, concurrency bug, debugging, atomicity violation, deadlock

1. Introduction

Transactional memory (TM) promises to simplify concurrent programming by reducing the burden on programmers and to improve performance or scalability through increased concurrency [21]. The simplicity benefit can be achieved by writing new programs using transactions [46] or by rewriting existing programs to use transactions [60]. However, this benefit could also be realized by applying transaction memory to problematic code in existing programs without a complete rewrite. This preserves the investment in existing code while potentially simplifying complex synchronization code.

Applying transactional memory to concurrency bugs raises three challenges. First, it focuses the effort on especially difficult problems and thus stresses TM's ability to express synchronization requirements. Second, it forces us to consider *concise* code changes, because we want to minimize the amount of code that must be rewritten throughout the program. Finally, it stresses the *integration* with existing code to avoid rewriting major portions of the program. Fortunately, extensions to TM allowing the use of locks [45, 53], condition variables [17, 22], and select system calls [39, 54] simplify this task by allowing most existing code to be moved into transactions.

We evaluate the utility of TM in complex concurrent programs by applying it as a fix for previously found concurrency bugs in three programs: the Mozilla web browser, the Apache httpd web server, and the MySQL database [30]. We explore four different approaches to using transactional memory in existing concurrent programs. To be as unobtrusive as possible, these four methods tailor the use of TM to existing lock-based synchronization code so they do not necessarily reflect how a programmer would use TM to write new programs. Two simple approaches place all conflicting code in transactions. While useful, we find this sometimes requires widespread code modifications. Two other, more sophisticated approaches compose transactions with locks and leverage the rollback mechanism of transactional memory to preempt locks causing a deadlock.

We find that transactional memory is not useful in 17 of 60 atomicity violations and deadlock bugs. This surprising result arises because many concurrency bugs are not about shared data; rather they concern synchronization, such as condition variables, or I/O, such as file or network access. However, we do find that straightforward uses of TM can fix 40 of the 60 bugs, and sophisticated uses of TM can fix 3 additional bugs and simplify the fixes of 20 of the 40 bugs. We judge that 34 out of the 43 TM-based fixes are simpler and preferable to developers' fixes. These results demonstrate that transactional memory, as proposed, is moderately useful in concurrent programs, but that it does not ameliorate enough predicaments to be a panacea. We also find that ad hoc synchronization, such as ownership flags put in place to avoid the overhead of locking, can be greatly simplified with TM, but requires hardware support to perform well enough.

2. Related Work

As the count of cores in commodity computers rises, researchers have devoted more effort to the problem of writing correct multithreaded code. Our work builds on past work investigating the

* Work done while a student at the University of Wisconsin – Madison

ASPLOS'12, March 3–7, 2012, London, England, UK.

usefulness of transactional memory, integrating transactions into existing code, and fixing concurrency bugs.

Usefulness of TM Our work explores the utility of TM as a useful tool for fixing concurrency bugs. Several recent studies have sought to quantify and explain the benefits of programming with transactions as compared to locks [37, 46]. These studies found that TM is measurably easier than fine-grained locks, and results in fewer bugs, less development time, or better performance. Compared to our work, these studies use TM for relatively simple programs with a small number of different thread types accessing a small number of data structures, and do not require synchronization around I/O. Thus they may not have encountered similarly difficult synchronization problems. Other work has questioned the utility of software TM due to its poor performance [6], despite work showing it can improve performance of existing multithreaded applications [54]. In contrast, our work targets transactional memory at solving complex synchronization problems in existing code rather than exploring the benefits of developing an entire program with transactions. Furthermore, we observe that large programs use many different synchronization mechanisms, while these studies focused on using just a single mechanism (locks or transactions).

Most similar to our work is the Atomic Quake project [60], which rewrote a game engine to use transactions. The authors sought to use transactions everywhere, and redesigned the application to better fit transactions. They found, similar to our results, that conditional synchronization remains a problem for transactions. In contrast to Atomic Quake, we use transactions as one of many synchronization tools, rather than applying it as the dominant synchronization method.

Transactional Memory Mechanisms Our work depends on high-quality transactional memory systems and seeks to apply them to existing code bases. There are many proposed and developed transactional memory mechanisms in hardware [14, 20, 34, 43] and software [12, 15, 16, 19, 21, 48]. IBM has integrated transactional memory into their Blue Gene/Q supercomputer processor [1], AMD has indicated it may implement limited transactional memory systems in hardware [3], and GCC provides extensions for using transactional memory [23]. Thus, transactional memory is reaching a maturity level where it can be used in deployed applications.

Access to non-memory resources is difficult for transactional memory systems. Past work on executing system calls within transactions has shown that system calls occur regularly within lock-based critical sections [4, 51]. Proposed mechanisms to handle system calls include making transactions inevitable [5, 50, 56] or executing them transactionally with library support [54] or with kernel transactions [39]. Our work leverages these mechanisms and shows that supporting system calls within transactions is useful even for the specific task of fixing concurrency bugs.

TM-enabled locks Our work relies on using transactions and locks cooperatively. Due to the difficulty of providing transactional semantics for system calls or I/O and the low performance of software TM systems, prior work such as TxLinux propose locks accelerated by transactions that provide the programmability and low overhead of coarse-grained locks but the concurrency of transactions [44, 45, 52]. In contrast, we seek the programmability of transactions more than their concurrency. However, transactions cannot normally coexist with the locks found in existing code without modifying the implementation of locks [53]. Fortunately, proposed transactional-memory semantics precisely define the interaction of locks and transactions and enable interoperability [2, 11, 49]. In this paper, we leverage the TxLock [53] design, which defers releasing locks until a transaction commits and automatically releases locks on abort.

Concurrency bugs While we apply transactions as a possible solution to concurrency bugs, other research has looked at automated methods to generate locking code [25] or to dynamically avoid concurrency bugs through scheduling [8, 8, 26, 31, 40, 41]. Our work focuses on the utility of transactional memory to express hard synchronization requirements, while those projects focus more specifically on fixing bugs, perhaps temporarily until a developer creates a permanent patch.

3. Applying TM to Concurrency Bugs

The goal of our work is to investigate whether transactional memory's simple interface can address challenging synchronization problems in concurrent programs. To that end, we apply TM to *concurrency bugs*, where developers either left out synchronization statements or coded them incorrectly. We do not attempt to rewrite the whole program using transactional memory for two reasons: the current performance of software TM is too low for some uses, and not all system calls can be handled transactionally. For example, state-of-the art TM systems fall back on a single global lock for difficult I/O operations, and cannot handle two-way communication.

Instead, we look at transactional memory as a tool that can be useful in solving difficult synchronization problems. Thus, our approach is to look for solutions that require a minimum of code changes and allow transactions to co-exist with existing lock-based synchronization code. To that extent, our approach to applying transactional memory to concurrency bugs does not necessarily reflect how a programmer would use transactional memory to write new programs.

3.1 Concurrency bugs

We focus on two classes of concurrency bugs that transactional memory was designed to address. In a *deadlock* (DL) the order of lock operations may lead to circular wait between threads. Deadlocks can also occur with condition variables, for example when waiting with a lock held. TM addresses deadlock by (i) removing the use of multiple locks that enable deadlock, and (ii) automatically aborting one or more waiting threads. In an *atomicity violation* (AV), code is not protected from interleaving with other threads accessing the same shared data. TM addresses atomicity violations by making it simple to declare atomicity without having to select the right lock: TM detects conflicts with all other threads, not just those holding the same locks. TM alone does not address *ordering violations*, which occur when the program requires that events in two threads happen in a certain order but does not enforce the ordering, so we do not consider these bugs.

Writing correctly synchronized code can be challenging: it may require the addition of synchronization code throughout a program when a variable becomes shared. More importantly, it requires *non-local reasoning* to understand how introducing new synchronization code in one location can affect code elsewhere. For example, adding a new lock requires considering whether it can introduce deadlock with all existing locks.

The difficulty in fixing a bug comes from the *conceptual effort* of creating the patch, which is how difficult it is to find a solution, and the *implementation effort*, the amount of code that must be changed, both of which we evaluate with transactional memory. Due to the non-local nature of concurrency bugs, the conceptual effort can be harder than the implementation effort, as it requires finding all the code regions that have contributed to the bug, and making sure that the new fix will not introduce new correctness problems (*e.g.*, no deadlock, no double-acquire of locks). In contrast, the implementation effort is largely mechanical and relates to how many code locations must change. Ideally, transactional memory will prove to have less conceptual effort, because of its simple interface and strong semantics, as well as less implementation effort, because less code needs to be changed.

Indeed, evidence suggests that concurrency bug fixes frequently take a long time to produce and often fail to fix the problem or introduce new bugs as a result of the above challenges. Consider atomicity violations, where the logic of the fix is straightforward: hold a lock while executing critical regions of code. In studying concurrency bug fixes, we have seen that the reality of fixing these bugs is far more complex:

- In Mozilla, programmers used the wrong lock to fix an atomicity violation (Mozilla#18025), which was not discovered until diagnosing another atomicity violation four years later (Mozilla#133773).
- In an Apache bug, although the buggy code involved only one function, developers had to make code changes in another two places to declare new lock variables and initialize these locks (Apache#25520).
- Performance concerns further complicate the fixing process in a MySQL bug: programmers implemented their own conflict checking, abort, rollback, and re-execution mechanisms to fix an atomicity violation bug without using locks (MySQL#16582).

Deadlock bugs lead to similar problems. Their fixes frequently require re-ordering, adding and removing synchronization code.

- In several cases, fixing one deadlock bug introduced another deadlock bug, taking months or even a year to completely fix the problem (Mozilla#54743,#79054, #60303,#90994).
- In a Mozilla deadlock bug, the developers were so frustrated that they intentionally introduced a data-race bug in order to fix the original deadlock bug (Mozilla#123930).

These experiences demonstrate that writing correctly synchronized concurrent code is hard, and easier coding techniques would be welcomed.

3.2 Transactional Memory

Transactional memory allows a programmer to declare a block of code as an *atomic region* with the `atomic` keyword, and the TM system ensures that each atomic region executes to completion or not at all (atomicity), and that intermediate states of memory are not visible to other atomic regions (isolation). This simple interface aims to ease concurrent programming as compared to alternatives by helping the programmer to avoid correctness pitfalls.

A speculation-based implementation of atomic regions allows multiple regions to execute concurrently through memory transactions. [1] The implementation must detect and resolve conflicts between concurrent atomic regions by aborting and re-executing one of the transactions involved.

Both software and hardware implementations have been proposed. Software TM implementations instrument code to record the locations read and written and detect conflicts either at commit or while the transaction executes. As a result, software TM implementations may slow down critical sections by 3-5x [12]. Proposed hardware TM implementations, in contrast, perform these operations in hardware with less slowdown to critical-section code [20, 34]. However, feasible hardware TM implementations often bound the number of distinct memory locations that can be accessed within a transaction. Thus, they are best paired with a software TM for fallback when transactions exceed hardware limits [10, 13, 29].

[1] In this paper, we use the term *atomic region* to refer to the language level construct and the term *memory transaction* to refer to the implementation of an atomic region with a speculation-based transactional memory system.

4. Bug-Fix Methodology

We develop a set of different uses of transactional memory to solve hard concurrency problems. We present our mechanisms for fixing concurrency bugs as a set of recipes: the *ingredients* are the underlying mechanisms provided by transactional memory, while *recipes* describe how to combine the mechanisms to fix specific classes of bugs.

4.1 Transactional Memory Ingredients

Our fix recipes rely on four mechanisms, each of which we describe below. We describe possible implementations below, and defer discussion of specific mechanisms used in experiments to Section 5.1. Not all proposals for transactional memory support all these mechanisms, and this study demonstrates the added value of such support.

Atomic regions allow a programmer to declare a region of code `atomic`, and the underlying implementation ensures that it executes atomically in isolation. Thus, other atomic regions cannot view updates performed by the code region until it has executed entirely and this region cannot see changes made by other regions during its own execution. Atomic regions may be implemented through either memory transactions or locks. All transactional memory systems support atomic regions, although they may be limited in size and complexity for some hardware proposals, for example to the size of the write buffer, cache or a fixed number of cache lines [9, 42]. Lock implementations have unlimited size, and use either a global lock or perform lock inference, which (semi-)automatically assigns distinct fine-grain locks to atomic regions [7, 18, 33]. Locks remove the need for rollback and thus can easily support I/O operations.

Explicit rollback leverages the ability of transactional memory implementations to rollback partially executed transactions. It can be used for retry-style synchronization [22], akin to condition variables: a thread aborts the current transaction and suspends until a variable the transaction read has changed, at which point the thread retries the transaction. This allows a thread to wait until a condition is satisfied as a result of another thread's actions. Not all TM mechanisms support rollback, as atomic regions implemented with locks cannot roll back.

In addition to these two basic mechanisms, which have been explored in the past, we also identify two additional mechanisms that use transactions and locks cooperatively to simplify synchronization.

Preemptible resources can safely be acquired inside a memory transaction and automatically released if the transaction aborts. With this mechanism, the no-preemption requirement for deadlock can be removed if one thread is in a transaction and aborts and releases contested resources. Several proposed designs allow standard locks to be acquired and preempted within a transaction [27, 45, 53]. Reversible I/O operations extend the set of operations that can take place within a transaction to include system calls. Transactional system interfaces such as TxOS [39] or xCalls [54] may be used to enable reversible I/O. Unfortunately, some forms of I/O, such as two-way communication, cannot be made reversible with these techniques.

Atomic/lock serialization properly synchronizes accesses protected under an atomic region with accesses protected under a lock so that code protected using locks cannot see intermediate state of an atomic section that has not yet completed, and vice-versa. The *cxspinlock* construct from TxLinux [45] and speculative lock elision using transactions [38, 42, 47] provide this by beginning transactions in all critical sections. Another possible implementation is to grab a global reader/writer lock in shared mode when acquiring a lock, and exclusively when executing a transaction.

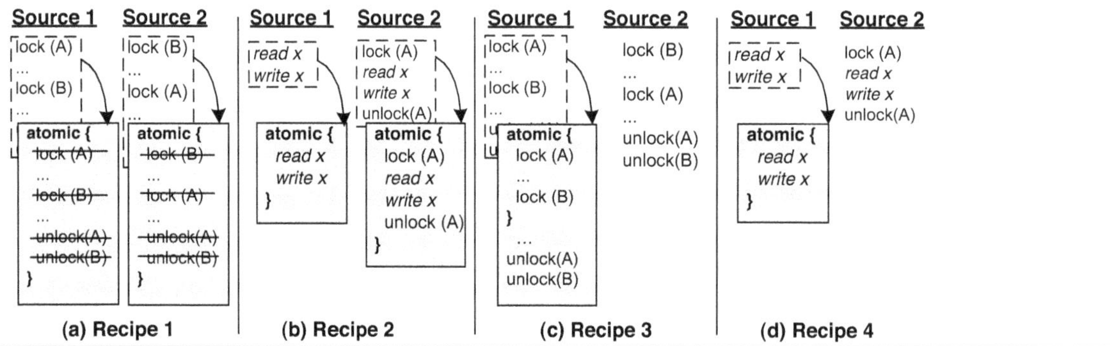

Figure 1. Example uses of our fix recipes.

This construct ensures that code synchronized with transactions correctly interoperates with code using locks, and therefore allows any atomicity violation to be fixed by placing the relevant code in a transaction, whether or not other code uses locks for atomicity. We stress that we evaluate this mechanism to see whether it is useful, not because it is efficient in software.

4.2 Recipes

We use two *straightforward* fix methods (recipes 1 and 2) that rely primarily on atomic regions and have broad applicability. In addition, we describe two *sophisticated* methods (recipes 3 and 4) that use additional ingredients beyond atomic regions, have limited applicability but require less effort to apply.

4.3 Simple Approaches

Recipe 1: Replacement of Deadlock-prone Locks

Remove all locks contributing to a deadlock and insert atomic regions in their places. Similarly to lock coarsening, this fixes deadlock bugs by preventing circular wait.

This approach can solve a large set of deadlocks and simplify complex locking protocols. When deadlock would occur, the transactional memory system either prevents deadlock by serializing the threads involved (similar to lock coarsening), or automatically aborts one or more transactions and allows the others to make progress. Unlike lock coarsening, a transactional solution preserves the concurrency of fine-grained locking if independent atomic regions can execute concurrently. However, the overhead of software TM may degrade performance unacceptably if transactions occur in critical-path code. In addition, this approach cannot solve deadlocks involving non-lock resources (*e.g.*, conditional variables, pipes), because transactions only protect concurrent access to memory.

Conceptually, replacing deadlock-prone locks with transactions is simple because the identity of the locks is available when a deadlock occurs. Compared to fixing the locks, the developer does not need to reason about how to change the order in which locks are acquired or whether a lock can be removed. In addition, a developer needs not reason about which code path leads to locks being acquired out of order. This fix is largely mechanical, but may be time-consuming to apply to existing code if the locks protecting data are acquired in many places.

Recipe 2: Wrap All

Wrap all conflicting code regions in atomic regions, effectively fixing atomicity violation bugs.

Atomicity violations can be fixed by placing all conflicting code regions (regions that access shared data where at least one region performs a write) in atomic regions. This ensures that the memory accesses of those regions are protected under a common synchronization mechanism. For code with completely missing synchronization all synchronization is done with transactions. When some code already uses locks, this fix can be applied by either replacing existing locks with transactions, or acquiring those locks within transactions (using a transaction-safe lock such as TxLocks [53] or cxspinlocks [45]).

Compared to locks, fixing atomicity violations with atomic regions has low conceptual effort: a programmer introduces atomic regions by placing begin/end transaction markers around a portion of code, without worrying about lock granularity for concurrency and whether the fix introduces new deadlocks. In contrast, a programmer relying on locks to solve an atomicity bug must identify the right lock to use. If such lock does not exist, the programmer must introduce a new lock, and reason where the new lock falls into the lock hierarchy to avoid deadlocks with existing locks

The effort to wrap code in atomic regions is largely mechanical, but requires identifying all code that accesses the protected data. If a lock exists and is known, the effort to use transactions is similar to using existing locks. However, if a lock does not exist, using TM is simpler, because a programmer introducing a new lock to fix the bug has to add code to manage the new lock.

4.4 Sophisticated Approaches

The preceding approaches relied on the normal application of transactional memory: place all access to a subset of shared data within transactions to reap the benefits. However, we have identified two further methods that use TM's mechanisms in different ways.

Recipe 3:(Asymmetric) Deadlock Preemption

Make at least one thread (dynamic path) involved in the deadlock preemptible by wrapping the corresponding static code regions in a single abortable atomic region (memory transaction).

This recipe fixes deadlock bugs by removing the *non-preemption* requirement for deadlock. At least one of the threads involved in the deadlock must begin a transaction before acquiring the locks involved with the deadlock. When deadlock occurs, the transaction aborts, and releases any locks it acquired before retrying. This allows at least one thread to proceed. Note that not all threads need to execute transactions: as long as one thread involved with the deadlock can abort, it can break the circular wait for all threads. Thus, this solution can be efficient, because most threads can execute unchanged with locks. Preferably, the preemptible thread should be low priority or infrequently run to minimize the performance impact of executing its critical sections within a transaction.

For this fix to work, all resources acquired transactionally must be revocable: locks must be released on abort, and I/O operations must be undone. It also requires a deadlock detector to determine when to abort the transaction. Furthermore, this recipe is unique in that transactions are used only for rollback and not isolation; locks still provide mutual exclusion between threads.

Deadlock preemption can cause livelock if the preempted thread restarts and acquires locks before the other threads finish. Exponential backoff before retry, already used for contention management in TM systems, can prevent this livelock. However, livelock can also occur if useful work performed by a transaction before the deadlock is needed to make progress, as in the work performed in a monitor before waiting on a condition variable. Thus, this recipe is not useful in such cases.

Like Recipe 1, this recipe requires identifying a deadlocked thread. Unlike Recipe 1, it also requires ensuring that all resources acquired in a transaction are revocable, making it slightly more difficult to reason about than Recipe 1, which can use inevitability mechanisms to handle complex I/O. However, this fix recipe is simple to implement, as it keeps existing locks in place and wraps them in a transaction.

Recipe 4: Wrap Unprotected

Wrap the code region intended to be executed atomically in an atomic section that is serialized with all other lock critical sections.

Recipe 2 requires a developer to wrap *all* conflicting code regions in atomic regions, even if they already use locks. This in effect duplicates any existing effort put into using locks. In contrast, this recipe approach modifies only the buggy code regions that actually contribute to the atomicity violation, and leaves unmodified the code that correctly uses locks. This method is useful for *asymmetric atomicity violations*: when most code regions properly use the intended locking discipline to correctly express their atomicity objective but some do not. While atomic regions are conceptually serialized with all other lock critical section in this recipe, atomic and lock critical sections may execute concurrently if a scalable implementation of atomic/lock serialization is available. As suggested earlier, such an implementation is possible on TM systems that support transactionally executing critical sections such as TxLinux [45] and speculative lock elision using transactions [38,42,47].

This approach is conceptually simpler to apply than either Recipe 2 (wrap all accesses to the shared data in transactions) or to using locks, as it requires the developer to identify only the code regions that do not correctly express their atomicity objective. Furthermore, this approach has the same implementation effort as using an existing lock, assuming it is known. Compared to Recipe 2 it effectively saves the developer from distributed code changes.

5. Effectiveness of TM on Concurrency Bugs

In this section, we evaluate our bug-fix methods in the context of previously found and fixed bugs in Mozilla, Apache httpd, and MySQL [30]. The existence of fixes allows us to compare a TM solution against the developer solution, and the log of changes allows us to gauge the complexity of the fix, such as whether it took multiple tries.

Our study has three main goals. First, we want to determine whether TM has the expressive power to solve a synchronization bug (*Can TM fix the bug?*). Second, we want to find whether TM offers value to a developer when compared against locks (*Can TM fix the bug simply?*). We answer these two questions first. Finally, we give a set of examples of showing how TM can address synchronization problems and evaluate whether the performance of the fix using TM is satisfactory (*Can TM fix the bug efficiently?*).

5.1 Recipe Ingredients: Implementation

Section 4.1 presented a high-level description of the basic mechanisms required by the fixes. We now describe the specific implementation of each mechanism used in our study. We use Intel's software transactional memory (STM) compiler and runtime framework as our main TM platform [24], as it runs on real hardware, can compile the code in many open-source projects, and automatically instruments the code placed in atomic regions with calls to the STM runtime. This greatly reduces the implementation effort needed to use transactions.

Atomic Regions. The Intel STM uses memory transactions to execute atomic regions but it reverts to a global lock [5, 50, 56], when there are calls to unsafe operations that have visible side-effects before the transaction commits, such as un-instrumented legacy code, synchronization and I/O [36]. Recent work on defining TM semantics [2, 49] captures this dual notion of execution by differentiating between two types of atomic regions: atomic transactions and relaxed transactions. Atomic transactions can only be used when there are no unsafe operations, and they appear to execute atomically in a data-race-free program. In contrast, relaxed transactions are allowed to contain unsafe operations, in which case they may appear to interleave with non-transactional operations from other threads. The implication to our recipes is that memory transactions in the form of atomic transactions may only be used when unsafe operations are replaced with their transactionally safe equivalent ones as we describe in the *preemptible resources* section below.

Explicit Rollback. The Intel STM provides an `abort` statement, which can be used to explicitly roll back a transaction. We use this statement to provide a limited version of the `retry` mechanism, by aborting and immediately retrying a deadlocking transaction. The use of this mechanism precludes the use of atomic regions that do not utilize speculation and cannot roll back. In light of the work on TM semantics, this mechanism is only safe with atomic transactions as implementations of relaxed transactions may not always utilize speculation.

Preemtible Resources. We implement two classes of preemptible resources: revocable locks and reversible I/O. We implement revocable locks with TxLocks [53]. When acquired within a transaction, these locks are held until the transaction commits and released if the transaction aborts. In addition, they detect deadlock both among locks and between locks and transactions, and will abort the transaction if deadlock occurs. We enable reversible I/O via xCalls [54]. xCalls provide a library-based implementation of transactional semantics for common system calls. The xCall library defers until commit time those system calls that can be delayed. When that is not possible, system calls are executed as part of the transaction and their side effects are reversed on abort atomically with respect to all other transactions. xCalls reverts to inevitable transactions for system calls that are not reversible and cannot be deferred. Such calls produce side effects and either have ambiguous/variable semantics (*e.g.*, `ioctl`) or require two-way communication with a non-transactional device or service. Finally, since xCalls is a library-based approach, it enables transactional semantics only for threads running in the same process. In consideration of TM semantics, preemptible resources extend the use of atomic transactions into code that otherwise would have to rely on relaxed transactions to perform unsafe operations, namely acquire locks or do I/O.

Atomic/lock Serialization. We augment both the STM's atomic regions and POSIX mutex locks with a special global reader/writer lock that provides mutual exclusion between atomic regions and lock-based critical sections. Mutex locks acquire the global lock in shared mode, while atomic regions acquire it exclusively. We note this approach prevents transactions from having any concurrency and slows down other uses of locks. This limitation however is an artifact of this implementation. As we suggested earlier in section 4.1, other more scalable approaches such as *cxspinlock* may be used.

Bug	App	All	Transactional Memory Fixes				
			Total	R1	R2	R3	R4
DL	Mozilla	13	9	8(2)	-	7(1)	-
	Apache	4	2	1(1)	-	1(1)	-
	MySQL	5	1	0	-	1(1)	-
AV	Mozilla	25	20	-	20(12)	-	8(0)
	Apache	7	5	-	5(3)	-	2(0)
	MySQL	6	6	-	6(2)	-	4(0)
	Total	60	43	9(2)	31(17)	9(3)	14(0)

Table 1. Applications and the number of concurrency bugs in each category together with a breakdown of how many bugs each recipe can help fix.

5.2 Methods

To evaluate whether TM *can* fix a bug and can *simply* fix a bug, we obtained the buggy source code from application repositories and used our recipes to apply transactions to fix the bug. We used a set of found and fixed concurrency bugs in Mozilla, Apache httpd, and MySQL [30], excluding order-violation bugs because TM does not fit naturally to such bugs. For a subset of the bugs, we implemented and tested a fix. For the remainder, which had no reproduction scenario, we examined the code, determined what library or function calls were made within the transaction and sketched how to apply transactions.

For each TM fix we implement, we ensure the bug is fixed by running either tests cases provided with the bug report or ones we wrote. Fixing a bug raises the risk of introducing a new bug. We ensure the correctness of our fixes by comparing them against the existing developer fixes and ensure that they provide the same atomicity properties. Furthermore, we ensure our changes do not break any regression tests. While this approach to correctness does not represent a formal proof, it provides us a degree of confidence comparable to the developers'.

To evaluate whether TM fixes a bug simply, we qualitatively compare our fix against the developers' final fix, in which the bug is actually resolved. We note that, in many places, developers chose to fix bugs without the use of locks or by removing portions of the code. As a result, our evaluation is not a comparison of using locks and transactions to fix a bug but rather of comparing what application developers currently do against transactions. To be as objective as possible, we rate the difficulty of each TM and developers' fix by considering the implementation and conceptual effort of the fix, and then pick the fix with the lowest difficulty. In general, logic or design changes are rated as hard; changes that require checking whether resources can be safely preempted or dropped are rated as medium or hard; changes that require adding a new lock in the lock hierarchy are rated as medium; and changes that require large scale code changes such as adding multiple atomic blocks are rated as medium or hard.

To evaluate whether TM *efficiently* fixes the bugs, we performed several case study experiments where we compare the performance of representative TM fixes to the performance of the developers' fixes using Intel's STM [24]. We ran tests on an Intel Core 2 2.5GHz quad-core based machine running CentOS Linux. We note that this is not the best performing transactional memory system, particularly given some of caveats noted above, so performance numbers should be treated as a lower bound.

5.3 Effectiveness

In this section, we discuss our findings of whether transactional memory is useful as a concurrency-bug fixing mechanism. We summarize our findings in Table 1: for each application and bug type, it lists the number of bugs that each recipe can fix. Each number in parentheses indicates how many bugs can be fixed only using the specific recipe.

App	Difficulty	Dev' fixes		Transactional Memory fixes			
		DL	AV	R1	R2	R3	R4
Mozilla	Easy	1	5	2	4	4	6
	Medium	1	6	4	13	2	2
	Hard	7	9	2	3	1	0
Apache	Easy	0	1	1	3	0	2
	Medium	0	2	0	1	0	0
	Hard	2	2	0	1	1	0
MySQL	Easy	0	1	0	2	0	4
	Medium	0	3	0	4	1	0
	Hard	1	2	0	0	0	0

Table 2. Characterization of developers' and TM fixes in terms of easy, medium, and hard difficulty. We characterize only fixes solved by both developers and TM.

Bug type	Application	Downcalls			
		CV	I/O	LongAction	Other
Deadlock	Mozilla	3	2	3	3
	Apache	1	0	0	0
	MySQL	0	0	0	0
Atomicity	Mozilla	3	3	3	0
	Apache	0	2	0	0
	MySQL	0	1	1	0
	Total	7	8	7	3

Table 3. Characterization of our TM fixes based on the number and type of function calls inside atomic blocks (*downcalls*).

Overall, we found that the TM can fix 43 out of the 60 bugs (71 percent) we investigated. As we could not reproduce all the bugs, we implemented and thoroughly tested 18 of the 43 fixes: 7 deadlock and 11 atomicity violation fixes. The *straightforward* recipes (Recipes 1 and 2) are sufficient to tackle 40 of the 43 bugs. The *sophisticated* recipes can fix 3 more bugs: Recipe 3 (deadlock preemption) can repair three deadlock bugs involving condition variables operations that could not be fixed using Recipe 1 (replace deadlock-prone locks). These results demonstrate that straightforward TM has the expressive power to capture the synchronization requirements regarding locks and the flexibility to execute all the code necessary for many concurrency bugs. Furthermore, extensions for failure atomicity (such as rolling back on failure) provide an easy "out" from complex deadlocks involving locks and condition variables. We describe one of these bugs in more detail in Section 5.4.

We judge that 34 out of the 43 TM-based fixes are simpler and preferable to developers' fixes. Table 2 lists the number of easy, medium, and hard fixes for each application based on the criteria of Section 5.2. In the next two sections, we further discuss the relative difficulty of our and the developer' fixes.

Many TM systems have limited support for *downcalls*, calls to non-transactional code in system services or other modules. Table 3 lists how many fixes have atomic blocks making direct or indirect calls to: condition variables (*CV*), I/O, long actions such as garbage collection (*LongAction*), and other library/module functions. Five fixes (all in Mozilla) required support for condition variables in transactions [17], two required a `retry`, eight required I/O [54], and seven required very long transactions encompassing millions of instructions. Thus, we found that incorporating memory transactions into a concurrent program requires supporting many actions beyond memory access within a transaction, which is similar to the experience of the AtomicQuake developers [60].

5.3.1 Deadlock Bugs

As shown in Table 1, TM can be used to fix 12 of the 22 deadlock (DL) bugs. We further break down the 12 bugs where TM can be used to evaluate whether a TM fix is simpler than the fix chosen by the application developers. Overall, we judge that a TM-based fix is simpler than the developers' for 10 deadlock bugs.

In analyzing the results, we found it useful to classify bugs by the state they access and the location of the code. *Preemptible* bugs occur when there are no changes to unrelated shared state while holding the deadlocking locks; otherwise the bug is *non-preemptible* because state unrelated to the locks has changed and cannot be reverted. For example, calls to non-transactional functions or system calls are non-preemptible when executed with inevitable transactions. Similarly, code that acquires a lock and then returns to a caller in a different module is not preemptible, as it would require executing the caller's code within a transaction. *Single-module* deadlock bugs involved locks defined in a single module, while *multi-module* bugs involve locks from more than one module.

When TM does not work Most importantly, transactional memory in its pure atomic-region form (Recipe 1) cannot help deadlocks caused by condition-variable wait operations. Such deadlocks can only be approached using a combination of preemption and `retry` as described in Recipe 3. However, preemption and `retry` cannot help with deadlocks involving two-way communication such as in nested monitor lockouts [28]. In such a case, one thread holds a lock, and waits for a signal from a second thread that can only be sent after acquiring the lock held by the first thread. Such deadlocks may be only approached through design changes [28, 57]. This occurred for example in Mozilla#65146.

We also found deadlocks that span multiple modules were difficult to fix with TM, because of the large-scale changes required to modify multiple modules. Furthermore, in one case deadlock involved a third-party plugin where it was impossible to apply TM. As a result, we were not able to use TM to fix any bugs that spanned non-preemptible code in multiple modules, which represent 5 deadlock bugs. Nevertheless, it is interesting to note that in nearly all cases the developer's fix was to release a lock before continuing down the deadlocked path, which presents a dangerous decision often accompanied with significant conceptual effort to determine the correctness.

Other deadlocks were design bugs, for example when one thread waits for a signal from a component that has already been destroyed (Mozilla#27486). Thus, for problems that do not relate to circular wait of locks, or locks with a single condition variable, transactional memory provides little value. In addition, transactional memory cannot help solve deadlocks that arise through fundamental design errors rather than the mechanisms for enforcing mutual exclusion.

When TM works well Simple memory-only transactions fixed 9 of the 12 deadlock bugs fixed. These 9 all involved acquiring pairs of locks out of order. Applying Recipe 1 addressed this by removing the possibility of deadlock. We found bugs involving non-preemptible code (*e.g.*, code that can only execute as an inevitable transaction) can only be fixed by replacing deadlock-prone locks with transactions, because Recipe 3 relies on the ability to roll back at least one thread.

We rate these fixes as easy if they required few code changes and otherwise as medium or hard depending on the code changes required. In one case described below (Section 5.4.1), we replaced code that held locks for an extended period with code that instead executes a series of short transactions, with the non-preemptible code occurring between transactions. Thus, the non-preemptible lock that was held for a long period was changed to shorter transactions that could abort to prevent deadlock. This fix we rated as hard.

In contrast, the developers' fix in all cases except one was to remove the acquisition of one of the locks held to break deadlock. Switching the acquisition order was not possible in many cases as it would require drastic changes in the design of the lock hierarchy. Giving up a lock is a conceptually challenging task as it requires deep understanding of the code to reason about the safety of this action so we judge such fixes as hard. In one case, the developer's fix was as simple as switching the acquisition order of locks as the locks were acquired locally in a single function. We judge this fix as easy and favor it compared to TM that requires replacing locks with transactions.

The remaining 3 bugs required using revocable locks with Recipe 3 to acquire locks within a transaction. Two of those bugs involve condition variable operations that could not be fixed using transactional condition variables, which commit the transaction before waiting, but could be fixed via a `retry`, which aborts. We rate these fixes as hard as they require reasoning that is safe to replace the condition variable with a `retry`. In addition, we found that Recipe 3 can reduce the implementation effort to fix 6 of the 9 bugs fixed using Recipe 1 by localizing fixes to the bug sites instead of modifying all uses of the deadlocking locks.

Overall, we favor 2 developers' fixes as they are as easy as TM or easier, and favor 10 TM fixes as conceptual and implementation effort is less than with the developer's fix. The 2 developers' fixes include the one easy fix described above, and another of medium difficulty, which requires a simple design change.

5.3.2 Atomicity-Violation Bugs

As shown in Table 1, TM can be used to fix 31 of 38 atomicity-violation (AV) bugs. Overall, we judge that a TM-based fix is simpler than the developers' for 24 bugs.

When TM does not work There were 7 atomicity bugs that could not be fixed with transactions for a variety of reasons. One situation occurs when the application must atomically issue a long-latency operation and process a callback event when the operation completes. For example, Mozilla holds a lock while loading a URL and invokes a callback once the URL is fetched (bug#19421), which can take an arbitrarily long time. Contention for the lock is not high so its use is acceptable. However, a memory transaction is global to the process, particularly if it uses inevitability mechanisms that acquire a global lock. Therefore, using transactions around a long-latency operation would prevent all other transactions from making progress. Having support to issue asynchronous I/O and execute a callback upon I/O completion within a transaction would help fixing this problem.

In other cases, the bugs were not simply atomicity violations, but required additional semantics: in Mozilla, one code section required both atomicity and that only one thread executed the code (exactly-once semantics). This requirement is beyond TM's guarantees.

Finally, there were several atomicity violations regarding I/O: lost notifications waiting for I/O to arrive (Mozilla#72965) and races between two processes reading from the same pipe (Apache #7617). Like the last two problems, these problems arise not from the atomicity of memory operations but from the atomicity of I/O operations across multiple processes (the kernel and a process, or two separate processes), which current TM systems do not address.

When TM works well Atomicity violations caused by code with completely missing synchronization are the best-case scenario for TM. Such bugs are fixed using Recipe 2. In our study, this type of violation included 22 out of the 38 atomicity-violation bugs, 17 of which could be fixed using Recipe 2. In 12 of the 17 fixes, bugs could be fixed with a single atomic block. We judge 9 of the 12 as easy fixes, while we judge the remaining 3 fixes as medium difficulty because we had to reason that wrapping downcalls inside the atomic block was safe.

Bug ID	Cause	Characteristics	Fix	Perf.	Lines of Code	
					Dev	TM
Mozilla-I	DL	Involves locks only	1	21%	23	1039
			3	85%	23	16
Apache-I	DL	Involves lock and wait	3	78%	32	14
Apache-II	AV	Complete missing synchronization	2	96.5%	20	5
MySQL-I	AV	Partial missing synchronization	4	50%	103	4

Table 4. Bugs and corresponding fix recipes applied for demonstration purposes. Performance is relative to that of developer's fix. Lines of code (LOC) includes both lines added and lines modified.

In 3 of these 12 cases, the developers' fix was to wrap actions inside a critical section by adding a new lock, which we judge as medium difficulty because it requires reasoning that the new lock does not introduce a deadlock. The remaining 9 developer's fixes require profound understanding of the application to develop a specialized local fix, such as switching the order of statements in the source code [30]. We judge 2 of them as easy, though, because the fix is replacing a global variable with a local one, while we judge the rest as hard. As an example of a hard case, the developer implemented a custom optimistic concurrency protocol by copying shared data locally, updating the copy, and then updating the shared data atomically with a single store instruction. This is essentially a form of optimistic concurrency control that suits TM well. The remaining 5 of the 17 fixes required us to find all the places where synchronization is missing and place multiple atomic blocks. We judge these fixes as medium. We find though that using TM to fix these is a bit simpler than the developer fixes, again because a developer does not have an already existing synchronization mechanism to exploit.

The remaining 16 of the 38 atomicity violations include asymmetric atomicity-violation bugs, where most accesses to shared data use the correct lock but some do not. Of these, 14 could be fixed either using Recipe 2 or Recipe 4. Such bugs though are easier to fix by wrapping the code region intended to be executed atomically in an atomic section that is serialized to any other lock-based critical section (Recipe 4), because this recipe requires fewer changes compared to Recipe 2. Developers commonly fix such bugs by acquiring an existing lock either because they forgot to use it before or they used the wrong one. In 5 cases the fix was as easy as extending the coverage of an existing lock critical section without wrapping calls to functions that may be deadlock prone. In these cases the developer's fix is clearly simpler than a TM fix that replaces existing locks with transactions. Even when the correct lock is hard to identify, using TM is no simpler because the developer must still identify all places where the data are accessed. Nevertheless, Recipe 4 significantly simplifies the fix, making TM competitive with the developer's fix.

Overall, we favor 7 developer's fixes as they are as easy as TM or easier, and favor 24 TM fixes as the conceptual and implementation effort is less than with the developer's fix.

5.4 Demonstrating Applicability

To further clarify the application of transactional memory to concurrency bugs and to evaluate its performance, we demonstrate its application to a subset of the bugs we studied. We selected this subset to cover the spectrum of the bugs targeted by our fix recipes. For each bug, we give a description of the bug, present both the developer's and TM fix, and finally compare the two fixes. Table 4 summarizes the bugs we used.

```
1  js_SetProtoOrParent (...)
2  {
3    LOCK (rt->setSlotLock);
4    obj2 = pobj;
5    while (obj2) {
6      if (obj2 == obj) {
7        ...
8      }
9      LOCK_SCOPE (obj2);
10     next_obj2 = OBJ_GET_PROTO(obj2);
11     UNLOCK_SCOPE (obj2);
12     obj2 = next_obj2;
13   }
14   /* Proceed with setting */
15   ...
16   UNLOCK (rt->setSlotLock);
17 }
```

(a) Buggy code

```
1  js_SetProtoOrParent (...)
2  {
3    atomic {
4      obj2 = pobj;
5      while (obj2) {
6        if (obj2 == obj) {
7          ...
8        }
9        atomic {
10         next_obj2 =
11           OBJ_GET_PROTO(obj2);
12       }
13       obj2 = next_obj2;
14     }
15     /* Proceed with setting */
16     ...
17   }
   }
```

(b) Fixed with TM

Figure 2. A deadlock code sample from Mozilla (SpiderMonkey: jsobj.c) modified for legibility.

5.4.1 Case Study 1: *Mozilla-I: Deadlock*

Figure 2 illustrates a deadlock bug found in SpiderMonkey, Mozilla's JavaScript engine, that involves locks only. SpiderMonkey uses an ownership-based mechanism to synchronize accesses to an object by multiple threads. Under this mechanism, objects are protected by a "scope lock" and an owner field. If a thread owns an object, it can access the object with a simple test of the owner field and without acquiring any locks. If a thread accesses objects owned by another thread, then SpiderMonkey follows a complex revocation protocol to switch the object from using the owner field to using the scope lock. Switching to a scope lock is a blocking operation because the owning thread could be actively accessing the object. The motivation behind this complex synchronization mechanism, is that most objects are only ever locked by a single thread [35].

The deadlock bug occurs when two threads try to lock the same set of objects in different orders. Suppose a first thread executing the function in Figure 2(a) owns `setSlotLock` and needs to lock an object's scope in line 9. But that scope is exclusively owned by a second thread, which is blocked behind `setSlotLock`. The first thread cannot claim the scope from thread 2 so the threads deadlock.

Developer fix SpiderMonkey developers solved this bug by forcing threads to drop ownership of objects before blocking. This required the addition of a new condition variable and small changes in three files. This fix adds overhead to drop and reacquire ownership, yet was adopted because it reliably prevents the deadlock. We judge this fix as hard, as the developers had to reason that dropping ownership was safe and would not violate atomicity.

TM fixes As this deadlock involves locks only, we may fix it using either Recipe 1 or Recipe 3 if locks can be made revocable. When using Recipe 1, we fix this bug by replacing the deadlock-prone locks with atomic sections as shown in Figure 2(b), deprecating the notion of ownership, and thus eliminating the complex revocation protocol. As there is no longer the notion of long-lived ownership, atomic sections, which synchronize access to objects, are shorter. While this fix is conceptually straightforward to reason about, it has a moderate implementation complexity as it requires modifications across 15 files to replace locks with atomics. However, as we demonstrate below it requires hardware support to perform well. We judge this fix as hard, similarly to the developers' fix.

When using Recipe 3, we fix this bug by making the locks involved in the deadlock revocable. We first interpose all calls to `lock/unlock` and `lock_scope/unlock_scope` with calls to the lock/unlock routines of our revocable lock implementation. We then fix the deadlock bug by wrapping the single deadlocking site inside a transaction. The deadlock-prone code executes within a

```
worker_thread(...)
{
  ...
  LOCK (timeout);
  ...
  UNLOCK (timeout);
  ...
  LOCK (idlers)
  ...
  SIGNAL (wait_for_idlers)
  ...
  UNLOCK (idlers)
}
```

```
listener_thread (...)
{
  ...
  LOCK (timeout);
  ...
  LOCK (idlers);
  ...
  COND_WAIT (wait_for_idler,
             idlers)
  UNLOCK (idlers)
  ...
  UNLOCK (timeout)
}
```

(a) Buggy code

```
listener_thread (...)
{
  ...
  atomic {
    LOCK (timeout);
    ...
    LOCK (idlers);
    ...
    if (!COND_TRY_WAIT(...))
      retry;
    UNLOCK (idlers)
  }
  ...
  UNLOCK (timeout)
}
```

(b) Fixed with TM

Figure 3. A deadlock code sample from Apache (httpd-2.2.0: event.c, fdqueue.c), modified for legibility.

transaction and acquires locks revocably; if the transaction cannot acquire a lock it aborts and retries, thus preventing any deadlock. We judge this fix as medium difficulty, as we had to reason about the safety of preemption.

Comparison While the first fix based on Recipe 1 has a moderate implementation complexity, it substantially simplifies the locking protocol. This results in more maintainable code and additionally has the advantage that it *solves another **four** reported deadlock bugs as a side effect* of removing scope locks, which overall took the developers a year to fix. So while hard to implement, we favor it compared to the developers' fix. In comparison, the second fix based on Recipe 3 requires far fewer code changes: only to interpose calls to lock/unlock routines (which could be done automatically by redefining macros) and the deadlocking code. However, it requires some conceptual effort to determine that is safe to revoke any resources used while executing in the transaction. Furthermore, this approach only fixes one bug, while the first fix fixed many other deadlock bugs found later by the developers.

We measured the performance of our fixes and compared it to the performance of the developers' fix using the SunSpider JavaScript benchmark [55]. We run tests in four threads running the same SunSpider script. Even if scripts do not share data, we are still able to exercise the multithreaded code path because all threads run within the same runtime. The first fix performs 79% worse than the developers' fix. This occurs because the code is on the critical path, as evidenced by the effort put in by developers to avoid acquiring a lock. The second fix improves performance significantly as it performs only 15% slower than the developer's fix. This performance improvement arises because critical path code can execute without transactions or atomic operations. As there is still non-critical path code that executes transactionally the workload experiences some drop in performance. These results show that avoiding synchronization is important and that asymmetric deadlock preemption can provide the benefit of transactions without hurting performance too much.

To gauge the benefit of hardware support for TM, we ran the code on the proposed hardware TM platform LogTM-SE [2] [59]. The performance of the first fix increases to 99.3% of the developer's fix. Thus, the performance of hardware TM is good enough that transactions can take the place of ad hoc locking protocols [58], such as SpiderMonkey's ownership protocol, and thereby greatly simplifies code.

5.4.2 Case Study 2: *Apache-I: Deadlock between lock and wait*

Figure 3(a) depicts a deadlock bug between lock and wait operations. This is a section of code taken from Apache in which the listener thread holds the `timeout` mutex protecting the timed-out sockets list while waiting for an idle worker thread. The worker thread block waits for the timeout mutex before signaling to the listener thread its availability, thus leading to a deadlock. The listener holds this mutex while waiting to ensure that it atomically removes a timed-out socket from the list and hands the socket off to an idle worker.

Developer fix The Apache developer's fix removes the circular wait by releasing the timeout mutex before calling through the conditional wait. The developers reached this fix after three failed attempts. To make this fix correct, they wrote code that compensates for breaking atomicity. We judge this fix as hard, given its history and the compensation required.

TM fix As this deadlock does not involve only locks, we use preemption to fix the bug as suggested by Recipe 3. While this at first sight might appear as a nested monitor lockout, which as discussed in Section 5.3.1 cannot be fixed with TM, careful inspection reveals that there is no two-way communication between the worker and listener: the worker needs to communicate to the listener its availability but the listener does not need to assign work to the worker immediately. We therefore modify the listener thread to acquire locks and perform any wait operations revocably inside a transaction, as shown in Figure 3(b). If the listener thread executing inside the transaction does not find an idle worker, it aborts the transaction, releases any locks it acquired, and retries the transaction. This allows the worker thread to acquire the locks it needs and make progress. We judge this fix as hard.

Comparison We judge this fix to be simpler than the developer fix, because it leverages transactions to automatically guarantee the atomicity of the listener's operation without having to reason and write compensating code. We measure the performance of the two fixes using `ab`, the Apache HTTP server-benchmarking tool, running on the same machine as the web server to avoid any network bottlenecks. We saturated the machine by performing 128 multiple requests at a time. We find that the TM fix performs 22% slower than the developer's fix, but that overhead could be reduced by making `retry` block rather than spin. Since this is performance under a stress test workload, we expect the performance difference between the two fixes to be less under realistic workloads. Thus, we believe the TM fix offers a good balance between effort and performance.

```
1  void ap_buffered_log_writer (...)
2  {
3    ...
4    s = &buffer[buf->outputCount];
5    memcpy (s, str, len);
6    temp = buf->outputCount + len;
7    buf->outputCount = temp;
8    apr_file_write(buf->handle);
9    ...
10 }
```

(a) Buggy code

```
1  void ap_buffered_log_writer (...)
2  {
3    ...
4    atomic {
5      s = &buffer[buf->outputCount];
6      memcpy (s, str, len);
7      temp = buf->outputCount + len;
8      buf->outputCount = temp;
9      apr_file_write(buf->handle);
10   }
11   ...
12 }
```

(b) Fixed with TM

Figure 4. An unsynchronized code sample from Apache (httpd-2.0.45: mod_log_config.c), modified for legibility.

5.4.3 Case Study 3: *Apache-II: Missing Synchronization Atomicity Violation*

Figure 4 illustrates a case of an atomicity violation caused by missing synchronization. This code, taken from the Apache web server, has a race condition in which two threads may compete over the buffer, independently advancing `outputCount` and producing either garbage in the log or buffer overflow. The race condition is prevented by executing all the logic of the function from line 2 onwards as a critical section.

[2] We simulated LogTM-SE using Wisconsin GEMS [32]. The configuration we used is a 1GHz 8-core SPARC CMP. The operating system is Solaris 9 and the compiler we used is GCC 3.4.4.

Developer Fix Apache developers fixed this bug by assigning a lock to each log device (`buffered_log`) that they acquire on entry to the function `ap_buffered_log_writer`. While a single static lock could protect the entire function, concurrency favors the more scalable solution at the expense of introducing several new locks to the system. We judge this fix as medium difficulty.

TM Fix By following Recipe 2, we insert a single atomic block from line 4 to 10 to protect the critical section, effectively fixing the bug with only five lines of code. The file I/O is performed using an xCall that defers the actual I/O until the transaction commits. We judge this fix as easy.

Comparison Compared to the developers' fine-grained locks, the TM fix for this bug provides equal concurrency, as writes to different logs can proceed in parallel. In addition, the TM fix is local: the only code that changes is within a single function, whereas the developers' fix required changes elsewhere in Apache to add a lock to the `buffered_log` structure and manage its creation. We measure the performance of the two fixes using `ab` as described earlier in Section 5.4.2. Our TM fix performs comparable to the developer's fix, being only 4% slower. Overall, we believe our TM fix offers a simpler fix compared to the developer's one without penalizing performance.

5.4.4 Case Study 4: *MySQL-I: Partially Missing Synchronization Atomicity Violation*

This MySQL atomicity violation bug occurs when the following two queries execute in parallel:

```
INSERT INTO table VALUES (...);
DELETE FROM table;
```

The first query inserts values into a table while the second deletes the entire table. Within MySQL, the code in Figure 5 to execute the second command is not correctly synchronized with the query logging code: the two queries may execute in one order while the log lists the queries in the opposite order. This happens when an optimized delete function releases logical isolation over the table too early, unlocking `lock_open` before logging and allowing the entire insert function to begin and end before the delete is logged. In contrast, the insert operation holds a logical lock for both the insert and the log write.

Developer fix In the next working version of the code, this optimization disappeared completely, and the surrounding code was restructured. It is unclear whether the developer was unable to fix the bug or whether s/he recognized a fix and removed the code for other reasons. An obvious lock-based fix is to extend the global `lock_open` to cover both operations, but this requires an understanding of that lock's purpose as well as an understanding of the performance implications; `lock_open` is the most contended lock in old versions of MySQL. We judge this fix as hard.

TM Fix Transactional memory fixed this bug with little effort and without requiring a deep understanding of table synchronization, as illustrated in Figure 5. An atomic/lock serializable section (Recipe 4), on the right, wraps the physical operation of the delete query together with logging. This atomic section is serializable against any lock-based critical section. This includes the critical section of thread 1 that uses `lock_open` so any concurrent table-modifying operation is prevented. Overall, this change is local to the (very rare) delete-all-rows operation and obviates any need to understand the correct logical locking to apply in this scenario. We judge this fix as easy.

Comparison We measured the performance of our fix with two tests: repeatedly deleting all rows from different tables, and repeatedly inserting rows into a table. The performance of our fix is identical to that of the buggy version. Thus, the TM fix is simple, expressive and non-invasive, and therefore preferable to a rewrite of the code.

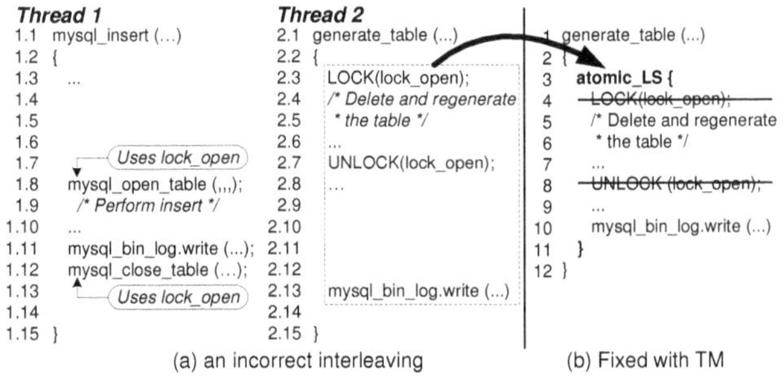

Figure 5. An unsynchronized code sample from MYSQL, modified for legibility.

6. Summary and Conclusions

With this study, we find that current TM is not useful in 17 of 60 atomicity-violation and deadlock bugs examined. This surprising result arises because many concurrency bugs are not about shared data; rather than they concern synchronization, such as condition variables, or I/O, such as file or network access. However, we do find that straightforward uses of TM can fix 40 of the 60 bugs, and sophisticated uses of TM can fix 3 additional bugs and simplify the fixes of 20 of the 40 bugs. Overall, we found that among the 43 bugs that could be fixed by TM, the TM fix may be preferable in 34 cases. These results demonstrate that transactional memory, as proposed, is moderately useful in concurrent programs, but that it does not address enough of the problems that cause bugs.

While replacing existing locks with transactions may require some non-trivial implementation effort, we have seen that transactions can simplify existing logic and fix other bugs as a side effect. Furthermore, the resulting code, structured as clearly identified atomic blocks, may be easier for developers to understand as demonstrated in Case Study 1.

On the other hand, some bugs are trivially fixed with locks, for example when extending an existing critical section to include more code. In such cases, applying transactions yields little value. Finally, even for bugs that can be more simply fixed with TM, the performance overhead of TM may be too large in the absence of hardware support, because software TM is generally more expensive than locking when there is no lock contention [52].

For some bugs, the primitive of atomic execution may not have sufficient expressive power to solve the problem. We identify three such deficiencies. First, deadlocks regarding I/O channels, such as pipes, are not addressed by memory transactions, as the contended resource (the I/O channel) is outside the process. Second, asynchronous I/O allows the OS to write to memory at a later time, possibly after the transaction commits or aborts, thus making it work poorly with transactional memory. Third, shared memory similarly allows other processes to access memory, while current STMs only enforce isolation for threads in the same process. Extending TM along these dimensions might be a fruitful research topic. At least for our work, such extensions would allow TM to fix five more bugs.

Finally, in several bugs the use of STM slowed down performance, especially when TM was used to replace ad hoc synchronization where performance is critical. While low-performance cases could be considered as non-applicable for TM, we believe that as STM systems mature or as TM becomes available in hardware, the performance for those cases will greatly improve, thus making them more suitable for TM.

Acknowledgements

This work is supported in part by National Science Foundation (NSF) grants CNS-0720565 and CNS-0834473. We would like to thank Wei Zhang for help with the reproduction of bugs. We would also like to thank our shepherd, Michael Scott, and the anonymous reviewers for their invaluable feedback. Swift has a significant financial interest in Microsoft.

References

[1] The IBM Blue Gene/Q compute chip with SIMD floating-point unit. Hot Chips 23, Aug. 2011.

[2] A.-R. Adl-Tabatabai and T. Shpeisman. Draft specification of transactional language constructs for C++, version 1.0. `http://software.intel.com/file/21569`, Aug. 2009.

[3] AMD Corporation. Advanced synchronization facility: Proposed architectural specification, rev. 2.1. `http://developer.amd.com/assets/45432-ASF\_Spec\_2.1.pdf`, Mar. 2009.

[4] L. Baugh and C. Zilles. An analysis of I/O and syscalls in critical sections and their implications for transactional memory. In *Proc. of the 2nd ACM SIGPLAN Workshop on Languages, Compilers, and Hardware Support for Transactional Computing*, Aug. 2007.

[5] C. Blundell, J. Devietti, E. C. Lewis, and M. M. Martin. Making the fast case common and the uncommon case simple in unbounded transactional memory. In *Proc. of the 34th Annual Intnl. Symp. on Computer Architecture*, June 2007.

[6] C. Cascaval, C. Blundell, M. Michael, H. W. Cain, P. Wu, S. Chiras, and S. Chatterjee. Software transactional memory: Why is it only a research toy? *Commun. ACM*, 51(11):40–46, 2008.

[7] S. Cherem, T. Chilimbi, and S. Gulwani. Inferring locks for atomic sections. In *Proc. of the SIGPLAN 2008 Conf. on Programming Language Design and Implementation*, June 2008.

[8] L. Chew and D. Lie. Kivati: Fast detection and prevention of atomicity violations. In *Proc. of the 5th ACM European Conf. on Computer Systems*, Apr. 2010.

[9] D. Christie, J.-W. Chung, S. Diestelhorst, M. Hohmuth, M. Pohlack, C. Fetzer, M. Nowack, T. Riegel, P. Felber, P. Marlier, and E. Riviere. Evaluation of AMD's advanced synchronization facility within a complete transactional memory stack. In *Proc. of the 5th ACM European Conf. on Computer Systems*, Apr. 2010.

[10] L. Dalessandro, F. Carouge, S. White, Y. Lev, M. Moir, M. L. Scott, and M. F. Spear. Hybrid NOrec: A case study in the effectiveness of best effort hardware transactional memory. In *Proc. of the 16th Intnl. Conf. on Architectural Support for Programming Languages and Operating Systems*, Mar. 2011.

[11] L. Dalessandro, M. L. Scott, and M. F. Spear. Transactions as the foundation of a memory consistency model. In *Proc. of the 24th International Symp. on Distributed Computing*, Sept. 2010.

[12] L. Dalessandro, M. F. Spear, and M. L. Scott. NOrec: Streamlining STM by abolishing ownership records. In *Proc. of the 15th ACM SIGPLAN Symposium on Principles and Practice of Parallel Programming*, Jan. 2010.

[13] P. Damron, A. Fedorova, Y. Lev, V. Luchango, M. Moir, and D. Nussbaum. Hybrid transactional memory. In *Proc. of the 12th Intnl. Conf. on Architectural Support for Programming Languages and Operating Systems*, Oct. 2006.

[14] D. Dice, Y. Lev, M. Moir, and D. Nussbaum. Early experience with a commercial hardware transactional memory implementation. In *Proc. of the 14th Intnl. Conf. on Architectural Support for Programming Languages and Operating Systems*, Mar. 2009.

[15] D. Dice, O. Shalev, and N. Shavit. Transactional locking II. In *Proc. of the 20th International Symp. on Distributed Computing*, Sept. 2006.

[16] A. Dragojević, R. Guerraoui, and M. Kapalka. Stretching transactional memory. In *Proc. of the SIGPLAN 2009 Conf. on Programming Language Design and Implementation*, June 2009.

[17] P. Dudnik and M. M. Swift. Condition variables and transactional memory: Problem or opportunity? In *Proc. of the 4rd ACM SIGPLAN Workshop on Languages, Compilers, and Hardware Support for Transactional Computing*, Feb. 2009.

[18] M. Emmi, J. S. Fischer, R. Jhala, and R. Majumdar. Lock allocation. In *Proc. of the 34th ACM SIGPLAN/SIGACT Symp. on Principles of Programming Languages*, 2007.

[19] P. Felber, C. Fetzer, and T. Riegel. Dynamic performance tuning of word-based software transactional memory. In *Proc. of the 13th ACM SIGPLAN Symp. on Principles and Practice of Parallel Programming*, Feb. 2008.

[20] L. Hammond, V. Wong, M. Chen, B. D. Carlstrom, J. D. Davis, B. Hertzberg, M. K. Prabhu, H. Wijaya, C. Kozyrakis, and K. Olukotun. Transactional memory coherence and consistency. In *Proc. of the 31st Annual Intnl. Symp. on Computer Architecture*, June 2004.

[21] T. Harris, J. R. Larus, and R. Rajwar. *Transactional Memory, 2nd edition*. Morgan & Claypool Publishers, 2010.

[22] T. Harris, S. Marlow, S. P. Jones, and M. Herlihy. Composable memory transactions. In *Proc. of the 10th ACM SIGPLAN Symp. on Principles and Practice of Parallel Programming*, June 1991.

[23] HIPEAC. Gcc for transactional memory. `http://www.hipeac.net/node/2419`.

[24] Intel. Intel C++ STM compiler, Prototype edition. `http://software.intel.com/en-us/articles/intel-c-stm-compiler-prototype-edition/`, 2009.

[25] G. Jin, L. Song, W. Zhang, S. Lu, and B. Liblit. Automated atomicity-violation fixing. In *Proc. of the SIGPLAN 2011 Conf. on Programming Language Design and Implementation*, June 2011.

[26] H. Jula, D. M. Tralamazza, C. Zamfir, and G. Candea. Deadlock immunity: Enabling systems to defend against deadlocks. In *Proc. of the 8th USENIX Symp. on Operating Systems Design and Implementation*, Dec. 2008.

[27] E. Koskinen and M. Herlihy. Dreadlocks: Efficient deadlock detection. In *Proc. of the 20th ACM Symp. on Parallel Algorithms and Architectures*, June 2008.

[28] B. W. Lampson and D. D. Redell. Experience with processes and monitors in Mesa (summary). In *Proc. of the 7th Symp. on Operating System Principles*, Dec. 1979.

[29] Y. Lev, M. Moir, and D. Nussbaum. PhTM: Phased transactional memory. In *Proc. of the 2nd ACM SIGPLAN Workshop on Languages, Compilers, and Hardware Support for Transactional Computing*, Aug. 2007.

[30] S. Lu, S. Park, E. Seo, and Y. Zhou. Learning from mistakes: A comprehensive study on real world concurrency bug characteristics. In *Proc. of the 13th Intnl. Conf. on Architectural Support for Programming Languages and Operating Systems*, Mar. 2008.

[31] B. Lucia, J. Devietti, K. Strauss, and L. Ceze. Atom-aid: Detecting and surviving atomicity violations. In *Proc. of the 35th Annual Intnl. Symp. on Computer Architecture*, June 2008.

[32] M. M. K. Martin, D. J. Sorin, B. M. Beckmann, M. R. Marty, M. Xu, A. R. Alameldeen, K. E. Moore, M. D. Hill, and D. A. Wood. Multifacet's general execution-driven multiprocessor simulator (GEMS) toolset. *Computer Architecture News*, pages 92–99, Sept. 2005.

[33] B. McCloskey, F. Zhou, D. Gay, and E. Brewer. Autolocker: Synchronization inference for atomic sections. In *Proc. of the 33rd ACM SIGPLAN/SIGACT Symp. on Principles of Programming Languages*, 2006.

[34] K. E. Moore, J. Bobba, M. J. Moravan, M. D. Hill, and D. A. Wood. Logtm: Log-based transactional memory. In *Proc. of the 12th IEEE Symp. on High-Performance Computer Architecture*, Feb. 2006.

[35] Mozilla. Performance: Page load and DHTML performance. `http://wiki.mozilla.org/Performance:Home_Page`, Mar. 2010.

[36] Y. Ni, A. Welc, A.-R. Adl-Tabatabai, M. Bach, S. Berkowits, J. Cownie, R. Geva, S. Kozhukow, R. Narayanaswamy, J. Olivier, S. Preis, B. Saha, A. Tal, and X. Tian. Design and implementation of transactional constructs for c/c++. In *Proc. of the 23rd SIGPLAN Conf. on Object-Oriented Programming, Systems, Languages and Application*, Oct. 2008.

[37] V. Pankratius. Does transactional memory keep its promises? Results from an empirical study. Technical Report 2009-12, University of Karlsruhe, Germany, Sept. 2009.

[38] M. Pohlack and S. Diestelhorst. From lightweight hardware transactional memory to lightweight lock elision. In *Proc. of the 6th ACM SIGPLAN Workshop on Languages, Compilers, and Hardware Support for Transactional Computing*, June 2011.

[39] D. E. Porter, O. S. Hofmann, C. J. Rossbach, A. Benn, and E. Witchel. Operating systems transactions. In *Proc. of the 22nd ACM Symp. on Operating System Principles*, Oct. 2009.

[40] F. Qin, J. Tucek, J. Sundaresan, and Y. Zhou. Rx: Treating bugs as allergies — a safe method to survive software failure. In *Proc. of the 20th ACM Symp. on Operating System Principles*, Oct. 2005.

[41] S. Rajamani, G. Ramalingam, V. P. Ranganath, and K. Vaswani. ISOLATOR: Dynamically ensuring isolation in concurrent programs. In *Proc. of the 14th Intnl. Conf. on Architectural Support for Programming Languages and Operating Systems*, Mar. 2009.

[42] R. Rajwar and J. R. Goodman. Transactional lock-free execution of lock-based programs. In *Proc. of the 10th Intnl. Conf. on Architectural Support for Programming Languages and Operating Systems*, 2002.

[43] R. Rajwar, M. Herlihy, and K. Lai. Virtualizing transactional memory. In *Proc. of the 32nd Annual Intnl. Symp. on Computer Architecture*, June 2005.

[44] H. E. Ramadan, C. J. Rossbach, D. E. Porter, O. S. Hofmann, A. Bhandari, and E. Witchel. MetaTM/TxLinux: Transactional memory for an operating system. In *Proc. of the 34th Annual Intnl. Symp. on Computer Architecture*, June 2007.

[45] C. J. Rossbach, O. S. Hofmann, D. E. Porter, H. E. Ramadan, A. Bhandari, and E. Witchel. TxLinux: Using and managing hardware transactional memory in an operating system. In *Proc. of the 21st ACM Symp. on Operating System Principles*, Oct. 2007.

[46] C. J. Rossbach, O. S. Hofmann, and E. Witchel. Is transactional programming actually easier? In *Proc. of the 15th ACM SIGPLAN Symposium on Principles and Practice of Parallel Programming*, Jan. 2010.

[47] A. Roy, S. Hand, and T. Harris. A runtime system for software lock elision. In *Proc. of the 4th ACM European Conf. on Computer Systems*, Apr. 2009.

[48] B. Saha, A.-R. Adl-Tabatabai, R. L. Hudson, C. C. Minh, and B. Hertzberg. McRT-STM: A high performance software transactional memory system for a multi-core runtime. In *Proc. of the 11th ACM SIGPLAN Symp. on Principles and Practice of Parallel Programming*, Mar. 2006.

[49] T. Shpeisman, A.-R. Adl-Tabatabai, R. Geva, Y. Ni, and A. Welc. Towards transactional memory semantics for C++. In *Proc. of the 21st ACM Symp. on Parallel Algorithms and Architectures*, June 2009.

[50] M. F. Spear, M. Silverman, L. Dalessandro, M. M. Michael, and M. L. Scott. Implementing and exploiting inevitability in software transactional memory. In *Proc. of the 37th Intnl. Conf. on Parallel Processing*, Sept. 2008.

[51] M. M. Swift, H. Volos, N. Goyal, L. Yen, M. D. Hill, and D. A. Wood. OS support for virtualizing hardware transactional memory. In *Proc. of the 3rd ACM SIGPLAN Workshop on Languages, Compilers, and Hardware Support for Transactional Computing*, Feb. 2008.

[52] T. Usui, Y. Smaragdakis, and R. Behrends. Adaptive locks: Combining transactions and locks for efficient concurrency. In *Proc. of the 4rd ACM SIGPLAN Workshop on Languages, Compilers, and Hardware Support for Transactional Computing*, Feb. 2009.

[53] H. Volos, N. Goyal, and M. M. Swift. Pathological interaction of locks with transactional memory. In *Proc. of the 3rd ACM SIGPLAN Workshop on Languages, Compilers, and Hardware Support for Transactional Computing*, Feb. 2008.

[54] H. Volos, A. J. Tack, N. Goyal, M. M. Swift, and A. Welc. xCalls: Safe I/O in memory transactions. In *Proc. of the 4th ACM European Conf. on Computer Systems*, Apr. 2009.

[55] Webkit. Sunspider javascript benchmark. `http://www2.webkit.org/perf/sunspider-0.9/sunspider.html`.

[56] A. Welc, B. Saha, and A.-R. Adl-Tabatabai. Irrevocable transactions and their applications. In *Proc. of the 20th ACM Symp. on Parallel Algorithms and Architectures*, June 2008.

[57] H. Wettstein. The problem of nested monitor calls revisited. *SIGOPS Operating Systems Review*, January 1978.

[58] W. Xiong, S. Park, J. Zhang, Y. Zhou, and Z. Ma. Ad hoc synchronization considered harmful. In *Proc. of the 9th USENIX Symp. on Operating Systems Design and Implementation*, Oct. 2010.

[59] L. Yen, J. Bobba, M. R. Marty, K. E. Moore, H. Volos, M. D. Hill, M. M. Swift, and D. A. Wood. LogTM-SE: Decoupling hardware transactional memory from caches. In *Proc. of the 13th IEEE Symp. on High-Performance Computer Architecture*, Feb. 2007.

[60] F. Zyulkyarov, V. Gajinov, O. S. Unsal, A. Cristal, E. Ayguadé, T. Harris, and M. Valero. Atomic Quake: Using transactional memory in an interactive multiplayer game server. In *Proc. of the 14th ACM SIGPLAN Symp. on Principles and Practice of Parallel Programming*, Feb. 2009.

Bottleneck Identification and Scheduling in Multithreaded Applications

José A. Joao
ECE Department
The University of Texas at Austin
joao@ece.utexas.edu

M. Aater Suleman
Calxeda Inc.
aater.suleman@calxeda.com

Onur Mutlu
Computer Architecture Lab.
Carnegie Mellon University
onur@cmu.edu

Yale N. Patt
ECE Department
The University of Texas at Austin
patt@ece.utexas.edu

Abstract

Performance of multithreaded applications is limited by a variety of bottlenecks, e.g. critical sections, barriers and slow pipeline stages. These bottlenecks serialize execution, waste valuable execution cycles, and limit scalability of applications. This paper proposes *Bottleneck Identification and Scheduling* (BIS), a cooperative software-hardware mechanism to identify and accelerate the most critical bottlenecks. BIS identifies which bottlenecks are likely to reduce performance by measuring the number of cycles threads have to wait for each bottleneck, and accelerates those bottlenecks using one or more fast cores on an Asymmetric Chip Multi-Processor (ACMP). Unlike previous work that targets specific bottlenecks, BIS can identify and accelerate bottlenecks regardless of their type. We compare BIS to four previous approaches and show that it outperforms the best of them by 15% on average. BIS' performance improvement increases as the number of cores and the number of fast cores in the system increase.

Categories and Subject Descriptors C.1.2 [*Processor Architectures*]: Multiple Data Stream Architectures (Multiprocessors)

General Terms Design, Performance

Keywords Critical sections, barriers, pipeline parallelism, multicore, asymmetric CMPs, heterogeneous CMPs

1. Introduction

Speeding up a single application using Chip Multi-Processors (CMPs) requires that applications be split into *threads* that execute concurrently on multiple cores. In theory, a CMP can provide speedup equal to the number of cores, however, the speedup is often lower in practice because of the thread waiting caused by serializing bottlenecks. These bottlenecks not only limit performance but also limit application scalability, e.g., performance of the *mysql* database peaks at 16 threads (Section 5.1.1).

Programmers are often burdened with the task of identifying and removing serializing bottlenecks. This solution is too costly because (a) writing correct parallel programs is already a daunting task, and (b) serializing bottlenecks change with machine configuration, program input set, and program phase (as we show in Section 2.2), thus, what may seem like a bottleneck to the programmer may not be a bottleneck in the field and vice versa. Hence, a solution that can identify and remove these bottlenecks at run-time (without requiring programmer effort) can not only increase parallel program performance and scalability but also reduce the work of the programmers.

An Asymmetric CMP (ACMP) consists of at least one large, fast core and several small, slow cores.[1] Previous research has shown that faster cores on an ACMP can be used to accelerate serializing bottlenecks. However, these proposals lack generality and fine-grained adaptivity. For example, several proposals [5, 13, 21, 26] use the fast core to accelerate Amdahl's serial portions (i.e., portions of a program where only one thread exists) but they do not handle serializing bottlenecks that happen in the parallel portions of the code. Accelerated Critical Sections (ACS) [36] accelerates critical sections –code regions that only one thread can execute at a given time–, but it does not always accelerate the critical sections that are currently *most critical* for performance and is limited to ACMPs with a single large core. Meeting Points [8] accelerates the thread with the longest expected completion time in the parallel region to reduce barrier synchronization overhead. However, it only applies to barriers in statically scheduled workloads, where the work to be performed by each thread is known before runtime. Feedback-Directed Pipelining (FDP) [34, 37], a software-only library, assigns threads to cores to balance stage throughput on pipelined workloads and improve performance or reduce power consumption, but it is slow to adapt to phase changes because it is software-based. Realistic workloads contain multiple different bottlenecks that can become critical at different execution phases, as we show in this paper. Therefore, it is important to have a single mechanism that is general and adaptive enough to accelerate the *most critical* bottlenecks at any given time.

We propose *Bottleneck Identification and Scheduling* (BIS), a general cooperative software-hardware framework to *identify* the most critical serializing bottlenecks at runtime, and *accelerate* them using one or multiple large cores on an ACMP. The key insight for identification is that *the most critical serializing bottlenecks are likely to make other threads wait for the greatest amount of time.* The programmer, compiler or library delimits potential bottlenecks using BottleneckCall and BottleneckReturn instructions, and replaces the code that waits for bottlenecks with a BottleneckWait instruction. The hardware uses these instructions to measure thread waiting cycles (i.e., number of cycles threads wait due to the bottleneck) for each bottleneck and tracks them in a *Bottleneck Table.* The bottlenecks with the highest number of thread waiting cycles are selected for acceleration on one or more large cores. On executing a BottleneckCall instruction, the small core checks if the bottleneck has been selected for acceleration. If it has, the small core enqueues an execution request into the *Scheduling Buffer* of a large core. The large core dequeues each request from its Scheduling Buffer, executes the bottleneck and notifies the small core once it encounters the BottleneckReturn instruction.

[1] We use the terms fast and large, and slow and small, interchangeably, to refer to the two types of cores on an ACMP.

ASPLOS'12. March 3–7, 2012, London, England, UK.

This paper makes three main **contributions**:

1. We propose a cooperative hardware-software mechanism to identify the most critical bottlenecks of different types, e.g., critical sections, barriers and pipeline stages, allowing the programmer, the software or the hardware to remove or accelerate those bottlenecks. To our knowledge, this is the first such proposal.
2. We propose an automatic acceleration mechanism that decides which bottlenecks to accelerate and where to accelerate them. We use the fast cores on an ACMP as hardware-controlled fine-grain accelerators for serializing bottlenecks. By using hardware support, we minimize the overhead of execution migration and allow for quick adaptation to changing critical bottlenecks.
3. This is the first paper to explore the trade-offs of bottleneck acceleration using ACMPs with multiple large cores. We show that multiple large cores improve performance when multiple bottlenecks are similarly critical and need to be accelerated simultaneously.[2]

Our evaluation shows that BIS improves performance by 37% over a 32-core Symmetric CMP and by 32% over an ACMP (which only accelerates serial sections) with the same area budget. BIS also outperforms recently proposed dynamic mechanisms (ACS for non-pipelined workloads and FDP for pipelined workloads) on average by 15% on a 1-large-core, 28-small-core ACMP. We also show that BIS' performance improvement increases as the number of cores and the number of large cores increase.

2. Motivation

2.1 Bottlenecks: What They Are and Why They Should Be Accelerated

We define *bottleneck* as any code segment for which threads contend. A bottleneck may consist of a single thread or multiple threads that need to reach a synchronization point before other threads can make progress. We call the threads that stall due to a bottleneck *waiters* and the threads executing a bottleneck *executers*. A single instance of a bottleneck can be responsible for one or many waiters. The effect of bottlenecks on performance can be substantial because every cycle a bottleneck is running is a cycle wasted on *every one of the waiters* of that bottleneck. Bottlenecks cause thread serialization. Thus, a parallel program that spends a significant portion of its execution in bottlenecks can lose some or even all of the speedup that could be expected from parallelization. Next we describe examples of bottlenecks.

2.1.1 Amdahl's Serial Portions

When only one thread exists [4], it is on the critical path and should be scheduled on the fastest core to minimize execution time. Meanwhile, all other cores are idle.

2.1.2 Critical Sections

Critical sections ensure mutual exclusion, i.e. only one thread can execute a critical section at a given time, and any other thread wanting to execute the critical section must wait. That is, there is only one executer and possibly multiple waiters. Figure 1(a) shows the execution of four threads (T1-T4) that run a simple loop that consists of a critical section C1 and a non-critical section N. Threads can execute in parallel until time 30, at which T3 acquires the lock and prevents T1 and T4 from doing so. Then, T1 and T4 become idle, waiting on T3. Accelerating the execution of C1 on T3 during this time would not only accelerate T3 and reduce the total execution time (because this instance of code segment C1 is on the critical path), but also reduce the wait for both T1 and T4. However, accelerating the same C1 on T2 between times 20 and 30 would not help because all the other threads are running useful work and no thread is waiting for the lock.

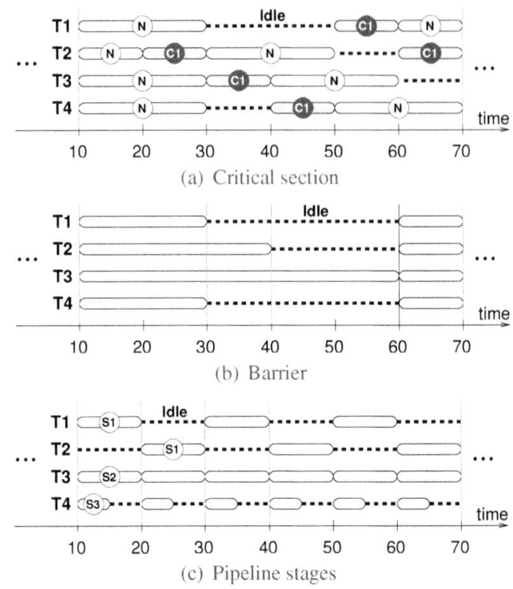

(a) Critical section

(b) Barrier

(c) Pipeline stages

Figure 1. Examples of bottleneck execution.

2.1.3 Barriers

Threads that reach a barrier must wait until all threads reach the barrier. There can be multiple executers and multiple waiters. Figure 1(b) shows the execution of four threads reaching a barrier. T1 and T4 reach the barrier at time 30 and start waiting on T2 and T3. T2 reaches the barrier at time 40, leaving T3 as the only running thread until time 60, when T3 reaches the barrier and all four threads can continue. Therefore, every cycle saved by accelerating T3 gets subtracted from the total execution time, up to the difference between the arrivals of T2 and T3 at the barrier.

2.1.4 Pipeline Stages

In a pipelined parallel program, loop iterations are split into stages that execute on different threads. Threads executing other pipeline stages wait for the slowest pipeline stages. There can be multiple executers and multiple waiters. Figure 1(c) shows the execution of a pipelined program with three stages (S1-S3) on four threads. S1 is scalable and runs on both T1 and T2. S2 is not scalable, so it runs on a single thread (T3). S3 is shorter and runs on T4. The throughput of a pipeline is the throughput of the slowest stage. Since S2 has a smaller throughput than S1, S2's input queue gets full and S1 has to stall to produce work for S2 at the pace S2 can deal with it, which introduces idle time on T1 and T2. On the other side, S3 is faster than S2 and finishes each iteration before S2 can feed it more work to do, which introduces idle time on T4. Therefore, T1, T2 and T4 are all waiters on T3 at some point. If S2 could be accelerated by a factor of 2, the pipeline throughput would be balanced (i.e., each stage would deal with one iteration every 5 time units) and all idle time would be eliminated. Since S2 is not scalable, this acceleration is only feasible with higher single-thread performance on T3. Note that only accelerating the actual slowest stage improves performance. Accelerating any other stage does not. Also note that the best way to accelerate a *scalable* stage is to add more threads (cores) to work on it.

From these examples, we can conclude that *accelerating the bottlenecks that are making other threads wait is likely to improve multithreaded program performance*.

[2] We also evaluate large cores with Simultaneous Multithreading (SMT) in Section 5.2.

2.2 How Bottlenecks Change Over Time

Let's first consider a simple example, Program 1, where elements X are moved from linked list A to linked list B. Removal from A and insertion into B are protected by critical sections to avoid races that could corrupt the lists. The amount of work performed inside each of those critical sections varies over time, because list A is shrinking while list B is growing. Figure 2 shows that contention (i.e. the number of threads waiting to enter each critical section) with 32 threads changes as follows: in the first phase, critical section A is the bottleneck, while in the second phase, critical section B becomes the bottleneck. Successful acceleration of this program at runtime requires dynamic identification of which code is the current critical bottleneck and then running it on a fast core.

Program 1 Example of time-variant critical sections

```
A=full linked list; B=empty linked list
repeat
  Lock A
    Traverse list A
    Remove X from A
  Unlock A
  Compute on X
  Lock B
    Traverse list B
    Insert X into B
  Unlock B
until A is empty
```

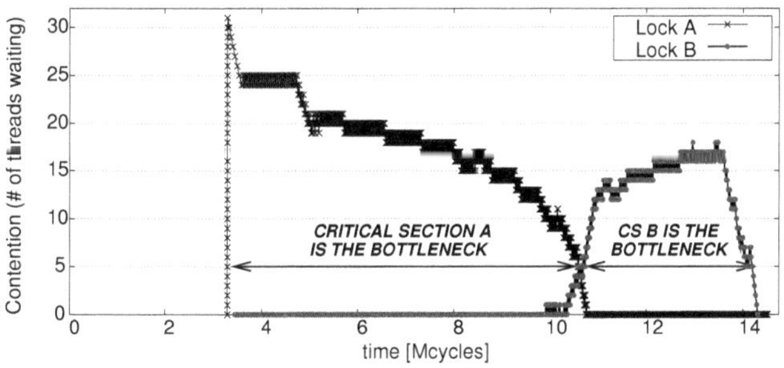

Figure 2. Contention for each critical section on Program 1.

Similar examples exist in important real-life workloads. For example, the most contended critical section in the widely used *mysql* database changes over short periods of time. The two most contended critical sections in *mysql* with the OLTP-nontrx input set are *LOCK_open* and *LOCK_log*. *LOCK_open* is used to ensure mutual exclusion while opening and closing tables in the *open_table* and *close_thread_tables* functions. *LOCK_log* is used to protect access to the log file, which happens in the *MYSQL_LOG::write* function.

Figure 3 shows contention for *LOCK_open* and *LOCK_log* over the first 8M cycles of *mysql* with 16 threads (the optimal number of threads) while being driven by SysBench [3] with the OLTP-nontrx input set[3] (*mysql-3* in our benchmark set, Table 6). The graph shows three clearly different phases: A) the initial use of *LOCK_log* by every thread, B) the heavy use of *LOCK_open* while all threads simultaneously want to open the tables they need, C) the steady state period where transactions continue executing and *LOCK_log* is usually the most contended, but *LOCK_open* sporadically gets highly contended (e.g., see arrows around 4.8Mcycles and 7.7Mcycles). This last phase continues for the rest of the program: the most contended lock changes intermittently for the duration of this phase. The temporal behavior of the critical sections depends entirely on the database operations that are executed, i.e., the input set. For example, with the OLTP-complex input set, *LOCK_open* gets highly contended even more often.

[3] SysBench is a widely used multi-threaded benchmark to measure system and database performance.

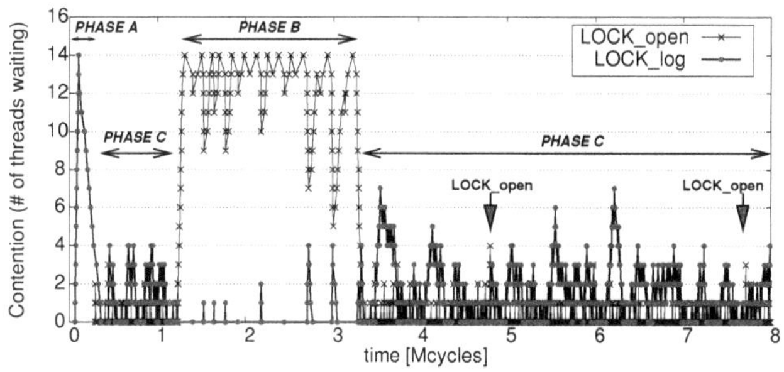

Figure 3. Most contended critical sections on *mysql*.

Previously proposed ACS [36] can accelerate only one critical section at a time on a single large core (or two critical sections on a 2-way SMT large core, but this reduces the benefit of acceleration due to resource sharing between SMT threads). When there are multiple critical sections contending to be accelerated, ACS disables acceleration of critical sections that are less frequent, in order to avoid false serialization (i.e., serialized execution of different critical sections at the large core). Periodically (every 10M instructions in [36]), ACS re-enables acceleration of all critical sections, allowing for some false serialization while it relearns which critical sections should be disabled. This mechanism works well when contention for critical sections is stable for long periods but it is suboptimal for applications like *mysql*, because it ignores the frequent changes on which critical section is currently the most limiting bottleneck, as shown in Figure 3. In addition, ACS is specific to critical sections and cannot handle other types of bottlenecks such as barriers and slow pipeline stages.

Our goal is to design a mechanism that identifies at any given time which bottlenecks of any type are currently limiting performance, and accelerates those bottlenecks.

3. Bottleneck Identification and Scheduling

3.1 Key Insight

The benefit of parallel computing comes from concurrent execution of work; the higher the concurrency, the higher the performance. Every time threads have to wait for each other, less work gets done in parallel, which reduces parallel speedup and wastes opportunity. To maximize performance and increase concurrency, it is pivotal to minimize thread waiting as much as possible. Consequently, a large amount of effort is invested by parallel programmers in reducing bottlenecks that can lead to thread waiting. For example, programmers spend an enormous amount of effort in reducing false sharing, thread synchronization, thread load imbalance, etc. Previous research on computer architecture also targets thread waiting, e.g., transactional memory [12], primitives like test-and-test-and-set [31], lock elision [29], speculative synchronization [24], etc. We use this conventional wisdom –that reducing thread waiting improves performance– to identify the best bottlenecks for acceleration. Our key idea is thus simple: measure the number of cycles spent by threads waiting for each bottleneck and accelerate the bottlenecks responsible for the highest thread waiting cycles.

Our proposal, BIS, consists of two parts: identification of critical bottlenecks and acceleration of those bottlenecks.

3.2 Identifying Bottlenecks

Identification of critical bottlenecks is done in hardware based on information provided by the software. The programmer, compiler or library assigns a unique bottleneck ID (*bid*) to each potential serializing bottleneck, and encapsulates the bottleneck code between *BottleneckCall* and *BottleneckReturn* instructions. Using these instructions, the hardware keeps track of the bottlenecks and which hardware threads (core ID and SMT context) they execute on.

```
...
BottleneckCall bid, targetPC
...
targetPC: while cannot acquire lock
              BottleneckWait bid
          acquire lock
          ...
          release lock
          BottleneckReturn bid
```

(a) Critical section

```
...
BottleneckCall bid, targetPC
...
targetPC: code running for the barrier
          ...
          enter barrier
          while not all threads in barrier
              BottleneckWait bid
          exit barrier
          BottleneckReturn bid
```

(b) Barrier

```
while not done
    BottleneckCall bid, targetPC
...
targetPC: while empty queue                  // previous stage
              BottleneckWait prev_bid        // caused the waiting
          dequeue work
          do the work ...
          while full queue                   // next stage
              BottleneckWait next_bid        // caused the waiting
          enqueue next work
          BottleneckReturn bid
```

(c) Pipeline

Figure 4. Modifications to code implementing bottlenecks.

To identify which bottlenecks cause thread waiting, we use a new instruction *BottleneckWait*. The purpose of this instruction is twofold: it implements waiting for a memory location to change (similarly to existing instructions like *mwait* in x86 [17]), and it allows the hardware to keep track of how many cycles each thread is waiting for each bottleneck. Typically, when threads are waiting for a bottleneck, they are waiting for the value of a particular memory location *watch_addr* to satisfy a condition. For example, for critical sections, *watch_addr* can be the lock address; for barriers it can be the address of the counter of threads that have reached the barrier; and for pipeline stages it can be the address of the size of the queue where work quanta are read from [37]. In most cases *bid* can be the same as *watch_addr*, but we separate them to provide the flexibility required for some implementations, e.g. MCS locks [25]. Table 1 summarizes the format and purpose of the new instructions required by BIS.

BottleneckCall bid, *targetPC*
Marks the beginning of the bottleneck identified by *bid* and calls the bottleneck subroutine starting at targetPC
BottleneckReturn bid
Marks the end of the bottleneck identified by *bid* and returns from the bottleneck subroutine
BottleneckWait bid[, *watch_addr*[, *timeout*]]
Waits for a maximum of *timeout* cycles for the content of memory address *watch_addr* associated with bottleneck *bid* to change, while keeping track of the number of waiting cycles

Table 1. ISA support for BIS.

The new instructions required by BIS do not affect the semantics or the implementation of the bottlenecks and can be easily added to any existing bottleneck implementation. The compiler encapsulates potential bottlenecks into functions using *function outlining* [40] and inserts BottleneckCall, BottleneckReturn and BottleneckWait instructions. Figure 4 shows the use of these instructions for critical sections, barriers and pipeline stages. Since programming primitives that become bottlenecks are usually implemented inside libraries, the changes can be hidden so that the programmer does not need to change the program.

We track waiting cycles for each bottleneck, and identify the critical bottlenecks with low overhead in hardware using a **Bottleneck Table (BT)**. Each BT entry corresponds to a bottleneck and includes a thread waiting cycles (TWC) field. TWC is computed by aggregating the number of waiters on the bottleneck (i.e., the number of threads currently running a BottleneckWait instruction) over time. The exact computation is described in Sections 3.5.1 and 3.5.2. The number of waiters is another field in the BT entry, and is incremented when a BottleneckWait instruction starts executing for that *bid* and decremented when the BottleneckWait instruction commits, i.e., after the wait for the bottleneck ends. The Bottleneck Table contains logic to identify the most critical bottlenecks, i.e. the entries with top N highest thread waiting cycles. We provide more details about the implementation of the BT in Section 3.5.2.

3.3 Accelerating Bottlenecks

There are multiple ways to accelerate a bottleneck, e.g. increasing core frequency [5], giving a thread higher priority in shared hardware resources [9], or migrating the bottleneck to a faster core with a more aggressive microarchitecture or higher frequency [26, 36]. The bottleneck identification component of BIS can work with any of these schemes. As an example, we show how our identification mechanism can use the fast/large cores of an ACMP as fine-grain hardware-controlled bottleneck accelerators, and the slow/small cores for running the remaining parallel code. We first assume a single large core context and in Section 3.4 we extend the design to multiple large core contexts.

When the BT updates thread waiting cycles (TWC), bottlenecks with TWC greater than a threshold are enabled for acceleration and the rest are disabled.[4]

When a small core encounters a BottleneckCall instruction, it checks whether or not the bottleneck is enabled for acceleration. To avoid accessing the global BT on every BottleneckCall, each small core is augmented with an **Acceleration Index Table** (AIT) that caches the *bid* and acceleration enable bit of bottlenecks.[5] If a *bid* is not present in the AIT, it is assumed to be disabled for acceleration. If the bottleneck is disabled for acceleration, the small core executes the bottleneck locally. If acceleration is enabled, the small core sends a bottleneck execution request to the large core and stalls waiting for a response.

When the large core receives a bottleneck execution request from a small core, it enqueues the request into a new structure called **Scheduling Buffer** (SB). Each SB entry has: *bid*, originating small core/hardware thread ID, target PC, stack pointer and thread waiting cycles (TWC, copied from the BT entry). The SB works as a priority queue based on TWC: the first bottleneck that runs on the large core is the oldest instance of the bottleneck with the highest TWC. When the large core executes the BottleneckReturn instruction, it sends a BottleneckDone signal to the small core. On receiving BottleneckDone, the small core continues executing the instruction after the BottleneckCall. As we will explain in Section 3.3.2, the large core may also abort the request while it is on the SB. If that happens, the large core removes the request from the SB and sends a BottleneckCallAbort signal to the small core. On receiving BottleneckCallAbort, the small core executes the bottleneck locally.

3.3.1 Threads Waiting on the Scheduling Buffer

A thread executing a BottleneckCall instruction that was sent to the large core and is waiting on the SB also incurs thread waiting cycles that must be attributed to the bottleneck. To account for these waiting cycles, when a bottleneck execution request is enqueued into the SB, the large core sends an update to the BT, incrementing waiters. It also increments a new field waiters_sb, which separately

[4] A threshold of 1024 works well for our workloads.

[5] When a bottleneck gets enabled or disabled for acceleration, the BT broadcasts the updates to the AITs on all small cores.

keeps track of the number of waiters on the Scheduling Buffer for purposes we explain in Section 3.3.2. When the bottleneck execution request is dequeued from the SB, to be executed or aborted, the large core updates the BT, decrementing waiters and waiters_sb.

3.3.2 Avoiding False Serialization and Starvation

Since multiple bottlenecks can be scheduled on a large core, a bottleneck may have to wait for another bottleneck with higher priority (i.e. higher thread waiting cycles) for too long, while it could have been executing on the small core. This problem is called *false serialization*[6] and BIS mitigates it by aborting a request enqueued on the SB if the bottleneck: (a) does not have the highest thread waiting cycles in the SB, and (b) would be *ready to run* on its original small core. A bottleneck is considered *ready to run* if no other instance of that bottleneck is currently executing and all the waiters are on the SB. This situation results in unnecessary delaying of all those waiters and can be easily detected when the BT is updated. To perform this detection, each BT entry keeps the number of executers (incremented by BottleneckCall and decremented by BottleneckReturn), the number of waiters (incremented while a BottleneckWait instruction is executing or a bottleneck is waiting on the SB), and the number of waiters on the SB (waiters_sb, incremented while a request is waiting on the SB). If executers is zero and waiters is non-zero and equal to waiters_sb, the BT sends a BottleneckReady signal to the SB. Upon receiving this signal, the SB dequeues the oldest request for the bottleneck and sends a BottleneckCallAbort to the originating small core. This mechanism also prevents starvation of requests in the SB. As a failsafe mechanism to avoid starvation, the SB also aborts requests that have been waiting for more than 50K cycles.

3.3.3 Preemptive Acceleration

Bottleneck instances can vary in length. Since our mechanism uses history to decide whether or not to accelerate a bottleneck, it is possible for a long instance to get scheduled on a small core and later become responsible for high thread waiting cycles. To fix this problem, we introduce a preemptive mechanism: if upon updating thread waiting cycles, the BT detects that a bottleneck running on a small core has become the bottleneck with the highest thread waiting cycles, the bottleneck is shipped to the large core. BT sends a preempt signal to the small core informing it to stall execution, push the architectural state on the stack and send a request to the large core to continue execution. The large core pops the architectural state from the stack and resumes execution until BottleneckReturn. Acceleration of barriers relies on this preemptive mechanism.

3.4 Support for Multiple Large Core Contexts

Our mechanism can scale to multiple large cores or a large core with multiple hardware contexts (Simultaneous Multithreading, SMT) with only three modifications:

First, each large core has its own Scheduling Buffer. SMT contexts at a large core share the Scheduling Buffer but execute different bottlenecks because otherwise they would wait for each other.

Second, each bottleneck that is enabled for acceleration is assigned to a fixed large core context to preserve cache locality and avoid different large cores having to wait for each other on the same bottlenecks. To that effect, each BT entry and Acceleration Index Table entry is augmented with the ID of the large core the bottleneck is assigned to. If there are N large core contexts, the Bottleneck Table assigns each of the top N bottlenecks to a different large core context to eliminate false serialization among them. Then, the rest of the bottlenecks that are enabled for acceleration are assigned to a random large core.

[6] False serialization can also introduce deadlocks on a deadlock-free program [36].

Third, the preemptive mechanism described in Section 3.3.3 is extended so that in case a bottleneck scheduled on small cores (a) becomes the top bottleneck, and (b) its number of executers is less than or equal to the number of large core contexts, the BT sends signals to preemptively migrate those threads to the large cores. This mechanism allows acceleration on N large core contexts of the last N threads running for a barrier.

3.5 Implementation Details

3.5.1 Tracking Dependent and Nested Bottlenecks

Sometimes a thread has to wait for one bottleneck while it is executing another bottleneck. For example, in a pipelined workload, a thread executing stage S2 may wait for stage S1. Similar situations occur when bottlenecks are nested. For example, a thread T1 is running B1 but stalls waiting for a nested bottleneck B2. Concurrently, T2 also stalls waiting for B1, which means it is indirectly waiting for B2. In these scenarios, the thread waiting cycles should be attributed to the bottleneck that is the root cause of the wait, e.g., waiting cycles incurred by T2 should not be attributed to bottleneck B1 which is not really running, but to bottleneck B2.

In general, to determine the bottleneck Bj that is the root cause of the wait for each bottleneck Bi, we need to follow the dependency chain between bottlenecks until a bottleneck Bj is found not to be waiting for a different bottleneck. Then, the current number of waiters for Bi, i.e. the required increment in TWC, is added to the TWC for Bj. To follow the dependency chain we need to know (a) which threads is executing a bottleneck and (b) which bottleneck, if any, that thread is currently waiting for. To know (a), we add an executer_vec bit vector on each BT entry (one bit per hardware thread) that records all current executers of each bottleneck (set on BottleneckCall and reset on BottleneckReturn). To know (b), we add a small **Current Bottleneck Table** (CBT) associated with the BT and indexed with hardware thread ID that gives the *bid* that the thread is currently waiting for (set during the execution of BottleneckWait, or zero at all other times). To summarize, the BT updates TWC for each bottleneck Bi with the following algorithm:

```
foreach Bi in BottleneckTable:
  B = Bi; done = false
  while (not done):
    Bj = B
    E = randomly picked Executer of B // uniformly distribute TWC
    B = CurrentBottleneck(E)
    done = (B == 0) or // Bj is running or
           (B == Bj)   // waiting for another instance of itself
  TWC(Bj) += waiters(Bi)
```

The basic idea of the algorithm is to follow the dependence chain between bottlenecks until a bottleneck Bj is found not to be waiting for a different bottleneck. This algorithm is also applicable when there are no dependencies, i.e. the loop will execute once and will result in Bj = Bi. Note that the algorithm is not exact and only attempts to assign thread waiting cycles to a bottleneck that is actually running and making other threads wait, so that if that bottleneck were accelerated, the cycles spent by other threads waiting would also be reduced. The computation of TWC does not need to be perfect because BIS is solely for performance and does not affect correctness.

3.5.2 Bottleneck Table

The new instructions update the Bottleneck Table after committing and off the critical path of execution. Table 2 describes each BT entry. When a BottleneckCall or BottleneckWait instruction is executed with a *bid* that is not in the BT, a new entry is inserted in the BT. Since BIS is solely for performance and not for correctness, the BT only needs enough entries to track the major bottlenecks in each phase of a program. Our studies (not included here due to space constraints) show that a BT with 32 entries is sufficient for our workloads.

Field	Description
bid	Bottleneck ID
pid	Process ID
executers	Current number of threads that are running the bottleneck, i.e., executing between a BottleneckCall and a BottleneckReturn
executer_vec	Bit vector of threads executing the bottleneck, each bit set on BottleneckCall and reset on BottleneckReturn
waiters	Current number of threads that are waiting for the bottleneck, i.e. executing a BottleneckWait or enqueued on the SB
waiters_sb	Current number of threads that are waiting on the SB, i.e. executing a BottleneckCall that was sent to a large core
TWC	Thread waiting cycles
large_core_id	ID of the large core assigned for acceleration

Table 2. Bottleneck Table entry.

We implement the BT as an associative cache. The replacement algorithm evicts the entry with the smallest thread waiting cycles. We update thread waiting cycles for each bottleneck by incrementing it by the number of waiters every cycle (for practicality we add 32 * number of waiters every 32 cycles). We halve the thread waiting cycles for all entries every 100K cycles to allow for the replacement of stale entries. We find that a centralized BT structure is not a bottleneck, however, if need arises, the BT can be partitioned without much effort using the principles of a distributed directory.

3.5.3 Hardware Cost

Figure 5 shows the location of the new structures required by BIS on an ACMP, and Table 3 describes their storage cost, which is only 18.7 KB for a CMP with 2 large cores and 56 small cores (area budget of 64). The storage cost for a CMP with 2 large cores and 120 small cores (area budget of 128) would be 39.6 KB.

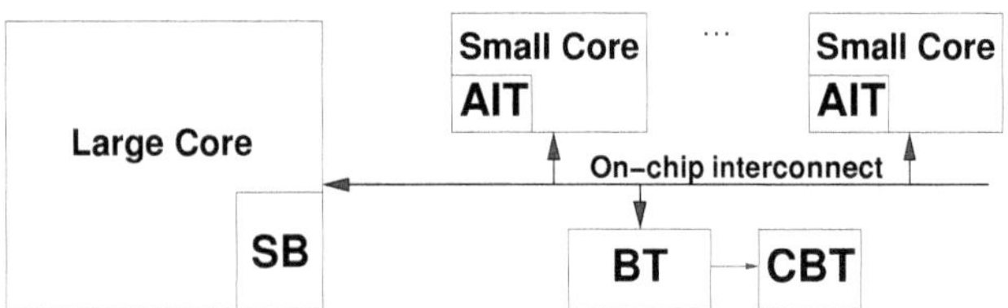

Figure 5. Hardware structures for BIS.

3.5.4 Handling Interrupts

The Operating System may interrupt the cores, e.g., on time quantum expiration or for I/O. If a small core gets an interrupt while waiting for a large core to execute a bottleneck, it does not service the interrupt until a BottleneckDone or BottleneckCallAbort is received. If a small core gets an interrupt while executing a BottleneckWait instruction, the BottleneckWait instruction is forced to finish, which removes the waiter from the BT, but it is reexecuted after returning from the interrupt. If a large core gets an interrupt while accelerating a bottleneck, it aborts all bottlenecks in its Scheduling Buffer, finishes the current bottleneck, and then services the interrupt.

3.5.5 Transfer of Cache State to the Large Core

A bottleneck executing remotely on the large core may require data that resides in the small core, thereby producing cache misses that reduce the benefit of acceleration. Data Marshaling [35] (DM) has been proposed to reduce these cache misses, by identifying and marshaling the cache lines required by the remote core. It is easy to integrate DM with our proposal and we evaluate our proposal with and without DM in Section 5.4.

3.5.6 Compiler Support

The compiler can trivially convert bottlenecks that start and end in the same scope to use BottleneckCall/BottleneckReturn. Complex bottlenecks spanning multiple functions or modules may require programmer intervention and certainly BIS may not be applicable when not even the programmer can perform function outlining on the bottlenecks. A more flexible ISA with two separate instructions BottleneckBegin and BottleneckEnd to delimit bottlenecks without encapsulating them in functions can expand the applicability of BIS at the expense of potentially higher overheads, but we have not explored it. The consequences of failing to mark code segments as potential bottlenecks depend on their actual criticality. There is no penalty for failing to mark non-critical bottlenecks. However, if critical bottlenecks are not marked, BIS misses the opportunity to improve performance. Marking too many non-critical bottlenecks does not significantly reduce performance because the Bottleneck Table retains only the currently most critical bottlenecks.

We have targeted same-ISA ACMPs. However, BIS could be extended to heterogeneous-ISA ACMPs by including two binary implementations for each bottleneck in the executable image, one to be executed on the small core and the other to be executed on the large core. This is part of our future work.

3.5.7 Support for Program Tuning

BIS can increase programmer productivity by providing feedback to programmers about the most critical bottlenecks. Programmers can then decide which bottlenecks to optimize to get the best results from their effort. We propose adding a set of performance counters to the BT to store *bid* and cumulative thread waiting cycles (TWC) for the bottlenecks with highest TWC. These counters can be accessed by tools such as Vtune and Intel Parallel Studio [18] to guide the programmer. Due to space limitations we do not describe the structure and the interface, but these are straightforward since the BT already has the required information.

4. Experimental Methodology

We use an x86 cycle-level simulator that models symmetric and asymmetric CMPs. Symmetric CMPs (SCMPs) consist of only small cores. The small in-order cores are modeled after the Intel Pentium processor and the fast cores are modeled after the Intel Core 2 architecture. Details are shown in Table 4. We model all latency overheads associated with our mechanism faithfully. We evaluate our proposal on different processor configurations with equal area budget. We compare our proposal to previous work, summarized in Table 5. SCMP and ACMP use different thread scheduling policies for non-pipelined and pipelined workloads. We apply ACS and MC-ACS only to non-pipelined workloads, while FDP only applies to pipelined workloads by design. BIS is general and applies to both. Our evaluation is based on the 12 workloads shown in Table 6, which we simulate to completion. We use *mysql* with three different input sets because (a) *mysql* is a widely used commercial workload, and (b) its behavior significantly depends on the input set.

5. Evaluation

5.1 Single Large Core

It is difficult to determine before runtime the optimal number of threads (and this number varies dynamically), thus it is common practice to run applications with as many threads as available cores [16, 28]. On applications that are not I/O-intensive, this policy can maximize resource utilization without oversubscribing the cores, but may result in inferior performance if the application performance peaks at fewer threads than the number of cores. Thus, we evaluate two situations: number of threads equal to the number of cores and optimal number of threads, i.e., the number of threads at which performance is maximum. Table 7 summarizes the average speedups of BIS over other techniques in both situations for different area budgets.

Structure	Purpose	Location and entry structure (field sizes in parenthesis)	Cost
Bottleneck Table (BT)	To decide which bottlenecks are more critical and where to accelerate them	One global 32-entry table for the CMP. Each entry has 192 bits: *bid*(64), pid(16), executers(6), executer_vec(64), waiters(6), waiters_sb(6), TWC(24), large_core_id(6)	768 B
Current Bottleneck Table (CBT)	To help track the root cause of thread waiting on nested or dependent bottlenecks	Attached to the BT, 64-entries. Each entry has 64 bits, the *bid* of the bottleneck the thread is waiting for, and is indexed by hardware thread ID.	512 B
Acceleration Index Tables (AIT)	To reduce global accesses to BT to find if a bottleneck is enabled for acceleration	One 32-entry table per small core. Each entry has 66 bits: *bid*(64), enabled (1), large core ID (1). Each AIT has 264 bytes.	14.4 KB
Scheduling Buffers (SB)	To store and prioritize bottleneck execution requests on each large core	One 56-entry buffer per large core. Each entry has 222 bits: *bid*(64), small core ID (6), target PC(64), stack pointer (64), thread waiting cycles (24). Each SB has 1554 bytes.	3.1 KB
		Total	18.7 KB

Table 3. Description of hardware structures for BIS and storage cost on a 56-small-core, 2-large-core CMP.

Small core	2-wide, 5-stage in-order, 4GHz, 32 KB write-through, 1-cycle, 8-way, separate I and D L1 caches, 256KB write-back, 6-cycle, 8-way, private unified L2 cache
Large core	4-wide, 12-stage out-of-order, 128-entry ROB, 4GHz, 32 KB write-through, 1-cycle, 8-way, separate I and D L1 caches, 1MB write-back, 8-cycle, 8-way, private unified L2 cache
Cache coherence	MESI protocol, on-chip distributed directory, L2-to-L2 cache transfers allowed, 8K entries/bank, one bank per core
L3 cache	Shared 8MB, write-back, 16-way, 20-cycle
On-chip interconnect	Bidirectional ring, 64-bit wide, 2-cycle hop latency
Off-chip memory bus	64-bit wide, split-transaction, 40-cycle, pipelined bus at 1/4 of CPU frequency
Memory	32-bank DRAM, modeling all queues and delays, row buffer hit/miss/conflict latencies = 25/50/75ns
	CMP configurations with area equivalent to N small cores.
SCMP	N small cores
ACMP	1 large core and N-4 small cores, the large core always runs any single-threaded code
ACS	1 large core and N-4 small cores, the large core always runs any single-threaded code and accelerates critical sections as proposed in [36]
BIS	L large cores and S=N-4*L small cores, one large core always runs any single-threaded code, 32-entry Bottleneck Table, N-entry Current Bottleneck Table, each large core is equipped with an S-entry Scheduling Buffer, each small core is equipped with a 32-entry Acceleration Index Table

Table 4. Baseline processor configuration.

Mechanism	Non-pipelined workloads	Pipelined workloads
SCMP	One thread per core	Best static integer schedule described in [37]
ACMP	Serial portion on large core, parallel portion on all cores [5, 26]	Best static integer schedule including large cores [34]
ACS	Serial portion and critical sections on large core, parallel portion on small cores [36]	Not used, because in our workloads it is more profitable to schedule the large core/s to accelerate pipeline stages using FDP, as described in [34], instead of critical sections within stages
MC-ACS	To compare to the best possible baseline, we extend ACS to multiple large cores by retrying once more the acceleration of falsely serialized critical sections on a different large core before disabling their acceleration	
FDP	Not applicable (designed for pipelined workloads)	Dynamic scheduling of all cores to stages described in [34]
BIS	Our proposal	

Table 5. Experimental configurations.

Workload	Description	Source	Input set	# of Bottl.	Bottleneck description
iplookup	IP packet routing	[39]	2.5K queries	# of threads	Critical sections (CS) on routing tables
mysql-1	MySQL server [1]	SysBench [3]	OLTP-complex	29	CS on meta data, tables
mysql-2	MySQL server [1]	SysBench [3]	OLTP-simple	20	CS on meta data, tables
mysql-3	MySQL server [1]	SysBench [3]	OLTP-nontrx	18	CS on meta data, tables
specjbb	JAVA business benchmark	[33]	5 seconds	39	CS on counters, warehouse data
sqlite	sqlite3 [2] DB engine	SysBench [3]	OLTP-simple	5	CS on database tables
tsp	Traveling salesman	[20]	11 cities	2	CS on termination condition, solution
webcache	Cooperative web cache	[38]	100K queries	33	CS on replacement policy
mg	Multigrid solver	NASP [6]	S input	13	Barriers for omp single/master
ft	FFT computation	NASP [6]	T input	17	Barriers for omp single/master
rank	Rank strings based on similarity to another string	[37]	800K strings	3	Pipeline stages
pagemine	Computes a histogram of string similarity	Rsearch [27]	1M pages	5	Pipeline stages

Table 6. Evaluated workloads.

Num. of threads	Equal to number of cores				Optimal			
Area Budget	8	16	32	64	8	16	32	64
SCMP	-20	10	45	75	-20	10	37	43
ACMP	6.9	13	43	70	1.4	12	32	36
ACS/FDP	2.4	6.2	17	34	2.4	6.2	15	19

Table 7. Average speedups (%) of BIS over SCMP, ACMP and ACS/FDP.

5.1.1 Number of Threads Equal to Number of Cores

Figure 6 shows speedups over a single small core for different area budgets (measured in equivalent number of small cores). The figure shows the speedups of SCMP, ACMP and ACS (for non-pipelined workloads) or FDP (for pipelined workloads) and BIS. Our proposal improves performance over ACMP and SCMP and matches or improves over ACS/FDP on all benchmarks for an area budget of 32 cores. On average, it improves performance by 43% over ACMP, 45% over SCMP and 17% over ACS/FDP. Three key observations are in order.

First, as the number of cores increases, so does the benefit of BIS. On average, BIS outperforms ACS/FDP by 2.4%/6.2%/17%/34% for 8/16/32/64-core area budget. Recall from Table 4 that the large core replaces 4 small cores, reducing the maximum number of threads by 3 for ACMP and FDP (because they run only one thread on the large core), and by 4 for ACS and BIS (because they dedicate the large core for critical sections and bottlenecks) with respect to SCMP. With a small area budget, this loss of parallel throughput cannot be offset by the benefit of acceleration because contention for bottlenecks is smaller at fewer threads. Therefore, with a small area budget, BIS performs similar to ACS/FDP and underperforms SCMP (e.g. for an 8-core area

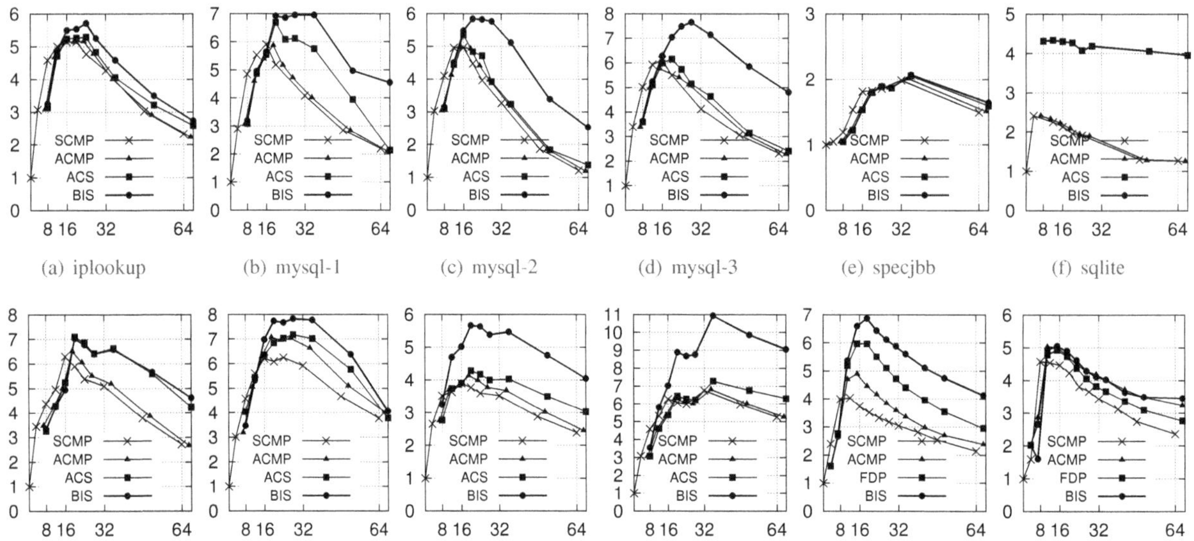

(a) iplookup (b) mysql-1 (c) mysql-2 (d) mysql-3 (e) specjbb (f) sqlite

(g) tsp (h) webcache (i) mg (j) ft (k) rank (l) pagemine

Figure 6. Speedup over a single small core, x-axis is area budget (in equivalent small cores).

budget). As the area budget increases, the marginal loss of parallel throughput due to the large core becomes relatively smaller, and with more threads running, contention for serializing bottlenecks increases. Therefore, the dynamic mechanisms that accelerate those bottlenecks (ACS, FDP and BIS) start to prevail.

Second, with more threads, the benefit of BIS over ACS/FDP increases on workloads where the critical bottlenecks change over time (*iplookup*, all *mysql*, *webcache*, *mg*, *ft* and *rank*), because BIS is better at choosing which bottlenecks to accelerate and quickly adapts to changes. Additionally, both critical sections and barriers are limiting bottlenecks in *mg* and *ft* at different times, and BIS accelerates both types of bottlenecks, unlike ACS. On workloads where the critical bottlenecks do not change over time (*specjbb*, *sqlite* and *tsp*), BIS matches the performance of ACS. *Pagemine* has two very similar non-scalable pipeline stages (the reduction of local histograms into a global histogram) that are frequently the limiting bottlenecks. Therefore, BIS with a single large core is unable to significantly improve performance over FDP because that would require both stages to be simultaneously accelerated. However, BIS is able to improve performance when multiple large cores are employed, as we will show in Section 5.2.

Third, BIS increases the scalability (the number of threads at which performance peaks) of four of the workloads (all versions of *mysql* and *rank*) beyond the already-improved scalability of ACS/FDP over ACMP or SCMP. By accelerating bottlenecks more effectively than previous proposals, BIS reduces contention and thread waiting, allowing the workloads to take advantage of a larger number of threads before performance gets limited by bottlenecks.

We conclude that BIS improves performance and scalability of applications over ACS/FDP. As the area budget increases, so does the performance benefit of BIS.

5.1.2 Optimal Number of Threads

Figure 7 shows the speedups of our proposal for different area budgets with the optimal number of threads, relative to the ACMP configuration. We determine the optimal number of threads for each application-configuration pair by simulating all possible numbers of threads and reporting results for the one that minimizes execution time. For example, the optimal number of threads for iplookup-BIS on the 32-core area budget is 20.

With an area budget of 8 cores, all benchmarks except *sqlite* run with the maximum number of threads (8 for SCMP, 5 for ACMP/FDP and 4 for ACS and BIS) and with low contention for bottlenecks. Therefore, SCMP performs the best because the loss of throughput on the configurations with a large core is greater than the benefit of acceleration. The exception is *sqlite*, which becomes critical-section limited at 4 threads and can take full advantage of the acceleration mechanisms. Since *sqlite* has only one dominant critical section during the whole execution, both ACS and BIS provide the same performance improvement. On average, ACS, BIS and ACMP perform within 2% of each other.

With higher area budgets, the relative impact of running fewer threads due to the presence of a large core becomes less significant, which progressively reduces the advantage of SCMP and favors ACMP, ACS/FDP and BIS. On average, BIS outperforms SCMP by 10%/37%/43%, ACMP by 12%/32%/36% and ACS/FDP by 6.2%/15%/19% on a 16/32/64-core budget. As contention increases, it becomes more important to focus the acceleration effort on the *most critical* bottlenecks. While BIS actively identifies and accelerates the bottlenecks that are stopping more threads from making progress, ACS disables acceleration of critical sections that suffer from false serialization, even though such critical sections can be causing the most thread waiting. Additionally, BIS is more adaptive to changes in the important bottlenecks, while both ACS and FDP maintain the decisions they make for a fixed and relatively long period (10Mcycles for ACS and until the next major phase change for FDP). As a result of these two factors, BIS significantly outperforms ACS and FDP.

The only benchmark where BIS does not outperform ACS is *tsp* because BIS accelerates many more bottlenecks than ACS, increasing core-to-core cache misses. Since those bottlenecks are only 52-instruction long on average, the benefit of accelerating them does not overcome the cache miss penalty, which causes BIS' performance to be lower than that of ACS. BIS is able to improve performance of *tsp* over ACS with the Data Marshaling mechanism [35] that reduces cache misses incurred by the bottlenecks, as we show in Section 5.4.

We conclude that even with optimal number of threads, BIS improves performance and its benefit over all other mechanisms increases as the number of cores (area budget) increases.

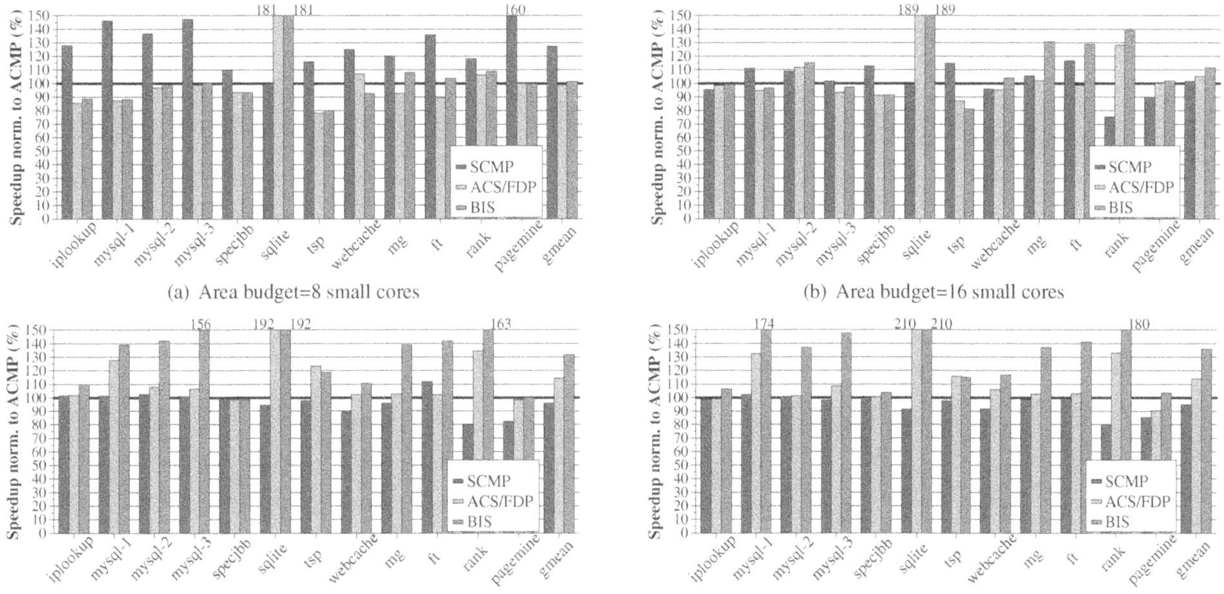

(a) Area budget=8 small cores

(b) Area budget=16 small cores

(c) Area budget=32 small cores

(d) Area budget=64 small cores

Figure 7. Speedup for optimal number of threads, normalized to ACMP.

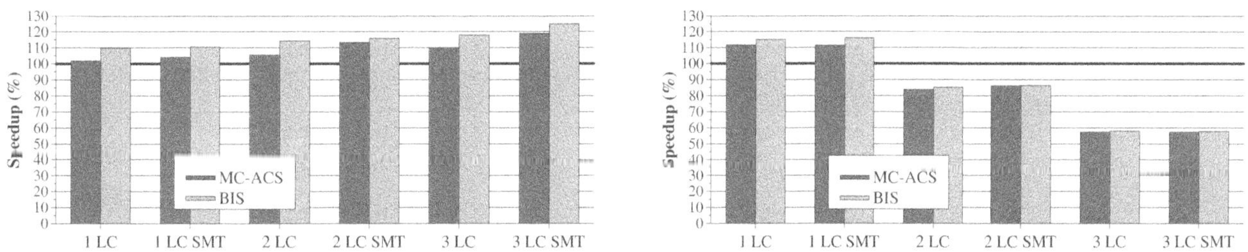

(a) iplookup at 32-core area budget

(b) mysql-2 at 16-core area budget

Figure 8. Speedup with multiple large core contexts, normalized to ACMP with a single large core (LC: large core).

5.2 Multiple Large Core Contexts

We first explain the trade-offs of multiple large cores with two examples. Figure 8(a) shows the performance of *iplookup* with optimal number of threads as we increase the number of large cores while keeping the same area budget. The figure also shows results for large cores with 2-way Simultaneous Multithreading. *Iplookup* executes a large number of independent critical sections that are contended. Therefore, it can significantly benefit from extra large cores that can simultaneously accelerate more of those equally-critical bottlenecks. The performance improvement of BIS over ACMP steadily grows from 10% for one large core to 25% with three large 2-way SMT cores. On the other hand, Figure 8(b) shows that for *mysql-2* additional large cores decrease performance with MC-ACS or BIS because the benefit of simultaneously accelerating multiple critical sections that are not heavily contended is much smaller than the cost of reducing the number of threads that can be executed concurrently to accommodate the additional large cores. The conclusion is that the best number of large cores dedicated to bottleneck acceleration significantly depends on the application and number of threads. Therefore, achieving the best performance requires either software tuning to tailor bottleneck behavior to what the available hardware configuration can efficiently accelerate, or building reconfigurable "large" cores that can either run more threads with lower performance or a single thread with higher performance. Both are interesting avenues for future work.

Figure 9 shows the geometric mean of speedups for all of our benchmarks on different core configurations with the same area budget, ranging from an area budget of 8 small cores to 64 small cores. The workloads run with the optimal number of threads for each configuration. An area budget of 8 small cores only allows for a single-large-core ACMP configuration, and on average there is not much contention for bottlenecks that either ACS/FDP or BIS can provide benefit for. With an area budget of 16 cores, performance decreases with additional large cores because the benefit of acceleration on the extra large cores is not enough to compensate for the loss of parallel performance due to the reduced number of threads. When the area budget is 32 cores, the average performance benefit of BIS remains stable for different numbers of large cores. With an area budget of 64 cores, there is no loss of parallel throughput with 2 or 3 large cores, because Figure 6 shows that performance peaks at fewer than 40 threads on all workloads. Therefore, BIS' performance increases by 3.4% and 6% with 2 and 3 large cores, respectively, with respect to a single large core. We conclude that having more large cores increases the benefit of BIS at large area budgets.

Having SMT on the large core does not change BIS' performance by more than 2% in any configuration. The trade-off is that a 2-way SMT large core can accelerate two different bottlenecks concurrently, but the two hardware threads share all processor resources and therefore the acceleration benefit of each thread is lower than if the thread were running alone on the large core. Two effects reduce the acceleration benefit when SMT is used on the large core. First, since local data is frequently accessed inside critical sections and pipeline stages and stays resident in the cache, our

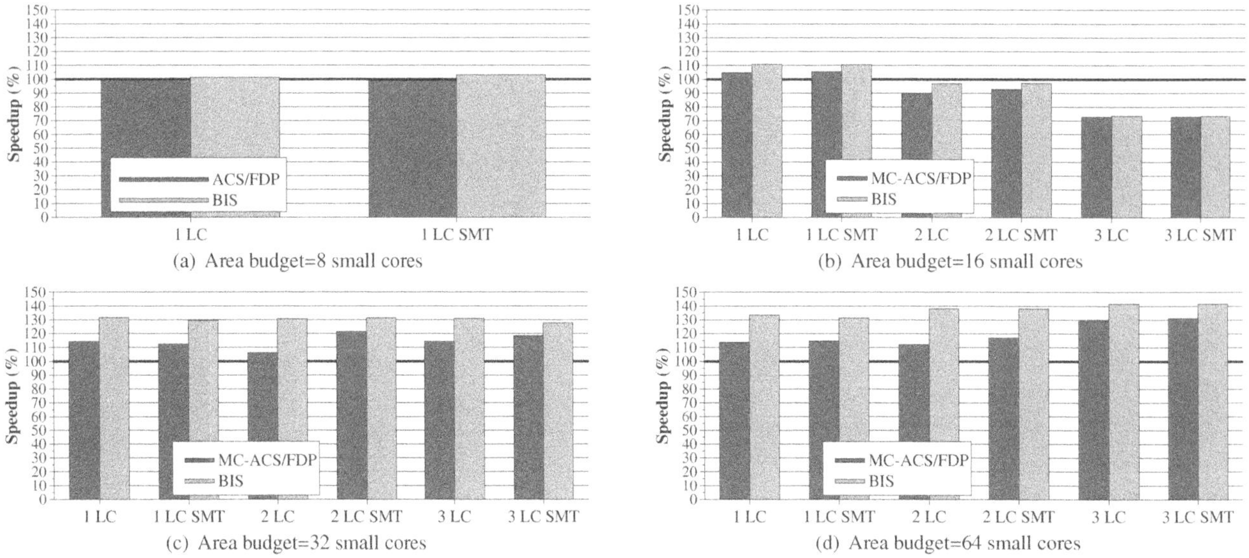

Figure 9. Speedup with multiple large core contexts, normalized to ACMP with a single large core (LC: large core).

workloads rarely need to access main memory (average L3 MPKI is 0.79 on BIS with the 32-core budget), hence SMT's main benefit on an out-of-order core, cache miss latency tolerance, rarely gets exercised. Second, tight resource sharing between threads degrades performance of each thread. We conclude that using SMT to increase the number of large core contexts available for bottleneck acceleration is not useful for BIS.

5.3 Analysis

Figure 10 shows the normalized execution time spent accelerating code segments on and off the critical path for ACS/FDP and BIS on a 32-core area budget running 28 threads. To avoid changing the critical path on the fly due to acceleration, we disable acceleration and only perform bottleneck identification in this experiment. Then the actual critical path is computed off-line and compared to the code segments identified as bottlenecks by ACS/FDP and BIS. We define *coverage* as the fraction of the critical path that is actually identified as bottleneck. BIS matches or improves coverage of ACS/FDP on every benchmark and the average coverage of BIS (59%) is significantly better than the average coverage of ACS/FDP (39%). We define *accuracy* as the fraction of execution time of identified bottlenecks that is actually on the critical path. The average accuracy of BIS (73.5%) is slightly better than that of ACS/FDP (72%). We conclude that the significantly better coverage and similar accuracy of BIS vs. ACS/FDP results in the performance improvements we showed in Sections 5.1 and 5.2.

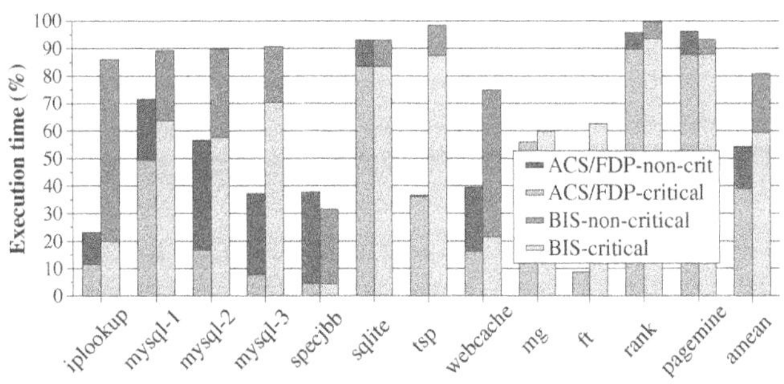

Figure 10. Bottleneck identification on and off the critical path.

Table 8 shows the number of dynamic instances of annotated bottlenecks that are executed and identified for acceleration, along with their average length in number of instructions. Bottlenecks are most numerous and only 52-instruction long on *tsp*, which increases the overhead since even a single cache-to-cache transfer due to migration introduces a penalty in the same order of magnitude as the benefit of acceleration, resulting in a performance loss unless Data Marshaling is used, as we will show next.

Workload	Annotated Bottlenecks Executed	Annotated Bottlenecks Identified	Average Length (Instructions)
iplookup	19184	888 (4.6%)	2130
mysql-1	18475	9342 (50.6%)	391
mysql-2	11761	1486 (12.6%)	378
mysql-3	25049	2593 (10.4%)	453
specjbb	1652	1008 (61.0%)	1468
sqlite	174	116 (66.7%)	29595
tsp	21932	12704 (57.9%)	52
webcache	15118	2099 (13.9%)	1908
mg	516	515 (99.8%)	11585
ft	228	227 (99.6%)	39804
rank	3003	1024 (34.1%)	1800
pagemine	5005	1030 (20.6%)	1160

Table 8. Bottleneck characterization.

5.4 Interaction with Data Marshaling

Bottlenecks that are accelerated on a large core may need to access data that was produced in the code segment running on the small core before execution migrated to the large core. These *inter-segment* memory accesses become cache misses that may limit the performance benefit of acceleration. To reduce these cache misses, Suleman et al. [35] proposed Data Marshaling (DM), which can be easily integrated with BIS. DM identifies and marshals the data needed by a bottleneck to the large core using compiler and hardware support. The compiler uses profiling to find the store instructions that generate the data to be produced in the small core and consumed by a bottleneck. The hardware keeps track of the cache lines modified by those special store instructions and pushes those cache lines into the large core's cache as soon as the bottleneck is shipped to the large core. When the bottleneck starts executing, after waiting in the Scheduling Buffer, the inter-segment data is likely to be available in the large core's cache.

Figure 11 shows performance of BIS and ACS/FDP with and without DM on 32-core area budget with 28 threads, normalized to ACMP. In general, DM improves ACS and BIS, but it improves BIS more, because BIS migrates bottlenecks to a large core more frequently than ACS. In particular, BIS underperforms ACS on *tsp*

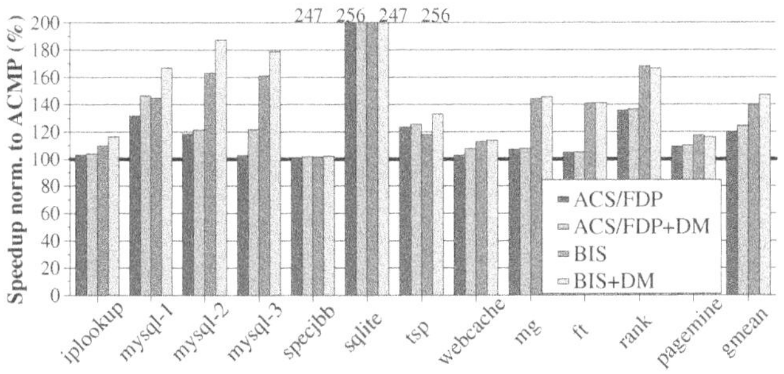

Figure 11. Speedup with and without Data Marshaling.

due to inter-segment cache misses, which are eliminated by DM, which results in BIS+DM outperforming ACS+DM. On average on the 32-core budget, BIS+DM improves performance by 5.2% over BIS, while ACS+DM improves by 3.8% over ACS. We conclude that BIS interacts positively with techniques that can reduce cache misses incurred due to bottleneck acceleration.

6. Related Work

Our proposal is a comprehensive mechanism to identify and accelerate bottlenecks (using heterogeneous cores) in a multithreaded program. To our knowledge, this is the first proposal that reduces thread waiting caused by bottlenecks regardless of bottleneck type. The mechanism is unique as it requires no significant programmer support and uses the fast cores on the ACMP to accelerate the bottlenecks. Most related to our work are previous proposals to reduce the performance impact of bottlenecks and other techniques to accelerate specific bottlenecks using heterogeneous cores.

6.1 Reducing the Impact of Bottlenecks

Removing or alleviating serializing bottlenecks has been a topic of wide interest for decades. For example, test-and-test-and-set [31] was proposed to reduce the serialization caused by thread communication. These primitives are only used at the start and the end of the bottleneck (lock acquire/release). As such, they are orthogonal to BIS since BIS accelerates the code inside the bottleneck.

Several mechanisms have been proposed to overlap execution of bottlenecks as long as they do not modify shared data. The first of these approaches is Transactional Memory (TM) [12], which targets critical sections. TM's benefit heavily depends on bottlenecks not having data conflicts, i.e. if two instances of a transaction have a data conflict, TM cannot execute them in parallel. In contrast, BIS speeds up bottlenecks regardless of their data access patterns. BIS can also complement TM as it can be used to accelerate transactions that cannot be overlapped due to their length or conflicts.

Other proposals like Speculative Lock Elision [29], Transactional Lock Removal [30], and Speculative Synchronization (SS) [24] can overlap the execution of non-conflicting instances of the same critical section without requiring programmers to write code using transactions. In addition to critical sections, SS can also reduce the overhead of barriers by speculatively allowing threads to execute past the barrier as long as there are no data conflicts. These approaches fundamentally differ from BIS for four reasons. First, they cannot hide the latency of bottlenecks that have data conflicts, whereas BIS can accelerate such bottlenecks. Second, they best apply to short bottlenecks as long bottlenecks complicate conflict detection hardware and are more likely to conflict, while BIS can accelerate arbitrarily long bottlenecks. Third, these techniques do not take criticality of the bottleneck into account, which is a main feature of BIS. Fourth, they are limited to particular types of bottlenecks (e.g., these approaches cannot be applied to bottleneck pipeline stages), whereas BIS is more general. BIS can complement these proposals by accelerating bottlenecks to which they are not applicable.

Previously proposed techniques [15, 37] to reduce load imbalance among stages of a parallel pipeline do so by either re-pipelining the workload via compiler/programmer support or by choosing the thread-to-stage allocation to reduce imbalance. Their performance benefit is limited because the decisions are coarse-grain and they are unable to speedup stages that do not scale with the number of cores. In BIS, we can leverage these previous mechanisms to manage our thread-to-core allocation but we also identify and accelerate the critical bottlenecks using a large core at a fine granularity. Using the faster cores allows us to improve performance even if the bottleneck pipeline stage does not scale.

In general, our proposal is complementary to mechanisms that reduce the impact of bottlenecks. Evaluating their interactions is part of our future work.

6.2 Accelerating Bottlenecks

Annavaram et al. [5] proposed to make the core running the serial bottleneck faster using frequency throttling. Morad et al. [26] proposed accelerating Amdahl's serial bottleneck [4] using the fast core of an ACMP while running the parallel phases on the small cores. While accelerating the single-threaded bottleneck is provably beneficial for performance, it does not reduce serialization in parallel portions of programs. We use their mechanism as a baseline and provide significant performance improvement on top of it by also accelerating bottlenecks in the parallel portions.

Suleman et al. [36] use the faster cores to accelerate critical sections. Their scheme differs from ours because (1) it is limited to critical sections while BIS targets thread waiting for any bottleneck, (2) it does not consider critical section criticality when deciding which critical sections to accelerate while BIS prioritizes bottlenecks that are predicted to be most critical, and (3) it only supports a single large core (which can execute only a single bottleneck) while BIS can schedule multiple bottlenecks for acceleration on any arbitrary number of fast cores. The generality and fine-grained adaptivity of BIS allow it to significantly outperform ACS, as we showed in Section 5.

Meeting Points [8], Thread Criticality Predictors (TCP) [7] and Age-Based Scheduling [22] try to reduce the overhead of barriers by detecting and accelerating the threads which are likely to reach the barrier last. Age-Based Scheduling uses history from the previous instance of the loop to choose the best candidates for acceleration. Thus, their scheme is restricted to iterative kernels that have similar behavior across multiple invocations. TCP uses a combination of L1 and L2 cache miss counters to predict which threads are likely to arrive early at a barrier and slows them down to save power, but it can also be used to guide acceleration of the thread that is lagging. Meeting Points uses hints from the software to determine which thread is lagging (thus likely to be a bottleneck). We can leverage these schemes to enhance our bottleneck identification mechanism, because they may be able to identify threads that need acceleration before they start making other threads wait, allowing their acceleration to start earlier and be more effective.

6.3 Critical Path Prediction

Hollingsworth [14] was the first to propose an online algorithm to compute the critical path of a message-passing parallel program. Fields et al. [10, 11] proposed a data- and resource-dependency-based token-passing algorithm that predicts instruction criticality and slack in single-threaded applications. In contrast, our approach predicts criticality at the code segment (i.e., bottleneck) granularity in multithreaded applications by only focusing on thread waiting. Dependencies between instructions in a single-threaded application and between bottlenecks in a multithreaded application are conceptually different. While instructions obey well-defined data-flow dependencies, bottlenecks have more complicated and dynamic dependencies. For example, critical sections with the same lock can execute in any order as long as they do not execute concurrently, e.g., block A may wait for block B in one dynamic instance while block B may wait for block A in another instance of execution, depending on the timing of each thread's execution. With many threads, dependencies between bottlenecks become more complicated and their execution order becomes less repeatable. Therefore, we found that methods to predict instruction criticality in single-threaded applications similar to Fields et al. [11] are not straightforwardly applicable to predict bottlenecks in multithreaded applications, although future work may find a way of doing it. Li et al. [23] proposed an efficient *off-line* DAG-based algorithm to find instruction-level criticality in multithreaded applications. Our problem is different in that it requires *online* prediction of critical bottlenecks to enable their acceleration.

6.4 Coarse-Grain Thread Scheduling

Several proposals schedule threads to large cores of an ACMP at coarse granularity, i.e. the operating system level. For example, Saez et al. [32] proposed running on large cores the threads that can make better use of them, according to a utility factor that considers both memory-intensity and thread-level parallelism. Koufaty et al. [19] proposed assigning a large core to the thread that is expected to have a larger speedup running on the large core, i.e. those that have fewer off-core memory requests and fewer core front-end stalls. In contrast, BIS does fine-grain code segment scheduling in hardware, running only serial and parallel bottlenecks on large cores, i.e. the portions of *any thread* that are adaptively identified as performance limiters.

7. Conclusion

We propose *Bottleneck Identification and Scheduling* (BIS), the first generalized mechanism to identify the most critical bottlenecks that cause thread waiting on multithreaded applications and to accelerate those bottlenecks using one or more large cores of an ACMP. We show that BIS improves performance of a set of bottleneck-intensive applications on average by 15% over ACS, which is the state-of-the-art technique for critical section acceleration, and FDP, a software technique to dynamically assign pipeline stages to cores, on a 1-large-core, 28-small-core ACMP. The benefit of BIS increases with the number of cores and BIS improves scalability of 4 out of 12 workloads compared to ACS/FDP. We are also the first to propose bottleneck acceleration using multiple large cores and find that performance improves with multiple large cores since there are independent bottlenecks that need to be simultaneously accelerated. We conclude that BIS provides a comprehensive approach to fine-grain bottleneck acceleration on future ACMPs that can help existing and future applications take advantage of a larger number of cores while reducing programmer effort.

Acknowledgments

We thank Eiman Ebrahimi, Veynu Narasiman, Santhosh Srinath, other members of the HPS research group, our shepherd Ras Bodik and the anonymous reviewers for their comments and suggestions. We gratefully acknowledge the support of the Cockrell Foundation, Intel Corporation, Oracle Corporation and the Gigascale Systems Research Center. José Joao was supported by an Intel PhD Fellowship.

References

[1] MySQL database engine 5.0.1. http://www.mysql.com.

[2] SQLite database engine version 3.5.8. 2008.

[3] SysBench: a system performance benchmark v0.4.8. http://sysbench.sourceforge.net.

[4] G. M. Amdahl. Validity of the single processor approach to achieving large scale computing capabilities. In *AFIPS*, 1967.

[5] M. Annavaram, E. Grochowski, and J. Shen. Mitigating Amdahl's law through EPI throttling. In *ISCA*, 2005.

[6] D. H. Bailey et al. The NAS parallel benchmarks. Technical Report RNR-94-007, NASA Ames Research Center, 1994.

[7] A. Bhattacharjee and M. Martonosi. Thread criticality predictors for dynamic performance, power, and resource management in chip multiprocessors. In *ISCA*, 2009.

[8] Q. Cai, J. González, R. Rakvic, G. Magklis, P. Chaparro, and A. González. Meeting points: using thread criticality to adapt multicore hardware to parallel regions. In *PACT*, 2008.

[9] E. Ebrahimi, R. Miftakhutdinov, C. Fallin, C. J. Lee, J. A. Joao, O. Mutlu, and Y. N. Patt. Parallel application memory scheduling. In *MICRO*, 2011.

[10] B. Fields, R. Bodik, and M. Hill. Slack: maximizing performance under technological constraints. In *ISCA*, 2002.

[11] B. Fields, S. Rubin, and R. Bodik. Focusing processor policies via critical-path prediction. In *ISCA*, 2001.

[12] M. Herlihy and J. E. B. Moss. Transactional memory: architectural support for lock-free data structures. In *ISCA*, 1993.

[13] M. D. Hill and M. R. Marty. Amdahl's law in Multicore Era. Technical Report CS-TR-2007-1593, Univ. of Wisconsin, 2007.

[14] J. K. Hollingsworth. An online computation of critical path profiling. In *SIGMETRICS Symposium on Parallel and Distributed Tools*, 1996.

[15] A. H. Hormati, Y. Choi, M. Kudlur, R. Rabbah, T. Mudge, and S. Mahlke. Flextream: Adaptive compilation of streaming applications for heterogeneous architectures. In *PACT*, 2009.

[16] Intel. Source code for Intel threading building blocks.

[17] Intel. IA-32 Intel Architecture Software Dev. Guide, 2008.

[18] Intel. Getting Started with Intel Parallel Studio, 2011.

[19] D. Koufaty, D. Reddy, and S. Hahn. Bias scheduling in heterogeneous multi-core architectures. In *EuroSys*, 2010.

[20] H. Kredel. Source code for traveling salesman problem (tsp). http://krum.rz.uni-mannheim.de/ba-pp-2007/java/index.html.

[21] R. Kumar, D. Tullsen, N. Jouppi, and P. Ranganathan. Heterogeneous chip multiprocessors. *IEEE Computer*, 2005.

[22] N. B. Lakshminarayana, J. Lee, and H. Kim. Age based scheduling for asymmetric multiprocessors. In *SC*, 2009.

[23] T. Li, A. R. Lebeck, and D. J. Sorin. Quantifying instruction criticality for shared memory multiprocessors. In *SPAA*, 2003.

[24] J. F. Martínez and J. Torrellas. Speculative synchronization: applying thread-level speculation to explicitly parallel applications. In *ASPLOS*, 2002.

[25] J. M. Mellor-Crummey and M. L. Scott. Synchronization without contention. In *ASPLOS*, 1991.

[26] T. Morad, U. C. Weiser, A. Kolodny, M. Valero, and E. Ayguade. Performance, power efficiency and scalability of asymmetric cluster chip multiprocessors. *Computer Architecture Letters*, 2006.

[27] R. Narayanan, B. Ozisikyilmaz, J. Zambreno, G. Memik, and A. Choudhary. MineBench: A benchmark suite for data mining workloads. In *IISWC*, 2006.

[28] Y. Nishitani, K. Negishi, H. Ohta, and E. Nunohiro. Implementation and evaluation of OpenMP for Hitachi SR8000. In *ISHPC*, 2000.

[29] R. Rajwar and J. Goodman. Speculative lock elision: Enabling highly concurrent multithreaded execution. In *MICRO*, 2001.

[30] R. Rajwar and J. R. Goodman. Transactional lock-free execution of lock-based programs. In *ASPLOS*, 2002.

[31] L. Rudolph and Z. Segall. Dynamic decentralized cache schemes for MIMD parallel processors. In *ISCA*, 1984.

[32] J. C. Saez, M. Prieto, A. Fedorova, and S. Blagodurov. A comprehensive scheduler for asymmetric multicore systems. In *EuroSys*, 2010.

[33] The Standard Performance Evaluation Corporation. *Welcome to SPEC*. http://www.specbench.org/.

[34] M. A. Suleman. *An Asymmetric Multi-core Architecture for Efficiently Accelerating Critical Paths in Multithreaded Programs*. PhD thesis, UT-Austin, 2010.

[35] M. A. Suleman, O. Mutlu, J. A. Joao, Khubaib, and Y. N. Patt. Data marshaling for multi-core architectures. *ISCA*, 2010.

[36] M. A. Suleman, O. Mutlu, M. K. Qureshi, and Y. N. Patt. Accelerating critical section execution with asymmetric multi-core architectures. *ASPLOS*, 2009.

[37] M. A. Suleman, M. K. Qureshi, Khubaib, and Y. N. Patt. Feedback-directed pipeline parallelism. In *PACT*, 2010.

[38] Tornado Web Server. Source code. http://tornado.sourceforge.net/, 2008.

[39] M. Waldvogel, G. Varghese, J. Turner, and B. Plattner. Scalable high speed IP routing lookups. In *SIGCOMM*, 1997.

[40] P. Zhao and J. N. Amaral. Ablego: a function outlining and partial inlining framework. *Softw. Pract. Exper.*, 37(5):465–491, 2007.

Optimal Task Assignment in Multithreaded Processors: A Statistical Approach

Petar Radojković
Barcelona Supercomputing Center (BSC), Barcelona, Spain
petar.radojkovic@bsc.es

Vladimir Čakarević
Barcelona Supercomputing Center, Barcelona, Spain
vladimir.cakarevic@bsc.es

Miquel Moretó
Universitat Politècnica de Catalunya (UPC) & BSC, Barcelona, Spain
mmoreto@ac.upc.edu

Javier Verdú
Universitat Politècnica de Catalunya, Barcelona, Spain
jverdu@ac.upc.edu

Alex Pajuelo
Universitat Politècnica de Catalunya, Barcelona, Spain
mpajuelo@ac.upc.edu

Francisco J. Cazorla
BSC & Spanish National Research Council (IIIA-CSIC), Barcelona, Spain
francisco.cazorla@bsc.es

Mario Nemirovsky
ICREA Research Professor at BSC, Barcelona, Spain
mario.nemirovsky@bsc.es

Mateo Valero
BSC & UPC, Barcelona, Spain
mateo@ac.upc.edu

Abstract

The introduction of massively multithreaded (MMT) processors, comprised of a large number of cores with many shared resources, has made task scheduling, in particular task to hardware thread assignment, one of the most promising ways to improve system performance. However, finding an optimal task assignment for a workload running on MMT processors is an NP-complete problem.

Due to the fact that the performance of the best possible task assignment is unknown, the room for improvement of current task-assignment algorithms cannot be determined. This is a major problem for the industry because it could lead to: (1) A waste of resources if excessive effort is devoted to improving a task assignment algorithm that already provides a performance that is close to the optimal one, or (2) significant performance loss if insufficient effort is devoted to improving poorly-performing task assignment algorithms.

In this paper, we present a method based on Extreme Value Theory that allows the prediction of the performance of the optimal task assignment in MMT processors. We further show that executing a sample of several hundred or several thousand *random* task assignments is enough to obtain, with very high confidence, an assignment with a performance that is close to the optimal one. We validate our method with an industrial case study for a set of multithreaded network applications running on an UltraSPARC T2 processor.

Categories and Subject Descriptors D4 [*Operating systems*]: Process management—Scheduling

General Terms Performance, experimentation

Keywords Scheduling, Task assignment, Multithreading, Statistical estimation, Extreme value theory

1. Introduction

The main purpose of Lightweight Kernel (LWK) implementations is to provide maximum access to the hardware resources for the applications, as well as providing predictable system performance. In order to achieve these goals, system services are restricted only to the ones that are essential. Furthermore, the services are streamlined, thus reducing the overhead of LWKs to the minimum. Also, LWKs usually apply simplified algorithms for task scheduling and memory management that provide a significant and predictable amount of the processor resources to the running applications.

Dynamic scheduling may potentially vary the amount of processing time made available to applications during their execution, which can significantly affect the performance of HPC applications [26, 42] and reduce the performance provided by commercial network processors. Maximizing the amount of computation power delivered to running parallel applications is critical to achieving high performance and scalability. As a result, many commercial systems already use LWKs with static scheduling, such as CNK [48] in BlueGene HPC systems, and Netra DPS [3, 4] which is mainly used in networking.

Multithreaded processors[1] comprised of several cores, where each core supports several simultaneously running threads, have different *levels of resource sharing* [56]. For example, in a CMP processor where each core supports the concurrent execution of several tasks through SMT, all simultaneously running tasks share global resources such as the last level of cache or the I/O. In addition to this, tasks running in the same core share core resources such as the Instruction Fetch Unit, or the L1 instruction and data cache. Therefore, the way that tasks are assigned to cores determines which resources they share, which, in turn, may significantly affect the system performance. In processors with several levels of resource sharing, task scheduling is comprised of two steps. In the first step, usually called *workload selection*, the OS selects the set of tasks (workload) that will be executed in the processor in the next time slice, from a set of ready-to-run tasks. In the second step, called *task assignment*, each task in the workload is assigned to a hardware context (virtual CPU) of the processor.

[1] In this paper, we use the term "multithreaded processor" to refer to any processor that has support for more than one thread running at a time. Chip Multiprocessors (CMPs), Simultaneous Multithreading (SMT), Coarse-grain Multithreading, Fine-Grain Multithreading processors, or any combination of them are multithreaded processors.

In Massively Multithreaded (MMT) processors with large numbers of cores and several levels of resource sharing that increase in each generation [5], finding a good task assignment becomes an intractable problem. As the number of possible task assignments is vast (*e.g.* 10^{50}) [18, 20, 33, 44], it is unfeasible to do an exhaustive search in order to find the task assignment with the highest performance. Also, the analytical analysis of optimal task assignment is an NP-complete problem [24].

Therefore, current task assignment approaches can not guarantee that the performance of the predicted best assignment is either the optimal one, or close to it. As the performance of the optimal task assignment for a workload is unknown, the room for improvement of current task assignment techniques cannot be determined. Thus, it is difficult to properly determine the effort needed to invest in the task assignment process. This may lead to overspending if a good task assignment algorithm is constantly improved, or sub-optimal performance if a poor-performing algorithm is not enhanced.

In this paper, we present a method based on Extreme Value Theory (EVT) that allows the prediction of the performance of the optimal task assignment. We also show that, in environments in which the workload infrequently changes, the system designer can simply execute a sample of several hundred or several thousand *random* task assignments of a given workload and measure the performance of each assignment. According to this analysis, there is a very high probability that the performance of the best observed assignment will be close to the optimal system performance. This removes the need for any application profiling or an understanding of the increasingly complex MMT architectures. Unlike other task assignment proposals that use performance predictors to find the best task assignment, our method is application and architecture independent. The method can be applied directly and without any change to any architecture running any set of applications. Our study makes the following contributions:

1. We show that running a sample of several hundred or several thousand random task assignments will most probably capture an assignment within 1% or 2% of the best performing ones.
2. We present a statistical method that, based on the measured performance of a sample of random assignments, estimates the performance of the best task assignment *i.e.* the optimal system performance for a given workload.
3. We present an iterative algorithm that, based on the previous analysis, samples random task assignments until it captures an assignment with the acceptable performance difference with respect to the estimated optimal system performance.

We applied the presented analysis and the iterative tasks-assignment algorithm to an industrial case study in which we scheduled multithreaded network applications running on the UltraSPARC T2 processor. For all five applications used in the study, just several thousand random task assignments were enough to capture an assignment with a performance loss below 2.5% with respect to the estimated optimal system performance (the estimated performance of the best task assignment). When the acceptable performance loss increased to 10%, for all the benchmarks in the suite, running less than 1300 random assignments was enough to provide the required performance. In addition to being architecture and application independent, our method required, in the worst case, around two hours of experimentation on the target systems to find the task assignments with performance very close to the optimal one.

The rest of the paper is organized as follows. Section 2 motivates the need for systematic task assignments and quantifies the number of possible different assignments in modern MMT processors. Section 3 presents a statistical analysis that we use to estimate the optimal system performance based on a small sample of random task assignments. Section 4 describes the experimental environment used in the case study. In Section 5, we present the results of experiments in which we applied the presented analysis to the industrial case study for the assignment of multithreaded network applications. Section 6 presents the related work, while Section 7 lists the conclusions of the study.

2. Motivation and background

In this paper, we focus on the problem of task assignment for network applications running on massively multithreaded processors. The importance of network applications increases with the number and the complexity of services that these applications provide and with the tremendous growth of Internet traffic. Providing high performance in networking services is critical to sustain these services and avoid dropping packets, since network processors are saturated by a high network bandwidth that is constantly increasing.

In order to provide high-speed processing and high throughput, network applications have specific hardware and operating system requirements. Massively multithreaded processors are the best alternative to exploit the multiple levels of parallelism exposed by network applications [57]. These processors support simultaneous execution of multiple threads that can process numerous packets at the same time. Network-oriented systems require run-time environments that provide high performance, high-speed packet processing, and execution time predictability. To that end, these systems use low-overhead runtime environments that reduce the performance impact of the system overhead because of execution of management tasks [4].

In networking environments, applications continuously process different packets, repeating a similar processing algorithm for each packet. As the applications running on network processors provide a constant set of services and process different packets in a similar manner, dynamic task scheduling is not essential. In addition to this, the workload running on network processors is usually known beforehand and seldom changes at runtime. Hence, the most promising way to increase the performance of network applications running in MMT processor is by finding a task assignment with a performance that is close to the optimal (close-to-the-optimal task assignment), which is the focus of our study.

Doing optimal task assignment requires a deep knowledge of the resource requirements of each running task and an understanding of how the tasks interact in each shared processor resource. Therefore, it is difficult to determine the optimal task assignment without a previous analysis of a large number of experiments that exponentially increases with the number of processor hardware contexts (virtual CPUs), number of different levels of resource sharing, and number of simultaneously running tasks. The problem becomes even more complex for multithreaded applications. When an application comprises several threads, it is not enough to understand how sharing hardware resources affects the execution time of each thread independently. The designer also has to be aware of the way that the threads communicate and to understand which application threads are the bottlenecks that determine application performance. Currently, task assignment is done in one of two ways:

(1) **Manual assignment:** A skilled designer determines the optimal task assignment based on a detailed analysis of the target architecture and an off-line application profiling. This analysis is complex and its complexity increases with the number of processor hardware contexts, number of levels of resource sharing, and number of simultaneously running tasks. In addition to this, any change in the application or in the hardware platform requires the repetition of the whole analysis. Manual task assignment is not a systematic

approach, its performance depends on the designer's skills, and, in general, does not provide the optimal solution.

(2) **Performance predictors:** Several studies [20, 44, 46] propose approaches that predict the performance of different task assignments for a given workload based on some architecture-dependent heuristics. As the number of all possible task assignments is vast (over 10^{50} in current architectures), predicting the performance of all assignments is unfeasible. Therefore, the predictors are used to estimate performance for a sample of assignments, and to determine the best task assignment in the given sample. In addition to this, as predictors introduce an error when estimating the performance of task assignments, the best predicted assignment in the sample may not be the actual best one. Another drawback of most of the currently available performance predictors is that they are not designed with multithreaded applications in mind.

In both manual task assignment and performance predictors, any change in the architecture or applications may require significant extra time and effort to find good task assignments under new conditions. If task assignment is done manually, a change in the set of running applications or target architecture requires the designer to repeat the whole analysis. In the case of performance predictors, the whole process of application profiling and performance estimation has to be re-analyzed, and the prediction algorithm may require significant changes.

Number of possible task assignments in current MMT processors: In current multithreaded processors comprised of several cores where each core supports several simultaneously-running tasks, the total number of possible task assignments is vast [18, 20, 33, 44]. This number will grow hugely in future massively multithreaded processors in which the number of cores and number of different levels of resource sharing increase [5]. In order to illustrate this, we study the number of possible assignments when several tasks simultaneously execute on the UltraSPARC T2 processor. The UltraSPARC T2 processor comprises eight cores, and each core contains two hardware pipelines. Each (hardware) pipeline can execute up to four tasks at a time, meaning that the maximum number of simultaneously running tasks is 64. The number of possible task assignments for different workload size is shown in Table 1. The first column of the table shows the number of tasks in the workload. We present results for 3, 6, 9, 12, 15, 18, and 60 tasks. The second column presents the number of different task assignments for a given workload size. When the workload is comprised of 3 tasks, *a*, *b* and *c*, the number of possible task assignments is 11. For example, in one assignment, *a* is executed alone on *Core 0*, while *b* and *c* run inside the same hardware pipeline of Core 1: {*[a][]*}{*[bc][]*} [2]. In the second assignment, *a* executes alone on *Core 0*, and *b* and *c* are distributed among two hardware pipelines of Core 1, {*[a][]*}{*[b][c]*}, *etc.* The third column of the table shows the time needed to execute all possible task assignments assuming that each assignment can be executed in only one second. Finally, in the last column, we present the time needed to predict the performance of all task assignments. We make an optimistic assumption that the performance of a single assignment can be predicted in $1\mu s$ that is in the order of 1000 cycles of a processor running at 1GHz frequency.

Overall, we observe that the number of possible tasks assignments as well as the time needed to execute them grows exponentially with the number of tasks in the workload. The point where running all assignments is unfeasible is reached very fast. For 9 tasks in the workload, the time needed to execute all assignments is 7 days, for 12 tasks, the execution time is more than 15 years. For 60-task workloads that use 94% of hardware contexts of the processor, the time needed to execute all possible task assignments is 1.75×10^{51} years. The results presented in Table 1 clearly show that, in general, running all task assignments is unfeasible, and that an exhaustive search cannot be used to find the optimal system performance for a given workload.

Number of tasks	Number of possible task assignments	Time needed to execute all task assignments	Time needed to predict all task assignments
3	11	11 seconds	11 μs
6	1,526	25 minutes	1.5 ms
9	591×10^3	7 days	0.6 seconds
12	458×10^6	15 years	8 minutes
15	600×10^9	19 thousand years	7 days
18	971×10^{12}	30 million years	31 years
60	550×10^{56}	1.75×10^{51} years	1.75×10^{45} years

Table 1. Number of different task assignments for applications running on the UltraSPARC T2 processor

From Table 1, we also see that the prediction of all possible tasks assignments is unfeasible. The last column shows that, for example, for the case of 15-task workloads, the time needed to predict all assignments is 7 days. For 18 tasks, the prediction time is measured in years. Therefore, performance predictors can be used only to determine the close-to-the-optimal task assignment in a limited sample. But, as the number of possible task assignments in modern processors is vast, the effectiveness of performance predictors is questionable [18, 20]; even if we assumed that a performance predictor would be able to find the best assignment in the sample, it would not be clear what the performance difference between the best assignment in the sample and the actual global best assignment (the optimal system performance) would be.

Importance of knowing the optimal system performance: Numerous studies present the algorithms for task assignments on multithreaded processors (see Section 6). Given that, in general, running all possible task assignments is unfeasible, several authors [6, 20, 44] verify their proposals with respect to a naive task assignment, in which tasks are randomly assigned to the virtual CPUs of the processor, or Linux-like assignments, in which the number of tasks per core or *scheduling domain* is balanced. It is our position that the evaluation of those proposals could significantly improve if they were also compared to the performance of the optimal task assignment.

We use an example to show how the evaluation of task assignments techniques can be misleading if the optimal system performance is unknown. Figure 1 presents the performance of two multithreaded network benchmarks running on the UltraSPARC T2 processor. Both benchmarks used in the experiment, *IPFwd-intadd* and *IPFwd-intmul*, are based on a generic 3-thread pipelined IP Forwarding network application [44]. Figure 1 shows the results for two instances of the 3-thread benchmark (six threads) simultaneously running on the processor. As, in this specific case, the total number of possible task assignments is around 1500, we can obtain the performance for all assignments. The X axis lists the benchmarks that are used in the experiment and the Y axis shows the performance measured in processed Packets Per Second (PPS). The chart is divided into two parts. In the left part, we only plot the results for *Naive* and the *Linux-like* task assignment. In the right part, we also include the bar that corresponds to the optimal system performance.

Based on the results presented in Figure 1, we want to analyze whether the Linux-like scheduler provides a good performance for *IPFwd-intadd* and *IPFwd-intmul* benchmarks running on the UltraSPARC T2 processor. First, we compare only the Linux-like and Naive scheduler (see the left part of the chart). The improve-

[2] The rest of the cores are not shown for the sake of simplicity.

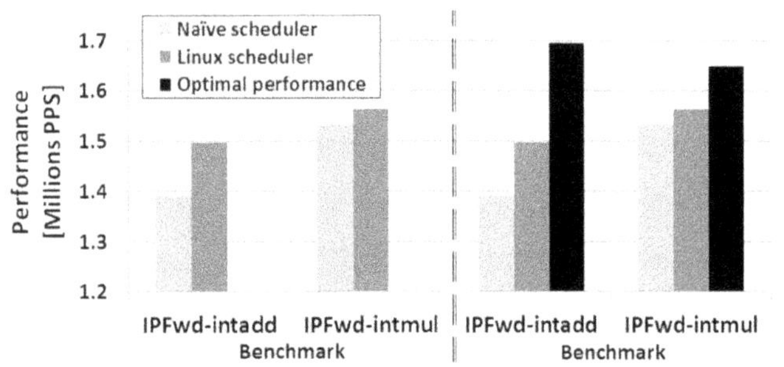

Figure 1. Comparison of a naive, Linux-like, and optimal task assignment

ment of the Linux-like scheduler with respect to naive scheduling is around 110,000 PPS (8%) for *IPFwd-intadd* benchmark, and around 30,000 PPS (2%) for *IPFwd-intmul* benchmark. Based on these results, we could conclude that the Linux-like scheduler provides much better performance for *IPFwd-intadd* than for *IPFwd-intmul* benchmark.

However, when we also consider the performance of the optimal task assignment, the conclusions of the analysis change. From the results presented in the right part of the chart, we see that the difference between the optimal performance and performance provided by the naive scheduler is much larger for *IPFwd-intadd* than for *IPFwd-intmul* benchmark, 305,000 PPS (22%) and 115,000 PPS (7%), respectively. Therefore, we conclude that the improvement of the Linux-like scheduler for *IPFwd-intadd* benchmark is higher because the room for the improvement is larger, and not because the Linux-like scheduler fits better with this benchmark. Actually, for the *IPFwd-intmul* benchmark, the Linux-like scheduler provides a performance much closer to the optimal one. For *IPFwd-intmul*, the performance loss of the Linux-like scheduler with respect to optimal performance is only 85,000 PPS (5%). For *IPFwd-intadd*, the performance loss is 200,000 PPS (12%).

Overall, knowing the optimal system performance not only improves the evaluation of different task assignment techniques, but it also shows the performance difference between the proposed task assignments and the optimal one. This performance difference determines the upper limit for improvement of a given task assignment algorithm, which is the most important piece of information for the system designer when deciding whether the algorithm should be enhanced.

3. A statistical approach to the task assignment problem

In this paper, we present a statistical method that overcomes the limitations of the approaches currently used for task assignment in multithreaded processors. The analysis is comprised of three parts. First, we execute a sample of random task assignments on the target processor and measure the performance of each one of them. We analyze whether the best performing assignment in the random sample exhibits performance close to the optimal one. In order to do this, we analyze the probability that a sample of randomly selected n task assignments contains at least one from the $P\%$ (*e.g.*, $P = 1$, 2, or 5%) of the best-performing assignments. Second, we show how the cumulative distribution function can be used to identify which portion of all task assignments has good performance. Thirdly, we use Extreme Value Theory to statistically estimate the performance of the best task assignment, *i.e.* the optimal system performance for the given workload. We also use the estimated optimal system performance to determine the possible room for the performance improvement of the proposed task assignment method.

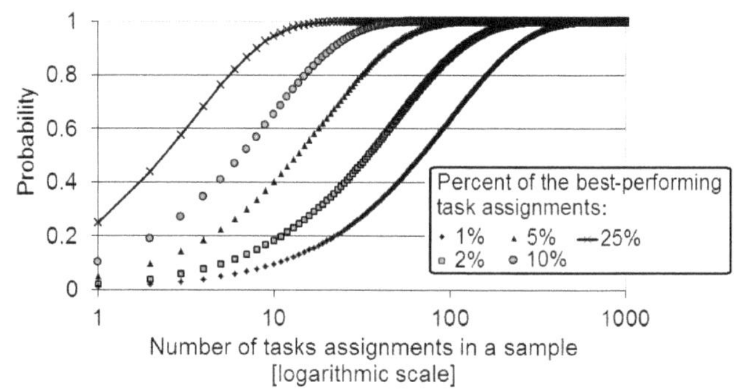

Figure 2. Probability that a sample contains a task assignment from P% of the best-performing assignments

3.1 Finding task assignments with a good performance

The probability that a sample of random assignments selected from a vast population contains the assignment with *the best* performance is low. However, it is not clear what the probability is that a sample of random assignments contains at least one of the assignments with *a good* performance.

Assume that event A is the probability that a sample contains at least one task assignment from the $P\%$ of best-performing assignment. Event A' is the opposite of event A, representing the probability that the random sample contains zero task assignments from $P\%$ of the best-performing assignments. If the number of possible task assignments is large (*i.e.* the population is large), the probability that a single assignment is in the lower $(100 - P)\%$ of the population is $\frac{100-P}{100}$. We assume that the sample is selected from a finite population of all task assignments using sampling with replacement. Sampling with replacement means that at any draw, all assignments in the population are given an equal chance of being drawn, no matter how often they have already been drawn [16]. In addition to this, we assume that the selected task assignments in the sample are mutually independent and uniformly distributed. Taking into account these assumptions, the probability that all n assignments in the sample are contained in the lower $(100 - P)\%$ of the population is computed as: $P(A') = (\frac{100-P}{100})^n$. As A and A' are opposite events, the sum of probabilities that they occur is equal to 1: $P(A) + P(A') = 1$. Therefore, the probability of the event A can be computed as:

$$P(A) = 1 - P(A') = 1 - \left(\frac{100\text{-P}}{100}\right)^{n}$$

We observe that the probability that a sample of random task assignments contains at least one of the $P\%$ of the best-performing assignment is independent of the population size (*i.e.* the number of possible task assignments). However, we have to be aware that this is valid only for large populations, which is satisfied in the case of task scheduling problems in MMT processors, as we have shown in Table 1.

Figure 2 plots the probability $P(A)$ for the samples of different size and for different percentages of the best-performing task assignments. The X axis of the figure shows the number of assignments in the sample (n), while the Y axis presents the probability that the sample contains at least one from $P\%$ of the best-performing task assignments. The figure shows data for $P =$ 1, 2, 5, 10, 25. We derive three conclusions from Figure 2. First, that the probability asymptotically approaches 1 as the number of task assignments in the sample increases. Second, as the fraction of the best-performing assignments decreases (from 25% to 1% in the figure) the probability approaches 1 slower (more task assignments are required to reach a high probability). Finally, we observe

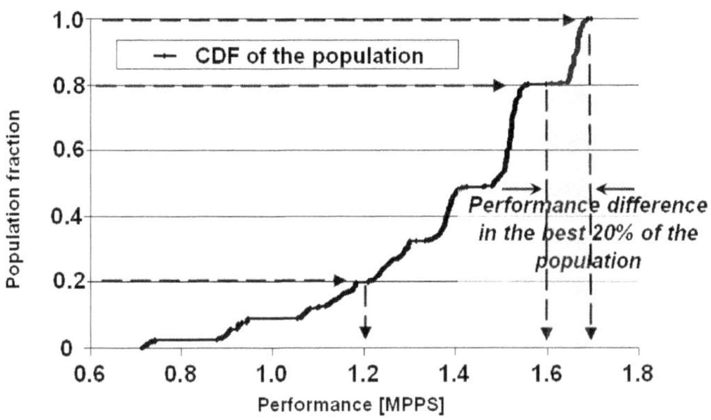

Figure 3. An example of Cumulative Distribution Function

that small samples of below 10 elements are unlikely to capture any task assignment from 1%, 2%, and 5% of the best-performing ones. However, a sample of several hundred random observations is sufficient to capture at least one of 1% or 2% of the best-performing task assignments with a very high probability. This means that, if we assume that 1% or 2% of the best-performing assignments have a good performance, simply running several hundred or several thousand randomly selected task assignments is sufficient to capture at least one assignment with a good performance.

3.2 Cumulative Distribution Function

One way to determine which portion of the population of all task assignments exhibits a good performance is by plotting the Cumulative Distribution Function (CDF). We illustrate CDF with the following example. Figure 3 shows the CDF of all 1500 task assignments for a network processing a workload of six threads. The details of the experimental framework are described in Section 4. The X axis of the figure shows the measured performance in Millions of Packets processed Per Second (MPPS). The Y axis shows the portion of all task assignments (the population) that exhibit a performance lower or equal to the corresponding value on the X axis.

The presented CDF plot also shows the importance of task assignment. The performance of the task assignments ranges from 0.715 MPPS to 1.7 MPPS, meaning that non-optimal assignment could lead to $\frac{1,700,000-715,000}{1,700,000} = 58\%$ of performance loss. The performance difference in $P\%$ of the best-performing task assignments can be directly determined from the CDF of the population. For the data presented in Figure 3, the performance difference in 1% of the best-performing task assignments is very low, below 10,000 PPS which is only 0.6% of the optimal system performance. However, in general, since running all task assignments is not feasible, CDF based on the performance of all assignments cannot be constructed. In that case, the measured performance of a sample of task assignments can be used to construct an Empirical CDF (ECDF) that estimates the CDF of the whole population [27, 34]. ECDF is a very good method to estimate the median part of the actual CDF, but it cannot be used to infer the performance of the best task assignments in the tails of CDF of vast populations. Therefore, ECDF cannot be used to estimate (with a hard confidence level) the optimal system performance, nor the performance difference in $P\%$ of the best-performing task assignments, which are the main goals of our study.

3.3 Estimation of the optimal performance

One way to evaluate any task assignment approach is to compare the performance of the task assignments provided by the approach

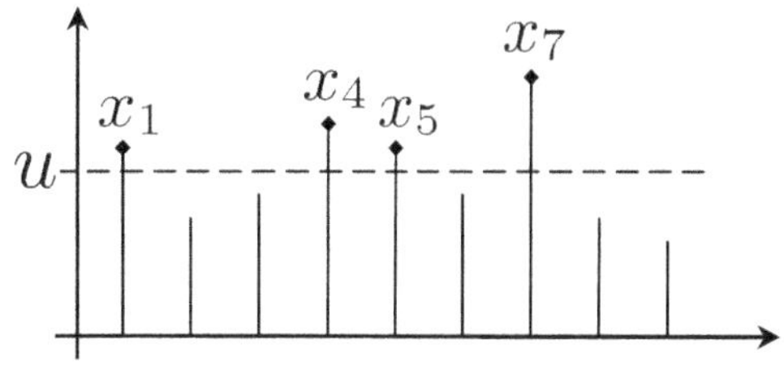

Figure 4. Exceedances over the threshold u

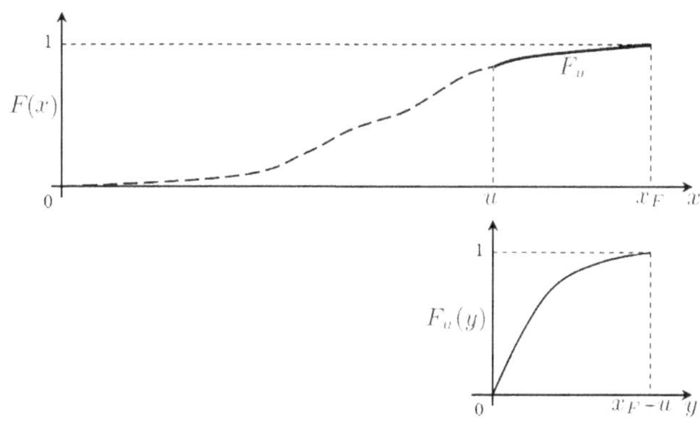

Figure 5. Cumulative distribution function $F(x)$ and and corresponding conditional excess distribution function $F_u(y)$

with the performance of the best assignment, *i.e.* with the optimal system performance. This performance difference shows the room for possible improvement of the proposed scheduling approach. However, as in general the number of possible task assignments is vast, the optimal system performance cannot be determined [33]. In this paper, we propose using statistical inference methods to estimate the optimal system performance based on the measured performance of a sample of random task assignments.

3.3.1 Extreme value theory

We estimate the performance of the best task assignment using Extreme Value Theory (EVT). EVT is a branch of statistics that studies extreme deviations from the median of distributions [10, 11]. One of the EVT approaches is the *Peak Over Threshold* (POT) method. The POT method takes into account the distribution of the observations that exceed a given (high) threshold. For example, in Figure 4, the observations x_1, x_4, x_5, and x_7 exceed the threshold u and constitute extreme values that can be used in POT analysis.

The POT method can also be explained using cumulative distribution function (CDF). For example, assume that F is the CDF of a random variable X. The POT method can be used to estimate the cumulative distribution function F_u of values of x above a certain threshold u. The function F_u is called the *conditional excess distribution function* and it is defined as

$$F_u(y) = P(X - u \leq y \mid X > u), \quad 0 \leq y \leq x_F - u,$$

where X is the observed random variable, u is the given threshold, $y = x - u$ are the exceedances over the threshold, and $x_F \leq \infty$ is the right endpoint of the cumulative distribution function F. Figure 5 shows a CDF of a random variable X (upper chart) and the corresponding conditional excess distribution function $F_u(y)$ (bottom chart).

The POT method is based on the following theorem [9, 43]:

THEOREM 1. *For a large class of underlying distributions functions F, the conditional excess distribution function $F_u(y)$, for u large, is well approximated by $F_u(y) \approx G_{\xi,\sigma}(y)$ where*

$$G_{\xi,\sigma}(y) = \begin{cases} 1-(1+\frac{\xi}{\sigma}y)^{-1/\xi} & \text{for} \quad \xi \neq 0 \\ 1-e^{-y/\sigma} & \text{for} \quad \xi = 0 \end{cases}$$

for $y \in [0, (x_F - u)]$ if $\xi \geq 0$ and $y \in [0, -\frac{\sigma}{\xi}]$ if $\xi < 0$, where $G_{\xi,\sigma}$ is called Generalized Pareto Distribution (GPD).

This means that the F_u of numerous distributions that present real-life problems can be approximated with GPD. For each particular problem, the decision as to whether GPD can be used to model the problem, is made based on how well the sample of observations can be fitted to GPD. We describe the goodness of fit of observations to GPD in Section 3.3.2 in Step 2 and Step 3 of the presented analysis. GPD is defined with two parameters: shape parameter ξ and scaling parameter σ. One of the characteristics of GPD is that for $\xi < 0$ the upper bound of the observed value (in our study, the performance of the best task assignment) can be computed as $u - \frac{\sigma}{\xi}$, where σ and ξ are the GPD parameters and u is the selected threshold [25, 35].

In Theorem 1, the definition of $G_{\xi,\sigma}(y)$ for parameter $\xi = 0$ can only be used to model problems with an infinite upper bound [25, 35]. As in this study we use GPD to estimate application performance when running in a real computer system, the upper bound of the observed value is finite and the estimated values of the parameter ξ are always $\hat{\xi} < 0$. Therefore, for the sake of the simplicity of the presented mathematical formulas, in the rest of the paper we do not present $G_{\xi,\sigma}(y)$ formulas for parameter $\xi = 0$.

3.3.2 Application of Peak Over Threshold method

We use the POT method to estimate the optimal system performance for a given workload (*i.e.* the performance of the best task assignment) based on the measured performance of the sample of random task assignments. The application of the POT method involves the following steps:

Step 1: Generate the sample of random task assignments, execute the assignments on the target machine, and measure the performance of each assignment. A requisite of the presented statistical analysis is that the selected task assignments in the sample are independent and identically distributed (*iid*): they have to be independent and have to have the same marginal distribution. The sample assignments have to be taken from a single population using sampling with replacement [55]. The method we use to generate *iid* task assignments is described next.

For example, assume that a workload of T tasks would be assigned on a processor comprising V hardware contexts, where $T \leq V$. We enumerate the hardware contexts of the processor with integers from 1 to V and for each task in the workload we randomly select an integer from this interval. The number assigned to each running task represents the hardware context to which the task is mapped to in a given task assignment. After mapping all tasks, we check if the generated task assignment is valid. An assignment is not valid if two or more tasks are mapped to the same hardware context. If this is the case, we simply discard the invalid assignment and repeat the whole process until the sample contains the required number of task assignments. As assignments in the sample are independent and they are sampled from a single population using sampling with replacement, the generated sample is comprised of *iid* task assignments.

Step 2: Select the threshold u. The selection of the threshold u is an important step in POT analysis. Gilli and Këllezi [25, 35] propose using *sample mean excess plot*, a graphical tool for

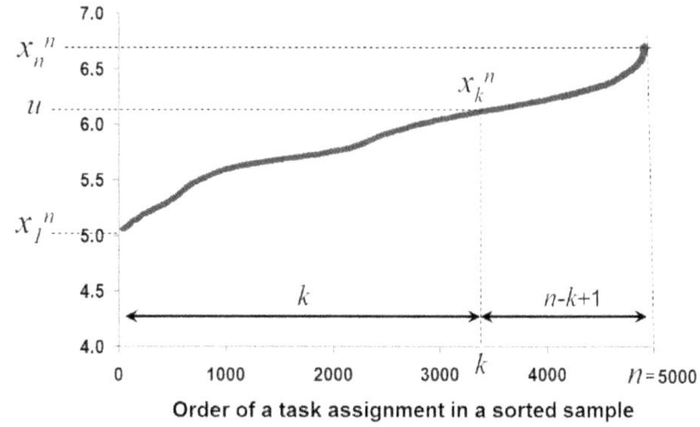

(a) Ordered sample of task assignments

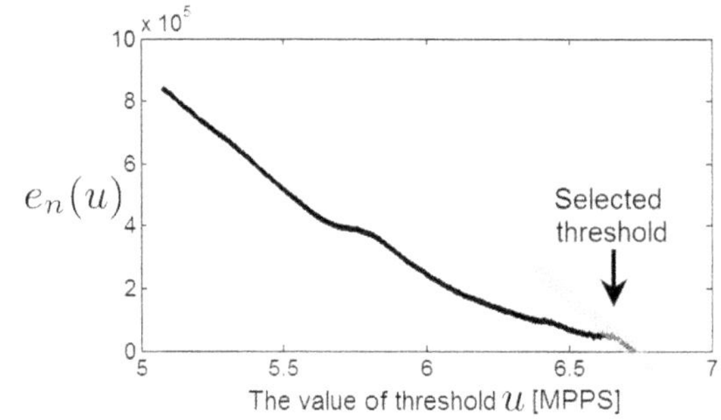

(b) Sample mean excess plot

Figure 6. Selection of the threshold u

threshold selection. This method first sorts all task assignments in a sample in non-decreasing performance order: $x_1^n \leq x_2^n \leq \cdots \leq x_n^n$. Figure 6(a) shows the sorted performance of 5000 random task assignments for a workload comprised of 24 threads of the *IPFwd-L1* application (see Section 4). Then, the possible threshold u takes the values from x_1^n to x_n^n ($x_1^n \leq u \leq x_n^n$) and for each value we compute the sample mean excess function $e_n(u)$:

$$e_n(u) = \frac{\sum_{i=k}^{n}(x_i^n - u)}{n-k+1}, \text{ where } k = min\{\ i \mid x_i^n > u\}.$$

In this formula, the factor $n - k + 1$ is the number of observations that exceed the threshold. Finally, the sample mean excess plot is defined by the points $(u, e_n(u))$ for $x_1^n \leq u \leq x_n^n$. Figure 6(b) shows the example of the sample mean excess plot for 24 threads of *IPFwd-L1* application.

As we are interested in the upper performance bound estimation, the estimated parameter ξ of GPD has to be negative ($\hat{\xi} < 0$). One of the characteristics of the GPD with parameter $\xi < 0$ is that it has linear mean excess function plot. In order to have a good fit of the conditional distribution function F_u to GPD, the threshold should be selected so that the observations that exceed the threshold have a roughly linear sample mean excess plot. As an example, for the data presented in Figure 6, the threshold should be selected to be around 6.6×10^6. Sample mean excess plot is also a very good tool to test whether GPD can be used to model a particular set of observations. If the right portion of the mean excess plot for the sample of measured task assignments performance is not (roughly) linear, that particular problem cannot be modeled using GPD.

Another important tool that can be used to understand if a given sample of observations can be modeled with a Generalized Pareto Distribution is a *quantile plot* [10, 35]. In a quantile plot, the sample quantiles x_i^n are plotted against the quantiles of a target distribution $F^{-1}(q_i)$ for $i = 1, \ldots, n$. If the sample data originates from the family of distributions F, the plot is close to a straight line. For all experiments presented in this paper, we plot the quantiles of the samples of observations against the quantiles of GPD. In all experiments, the form of quantile plots strongly suggest that that samples of observations follow a Generalized Pareto Distribution.

The linear sample mean excess plot and the quantile plot are not the only constraints that should be considered when selecting the threshold. If the threshold is too low, the estimated parameters of GPD may be biased to the median values of the cumulative distribution function instead of to the maximum values. In order to avoid this bias, when selecting a threshold we have to ensure that the number of observations that exceed the selected threshold is not higher than 5% of the task assignments in the whole sample. This is a commonly used limit in studies that use POT analysis [25, 35].

Step 3: Fit the GPD function to the observations that exceed the threshold and estimate parameters ξ and σ.

Once the threshold u is selected, the observations over the threshold can be fitted to GPD, and the parameters of the distribution can be estimated. For the sake of simplicity, we assume that observations from x_k^n to x_n^n in the sorted sample presented in Figure 6(a) exceed the threshold. We rename the exceedances $y_{i-k+1} = x_i^n - u$ for $k \leq i \leq n$ and use the set of elements $\{y_1, y_2, ..., y_m\}$ to estimate the parameters of GPD. The number of elements in the set, $m = n - k + 1$, is the number of exceedances over the threshold.

Different methods can be used to estimate the parameters of GPD from a sample of observations [12, 28, 30, 52]. In our study, we used the estimation based on the *likelihood* function. The likelihood is a statistical method that estimates distribution parameters based on a set of observations [8]. The GPD is defined with parameters ξ and σ. The likelihood that a set of observations $\{y_1, y_2, ..., y_m\}$ is the outcome of a GPD with parameters $\xi = \xi_0$ and $\sigma = \sigma_0$ is equal to the probability that GPD with parameters ξ_0 and σ_0 has the outcome $\{y_1, y_2, ..., y_m\}$.

We will use the likelihood function to compute the probability that different values of GPD parameters have for a given set of observations $\{y_1, y_2, ..., y_m\}$. As the logarithm is a monotonically increasing function, the logarithm of a positive function achieves the maximum value at the same point as the function itself. This means that instead of finding the maximum of a likelihood function, we can determine the maximum of the logarithm of the likelihood function - the *log-likelihood* function. In statistics, log-likelihood is frequently used instead of the likelihood function because it simplifies the computation. The estimation of parameters ξ and σ of $G_{\xi,\sigma}(y)$ involves the following steps:

(i) Determine the corresponding probability density function as a partial derivate of $G_{\xi,\sigma}(y)$ with respect to y:

$$g_{\xi,\sigma}(y) = \frac{\partial G_{\xi,\sigma}(y)}{\partial y} = \frac{1}{\sigma}(1 + \frac{\xi}{\sigma}y)^{-\frac{1}{\xi}-1}$$

(ii) Find the logarithm of $g_{\xi,\sigma}(y)$:

$$log\ (g_{\xi,\sigma}(y)) = -log\ \sigma - (\frac{1}{\xi} + 1)\ log(1 + \frac{\xi}{\sigma}y)$$

(iii) Compute the log-likelihood function $L(\xi, \sigma|y)$ for the GPD as the logarithm of the joint density of the observations $\{y_1, y_2, ..., y_m\}$:

$$L(\xi, \sigma|y) = \sum_{i=1}^{m} log\ g_{\xi,\sigma}(y_i)$$

$$L(\xi, \sigma|y) = -m\ log\ \sigma - (\frac{1}{\xi} + 1)\sum_{i=1}^{m} log(1 + \frac{\xi}{\sigma}y_i)$$

We compute estimated values of parameters $\hat{\xi}$ and $\hat{\sigma}$, to *maximize* the value of the log-likelihood function $L(\xi, \sigma|y)$ for observations $\{y_1, y_2, ..., y_m\}$:

$$L(\hat{\xi}, \hat{\sigma}|y) = \max_{\xi,\sigma}(L(\xi, \sigma|y))$$

$$L(\hat{\xi}, \hat{\sigma}|y) = \max(-m\ log\ \sigma - (\frac{1}{\xi} + 1)\sum_{i=1}^{m} log(1 + \frac{\xi}{\sigma}y_i))$$

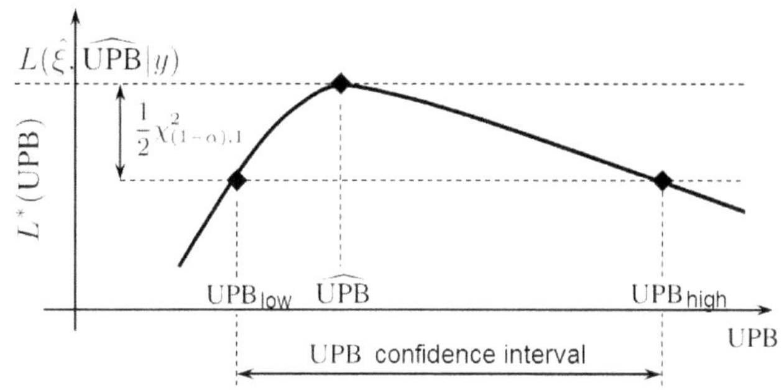

Figure 7. UPB confidence interval

In order to determine the parameters $\hat{\xi}$ and $\hat{\sigma}$, we find the minimum of the negative log-likelihood function, $\min_{\xi,\sigma}(-L(\xi, \sigma|y))$, using the procedure *fminsearch()* included in Matlab® R2007a [14]. The values $\hat{\xi}$ and $\hat{\sigma}$ are called the point estimate of the parameters ξ and σ, respectively.

Step 4: Estimate the optimal system performance (the upper performance bound of all task assignments). The upper bound of the observed value can be determined only for $\hat{\xi} < 0$ which is satisfied for all data sets that are presented in this paper. The point estimate of the Upper Performance Bound (UPB) is computed as $\widehat{\text{UPB}} = u - \hat{\sigma}/\hat{\xi}$.

In order to indicate the confidence of the estimate, we compute the confidence intervals of the estimated $\widehat{\text{UPB}}$. UPB confidence interval is computed using *likelihood ratio test* [8] which consists of the following steps:

(i) Define GPD as a function of ξ and UPB:

$$G_{\xi,\text{UPB}}(y) = 1 - (1 - \frac{1}{\text{UPB}-u}y)^{-1/\xi}$$

(ii) Determine the corresponding probability density function:

$$g_{\xi,\text{UPB}}(y) = \frac{\partial G_{\xi,\text{UPB}}(y)}{\partial y} = -\frac{1}{\xi(\text{UPB}-u)}(1 - \frac{1}{\text{UPB}-u}y)^{-\frac{1}{\xi}-1}$$

(iii) Compute the joint log-likelihood function for observations $\{y_1, ..., y_m\}$:

$$L(\xi, \text{UPB}|y) = \sum_{i=1}^{m} log\ g_{\xi,\text{UPB}}(y_i)$$

$$L(\xi, \text{UPB}|y) = -n\ log(-\xi(\text{UPB} - u)) - (1 + \frac{1}{\xi})\sum_{i=1}^{n} log(1 - \frac{1}{\text{UPB} - u}y_i)$$

(iv) Find the UPB confidence interval. We determine the confidence interval for UPB using likelihood ratio test [8] and Wilks's theorem [15, 59, 60]. The maximum log-likelihood function is determined as $L(\hat{\xi}, \widehat{\text{UPB}}|y) = \max_{\xi,\text{UPB}}(L(\xi, \text{UPB}))$.

The function $L(\hat{\xi}, \widehat{\text{UPB}}|y)$ has two parameters that are free to vary (ξ and UPB), hence it has two degrees of freedom, $df_1 = 2$. As UPB is our parameter of interest, the profile log-likelihood function is defined as $L^*(\text{UPB}) = \max_{\xi} L(\xi, \text{UPB})$.

The function $L^*(\text{UPB})$ has one parameter that is free to vary *i.e.* one degree of freedom, $df_2 = 1$. Wilks's theorem applied to the problem that we are addressing claims that, for large number of exceedances over the threshold, distribution of $2(L(\hat{\xi}, \widehat{\text{UPB}} - L^*(\text{UPB}))$ converges to a χ^2 distribution with $df_1 - df_2$ degrees of freedom. Therefore, the confidence interval of UPB includes all values of UPB that satisfy the following condition:

$$L(\hat{\xi}, \widehat{\text{UPB}}) - L^*(\text{UPB}) < \frac{1}{2}\chi^2_{(1-\alpha),1} \quad (1)$$

$\chi^2_{(1-\alpha),1}$ is the $(1 - \alpha)$-level quantile of the χ^2 distribution with one degree of freedom ($df_1 - df_2 = 1$). α is the confidence level for which we compute UPB confidence intervals.

We illustrate the computation of the UPB confidence interval in Figure 7. The figure plots $L^*(\text{UPB})$ for different values of UPB. For UPB $= \widehat{\text{UPB}}$, L^* reaches its maximum. The confidence interval of UPB includes all values of UPB that satisfy the condition $L^*(\text{UPB}) > L(\hat{\xi}, \widehat{\text{UPB}}) - \frac{1}{2}\chi^2_{(1-\alpha),1}$ which corresponds to the Equation 1. We computed the UPB confidence interval using an iterative method based on the *fminsearch()* function included in Matlab® R2007a.

The code that generates the sample mean excess plots, infers the parameters of the GPD distribution, and estimates the optimal system performance was developed in Matlab® R2007a.

3.4 Summary

In this section, we have presented two statistical methods. The first method computes the probability that a sample of n randomly selected task assignments captures at least one out of $P\%$ (*e.g.* 1%) best performing assignments. The results of this method show that running several hundred or several thousand random tasks assignments is enough to capture at least one out of 1% of the best performing assignments with a very high probability. The second method estimates the performance of the best-performing task assignment, *i.e.* the optimal system performance for a given workload. The method infers the optimal system performance with the hard statistical confidence based on a measured performance of the sample of random task assignments. The presented method is completely independent of the hardware environment and target applications. The method scales to any number of cores and hardware contexts per core and it does not require any profiling of the application nor does it require knowledge of the architecture of the target hardware.

4. Experimental environment

We evaluated the presented statistical analysis for the case study of multithreaded network applications running in a real industrial environment. The environment comprised two T5220 machines that managed the generation and the processing of network traffic. Each T5220 machine comprised one UltraSPARC T2 processor. One T5220 machine executed the Network Traffic Generator (NTGen) [4]. NTGen is a software tool, developed by Oracle that generates IPv4 TCP/UDP packets with configurable options to modify various packet header fields. NTGen transmitted network packets through a 10Gb link to the second T5220 machine in which we executed the task assignments selected by our method. In all the experiments presented in the study, NTGen generated enough traffic to saturate the network processing machine. Thus, in all experiments, the performance bottleneck was the speed at which the packets were processed, which is determined by the performance of the selected task assignment.

4.1 UltraSPARC T2 processor

The UltraSPARC T2 is a multithreaded processor [1][2] that comprises eight cores connected through the crossbar to the shared L2 cache (see Figure 8). Each of the cores supports eight hardware contexts, thus up to 64 tasks can be simultaneously executed on the processor. Strands inside each hardware core are divided into two groups of four strands, forming two hardware execution pipelines. Therefore, tasks simultaneously running on the UltraSPARC T2 processor can share (and compete for) different resources in three different levels depending on how they are distributed on the processor. Resources at the *IntraPipe* level, such as the Instruction Fetch Unit (IFU) and the Integer Execution Units (IEU) are shared among tasks running in the same hardware pipeline. The *IntraCore* resources, such as the L1 instruction cache, L1 data cache, instruction and data TLBs, Load Store Unit (LSU), Floating Point

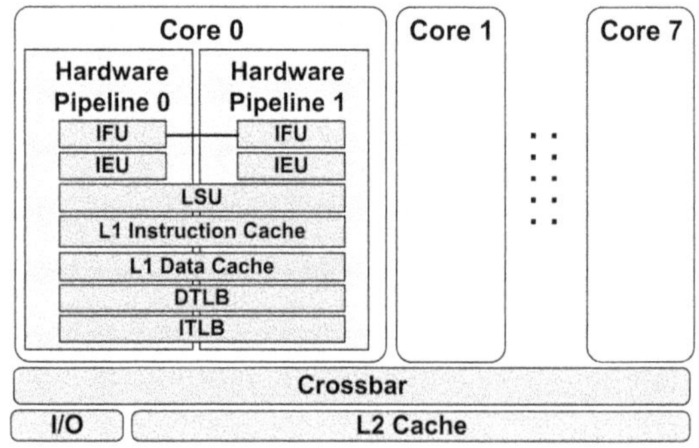

Figure 8. Schematic view of the three resource sharing levels of the UltraSPARC T2 processor

and Graphic Unit (FPU), and Cryptographic Processing Unit are shared among tasks running on the same core. Finally, the resources shared among all tasks simultaneously running on the processor (*InterCore* sharing level) are mainly the L2 cache, the on-chip interconnection network (crossbar), the memory controllers, and the interface to off-chip resources [56].

4.2 Netra DPS

Networking systems use lightweight runtime environments to reduce the overhead introduced by fully-fledged OSs. One of these environments is Netra DPS [3, 4] developed by Oracle. Netra DPS does not incorporate virtual memory nor a run-time process scheduler, and performs no context switching. The assignment of running tasks to processor hardware contexts (virtual CPUs) is performed statically at the compile time. It is the responsibility of the programmer to define the hardware context in which each particular task will be executed. Netra DPS does not provide any interrupt handler nor daemons. A given task runs to completion on the assigned hardware context without any interruption.

4.3 Benchmarks

Netra DPS is a specific lightweight runtime environment that does not provide functionalities of fully-fledged OSs such as system calls, dynamic memory allocation, or file management. Therefore, benchmarks included in standard benchmark suites have to be adopted in order to execute in this environment. The benchmarks used are described next:

(1) IP Forwarding (IPFwd) is one of the most representative Layer2/Layer3 network applications. IPFwd application makes the decision to forward a packet to the next hop based on the destination IP address. Depending on the size of the lookup table and destination IP addresses of the packets that are to be processed, the IPFwd application may have significantly different memory behavior. In order to cover different cases of IPFwd memory behavior, we created two variants of the IPFwd application that are based on the IPFwd application included in the Netra DPS distribution [3]:

(i) The lookup table fits in the L1 data cache (**IPFwd-L1**);

(ii) The lookup table entries are initialized to make IPFwd continuously access the main memory (**IPFwd-Mem** benchmark).

IPFwd-L1 is representative of the best case of IPFwd memory behavior, since it shows high locality in data cache accesses. On the other hand, IPFwd-Mem represents the worst case of IPFwd memory behavior used in network processing studies, in which there is no cache locality between accesses to the lookup table [47].

(2) Packet analyzer is a program that can intercept and log traffic passing over a network or part of a network [17]. Packet analyzers are primary tolls for network monitoring and management used to troubleshoot network problems, examine security issues, gather and report network statistics, detect suspect content, and filter it from the network traffic [51, 54, 61].

The packet analyzer that we used in the experiments captures each packet that passes through the Network Interface Unit (NIU), decodes the packet, and analyzes its content according to the appropriate RFC specifications [31]. The packet analyzer can display the information about different fields of packet headers at Layer 2, Layer 3, and Layer 4, and about the packet payload. A user can decide to log all traffic that passes through the NIU, or to define filters based on many criteria. In the experiments presented in this paper, we used the packet analyzer to log MAC source and destination address, time to live field, Layer 3 protocol, source and destination IP address, and source and destination port number of all packets passing through the NIU of the processor under study.

(3) Aho-Corasick is a string matching algorithm. String matching is the basic technique to analyze the network traffic at the application layer [29]. In networking, string matching algorithms search for a set of strings (keywords) in the payload of the network packets. Aho-Corasick is an efficient algorithm that locates all occurrences of a given set of keywords in a string of text (packet payload in case of packet processing). The algorithm constructs a finite state pattern matching machine from the keywords and then uses the pattern matching machine (finite automata) to process the string of text in a single pass [7]. The Aho-Corasick string matching algorithm has proven linear performance, and it is suitable for searching of a large set of keywords concurrently. This is why the Aho-Corasick algorithm is used in state-of-the art network intrusion detection systems such as Snort [40].

In the experiments presented in the paper, we used the Aho-Corasick algorithm to search for keywords from Snort Denial-of-Service set of intrusion detection rules (version 2.9, November 2011) in the payloads of the packets that were processed.

(4) Stateful packet processing is an important component of state-of-the art network monitoring tools [41, 58] and intrusion prevention and detection system [51]. Unlike stateless applications that process each packet independently (like the IPFwd, Packet analyzer, and Aho-Corasick benchmarks used in this study), stateful packet processing keeps the information of previous packet processing.

The packets that belong to the same *flow*, *i.e.* have the same *flow-keys* [3], share the common information called the *flow-record* [19]. The record of a given flow contains the information as to whether the flow is open (the connection is established), safe, malicious, *etc.* The information about the active flows is stored in a hash table that is indexed based on the flow-keys. The common main components of stateful packet processing are: (1) Read the flow-keys of a packet; (2) Use a hash function to determine the corresponding hash table entry based on the packet flow-keys; (3) Access the hash table. Lock, read, and update the flow-record of an already-existing flow, or create a flow-record for a new flow.

The stateful packet processing benchmark that we used in the experiments is comprised of these three components. The stateful benchmark uses the same hash function as the one that is implemented in *nProbe* network monitor [19, 41]. The hash table contains 2^{16} entries, which is sufficient to store the records of active flows of fully-utilized 10Gb link [57], and it is the hash table size that was already used to test different network monitoring tools [19].

[3] The flow-keys are typically the source and destination IP address, the source and destination port, and protocol used.

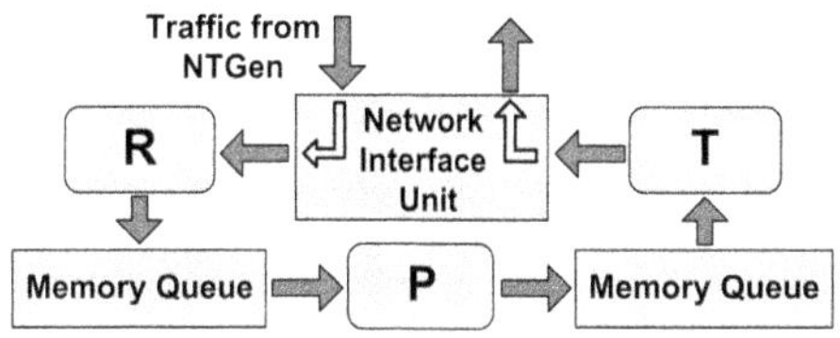

Figure 9. The schematic view of the benchmarks

4.3.1 Benchmark implementation

Each benchmark is divided into three threads that form a software pipeline (see Figure 9). This is a commonly-used approach in the development of the network applications [4, 62]:

- The receiving threads (R) of all benchmarks read the packets from the Network Interface Unit (NIU) associated with the receiver 10Gb network link, and write the pointers to the packets into the R→P memory queues.
- The processing threads (P) read the pointer to the packets from the memory queues, process the packets, and write the pointers to the P→T memory queues. The packet processing is different for each benchmark, *e.g.* P threads of the *IPFwd-L1* and *IPFwd-Mem* benchmarks read the destination IP address, call the hash function, and access the lookup table; P threads of the *Aho-Corasick* benchmark search for the keywords in the packet payload, *etc.*
- Finally, the transmitting threads (T) of all benchmarks read the pointers from the P→T memory queues, and send the packets to the network through the NIU associated to the 10Gb network link.

To summarize, the presented benchmarks represent a good testbed for the analysis of tasks assignment techniques because:

(1) Each benchmark is divided in three different threads, thus the systems deal with heterogeneous tasks even when several instances of the same application are executed simultaneously.

(2) The benchmarks stress the hardware resources of the UltraSPARC T2 processor at all three sharing levels [56].

(3) Each instance of the benchmarks comprises interconnected threads that communicate through shared memory queues. The performance of the benchmarks also depend on the distribution of interconnected threads among processor cores (L1 cache domains).

(4) The impact of task assignment to the performance is significant. We detect performance variation of up to 49% between different task assignments of the same workload.

4.4 Methodology

In order to assure stable results, we measured the performance of task assignments when each application instance processed three million network packets. This means that each application thread was executed three million times. The execution time of each experiment was around 1.5 seconds, and the duration depended on the benchmark and on the distribution of the simultaneously running threads.

5. Results

In this section, we apply the presented statistical approach to the task assignment of multithreaded network applications running on the UltraSPARC T2 processor. We start by analyzing whether a sample of random task assignments can capture an assignment with a good performance. Next, we estimate the optimal system performance for a given workload, and compare it with the measured performance of the observed best task assignment in the sample.

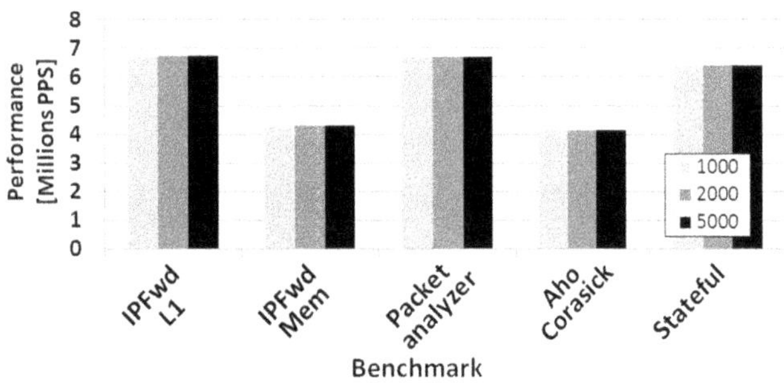

Figure 10. Performance of the best task assignment in the random sample

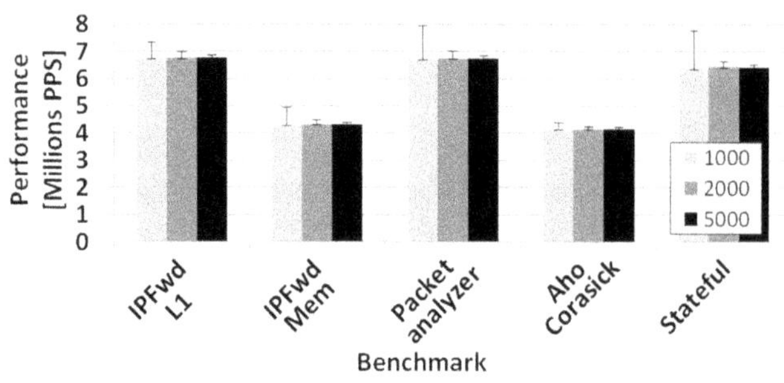

Figure 11. Estimated best-performing schedule performance

Finally, we show how the presented analysis can be applied in the industrial case study for task assignment of network applications.

In all presented experiments, we simultaneously executed eight benchmark instances (24 threads). We could not execute more than eight benchmark instances because of the limitation in the experimental environment: the on-chip Network Interface Unit (NIU) of the UltraSPARC T2 used in the study can split the incoming network traffic into up to eight DMA channels and Netra DPS binds at most one receiving thread to each DMA channel. As a part of future work, we plan to apply the presented statistical approach to applications with several processing threads and to workloads with a higher number of simultaneously-running tasks.

5.1 Finding task assignments with good performance

In Section 3.1, we presented a method to compute the probability that a sample of randomly selected task assignments contains at least one of $P\%$ of best-performing assignments. We showed that samples containing more than several hundred random task assignments capture at least one in 1% or 2% of the best performing task assignments with a probability higher than 99%. We also showed that the probability that a sample of random assignments contains at least one out of 1% of the best-performing task assignments asymptotically approaches 1 as the number of task assignments in the sample exceeds 1000 (see Figure 2).

In order to analyze if further increasing the number of task assignments in the sample increases the performance of the captured best-performing assignment, we executed experiments for 1000, 2000, and 5000 random task assignments. The results of the experiment are plotted in Figure 10, in which the X axis lists different benchmarks and the Y axis shows the performance of the best task assignment in the sample, measured in processed Packets Per Second (PPS). We observed that increasing the sample size from 1000 to 5000 only negligibly improves the performance of the captured best task assignment. The highest performance improvement we detect is only 0.6% for the *IPFwd-Mem* benchmark. For the remaining four benchmarks, the performance improvement when the sample increases from 1000 to 5000 assignments is below 0.25%.

We repeated the same set of experiments for different workloads each having a different number of simultaneously running threads. The conclusions that we reached are the same - increasing sample size from 1000 to 5000 insignificantly improves the performance of the captured best-performing task assignment.

In order to analyze how good the performance of the captured best task assignment in the sample is, and what its performance loss with respect to the optimal one is, we used the statistical inference method that estimates the performance of the optimal task assignment.

5.2 Estimation of the optimal performance

In Section 3.3, we described the statistical approach for the estimation of the optimal system performance for a given workload. The presented statistical method estimates the performance of the best task assignment based on the measured performance of a sample of random assignments. Figure 11 shows the estimated optimal system performance for all five benchmarks in the suite which are listed along X axis. In order to understand the impact of sample size to the estimated optimal system performance, we executed experiments and present data for 1000, 2000, and 5000 random task assignments in the sample. The height of the solid bar corresponds to the point estimation of the optimal system performance, while the error bars show the confidence interval for the 0.95 confidence level.

From the data presented in Figure 11, we can see that the point estimation is roughly the same for all three sample sizes. On the other hand, we see that for four out of five benchmarks (all except *Aho-Corasick*) increasing the sample size significantly narrows the confidence interval, *i.e.* it improves the precision of the estimation. As we increase the number of assignments in the sample, more task assignments in the right tail of the cumulative distribution function (see Figure 5) are used to estimate the parameters of the Generalized Pareto Distribution (GPD). As we stated in Section 3, in order to avoid the bias of the GPD to median values in the cumulative distribution function, no more than 5% of the best performing assignments should be considered when the right tail of the cumulative distribution function is fitted to GPD. Therefore, the maximum number of observations we use to estimate a performance of the optimal system performance is 50, 100, and 250 for the sample of 1000, 2000, and 5000 task assignments, respectively. As we increase the number of task assignments in the sample, more observations can be used to estimate the optimal system performance, which, in turn, leads to more precise estimations.

Figure 12 shows the performance difference between the best-performing assignment in the sample and the estimated optimal system performance. This chart shows how good the performance of the captured best assignment in the given sample is. The benchmarks that are used in the case study are listed along the X axis. Different bars present results for 1000, 2000, and 5000 random assignments in the sample. The height of the solid bar corresponds to the point estimation of the optimal system performance, while the error bars correspond to the confidence interval for the 0.95 confidence level. We reach several conclusions from the results that are presented in Figure 12. For 1000 task assignments in the sample, the estimated possible performance improvement is considerable and significantly different for different benchmarks. For *Aho-Corasick* and *IPFwd-L1* benchmarks, the detected possible performance improvement ranges up to 7% and 9%. For *IPFwd-Mem, Packet analyzer,* and *Stateful* benchmarks, the possible performance improvement ranges up to 16%, 19%, and 23%, respec-

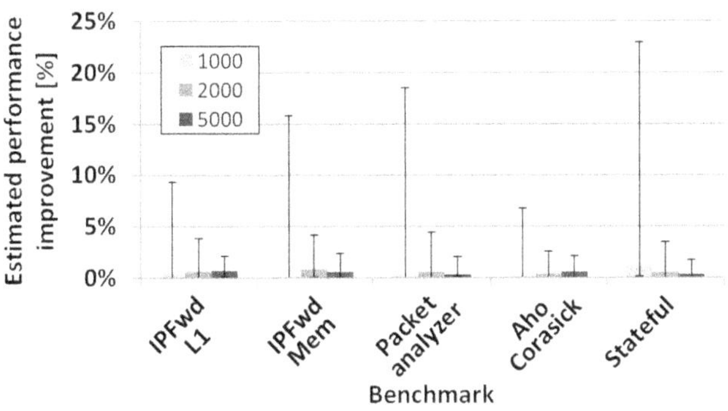

Figure 12. Estimated performance improvement

tively. For 2000 assignments in the sample, the performance difference between the best assignment in the sample and the estimated optimal performance is below 5% for all five benchmarks in the suite. Finally, for the 5000 task assignments in the sample, the best measured performance in the random sample is very close to the estimated optimal performance, for all five benchmarks in the suite. The highest possible performance improvement is only 2.4% (*IPFwd-Mem* benchmark).

Overall, in this section, we applied the method presented in Section 3 to estimate the optimal system performance for a given workload. We used the estimated performance to understand how good the best task assignments captured in the random samples are. In our experiments, running only several thousand random task assignments from a vast population was enough to detect assignments with performance very close to the optimal ones. We also showed that increasing the sample size from 1000 to 5000 significantly improved the precision of the estimation, though it only insignificantly improved the performance of the captured best task assignment.

5.3 Case study

Next, we show how the presented analysis can be applied to an industrial case study for the task assignment of network applications. In the presented scenario, the main objective is to satisfy the given performance requirement of the best task assignment that is captured in the random sample. In this scenario, the customer requires that the performance difference between the captured best task assignment and the optimal system performance for the given workload is below $X\%$.

In order to address this problem, we developed an iterative algorithm that converges to the performance required by the customer by increasing the number of random assignments in the sample. The schematic view of the algorithm is shown in Figure 13. The algorithm is comprised of four steps.

In **Step 1**, we select the initial sample size N_{init}, generate a sample of N_{init} random task assignments, execute them on the target processor, and measure the performance of each assignment in the sample. The output of Step 1 is the measured performance of all task assignments that are executed on the target processor.

In **Step 2**, we apply the described statistical method to estimate the optimal system performance. There are two outputs from Step 2: the performance of the best assignment in the sample and the estimated optimal system performance, *i.e.* the performance of the optimal assignment for a given workload.

In **Step 3**, we compute the performance difference between the observed best assignment in the random sample and the estimated optimal system performance. If this performance difference is acceptable for the customer (it is below $X\%$), then the iterative process ends. The final outcome of this process is the observed best assignment in the sample and the estimated performance difference with respect to the optimal assignment. On the other hand, if the difference between the performance of the best task assignment in the sample and the estimated optimal system performance is not acceptable (it is higher than $X\%$), the iterative process continues.

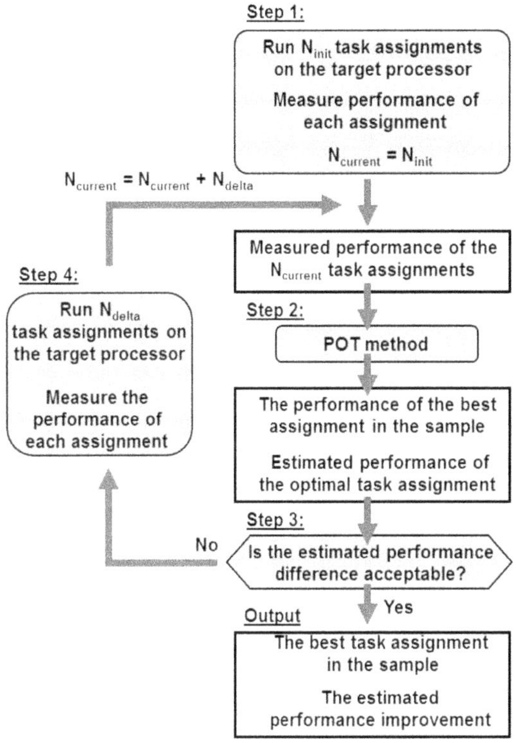

Figure 13. Case study: The schematic view of the algorithm

In **Step 4**, we generate a sample of N_{delta} random assignments, execute the assignments on the target processor, and measure the performance of each of them. The set of N_{delta} measured values is included in the set of measurements that are the input to the statistical analysis in Step 2 ($N_{current} = N_{current} + N_{delta}$) and the statistical analysis is repeated, this time for a larger input dataset. As the number of task assignments in the random sample increases, the performance of the captured best assignment increases as well. But, more importantly, the input dataset for statistical analysis increases, which provides a more precise estimation of optimal system performance.

Step 2, **Step 3**, and **Step 4** of the algorithm are repeated as long the best task assignment in the sample does not satisfy performance requirements specified by the customer.

We appled the presented algorithm to the set of network benchmarks executing in Netra DPS low-overhead runtime environment on the UltraSPARC T2 processor. We started the algorithm with $N_{init} = 1000$ task assignments and in each iteration we executed $N_{delta} = 100$ assignments more. We analyzed three cases, when the acceptable performance loss is 2.5%, 5%, and 10%. In Step 2 of the algorithm, the optimal system performance was estimated for the 0.95 confidence level. The number of task assignments in the sample needed to capture an assignment with the acceptable performance loss is presented in Figure 14. We present data for all five benchmarks in the suite that are listed along the X axis. From the results presented in the figure we see that: (1) Running several

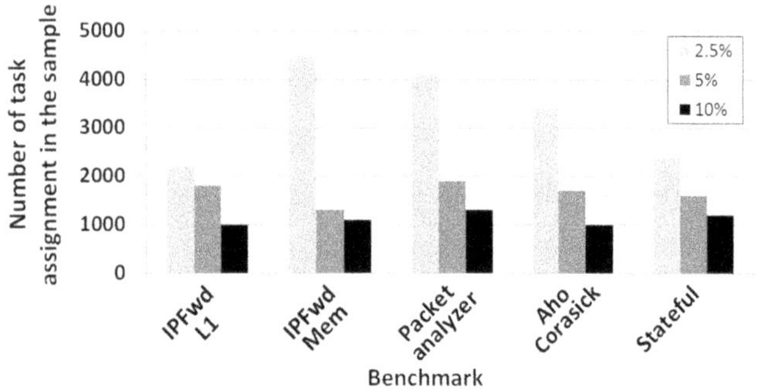

Figure 14. Case study: Required number of task assignments

thousand random task assignments was enough to capture an assignment with a performance loss of below 2.5% with respect to the estimated optimal performance. The required number of task assignments range from 2200 for *IPFwd-L1* to 4500 for *IPFwd-Mem* benchmark. (2) As the acceptable performance loss increased, less assignments in the sample were needed. For example, when the acceptable performance loss was 10%, running less then 1300 random task assignments was sufficient to provide the required performance for all five benchmarks. (3) Required number of tasks assignments in the sample depends on the concrete benchmark.

One of the main strengths of the presented approach is that it is application and architecture independent, and that it can be applied to find task assignments that satisfy different performance requirements. The number of assignments in the sample depends on the characteristics of the benchmarks, characteristics of the target architecture, and also on the performance requirements.

5.4 Other Considerations

There are a couple of aspects to consider regarding the presented approach.

Experimental time: Our method requires execution on the target architecture of all task assignments in the sample. In our target networking environment, as described in Section 4.4, around 1.5 seconds were enough to take a stable measurements of the performance of each task assignment. Hence, the time needed to execute all experiments for samples of 1000, 2000, and 5000 task assignments, for which we have obtained close-to-the-optimal performance, was approximately 25 minutes, 50 minutes, and 2 hours, respectively. This experimentation time is reasonable considering that the selected task assignment can be used during the lifetime of the system.

However, it may be the case that in some environments the time required to execute thousands of experiments on the target architecture is large or unfeasible. In that case, instead or execution of random task assignments on a target processor, the performance of each assignment in the sample can be predicted using a performance predictor. For that matter, the input data to the statistical model is the predicted performance for a sample of task assignments. Performance predictors are models that estimate the performance of task assignments based on the analysis of the target architecture and resource requirements of each task in a workload (see Section 6). It is important to note that the accuracy of the integrated approach that combines performance predictors and statistical analysis depends on the accuracy of the predictor that is used. Design and evaluation of such an integrated approach is part of our future work.

Workload selection: As we mentioned in Section 1, for processors with one level of resource sharing, the task scheduling is done in a single step, called *workload selection*: out of all ready-to-run tasks, the OS selects a set of tasks (workload) that will concurrently execute on the processor [32]. As all tasks share the same processor resources homogeneously, the way they interfere is independent of their distribution. In processors with several levels of resource sharing, task scheduling requires an additional step, called *task assignment*. Once the workload is selected, the tasks have to be distributed among different hardware context of the processor.

In the industrial networking environment used in our experimental setup, the workload is known beforehand and cannot be changed at runtime (see Section 4). Hence, in this kind of environment, the workload selection is not an issue and the optimal task assignment is the only scheduling problem. In this paper, we have shown how our statistical approach can be applied to the problem of the optimal task assignment. In processors with one level of resource sharing, the presented methodology can be directly applied to address the workload selection problem. The designer has to generate a sample of random workloads, run them on the target machine, measure the performance of each workload, and follow the methodology we presented in Section 3.

The application of the presented statistical approach becomes more complex for processors with several levels of resource sharing. In this case, the processor may execute different workloads, and each workload may have a different performance for different task assignments. The development of a statistical approach that addresses a combined *workload selection and task assignment* problem is part of our future work.

6. Related work

Workload Selection: Several approaches that address the workload selection problem propose models that predict the impact of interferences among co-running tasks to system performance. Snavely et al. [49, 50] present the SOS scheduler, which is, to the best of our knowledge, the first scheduler that uses profile-based information to compose workloads. The SOS scheduler uses hardware performance counters to find schedules that exhibit good performance. Eyerman and Eeckhout [22] propose probabilistic job symbiosis model that enhances the SOS scheduler. Based on the cycle accounting architecture [21], the model estimates the single-threaded progress for each job in a multithreaded workload. Other approaches [13, 23, 36, 45] propose techniques to construct workloads of tasks that exhibit good symbiosis in shared caches solving problems of cache contention.

Task Assignment: Several studies show that the performance of applications running on multithreaded processors depends on the interference in hardware resources, which, in turn, depends on task assignment [6, 20, 44]. Acosta et al. [6] propose a task assignment algorithm for CMP+SMT processors that takes into account not only the workload characteristics, but also the underlying instruction fetch policy. El-Moursy el al. [20] also focus on CMP+SMT processors and propose an algorithm that uses hardware performance counters to profile task behavior and assign compatible tasks on the same SMT core. Radojković et al. [44] present a model for task assignment of applications running on multithreaded processors. The solution can be used when the number of tasks is low, and it requires profiling information from the application and knowledge about the target architecture.

Other studies analyze task scheduling for platforms comprised of several multithreaded processors [39, 53]. McGregor et al. [39] introduce new scheduling policies that use run-time information from hardware performance counters to identify the best mix of tasks to run across processors and within each processor. Tam el al. [53] present a run-time technique for the detection of data sharing among different tasks. The proposed technique can be used by an operating system job scheduler to assign tasks that share data to the same memory domain (same chip or the same core on the chip).

Kumar et al. [38] and Shelepov et al. [46] propose algorithms for scheduling in *heterogeneous* multicore architectures. The focus of these studies is to find an algorithm that matches the application's hardware requirements with the processor core characteristics. In our study, we explore interference among tasks that are distributed among the *homogeneous* hardware domains (processor cores and hardware pipelines) of a processor.

Other studies propose solutions for optimal assignment of multithreaded network workloads in parallel processors, specifically in network processors. Kokku et al. [37] propose an algorithm that assigns network processing tasks to processor cores with the goal of reducing the power consumption. Wolf et al. [62] propose run-time support that considers the partitioning of applications across processor cores. The authors address the problem of dynamic threads re-allocation because of network traffic variations, and provide task assignment solutions based on the application profiling and traffic analysis.

Optimal performance analysis: To the best of our knowledge, the work of Jiang et al. [33] is the only systematic study devoted to find the optimal task assignment of applications running on multithreaded processors. First, the authors analyze the complexity of the task assignment for multithreaded processors. Later, they propose several task assignment algorithms. The authors use graphs to model interaction between simultaneously-running tasks and use graph search to find the optimal solution. The main drawback of this study is that it assumes that the impact of task interaction to system performance is known beforehand for all possible assignments.

We present a different approach for finding the performance of the optimal task assignment. We do not try to find the best-performing assignment, but to capture a task assignment with performance close to the optimal one. In our approach, the optimal system performance is estimated using statistical inference based on measured performance of a sample of random task assignments.

7. Conclusions

Optimal task assignment is one of the most promising ways to improve the performance of applications running on massively multithreaded processors. However, finding an optimal task assignment on modern multithreaded processors is an NP-complete problem.

In this paper, we proposed a statistical approach to the problem of optimal task assignment. In particular, we showed that running a sample of several hundred or several thousand random task assignments is enough to capture at least one out of 1% of the best-performing assignments with a very high probability. We also described the method that estimates, with a given confidence level, the optimal system performance for given workload. Knowing the optimal system performance improves the evaluation of any task assignment technique and it is the most important piece of information for the system designer when deciding whether any scheduling algorithm should be enhanced.

The presented approach is completely independent of the hardware environment and target applications. The approach scales to any number of cores and hardware contexts per core and it does not require any profiling of the application nor does it require knowledge of the architecture of the target hardware.

We successfully applied our proposal to a case study of task assignment of multithreaded network applications running on the UltraSPARC T2 processor. Our results showed that running several thousand random task assignments provided enough information for the precise estimation of the performance of the optimal task assignment, and that it was sufficient to capture the assignments with performance very close to the optimal ones (less than 2.5% of the performance loss), requiring around two hours of experimentation in the target architecture in the worst case.

Acknowledgments

This work has been supported by the Ministry of Science and Technology of Spain under contract TIN-2007-60625. Petar Radojković and Vladimir Čakarević hold the FPU grant (Programa Nacional de Formación de Profesorado Universitario) under contracts AP2008-02370 and AP2008-02371, respectively, of the Ministry of Education of Spain. This work has been partially supported by the Department of Universities, Research and Information Society (DURSI) of the Catalan Government (grant 2010-BE-00352). The authors wish to thank to Liliana Cucu-Grosjean and Luca Santinelli from INRIA, and Jochen Behrens and Aron Silverton from Oracle for their technical support.

References

[1] *OpenSPARC^{TM} T2 Core Microarchitecture Specification.* Sun Microsystems, Inc, 2007.

[2] *OpenSPARC^{TM} T2 System-On-Chip (SOC) Microarchitecture Specification.* Sun Microsystems, Inc, 2007.

[3] *Netra Data Plane Software Suite 2.0 Update 2 Reference Manual.* Sun Microsystems, Inc, 2008.

[4] *Netra Data Plane Software Suite 2.0 Update 2 User's Guide.* Sun Microsystems, Inc, 2008.

[5] *Software. Hardware. Complete.* http://www.oracle.com/ocom/groups /public/@ocom/documents /webcontent/044518.pdf, 2010.

[6] C. Acosta, F. Cazorla, A. Ramirez, and M. Valero. Thread to Core Assignment in SMT On-Chip Multiprocessors. In *SBAC-PAD '09: Proceedings of the 21st International Symposium on Computer Architecture and High Performance Computing*, 2009.

[7] A. V. Aho and M. J. Corasick. Efficient String Matching: An Aid to Bibliographic Search. *Commun. ACM*, 18, 1975.

[8] A. Azzalini. *Statistical Inference Based on the Likelihood.* Chapman and Hall, London, 1996.

[9] A. A. Balkema and L. de Haan. Residual life time at great age. *Annals of Probability*, 2:792–804, 1974.

[10] J. Beirlant, Y. Goegebeur, J. Segers, and J. Teugels. *Statistics of Extremes: Theory and Applications.* John Wiley and Sons, Ltd, 2004.

[11] E. Castillo. *Extreme value theory in engineering.* Academic Press, Inc., 1988.

[12] E. Castillo and A. Hadi. Fitting the Generalized Pareto Distribution to data. *Journal of the American Statistical Association*, 92, 1997.

[13] D. Chandra, F. Guo, S. Kim, and Y. Solihin. Predicting inter-thread cache contention on a chip multi-processor architecture. In *HPCA '05: Proceedings of the 11th International Symposium on High-Performance Computer Architecture*, 2005.

[14] S. J. Chapman. *Essentials of MATLAB Programming.* Cengage Learning, 2009.

[15] H. Chernoff. On the distribution of the likelihood ratio. *Annals of Mathematical Statistics*, 25, 1954.

[16] W. G. Cochran. *Sampling techniques.* Wiley, 1977.

[17] K. J. Connolly. *Law of Internet Security and Privacy.* Aspen Publishers, 2003.

[18] M. De Vuyst, R. Kumar, and D. Tullsen. Exploiting unbalanced thread scheduling for energy and performance on a CMP of SMT processors. In *IPDPS '06: Proceedings of the 20th IEEE International Parallel and Distributed Processing Symposium*, 2006.

[19] D. Eckhoff, T. Limmer, and F. Dressler. Hash Tables for Efficient Flow Monitoring: Vulnerabilities and Countermeasures. In *LCN '09: Proceedings of the 34th Conference on Local Computer Networks*, 2009.

[20] A. El-Moursy, R. Garg, D. Albonesi, and S. Dwarkadas. Compatible phase co-scheduling on a CMP of multi-threaded processors. In *IPDPS '06: Proceedings of the 20th IEEE International Parallel and Distributed Processing Symposium*, 2006.

[21] S. Eyerman and L. Eeckhout. Per-thread cycle accounting in SMT processors. In *ASPLOS '09: Proceeding of the 14th international conference on Architectural support for programming languages and operating systems*, 2009.

[22] S. Eyerman and L. Eeckhout. Probabilistic job symbiosis modeling for SMT processor scheduling. In *ASPLOS '10: Proceeding of the 15th international conference on Architectural support for programming languages and operating systems*, 2010.

[23] A. Fedorova, M. Seltzer, C. Small, and D. Nussbaum. Performance of multithreaded chip multiprocessors and implications for operating system design. In *ATEC '05: Proceedings of the annual conference on USENIX Annual Technical Conference*, 2005.

[24] M. R. Garey and D. S. Johnson. *Computers and Intractability: A Guide to the Theory of NP-Completeness*. W.H. Freeman and Company, 1979.

[25] M. Gilli and E. Këllezi. An application of extreme value theory for measuring financial risk. *Computational Economics*, 27, 2006.

[26] R. Gioiosa, F. Petrini, K. Davis, and F. Lebaillif-Delamare. Analysis of system overhead on parallel computers. In *ISSPIT '04: 4th IEEE International Symposium on Signal Processing and Information Technology*, Rome, Italy, 2004.

[27] M. Greenwood. The natural duration of cancer. *Reports on Public Health and Medical Subjects*, 33:1–26, 1926.

[28] S. Grimshaw. Computing the maximum likelihood estimates for the Generalized Pareto Distribution to data. *Technometrics*, 35, 1993.

[29] F. Guo and T. Chiueh. Traffic Analysis: From Stateful Firewall to Network Intrusion Detection System. In *RPE Report*, 2004.

[30] J. R. M. Hosking and J. R. Wallis. Parameter and quantile estimation for the generalised pareto distribution. *Technometrics*, 29, 1987.

[31] Internet Engineering Task Force (IETF). Request for Comments (RFC), http://www.rfc-editor.org/.

[32] R. Jain, C. J. Hughes, and S. V. Adve. Soft real- time scheduling on simultaneous multithreaded processors. In *RTSS '02: Proceedings of the 23rd IEEE Real-Time Systems Symposium*, 2002.

[33] Y. Jiang, X. Shen, J. Chen, and R. Tripathi. Analysis and approximation of optimal co-scheduling on chip multiprocessors. In *PACT '08: Proceedings of the 17th international conference on Parallel architectures and compilation techniques*, 2008.

[34] E. L. Kaplan and P. Meier. Nonparametric estimation from incomplete observations. *Journal of the American Statistical Association*, 52 (282):457–481, 1958.

[35] E. Këllezi and M. Gilli. Extreme value theory for tail-related risk measures. Fame research paper series, International Center for Financial Asset Management and Engineering, 2000.

[36] J. Kihm, A. Settle, A. Janiszewski, and D. A. Connors. Understanding the impact of inter-thread cache interference on ILP in modern SMT processors. *The Journal of Instruction Level Parallelism*, 7, 2005.

[37] R. Kokku, T. L. Riché, A. Kunze, J. Mudigonda, J. Jason, and H. M. Vin. A case for run-time adaptation in packet processing systems. *SIGCOMM Comput. Commun. Rev.*, 34(1), 2004.

[38] R. Kumar, D. M. Tullsen, P. Ranganathan, N. P. Jouppi, and K. I. Farkas. Single-ISA heterogenous multi-core architectures for multithreaded workload performance. In *ISCA '04: Proceedings of the 31st Annual International Symposium on Computer Architecture*, 2004.

[39] R. L. McGregor, C. D. Antonopoulos, and D. S. Nikolopoulos. Scheduling algorithms for effective thread pairing on hybrid multiprocessors. In *IPDPS '05: Proceedings of the 19th IEEE International Parallel and Distributed Processing Symposium*, 2005.

[40] M. Norton. Optimizing Pattern Matching for Intrusion Detection, http://docs.idsresearch.org/OptimizingPatternMatchingForIDS.pdf, 2004.

[41] nProbe network monitor. http://www.ntop.org.

[42] F. Petrini, D. Kerbyson, and S. Pakin. The case of the missing supercomputer performance: Achieving optimal performance on the 8,192 processors of ASCI Q. In *SC '03: Proceedings of the 2003 ACM/IEEE conference on Supercomputing*, 2003.

[43] J. I. Pickands. Statistical inference using extreme value order statistics. *Annals of Statististics*, 3:119–131, 1975.

[44] P. Radojković, V. Čakarević, J. Verdú, A. Pajuelo, F. J. Cazorla, M. Nemirovsky, and M. Valero. Thread to strand binding of parallel network applications in massive multi-threaded systems. In *PPoPP-2010: Proceedings of the 15th ACM SIGPLAN Symposium on Principles and Practice of Parallel Programming, Bangalore, India*, 2010.

[45] A. Settle, J. Kihm, A. Janiszewski, and D. Connors. Architectural support for enhanced SMT job scheduling. In *PACT '04: Proceedings of the 13th International Conference on Parallel Architectures and Compilation Techniques*, 2004.

[46] D. Shelepov, J. C. S. Alcaide, S. Jeffery, A. Fedorova, N. Perez, Z. F. Huang, S. Blagodurov, and V. Kumar. Hass: A scheduler for heterogeneous multicore systems. In *ACM SIGOPS Operating Systems Review*, 2009.

[47] T. Sherwood, G. Varghese, and B. Calder. A Pipelined Memory Architecture for High Throughput Network Processors. In *ISCA '03: Proceedings of the 30th Annual International Symposium on Computer Architecture*, 2003.

[48] E. Shmueli, G. Almasi, J. Brunheroto, J. Castanos, G. Dozsa, S. Kumar, and D. Lieber. Evaluating the effect of replacing CNK with Linux on the compute-nodes of Blue Gene/L. In *ICS '08: Proceedings of the 22nd Annual International Conference on Supercomputing*, 2008.

[49] A. Snavely and D. M. Tullsen. Symbiotic jobscheduling for a simultaneous multithreaded processor. In *ASPLOS 2000: Proceedings of the 9th International Conference on Architectural Support for Programming Languages and Operating Systems*, 2000.

[50] A. Snavely, D. M. Tullsen, and G. Voelker. Symbiotic jobscheduling with priorities for a simultaneous multithreading processor. In *Proceedings of the 2002 ACM SIGMETRICS International Conference on Measurement and Modeling of Computer Systems*, 2002.

[51] Snort network intrusion prevention and detection system. http://www.snort.org/.

[52] N. Tajvidi. Design and implementation of statistical computations for Generalized Pareto Distributions. *Technical Report, Chalmers University of Technology*, 1996.

[53] D. Tam, R. Azimi, and M. Stumm. Thread clustering: sharing-aware scheduling on SMP-CMP-SMT multiprocessors. In *EuroSys '07: Proceedings of the 2nd ACM SIGOPS/EuroSys European Conference on Computer Systems*, 2007.

[54] TCPDUMP/LIBPCAP public repository. http://www.tcpdump.org/.

[55] S. B. Vardeman. *Statistics for Engineering Problem Solving*. PWS publishing company, 1993.

[56] V. Čakarević, P. Radojković, J. Verdú, A. Pajuelo, F. Cazorla, M. Nemirovsky, and M. Valero. Characterizing the resource-sharing levels in the UltraSPARC T2 processor. In *MICRO-42: Proceedings of the 42nd Annual IEEE/ACM International Symposium on Microarchitecture, NY, USA*, 2009.

[57] J. Verdú. *Analysis and Architectural Support for Parallel Stateful Packet Processing, PhD Thesis*. Universitat Politècnica de Catalunya, 2008.

[58] Vermont (VERsatile MONitoring Toolkit). http://vermont.berlios.de/.

[59] S. S. Wilks. The large-sample distribution of the likelihood ratio for testing composite hypotheses. *Annals of Mathematical Statistics*, 9, 1938.

[60] S. S. Wilks. *Mathematical Statistics*. Princeton University Press, 1943.

[61] Wireshark network protocol analyzer. http://www.wireshark.org/.

[62] T. Wolf, N. Weng, and C.-H. Tai. Design considerations for network processor operating systems. In *ANCS '05: Proceedings of ACM/IEEE Symposium on Architectures for Networking and Communication Systems*, Princeton, NJ, 2005.

CRUISE: Cache Replacement and Utility-aware Scheduling

Aamer Jaleel[†], Hashem H. Najaf-abadi[*], Samantika Subramaniam[†], Simon C. Steely Jr.[†], and Joel Emer[†‡]

[†]Intel Corporation, VSSAD
Hudson, MA

[*]Intel Corporation, VPG
Folsom, CA

[‡]Massachusetts Institute of Technology (MIT)
Cambridge, MA

{aamer.jaleel, hashem.hashemi, samantika.subramaniam, simon.c.steely.jr, joel.emer}@intel.com

Abstract

When several applications are co-scheduled to run on a system with multiple shared LLCs, there is opportunity to improve system performance. This opportunity can be exploited by the hardware, software, or a combination of both hardware and software. The software, i.e., an operating system or hypervisor, can improve system performance by co-scheduling jobs on LLCs to minimize shared cache contention. The hardware can improve system throughput through better replacement policies by allocating more cache resources to applications that benefit from the cache and less to those applications that do not.

This study presents a detailed analysis on the interactions between intelligent scheduling and smart cache replacement policies. We find that smart cache replacement reduces the burden on software to provide intelligent scheduling decisions. However, under smart cache replacement, there is still room to improve performance from better application co-scheduling. We find that co-scheduling decisions are a function of the underlying LLC replacement policy. We propose Cache Replacement and Utility-aware Scheduling (CRUISE)—a hardware/software co-designed approach for shared cache management. For 4-core and 8-core CMPs, we find that CRUISE approaches the performance of an ideal job co-scheduling policy under different LLC replacement policies.

Categories and Subject Descriptors D.4.1 [Process Management]: Scheduling, B.3.2 [Design Styles]: Cache memories, C.1.4 [Parallel architectures]: Distributed architectures

General Terms Algorithms, Measurement, Performance, Design.

Keywords Scheduling, Cache Replacement, Shared Cache

1. Introduction

Emerging technologies such as virtualization, multi-core, and multi-socket systems have enabled the consolidation of multiple applications onto a single system. In doing so, a wide variety of applications with differing memory demands can concurrently execute and compete for shared resources in the system. Since modern multi-core and multi-socket CMP systems typically contain one or more shared last-level caches (LLC), system performance is typically determined by how well the shared LLC is managed.

Traditionally, there have been two approaches to manage shared LLCs: intelligent software scheduling [37, 38, 31, 32, 7, 15, 17, 18, 21] and smart hardware cache replacement [4, 12, 10, 11, 14, 25, 34, 36]. Software scheduling puts the onus of co-scheduling applications on a layer between the hardware and the applications themselves, like the operating system or a hypervisor. The advantage of software scheduling is that the underlying hardware is agnostic to the scheduling of applications and can be designed independently. However, the drawback is that the scheduler is unaware of the runtime memory requirements of the applications scheduled. To address this problem, researchers have proposed using existing hardware performance counters (or adding new counters) to guide scheduling [31, 21, 38]. For example, a recent proposal measures per-application miss-rate using performance counters and then co-schedules applications based on the degree of memory intensity [38]. However, this approach can cause sub-optimal co-scheduling decisions since per-application miss-rate while sharing a cache can be significantly different from the miss-rate while running in isolation. Nonetheless, hardware performance counter based scheduling algorithms, to some degree, have addressed shared cache contention.

Researchers from the hardware community, on the other hand, have addressed heterogeneity in memory demand by proposing to build resource sharing decisions directly into the cache replacement policy. Such smart replacement policies dynamically allocate more cache resources to applications that benefit from the cache and less cache resources to applications that do not benefit from the cache. While cache replacement does not specify which applications can be co-scheduled to share a cache resource, it can change the impact that these applications have on shared cache usage. Consequently, we believe that it is important to study the interaction between the software and hardware approaches to shared cache management.

This paper presents the first comprehensive study on the interactions between intelligent software scheduling and smart cache replacement. In general, we find that smart cache replacement policies minimize the burden on software to provide intelligent scheduling decisions. However, they do not eliminate the need for intelligent scheduling decisions. Based on our observations, we propose a hardware/software co-designed approach for shared cache management called *Cache Replacement and Utility-aware Scheduling (CRUISE)*. We also propose a novel hardware mechanism, *Runtime Isolated Cache Estimator (RICE)*, which provides a low overhead mechanism to dynamically estimate the isolated cache performance of an application while still sharing the cache with other applications. RICE requires no changes to the existing shared cache structure and merely requires two counters per application. The software component of our proposal uses cache utility information provided by RICE *and* the knowledge of the underlying LLC replacement policy to intelligently co-schedule

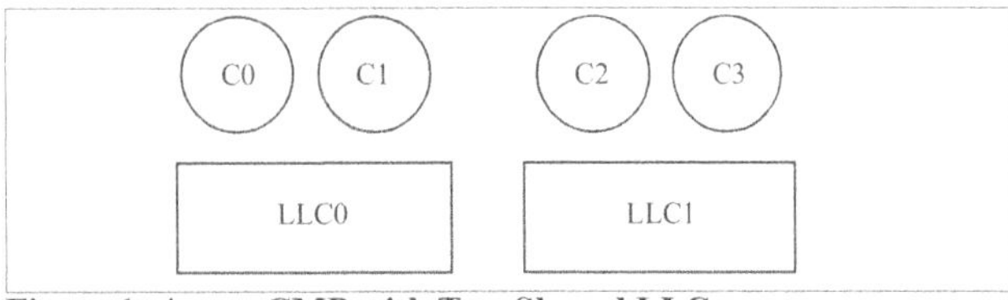

Figure 1: 4-core CMP with Two Shared LLCs.

applications. Our evaluations on 4-core and 8-core CMPs with two and four threads sharing an LLC show that CRUISE consistently provides *near-optimal* co-scheduling decisions.

2. Motivation

Recent studies have shown that the commonly used LRU replacement policy (and its approximations) perform poorly on shared caches [12, 34, 10, 30, 29, 25]. This is because LRU replacement allocates cache resources based on demand instead of cache utility [30, 25, 12]. To improve shared cache performance, researchers from the computer architecture community propose smart replacement policies to improve upon LRU [12, 34, 10, 30, 29, 25]. On the other hand, other researchers have proposed intelligent co-scheduling policies [37, 38, 32, 31, 21] that an operating system or hypervisor can use to minimize shared cache contention.

Figure 2 illustrates a 4-core CMP with two shared LLCs. When four applications (A, B, C, and D) concurrently execute on this CMP, there are three possible *application schedules*: AB|CD, AC|BD, and AD|BC. Depending on the amount of shared cache contention, the three application schedules may observe different system and per-application performance. For a given performance metric (e.g., throughput, weighted speedup), we refer to the application schedule that yields the best system performance as *Optimal Application Schedule (OAS)* and the application schedule that yields the lowest system performance as *Worst Application Schedule (WAS)*.

In our 4-core CMP system, application performance and system performance is largely dependent on the degree of cache contention between the two applications *co-scheduled* (i.e. share) on the same LLC. To avoid the worst application schedule, conventional wisdom prevents co-scheduling a CPU bound application with a memory bound application. However, such practice is only necessary for an LRU managed LLC. In an LLC managed by smart cache replacement, co-scheduling a CPU bound application with a memory bound application no longer hurts the performance of a CPU bound application. This is because smart cache replacement policies allocate cache resources based on utility instead of demand. Since the majority of existing intelligent scheduling studies have been evaluated in the presence of an inefficient LLC replacement policy (i.e., LRU), the question arises as to whether intelligent application scheduling is necessary in the presence of smart cache replacement.

In efforts to understand the interaction between cache replacement and application scheduling, Figure 2 illustrates the effects of optimal scheduling in the presence and absence of smart cache replacement. The study is based on 1365 4-core heterogeneous SPEC CPU2006 application mixes simulated on our 4-core CMP illustrated in Figure 1. We use DRRIP [10], a recently proposed low overhead, high performing shared cache replacement policy.

In the figure, the x-axis represents the system performance ratio OAS_{LRU}/WAS_{LRU} while the y-axis represents the system performance ratio OAS_{DRRIP}/WAS_{DRRIP}. This ratio (illustrated as a percent) represents the performance variability that intelligent scheduling policies attempt to minimize. We use system throughput as our performance metric. Each data point in the figure represents a 4-core workload mix. Some mixes are emphasized using large shapes (circle, square, diamond, and triangle) to highlight representative behavior. Circles are in "Region I", squares are in "Region II", diamond in "Region III", and finally triangle in "Region IV".

An interesting observation from the figure is the behavior of workloads in Region II (emphasized by squares). Under LRU replacement, these workloads have significant performance variation (up to 28% on the x-axis). Hence, under LRU, these workloads significantly benefit from intelligent scheduling decisions. However, under a smarter replacement policy, like DRRIP, these workloads have lesser performance variation (<4% on the y-axis). Consequently, under DRRIP, there is little benefit from improving scheduling decisions. Upon inspection, these workload mixes consist of memory bound applications paired with CPU bound applications. Smart cache replacement policies, such as DRRIP, are particularly designed to address such workload mixes.

In general, the figure shows that the majority of workload mixes lie below the linear bisector. Such behavior suggests that smarter cache replacement policies minimize the burden on software (i.e. operating system or hypervisor) to provide intelligent co-scheduling decisions. However, note that smarter replacement policies do not eliminate the need for intelligent scheduling decisions. For example, workloads in Region IV (emphasized by triangle) can have as much as 20% performance variation under both LRU and DRRIP. Furthermore, for workload mixes in region III, smart replacement policies introduce up to 20% performance variation. Note that these workload mixes had less than 4% performance variation under LRU replacement. Upon inspection, these workload mixes consist of several non-memory bound applications that benefit from more intelligent co-scheduling decisions.

For the workloads studied, we find that DRRIP alone improves performance over LRU by roughly 4.8%. Intelligent scheduling by itself in an LRU-managed cache improves performance by 4.4%. We find there is up to 8.4% performance potential when intelligent scheduling is employed in a DRRIP-managed cache. This shows that

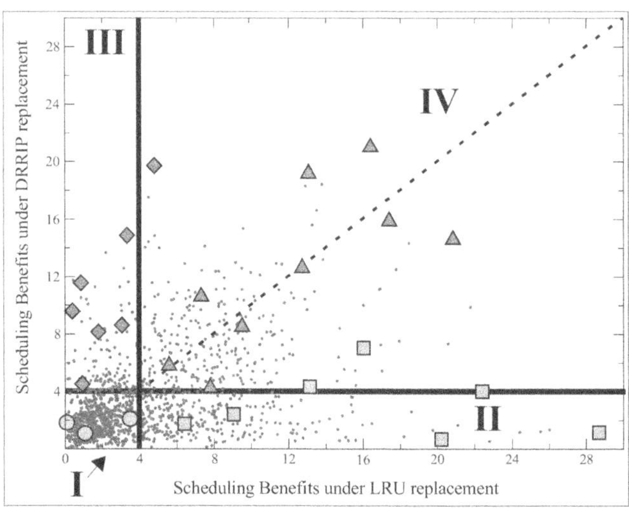

Figure 2: Behavior of Optimal Co-Scheduling in Presence and Absence of Intelligent Replacement. Some workload mixes are emphasized with different sized shapes and are analyzed more closely in the results section of this paper.

the underlying replacement policy *and* intelligent scheduling combined can together improve performance significantly. The next section proposes such an intelligent scheduling policy.

3. Cache Replacement and Utility-aware Scheduling (CRUISE)

Determining a suitable application co-schedule requires runtime knowledge on the cache requirements of an application in isolation [31, 38]. The next section describes our run-time mechanism to determine isolated cache *utility* of an application. Given the cache utility information, we then present our *Cache Replacement and Utility-aware Scheduling (CRUISE)* proposal that co-schedules applications based on knowledge of the underlying LLC replacement policy. Finally, we discuss how an operating system (or hypervisor) can incorporate CRUISE to improve system performance.

3.1. Classifying Application Cache Utility

Recent work used *colors* [18] and *animals* [35] as analogies to characterize the memory intensity of applications. Instead of using analogies, we propose to classify applications based on their cache performance on the available CMP cache hierarchy. We categorize application cache utility into four different categories:

- "Core Cache Fitting" (CCF) Applications: These applications have a working set size that fits in the smaller levels of the cache hierarchy. CCF applications have no benefit from the shared LLC.
- "LLC Thrashing" (LLCT) Applications: These applications have a working set size that is greater than the available LLC. We consider *streaming* applications as LLCT applications. Under LRU, LLCT applications degrade performance of any application that benefits from the shared LLC.
- "LLC Fitting" (LLCF) Applications: These applications require the majority of the available shared LLC capacity to perform well. If these applications do not receive the bulk of the shared LLC, like LLCT applications, their performance degrades significantly due to cache thrashing. As such, LLCF applications perform best when running in isolation or when sharing the LLC with CCF applications. LLCF application performance degrades when co-executed with any other application.
- "LLC Friendly" (LLCFR) Applications: These applications benefit from the available shared LLC and continue to do so as they are given more cache resources. Unlike LLCF applications, LLCFR application performance does not degrade significantly when they do not receive the bulk of the shared LLC. LLCFR application performance degrades only when co-executed with LLCT or LLCF applications.

Based on the above application classifications, intelligent scheduling decisions can be developed to manage a system with multiple shared LLCs. For example, since CCF applications do not require the shared LLC, co-scheduling them with LLCF applications can significantly improve LLCF application performance. Similarly, it is best to co-schedule LLCFR applications with LLCFR applications.

Before we provide a detailed description of our proposed application co-scheduling policies, we first discuss mechanisms to classify application cache *utility*.

3.1.1 Profiling based Classification of Applications

Cache utility of an application can be determined statically using profile information. Applications can be executed beforehand and classified into one of the four categories described above. However,

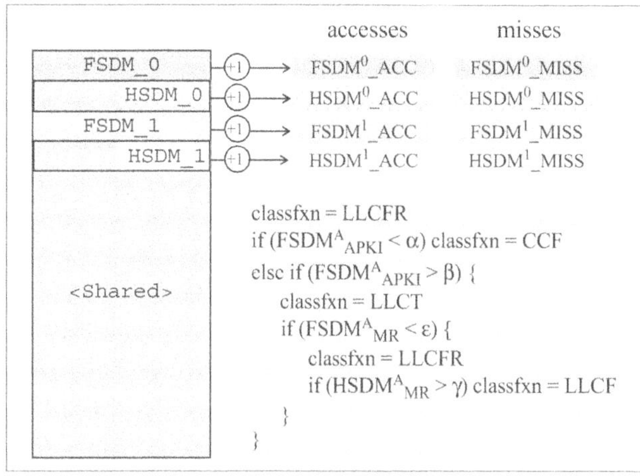

Figure 3: Runtime Isolated Cache Estimator (RICE) and Classification Algorithm. In the classification algorithm, to compute APKI, we multiply $FSDM^A\_ACC$ by (total sets / SDM size). For this paper, we use $\alpha = 1$, $\beta = 4$, $\varepsilon = 25$, $\gamma = 50$.

the primary drawback of a profiling based approach is that the information gathered is highly sensitive to the choice of input sets (which is only available at run time), application phase, and also varies across different types of applications.

3.1.2 Runtime Classification of Applications

A straightforward way of classifying application cache utility in isolation is to periodically pause all cores on a CMP and measure the application cache performance. However, this approach degrades performance of all other concurrently executing applications. Alternatively, external shadow tags can be used to monitor cache utility [25, 35]. However, such approaches require extra hardware and power overhead for the shadow tags. To avoid additional hardware overhead and changes to the existing shared cache structure, we propose a *Runtime Isolated Cache Estimator (RICE)*. RICE *estimate*s cache utility of an application by using a *Set Dueling Monitor (SDM)* [24]. An SDM estimates the misses for any given policy by permanently dedicating a few sets[1] of the cache to follow that policy. RICE dedicates two SDMs per application in the cache. For each SDM, two 32-bit counters track the number of accesses and misses to that SDM (illustrated in Figure 3). The first SDM, referred to as Full-SDM (FSDM) estimates the caching behavior of an application if it were to have sole access to the cache. The FSDM for an application A ($FSDM^A$) only allows A to allocate lines in these cache sets. All other applications are required to *bypass*[2] these cache sets. The second SDM, referred to as Half-SDM (HSDM) estimates the caching behavior of an application if it were to have sole access to only half the cache. All other applications can share the remaining ways in the HSDM. An HSDM can be implemented using way partitioning [25]. For example, in $HSDM^A$ of a 4-way set associative cache, application A only allocates lines in way 0 and way 1 while all other applications allocate lines in way 2 and way 3.

---

1. Prior work has shown that 32 sets are sufficient to estimate cache performance [25, 24]. Throughout the paper an SDM consists of 32 sets.
2. For an inclusive LLC, a single way in each set can be dedicated for all other applications. This effectively causes the SDM to behave like a direct mapped cache for all other applications.

RICE can be enabled permanently or can be software controlled through privileged instructions. Providing the dynamic on/off ability reduces RICE overhead especially when the FSDM or HSDM tend to be "hot" sets for other applications. The drawback however is that privileged instructions must be introduced into the instruction set architecture (ISA) to explicitly enable or disable RICE.

When RICE is enabled, periodically sampling the RICE counters and calculating the accesses per kilo instructions (APKI) and miss rate (MR) metrics in each SDM can be used to classify the cache utility of application A at runtime. For example, if the $FSDM^{A}_{APKI}$ of the application is small (e.g. < 1), then the application is a CCF application. On the other hand, if the $FSDM^{A}_{APKI}$ of the application is high, the $FSDM^{A}_{MR}$ is small but the $HSDM^{A}_{MR}$ miss rate is high, then the application is a LLCF application. However, if the $FSDM^{A}_{APKI}$ of the application is high and the $FSDM^{A}_{MR}$ is also very high, then the application is an LLCT application. If none of the above conditions apply, then the application can be classified as a LLCFR application. Note that the primary use of the HSDM is to classify an LLCF application. Without the HSDM, an LLCF application would incorrectly be classified as an LLCFR application. Since LLCF applications behave like LLCT applications in the presence of any other application, it is imperative that such applications be classified correctly. A summary of our runtime application classification algorithm is provided in Figure 3.

3.2. Cache Replacement and Utility-aware Scheduling

Given statically profiled or dynamically gathered cache utility information of all concurrently executing applications, we now discuss the design of an intelligent scheduling algorithm that is *co-designed* to the underlying shared LLC replacement policy.

3.2.1 CRUISE for Demand-based Cache Replacement

LRU-managed shared caches allocate cache resources based on demand instead of cache utility. As a result, under LRU replacement, LLCT applications receive more cache resources despite the fact that they do not benefit from the cache. Since LLCT applications can degrade the performance of LLCF and LLCFR applications, it is best to co-schedule them with LLCT or CCF applications.

When scheduling CCF applications, it is best to separate these applications across all available shared LLCs. Since CCF applications require little LLC resources, such a strategy allows co-scheduled applications to utilize more of the LLC.

When scheduling LLCF applications, it is best to co-schedule them with CCF applications. This is because an LLCF application requires majority of the shared cache while a CCF application requires little LLC resources. In the absence of CCF applications, LLCF applications behave like LLCT applications and thus should be scheduled in a similar fashion as LLCT applications.

Finally, LLCFR applications perform well when co-scheduled with other applications that benefit from the cache. Once LLCT, CCF, and LLCF applications are scheduled onto the appropriate LLCs, LLCFR applications can be co-scheduled anywhere.

Since an LRU-managed shared LLC allocates cache resources on demand, we propose *CRUISE-LRU (CRUISE-L)*. To ensure a proper schedule, steps must be followed in the order listed below:

1. <u>Group</u> LLCT applications on the same LLC
2. <u>Spread</u> CCF applications across all LLCs
3. <u>Co-schedule</u> LLCF with CCF applications
4. <u>Fill</u> in the LLCFR applications

During the scheduling process, if all computing resources on one shared LLC are occupied, then the scheduling algorithm overflows onto the next available LLC (selected at random). Additionally, if there exists more than one application from the same category, then the scheduling algorithm selects an application at random.

3.2.2 CRUISE for Utility-based Cache Replacement

Unlike LRU, DRRIP-managed shared caches allocate cache resources based on utility instead of demand. As a result, LLCT applications receive very few cache resources when co-scheduled with applications that benefit from the shared cache. Consequently, in a DRRIP-managed cache, LLCT applications can be treated like CCF applications that do not benefit from the available cache.

When co-designing the scheduling policy for an LRU-managed cache, an entire shared cache was used to "contain" LLCT applications and prevent them from hurting LLCFR and LLCF applications. In doing so, CRUISE-L is inefficient since it can "waste" one or more shared caches. However, in a system with more than one DRRIP-managed shared cache, we propose *CRUISE-DRRIP* (*CRUISE-D)* to efficiently utilize all available shared caches. Again, to ensure a proper schedule, steps must be followed in the order listed below:

1. <u>Spread</u> LLCT applications across all LLCs
2. <u>Spread</u> CCF applications across all LLCs
3. <u>Co-schedule</u> LLCF with CCF/LLCT applications
4. <u>Fill</u> in the LLCFR applications

Note that CRUISE-D is similar to the recently proposed *Distributed Intensity (DI)* proposal [38]. Like DI, CRUISE-D separates LLCT applications onto separate LLCs. However, CRUISE-D differs from DI in that it explicitly detects LLCF applications and co-schedules them intelligently to maximize system performance.

3.2.3 CRUISE-L vs. CRUISE-D

CRUISE-L and CRUISE-D primary differ in how they co-schedule LLCT applications. CRUISE-D treats LLCT applications like CCF applications. This is because a DRRIP managed cache naturally allocates fewer cache resources to LLCT applications since they do not benefit from cache.

Note that while CRUISE-L is co-designed for an LRU-managed cache, CRUISE-L is applicable for any un-managed cache replacement policy. Similarly, though CRUISE-D is co-designed for a DRRIP-managed cache, CRUISE-D is applicable for any utility-based cache replacement policy. Therefore, applying CRUISE-L to a utility-managed cache or applying CRUISE-D to an un-managed cache will yield suboptimal co-schedules.

3.3. Integrating CRUISE into Existing Software

Existing software (i.e., operating systems or hypervisor) can utilize CRUISE by using statically profiled utility information or by dynamically learning the application utility if RICE hardware is available. If an operating system implements CRUISE using statically profiled cache utility information, then the natural opportunity to determine the best application co-schedule is when the operating system (or hypervisor) schedules a new application onto a CPU (e.g., after a context switch). With statically profiled cache utility information, co-scheduling decisions are limited to context switches and/or when an application finishes execution. As a result, the operating system (or hypervisor) cannot adapt to dynamic application phases.

Table II. MPKI of Representative SPEC CPU2006 Applications In the Absence of Prefetching

	ast	bzi	cal	dea	gob	h26	hmm	lib	mcf	per	pov	sje	sph	wrf	xal
L1 MPKI (64KB)	29.29	19.48	21.19	0.95	10.56	11.26	4.67	38.83	21.51	0.42	15.08	0.99	19.03	16.50	27.80
L2 MPKI (256KB)	17.02	17.44	14.06	0.22	7.91	1.57	2.76	38.83	20.43	0.20	0.18	0.37	16.20	15.18	3.38
LLC MPKI (4MB)	2.02	1.05	0.51	0.05	7.70	0.03	0.80	34.28	18.72	0.60	0.01	0.30	1.21	8.23	1.72
Classification (4MB)	LLCFR	LLCFR	LLCFR	CCF	LLCT	LLCFR	LLCFR	LLCT	LLCT	CCF	CCF	CCF	LLCF	LLCT	LLCFR

Alternatively, if the underlying processor supports RICE, then an operating system (or hypervisor) can dynamically adapt to application phase behavior. To do so, the operating system can periodically read and classify all applications using the RICE counters. Upon classifying application cache utility, the operating system (or hypervisor) can periodically apply CRUISE.

4. Experimental Methodology

We use CMP$im [9], a Pin [19] based trace-driven x86 simulator for our performance studies. Our baseline system is a 4-core CMP with two shared LLCs (see Figure 1). Each core in the CMP is a 4-way out-of-order processor with a 128-entry reorder buffer and a three level cache hierarchy. We assume single-threaded cores with the L1 and L2 caches private to each core. The L1 instruction and data caches are 4-way 32KB each while the L2 cache is unified 8-way 256KB. The L1 and L2 cache sizes are kept constant in our study. We support two L1 read ports and one L1 write port on the data cache. Each last-level cache (LLC) is a unified 16-way 4MB cache that is shared by two cores in the CMP. We assume a banked LLC with as many banks as there are cores in the system. All caches in the hierarchy are non-inclusive and use a 64B line size. For replacement decisions, the L1 and L2 caches always use the Not Recently Used[3] (NRU) replacement policy. To evaluate interactions with intelligent scheduling, we only vary the LLC replacement policy between NRU and DRRIP [10]. We model a stream prefetcher that trains on L2 cache misses and prefetches lines into the L2 cache (i.e. the prefetcher is private to each core). The prefetcher has 16 stream detectors. The load-to-use latencies for the L1, L2, and LLC are 1, 10, and 24 cycles respectively. We model an interconnect with a fixed average latency. Bandwidth onto the interconnect is modeled using a fixed number of MSHRs. Contention for the MSHRs models the increase in latency due to additional traffic introduced into the system. We use a queuing model to model off chip contention. We model a 150 cycle unloaded latency penalty to main memory and support 16 outstanding misses to memory. The cache hierarchy organization and latencies are based on the Intel Core i7 processor [2]. Note that our proposed scheduling policies do not rely on the specific latencies used.

We do not use an operating system, but instead augment our CMP$im model with an application scheduler. Applications are initially assigned to the first available free CPU at the beginning of simulation. Our dynamic scheduler periodically (every 1ms) determines whether applications need to be re-scheduled. When classifying an application at runtime, RICE uses hysteresis to ensure steady state. This is to prevent CRUISE from doing frequent reschedules due to slight phase changes in the application. When an application is re-scheduled to a new CPU, we model all compulsory misses to warm up all levels of the cache hierarchy on the new CPU (and possibly new LLC). Additionally, when CRUISE attempts to reschedule applications, CRUISE tries to minimize the number of applications that need to be rescheduled. This is to minimize the compulsory miss overhead for all applications.

3. NRU is the hardware approximation for LRU replacement. NRU performs similar to LRU for a wide variety of workloads [10] and is the commonly used LLC replacement policy in majority of microprocessors today [10].

4.1. Benchmarks

For our study, we use benchmarks from the SPEC CPU2006 suite. We first grouped the SPEC CPU2006 benchmarks into four different categories based on their L1, L2, and LLC cache hit behavior. Of all the SPEC CPU2006 benchmarks, we selected few applications from each category to cover the spectrum of hit/miss behavior in the different levels of the cache hierarchy. A total of 15 representative SPEC CPU2006 benchmarks were selected. Each benchmark was compiled using the *icc* compiler with full optimization flags. Representative regions for the SPEC benchmarks were all collected using PinPoints [23]. Table II lists the 15 SPEC CPU2006 benchmarks and their misses per 1000 instructions (MPKI) in the L1, L2, and LLC when run in isolation. To illustrate application cache utility, the MPKI numbers are reported in the absence of a prefetcher.

To evaluate our proposed scheduling algorithms, we ran all possible four-threaded combinations of the 15 SPEC CPU2006 benchmarks, i.e. 15 choose 4—1365 workloads. To provide insights on when scheduling policies are beneficial, we selected 26 workload mixes (listed in Table I) to showcase results. These 26 workload mixes correspond to the same workload mixes emphasized with different shapes in Regions I, II, III, and IV of Figure 2. Recall that Region I workload mixes have no performance variation under different application schedules. Region II workload mixes have significant performance variation under LRU-managed shared caches. These workload mixes mostly consist of LLCT applications. Region III workload mixes have significant performance variation under DRRIP-managed shared caches. These workload mixes mostly consist of LLCFR applications. Finally Region IV workload mixes

Table I. Workload Mixes and Their Types

Name	Apps	Type	Name	Apps	Type
MIX_00	mcf,pov,sje,wrf	I	**MIX_13**	bzi,cal,h26,mcf	III
MIX_01	bzi,dea,per,xal	I	**MIX_14**	bzi,hmm,mcf,sph	III
MIX_02	ast,bzi,gob,hmm	I	**MIX_15**	ast,cal,sph,wrf	III
MIX_03	bzi,dea,gob,mcf	II	**MIX_16**	ast,cal,mcf,sph	III
MIX_04	ast,h26,hmm,lib	II	**MIX_17**	cal,per,sph,xal	IV
MIX_05	lib,sje,sph,wrf	II	**MIX_18**	ast,cal,dea,sph	IV
MIX_06	gob,lib,mcf,sph	II	**MIX_19**	hmm,lib,mcf,wrf	IV
MIX_07	lib,sph,wrf,xal	II	**MIX_20**	hmm,mcf,per,sph	IV
MIX_08	lib,mcf,sph,xal	II	**MIX_21**	ast,lib,sph,gob	IV
MIX_09	lib,mcf,pov,sph	II	**MIX_22**	ast,lib,sph,wrf	IV
MIX_10	ast,cal,sph,xal	III	**MIX_23**	ast,lib,sph,mcf	IV
MIX_11	cal,h26,mcf,sph	III	**MIX_24**	ast,lib,sph,per	IV
MIX_12	bzi,h26,wrf,xal	III	**MIX_25**	ast,lib,sph,pov	IV

have performance variation under both replacement policies. These workload mixes consist of both LLCT and LLCFR applications. To provide a thorough analysis, we also provide results for all 1365 workloads wherever applicable.

We simulated half billion instructions for each benchmark. Simulations continue to execute until all benchmarks in the workload mix execute at least half billion instructions. If a faster thread finishes its required instructions, it continues to execute to compete for cache resources. We only collect statistics for the half billion instructions committed by each application. This methodology is similar to existing work on shared cache management [25, 12, 34].

4.2. Metrics

For our studies we use the three metrics commonly used in literature for measuring the performance of multiple concurrently executing applications: throughput, weighted speedup, and fairness. The weighted speedup metric indicates reduction in execution time [28]. The "harmonic mean fairness" metric (which is harmonic mean of normalized IPCs) balances both fairness and performance [20]. The different metrics are defined as follows:

$$\text{Throughput} = \Sigma \text{IPC}_i \quad \text{(Eq. 1)}$$

$$\text{Weighted Speedup} = \Sigma(\text{IPC}_i/\text{SingleIPC}_i) \quad \text{(Eq. 2)}$$

$$\text{Harmonic Mean Fairness} = N/\Sigma(\text{SingleIPC}_i/\text{IPC}_i) \quad \text{(Eq. 3)}$$

where IPC_i is the IPC of the ith application when it concurrently executes with other applications and SingleIPC_i is IPC of the same application in isolation.

5. Results and Analysis

5.1. Throughput

To decouple the performance of CRUISE and the accuracy of our application classifier RICE, we first illustrate CRUISE using cache utility information from static profiling. In doing so, we can measure the overall accuracy of the CRUISE algorithm that is specifically co-designed to the replacement policy. RICE is just our low overhead hardware classification mechanism.

Figure 4 presents the relative throughput of five different application scheduling policies (*random*, *CRUISE-L*, *CRUISE-D*, *Distributed Intensity (DI)*[4] [38], and *Optimal Application Schedule (OAS)*) normalized to the *Worst Application Schedule (WAS)*. Random schedule refers to selecting a co-schedule at random from the different possible co-schedules. The x-axis represents the different workload mixes. The bar labeled geomean is the geometric mean of all 26 workloads. In an LRU-managed LLC (Figure 4a), as expected, workload mixes from category 'I' do not benefit from scheduling since all applications in these workload mixes do not benefit from the shared LLC. Workload mixes from category III also do not benefit from scheduling because they mostly consist of LLCFR applications. For such applications, LRU works best. Workload mixes from categories II and IV benefit from intelligent scheduling decisions because they consist of LLCT applications. In these workloads, we find that CRUISE-L performs very similar to OAS. In some scenarios CRUISE-L does not perform as well as OAS (e.g. MIX_04, MIX_06, MIX_19). CRUISE-L reaches suboptimal decision because these workload mixes consist of multiple applications that belong to the same cache utility category (e.g.,

4. For DI, we use isolated cache miss rate based on profile information.

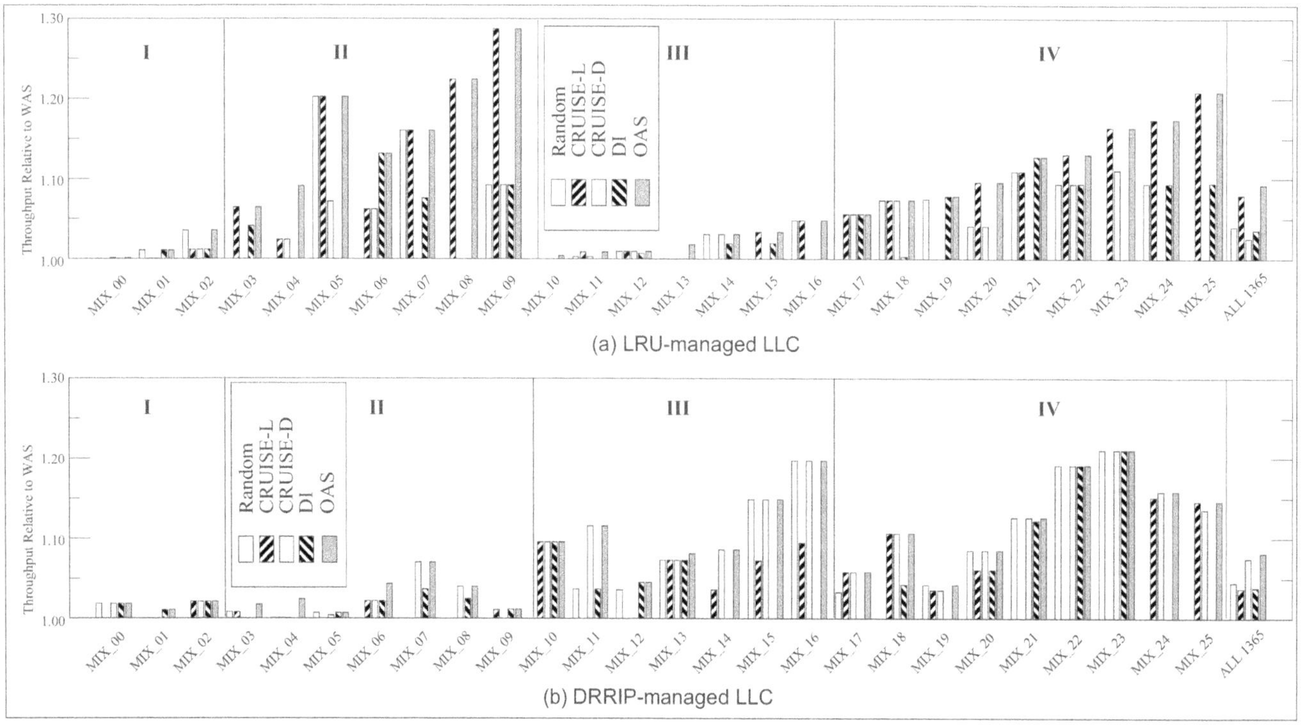

Figure 4: Throughput Comparison of Scheduling Policies to Worst Application Schedule (WAS) on a 4-core CMP. (a) LRU-managed LLC (b) DRRIP-managed LLC

multiple LLCFR applications). When co-scheduling applications, CRUISE randomly selects an application and does not distinguish between applications that belong to the same cache utility category. Though further enhancements can be made to CRUISE to make this distinction, the first order benefits are from distinguishing applications that belong to different cache utility categories.

Additionally, the figure also shows that in an LRU-managed cache, CRUISE-D is not as high performing as CRUISE-L (e.g. MIX_05, MIX_07, MIX_20). Unlike CRUISE-L, CRUISE-D is specifically designed for a utility managed cache and thus does not perform well on a demand managed cache.

The figure also shows that DI scheduling does not perform as well as CRUISE-L (e.g. MIX_05, MIX_07, MIX_09). This is because these workload mixes consist of an LLCF application, and DI incorrectly co-schedules LLCF applications. For example, consider MIX_05, the workload mix consists of applications *lib,sje,sph,wrf*. Based on cache miss rates, DI co-schedules these applications as *lib,sje|sph,wrf*. However, the OAS is *sph,sje|lib,wrf*. This is because *sph* is an LLCF application that benefits from being co-scheduled with *sje*, a CCF application. Furthermore, DI has suboptimal performance under LRU because it co-schedules memory bound applications with CPU bound applications. In doing so, DI degrades CPU bound application performance. As a result, DI is unable to arrive at the OAS.

On average in an LRU-managed cache, DI performs similar to random scheduling, both performing roughly 4% better than WAS. CRUISE-D and CRUISE-L perform roughly 3% and 8% better than WAS respectively. CRUISE-L bridges 90% of the gap between WAS and OAS—OAS performs roughly 9% better than WAS.

Figure 4b shows the performance of the different scheduling policies on a DRRIP-managed cache. Recall that DRRIP allocates cache resources based on utility instead of demand. We again observe that workloads from category 'I' do not benefit from scheduling since these mixes do not benefit from the shared LLC. Unlike an LRU-managed cache, workload mixes in category II do not benefit from scheduling because DRRIP inherently *knows* how to handle LLCT applications in a workload mix. However, CRUISE-D finds opportunity to improve workload mixes from categories III and IV because they consist of multiple LLCFR and LLCT applications. In a DRRIP-managed cache, we again observe CRUISE-D almost always outperforms CRUISE-L. In a utility managed shared LLC, random, DI, CRUISE-L, and CRUISE-D improve performance over WAS by 4.4%, 3.7%, 3.8%, and 7.5% respectively. Again, note that CRUISE-D bridges 90% of the performance gap between WAS and OAS—OAS performs roughly 8% better than WAS.

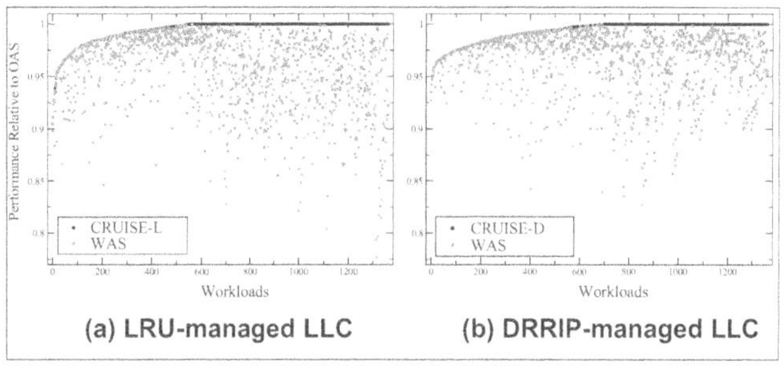

Figure 5: Per workload Comparison of CRUISE to WAS.

To illustrate the behavior of CRUISE-L and CRUISE-D across a much wider set of workload mixes, Figure 5 shows per-workload performance comparison of each scheduling policy on an LRU-managed and DRRIP-managed cache. The x-axis in the figures show the 1365 workload mixes and the y-axis shows the performance relative to OAS. Values at 1 imply that CRUISE application schedule is identical to OAS, and values below 1 illustrate the relative throughput difference between CRUISE and OAS. Each graph is sorted in ascending order based on the CRUISE algorithm. Both figures show that CRUISE significantly reduce the performance variation between WAS and OAS. For workload mixes where the performance variation is significantly high, CRUISE frequently arrives at an optimal schedule. In both LRU-managed and DRRIP-managed shared caches, the majority of performance variation is less than 5%. For cases where the performance variation is greater than 5%, further refinement can be made by intelligently selecting between applications that belong to the same cache utility category.

5.2. Weighted Speedup and Fairness

Again, assuming statically profiled utility information, Figure 6 and Figure 7 presents the throughput, weighted speedup, and fairness comparison of CRUISE on both LRU-managed and DRRIP-managed caches. Each figure shows the workloads on the x-axis and the corresponding performance metric on the y-axis. Like Figure 5, the throughput and weighted speedup metrics in these figures are normalized to OAS. The throughput and weighted speedup figures compare five different scheduling policies: *WAS, random, CRUISE-L, CRUISE-D, and DI*. We present 's-curves' independently sorted for each scheduling algorithm.

In an LRU-managed cache, across all 1365 workloads, for the throughput and weighted speedup metrics, there is roughly 0.5%

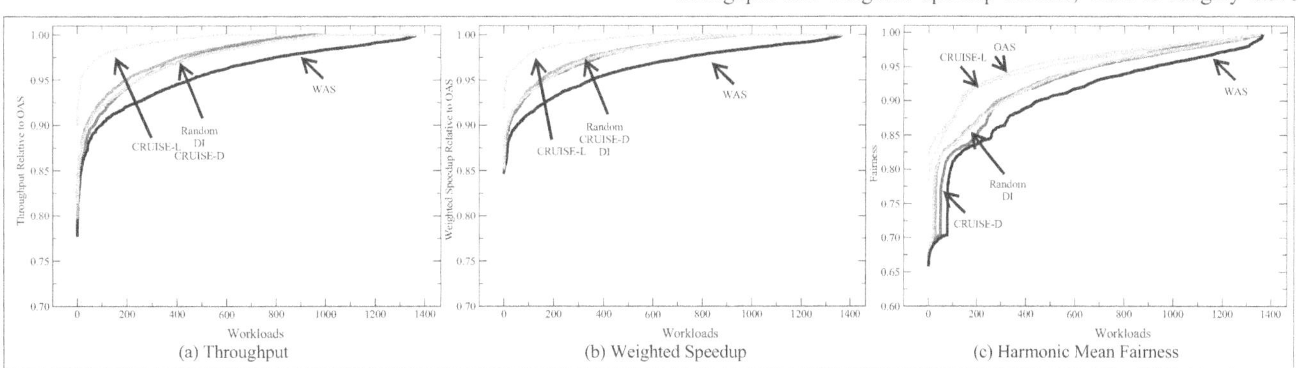

Figure 6: Throughput, Weighted Speedup, and Fairness of Scheduling Policies on a 4-core CMP for an LRU-managed LLC. Note that these curves are independently sorted for each scheduling policy.

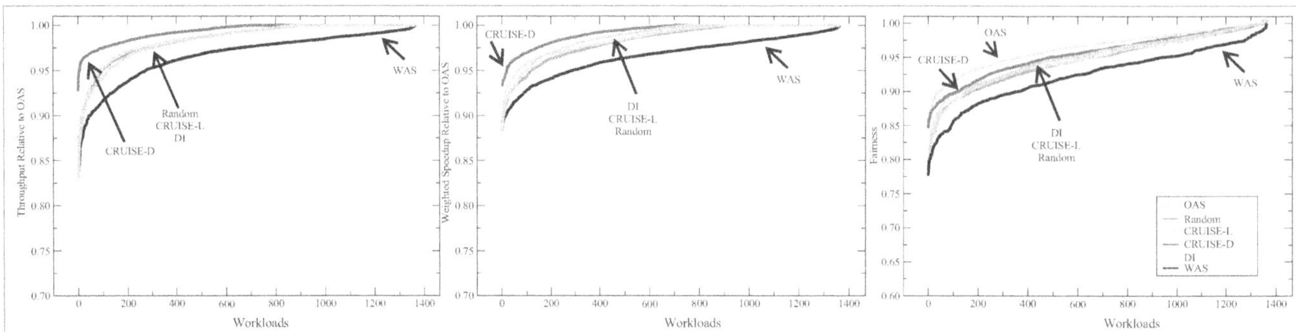

(a) Throughput (b) Weighted Speedup (c) Harmonic Mean Fairness

Figure 7: Throughput, Weighted Speedup, and Fairness of Scheduling Policies on a 4-core CMP for a DRRIP-managed LLC. . Note that these curves are independently sorted for each scheduling policy.

performance variation for CRUISE-L, roughly 2.5% for CRUISE-D, random, and DI scheduling, and finally roughly 4% for WAS. Similarly, for a DRRIP-managed cache, we observe roughly 0.8% performance variation for CRUISE-L, roughly 1.8% for CRUISE-D, random, and DI scheduling, and finally roughly 3.5% for WAS. Also, note that a randomly selected co-schedule tends to always be better than the WAS. However, CRUISE-D and CRUISE-L always provide better performance than a random schedule. Additionally, both CRUISE-L and CRUISE-D are within 1% of OAS for the fairness metric. In summary, Figure 6 and Figure 7 reveal that CRUISE performs similar to OAS for the throughput, weighted speedup, and fairness metrics—essentially CRUISE is robust across all metrics.

5.3. Scalability

We now discuss scalability of CRUISE by varying the number of shared LLCs and also varying the number of threads sharing an LLC. We construct 8-core workload mixes and consider two 8-core systems (a) four shared LLCs—two cores each sharing an LLC (b) two shared LLCs—four cores each sharing an LLC. For both these systems, we evaluate the performance of different scheduling policies for LRU and DRRIP-managed caches. We evaluate all possible 8-core combinations of the 15 applications—6435 workload mixes. For each system, we also evaluate all possible co-schedules. For a four LLC system with two cores per LLC, there are 105 possible co-schedules while for a two LLC system with eight cores per LLC, there are 35 possible co-schedules. Since we have already illustrated that CRUISE performs well across all performance metrics, we now limit ourselves to the throughput metric. We observe similar behavior for both the weighted speedup and fairness metrics.

Figure 8 illustrates CRUISE performance for the different 8-core configurations. As the number of shared LLCs increase, CRUISE consistently bridges the performance variation between OAS and WAS (Figure 8 (a) and (b)). Similarly, when increasing the number of threads per LLC, CRUISE still manages to bridge the performance variation (Figure 8 (c) and (d)). In these larger systems, CRUISE consistently performs better than all other scheduling policies.

5.4. Dynamic Classification

Thus far we have investigated the accuracy of CRUISE using profiled utility information. We now evaluate CRUISE with dynamically observed utility information gathered by RICE. Note that any performance deviation from OAS can primarily be attributed to the accuracy and sampling overhead of RICE. Figure 9 illustrates CRUISE-L and DI performance compared to OAS for our baseline 4-core CMP with two shared LLCs. We do not account for the RICE overhead due to sampling for OAS. We observe that CRUISE-L consistently tracks the performance of OAS, thereby showing that RICE performs well in dynamically classifying the application. We also observe that CRUISE-L consistently outperforms DI. On average, we find that CRUISE-L, DI, and OAS improve performance over WAS by roughly 2%, -0.2%, and 4% respectively. The difference between CRUISE-L and OAS is roughly 2% due to the sampling overheads of RICE (we observed similar comparison of CRUISE-D to OAS in DRRIP-managed caches). Note that these single digit performance gains are not insignificant since our studies span more than 1000 workload mixes that include a significant number of workloads that do not benefit from intelligent scheduling.

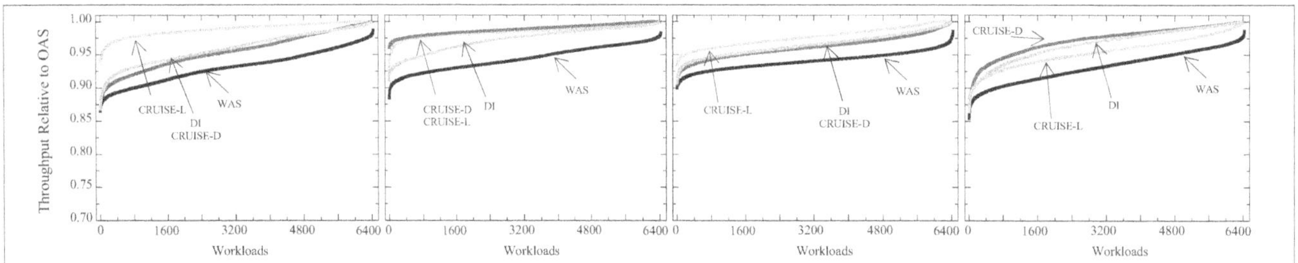

(a) 8-cores, 4 LLCs, 2C/LLC (LRU) (b) 8-cores, 4 LLCs, 2C/LLC (DRRIP) (c) 8-cores, 2 LLCs, 4C/LLC (LRU) (d) 8-cores, 2 LLCs, 4C/LLC (DRRIP)

Figure 8: Performance of CRUISE when Increasing Number of Shared LLCs or when Increasing Number of Cores Per LLC (C/LLC). Note that these curves are independently sorted for each scheduling policy.

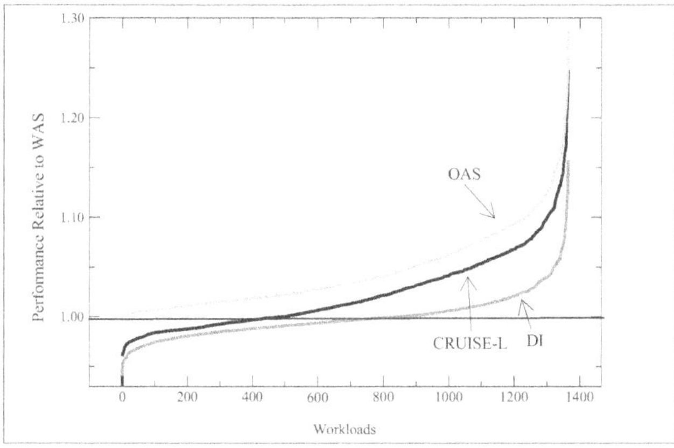

Figure 9: CRUISE Using Dynamic Classification From RICE for LRU-managed caches. Note that these curves are independently sorted for each scheduling policy.

Both CRUISE-L and DI degrade performance slightly (less than 5%) compared to WAS. The negative outliers can be attributed to the sampling overhead of RICE (for CRUISE-L) or the overhead of compulsory misses from to context switches. Our investigations revealed that for the duration of the runs, the application classification reaches steady state and the number of context switches are low. This indicates that there is opportunity to reduce the negative overheads and improve CRUISE performance by periodically sampling RICE counters. Investigating this is part of on-going work.

5.5. Sensitivity to Cache Size

CRUISE performance is dependent on the accuracy of the per-application cache utility. We evaluated CRUISE using profile based cache utility information on our baseline CMP system with smaller shared caches (2MB) and larger shared caches (8MB). With perfect cache utility knowledge, we found that CRUISE behaves similar to results illustrated in Figure 7 for all performance metrics. Similarly, when using RICE to dynamically classify applications, CRUISE behaves similar to results in Figure 9.

With regards to RICE-based dynamic *utility* classification, we found that classification of applications is a function of the available LLC size. For example, RICE correctly classifies *sphinx* as a LLCF application on a 4MB and an LLCT application on a 2MB cache. This is because *sphinx* has a roughly 4MB working-set size. Similarly, RICE correctly classifies *h264ref* as a LLCFR application on a 4MB cache but a LLCF application on a 2MB cache. This is because *h264ref* has a roughly 2MB working-set size. In general, as expected, we observe transitions in application classification from cache fitting/friendly to cache thrashing/fitting when the LLC size is reduced. Similarly, we see transitions in application classification from cache thrashing/fitting to cache fitting/friendly as the LLC size is increased. This shows that RICE can dynamically classifying the isolated application cache utility regardless of the available LLC size.

6. Related Work

Several researchers from the software and hardware community have independently studied and proposed ways to mitigate contention in shared caches. In this section we briefly describe recent work that is relevant to our proposal.

Perhaps the effort that closely resembles our work is the recent *Distributed Intensity (DI)* proposal [38]. Unlike our simulation based study, DI was evaluated on real hardware composed of Intel and AMD systems with shared LLCs. To the best of our knowledge, these LLCs use a pseudo-LRU replacement policy [10]. DI proposes to capture runtime cache miss rates of applications (using hardware performance counters), sort the miss rates, and then separate the memory intensive applications onto different LLCs, in effect co-scheduling memory intensive applications with non-memory bound applications. For an LRU managed cache, this co-scheduling strategy is at odds with all recent work on shared cache management [12, 25, 34, 8]. These studies have illustrated that in an LRU managed cache, memory intensive applications significantly degrade the performance of non-memory intensive applications. Perhaps the primary difference is because the authors correlate performance degradation to not only sharing the LLC but also from sharing prefetchers and the DRAM memory controller. More recent Intel and AMD processors, however, use a three-level hierarchy, where the prefetchers are private and located at the L2 cache [2]. Furthermore, the DRAM controller is on-die and more sophisticated than earlier designs [2]. Thus, the sharing effects of the prefetcher and DRAM controller is less pronounced in modern day processors with LRU replacement. As such, we show that DI does not perform well on LRU-managed caches. Furthermore, while CRUISE-D is similar to DI, it outperforms DI on DRRIP-managed caches as well.

There has been considerable work in shared cache management via software cache partitioning [6, 17, 36]. The general idea in these designs is to allocate a portion of the cache to each of the applications and modify physical memory allocation such that every application's cache lines map into its reserved cache space. These schemes have non-trivial and intricate interactions with the operating system kernel and require complicated changes to virtual memory management.

Some software-centric scheduling algorithms attempt an ad-hoc approach to choosing which threads should be co-scheduled by attempting several thread allocation strategies and picking the best-performing ones [28]. This period during which the algorithm is sampling and learning can have sub-optimal system performance to dynamic phase changes. Furthermore, such a scheme is impractical for large number of threads since the number of permutations of co-schedules exponentially increases.

Recent work in understanding the software co-scheduling of threads has also shown that data sharing is an important parameter by which to classify threads [32]. Tang et al. focus on datacenter application workloads and use a heuristic based algorithm to predict which threads should be mapped to which cores. Since our runtime classification is based on miss rates it works in the same manner as a heuristic based algorithm.

More recent efforts attempt to design an intelligent scheduler that is aware of underlying caches and that can differentiate between applications with differing memory demands [7, 37, 38]. These proposals, however do not consider the impact that the underlying hardware replacement and allocation policies may have on the benefit of the scheduling decisions. Additionally, to differentiate between and classify the applications, these mechanisms do not take into account that hardware cache contention between the threads can lead to misguided classifications.

In the hardware management of shared caches, some of the earlier work focused on hardware cache partitioning [30, 25]. Hardware cache partitioning allocates cache resources to competing applications either statically or dynamically. These proposals use way partitioning in the cache and extra identifying bits per cache line to reserve portions of the cache for each application. Such designs work well independently to manage caches at a hardware level but cannot reach optimal performance since they do not guide the software scheduler to make intelligent decisions in the first place.

More recent work in hardware management of caches has focused on smart insertion and replacement policies. These policies do not influence application co-schedules, but instead can mitigate the impact that thrashing and scans have on the performance of individual applications [12, 24].

The recent state-of-the-art work in smart hardware cache management focuses on more fine-grained classification of each application by differentiating between references that have near and distant re-reference intervals [10]. The RRIP and DRRIP proposals improve the performance of shared caches considerably and are good starting points to consider a hardware-software co-design where a smart cache replacement removes some of the inefficiencies of shared caches such that intelligent software scheduling is able to reach near optimal performance as we showed in this paper.

There has also been some independent work done in classifying the memory intensity of applications [5, 15, 35, 31]. These proposals draw analogies to differentiate between the memory requirements of several competing applications. However, the proposed mechanisms are more complex than our RICE proposal. As we show in this paper, RICE has negligible hardware overhead, and is practical design that can obtain online and dynamic classification information of concurrently executing applications.

7. Summary and Future Work

The use of virtualization, multi-core, and multi-socket systems have enabled multiple concurrently executing applications on the same system. In doing so, applications with varying memory demands contend for shared resources. Since the on-chip shared LLC serves as the last-line of defense before the long-latency penalty to memory, it is crucial that shared LLCs be efficiently managed.

Shared LLCs commonly found in microprocessors today use the LRU replacement policy. Several studies have shown that LRU performs poorly for shared LLCs because LRU allocates cache resources based on demand instead of benefit. To address the LRU problem, shared LLCs have been managed independently by the software or the hardware. Software tries to intelligently co-schedule applications to avoid shared cache contention while hardware tries to reduce shared cache contention by improving the replacement policy. However, to-date there exists no comprehensive study that evaluates the interaction between improved cache replacement and intelligent scheduling decisions. With this in mind, this paper makes the following contributions:

- We conduct a detailed study on the interactions between intelligent scheduling and smart cache replacement. We find that smart cache replacement reduces the burden on software for intelligent scheduling but does not completely eliminate the need for finding optimal application co-schedules.
- We propose *Cache Replacement and Utility-aware Scheduling (CRUISE)*, a hardware/software co-designed application scheduling policy that uses knowledge of the underlying LLC replacement policy *and* application cache utility information to determine how best to co-schedule applications.
- Finally, we propose a *Runtime Isolated Cache Estimator (RICE)*, a hardware mechanism that dynamically determines isolated LLC performance while concurrently sharing the LLC with other applications. RICE requires no changes to the existing cache structure and requires storage overhead of only eight bytes per hardware-thread in the system.

For a large number of heterogeneous workload mixes, we evaluate CRUISE for a variety of systems with multiple shared LLCs. Our evaluations included LLCs shared by two and four applications. We show that CRUISE significantly reduces the performance variation between different static application co-schedules. In the majority of cases, CRUISE provides *near-optimal* performance for the throughput, weighted speedup, and fairness metrics.

In this paper, we evaluated CRUISE assuming as many cores as there are running applications. However, CRUISE is also applicable when the number of running applications is significantly larger than the number of cores. In such a system, the operating system or hypervisor can utilize CRUISE and RICE to dynamically select applications from the waiting queue while guaranteeing some degree of Quality of Service (QoS). Furthermore, we find that there is opportunity to reduce RICE overhead by dynamically controlling when to gather cache utility information. Exploring these extensions is part of our on-going work.

Acknowledgements

The authors would like to thank Bushra Ahsan, Malini Bhandaru, Jaideep Moses, Moinuddin Qureshi, Paul Racunas, Puneet Zaroo, and the anonymous reviewers for their feedback in improving the quality of this paper.

References

[1] Intel Corporation. Next leap in microprocessor architecture: Intel core duo. White paper. http://ces2006.akamai.com.edgesuite.net/yonahassets/CoreDuo_WhitePaper.pdf.

[2] Intel. Intel Core i7 Processor. http://www.intel.com/products/processor/corei7/specifications.htm

[3] H. Al-Zoubi, A. Milenkovic and M. Milenkovic. Performance evaluation of cache replacement policies for the SPEC CPU2000 benchmark suite. In ACMSE, 2004.

[4] J. Chang and G. S. Sohi. Cooperative cache partitioning for chip multiprocessors. ICS-21, 2007.

[5] D. Chandra, F. Guo, S. Kim, and Y. Solihin. Predicting Inter-thread Cache Contention on a CMP. In HPCA, 2005.

[6] S. Cho and L. Jin. Managing distributed shared L2 caches through OS-level Page Allocation. In MICRO-39, 2006.

[7] A. Fedorova, M. I. Seltzer, and M. D. Smith. Improving Performance Isolation on Chip Multiprocessors via an Operating System Scheduler. In PACT, 2007.

[8] R. Iyer. CQoS: a framework for enabling QoS in shared caches of CMP platforms. In ICS-18, 2004.

[9] A. Jaleel, R. S. Cohn, C. K. Luk, and B. Jacob. CMP$im: A Pin-Based On-The-Fly Multi-Core Cache Simulator. In MoBS, 2008.

[10] A. Jaleel, K. Theobald, S. Steely, and J. Emer. High Performance Cache Replacement Using Re-Reference Interval Prediction (RRIP). In ISCA-2010.

[11] A. Jaleel, E. Borch, M. Bhandaru, S. Steely, and J. Emer. Achieving Non-Inclusive Cache Performance With Inclusive Caches -- Temporal Locality Aware (TLA) Cache Management Policies, In MICRO, 2010.

[12] A. Jaleel, W. Hasenplaugh, M. Qureshi, J. Sebot, S. Steely, and J. Emer. Adaptive Insertion Policies for Managing Shared Caches. In PACT, 2008.

[13] R. Kalla, B. Sinharoy, and J. M. Tendler. IBM Power5 chip: A Dual-Core Multi-Threaded Processor. IEEE Micro, 2004.

[14] S. Kim, D. Chandra, and Y. Solihin. Fair cache sharing and partitioning in a CMP architecture. In PACT-13, 2004.

[15] R, Knauerhase, P. Brett, B. Hohlt, T. Li, and S. Hahn. Using OS Observations to Improve Performance in Multicore Systems. In IEEE-MICRO 2008.

[16] P. Kongetira, K. Aingaran, and K. Olukotun. Niagara: A 32-way multithreaded sparc processor. IEEE Micro, March/April 2005.

[17] J. Liedtke, H. Haertig, and M. Hohmuth. OS-Controlled Cache Predicatbility for Real-Time Systems. In RTAS-97.

[18] J. Lin, Q. Lu, X. Ding, Z. Zhang, and P. Sadayappan. Gaining Insights into Multicore Cache Partitioning: Bridging the Gap between Simulation and Real Systems. In HPCA, 2008.

[19] C.-K. Luk, R. Cohn, R. Muth, H. Patil, A. Klauser, G. Lowney, S.Wallace, V. J. Reddi, and K. Hazelwood. Pin: building customized program analysis tools with dynamic instrumentation. In PLDI, 2005.

[20] K. Luo, J. Gummaraju, and M. Franklin. Balancing throughput and fairness in smt processors. In ISPASS, pages 164–171, 2001.

[21] J. Moses, K. Aisopos, A. Jaleel, R. Iyer, R. Illikkal, D. Newell, and S. Makineni. CMPSched$im: Evaluating OS/CMP Interaction on Shared Cache Management, In ISPASS, 2009.

[22] K. J. Nesbit, J. Laudon, and J. E. Smith. Virtual private caches. In ISCA-34, pages 57–68, 2007.

[23] H. Patil, R. Cohn, M. Charney, R. Kapoor, and A. Sun. Pinpointing Representative Portions of Large Intel Itanium Programs with Dynamic Instrumentation. In MICRO, 2004.

[24] M. K. Qureshi, A. Jaleel, Y. N. Patt, S. C. Steely Jr., and J. Emer. Adaptive insertion policies for high-performance caching. In ISCA-34, 2007.

[25] M. K. Qureshi and Y. Patt. Utility Based Cache Partitioning: A Low Overhead High-Performance Runtime Mechanism to Partition Shared Caches. In MICRO-39, 2006.

[26] M. K. Qureshi, D. N. Lynch, O. Mutlu, and Y. N. Patt. A Case for MLP-Aware Cache Replacement. In ISCA-33, 2006.

[27] S. Srinath, O.Mutlu, H. Kim, and Y. N. Patt. Feedback directed prefetching: Improving the performance and bandwidth-efficiency of hardware prefetchers. In HPCA-13, 2007.

[28] A. Snavely and D. Tullsen. Symbiotic Jobscheduling for a Simultaneous Multithreading Processor. In ASPLOS IX, 2000.

[29] H. S. Stone, J. Turek, and J. L. Wolf. Optimal partitioning of cache memory. IEEE Transactions on Computers, 1992.

[30] G. E. Suh, L. Rudolph, and S. Devadas. Dynamic partitioning of shared cache memory. In Journal of Supercomputing, 2004.

[31] G. E. Suh, S. Devadas, and L. Rudolph. A New Memory Monitoring Scheme for Memory-Aware Scheduling and Partitioning. In HPCA'2002.

[32] L. Tang, J. Mars, N. Vachharajani, R. Hundt, M. Soffa. The Impact of Memory Subsystem Resource Sharing on Datacenter Applications. In ISCA, 2011.

[33] J. Tendler, S. Dodson, S. Fields, H. Le, and B. Sinharoy. POWER4 system microarchitecture. IBM Paper, Oct. 2001.

[34] Y. Xie and G. H. Loh. PIPP: Promotion/Insertion Pseudo-Partitioning of Multi-Core Shared Caches. In ISCA, 2009.

[35] Y. Xie and G. H. Loh. Dynamic Classification of Program Memory Behaviors in CMPs. In CMP-MSI, 2008.

[36] X. Zhang, S. Dwarkadas, and K. Shen. Towards practical page coloring - based multicore cache management. In EuroSys, 2009.

[37] S. Zhuravlev, S. Blagodurov and A. Fedorova. AKULA: A Toolset for Developing Scheduling Algorithms on Multicore Systems. In PACT, 2010.

[38] S. Zhuravlev, S. Blagodurov and A. Fedorova. Addressing Shared Resource Contention in Multicore Processors via Scheduling. In ASPLOS, 2010.

Execution Migration in a Heterogeneous-ISA Chip Multiprocessor

Matthew DeVuyst Ashish Venkat Dean M. Tullsen
University of California, San Diego
{mdevuyst | asvenkat | tullsen}@cs.ucsd.edu

Abstract

Prior research has shown that single-ISA heterogeneous chip multiprocessors have the potential for greater performance and energy efficiency than homogeneous CMPs. However, restricting the cores to a single ISA removes an important opportunity for greater heterogeneity. To take full advantage of a heterogeneous-ISA CMP, however, we must be able to migrate execution among heterogeneous cores in order to adapt to program phase changes and changing external conditions (e.g., system power state).

This paper explores migration on heterogeneous-ISA CMPs. This is non-trivial because program state is kept in an architecture-specific form; therefore, state transformation is necessary for migration. To keep migration cost low, the amount of state that requires transformation must be minimized. This work identifies large portions of program state whose form is not critical for performance; the compiler is modified to produce programs that keep most of their state in an architecture-neutral form so that only a small number of data items must be repositioned and no pointers need to be changed. The result is low migration cost with minimal sacrifice of non-migration performance.

Additionally, this work leverages binary translation to enable instantaneous migration. When migration is requested, the program is immediately migrated to a different core where binary translation runs for a short time until a function call is reached, at which point program state is transformed and execution continues natively on the new core.

This system can tolerate migrations as often as every 100 ms and still retain 95% of the performance of a system that does not do, or support, migration.

Categories and Subject Descriptors D.3.4 [*Programming Languages*]: Processors – Compilers; Code Generation

General Terms Design, Performance, Languages

Keywords Heterogeneous CMP, Thread migration

1. Introduction

Modern general-purpose processors contain multiple cores on a single die, and industry roadmaps call for increasing core counts. Current industry offerings are homogeneous CMPs (all cores on a die are identical); however, research has shown that single-ISA (instruction set architecture) heterogeneous CMPs can achieve even greater performance and power efficiency [12, 16]. Restricting the cores to a single ISA, however, eliminates an important dimension of potential heterogeneity. ISAs are already designed to meet different goals: some are designed to make hardware implementation simple, to reduce code size, to reduce memory accesses, to enable more energy-efficient hardware design, or to support domain-specific instructions. Heterogeneous-ISA CMPs would allow architects flexibility to create more efficient multicore microprocessors for mixed workloads. Additionally, support for multi-ISA execution enables the design and use of ISAs that are less general-purpose, targeted at a particular application domain or desired execution characteristics.

There are several obstacles that must be overcome to make general-purpose heterogeneous-ISA CMPs feasible. This paper proposes a solution to the most significant barrier: process migration. The ability to migrate a running program among heterogeneous cores is critical because it allows the system to capitalize on the available heterogeneity by being able to adapt to both phase changes and environmental changes. Reasons that a thread may want to migrate include:

- When the power state of the computer changes (e.g., a laptop going from normal to low-battery operation), programs running on a core designed for high performance could be migrated to a core designed for energy efficiency.
- When a new process with high priority and high performance demands enters the run queue, other processes could be migrated away from the most powerful core.
- If a program enters a new phase of execution with different computational demands (e.g., floating-point intensive code or cryptographic code), execution could migrate to a core with strong support for the new computation type (e.g., dedicated vector hardware or cryptographic instructions).
- If a part of the chip becomes too hot, programs executing on cores in that region could migrate away. If the cooler cores are a different ISA, threads can still make progress.

Many special-purpose heterogeneous multiprocessors have been produced [5, 9, 27]. Called heterogeneous multiprocessor systems-on-chips (MPSoCs), these architectures are designed for computation in specific domains that require a diverse set of algorithms to solve a problem. This paper focuses on migration in the context of general-purpose heterogeneous CMPs. Migration in this context is more important than on embedded systems where hardware-software co-design is more common and flexibility is less important. Nevertheless, migration can benefit heterogeneous MPSoCs as well by easing programmer burden.

Execution migration on a heterogeneous-ISA CMP is much more challenging than on a homogeneous CMP because program state (in registers and memory) is kept in an architecture-specific form. This requires state transformation during migration, which can be very expensive.

The goal of this research is dramatic reduction in the cost of state transformation at migration time. Prior work on migration among heterogeneous systems has only considered migration among heterogeneous machines (e.g., among nodes in a grid), not among heterogeneous cores in a CMP. In all of those cases, migration cost was dominated by state copy between nodes; however, on a multicore, that copy is unnecessary because cores share memory, opening the door for fast and frequent migration. But this now exposes the cost of the state transformation step. Because this cost was a small factor in cross-machine migration, the optimizations and transformations studied in this work are largely unique to our approach.

Thus, to minimize migration time, it is essential that as little transformation as possible be done. We accomplish this by ensuring that the memory state of the program, at particular points throughout execution, is nearly identical across compilations for different architectures. During migration, most data objects do not need to be copied or repositioned. As a result, pointers remain correct after migration, avoiding the cost and complexity of finding and fixing pointers at migration time.

We cannot maintain points of equivalence (where memory state is consistent between the executables) at all instructions in the program without serious performance consequences (e.g., worse than unoptimized code). We relax the equivalence constraint to only those points in execution that represent function call sites. However, we still allow for instantaneous migration (i.e., at any instruction) by performing binary translation on the migrated process until a function call is reached, at which point the program state is quickly transformed and execution is resumed natively. Thus, by adding the ability to do binary translation, we decouple the two aspects of migration—we can restrict migration between ISAs to specific equivalence points (call sites), yet still support migration between cores at any arbitrary point in the program.

In addition to the challenges presented by ISA diversity, the fact that migration, and hence binary translation, can start at random points of execution and run for a short duration (until a function call is reached) poses a challenge to efficient binary translation. We discuss these challenges and present an efficient dynamic binary translation and optimization technique in this paper.

If we can limit the incremental performance cost for cross-ISA migration to a few percent, even assuming very frequent migration (e.g., every few hundred milliseconds), then there is no significant performance barrier to using multi-ISA heterogeneous cores, making the full spectrum of heterogeneity available to processor designers. Besides minimizing performance cost (both for migrating code as well as steady-state non-migrating code), we have the following additional goals for this design. The technique should not require type-safe code, should not require special effort by the programmer, and should not require any special hardware. Migration should be possible at any instruction.

The level of ISA heterogeneity between cores could vary widely, from ISA extensions that are specific to a subset of the cores, to completely different ISAs. To maximize the generality of our system, we tackle the hardest problem, of completely disjoint ISAs. However, most of the techniques and principles of this work would also apply when the degree of heterogeneity is more moderate.

The next section discusses related work in the area of execution migration as it has been applied to other heterogeneous domains. In Section 3 we give an overview of the migration strategy. Section 4 describes how we ensure a nearly identical memory image across compilation for different architectures to make migration fast. Section 5 describes migration itself. Section 6 describes the binary translation techniques used to allow for instantaneous migration. Section 7 details our experimental methodology, while Section 8 shows the performance of migration. Section 9 concludes.

2. Related Work

Kumar, et al. [15, 17] demonstrate that a CMP of heterogeneous cores (with a homogeneous ISA) is often the best use of die area for better performance and power efficiency on mixed workloads. Removing the restriction of a single ISA among all cores allows for greater heterogeneity and the potential for more efficiency. In the embedded world heterogeneous-ISA multiprocessors (MP-SoCs) are not uncommon [5, 9, 27], but no truly general-purpose heterogeneous-ISA CMPs are on the market at this time. The Cell processor [13] lies somewhere in the middle—more general-purpose than most embedded systems, but not designed for mainstream mixed workloads. It has no ability to migrate code between core types dynamically.

To our knowledge, no previous work has addressed the problem of migrating a process among heterogeneous-ISA cores on a chip multiprocessor. However, there are two closely related problems, both potentially involving machines of different architectures: process migration on a cluster, grid, or distributed system; and checkpointing and recovery (CPR). The related works described in this section address one or both of these problems. In every proposed solution, large-scale state copy is necessary and dominates latency. Thus, it is typically the primary performance concern.

Von Bank, et al. [29] put forth a theoretical model, including a formal definition of heterogeneous process migration. They assert that the language system (i.e., compiler, assembler, linker, etc.) can be designed to ensure points of equivalence at a desired granularity; but the finer the granularity, the more performance will suffer because the compiler will be more constrained and less able to make machine-dependent optimizations—a conclusion that we confirm empirically in this research.

Dubach and Shub [8, 21] produce some of the earliest work on process migration. Their solution is meant to work on the equivalent of a strongly-typed language to facilitate low-cost state transformation. They follow a principle they call "greatest common denominator" (GCD), where data is placed in memory with extra padding, if necessary, to accommodate the largest data representation among architectures to which execution might be migrated. This allows most pointers to work without the need for correction. We apply the same GCD principle to our work; only in our case, the migrated process uses the exact same memory image instead of a copy of it. Also, our compiler ensures that function entry points appear at the same offsets within the code sections so that function pointers do not need to be located and fixed.

Several researchers have proposed migration techniques designed to work with strongly-typed programming languages, like Java [28] and Emerald [24]. Many more have proposed migration and/or CPR through the instrumentation of well-typed C code [4, 10, 11, 14, 19, 23, 25, 26]. The definition of well-typed code is different among these works, with some work supporting certain type-unsafe constructs. In contrast, the migration technique this paper proposes does not place any such restrictions on the code.

Pointers in languages like C present a difficult problem for heterogeneous migration because they are machine-dependent, allowing direct access to any object in the address space of a process. No prior work has been able to efficiently deal with the problem of pointers. Either runtime performance [14] or migration performance [10, 11, 19, 23, 25, 26] is sacrificed.

One of the main contributions of our work is to demonstrate an effective method of dealing with pointers (by ensuring all pointed-to objects remain at fixed locations).

Traditionally, binary translation has been used to convert legacy binaries from one ISA to another. Chen, et al. [6] describe a translation technique for translating ARM binaries for execution on a MIPS-like architecture. This work deals with similar challenges of ISA diversity. However, their work describes static translation while our work proposes dynamic translation, requiring different approaches in many cases.

Some examples of dynamic translators used for emulation include Digital's FX!32 [20] (which translates x86 applications to Alpha) and HP's Aries [30] (which translates PA-RISC applications to IA-64). These translators use a two-phase translation, where the first phase does emulation and collects runtime profile information, and the second performs optimization. We cannot afford to have a two-phase translation, as binary translation in our case typically runs for far fewer instructions, rather than the entire program—the extra time for profiling and a two-phase translation process cannot be amortized. QEMU [2] is the closest dynamic translator to the one described in our work. However, it is optimized for system emulation and our binary translator is optimized for the migration use case.

3. Overview of Migration

When migration is requested (by some entity), the operating system must perform four actions to facilitate migration. It must reschedule the process on another core, change page table mappings to facilitate access to the code for the migrated-to core, perform binary translation until a program transformation point, and transform program state for execution on the new architecture. The first two tasks—process scheduling and page table manipulation—are common operating system responsibilities and require no further discussion here. The final two tasks—binary translation and state transformation—are unique to heterogeneous-ISA migration. We describe these in Sections 6 and 5, respectively.

In this paper, we study in detail a specific instance of the general problem of heterogeneous core migration. In the following paragraphs we describe the language and ISAs/cores we compile for.

We assume that the process to be migrated is written in C, free of inline assembly code. We also assume that externally-linked libraries are compiled for migration (following a similar process to that described in this paper). For libraries that are tuned to specific architectures, this will require some code changes. The C library, for example, because it contains a significant amount of architecture-specific code, will require significant refactoring to be migration-safe. For the testing of our migration technique on programs which are linked to C library code (because we have not yet accomplished the transformation of the libraries), we restrict migration to occur only within non-library code. Finally, we assume some similarities in the ISAs: the same endianness and fundamental data size.

For this study, we model a small, low-power ARM [1] core and a large, high-performance MIPS [18] core. ARM and MIPS are both 32-bit, (typically configured) little-endian, RISC ISAs. However, they represent a significant element of diversity in terms of their memory layout and register access patterns. Diversity in these areas pose more of a problem to migration than diversity of instruction type. The primary contribution of our work is to perform efficient memory transformation during migration, despite this element of diversity.

ARM is most commonly used in highly power-constrained devices, and specific microarchitecture implementations of the ARM core typically reflect this emphasis. MIPS cores, while also commonly used in power-constrained devices, have also been used in more performance-focused devices (like the Origin series of SGI supercomputers). Fundamental differences between these ISAs are discussed in Section 6.2.

We experiment with only two ISAs, but our migration technique should extend in a very straightforward manner to more ISAs on a single CMP. Because we do not create a direct mapping of program state between binaries of each ISA, but rather to a shared compiler front-end intermediate representation, the amount of compiler meta-data used in migration is linear with the number of ISAs.

Fast migration calls for minimal state transformation. This hinges on memory image consistency—the memory image at a point *P* in the execution of a program on ISA A should be nearly identical to the memory image at *P* on ISA B so that very little state must be transformed to a machine-dependent form during migration. This is the heart of our migration strategy. The next section describes how memory image consistency is achieved, and the sections following that describe the mechanics of migration, including both the state transformer and the binary translator.

4. Memory Image Consistency

To facilitate fast execution migration, each binary representation of a program (compiled for different ISAs) should expect to find each item of program data at the same virtual address. This makes it possible to perform the migration without having to rearrange data items in memory, greatly reducing the latency of the migration process. In prior systems targeting inter-machine heterogeneous migration, state copy dominates migration overhead and the cost of reordering and transforming memory is inconsequential. Migration on a CMP does not involve memory state copy, so keeping transformation overhead (now the dominant cost) low is critical to good performance.

To achieve memory image consistency, within each section the number of objects, their sizes, their relative order in memory, and their alignment and padding rules must be identical in order for their virtual addresses to be consistent across ISAs. This not only applies to data sections, but also to sections containing code—function definitions must begin at the same virtual address so that function pointers will be correct after a migration. The dynamic portions of memory—the heap and the stack—also need to be consistent.

Although this would best be done by a single compiler with two backends, for this initial study we use two GCC-based compilers and merge the results. Once the compilers agree on memory image layout, we can create a single binary composed of two coordinated text sections and a single version of each compiled data section (since the static data sections created by the two compilers are identical).

4.1 Global Data Consistency

ISAs may utilize entirely different sections for the same data. This is the case for the *small* data sections in MIPS: the *.sbss*, *.sdata*, and *.scommon* sections. Data objects below a certain size are placed in the small data sections; this allows for faster access to these data objects since it takes fewer instructions to reach these items from a base pointer (like the global pointer). This is a consequence of the limited amount of space (16 bits) in a MIPS instruction to specify the offset from the base pointer. ARM overcomes this problem, primarily, by supporting PC-relative addressing. To avoid copying data in or out of small data sections at migration time, we add support for small data sections to the GCC ARM back-end. However, we do not change the compiler to generate ARM code that can take advantage of the small data section by generating code to access data in these sections with fewer instructions—so the performance of ARM code is not improved, but is not degraded either.

4.2 Code Section Consistency

Another program section that must be modified to reduce migration cost is the code (*.text*) section because fixing function pointers during migration is expensive. To eliminate the cost of finding and fixing all function pointers, function bodies should be placed at identical virtual addresses across each ISA. This implies that the order of function definitions in memory be identical. The compiler, therefore, emits function definitions in the order they are encountered in the source files. The size of each function must also be identical; so the assembler adds NOP instructions, when necessary, to pad functions to the appropriate size. While this increases code size a little, we measure no performance loss.

Note that while each function body begins at the same virtual address across binaries, the location of each function call *site* is not identical. Since the address of the call site can vary, the return address will vary—the cost of translating return addresses is incurred at migration time because the constraint of placing call sites at consistent addresses would be too limiting for the compiler and would impact performance.

4.3 Heap Consistency

Code that accesses the heap must be consistent—we call this *heap consistency*—but for different reasons. Heap consistency is not necessary because of pointers—pointers to the heap will work correctly after migration because the addresses of heap objects in the shared space are created dynamically, not hard-coded into the binary. Instead, heap consistency is necessary to ensure that after migration the program has an accurate record of what heap memory is allocated and what is free. This requires that the same implementation of *malloc* be used for all ISAs. Then, at migration time, because all *malloc*'s internal data structures are preserved, a consistent view of the heap will be maintained. The same principle applies to any memory management library a program uses.

In the Linux system that we model, *malloc* acquires memory on behalf of the caller in two ways: through the *brk* system call, which grows the heap, and through the *mmap* system call. The *mmap* system call does not return heap memory, but pages of virtual memory that the operating system has allocated to the process. Since a single operating system instance governs all the cores, a common page table is used, and page allocations will not change, despite the migration.

4.4 Stack Consistency

Objects on the stack may need to be adjusted or reordered for two reasons. First, many instructions have hard-coded stack offsets. Either these instructions must be changed during migration, the objects must be moved during migration, or the objects must be consistently placed by the code (compiled for each ISA) in the first place—we implement a combination of the latter two. Second, some stack objects may have pointers to them; these pointers would need to be fixed during migration if the objects are not placed at identical addresses.

The stack is especially difficult to make consistent without sacrificing performance because stack interaction is carefully optimized for each ISA. For example, in an ISA with a large number of registers, many function arguments may be passed through registers to avoid loads and stores to stack memory. But for an ISA with a small number of registers, most function arguments must be passed on the stack. Our goal is to find the right balance between good runtime performance and low migration overhead. We must change stack memory as little as possible at migration time without eliminating performance-critical ISA-specific stack optimizations. This section describes what we change (and what we do not change) in the stack organization to strike this balance.

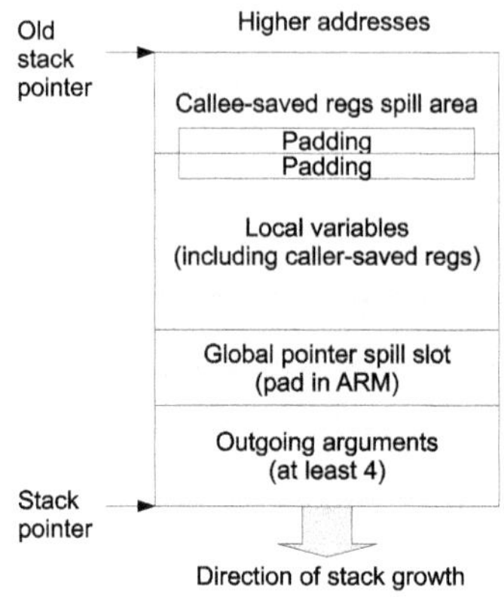

Figure 1. The organization of a non-leaf stack frame in a migration-capable program.

To avoid major changes to the stack during migration, the following properties of the stack must be made identical across ISAs: (1) direction of growth, (2) size, (3) ordering, and (4) alignment. First, the stack's direction of growth should be the same: in both ARM and MIPS, the stack grows downward. Also, for every function in a given program, we make the stack frame size the same for each ISA (by adding padding), making the overall stack size consistent. It is also necessary to have a consistent ordering of regions within each frame. The cross-architectural layout of a non-leaf stack frame is shown in Figure 1. In order to achieve identical frame size, it is also necessary to maintain consistent alignment and padding rules between regions. In our implementation, each region is 8-byte aligned.

In addition to the changes to the overall structure of the stack, we must make changes to each major frame sub-component to avoid costly stack transformations during migration. The major frame sub-components are: (1) the function arguments region, (2) the callee-saved register spill area, and (3) slots for local variables.

Function Arguments. After migration, the program must be able to locate arguments to open functions—we desire to do this with minimal transformation during migration. We recognize that forcing arguments on the stack that would otherwise have been passed through registers can hurt performance, so we are careful to avoid such a change. Both ARM and MIPS pass the first four arguments through registers, but MIPS also allocates stack space for these arguments in case the callee needs to spill them. We force ARM to do the same—space is allocated for the first four arguments, though the arguments are always passed through registers. This increases memory usage by about 16 bytes per frame; however we observe no noticeable effect on performance.

Callee-saved Register Spills. For a given function, the number of callee-saved registers that need to be overwritten depends heavily on the number of registers the ISA supports (affecting register pressure), constraints placed on ISA-specific special-purpose registers, and low-level code transformations. Because all of these factors are architecture-specific, the size of the callee-saved register spill area differs greatly across ISAs. We therefore modify the compiler to add padding, as necessary, to the callee-saved register spill area of each stack frame. This change has no noticeable effect on performance.

Local Variables. The last frame sub-component that requires modification is the area reserved for local variables. Our changes ensure consistent ordering and identical size (requiring padding). For MIPS, GCC allocates variables in this region from low address to high; for ARM from high address to low. Large aggregate objects (like structs and arrays) and objects whose addresses are taken are allocated to the stack first. The different allocation directions cause these objects to be allocated at different addresses on the stack. For pointers to these objects to work after migration, we require all of these objects to be allocated to the same addresses across ISAs. To enforce this requirement we change the allocation direction; when GCC compiles ARM code it now allocates stack objects from low address to high. Like the other regions of a stack frame described above, this region may require padding because the number and choice of local variables to allocate depends on the number of registers in the ISA, resulting in different frame size.

5. Migration Process

When all of the compiler/assembler/linker changes described in the previous section are applied, all program sections, except for some portions of the stack, are migratable without any transformation. To facilitate the transformation of a process' memory image (specifically, the stack portion) we introduce a small program called the Stack Transformer (ST). The ST has three jobs: (1) It creates the register state for the migrated-to core. (2) It fixes all the return addresses on the stack. (3) It moves the values of local variables in open function activations to the right stack offsets. The ST must ensure that the value of every stack-based variable is at the address where code for the migrated-to core expects it.

The Stack Transformer (ST) needs detailed information about the compilation of the program from source code in order to prepare the stack for execution on the migrated-to core. We modify GCC to record the necessary information during compilation. This information includes the frame layout for each function, details about function call sites, the locations of local variables, and the sets of spilled caller-saved and callee-saved registers. This compilation meta-data can easily be placed in a new ELF section and bundled with the binary (in the same way debugging information is) to make the executable self-contained.

5.1 Optimizations that Interfere with Variable Location

A few late optimization passes in GCC expose new live registers across call sites. They do so in such a way that these new live registers do not always correspond to a high-level variable name; moreover, the transformations are not always applied uniformly across all architectures, resulting in architecture-specific state that cannot be transformed at migration time. The incompatibility of these passes with migration is not inherent to the optimization algorithms, but an artifact of their implementation in GCC. To make these optimizations compatible with migration, one of two things may be done. First, the optimizations can be converted from RTL passes to tree passes because the tree intermediate representation is architecture-independent. In this way, optimization can be applied consistently during compilation for both architectures, and intermediate state that is exposed can be assigned labels that are carried in the intermediate representation until register assignment. Second, the optimization passes can be modified to avoid applying the optimization across call sites—we do this for the common subexpression elimination pass. How this is to be done depends on the operation of the optimization. If the optimization moves code, then code motion across call sites should be avoided. If the optimization deletes instructions, it should avoid deleting an instruction that exposes a new live register at any call site.

Both solutions—converting RTL passes to tree passes and introducing optimization barriers at call sites—may result in less than ideal performance over the current implementations. But given the minimal performance degradations we observe with these optimizations completely disabled, we expect the performance tradeoff to be minimal and acceptable. Either solution would require a significant refactoring of the code; so for this study, we have chosen to disable the problematic RTL optimization passes, including loop invariant motion, global common subexpression elimination, forward propagation, post-reload instruction scheduling, temporary expression elimination, and tail call elimination. Disabling most of these passes results in negligible performance loss. For the benchmarks we use in this study, we observe some performance degradation when the following passes are disabled: global common subexpression elimination (less than 1%), forward propagation (less than 1%), post-reload instruction scheduling (less than 0.5%), and temporary expression elimination (less than 1%). Turning off all these passes results in a performance loss of 3.1% in ARM code and 1.6% in MIPS code.

A compiler designed from the ground up to emit multiple-ISA code would not have these problems, and these passes would not have to be deactivated. In that case, we believe the performance cost of restricting a few optimizations across call sites would be close to zero.

5.2 Operation of the Stack Transformer

The job of the Stack Transformer is to transform the architecture-specific program state (mainly stack data, but also register state) from ISA A to ISA B, so that the program running on ISA B will find all of its data after migration where it expects it. At migration time multiple functions may be open at once (represented by a sequence of frames on the stack). The value of each local variable in each open function may be in one of three locations: a register, a fixed stack slot allocated on function entry, or a register spill location on the stack (either in the owning function's frame or in the frame of a descendant function). The code compiled for the destination core will likely expect the value of each variable at a different location (due to differences in the type and number of registers). For example, register pressure may have forced the compiler to allocate variable 'x' to stack offset 20 in code for ISA A, but code for ISA B (which has more registers) put 'x' in register 18. The ST must move the values of all live variables in all open functions to the locations expected by the code for the destination core. It walks the stack, one frame at a time, locating and repositioning live local variables.

From a high level, the ST performs two quick passes over the call stack. Two passes are necessary because we do not know which variable's value should be placed in a callee-saved spill location until we discover the ancestor function that keeps one of its local variables in the callee-saved register. The first pass goes from innermost frame (the frame in which execution was stopped) to outermost frame and finds values for caller-saved spill locations and simple stack-bound variables. The second pass works in the reverse direction—from outermost frame back to innermost frame—finding values for callee-saved spill locations and determining final register state. We describe each of these passes in turn.

First Pass. The first pass examines and transforms each stack frame from the most recently opened frame to the first frame created. Before it can start locating live local variables, the ST must discover which function execution stopped in, and which call site it stopped at (since different variables may be live at different call sites). Therefore, when the ST begins, it is given the value of the PC on the source core. Using the PC, the ST looks up information about the call site (recorded during compilation). The ST then looks up information on the function containing the call site (also recorded during compilation). Finally, the ST looks up records for the same call site (using the call site UID) and function for the other ISA (the ISA of the destination core). With these four records—call site information and function information for each ISA—the ST goes to work transforming the stack frame.

First, it processes the list of registers that are live across the call site. It looks for the values of these registers (by variable name) in three places: (1) live registers on the source core, (2) caller-saved spill locations, and (3) fixed stack slots. When checking fixed stack slots, associated scope information for each variable may be used; the scope of the call site must be contained within the scope that the variable is defined in. Once the ST has located the value that the register should have at the current call site, it copies the value to a list of live register values for the current function. It will keep such a list of live register values for every frame encountered, to be used later in the reverse call stack traversal. In some special cases, the value for the live register will be a constant (which would have been recorded during compilation) or the address of a global variable (which can be looked up in the program's symbol table).

Next, the ST finds the values of variables in the caller-saved spill slots and variables at fixed locations on the stack. The ST checks the same three sources that it used to find values for the live registers on the destination core. Only small variables whose addresses are never taken are moved. Large variables on the stack (like arrays and structs) and variables whose addresses are taken are given identical stack locations by the compiler, so no copying of these values is needed, and pointers to these variables will remain valid after migration.

When the ST is done processing a frame it will determine the live register state on the source core as it existed immediately before the current function was entered. It will carry over this register state when it transforms the next frame. It updates its snapshot of the register state on the source core by reading from the callee-saved register spill locations in the current frame.

Besides moving local variables to their expected locations, the ST is also tasked with fixing all the return addresses saved on the stack. Each stack frame stores the return address of the call site of its caller. Because only function heads, not call sites within functions, are placed at identical addresses by the compiler, return addresses need to be fixed so that return instructions that are eventually executed on the destination core will work properly. When the ST visits each frame to move local variables, it also fixes return addresses. Since the compiler records the size of each frame and the offset where the return address is saved, the ST can find the saved return address. The ST looks up compiler-recorded data on the parent function and repeats the transformation procedure for the next frame up the call stack.

Second Pass. After the ST has passed over all the stack frames from innermost to outermost, it has enough information about the live register state at each call site to determine the values of the important callee-saved spill locations. The ST starts with live registers in the outermost frame (which it recorded in the previous pass) and moves to the next (inner) frame. For each callee-saved register, it copies the value from its snapshot of the current register state to the appropriate location on the stack. Then it updates the current register state with the live register values at the next call site (which it recorded in the previous pass). The ST moves to the next frame and repeats the process until all the important callee-saved spill slots are full. The register state at the end of this process is the register state that should be instated on the destination core when the ST is done and the core is ready for native execution of the program.

There are two important things to note about this process. First, it handles the case where a live register at a particular call site is not saved immediately by the callee (because the callee doesn't recycle that register), but is instead saved in some distant frame or is never saved—with the value remaining in the register at the time of migration. This would not be possible with only one pass from innermost to outermost frame. Second, if the callee spills a register that is not live at the call site, the ST may not have a value to place in that spill slot; but this does not cause any problems after migration because when the called function is returned and the register is filled, it is not live, so it will not be read before being overwritten.

6. Binary Translation

Binary translation is performed on a migrated process until it reaches an equivalence point, at which point the stack transformer described in the previous section transforms program state for native execution. Our binary translator uses the following scheme of classic just-in-time (JIT) [7] dynamic translation:

- Starting from the instruction at the point of migration, each instruction is translated to the ISA of the migrated-to core and placed in a code cache until we encounter a function call site or an indirect/conditional jump instruction (whose target address is not known until execution).
- Next, a stub (a short group of additional instructions) is added to the end of this translated block of instructions. The stub contains a jump to the stack transformer if we've reached a function call site. Otherwise, the stub saves the target address at a known location and jumps to a translator core function called the *translation engine*.
- Control is then transferred to the translated code in the code cache. If the code eventually relinquishes control back to the translation engine, we repeat the above steps from the instruction at the target address until we finally reach a function call site.

6.1 Translation Block Chaining

The translation engine, before translating the next block of instructions, checks if the block is already available in the code cache. If it is available, it links the end of the previous block to the beginning of the next block, with a direct branch instruction. This process is known as translation block (TB) chaining and has been extensively applied in emulators and virtual machines [22].

We extend this idea by allowing translation block chaining from any instruction in the middle of a TB to any instruction in another TB. This allows for a TB to be chained to more than one TB at different instructions (the most common case is a conditional branch). For example, TB X can be chained with TB Y at $X.i$, with Z at $X.j$ and with itself at $X.k$, where $X.i,j,k$ represent three different instructions in X. The converse is also true: TBs X and Y can both chain to Z at $Z.i$ and $Z.j$ respectively. In this case, however, $Z.i$ and $Z.j$ can be the same. Merge point is a classic example for such a scenario, wherein the "if" part can be in TB X, "else" part in TB Y, and they both chain to TB Z at their merge instruction $Z.i$.

We call this *Multiple-Entry Multiple-Exit (MEME) translation block chaining*. The following issues need to be addressed by such a design:

Condition Codes. In a MEME TB, any instruction can have multiple entry points, including those that check condition codes. To improve performance, our binary translator performs lazy condition code evaluation, which defers evaluation of a condition code until it is checked. Any instruction that checks a condition code (CC) evaluates it first, if it has not already been evaluated by an instruction prior to that in the same TB. With MEME chaining, we can never be sure whether a CC has been evaluated or not, due to multiple entry points. Also, we do not know which instruction modified the CC in the first place, to perform lazy evaluation accordingly. To overcome these issues, we update a dirty CC map register at every exit point. The dirty map can be used by instructions to check if a CC has been already evaluated. In addition to this, we also store the opcode of the last CC modifier instruction in a register, so that at the time of lazy evaluation, we would know which instruction modified the CC.

Program Counter Updates. ARM allows instructions to use the program counter as a general-purpose register. For performance reasons, the (virtual) program counter is not updated after executing every block of target instructions that emulates a source instruction. It is instead updated whenever necessary. We further optimize this by adding an offset from the last-calculated PC rather than moving the entire 32 bit address (32 bit move takes at least two MIPS instructions). With MEME chaining, the last-calculated PC can be different for different entry points. To overcome this, we maintain a map of the last-calculated PC at every instruction in a TB. Using this map, the last-calculated PC is updated at the end of every exit point.

Instruction Scheduling. Instructions within a translation block might be reordered. We do not do instruction scheduling optimizations, but we do fill branch delay slots. Branch delay slots are filled with an independent instruction prior to the branch in the same TB. This is not always correct if the branch has multiple entry points. We handle branch delay slots in ARM to MIPS translation as follows:

- All register indirect branches trap into the translation engine.
- All direct branches are evaluated by the translator, which translates instructions at the target address and inserts them inline. If they are already translated, we do MEME chaining with the lazy PC update instruction in the branch delay slot, which has to be executed regardless of the entry point.
- All conditional branches are only dependent on condition codes which are taken care of by lazy CC evaluation. So the instruction just before the branch is not dependent on the branch and hence always goes into the delay slot. When MEME chaining happens at a conditional branch, we move back any instruction in the delay slot and insert a NOP into the delay slot instead. Performance reduction due to this is negligible compared to the significant gain in performance due to TB chaining.

Delay slots are not a problem in MIPS to ARM translation because ARM does not have delay slots.

As a further optimization, we have the ability to preserve the code cache across migrations, so that if the process is migrated to the same core type again, there is a good chance that the code we need is already present in the cache and can be directly used. However, we do not employ this optimization in our presented results.

6.2 ISA-Specific Challenges

Despite high-level similarities, ARM and MIPS represent significant diversity. ARM has many features that MIPS lacks: condition codes and an abundance of predicated instructions, load multiple and store multiple instructions, a program counter that is accessible as a general-purpose register, and finally PC-relative load instructions to access data embedded in the text section. MIPS, on the other hand, has double the number of integer registers that are accessible to programmers and allows for 16-bit immediates as opposed to the 8-bit immediate restriction in ARM. Finally, each ISA has a different *application binary interface* (ABI); they use different system call numbers and follow different conventions to make system calls. We discuss several of these challenges in this section.

Register Allocation. *Mapping from ARM to MIPS:* ARM has 16 general-purpose registers visible to the programmer, while MIPS has 31 general-purpose registers (excluding R0). Hence, all 16 registers in ARM are easily mapped to registers in MIPS. In addition, we reserve four MIPS registers for the ARM condition codes (Zero, Negative, Carry, and Overflow) and an extra register for inverse carry. Of the remaining 10 registers, four are used for lazy condition code evaluation as described below, three are used as temporary registers, and the remaining three are reserved for future use.

Mapping from MIPS to ARM: All 31 MIPS general-purpose registers cannot be mapped onto registers in ARM. Hence, we map frequently used MIPS registers (R1–R7, global pointer, stack pointer, frame pointer and link register, collectively called the "mapped" registers) to registers in ARM. One register points to an in-memory register context block where the "unmapped" MIPS registers are placed. In addition to this, we reserve three registers as cache registers that contain the three most frequently used unmapped registers for faster access.

Condition Codes and Predicated Instructions. Most translators use a global data flow analysis technique to perform a lazy evaluation of condition codes. However, since we perform binary translation for a relatively small number of instructions until we reach an equivalence point, a data flow analysis would increase migration overhead significantly. Hence, we use a lazy condition code evaluation scheme similar to the one used in QEMU [2]: for every instruction that updates a condition code, we store the opcode, operands, and result in temporary registers reserved for the lazy evaluation, and compute the condition codes using this information whenever required. In addition to this, a dirty map register is used to support MEME TB chaining as described above.

Once the condition codes necessary for a predicated instruction are evaluated, a branch instruction is used to test the condition, which skips the operation performed by the instruction if the condition is false. The conditional move instruction in MIPS is used to translate conditional move instructions in ARM, but we use a conditional branch around arithmetic instructions for more complex predicated instructions.

Immediate Instructions. MIPS restricts the size of immediates to 16 bits while ARM limits them to 8 bits. This necessitates two ARM instructions to construct a MIPS immediate, store it in a register, and then perform the actual operation. The problem worsens with 32 bit immediate updates like link register or program counter updates, where four ARM instructions are needed to perform the move. To overcome this, we extend the register context block to also include a "cache of immediates", so that one load instruction will suffice for the entire operation, as opposed to the four mutually dependent shift-OR instructions.

System Calls. In this work, we assume a single operating system instance running on both the cores. This guarantees that a system call works in the same way on both the cores. However, the system call numbers and calling conventions are dictated by the ISA's ABI, which requires a remapping step when in binary translation mode.

One approach would be to provide system call emulation during translation. As an alternative, it is a minor change to our system to also make system calls equivalence points, like function calls. This eliminates the need for system call emulation, but also increases the frequency of equivalence points, which is also a useful feature. To support migration while executing a system call, we would need to apply our techniques and methodology to the operating system itself.

7. Experimental Methodology

To test migration and measure the runtime performance effects of compilation for migration, we use the SPEC2000 Integer benchmarks written in C (i.e., all but the C++ benchmark, *eon*). From this set of benchmarks we exclude the *gcc* benchmark because it uses the non-standard *alloca* C library function to dynamically allocate memory on the stack instead of on the heap—at this time our migration technique does not support variable-size stack frames. All benchmarks are compiled with GCC at optimization level -O2. In all simulations the reference inputs are used. We use the M5 processor simulator [3] (configured to execute ARM binaries and MIPS binaries). The architectural model of the ARM core is based on the low-power Cortex-A8 core, while the MIPS core is modeled with

	ARM core		
Frequency	833 MHz	I cache	32 KB, 4 way
Fetch/commit width	2	D cache	32 KB, 4 way
Branch predictor	local	L2 cache	2 MB, 8 way
	MIPS core		
Frequency	2 GHz	I cache	64 KB, 4 way
Fetch/commit width	4	D cache	64 KB, 4 way
Branch predictor	tournament	L2 cache	4 MB, 8 way

Table 1. Architecture detail for ARM and MIPS cores

performance as the primary design objective. The details of each core are given in Table 1.

To evaluate the steady-state behavior of each benchmark on each core type, we simulate a portion of execution for each benchmark. To ensure that we measure the performance of the modeled cores on the same unit of work even after benchmark recompilation, we insert two marks in the source code of each benchmark—one to indicate where detailed simulation should start and one to indicate where it should stop. The first mark is made at the point in the code after approximately one billion instructions have passed (to skip over initialization code) and the second mark is made after approximately 500 million more instructions have passed. So the simulation interval is approximately 500 million dynamic instructions, the exact number of dynamic instructions depending on the ISA and compilation options.

To evaluate the average cost of migration, we cross-compile both the Binary Translator and the Stack Transformer for ARM and MIPS and run them in the M5 simulator on sample migration points taken from the benchmarks. For these experiments, we venture further into the executable than in the steady-state experiments, to gather more samples of potential migrations points. We collect 10 samples for each benchmark in each direction of migration. The samples are collected at intervals of 100 million dynamic instructions starting one billion instructions into execution. We first run the binary translator on each sample, and perform stack transformation as soon as execution reaches the nearest function call site. In a few cases migration at the nearest call site is not possible due to issues like executing in migration-unsafe library code; so in those cases, a nearby sample that is suitable is used.

The Stack Transformer is written in C++. Designed as a proof-of-concept, there is still plenty of room for performance optimization, and the performance results for the ST presented in this paper should be considered conservative estimates of potential performance.

8. Results

The goal of this research is to enable multi-ISA heterogeneous architectures. Such an architecture will be most useful if we can migrate threads often enough, with low enough overhead, to actually exploit that heterogeneity within a single process execution. This section outlines the costs of migration, including the runtime (migration-free) cost, the stack transformer, and the binary translator.

8.1 Runtime Performance of Migratable Code

A key goal of this work is to enable fast migration without compromising runtime performance—that is, performance when no migration is occurring. Throughout the toolchain changes to ensure a nearly identical memory image across architectures, care must be taken that performance is not compromised. Among our benchmarks no performance is lost due to changes to make the memory image consistent, including the addition of padding (which is too little to cause more instruction cache misses).

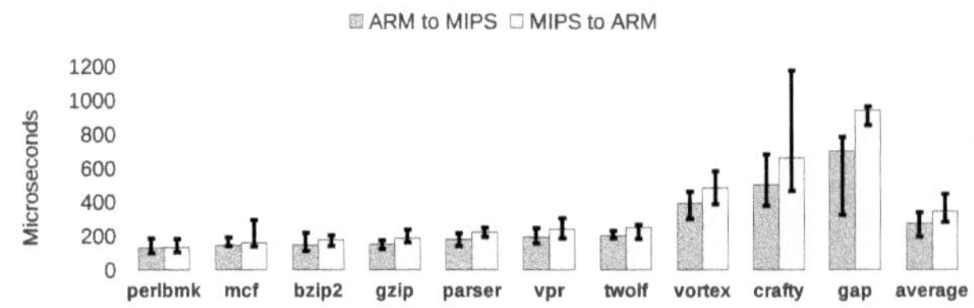

Figure 2. The average costs of state transformation for migration. Lines indicate the minimum and maximum measured transformation times.

There is, however, some performance loss due to optimizations in GCC that are disabled because they inconsistently move code across call sites (that is, call-crossing code motion is applied in only one ISA) and/or they impair the association of variable names with locations (preventing the ST from being able to move some data values). The specific changes that result in performance loss are described in Section 5.1. On average, runtime performance only suffers by 3.1% in ARM code and 1.6% in MIPS code. Again, these are an artifact of a compilation system not intended to create dual executables, and we expect these costs would disappear in a native dual-ISA compiler.

8.2 Migration Cost

The cost of performing a migration is a combination of binary translation overhead, overhead from the involvement of the operating system, and the execution time of the Stack Transformer. Since we do not have an OS for a heterogeneous-ISA CMP, we focus only on the migration cost incurred by binary translation and the Stack Transformer. However, we expect the incremental OS overhead to be relatively small, since its role is to add the thread to the run queue of another core and change some page table entries (to swap out code sections).

For our benchmarks, state transformation (i.e., ST execution time) on our detailed architectural models for ARM and MIPS cores takes (on average) 272 microseconds for migration from ARM to MIPS and 344 microseconds for migration from MIPS to ARM. Figure 2 shows the average transformation costs for each benchmark for migration in each direction. It also shows the fastest and slowest transformation times we measure, as error bars. We do not compare the overhead of the ST (which, due to compiler support, has very little to transform) to a naïve transformer (that must transform most of the memory image, including all pointers) because it would be several orders of magnitude slower.

For migration in either direction, the transformation overheads for the benchmarks *vortex*, *crafty*, and *gap* are the greatest. These three benchmarks also have the highest average stack depths. The average stack depth is the average number of frames on the call stack at any given point in execution. *Gap* has an average stack depth of just under 30. On the other end of the spectrum, *perlbmk* has an average stack depth of three. The average stack depth across all the benchmarks is nine. Stack depth has the greatest influence on migration cost in our migration technique; the deeper the stack, the more state needs to be transformed.

Figure 3 shows the relationship between performance and migration frequency. The performance results presented in this graph account for both performance costs due to compilation for migration (discussed in the previous section) and transformation overhead. In this graph, migration frequency refers to how frequently migrations take place. For example, a frequency of 20 milliseconds means that every 20 milliseconds the program switches cores.

We assume in this graph that we can migrate at any time—that potential migration points (call sites) occur frequently (Section 8.4

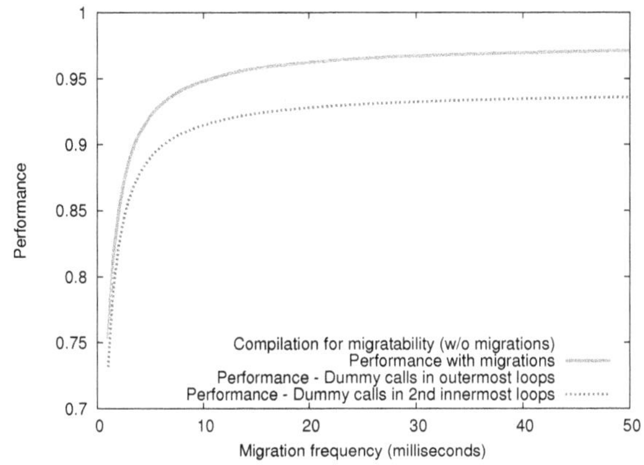

Figure 3. Performance (without binary translation) vs. migration frequency when migrating back and forth between an ARM core and a MIPS core.

quantifies the additional cost of binary translation). The straight line in the graph represents the performance if no migration occurs, and accounts only for the overhead of compilation for migratability. The line below that shows performance when migrations occur. When migrations happen every 10 milliseconds or less the effect on performance is significant. But above 10 milliseconds, performance remains above 95%, as compilation cost dominates migration overhead. The other two lines will be discussed in the next section.

8.3 Frequency of Potential Migration Points

In a system without binary translation, we would have to postpone migrations until the next function call is encountered. Even with binary translation, the latency to reach the next function call site is important because it determines how many instructions must be executed by our binary translator, which incur a performance overhead.

The distribution of function calls is highly irregular. During some phases of execution, function calls are frequent; in other phases, calls are much less frequent. Consequently, the average time between calls and the median time between calls are poor metrics for evaluating call frequency. Instead, we select as our metric the expected time to transformation (ETTT). This is the average time (measured in dynamic instructions) until the next call site is reached from any randomly-selected point in execution.

Figure 4 (first two bars) shows the ETTT for each benchmark. From this graph it is clear that call frequency varies dramatically across benchmarks. Among the ARM binaries, on one end of the spectrum is *vpr* where, on average, one must wait only 84 dynamic instructions until the next possible transformation opportunity. On the other end of the spectrum is *mcf* where, on average, one must wait over 48 million instructions until the next possible transformation opportunity. For seven of the ten benchmarks, the ETTT is under 130,000 dynamic instructions; but for *bzip2*, *crafty*, and *mcf* the ETTT is much higher.

One way to increase the frequency of migration opportunities is to add more function calls. The long gaps between calls result from long-running loops that do not contain any function calls (or have had their function calls inlined). We modify GCC to inject dummy function calls (calls to an empty function that returns immediately) into loops. We experiment with two loop selection policies following two simple heuristics: inject dummy calls in outermost loops and inject dummy calls in second-innermost loops (parents of innermost loops). We never select innermost loops because the performance impact is too severe [11].

The impact on ETTT of these policies is shown in the last four bars in Figure 4. For the three benchmarks with the longest ETTT, inserting function calls in outermost loops dramatically improves call frequency. For example, in the MIPS binaries, the ETTT for *bzip2* drops from over 19 million to about 3.1 million dynamic instructions; for *gap*, the ETTT drops from about 7.4 million to about 4 million dynamic instructions; and *mcf* sees its ETTT reduced from almost 60 million to under 200,000 dynamic instructions. Using the second loop selection policy (second-innermost) results in only marginal gains—most benchmarks only see a slight decrease in ETTT. *Bzip2* is an exception, dropping by a factor of 7.9 on ARM and 4.5 on MIPS.

The additional transformation opportunities that these changes bring comes at the cost of performance. Injecting dummy calls adds instructions that do not do any useful work and may interfere with some compiler optimizations. Performance drops 1.4% on ARM and 4.7% on MIPS when dummy calls are added to outermost loops for all applications. When calls are added to second-innermost loops, performance drops 2.3% on ARM and 5.4% on MIPS. For some programs (ones with infrequent calls) the performance degradation may be justified if the migration policy demands it. Note that if we assume the compiler is smart enough to only apply dummy calls for applications that need them, the cost would be significantly lower.

The two lowest bars in Figure 3 show the performance of code compiled with dummy calls inserted. Migration overhead is the same, but due to the additional compilation costs, performance is lower at every migration frequency. If migration never occurs, performance remains below 95%.

For the results in the next section, we do not assume the presence of dummy procedures calls. This preserves some non-migration performance, but produces very conservative, worst-case numbers for expected binary translation overhead.

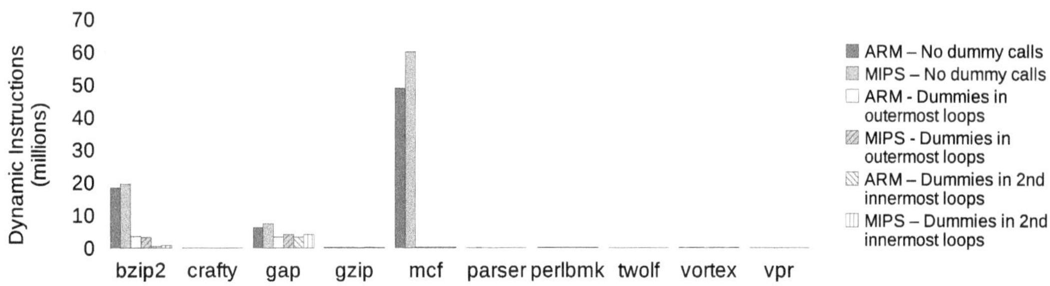

Figure 4. The expected time to the next call, under three situations: no dummy calls have been added, dummy calls to outermost loops have been added, and dummy calls to second-innermost loops have been added.

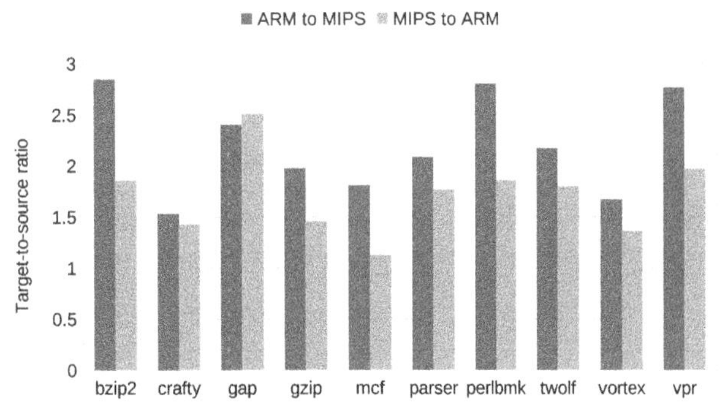

Figure 5. The ratio of the number of target instructions executed during binary translation to the number of source instructions during native execution.

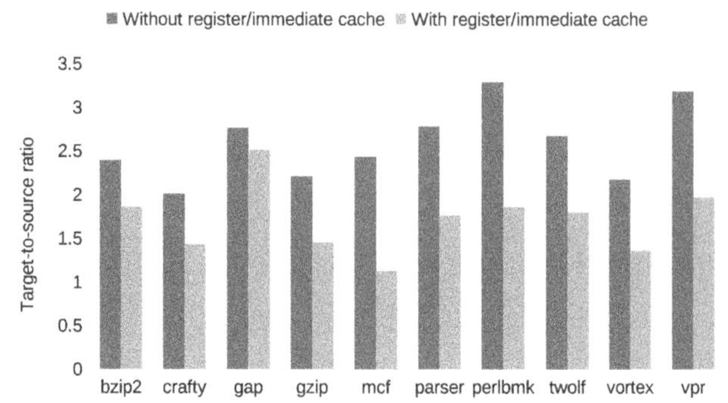

Figure 7. Target-to-Source ratio during Binary Translation from ARM to MIPS—with and without Register and Immediate caches

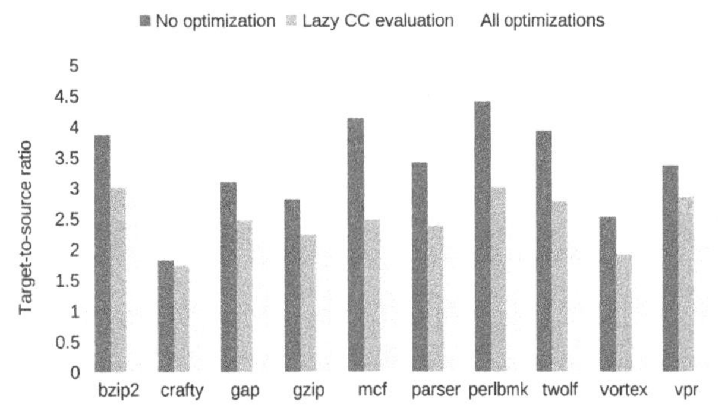

Figure 6. Target-to-Source ratio during Binary Translation from ARM to MIPS—without optimization, with lazy condition code evaluation and with full optimization.

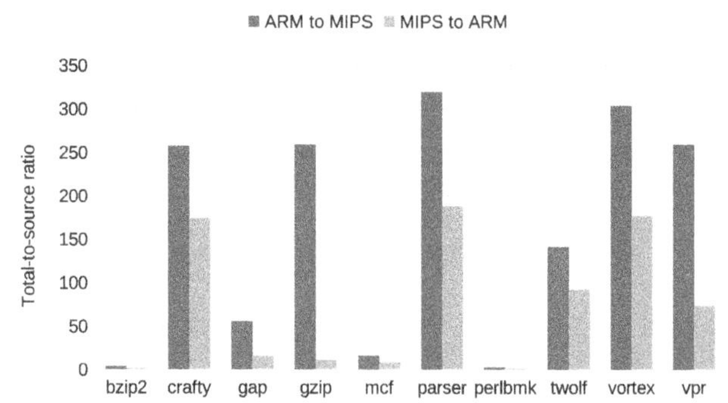

Figure 8. The ratio of the number of dynamic instructions executed (including the ones used for translation) during binary translation to the number of source instructions during native execution.

8.4 Binary Translator Performance

We characterize the performance of our binary translator based on the following three metrics:

- **Target-to-Source Ratio:** The ratio of the number of dynamic target instructions executed on the migrated-to core to the number of dynamic source instructions executed on the native core. Most static binary translators report a target-to-source ratio between one and two. Dynamic binary translators tend to have a higher target-to-source ratio because they have less scope for optimization.
- **Total-to-Source Ratio:** The ratio of the number of dynamic instructions inclusive of both the target instructions and the instructions used for translation (as executed on the migrated-to core) to the number of dynamic source instructions executed on the native core. This is the ratio we address with our translation block chaining algorithms.
- **Overhead due to binary translation:** Time taken for binary translation compared against time taken on native core, in microseconds.

Figure 5 shows the target-to-source ratio for each benchmark in both directions of migration. The target-to-source ratio for MIPS to ARM translation is generally less than that from ARM to MIPS, due to the more complex instructions in ARM. One exception to this is *gap*, which has a higher ratio for MIPS to ARM translation. This is because *gap* is characterized by tight loops with multiply instructions, which takes additional instructions in ARM to perform stores to "hi" and "lo" memory locations. In both directions, *bzip2*, *perlbmk*, and *vpr* have high target-to-source ratios because of a large number of branches in MIPS code and large number of predicated instructions in ARM code.

Figure 6 shows the target-to-source ratio for ARM to MIPS translation without optimization and then with each optimization applied incrementally. The leftmost bar shows the performance of a naïve binary translator without any optimizations. The middle bar shows the performance of the binary translator doing lazy condition code evaluation. This optimization significantly reduces the dynamic instruction count. The rightmost bar shows the binary translator with all optimizations enabled. This includes grouping predicate instructions and certain constant-folding optimizations. Lazy condition code evaluation contributes the most to the overall translation speedup.

Figure 7 shows the performance of the MIPS to ARM translator with and without the use of the register cache and immediate cache. Dynamic instruction count is significantly lower with these optimizations. Our register cache is made up of only three temporary registers. We expect that a larger cache with an adaptive register allocation strategy should give even greater speedups.

Figure 8 shows the total-to-source ratio for each benchmark in both directions of migration. Again the MIPS to ARM translator has a lower translation cost than ARM to MIPS, because it does not have to make complex decisions like lazy condition code evaluation and lazy PC update during translation. However, there is a high irregularity in the total-to-source ratios of different benchmarks—

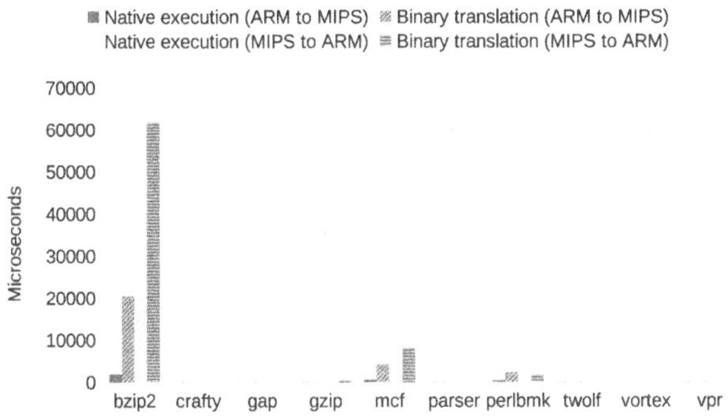

Figure 9. Comparison of Binary Translation time with Native Execution time in microseconds

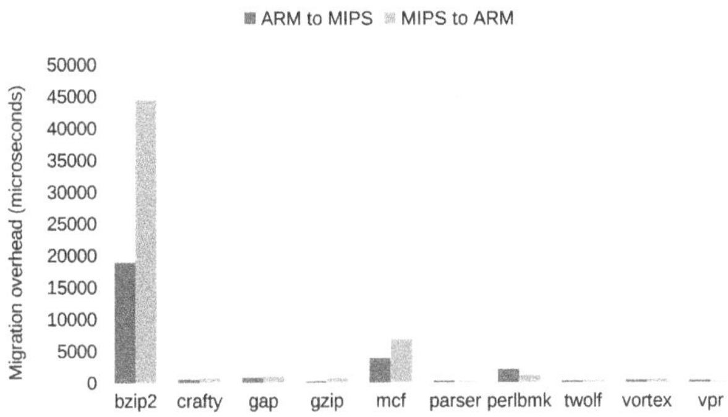

Figure 10. Migration Overhead due to Binary Translation and Stack Transformation in microseconds

some are as high as 300 while some are close to one. This is heavily impacted by the number of instructions to the next equivalence point (call site). If it is 84 instructions (the average for *vpr*), the cost of translation is not amortized. If it is hundreds of millions of instructions, the vast majority of execution is in code cache and the translation cost is insignificant. The latter is due, in large part, to the MEME chaining which allows execution to remain in the code cache once a steady state is reached. Table 2 shows the percentage of dynamic instructions executed in the code cache during binary translation.

We next compare the performance of our binary translator with native execution in Figure 9. Within the migration points we sample, the average execution time for an ARM binary on an ARM core from the time migration is requested until an equivalence point is reached is 284 microseconds, while the average binary translation time of the ARM binary on a MIPS core is 2745 microseconds. For ARM to MIPS, the average execution time on a MIPS core is 1981 microseconds while binary translation time on an ARM core is 7240 microseconds. Thus, binary translation costs us 2461 microseconds while migrating from ARM to MIPS and 5259 microseconds while migrating from MIPS to ARM. All benchmarks except *bzip2*, *perlbmk*, and *mcf* complete binary translation in tens or hundreds of microseconds. These three benchmarks show a high binary translation overhead because they have to translate millions of instructions before reaching an equivalence point.

Finally, we evaluate the performance of our migration strategy by looking at the total migration overhead—time taken by both binary translation and stack transformation. This is shown in Figure 10. The average migration overhead for ARM to MIPS migration is 2734 microseconds, while it is 5602 microseconds for MIPS to ARM migration. It should be noted that this average is dominated by a few outliers. If we ignore *bzip2*, *mcf*, and *perlbmk*, the average overhead drops by about a factor of 10.

Benchmark	ARM to MIPS	MIPS to ARM
bzip2	99.9992	99.993
crafty	0.0	0.0
gap	85.9	94.0
gzip	18.1	99.9
mcf	99.96	99.1
parser	15.7	30.7
perlbmk	99.997	99.99
twolf	58.9	65.4
vortex	0.0	0.0
vpr	36.6	67.1

Table 2. Percentage of instructions used from code cache

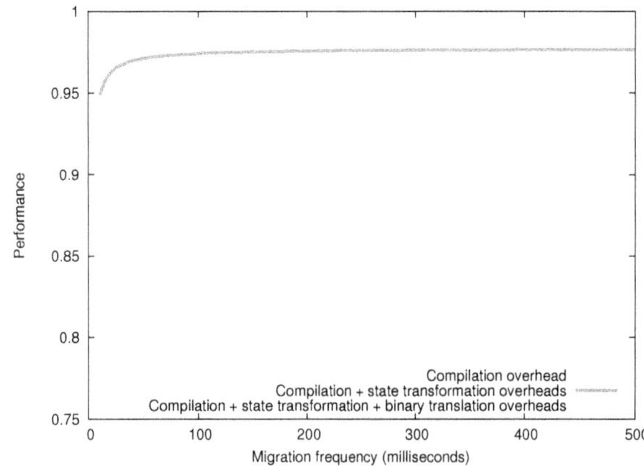

Figure 11. Performance vs. migration frequency when migrating back and forth between an ARM core and a MIPS core. Performance includes overheads due to compilation for migratabiltity, state transformation, and binary translation.

Figure 11 shows performance (relative to native execution without migration) at different migration frequencies (when migrating back and forth between cores at fixed time intervals), assuming average cost values. It breaks down the costs due to compilation for migratability, state transformation, and binary translation. With all costs considered, execution is 95% as fast as native execution when migration occurs, on average, every 87 milliseconds. This would be an extremely high rate of migration for most foreseeable applications. Also recall that much of that 5% lost performance is an artifact of the compiler not being designed from the ground up to emit multi-ISA code.

We believe this level of performance crosses a critical threshold. Unless the code is migrating between cores nearly every timer interrupt, the cost of migration is very small. This means that the difference in migration cost between a single-ISA heterogeneous CMP and a multi-ISA CMP is negligible for most reasonable assumptions about desired migration frequency. Thus, there is no significant performance barrier to fully exploiting heterogeneity in a multicore architecture, including both microarchitecture heterogeneity and ISA heterogeneity. For comparison, recall that prior work typically measured migration time in hundreds of milliseconds [11], if not worse, and that migration could not occur at an arbitrary point in execution.

9. Conclusion

In this paper we present a new technique for execution migration in a heterogeneous-ISA CMP. This environment affords a unique opportunity for fast migration because migration overhead is not dominated by state copying since memory is shared among all cores. Our migration technique takes advantage of this opportunity by compiling programs to maintain memory state in a way that is nearly identical to its representation on every core type. As a result, migration requires only minimal transformation—only portions of the stack and register state need to be transformed. All pointers remain valid after migration without any transformation, eschewing the need for expensive pointer fixing during migration. We demonstrate that with strategic compiler changes, runtime performance does not have to be compromised for migratability—on average, non-migration performance is reduced by 1.6% for MIPS and 3.1% for ARM. The state transformation cost for migration is, on average, 272 microseconds for ARM to MIPS migration and 344 microseconds for MIPS to ARM migration. We support migration at all points of execution in the program with the help of binary translation. We incur an average binary translation cost of 2.75 milliseconds for ARM to MIPS migration and 7.24 milliseconds for MIPS to ARM. Finally, we show that even if we were to migrate every few hundred milliseconds, we experience a total loss in performance of well under 5%.

Acknowledgements

The authors would like to thank the anonymous reviewers for their helpful insights. This research was supported in part by NSF grant CCF-1018356.

References

[1] ARM Limited. *ARM Architecture Reference Manual.*

[2] F. Bellard. Qemu, a fast and portable dynamic translator. In *USENIX Technical Conference*, Apr. 2005.

[3] N. L. Binkert, R. G. Dreslinski, L. R. Hsu, K. T. Lim, A. G. Saidi, and S. K. Reinhardt. The M5 simulator: Modeling networked systems. *International Symposium on Microarchitecture*, Dec. 2006.

[4] G. Bronevetsky, D. Marques, K. Pingali, and P. Stodghill. Automated application-level checkpointing of MPI programs. In *Symposium on Principles and Practice of Parallel Programming*, June 2003.

[5] C-Port Corp. *C-5 Network Processor Architecture Guide.*

[6] J.-Y. Chen, W. Yang, T.-H. Hung, H.-M. Su, and W.-C. Hsu. A static binary translator for efficient migration of ARM-based applications. In *Workshop on Optimizations for DSP and Embedded Systems*, Apr. 2008.

[7] L. P. Deutsch and A. M. Schiffman. Efficient implementation of the smalltalk-80 system. In *Symposium on Principles of Programming Languages*, Jan. 1984.

[8] F. B. Dubach, R. M. Rutherford, and C. M. Shub. Process-originated migration in a heterogeneous environment. In *ACM Annual Computer Science Conference*, Feb. 1989.

[9] S. Dutta, R. Jensen, and A. Rieckmann. Viper: A multiprocessor SoC for advanced set-top box and digital TV systems. *Design & Test of Computers, IEEE*, 18(5), 2001.

[10] R. Fernandes, K. Pingali, and P. Stodghill. Mobile MPI programs in computational grids. In *Symposium on Principles and Practice of Parallel Programming*, Mar. 2006.

[11] A. Ferrari, S. J. Chapin, and A. Grimshaw. Heterogeneous process state capture and recovery through process introspection. *Cluster Computing*, 3(2), 2000.

[12] M. Hill and M. Marty. Amdahl's law in the multicore era. *Computer*, July 2008.

[13] J. A. Kahle, M. N. Day, H. P. Hofstee, C. R. Johns, T. R. Maeurer, and D. Shippy. Introduction to the cell multiprocessor. *IBM Journal of Research and Development*, July 2005.

[14] F. Karablieh, R. Bazzi, and M. Hicks. Compiler-assisted heterogeneous checkpointing. Oct. 2001.

[15] R. Kumar, K. I. Farkas, N. P. Jouppi, P. Ranganathan, and D. M. Tullsen. Single-ISA Heterogeneous Multi-core Architectures: The Potential for Processor Power Reduction. In *International Symposium on Microarchitecture*, Dec. 2003.

[16] R. Kumar, D. M. Tullsen, N. Jouppi, and P. Ranganathan. Heterogeneous chip multiprocessors. *Computer*, 38(11), 2005.

[17] R. Kumar, D. M. Tullsen, P. Ranganathan, N. P. Jouppi, and K. I. Farkas. Single-ISA Heterogeneous Multi-core Architectures for Multithreaded Workload Performance. In *International Symposium on Computer Architecture*, June 2004.

[18] MIPS Technologies, Inc. *MIPS32 Architecture for Programmers Volume II: The MIPS32 Instruction Set.*

[19] B. Ramkumar and V. Strumpen. Portable checkpointing for heterogeneous archtitectures. *International Symposium on Fault-Tolerant Computing*, June 1997.

[20] A. C. Ray and R. Hookway. DIGITAL FX!32 running 32-bit x86 applications on alpha NT. In *USENIX Windows NT Workshop*, Aug. 1997.

[21] C. M. Shub. Native code process-originated migration in a heterogeneous environment. In *ACM Conference on Cooperation*, Feb. 1990.

[22] J. Smith and R. Nair. *Virtual Machines: Versatile Platforms for Systems and Processes.* Morgan Kaufmann Publishers Inc., June 2005.

[23] P. Smith and N. C. Hutchinson. Heterogeneous process migration: the Tui system. *Software — Practice and Experience*, May 1998.

[24] B. Steensgaard and E. Jul. Object and native code thread mobility among heterogeneous computers (includes sources). In *Symposium on Operating Systems Principles*, Dec. 1995.

[25] V. Strumpen. Compiler technology for portable checkpoints. Technical report, Laboratory for Computer Science, Massachusetts Institute of Technology, 1998.

[26] V. Strumpen and B. Ramkumar. Portable checkpointing and recovery in heterogeneous environments. Technical report, University of Iowa, June 1996.

[27] Texas Instruments Inc. *OMAP5912 Multimedia Processor Device Overview and Architecture Reference Guide.*

[28] R. Veldema and M. Philippsen. Near overhead-free heterogeneous thread-migration. In *Cluster Computing*, Sept. 2005.

[29] D. G. von Bank, C. M. Shub, and R. W. Sebesta. A unified model of pointwise equivalence of procedural computations. *ACM Transactions on Programming Languages and Systems*, 16(6), 1994.

[30] C. Zheng and C. Thompson. PA-RISC to IA-64: Transparent execution, no recompilation. *Computer*, Mar. 2000.

Efficient Sequential Consistency via Conflict Ordering

Changhui Lin
University of California Riverside
linc@cs.ucr.edu

Vijay Nagarajan
University of Edinburgh
vijay.nagarajan@ed.ac.uk

Rajiv Gupta
University of California Riverside
gupta@cs.ucr.edu

Bharghava Rajaram
University of Edinburgh
r.bharghava@ed.ac.uk

Abstract

Although the sequential consistency (SC) model is the most intuitive, processor designers often choose to support relaxed memory consistency models for higher performance. This is because SC implementations that match the performance of relaxed memory models require post-retirement speculation and its associated hardware costs. In this paper we propose an efficient approach for enforcing SC without requiring post-retirement speculation. While prior SC implementations guarantee SC by explicitly completing memory operations within a processor in program order, we guarantee SC by completing conflicting memory operations, within and across processors, in an order that is consistent with the program order. More specifically, we identify those conflicting memory operations whose ordering is critical for the maintenance of SC and explicitly order them. This allows us to safely (non-speculatively) complete memory operations past pending writes, thus reducing memory ordering stalls. Our experiments with SPLASH-2 programs show that SC can be achieved efficiently, with performance comparable to RMO (relaxed memory order).

Categories and Subject Descriptors C.1.2 [*Processor Architectures*]: Multiple Data Stream Architectures (Multiprocessors)—Parallel processors

General Terms Design, Performance, Experimentation

Keywords Sequential consistency, Conflict ordering

1. Introduction

While parallel architectures are becoming ubiquitous, extracting performance from them is contingent on programmers writing parallel software. To this end, there has been significant research on developing programming models, memory models, and debugging tools for making programmers' tasks easier. In particular, one reason why programmers find parallel programming hard is because of the intricacies involved in the underlying memory consistency models. The complexity of the memory models is well illustrated in recent work by Sewell *et al.* [28] in which they describe how the recent Intel and AMD memory model specifications do not match with the actual behavior observed in real machines. Among the various memory consistency models, the *sequential consistency* (SC) model in which memory operations appear to take place in the order specified by the program is most intuitive to programmers. Indeed, most works on semantics and software checking that strive to make concurrent programming easier assume SC [28]; several debugging tools for parallel programs, e.g. *RaceFuzzer* [27], also assume SC. Finally, SC would simplify the memory models of languages such as Java and C++ by enabling simpler implementations of Java `volatile` or C++ `atomic`.

(Prior SC implementations). In spite of the advantages of the SC model, processor designers typically choose to support relaxed consistency models; none of the Intel, AMD, ARM, Itanium, SPARC, or PowerPC processor families choose to support SC. This is because SC requires reads and writes to be ordered in program order, which can cause significant performance overhead. Indeed, SC requires the enforcement of all four possible program orderings: $r \rightarrow r$, $r \rightarrow w$, $w \rightarrow w$, $w \rightarrow r$, where r denotes a read operation and w denotes a write operation. A straightforward SC implementation enforces these orderings by delaying the next memory operation until the previous one completes, introducing a significant number of program ordering stalls. Some of these stalls can be reduced in a dynamically scheduled ILP processor, where *in-window speculation* support can be used to execute memory operations out-of-order while completing them in program order [12]. Nonetheless, enforcing the $w \rightarrow r$ (and $w \rightarrow w$) order necessitates that the write-buffer is drained before a subsequent memory operation can be completed. Thus, a high latency write can still cause significant program ordering stalls – which in-window speculation is unable to hide. Recent works have utilized *post-retirement speculation* – speculation beyond instruction window – to eliminate these program ordering stalls [6–8, 11, 13–15, 23, 31]. While this approach is promising, the significant hardware complexity associated with post-retirement speculation could hinder its wide-spread adoption [3].

(Our Approach). SC requires memory operations of all processors to appear to perform in some *global memory order*, such that, memory operations of each processor appear in this global memory order in the order specified by the program [17]. Prior SC implementations ensure this by enforcing program ordering by explicitly completing memory operations in program order. More specifically, if m_1 and m_2 are two memory operations with m_1 pre-

ASPLOS'12, March 3–7, 2012, London, England, UK.

ceding m_2 in the program order, prior SC implementations ensure $m_1 \rightarrow m_2$ by allowing m_2 to complete only after m_1 completes; in effect, m_2 is made to wait until m_1 and all of m_1's predecessors in the global memory order have completed. In other words, if $pred(m_1)$ refers to m_1 and its predecessors in the global memory order, m_2 is allowed to complete only when all memory operations from $pred(m_1)$ have completed.

While enforcing program ordering is a sufficient condition for ensuring SC [26], it is not a necessary condition [19, 25, 29]. In contrast with prior SC implementations, we ensure SC by *explicitly ordering only conflicting memory operations* – where conflicting memory operations are pairs of memory operations that access the same address, with one of them being a write. More specifically, we observe that m_1 *appears* to be ordered before m_2, as long as those memory operations from $pred(m_1)$ which conflict with m_2, complete before m_2. In other words, if $pred_p(m_1)$ refers to memory operations from $pred(m_1)$ which are pending completion, m_2 can safely complete before m_1 as long as m_2 does not conflict with any of the memory operations from $pred_p(m_1)$. It is worth noting that the above condition generally evaluates to true, since in well-written parallel programs conflicting accesses are relatively rare and staggered in time [14, 19].

Our SC implementation, which allows for memory operations to be safely (and non-speculatively) completed past pending writes, is considered in the context of a scalable CMP with local caches kept coherent using an invalidation based cache coherence protocol. When a write-miss w is encountered, we conservatively estimate $pred_p(w)$ to be the set of write misses that are currently being serviced by the coherence controller. This lets us safely complete subsequent memory operations which do not conflict with $pred_p(w)$, even while w is pending.

The main contribution of this paper is an efficient and lightweight approach for SC using conflict ordering. More specifically, our SC implementation is:

- **Efficient.** Our experiments with SPLASH-2 programs show that SC can be achieved efficiently, with performance comparable to RMO (relaxed memory order).
- **Lightweight.** Ours is the first SC implementation that performs almost as well as RMO, while requiring no post-retirement speculation.
- **Scalable.** Our SC implementation scales well, with performance that is comparable to RMO even with 32 cores.

2. Background

Memory consistency models [4] constrain memory behavior with respect to read and write operations from multiple processors, providing formal specifications of how the memory system will appear to the programmer. Each of these models offers a trade-off between programming simplicity and high performance. Sequential consistency (SC) is the simplest model that is easy to understand but can potentially affect the performance of programs. The strict memory ordering imposed by SC can potentially restrict both compiler and hardware optimizations that are possible in uniprocessors [4]. For performance reasons, researchers have proposed relaxed memory consistency models at the cost of programming complexity [4, 5]. Such memory models provide fence instructions to enable programmers to explicitly provide memory ordering. For instance, the SPARC RMO model (relaxed memory order) relaxes all four program orderings – but provides memory fence instructions that the programmer can use for overriding the relaxations and enforce memory orderings on demand. The complexities of specifying relaxed memory models, however, combined with the additional burden it places on the programmers have rendered relaxed memory models inadequate [3]. Next, we discuss different approaches for achieving SC.

2.1 SC via program ordering

In program ordering based SC implementations the hardware directly ensures all four possible program ordering constraints [6, 12–14, 23]; they are based on the seminal work by Scheurich and Dubois [26], in which they state the sufficient conditions for SC for general systems with caches and interconnection networks.

(Naive). A naive way to enforce program ordering between a pair of memory operations is to delay the second until the first fully completes. However, this can result in a significant number of memory ordering stalls; for instance, if the first access is a miss, then the second access has to wait until the miss is serviced.

(In-window speculation). Out-of-order processing capabilities of a modern processor can be leveraged to reduce some of these stalls. This is based on the observation that memory operations can be freely reordered as long as the reordering is not observed by other processors. Instead of waiting for an earlier memory operation to complete, the processor can use hardware prefetching and speculation to execute memory operations out of order, while still completing in order [12, 33]. However, such reordering is within the instruction window – where the instruction window refers to the set of instructions that are in-flight. If the processor receives an external coherence (or replacement) request for a memory operation that has executed out of order, the processor's recovery mechanism is triggered to redo computation starting from that memory operation. Nonetheless, enforcing the $w \rightarrow r$ (and $w \rightarrow w$) order necessitates that the write-buffer is drained before a subsequent memory operation can be completed. Thus, a high latency write can still cause significant program ordering stalls – which in-window speculation is unable to hide. Our experiments with the SPLASH-2 programs show that programs spend more than 20% of their execution time on average waiting for the write buffer to be drained. For our work, we assume in-window speculation support as part of baseline implementations of SC as well as fences in RMO.

(Post-retirement speculation). Since in-window speculation is not sufficiently able to reduce program ordering stalls, researchers have proposed more aggressive speculative memory reordering techniques [6–8, 11, 13–15, 23, 31]. The key idea is to *speculatively retire* instructions neglecting program ordering constraints while maintaining the state of speculatively-retired instructions separately. One way to do this is to maintain the state of speculatively-retired instructions at a fine granularity, which enables precise recovery from misspeculations [13, 14, 23]. This obviates the need for a load to wait until the write buffer is drained and is made to retire speculatively. More recently, researchers have proposed *chunk based* techniques [6–8, 11, 15, 31] which again use aggressive speculation to efficiently enforce SC at the granularity of coarse-grained chunks of instructions instead of individual instructions. While the above approaches show much promise, hardware complexity associated with aggressive speculation, being contrary to the design philosophy of multi-cores consisting of simple energy-efficient cores [1, 2], can hinder wide-spread adoption. Through our work, we seek to show that a lightweight SC implementation is possible without sacrificing performance.

2.2 Other SC approaches

Shasha and Snir, in their seminal work [29], observed that not all pairs of memory operations need to be ordered for SC; only those pairs which conflict with others run the risk of SC violation and consequently need to be ordered. To ensure memory operation pairs are not reordered, memory fences are inserted. They then propose *delay set analysis*, a compiler based algorithm for minimizing the number of fences inserted for ensuring SC. This work led to other compiler based algorithms that implement various fence insertion and optimization algorithms [10, 18]. Recently, we proposed *conditional fence* [19], a novel fence mechanism that dynamically decides if a fence needs to stall; we show that with conditional fences, the number of fences that actually need to stall is reduced significantly. The limitation of compiler-based SC implementations is that they rely on alias analysis for identifying conflicts, and so are overly conservative for programs that employ pointers and dynamic data structures [3, 19].

In developing delay set analysis, Shasha and Snir introduced a precise formalism for SC in terms of the program order being consistent with the execution order. Their SC formalism reflects the notion that SC does not actually require memory operations to be performed in program order; it merely requires the execution to be consistent with program order. Gharachorloo *et al.*later built on Shasha and Snir's formalism to derive aggressive SC specifications [25] which relaxes program ordering constraints. While our idea of conflict ordering and its formalization is strongly influenced by Shasha and Snir's SC formalism, we additionally leverage this idea and propose a lightweight and efficient SC implementation, that performs almost as well as RMO.

Mainstream programming languages like C++ and Java use variants of the data-race-free memory model [4, 5] which guarantee SC as long as the program is free of data races. However, if the programs do have data races then these models provide much weaker semantics. To redress this there have been works that employ dynamic race detection [9] in order to stop execution when semantics become undefined. Since dynamic data race detection can be slow, recent works [20, 21, 30] propose raising an exception upon encountering an SC violation as this can be done more efficiently.

Finally, recent work has shown that it is possible to support high performance compiler that preserves SC [22]. Their SC-preserving compiler, however, cannot prevent the hardware from exposing non-SC behaviour. Thus, our work which proposes an efficient and lightweight hardware SC implementation, is complementary to the above work.

3. SC via conflict ordering

In this section, we first informally describe our approach of enforcing SC using conflict ordering with a motivating example. We then formally prove that our approach correctly enforces SC.

3.1 A motivating example

SC requires that memory operations appear to complete in program order. To ensure this, prior SC implementations force memory operations to *explicitly* complete in program order. However, is program ordering necessary for ensuring SC? Let us consider the example in Fig. 1, which shows memory operations a_1, a_2, b_1 and b_2 from processors A and B. They are two pairs of conflicting accesses. Can a_2 complete before a_1 in an execution without breaking SC? Prior SC implementations forbid this and force a_2 to wait until a_1 completes. In this work, we observe that a_1 *appears* to complete before a_2, as long as a_2 is made to complete after b_1, with which a_2 conflicts. In other words, a_2 can complete before a_1 without breaking SC, as long as we ensure that a_2 waits for b_1 to complete. Indeed, if b_1 and b_2 have completed before a_1 and a_2, the execution order (b_1, b_2, a_2, a_1) is equivalent to the original SC order (b_1, b_2, a_1, a_2) as the values read in the two executions are identical.

We propose *conflict ordering*, a novel approach to SC, in which SC is enforced by explicitly ordering only conflicting memory operations. Conflict ordering allows a memory operation to complete, as long as all conflicting memory operations prior to it in the global memory order have completed. More specifically, let m_1 and m_2 be consecutive memory operations; furthermore let $pred(m_1)$ refer to memory operations that include m_1 and those before m_1 in the global memory order. Conflict ordering allows m_2 to safely complete as long as those memory operations from $pred(m_1)$, which conflict with m_2, have completed.

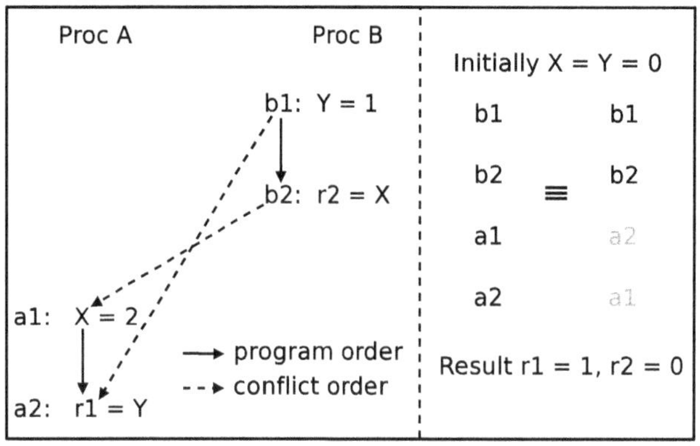

Figure 1. A motivating example: As long as a_2 is made to wait until the conflicting access b_1 completes, a_2 can be safely reordered before a_1, without breaking SC

3.2 Conflict ordering enforces SC

In this section, we prove that conflict ordering enforces SC using the formalism of Shasha and Snir [29]. For the following discussion, we assume an invalidation based cache coherence protocol for processors with private caches. A read operation is said to complete when the returned value is bound and can not be updated by other writes; a write operation is said to complete when the write invalidates all cached copies, and the generated invalidates are acknowledged [12]. Furthermore, we assume that the coherence protocol serializes writes to the same location and also ensures that the value of a write not be returned by a read until the write completes – in other words, we assume that the coherence protocol ensures *write atomicity* [4].

Definition 1. *The program order* **P** *is a local (per-processor) total order which specifies the order in which the memory operations appear in the program. That is,* $m_1 \mathbf{P} m_2$ *iff the memory operation* m_1 *occurs before* m_2 *in the program.*

Definition 2. *The conflict relation* **C** *is a symmetric relation on* **M** *(all memory operations) that relates two memory operations (of which one is a write) which access the same address.*

Definition 3. *An execution* **E** *(or execution order or conflict order) is an orientation of* **C**. *If* $m_1 \mathbf{C} m_2$, *then either* $m_1 \mathbf{E} m_2$ *or* $m_2 \mathbf{E} m_1$ *holds.*

Definition 4. *An execution* **E** *is said to be atomic, iff* **E** *is a proper orientation of* **C**, *that is, iff* **E** *is acyclic.*

Definition 5. *An execution* **E** *is said to be sequentially consistent, iff* **E** *is consistent with the program order* **P**, *that is, iff* $\mathbf{P} \cup \mathbf{E}$ *has no cycles.*

Definition 6. *The global memory order* **G** *is the transitive closure of the program order and the execution order,* $\mathbf{G} = (\mathbf{P} \cup \mathbf{E})^+$.

Remark. In the scenario shown in Fig. 1, b_1 appears before a_1 in the global memory order, since b_1 appears before b_2 in program order, and b_2 is ordered before a_1 in the execution order. That is, $b_1 \mathbf{G} a_1$ since $b_1 \mathbf{P} b_2$ and $b_2 \mathbf{E} a_1$.

Definition 7. *The function* $pred(m)$ *returns a set of memory operations that appear before* m *in the global memory order* **G**, *including* m. *That is,* $pred(m) = \{m\} \cup \{m' : m' \mathbf{G} m\}$.

Definition 8. *An SC implementation constrains the execution by enforcing certain conditions under which a memory operation can be completed. An SC implementation is said to be correct if it is guaranteed to generate an execution that is sequentially consistent.*

Definition 9. *Conflict ordering is our proposed SC implementation in which a memory operation m_2 (whose immediate predecessor in program order is m_1) is allowed to complete iff those memory operations from $pred(m_1)$ which conflict with m_2 have completed. That is, m_2 is allowed to complete iff $\{m \in pred(m_1) : m\mathbf{C}m_2\}$ have already completed.*

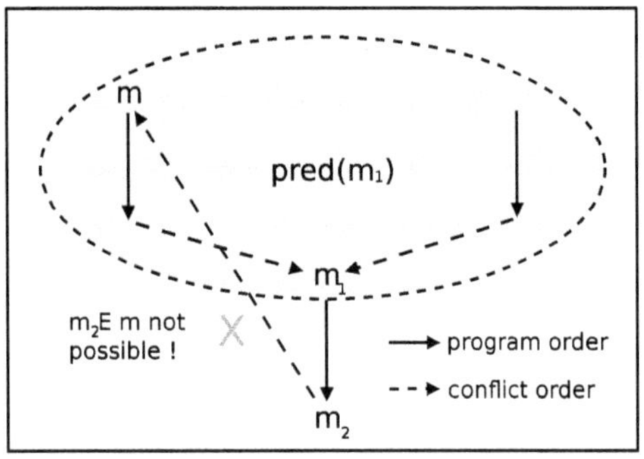

Figure 2. Conflict ordering ensures SC

Lemma 1. *Any execution* **E** *(Definition 3) is atomic.*

Proof. Let w and r with a subscript be a write operation and a read operation. Write-serialization ensures that $w_1\mathbf{E}w_2$ iff w_1 completes before w_2; furthermore, $w_1\mathbf{E}w_2$ and $w_2\mathbf{E}w_3$ result in $w_1\mathbf{E}w_3$. Write-atomicity also ensures that $w_1\mathbf{E}r_2$ iff w_1 completes before r_2. Since reads are atomic, $r_1\mathbf{E}w_2$ iff r_1 completes before w_2. Furthermore, $w_1\mathbf{E}r_2$ and $r_2\mathbf{E}w_3$ result in $w_1\mathbf{E}w_3$. Thus, **E** is acyclic; therefore, from Definition 4, **E** is atomic. □

Theorem 1. *Conflict ordering is correct.*

Proof. We need to prove that any execution **E** generated by conflict ordering is sequentially consistent. That is, to prove that the graph $\mathbf{P} \cup \mathbf{E}$ is acyclic (from Definition 5). Let us attempt a proof by contradiction, and assume that there is a cycle in $\mathbf{P} \cup \mathbf{E}$. Since **E** is acyclic (from Lemma 1), the assumed cycle should contain at least one program order edge. Without loss of generality, let us assume that the program order edge that contains a cycle is $m_1\mathbf{P}m_2$ as shown in Fig. 2. To complete the cycle, there must be a conflict order edge $m_2\mathbf{E}m$, where $m \in pred(m_1)$. Conflict ordering, however, ensures that those memory operations from $pred(m_1)$, which conflict with m_2 would have completed before m_2 (from Definition 9). Since $m \in pred(m_1)$, m would have completed before m_2. Thus, the conflict order edge $m_2\mathbf{E}m$ is not possible, which results in a contradiction. Thus, conflict ordering is correct. □

4. Hardware Design

In this section we describe our hardware design that incorporates conflict ordering to enforce SC efficiently. We first describe our basic design in which all memory operations will have to check for conflicts before they can complete. We then describe how we can determine phases in program execution where memory operations can complete without checking for conflicts.

(System Model). For the following discussion we assume a tiled chip multiprocessor, with each tile consisting of a processor, a local L1 cache and a single bank of the shared L2 cache. We assume that the local L1 caches are kept coherent using a directory based cache coherence protocol, with the directory distributed over the L2 cache. We assume that addresses are distributed across the directory at a page granularity using the first touch policy. We assume a directory protocol in which the requester notifies the directory on transaction completion, so each coherence transaction can have a maximum of four steps. Thus, each coherence transaction remains active in the directory until the time at which it receives the notification of transaction completion. Furthermore, we assume that the cache coherence protocol provides write atomicity. We assume each processor core to be a dynamically scheduled ILP processor with a reorder buffer (ROB) which supports in-window speculation. All instructions, except memory writes, are made to complete in program order, as and when they retire from the ROB. Writes on the other hand, are made to retire into the write-buffer, so that the processor need not wait for them to complete. Finally, it is worth noting that our proposal is also applicable to bus based coherence protocols; indeed, we report experimental results for both bus based and directory based protocols.

4.1 Basic conflict ordering

We describe our conflict ordering implementation which allows memory operations (both reads and writes) to complete past pending writes, while ensuring SC; it is worth noting, however, that our system model does not allow memory operations to complete past pending reads. Recall that conflict ordering allows a memory operation m_2, whose immediate predecessor is m_1, to complete as long as m_2 does not conflict with those memory operations from $pred(m_1)$ which are pending completion – let us call such pending operations as $pred_p(m_1)$. Thus, for m_2 to safely complete, we need to be sure that m_2 does not conflict with any of the memory operations from $pred_p(m_1)$. Alternatively, if $addr_p(m_1)$ refers to the set of addresses accessed by memory operations from $pred_p(m_1)$, we can safely allow m_2 to complete if its address is not contained in $addr_p(m_1)$. The challenge is to determine $addr_p(m_1)$ as quickly as possibly – and in particular without waiting for m_1 to complete. Next, we show how we compute $addr_p(m_1)$ for a write-miss, cache-hit, and a read-miss respectively.

(Write-misses). Our key idea for determining $addr_p(m_1)$ for a write-miss m_1 is to simply get this information from the directory. We show that those memory operations from $pred_p(m_1)$, if any, would be present in the directory (as pending memory operations that are currently being serviced in the directory), provided write-misses such as m_1 are issued to the directory, before subsequent memory operations are allowed to complete. In other words, if *addr-list* refers to the set of addresses of the cache misses being serviced in the directory, $addr_p(m_1)$ would surely be contained in *addr-list*. In addition to this, since our system model does not allow memory operations to complete past pending reads, we are able to show that $addr_p(m_1)$ would surely be contained in *write-list* – where *write-list* refers to the set of memory addresses of the write-misses being serviced in the directory. Consequently, when the write-miss m_1 is issued to the directory, the directory replies back with the *write-list*, containing the addresses of the write-misses which are currently being serviced by the directory (to minimize network traffic we safely approximate the write-list by using a bloom filter). A subsequent memory operation m_2 is allowed to complete, only if m_2 does not conflict with any of the writes from the write-list. If m_2 does conflict, then the local cache block m_2 maps to is invalidated, and the memory operation m_2 and its following instructions are replayed when necessary. During replay, m_2 would turn out to be a cache miss and hence the miss request would be sent to the directory. This would ensure that m_2 would be ordered after its conflicting write that was pending in the directory. *It is worth noting that memory operations that follow a pending write, will now need to wait only until the write is issued to the directory and get a reply back from the directory, as opposed to waiting for the write-miss to complete.* While the former takes as much time as the round trip latency to the directory, the latter can take a significantly longer time – since it may involve the time taken to invalidate all shared copies, and also access memory if it is a miss.

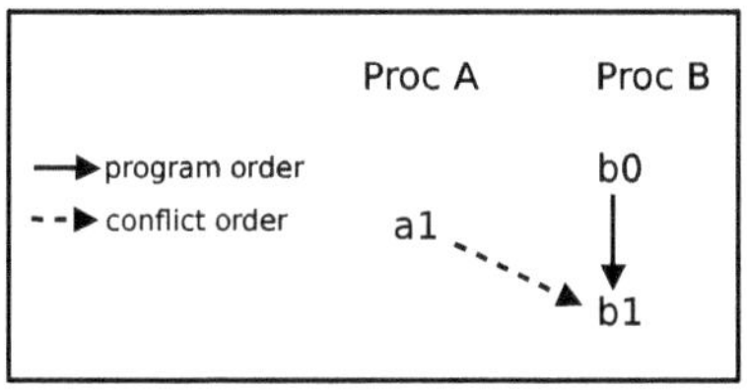

Figure 3. $pred_p(b_1) = \{b_1\} \cup pred_p(b_0) \cup pred_p(a_1)$.

(Cache-hits). Fig. 3 shows how $pred_p(b_1)$ relates to $pred_p(b_0)$, where b_0 is the immediate predecessor of b_1 in the program order, and a_1 is the immediate predecessor of b_1 in the conflict order. As we can see, $pred_p(b_1) = \{b_1\} \cup pred_p(b_0) \cup pred_p(a_1)$; this is because the global memory order is the union of the program order and the conflict order. If, however, b_1 is a cache hit, then its immediate predecessor in the conflict order must have completed and hence cannot be pending; if it were pending, b_1 would become a cache-miss. Thus $pred_p(b_1) = \{b_1\} \cup pred_p(b_0)$. Since memory operations that follow a cache-hit are allowed to complete only after the cache hit completes, $pred_p(b_1)$ remains the same as $pred_p(b_0)$. Consequently, $addr_p(b_1)$ remains the same as $addr_p(b_0)$ and thus, the write-list for a cache-hit need not be computed afresh.

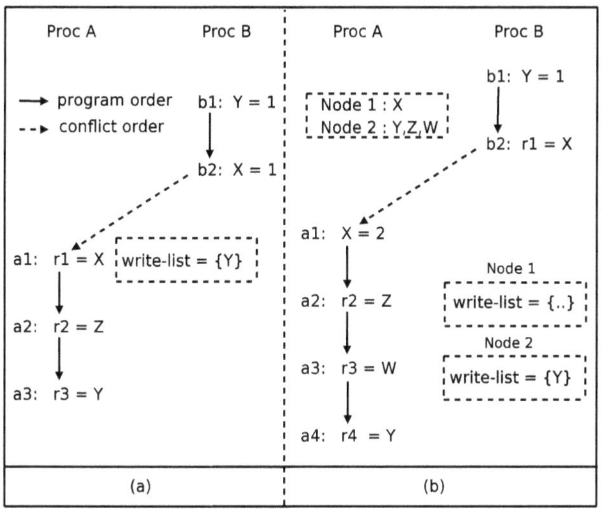

Figure 4. Basic Conflict Ordering: Example

(Read-misses). One important consequence of completing memory operations past pending writes is that, when a read-miss completes, there might be writes before it in the global memory order that are still pending. As shown in Fig. 4(a), if b_2 is allowed to complete before b_1, b_1 might still be pending when a_1 completes. Now, conflict ordering mandates that memory operations that follow a_1 can complete, only when they do not conflict with $pred_p(a_1)$. To enable this check, read-misses are also made to consult the directory and determine the write-list. Accordingly, when read-miss a_1 consults the directory, it fetches the write-list and replies to the processor. Having obtained the write-list, a_2 which does not conflict with memory operations from the write-list, is allowed to complete. Memory operation a_3, since it conflicts, is replayed obtaining its value from b_1 via the directory.

4.1.1 Handling distributed directories

To avoid a single point of contention, directories are typically distributed across the tiles, with the *directory placement policy* deciding the mapping from the address to the corresponding *home* directory; we assume the *first touch* directory placement policy. With a distributed directory, a write-miss (or a read-miss) m_1 is issued to its home directory and can only obtain the list of pending writes from *that* directory. This means that a memory operation m_2 that follows m_1 can use the write-list to check for conflicts only if m_2 maps to the same home directory as m_1. If m_2 does not map to the same home node as m_1, then m_2 will have to be conservatively assumed to be conflicting. Consequently m_2 will have to go to its own home directory to ensure that it does not conflict. If it does not conflict, then m_2 can simply commit like a cache hit; otherwise, it is treated like a miss and replayed. When m_2 goes to its home directory to check for conflicts, we take this opportunity to fetch the write-list from m_2's home directory, so that future accesses to the same node can check for conflicts locally. To accommodate this, the local processor has multiple write-list registers which are tagged by the tile id.

The scenario shown in Fig. 4(b) illustrates this. Let us assume that the variable X maps to Node 1, while variables Z, W and Y map to Node 2. Note that the processor also has two write-list registers. When a_1 is issued to its directory, it returns the pending write-misses from Node 1. Consequently, this is put into one of the write-list register which is tagged with the id of Node 1. The contents of the other write-registers are invalidated as they might contain out-of-date data. When a_2 tries to commit, the tags of the write-list registers are checked to see if any of the write-list registers is tagged with the id of Node 2, which is the home node for a_2. Since none of the write-list registers have the contents of Node 2, a_2 is sent to its home directory (Node 2) to check for conflicts. After ensuring that a_2 does not conflict, the pending stores of the home directory (from Node 2) are returned and inserted into the write-list register. This allows us to commit a_3 which maps to the same node. Likewise, when a_4 tries to commit, it is found to be conflicting and hence replayed.

Although the distributed directory could potentially reduce the number of memory operations that can complete past pending writes, our experiments show that, due to locality, most of the nearby accesses tend to map to the same home node, which allows us to complete most memory operations past pending writes.

4.1.2 Correctness

The correctness of our conflict ordering implementation hinges on the fact that when a cache-miss m_1 is issued to the directory, the write-list returned by the directory is correct; that is, the write-list should include $addr_p(m_1)$, the addresses of all pending memory operations that occur before m_1 in the global memory order. We prove this formally, next.

Lemma 2. *When a cache-miss m_1 is issued to the directory, all pending memory operations prior to it in the global memory order must be present in the directory. That is, when m_1 is issued to the directory, $\{m : m\mathbf{G}m_1\}$ must be present in the directory.*

Proof. (1) m_1 is a write-miss. When m_1 is issued to the directory, conflict ordering ensures that all pending memory operations prior to m_1 in the program order must have been issued to the directory. (2) m_1 is a read-miss. m_1 is issued to the directory to fetch the

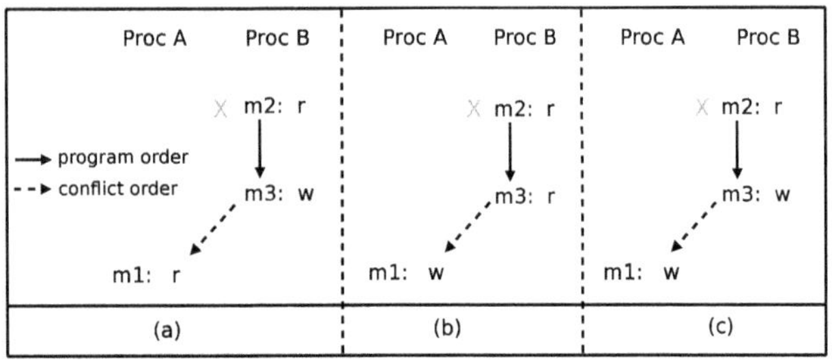

Figure 5. Correctness of conflict ordering implementation: m_2 cannot be a read in each of the 3 scenarios

write-list only when it is retired, and all memory operations prior to it have in turn been issued. Thus, whether m_1 is a write-miss or a read-miss, when m_1 is issued to the directory, $\{m : m\mathbf{P}m_1\}$ must be present in the directory. Likewise, when m_1 is issued to the directory all memory operations prior to m_1 in the conflict order, $\{m : m\mathbf{E}m_1\}$ must have been issued to the directory. Thus, when m_1 is issued to the directory, $\{m : m\mathbf{G}m_1\}$ must be present in the directory. □

Lemma 3. *When a read-miss m_1 is issued to the directory (to obtain the write-list), none of the pending memory operations prior to it in the global memory order are read-misses.*

Proof. Let us attempt a proof by contradiction and assume that such a pending read-miss exists. Let m_2 be the assumed read-miss such that $m_2 \in pred_p(m_1)$. Now the read-miss m_2 cannot occur before m_1 in the program order, as all such read-misses would have retired and hence cannot be pending. m_2 cannot occur before m_1 in the conflict order, as two reads do not conflict with each other. Thus, the only possibility is as shown in Fig. 5(a), where there is a write-miss m_3 such that $m_2\mathbf{P}m_3$ and $m_3\mathbf{E}m_1$ (without loss of generality). This again, however, is impossible since the write m_3 will be issued only after all reads before it (including m_2) complete. □

Lemma 4. *When a write-miss m_1 is issued to the directory, all pending read-misses prior to it in the global memory order, conflict with m_1.*

Proof. As shown in Fig. 5(b), it is possible that there exists m_3, a read-miss, such that $m_3\mathbf{G}m_1$ since $m_3\mathbf{E}m_1$. There cannot be, however, any read-miss m_2 such that $m_2\mathbf{G}m_1$ with m_2 not conflicting with m_1. Proof is by contradiction, along similar lines to Lemma 3 (m_2 in Fig. 5 (b) and Fig. 5 (c) cannot be reads). □

Theorem 2. *When a cache-miss m_1 is issued to the directory, the write-list returned will contain $addr_p(m_1)$, the addresses of all pending memory operations that occur before m_1 in the global memory order.*

Proof. When a cache-miss m_1 is issued to the directory, the addresses of the memory operations serviced in the directory (addr-list) will contain $addr_p(m_1)$ (from lemma 2). All pending read-misses which occur before m_1 in the global memory order, if any, would conflict with m_1 and hence access the same address as m_1. (from Lemma 3 and Lemma 4). Thus, the write-list is guaranteed to contain $addr_p(m_1)$. □

4.2 Enhanced conflict ordering

In this section, we describe our enhanced conflict ordering design, in which we identify phases in program execution where memory operations can complete without checking for conflicts. But first, we discuss the limitations of basic conflict ordering, to motivate our approach.

4.2.1 Limitations of basic conflict ordering

We illustrate the limitations of basic conflict ordering with the example shown in Fig. 6(a) and (b). As we can see, in Fig. 6(a), the write-miss a_1 estimates $pred_p(a_1)$ by consulting the directory and obtaining the write-list. All memory operations that follow the pending write miss a_1 need to be checked with the write-list for a conflict, before they can complete. It is important to note that even after a_1 completes, memory operations following a_1 will still have to be checked for conflicts. This is because b_1, which precedes a_1 in the global memory order, could still be pending when a_1 completes. In other words, the completion of the store a_1 is no longer an indicator of all memory operations belonging to $pred(a_1)$ completing. Thus, in basic conflict ordering, all memory operations that follow a write miss (or a read miss) need to be continually checked for conflicts before they can safely complete.

Another limitation stems from the fact that a read-miss (or a write-miss) *conservatively* estimates its predecessors in the global memory order by accessing the directory. Let us consider the scenario shown in Fig. 6(b), in which the read-miss a_1 estimates $pred_p(a_1)$ from the directory. However, if b_2 and a_1 are sufficiently staggered in time, which is typically common [19], then all memory operations belonging to $pred(b_2)$ (including b_1) might have already completed by the time a_1 is issued. In such a case, there is no need for a_1 to compute its write list; indeed, memory operations such as a_2 can be safely completed past a_1.

4.2.2 Our approach

(HW support and operation). Our approach is to keep track of the (local) memory operations that have retired from the ROB, but whose predecessors in the global memory order are still pending. We call such memory operations as *active* and we track such memory operations in a per-processor *augmented write buffer* (AWB). The AWB is like a normal write-buffer, in that, it buffers write-misses; unlike a conventional write-buffer, however, it also buffers the addresses of other memory operations (including read-misses, read-hits and write-hits) that are active. Therefore, an empty AWB indicates an executing phase in which all preceding memory operations in the global memory order have completed; this allows us to complete succeeding memory operations without checking for conflicts. To reduce the space used by AWB, the consecutive cache hits to the same block are merged.

We now explain how we keep track of active memory operations in the AWB. A write-miss that retires from the ROB is marked active by inserting it into the AWB, as usual. The write-miss, however, is not necessarily removed from the AWB (i.e. marked *inactive*) when it completes; we will shortly explain the conditions under which a write-miss is removed from the AWB.

A memory operation which retires from the ROB while the AWB is non-empty is active by definition. Consequently, a cache hit which retires while the AWB is non-empty is marked active by inserting its cache block address into the AWB; it is subsequently removed when the memory operation becomes *inactive* – i.e., when all prior entries in the AWB have been removed.

A cache miss which retires while the AWB is non-empty, like a cache hit, is marked active by inserting its cache block address into the AWB. However, unlike a cache hit, its block address is not necessarily removed when all prior entries in the AWB have been removed. Indeed, a cache miss remains active, and hence its cache block address remains buffered in the AWB, until its predecessors in the conflict order become inactive. Accordingly, even if a write-miss completes, it remains buffered in the AWB until all the cache blocks that it invalidates turn inactive. Likewise, a read-miss that completes is inserted into the AWB, if it gets its value from a cache block that is marked active. Here, a cache block is said to be active

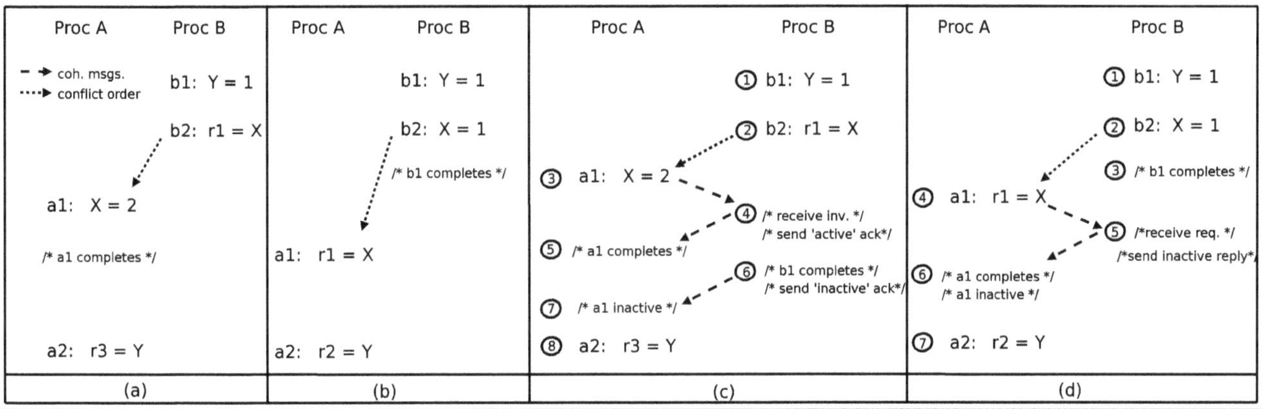

Figure 6. (a) and (b): Limitations of basic conflict ordering; (c) and (d): Our approach

if the corresponding cache block address is buffered in the AWB, and inactive otherwise.

Thus, to precisely keep track of cache misses that are active, we need to somehow infer whether its predecessors in the conflict order are active. We implement this by tagging coherence messages as active or inactive. When a processor receives a coherence request for a cache block, we check the AWB to see if it is marked active. If it is marked active, the processor responds to this coherence request with a coherence response that is tagged active. This would enable the recipient (cache miss) to infer that the coherence response is from an active memory operation. At the same time, when a processor receives a coherence request to an active cache block, it is buffered; when the cache block eventually becomes inactive, we again respond to the buffered coherence request with a coherence response that is tagged *inactive*. This would enable the recipient (cache miss) to infer that the response is from a block that has transitioned to inactive. A cache miss, when it receives a coherence response, is allowed to complete irrespective of whether it receives an active or an inactive coherence response; however, it remains active (and hence buffered in the AWB) until it gets an inactive response. Finally, by not allowing an active cache block to be replaced, we ensure that if a cache miss has predecessors in the conflict order, it will surely be exposed via the tagged coherence messages.

(Write-Miss: Example). We now explain the operation with the scenario shown in Fig. 6(c) which addresses the limitation shown in Fig. 6(a). First, the write-miss b_1 is issued from the ROB of processor B and is inserted into the AWB (step 1), after which the read-hit b_2 is made to complete past it. Since, the AWB is non-empty when b_2 completes, b_2 is marked active by inserting the cache block address X into the AWB (step 2). Then, write-miss a_1 to same address X is issued in processor A, inserted into the AWB, and issued to the directory (step 3). The directory then services this write-miss request, sending an invalidation request for cache block address X to processor B. Since cache block address X is active in processor B (cache block address X is buffered in processor B's AWB), processor B sends an active invalidation acknowledgement back to processor A (step 4); at the same time, processor B buffers the invalidation request so that it would be able to respond again when cache block address X eventually becomes inactive. When processor A receives the invalidation acknowledgement, a_1 completes (step 5), and so it sends a completion acknowledgement to the directory. It is worth noting that a_1 has completed at this point, but is still active and hence is still buffered in processor A's AWB. Let us assume that b_1 completes at step 6; furthermore let us assume that at this point all the predecessors of b_1 in the global memory order have also completed – in other words, b_1 has becomes inactive. Since b_1 has become inactive, cache block address Y is removed from the AWB. This, in turn, causes b_2 (cache block address X) to be removed from the AWB, because all those entries that preceded b_2 (including b_1) have been removed from the AWB. Since cache block address X has become inactive, processor B again responds to the buffered invalidation request by sending an inactive invalidation acknowledgement to processor A. When processor A receives this inactive acknowledgement, the recipient a_1 is made inactive and hence removed from the AWB (step 7). This will allow succeeding memory operations like a_2 to safely complete without checking for conflicts (step 8).

(Read-Miss: Example). Fig. 6(d) addresses the limitation shown in Fig. 6(b). First, the write-miss b_1 is issued and made active by inserting it into the AWB (step 1). Then, the write-hit b_2 which completes past it is made active by inserting address X into the AWB (step 2). Let us assume that b_1 then completes, and also becomes inactive (step 3). This causes b_1 to be removed from the AWB, which in turn causes b_2 (cache block address X) to be removed. When the read-miss a_1 is issued to the directory (step 4), it sends a data value request for address X to processor B. Since the cached block address X is inactive, processor B responds with an inactive data value reply to processor A (step 5). Upon receiving this value reply, a_1 completes. Furthermore, since the reply is inactive, it indicates that all the predecessors of a_1 in the conflict order have completed. Thus, the write-list is not computed and a_1 is not inserted into the AWB. Indeed when a_2 is issued (step 8), assuming the AWB is empty, it can safely be completed.

(Misses to uncached blocks). When a cache-miss is issued to the directory and it is found to be uncached in each of the other processors, this indicates that the particular cache block is inactive in each of the other processors. This is because an active block is not allowed to be replaced from the local cache. This allows us to handle a miss to an uncached block similar to a cache hit, in that, we do not need to compute a new write-list for such misses. Indeed, if there are no other pending entries in the AWB, then memory operations that come after a miss to an uncached block can be completed without checking for conflicts. It is worth noting that misses to local variables, which account for a significant percentage of misses, would be uncached in other processors. This optimization would allow us to freely complete memory operations past such local misses.

(Avoiding AWB snoops). In the above design, all coherence requests and replacement requests must snoop the AWB first to see if the corresponding cache block is marked active. To avoid this, we associate an *active bit* with every cache block; the active bit is set whenever the corresponding cache block address is inserted into the AWB and reset, whenever the cache block address is not contained in the AWB.

(Deadlock-freedom). Deadlock-freedom is guaranteed because memory operations that have been marked active will eventually become inactive. It is worth recalling that a memory operation becomes inactive when all its predecessors in the global memory order in turn become inactive. In theory, since conflict ordering guarantees SC, there cannot be any cycles in the global memory order, which ensures deadlock-freedom. The fact that an active cache block is not allowed to be replaced, however, can potentially cause the following subtle deadlock scenario. In this scenario, an earlier write-miss is not allowed to bring its cache block into its local cache, since all the cache blocks in its set have been marked active by later memory operations which have completed. In such a scenario, the later memory operations that have completed are marked active, and are waiting for the earlier write-miss to turn inactive; the earlier write-miss, however, cannot complete (and become inactive), since it is waiting for the later memory operations to turn inactive. We avoid such a scenario by forcing a write-miss to invalidate the cache block chosen for replacement and set its active bit, before the write-miss is issued to the directory. This will ensure that later memory operations which complete before the write-miss will not be able to use the same cache block used by the write-miss, as this cache block has been marked active by the write-miss. Thus, the deadlock is prevented.

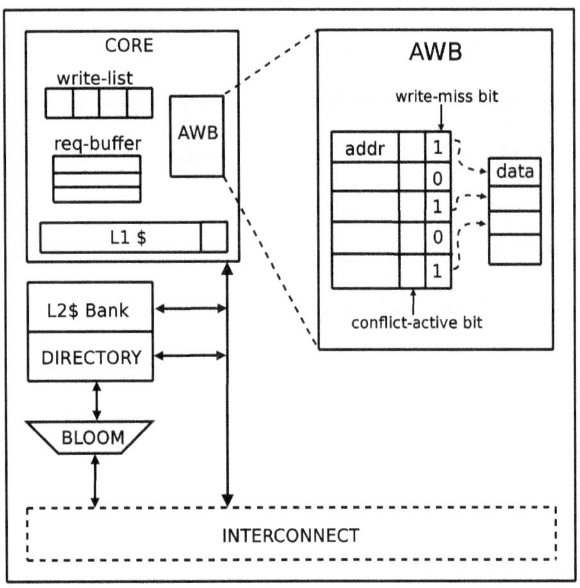

Figure 7. Hardware Support: Conflict Ordering

4.3 Summary

(Hardware support). Fig. 7 summarizes the hardware support required by conflict ordering. First, each processor core is associated with a set of write-list registers. Second, each processor core is associated with an augmented write buffer (AWB), which replaces a conventional write-buffer. Like a conventional write-buffer, each entry of the AWB is tagged by the cache block address; unlike a conventional write buffer, however, it also buffers read-misses, read-hits and write-hits. To distinguish write-misses from other memory operations, each entry of the AWB is associated with a *write-miss bit*. If the current entry corresponds to a write-miss, i.e. the write-miss bit is set, the entry additionally points to the data that is written by the current write-miss. Each entry is also associated with a *conflict-active* bit, which is set if any of its predecessors which conflict with it are active. Third, an *active* bit is added to each local cache block, which indicates whether that particular cache block is active. Lastly, conflict ordering requires minor extensions to the cache coherence subsystem. Each processor is associated with a *req-buffer* which is used to buffer coherence requests to active cache blocks. Each coherence response message (data value reply and invalidation acknowledgement) is tagged with an active bit, to indicate whether it is an active response or an inactive response. Also, conflict ordering involves the exchange of additional coherence message. While additional coherence messages are exchanged as part of conflict ordering, it is worth noting that the coherence protocol and its associated transactions for maintaining coherence are left unchanged. We summarize the additional transactions next.

(Write-miss actions). The actions performed when the write-miss retires from the ROB are as follows:

- Insert into the AWB. The write-miss is first inserted into the AWB as follows: the inserted entry is tagged with the cache block address of the write-miss; since the entry corresponds to a write-miss, the write-miss bit is set to 1 and the entry points to the data written by the write-miss; the conflict-active bit is set to 1 since its predecessor in the conflict order may be active.
- Invalidate replacement victim. Once the write-miss is inserted into the AWB, the cache block chosen for replacement is invalidated and its active bit is set to 1 – it is worth recalling that this is done to prevent the deadlock scenario discussed earlier.
- Issue request to home-directory. Now, the write-miss is issued to its home directory. If the corresponding cache block is found to be uncached in any of the other processors, the directory replies with an empty write-list. If the cache block is indeed cached in some other processor, the directory replies with the list of pending write-misses being serviced in the directory. To minimize network traffic, before sending the write-list, a bloom filter is used to compress the list of addresses.
- Process response. Once the processor receives the write-list, if it indeed receives a non-empty write-list, it updates the local write-list register. When the write-miss receives all of its invalidation acknowledgements, it completes. When the write-miss completes, it sends a completion message to the directory, so that the directory knows about its completion. When a write-miss receives all of its acknowledgements and each of the acknowledgements are tagged inactive, its corresponding conflict-active bit (in the AWB) is reset to 0. When the conflict-active is reset, the write-miss checks the AWB to see if there are any entries prior to it. If there are none, it implies that the write-miss has become inactive and can be removed from the AWB.
- Remove write-miss and other inactive entries from the AWB. Before removing the write-miss entry, we first identify those memory operations which follow the original write-miss that have also become inactive. To identify such inactive memory operations, the AWB is scanned sequentially starting from the original entry, selecting all those entries whose conflict-active bit is reset to 0; the scanning is stopped when an entry whose conflict-active bit is set to 1 is encountered. All such selected entries are removed from the AWB, and the active bits of their respective cache blocks are reset to 0.

(Cache-hit actions). The actions performed when a cache-hit reaches the head of the ROB are as follows:

- AWB empty. The AWB is first checked to see if it is empty. If the AWB is empty, the cache-hit completes without checking for conflicts.
- Check for conflicts. If the AWB is not empty, the write-list registers are checked to see if the cache-hit conflicts with it. If the cache-hit conflicts (or if write-list register does not cache the directory entries of the cache-hit's home node), the cache-hit is treated like a miss and is issued to its home directory.
- No conflicts. If the cache-hit does not conflict, it is allowed to safely complete. Since the AWB is non-empty, the cache-hit is marked active by inserting it into the AWB with the write-miss bit set to 0, the conflict-active bit set to 0 (since it is a cache-hit, its predecessors in the conflict order must have completed), and the active bit of the cache block is set to 1.

(Read-miss actions). The actions performed when a read-miss reaches the head of the ROB are as follows:

- AWB empty. The AWB is first checked to see if it is empty. If the AWB is empty, the read-miss completes without checking for conflicts. Then, the data value reply that the read-miss received as a coherence response is examined. If it is tagged active, it is inserted into the AWB with the write-miss bit set to 0, the conflict-active bit set to 1 (since it obtained an active response), and the active bit of the cache block is set to 1. Later, when the read-miss receives its inactive response, the read-miss entry is removed along with subsequent inactive entries, as discussed earlier.
- Check for conflicts. If the AWB is not empty, the write-list registers are checked to see if the read-miss conflicts with it. If the read-miss conflicts (or if write-list register does not cache the directory entries of the read-miss' home node), the cache-miss is re-issued to its home directory.
- No conflicts. If the read-miss does not conflict, the read-miss is allowed to safely complete. Since the AWB is non-empty, the read-miss is marked active by inserting into the AWB with the write-miss bit set to 0. The conflict-active bit is set to 0 or 1 depending on whether the read-miss received an inactive or an active data value response, respectively. If it received an active response – later, when the read-miss receives the inactive response, the read-miss entry is removed along with subsequent inactive entries, as discussed earlier.

(Coherence and replacement requests). When a coherence request (invalidate or data value request) is received for a cache block that is marked active/inactive, the coherence response is in turn tagged active/inactive. Additionally, if the coherence request is for an active cache block, the coherence request is buffered in the req-buffer. When the cache block is eventually reset to inactive, the corresponding entry is removed from the req-buffer and the processor again responds to the buffered request – but now with an inactive response. When a coherence request is received for an active cache block and the req-buffer is full, the coherence response is delayed until a space in the req-buffer frees up. As discussed earlier, this cannot cause a deadlock, since active cache blocks will eventually turn inactive. Finally, a cache block that is marked active is not allowed to be replaced. When a replacement request is received, and all cache blocks in the set are marked active, the response is delayed until once of the blocks in the set turns inactive – again, without the risk of a deadlock.

5. Experimental Evaluation

We performed our experiments with several goals in mind. First and foremost, we want to evaluate the benefit of ensuring SC via conflict ordering in comparison with the baseline SC and RMO implementations. We then study the effect of varying the values of the parameters in our HW implementation, on the performance. Since the performance of our approach is dependent on how fast requests can get back replies from directories, we study the sensitivity towards the network latency. We also vary the size of write-lists to evaluate their effects on performance. We then study the characterization of conflict ordering to see how it reduces the overhead of using in-window speculation technique. Furthermore, we measure the additional network bandwidth that is used up and finally, we also measure the on-chip hardware resources that conflict ordering utilizes. However, before we present the results of our evaluation, we briefly describe our implementation.

5.1 Implementation

Processor	8, 16 and 32 core CMP, out of order
ROB size	176
L1 Cache	private 32 KB 4 way 2 cycle latency
L2 Cache	shared 8 MB 8 way 9 cycle latency
Memory	300 cycle latency
Coherence	directory based invalidate
# of AWB entries	50 per core
# of req-buffer entries	8 per core
# of write-list registers	6 per core
write-list size	160 bits
Interconnect	2D torus (2×4 for 8-core, 4×4 for 16-core, 4×8 for 32-core) 5 cycle hop latency

Table 1. Architectural Parameters.

Benchmark	Inputs
barnes	16K particles
fmm	16K particles
ocean	258× 258
radiosity	batch
raytrace	car
water-ns	512 molecules
water-sp	512 molecules
cholesky	tk15.O
fft	64K points
lu	512×512
radix	1M integers

Table 2. Benchmarks.

We implemented conflict ordering using SESC [24] simulator, targeting the MIPS architecture. The simulator is a cycle-accurate, execution-driven multi-core simulator with detailed models for the processor and the memory systems. To implement conflict ordering, we added the associated control logic to the simulator. We considered conflict ordering in the context of a CMP with local caches kept coherent using a distributed directory based protocol. The architectural parameters for our implementation are presented in Table 1. The default architectural parameters were used in all experiments unless explicitly stated otherwise. We measured performance with 8, 16 and 32 processors in Section 5.2, and for other studies, we assumed 32 processors. We used the SPLASH-2 [32], a standard multithreaded suite of benchmarks for our evaluation. We could not get the program *volrend* to compile using the compiler infrastructure that targets the simulator and hence we omitted it. We used the input data sets described in Table 2 and ran the benchmarks to completion.

(Our baseline SC implementation). Our SC baseline, referred to as conventional SC in the experiments below, uses in-window speculation support. It is an aggressive implementation that uses hardware prefetching and support for speculation in modern processors to speculatively reorder memory operations while guaranteeing SC ordering using replay. However, such speculation is within the instruction window – where the instruction window refers to the set of instructions that are in-flight. The implementation we use is similar to ones used as SC baselines in proposals such as [6, 14, 31].

(Our baseline RMO implementation). Our baseline RMO implementation allows memory operations to be freely reordered, enforcing memory ordering only when fences are encountered. Even when fences are encountered, in-window speculation support (as used in the SC baseline) is used to mitigate the delays. The RMO implementation is similar to ones used in recent works such as [6, 14, 31].

5.2 Execution time overhead

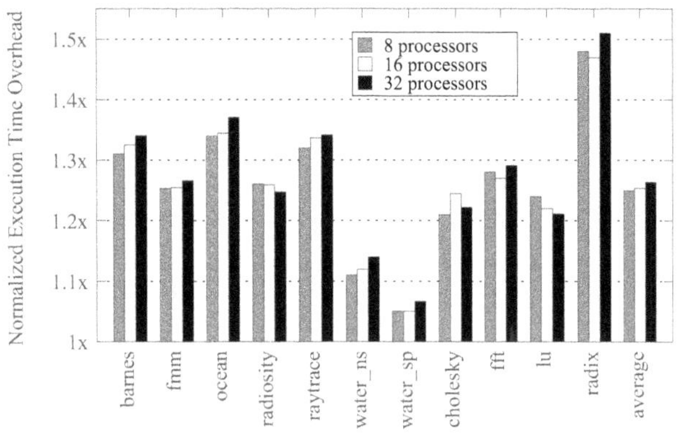

Figure 8. Conventional SC normalized to RMO

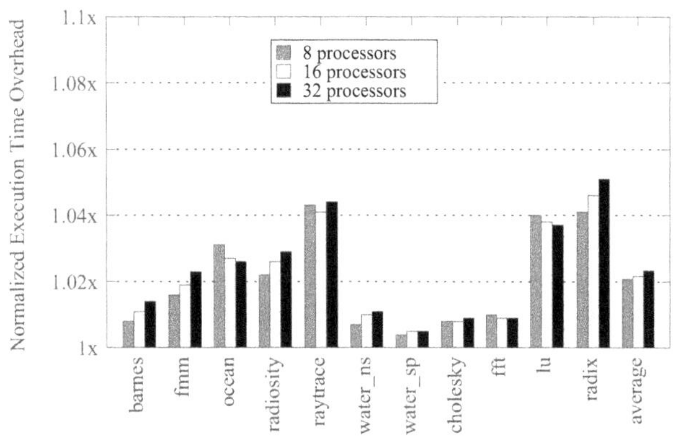

Figure 9. Conflict ordering normalized to RMO

We measure the execution time overhead of ensuring SC via our approach conflict ordering and compare it with the corresponding overhead for conventional SC. We conducted this experiment for 8, 16 and 32 processors using the default hardware implementation presented in Table 1. Fig. 8 and Fig. 9 show the execution time overheads for conventional SC and conflict ordering, respectively. The execution time overheads are normalized to the performance achieved using RMO. As we can see, most benchmark programs experience significant slowdown for conventional SC (more than 20% overhead on average for all numbers of processors). In particular, *radix* has the highest overhead. This is because *radix* has a relatively high store-miss rate which forces the following loads to wait longer before they can be retired. As we can see, with conflict ordering the overhead of ensuring SC is significantly reduced. On average, the overhead is just 2.0% for 8 processors, 2.2% for 16 processors and 2.3% for 32 processors, and thus the performance of our approach is comparable to RMO. With conflict ordering loads and stores do not need to wait until outstanding stores complete; they can mostly retire as soon as the pending stores get replies back from directories. Since the time to get replies from directories is significantly less than the time for outstanding stores to complete, loads do not end up causing stalls and stores can also be performed out of order. This explains why the performance with conflict ordering is significantly better than conventional SC. Furthermore, it is worth noting that, with different numbers of processors, the performance does not vary significantly. Therefore, our approach appears scalable.

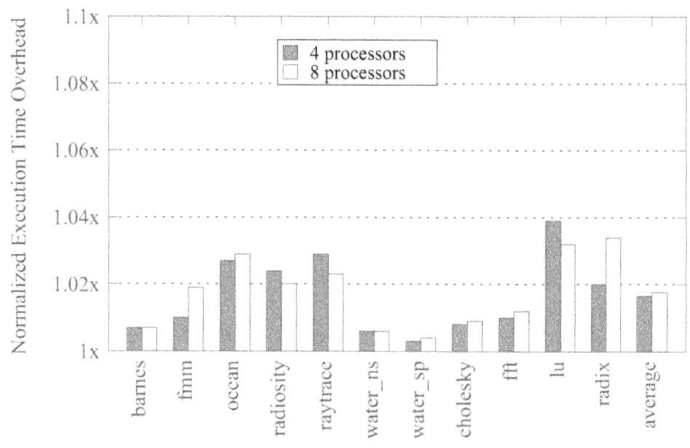

Figure 10. Performance for bus-based implementation.

(Bus-based implementation). In addition to the distributed directory-based implementation, we also evaluated a bus-based implementation to find out if conflict ordering is applicable to current multi-core processors which are predominantly bus based. For our bus based implementation, we just implement basic conflict ordering; we maintain a centralized on-chip structure called *write-list-buffer* (WLB), which records the addresses of the write-misses which are currently pending. When a write-miss retires into a local write-buffer it is sent to the WLB; upon receiving the write-miss, the WLB inserts its address into the WLB and replies back with the write-list – containing all the addresses that are currently present in the WLB except the addresses from the source processor. Similar to the directory-based implementation, a bloom filter is used to compress the addresses. Memory operations which attempt to complete past the write-miss, check the received write-list to decide whether they can be completed safely, without violating SC. We conducted experiments for bus-based implementation with 4 and 8 processors, and set the round-trip latency for accessing WLB as 5 cycles. Fig. 10 shows the execution time normalized to RMO. As we can see, the execution time of our technique is close to RMO for both 4 and 8 processors, with the overhead less than 2% on average. This shows that conflict ordering is also applicable to small scale multi-core processors that use a bus for coherence.

5.3 Sensitivity studies

(Sensitivity towards network latency). The performance of conflict ordering hinges on the time for a miss to get replies from the directory. It is desirable that conflict ordering is reasonably tolerant to the network latency. In our experiments, we used 2D torus network and varied the latency of each hop with values of 3 cycles,

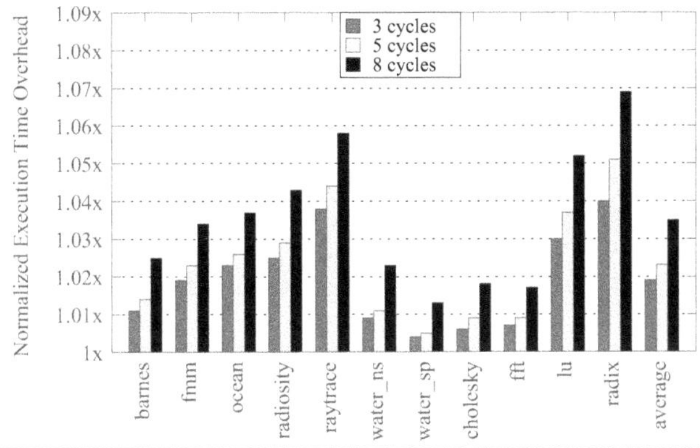

Figure 11. Varying the latency of network.

5 cycles, and 8 cycles, as shown in Fig. 11. The performance is measured with 32 processors. As we can see, the overhead does not vary significantly when the latency is increased from 3 cycles to 5 cycles. Even when the latency is increased to 8 cycles, the average performance drops only slightly, to 3.5%. This shows conflict ordering is reasonably tolerant to the network latency. In our default design, we choose 5 cycles as each hop latency, assuming 2 cycle wire delay between routers and 3 cycle delay per pipelined router.

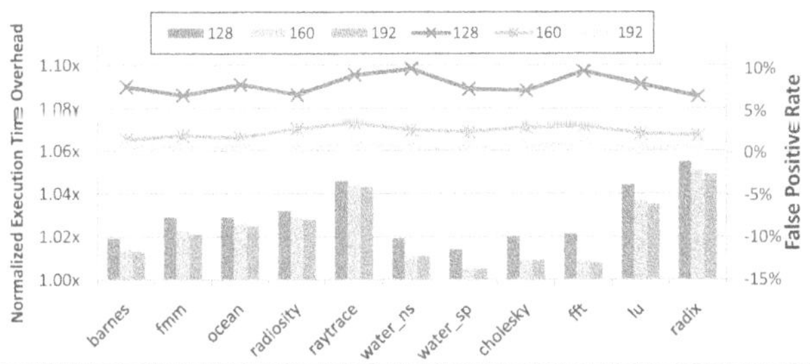

Figure 12. Varying number of bits of write-list.

(Sensitivity towards size of write-list). Recall that, to minimize network bandwidth, the addresses within replies to cache miss requests are compressed to form a write-list using a bloom filter. While a smaller size is beneficial as far as saving network bandwidth is concerned, it could also result in false positives. A false positive can lead us to falsely conclude that a load or store conflicts with a pending store, causing the load to re-execute or the store to stall. In this experiment, we evaluated the minimum size of the write-list that does not result in performance loss. We varied the number of bits of write-list with the value 128, 160, and 192 to evaluate the performance and corresponding false positive rates with 32 processors. In our implementation, we used a bloom filter with 4 hash functions. Fig. 12 shows the results, where lines represent false positive rates and bars represent execution time overheads. As the number of bits increases from 128 to 192, the false positive rate decreases (on average, 8.01%, 2.42%, and 0.69% respectively), and the execution overhead also decreases (on average, 2.97%, 2.33% and 2.29% respectively). A size of 160 bits performs slightly better than 128 bits and very close to 192 bits. Therefore, we choose 160 bits (20 bytes) as the size of the write-list in our implementation.

5.4 Characterization of conflict ordering

In this experiment, we wanted to examine how conflict ordering reduces the overhead of using conventional SC. Recall that, in the conventional SC implementation, loads cannot be retired if there are pending stores and stores cannot be performed out of order, which leads to the gap between the performance of SC and RMO. On the other hand, using conflict ordering, we can safely retire loads and complete stores past pending stores by checking the write-list. Hence, performance hinges on how often loads and stores can be reordered with their prior pending stores.

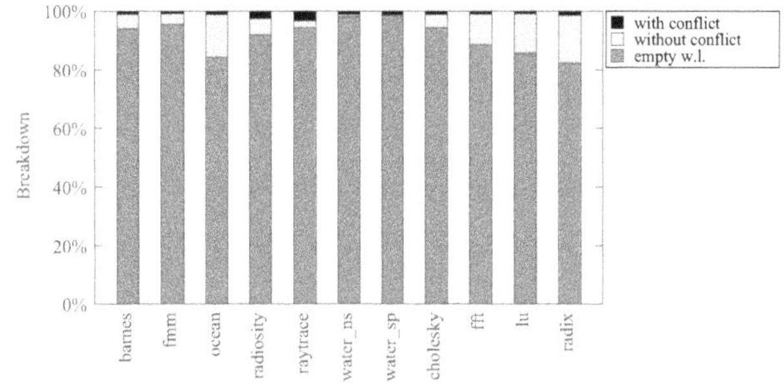

Figure 13. Breakdown of checks against write-lists.

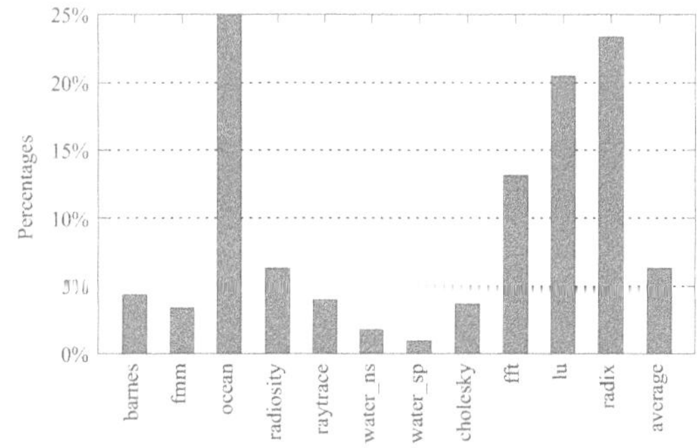

Figure 14. Reduced accesses to directories.

Fig. 13 shows the breakdown for all checks against write-lists. We categorize these checks into three types: checks against empty write-lists, checks against non-empty write-lists without finding any conflict, and checks against non-empty write-lists with finding a conflict. When a request to the directory finds that the targeted block is not cached, it indicates that no active memory operation has accessed the block and the requesting processor can get a reply with an empty write-list. As we can see, most checks are against empty write-lists (around 90% on average). For the checks against non-empty write-lists, there is almost no conflict. Hence, our approach allows almost all memory operation to be reordered, achieving performance comparable to RMO.

Fig. 14 shows the reduced directory accesses using enhanced conflict ordering, compared to basic conflict ordering. The performance of our approach also hinges on the frequency of directory accesses. Hence, it is important to have fewer directory accesses. As we can see, using enhanced conflict ordering, on average we only have about 6% directory accesses of basic conflict ordering. This is because, for most benchmark programs, AWB is empty most of the time. For some benchmarks, such as *ocean*, the access frequency does not reduce as much as other benchmarks. However, the access frequency for these benchmarks in basic conflict ordering is already low. Therefore, their overhead is still low.

5.5 Bandwidth increase

In this experiment, we measure the bandwidth increase due to write-lists that need to be transferred and extra traffic introduced by

Benchmark	Bandwidth increase (%)
barnes	2.49
fmm	0.98
ocean	2.64
radiosity	8.36
raytrace	1.21
water-ns	2.08
water-sp	2.21
cholesky	0.24
fft	1.16
lu	1.96
radix	1.71

Table 3. Bandwidth Increase.

conflict ordering for 32 processors. Table 3 shows the bandwidth increase compared to RMO. As we can see, for most benchmarks, the bandwidth increase is less than 3% (2.27% on average). *radiosity* has relatively higher bandwidth increase. This is because its write miss rate is relatively higher and requests to directories usually get non-empty write-lists, resulting in write-lists taking up a relatively high proportion of bandwidth.

5.6 HW resources utilized

Recall that the additional HW resources utilized by conflict ordering are AWB, req-buffers, write-list registers, and the active bits added to each cache block. Each AWB entry contains the cache block address, the conflict-active and the write-miss bits; we do not count the storage required for data written by the write-miss, since it is already present in conventional write buffers. Since we use 50 AWB entries per core, each of size 5 bytes, the total size per processor core amounts to 250 bytes for the AWB. Since we use 8 entries for the req-buffer, each of size 6 bytes (for storing the cache block address and the processor id), the total size per processor core amounts to 48 bytes. With 6 write-list registers per core, each of size 20 bytes, the total size per processor core amounts to 120 bytes. In addition, we also require active bits to be added to each cache block in the L1 cache. This amounts to an additional 64 bytes of on-chip storage per processor core. Thus the total additional on-chip storage space amounts to 482 bytes per processor core. In addition to this we require the hardware resources needed for in-window speculation which is also required by our SC and RMO baselines. Thus, the additional hardware resources utilized for conflict ordering is nominal.

6. Conclusion

Should hardware enforce SC? Researchers have examined this question for over 30 years, with no definite answers, yet. While there has been no clear consensus on whether hardware should support SC [3, 16], it is important to note, however, that the benefits of supporting SC are widely acknowledged [3]. Indeed, critics of hardware enforced SC, question it based on whether the costs of supporting SC justify its benefits – all prior SC implementations needing to employ aggressive speculation and its associated complexity for supporting SC.

In this paper we demonstrate that the benefits of SC can indeed be realized using nominal hardware resources. While prior SC implementations guarantee SC by explicitly completing memory operations within a processor in program order, we guarantee SC by completing conflicting memory operations, within and across processors, in an order that is consistent with the program order. More specifically, we identify those shared memory dependencies whose ordering is critical for the maintenance of SC and intentionally order them. This allows us to non-speculatively complete memory operations past pending writes and thus reduce the number of stalls due to memory ordering. Our experiments with SPLASH-2 suite showed that SC can be achieved efficiently, incurring only 2.3% additional overhead compared to RMO.

Acknowledgments

We would like to thank the reviewers and our shepherd for their helpful comments and advice for improving this paper. This work is supported by NSF grants CCF-0963996 and CCF-0905509 to the University of California, Riverside, and by the Centre for Numerical Algorithms and Intelligent Software, funded by EPSRC grant EP/G036136/1 and the Scottish Funding Council to the University of Edinburgh.

References

[1] Intel Single-Chip Cloud Computer. http://techresearch.intel.com/articles/Tera-Scale/1826.htm.

[2] Telera Tile-Gx processor. http://www.tilera.com/products/processors.

[3] S. V. Adve and H.-J. Boehm. Memory models: a case for rethinking parallel languages and hardware. *Communications of the ACM*, 53(8):90–101, 2010.

[4] S. V. Adve and K. Gharachorloo. Shared memory consistency models: A tutorial. *IEEE Computer*, 29:66–76, 1995.

[5] S. V. Adve and M. D. Hill. Weak ordering - a new definition. In *Proceedings of the 17th Annual International Symposium on Computer Architecture*, ISCA '90, pages 2–14, 1990.

[6] C. Blundell, M. M. Martin, and T. F. Wenisch. InvisiFence: performance-transparent memory ordering in conventional multiprocessors. In *Proceedings of the 36th Annual International Symposium on Computer Architecture*, ISCA '09, pages 233–244, 2009.

[7] L. Ceze, J. Tuck, P. Montesinos, and J. Torrellas. BulkSC: bulk enforcement of sequential consistency. In *Proceedings of the 34th Annual International Symposium on Computer Architecture*, ISCA '07, pages 278–289, 2007.

[8] H. Chafi, J. Casper, B. D. Carlstrom, A. McDonald, C. C. Minh, W. Baek, C. Kozyrakis, and K. Olukotun. A scalable, non-blocking approach to transactional memory. In *Proceedings of the IEEE 13th International Symposium on High Performance Computer Architecture*, HPCA '07, pages 97–108, 2007.

[9] T. Elmas, S. Qadeer, and S. Tasiran. Goldilocks: a race and transaction-aware java runtime. In *Proceedings of the ACM SIGPLAN Conference on Programming Language Design and Implementation*, PLDI '07, pages 245–255, 2007.

[10] X. Fang, J. Lee, and S. P. Midkiff. Automatic fence insertion for shared memory multiprocessing. In *Proceedings of the 17th Annual International Conference on Supercomputing*, ICS '03, pages 285–294, 2003.

[11] M. Galluzzi, E. Vallejo, A. Cristal, F. Vallejo, R. Beivide, P. Stenström, J. E. Smith, and M. Valero. Implicit transactional memory in kilo-instruction multiprocessors. In *Asia-Pacific Computer Systems Architecture Conference*, pages 339–353, 2007.

[12] K. Gharachorloo, A. Gupta, and J. Hennessy. Two techniques to enhance the performance of memory consistency models. In *Proceedings of the International Conference on Parallel Processing*, ISCA '91, pages 355–364, 1991.

[13] C. Gniady and B. Falsafi. Speculative sequential consistency with little custom storage. In *Proceedings of the International Conference on Parallel Architectures and Compilation Techniques*, PACT '02, pages 179–188, 2002.

[14] C. Gniady, B. Falsafi, and T. N. Vijaykumar. Is SC + ILP = RC? In *Proceedings of the 26th Annual International Symposium on Computer Architecture*, ISCA '99, pages 162–171, 1999.

[15] L. Hammond, V. Wong, M. Chen, B. D. Carlstrom, J. D. Davis, B. Hertzberg, M. K. Prabhu, H. Wijaya, C. Kozyrakis, and K. Olukotun. Transactional memory coherence and consistency. In *Proceedings of the 31st Annual International Symposium on Computer Architecture*, ISCA '04, page 102, 2004.

[16] M. D. Hill. Multiprocessors should support simple memory-consistency models. *Computer*, 31(8):28–34, 1998.

[17] L. Lamport. How to make a multiprocessor computer that correctly executes multiprocess program. *IEEE Transactions on Computers*, 28(9):690–691, 1979.

[18] J. Lee and D. A. Padua. Hiding relaxed memory consistency with a compiler. *IEEE Transactions on Computers*, 50(8):824–833, 2001.

[19] C. Lin, V. Nagarajan, and R. Gupta. Efficient sequential consistency using conditional fences. In *Proceedings of the 19th International Conference on Parallel Architectures and Compilation Techniques*, PACT '10, pages 295–306, 2010.

[20] B. Lucia, L. Ceze, K. Strauss, S. Qadeer, and H.-J. Boehm. Conflict exceptions: simplifying concurrent language semantics with precise hardware exceptions for data-races. In *Proceedings of the 37th Annual International Symposium on Computer Architecture*, ISCA '10, pages 210–221, 2010.

[21] D. Marino, A. Singh, T. Millstein, M. Musuvathi, and S. Narayanasamy. DRFx: a simple and efficient memory model for concurrent programming languages. In *Proceedings of the ACM SIGPLAN Conference on Programming Language Design and Implementation*, PLDI '10, pages 351–362, 2010.

[22] D. Marino, A. Singh, T. Millstein, M. Musuvathi, and S. Narayanasamy. A case for an SC-preserving compiler. In *Proceedings of the 32nd ACM SIGPLAN Conference on Programming Language Design and Implementation*, PLDI '11, pages 199–210, 2011.

[23] P. Ranganathan, V. S. Pai, and S. V. Adve. Using speculative retirement and larger instruction windows to narrow the performance gap between memory consistency models. In *Proceedings of the 9th Annual ACM Symposium on Parallel Algorithms and Architectures*, SPAA '97, pages 199–210, 1997.

[24] J. Renau, B. Fraguela, J. Tuck, W. Liu, M. Prvulovic, L. Ceze, S. Sarangi, P. Sack, K. Strauss, and P. Montesinos. SESC simulator, January 2005. http://sesc.sourceforge.net.

[25] K. G. Sarita, S. V. Adve, A. Gupta, J. L. Hennessy, and M. D. Hill. Specifying system requirements for memory consistency models. *Technical Report CSL-TR-93-594, Stanford University*, 1993.

[26] C. Scheurich and M. Dubois. Correct memory operation of cache-based multiprocessors. In *Proceedings of the 14th Annual International Symposium on Computer Architecture*, ISCA '87, pages 234–243, 1987.

[27] K. Sen. Race directed random testing of concurrent programs. In *Proceedings of the ACM SIGPLAN Conference on Programming Language Design and Implementation*, PLDI '08, pages 11–21, 2008.

[28] P. Sewell, S. Sarkar, S. Owens, F. Z. Nardelli, and M. O. Myreen. x86-TSO: a rigorous and usable programmer's model for x86 multiprocessors. *Communication of the ACM*, 53(7):89–97, 2010.

[29] D. Shasha and M. Snir. Efficient and correct execution of parallel programs that share memory. *ACM Transactions on Programming Languages and Systems*, 10(2):282–312, 1988.

[30] A. Singh, D. Marino, S. Narayanasamy, T. Millstein, and M. Musuvathi. Efficient processor support for DRFx, a memory model with exceptions. In *Proceedings of the 16th International Conference on Architectural Support for Programming Languages and Operating Systems*, ASPLOS '11, pages 53–66, 2011.

[31] T. F. Wenisch, A. Ailamaki, B. Falsafi, and A. Moshovos. Mechanisms for store-wait-free multiprocessors. In *Proceedings of the 34th Annual International Symposium on Computer Architecture*, ISCA '07, pages 266–277, 2007.

[32] S. C. Woo, M. Ohara, E. Torrie, J. P. Singh, and A. Gupta. The SPLASH-2 programs: characterization and methodological considerations. In *Proceedings of the 22nd Annual International Symposium on Computer Architecture*, ISCA '95, pages 24–36, 1995.

[33] K. C. Yeager. The MIPS R10000 superscalar microprocessor. *IEEE Micro*, 16(2):28–40, 1996.

HICAMP: Architectural Support for Efficient Concurrency-safe Shared Structured Data Access

David Cheriton * Amin Firoozshahian Alex Solomatnikov John P. Stevenson † Omid Azizi

Hicamp Systems, Inc.

{cheriton, aminf13, sols, jps, oazizi}@hicampsystems.com

Abstract

Programming language and operating system support for efficient concurrency-safe access to shared data is a key concern for the effective use of multi-core processors. Most research has focused on the software model of multiple threads accessing this data within a single shared address space. However, many real applications are actually structured as multiple separate processes for fault isolation and simplified synchronization.

In this paper, we describe the HICAMP architecture and its innovative memory system, which supports efficient concurrency safe access to structured shared data without incurring the overhead of inter-process communication. The HICAMP architecture also provides support for programming language and OS structures such as threads, iterators, read-only access and atomic update. In addition to demonstrating that HICAMP is beneficial for multi-process structured applications, our evaluation shows that the same mechanisms provide substantial benefits for other areas, including sparse matrix computations and virtualization.

Categories and Subject Descriptors B.3.2 [*Hardware*]: Memory Structures—associative memories, cache memories; C.1.2 [*Processor Architectures*]: Multiple Data Stream Architectures (Multiprocessors)—parallel processors

General Terms Design, Performance, Reliability

Keywords Parallel Programming, Parallel Architecture, Memory Model, Snapshot Semantics, Memory Sharing, Fault Isolation, Memory Deduplication, Iterator Register

1. Introduction

Programming language and operating system support for efficient concurrency-safe access to shared data is a key issue to address to achieve the effective use of multi-core processors. Most of the focus in this area has been on the multithreaded model, where multiple threads within a single address space concurrently access shared data in memory. However, this model introduces *non-deterministic* execution because of arbitrary interleaving of threads accessing shared memory [25]. The programmer thus needs to carefully orchestrate access to shared data using mechanisms such as locks, monitors or transactions to prevent corruption of shared state. Various programming language constructs and checking tools have been developed to reduce the associated problems. However, software bugs can still cause the entire application or system to fail and these bugs are hard to reproduce and thus difficult to track down.

A common approach is to partition the application system into multiple separate client processes and one or more shared state-managing processes, connected by an *inter-process communication* (IPC) mechanism such as sockets. For example, a web site is usually implemented as multiple web server processes accessing shared state stored in a database server, running as a separate process. To provide sufficient read bandwidth, many high traffic websites extend this model further by instantiating one or more memcached [15] processes that serve as a fast cache of common database queries, i.e., the common parts of dynamically generated web-pages[1]. A similar structure is found in many other web and database applications as well as embedded systems [5].

This multi-process structure provides strong fault isolation between the client processes and the servers, preventing the clients from corrupting the shared state and allowing restart of a failed client. This structure also allows client application code to be sequential, delegating concurrency control to these database/memcached servers, reducing the cost of development and improving the reliability of this software. It also allows the application to scale seamlessly across a cluster of networked processors, beyond the limits of a single physical server.

The disadvantage of this approach is the overhead: a client process needs to generate a message from its internal state, transmit the message over the socket to the server process, wait for the server's reply, extract information from server message and transform it back to the internal representation. Similar overhead is incurred on the server side as well as overheads for concurrency control, logging and buffer management. In fact, Stonebraker and Catte [28] estimate that only 13 percent of CPU cycles perform the actual work of a database when it is running completely in memory. As the number of cores on a chip increases, it becomes possible to run many processes on the same chip, yet these overheads, being memory-intensive, can be expected to become proportionally worse.

The **HICAMP (Hierarchical Immutable Content Addressable Memory Processor)** architecture provides an alternative to both shared memory and "database" models by implementing, in hardware, a memory abstraction of protected sharable segments

* also a professor at Stanford University

† also a Ph.D candidate at Stanford University

[1] memcached is widely used by many popular high-traffic web-sites (Facebook [27], YouTube, Wikipedia, LiveJournal, etc.).

ASPLOS'12, March 3–7, 2012, London, England, UK.

that can be "snapshotted" and atomically updated efficiently. This abstraction allows efficient, fault-tolerant, concurrency-safe access to shared data by multiple threads without the loss of hardware-enforced isolation, yet without the conventional overheads of an application structured as multiple processes. HICAMP also incorporates memory ***deduplication***, which further reduces copy overhead and improves cache and DRAM utilization.

In this paper, we describe the HICAMP architecture: how it supports key programming language constructs, including shared objects, iterators and atomic updates, how it simplifies operating systems for multi-core processors, and how it is amenable to a cost-effective implementation. We further describe how this novel memory architecture provides substantial benefits to other application domains, providing significant improvements in memory performance of applications ranging from web software to sparse matrix computations and virtual machine hosting. The latter allows HICAMP to run legacy software.

2. HICAMP Architecture

The HICAMP memory architecture introduces three key concepts:

1. *Content-unique lines:* memory is considered to be an array of small, fixed-size lines, where each line is addressed by a *Physical Line ID* (PLID), and has unique content that is immutable over its lifetime.
2. *Memory segments:* memory is accessed as a number of segments, where each segment is structured as a *Directed Acyclic Graph* (DAG) of memory lines, i.e. logically a tree but with potentially shared lines due to the content-uniqueness property of lines.
3. *Virtual segment map:* a mapping from *Virtual Segment IDs* (VSID) that identify memory segments for applications, to the root PLID of the DAG representing the segment contents.

The following subsections elaborate on these concepts.

2.1 Content-Unique Lines

The HICAMP main (DRAM) memory is divided into *lines*, each with a fixed size, such as 16, 32 or 64 bytes. Each line has unique content that is immutable during its lifetime. Uniqueness and immutability of lines is guaranteed and maintained by a duplicate suppression mechanism in the memory system. In particular, the memory system can either read a line by its PLID (similar to a reading a line in a conventional memory system using its address) or lookup a line by content (instead of writing), returning the PLID. The lookup-by-content operation allocates a line and assigns it a new PLID if a line with the specified content is not already present. When the processor needs to modify a line to effectively write new data into memory, it requests a PLID for a line with the specified (modified) content[2]. The *zero PLID* corresponds to *zero line* making it easy to identify any zero line references. It also provides a space-efficient representation of sparse data structures.

The PLIDs are a hardware-protected data type that can only be created in memory or registers from the return value of a lookup-by-content operation or by copying an existing PLID value. This protection is implemented by per-word tags that indicate whether the content contains a PLID[3]. This protection of PLIDs is necessary so that hardware can track the sharing of lines accurately. It has the further benefit of providing protected references; an application thread can only access content that it has created or for which the PLID has been explicitly passed to it.

2.2 Segments

A *segment* in HICAMP is a variable-sized, logically contiguous region of memory. It is represented as a DAG of fixed size lines with data elements stored at the leaf nodes, as illustrated in Figure 1. Figure 1a shows two memory segments representing two strings, labeled "First string" and "Second string" with the second one being a substring of the first. Note that the second string shares all the lines of the first string, given the latter is a substring of the former.

Each segment follows a canonical representation in which leaf lines are filled from the left to right. As a consequence of this rule and the duplicate suppression by the memory system, each possible segment content has a unique representation in memory. In particular, if the character string of Figure 1a is instantiated again by software, the result is a reference to the same DAG, which already exists. In this way, HICAMP extends the content-uniqueness property from lines to segments. Furthermore, two segments in HICAMP can be compared for equality by a simple comparison of their root PLIDs, independent of segment size. For example, two web pages represented as HICAMP strings (array of characters) can be compared in a single compare instruction.

When content of a segment is modified by creating a new leaf, the PLID of the new leaf replaces the old PLID in its parent line, requiring the content of parent line to change, and thus a different PLID for the parent line, thus requiring the parent of the parent to change, and so on. Consequently new PLIDs replace the old ones all the way up to the root of the DAG.

Each segment in HICAMP is *copy-on-write* because of the immutability of the memory lines. Consequently, passing a segment reference to another thread effectively guarantees a stable snapshot of the segment content at essentially no cost. Exploiting this property, concurrent threads can efficiently execute with *snapshot isolation* [6]; each thread simply needs to save the root PLIDs of all segments of interest. This isolation means that atomic updates do not have read-write conflicts, only write-write conflicts, which are substantially less common. In particular, it allows long running, read-only transactions to be executed without serialization overhead. For example, consider the task of calculating the balance of all bank accounts by bank database for audit or management purposes, by iterating over all accounts, using the state of the accounts at a given point in time. Concurrently, the state of accounts may be changing by ongoing customer transactions, a process which cannot be stalled. Modern databases support this form of query using the *consistent read* capability (effectively providing *snapshot semantics*) at the cost of copying and reverting database blocks to the start time of the long-running transaction. HICAMP supports a comparable facility in hardware largely eliminating this overhead.

A thread in HICAMP uses *non-blocking synchronization* to perform an atomic update of a segment by:

1. saving the root PLID for the original segment
2. modifying the segment and producing a new root PLID
3. using a *compare-and-swap* (CAS) instruction to atomically replace the original root PLID with the new root PLID, if the root

[2] A portion of the memory can operate in a conventional, non-deduplicated mode for memory regions that are expected to be modified frequently, such as thread stacks, which can be accessed with conventional read and write operations.

[3] The tags for words in the memory lines are stored in the ECC bits, using bits that are not needed for ECC at a line granularity (e.g. commodity DRAM chips with ECC contain 8 ECC bits per 64-bit of data yet for 16-byte lines 9 ECC bits are sufficient to implement standard *single-error-correcting-double-error-detecting* (SEC-DED) code [20]). Error detection can be further improved using the intrinsic properties of the HICAMP memory system as described in Section 3.1.

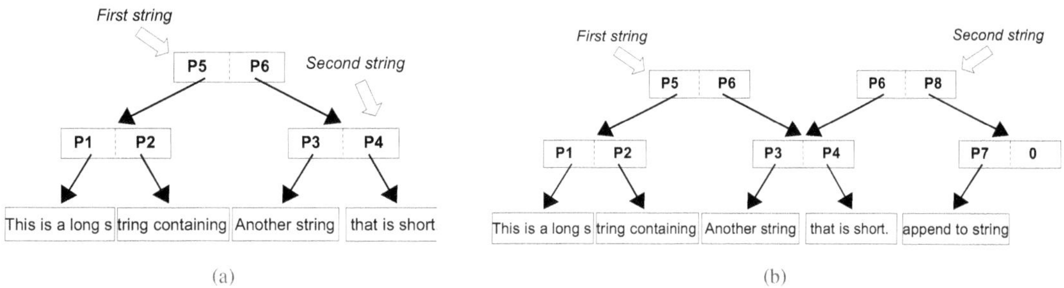

Figure 1: Two segment DAGs representing two strings

PLID for the segment has not been changed by another thread (and otherwise retrying as with conventional CAS).

In effect, the inexpensive (logical) copy and copy-on-write in HICAMP makes Herlihy's theoretical construction showing CAS as sufficient [21] actually practical to use in real applications. Because of the line-level duplicate suppression, HICAMP also maximizes the sharing between the original version of the segment and the new one. If the second string in Figure 1a is modified to add the extra characters "append to string", the memory then contains the segment corresponding to the second string, sharing all the lines of the original segment, simply extended with new lines to store the additional content and the extra parent lines necessary to form the DAG, as shown in Figure 1b.

2.3 Virtual Segment Map

A HICAMP segment is referenced in software using a *Virtual Segment ID* (VSID) that is mapped to the segment's root PLID, through a virtual segment map. Each virtual segment map is implemented either as a HICAMP array or in the conventional part of the memory, indexed by VSID and containing the following fields: `[rootPLID,height,flags]`. Flags are used to indicate read-only access, merge-update (described later) or to indicate a weak reference, i.e. a reference that should be zeroed when the segment is reclaimed, rather than prevent its reclamation.

Each software object corresponds to a segment. Software asks the memory system for a segment whenever it wants to create an object. When software needs one data structure to refer to another (e.g. object O1 needs to refer to O2), then an object's VSID is stored as the reference (O2 is represented by VSID S2; O1 stores S2 as one of its data members). When the contents of O2 are updated, the entry in the virtual segment map corresponding to S2 is updated to point to the new root PLID, and thus the other referencing objects (e.g. O1) do not have to change their references. VSIDs are protected by tags in memory, similar to PLIDs.

When the segment map itself is implemented as a HICAMP segment indexed by VSID, multiple segments can be updated by one atomic update/commit of the segment map. In particular, the revised segments are not visible to other threads until the commit of the revised segment map takes place. A segment map can be implemented in conventional memory, updating individual entries directly, when this property is not required.

There is no need for conventional address translation in HICAMP because inter-process isolation is achieved by the protected references. In particular, a process can only access data that it creates or to which it is passed a reference. Moreover, a reference (VSID) can be passed as read-only, restricting the process from updating the root PLID in the corresponding virtual segment map entry. Thus, a thread can efficiently share objects with other threads by simply passing the VSID, achieving the same protection as separate address spaces but without the IPC communication overheads forced by conventional virtual memory systems. Here, the segment mapping acts similar to a page table and virtual memory mechanism in a conventional architecture, but the "address translation" only occurs on the first access to the segment, not on every access to each data element.

3. Implementation

The HICAMP architecture is implementable using *conventional* DRAM, with reasonable hardware complexity and performance, avoiding any need for power-intensive hardware CAM memory, as is described in the following subsections.

3.1 Memory System

To implement *lookup by content*, the main memory is divided into hash buckets and each line is stored in a bucket corresponding to a hash of its contents (Figure 2). Each hash bucket is mapped to a single DRAM row. To further optimize the fetch by content, each hash bucket includes a secondary hash map of the line content to 8-bit *signatures* indicating the entries in the hash bucket, which could possibly contain the specified content. Signatures are stored in one line to reduce access latency (Figure 2). The lookup by content operation consists of the following steps:

1. calculate the hash and signature values
2. read the signature line in the corresponding hash bucket
3. compare the calculated and read signatures
4. if one or more signatures match, the corresponding data lines are read from memory and compared to the given content
5. if a data line matches, its PLID is returned
6. if there is no signature/data line match, the line is allocated and assigned a PLID, as follows:
   (a) an empty way in the hash bucket is found by checking the signature line for a zero signature
   (b) the PLID is assigned to be the *concatenation* of the way number and the hash bucket number (Figure 2)
   (c) the signature line is updated and written back to DRAM
   (d) the data content of the line is placed in the HICAMP cache

The common case of lookup by content incurs two line reads from DRAM when the line is present, i.e. read of the signature line and data line, because the probability of signature match for lines with different content is small[4]. When the line is not present, the common case of lookup by content requires a read of the signature line and a write of the signature byte. The data line itself is written

[4] For example, with twelve 16-byte data lines per hash bucket and 8-bit signatures the probability of false positives, i.e. a signature match without data line match, is less than 5%.

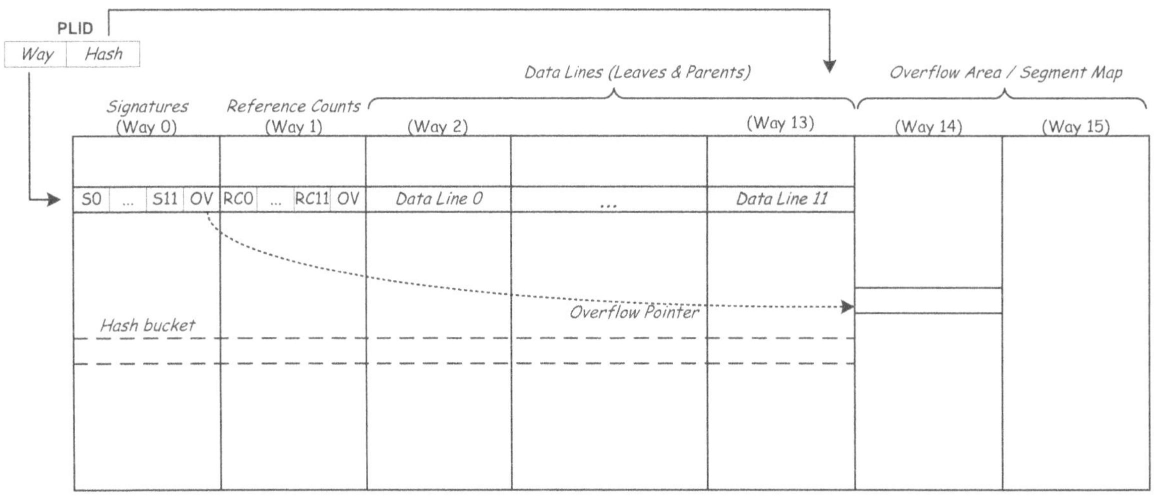

Figure 2: Main memory organization (16-byte lines)

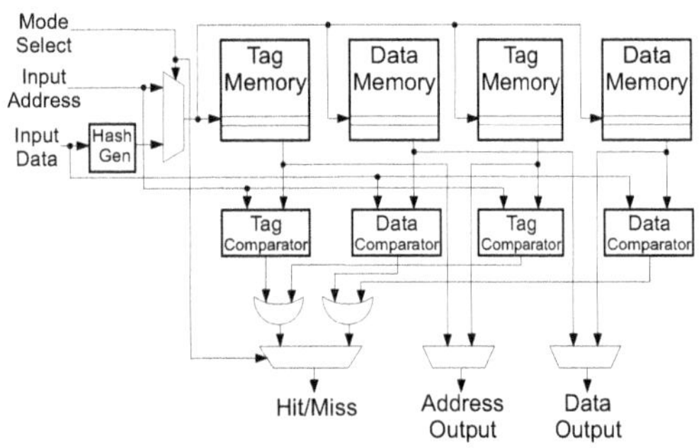

Figure 3: HICAMP cache

into the last level cache (LLC) and written into the main memory upon eviction from LLC if it is not de-allocated before then. Note that DRAM commands for performing the lookup operation access the same DRAM row, thereby minimizing DRAM command bandwidth, energy and latency. The line is written to a separate overflow area when the designated hash bucket is full.

Additionally, by recomputing the hash of the contents when a line is read from memory and comparing it to the hash bucket number where the line is read from, HICAMP can effectively increase the error-detection capabilities of the memory system.

The HICAMP cache, like the main HICAMP memory, supports two fundamental operations: read and lookup-by-content. Figure 3 shows the structure of the cache. The read operation accepts a PLID (i.e. the address) and returns a cache line of content. Thus, the read operation is essentially the same as in a conventional cache: the PLID is used to generate an index into the cache, tags of all ways within the indexed set are compared, and if a tag matches, the data is returned.

To support an efficient lookup-by-content operation, the HICAMP cache is designed such that each main memory hash bucket maps to only one cache set (lines from multiple hash buckets may map to a single cache set, but lines from a single hash bucket cannot map to multiple cache sets). This mapping is achieved simply by indexing the cache with a subset of the hash bits contained in the PLID. Because this indexing maps a hash bucket to exactly one cache set, the following key property is achieved: given the hash of a line content, only a single index in the cache needs to be searched. Thus, when a lookup operation is issued to the HICAMP cache, the hash of the line is first computed, and this provides an index into the cache set in which that data could be found. The data lines within that cache set are then compared with the provided content. If a match is found, the tag of the matching way is read and used to recompose the PLID, which is returned in response to the lookup-by-content operation.

For caches with high associativity, the lookup-by-content operation in the cache can be optimized by using tag bits to reduce the number of wide content comparisons required. Only a subset of the computed hash bits are used for indexing into the cache, thus the remaining hash bits are part of the cache tags. By comparing these tag bits to the calculated hash bits, the HICAMP cache can efficiently filter out ways that cannot contain the content.

Lines in HICAMP are reference counted by hardware, managed similar to a software implementation of reference counting. In particular, when a line reference count goes to zero, it is de-allocated by writing zeros to the corresponding signature. The line reference count is set to one when the line is created and is incremented by each lookup by content operation that matches to that line. The reference count of a line is decremented when a PLID reference to the line is overwritten, either in another line or in the virtual segment map. The most challenging aspect to implement in hardware is de-allocation of a line that recursively causes many other lines to be de-allocated; this is handled with a hardware state machine.

To reduce the number of DRAM operations, reference counts are also cached in the HICAMP cache. For example, when the line is allocated by lookup operation its reference count is written in the LLC and propagated to DRAM only when the line is evicted, if it was not de-allocated before that.

There is no traditional cache coherence problem for data lines because lines are immutable and can thus exist in multiple caches without conventional coherence protocol overheads. However, before an immutable data line can be de-allocated, it must be invalidated in all caches (e.g. using a protocol similar to invalidation-based broadcast or directory protocol). De-allocation is performed in the background and is not on the critical execution path; therefore, unlike cache coherent architectures, cache-line invalidation will not limit HICAMP's performance. However, the virtual segment map is mutable and will require a cache coherence protocol.

The question of scalability is a topic for future work. With no need for locks, semaphores, or cache coherence for data lines,

HICAMP accrues a significant scalability advantage over conventional shared memory architectures.

3.2 Path and Data Compaction

HICAMP applies both path and data compaction to each segment DAG to reduce the access cost (path length through the DAG) as well as the memory overhead of the segment DAG structure. *Path compaction* encodes the path to the line along with the PLID, storing it in the parent node, when a parent DAG node would otherwise have only one non-zero element (PLID). For example, in Figure 4a, the path to the leaf "Data" line is compacted into one entry in the root line, eliminating P2 and P3. The path is encoded using the unused bits of the non-zero PLID[5]. Note that the logical height of the DAG is stored in the corresponding virtual segment map entry and is not affected by such compaction.

HICAMP *data compaction* removes the most significant zero bytes from a word and inlines the resulting value directly into the parent line when possible. For example, in Figure 4b, S1 and S0 are values that can be represented as 32-bit values, and so are compacted into a 64-bit field in the parent line. More significantly, an array of small integers (less than 255) is compacted so that each element is stored in a single byte. Inserting a value that is larger only affects the compaction of that element and neighboring elements that can no longer be compacted.

Both forms of compaction can be applied multiple times in different levels and portions of the DAG, decreasing the number of memory reads to access data and reducing the DAG storage overhead. In particular, in a segment that contains a large number of zeroes, the interior nodes are compacted to provide an efficient sparse representation.

3.3 Iterator Registers

A HICAMP *iterator register* is an extended form of the conventional index or address register, extended to support efficient access to data in segments by storing the path through the DAG to its current line position (Figure 5). In HICAMP, each memory access is made through an iterator register. An ALU operation that specifies a source operand as an iterator register accesses the value of the current offset of the iterator register within the associated segment. A HICAMP processor ideally has a comparable number of iterator registers to the number of general-purpose registers in a conventional processor, e.g. 16 to 32 registers.

Upon initialization with a specific VSID and offset, an iterator register loads and caches the path to the element at the specified offset in the DAG. Upon increment of the iterator register, it moves to the next non-null element in the segment. In particular, the hardware detects if the next portion of the DAG refers to the zero line and moves the iterator register's position to the next non-zero memory line. The register only loads new lines on the path to the next element beyond those it already has cached. In the case of the next location being contained in the same line, no memory access is required to access the next element. Using the knowledge of the DAG structure, an iterator register can also automatically prefetch memory lines in response to sequential access to the segment.

Using an iterator register, sequential access to a segment representing a dense array is at most two times the number of lines of accessing the same segment stored in conventional memory system[6]. Moreover, in some cases, the overall cost of a HICAMP array can be less expensive because it does not need to be copied to be dynamically grown, as is typically the case in a conventional architecture. Also, with a sparse array such as a sparse matrix or associative array, the cache line references can be comparable or less, given the data and instruction overhead required for these software implementations and the deduplication of lines that HICAMP provides.

A store operation updates the current data element pointed to by the iterator register. To support efficient incremental updates, the iterator register caches an updated line as a *transient line*[7], namely a line in a pre-defined, per-processor area of the memory that operates outside of the normal duplicate-suppressed region. It also tags the update to indicate the requisite changes to the parent nodes on the path through the DAG. Then, after potentially multiple changes to a line (and potentially many lines), when the iterator register is "committed" by software, the transient lines are converted to permanent (duplicate-suppressed) lines using lookup by content operations, and a new root PLID for the modified segment is acquired, as described earlier. (An iterator register also supports an abort action, in which case the modifications are discarded, reverting the segment to the original state, i.e. old root PLID.)

Using the transient lines, the cost of allocating content-unique lines at the leaf and all the way up to the root of the DAG is deferred until the commit point, offering the ability to amortize this cost over many writes. In the extreme, a local temporary array can be created by a procedure using the transient lines, used and discarded and so never committed.

Overall, the iterator register provides a hardware construct that supports iterator concept in most modern programming languages as well as in SQL. Moreover, unlike conventional programming language constructs, it efficiently supports the *snapshot and atomic update semantics* of the SQL cursor.

3.4 Merge-update

HICAMP supports *merge-update* of segments to facilitate updates of high contention data structures such as maps, queues and counters. For example, if two non-conflicting entries are added concurrently to the same directory, represented as a segment, merge-update produces a segment that corresponds to the directory with these two entries added, rather than aborting one of the concurrent transactions. In more detail, if a segment is marked as merge-update, when a thread detects during a CAS that the root PLID has been modified by another thread (resulting in a new DAG for the segment), the system attempts to merge the thread's copy with the updated segment content by performing the following steps for each line offset:

1. compute the difference between the "original" segment line and the "modified" segment line
2. apply this difference to the "current" line content of the segment
3. add this line to the "merged" segment at the current offset

If the segment contains a PLID field, as would be the case with a directory, the field in the "current" segment is required to be either the same as the "original" segment or the same as the "modified" segment. That is, the two updates cannot store distinct PLIDs in the same field; otherwise the merge-update fails. The uniqueness of segments and subsegments allows merge-update to efficiently identify sub-DAGs of the "current" and "modified" segment that are identical, and skip the line-by-line actions above for such a sub-DAG.

[5] Here, "unused" refers to high-order bits of the PLID not used because they are not needed to address the available DRAM. For example, with a 32-byte line, a 32-bit PLID is sufficient to access 128 gigabytes of DRAM.

[6] For example, with 16-byte lines and 64-bit PLIDs, the DAG overhead is at most 2x in terms of memory space and line reads for sequential access. With longer 32-byte or 64-byte lines this overhead is smaller.

[7] Transient memory lines require no cache coherency because the lines are allocated per core and converted to immutable lines before they are made visible to other cores.

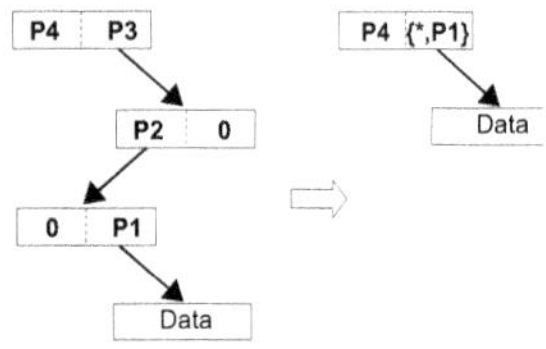

(a) Path compaction

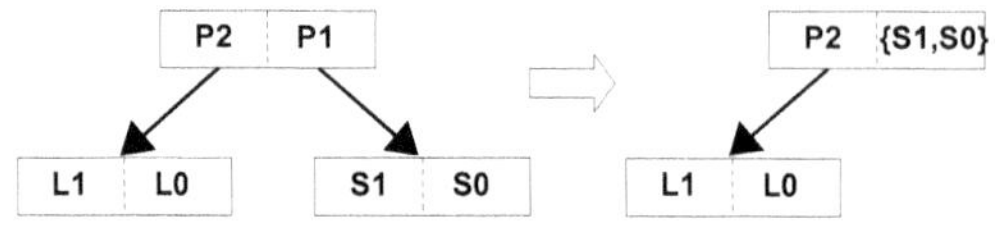

(b) Data compaction

Figure 4: Compaction

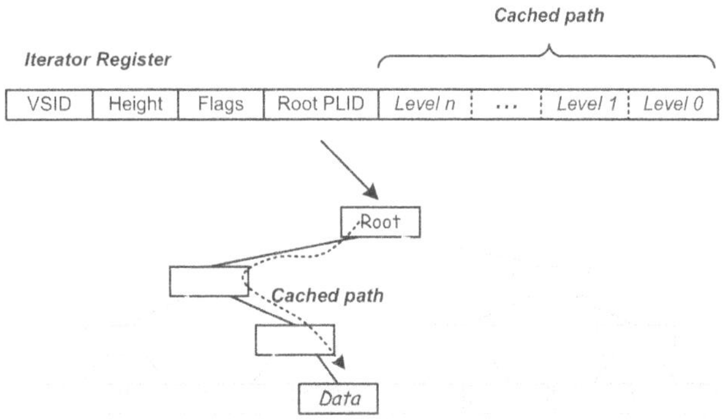

Figure 5: Iterator register

Merge-update can also apply to a segment of counters. In this case, the difference produces the increment applied by the thread, which is then added to the value in the "current" segment to produce the new count.

This capability can be exported to software level as an mCAS operation defined in pseudo-code as:

```
bool mCAS( old, curAddr, new ) {
   try {
     cur = *curAddr;
     while(!CAS(old,cur,new)) {
       new = merge(old,cur,new);
       old = cur;
     }
   } catch(...) {
      return false; /* merge failed */
   }
   return true;
}
```

Here, the merge operation performs the merge-update and returns true or else fails and returns false.

Merge-update addresses a recognized weakness of non-blocking synchronization (NBS) relative to lock-based synchronization, namely repeated aborts in the case of high contention structures. In particular, merge-update easily handles concurrent updates to maps, queues and counters, the most common high-contention data structures, only aborting when the updates are logically conflicting, which is expected to be rare.

4. HICAMP Programming Model

The HICAMP programming model is similar to a conventional *object oriented programming* (OOP) with minor changes for snapshotting/transactional behavior.

Each software object in HICAMP is mapped to a segment identified by a VSID and each pointer field in an object stores a VSID corresponding to the object to which it is pointing, or zero if a null reference. Each software iterator is implemented as an iterator register when the iterator is active.

4.1 Arrays and Maps

A software array is implemented as a HICAMP segment. Unlike an array in a conventional memory system, it can be extended in length dynamically without reallocation and copy; the DAG is simply extended with additional lines. This property also means that a *buffer overflow* bug or compromise cannot cause another object to be overwritten. If the array is sparse, it is automatically stored in a space-efficient form because of path and data compaction.

Thus, for example, an ordered collection of objects indexed by a 64-bit time stamp can be efficiently represented as a segment with the VSID of the object stored at the numeric index equal to its time stamp. In contrast, the same collection in a conventional memory system would require a red-black tree or similar data structure to handle the ordering, have a large index size and the sparsity of the data relative to the index, with attendant costs in memory accesses for performing lookup, rebalancing and locking for concurrency. An ordered collection indexed by a string value can be realized using two arrays, one mapping the root PLID of the string segment to the corresponding value and a second segment for storing the values in order for iteration. The memory deduplication minimizes the space overhead that this two-array solution would incur in a conventional memory.

A map is implemented as a sparse array, indexed by unique root PLID of the key, which can be an arbitrary byte string. Writing to the map entails storing through the iterator register. With HICAMP deduplication and path and data compaction, this structure incurs memory access overhead comparable to the various software tree data structures, which also require rebalancing. It entails more memory accesses than a map implemented as a contiguous array in a conventional architecture. However, it provides a far superior worst-case performance guarantee compared to a conventional implementation of a hash table. Moreover, it avoids the overhead incurred by the hash table for computing the hash on the key and further accessing the key to verify the match. Finally, iteration over the HICAMP map is significantly more efficient than over a conventional memory hash table that is sparsely populated (which is required to avoid collisions and chaining). In general, all the data structures we have considered have an efficient HICAMP implementation.

4.2 Iterators

The software concept of an iterator, an established design pattern for accessing data structures[8], maps directly onto the HICAMP iterator register. For example, iteration over a collection appears conventional:

```
for( it = obj.begin(); it != obj.end(); ++it ) {
  *it = newVal;
}
it->tryCommit();
```

[8] As provided in many programming languages and libraries such as C++ STL, Java and C#.

The ability to increment position pointed by the register to the next non-null element in the segment allows efficient iteration over sparse vectors and associative arrays. DAG prefetching and parent node caching in iterator register further support efficient access.

Moreover, the snapshot isolation provides superior *iterator semantics* compared to that feasible on a conventional architecture. Specifically, an iterator can iterate over the collection, being assured of visiting the collection exactly as it was when iterator register was loaded (snapshot was taken), independent of the actions of other threads. In contrast, conventional languages and systems resort to exceptions or undefined behavior when concurrent updates occur, a questionable approach for multi-core systems.

4.3 Using Merge-Update

A data structure for which merge-update semantics are acceptable can be updated using mCAS (Section 3.4) rather than CAS, thereby allowing many conflicts to be resolved more efficiently and eliminating an application level retry most of the time. For example, concurrent insert and delete operations on the key-value map that do not modify the same entry are resolved by merge-update rather than redoing the application-level operation (this is because an insert operation adds a value to a location which was zero and a delete operation sets a non-zero location to zero). Similarly, concurrent updates to counters can be resolved to produce the desired sum in a counter without application retry. High-contention queues can be implemented similarly, using the merge-update operation to store the queue data in a segment and merge-update of the counters to keep track of head and tail locations.

4.4 Example: Memcached Implementation

Memcached [15] is a practical example of how facilities provided by HICAMP can be effectively used to implement a real and performance-critical application. Memcached has a relatively simple API. The main commands are set key-value pair, get value corresponding to a key, and delete key-value pair. (There are also more complicated commands like add, replace, increment/decrement, and CAS but for brevity we limit our discussion to basic commands.) Its implementation on a conventional architecture is conceptually simple: a hash table is used for a key-value map.

However, in practice the implementation is complicated because the map is accessed as a separate process or processes over socket-based communication channels. Further complications arise from conventional memory management issues: the hash table needs resizing, which is performed by a separate thread. To avoid memory fragmentation and overheads of malloc() memcached pre-allocates user configured memory quota and uses a custom slab memory allocator. Reference counting is used to keep track of the allocated memory and to ensure that a chunk of data is not de-allocated before an I/O operation is completed. Additionally, a time-out mechanism is necessary to avoid memory leak that can arise from rare corner-case conditions of reference counting.

In contrast, a memcached implementation on HICAMP architecture is straightforward: the map of key-value pairs (KVP) is implemented as a HICAMP (sparse) array indexed by the root PLID of key strings. Each entry of the array stores the root PLID for the associated value or zero if no associated value is present in the map. HICAMP deduplication ensures the uniqueness of the root PLID for any given key.

At the beginning of processing a get command, a client thread (re)loads an iterator register with a read-only reference to the KVP map segment, at the offset corresponding to the desired key. Thus, for a memcached command that does not modify the map, access to the map does not require interprocess communication, locking or any other form of synchronization[9]. In a typical memcached workload such commands are 90-99% of all issued commands. Because of the HICAMP snapshot isolation, each client thread is completely isolated from any concurrent updates to the map. Moreover, because of the non-blocking synchronization, there is no interference between threads that can cause blocking or deadlock.

In the HICAMP implementation, a separate thread can perform updates, having a read-write reference to the map segment. Other threads queue update requests with this special thread. Alternatively, client threads can be trusted to update the map directly by providing them with a read-write reference to the map segment. In this case, an update is atomically committed when the new root PLID for the revised map is written to the corresponding segment map entry. Because this write is hardware-atomic, a client process cannot leave the map in an inconsistent state, even after being halted at an arbitrary point in its execution[10]. If the client fails before the root PLID is updated in the segment map, the reference to the revised DAG is eliminated and all the lines corresponding to the modifications are reclaimed, leaving the system in the original state. Thus, because of snapshot isolation and atomic update, HICAMP provides the hardware support equivalent to separate address spaces, while allowing direct access to shared data structures.

Memcached commands that update the key-value map can benefit from *merge-update* (Section 3.4), which eliminates re-execution of commands unless there is a true data conflict (Section 5.1.1).

Similar approaches can enhance access to shared state in applications beyond memcached, for example, an in-memory relational database. A client thread with a read-only reference to the database can access the state and process a query with its own private snapshot of the database state. It constructs a *view* as a new segment that specifies the result of the query, while referencing data directly in the database itself. Updates can be performed either by a designated updater thread or by the (trusted) client threads.

In summary, HICAMP provides substantial benefits to established software structures. Nevertheless, there is a long and sorry history of computer architectures that purport to do this, yet result in implementations that are slower than a careful software implementation on top of the conventional Von Neumann architecture, making these architectures unviable. Our evaluation in the next section addresses this legitimate concern.

5. Evaluation

Our preliminary evaluation of the HICAMP architecture uses both analytical techniques and software simulations with different data sets and traces, in various specific application domains. The three key measures that we consider are: off-chip memory traffic, reduction in memory footprint, and concurrency overhead. The conventional architecture was simulated using the PTLSim [33] cycle accurate processor simulator and DineroIV [1] memory hierarchy simulator, while the HICAMP memory system was simulated by a custom model. Both architectures used the same memory system parameters, namely: a 4-way 32 KB L1 data cache, a 16-way 4 MB L2 cache, and 16-byte cache lines. Some experiments use larger line sizes, as noted in the individual subsections.

[9] memcached does not have any ordering requirements for commands from different clients/network connections. Each client/connection is handled by a separate thread which processes commands in order and does not need to enforce any ordering with other connections (or threads that handle them).

[10] This implementation is appropriate when client software can be assumed to be *fail-stop*. If the client software is truly untrusted, i.e. can be malicious, a trusted updating process is required.

5.1 Memcached

The HICAMP implementation of memcached has significant performance advantages over the conventional "separate server" implementation because the socket communication and associated signaling, queuing, and context switching costs are eliminated. The following analysis shows how capabilities of the HICAMP architecture achieve *predictable* and efficient parallel performance.

5.1.1 Concurrent Performance

During execution of a set command, the write and commit of the new key/value pair and associated control state can be performed independent from other threads, because new segments are allocated for these data fields. However, update of the key/value map itself can cause conflict.

For conservative estimation we assume an 8-processor system that performs 200K commands per second [27] and a 10:1 get to set command ratio. One get command is executed every 5 microseconds and one set command is executed every 50 microseconds on average.

To update the key/value map, the software first reloads the iterator register with the root node of the DAG, fetching the path to the leaf node that is to be updated. The reload may well hit in the cache for several lines but assuming worst-case cache misses it would require $log_2(N)$ DRAM reads to access the leaf on average for N KVPs. The leaf line is then updated in the iterator register and the whole path from the leaf to root is regenerated. Because the leaf node is new content, all nodes up to the root of the map ($log_2(N)$ total for 16-byte lines) must be modified.

To perform a lookup for a line with new content, the memory controller reads the signature line and compares stored signatures with the signature of the new line (Section 3.1). If the new content is not present in the memory, the probability of a signature match is small (see footnote in Section 3.1). If there is no match, the memory controller assigns a new PLID for the line. Thus, signature read and compare are on the critical path of acquiring a PLID for new content, but other operations (updating signature line, etc.) are not and can be performed in parallel. Thus, the time to reload and update map segment is $2 \times log_2(N) \times (DRAM\ latency)$. Assuming that N is 10^6 and DRAM latency is 50ns, the total time to update the map is $2 \times 20 \times 50ns = 2\mu s$. The probability of a conflict can be estimated as $2\mu s/50\mu s = 0.04$. This result is not very sensitive to the number of KVPs in the map because of logarithmic dependence, e.g. for N equal to 10^9 the worst-case probability of conflict increases to 0.06. Moreover, for longer 32-byte or 64-byte lines the number of nodes that need to be updated and the probability of conflict decrease proportionally.

In case of a conflict, *merge-update* (Section 3.4) is used to merge changes to the map from the processor whose CAS operation failed with the new version of the map. In this case, the processor reloads the map and compares each level of the DAG with previous version (snapshotted by iterator register). Because two processors are unlikely to write into the same location in the map, new and previous versions have the same content at some level of the DAG. The merging processor reloads all nodes up to this level and regenerates the nodes above all the way to the root. Assuming that updates to the map are uniformly distributed, the probability of conflict one level below the root is 0.5, two levels below root is 0.25, etc. The average latency of merge-update therefore is the sum of a simple geometric series: $2 \times (DRAM\ latency) \times (1+0.5+0.25+...) \approx 4 \times (DRAM\ latency) = 200ns$, which is significantly smaller than the latency of original map update or application-level retry.

If contention on a map is high for merge-updates, the map can be split into an array of segments (i.e. a segment that points to the subsegments), indexed by several bits of the key PLID, while the rest of key PLID bits can be used as offset within the selected subsegment. Such a split would reduce probability of conflict and re-execution even further.

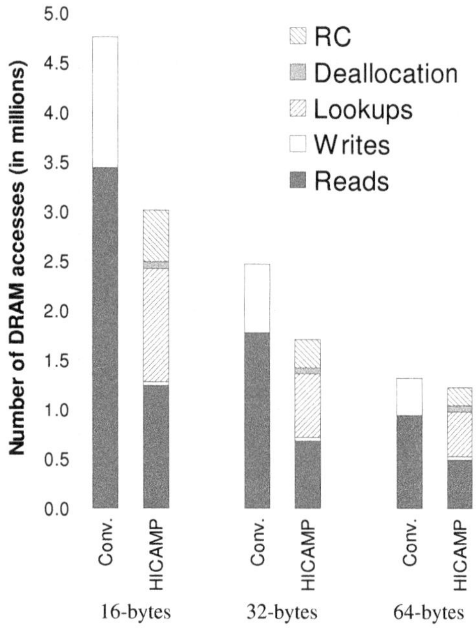

Figure 6: Memcached DRAM accesses

5.1.2 Off-Chip Memory Traffic

Figure 6 shows number of DRAM accesses for both HICAMP and a conventional memory system (using 16-, 32- and 64-byte line sizes) for memcached processing 15000 requests[11]. "Reads" is the number of DRAM reads due to cache misses. "Writes" is the number of DRAM writes due to cache writebacks. For HICAMP, Figure 6 also shows the number of DRAM operations necessary for content lookups[12], line de-allocation and reference counting. For the conventional memory system, we used trace option in VMware Workstation-7.0.0 (build 98145.x86_64) to generate the memory access trace, which includes more than 300 million loads and stores. It was processed by the DineroIV [1] cache simulator to generate DRAM access numbers. As shown in the figure, the number of off-chip DRAM accesses for HICAMP is comparable or smaller than for a conventional memory system.

Beyond these performance benefits, the HICAMP provides memory savings, as described next.

5.1.3 Memory Compaction

Table 1 shows HICAMP data compaction results for several types of data. For text data like HTML web pages and JavaScript scripts, compaction savings range from approximately 1.5x to more than 4x over conventional memory[13]. For binary data image files in compressed JPEG and GIF formats, which result in high-entropy data exhibiting few deduplication opportunities, HICAMP representation incurs a 10% overhead for short lines. Beyond these savings,

[11] These traces and statistics were generated after pre-loading 100000 items into memcached and processing another set of 15000 requests. Memcached items were generated from Facebook web-page dumps (downloaded from Stanford Infolab web-site) to emulate typical memcached dataset. The request trace was generated using a power-law distribution for item frequency and size which is typical for memcached workloads.

[12] Signature line reads/updates and data line reads/writes (Section 3.1).

[13] Compaction is defined as conventional memory requirement divided by the HICAMP memory requirement.

Dataset		Wikipedia webpages May'06	Facebook webpages May'08	Facebook webpages Sept'08	Facebook scripts May'08	Facebook scripts Sept'08	Facebook images May'08	Facebook images Sept'08
Number of items		99957	9741	65122	3106	1467	24827	31155
Total size, Mbytes		3249.58	179.38	3286.81	4.45	0.7	96.17	98.62
Compaction	LS=16	1.71	4.27	1.84	3.17	4.06	0.9	0.93
	LS=32	1.5	3.87	1.83	2.6	3.38	1.03	1.07
	LS=64	1.29	3.11	1.35	2.06	2.29	1.07	1.09

Table 1: Memcached data compaction (LS is line size)

HICAMP also eliminates duplication of data between processes and socket buffers, the size of which can be substantial [27].

We expect the HICAMP architecture to be compelling in other settings, including similar web and database-like applications. For example, some fault-tolerant embedded systems such as 10 Gbps Ethernet switches [5] incorporate a database and numerous client processes to achieve fault-tolerance and in-service software upgrade capability. These systems could use HICAMP to reduce communication overhead and memory duplication while retaining their robustness. Even in more restricted environments, such as hand-held devices, HICAMP could provide protected sharing of data between untrusted applications while providing memory compaction to reduce power demands.

In the completely different domain of high-performance computation, HICAMP also demonstrates substantial benefits, as described next.

5.2 Sparse Matrix Computation

Sparse matrix computations, and, in particular sparse matrix dense vector multiplication (SpMV) [32], are often the critical inner loop of certain applications including general high performance computing (HPC), embedded control systems, linear programming, and convex optimization. For SpMV, performance is limited by memory bandwidth, yet peak bandwidth is not achieved because of the unpredictability of the vector access sequence. Performance as low as 10% of peak FLOP rate has been observed [30]. Thus, the programming language and architecture challenge is supporting efficient execution of sparse matrix computations, particularly in a highly concurrent processing environment [29].

In HICAMP, a general (dense) matrix representation can be used to efficiently represent a sparse matrix, as described earlier, with an iterator providing efficient access to the data. Alternatively, a representation similar to the conventional *compressed sparse row (CSR)* format can also be used. To optimize further, one can recognize that many applications use sparse matrices with a high degree of self-similarity – they are either symmetric or have a high degree of symmetry, or have repeating patterns of non-zero values. To exploit matrix self-similarity, we have used the *symmetric quad-tree format* (QTS) that breaks a matrix into four regions, which have a dimension of an even power of two (and are zero padded if necessary). Sub-matrices A_{11} and A_{22} are stored in the left subtree of the DAG while sub-matrices with A_{12} and $A_{21}{}^T$ stored in the right subtree. If the sub-matrices are symmetric, A_{12} and $A_{21}{}^T$ are equal and hence have the same PLID as their root.

Some sparse matrices with little self-similarity in non-zero values are not compacted well by simple sparse array or quad tree representation, but still have a high degree of non-zero pattern similarity. In many of these cases, the underlying structure of this matrix can still be exploited using the *non-zero dense* (NZD) format where two HICAMP segments represent a matrix: one segment stores the non-zero pattern as a quad-tree and exploits pattern symmetry and self-similarity, while a separate segment is filled to be nearly dense with the original non-zero values.

Category	Matrices	Savings	StdDev
All	100	62.7%	36.5%
Non-symmetric	77	58.5%	33.9%
Symmetric	23	76.9%	41.8%
FEMs	29	70.7%	40.2%
LPs	15	43.0%	31.7%

Table 2: Sparse Matrix Compaction

The DAG structure lends itself to tree-recursive algorithms and many important operations in linear algebra can be naturally expressed in such form [18]. During tree traversal, zero and duplicate sub-matrices can be detected by PLID comparison. Such optimizations reduce number of memory accesses and increase the performance of the memory system.

5.2.1 Off-Chip Memory Traffic

The SpMV kernel was used to compare HICAMP to a conventional memory system in terms of number of accesses made to the off-chip memory. We compare a HICAMP SpMV algorithm with duplicate sub-matrix detection against a conventional CSR SpMV algorithm or against a symmetric CSR SpMV algorithm [24], as appropriate. In HICAMP, no distinction was made for symmetric matrices. Our test matrices were pulled from the University of Florida Sparse Matrix Collection [10] and represent a variety of application domains.

Considering only matrices that are larger than the L2 cache size, the results indicate that HICAMP reduces off-chip memory accesses on average by 20%.[14] Figure 7 plots the ratio of off-chip memory accesses in HICAMP to a conventional architecture using a $\log_2$ scale; matrix size is plotted on the abscissa. As shown in the figure, for most of the matrices HICAMP reduces main memory accesses by compacting the sparse matrix and reducing the storage requirements, as described next.

5.2.2 Memory Compaction

We compared the storage requirements for 100 large sparse matrices when stored in HICAMP versus the conventional memory, which uses CSR. In CSR, an m by n matrix with nnz non-zero entries requires $8 \times (1.5nnz + 0.5m)$ bytes (assuming 8 byte double precision floats and 4 byte integer indices). For a symmetric sparse matrix, the term nnz is replaced by $nnz_{\text{on-diagonal}} + 0.5nnz_{\text{off-diagonal}}$. We compare the best-known HICAMP format (QTS or NZD) against CSR, or symmetric CSR, as appropriate.

Table 2 lists the ratio of the matrix size in HICAMP versus conventional architecture, categorizing matrices in different classes and problem domains, while Figure 8 shows the same ratio for all matrices. Matrices are the same size or smaller in HICAMP except for a few having negligible increases due to the DAG overhead. The overall average is 62.7 bytes in HICAMP per 100 bytes on

[14] Excluding a matrix that was compacted by 4000x. Including this matrix the overall savings are 38%

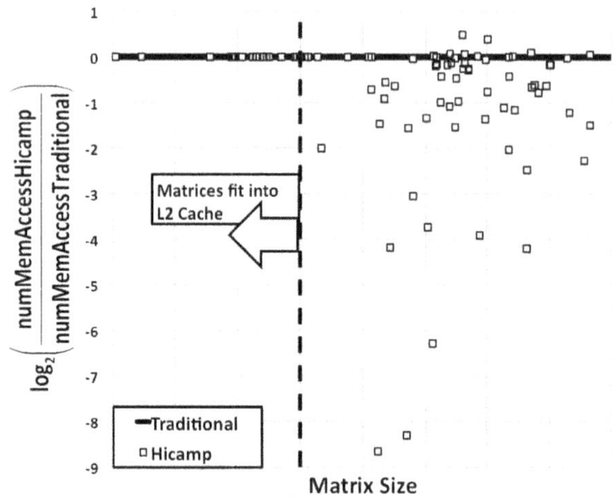

Figure 7: Main memory accesses for SpMV

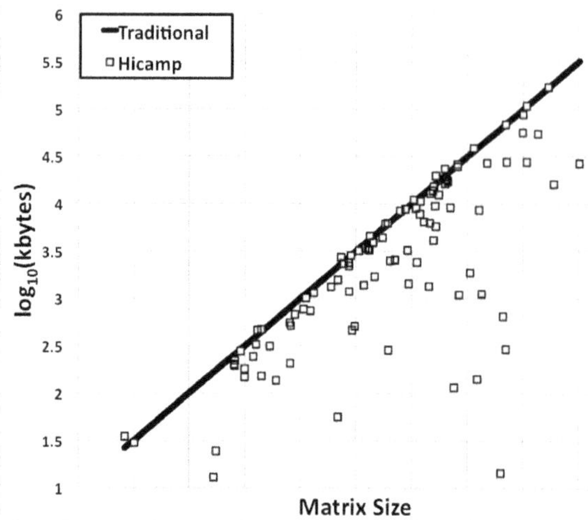

Figure 8: Sparse matrix memory footprint

a conventional architecture, indicating that HICAMP achieves significant data compaction over a broad range of matrices.

In addition to improving off-chip memory traffic and storage footprint, HICAMP also allows efficient, highly parallel execution of sparse matrix computations by partitioning the result matrix among K threads. Each thread computes from the previous matrix results, preserved by the snapshot isolation, generating the result partition it is assigned. At the end of a round, each partition is merged into the new result matrix, which is then made available as read-only data for the next round. Thus, the snapshot isolation, logical copy and merge-update provide architectural support for a simple but efficient programming model of concurrent matrix computation while ensuring protection between threads.

5.3 Virtual Machine Hosting

Virtual machine (VM) hosting is an important commercial application, which places significant demands on operating systems and hypervisors. It also provides a means for HICAMP to run legacy code, i.e. software designed for the conventional Von Neumann architecture. With an increasing number of cores and faster network connections allowing an increasing number of VMs per physical host, there can be a significant amount of duplication of code and data within the physical memory of the host, given duplicate copies of the same or similar operating systems and applications.

Some VM hypervisors such as VMware ESX server check for duplicate pages in software and replace multiple copies with a single shared copy in the machine memory [31]. Further research [17] has illustrated the benefits of sharing at finer granularity than a page. However, with the increasing size of physical memory, deduplication beyond just static code pages can incur significant software overhead. Moreover, with large (2 megabyte) pages, motivated by quadratic cost of nested page table lookup and reducing the size of page tables [7], the page-level sharing is significantly less effective.

HICAMP automatically provides fine-grain sharing at the line level without software overhead and reduces the memory footprint of hosted VMs. This compaction can potentially reduce the number of off-chip DRAM accesses, improving performance, reducing power and increasing overall efficiency.

To evaluate HICAMP for virtual machine hosting, we used the VMmark virtualization benchmark (version 1.1.1) [2] from VMware. VMmark organizes units of work in tiles, where each tile contains six virtual machines. There is a variety of 32-bit and 64-bit operating systems as well as various types of workloads in each tile (e.g. database, mail server, java server, etc.). We evaluate HICAMP's memory consumption when loading a number of virtual machines and tiles into the system.

We took snapshots of the memory of virtual machines while running benchmark workloads. These snapshots were then loaded into HICAMP's memory system simulator to compute the total number of memory lines required and were also analyzed to determine the number of duplicate pages. Figure 9 shows consumed memory when scaling number of VMs for each of the workloads in a VMmark tile and compares it to an ideal page sharing scheme where duplicate pages are detected and shared instantaneously. While not realistic, this provides an upper bound on how well a page sharing algorithm at the OS or hypervisor level can save memory. In practice, the benefits are less than this ideal scheme because scanning memory and detecting duplicate pages consumes processor cycles and occurs gradually over time.

Figure 10 shows the same comparison for VMmark tiles when loaded as a whole. HICAMP compacts memory footprint of VMs by a factor between 1.86x and 10.87x, while in ideal page sharing, the compaction ranges between 1.44x-5.21x. For tiles, HICAMP compacts the memory more than 3.55x while ideal page sharing compacts it only 1.8x.

Overall, HICAMP simplifies the OS/hypervisor, reduces processing overhead and improves the utilization of memory by providing transparent data sharing in hardware.

6. Related Work

Fresh Breeze [11] supports software structuring similar to HICAMP, providing protected "global" references and DAG structure support for sparse matrices. However, Fresh Breeze is focused primarily on supporting functional programming, not fault-tolerant thread isolation. It does not support a segment map or memory deduplication and compaction mechanisms of HICAMP. Fresh Breeze also does not appear to support an iterator register mechanism for efficient access to memory, instead relying exclusively on SMT to accommodate the additional latency to memory, and does not appear to support merge update.

Transactional Memory (TM) has been investigated by a variety of efforts, starting from the Herlihy and Moss paper [22]. However, TM does not provide isolation between threads. Moreover, TM uses the update-in-place approach to transactions so it suffers from read-write conflicts. For example, a transaction iterating over a large

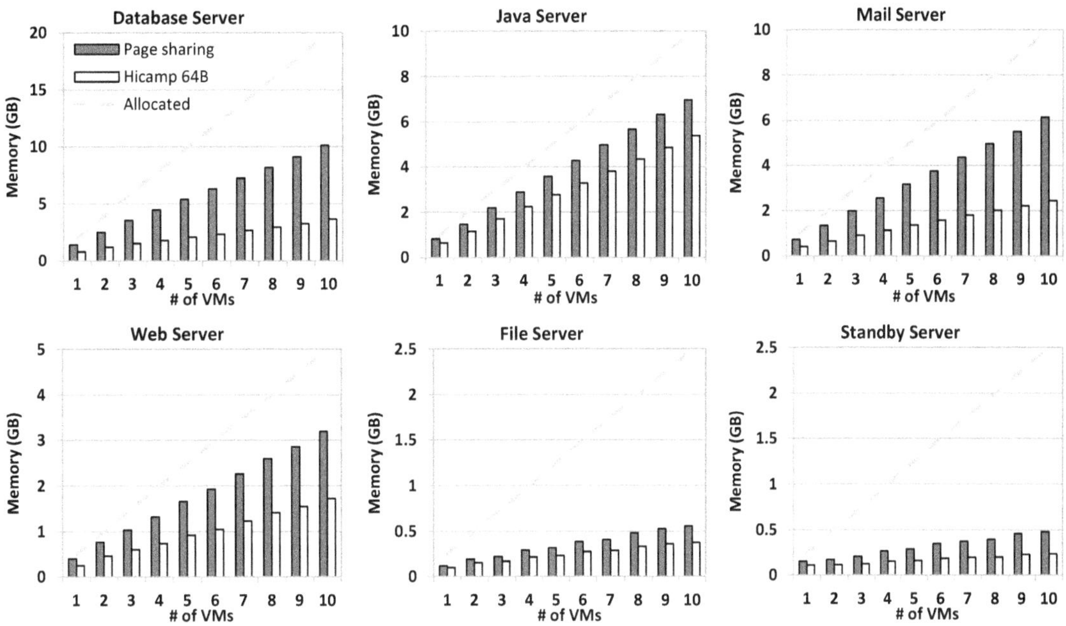

Figure 9: Memory consumption of individual VMs in a VMmark tile

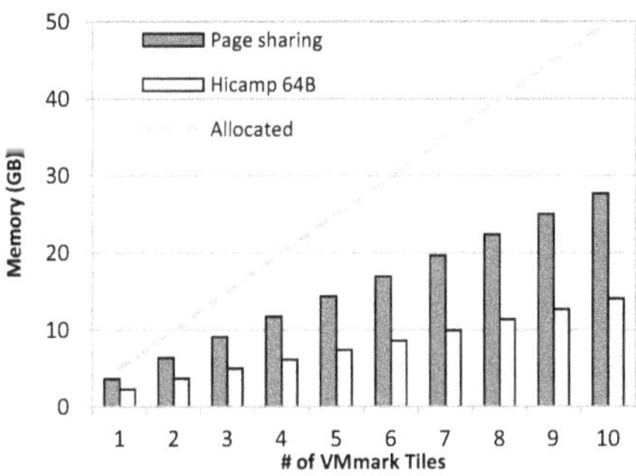

Figure 10: Memory consumption of VMmark tiles

collection can be repeatedly aborted by updates to the collection. In contrast, HICAMP implements an alternative approach based on snapshot isolation [6], so it only has write-write conflicts, which are far less frequent.

Hardware Snapshotting has been proposed separately [9]. However, the support in this case is coarse-grain, restricted in number of snapshots, and focused on actions such as checkpointing, not changing the application software execution semantics as in HICAMP. Snapshotting was also proposed as an extension of software transactional memory [26], however, it exhibits significant overheads of maintaining and tracking multiple versions of data in software.

Hardware support for *non-blocking synchronization* dates back many years to CAS on the early IBM computers and double-CAS on the Motorola 68040. It is known to have significant advantages over locking [16]. In HICAMP, a simple CAS suffices to update complex data structures and avoids the so-called ABA problem. Reference semantics, hardware support for data structures, and in particular the segment map mechanism allow atomic updates across multiple objects/data structures.

Memory Compression has been proposed for main memory [14], caches [4, 12] or both [13, 19]. A mergeable cache architecture was designed [8] to de-duplicate the content of second level cache. This approach only supports deduplication for cache lines that have the same virtual address, using page coloring to ensure that such lines are located in the same set. The HICAMP architecture supports general deduplication in main memory and caches, thereby reducing memory bandwidth and footprint.

VMware [31] provides transparent page sharing to reduce duplicate memory content at the page level. This process is configured by default to take place at a time scale of minutes in order to minimize processing overhead, so it only identifies static pages of long-running applications. The Difference Engine [17] project carries this direction further to detect intra-page differences, increasing software overhead and complexity. HICAMP provides finer-grain sharing in hardware without such overhead. However, we regard the key advantage HICAMP provides over software page sharing as providing line granularity in the presence of the trend to 2 megabyte pages [7].

There are some similarities between HICAMP and the Intel iAPX 432 project [3] including the protected segments and the support for higher-level programming constructs. However, the 432 was focused on providing protection with its segments and did not provide the functional and performance benefits HICAMP does of deduplication, snapshot semantics and atomic update. The 432 also suffered because of the limited gate count per chip that was available 30 years ago, forcing it to be implemented across multiple chips, with severe performance implications. In contrast, HICAMP appears to easily fit within current processor gate counts and tackles a key problem of modern applications and processors, namely the performance overhead/limitations arising from the memory system.

7. Conclusions

In this paper, we have presented HICAMP, a general-purpose computer architecture designed to address the key challenges facing programming languages and operating systems to support demanding complex, concurrent software on multi-core processors. It directly challenges conventional wisdom by providing hardware support for key programming language features, including variable-sized objects, iterators, "const" access, associative arrays and sparse matrices. It also supports non-blocking synchronization and structured data prefetching. It further supports snapshot semantics and atomic update, building on the proven benefits of these properties in database systems [6]. Finally, it provides memory deduplication at cache line granularity, complementing the page-sharing mechanisms in many operating systems and virtual machine hypervisors.

The protected segment references that arise in this architecture together with the concurrency-safe data structure support allow multiple threads to safely share structured data without the space and IPC overhead of separate address spaces and without the loss of isolation associated with conventional shared memory threads.

Even with these significant benefits, HICAMP is practical to implement with conventional DRAM, with an acceptable level of hardware complexity, and can achieve competitive, if not superior, performance for appropriately structured applications. We also show that it can provide performance benefits for existing software applications running in a virtualization environment, based on its deduplication capability.

HICAMP performance is a key focus of our results in this paper. Our evaluation shows that HICAMP provides significantly better DRAM bandwidth utilization for applications structured to take advantage of its features compared to conventional architectures. In particular, our measurements show that the reduced memory footprint provided by deduplication, together with the iterator register support, including data and path compaction, largely counterbalances the extra memory accesses required by the DAG representation of segments and the extra cost of content lookup in memory, both in terms of number of DRAM accesses and DRAM bandwidth. Moreover, certain cases such as sparse matrix applications show substantial reduction in memory size and access.

Beyond these advantages, the HICAMP memory deduplication and compaction reduces memory requirements, reducing capital cost and improving energy efficiency. Finally, studies [23] show that typical server utilization of DRAM bandwidth is less than 10 percent in many cases, so HICAMP can be viewed as exploiting this under-utilized resource to improve application properties, including performance.

In this comparison, the efficiency of HICAMP should be compared to the inefficiency of the established database process approach, where up to 87 percent of the performance is lost on a conventional architecture [28] to overheads that HICAMP largely eliminates by implementing necessary support in hardware. At the same time, we recognize that certain computing actions are significantly more expensive in HICAMP than a conventional Von Neumann architecture, such as randomly accessing data in a large, dense array. Our claim is that applications do not generally contain such behavior in the performance-critical portions, these performance pitfalls of HICAMP can be characterized and understood by the programmer, and there are reasonable alternatives in the cases that we have investigated. In general, HICAMP tackles macro-scale inefficiencies in applications such as interprocess communication overhead, lock synchronization overhead and memory copying, which we expect to become worse with increasing number of cores and have been somewhat neglected by the conventional focus on micro-benchmarks.

Overall, HICAMP offers a promising direction for future multi-core systems to properly support complex, concurrent, data-intensive software applications, simplifying operating systems and improving practical programming language semantics. It recognizes that access to shared structured data is a key problem in many demanding applications ranging from web servers to scientific computation to embedded systems, and demonstrates that memory system innovation can provide significant benefits to the software.

Acknowledgements

The authors would like to thank Min Xu, Rajat Goel, Steve Herrod and Vyacheslav (Slava) Malyugin of VMware for all their kind help and support regarding VMware Workstation product. The authors are also grateful for valuable comments on earlier versions of this paper from Al Davis and Stephen Richardson, and on the final version from Carl Waldspurger.

References

[1] `http://pages.cs.wisc.edu/~markhill/DineroIV/`.

[2] `http://http://www.vmmark.com/`.

[3] `http://wikipedia.org/wiki/Intel_iAPX_432`.

[4] A. R. Alameldeen and D. A. Wood. Adaptive Cache Compression for High-Performance Processors. *SIGARCH Comput. Archit. News*, 32(2):212, 2004.

[5] Arista Networks. EOS: An Extensible Operating System. `http://www.aristanetworks.com/en/EOSWhitepaper.pdf`.

[6] H. Berenson, P. Bernstein, J. Gray, J. Melton, E. O'Neil, and P. O'Neil. A Critique of ANSI SQL Isolation Levels. *SIGMOD Rec.*, 24(2):1–10, 1995.

[7] R. Bhargava, B. Serebrin, F. Spadini, and S. Manne. Accelerating Two-Dimensional Page Walks for Virtualized Systems. In *Proceedings of the 13th international conference on Architectural support for programming languages and operating systems*, ASPLOS XIII, pages 26–35, New York, NY, USA, 2008. ACM.

[8] S. Biswas, D. Franklin, A. Savage, R. Dixon, T. Sherwood, and F. T. Chong. Multi-Execution: Multicore Caching for Data-Similar Executions. In *ISCA '09: Proceedings of the 36th Annual International Symposium on Computer Architecture*, pages 164–173, 2009.

[9] J. Chung, W. Baek, and C. Kozyrakis. Fast Memory Snapshot for Concurrent Programming without Synchronization. In *ICS '09: Proceedings of the 23rd International Conference on Supercomputing*, pages 117–125, 2009.

[10] T. A. Davis and Y. Hu. The University of Florida Sparse Matrix Collection. *ACM Trans. Math. Softw.*, 38:1:1–1:25, Nov. 2011.

[11] J. B. Dennis. Fresh Breeze: A Multiprocessor Chip Architecture Guided by Modular Programming Principles. *SIGARCH Comput. Archit. News*, 31(1):7–15, 2003.

[12] J. Dusser, T. Piquet, and A. Seznec. Zero-Content Augmented Caches. In *ICS '09: Proceedings of the 23rd International Conference on Supercomputing*, pages 46–55, 2009.

[13] J. Dusser and A. Seznec. Decoupled Zero-Compressed Memory. In *Proceedings of the 6th International Conference on High Performance and Embedded Architectures and Compilers*, HiPEAC '11, pages 77–86. ACM, 2011.

[14] M. Ekman and P. Stenstrom. A Robust Main-Memory Compression Scheme. In *ISCA '05: Proceedings of the 32nd Annual International Symposium on Computer Architecture*, pages 74–85, 2005.

[15] B. Fitzpatrick. Distributed Caching with Memcached. *Linux Journal*, 2004(124):5, 2004.

[16] M. Greenwald and D. Cheriton. The Synergy Between Non-blocking Synchronization and Operating System Structure. In *OSDI '96: Proceedings of the second USENIX Symposium on Operating Systems Design and Implementation*, pages 123–136, 1996.

[17] D. Gupta, S. Lee, M. Vrable, S. Savage, A. Snoeren, G. Varghese, G. Voelker, and A. Vahdat. Difference Engine: Harnessing Memory Redundancy in Virtual Machines. In *8th USENIX Symposium on Operating Systems Design and Implementation*, pages 309–322, 2008.

[18] F. Gustavson, A. Henriksson, I. Jonsson, B. Kagstrom, and P. Ling. Recursive Blocked Data Formats and BLAS's for Dense Linear Algebra Algorithms. In *Applied Parallel Computing Large Scale Scientific and Industrial Problems*, Lecture Notes in Computer Science, pages 195–206. Springer Berline / Heidelberg, 1998.

[19] E. G. Hallnor and S. K. Reinhardt. A Unified Compressed Memory Hierarchy. In *HPCA '05: Proceedings of the 11th International*

Symposium on High-Performance Computer Architecture, pages 201–212, 2005.

[20] R. Hamming. Error Correcting and Error Detecting Codes. *Bell Sys. Tech. Journal*, 29(4):147–160, 1950.

[21] M. Herlihy. A Methodology for Implementing Highly Concurrent Data Structures. In *PPOPP '90: Proceedings of the second ACM SIGPLAN symposium on Principles & practice of parallel programming*, pages 197–206, 1990.

[22] M. Herlihy and J. E. B. Moss. Transactional Memory: Architectural Support for Lock-Free Data Structures. In *ISCA '93: Proceedings of the 20th Annual International Symposium on Computer Architecture*, pages 289–300, 1993.

[23] C. Kozyrakis, A. Kansal, S. Sankar, and K. Vaid. Server Engineering Insights for Large-Scale Online Services. *IEEE Micro*, 30:8–19, July 2010.

[24] B. C. Lee, R. W. Vuduc, J. W. Demmel, K. A. Yelick, M. de Lorimier, and L. Zhong. Performance Optimizations and Bounds for Sparse Symmetric Matrix-Multiple Vector Multiply. Technical Report UCB/CSD-03-1297, University of California, Berkeley, CA, November 2003.

[25] E. A. Lee. The Problem with Threads. *Computer*, 39(5):33–42, 2006.

[26] T. Riegel, C. Fetzer, and P. Felber. Snapshot Isolation for Software Transactional Memory. In *In Proceedings of the 1st Workshop on Languages, Compilers, and Hardware Support for Transactional Computing (TRANSACT 06)*, 2006.

[27] P. Saab. Scaling memcached at Facebook. `http://www.facebook.com/note.php?note_id=39391378919`, Dec 2008.

[28] M. Stonebraker and R. Cattell. 10 Rules for Scalable Performance in 'Simple Operation' Datastores. *Commun. ACM*, 54:72–80, June 2011.

[29] R. Vuduc, J. W. Demmel, and K. A. Yelick. OSKI: A Library of Automatically Tuned Sparse Matrix Kernels. In *Proceedings of SciDAC 2005*, Journal of Physics: Conference Series, June 2005.

[30] R. Vuduc, J. W. Demmel, K. A. Yelick, S. Kamil, R. Nishtala, and B. Lee. Performance Optimizations and Bounds for Sparse Matrix-Vector Multiply. In *Proceedings of Supercomputing*, 2002.

[31] C. A. Waldspurger. Memory Resource Management in the VMware ESX Server. In *OSDI '02: Proceedings of the 5th Symposium on Operating Systems Design and Implementation*, pages 181–194, 2002.

[32] S. Williams, L. Oliker, R. Vuduc, J. Shalf, K. Yelick, and J. Demmel. Optimization of Sparse Matrix-Vector Multiplication on Emerging Multicore Platforms. In *Supercomputing*, November 2007.

[33] M. Yourst. PTLSim: A Cycle Accurate Full System x86-64 Microarchitectural Simulator. In *Proceedings of ISPASS*, January 2007.

Architecture Support for Disciplined Approximate Programming

Hadi Esmaeilzadeh Adrian Sampson Luis Ceze
University of Washington
Department of Computer Science & Engineering
{hadianeh,asampson,luisceze}@cs.washington.edu

Doug Burger
Microsoft Research
dburger@microsoft.com

Abstract

Disciplined approximate programming lets programmers declare which parts of a program can be computed approximately and consequently at a lower energy cost. The compiler proves statically that all approximate computation is properly isolated from precise computation. The hardware is then free to selectively apply approximate storage and approximate computation with no need to perform dynamic correctness checks.

In this paper, we propose an efficient mapping of disciplined approximate programming onto hardware. We describe an ISA extension that provides approximate operations and storage, which give the hardware freedom to save energy at the cost of accuracy. We then propose Truffle, a microarchitecture design that efficiently supports the ISA extensions. The basis of our design is dual-voltage operation, with a high voltage for precise operations and a low voltage for approximate operations. The key aspect of the microarchitecture is its dependence on the instruction stream to determine when to use the low voltage. We evaluate the power savings potential of in-order and out-of-order Truffle configurations and explore the resulting quality of service degradation. We evaluate several applications and demonstrate energy savings up to 43%.

Categories and Subject Descriptors C.1.3 [*Other Architecture Styles*]; C.0 [*Computer Systems Organization*]: Hardware/software interfaces

General Terms Design, Performance

Keywords Architecture, disciplined approximate computation, power-aware computing, energy

1. Introduction

Energy consumption is a first-class concern in computer systems design. Potential benefits go beyond reduced power demands in servers and longer battery life in mobile devices; reducing power consumption is becoming a requirement due to limits of device scaling in what is termed the *dark silicon* problem [4, 11].

Prior work has made significant progress in various aspects of energy efficiency. Hardware optimizations include power gating, voltage and frequency scaling, and sub-threshold operation with error correction [10]. Software efforts have explored managing energy as an explicit resource [30], shutting down unnecessary hardware, and energy-aware compiler optimizations [28]. Raising energy concerns to the programming model can enable a new space of energy savings opportunities.

Trading off quality of service is one technique for reducing energy usage. Allowing computation to be approximate can lead to significant energy savings because it alleviates the "correctness tax" imposed by the wide safety margins on typical designs. Indeed, prior work has investigated hardware and algorithmic techniques for approximate execution [2, 12, 14, 16]. Most applications amenable to energy–accuracy trade-offs (e.g., vision, machine learning, data analysis, games, etc.) have approximate components, where energy savings are possible, and precise components, whose correctness is critical for application invariants [19, 23].

Recent work has explored language-level techniques to assist programmers in identifying *soft slices*, the parts of programs that may be safely subjected to approximate computation [23]. The hardware is free to use approximate storage and computation for the soft slices without performing dynamic safety checks. Broadly, we advocate co-designing hardware support for approximation with an associated programming model to enable new energy-efficiency improvements while preserving programmability.

In this paper, we explore how to map disciplined approximate programming models down to an approximation-aware microarchitecture. Our architecture proposal includes an ISA extension, which allows a compiler to convey what can be approximated, along with microarchitectural extensions to typical in-order and out-of-order processors that implement the ISA. Our microarchitecture proposal relies on a dual voltage supply for SRAM arrays and logic: a high V_{dd} (leading to accurate operation) and a low V_{dd} (leading to approximate but lower-power operation). We discuss the implementation of the core structures using dual-voltage primitives as well as dynamic, instruction-based control of the voltage supply. We evaluate the energy consumption and quality-of-service degradation of our proposal using a variety of benchmarks including a game engine, a raytracer, and scientific algorithms.

The remainder of this paper is organized as follows. Section 2 describes our ISA proposal and its support for an efficient microarchitecture via tight coupling with static compiler guarantees. Section 3 then explains microarchitecture implementation alternatives. Section 4 follows up with a detailed description of our dual-voltage microarchitecture and how the instruction stream can control dynamic voltage selection. Section 5 is our evaluation of power savings and quality-of-service degradation. Sections 6 and 7 discuss related work and conclude.

ASPLOS'12, March 3–7, 2012, London, England, UK.

2. An ISA for Disciplined Approximate Computation

With disciplined approximate programming, a program is decomposed into two components: one that runs *precisely*, with the typical semantics of conventional computers, and another that runs *approximately*, carrying no guarantees but only an expectation of best-effort computation. Many applications, such as media processing and machine learning algorithms, can operate reliably even when errors can occur in portions of them [8, 9, 18, 23, 27]. Floating-point data, for example, is by nature imprecise, so many FP-heavy applications have inherent tolerance to error. An architecture supporting disciplined approximation can take advantage of relaxed precision requirements to expose errors that would otherwise need to be prevented or corrected at the cost of energy. By specifying the portion of the application that is tolerant to error, the programmer gives the architecture permission to expose faults when running that part of the program. We propose an ISA that enables a compiler to communicate where approximation is allowed.

Our ISA design is defined by two guiding principles: the ISA should provide an *abstract* notion of approximation by replacing guarantees with informal expectations; and the ISA may be *unsafe*, blindly trusting the programming language and compiler to enforce safety invariants statically.

Replacing Guarantees with Expectations ISAs normally provide formal *guarantees* for operations (e.g., an "add" instruction must produce the sum of its operands). Approximate operations, however, only carry an *expectation* that a certain operation will be carried out correctly; the result is left formally undefined. For example, an approximate "add" instruction might leave the contents of the output register formally undefined but specify an *expectation* that the result will approximate the sum of the operands. The compiler and programmer may not rely on any particular pattern or method of approximation. Informally, however, they may expect the approximate addition to be useful in "soft" computation that requires summation.

The lack of strict guarantees for approximate computation is essential for *abstract* approximation. Instructions do not specify which particular energy-saving techniques are used; they only specify where approximation may be applied. Consequently, a fully-precise computer is a valid implementation of an approximation-aware ISA. Compilers for such ISAs can, without modification, take advantage of new approximation techniques as they are implemented. By providing no guarantees for approximate computation, the ISA permits a full range of approximation techniques.

By leaving the kind and degree of approximation unspecified, an approximation-aware ISA could pose challenges for portability: different implementations of the ISA can provide different error distributions for approximate operations. To address this issue, implementations can allow software control of implementation parameters such as voltage (see Section 3). Profiling and tuning mechanisms could then discover optimal settings for these hardware parameters at application deployment time. This tuning would allow a single application to run at the same level of quality across widely varying approximation implementations.

Responsibilities of the Language and Compiler An architecture supporting approximate computing requires collaboration from the rest of the system stack. Namely, the architecture relegates concerns of *safety and programmability* to the language and compiler. In order to be usable, approximate computation must be exposed to the programmer in a way that reduces the chance of catastrophic failures and other unexpected consequences. These concerns, while important, can be relegated to the compiler, programming language, and software-engineering tools.

EnerJ [23] is a programming language supporting disciplined approximation. Using a type system, EnerJ provides a static *non-interference* guarantee, ensuring that the approximate part of a program cannot affect the precise portion. In effect, EnerJ enforces separation between the error-tolerant and error-sensitive parts of a program, identifying and isolating the parts that may be subject to relaxed execution semantics. This strict separation brings safety and predictability to programming with approximation. Because it is static, the non-interference guarantee requires no runtime checking, freeing the ISA (and its implementation) from any need for safety checks that would themselves impose overheads in performance, energy, and design complexity.

In this paper, we assume that a language like EnerJ is used to provide safety guarantees *statically* to the programmer. The ISA must only expose approximation as an option to the compiler: it does not provide dynamic invariant checks, error recovery, or any other support for programmability. The ISA is thus unsafe *per se*. If used incorrectly, the ISA can produce unexpected results. It is tightly coupled with the compiler and trusts generated code to observe certain invariants. This dependence on static enforcement is essential to the design of a simple microarchitecture that does not waste energy in providing approximation.

2.1 Requirements for the ISA

An ISA extension for disciplined approximate programming consists of new instruction variants that leave certain aspects of their behavior undefined. These new instructions must strike a balance between energy savings and usability: they must create optimization opportunities through strategic use of undefined behavior but not be so undefined that their results could be catastrophic. Namely, approximate instructions should leave certain data values undefined but maintain predictable control flow, exception handling, and other bookkeeping.

To support a usable programming model similar to EnerJ, an approximation-aware ISA should exhibit the following properties:

- Approximate computation must be controllable at an *instruction granularity*. Approximation is most useful when it can be interleaved with precise computation. For example, a loop variable increment should likely be precise while an arithmetic operation in the body of the loop may be approximate. For this reason, it must be possible to mark individual instructions as either approximate or precise.
- The ISA must support *approximate storage*. The compiler should be able to instruct the ISA to store data approximately or precisely in registers, caches, and main memory.
- It must be possible to *transition* data between approximate and precise storage. (In EnerJ, approximate-to-precise movement is only permitted using an explicit programmer "endorsement," but this annotation has no runtime effect.) For full flexibility, the ISA must permit programs to use precise data approximately and vice-versa.
- Precise instructions, where approximation is not explicitly enabled, must carry traditional semantic guarantees. The effects of approximation must be constrained to where it is requested by the compiler.
- Approximation must be confined to predictable areas. For example, address computation for memory accesses must always be precise; approximate store instructions should not be allowed to write to arbitrary memory locations. Approximate instructions must not carry semantics so relaxed that they cannot be used.

Table 1. ISA extensions for disciplined approximate programming. These instructions are based on the Alpha instruction set.

Group	Approximate Instruction
Integer load/store	LDx.a, STx.a
Integer arithmetic	ADD.a, CMPEQ.a, CMPLT.a, CMPLE.a, MUL.a, SUB.a
Logical and shift	AND.a, NAND.a, OR.a, XNOR.a NOR.a, XOR, CMOV.a, SLL.a, SRA.a, SRL.a
Floating point load/store	LDF.a, STF.a
Floating point operation	ADDF.a, CMPF.x, DIVF.a, MULF.a, SQRTF.a, SUBF.a, MOV.a, CMOV.a, MOVFI.a, MOVIF.a

2.2 ISA Extensions for Approximation

Table 1 summarizes the approximate instructions that we propose adding to a conventional architecture. Without loss of generality, we assume an underlying Alpha ISA [1].

Approximate Operations The extended ISA provides approximate versions of all integer arithmetic, floating-point arithmetic, and bitwise operation instructions provided by the original ISA. These instructions have the same form as their precise equivalents but carry no guarantees about their output values. The approximate instructions instead carry the informal expectation of approximate adherence to the original instructions' behavior. For example, ADD.a takes two arguments and produces one output, but the ISA makes no promises about what that output will be. The instruction may be expected to typically perform addition but the programmer and compiler may not rely on any consistent output behavior.

Approximate Registers Each register in the architecture is, at any point in time, in either *precise mode* or *approximate mode*. When a register is in approximate mode, reads are not guaranteed to obtain the exact value last written, but there is an expectation that the value is likely the same.

The compiler does not explicitly set register modes. Instead, the precision of a register is implicitly defined based on the precision of the last instruction that wrote to it. In other words, a precise operation makes its destination register precise while an approximate operation puts its destination register into approximate mode.

While register precision modes are set implicitly, the precision of operand accesses must be declared explicitly. Every instruction that takes register operands is extended to include an extra bit per operand specifying the operand's precision. This makes precision level information available to the microarchitecture *a priori*, drastically simplifying the implementation of dual-voltage registers (see Section 4.1). It does not place a significant burden on the compiler as the compiler must statically determine registers' precision anyway. If the correspondence between register modes and operand accesses is violated, the value is undefined (see below).

With this design, data can move freely between approximate and precise registers. For example, a precise ADD instruction may use an approximate register as an operand; this transition corresponds to an *endorsement* in the EnerJ language. The opposite transition, in which precise data is used in approximate computation, is also permitted and frequently occurs in EnerJ programs.

Approximate Loads, Stores, and Caching The ISA defines a *granularity of approximation* at which the architecture supports setting the precision of cached memory. In practice, this granularity will likely correspond to the smallest cache line size in the processor's cache hierarchy.[1] For example, if an architecture has 16-byte L1 cache lines and supports varying the precision of every cache line, then it defines the approximation granularity to be 16 bytes. Each region of memory aligned to the granularity of approximation (hereafter called an *approximation line* for brevity) is in either approximate or precise mode at any given time.

An approximation line's precision mode is implicitly controlled by the precision of the loads and stores that access it. In particular, the ISA guarantees reliable data storage for precise accesses if, for every load from line x, the preceding store to line x has the same precision. (That is, after a precise store to x, only precise loads may be issued to x until the next store to x.) For the compiler and memory allocator, this amounts to ensuring that precise and approximate data never occupy the same line. Memory allocation and object layout must be adapted to group approximate data to line-aligned boundaries. Statically determining each line's precision is trivial for any language with sufficiently strong static properties. In EnerJ specifically, a type soundness theorem implies that the precision of every variable is known statically for every access.

The ISA requires this pattern of consistent accesses in order to simplify the implementation of approximation-aware caching. Specifically, it allows the following simple cache-approximation policy: a line's precision is set by misses and writes but is not affected by read hits. During read hits, the cache can assume that the precision of the line matches the precision of the access.

Approximate loads and stores may read and write arbitrary values to memory. Accordingly, precise stores always write data reliably, but a precise load only reads data reliably when it accesses a line in precise mode. However, any store (approximate or precise) can only affect the address it is given: address calculation and indexing are never approximated.

Approximate Main Memory While this paper focuses on approximation in the core, main memory (DRAM modules) may also support approximate storage. The refresh rate of DRAM cells, for example, may be reduced so that data is no longer stored reliably [19]. However, memory approximation is entirely decoupled from the above notion of approximate caching and load/store precision. This way, an approximation-aware processor can be used even with fully-precise memory. Furthermore, memory modules are likely to support a different granularity for approximation from caches—DRAM lines, for instance, typically range from hundreds of bytes to several kilobytes. Keeping memory approximation distinct from cache approximation decouples the memory from specific architecture parameters.

The program controls main-memory approximation *explicitly*, using either a special instruction or a system call to manipulate the precision of memory regions. Loads and stores are oblivious to the memory's precision; the compiler is responsible for enforcing a correspondence. When main-memory approximation is available, the operating system may store precision levels in the page table to preserve the settings across page evictions and page faults.

Preservation of Precision In several cases, where the ISA supports both precise and approximate operation, it relies on the compiler to treat certain data consistently as one or the other. For example, when a register is in approximate mode, all instructions that use that register as an operand must mark that operand as approximate. Relying on this correspondence simplifies the implementation of approximate SRAM arrays (Section 4.1).

The ISA does not enforce precision correspondence. No exception is raised if it is violated. Instead, as with many other situations in the ISA, the resulting value from any inconsistent operation is left undefined. Unlike other approximate operations, however, the *informal expectation* in these situations is also weaker: precise reads from approximate-mode registers, for example, should be expected to return random data. The compiler should avoid these situations even when performing approximate computation.

[1] Note that architects generally avoid tying cache line size to the ISA. However, we believe that in cases of strong co-design between architecture and compiler such as ours, it is acceptable to do so.

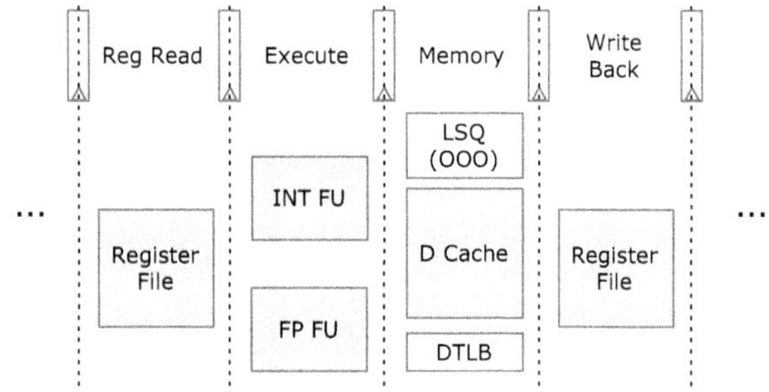

Figure 1. The data movement/processing plane of the processor pipeline. Approximation-aware structures are shaded. The instruction control plane stages (Fetch and Decode, as well as Rename, Issue, Schedule, and Commit in the OOO pipeline) are not shown.

These situations constitute violations of precision correspondence:

- A register in approximate mode is used as a precise operand to an instruction. (Note that a precise instruction can use an approximate operand; the operand must then be declared as approximate.)
- Conversely, a precise-mode register is used as an approximate operand.
- An approximate load (e.g., LDW.a) is issued to an address in an approximation line that is in precise mode.
- Conversely, a precise load is issued to an approximate-mode line.

In every case, these are situations where undefined behavior is already present due to approximation, so the ISA's formal guarantees are not affected by this choice. Consistency of precision only constitutes a recommendation to the compiler that these situations be avoided. These weak semantics keep the microarchitecture simple by alleviating the need for precision state checks (see Section 4.1).

3. Design Space

As discussed above, approximate instructions may produce arbitrary results. For example, ADD.a may place any value in its destination register. However, approximate instructions still have defined semantics: ADD.a cannot modify any register other than its output register; it cannot raise a divide-by-zero exception; it cannot jump to an arbitrary address. These guarantees are necessary to make our approximation-aware ISA usable.

Our microarchitecture must carefully distinguish between structures that can have relaxed correctness and those for which reliable operation is always required. Specifically, all fetched instructions need to be decoded precisely and their target and source register indices need to be identified without error. However, the content of those registers may be approximate and the functional units operating on the data may operate approximately. Similarly, memory addresses must be error-free, but the data retrieved from the memory system can be incorrect when that data is marked as approximate. Consequently, we divide the microarchitecture into two distinct planes: the *instruction control plane* and the *data movement/processing plane*. As depicted in Figure 1, the data movement/processing plane comprises the register file, data caches, load store queue, functional units, and bypass network. The instruction control plane comprises the units that fetch, decode, and perform necessary bookkeeping for in-flight instructions. The instruction control plane is kept precise, while the data movement/processing plane can be approximate for approximate instructions. Since the data plane needs to behave precisely or approximately depending on the instruction being carried out, the microarchitecture needs to do some bookkeeping to determine when a structure can behave approximately.

This paper explores voltage reduction as a technique for saving energy. (Other techniques, such as aggressive timing closure or reducing data width, are orthogonal.) Each frequency level (f_{max}) is associated with a minimum voltage (V_{min}) and lowering the voltage beyond that may cause timing errors. Lowering the voltage reduces energy consumption quadratically when the frequency is kept constant. However, we cannot lower the voltage of the whole processor as this would cause errors in structures that need to behave precisely. This leads to the core question of how to provide precise behavior in the microarchitecture.

One way to provide precise behavior, which we explore in this paper, is to run critical structures at a safe voltage. Alternatively, error correction mechanisms could be used for critical structures and disabled for the data movement/processing plane while executing approximate instructions. This way, the penalty of error checking would not be incurred for approximate operations. However, if V_{dd} were low enough to make approximation pay off, many expensive recoveries would be required during precise operations. For this reason, we propose using two voltage lines: one for precise operation and one for approximate operation. Below we describe two alternative designs for a dual-voltage microarchitecture.

Unchecked Dual-Voltage Design Our dual-voltage microarchitecture, called Truffle, needs to guarantee that (1) the instruction control remains precise at all times, and (2) the data processing plane structures lower precision only when processing approximate instructions. Truffle has two voltages: a nominal, reliable level, referred to as $V_{dd}H$, and a lower level, called $V_{dd}L$, which may lead to timing errors. All structures in the instruction control plane are supplied $V_{dd}H$, and, depending on the instruction being executed, the structures in the data processing plane are dynamically supplied $V_{dd}H$ or $V_{dd}L$. The detailed design of a dual-voltage data processing plane, including the register file, data cache, functional units, and bypass network, is discussed in the next section.

Checked Dual Voltage Design The energy savings potential of Truffle is limited by the proportion of power used by structures that operate precisely at $V_{dd}H$. Therefore, reducing the energy consumption of precise operations will lead to higher relative impact of using approximation. This leads to another possible design point, which lowers the voltage of the instruction control plane beyond $V_{dd}H$ but not as aggressively as $V_{dd}L$ and employs error correction to guarantee correct behavior using an approach similar to Razor [10]. We refer to this conservative level of voltage as $V_{dd}L_{high}$. The data plane also operates at $V_{dd}L_{high}$ when running the precise instructions and $V_{dd}L$ when running the approximate instructions. Since the instruction control plane operates at the reliable voltage level, the components in this plane need to be checked and corrected in the case of any errors. The same checking applies to the data movement/processing plane while running precise instructions. While this is an interesting design point, we focus on the unchecked dual-voltage design due to its lower complexity.

Selecting $V_{dd}L$ In the simplest case, $V_{dd}L$ can be set statically at chip manufacture and test time. However, the accuracy of approximate operations depends directly on this value. Therefore, a natural option is to allow $V_{dd}L$ to be set dynamically depending on the QoS expectations of the application. Fine-grained voltage adjustments can be performed after fabrication using off-chip voltage regulators as in the Intel SCC [13] or by on-chip voltage regulators as proposed by Kim et al. [15]. Off-chip voltage regulators have a high latency while on-chip voltage regulators provide lower-latency, fine-grained voltage scaling. Depending on the latency requirement of the application and the type of regulator available, $V_{dd}L$ can be selected at deployment time or during execution. Future work should explore software-engineering tools that assist in selecting per-application voltage levels.

4. Truffle: A Dual-Voltage Microarchitecture for Disciplined Approximation

This section describes Truffle in detail. We start with the design of a dual-voltage SRAM structure, which is an essential building block for microarchitectural components such as register files and data caches. Next, we discuss the design of dual-voltage multiplexers and level shifters. We then address the design of structures in both in-order and OOO Truffle cores, emphasizing how the voltage is selected dynamically depending on the precision level of each instruction. Finally, we catalog the microarchitectural overheads imposed by Truffle's dual-voltage design.

4.1 Dual-Voltage SRAM Array

We propose dual-voltage SRAM arrays, or DV-SRAMs, which can hold precise and approximate data simultaneously. Like its single-voltage counterpart, a DV-SRAM array is composed of mats. A mat, as depicted in Figure 2, is a self-contained memory structure composed of four identical subarrays and associated predecoding logic that is shared among the subarrays. The data-in/-out and address lines typically enter the mat in the middle. The predecoded signals are forked off from the middle to the subarrays. Figure 2 also illustrates a circuit diagram for a single subarray, which is a two-dimensional array of single-bit SRAM cells arranged in rows and columns. The highlighted signals correspond to a read access, which determines the critical path of the array.

For any read or write to a DV-SRAM array, the address goes through the predecoding logic and produces the one-hot `rowSelect` signals along with the `columnSelect` signals for the column multiplexers. During read accesses, when a row is activated by its `rowSelect` signal, the value stored in each selected SRAM cell is transferred over two complementary `bitline` wires to the sense amplifiers. Meanwhile, the `bitlines` have been precharged to a certain V_{dd}. Each sense amplifier senses the resulting swing on the `bitlines` and generates the subarray output. The inputs and outputs of the sense amplifiers may be multiplexed depending on the array layout. The sense amplifiers drive the `dataOut` of the mat for a read access, while `dataIn` drives the `bitlines` during a write access.

To be able to store both approximate and precise data, we divide the data array logic into two parts: the indexing logic and the data storage/retrieval logic. To avoid potential corruption of precise data, the indexing logic *always* needs to be precise, even when manipulating approximate data. The indexing logic includes the address lines to the mats, the predecoding/decoding logic (row and column decoders), and the `rowSelect` and `columnSelect` drivers. The data storage/retrieval logic, in contrast, needs to alternate between precise and approximate mode. Data storage/retrieval includes the precharge/equalizing logic, SRAM cells, bitline multiplexers, sense amplifiers, `dataOut` drivers and multiplexers, and `dataIn` drivers. For approximate accesses, this set of logic blocks operates at $V_{dd}L$.

In each subarray of a mat, a row of bits (SRAM cells) is either at high voltage ($V_{dd}H$) or low voltage ($V_{dd}L$). The precision column in Figure 2, which is a single-bit column operating at $V_{dd}H$, stores the voltage state of each row. The precision column is composed of 8-transistor cells: 6-transistor SRAM cells each augmented by two PMOS transistors. In each row, the output of the precision column drives the power lines of the entire row. This makes it possible to *route only one power line* to the data rows as well as the prechargers and sense amplifiers. This way, the extra $V_{dd}L$ power line is only routed to the precision column in each subarray and is distributed to the rows through the precision cells, which significantly reduces the overhead of running two voltage lines.

For a read access, the `bitlines` need to be precharged to the same voltage level as the row being accessed. Similarly, the sense amplifiers need to operate at the same voltage level as the subarray row being accessed. A `precision` signal is added to the address bits and routed to all the mats. The `precision` signal presets the voltage levels of the precharge and equalizing logic and the sense amplifiers before the address is decoded and the `rowSelect` and `columnSelect` signals are generated. This voltage presetting ensures that the sense amplifiers are ready when the selected row puts its values on the `bitlines` during a read. Furthermore, during a write, the value in the precision column is set based on the `precision` signal.

Since the precision cell is selected at the same time as the data cells, the state stored in the precision column cannot be used to set the appropriate voltage levels in the sense amplifiers and prechargers. Therefore, the precision information needs to be determined *before* the read access starts in the subarrays. This is why our ISA extensions (Section 2) include a precision flag for each source operand: these flags, along with the precision levels of instructions themselves, are used to set the `precision` signal when accessing registers and caches.

4.2 Voltage Level Shifting and Multiplexing

Several structures in the Truffle microarchitecture must be able to deal with both precise and approximate data. For this reason, our design includes *dual-voltage multiplexers*, which can multiplex signals of differing voltage, and *voltage level shifters*, which enable data movement between the high- and low-voltage domains.

Figure 3 illustrates the transistor-level design of the single-bit, one-input dual-voltage multiplexers (DV-Mux) as well as the high-to-low (H2L) and low-to-high (L2H) level shifters. The select line of the multiplexer and its associated inverter operate at $V_{dd}H$, while the input data lines can swing from 0 V to either $V_{dd}L$ or $V_{dd}H$. The L2H level shifter is a conventional differential low-to-high level shifter and the H2L level shifter is constructed from two back-to-back inverters, one operating at $V_{dd}H$ and the other operating at $V_{dd}L$. In addition to the `input` signal, the level shifters take an extra input, `precision`, to identify the voltage level of `input` and disengage the level-shifting logic to prevent unnecessary power consumption. For example, in the L2H level shifter, when `precision` is 0, `input` is precise (0 V or $V_{dd}H$) and does not require any level shifting, (`output` ← `input`). However, when `precision` is 1, the level shifter is engaged and generates the `output` with the required voltage level.

4.3 Truffle's Microarchitectural Constructs

This section describes the Truffle pipeline stage-by-stage, considering both in-order and out-of-order implementations. The out-of-order design is based on the Alpha 21264 [3] and uses a tag-and-index register renaming approach. We highlight whether a pipeline stage belongs to the instruction control plane or the data movement/processing plane. Importantly, we discuss how the voltage is dynamically selected in the structures that support approximation.

Fetch (OOO/in-order) [Instruction Control Plane] The fetch stage belongs to the instruction control plane and is identical to a regular OOO/in-order fetch stage. All the components of this stage, including the branch predictor, instruction cache, and ITLB, are ordinary, single-voltage structures. Approximate instructions are fetched exactly the same way as precise instructions.

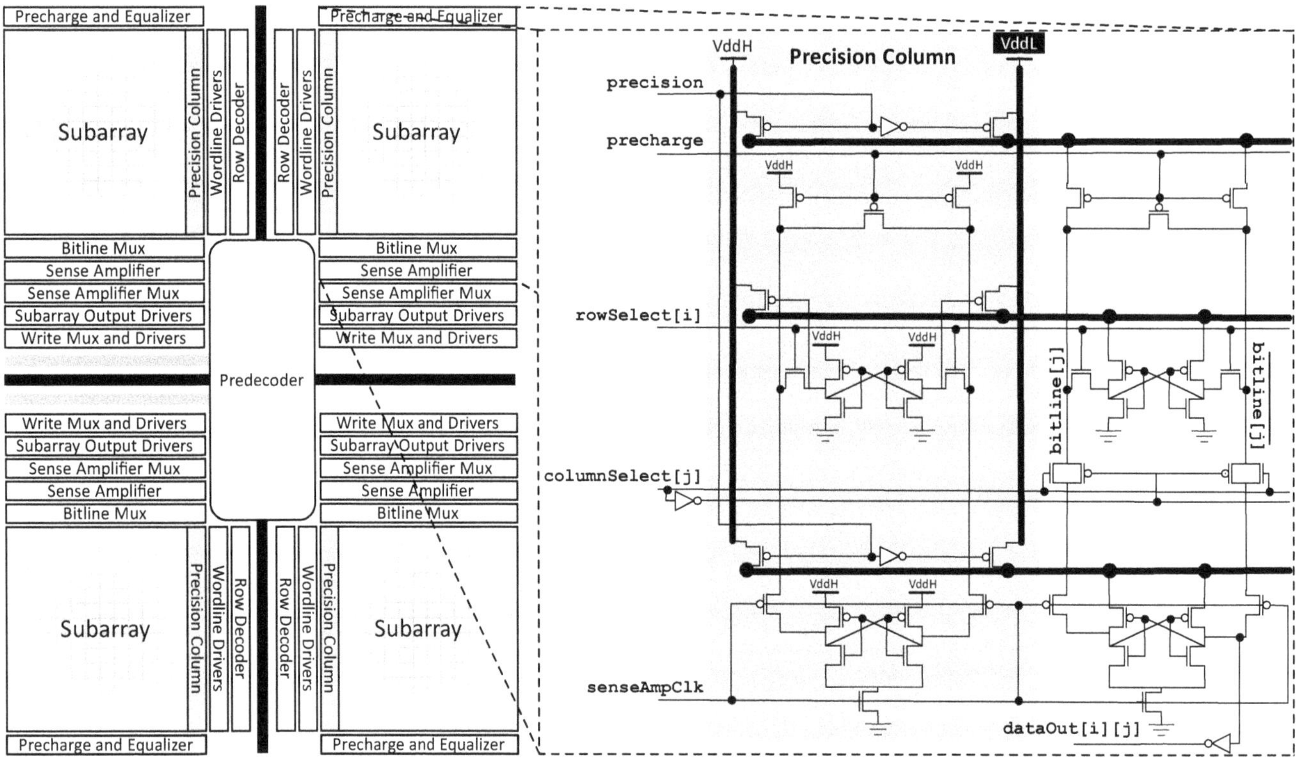

Figure 2. Dual-voltage mat, consisting of four identical dual-voltage subarrays, and partial transistor-level design of the subarrays and the *precision column*, which is shaded. The power lines during a read access are shown in bold.

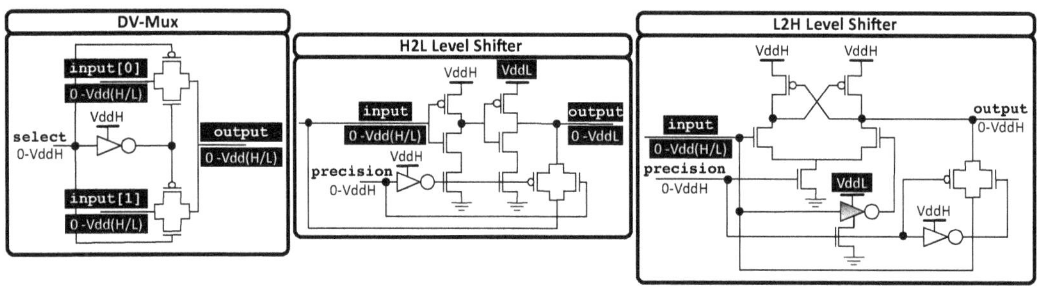

Figure 3. Transistor-level design of dual-voltage multiplexer (DV-Mux) and high-to-low (H2L) and low-to-high (L2H) level shifters.

Decode (OOO/in-order) [Instruction Control Plane] The instruction decoding logic needs to distinguish between approximate and precise instructions. The decode stage passes along one extra bit indicating the precision level of the decoded instruction.

In addition, based on the instruction, the decoder generates precision bits to accompany the indices for each register read or written. These register precision bits will be used when accessing the dual-voltage register file as discussed in Section 4.1. The precision levels of the source registers are extracted from the operand precision flags while the precision of the destination register corresponds to the precision of the instruction. For load and store instructions, the address computation must always be performed precisely, even when the data being loaded or stored is approximate. For approximate load and store instructions, the registers used for address calculation are always precise while the data register is always approximate. Recall that the microarchitecture does not check that precise registers are always used precisely and approximate registers are used approximately. This correspondence is enforced by the compiler and encoded in the instructions, simplifying the design and reducing the overheads of mixed-precision computation.

Rename (OOO) [Instruction Control Plane] For the OOO design, in which the register renaming logic generates the physical register indices/tags, the physical register tags are coupled with the register precision bits passed from the decode stage. The rest of the register renaming logic is the same as in the base design.

Issue (OOO) [Instruction Control Plane] The slots in the issue logic need to store the register index precision bits as well as the physical register indices. That is, each physical tag entry in an issue slot is extended by one bit. The issue slots also need to store the bit indicating the precision of the instruction. When an approximate load instruction is issued, it gets a slot in the load/store queue. The address entry of each slot in the load/store queue is extended by one extra bit indicating whether the access is approximate or precise. The precision bit is coupled with the address in order to control the precision level of the data cache access (as described above in Section 4.1).

Schedule (OOO) [Instruction Control Plane] As will be discussed in the execution stage, there are separate functional units for approximate and precise computation in Truffle. The approximate functional units act as *shadows* of their precise counterparts. The issue width of the processor is *not* extended due to the extra approximate functional units and no complexity is added to the scheduling logic to accommodate them. The coupled approximate/precise functional units appear to the scheduler as a single unit. For example, if an approximate floating-point operation is scheduled to issue, the precise and approximate FPUs are both considered busy. The bit indicating the precision level of the instruction is used to enable either the approximate or precise functional unit exclusively.

Register Read (OOO/in-order) [Data Movement/Processing Plane] The data movement/processing plane starts at the register read stage. As depicted in Figure 4, the pipeline registers are divided into two sets starting at this stage: one operating at $V_{dd}L$ (Approx Data Pipe Reg) and the other operating at $V_{dd}H$ (Precise Data Pipe Reg + Control). The approximate pipeline register holds approximate data. The precise pipeline register contains control information passed along from previous stages and precise program data. The outputs of the precise and approximate pipeline registers are multiplexed through a DV-Mux as needed.

The dual-voltage register file (physical in the OOO design and architectural in the in-order design) is made up of DV-SRAM arrays. Each register can be dynamically set as approximate or precise. While the precision levels of the general-purpose registers are determined dynamically, the pipeline registers are hardwired to their respective voltages to avoid voltage level changes when running approximate and precise instructions back-to-back.

The ISA allows precise instructions to use approximate registers as operands and vice-versa. To carry out such instructions with minimal error, the voltage levels of the operands need to be changed to match the voltage level of the operation. In the register read stage, the level shifters illustrated in Figure 4 convert the voltage level of values read from the register file. For example, if `reg1` is precise and used in an approximate operation, its voltage level is shifted from high to low through an H2L level shifter before being written to an approximate pipeline register. The precision level of `reg1`, denoted by `reg1Precision`, is passed to the level shifter to avoid unnecessary level shifting in the case that `reg1` is already approximate. Similarly, a low-to-high (L2H) level shifter is used to adjust the voltage level of values written to the precise pipeline register. Note that only *one* of the approximate or precise data pipeline registers is enabled based on the precision of the instruction.

Execute (OOO/in-order) [Data Movement/Processing Plane] As shown in Figure 4, all the functional units are duplicated in the execution stage. Half of them are hardwired to $V_{dd}H$, while the other half operate at $V_{dd}L$ as *shadows*. That is, the scheduler does not distinguish between a shadow approximate FU and its precise counterpart. Only the instruction precision bit controls whether the results are taken from the precise or approximate FU. Low-voltage functional units are connected to a low-voltage pipeline register. The outputs of the approximate FUs connect to the *same* broadcast network as their precise counterparts through a dual-voltage multiplexer driven by the approximate and precise pipeline register pair at the end of the execution stage.

The inputs of functional units may also be driven by the bypass network. Level shifters at the inputs of the functional units adjust the level of the broadcasted input data using the broadcasted precision bit. Only a single-bit precision signal is added to the broadcast network. Because the output of each FU pair is multiplexed, the extra FUs do not increase the size of the broadcast network beyond adding this single-bit precision line. While the data bypass network alternates between $V_{dd}L$ and $V_{dd}H$, the tag forwarding network in the OOO design always works at the high voltage level since it carries necessarily-precise register indexing information.

To avoid unnecessary dynamic power consumption in the functional units, the input to one functional unit is kept constant (by not writing to its input pipeline register) when its opposite-precision counterpart is being used.

An alternative design could use dual-voltage functional units and change the voltage depending on the instruction being executed. This would save area and static power but require a more complex scheduler design that can set the appropriate voltage level in the functional unit before delivering the operands to it. Since functional units can be large and draw a considerable amount of current while switching, a voltage-selecting transistor for a dual-voltage functional unit needs to be sized such that it can provide the required drive. Such transistors tend to consume significant power. Another possibility is lowering the FU voltage based on phase prediction. When the application enters an approximate phase, the voltage level of the functional unit is lowered. Phase prediction requires extra power and complicates the microarchitecture design. The main objective in the design of Truffle is to keep the microarchitectural changes to a minimum and avoid complexity in the instruction control and bookkeeping. Furthermore, since programs consist of a mixture of precise and approximate instructions, it is not obvious that phase-based voltage level adjustments can provide benefit that compensates for the phase prediction overhead. Additionally, static partitioning can help tolerate process variation by using defective functional units for approximate computations.

Memory (OOO/in-order) [Data Movement/Processing Plane] As previously discussed, the address field in each slot of the load/store queue is extended by one bit that indicates whether the address location is precise or approximate. The data array portion of the data cache is a DV-SRAM array, while the tag array is an ordinary single-voltage SRAM structure. The approximation granularity in the data cache is a cache line: one extra bit is stored in the tag array which identifies the precision level of each cache line. The extra bit in the load/store queue is used as the precision signal when accessing the DV-SRAM data array. The miss buffer, fill buffer, prefetch buffer, and write back buffers all operate at $V_{dd}H$. The DTLB also requires no changes.

The precision level of a cache line is determined by the load or store instruction that fills the line. If an approximate access misses in the cache, the line is fetched as approximate. Similarly, a precise miss fills the cache line as precise. Subsequent write hits also affect line precision: when a store instruction modifies the data in a cache line, it also modifies the line's precision level (see Section 2).

This paper focuses on the Truffle core and does not present a detailed design for approximation-aware lower levels of cache or main memory. The L1 cache described here could work with an unmodified, fully-precise L2 cache, but a number of options are available for the design of an approximation-aware L2. If the L2 has the same line size as the L1, then an identical strategy can be applied. However, L2 lines are often larger than L1 lines. In that case, one option is to control L2 precision at a sub-line granularity: if the L2 line size is n times the L1 line size, then the L2 has n precision columns. An alternative design could pair the lower-level caches with main memory, setting the precision of L2 lines based on the explicitly-controlled main-memory precision levels. These non-core design decisions are orthogonal to the core Truffle design and are an avenue for future work.

Write Back (OOO/in-order) [Data Movement/Processing Plane] The write back value comes from the approximate or precise

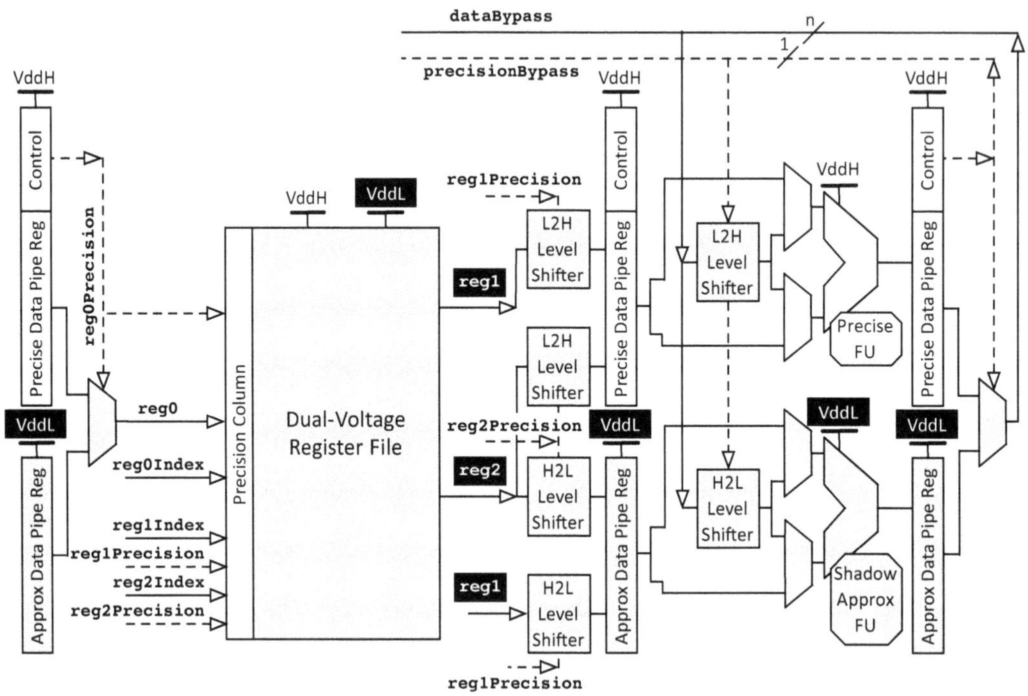

Figure 4. The register and execution stages in the Truffle pipeline along with the bypass network. The DV-Muxes and other approximation-aware units are shaded. The single-bit precision signals in the bypass network and in each stage are dashed lines.

pipeline register. As shown in Figure 4, the dual-voltage multiplexer driving `reg0` forwards the write back value to the data bypass network. The precision bit accompanying the write back value (`reg0Precision`) is also forwarded over the bypass network's precision line.

Commit (OOO) [Instruction Control Plane] The commit stage does not require any special changes and the reorder buffer slots do not need to store any extra information for the approximate instructions. The only consideration is that, during rollbacks due to mispredictions or exceptions, the precision state of the registers (one bit per register) needs to be restored. Another option is to restore all the registers as precise, ignoring the precision level of the registers during rollback.

4.4 Microarchitectural Overheads in Truffle

In this section, we briefly consider the microarchitectural overheads imposed by routing two power lines to structures in Truffle's data movement/processing plane. First, the data part of the pipeline registers is duplicated to store approximate data. An extra level of dual-voltage multiplexing is added after these pipeline registers to provide the data with the correct voltage for the next stage. The DV-SRAM arrays, including the register file and data array in the data cache, store one precision bit per row. In addition, a one-bit precision signal is added to each read/write port of the DV-SRAM array and routed to each subarray along with the $V_{dd}L$ power line. The tag for each data cache line is also augmented by a bit storing the precision state of the line. However, the tag array itself is an ordinary single-voltage SRAM structure. To adjust the voltage level of the operands accessed from the dual-voltage register file, one set of H2L and one set of L2H level shifters is added for each read port of the register file. Similarly, in the execution stage, one set of each level shifter type is added per operand from the data bypass network. The data bypass network is also augmented with a single-bit precision signal per operand. In addition, each entry in the issue queue is extended by one bit preserving the precision level of the instruction. Each physical tag entry in an issue slot is also extended by one precision bit. Similarly, the slots in the load/store queue are augmented by one extra bit indicating whether the access is approximate or precise. The pipeline registers also need to store the precision level of the operands and instructions.

5. Experimental Results

Our goals in evaluating Truffle are to determine the energy savings brought by disciplined approximation, characterize where the energy goes, and understand the QoS implications for software.

5.1 Evaluation Setup

We extended CACTI [21] to model the dual-voltage SRAM structure we propose and incorporated the resulting models into McPAT [17]. We modeled Truffle at the 65 nm technology node in the context of both in-order and out-of-order (based on the 21264 [3]) designs. Table 2 shows the detailed microarchitectural parameters.

Disciplined approximate computation represents a trade-off between energy consumption and application output quality. Therefore, we evaluate each benchmark for two criteria: energy savings and sensitivity to error. For the former, we collect statistics from the benchmarks' execution as parameters to the McPAT-based power model; for the latter, we inject errors into the execution and measure the consequent degradation in output quality.

For both tasks, we use a source-to-source transformation that instruments the program for statistics collection and error injection. Statistics collected for power modeling include variable, field, and array accesses, basic blocks (for branches), and arithmetic and logical operators. A cache simulator is used to distinguish cache hits and misses; the register file is simulated as a small, fully-associative cache. For error injection, each potential injection point (approximate operations and approximate memory accesses) is in-

Table 2. Microarchitectural parameters.

Parameter	OOO Truffle	In-order Truffle
Fetch/Decode Width	4/4	2/2
Issue/Commit Width	6/4	—/—
INT ALUs/FPUs	4/2	1/1
INT Mult/Div Units	1	1
Approximate INT ALUs/FPUs	4/2	1/1
Approximate INT Mult/Div Units	1	1
INT/FP Issue Window Size	20/15	—
ROB Entries	80	—
INT/FP Architectural Registers	32/32	32/32
INT/FP Physical Registers	80/72	—
Load/Store Queue Size	32/32	—
ITLB	128	64
I Cache Size	64 Kbyte	16 Kbyte
Line Width/Associativity	32/2	16/4
DTLB	128	64
D Cache Size	64 Kbyte	32 Kbyte
Line Width/Associativity	16/2	16/4
Branch Predictor	Tournament	Tournament

Table 3. List of benchmarks.

Application	Description	Type
fft	SciMark2 benchmark: scientific kernels	FP
sor		FP
mc		FP
smm		FP
lu		FP
zxing	Bar code decoder for mobile phones	FP/integer
jmeint	jMonkeyEngine game framework: triangle intersection kernel	FP
imagefill	ImageJ raster image processing application: flood-filling kernel	integer
raytracer	3D image renderer	FP

tercepted; each bit in the resulting value is flipped according to a per-component probability before being returned to the program.

Benchmarks We examine nine benchmark programs written in the EnerJ language, which is an extension to Java [23]. The applications are the same programs that were evaluated in [23]: existing Java programs hand-annotated with approximate type qualifiers that distinguish their approximate parts. Five of the benchmarks come from the SciMark2 suite. ZXing is a multi-format bar code recognizer developed for Android smartphones. jMonkeyEngine is a game development engine; we examine the framework's triangle-intersection algorithm used for collision detection. ImageJ is a library and application for raster image manipulation; we examine its flood-filler algorithm. Finally, we examine a simple 3D raytracer.

For each program, an application-specific *quality-of-service metric* is defined in order to quantify the loss in output quality caused by hardware approximation. For most of the applications, the metric is the root-mean-square error of the output vector, matrix, or pixel array. For jmeint, the jMonkeyEngine triangle-intersection algorithm, the metric is the proportion of incorrect intersection decisions. Similarly, for the zxing bar code recognizer, it is the proportion of unsuccessful decodings of a sample QR code image.

5.2 Unchecked Truffle Microarchitecture

Figure 5 presents the energy savings achieved in the core and L1 cache for the unchecked dual-voltage Truffle microarchitecture in both OOO and in-order configurations. In both designs, $V_{dd}H = 1.5$ V and $V_{dd}L$ takes values that are 50%, 62.5%, 75%, and 87.5% of $V_{dd}H$. The frequency is set constant at 1666 MHz. The Truffle

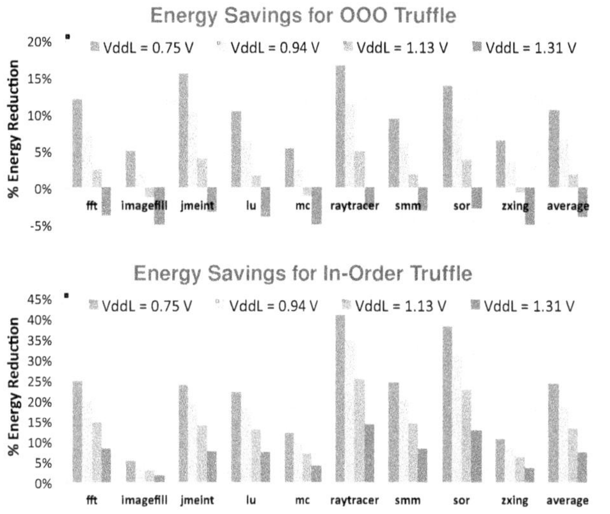

Figure 5. Percent energy reduction with unchecked OOO and in-order Truffle designs for various $V_{dd}L$ voltages.

cores include DV-SRAM arrays and extra approximate functional units. The baseline for the reported energy savings is the same core operating at the reliable voltage level of 1.5 V and 1666 MHz *without* the extra functional units or dual-voltage register files and data cache. Our model assumes that Truffle's microarchitectural additions do not prolong the critical path of the base design.

Depending on the configuration, voltage, and application, Truffle ranges from increasing energy by 5% to saving 43%. For the in-order configuration, all voltage levels lead to energy savings; the OOO design shows energy savings when $V_{dd}L$ is less than 75% of $V_{dd}H$. Our results suggest Truffle exhibits a "break even" point at which its energy savings outweigh its overheads.

The difference between the energy savings in OOO and in-order Truffle cores stems from the fact that the instruction control plane in the OOO core accounts for a much larger portion of total energy than in the in-order core. Recall that the instruction control plane in the OOO core includes instruction fetch and decode, register renaming, instruction issue and scheduling, load and store queues, and DTLB/ITLB, whereas in the in-order setting it includes only instruction fetch and decode and the TLBs. Since approximation helps reduce energy consumption in the data movement/processing plane only, the impact of Truffle in in-order cores is much higher. Furthermore, the OOO Truffle core is an aggressive four-wide multiple-issue processor whereas the in-order Truffle core is two-wide. Anything that can reduce the energy consumption of the instruction control plane indirectly helps increase Truffle's impact.

Figure 6 depicts the energy breakdown between different microarchitectural components in the OOO and in-order Truffle cores when $V_{dd}L = V_{dd}H$ (i.e., with fully-precise computation). Among the benchmarks, imagefill shows similar benefits for both designs. For this benchmark, 42% and 47% of the energy is consumed in the data movement/processing plane of the OOO and in-order Truffle cores, respectively. On the other hand, raytracer shows the largest difference in energy reduction between the two designs; here, the data movement/processing plane consumes 71% of the energy in the OOO core but just 50% in the in-order core. In summary, the simpler the instruction control plane in the processor, the higher the potential for energy savings with Truffle.

In addition to the design style of the Truffle core, the energy savings are dependent on the proportion of approximate computation in the execution. Figure 7 shows the percentage of approximate dynamic instructions along with the percentage of approxi-

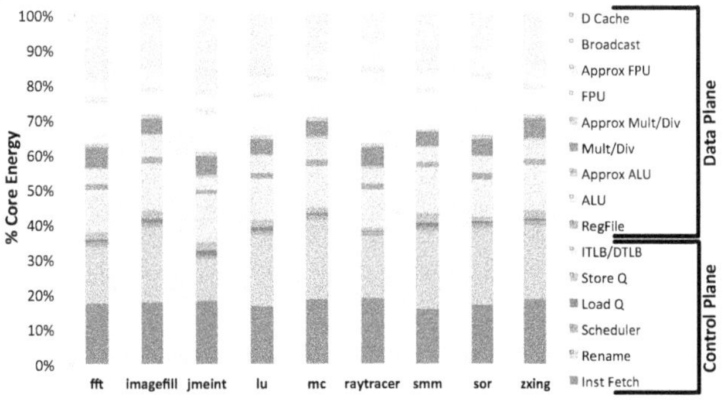

(a)

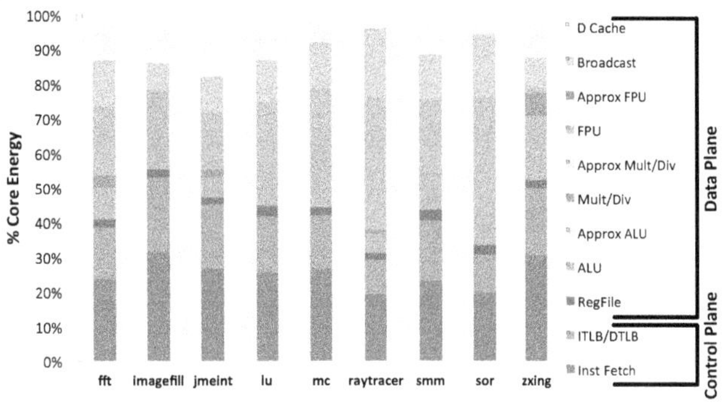

(b)

Figure 6. Percent energy consumed by different microarchitectural components in the (a) OOO and (b) in-order Truffle.

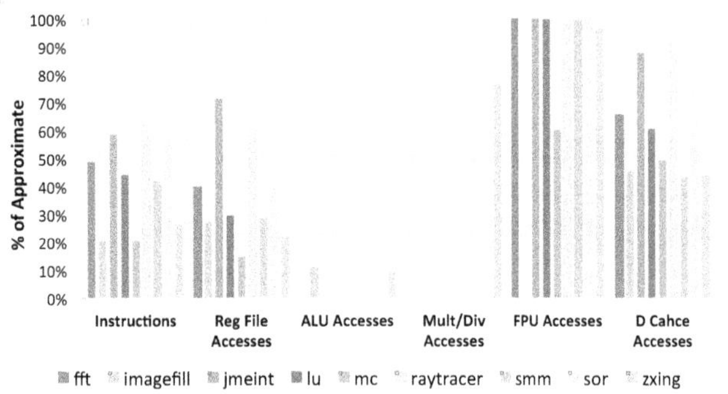

Figure 7. Percentage of approximate events.

mate ALU, multiply/divide, and floating point operations as well as the percentage of approximate data cache accesses. Among the benchmarks, imagefill has the lowest percentage of approximate instructions (20%) and no approximate floating point or multiplication operations—only 11% of its integer operations are approximate. As a fully integer application, it exhibits no opportunity for floating-point approximation, and its approximate integer operations are dwarfed by precise control-flow operations. imagefill also has a low ratio of approximate data cache accesses, 45%. These characteristics result in low potential for Truffle, about 5% energy savings for $V_{dd}L = 0.75$ V. Conversely, raytracer shows the highest ratio of approximate instructions in the group. Nearly all (98%) of its floating point operations are approximate. In addition, raytracer has the highest ratio of approximate data cache accesses in the benchmark set, 91%, which makes it benefit the most from Truf-

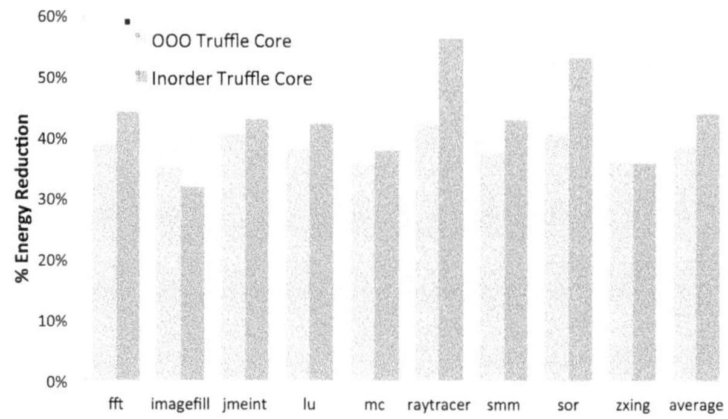

Figure 8. Percent energy reduction *potential* for checked in-order and OOO Truffle designs with $V_{dd}L = 0.75$ V.

fle. The high rate of floating-point approximation is characteristic of the FP-dominated benchmarks we examined: for many applications, more than 90% of the FP operations are approximate. This is commensurate with the inherently approximate nature of FP representations. Furthermore, for many benchmarks, FP data constitutes the application's error-resilient data plane while integers dominate its error-sensitive control plane.

These results show that, as the proportion of approximate computation increases, the energy reductions from the Truffle microarchitecture also increase. Furthermore, some applications leave certain microarchitectural components unexercised, suggesting that higher error rates may be tolerable in those components. For example, none of the benchmarks except imagefill exercise the approximate integer ALU, and the approximate multiply/divide unit is not exercised at all. As a result, higher error rates in those components may be tolerable. The results also support the utility of application-specific $V_{dd}L$ settings, since each of the benchmarks exercise each approximate component differently.

Overall, these results show that disciplined approximation has great potential to enable low-power microarchitectures. Also, as expected, the simpler the microarchitecture, the higher the energy savings potential.

Overheads We modified McPAT and CACTI to model the overheads of Truffle as described in Section 4.4. The energy across all the benchmarks increases by at most 2% when the applications are compiled with no approximate instructions. The approximate functional units are power-gated when there are no approximate instructions in flight. The energy increase is due to the extra precision state per cache line and per register along with other microarchitectural changes. CACTI models show an increase of 3% in register file area due to the precision column and a 1% increase in the area of the level-1 data cache. The extra approximate functional units also contribute to the area overhead of Truffle.

5.3 Opportunities in a Checked Design

As discussed above, reducing energy consumption of the instruction control plane (and the energy used in *precise* instructions) can increase the overall impact of Truffle. Section 3 outlines a design that uses a sub-critical voltage and error detection/correction for the microarchitectural structures that need to behave precisely. We now present a simple limit study of the potential of such a design. Figure 8 presents the energy savings potential when the voltage level of the instruction control plane is reduced to 1.2 V, beyond the reliable voltage level of $V_{min} = 1.5$ V, and $V_{dd}L = 0.75$ V. The results show only the ideal case in which there is no penalty associated with error checking and correction in the precise computation. As illustrated, the gap in energy savings potential between the OOO

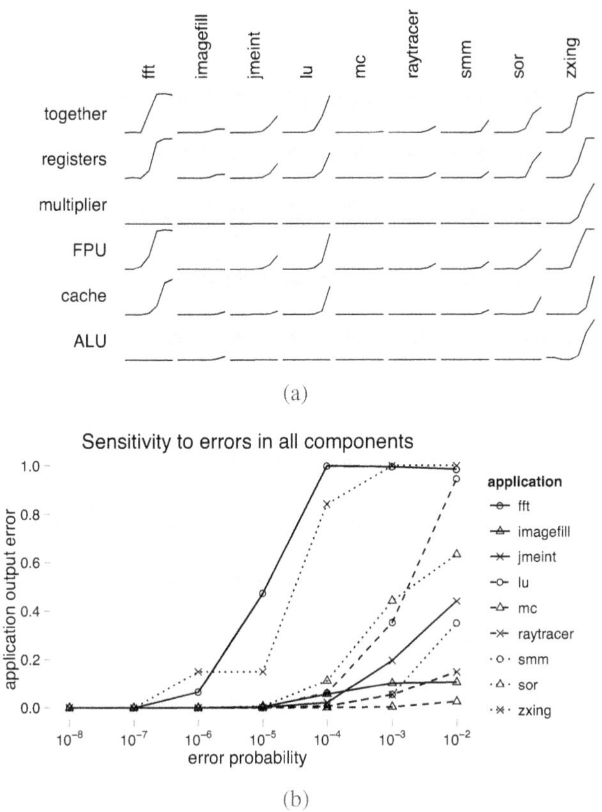

Figure 9. Application sensitivity to circuit-level errors. Each cell in (a) has the same axes as (b): application QoS degradation is related to architectural error probability (on a log scale). The grid (a) shows applications' sensitivity to errors in each component in isolation; the row labeled "together" corresponds to experiments in which the error probability for all components is the same. The plot (b) shows these "together" configurations in more detail. The output error is averaged over 20 replications.

and in-order designs is significantly reduced. In one case, imagefill, the checked OOO Truffle core shows higher potential compared to the checked in-order Truffle core. In this benchmark, the energy consumption of the instruction control plane is more dominant in the OOO design and thus lower voltage for that plane is more effective than in the in-order design. Note that in an actual design, energy savings will be restricted by the error rates in the instruction control plane and the rate at which the precise instructions fail, triggering error recovery. The overhead of the error-checking structures will further limit the savings.

5.4 Error Propagation from Circuits to Applications

We now present a study of application QoS degradation as we inject errors in each of the microarchitectural structures that support approximate behavior. The actual pattern of errors caused by voltage reduction is highly design-dependent. Modeling the error distributions of approximate hardware is likely to involve guesswork; the most convincing evaluation of error rates would come from experiments with real Truffle hardware. For the present evaluation, we thoroughly explore a space of error rates in order to characterize the range of possibilities for the impact of approximation.

Figure 9 shows each benchmark's sensitivity to circuit-level errors in each microarchitectural component. Some applications are significantly sensitive to error injection in most components (fft, for example); others show very little degradation (imagefill, raytracer, mc, smm). Errors in some components tend to cause more application-level errors than others—for example, errors in the integer functional units (ALU and multiplier) only cause output degradation in the benchmarks with significant approximate integer computation (imagefill and zxing).

The variability in application sensitivity highlights again the utility of using a tunable $V_{dd}L$ to customize the architecture's error rate on a per-application basis (see Section 3). Most applications exhibit a critical error rate at which the application's output quality drops precipitously—for example, in Figure 9(b), fft exhibits low output error when all components have error probability 10^{-6} but significant degradation occurs at probability 10^{-5}. A software-controllable $V_{dd}L$ could allow each application to run at its lowest allowable power while maintaining acceptable output quality.

In general, the benchmarks do not exhibit drastically different sensitivities to errors in different components. A given benchmark that is sensitive to errors in the register file, for example, is also likely to be sensitive to errors in the cache and functional units.

6. Related Work

A significant amount of prior work has proposed hardware that compromises on execution correctness for benefits in performance, energy consumption, and yield. ERSA proposes collaboration between discrete reliable and unreliable cores for executing error-resilient applications [16]. Stochastic processors encapsulate another proposal for variable-accuracy functional units [22]. Probabilistic CMOS (PCMOS) proposes to use the probability of low-voltage transistor switching as a source of randomness for special randomized algorithms [5]. Finally, algorithmic noise-tolerance (ANT) proposes approximation in the context of digital signal processing [12]. Our proposed dual-voltage design, in contrast, supports fine-grained, single-core approximation that leverages language support for explicit approximation in general-purpose applications. It does not require manual offloading of code to coprocessors and permits fully-precise execution on the same core as low-power approximate instructions. Truffle extends general-purpose CPUs; it is not a special-purpose coprocessor.

Relax is a compiler/architecture system for suppressing hardware fault recovery in certain regions of code, exposing these errors to the application [9]. A Truffle-like architecture supports approximation at a single-instruction granularity, exposes approximation in storage elements, and guarantees precise control flow even when executing approximate code. In addition, Truffle goes further and elides fault *detection* as well as recovery where it is not needed.

Razor and related techniques also use voltage underscaling for energy reduction but use error recovery to hide errors from the application [10, 14]. Disciplined approximate computation can enable energy savings beyond those allowed by correctness-preserving optimizations.

Broadly, the key difference between Truffle and prior work is that Truffle was co-designed with language support. Specifically, relying on *disciplined approximation* with strong static guarantees offered by the compiler and language features enables an efficient and simple design. Static guarantees also lead to strong safety properties that significantly improve programmability.

The error-tolerant property of certain applications is supported by a number of surveys of application-level sensitivity to circuit-level errors [8, 18, 27]. Truffle is a microarchitectural technique for exploiting this application property to achieve energy savings.

Dual-voltage designs are not the only way to implement low-power approximate computation. Fuzzy memoization [2] and bit-width reduction [26], for example, are orthogonal techniques for approximating floating-point operations. Imprecise integer logic blocks have also been designed [20]. An approximation-aware processor could combine dual-voltage design with these other techniques.

Previous work has also explored dual-V_{dd} designs for power optimization in fully-precise computers [6, 29]. Truffle's instruction-controlled voltage changes make it fundamentally different from these previous techniques.

Truffle resembles architectures that incorporate information flow tracking for security [7, 24, 25]. In that work, the hardware enforces information flow invariants dynamically based on tags provided by the application or operating system. With Truffle, the *compiler* provides the information flow invariant, freeing the architecture from costly dynamic checking.

7. Conclusion

Disciplined approximate programming is an effective and usable technique for trading off superfluous correctness guarantees for energy savings. Dual-voltage microarchitectures can realize these energy savings by providing both approximate and precise computation to be controlled at a fine grain by the compiler. We propose an ISA that simplifies the hardware by relying on the compiler to provide certain invariants statically, eliminating the need for checking or recovery at run time. We describe a high-level microarchitecture that supports interleaved high- and low-voltage operations and a detailed design for a dual-voltage SRAM array that implements approximation-aware caches and registers. We model the power of our proposed dual-voltage microarchitecture and evaluate its energy consumption in the context of a variety of error-tolerant benchmark applications. Experimental results show energy savings up to 43%; under reasonable assumptions, these benchmarks exhibit low or negligible degradation in output quality.

Acknowledgments

We would like to thank the anonymous reviewers for their valuable comments. We also thank Sied Mehdi Fakhraie, Jacob Nelson, Behnam Robatmili, and the members of the Sampa group for their feedback on the manuscript. This work was supported in part by NSF grant CCF-1016495, a Sloan Research Fellowship, and gifts from Microsoft and Google.

References

[1] *Alpha Architecture Handbook, Version 3*. Digital Equipment Corporation, 1996.

[2] C. Alvarez, J. Corbal, and M. Valero. Fuzzy memoization for floating-point multimedia applications. *IEEE Trans. Comput.*, 54(7), 2005.

[3] S. Y. Borkar and A. A. Chien. The Aplha 21264 Microprocessor. *MICRO*, 1999.

[4] S. Y. Borkar and A. A. Chien. The future of microprocessors. *CACM*, 54, May 2011.

[5] L. N. Chakrapani, B. E. S. Akgul, S. Cheemalavagu, P. Korkmaz, K. V. Palem, and B. Seshasayee. Ultra-efficient (embedded) SOC architectures based on probabilistic CMOS (PCMOS) technology. In *DATE*, 2006.

[6] C. Chen, A. Srivastava, and M. Sarrafzadeh. On gate level power optimization using dual-supply voltages. *IEEE Trans. VLSI Syst.*, 9, 2001.

[7] M. Dalton, H. Kannan, and C. Kozyrakis. Raksha: A flexible information flow architecture for software security. In *ISCA*, 2007.

[8] M. de Kruijf and K. Sankaralingam. Exploring the synergy of emerging workloads and silicon reliability trends. In *SELSE*, 2009.

[9] M. de Kruijf, S. Nomura, and K. Sankaralingam. Relax: An architectural framework for software recovery of hardware faults. In *ISCA*, 2010.

[10] D. Ernst, N. S. Kim, S. Das, S. Pant, R. Rao, T. Pham, C. Ziesler, D. Blaauw, T. Austin, K. Flautner, and T. Mudge. Razor: A low-power pipeline based on circuit-level timing speculation. In *MICRO*, 2003.

[11] H. Esmaeilzadeh, E. Blem, R. St. Amant, K. Sankaralingam, and D. Burger. Dark silicon and the end of multicore scaling. In *ISCA*, 2011.

[12] R. Hegde and N. R. Shanbhag. Energy-efficient signal processing via algorithmic noise-tolerance. In *ISLPED*, 1999.

[13] J. Howard et al. A 48-core IA-32 message-passing processor with DVFS in 45nm CMOS. In *ISSCC*, 2010.

[14] A. Kahng, S. Kang, R. Kumar, and J. Sartori. Designing a processor from the ground up to allow voltage/reliability tradeoffs. In *HPCA*, 2010.

[15] W. Kim, D. Brooks, and G.-Y. Wei. A fully-integrated 3-level DC/DC converter for nanosecond-scale DVS with fast shunt regulation. In *ISSCC*, 2011.

[16] L. Leem, H. Cho, J. Bau, Q. A. Jacobson, and S. Mitra. ERSA: Error resilient system architecture for probabilistic applications. In *DATE*, 2010.

[17] S. Li, J. H. Ahn, R. D. Strong, J. B. Brockman, D. M. Tullsen, and N. P. Jouppi. McPAT: An integrated power, area, and timing modeling framework for multicore and manycore architectures. In *MICRO*, 2009.

[18] X. Li and D. Yeung. Exploiting soft computing for increased fault tolerance. In *ASGI*, 2006.

[19] S. Liu, K. Pattabiraman, T. Moscibroda, and B. G. Zorn. Flikker: Saving refresh-power in mobile devices through critical data partitioning. In *ASPLOS*, 2011.

[20] H. R. Mahdiani, A. Ahmadi, S. M. Fakhraie, and C. Lucas. Bio-inspired imprecise computational blocks for efficient VLSI implementation of soft-computing applications. *Trans. Cir. Sys. Part I*, 57, 2010.

[21] N. Muralimanohar, R. Balasubramonian, and N. Jouppi. Optimizing NUCA organizations and wiring alternatives for large caches with CACTI 6.0. In *MICRO*, 2007.

[22] S. Narayanan, J. Sartori, R. Kumar, and D. L. Jones. Scalable stochastic processors. In *DATE*, 2010.

[23] A. Sampson, W. Dietl, E. Fortuna, D. Gnanapragasam, L. Ceze, and D. Grossman. EnerJ: Approximate data types for safe and general low-power computation. In *PLDI*, 2011.

[24] G. E. Suh, J. W. Lee, D. Zhang, and S. Devadas. Secure program execution via dynamic information flow tracking. In *ASPLOS*, 2004.

[25] M. Tiwari, H. M. Wassel, B. Mazloom, S. Mysore, F. T. Chong, and T. Sherwood. Complete information flow tracking from the gates up. In *ASPLOS*, 2009.

[26] J. Y. F. Tong, D. Nagle, and R. A. Rutenbar. Reducing power by optimizing the necessary precision/range of floating-point arithmetic. *IEEE Trans. VLSI Syst.*, 8(3), 2000.

[27] V. Wong and M. Horowitz. Soft error resilience of probabilistic inference applications. In *SELSE*, 2006.

[28] Q. Wu, M. Martonosi, D. W. Clark, V. J. Reddi, D. Connors, Y. Wu, J. Lee, and D. Brooks. A dynamic compilation framework for controlling microprocessor energy and performance. In *MICRO*, 2005.

[29] C. Yeh, Y.-S. Kang, S.-J. Shieh, and J.-S. Wang. Layout techniques supporting the use of dual supply voltages for cell-based designs. In *DAC*, 1999.

[30] H. Zeng, C. S. Ellis, A. R. Lebeck, and A. Vahdat. ECOSystem: Managing energy as a first class operating system resource. In *ASPLOS*, 2002.

DreamWeaver: Architectural Support for Deep Sleep

David Meisner
meisner@umich.edu

Thomas F. Wenisch
twenisch@umich.edu

Advanced Computer Architecture Lab
University of Michigan

Abstract

Numerous data center services exhibit low average utilization leading to poor energy efficiency. Although CPU voltage and frequency scaling historically has been an effective means to scale down power with utilization, transistor scaling trends are limiting its effectiveness and the CPU is accounting for a shrinking fraction of system power. Recent research advocates the use of full-system idle low-power modes to combat energy losses, as such modes provide the deepest power savings with bounded response time impact. However, the trend towards increasing cores per die is undermining the effectiveness of these sleep modes, particularly for request-parallel data center applications, because the independent idle periods across individual cores are unlikely to align by happenstance.

We propose DreamWeaver, *architectural support to facilitate deep sleep for request-parallel applications on multicore servers. DreamWeaver comprises two elements:* Weave Scheduling, *a scheduling policy to coalesce idle and busy periods across cores to create opportunities for system-wide deep sleep; and the* Dream Processor, *a light-weight co-processor that monitors incoming network traffic and suspended work during sleep to determine when the system must wake. DreamWeaver is based on two key concepts: (1) stall execution and sleep anytime any core is unoccupied, but (2) constrain the maximum time any request may be stalled. Unlike prior scheduling approaches, DreamWeaver will preempt execution to sleep, maximizing time spent at the systems' most efficient operating point. We demonstrate that DreamWeaver can smoothly trade-off bounded, predictable increases in 99th-percentile response time for increasing power savings, and strictly dominates the savings available with voltage and frequency scaling and timeout-based request batching schemes.*

Categories and Subject Descriptors C.5.5 [*Computer System Implementation*]: Servers

General Terms Design, Measurement

Keywords power management, servers

ASPLOS'12, March 3–7, 2012, London, England, UK.

1. Introduction

Modern data centers suffer from low energy efficiency due to endemic under-utilization [8]. The gap between average and peak load, performance isolation concerns, and redundancy all lead to low average utilization even in carefully designed data centers; conservative over-provisioning and improper sizing frequently result in even lower utilization. Low utilization leads to poor energy efficiency because current servers lack *energy proportionality*—that is, their power requirements do not scale down proportionally with utilization. Architects are seeking to improve server energy proportionality through low-power modes that conserve energy without compromising response time when load is low.

Unfortunately, the confluence of technology and software scaling trends is undermining the continued effectiveness of these low-power modes, particularly for interactive data center applications. On the one hand, device scaling trends are compromising the effectiveness of *voltage and frequency scaling* (VFS) [27, 30, 32, 51] due to the shrinking gap between nominal and threshold voltages [19], limiting both the range and leverage of voltage scaling. Recent research shows that, beyond the 45nm node, circuit delay grows disproportionately as voltage is scaled [15]. Figure 1 illustrates how the power-performance trade-off of VFS grows worse each generation. On the other hand, the prevalence of request-level parallelism in server software combined with the trend towards increasing cores per die is blunting the effectiveness of *idle low-power modes*, which place components in sleep states during periods of inactivity [3, 16, 21, 35, 37, 40, 41, 46]. In uniprocessors, the deep sleep possible with full-system idle low-power modes (e.g., PowerNap [40, 41]) can achieve energy-proportionality if mode transitions are sufficiently fast. However, for a request-parallel server application, full-system idleness rapidly vanishes as the number of cores grows—the busy and idle periods of individual cores (each serving independent requests) hardly ever align, precluding full-system sleep. Figure 2 illustrates the poor scalability of PowerNap for a Web serving workload when CPU utilization is fixed at 30% (i.e., load is scaled with the number of cores to maintain constant utilization; see Section 5.1 for methodology details).

In this paper, we propose *DreamWeaver*, architectural support to facilitate deep sleep for request-parallel applications on multicore servers. DreamWeaver comprises two elements: the *Dream Processor*, a light-weight co-processor that monitors incoming network traffic and suspended work during sleep to determine when the system must wake; and *Weave Scheduling*, a scheduling policy to coalesce idle and busy periods across cores to create opportunities for system-wide deep sleep while bounding the maximum latency increase observed by any request.

Like prior work on scheduling for sleep, DreamWeaver rests on the fundamental observation that system-wide idle periods will

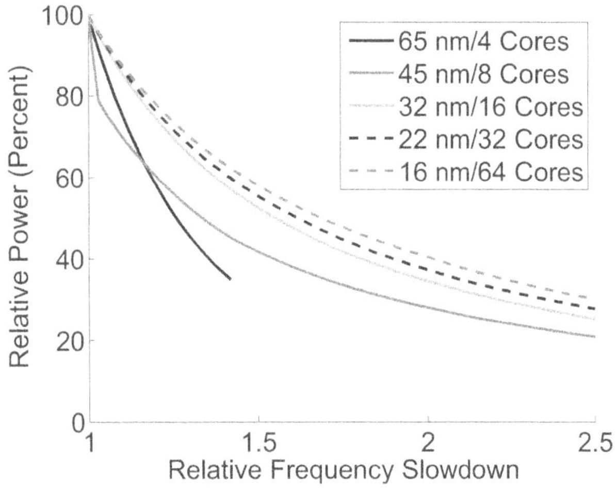

Figure 1: Voltage and frequency scaling. Future technology nodes require a disproportionate reduction in clock frequency for a given voltage reduction, breaking the classic assumption that dynamic power scales down cubically with frequency. Hence, VFS is becoming less effective: a 16nm processor requires a 2x slowdown for 50% power savings compared to 1.25x at 65nm. Data from [15].

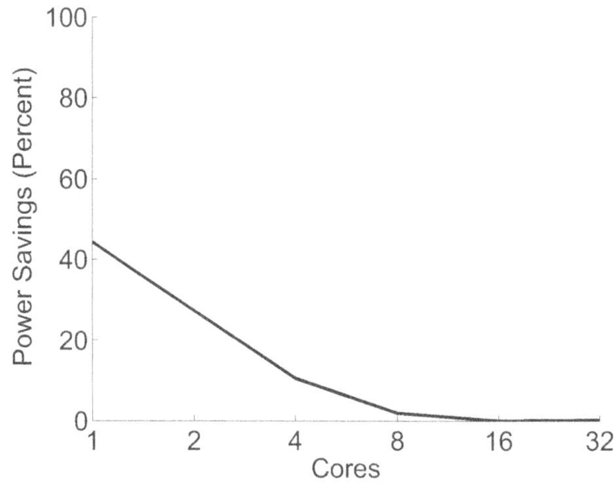

Figure 2: Full-system idle low-power mode. Power savings for a Web server at 30% utilization using a full-system idle low-power mode (e.g., PowerNap [41]). System-level idleness disappears with multicore integration, rendering coarse-grain power savings techniques ineffective.

not arise naturally in request-parallel systems; rather, per-core idle periods must be coalesced by selectively delaying and aligning requests. Prior work has proposed batching requests, using simple timeouts to control performance impact, to reduce the overhead of transitioning to/from sleep modes [5, 21, 46]. However, the fundamental flaw of timeout-based batching approaches is that they only align the *start* of a batch of requests. Since requests tend to have highly-variable long-tailed service times [25], there is nearly always a straggling request that persists past the rest of the batch, destroying the opportunity to sleep. A recent case study of request batching for Google's Web Search reveals an unappealing power-performance trade-off—even allowing a 5x increase in 95th-percentile Web search response time provides only $\sim$15% power savings for a 16-core system [42]. Naïve batching is not effective because it either (1) incurs too large an impact on response time if the batching timeout is too large, or (2) fails to align idle and busy times if the timeout is too small.

The central innovation that allows Weave Scheduling to solve the problems of batching is *preemptive sleep*; that is, DreamWeaver will interrupt and suspend in-progress work to enter deep sleep. Weave Scheduling is based on two simple policies: (1) stall execution and sleep any time that *any* core is unoccupied, but (2) constrain the maximum amount of time any request may be stalled. DreamWeaver will preempt execution to sleep when even a single core becomes idle (i.e., a request completes), provided that no active request has exhausted its allowable stall time. Thus, DreamWeaver tries to operate a server only when all cores are utilized—its most efficient operating point.

The Dream Processor is a simple microcontroller that tracks accumulated stall time for suspended requests and receives, enqueues, and counts incoming network packets during sleep. When enough packets arrive to occupy all idle cores, or when the allowable stall time for any request is exhausted, the Dream Processor wakes the system to resume execution. The Dream Processor bears similarities to the hardware support for Barely-alive Servers [6] and Somniloquy [3], but is simpler because it need not run a full TCP/IP stack.

We present a two-part evaluation of DreamWeaver. First, we analyze the performance impact of Weave Scheduling using a software prototype that emulates the Dream Processor on the system's primary CPU. Through a case study of the popular open-source Solr Web search system, we show that Weave Scheduling allows an 8-core system to sleep 40% of the time when allowed a 1.5x slack on 99th-percentile response time. We also use our prototype to validate the performance predictions of our simulation model. Second, we evaluate the power savings potential of DreamWeaver, examine its scalability, and contrast it with other power management approaches using *Stochastic Queuing Simulation (SQS)* [44], a validated methodology for rapidly simulating the power-performance behavior of data center workloads. Our simulation study demonstrates that DreamWeaver dominates the power-performance tradeoffs available from either VFS or batch scheduling on systems with up to 32 cores on four data center workloads, including Google Web search.

2. Background

We begin with a brief overview of the challenges that make power management for request-parallel data center workloads difficult. Then, we review related work on server power management.

2.1 Power Management Challenges

Power management for data center workloads is challenging because many of these workloads are latency-sensitive. Moreover, it is growing more challenging with multicore scaling [28]. Servers must meet strict *service level agreements* (SLAs), which prescribe per-request latency targets that must be met to prevent stringent penalties. SLAs are typically based on the 99th-percentile (or simi-

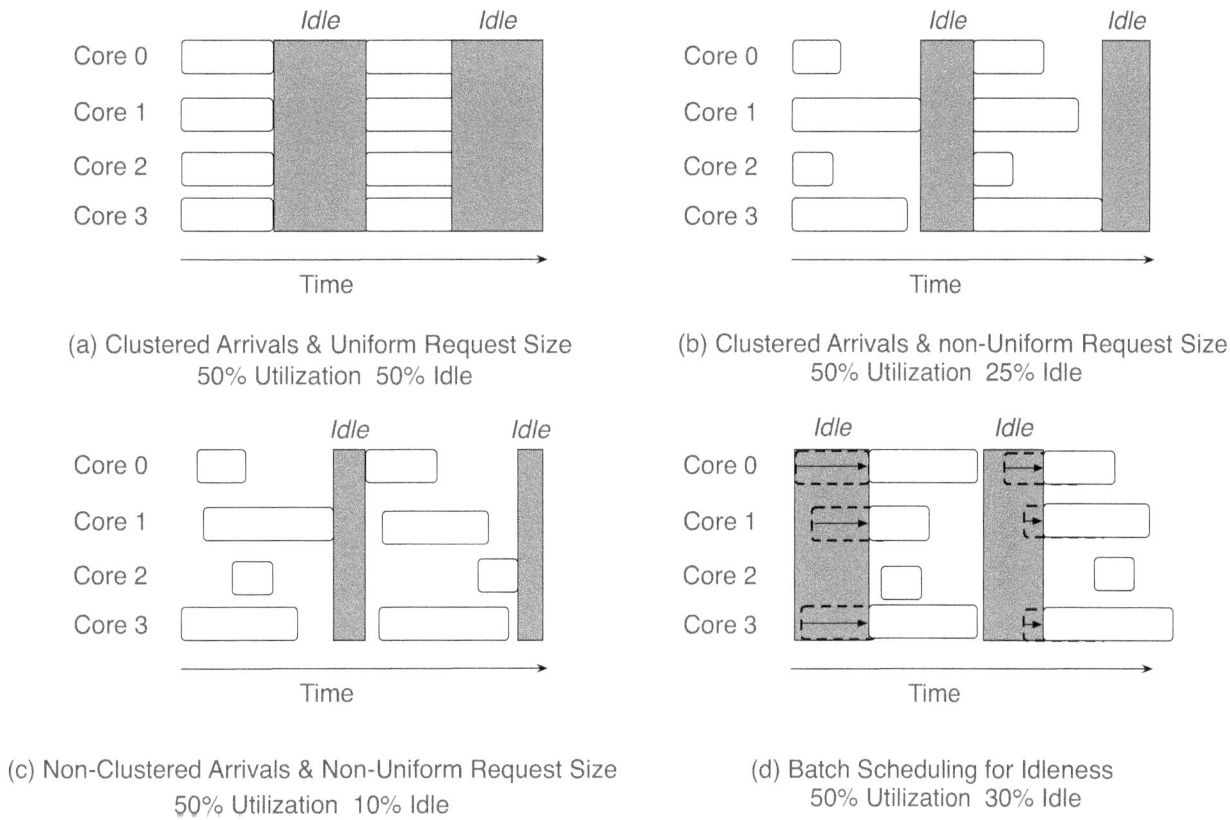

Figure 3: Full-system idleness varies widely as a function of arrival and request size patterns. As seen in (a), a workload with clustered arrivals (high coefficient of variation, or "C_v") and uniform request sizes (low C_v) maximizes idleness. Notice that in this case, core-level idleness and full-system idleness are the same (50%). If requests are non-uniform in size, as in (b), full-system idleness decreases (25%) although core-level idleness does not (50%). Similarly in (c), with both non-clustered request arrivals (low C_v) and non-uniform request sizes (high C_v), full-system idleness is significantly decreased. One technique to mitigate these effects is batching, shown in (d), which increases request latency and creates artificial idle periods.

lar high percentile) latency, not the mean. Meeting this requirement is complicated by workloads with long-tailed and unpredictable service times [25]. The majority of existing literature (particularly works that have focused on power management) has concentrated on the average latency of server systems; we instead set targets for 99th-percentile latency, but our results generalize to other high quantiles.

Furthermore, data center workloads are often highly variable. For instance, for Web serving, the difference between the mean and 99th-percentile latency is over a factor of four. This constraint means designers must take care: a change that has a small impact on mean response time may have a large effect on the 99th percentile.

2.2 Related Work

Previous literature has demonstrated that reducing power at low utilization is critical to increasing server efficiency [8, 41]. System designers use numerous approaches to improve energy efficiency of under-utilized systems. These approaches fall into three broad classes: cluster-grain approaches, active low-power modes, and idle low-power modes. Though our study is focused on idle low-power modes, we briefly discuss the merits and challenges of each.

Cluster-grain approaches to energy-proportionality. The cause of poor efficiency in servers is rooted in their low utilization and lack of energy-proportional components. Techniques such as dynamic cluster resizing and load dispatching [4, 12–14, 26, 33, 47] or server consolidation and virtual machine migration [10, 49] seek to increase average server utilization, which improves efficiency on non-energy-proportional hardware. By moving the work of multiple server onto a single machine, fixed power and capital costs may be amortized.

Though this approach is effective for many workloads, there are several data center workload paradigms for which consolidation/migration is inapplicable. For many workloads of increasing importance (e.g., Web search, MapReduce), large data sets are distributed over many servers and the servers must remain powered to keep data accessible in main memory or on local disks [39, 42]. In the case of Web search, clusters are sized based on memory capacity and latency constraints rather than throughput—the entire cluster must remain active to serve even a single search request with acceptable latency [42]. Task migration typically operates over too coarse time scales (minutes) to respond rapidly to unanticipated load. In latency-sensitive interactive workloads, compacting multiple services onto the same machine may make service increasingly vulnerable to the effects of variance (e.g., traffic spikes). Low utilization is common for this exact reason; well-designed services are intentionally operated at 20-50% utilization to ensure performance robustness despite variable load [8].

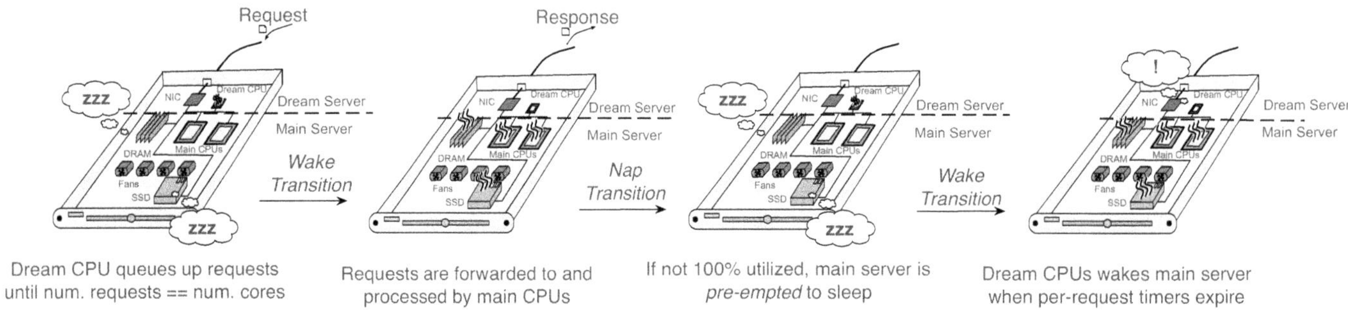

Figure 4: DreamWeaver. The DreamWeaver system is composed of a main server with PowerNap capabilities [41] and Dream Processor that implements Weave Scheduling. The Dream Processor is a modest microcontroller that is isolated from the power state of the rest of a server. It is responsible for modulating the power state of the main system, buffering incoming requests from the network, and tracking any delay of requests while in the nap state. The nap processor resembles hardware such as in Barely-alive Servers [6] or Somniloquy [3], but requires far less processing power because it does not directly process or respond to packets.

Server-level active low-power modes. Many hardware devices offer *active low-power modes*, which trade reduced performance for power savings while a device continues to operate. Active low-power modes (e.g., VFS) improve energy efficiency if they provide superlinear power savings for linear slowdown. VFS is well-studied for reducing CPU power [27, 30, 32, 38, 48, 51]. Unfortunately, the effectiveness of VFS is shrinking with technology scaling (see Figure 1) as decreases in voltage result in increasingly disproportionate increases in circuit delay [15]. Active low-power modes have also been proposed for disks [11, 24]. Whereas active low-power modes are largely orthogonal to our study, we compare the effectiveness of DreamWeaver to voltage and frequency scaling to provide a frame of reference for our results.

Sever-level idle low-power modes. Many devices also offer *idle low-power modes*, which provide even greater power savings than the most aggressive active low-power modes [22, 41]. One of the most attractive properties of idle low-power modes is that they offer fixed latency penalties. These modes are characterized by their transition time T_{tr}: the time to enter or leave the low-power mode. When T_{tr} is small relative to the average service time, requests only experience a slight delay [41]. Whereas active low-power modes can increase the 99th-percentile response time significantly, small T_{tr} minimally alters it.

The deepest component energy savings can typically be extracted only when a component is idle. Idle low-power modes have been explored in processors [39, 45], memory [17, 18, 37], network interfaces [3], and disk [11]. Unfortunately, current per-core power modes (e.g. ACPI C-states or "core parking") save less than 1/Nth of the power in an N core processor because support circuitry (e.g., last-level caches, integrated memory controllers) remain powered to serve the remaining active cores [29]. The Intel Nehalem processor provides a socket-grained idle low-power mode through its "Package C6" power state, which disables some of this circuitry, but the incremental power savings over the per-core sleep modes is small. Nevertheless, processors typically consume only 20-30% of a server's power budget, while 70% of power is dissipated in other devices (e.g., memory, disks, etc.) [41]. PowerNap [40, 41] proposes to use full-system sleep to save energy during system idle periods, however, the prior study did not consider the implications of multicore scaling on idleness.

Alternatively, some authors have proposed scheduling background tasks or other work during primary-application idle periods [20, 23]; these mechanisms are orthogonal to our study.

2.3 Scheduling for energy efficiency

Idleness depends heavily on the workload running on a server. The amount of idleness observed at individual cores and over the system as a whole can differ drastically depending on workload characteristics. We illustrate the factors affecting idleness in Figure 3 for a four core system with a fixed utilization. If all requests arrive at the server at the same time and are of equal length (Figure 3(a)), all core-level idle periods align. Only in this degenerate case are core-level and system-level idleness equal. In Figure 3(b), the timing of request arrivals remain the same, but the request lengths vary; the amount of system-level idleness is reduced. Additionally varying request arrival timing, in Figure 3(c), further reduces system-level idleness. Finally, Figure 3(d) illustrates the effect of batch scheduling; though it is not possible to change request sizes, it is possible to alter the effective arrival pattern by delaying requests.

Elnozahy et al investigated using request batching (similar to what is shown in Figure 3(d)) to leverage idle low-power modes in uniprocessors [21]. DreamWeaver's contribution differs in three regards. First, DreamWeaver's request alignment algorithm is different; it is based on per-request stall constraints, it initiates service immediately once sufficient requests have arrived to fill all processing slots, and it suspends/resumes in-progress execution. In contrast, Elnozahy et al implement a simpler algorithm: requests are accumulated during a predefined batching window and released upon timeout. Furthermore, rather than imposing a per-request latency constraint, their approach tunes the timeout period over coarse intervals in a control-loop. Second, we consider the consequences of idleness and request skew for multicore systems; the previous study seeks to reduce transition penalties in a uniprocessor. Finally, the previous study was concerned only with processor power; one of our key observations is that non-CPU power management is critical to achieve energy-proportionality. A recent case study of request batching for Google's Web Search concludes that it provides an unappealing power-performance trade-off [42].

Several other prior scheduling mechanisms bear similarities to DreamWeaver in that they seek to align or construct batches of requests, for example, ecoDB [34] and cohort scheduling [36]. EcoDB introduces two techniques: using DVFS and delaying requests to batch SQL requests with common operators that can be amortized. Cohort scheduling seeks to maximize performance by scheduling similar stages of multiple requests together to increase the effectiveness of data caching. In contrast, DreamWeaver introduces delays to increase usable idleness; it is agnostic of the underlying software (i.e., the requests need not be similar) and depends only on statistical effects. All of these techniques take advantage of

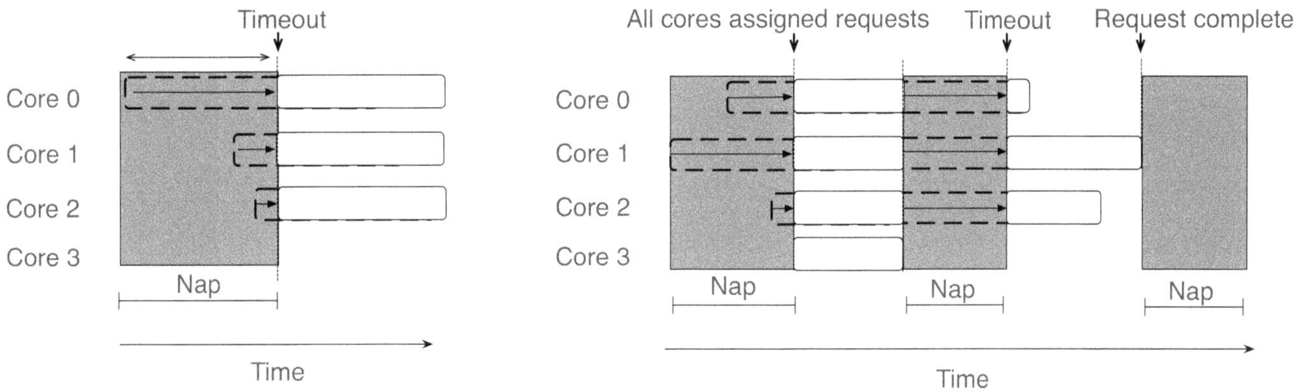

Figure 5: Weave Scheduling example. Weave Scheduling is an algorithm for intelligently delaying, preempting, and executing requests to maximize the fraction of time a multicore CPU is fully utilized while providing an upper-bound on per-request latency increase. The example on the left demonstrates an individual request exceeding its maximum delay. Although the system is underutilized, the system transitions out of the nap state because Core 0's request experienced a timeout. On the right, we demonstrate an example of preemption. At first, requests are delayed until all cores can be occupied and then the system transitions out of the nap state. The system remains active until Core 3's request finishes and then the system preempts the unfinished requests. Finally, Core 1's request experiences a timeout and the system resumes to meet the maximum delay constraint.

the insight that handling requests as they arrive may not be optimal for performance or energy efficiency.

3. DreamWeaver

DreamWeaver increases usable idleness by batching requests to maximize server utilization whenever it is active while ensuring that each request incurs at most a bounded delay. Our approach builds on PowerNap [40, 41], which allows a server to transition rapidly in and out of an ultra-low power nap state. PowerNap places an entire system (including memory, motherboard components, and peripherals) in an application-software–transparent deep sleep state during idle periods. PowerNap reduces power consumption by up to 95% while sleeping. Though PowerNap already approaches energy-proportionality (energy consumption proportional to utilization) in uniprocessor servers, it requires full-system idleness. As shown in Figure 2, there is little, if any, opportunity for PowerNap in lightly- to moderately-utilized large-scale multicore servers.

3.1 Hardware mechanisms: the Dream Processor

The baseline PowerNap design requires a sever (and, hence, all of its components) to transition between active and idle states in millisecond timeframes. Furthermore, it requires an operating system without a periodic timer tick, and software/hardware support to schedule wake-up in response to software timer expiration. The original PowerNap study [41] outlines these software and hardware requirements in greater detail, we focus here on new requirements.

DreamWeaver presents several additional implementation challenges. The largest challenge lies in handling the expiration of request timeouts and arrival of new work while the system is napping. Under PowerNap, handling the arrival of new work is simple—the system wakes up. Under DreamWeaver, however, the system must keep track of the number of idle cores and be able to defer arriving requests (while tracking their accumulated delay) without waking. A second challenge lies in preempting in-process execution to enter the nap state.

DreamWeaver addresses these requirements through the addition of a dedicated *Dream Processor* that coordinates with the operating system on the main processor(s) to manage sleep and wake transitions. The functionality of the Dream Processor is summarized in Figure 4. During operation, the primary OS uses the Dream Processor to track the assignment of requests to cores and the accumulated delay of each request. The primary OS notifies the Dream Processor each time a new request is created (e.g., because an incoming packet is processed), assigned one or more cores for execution, or completes. When a core becomes idle, the primary OS is responsible for preempting work on all cores and triggering a sleep transition. Upon transition, the primary OS passes the Dream Processor a list of active requests, the accumulated delay for each and the number of idle cores. Then, it hands control to the Dream Processor, which tracks the passage of time and continues to operate the network interface, while tracking the accumulated delay for each request. Using its own hardware timers, the Dream Processor wakes the system when any request's accumulated delay reaches the threshold.

Network packets that arrive during nap are received and queued by the Dream Processor. When the system wakes, the Dream Processor returns the accumulated delay of each request to the primary OS and then replays the delivery of queued packets through the network interface. Each arriving packet is assumed to create a new single-core request, and the Dream Processor wakes the system when the number of queued packets equals the number of idle cores. Hence, the number of queued packets is bounded by the number of cores and never grows large. While the Dream Processor could operate a complete TCP/IP stack, this is not necessary; only a layer-2 interface is needed to receive and log arriving packets. A more sophisticated Dream Processor may be able to identify packets that require minimal processing or can be deferred (e.g., TCP ack packets).

Since the Dream Processor operates continuously (including in the nap state), it is essential that its power requirements are low. Hence, it operates using its own dedicated memory and does not access any system peripherals except the network interface. The Dream and main processors communicate through programmed I/O (i.e., no shared memory). As the Dream Processor performs relatively simple tasks, it can be implemented with a low-power microcontroller. Several recent studies have evaluated auxiliary processors and network interfaces with similar capabilities, for example, Barely-alive Servers [6] and Somniloquy [3]. Our Dream Processor also is similar, albeit with considerably simpler requirements, to the service processors in existing IBM and HP server systems. These service processors perform a variety of environmental, temperature, and performance monitoring, maintenance, failure logging, and system management functions. They usually operate a complete TCP/IP stack to provide integrated lights-out functionality in contrast to the simple layer-2 and programmed I/O interfaces of the Dream Processor.

3.2 Weave Scheduling

Weave Scheduling improves energy efficiency by aligning service and idle times as much as possible, such that all cores are simultaneously active or idle. Our key intuition is to *stall service any time that any cores are unoccupied*, even if that means preempting requests that are in progress to go to sleep. During stalls, we invoke PowerNap to save energy. By allowing execution only when all cores are busy, DreamWeaver maximizes energy efficiency—the power required to operate the system is amortized over the maximum amount of concurrent work. If strictly implemented, this policy guarantees that all core-grain idleness is exploited at the system level.

Of course, such an approach could result in massive (potentially unbounded) increases in response time. To limit the impact on response time, we *constrain the maximum amount of time any request may be stalled*. Hence, if not all cores are occupied, but at least one request in the system has accrued its maximum allowable stall time, we resume service and allow all cores to execute until that request completes. When service proceeds due to exhausting a request's allowable stall time, some core-grain idleness is lost (cannot be used to conserve energy). However, the maximum stall threshold bounds the response time increase from Weave Scheduling; we simply choose this bound based on the amount of slack available between the current 99th-percentile response time and that required by the SLA.

We illustrate the operation of Weave Scheduling in a 4-core system in Figure 5. On the left, we demonstrate the stall threshold mechanism. Service is initially stalled and the system is napping. Then, the request at Core 0 reaches its maximum allowable delay (timeout). Request processing then resumes and all current requests are released (even though Core 3 is idle) until the request at Core 0 finishes. Subsequently, the system will again stall and nap. On the right, we demonstrate the behavior when all cores become occupied. The system is initially stalled and napping. Then a request arrives at Core 3, occupying all cores and starting service. As soon as the first request completes (at Core 3), the system again stalls and returns to nap. Shortly after, the request at Core 1 reaches timeout. Hence, service resumes and continues until the request at Core 1 is finished.

4. Prototype Evaluation

We evaluate DreamWeaver in two steps. In this section, we investigate its performance impact with a proof-of-concept prototype. We use these results to validate the performance predictions of our simulation approach. In Section 5, we use simulation to explore DreamWeaver's impact on power consumption.

4.1 Methodology

To assess the performance impact of DreamWeaver, we have constructed a software prototype that implements Weave Scheduling. Our prototype models the functionality of the Dream Processor with a software proxy that executes on the main CPU. Because servers with PowerNap capabilities are not currently commercially available, we cannot directly measure power savings from DreamWeaver; we defer this investigation to our simulation-based studies.

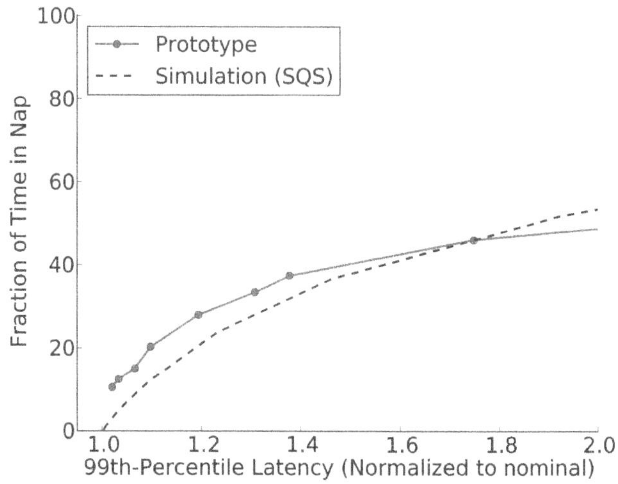

Figure 6: DreamWeaver prototype vs. simulation validation. This figure illustrates the accuracy of our simulation environment to predict the fraction of time a DreamWeaver server spends in the nap state. As we increase the predefined maximum delay a request can experience, the available full-system idleness increases as a function of 99th-percentile latency. One can see that the simulation ("Simulation") makes reasonable estimates of our prototype system ("Prototype").

We study the impact of DreamWeaver on a Web Search system modeled after that studied in [42] using the Solr Web Search platform. Solr is a full-featured Web indexing and search system used in production by many enterprises to add local search capability to their Web sites. Our system serves a Web index of the Wikipedia site [2], which we query using the AOL query set [1]. We believe this is the best approximation of a commercial Web search system that can be achieved using open source tools without access to proprietary binaries and data.

We emulate the behavior of the Dream Processor through a software proxy. Instead of sending queries directly to the Solr system, queries are sent to the proxy, which controls their admission to Solr. The software logic in the proxy mirrors that of the Dream Processor, however, the code runs on a core of the main CPU rather than a dedicated Dream Processor. The proxy tracks the number of active queries in the system and the accumulated delay of each query. When the system is awake, queries are passed immediately from the proxy to Solr via TCP/IP. We have confirmed that the addition of the proxy has negligible impact on the response time or throughput of Solr. When the system emulates nap, the proxy buffers incoming packets and uses timers to monitor accumulated delay. We implement the preemptive sleep called for by Weave Scheduling using Linux's existing process suspend capabilities; whenever the system enters the nap state, a suspend signal is sent to all Solr processes. The proxy assumes that all incoming TCP/IP packets correspond to a new query for the purposes of determining when to awake from nap. A Resume signal is sent to Solr upon a wake transition. Transition delays are emulated through busy waits in the proxy.

4.2 Results

We now present the results of our prototype system and compare it to our simulation infrastructure used in Section 5. Specifically we compare the sleep-latency tradeoff of the two evaluation methodologies. In Figure 6 we provide the time spent in sleep as a function of 99th-percentile latency as provided by our prototype ("Imple-

Table 1: Server Power Model. Based on data from Google [9] and HP [50].

Power (% of Peak)	CPU	Memory	Disk	Other
Max	40%	35%	10%	15%
Idle	15%	25%	9%	10%

mentation") and our simulation infrastructure ("SQS"). When allowed a 1.5x slack on 99th-percentile response time, DreamWeaver allows the prototype system to sleep 40% of the time. In contrast, the opportunity to sleep with PowerNap alone is negligible. Furthermore, the figure clearly demonstrates that the performance predictions of our simulation model agree well with the actual behavior of the prototype DreamWeaver system.

5. Power Savings Evaluation

While our prototype allows us to validate the performance impacts of DreamWeaver, the lack of PowerNap support in existing servers precludes measuring power savings. In this section, we use simulation to investigate DreamWeaver's power-performance impact on a variety of workloads over several multicore server generations.

5.1 Methodology

We evaluate the power savings potential of DreamWeaver and contrast it with other power management approaches using the BigHouse simulator [44]. This simulator leverages *Stochastic Queuing Simulation (SQS)*, a validated methodology for rapidly simulating the power-performance behavior of data center workloads. SQS is a framework for stochastic discrete time simulation of a generalized system of queuing models driven by empirical profiles of a target workload. In SQS, empirical interarrival and service distributions are collected from measurements of real systems at fine time-granularity. Using these distributions, synthetic arrival/service traces are generated and fed to a discrete-event simulation of a G/G/k queuing system that models server active and idle low-power modes through state-dependent service rates. SQS allows real server workloads to be characterized on one physical system, but then studied in a different context, for example on a system with vastly more cores (by varying k), or at different levels of load (by scaling the interarrival distribution). Furthermore, SQS enables analysis of queuing systems that are analytically intractable. Performance measures (e.g., 99th-percentile response time) are obtained by sampling the output of the simulation until each reaches a normalized half-width 95% confidence interval of 5%. Further details of the design and statistical methods used in SQS appear in [43, 44]. SQS has been previously used to model Google's Web search application [42], and its latency and throughput predictions have been validated against a production Web search cluster.

SQS does not model the details of what active system components are doing (e.g., which instructions are executing, what memory locations are accessed). However, these are not relevant to understanding idle periods and scheduling effects, hence, more detailed simulation models (e.g., instruction or cycle-accurate simulators) are unnecessary.

Low-Power Modes. Our power model assumptions for the system (Table 1) are based on the breakdowns from Google [9] and HP [50] and published characteristics of Intel Nehalem [29]. We model idle low-power modes through exceptional first service; that is, when a system is napping, the service rate of the corresponding server in the queuing model is set to zero and a latency penalty is incurred when the first request is serviced after idle.

As a point of comparison, we also model voltage and frequency scaling (VFS), by varying the service rate. We map core count to a corresponding technology node and power-performance scaling curve as shown in Figure 1, using data from [15]. We explore a range of power-performance settings by exhaustively sweeping static frequency and corresponding voltage settings. It is important to note that we optimistically allow the system to pick any arbitrary voltage/frequency setting although most processors only provide a few discrete points. Our VFS results should be viewed as an estimate of the potential of voltage and frequency scaling, they do not model any particular policy for selecting voltages. It is possible that a scheme that dynamically tunes frequency could improve slightly over our VFS estimates, though we expect such gains to be minimal because our experiments operate a server at a steady utilization.

Workloads. We collect empirical interarrival and service distributions from several production server workloads. These distributions are derived from week-long traces of departmental servers and from the Google Web Search test cluster as described in [42, 44]. Table 2 describes each workload and summarizes important interarrival and service statistics: for each distribution, we include the mean (Avg.), standard deviation (σ), and coefficient of variation (C_v).

Using these empirical distributions, we can independently scale arrival and service rates (i.e., without changing the distributions' shapes) to simulate higher and lower utilization. Moreover, we can replay stochastically-generated request sequences against arbitrary queuing models, including models for multicore chips far larger than are built today.

5.2 Results

Power-latency tradeoff compared to other techniques. We first contrast DreamWeaver with alternative power management approaches. We consider systems assuming a fixed throughput and evaluate the latency-power tradeoffs. It is important to note that nearly any power savings techniques will undoubtedly increase latency. If latency-at-any-cost is paramount, the best system design may discard power management. Instead, the question we pose is: Given an allowable threshold to increase 99th-percentile response time, what is the best way to save energy and how much can we save?

We contrast our mechanism ("DreamWeaver") with four other power management approaches. First, we compare against PowerNap as proposed in [41] ("PowerNap"). We initially assume an aggressive transition latency of 100 μs for both PowerNap and DreamWeaver because the goal of this work is to evaluate the ability of these techniques to exploit multicore idleness, not to mitigate transition latencies. We examine sensitivity to longer transition latencies below. Second, we compare it against Core Parking ("Core Parking"). We optimistically assume that cores can be parked during all core-grain idle time, ignoring transition penalties. Under this assumption, Core Parking subsumes approaches that consolidate tasks onto fewer cores to reshape core-grain idle periods (e.g., to lengthen them). Furthermore, we compare against a timeout-based batching mechanism ("Batch") based on the approach of Elnozahy et al [21]. Finally, we compare to voltage/frequency scaling ("VFS"), as described in Section 5.1.

4-Core Server. We first show the results for a server with four cores. The relative power savings of each of the considered power savings techniques is shown in Figure 7. Core Parking, Socket Parking, and PowerNap each yield only a single latency-performance point per system configuration and workload. In contrast, DreamWeaver, Batch, and VFS each produce a range of latency-power options. We present each of the four workloads with load scaled such that the server operates at 30% average utilization. The horizontal axis on each graph shows 99th-percentile latency

Table 2: Workload Characteristics.

Workload	Interarrival			Service			Description
	Avg.	σ	C_v	Avg.	σ	C_v	
DNS	1.1s	1.2s	1.1	194ms	198ms	1.0	DNS and DHCP server
Mail	206ms	397ms	1.9	92ms	335ms	3.6	POP and SMTP servers
Search	319μs	376μs	1.2	4.2ms	4.8ms	1.1	Google Web Search [42]
Apache	186ms	380ms	2.0	75ms	263ms	3.4	Web server

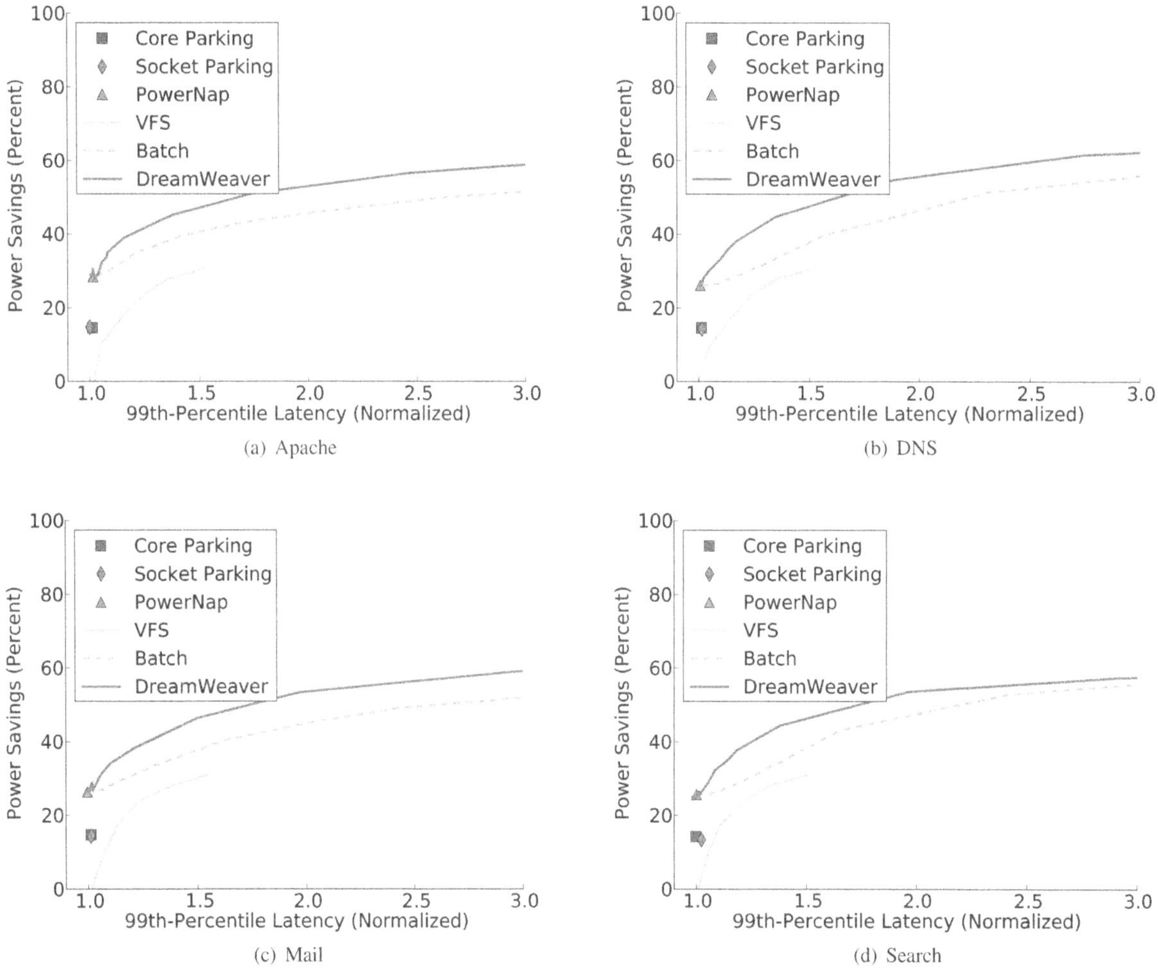

(a) Apache (b) DNS (c) Mail (d) Search

Figure 7: Comparison of power savings for 4-core system. This figure demonstrates the power savings of low-power modes as a function of 99th-percentile latency for a 4 core server. Per-core power gating ("Core Parking") can save a modest amount of power for a small latency increase because its transition latency is low, however it cannot reduce power in non-core components (e.g., last-level caches or the memory system). Attempting to put an entire socket into a low-power sleep mode ("Socket Parking") provides roughly the same benefit as per-core power gating; less idleness is available at socket granularity but this reduction is offset by the increase in power savings. Using a full-system low-power mode such as PowerNap ("PowerNap") exploits as much idle time as socket parking, but saves significantly more power. Processor voltage and frequency scaling ("VFS") provides significant savings for the CPU, but does not alter non-processor power (e.g., the memory system, I/O buses etc.). Greater power savings can be achieved by using a full-system idle low-power mode. Creating idleness by batching ("Batch"), provides even more power savings than PowerNap in exchange for increased latency due to delaying requests. An even better power-latency tradeoff is achieved by DreamWeaver ("DreamWeaver"), because of its hardware support to track requests and intelligent scheduling.

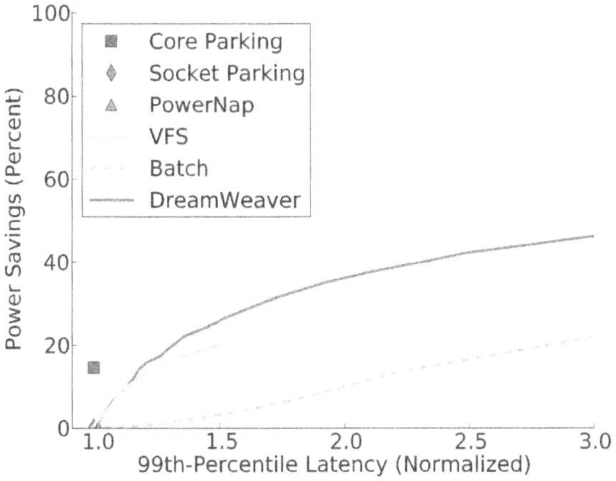

(a) Apache

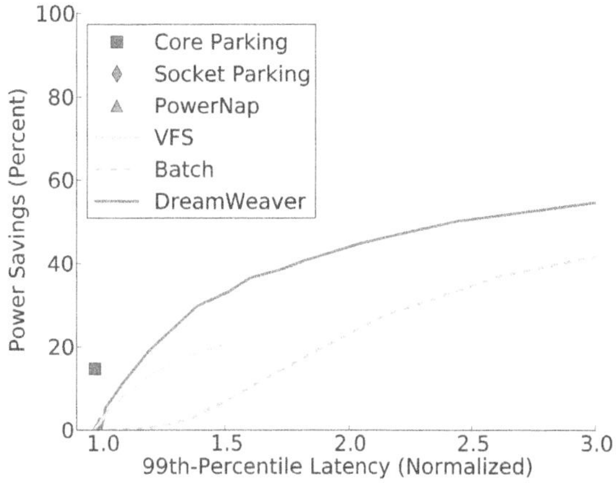

(b) DNS

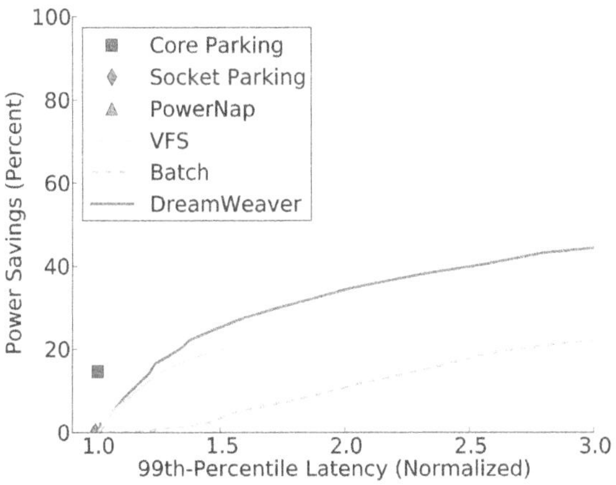

(c) Mail

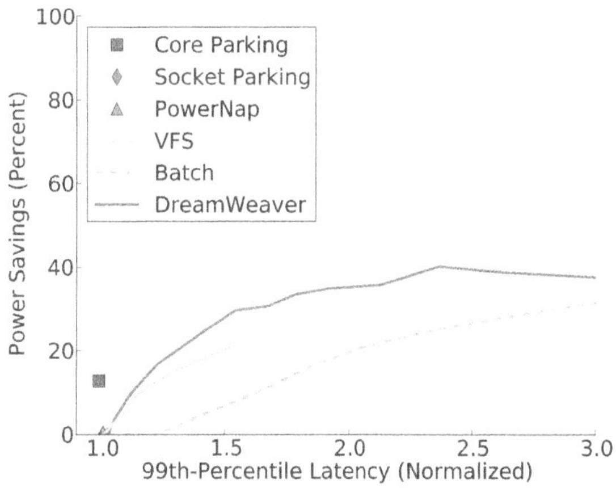

(d) Search

Figure 8: Comparison of power savings for 32-core system. Most low-power modes are less effective when moving to future systems (smaller transistor feature size and higher core count) because voltage scaling requires greater frequency reductions and coarse-grain idleness is more difficult to capture (See Figures 1 and 2). Per-core power gating ("Core Parking") does not rely on coarse-grain idleness and is just as effective as for a 4 core system (see Figure 6). However, both Socket Parking ("Socket Parking") and PowerNap ("PowerNap") require that all cores are simultaneously idle. At 32 cores, the system is almost never entirely idle and there is no opportunity to use these low-power modes. Voltage and frequency scaling ("VFS") saves less power because it requires a larger slowdown for a given voltage reduction. Batching ("Batch") at 32 cores is quite ineffective requiring inordinate latency increases to save appreciable power. DreamWeaver's effectiveness is reduced at 32 cores ("DreamWeaver"), but generally provides the greatest power savings for all but the tightest latency constraints.

normalized to the nominal latency (i.e., no power management). As discussed in Section 2, we focus our evaluation on 99th-percentile latencies as these are the more difficult constraints to meet; DreamWeaver's impact on mean latency follows the same trends. The vertical axis shows power savings relative to a nominal system without any of these power management features (but with clock gating on HLT instructions as in Nehalem); higher values indicate greater power savings.

Over the range from nominal to a 2x increase in 99th-percentile latency, DreamWeaver strictly dominates the other power management techniques. When the user configures DreamWeaver to allow no additional performance degradation on the 99th-percentile latency (i.e., a timeout of zero), DreamWeaver converges to PowerNap as expected; with a 2x increase in latency, DreamWeaver can offer roughly 25% better power savings than PowerNap and nearly 30% more than VFS. Also important, Batching can provide substantial power savings, and provides a roughly linear trade-off of 99th-percentile latency vs. power. However, its range of latency-power settings, while also better than VFS, is strictly inferior to DreamWeaver.

32-Core Server. Next, we consider a server with 32 cores. The results are presented in Figure 8 and parallel the previous study. First, as expected, we highlight that PowerNap is ineffective. Because there is no naturally occurring full-system idleness, there is no opportunity for PowerNap and it saves no power (nor incurs any latency). Next, we observe that Core Parking is still effective, but as before only provides power savings of less than 20%. A striking difference is that, unlike our four core study, Batch has become largely ineffective. The latency-power tradeoff for this technique is unattractive; it saves far less power than Core Parking,

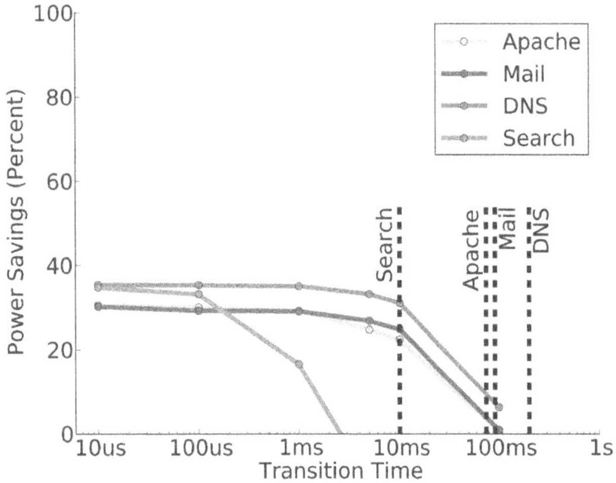

Figure 9: Sensitivity to transition time. DreamWeaver is less effective as the transition time in and out of PowerNap increases. Dotted vertical lines denote the average service time of each workload. The majority of power savings is realized by providing a transition time of about one order of magnitude less than the average service time of the workload.

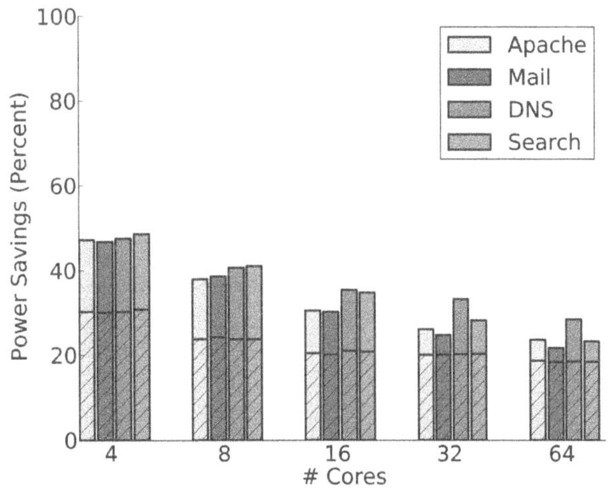

Figure 10: Sensitivity to number of cores. Solid bars represent DreamWeaver savings and hatched bars represent VFS savings. DreamWeaver is less effective as the number of cores increase, but always provides greater savings than VFS.

while incurring much greater delays. As with the 4-core system, DreamWeaver dominates the alternative approaches.

Sensitivity to transition time. To understand the utility of DreamWeaver for various server scenarios, we provide three sensitivity studies. First, we characterize the effectiveness of DreamWeaver for varying sleep transition times. Figure 9 illustrates how power savings diminishes for increasing transition time. We present results for a 16-core system at 30% utilization, with a performance constraint of 1.5x increase in 99th-percentile latency relative to nominal. We annotate the average service time of each workload

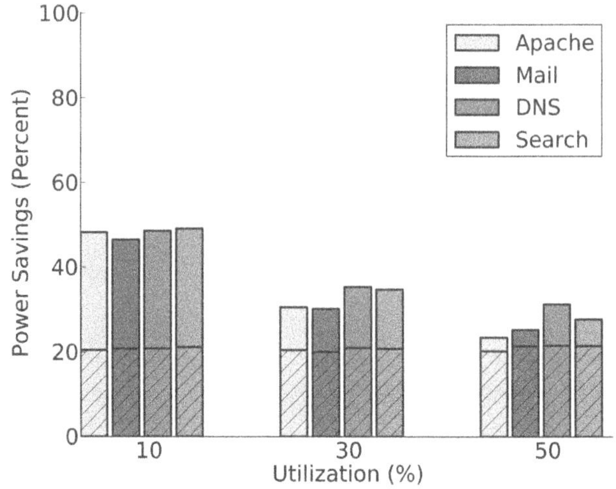

Figure 11: Sensitivity to utilization. Solid bars represent DreamWeaver savings and hatched bars represent VFS savings. DreamWeaver provides more savings in all cases.

along the time axis. As with PowerNap, when transition time becomes large relative to average service time, less power is saved. Ideally, transition time should be roughly an order of magnitude smaller than the average service time. Consistent with PowerNap [41], we find that the slowest transition time that is useful across all workloads is 1ms and designers should target the 100 μs to 1ms range.

Sensitivity to core count. In the next two sensitivity studies, we directly compare DreamWeaver to a system using VFS to save power. Figure 10 contrasts the power savings of DreamWeaver (solid bars) and VFS (hashed subset within each bar) when both are allowed a 1.5x slack on 99th-percentile latency. We vary the number of cores and the corresponding assumption for technology generation (65nm down to 16nm). Even for 64-core systems, DreamWeaver still provides power savings over 20%. DreamWeaver provides greater savings than VFS at all core counts, though its advantage shrinks as the number of cores grows.

Sensitivity to utilization. DreamWeaver is designed for low utilization, which is the common-case operating mode of servers [7]. Accordingly, DreamWeaver provides greater power savings at lower utilization. In Figure 11 we again contrast DreamWeaver (solid) and VFS (hashed) for a 16-core system as a function of utilization, under a 1.5x 99th-percentile response time slack. DreamWeaver still saves roughly 25% of power at utilization as high as 50%. Across the utilization spectrum, DreamWeaver saves more power than VFS, though its advantage is small for some workloads.

5.3 Discussion

Power Management in the 1000-Core Era. DreamWeaver is an effective means to enable full-system idle low-power modes for core counts that we foresee in the next three process generations (to 16nm). However, recent research has proposed 1000-core systems [31] and if transistor scaling beyond the 16nm node continues to double core counts, eventually, massively multicore architectures may become mainstream. The power management challenges we have identified will reach near-asymptotic limits in such a scenario. As we have observed, VFS effectiveness is shrinking at each technology node due to transistor scaling. Similarly, if servers continue to leverage weak scaling, full-system idleness will clearly disappear altogether with 1000 concurrent requests. The hardware and software models for 1000-core systems remain unclear; however, if we continue under current server software paradigms, we conclude that these power management techniques may become ineffective.

The Potential of Strong Scaling. Existing data center workloads rely on request-level parallelism to achieve performance scalability on multicore hardware. This parallelism strategy is a form of *weak scaling* (i.e, solving a larger problem size in a fixed amount of time, as opposed to *strong scaling* where a fixed problem size is solved in a reduced amount of time)—scalability is achieved by increasing request bandwidth rather than per-request speedup. A potential solution to the inefficacy of power management in a 1000-core system is for server software architectures to adopt strong scaling. Whereas in current systems each incoming request is assigned to a single core, under strong scaling multiple cores work together to service a single request faster. The aggregate throughput under strong scaling stays the same, but per-request latency is reduced; the downside is that the software engineering overhead for such architectures is likely to be significantly higher, as engineers must identify intra-request parallelism. Strong scaling makes power management easier because the number of concurrent independent requests is reduced—idle and busy periods naturally align across cooperating cores. As a result, the trends observed in Figure 2 will be reversed. In the limit, if all cores are used to service a single job, the system will behave (with respect to idleness) as if it were a uniprocessor. However, it is likely that Amdahl bottlenecks will preclude using 1000 cores for one request; instead clusters of cores might cooperate. Under this scenario, there will be a moderate number of clusters, and the effectiveness of DreamWeaver will resemble a weak-scaling system with the corresponding moderate number of cores. Unfortunately, the effectiveness of VFS does not change with better parallel software and its effectiveness will continue to decline unless better circuit techniques are developed.

6. Conclusion

As technology continues to scale and core counts increase, effective power management is becoming increasingly difficult. The effectiveness of voltage and frequency scaling is diminishing due to fundamental scaling trends. Because current-generation server software relies on weak scaling to use additional cores, full-system idleness is becoming increasingly scarce. DreamWeaver offers one mechanism to trade latency for power savings from idle low-power modes despite the challenges posed by multicore scaling. We show that DreamWeaver outperforms alternatives such as VFS, Core and Socket Parking, and past batching approaches while providing a smooth trade-off of 99th-percentile latency for power savings. Furthermore, should the community succeed in rearchitecting server systems to leverage strong scaling through intra-request parallelism, the advantages of DreamWeaver over other power management schemes grow even larger. We hope that our work serves as a warning that past approaches to power management are under threat given present scaling trends, and as a call to arms to redesign server software for strong scaling.

Acknowledgements

The authors would like to thank Ricardo Bianchini and Philip Wells for feedback on early drafts of the paper and the anonymous reviewers for their feedback. This work was supported in part by grants from Google and NSF grants CNS-0834403, CCF-0811320, and CCF-0815457.

References

[1] AOL Query Log, 2006.

[2] A Solr index of Wikipedia on EC2/EBS. 2010.

[3] Y. Agarwal, S. Hodges, R. Chandra, J. Scott, P. Bahl, and R. Gupta. Somniloquy: augmenting network interfaces to reduce PC energy usage. *NSDI '09: Networked Systems Design and Implementation*, 2009.

[4] F. Ahmad and T. Vijaykumar. Joint optimization of idle and cooling power in data centers while maintaining response time. *ASPLOS '10: Architectural Support for Programming Languages and Operating Systems*, 2010.

[5] H. Amur, R. Nathuji, M. Ghosh, K. Schwan, and H. Lee. IdlePower: Application-aware management of processor idle states. *MMCS '08: Workshop on Managed Many-Core Systems*, 2008.

[6] V. Anagnostopoulou, S. Biswas, A. Savage, R. Bianchini, T. Yang, and F. Chong. Energy Conservation in Datacenters through Cluster Memory Management and Barely-Alive Memory Servers. *WEED '09: Workshop on Energy-Efficient Design*, 2009.

[7] L. A. Barroso, J. Dean, and U. Hölzle. Web Search for A Planet: The Architecture of the Google Cluster. *IEEE Micro*, 2003.

[8] L. A. Barroso and U. Hölzle. The Case for Energy-Proportional Computing. *IEEE Computer*, (December):33–37, 2007.

[9] L. A. Barroso and U. Hölzle. The Datacenter as a Computer: An Introduction to the Design of Warehouse-Scale Machines. *Synthesis Lectures on Computer Architecture*, Morgan Claypool, 2009.

[10] C. Bash and G. Forman. Cool job allocation: Measuring the power savings of placing jobs at cooling-efficient locations in the data center. *USENIX Annual Technical Conference*, 2007.

[11] E. V. Carrera, E. Pinheiro, and R. Bianchini. Conserving disk energy in network servers. *ICS '03: Proceedings of the 17th annual international conference on Supercomputing*, 2003.

[12] J. S. Chase, D. C. Anderson, P. N. Thakar, A. M. Vahdat, and R. P. Doyle. Managing Energy and Server Resources in Hosting Centers. *SOSP '01: Symposium on Operating Systems Principles*, Dec. 2001.

[13] G. Chen, W. He, J. Liu, S. Nath, L. Rigas, L. Xiao, and F. Zhao. Energy-aware server provisioning and load dispatching for connection-intensive internet services. *NSDI '08: Networked Systems Design and Implementation*, 2008.

[14] Y. Chen, A. Das, W. Qin, A. Sivasubramaniam, Q. Wang, and N. Gautam. Managing server energy and operational costs in hosting centers. *SIGMETRICS '05: International Conference on Measurement and Modeling of Computer Systems*, 2005.

[15] M. Cho, N. Sathe, M. Gupta, S. Kumar, S. Yalamanchilli, and S. Mukhopadhyay. Proactive power migration to reduce maximum value and spatiotemporal non-uniformity of on-chip temperature distribution in homogeneous many-core processors. *Semiconductor Thermal Measurement and Management Symposium*, 2010.

[16] V. Delaluz, M. Kandemir, N. Vijaykrishnan, A. Sivasubramaniam, and M. Irwin. DRAM energy management using software and hardware directed power mode control. *HPCA '01: High-Performance Computer Architecture*, 2001.

[17] Q. Deng, D. Meisner, T. F. Wenisch, and R. Bianchini. MemScale : Active Low-Power Modes for Main Memory. *ASPLOS '11: Architectural Support for Programming Languages and Operating Systems*, 2011.

[18] B. Diniz, D. Guedes, W. Meira Jr., and R. Bianchini. Limiting the Power Consumption of Main Memory. *ISCA '07: International Symposium on Computer Architecture*, 2007.

[19] R. Dreslinski, M. Wieckowski, D. Blaauw, D. Sylvester, and T. Mudge. Near-threshold computing: Reclaiming Moore's law through energy efficient integrated circuits. *Proceedings of the IEEE*, 98(2), Feb. 2010.

[20] L. Eggert, J. D. Touch, and M. Rey. Idletime scheduling with preemption intervals. *SOSP '05: Symposium on Operating Systems Principles*, Oct. 2005.

[21] M. Elnozahy, M. Kistler, and R. Rajamony. Energy conservation policies for web servers. *USENIX Symposium on Internet Technologies and Systems-Volume 4*, 2003.

[22] A. Gandhi, M. Harchol-Balter, R. Das, J. Kephart, and C. Lefurgy. Power Capping Via Forced Idleness. *WEED '09: Workshop on Energy Efficient Design*, 2009.

[23] R. Golding, P. Bosch, C. Staelin, T. Sullivan, and J. Wilkes. Idleness is not sloth. *USENIX Annual Technical Conference*, 1995.

[24] S. Gurumurthi, A. Sivasubramaniam, and M. Kandemir. DRPM: dynamic speed control for power management in server class disks. *ISCA '03: International Symposium on Computer ArchitectureA*, 2003.

[25] M. Harchol-Balter and A. B. Downey. Exploiting process lifetime distributions for dynamic load balancing. *ACM Transactions on Computer Systems*, 15(3), Aug. 1997.

[26] T. Heath, B. Diniz, and E. Carrera. Energy conservation in heterogeneous server clusters. *PPoPP '05: Principles and Practice of Parallel Programming*, 2005.

[27] S. Herbert and D. Marculescu. Analysis of Dynamic Voltage/Frequency Scaling in Chip-Multiprocessors. *ISLPED '07: International Symposium on Low Power Electronics and Design*, 2007.

[28] U. Hölzle. Brawny cores still beat wimpy cores, most of the time. *IEEE Micro*, 30(4), 2010.

[29] Intel. Intel Xeon Processor 5600 Series. Datasheet, Volume 1. 2010.

[30] C. Isci, A. Buyuktosunoglu, C.-Y. Cher, P. Bose, and M. Martonosi. An Analysis of Efficient Multi-Core Global Power Management Policies: Maximizing Performance for a Given Power Budget. *Micro '06: International Symposium on Microarchitecture*, 2006.

[31] J. H. Kelm, D. R. Johnson, M. R. Johnson, N. C. Crago, W. Tuohy, A. Mahesri, S. S. Lumetta, M. I. Frank, and S. J. Patel. Rigel : An Architecture and Scalable Programming Interface for a 1000-core Accelerator. *ISCA '09: International Symposium on Computer Architecture*, 2009.

[32] W. Kim, M. S. Gupta, G.-Y. Wei, and D. Brooks. System level analysis of fast, per-core DVFS using on-chip switching regulators. *HPCA '08: High Performance Computer Architecture*, 2008.

[33] A. Krioukov, P. Mohan, S. Alspaugh, L. Keys, D. Culler, and R. Katz. NapSAC : Design and Implementation of a Power-Proportional Web Cluster. *Green Networking*, 2010.

[34] W. Lang and J. Patel. Towards eco-friendly database management systems. *CIDR '09: Conference on Innovative Data Systems Reasearch*, 2009.

[35] W. Lang and J. M. Patel. Energy Management for MapReduce Clusters. *VLDB*, 2010.

[36] J. Larus and M. Parkes. Using Cohort Scheduling to Enhance Server Performance. In *ACM SIGPLAN Notices*, volume 36, 2001.

[37] A. R. Lebeck, X. Fan, H. Zeng, and C. Ellis. Power Aware Page Allocation. *ASPLOS '00: Architectural Support for Programming Languages and Operating Systems*, 2000.

[38] C. Lefurgy, K. Rajamani, F. Rawson, W. Felter, M. Kistler, and T. Keller. Energy management for commercial servers. *Computer*, 36(12):39–48, Dec. 2003.

[39] J. Leverich, M. Monchiero, V. Talwar, P. Ranganathan, and C. Kozyrakis. Power Management of Datacenter Workloads Using Per-Core Power Gating. *IEEE Computer Architecture Letters*, 8(2):48–51, Feb. 2009.

[40] D. Meisner, B. T. Gold, and T. F. Wenisch. The PowerNap server architecture. *ACM Transactions on Computer Systems (TOCS)*, 29(1), 2011.

[41] D. Meisner, B. T. Gold, and T. F. Wenisch. PowerNap: Eliminating Server Idle Power. *ASPLOS '09: Architectural Support for Programming Languages and Operating Systems*, Feb. 2009.

[42] D. Meisner, C. M. Sadler, L. A. Barroso, W.-D. Weber, and T. F. Wenisch. Power Management of Online Data-Intensive Services. *ISCA '11: International Symposium on Computer Architecture*, 2011.

[43] D. Meisner, and T. F. Wenisch. Stochastic Queuing Simulation for Data Center Workloads. *EXERT '10: Exascale Evaluation and Research Techniques Workshop*, 2010.

[44] D. Meisner, J. Wu, and T. F. Wenisch. BigHouse: A simulation infrastructure for data center systems. *ISPASS '12: International Symposium on Performance Analysis of Systems and Software*, 2012.

[45] Microsoft. Improved data center power consumption and streamlining management. 2010.

[46] V. Pandey, W. Jiang, Y. Zhou, and R. Bianchini. DMA-Aware Memory Energy Management. *HPCA '06: High-Performance Computer Architecture*, 2006.

[47] E. Pinheiro, R. Bianchini, E. Carrera, and T. Heath. Load Balancing and Unbalancing for Power and Performance in Cluster-Based Systems. *Workshop on Compilers and Operating Systems for Low Power*, 2001.

[48] J. Sharkey, A. Buyuktosunoglu, and P. Bose. Evaluating design tradeoffs in on-chip power management for CMPs. *ISLPED 07: International symposium on Low power electronics and design*, 2007.

[49] N. Tolia, Z. Wang, M. Marwah, C. Bash, P. Ranganathan, and X. Zhu. Delivering Energy Proportionality with Non Energy-Proportional Systems Optimizing the Ensemble. *HotPower '08: Workshop on Power-Aware Computing Systems*, 2008.

[50] D. Tsirogiannis, S. Harizopoulos, and M. A. Shah. Analyzing the energy efficiency of a database server. *SIGMOD*, 2010.

[51] F. Xie, M. Martonosi, and S. Malik. Bounds on power savings using runtime dynamic voltage scaling: an exact algorithm and a linear-time heuristic approximation. *International Symposium on Low Power Electronics and Design*, page 287, 2005.

Automatic Generation of Hardware/Software Interfaces

Myron King, Nirav Dave, Arvind
Massachusetts Institute of Technology - Computer Science and Artificial Intelligence Laboratory
{mdk,ndave,arvind}@csail.mit.edu

Abstract

Enabling new applications for mobile devices often requires the use of specialized hardware to reduce power consumption. Because of time-to-market pressure, current design methodologies for embedded applications require an early partitioning of the design, allowing the hardware and software to be developed simultaneously, each adhering to a rigid interface contract. This approach is problematic for two reasons: (1) a detailed hardware-software interface is difficult to specify until one is deep into the design process, and (2) it prevents the later migration of functionality across the interface motivated by efficiency concerns or the addition of features. We address this problem using the Bluespec Codesign Language (BCL) which permits the designer to specify the hardware-software partition in the source code, allowing the compiler to synthesize efficient software and hardware along with transactors for communication between the partitions. The movement of functionality across the hardware-software boundary is accomplished by simply specifying a new partitioning, and since the compiler automatically generates the desired interface specifications, it eliminates yet another error-prone design task. In this paper we present BCL, an extension of a commercially available hardware design language (Bluespec SystemVerilog), a new software compiling scheme, and preliminary results generated using our compiler for various hardware-software decompositions of an Ogg Vorbis audio decoder, and a ray-tracing application.

Categories and Subject Descriptors B.6.3 [*LOGIC DESIGN*]: Hardware description languages; C.3 [*SPECIAL-PURPOSE AND APPLICATION-BASED SYSTEMS*]: Real-time and embedded systems; D.3.3 [*PROGRAMMING LANGUAGES*]: Language Constructs and Features

General Terms Design, Performance

Keywords Hardware/Software Codesign

1. Introduction

Modern mobile devices provide a large and increasing range of functionality, from high-resolution cameras, video and audio decoders, to wireless basebands that can work with a variety of protocols. For power and performance reasons much of this functionality relies on specialized hardware. Often designers start with a pure software (SW) implementation of an algorithm written in C (or Matlab), and identify computationally intensive parts which need to be implemented in hardware in order to meet the design constraints. Hardware (HW) accelerators come in three different forms. Hardware can be synthesized as an ASIC for the application at hand, in which case the problem reduces to whether the source description is amenable to generation of good quality hardware. The accelerator may also be available in the form of a standardized IP block, like FFT, to be called from the application code. Lastly, the accelerator could be in the form of a programmable processor like a DSP with its own tool chain and distinct programming model. In all three cases, the designer must modify some parts of the application code to make use of the accelerator.

Regardless of what kind of accelerator is eventually used, some software is always required to drive it. Since the time to market is of paramount importance, the hardware and the associated software driver are almost always developed in parallel by two separate design teams. The two teams agree upon a hardware-software decomposition and the associated interface early on to make the final integration as seamless as possible. However, in practice the interface rarely matches the specification precisely. This happens because the early hardware specifications are often incomplete, and either leave room for misinterpretation, or are simply unimplementable. This integration problem has a large negative impact on the time-to-market. Worse, by prematurely restricting the design, lower-cost or higher-performance alternatives may be ignored.

In our approach, the complete module, as well as the partition boundaries, are specified in the Bluespec Codesign Language (BCL), which is suitable for both hardware and low-level software design. BCL is a semantic extension of Bluespec SystemVerilog (BSV) [1], a commercial language for hardware synthesis. The BCL compiler uses the BSV compiler to generate the special purpose hardware (Verilog) for the hardware partition and it compiles the software partition into C++. It also generates the infrastructure code for communication between the partitions. Crucially, the generated implementations can interoperate with *any* other implementation which conforms to the generated interface. Our approach therefore supports the following design methodologies:

- **Fully Automatic:** The system implementers use the automatically generated implementations directly for both the hardware and software partitions. A major advantage of this approach is that the hardware and software decompositions can be redone with little or no effort to meet changing system requirements as the system design evolves.
- **Partially Automatic:** The system implementers use the automatically generated implementations for either the hardware or software components, choosing some other approach for the remaining parts. While this approach limits the ability to change the partition late in the design process, it does provide implementers with a reference design they can use during testing and development.
- **Interface Only:** The system implementors develop both the hardware and software pieces using alternative approaches, *but use the communication infrastructure code generated by the*

ASPLOS'12, March 3–7, 2012, London, England, UK.

BCL compiler to define the HW/SW interface. Because the interfaces are backed by fully functional reference implementations, there is no need to build simulators for testing and development purposes.

The primary contributions of this paper are (1) the BCL language, including a method of specifying hardware-software partition at the source level; (2) a compilation strategy for generating efficient code for software partitions; (3) the specification of transactors needed to communicate with the hardware partitions; and (4) a demonstration of the viability of our approach by applying it to concrete examples. We think this is the first demonstration of multiple versions of a hardware-software codesign from the same source code working on an FPGA.

Paper organization: In Section 2 we illustrate HW/SW design complications with an example. After a discussion of related work in Section 3, we give an introduction to BCL in Section 4, using Vorbis as a running example. In Section 5 we discuss the operational semantics of the kernel of BCL informally. In Sections 6 we present our compilation strategy, and conclude with a presentation of the experimental results in Section 7.

2. A Motivating Example

Ogg Vorbis is an open-source psychoacoustically-aware audio CODEC aimed at simple low-complexity decoding (see Figure 1). We have chosen this example for its relative simplicity, but the analysis we do applies equally to video CODECs and radio baseband processing [2] which are much more complex.

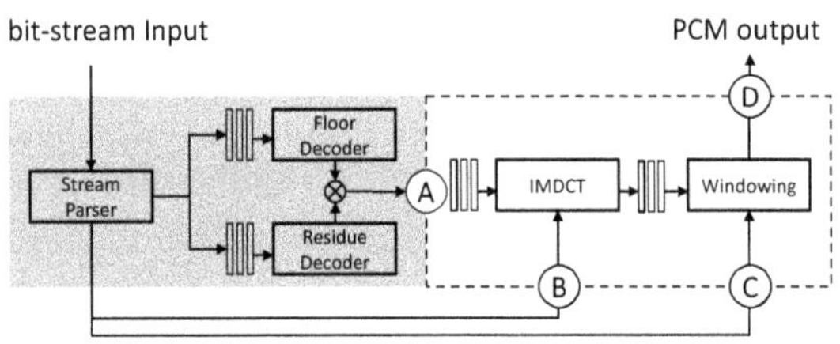

Figure 1. Ogg Vorbis pipeline diagram. The HW accelerator is delimited by the dotted line, and the original SW is shaded

The front end of the pipeline consists of a stream parser and various decoders though which the audio frequency spectra are reconstructed. Due to the compression schema, these modules have complex control, but are relatively lightweight from a computational standpoint. We will assume the front end of the pipeline generates frames, which are then sent to the back-end by invoking the back-end method with a pointer to the frame and the frame size as arguments. The back-end of the pipeline transforms the signal from the frequency to the time domain through the use of an IMDCT which internally uses the computationally intensive IFFT. The frames in the final output are overlapped using a sliding window function to compensate for spectral leakage at the frame boundaries, after which the PCM frames are sent directly to the speaker through memory-mapped IO. The C++ pseudocode for the back-end is shown in Figure 2.

To accelerate this application, it is quite clear that the back-end will require some HW acceleration. However, it is not clear if the entire back-end or just the IFFT should end up in hardware.

2.1 Restructuring Software to Interact with the Accelerator

Let us assume that we are able to implement an efficient IFFT HW accelerator which has an input port and an output port which transfer serialized frames one word at a time. The HW implementation keeps track of the number of words that have been received, and once a full frame is present, it computes the IFFT and subsequently

```
void backend(int* frame, int N){
 int a[2*N], b[2*N], *tmp, i;
 for(i = 0; i < N; i++){
   a[i]   = imdctPreLo(i,N,frame[i]);
   a[i+N] = imdctPreHi(i,N,frame[i]);}
 swIFFT.ifft(2*N, a, a);
 for(i = 0; i < N; i++)
   b[bitReverse(i)] = imdctPost(i,N,a[i]);
 tmp = swWindow.nextFrame(b,2*N);
 for(i = 0; i < N; i++)
   memcpy(AUDIO_DEV, tmp[i], 4);}
```

Figure 2. Vorbis back-end in C++

makes the data available on the output port. Let us also assume that the bus protocol permits blocking reads and blocking writes, so if we attempt to read a word from the output port before the answer has been computed, the SW will block. Likewise if we attempt to write a word to the input port before the prior word has been consumed, the write will also block. The invocation of the IFFT in Figure 2 (`swIFFT.ifft(2*N, a, a)`) can be replaced by the code shown in Figure 3 to exploit such HW.

```
...
hwIFFT.setSize(2*N);
for(i = 0; i < 2*N; i++)
  hwIFFT.put(a[i]);
for(i = 0; i < 2*N; i++)
  a[i] = hwIFFT.get();
...
```

Figure 3. Acceleration using blocking HW

Given the latency introduced by transferring the data to and from the accelerator over the bus, it is highly unlikely that the overall algorithm will be sped up by using the accelerator in this manner. In almost all such HW designs where significant data transfer is involved, it is important to find ways to speed up the communication, it is often not possible to change the *latency* of communication because it is tied to system components like BUS and networks which are typically fixed. Several potential solutions exist to hide this latency:

Communication Granularity: Transferring data one word at a time is inefficient, given the overhead of a bus transaction. This cost can be amortized by transferring larger blocks of data directly into the accelerator memory. At the BUS protocol level, this means exploiting burst transfers. The two loops in Figure 3 which invoke `hwIFFT.put()` and `hwIFFT.get()` respectively will be replaced by two invocations to a burst transfer (see Figure 4). Many systems have dedicated DMA hardware which efficiently implements the desired behavior. Another way to halve the BUS traffic would be to implement the windowing function in the same accelerator and connect the accelerator directly to the speaker.

Pipelining: Often the use of DMA can saturate the BUS bandwidth, and when this happens, the accelerator can become the bottleneck. Pipelining the accelerator hardware can further improve the throughput, and we exploit this concurrency through the use of multithreading, as shown in Figure 4. Though the putFrame() and getFrame() calls to the HW are still blocking, the pipelined HW implementation can now begin receiving new frames even though it may not have completed the transformation of the previous ones. A separate thread is started at the beginning of time which invokes `backend_complete()` in a `while(true)` loop to drain the HW accelerator and drive the final audio pipeline stages. When running under a traditional OS, this code is actually quite convenient to write, though many embedded operating systems do not support multithreading, requiring the application to simulate this behavior manually.

```
void backend(int* frame, int N){
 int a[2*N], i;
 for(i = 0; i < N; i++){
   a[i]   = imdctPreLo(i,N,frame[i]);
   a[i+N] = imdctPreHi(i,N,frame[i]);}
 hwIFFT.setSize(2*N);
 hwIFFT.putFrame(a,2*N);
}
void backend_complete(int N){
 int a*, b[2*N], i, *tmp;
 a = hwIFFT.getFrame(2*N);
 for(i = 0; i < N; i++)
   b[bitReverse(i)] = imdctPost(i,N,a[i]);
 tmp = swWindow.nextFrame(b,2*N);
 for(i = 0; i < N; i++)
   memcpy(AUDIO_DEV, tmp[i], 4);}
```

Figure 4. Multithreaded use of pipelined HW (`backend_complete()` is repeatedly invoked by a separate thread)

Nonblocking Interface: Suppose that the accelerator is not pipelined, we can still improve the overall efficiency by doing useful work while waiting for the accelerator to complete its work. This requires making the IFFT interface non-blocking, as shown in Figure 5. Nonblocking interfaces require exposing some internal details of the accelerator, *e.g.,* the status of internal state machines or memory buffers. For example, a protocol might require the HW to first indicate that it has enough buffering to receive an entire frame, so that individual puts will never block waiting for space to become available. This information invariably percolates up to the front of the audio pipeline, since we now need to change the interface type of `backend` to return `bool` (see Figure 5). Related, but more complicated issues arise when an accelerator is shared among several threads.

```
volatile int* hw_status, *hw_fbuff, *hw_sz;
bool backend(int* frame, int N){
 if(*hw_status == RDY){return false;}
 ...
 *hw_size = (2*N);
 memcpy(*hw_fbuff, a, 2*N*4);
 *hw_status = GO;
 while(*hw_status != RDY){;}
 memcpy(a, *hw_fbuff, 2*N*4);
 ...
 return true;}
```

Figure 5. Acceleration using non-blocking hardware

The software now has much greater control over the hardware, but as a result, the clean get/put interface has now been polluted by implementation detail. Exposing this level of details violates the important design principle of isolation; now if the HW needs to be refined, the SW must be re-validated since it can observe the internal state of the HW.

2.2 Synthesis of the Accelerator

It should be clear from the previous discussions that several different hardware designs – pipelined versus non-pipelined, blocking versus nonblocking – are possible for the IFFT accelerator. Given the state of the art in hardware synthesis, it is not possible to generate efficient hardware from typical software codes written in C or C++. The designer must describe the architecture for the accelerator in some HDL like Verilog. To anyone who is familiar with HDL's, it should be clear that this is a radical change in the way one thinks about programming. Furthermore, any verification effort performed on the original implementation must be repeated in a new language with completely different semantics, and since the IFFT interface has changed, the SW partition will need to be modified and re-verified as well.

2.3 Data Format Issues

Mismatch of data representation is one of the more common source of errors in HW/SW codesign. The objects generated by the application must be correctly converted to the bit representation expected by the accelerator. This problem is compounded by the fact that the C++ compiler and the Verilog compiler may have completely different layouts for the "same" data structure:

```
C++:
template<typename F, typename I>
 struct FixPt{ F fract; I integer; };
template<typename T>
 struct Complex{T rel; T img;};

Verilog:
typedef struct {bit[31:0] fract; bit[31:0] int;} FixPt;
typedef struct {FixPt rel; FixPt img;}; Complex_FixPt;
```

The two languages may have different endian conventions, and even two compilers for the same language can use different conventions depending on the targeted substrate. Many SW representations do not even have a natural HW analog. In general, keeping HW and SW representations of shared data structures is both tedious and error prone.

2.4 A Language-Based Solution

A fundamental difficulty of hardware-software codesign stems from the fact that the software and hardware continue to be developed in two separate languages, each with its own semantics and programming idioms. We believe that what is needed instead is a common language for hardware-software codesign with the following properties:

1. *Fine-grain parallelism:* Hardware is inherently parallel and any codesign language must be flexible enough to express meaningful hardware structures. Low-level software which drives the hardware does so via highly concurrent untimed transactions, which must also be expressible in the language.
2. *Easy specification of partitions:* In complex designs it is important for the designer to retain a measure of control in expressing his insights about the partitioning between hardware and software. Doing so within suitable algorithmic parameters should not require any major changes in code structure.
3. *Generation of high-quality hardware:* Digital hardware designs are usually expressed in RTL languages like Verilog from which low-level hardware implementations can be automatically generated using a number of widely available commercial tools. (Even for FPGAs it is practically impossible to completely avoid RTL). The codesign language must compile into efficient RTL code.
4. *Generation of efficient sequential code:* Since the source code is likely to contain fine-grain transactions, it is important to be able to interleave partially executed transactions without introducing deadlocks while waiting for external events.
5. *Shared communication channels:* Often the communication between a hardware device and a processor is accomplished via a shared bus. The high-level concurrency model of the codesign language should permit sharing of such channels without introducing deadlocks.

The design of BCL was motivated by these goals, and in BCL it is possible to describe any subset of the Vorbis pipeline in such a way that efficient hardware may be synthesized. Different microarchitectures for implementing [say] IFFT can also be described by writing different BCL programs [2], and at the same time, the whole design can be compiled into sequential software. What makes BCL unique is that by using the idea of *computational domains* (Section 4.2), it is possible to specify which part of the BCL program should be run in HW (*i.e.*, compiled to Verilog) and which in SW (*i.e.*, compiled to C++). Thus, moving any code across the HW/SW boundary is as simple as specifying a different partition, a feature that is especially useful when experimenting with how much of the code surrounding IFFT in the back-end should be implemented as hardware. The use of a single language automatically avoids the data formatting issues mentioned previously, and the code generated by compiling BCL can interface both with other system hardware such as the audio device, and software up the stack starting from the Ogg Vorbis front end.

The computational domains specified in BCL let the compiler automatically deduce the communication between hardware and software. If the accelerator is connected to the microprocessor by a BUS, the compiler will use this underlying substrate through low-level library elements. Note that the interface given for the back-end of the pipeline (behind which all HW/SW codesign exploration takes place) is a much more stable interface than any traditional BUS-based interface used by device drivers.

3. Related Work

We are not aware of any language which satisfies all the goals enumerated in Section 2, however there is a substantial body of work, both academic and commercial, relevant to various aspects of hardware-software codesign.

Implementation-agnostic parallel models: There are several parallel computation models whose semantics are agnostic to implementation in hardware or software. In principle, any of these can provide a basis for hardware-software codesign.

Threads and locks are used extensively in parallel programming and also form the basis of SystemC [3] – a popular C++ class library for modeling embedded systems. While these libraries provide great flexibility in specifying modules, the language itself lacks proper compositional semantics, producing unpredictable behaviors when connecting modules. Synthesis of high-quality hardware from SystemC remains a challenge.

Dataflow models, both at macro-levels (Kahn [4]) and fine-grained levels (Dennis [5], Arvind [6]), provide many attractive properties but abstract away important resource-level issues that are necessary for expressing efficient hardware or software. Nevertheless dataflow models where the rates at which each node works are specified statically have been used successfully in signal processing applications [7, 8].

Synchronous dataflow is a clean model of concurrency based on synchronous clocks, and forms the basis of many programming languages (*e.g.*, Esterel [9], Lustre [10], Signal [11], Rapide [12], Shim [13], Polysynchrony [14]). Scade [15], a commercial tool for designing safety-critical applications, is also based on this model.

We have chosen *guarded atomic actions* (or rules) as the basis for *BCL*. All legal behaviors in this model can be understood as a series of atomic actions on a state. This model was used by Chandy and Misra in Unity [16] to describe software, and then by Hoe and Arvind to generate hardware [17]. Dijsktra's Guarded Commands [18] and Lynch's IO Automata [19] are also closely related. BCL extends the idea of multiple clock domains [20] from Bluespec SystemVerilog (BSV) [21] to specify how a design should be split between hardware and software. Hardware compilation from BCL is a straightforward translation into BSV, whose subsequent compilation to Verilog is a mature and proven technology [17, 21]. Guarded atomic actions also provide a good foundation to build analysis and verification tools [22].

Generation of software from hardware descriptions: Hardware description languages (HDLs) like Verilog and VHDL provide extremely fine-grain parallelism but lack an understandable semantic model [23] and are also impractical for writing software. Nevertheless, these languages can compile to a software simulator, which can be viewed as a software implementation. Popular commercial products like Verilator [24] and Carbon [25] show significant speedup in the performance of these simulators, though the requirement to maintain cycle-level accuracy (at a gate-level) is a fundamental barrier; the performance is often several factors slower than natural software implementations of the same algorithm.

The Chinook [26, 27] compiler addressed an important aspect of the hardware/software interface problem, by automating the task of generating a software interface from the RTL description and the timing information of the hardware blocks.

Lastly, Bluespec's Bluesim [21] can exploit the fact that the cycle-level computation can be represented as a sequence of atomic actions. This permits dramatic improvement in performance but the underlying cost of cycle-accuracy remains.

Generation of hardware from sequential software specifications: To avoid the burden of using low-level HDLs, the idea of extracting a hardware design from a familiar software language, *e.g.*, C, Java, or Haskell, has great appeal. Liao et al. [28] present one of the earliest solutions to mitigate the difficulty of the hardware-software interface problem by describing the interface in C++ and generating an implementation using hand coded libraries that interact with automatically synthesized hardware. Many systems like CatapultC [29], Pico Platform [30], or AutoPilot have been effective at generating some forms of hardware from C code. However, constructing efficient designs with dynamic control can be very hard, if not impossible, using such tools [31].

A related effort is the Liquid Metal project [32] which compiles an extension of Java into hardware. It lets the programmer specify parts of the program in a manner which eases the analysis required for efficient hardware generation. In contrast to BCL which relies on explicit state and guarded atomic actions, Liquid Metal exploits particular extensions to the Java type system.

Frameworks for simulating heterogeneous systems: There are numerous systems that allow co-simulation of hardware and software modules. Such systems, which often suffer from both low simulation speeds and improperly specified semantics, are typically not used for direct hardware or software synthesis.

Ptolemy [33] is a prime example of a heterogeneous modeling framework, which concentrates more on providing an infrastructure for modeling and verification, and less on the generation of efficient software; it does not address the synthesis of hardware at all. Metropolis [34], while related, has a radically different computational model and has been used quite effectively for hardware/software codesign, though primarily for validation and verification rather than the synthesis of efficient hardware.

Matlab and Simulink generate production code for embedded processors as well as VHDL from a single algorithmic description. Simulink employs a customizable set of block libraries which allow the user to describe an algorithm by specifying the component interactions. Simulink does allow the user to specify modules, though the nature of the Matlab language is such that efficient synthesis of hardware would be susceptible to the same pitfalls as C-based tools. A weakness of any library-based approach is the difficulty for users to specify new library modules.

In summary, while all these frameworks may be effective for modeling systems, we do not believe they solve the general problem of generating efficient implementations.

Algorithmic approaches to hardware/software partitioning: There is an extensive body of work which views hardware-software partitioning as an optimization problem, similar to the way one might look at a graph partitioning problem to minimize communication [35, 36]. The success of such approaches depends upon the quality of estimates for various cost functions as well as the practical relevance of the optimization function. Since these approaches do not generate a working hardware/software design, they need to make high-level approximations, often making use of domain-specific knowledge to improve accuracy. Such analysis is complementary to real hardware-software codesign approaches.

4. Introduction to BCL via Vorbis

BCL is a modern statically-typed language with the flexibility to target either hardware or software. It contains higher-order functions and the rich data structures required to express fine-grain parallelism. Any language with hardware as a target must be restricted so that it is compilable into efficient FSMs. Consequently BCL can be used for writing only the type of software which does not require dynamic heap storage allocation and where the stack depth is known at compile-time. In fact, in a BCL program all state must be declared *explicitly*, and the type system prohibits dynamic allocation of objects. Because BCL's intended use is for describing software primarily at the bottom of the stack, this restriction is not burdensome.

BCL is an extension of Bluespec SystemVerilog (BSV) and borrows BSV's syntax and its powerful Haskell inspired meta-programming features. In the rest of this section we will explain BCL using the Vorbis pipeline and its partitioning between hardware and software.

4.1 The Vorbis Pipeline

Below we have given a simplified version of the code implementing the back-end of the Vorbis pipeline. The reader will notice that the high-level organization is very similar to the code example given in Figure 2:

```
module mkVorbisBackEnd(VorbisBackEnd#(k,t))
  IFFT#(2*k, Complex#(t)) ifft <- mkIFFT;
  Window#(2*k, t)         window <- mkWindow;
  method Action input(Vector#(k,Complex#(t)) vx)
    Vector#(2*k,Complex#(t)) v;
    for(int i = 0; i < k; i++)
      v[i]   = preTable1[i]*vx[i];
      v[K+i] = preTable2[i]*vx[i];
    ifft.input(v);
  rule xfer
    let x = ifft.output() in (ifft.deq();
    Vector#(2*k,t) v;
    for(int i = 0; i < 2*k; i++)
      v[i] = x[bitReverse(i)].real;
    window.input(v))
  rule output
    let rv = window.output();
     window.deq(); AUDIO_DEV.output(rv)
```

A BCL program consists of a hierarchy of modules, and as with any object-oriented language, all interactions with modules occur through their interface methods. The `mkVorbisBackend` module definition instantiates two sub-modules: `ifft` and `window`. Each module is potentially stateful, but ultimately all state is built up from primitive elements called *registers*. It is important not to confuse the state elements with ordinary variables such as "x" or "v", which are just names. Like functional languages, "`x = exp`" simply assigns the name `x` to the expression `exp`.

Module interfaces are declared separately from the implementation to encourage reuse; the following code defines the polymorphic IFFT interface, parametrized by the type variable `t`, where `t` is used to indicate the type of components (*e.g.*,`Fix32`, `Fix16`, `Float63`) used to construct the complex numbers:

```
interface IFFT#(numeric type k, type t)
  method Action input(Vector#(k,Complex#(t)) x)
  method Vector#(k,Complex#(t))) output()
  method Action deq()
```

In BCL, state change is indicated by the `Action` type. The `input` method is of type `Action` and takes as arguments an input frame of size k. This was declared under the assumption that any *implementation* of this interface will store the frame in some internal buffering, changing its state and necessitating the `Action` type. Methods such as `output` which are not of type `Action` may only read state and compute the return value with a pure function.

The `VorbisBackend` interface (not shown) contains a single action method, `input`. (This interface has no output because the final effect of inputting a frame is the transmission of PCM packets to the audio device.) In contrast to other object-oriented languages, in BCL every method has an associated *guard*, which indicates whether that method is ready to be called. An action method whose guard is false will have no effect, and a value method whose guard is false produces values which cannot be used in further computation; any computation which calls an unready method is itself not valid to be executed. The generation of control logic in the HW implementations is directly based on guard composability.

In our example, the `input` method is only ready to be called once `ifft` is ready to accept the next frame, that is when the internal guard of `ifft.in` is true. We refer to this style of guard as *implicit*, though it is also possible to introduce guards *explicitly* with the **when** keyword. There is no semantic distinction between implicit and explicit guards. Since we cannot determine from outside a module when a particular method will be ready, guarded methods provide a natural abstraction for refining the timing of internal modules.

In addition to the interface methods, the behavior of a module can also be affected by its rules. The module `mkVorbisBackEnd` contains two such rules, one to transfer data between the `ifft` and `window` modules, and another to transmit PCM packets to the audio device. The invocation of a rule is a *guarded atomic action* and is the only way to modify program state. Just as with action methods, every rule produces a side-effect (state change) which is applied only when the rule's guard evaluates to true. As will become clear in the next section, the rule's guard is the conjunction of all the explicit and implicit guards contained within the constituent actions and expressions.

Rules also provide a natural way to express concurrency. For example the rules `xfer` and `output` may both be executable simultaneously, that is their guards both evaluate to true. Ultimately, all observed behaviors of the rule-based system must be understandable in terms of the execution procedure shown below:

Repeatedly:

1. Choose a rule to execute.
2. Compute the set of state updates and the value of the rule's guard.
3. If the guard is true, apply the updates.

Every rule modifies the state deterministically; non-determinism is introduced through the choice of which rule to fire. This makes a BCL program more like a design specification, and how we resolve this nondeterminism is very important for the quality of the implementation. For example, in hardware we often execute many enabled rules concurrently as long as one-rule-at-a-time semantics are not violated. In sequential SW, on the other hand, we want to compose long sequences of rules in order to exploit data locality. BCL also has the power to let the user specify any level of scheduling constraints [37], but experience shows that designers tend to leave all scheduling decisions to the compiler, except in extremely performance-critical modules.

4.2 Computational Domains

Computational domains, a part of the type system, is the mechanism by which we partition BCL designs between hardware and software. Domains are enforced by annotating every method with a domain name; each rule (or method) can refer to methods in only *one* domain. If a rule refers to methods from domain D, we can say that the rule *belongs* to domain D, and a simple type invariant can determine if the domain annotations are consistent.

This one-domain-per-rule restriction would seem to preclude inter-domain communication since all data flow occurs through rules. To enable inter-domain communication, primitive modules called *synchronizers*, which have methods in more than one domain, are provided. Inter-domain communication is possible only through synchronizers, thereby ensuring the absence of inadvertent inter-domain communication (a common pitfall in HW/SW codesign). As we show below, inserting synchronizers *is* the mechanism we provide to specify a program partition. The correct use of synchronizers allows the compiler to automatically infer the domain types on all rules and methods and safely partition a design, while an incorrect use will fail to type check, causing a compilation error.

Suppose we want to implement the IFFT in hardware and the remainder of the Vorbis backend in software. The input and output methods of IFFT must be in the hardware domain (HW) but all other methods must be in the software domain (SW). This can be specified by introducing two synchronizing FIFOs with the following interfaces:

```
interface SyncHtoS#(type t)
 (HW) Action enq(t val)
 (SW) Action deq()
 (SW) t first()
```

```
interface SyncStoH#(type t)
 (SW) Action enq(t val)
 (HW) Action deq()
 (HW) t first()
```

These synchronizing FIFOs are inserted in the original Vorbis code, and two new rules are introduced in the HW domain to transmit data to and from the IFFT as shown below:

```
module mkPartitionedVorbisBackEnd(VorbisBackEnd#(t))
 IFFT#(Complex#(t)) ifft <- mkIFFT();
 Window#(t)         window <- mkWindow();
 SyncS2H#(Vector#(2*MAX, Complex#(t)))inSync<-mkSyncS2H;
 SyncH2S#(Vector#(2*MAX, Complex#(t)))outSync<-mkSyncH2S;
 method Action input(vx)
   Vector#(2*K,Complex#(t)) v;
   for(int i = 0; i < K; i++)
     v[i]   = preTable1[i]*vx[i];
     v[K+i] = preTable2[i]*vx[i];
   inSync.in(2*K,v)
 rule feedIFFT
   let rv = inSync.first(); inSync.deq();
   ifft.input(rv);
 rule drainIFFT
   let rv = ifft.output(); ifft.deq();
   outSync.enq(rv);
 rule xfer
   let x = outSync.first(); outSync.deq();
   Vector#(2*K,t) v;
   for(int i = 0; i < 2*K; i++)
     v[i] = x[bitReverse(i)].real;
   window.input(v);
 rule output
   let rv = window.output(); window.deq();
   AUDIO_DEV.output(rv);
```

Though moving the design from a single domain to multiple domains required modifying only a few lines to code, we have introduced buffering along the HW/SW cut. In general such buffering can change the behavior of the design. However if we restrict such changes to interfaces that are *latency-insensitive*, then such changes are correct by construction. This property of interfaces also enables modular refinement of a design; moving a module from hardware to software *is* modular refinement [38]. A method to automatically verify these types of refinements is discussed by Dave et al [22].

Domain Polymorphism: BCL also allows domain names to be passed as (type) parameters. This permits us to write very general partitioned codes where a domain can be moved from software to hardware or vise versa without changing the source code. We illustrate this next.

```
interface Sync#(type t, domain a, domain b)
 (a) Action enq(t val)
 (b) t first()
 (b) Action deq()
```

We can then declare the internal synchronizers in the following manner, where **a** is a free type variable:

```
Sync#(Vector#(2*MAX, Complex#(t)), a, HW)
     inSync  <- mkSync();
Sync#(Vector#(2*MAX, Complex#(t)), HW, a)
     outSync <- mkSync();
```

The resulting Vorbis module is fully polymorphic in its domain type. If the parameter **a** is instantiated to HW, the compiler will replace the synchronizers with lightweight FIFOs since no actual synchronization is necessary. If the domain type variable **a** is instantiated as "SW" then the synchronizers would become mkSyncHtoS and mkSyncStoH respectively. In other words, a very general partitioned code may insert more synchronizers than necessary for a specific partition, but these can be optimized by the compiler in a straightforward manner.

4.3 Generating Partitions

We can extract the code for a particular domain D by removing all the *rules* not annotated with D from the partitioned code once type checking has completed. As shown in Figure 6, the hardware partition of the mkPartitionedVorbisBackEnd module will contain the rules `feedIFFT`, and `drainIFFT`, and the software partition will contain the rest. Once separated, *each partition can now be treated as an distinct BCL program, which communicates with other partitions using synchronizer primitives.* The overall semantics of the original (un-partitioned) program will preserved, since the synchronizers enforce the property of *latency-insensitivity*. We refer to the data-flow graphs describing such partitioned programs as LIBDNs (Latency-Insensitive Bounded Dataflow Graphs)[39]. If used correctly, the Sync FIFOS in the BCL programs are equivalent to LIBDN FIFOs.

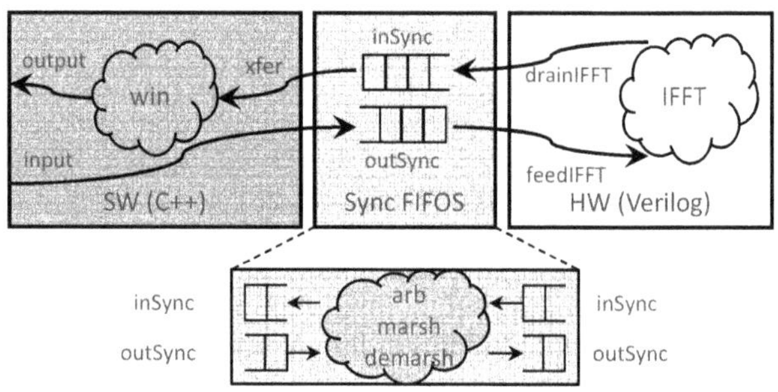

Figure 6. Each BCL program compiles into three partitions: HW,SW,and Interface. Each synchronizer is "split" between hardware and software, and arbitration, marshaling, and de-marshaling logic is generated to connect the two over the physical channel.

4.4 Mapping Synchronizers

In addition to the generation of the HW and SW partitions as shown in Figure 6, the compiler must generate code to connect the two on a particular platform. A partitioned code often requires more synchronizers than the number of physical channels available in a system (typically *one*, in the form of a bus). In addition to arbitration of the physical communication substrate among multiple LIBDN FIFOs, the compiler handles the problem of marshaling and demarshaling messages. For example, in our program we specified atomic transfers at the audio-frame granularity, but the transmission of these "messages" occurs at a granularity which is dictated by the physical substrate. Through analysis, the compiler is sometimes able to transform the marshaling and demarshaling loops into more efficient burst transfers.

The low-level details of bus transactions or on-chip networks are tedious and ever-changing. For each "supported" platform, these must be manually abstracted as simple get/put interfaces. Using such interfaces, the BCL compiler synthesizes the appropriate hardware and software to map the LIBDN FIFOs onto the available physical channels. With the use of sufficient buffering and virtual channels representing each LIBDN FIFO, we can guarantee that no new deadlocks or head-of-line blocking will be introduced. Our compiler generates the necessary software and hardware infrastructures, assuming that the HW partition fits on a single FPGA. Fleming et al. have synthesized a a similar communication infrastructure for multiple FPGA platforms [40]. It is possible to generalize either scheme to handle multiple computational domains for arbitrary physical topologies.

4.5 Implementing the IFFT Module in BCL

Our partitioned example now assumes that the IFFT functionality will run in hardware, but we have not yet shown how BCL can be used to design efficient HW. There is substantial literature on this topic, but here we provide a short discussion in terms of IFFT which also illustrates the tradeoffs between hardware and software quality. Though the IFFT interface was specified to operate on dynamic sizes, the resulting mechanism needlessly obscures the discussion. Therefore, we present the subsequent designs assuming a fixed frame size of sixty-four, though the reasoning applies equally to the fully flexible design.

Unpipelined: Perhaps the most natural description of the IFFT is the nested **for** loop contained within a single rule, shown below:

```
module mkIFFTComb(IFFT#(k, t))
  FIFO#(Vector#(k, t))  inQ <- mkFIFO()
  FIFO#(Vector#(k, t)) outQ <- mkFIFO()
  method Action input(Vector#(k,t) x)
    inQ.enq(x)
  rule doIFFT
    let x = inQ.first(); inQ.deq();
    for(int stage = 0; stage < 3; stage++)
      for(int pos = 0; pos < 16; pos++)
        x = applyRadix(stage, pos, x);
    outQ.enq(x);
  method Vector#(k,t)) output()
   return outQ.first();
  method Action deq()
   outQ.deq();
```

In this module, all the computation is done by the `doIFFT` rule, but to correctly implement the asynchronous interface, two FIFOs are used to buffer values. In software, the rule will compile into efficient loops, while in hardware they will be fully unrolled into a single block of combinational logic. Anyone with experience in hardware design will recognize that this circuit will produce an extremely long combinational path which will need to be clocked very slowly.

Pipelined: A better implementation would compute each stage of the IFFT in separate cycles. This cuts the critical path in hardware and introduces interesting pipelining opportunities. To do this we need to add some extra buffering in the form of additional FIFOs:

```
module mkIFFTPipe(IFFT#(k, t))
  Vector#(4,FIFO#(Vector#(k, t))) buff <- replM(mkFIFO);
  method Action input(Vector#(k,t) x)
    buff[0].enq(x);
  for(stage = 0; stage < 3; stage++) // gen. the rules
    rule stageN
      let x = buff[stage].first(); buff[stage].deq();
      for(int pos = 0; pos < 16; pos++)
        x = applyRadix(0, pos, x);
      buff[stage+1].enq(x);
  method Vector#(k,t) output()
   return buff[3].first();
  method Action deq()
   buff[3].deq();
```

The for-loop which encloses the rule `stageN` is meta-syntax for writing three rules manually. These rules are generated by unfolding the loop. Consequently, in this module each stage is represented by a single rule which can fire independently. The implicit conditions (formed by the internal conditions on the FIFOs) in each stage rule enforces the necessary data dependencies to guarantee correct results are generated.

When compiling `mkIFFTPipe` to software we want to exploit data locality and process a single frame at a time, a task which can be accomplished by executing each IFFT stage in data-flow order. This reconstruction of the original outer-level loop and has the effect of "passing the algorithm over the data". In hardware, on the other hand, we want to exploit pipeline parallelism and in each clock cycle run each rule once on different data, an approach which can be characterized as "passing the data through the algorithm". There are a host of other variations on this pipeline which are easily specified in BCL which we do not discuss for the sake of brevity. It should be noted that as the implementations become more "hardware-friendly" the task of synthesizing efficient software often becomes increasingly challenging.

5. Kernel of BCL

The kernel of BCL that we describe in this section consists of the language once type checking has been performed, all modules have been instantiated, and all meta-linguistic features have been eliminated by a compiler phase known as *static elaboration*. We explain the main features of kernel BCL intuitively; an SOS-style semantics of kernel BCL can be found in [37].

BCL Grammar: The grammar for BCL is given in Figure 7. A BCL *module* consists of 3 major parts: a set of state element variables (*i.e.*,registers or other module instantiations), a set of guarded atomic actions or *rules* which describe the internal state changes, and a set of *methods* which implement the interface through which the rest of the design interacts with this module. The Module definition includes a constructor argument list $[t]$, and each module instantiation *Inst* contains a list of values $[v]$ to be passed to the module constructor when building a module hierarchy. A BCL *program* consists of a list of module definitions with one module specified as the root or the main program. Instantiating the root recursively instantiates the entire program state.

<table>
<tr><td>m ::=</td><td>Module mn $[t]$</td><td>// Name, Argument list</td></tr>
<tr><td></td><td>[Inst mn n $[c]$]</td><td>// Instantiate state</td></tr>
<tr><td></td><td>[Rule n a]</td><td>// Rules</td></tr>
<tr><td></td><td>[ActMeth n $\lambda t.a$]</td><td>// Action methods</td></tr>
<tr><td></td><td>[ValMeth n $\lambda t.e$]</td><td>// Value methods</td></tr>
<tr><td>v ::=</td><td>c</td><td>// Constant Value</td></tr>
<tr><td>||</td><td>t</td><td>// Variable Reference</td></tr>
<tr><td>a ::=</td><td>r := e</td><td>// Register update</td></tr>
<tr><td>||</td><td>if e then a</td><td>// Conditional action</td></tr>
<tr><td>||</td><td>$a \mid a$</td><td>// Parallel composition</td></tr>
<tr><td>||</td><td>a ; a</td><td>// Sequential composition</td></tr>
<tr><td>||</td><td>a when e</td><td>// Guarded action</td></tr>
<tr><td>||</td><td>(t = e in a)</td><td>// Let action</td></tr>
<tr><td>||</td><td>loop e a</td><td>// Loop action</td></tr>
<tr><td>||</td><td>localGuard a</td><td>// Local guard action</td></tr>
<tr><td>||</td><td>$m.g(e)$</td><td>// Action method call g of m</td></tr>
<tr><td>e ::=</td><td>r</td><td>// Register Read</td></tr>
<tr><td>||</td><td>c</td><td>// Constant Value</td></tr>
<tr><td>||</td><td>t</td><td>// Variable Reference</td></tr>
<tr><td>||</td><td>e op e</td><td>// Primitive Operation</td></tr>
<tr><td>||</td><td>e ? e : e</td><td>// Conditional Expression</td></tr>
<tr><td>||</td><td>e when e</td><td>// Guarded Expression</td></tr>
<tr><td>||</td><td>(t = e in e)</td><td>// Let Expression</td></tr>
<tr><td>||</td><td>$m.f(e)$</td><td>// Value method call f of m</td></tr>
<tr><td>op ::=</td><td>&& | || | ...</td><td>// Primitive operations</td></tr>
<tr><td>pr ::=</td><td>$[m]$ (mn,$[c]$)</td><td>// BTRS program</td></tr>
</table>

Figure 7. BCL Grammar

Rules: A rule in BCL is a guarded atomic action, and whenever a rule is evaluated it yields a Boolean guard value and a set of state (register) updates. If the guard is true then the system is allowed

A.1	$(a_1 \textbf{ when } p) \mid a_2$	$\equiv$	$(a_1 \mid a_2) \textbf{ when } p$
A.2	$a_1 \mid (a_2 \textbf{ when } p)$	$\equiv$	$(a_1 \mid a_2) \textbf{ when } p$
A.3	$(a_1 \textbf{ when } p) \,;\, a_2$	$\equiv$	$(a_1 \,;\, a_2) \textbf{ when } p$
A.4	$\textbf{if } (e \textbf{ when } p) \textbf{ then } a$	$\equiv$	$(\textbf{if } e \textbf{ then } a) \textbf{ when } p$
A.5	$\textbf{if } e \textbf{ then } (a \textbf{ when } p)$	$\equiv$	$(\textbf{if } e \textbf{ then } a) \textbf{ when } (p \vee \neg e)$
A.6	$(a \textbf{ when } p) \textbf{ when } q$	$\equiv$	$a \textbf{ when } (p \wedge q)$
A.7	$r := (e \textbf{ when } p)$	$\equiv$	$(r := e) \textbf{ when } p$
A.8	$m.h(e \textbf{ when } p)$	$\equiv$	$m.h(e) \textbf{ when } p$
A.9	$\textbf{Rule } n \textbf{ if } p \textbf{ then } a$	$\equiv$	$\textbf{Rule } n\ (a \textbf{ when } p)$

Figure 8. When-Related Axioms on Actions

to make a transition to the new state, *i.e.*, update the state. If the guard is false then the rule has no effect. As discussed in Section 4, a scheduler selects a rule to execute. Since several different rules can have their guards true in a given state, the choice of which rule to execute can lead to different execution paths. This source of non-determinism is an important aspect of BCL.

Actions: The primitive action in BCL is the assignment of a value to a register, written as "`r := e`". Since expressions are guarded, it is possible that in a given state, `e`'s guard may be false, that is, `e` is not ready to be evaluated. By the axioms described in Figure 8, the guard on entire assignment action is false, and the value stored in `r` is not updated.

Two actions can be composed either in *parallel* or in *sequence* to form a bigger atomic action. If $A_1|A_2$ are composed in parallel both observe the same initial state and do not observe each other's updates. Thus the action r_1**:=**$r_2 \mid r_2$**:=**r_1 swaps the values in registers r_1 and r_2. If both A_1 and A_2 try to update the same register, the parallel action is illegal and generates a DOUBLE_WRITE_ERROR. Sequential composition is more in line with other languages with atomic actions. The action $A_1; A_2$ represents the execution of A_1 followed by A_2. A_2 observes the full effect of A_1. No other action observes A_1's updates without also observing A_2's updates. In both cases, a guard failure in the evaluation of either action invalidates the composed action.

Conditional versus Guarded Actions: BCL has both conditional actions (**if**s) as well as guarded actions (**when**s). These are similar as they both restrict the evaluation of an action based on some condition. The difference is their scope of effect: conditional actions have only a local effect whereas guarded actions have a global effect. If an **if**'s predicate evaluates to false, then that action doesn't happen (produces no updates). If a **when**'s predicate is false, the subaction (and as a result the whole atomic action that contains it) is invalid. One of the best ways to understand the differences between **if**s and **when**s is to examine the axioms in Figure 8.

Axioms A.1 and A.2 collectively state that a guard on one action in a parallel composition affects all the other actions. Axiom A.3 deals with a particular sequential composition. Axioms A.4 and A.5 state that guards in conditional actions are reflected only when the condition is true, but guards in the predicate of a condition are always evaluated. A.6 deals with merging **when** clauses. A.7 and A.8 translate expression **when**-clauses to action **when**-clauses. Axiom A.9 states that top-level **when**s in a rule can be treated as an **if** and vice versa.

`localGuard(a)`, instead of propagating a guard failure in action `a` to the enclosing rule, effectively converts `a` to `noAction`. This gives the programmer the power to indirectly predicate behavior upon implicit guard failures and can be used to construct a dynamic-length *sequence* of atomic actions. For example, we might want to implement a "non-atomic atomic loop", in which the loop body itself is atomic, but loop termination is triggered by the final guard failure as shown below:

```
cond_reg := true;
loop (cond_reg = true)
  cond_reg := false;
  localGuard {<loop_body> | cond_reg := true}
```

Expressions: The only thing special about expressions in BCL is guards. However guards in expressions can be lifted to the top expression using axioms which are similar to the when-axioms for actions in Figure 8. After **when** lifting, we end up with "`e` **when** `g`" where both `e` and `g` are free of guards.

Module boundaries represent a slight complication in lifting guards. It is best of think of every method call $f(e)$ as a pair of unguarded method calls $f_b(e)$ and $f_g(e)$ containing the method body and guard respectively. Any invocation of $f(e)$ can be replaced with the expression "$f_b(e)$ **when** $f_g(e)$".

Strict Method Calls and Non-Strict Lets: BCL has non-strict (sometimes called lazy) lets and procedure calls. Consequently spurious let bindings have no effect and we have more powerful algebraic laws for program transformation. However, BCL has strict method calls because each method represents a concrete resource, a *port*, in our implementation. Thus we expect the semantics of the program to be affected if a module is merged with the surrounding module.

6. Implementing BCL

We have implemented a compiler which generates a C++ implementation of the software partition of a BCL specification. This is then compiled, along with some libraries, into an executable program. For hardware partitions, our compiler generates BSV, which is compiled into Verilog using BSC from Bluespec Inc. We discuss software generation at length but describe hardware generation only briefly because it has been published elsewhere.

6.1 Shadowing State

At a high level, the software implementation of BCL can be explained by pointing out the differences between rule-based systems and Transactional Memory. Both these systems have the *linearizability* property, that is, the semantics of the system are understandable by executing rules (transactions) in some sequential order. However, the implementation techniques for the two systems are quite different. In TM systems, multiple transactions are executed eagerly, and all except one are aborted if a conflict is detected. Upon failure, TM systems transfer control back to the transaction's boundary, and the transaction is re-executed. In TM systems, conflicts are typically defined in terms of read/write conflicts, though more sophisticated schemes exist. The challenge in the implementation of TM systems is to find low-cost mechanisms for detecting conflicting transactions and rolling back the computation in case of an aborted transaction. The possibility of a rollback invariably requires shadow states or check-points.

The implementation of rule-based systems such as BSV and BCL, on the other hand, pre-schedule rules in such a way that conflicting rules are never executed simultaneously. Thus, there is no need for dynamic conflict detection. Typically, many rule guards are evaluated in parallel, and among the rules whose guards are *true*, all non-conflicting rules are scheduled simultaneously. The compiler does pair-wise static analysis to conservatively estimate conflicts between rules. Thus, compilers for rule-based systems construct a scheduler for each design using the static conflicts, as well as dynamic information about which rules are ready to *fire*.

Even though we never simultaneously schedule conflicting rules, our implementation still requires shadow states. In simple designs all guards can be lifted out of the rule, and the scheduler executes a rule only when its guard is true. In complex rules, not all guards can be lifted, which leaves the possibility of internal guard failure. It is this possibility of failure which necessitates shadows in our system.

Parallel Composition: There is a complication which arises from the fact that GAAs might contain internal concurrency (due to the use of parallel action composition). In general, "`A1 | A2`" will require creating two shadows of the incoming state to execute A1 and A2 in isolation. After the execution of A1 and A2, the copies will have to be merged into a single shadow. This merge may produce a dynamic error if A1 and A2 modify the same state element; such actions are illegal. The following example illustrates this, where c1 and c2 are dynamic boolean expressions, f is a fifo, and a and b are registers:

```
(if (c1) then a := f.first(); f.deq()) |
(if (c2) then b := f.first(); f.deq())
```

If c1 and c2 both evaluate to true and f is not empty then both the sub-actions will attempt to dequeue the same element, which is an error. Even if there is no danger of parallel merge errors, shadow state is required, as illustrated by the following simple example, which swaps the values of two registers: "a := b | b := a".

6.2 Control Transfer

The C++ implementation of BCL programs can be described informally as follows: Each BCL module is implemented as a C++ class definition. The user-specified rules and methods are implemented as class member functions, and the sub-modules are implemented as member variables. Each class definition is augmented with a number of additional member functions and variables, which together constitute light-weight transactional run-time, and execution strategy.

A copy of the original state is allocated at program start-up time, and is referred to as the *persistent* shadow. This shadow is populated (in a change-log manner) as the rule executes. When a rule executes to completion, the shadow state is committed to the original program state. Consistency with the original state is maintained by executing a rollback if a rule fails. Unlike the shadows for rule execution, those required for parallel action execution are allocated and de-allocated dynamically. We chose this approach because after optimizations, parallel compositions are relatively infrequent.

Because of the need for compositional method invocations, guard failure is implemented using the C++ throw command, which is always caught by the rule in which the action is being executed. Hence, the structure of rule bodies is always a try/catch block, with commit routines at the end of the try block and the necessary rollback code in the catch block. The *localGuard* construct also requires dynamic shadow creation and because it doesn't propagate rule failures, the C++ implementation of this construct also uses try/catch blocks.

6.3 Code Transformation: Reducing the Cost

In this section, we discuss some simple transformations which can drastically improve the code quality.

Lifting Guards: When executing a rule whose guard might fail, it is preferable that it happen as early in the execution as possible, since early failure avoids the useless execution of the remainder of the rule body. Consider the following transformation of a BCL expression:

$$(A1\ \mathtt{when}\ A1_g \mid A2\ \mathtt{when}\ A2_g) \Rightarrow$$
$$(A1 \mid A2)\ \mathtt{when}\ (A1_g \wedge A2_g)$$

By rules given in [37], it is possible to lift most guards to the top level. In some cases, we can transform rules to the form "A **when** E" where A and E are themselves guard-free. In this form, we can guarantee that if E evaluates to 'True', A will execute without any guard failures. With this knowledge, we can avoid the cost of using a try/catch block to detect guard failures in sub-module method invocations, and also perform the computation *in situ* to avoid the cost of commit entirely. The when-axioms (Figure 8) state that guards cannot be lifted through the sequential composition of actions or loops, which is why we cannot do away with state shadowing all together.

Avoiding Try/Catch: Even when guards cannot be lifted completely, we can still improve the quality of code when all methods in a rule are inlined, or at least determine through static analysis that those remaining (methods on primitive modules) will not fail. In this case, we can dispense with the top-level try/catch block and instead handle all constituent **when** clauses explicitly, branching directly to the rollback code. Try/catch blocks in C++ are not cheap, and this analysis proves to be quite effective. To illustrate this optimization, consider the BCL rule "**Rule** foo {a := 1; f.enq(a); a := 0}". The code generated without method inlining is give in Figure 9, while the (far more efficient) code generated after method inlining is given in Figure 10.

```
void foo(){
  try{
    a_s.write(0);
    f_s.enq(a_s.read());
    a_s.write(1);
    f.commit(f_s);
    a.commit(a_s);
  }catch{
    a_s.rollback(a);
    f_s.rollback(f);
  }
}
```

Figure 9. without inlining

```
void foo(){
  a_s.write(0);
  if(f_s.can_enq()){
    f_s.enq(a_s.read());
  else
    goto rollback;
  a_s.write(1);
  f.commit(f_s);
  a.commit(a_s);
rollback:
  a_s.rollback(a);
}
```

Figure 10. with inlining

Sequentialization of Parallel Actions: The cost of shadowing for parallel actions can be reduced by transforming them into an equivalent sequential composition of actions. For example, (A | B) is equivalent to (A ; B) if the intersection of the write-set of action A and the read set of action B is empty. The equivalence of (A | B) and (B | A) gives us even more flexibility in finding an equivalent sequential form. In addition, action methods invoked on the same module but in parallel branches can be invoked in sequence if they modify disjoint internal states. In both cases, since the two actions were originally composed in parallel, their respective guards may be lifted, giving us a sequential composition *and* the ability to guarantee that the second action will complete without a guard failure. Since parallel composition is most naturally expressed in hardware and sequential composition in software, recognizing these patterns is important when implementing a "hardware" module in software. Sometimes sequentialization of parallel actions is made possible by introducing some shadow state (consider the swap example). Even this turns out to be a win because static allocation of state is more efficient than *dynamic* allocation.

Partial Shadowing: When we must create shadow state for an action, we need not shadow the entire module: only those state elements which can *actually* be modified by the action need to be shadowed. This selective shadowing provides substantial savings in many cases, and opportunities for these savings increase if we inline methods or perform some static analysis. Loops and localGuard provide additional opportunities for partial shadowing.

Scheduling: In both hardware and software, the execution strategy has a great impact on performance. The most important concern in scheduling software is to choose a rule which will not fail, since partial execution of any rule is wasted work (the cost of partial execution and rollback). We are investigating the use of user-provided scheduling annotations to improve compiler analysis, but do not discuss it in this paper.

Parts of programs are sometimes identifiable as synchronous regions in which case well-known static scheduling techniques are applied [7]. When available, these synchronous guarantees can lead to very efficient code generation in both hardware and software implementations. Even without such synchronous guarantees, the compiler can exploit data-flow analysis which may reveal that the execution of one rule may enable another, permitting the construction of longer sequences of rule invocations which successfully execute without guard failures, an important element in efficient software. This strategy is most effective when the program data-flow graph is sparse.

To illustrate the scheduling challenge, consider the following rule, which transfers a single audio frame between a producer module (p) and consumer module (c) non-atomically. If p empties or c is full before the complete frame has been transferred, the scheduler will attempt to complete the transfer during a subsequent rule invocation:

```
rule xferSW when(True)
  cond_reg := true;
  loop (cond_reg = true && cnt < frameSz)
    cond_reg := false;
    localGuard
      cond_reg := true ; cnt := cnt+1;
      let w = p.output(); p.deq(); c.input(w)
```

The sequential composition inherent in loops is not directly implementable in HW. For a hardware implementation, we might instead use a rule which transmits one word at a time, and rely on the scheduler to attempt to execute it once every HW clock cycle. The effects of the resulting non-atomic transfer of a single frame is identical, though the schedules are completely different:

```
rule xferHW when(cnt < frameSz)
  let w = p.output(); p.deq();
  c.input(w); cnt := cnt+1
```

Since one of our goals is to write code which can be moved between HW and SW with minimal changes, we need some way of resolving these two very different idioms. In essence, we would like to transfer a frame from p to c using xferHW with the same efficiency as if we had used xferSW. If the SW scheduler invokes xferHW in a loop, the overall performance of the transfer will not suffer. If the rules in c require a complete frame before they are enabled, any attempts to execute those rules by the scheduler before xferHW has been invoked 'frameSZ' times will be wasted effort. By employing completely different schedules, we are able to generate both efficient HW and SW from the same rules.

Finally, the software implementation presented in this paper is single-threaded: an obvious scheduling improvement would be to use multithreading to exploit rule-level parallelism. Work on this front is ongoing, but beyond the scope of this paper.

6.4 HW Generation

Techniques for hardware generation from rules are well understood and used successfully in the BSV compiler. The initial implementation of this tool was done by Lennart Augustsson, and was then commercialized by Bluespec Inc. With the exception of loops and sequential composition, BCL can be translated to legal BSV, which is then compiled to Verilog using the BSV compiler. We give a short sketch of the BSV compiler, and leave the reader to follow the references for further details.

To implement a rule directly in hardware, we require some notion of shadow state so that we can unwind a computation if we encounter a guard failure in the evaluation. These shadows can require a substantial hardware cost if they are implemented via stateful constructs. However, if we store them ephemerally in wires, they become cheap. The guard drives a multiplexer on the registers holding the module state, which updates them only if the guard evaluates to true. In synchronous hardware, we can guarantee that all shadows are implementable in wires as long as each rule is executed in a single clock cycle. This is the primary optimization which enables the compilation of guarded atomic actions into efficient synchronous circuits [17, 41, 42].

Since, loops with dynamic bounds can't be executed in a single cycle, such loops are not directly supported in BSV. A technique has been proposed to introduce rules which can be executed over multiple cycles [43] which provides a solution to this limitation.

7. Experiment and Results

The compiler we have implemented takes a BCL program as input, partitions the design based on the use of synchronizer modules, and outputs the following three components: (1) a C++ implementation of the SW partition, complete with a concrete rule schedule and a driver, (2) a BSV implementation of the HW partition, and (3) infrastructural code to connect the two partitions on supported platforms.

Mobile devices use ASIC implementations for HW acceleration, and our compiler generates Verilog from which such ASIC implementations can be synthesized. Since we do not synthesize ASICs, HW/SW co-simulation is required to test our designs. This type of simulation is very slow, so instead we have chosen an FPGA platform on which to demonstrate our techniques. The conclusions about the quality of the partitions are slightly skewed by the inferior performance of an FPGA when compared to ASIC, but the goal of this paper is not *necessarily* to determine the best partition for these examples, but rather to demonstrate a technique. In spite of this, the *relative* performance of modules running on the FPGA versus the microprocessor gives us valuable insight.

We explored six different HW/SW partitions of the Vorbis decoder, as well as four different partitions of a realistic ray-tracer, both implemented entirely in BCL. The performance numbers were generated in the *fully automatic* mode to demonstrate the efficiency of all components. We show that not only does the relative performance of the various decompositions match our intuition, but that the absolute performance of the full-software partition is competitive with hand-written software. The performance of the generated hardware has already been shown to be as good as hand-written versions [2]. The quality of these results demonstrate the suitability of BCL for all the use cases discussed in Section 1.

Experimental Platform: Our experimental setup is shown in Figure 11. The synchronizer modules operate on the PCI Express bus as well as the internal Xilinx bus connecting the PPC440 to the FPGA, and we ran the experiments in both contexts. Since the performance characteristics of the embedded configuration are more closely aligned with mobile platforms, we use it to generate all the results reported in this section.

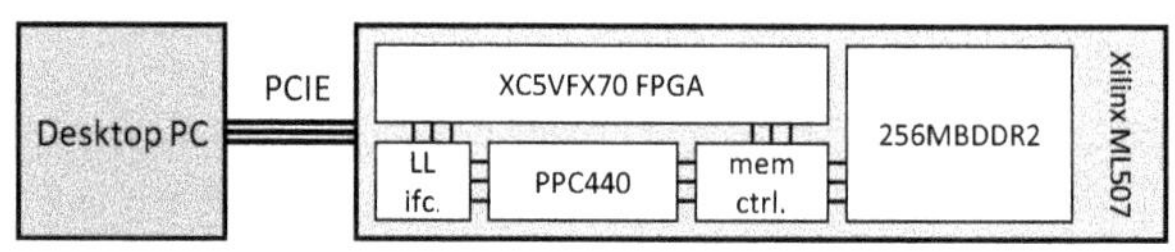

Figure 11. Experimental Setup

The software running on the microprocessor communicates directly to the hardware running on the FPGA through the LocalLink™ interface using embedded HDMA engines. The synchronizers themselves form a thin layer on top of this link to provide a FIFO abstraction. Through the synchronizers, we achieve a round-trip latency of approximately 100 FPGA cycles, and are able to stream up to 400 megabytes per second from DDR2 memory to the FPGA modules. For these tests, we clock the PPC440 at 400 Mhz and the FPGA at 100 Mhz.

7.1 Ogg Vorbis

The different HW/SW partitions are shown in Figure 12. The initial stages of the Vorbis pipelined were written manually in C++, and the back-end was specified in BCL. Once the code was written and tested, the specification of the partitions and generation of results required only a few hours.

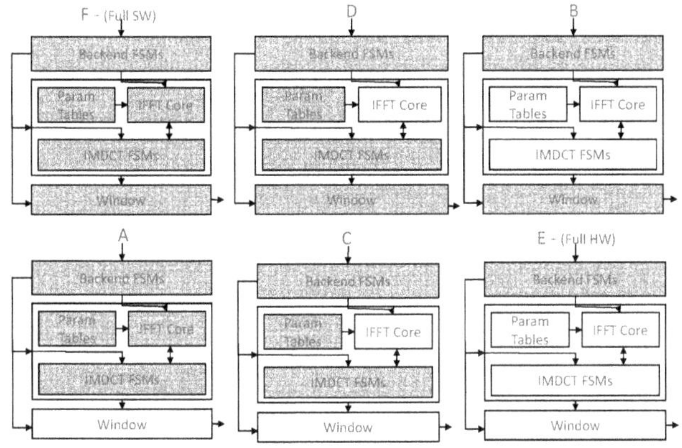

Figure 12. Ogg Vorbis partitions. (SW modules are shaded). The output from the windowing function is always in SW (not shown)

We constructed a test bench consisting of 10000 Vorbis audio frames, and all computation was done using 32-bit fixed point values with 24-bits of fractional precision. The performance results are shown in Figure 13. This graph shows us is that moving computation to the hardware does not always speed up the execution; the slowest partition is *not* the one which computes everything in SW (F). In fact, partitions A and C are both slightly slower than F. We know that each link between the HW and SW partitions has a cost, and in order for the net speedup from moving a module from SW to HW to be positive, the speedup observed in the module itself must outweigh the cost of the communication. The performance numbers show that moving the windowing function to HW is not worth the communication overhead. Additionally, notice that the effect of moving *only* the IFFT to HW is marginal. This is because IMDCT FSMs invoke IFFT repeatedly to compute a single output, and transferring this quantity of data between HW and SW is costly. It should be noted that if the audio output could be driven directly from a HW partition, the implementation of windowing in HW would *always* improve performance. These are by no means unexpected results; the novelty is that we are able to generate these numbers with such ease.

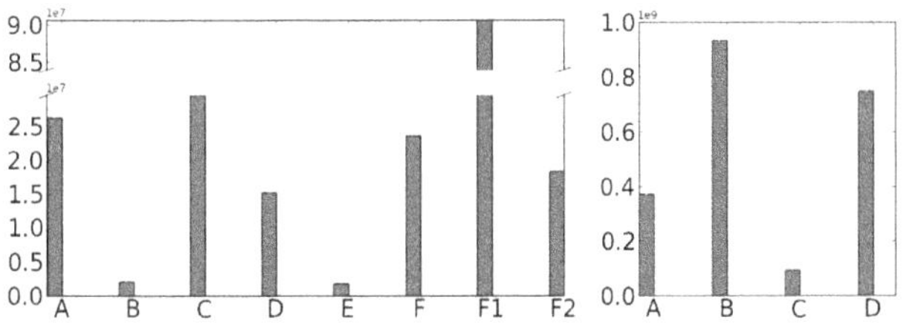

Figure 13. Execution times of OggVorbis (left) and RayTrace (right) partitions listed in FPGA cycles. SW implementations F1 and F2 are hand-coded SystemC and C++ respectively

To compare the performance of our language to more conventional methods of HW/SW codesign, we implemented the pure software partition (F) in SystemC and manually in C++. We chose SystemC to establish an upper bound since it is widely used in HW/SW codesign (though generally in the *modeling* of systems), and the performance is considered by some to be realistic enough to drive design decisions. We chose manual C++ as a lower bound, since this is how embedded devices are commonly written. The SystemC implementation is roughly 3x slower due to the required overhead of modeling all the simulation events. The manual C++ version is slightly faster than the generated one, as it avoids all discarded work or need for shadow state.

7.2 Ray Tracing

A realistic ray tracer was chosen as an additional application with which to evaluate the use of BCL. Since scene geometries can be quite large, memory bandwidth is often as important a concern as the actual compute required to detect ray/geometry intersections. Figure 14 shows the microarchitectural detail, as well as the four HW/SW decompositions considered in this experiment

Once the geometry has been loaded to memory, the module labeled "BVH Ctor" performs an initial pass to construct a bounding volume hierarchy (BVH). With the scene in this form, we can perform $\log(n)$ intersection tests instead of n in the number of scene primitives. The module labeled "Ray Gen" constitutes the first step of the pipeline, computing rays which originate at the camera position and pass through each point in the field of view at a specified granularity. The module labeled "BVH Trav" implements the core of the ray tracing pipeline. As the algorithm traces a ray through the scene, it traverses the BVH by repeatedly testing for intersection with the sub-volumes, and finally with the geometry primitives at the leaves of the tree. After a fixed number of reflections/refractions are calculated, the final color is stored in a bitmap. Unlike the Vorbis example, which is amenable to pipeline parallelism, efficient ray tracing requires us to exploit data parallelism.

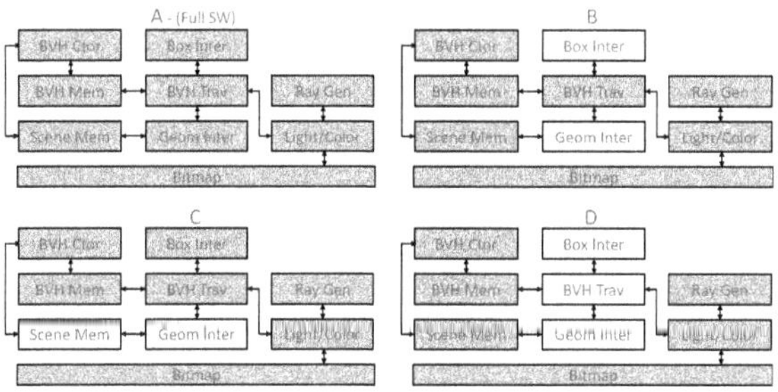

Figure 14. Ray tracing partitions with SW modules shaded

The performance numbers for ray tracing (Figure 13) were generated using a small benchmark consisting of 1024 geometry primitives. This application provides a multitude of different partitioning options, and we chose four which illustrate important properties of the program's data flow. The fastest partitioning given (C) has the ray/geometry intersection engine implemented in hardware, and the scene geometry stored in low-latency-access on-chip block RAMs. Collision testing requires a substantial amount of arithmetic, which we are able to accelerate through aggressive pipelining. Of course, if the number of geometry primitives falls below some threshold, a full SW implementation might be faster. Configurations B and D, though they both use HW acceleration, are slower than the pure software implementation because the savings in computation are outweighed by the incurred cost of communication.

8. Conclusion

In this paper we have explored a new method for HW/SW codesign, where instead of requiring precise interface specification a priori, the user specifies the entire design, *including* the HW/SW decomposition, in a single language. The resulting specification can be used to generate precise implementations which encapsulate low-level properties of the communication substrate inside the synchronizer modules. We have implemented a complete system, including a compiler and run-time, and have illustrated our approach using examples written in BCL. We have shown that partitioning designs in BCL is natural and easy and that the reduced effort of partitioning allows the programmer to concentrate exclusively on the performance implications of the partitioning choices. BCL concedes nothing in the quality of hardware or software that is generated. The same exercise using conventional multi-language methodologies would require far greater effort.

Future work includes applying BCL to exploit multiple software threads and multiple hardware substrates, the improvement of generated software through more complex analysis, the investigation of additional HW/SW codesign platforms for *exploring* HW/SW tradeoffs, and gaining more insight into which BCL patterns are best suited for generating both efficient HW and SW.

Acknowledgments

This work was supported by the NSF (#CCF-0541164), and a NRF grant from the Korean Government (MEST) (#R33-10095). The authors thank Jamey Hicks and John Ankorn of NRC-Cambridge for their input at the start of this project, the team at Bluespec Inc. for their technical support, Asif Khan of CSAIL for his invaluable help with FPGA platforms, and Martin Rinard of CSAIL for his input in the writing process. Discussions with fellow CSG members and Professor Jihong Kim of Seoul National University have also improved this work.

References

[1] L. Augustsson, J. Schwarz, and R. S. Nikhil, "Bluespec Language definition," p. 95, 2001, Sandburst Corp.

[2] M. C. Ng, M. Vijayaraghavan, G. Raghavan, N. Dave, J. Hicks, and Arvind, "From WiFI to WiMAX: Techniques for IP Reuse Across Different OFDM Protocols," in *Proceedings of Formal Methods and Models for Codesign (MEMOCODE)*, Nice, France, 2007.

[3] S. Y. Liao, "Towards a new standard for system level design," in *Proceedings of the Eighth International Workshop on Hardware/Software Codesign*, San Diego, CA, May 2000, pp. 2–7.

[4] G. Kahn, "The semantics of simple language for parallel programming," in *IFIP Congress*, 1974, pp. 471–475.

[5] J. B. Dennis, J. B. Fosseen, and J. P. Linderman, "Data flow schemas," in *International Sympoisum on Theoretical Programming*, 1972.

[6] Arvind and R. Nikhil, "Executing a program on the MIT Tagged-Token Dataflow Architecture ," *Computers, IEEE Transactions on*, vol. 39, no. 3, pp. 300 –318, Mar. 1990.

[7] E. A. Lee and D. G. Messerschmitt, "Static scheduling of synchronous data flow programs for digital signal processing," *IEEE Trans. Computers*, vol. 36, no. 1, pp. 24–35, 1987.

[8] W. Thies, M. Karczmarek, and S. P. Amarasinghe, "Streamit: A language for streaming applications," in *CC*, ser. Lecture Notes in Computer Science, R. N. Horspool, Ed., vol. 2304. Springer, 2002.

[9] G. Berry and L. Cosserat, "The ESTEREL Synchronous Programming Language and its Mathematical Semantics," in *Seminar on Concurrency*, 1984, pp. 389–448.

[10] N. Halbwachs, P. Caspi, P. Raymond, and D. Pilaud, "The synchronous data flow programming language lustre," *Proceedings of the IEEE*, vol. 79, no. 9, pp. 1305 –1320, sep 1991.

[11] J.-L. Colaço, G. Hamon, and M. Pouzet, "Mixing signals and modes in synchronous data-flow systems," in *Proceedings of the 6th ACM & IEEE International conference on Embedded software*, ser. EMSOFT '06. New York, NY, USA: ACM, 2006, pp. 73–82.

[12] D. C. Luckham, "Rapide: A language and toolset for causal event modeling of distributed system architectures," in *WWCA*, 1998.

[13] S. A. Edwards and O. Tardieu, "Shim: a deterministic model for heterogeneous embedded systems," *IEEE Trans. VLSI Syst.*, vol. 14, no. 8, pp. 854–867, 2006.

[14] J.-P. Talpin, C. Brunette, T. Gautier, and A. Gamatié, "Polychronous mode automata," in *EMSOFT*, 2006, pp. 83–92.

[15] P. A. Abdulla and J. Deneux, "Designing safe, reliable systems using scade," in *In Proc. ISoLA 2004*, 2004.

[16] K. M. Chandy and J. Misra, *Parallel Program Design: A Foundation*. Reading, Massachusetts: Addison-Wesley, 1988.

[17] J. C. Hoe and Arvind, "Operation-Centric Hardware Description and Synthesis," *IEEE TRANSACTIONS on Computer-Aided Design of Integrated Circuits and Systems*, vol. 23, no. 9, September 2004.

[18] E. W. Dijkstra, "Guarded commands, nondeterminacy and formal derivation of programs," *Commun. ACM*, vol. 18, no. 8, 1975.

[19] N. A. Lynch and M. R. Tuttle, "An introduction to input/output automata," *CWI Quarterly*, vol. 2, pp. 219–246, 1989.

[20] E. Czeck, R. Nanavati, and J. Stoy, "Reliable Design with Multiple Clock Domains," in *Proceedings of Formal Methods and Models for Codesign (MEMOCODE)*, 2006.

[21] *Bluespec SystemVerilog Version 3.8 Reference Guide*, Bluespec, Inc., Waltham, MA, November 2004.

[22] N. Dave, M. Katelman, M. King, J. Meseguer, and Arvind, "Verification of Microarchitectural Refinements in Rule-based systems," in *MEMOCODE*, Cambridge, UK, 2011.

[23] P. O. Meredith, M. Katelman, J. Meseguer, and G. Roşu, "A formal executable semantics of Verilog," in *Eighth ACM/IEEE International Conference on Formal Methods and Models for Codesign (MEMOCODE'10)*. IEEE, 2010, pp. 179–188.

[24] W. Snyder and P. Wasson, and D. Galbi, "Verilator," `http://www.veripool.com/verilator.html`, 2007.

[25] "Carbon Design Systems Inc," `http://carbondesignsystems.com`.

[26] P. Chou, R. Ortega, and G. Borriello, "Synthesis of the hardware/software interface in microcontroller-based systems," in *In Proceedings of the International Conference on Computer Aided Design*, 1992, pp. 488–495.

[27] P. H. Chou, R. B. Ortega, and G. Borriello, "The chinook hardware/software co-synthesis system," in *In International Symposium on System Synthesis*, 1995, pp. 22–27.

[28] S. Y. Liao, S. W. K. Tjiang, and R. K. Gupta, "An efficient implementation of reactivity for modeling hardware in the scenic design environment," in *DAC*, 1997, pp. 70–75.

[29] *Catapult-C Manual and C/C++ style guide*, Mentor Graphics, 2004.

[30] Synfora, "PICO Platform," `http://www.synfora.com/`.

[31] A. Agarwal, M. C. Ng, and Arvind, "A comparative evaluation of high-level hardware synthesis using reed-solomon decoder," *Embedded Systems Letters, IEEE*, vol. 2, no. 3, pp. 72 –76, 2010.

[32] S. S. Huang, A. Hormati, D. F. Bacon, and R. Rabbah, "Liquid metal: Object-oriented programming across the hardware/software boundary," in *ECOOP '08: Proceedings of the 22nd European conference on Object-Oriented Programming*, Berlin, Heidelberg, 2008.

[33] J. T. Buck, S. Ha, E. A. Lee, and D. G. Messerschmitt, "Ptolemy: A framework for simulating and prototyping heterogenous systems," *Int. Journal in Computer Simulation*, vol. 4, no. 2, pp. 0–, 1994.

[34] F. Balarin, Y. Watanabe, H. Hsieh, L. Lavagno, C. Passerone, and A. Sangiovanni-Vincentelli, "Metropolis: An integrated electronic system design environment," *Computer*, vol. 36, pp. 45–52, 2003.

[35] K. S. Chatha and R. Vemuri, "Magellan: multiway hardware-software partitioning and scheduling for latency minimization of hierarchical control-dataflow task graphs," in *CODES*, 2001, pp. 42–47.

[36] P. Arató, Z. A. Mann, and A. Orbán, "Algorithmic aspects of hardware/software partitioning," *ACM Trans. Des. Autom. Electron. Syst.*, vol. 10, pp. 136–156, January 2005. [Online]. Available: http://doi.acm.org/10.1145/1044111.1044119

[37] N. Dave, Arvind, and M. Pellauer, "Scheduling as Rule Composition," in *Proceedings of Formal Methods and Models for Codesign (MEMOCODE)*, Nice, France, 2007.

[38] N. Dave, M. C. Ng, M. Pellauer, and Arvind, "A design flow based on modular refinement," in *Formal Methods and Models for Codesign (MEMOCODE 2010)*.

[39] M. Vijayaraghavan and Arvind, "Bounded dataflow networks and latency-insensitive circuits," in *MEMOCODE*, 2009, pp. 171–180.

[40] K. Fleming, M. Adler, M. Pellauer, A. Parashar, Arvind, and J. Emer, "Leveraging latency-insensitivity to ease multiple fpga design," in *FPGA*, February 2011.

[41] T. Esposito, M. Lis, R. Nanavati, J. Stoy, and J. Schwartz, "System and method for scheduling TRS rules," United States Patent US 133051-0001, February 2005.

[42] J. C. Hoe, "Operation-Centric Hardware Description and Synthesis," Ph.D. dissertation, MIT, Cambridge, MA, 2000.

[43] M. Karczmarek and Arvind, "Synthesis from multi-cycle atomic actions as a solution to the timing closure problem," in *ICCAD*, 2008.

Path-Exploration Lifting: Hi-Fi Tests for Lo-Fi Emulators

Lorenzo Martignoni
UC Berkeley
martignlo@gmail.com

Stephen McCamant
UC Berkeley
smcc@cs.berkeley.edu

Pongsin Poosankam
CMU & UC Berkeley
ppoosank@cmu.edu

Dawn Song
UC Berkeley
Berkeley, CA, USA
dawnsong@cs.berkeley.edu

Petros Maniatis
Intel Labs
Berkeley, CA, USA
petros.maniatis@intel.com

Abstract

Processor emulators are widely used to provide isolation and instrumentation of binary software. However they have proved difficult to implement correctly: processor specifications have many corner cases that are not exercised by common workloads. It is untenable to base other system security properties on the correctness of emulators that have received only ad-hoc testing. To obtain emulators that are worthy of the required trust, we propose a technique to explore a high-fidelity emulator with symbolic execution, and then lift those test cases to test a lower-fidelity emulator. The high-fidelity emulator serves as a proxy for the hardware specification, but we can also further validate by running the tests on real hardware. We implement our approach and apply it to generate about 610,000 test cases; for about 95% of the instructions we achieve complete path coverage. The tests reveal thousands of individual differences; we analyze those differences to shed light on a number of root causes, such as atomicity violations and missing security features.

Categories and Subject Descriptors D.2.5 [*Testing and Debugging*]: Testing tools

General Terms Reliability, Security, Verification

Keywords Symbolic binary execution, CPU emulators, cross-validation

1. Introduction

Processor emulators are widely used in systems, to provide privacy [29], integrity [17], instrumentation, replay, sandboxing [9], and program analysis [3, 27]. In principle, any component meant to *mediate transparently* between an operating system and the hardware needs to emulate the hardware to some degree; consequently, processor emulators have been linchpin components for a large class of critical applications.

Unfortunately, our critical reliance on emulators has not been met by a commensurate assurance of their correctness. Emulators are just too hard to implement correctly, for several reasons. First, emulators are large, complex pieces of software meant to mirror complex emulated layers such processors. Second, as components that often appear in the critical path of applications, emulators must be optimized aggressively, often using pervasive, brittle optimizations involving self-modifying code and multiple intermediate representations. Third, typical emulated systems exhibit great variance in how their different features are exercised, which leads to emulators with many corner cases that are infrequently exercised by common workloads.

In this paper, we tackle the problem of increasing the assurance of processor emulators, hoping to generalize what we learn to broader emulation assurance. Specifically, we present PokeEMU, a systematic framework for high-coverage testing and cross-validation of processor emulators such as Bochs[1] and QEMU[2]. Our work is inspired by two observations. First, there are several emulators for common processor architectures such as IA-32, each of which achieves a different point in the complexity-fidelity spectrum. For example, the Bochs interpreter is a faithful but relatively slow implementation of the processor (a "Hi-Fi" emulator), whereas QEMU, a dynamic binary translator, is faster but much more complex, buggier, and less complete ("Lo-Fi")[3]. Second, exploration based on symbolic execution has matured significantly in recent years, allowing us to leverage such techniques to enable high-coverage path exploration and test-case generation.

We capitalize on these observations by exploiting the following insight: one can use symbolic execution on a Hi-Fi emulator to generate high-quality test cases for a Lo-Fi emulator. Analysis of the Hi-Fi emulator extracts all the distinct behaviors and corner cases it implements; those are useful because we assume the Hi-Fi emulator's behavior is closer to the ideal processor specification than the behaviors implemented by the Lo-Fi emulator. Using then the Hi-Fi emulator's behaviors to generate automatically a test suite for the Lo-Fi emulator, one can detect and fix deviations of the Lo-Fi emulator from the behavior of the (presumed "more correct") Hi-Fi emulator or the emulated hardware. We call this methodology *path-exploration lifting*, since it automatically "lifts" definitions of program behaviors—as captured by distinct *code paths*—from one emulator to another.

ASPLOS'12, March 3–7, 2012, London, England, UK.

[1] `http://bochs.sourceforge.net/`.

[2] `http://www.qemu.com/`.

[3] We use *fidelity* loosely to denote how closely an emulator approximates the target architecture; a buggier, less complete emulator has lower fidelity than a more correct, more complete emulator.

Interestingly, although in this paper we use path-exploration lifting from a Hi-Fi emulator to a Lo-Fi emulator, hoping to "rub off" some of the higher fidelity of the Hi-Fi emulator to the Lo-Fi one, the technique is more general. It can be used in the opposite direction, from Lo-Fi to Hi-Fi, to see how the Hi-Fi emulator would behave for the distinct cases implemented by the Lo-Fi emulator developers. Beyond emulation, for any two implementations of the same precise specification (e.g., SQL query engines, SSL implementations, etc.), it makes sense to analyze one implementation to generate test cases for comparison to the other implementation.

Certainly neither cross-validation nor path exploration via symbolic execution are new. However, path exploration on an artifact to test that same artifact can at best trigger its own corner cases, but not capture those unimplemented in it, which our approach can achieve. More importantly, cross-validation alone can, at best, do random directed testing ("fuzzing") without capitalizing on the fundamental differences between the different tested artifacts. In contrast, applying systematic program analysis for path exploration, such as symbolic execution, to amplify the benefits of cross-validation is novel to our knowledge. Ideally, one would want to apply path-exploration lifting to a hardware specification (e.g., the register-transfer language specification of a circuit); unfortunately, such specifications for commodity hardware are proprietary and extremely well guarded. By applying the methodology to a Hi-Fi emulator, we capture corner cases from the next best thing. Conveniently, the Hi-Fi emulator need not be perfect, only complete: we use the actual hardware to test our emulators against, so correctness bugs in the Hi-Fi emulator do not impact our results, and can be discovered through our approach as side effects.

Although path-exploration lifting is a general concept, its implementation is challenging, often losing generality. In this paper we apply and customize the technique for Bochs and QEMU, dealing with several fundamental challenges. While in the past others have used symbolic execution to generate high-coverage test cases for programs, those programs were applications with scalar or other simple input types. In contrast, PokeEMU must generate test cases for emulators, whose input is a starting machine state and a test instruction, a staggeringly large state space to explore. Furthermore, even after PokeEMU makes sense out of the state space and generates some test cases with starting states for a given test instruction, we must figure out how to *lead* the emulated system to the desired start state: how to get it to set its registers, configuration, program counter, and execution mode to the values required, which is not straightforward since certain parts of the machine state cannot be set directly and most instructions have multiple side effects that may undo prior state setup. Finally, it may not always be possible to analyze the source code of an emulator due to intellectual property restrictions and, even without such restrictions, the emulator may manipulate system state through multiple intermediate representations, via just-in-time compilers, etc.; operating on the binary executable may be the only option for testing system emulators.

Contributions. This paper proposes path-exploration lifting, a new methodology for *exhaustively* exploiting the correctness of one artifact to improve the correctness of another. The paper presents the design, implementation, and evaluation of the methodology in the PokeEMU system for processor emulators. PokeEMU consists of several key components. First, the paper presents a symbolic execution engine for x86 binaries, FuzzBALL, used to explore paths from binaries, as opposed to source code. Second, it describes a novel exploration strategy for processor emulators, which starts with the instruction decoders, generating instructions to iterate over, and then explores the instruction emulator to identify paths per instruction, with optimizations to reduce the state space. Third, it details an essential tool for processor testing: an input-state generator that, given an input state for a test case, automatically creates a program to bring an emulator or physical system to that state, so that the test can take place. Finally, it conducts the first systematic study of the approach using symbolic execution, assessing QEMU's emulation fidelity using test cases lifted from Bochs and comparing it to both Bochs and real hardware, identifying several deviations from expected behavior.

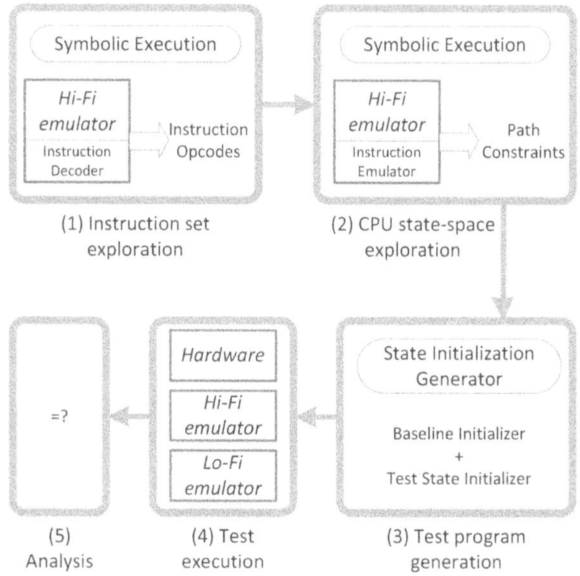

Figure 1. Overview

Our evaluation establishes four key points. First, for more than 95% of the instructions, PokeEMU achieved complete path coverage. Second, PokeEMU found a large number of deviations among the emulators tested and real hardware: out of about 610,000 programs, more than 72,000 triggered differences, and we have identified a number of root causes, some of which affect many instructions. Third, many of the deviations found could not have been found by prior emulator-testing approaches, such as random testing. Finally, at least two of the deviations found could lead to significant security problems, when those emulators are used as the basis for a security tool.

2. Overview

A CPU or instruction-set emulator is a program that runs on one architecture (*host*), but whose functionality is to simulate the processor of a potentially different architecture (*guest*). Our goal in this work is to discover differences between the behavior of a CPU emulator, and the behavior of another emulator or real hardware: such a difference enables us to find bugs in emulators.

To be precise, we define the *(machine) state* of a CPU emulator or hardware system to be all the values, such as in general purpose registers, control registers, flags, or memory, that can affect the execution of a future instruction. We say that systems show a behavioral difference if we start them in the same machine state (called the *test state*), and they execute the same instruction (called the *test instruction*), but after the instruction executes they are in different machine states (called the *final states*). Example differences include having a different value in a register, or not raising an exception when the hardware would.

Approach. At a high level, our approach is to discover differences by constructing high-coverage tests that trigger them, using the methodology of *path-exploration lifting*. Furthermore, unlike traditional program testing where the tests are simply scalar test input values, a test for the emulator would specify a test state and a test instruction. And in practice, we generate *test programs*: stand-alone programs that can run on an emulator to set up the test states and then execute the test instructions.

Our design goals are (1) to maximize the coverage of our testing, subject to the constraints of (2) producing a practical number of tests, while (3) requiring relatively little human guidance in modifying the emulators or configuring the tests. Next we discuss how we apply these principles to the key technical challenges.

Challenges and Techniques. First, the space of possible instructions and machine states is astronomically large, so it would not be practical to individually test every possible instruction and initial state. However this space also has complex structure, so choosing instructions and states at random, or based on typical usage, would miss differences that occur in corner cases. We address this challenge by using symbolic execution to explore the space based on how components of the state are used by a tested emulator. First, we apply symbolic execution on the instruction decoder of an emulator to select test instructions. Then for each test instruction, we apply symbolic execution to the emulator's implementation of that instruction. Specifically, we choose a subset of the machine state as relevant (this choice is discussed in detail in Section 3.3.1 and Figure 3). Symbolic execution determines a test state for each execution path through the implementation that can be triggered by some assignment of values to the selected state components.

A second challenge is that CPU architectures do not provide a uniform interface to initialize all the components of their state. For instance control registers must be initialized using specialized instructions, and some kinds of initialization are either prerequisites for or conflict with other kinds. To address these challenges, we write a fixed piece of code to initialize a machine to a baseline state. Then our tool automatically instantiates a sequence of *test state initializers* to set the remaining parts of the state. Thus the test program consists of the baseline state initializer, then the test state initializers, then the test instruction.

A third challenge is that many emulators use inline assembly code or perform just-in-time (JIT) compilation, so they cannot be properly analyzed at the source code level. We address this challenge by using binary-level symbolic execution, which applies uniformly to an interpreter compiled from source code and the machine code created by a just-in-time compiler. Although we did have source code for the emulators we studied, we took on this challenge so as to prepare for also studying closed-source, commercial emulators and VMMs.

System Architecture. Our approach has four steps: exploration, test program generation, test program execution, and difference analysis (Figure 1).

In the first step, exploration, we use symbolic execution to explore an emulator. To efficiently partition the space of possible instruction executions, we do the exploration in two steps: we first explore to generate legal instructions (Figure 1(1)), and then explore the execution of each instruction separately (Figure 1(2)). We progressively explore all the execution paths of an instruction implementation, given a selected set of symbolic state components, and generate one test for each path. Thus the output of this step is a set of pairs of test instructions and test states. The symbolic execution is implemented using our tool FuzzBALL, which we have extended with optimizations for this problem domain. The second step, test program generation, constructs complete test programs from the results of exploration. For each input pair of a test instruction and an test state found in the exploration phase, we construct as output a test program consisting of the baseline initializer, the test state initializer for the test state, and the test instruction (Figure 1(3)). In the third step, test program execution, we take the test programs as input and run them on emulators and real hardware (Figure 1(4)). We instrument the emulators and a hardware-based virtual machine to save as output the machine state after executing the test program (the *final state*). In the fourth step, difference analysis, we compare the final states from the different executions of a test (Figure 1(5)). If the results differ between emulators or between an emulator and the real hardware, we have triggered a behavior difference.

For our evaluation, we have selected two emulators that support x86 guest code: Bochs is an interpreter, and QEMU is a JIT compiler. We compile the emulators for the Linux/x86 host platform. In our experiments, we apply symbolic execution to Bochs, and then use the generated tests for a three-way behavior comparison of Bochs, QEMU, and an Intel® Core™ i5 * workstation virtualized by KVM. We test the processor's 32-bit protected mode.

3. Path-Exploration Lifting

In this section we describe the main technical aspects of how our system explores the space of possible instruction executions in an emulator. We start by describing our core technology of lightweight binary-level symbolic execution (Section 3.1). Then we describe the two ways we apply it: first, to discover possible instructions (Section 3.2), and then to find machine states that trigger various behaviors in an emulated instruction (Section 3.3). Finally, we describe a difference-minimization technique that we use to simplify the machine states discovered by symbolic execution (Section 3.4).

3.1 Lightweight Symbolic Execution

The core of our system's state-space exploration is a lightweight engine for binary-level symbolic execution, named FuzzBALL. We start our description with a review of the key concepts of symbolic execution in general, then describe the *online* approach our tool takes, and some of the particular challenges that arise when operating on binaries. At a high level, FuzzBALL implements similar functionality to previous symbolic execution systems such as KLEE [6]. But in contrast, it takes a simpler approach in some areas that can be performance or code complexity challenges in other systems, and it is designed for a binary-level, rather than a source-level, program representation.

3.1.1 Background: Symbolic Execution

The basic principle of symbolic execution is to replace certain *concrete* values in a program's state with *symbolic variables*. As these symbolic values are used in later computations, they produce more complex symbolic expressions. These symbolic expressions are valuable because they can summarize the effect of many concrete executions.

When a symbolic expression is used in a control-flow instruction, we call the formula that controls the target a *branch condition*. On a complete program run, the conjunction of the conditions for all the symbolic branches is the *path condition*. Thus the values for the symbolic variables that satisfy a path condition are ones that would cause the program to execute the same control-flow path as the one executed symbolically. Similarly, by taking a prefix of the path condition with the final branch condition negated, we obtain a condition corresponding to a different control-flow path. Solving such a path condition lets us obtain a new set of concrete values that would cause the corresponding path to be executed.

* Intel® Core™ i5 is a trademark of Intel Corporation in the U.S. and/or other countries. Other names and brands may be claimed as the property of others.

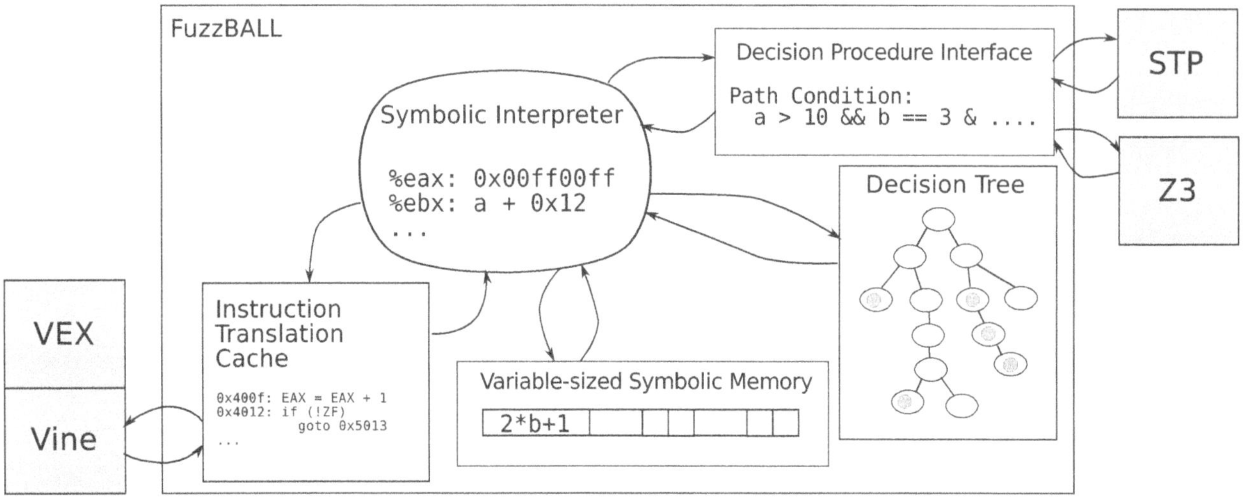

Figure 2. An overview of some of the key components of our symbolic execution engine FuzzBALL. The interior components are described in Section 3.1; the gray-shaded components are off-the-shelf libraries.

3.1.2 Lightweight, Online Approach

At its core, FuzzBALL is an interpreter for x86 instructions, but one in which the values in registers and memory can be symbolic expressions rather than just concrete bit patterns. A graphical overview of FuzzBALL's architecture is shown in Figure 2. As it executes an x86 binary program, FuzzBALL translates each instruction into a streamlined intermediate representation (IR), then performs each action specified by this IR on a symbolic state representation. For instance, suppose that `%eax` has the symbolic value $a - 20$, and the location pointed to by `%ebx` has the value 5. Then after FuzzBALL interprets the instruction `add (%ebx),%eax`, the symbolic value of `%eax` will be $a - 15$.

Suppose that the following instruction is `jz a04`, a conditional branch that checks whether `%eax` is zero. The branch condition $a - 15 = 0$ depends on the symbolic variable a, so to decide which instruction to execute next, FuzzBALL checks whether either of the formulas $a - 15 = 0$ or $a - 15 \neq 0$ is satisfiable, using a decision procedure. In this case both are, so FuzzBALL can choose freely. Suppose it chooses to take the true case ($a - 15 = 0$); then it will record that the false case is available to explore later, and go on to the instruction at address `0xa04`. As it encounters other symbolic branches, it makes similar choices and records them. When it reaches the end of the program or another specified stopping point, FuzzBALL will mark that state as explored, and start again from the beginning of the program or a specified starting point. On the next run, FuzzBALL uses recorded decisions to ensure that the path it executes is different from those explored before. FuzzBALL continues in a loop, executing new paths, until all the possible paths have been executed. The choice of which program values are marked symbolic (typically the inputs to some computation) controls how many paths FuzzBALL explores: more symbolic values mean more execution paths.

Many uses of symbolic execution start by running a program with a pre-existing concrete input. In such applications, a simplification is to have the symbolic execution run in parallel with, but not modify, a concrete execution, so that the path condition describes the path the concrete execution took. In our context, by contrast, we wish to completely explore an execution space, so it does not matter which path we execute first. On the other hand, it is useful to have more flexibility in choosing which paths to symbolically execute. Therefore our system performs *online* symbolic execution. During execution we start with no commitment to a concrete value for any symbolic variable; when the value at a memory location has a symbolic expression, this is instead of, rather than in addition to, a concrete value. This gives the system the flexibility to choose either direction for a symbolic branch, subject only to feasibility.

Thus FuzzBALL is an interpreter for machine instructions, where registers and memory contain symbolic formulas. The representation of memory uses a two-level data structure similar to a page table, in which each page of memory is an array of formulas rather than an array of integers.

Online Decision Making. When a branch condition is symbolic, an online symbolic execution tool can execute either the true or false side of the branch, but to make this decision it must reason about the path condition before execution can proceed. Our symbolic execution engine can choose directions subject to two constraints: the branch direction must be *feasible*, and it should lead to a path that has not been explored before. A branch direction is feasible if it is logically consistent with the previous branches in the path. For instance, in `if (x>y) x=y; if (x>y) abort();`, there is no feasible path in which both `if` conditions are true. FuzzBALL checks feasibility by giving the path condition to a decision procedure, which determines whether the condition is satisfiable, and if so, supplies a satisfying assignment.

Specifically, FuzzBALL interfaces with the decision procedures STP [13] and Z3 [12]. After simplifying symbolic expression, it translates them into STP or Z3's syntax for quantifier-free formulas over fixed-sized bit-vectors (representing bounded machine arithmetic). STP and Z3 are well tuned for applications like FuzzBALL: their results are precise but produced quickly, with most queries completing in a fraction of a second. When using Z3, FuzzBALL can also solve path conditions incrementally: i.e., if it previously solved $b_1 \wedge b_2$, Z3 can reuse information from that solving process when solving $b_1 \wedge b_2 \wedge b_3$.

Decision Tree. To avoid exploring the same paths repeatedly, FuzzBALL uses a *decision tree*. The decision tree is a binary tree in which each node represents the occurrence of a symbolic branch on a particular execution path, and a node has children labeled "false" and "true" representing the next symbolic branch that will occur in either case. Each tree node records whether the false and true branches have been checked for feasibility, as well as whether any additional unexplored branches appear below this node in the tree.

On each execution, FuzzBALL examines the decision tree to choose a random path within the part of the tree that has not been completely explored, then adds on to the tree for the part of the path being explored that is new. When creating a new node, FuzzBALL checks whether both the false and true branch directions are feasible, and if so, it can choose arbitrarily (either randomly or according to a supplied heuristic). After reaching the end of the path, FuzzBALL propagates the bit indicating that a subtree has been fully explored back up the tree until it reaches a node with an unexplored branch. The decision tree grows as more paths are explored, so FuzzBALL uses a compact in-memory representation and can optionally store it on disk instead, but this is not needed for runs of the length used in this project.

Branches that come from `if` statements and branches for loop exit conditions are treated uniformly, since at the instruction level they look the same. Thus FuzzBALL considers a different number of executions of a loop as distinguishing a different execution path. In other applications, this can lead to a significant state-space explosion to manage, but it is not a major obstacle to PokeEMU because instructions usually do not contain unbounded input-dependent loops.

Thus the decision tree ensures that each path FuzzBALL explores is different, and that exploration stops if no further paths are possible. Similarly to systems that duplicate execution state at a symbolic branch [6, 8], the decision tree saves (expensive) invocations of the decision procedure when the tool already knows which branch direction is feasible. As a tradeoff, our approach repeats (relatively inexpensive) concrete and symbolic execution on the repeated path, to avoid keeping multiple states at once, which would increase memory usage and implementation complexity.

Extension to Word-sized Values. When execution requires a concrete value for a word-sized expression, like a `switch` statement argument or an array index, FuzzBALL applies the same mechanisms described above for two-way branches, once for each bit in the word, most-significant first. This reduction carries over the key properties from two-way branches: FuzzBALL chooses only feasible values, and eventually tries all feasible values.

3.1.3 Operating at the Binary Level

Since FuzzBALL targets binaries rather than source, it must address challenges including instruction-set complexity and variable-sized memory accesses.

To factor out instruction-set complexity, FuzzBALL uses the BitBlaze[4] Vine library [27], which in turn builds on the VEX library which is also used by the Valgrind debugging tool [25]. First VEX translates an x86 instruction into the VEX intermediate representation, and then Vine translates from this into its own language which is even simpler; these translations are cached for efficiency. To handle memory accesses of different operand sizes (bytes, words, etc.), FuzzBALL tries when possible to represent values in their natural size, so that splitting and reassembly are required only when the program itself accesses memory in an inconsistent way. To achieve this, FuzzBALL's representation of memory can contain symbolic values of differing sizes. We describe some additional implementation challenges that, in particular, are inspired by use with emulators in Section 3.3.2.

3.1.4 Impact of FuzzBALL's Correctness

At this point, one might worry about seemingly circular reasoning in our approach. Our goal is to check the correctness of one x86 interpreter (that in an emulator), but our technique relies on another x86 interpreter (that inside FuzzBALL). What if FuzzBALL has bugs similar to those we find (Section 6) in other emulators?

In fact there are several reasons why our approach is still effective. First, any such bugs in FuzzBALL would be unlikely to significantly affect our results, because emulators *use* in their own implementation a much smaller and better-exercised subset of processor functionality than they *emulate*. Second, the differences we discover are real, independent of the test generation process. We use symbolic execution to improve coverage, but the behavior differences are validated by test cases that run on their own. Third, FuzzBALL can be used to validate many emulators, so efforts towards strengthening or verifying the correctness of FuzzBALL would be amplified through its use in a tool such a PokeEMU.

3.2 Instruction Set Exploration

The x86 instruction set is complex enough that even just enumerating all the possible instructions is non-trivial. But we would like exactly such an enumeration, in order to partition the later exploration so that we consider each instruction separately and exactly once. Therefore our first, and relatively simpler, application of symbolic execution is to discover a set of byte sequences representing instructions to test.

We observe that emulators contain *instruction-decoding functionality* to parse a byte sequence, check whether the sequence is a legal instruction, and if so, decide which code in the emulator will process it. This later code might be the implementation itself in an interpreter, or a code-generation routine in an IR-based or JIT-compiler emulator; we will refer to it as *per-instruction code*. By exploring the instruction decoder with symbolic execution, we can discover which byte sequences the emulator considers to be instructions, and group byte sequences that are the "same" instruction in the sense that they have common per-instruction code in the emulator. In particular, we start symbolic execution at the entry point of the emulator's instruction parser, mark the bytes that are the input to this parser as symbolic, and explore execution paths up to the selection of the per-instruction code.

An x86 instruction is between 1 and 15 bytes, consisting of optional prefix bytes, an opcode that is usually 1 or 2 bytes, and trailing fields. Those trailing fields can specify a sub-opcode, register operands, addressing modes, and immediate values. The total number of possible instruction byte sequences is astronomical (though less than $2^{8 \cdot 15} \approx 1.3 \cdot 10^{36}$, because not all instructions allow all possible prefixes and operands). To select a more manageable number of byte sequences, we conceptually partition the byte sequences according to which per-instruction code they trigger, and select a bounded number of byte sequences (currently 1) from each cell of the partition. Intuitively, we select one byte sequence per instruction, for the definition of "instruction" given by the emulator's per-instruction code. Selecting more byte sequences per instruction would slightly improve our coverage of functionality selected by flags within the instruction, such as different addressing modes, but we estimate that the incremental benefit would be relatively low.

The instructions defined by emulator implementations are not in one-to-one correspondence with the 1-2 byte instruction opcode field: some opcode values correspond to multiple implementations depending on prefixes or an extra sub-opcode field, and some distinct opcodes share a single implementation. But we observe that generally at most either a single prefix byte or the sub-opcode within the next byte after the opcode is also relevant, and any other prefix bytes are optional, so every implementation has a unique representative based on the first three bytes of an instruction byte sequence. As shown in the results of Section 6, this approach allows us to cut down an original space of 2^{24} (16.8 million) three-byte sequences into less than 1000 unique instructions.

[4] `http://bitblaze.cs.berkeley.edu/`

3.3 Machine State-Space Exploration

Our system's more critical (and more complex) use of symbolic execution is to explore how the state of the emulated machine before execution of an instruction (the *input state*) affects the instruction execution of the Hi-Fi emulator, and the state after its execution (the *output state*). At a high level, we mark the input state as symbolic, symbolically execute the instruction implementation, and for each execution path record the behavior and output state. Specifically, each execution path starts at the beginning of the code implementing an instruction and ends when the Hi-Fi emulator is about to raise an exception or execute the next instruction. Here we discuss how we select and mark machine state as symbolic, and some optimizations that make this state space manageable.

3.3.1 Machine State

Our key control over the exploration performed by symbolic execution is the choice of which parts of the machine state we treat as symbolic. Symbolic execution will explore all of the code paths that can be reached for some assignment of values to the symbolic parts of the input state. On the other hand, those parts of the machine state that are left concrete will be treated as fixed in exploration. Thus the more state we mark as symbolic, the larger a state space we will explore. We would generally like to explore as large a state space as possible, except that we would like to avoid repeatedly exploring large numbers of executions that are effectively identical. For instance the page table can have 2^{20} possible base addresses, but while the contents of the page table are significant, its location is not, so it is enough to use only one such position for exploration.

The state of the guest machine is represented by data structures in the memory of the host program, so it is with respect to these data structures that we specify symbolic locations. FuzzBALL supports a mode in which the entire state of the host machine is symbolic, and we also considered inferring this data layout from execution. However, neither of those approaches has proved necessary so far: in our observation the data structures that represent the machine state have a straightforward layout in the Hi-Fi emulator.

Symbolic values are specified to FuzzBALL by giving their address, so we write C test code to print the locations of the fields that we make symbolic. For uniformity, all of the symbolic locations are specified as bytes, but specifying 4 consecutive bytes as symbolic is equivalent to specifying a single symbolic word. Conversely, we can make a subset of the bits in a byte symbolic by marking the entire byte as symbolic, and then adding a side constraint that fixes the concrete bits.

Overall, our strategy has been to mark as much of the machine state as symbolic as possible, except for locations that have many effectively equivalent values. Thus we make most of the machine registers and tables such as the page table and the global descriptor table (used for segment accesses) symbolic. A graphical presentation of the registers we mark symbolic is shown in Figure 3. However, we keep concrete values for parts of registers that are effectively just pointers to other data in memory, such as the portion of the CR3 register that is a pointer to the page table, as described above. We also leave concrete the flags that specify the CPU is operating in 32-bit protected mode, since that is the target of our testing. And of course the instruction pointer (EIP in x86 terminology) needs to be concrete along with the bytes of the instruction to be executed. In total, our symbolic machine state consists of approximately 400 bytes in registers and tables, along with all of the unused bytes in physical memory.

3.3.2 Optimizations for Exploration

Even after restricting to a single instruction and carefully selecting which machine state should be symbolic, the space of possible executions is still quite large. Here we discuss two classes of further optimizations that make our symbolic execution more effective by avoiding repeated exploration of similar paths.

Summarizing Common Computations. Some parts of instruction execution involve multiple execution paths, but are consistent over a large number of instructions. We would like to avoid repeated execution of these code regions, particularly since each such multipath region has a multiplicative effect on the total number of paths. To avoid path explosion, we take a divide and conquer approach: we identify the common code region, perform symbolic execution on it separately to build a precise summary, and then use that summary in place of the common code.

Using a preliminary run of symbolic execution, we explore all the paths of a computation and record the outputs as a function of the inputs. Next, we combine the symbolic expressions for the path conditions and the output values for a value into a single large formula: for instance, if such a computation had an output v_i on the path with path condition p_i, the summary formula is `p1 ? v1 : (p2 ? v2 : ...)`. Then, in the main symbolic execution runs, we skip execution of the computation and instead add the pre-computed constraint to the path condition.

For instance, we use this treatment for code in Bochs that computes a cached copy of a segment descriptor. An x86 processor allows the specification of six memory regions, called segments, each with a chosen base address and size (these were once used for memory management, and are still used for thread-local memory regions and some security applications). The locations and other attributes of each segment are stored in a packed data structure called the *segment descriptor*, but since this descriptor rarely changes, emulators often cache its information in a data structure with their own choice of layout. The layout of the cache is emulator-specific, so we mark the state symbolic in the emulator-independent descriptor structure and let the emulator recompute its cache. However the code that updates the cache has 23 paths, so executing all the possible paths through all of the possible cache updates would increase the search space by a factor of $23^6 = 148035889$. Instead, we summarize the cache-update computation with a single set of symbolic expressions, automatically computed from an exploration, in advance, of just the cache-update function.

Indexing Memory and Tables. As described in Section 3.1.2 above, FuzzBALL's default behavior, when a symbolic value is used as an index, is to exhaustively explore each index value. While this would be suitable for a small table in which each entry is different, it is impractical for large arrays such as the page table or the guest memory (which is generally represented as a single or multi-level table in the host). For these arrays, we instead direct FuzzBALL to select a single index value at random, and not explore any other values. Like making a pointer in the initial state concrete rather than symbolic, this on-the-fly concretization narrows the search space that FuzzBALL explores, but it is justified by the observation that for most purposes, all 2^{32} locations in memory are equivalent.

Another important consideration for large tables in the machine state is how they are initialized for symbolic execution. For the page table, we concretely initialize the parts of the table that are pointers to sub-tables or page frames, but make all of the flag bits symbolic. For main memory, we treat each byte as a separate symbolic variable, but we modify FuzzBALL to create those variables on demand only when a location is accessed.

3.4 State Difference Minimization

For each path explored in symbolic execution, the decision procedure computes an assignment of bits to the symbolic variables that would cause the emulator to execute that path: this assignment is then the basis for constructing a test state. If any bits are symbolic,

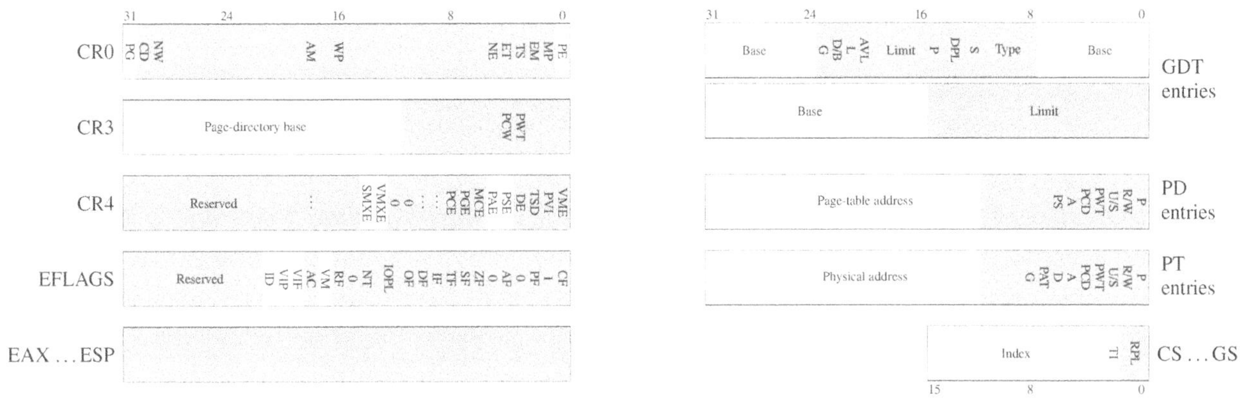

Figure 3. Symbolic machine state (grayed bits are symbolic, the remaining ones are concrete).

but not constrained by checks on the explored path, the decision procedure will choose values for them arbitrarily. However, this flexibility is inconvenient for two reasons. First, it makes the generated tests harder to understand, because they contain extra state differences that are irrelevant to the execution of the emulator, and caused only by the decision procedure's arbitrary choices. Second, these irrelevant differences can cause test execution to fail when they affect state that is checked in the test execution but not during the symbolic execution. As an example, we start symbolic execution in Bochs after it has fetched and decoded an instruction, so the permissions on the code segment CS are not relevant for most instructions. But in a real execution, the test instruction must be fetched using CS, so a change that makes that segment inaccessible will cause the test to fail before executing the instruction.

To avoid these problems, we wish to base test states not on an assignment where unconstrained bits are arbitrary, but on one where unconstrained bits are left the same as in a baseline machine state that "just works." In other words we want to find an assignment that is minimally different from the baseline state. We implement this minimization using a simple and efficient greedy approach. Starting with a working assignment equal to the one produced by the decision procedure, we iterate over each of the bits that are different from the baseline state. For each bit that is different, we check whether setting it to its value in the baseline state still satisfies the path condition; if so, we make the change in the working assignment. Potentially making multiple passes could further reduce the size of the difference, but a single pass is sufficient for the problem of unconstrained variables, which is our main motivation.

We also explored implementing this minimization by excluding variables from the assignment that do not appear in the path condition. However, particularly in the presence of bitwise operations, FuzzBALL's symbolic expressions sometimes retain irrelevant variables. It would have required a complex additional analysis to reliably remove such variables. By comparison our current approach based on evaluation was simple to implement and requires no approximation.

4. Generating Test Programs

Figure 4 shows the execution of a test program, which is a standalone disk image that boots an emulator, initializes a test state, executes a test instruction, and either halts normally or raises an exception. To simplify the process of constructing code to set up the test state, we divide it into two steps. First we write a *baseline state initializer*, code that sets up a single baseline state that is a starting point for any state in a given processor mode. Then we use an automated code generation process to construct, for each spe-

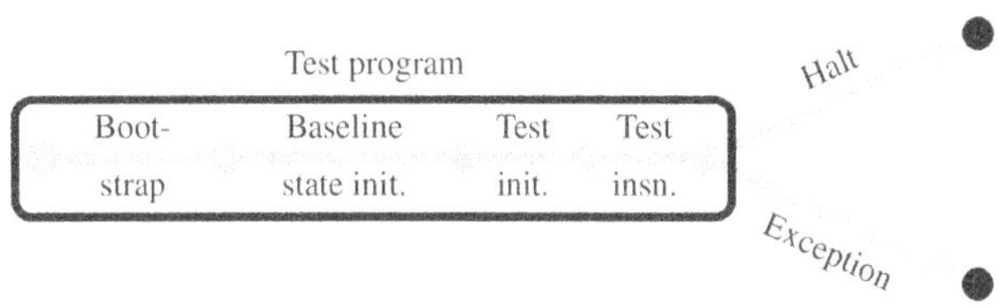

Figure 4. Execution of a test (the black circles denote when we take a snapshot of the CPU state and of the physical memory; the rectangle delimits the test program).

cific test state, the additional initializations needed to reach the test state from the baseline state: we call these the *test state initializers*. The advantage of this two-step approach is that because the test states are similar to the baseline state, we require relatively little new code specific to each test.

We choose a bootable disk image as the easiest way to load and run code in an emulator. So in summary, a test consists of a bootable disk image containing an off-the-shelf boot loader, the fixed baseline state initializer, the test state initializers for a particular test state, and the test instruction.

Next we describe in detail baseline-state initialization and test-state initializer generation.

4.1 Baseline State Initialization

The baseline state is a minimalist execution environment necessary for successfully running all possible tests in a specific operating mode. This baseline state corresponds to the concrete state used during the exploration stage (described in Section 3.3). We now describe specifically the baseline initializer we use for 32-bit protected mode with paging enabled, the most common mode for x86 processors and the one used in our evaluation. We could construct similar baseline initializers for other modes.

The off-the-shelf boot loader we use happens to already configure the machine in 32-bit protected mode. The remainder of the initialization consists of populating the global descriptor table, the page table, the interrupt descriptor table, and enabling paging and interrupts. More precisely we initialize the global descriptor table to use a flat segmentation model. That is, the code, data, and stack segments have a zero base and a 4-GByte limit. We configure the page table to map the 4-GByte virtual address space linearly to a 4-MByte physical memory, repeating every 4-MBytes so that each physical page backs 1024 virtual pages. All pages are initially marked as readable and writable and accessible to both user and kernel mode. This configuration ensures that, unless the global descriptor table or the page table are modified later during the execution, any access to the memory will succeed. The interrupt descriptor table is configured to dispatch exceptions to handlers that halt the CPU, and interrupts to handlers that effectively ignore the interrupt by resuming execution immediately.

4.2 Building Test Programs

Each output of the exploration phase is a test instruction and a test state: a precise configuration for a subset of the CPU state and of the physical memory, necessary to trigger a specific path during the emulation of the test instruction. In order to exercise the same behavior at run-time, we need to run the test instruction starting from the same machine state discovered during the exploration. To do so, we need to generate code that, starting from the baseline state described in the previous section, sets up the machine state for running the test instruction. This code, the *test state initializer*, will be executed immediately after the baseline state has been initialized. The test program then executes the test instruction. If the test program is executed successfully the CPU halts; otherwise an exception is raised.

To organize the process of constructing the test state initializer, we divide it according to the various parts of the machine state we initialize. For each part of the state that must be initialized, we design a *gadget*, a short code snippet, that encapsulates how to initialize the state component. Then we have an algorithm that automatically selects and instantiates appropriate gadgets and assembles them into a complete test state initializer.

In more detail, each gadget consists of an assembly-language instruction sequence that initializes a specific state component, plus additional constraints specifying its prerequisites and side effects. The prerequisites specify that one gadget must execute before another. The side effects specify that in addition to the intended initialization, a gadget has other effects such as modifying scratch registers or causing a cache to become out of date. We have built gadgets to initialize general purpose registers, segment registers, control registers, and memory locations.

Then, our algorithm to generate the test state initializer operates as follows. First we instantiate a gadget for each component of the test state. Next, for each side effect of this first set of gadgets, we instantiate an additional gadget to correct the side effect, and we continue this process until there are no more outstanding side effects. Then, based on the prerequisite structure between all of these gadgets, we construct a dependency graph, and topologically sort the gadgets to respect the dependencies among them. Finally we append to this initializer sequence the test instruction itself and a halt instruction, and assemble the whole sequence to a binary. If our mechanism fails to find an initializer (e.g., because of a cyclic dependency or a side effect for which no gadget exists), we abort and ask for user assistance. A benefit of state-difference minimization (Section 3.4) is that none of the test cases generated by our system caused the initializer generator to fail.

Figure 5 shows a sample test program (without the baseline initializer) generated by our system for the instruction `push %eax`. The left hand side (Figure 5(a)) shows the output of the machine state space exploration. The system returned an assignment for the stack pointer and for two bytes of the physical memory, corresponding respectively to the fifth and sixth byte of the tenth entry in the global descriptor table. This descriptor is used for the stack segment, thus the purpose of the test is to exercise checks on the type and on the limit of the stack segment. The right hand side of the figure (Figure 5(b)) shows the code generated by our system to initialize the state, to execute the `push` instruction, and to mark the end of the execution. Line 1 initializes the stack pointer. Lines 2 and 3 overwrite the type and the default operand size attributes of the tenth segment descriptor in the global descriptor table. Lines 4 and 5 force the CPU to reload the descriptor of the stack segment (the tenth descriptor). Line 6 restores the original value of the `%eax` register, used by the previous instructions. Line 7 is the test instruction and line 8 halts the CPU. Our sequence generation algorithm automatically determines that lines 2 and 3 require lines 4 and 5, and that lines 4 and 5 require line 6.

5. Executing Test Programs

In the test program execution step, we take as input a test program as constructed in the previous step, and execute it on either an emulator or the real hardware. We monitor its execution to catch any exceptions raised by the test instruction, and to record the final state; these are the outputs that we will then compare. We now explain how we implement this execution step for emulators and for real hardware.

5.1 Emulator Execution

To run a test on a given emulator, we boot the emulator using the virtual disk image created for the test. After booting, the test runs automatically. The execution of the test can terminate in two different ways: the CPU either halts or throws an exception. To detect the termination of a test, we intercept those events; when one occurs, we generate a snapshot of the state of the CPU and of the physical memory. We achieve this by instrumenting the main execution loop of the emulator, enabling the interception after the baseline initialization has completed.

The test state initialization might modify critical portions of the CPU state (e.g., the page table or the global descriptor table). If any hardware interrupt is delivered during this stage of the initialization, the CPU might be unable to execute the interrupt handler successfully and will throw an exception. Different emulators simulate different devices and adopt different strategies to deliver hardware interrupts. Therefore, to prevent a spurious difference in the state, we ignore all interrupts after the baseline state has been initialized, again by instrumenting the main execution loop of the emulator.

We have had to implement very little instrumentation to intercept hardware interrupts, exceptions, and halt requests. Bochs already offers an API to instrument various types of events. QEMU does not provide an API, but we only needed to write a 10-line patch to intercept the events.

We create snapshots of the CPU state and of the physical memory with instrumentation code in the emulator that uses the emulator's APIs for memory access. The advantage of this approach, as opposed to attempting to create the snapshot as part of the test program, is that it is effective even if the emulated CPU is in an invalid state. Bochs and QEMU have similar built-in snapshot capabilities, but we implement our own file format to simplify comparison.

5.2 Hardware Execution

As with the emulator, we would like to record the state of the CPU and of the physical memory obtained at the end of the test program on real hardware Unfortunately, this is not easy to do because the execution environment would require special support for creating snapshots of the state at the end of the execution and because each test would have to reset the hardware.

Our strategy to overcome this problem is to leverage the closest approximation of the real hardware available: a hardware assisted virtual machine. With a hardware assisted virtual machine, based on Intel® VT-x, or AMD-V* [1, 24], we can execute tests in a guest virtual machine and supervise the execution of the guest from the virtual machine monitor. The majority of the instructions (including most privileged ones) can be executed directly on the hardware from the guest. The mediation of the virtual machine monitor is required only for a small subset of the instructions and events,

```
%esp     : 0x002007dc
00208055: 0x13   (gdt 10)
00208056: 0xcf   (gdt 10)
```

(a)

```
movl $0x002007dc,%esp
movb $0x13,0x00208055       // modify segment type and
movb $0xcf,0x00208056       //    default operation size (gdt 10)
movw $0x0050,%ax            // force reload of stack segment
movw %ax,%ss
movl $0x00000000,%eax       // restore killed %eax
.byte 0xff,0xf0             // push %eax
hlt                         // the end
```

(b)

Figure 5. Sample test-case generated by FuzzBALL (a) and corresponding x86 code of the test program (b), for the instruction `push %eax`.

and is triggered by traps. Hardware interrupts, exceptions, and halt requests that occur while executing guest code directly on the hardware can be intercepted by configuring the CPU to trap into the virtual machine monitor whenever they occur. When a trap occurs, the virtual machine monitor, having complete visibility to the state of the guest virtual machine, can create a snapshot of the state of the CPU and of the physical memory. Finally, the hardware guarantees a separation of the guest from the virtual machine monitor. Thus, the virtual machine monitor is always able to regain control of the execution, it can reset the state of the guest, and multiple tests can be run without having to reset the machine physically.

All the guest instructions in the test program that can be directly executed on the hardware are guaranteed to be correct. In other words, the state at the end of their execution corresponds to the state we would obtain if we executed the same instructions without the virtualization layer. On the other hand, for the instructions that require the mediation of the virtual machine monitor we do not have the same guarantee. However the number of such instructions is very small (just those that load and store a few privileged control registers), and their semantics simple, so we have checked by hand that the code in the virtual machine monitor responsible for the mediation complies with the real semantics.

Our implementation is based on KVM [19] (Kernel-based Virtual Machine), a virtual machine monitor for GNU/Linux. Only a few modifications were necessary to the original KVM codebase in order to intercept all traps that occur after the baseline state has been initialized. We handle different types of traps differently. If the trap originates from an exception or a halt request, we take a snapshot of the guest CPU state and physical memory and terminate the guest. If the trap originates from a hardware interrupt, we ignore the trap and resume the execution of the guest. Another class of traps are used to simulate exceptions: these occur when an instruction that would normally cause an exception (in the absence of the virtualization layer), instead generates a virtualization trap. Thus for all other types of trap, we let the virtual machine monitor handle the trap, but, before resuming the execution of the guest, we check whether an exception will be injected into the guest at the next resume. If so, this indicates that the trap was simulating an exception, so we take a snapshot and terminate as for a direct exception.

6. Evaluation

We evaluated PokeEMU by comparing the behaviors of the latest versions of QEMU (0.14.0) and Bochs (2.4.6), with the behavior of an Intel® Core™ i5 processor. On the latter we used a customized version of KVM (2.6.37) to automate the execution of the experiments. Since the i5 processor has hardware support for memory virtualization (extended, or nested, page tables), the vast majority of the instructions could be executed natively by the hardware without the need for software emulation.

As the Hi-Fi emulator we used a slightly earlier version of Bochs (2.4.5), the latest available at the time we started working on this project. We slightly customized this emulator to ease symbolic execution (e.g., we disabled the devices and the user interface).

We generated test cases using virtual machines running on Amazon EC2. We then used the same virtual machines to run the test cases in QEMU and Bochs and to compare their behaviors. The generation of the test cases required 545.4 CPU hours on 3 8-core instances on EC2 (total cost was about 135 US dollars in Amazon EC2 charges during the summer of 2011). Generation is highly parallelizable, since the bulk of its execution cost lies in the invocations of the solver, and multiple paths can be explored at the same time. We estimate that, with proper scheduling, test-case generation would take about 33.0 hours on 3 instances.

Test-case execution took totals of 198.7, 391.9, and 48.5 CPU hours on QEMU, Bochs, and the real hardware, respectively, and results comparison took 175.9 CPU hours. Test execution is also highly parallel, but our real-hardware testing approach is incompatible with EC2's para-virtualization; for the present results we used a local workstation. By combining 13 EC2 instances and 3 bare-metal instances from another provider, and accounting for the network transfer between them, we estimate that a complete set of test executions and the comparison of their results would take 7.8 hours and $100.19. This is already fast enough to use for nightly regression testing, so we believe that execution time is not a limiting factor for our approach or the PokeEMU prototype.

Our system was able to identify several differences in the behaviors of the emulators, some of which were not known before. We argue that our system can successfully be used in the future to validate the implementation of the currently missing security features in QEMU (i.e., the enforcement of segments' limits and rights) and the other issues (such as those caused by the lack of atomicity during emulation) we found.

6.1 Completeness of the Testing

To generate test instructions we explored the instruction set using a 15 byte input buffer. The first three bytes of this buffer were made symbolic (for the reasons explained in Section 3.2) and the remaining ones were set to zero. We identified 68,977 candidate byte sequences encoding valid instructions and then selected 880 unique instructions. This set of instructions covered all the unique instructions supported by the emulator, with the exception of a few SIMD instructions whose opcodes are longer than three bytes; we also excluded floating point instructions since our symbolic execution engine does not support them.[5]

We used each of these instructions to explore the machine state-space and to generate test programs. For the exploration we treated the entire machine state as symbolic, with the exception of the bytes in memory representing pointers (as shown in Figure 3), the FPU state, the MMX registers, and the contents of the interrupt descriptor table. As concrete inputs we used a snapshot of the

[5] Some of the techniques used for floating-point equivalence checking by Collingbourne et al. [11] might help us remove the floating-point restriction from PokeEMU in our future work.

baseline machine state. For each test instruction we executed the emulator until we explored all paths or we reached a limit on the maximum number of paths (currently 8192).

In this setting, our system explored 610,516 different paths. We observed that the number of explored paths per instruction mainly depends on the type of instructions and on the type of operands (e.g., whether the operand represents a register or a memory location). We exhaustively explored the machine state-space for about 95% of the instructions. The remaining 5% of the test instructions were not exhaustively explored because we either hit the limit on the maximum number of paths or because of a limitation of our current concretization strategy. Thus, for the exhaustively explored instructions, our system generated test programs that covered *all the possible behaviors* of the Hi-Fi emulator that can be triggered by varying the symbolic machine state. (It does not follow that our tests achieved 100% block or branch coverage of all of the code within the exhaustively-explored instructions, because for instance code that would only execute outside of protected mode was not included in the exploration. But in the cases we examined manually the static coverage appeared very high.)

6.2 Analysis of Differences

Overall, we observed quite a high number of differences: out of the 610,516 test programs generated by our system, 60,770 of these programs produced distinguishable behaviors in QEMU and 15,219 of them produced distinguishable behaviors in Bochs.

Not all discovered differences represent a distinct bug. Some are caused by undefined CPU behaviors; since those behaviors are undocumented, there may be no single correct behavior (and even different physical CPUs may produce different results). Among the remaining differences, many are imputable to the same root cause. We used scripts to filter out differences due to undefined behaviors (we reused filters from our prior work [20, 21]). We then clustered the differences according to root cause; this clustering identified different executed paths that triggered the same behavior difference. We then examined representative tests to understand each root cause. In the remainder of this section we briefly summarize some of the root causes we identified, and we discuss their implications.

Hardware CPUs execute instructions atomically. On the other hand, in a software emulated CPU, the execution of an instruction requires executing multiple instructions on the real hardware. Thus, to emulate the execution of an instruction atomically, special care is needed to ensure that the original state is preserved (or restored) when the execution of an instruction is interrupted by an exception. Non-atomic execution of instruction can produce incorrect program behaviors and open opportunities for attacks. The test programs generated by our system confirmed that both emulators execute the majority of the instructions atomically. However, our system identified instructions for which the atomicity property is not guaranteed in QEMU. More precisely, our system found that this problem occurs with the instructions `leave` (high level procedure exit) and `cmpxchgw` (compare and exchange). The former corrupts the stack pointer when the page containing the top of the stack is not accessible. The latter corrupts the source operand when the destination operand represents a memory location and this memory location is read-only. Indeed, the lack of write permissions is detected only after the source operand has been updated, and the original value of the source operand is not checkpointed. We speculate that such issues, although not easy to trigger, might lead to serious security consequences.

Paging and segmentation are the two main security mechanisms provided by the CPU; an emulator has to support these mechanisms to be considered trustworthy. Our system identified that QEMU does not implement segmentation properly because it does not enforce segment limits and rights with the majority of instructions, which can have serious security implications. The lack of segmentation support renders security mechanisms that rely on this feature [28] completely useless. This problem is known to QEMU's developers and was previously, in part, found by applying random fuzzing to manually written test programs [21]. However, our system was able to generate test programs to exercise all the checks the CPU could possibly do and to identify all the cases in which limits and rights are not properly enforced. Thus, the test programs we have generated can be used again in the future to validate the implementation when this currently missing feature is available.

We also found other less dangerous discrepancies in the behaviors of the tested emulators. For example our system generated test programs showing that QEMU does not raise a general protection fault exception when the `rmsr` (read machine specific register) instruction is used to read the value of an invalid machine status register. Moreover, our system found that QEMU, Bochs, and the hardware fetch data from memory in different orders. For example, the order in which the emulators pop items from the stack while emulating the `iret` (interrupt return) instruction differs (QEMU accesses stack items from the outermost to the innermost, Bochs and the hardware in the opposite order). Similarly, for the `lfs` instruction (load far pointer), Bochs fetches the two operands from the memory in the opposite order as QEMU and the hardware. This difference could cause different exceptions. Again, we found that QEMU does not consider valid certain instruction encodings and that it does not properly update the segments' "accessed" flag. Finally, both in QEMU and Bochs, some arithmetic and logical instructions differently update some status flags (documented as undefined). Since emulators are widely used to dynamically analyze malicious software, malicious developers could embed into their software anti-emulation tricks that fingerprint emulators by exploiting these subtle differences in their behaviors.

Many of these differences would have been difficult to find using purely random testing, and were in fact not found by a previous such study [20]. For instance, the difference in `iret` read ordering can be significant only if the values read lie on different pages or across a segment boundary, either of which would have a very low probability if the address and segment limit were chosen uniformly at random. Random testing can generate tests more quickly than PokeEMU, but this would leave the cost dominated by the time to execute the tests.

7. Limitations and Future Work

By necessity, our work reduced the size of the problem by narrowing its scope. We examine the resulting limitations and the direction of our future work next.

Other operating modes and extended instruction sets. Although x86 CPUs support multiple operating modes, we focus on testing only the 32-bit protected mode with paging enabled. Other operating modes (e.g. real and virtual 8086) are more prone to buggy behavior, since they are less commonly used. Our system could be easily extended for testing these operating modes as well. We plan to do that in the future. We also plan to extend our system to support floating-point, MMX, and SSE instructions.

Multiple-Instruction Sequences. We focus on testing each instruction separately, rather than sequences of several instructions together. In principle, doing so is completely sufficient if we can construct an initializer for every possible machine state, and the execution of every instruction is independent, properties that have held in our experiments so far. Under these observations, any difference caused by a multi-instruction sequence can be divided into one or more single-instruction differences.

In practice, however, emulators may themselves compose individual instructions incorrectly, especially in the case of QEMU, which performs dynamic binary translation for multi-instruction sequences. In our future work, we plan on studying how multi-instruction sequences are treated by emulators.

Symbolic Execution of JIT Compilers and Hardware Specifications. We have based our system on binary-level symbolic execution so that in the future we can apply it to emulators based on just-in-time compilation, such as QEMU. For example, it would be interesting to perform the converse of the comparison in Section 6 by generating tests from QEMU and using them to evaluate Bochs. Since Bochs is generally more complete, our expectation is that this would produce only a few more differences than our current experiments, but it is important if there are cases where QEMU implements a check and Bochs fails to.

In the limit, it may be possible to apply our path-exploration lifting methodology to the highest-Fi emulator there is: the hardware specification itself. Although we have no hope of obtaining (and publishing about) specifications of commercial hardware, it might be possible to apply this methodology to open-source hardware architectures, like the SPARC Leon processor.

Before we reach that desirable remote limit, we hope to study higher-level interpreters, e.g., for high-level languages such as Java.

Other Virtual Machines. We currently make some use of source code to simplify the workflow of our study, but our binary approach allows us to tackle emulators for which we have no source code at all, e.g., commercial virtual machine monitors that incorporate emulation in one or more execution modes. To facilitate this, we would like to further automate the process of determining which host locations hold guest machine state. For instance the location of `%eax` is the one where the emulator writes 42 when executing the instruction `mov $42, %eax`.

Equivalence Checking. Despite its promise, our approach only provides tests, not proofs of correctness. A further direction to improve the completeness of our emulator checking would be to perform a complete equivalence check between our set of symbolic execution results. Starting with a single Hi-Fi emulator path, we could identify all paths in the Lo-Fi emulator exercised by the same input states. Then we could symbolically combine the results for all Lo-Fi paths into a single large formula (as in the summary-building technique described in Section 3.3.2). Then we would check with a decision procedure whether the formula for the single Hi-Fi path is equivalent to the formula for the few Lo-Fi paths on all possible inputs. It may be difficult to make such an approach scale to all instructions, but when it works it provides a very strong statement about the absence of differences. This has been tried successfully for smaller, restricted programs, like processor microcode [2].

8. Related Work

Next we discuss two classes of previous research that are related to our work here: first, other projects that have searched for bugs in emulators, and then other systems for symbolic execution.

Testing of Emulators. Emulator authors presumably perform testing internally, but there has been relatively little research on techniques to make that testing more automated and effective. A series of two recent papers by Martignoni et al. show the practical value of third-party comparative testing of emulators. They first tested CPU emulators specifically, with randomly generated instructions [20]. Later they tested whole-system virtual machines (based on emulation and other technologies) using hand-written templates that were then automatically expanded to create a larger number of instruction sequences [21]. To generate a set of legal instruction byte sequences (the same challenge we face in Section 3.2), they perform a concrete exploration using the CPU as a black-box correctness oracle. They also execute tests using techniques similar to the ones we describe in Section 4: either with a user-space program [20] or a custom-written kernel [21]. However, random testing on its own does not provide the same kind of coverage guarantees that symbolic execution does. First, PokeEMU completed test generation with measurable path coverage: complete path coverage for 95% of the tested instructions, a precise quantitative measure of coverage, which random-testing methods cannot provide. Second, as shown by the comparison of Section 6, our approach revealed some bugs that these previously state-of-the-art studies based on random testing did not find. Therefore, we consider PokeEMU a demonstrated improvement over the state of the art.

Symbolic Execution. Though our primary motivation in this work is the practical problem of trustworthy emulation, our results there are made possible in part by improvements in the underlying technology of symbolic execution.

Symbolic execution was first proposed in the 1970s [18]. It has been the subject of renewed interest in the last decade thanks to a new generation of approaches [7, 15] and advances in constraint solving and increased computing power that have allowed it to be more widely applied. We can classify symbolic execution systems according to the relationship between concrete and symbolic execution. In systems that are called trace-based, dynamic, or concolic [26], the program chooses branch directions based on a concrete input, but records a path so that it can generate an different input later. By contrast online systems, of which FuzzBALL is an example, maintain symbolic values without a corresponding concrete value, and so can be free to choose either direction at a branch.

Another online symbolic execution tool is KLEE [6], which generates test cases for C programs using a symbolic interpreter for LLVM byte code. KLEE is similar to FuzzBALL in many ways, but has two key design differences. First, KLEE "forks" and maintains multiple execution states at once when both sides of a branch are feasible, whereas FuzzBALL executes just one path to completion and returns to other paths later. Second, KLEE's symbolic constraints can contain array expressions, while FuzzBALL avoids them by choosing concrete values for indexes. KLEE's approach produces fewer execution paths, but it requires additional knowledge and assumptions about the way a program manages memory. Also, decision procedure queries that contain large arrays can be significantly difficult to solve. Though a more symbolic approach could be added to FuzzBALL, our current approach works sufficiently well for many applications, including the present one.

Particularly for security applications, it is important to be able to perform symbolic execution at the binary level, as we do. SAGE [16] is a trace-based symbolic execution system for x86 that is used for extensive testing within Microsoft, but is not publicly available; SmartFuzz [22] is open-source and based on Valgrind. However trace-based systems tend to be geared to exploring just a few paths in a program, rather than the exhaustive exploration we perform. Another capability that is important in some security applications is to be able to symbolically execute a program in the context of a complete operating system. In a trace-based tool one can collect traces with a whole system emulator, but maintain symbolic information for a single process, as in the BitFuzz [5] system, based on QEMU. Most recently, S^2E [10] is an online system that integrates KLEE with QEMU, allowing more flexible combination of symbolic and concrete execution across multiple components. However, our emulators do not make significant use of the operating system when executing instructions, so a lighter-weight single-process approach was appropriate for us.

Some of the optimizations we perform are also related to previous approaches in symbolic execution. For instance, the technique of summary construction described in Section 3.3.2 is similar in spirit to compositional symbolic execution techniques [14].

It is important to distinguish our work on validating processor emulators (using symbolic execution) from work on using processor emulators (possibly to implement symbolic execution). For example, Anubis [3] uses a CPU emulator (based on QEMU) to analyze malware and can perform symbolic path exploration [23]. Similarly, Minesweeper [4] uses an emulator to discover trigger-based behaviors in malware. Although our work concerns itself with security, emulators, and symbolic execution, it aims instead to provide assurances that the emulator itself is correct. The challenges of executing an emulator symbolically may have some similarities to executing malware symbolically. However, we have two additional problems to address: mapping a CPU state identified by symbolic execution to a sequence of instructions that allow to reach the state, and identifying anomalous behaviors in an emulator.

9. Conclusion

We perform high-coverage testing of emulators by using binary-level symbolic execution to explore the space of legal instructions and machine state that could influence their execution in a high-fidelity emulator (Bochs). The system generates a test, in the form of a bootable disk image, for each of the 610,516 explored paths. We can use these tests to lift the exploration to test a low-fidelity emulator (QEMU), and to cross-validate with a hardware processor. In analyzing the differences, we see that many reveal systematic implementation oversights, such as atomicity violations in QEMU: the tests will be valuable both for understanding the failures and verifying that the problems have been fixed. Though this is only the first application, it demonstrates a practical and powerful tool to make emulators more trustworthy.

Acknowledgments: We thank the anonymous reviewers, as well as our shepherd, Jim Larus, for their comments and helpful suggestions. We are grateful to Jim Grundy for his detailed feedback on our drafts. This work was in part supported by a gift from Intel Corporation, by the Air Force Office of Scientific Research (AFOSR) under MURI award FA9550-09-1-0539, by the Air Force Research Laboratory under grant no. P010071555, by DARPA under award HR0011-12-2-005, and by the National Science Foundation under grants CCF-0424422 and 0842695. Our use of Amazon EC2 was supported by the Amazon Web Services in Education research grant program. Any opinions, findings, and recommendations expressed herein are those of the authors and do not necessarily reflect the views of Intel or the US Government.

References

[1] Advanced Micro Devices. AMD64 virtualization: Secure virtual machine architecture reference manual. AMD Publication no. 33047 rev. 3.01, 2005.

[2] T. Arons, E. Elster, L. Fix, S. Mador-Haim, M. Mishaeli, J. Shalev, E. Singerman, A. Tiemeyer, M. Vardi, and L. Zuck. Formal Verification of Backward Compatibility of Microcode. In *Computer Aided Verification (CAV)*, 2005.

[3] U. Bayer, C. Kruegel, and E. Kirda. TTAnalyze: A Tool for Analyzing Malware. In *European Institute for Computer Antivirus Research (EICAR)*, 2006.

[4] D. Brumley, C. Hartwig, Z. Liang, J. Newsome, D. Song, and H. Yin. Automatically identifying trigger-based behavior in malware. In W. Lee, C. Wang, and D. Dagon, editors, *Botnet Detection*, volume 36 of *Advances in Information Security*. Springer, 2008.

[5] J. Caballero, P. Poosankam, S. McCamant, D. Babic, and D. Song. Input generation via decomposition and re-stitching: Finding bugs in malware. In *CCS*, 2010.

[6] C. Cadar, D. Dunbar, and D. Engler. KLEE: Unassisted and automatic generation of high-coverage tests for complex systems programs. In *OSDI*, 2008.

[7] C. Cadar and D. Engler. Execution generated test cases: How to make systems code crash itself. In *Model Checking Software (SPIN Workshop)*, 2005.

[8] C. Cadar, V. Ganesh, P. M. Pawlowski, D. L. Dill, and D. Engler. EXE: automatically generating inputs of death. In *CCS*, 2006.

[9] X. Chen, T. Garfinkel, E. C. Lewis, P. Subrahmanyam, C. A. Waldspurger, D. Boneh, J. Dwoskin, and D. R. K. Ports. Overshadow: A Virtualization-Based Approach to Retrofitting Protection in Commodity Operating Systems. In *ASPLOS*, 2008.

[10] V. Chipounov, V. Kuznetsov, and G. Candea. S2E: A platform for in-vivo multi-path analysis of software systems. In *ASPLOS*, 2011.

[11] P. Collingbourne, C. Cadar, and P. H. J. Kelly. Symbolic Crosschecking of Floating-Point and SIMD Code. In *EuroSys*, 2011.

[12] L. de Moura and N. Bjørner. Z3: An efficient SMT solver. In *Tools and Algorithms for the Construction and Analysis of Systems (TACAS)*, 2008.

[13] V. Ganesh and D. L. Dill. A decision procedure for bit-vectors and arrays. In *Computer Aided Verification (CAV)*, 2007.

[14] P. Godefroid. Compositional dynamic test generation. In *POPL*, 2007.

[15] P. Godefroid, N. Klarlund, and K. Sen. DART: directed automated random testing. In *PLDI*, 2005.

[16] P. Godefroid, M. Y. Levin, and D. A. Molnar. Automated whitebox fuzz testing. In *Network and Distributed System Security (NDSS)*, 2008.

[17] A. Ho, M. Fetterman, C. Clark, A. Warfield, and S. Hand. Practical Taint-Based Protection using Demand Emulation. In *EuroSys*, 2006.

[18] J. C. King. Symbolic execution and program testing. *Communications of the ACM*, 19(7), 1976.

[19] Kernel-based Virtual Machine (KVM). `http://linux-kvm.org/`.

[20] L. Martignoni, R. Paleari, G. F. Roglia, and D. Bruschi. Testing CPU emulators. In *International Symposium on Software Testing and Analysis (ISSTA)*, 2009.

[21] L. Martignoni, R. Paleari, G. F. Roglia, and D. Bruschi. Testing system virtual machines. In *International Symposium on Software Testing and Analysis (ISSTA)*, 2010.

[22] D. Molnar, X. C. Li, and D. A. Wagner. Dynamic test generation to find integer bugs in x86 binary Linux programs. In *USENIX Security Symposium*, 2009.

[23] A. Moser, C. Kruegel, and E. Kirda. Exploring Multiple Execution Paths for Malware Analysis. In *IEEE Symposium on Security and Privacy (Oakland)*, 2007.

[24] G. Neiger, A. Santoni, F. Leung, D. Rodgers, and R. Uhlig. Intel Virtualization Technology: Hardware support for efficient processor virtualization. *Intel Technology Journal*, 10(3), 2006.

[25] N. Nethercote and J. Seward. Valgrind: a framework for heavyweight dynamic binary instrumentation. In *PLDI*, 2007.

[26] K. Sen, D. Marinov, and G. Agha. CUTE: A concolic unit testing engine for C. In *European Software Engineering Conference / Foundations of Software Engineering (ESEC/FSE)*, 2005.

[27] D. Song, D. Brumley, H. Yin, J. Caballero, I. Jager, M. G. Kang, Z. Liang, J. Newsome, P. Poosankam, and P. Saxena. BitBlaze: A new approach to computer security via binary analysis. In *International Conf. on Information Systems Security (ICISS)*, 2008. Keynote.

[28] B. Yee, D. Sehr, G. Dardyk, J. B. Chen, R. Muth, T. Ormandy, S. Okasaka, N. Narula, and N. Fullagar. Native client: A sandbox for portable, untrusted x86 native code. In *IEEE Symposium on Security and Privacy (Oakland)*, 2009.

[29] Q. Zhang, J. McCullough, J. Ma, N. Schear, M. Vrable, A. Vahdat, A. C. Snoeren, G. M. Voelker, and S. Savage. Neon: system support for derived data management. In *Virtual Execution Environments (VEE)*, 2010.

Green-Marl: A DSL for Easy and Efficient Graph Analysis

Sungpack Hong
Pervasive Parallelism Laboratory
Stanford University
hongsup@stanford.edu

Hassan Chafi
Pervaisve Parallelism Laboratory
Stanford University
and Oracle Labs
hassan.chafi@oracle.com

Eric Sedlar
Oracle Labs
eric.sedlar@oracle.com

Kunle Olukotun
Pervasive Parallelism Laboratory
Stanford University
kunle@stanford.edu

Abstract

The increasing importance of graph-data based applications is fueling the need for highly efficient and parallel implementations of graph analysis software. In this paper we describe Green-Marl, a domain-specific language (DSL) whose high level language constructs allow developers to describe their graph analysis algorithms intuitively, but expose the data-level parallelism inherent in the algorithms. We also present our Green-Marl compiler which translates high-level algorithmic description written in Green-Marl into an efficient C++ implementation by exploiting this exposed data-level parallelism. Furthermore, our Green-Marl compiler applies a set of optimizations that take advantage of the high-level semantic knowledge encoded in the Green-Marl DSL. We demonstrate that graph analysis algorithms can be written very intuitively with Green-Marl through some examples, and our experimental results show that the compiler-generated implementation out of such descriptions performs as well as or better than highly-tuned hand-coded implementations.

Categories and Subject Descriptors D.1.3 [*Software*]: Programming Techniques—Concurrent Programming

General Terms Algorithms, Design, Performance

Keywords Graph, Domain-Specific Language, Parallel Programming

1. Introduction

A graph is a fundamental data structure that captures relationships between different data entities. Graphs are used to represent data sets in a wide range of application domains, such as social science, astronomy and computational biology. In a social graph, for example, nodes correspond to people while friendship relationships between them are represented as edges. In addition, nodes or edges in a graph are typically associated with a certain set of values. For example, the edges of a social graph might be associated with the average number of phone calls per month between two people. Graph analysis involves extracting information from a given data-set which is represented as a graph. For example, one might be interested in finding groups of people who call each other frequently.

The enormous growth in data leads to large underlying graphs which require huge amounts of computational power to analyze. While modern commodity computer systems provide a significant amount of computational power measured in the tera-flops, efficient execution of graph analysis algorithms on large datasets remains difficult on these systems [26]. Some of the challenges include:

- Capacity – for very large datasets, the graph will not fit into a single physical memory address space.
- Performance – Some graph algorithms often perform poorly when applied to large graph instances.
- Implementation – it is not easy to develop a correct and efficient implementation for many graph algorithms.

In this paper, we tackle the performance and implementation challenges, and focus on the case when the graph fits into physical memory. This is practical– as recent work [4] has demonstrated that fairly large-sized graph problems can be processed in the physical memory of a modern high-end server machine. In Section 5, however, we do discuss some future work to deal with the capacity challenge.

Even in a single memory address space, graph applications often suffer from poor performance on large problems. Poor performance is due to the random memory access behavior of most graph analysis algorithms – as soon as the working-set size exceeds the size of the various levels of caches in the system, performance becomes dominated by memory latency.

One common approach to address the performance challenge is to exploit the data parallelism which is typically abundant in analysis algorithms on large graphs. This approach leverages both the increasing number of parallel implementations proposed for common graph-theory algorithms, and the recent advances and proliferation of parallel computing systems By properly utilizing this hardware, we hide this memory latency problem by using parallelism and are only limited by the available memory bandwidth in the system.

However, adopting parallelism exacerbates the third challenge – implementation. Even without parallelism, it is often challenging to implement a graph analysis algorithm in an efficient way. The application developer has to carefully consider which data structure

ASPLOS'12 March 3–7,2012, London, England, UK.

to use and has to reason about the algorithm's memory access patterns. Parallel programming introduces a whole set of other issues to be carefully considered – race-conditions, dead-lock, etc.

Even the same algorithm may show drastically different performance depending on its implementation. For instance, many different parallel implementations [4, 21, 38] have been proposed for a simple breadth-first search algorithm, all with different performance results. As we will show in Section 1.1, achieving an efficient implementation requires both a clear understanding of the graph algorithm and a deep knowledge of the underlying hardware architecture. This also introduces a tight coupling to the underlying architecture which decreases the portability of the resulting implementation.

In this paper, we take a different approach on how to tackle the performance and implementation challenges we have identified. We propose Green-Marl[1], a domain-specific language (DSL) designed specifically for graph analysis algorithms. Users of Green-Marl can describe their graph algorithm intuitively using high-level graph constructs which expose the inherent parallelism in the algorithm. A compiler for Green-Marl can exploit this high-level information by applying a series of high-level optimizations and parallelizing the algorithm, and finally producing a (correct) optimized parallel implementation of the given algorithm. By using the DSL, the users can concentrate on their algorithm rather than its implementation. The Green-Marl compiler final output is an implementation written in a general-purpose language, e.g. C++, rather than a machine language, e.g. x86 instructions (Section 3).

Our specific contributions are as follows:

- Green-Marl, a DSL in which a user can describe a graph analysis algorithm in a very intuitive way. This DSL captures the high-level semantics of the algorithm as well as its inherent parallelism.
- The Green-Marl compiler which applies a set of optimizations and parallelization enabled by the high-level semantic information of the DSL and produces an optimized parallel implementation targetted at commodity SMP machines.
- An interdiscipliary DSL approach to solving computational problems that combines graph theory, compilers, parallel programming and computer architecture.

The rest of this paper is organized as follows: we present the overall language design of Green-Marl in Section 2. In Section 3, we describe the Green-Marl compiler which produces high-performing parallel implementations of algorithms described in Green-Marl. Our experimental results (Section 4) show that while graph analysis algorithms can be written using Green-Marl in a simple way, their compiler-generated implementation performs equally as well as or better than a highly-tuned hand-coded library implementations. In Section 5, we discuss how Green-Marl can be used with minimal disruption in existing development environments, and how we plan to solve the capacity issue using Green-Marl. Section 6 highlights related work and we conclude in Section 7.

1.1 A Motivating Graph Example

Before discussing the details of the Green-Marl language and compiler, we present a well known social network analysis algorithm, "betweenness centrality" (BC), written in Green-Marl. BC measures the centrality (or relative importance) of nodes in a given graph. BC is widely used in social network analysis. Brandes [13] first proposed a fast sequential algorithm to compute BC values for all nodes in a graph.

[1] Green-Marl is a transliteration of Korean words meaning 'pictured language'.

```
1  Procedure Compute_BC(
2   G: Graph, BC: Node_Prop<Float>(G)) {
3    G.BC = 0;          // initialize BC
4    Foreach(s: G.Nodes) {
5     // define temporary properties
6      Node_Prop<Float>(G) Sigma;
7      Node_Prop<Float>(G) Delta;
8      s.Sigma = 1; // Initialize Sigma for root
9     // Traverse graph in BFS-order from s
10     InBFS(v: G.Nodes From s)(v!=s) {
11       // sum over BFS-parents
12       v.Sigma = Sum(w: v.UpNbrs) {w.Sigma};
13     }
14    // Traverse graph in reverse BFS-order
15     InRBFS(v!=s) {
16       // sum over BFS-children
17       v.Delta = Sum (w:v.DownNbrs) {
18          v.Sigma / w.Sigma * (1+ w.Delta)
19       };
20       v.BC += v.Delta @s; //accumulate BC
21 } } }
```

Figure 1. Betweenness Centrality algorithm described in Green-Marl

Although the original BC computation algorithm was written for sequential execution, the algorithm contains an abundant amount of inherent parallelism. Bader and Madurri [7] leveraged this fact and presented an initial parallel implementation. A few years later, the same researchers presented a significantly improved implementation of the same algorithm [28]; the implementation adopted different meta-data structures, used a better iteration scheme, and eliminated lock contention. This resulted in more than 2x speedup over their previous parallel implementation when measured on a Cray XMT machine.

Figure 1 shows the same algorithm written in Green-Marl. The procedure takes two arguments `G`, a graph, and `BC`, a node property (a piece of data associated with each node) of graph `G`, which is to be computed (line 2). At line 3, the `BC` value is initialized to 0 for all nodes in the graph `G`. Line 4 begins an iteration over every node `s` in graph `G`. At each iteration step, two temporary node properties, `Sigma` and `Delta`, are defined. After initializing `Sigma` for node `s` (line 8), we do a breadth-first (BFS) order iteration over the nodes in graph `G`, where `s` is the root of the search (line 10). During the BFS iteration over every node `v` other than `s`, `Sigma` of `v` is computed by summing up `Sigma` values of its BFS-parents (line 12). When the BFS iteration concludes, at line 15 we then perform a reverse order BFS traversal (i.e. we start iterating at the farthest nodes from `s`). During this traversal we compute `Delta` from the BFS-children nodes for each node `v` (line 17). Finally, `Delta` is accumulated into `BC` during every iteration of s (line 20).

Note that the Green-Marl implementation is much shorter than Brandes' original description, which included implementation details related to performing the BFS iteration using queues and lists. Bader and Madduri's implementation [7], on the other hand, available in a library [9] is more than 400 lines long. Note that the library is implemented using OpenMP [31] which is a concise way of writing parallel code.

Although written in an intuitive way, the Green-Marl implementation fully exposes the parallelism inherent in the algorithm. Initialization at Line 3 is a trivial data-parallel operation, while BFS and RBFS (line 10 and line 15 can be parallelized at each level of the iteration. Finally, even the outer loop 4 can be parallelized. The compiler's analysis phase (Section 3) ensures that there are no data accesses that conflict (otherwise the compiler emits an error or a warning). The Green-Marl compiler exploits the available parallelism to generate an efficient implementation in a general-purpose language (e.g. C++). In Section 4, we will show that this Green-Marl implementation performs as well as the hand-optimized implementation [28].

2. Green-Marl Language Design

2.1 Scope of the Language

Mathematically, a graph is an ordered pair $G = (N, E)$ comprising a set, N, of nodes and E, a set of edges or optionally ordered pairs of two nodes. The data associated with each node or edge can be defined as a mapping P from N (or E) to some codomain (e.g. $P_{phone} : E \rightarrow \mathbb{R}$). In this paper, we refer to such a mapping as a *node (or edge) property*.

Given a graph, $G = (V, E)$, and a set of properties defined on the graph, $\Pi = \{P_1, P_2, ...P_n\}$, our language is specifically designed for the following types of graph analysis:

- Computing a scalar value from (G, Π), e.g. the conductance of a sub-graph
- Computing a new property P_{n+1} from (G, Π), e.g. the pagerank of each node of a graph
- Selecting a subgraph of interest out of the original graph $(V', E') \subset (V, E)$, e.g. strongly connected components of a graph

Note that the last type of analysis can be also be formulated as computing two new properties $P_{node} : N \rightarrow \{true, false\}$ and $P_{edge} : E \rightarrow \{true, false\}$ which captures the membership of the original nodes and edges in the resulting subgraph.

The above mathematical descriptions imply two important assumptions that Green-Marl makes:

1. The graph is immutable and is not modified during analysis.
2. There are no aliases between graph instances nor between graph properties.

We assume an immutable graph so that we can focus on the task of graph analysis, rather than worry about orthogonal issues such as how graphs are constructed or modified. Since Green-Marl is designed to be used in re-writting only parts of the user application (Section 3.1), one can construct or modify the graph in their own preferred way (e.g. from data file, from a database, etc.) but when a Green-Marl generated implementation is handed a graph, the assumption is that the graph will not be modified while a Green-Marl procedure is analyizing it.

2.2 Parallelism in Green-Marl

The Green-Marl language design is based on a few paradigms. First, it includes language constructs for *implicit parallelism*, e.g. group assignment (line 3 in figure 1) and in-place reductions (line 12). Second, it allows users to explicitly demarcate parallel execution regions. For example, the `foreach` statement used in line 4 specifies a parallel region. The compiler analysis enabled by the domain-specific knowledge encoded in Green-Marl applications can detect possible conflicts in parallel regions. Finally, the domain-specific data analyses increase the likelihood that the compiler can apply speculative or automatic parallelization. For example, while the `for` statement, in contrast to a `foreach` statement, specifies sequential execution of the iteration steps in no particular order, the compiler may parallelize the iteration as long as the parallelization can guarantee a serializable execution of iteration steps. [2]

The language adopts a fork-join style of parallelism, where iteration steps in a `foreach` are forked and execute in parallel and then are synchronized at a join point which is inserted right after the `foreach`. Note that this is the same widely used mechanism adopted in successful parallel frameworks such as OpenMP [31], CUDA [30], and Pregel [29]. Green-Marl also allows the users to express nested parallelism. The following example[3] shows nested parallel regions: line 23 is a parallel iteration over all the nodes in the graph `G`, while line 26 is a nested parallel iteration over all the neighbors of node s. Forked iteration steps are joined at the end of a parallel iteration. All the forked iteration steps of line 26 from a single `s` have to synchronize before execution proceeds to line 27. However, forked iteration steps do not need to synchronize with other nested parallel execution regions (i.e., those iteration steps which are forked from a different `s`).

```
22  Int sum=0;
23  Foreach(s: G.Nodes) {
24    Int p_sum = u.A;
25    Foreach(t: s.Nbrs)
26       p_sum *= t.B;
27    sum += p_sum;
28  }
29  Int y = sum / 2;
```

Green-Marl uses static scoping rules. Local variables are private to the current iteration step, but are shared by any parallel region in the same scope as the variables. In our previous example, `p_sum` is private to each parallel iteration step of the iteration at line 23 (*s-iteration*) but shared by every parallel iteration step at line 26 (*t-iteration*) originated from the same `s`.

Finally, Green-Marl's memory consistency model for parallel execution is similar to that of OpenMP's:

1. a write to a shared variable is not guaranteed to be visible to other concurrent iteration steps during the parallel execution.
2. a write to a shared variable is guaranteed to be visible to the later statements of the current iteration step, unless another write to the same variable from a concurrent iteration step becomes visible beforehand.
3. a write to a shared variable becomes visible at the end of a parallel iteration; if there have been multiple concurrent iteration steps that wrote to the same, only one write (chosen non-deterministically).

On the other hand, Green-Marl ensures each write is atomic (i.e. no data is partially written) and operations on a collection (i.e. adding an item to a set) are also atomic.

Thus, the following Green-Marl example suffers from data-races under the above consistency model. Line 32 is a write-write conflict because multiple s-iteration steps can write to the same t-node. Similarly the read at line 33 and the write at line 32 is a read-write conflict. We encourage the readers to visualize these cases using Figure 2.(a). A Green-Marl compiler would detect such data-races at compile time (Section 3.2).

```
30  Foreach(s:G.Nodes)
31    Foreach(t:s.OutNbrs)
32      t.A =                // write-write conflict
33         t.A + s.B;        // read-write conflict
```

Fundamentally, Green-Marl prevents users from writing algorithms that communicate between concurrent iteration steps. Instead, it expects users to use proper *reductions* (Section 2.3.4) to get deterministic results. This design decision was made to allow the language to work in distributed environments as well (Section 5.2).

2.3 Language Constructs

2.3.1 Data-Types and Collections

Green-Marl has a simple type system. First, there are five primitive types (`Bool`, `Int`, `Long`, `Float` and `Double`). Green-Marl also

[2] Our current Green-Marl compiler (Section 3) does not attempt to parallelize `for` iterations; however, future implementations may safely parallelize them via conventional schemes such as fine-grained locking, graph coloring, or transactional memory.

[3] In our examples, our convention is to use 'G' for graphs, 'x,y,z' for scalar variables, 'A,B,C' for propertes, 's,t,u' for loop variables, 'F(),G()' for Boolean functions, and 'X(),Y()' for numeric functions.

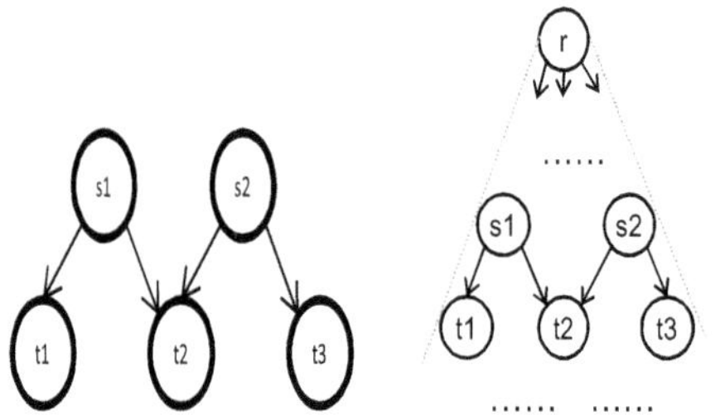

(a) (b)

Figure 2. Simple graph instances. (a) is a small bipartite graph, while (b) is showing only a portion of the graph in the middle of BFS traversal rooted from r.

		sequential			parallel		
Group	Op-Name	*S*	*O*	*Q*	*S*	*O*	*Q*
Grow	Add	v			v		
	Push(Front/Back)		v	v		v	v
Shrink	Remove	v			v		
	Pop(Front/Back)		v	v		?	?
	Clear	v	v	v	v	v	v
Lookup	Has	v	v	v	v	v	v
	Front(Back)		v	v		v	v
	Size	v	v	v	v	v	v
Copy	=	v	v	v	X	X	X
Iteration	Items	v	v	v	v	v	v

Modification under iteration → Shrink, Grow, or Copy: X

Conflicts under parallel execution →
Grow-Shrink: X Lookup-Shrink: ? Lookup-Grow: ?

Table 1. Operations on Collections: S,O,and Q denotes set, order and sequence, respectively. In the table, 'v', 'X', '?' stands for the operation being valid, invalid, and undefined for the selected collection type under the selected execution context.

defines two graph types (`DGraph` and `UGRaph`) which denote a directed graph and an undirected graph respectively[4]. Second, there is a node type and an edge type both of which are always bound to a graph instance, as in the `n1` and `n2` in following code example. Third, there are node properties and edge properties which are bound to a graph but have base-types as well (`A` in the following code example).

Finally, Green-Marl provides three types of collection types (for both node and edge types): Set, Order, and Sequence. Elements in a Set are *unique* while a Set is *unordered*. Elements in an Order are *unique* while an Order is *ordered*. Elements in a Sequence are *not unique* while a Sequence is *ordered*. All of these type are also bound to a graph: e.g., `S` in the following code example.

```
Procedure foo(G1, G2:Graph, n:Node(G1)) {
    Node(G2) n2; // a node of graph G2
    n2 = n;  // type-error (bound to different graphs)
    Node_Prop<Int>(G1) A; //integer node property for G1
    n.A = 0;
    Node_Set(G1) S; // a node set of G1
    S.Add(n);
}
```

Table 1 summarizes the operations defined on collection types in a sequential and parallel execution context. Here are a few highlights: (a) The semantics of assignment to a collection is to create a copy of the collection. During parallel execution, assignment to a shared collection variable is not allowed. (b) Parallel `Push` to an `Order` is allowed – the relative order of pushes in a parallel context is non-deterministic and the pushed elements may not be visible to other iteration steps. Support for parallel `Pop` is dependent on each compiler implementation. (c) Every collection can be iterated on, in sequential or in parallel. When iterating in parallel on a Sequence or an Order, however, ordering information is lost. (d) It is prohibited to modify the collection while iterating over it. (e) During parallel execution, a collection should either grow or shrink, but cannot do both.

[4] `Graph` is a type alias for `DGraph`. Both `DGraph` and `UGraph` can be multi-graphs.

2.3.2 Iterations and Traversals

Iteration in Green-Marl has the following form:

`Foreach` (*iterator*`:`*source*`(-).`*range*) (*filter*)
  body_statement

The keyword `Foreach` implies parallel execution; it can be replaced with `For` which implies sequential execution. *iterator* defines an iterator symbol for this iteration, while *source* and *range* determines over what is being iterated on and how. *filter* is an optional boolean expression, which dictates whether to apply *body_statement* on the current iteration step or not. The following table summarizes the possible iteration range defined on each source type.[5]

Source Type	Range	Access
`D/UGraph`	`Nodes`	Linear
`Node(D/UGraph)`	`Nbrs`	Random
`Node(DGraph)`	`OutNbrs`	Random
`Node(DGraph)`	`InNbrs`	Random
`Node(D/UGraph)`	`UpNbrs`	Random/-1
`Node(D/UGraph)`	`DownNbrs`	Random/+1
`Node_Set`	`Items`	Linear
`Node_Order`	`Items`	Linear
`Node_Seq`	`Items`	Random

One can iterate on all the nodes in a graph (`Nodes`), or all the items in a collection (`Items`). From a node, one can iterate on its neighborhood nodes in several different ways. `InNbrs` and `OutNbrs` are defined for directed graphs using the edge directions – neighbors that are connected by incoming/outgoing edges. For undirected graphs `InNbrs` and `OutNbrs` become synonym to `Nbrs`. `UpNbrs` and `DownNbrs` and are defined only during a BFS from a specific node: `UpNbrs` of a node are `InNbrs` of the node whose hop-distance from the root is smaller by one. See Figure 2.(b) to visualize `UpNbrs` and `DownNbrs`.

The *access* column in the previous table indicates the nature of the iteration. *Linear* iteration means that every iterator points to a unique item, i.e. each item will be accessed once and only once via the iterator. On the other hand, *Random* indicates the possibility of aliasing; Random/+-1 will be discussed when we discuss BFS traversal.

Sequential(i.e. `For`) iteration on an `Order` or a `Set` preserves the order in which items were appended to the collection. Reverse order iteration is also possible as shown in the following example:

```
Node_Order(G) O; ...
For(o: O-.Items) // reverse order iteration on O
    ...
```

Green-Marl also provides two graph traversal schemes – Breadth-First Search (BFS) order traversal and Depth-First Search (DFS) order traversal. The syntax takes the following form:

`InBFS` (*iter*`:`*src*`^.Nodes From` *root*) [*navigator*] (*filter1*)
  forward_body_statement
`InRBFS` (*filter2*)
  backward_body_statement

[5] For the sake of brevity, the table only shows iteration types for node-wise iteration. Similar iteration types are also defined for edge-wise iteration.

The above syntactic form is similar to that of normal iteration with a few differences. First, *root* defines the root node of the BFS traversal. Second, the optional ^ character means that we first create a transposed version of the graph and then traverse it along the transposed edges. Third, *navigator* is another optional boolean expression that dictates which nodes will be pruned for traversal. For example, if a node does not satisfy the navigator condition, the node is not further expanded during traversal. On the other hand, a node that satisfies the navigator condition is still expanded, even if it does not satisfy the filter condition.

The following code example specifies a BFS traversal on the transposed graph of G, traversing only through nodes whose flag have not been set.

```
Node_Prop<Bool>(G) flag;
InBFS(s: G^.Nodes From r)[!s.flag]
{...}
```

Also, note that the BFS syntax has two body statement blocks. The first body statement block is executed while in forward BFS expansion (i.e. traversing nodes from closest to farthest from the root). If the optional second sentence block is specified, the reverse order BFS traversal (i.e. from the farthest to the closest nodes to the root) is also performed.

DFS has the same syntactic form as BFS except that `InDFS` and `InPost` are used in place of `InBFS` and `InRBFS`; the first body statement block specifies the statements to be executed while in pre-order execution while the second is for post-order execution.

DFS and BFS have different parallel execution semantic. DFS implies sequential execution, while BFS implies level-synchronous parallel execution. That is to say, during BFS, all the nodes that have the same distance from the root node are visited concurrently but parallel execution contexts are synchronized before moving on to the next level. Therefore there are no data conflicts in the following code example, as nodes accessed via `s` are disjoint with repect to the nodes accessed via `t`.

```
InBFS(s: G.Nodes From r) {
  Foreach(t: s.UpNbrs)      // t: Random/-1 access
    s.A += t.A;   // s.A does not conflict with t.A
}
```

2.3.3 Deferred Assignment

Green-Marl also supports bulk synchronous consistency [34] via deferred assignments. Deferred assignments are denoted by `<=` and followed by a binding symbol as in the following example. When a symbol is written using a deferred assignment, a read from the symbol always gives an 'old' value and a write to the symbol becomes effective at the end of the binding iteration.

```
Foreach(s:G.Nodes) {
    // no conflict. t.X gives 'old' value
    s.X <= Sum(t:s.Nbrs) {t.X} @ s
}
// All the writes to X becomes visible simultaneously
// at the end of the s iteration.
```

2.3.4 Reductions

Green-Marl heavily relies on reductions to achieve deterministic results despite its non-sequential memory consistency model (Section 2.2). There are two (slightly) different kinds of reductions: one assumes an expression form (or *in-place* from), the other an assignment form. In the following example, `Sum` is in-place reduction and `+=` is reduction assignment. Note that initialization is required for the reduction assignment; in the case of `G` being an empty graph, x becomes zero, but `y` would have become a non-deterministic value without proper initialization.

```
Int x,y;
x = Sum(t:G.Nodes){t.A}; // equivalent to next 3 lines.
y = 0;
Foreach(t:G.Nodes)
  y+= t.A;
```

The following lists all the reduction operators in Green-Marl; we list both in-place form and assignment form[6]. Note that in-place reductions can have filters just like the `foreach` statement.

In-place	Assignment	In-place	Assignment
All	&&=	Sum	+=
Any	||=	Product	*=
Min	min=	Count	++
Max	max=		

Min and Max are especially interesting forms of reduction because they can be accompanied with *argmax* and *argmin* assignment. In the following example, line 67 stores not only the minimum value of the expression `t.A + u.b` but also the arguments minimizing the expression. Note that all three LHS symbols will be written atomically.

```
63  Int X=INF;
64  Node(G) from, to;
65  Foreach(t:G.Nodes)
66      Foreach(u:t.Nbrs)
67        X <from, to> min= (t.A + u.B) <t, u>;
```

Similarly to deferred assignments, reduction assignments can be accompanied with a bound symbol, denoted as an iteration variable followed by `@` character, which indicates the iteration scope where the reduction happens. This syntax is designed to clarify the user's intention in the presence of nested iterations. For example, x+=..@s means that variable x is reduced by addition during the s-iteration and therefore x should not be read or written otherwise inside the s-iteration. The concept is not far from OpenMP's reduction pragma.

However, specifying a bound symbol is optional for reduction assignments, as in the following example; if omitted, a Green-Marl compiler should try finding appropriate bound for the user, or give an error if it can't.

```
Int sum = 0;
Foreach(s:G.Nodes) {
    Foreach(t:s.Nbrs)
       sum += t.A @s; // accumulate over s-iteration
    if (s.A > THRESHOLD)
       sum += s.B ; // @s is implied
    s.C = sum; // this is an read-reduce conflict.
}              // (sum is still being reduced)
```

Although this section introduced key features of the Green-Marl language, we are in the process of adding formalism in our language specification. The current draft of Green-Marl language specification is publicly available on our website. [1].

3. Compiler

3.1 Compiler Overview

Figure 3 shows how Green-Marl fits in the overall application development process. We envision that the user application is composed of graph analysis components and also other components like data acquisition and UI. We expect that the application developer would extract the graph analysis components and use Green-Marl to express them. The Green-Marl compiler is used to generate an equivalent implementation of the graph analysis component in a lower level general purpose language such as C++. The generated code assumes certain data structures for graph representation. The definition and implementation of these required data structures is

[6] We're investigating adding custom reduction operators in the next version of the language.

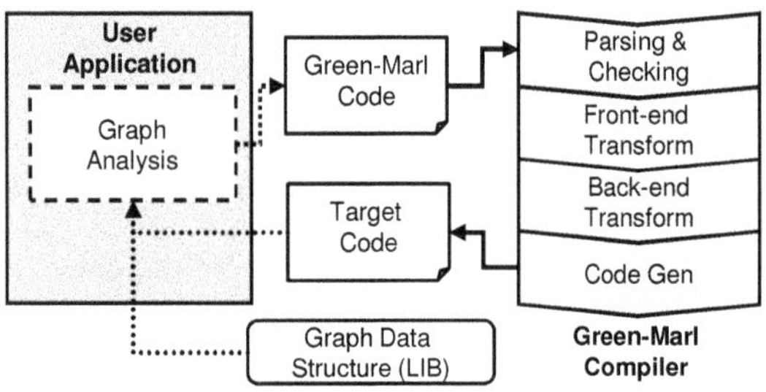

Figure 3. Overview of Green-Marl DSL-compiler Usage

supplied as a library to be linked into the final executable. Therefore each Green-Marl compiler should specify a one-to-one mapping between Green-Marl types and target language types.

The figure also shows the four phases of Green-Marl compilation. In the first phase, the compiler conducts syntactic checks, runs a type-checker, and ensures that the application developer is not violating the semantics of Green-Marl's parallel constructs. If all checks pass successfully, the compiler applies a set of transformations that are target independent. These are followed by target dependent transformations and optimizations. The fourth phase handles the task of code generation. In this paper, we discuss our first implementation of a Green-Marl compiler which targets coherent shared-memory multi-processor systems and emits C++ code. Note that, however, the first two phases can be re-used for our future compiler implementations that will target completely different systems (Section 5.2). Each of the four different phases will be discussed in more detail in the following sections:

3.2 Parsing and Checking

The first phase of compilation involves checking the validity of the user input. The compiler checks for three things: (1) syntax, (2) types, and (3) valid parallel semantics.

Syntax checking and type checking in Green-Marl is no different than what is found in traditional general-purpose compilers. Green-Marl is a statically typed language; the type of each expression is determined at compile time. The type checking phase of a Green-Marl compiler is much simpler than that of a general purpose language,since Green-marl is composed of a handful of primitive and built-in types.[7]

While Green-Marl's type system is quite rudimentary, the high-level semantics it encodes enable powerful program analysis, which can be used to check for incorrect use of parallel constructs. Let us consider the following example Green-Marl code snippet:

```
76  Int y=0;
77  Foreach(s:G.Nodes)(s.C>3){
78    Foreach(t:s.Nbrs){
79      Int x = y * s.B;
80      s.A += t.B * X @ t;
81    }
82    s.B = 4;
83  }
```

Table 2 shows how the above code can be analyzed. The table should be read from top to bottom, where each row represents a step in the semantics analysis phase. The analysis happens through post-order iteration of the abstract syntax tree; thus, we first analyze the body of a `foreach` iteration before finishing the analysis of the `foreach` itself. First, the analyzer identifies at line 76 that scalar symbol `y` is being written. Then the analysis continues two levels deeper and reaches line 79, where it detects a read of `y`, a read of `B` driven by `s`, and a write to `x`. Similar analysis happens at line 80, where `x` is being read, `B` is being read driven-by `t`, but this time symbol `A` is being reduced with a plus, driven-by `s`, and bound to `t`.

Line	type	target symbol	driver/ access.	cond?	reduce op	binding symbol
76	W	y	-	N	-	-
79	R	y	-	N	-	-
	R	B	s	N	-	-
	W	x	-	N	-	-
80	R	x	-	N	-	-
	R	B	t	N	-	-
	D	A	s	N	+	t
78 (during	R	y	-	N	-	-
inspect-	R	B	s	N	-	-
ion)	R	B	t	N	-	-
	D	A	s	N	+	t
78 (after	R	y	Rand	N	-	-
abst-	R	B	s	N	-	-
raction)	R	B	Rand	N	-	-
	W	A	s	N	-	-
82	W	B	s	N	-	-
77 (after	R	y	Rand	Y	-	-
abst-	R	B	Linear	Y	-	-
raction)	R	B	Rand	Y	-	-
	R	C	Linear	N	-	-
	W	A	Linear	Y	-	-
	W	B	Linear	Y	-	-

Table 2. Read-Write Analysis Example

When all the statements of the *foreach(t)* have been analyzed, the parallel semantics of this loop are analyzed. First, all the read, write, and reduce sets of body block are merged while references to the local scope variables (e.g. `x`) are eliminated. The compiler checks (1) if the reduced symbol (i.e. `A`) is not being written, read, or reduced by other operations. Then, (2) it compares every symbol in the merged read-set against the write-set, and a check is made for conflicting writes. In this example, there are no errors.

If the data conflict checks do not generate errors, the result of current iteration analysis is computed in the following way: (a) reduction bound to the current iterator is changed into a write and (b) access through the current iterator is abstracted according to the iterator's type. In the example in table 2, the reduction to symbol `A` is changed to a write, and the read of `B` driven by t is now labeled as a *Random* read of `B`, as `t` is a neighborhood iterator.

Now, the analysis goes up one level and reaches line 82, where it sees the write to `B`, driven by `s`. Then, parallel semantic checking can be performed for the iteration at line 77. This time the analysis will find a conflict between the write to `B` driven by `s` (line 82 and the Random read of `B` (line 80). The current default action for a Read-Write conflict is to warn the users – In contrast, Read-Reduce, Write-Reduce, or Reduce-Reduce conflicts cause compilation to terminate in error. When no errors have been detected, the data-access of the s-iteration can be computed, as in the last row of table 2. Note how the filter at line 77 adds a conditional flag.

This analysis proceeds until all the statements in a procedure are analyzed. The parallel semantic analysis is not only used to flag errors, but its results are also used during the code transformation phase as it will become clear in the following section.

3.3 Architecture Independent Optimizations

Once a Green-Marl application successfully emerges from the type-checking and data-access analysis phases, the compiler can apply to it a set of transformations that are target independent.

In this phase, the compiler first transforms all the syntactic sugar into explicit iterations (*Group Assignments* and *In-place Reduction*). Then it applies optimizations that are effective regardless of the target architecture. (*Loop Fusion*, *Hoisting Definitions*, *Reduc-*

[7] User defined types are supported via foreign syntax (Section 5.1).

tion Bound Relaxation). In addition, the compiler might use additional knowledge on the domain-specific properties of the data-set, possibly controlled by command-line options (*Flipping Edges*).

Group Assignment: Group assignment can be trivially expanded into a parallel or sequential iteration, depending on the type of source collection.

```
Node_Set S(G);
Node_Seq Q(G); //may not be unique
S.A = S.A + S.size();
Q.A = Q.A + Q.size();
```

becomes

```
Foreach(s:S.Items) // parallel iteration
  s.A = s.A + S.Size();
For(q:Q.Items) // sequential iteration
  q.A = q.A + Q.size();
```

In-place Reduction: *In-place Reductions* are expanded into loop and reduction assignments.

```
Int y = Sum(s:G.Nodes){
           Product(t:s.Nbrs)(f(t)){X(t,s)}};
```

becomes

```
Int y;
Int _s0 = 0;
Foreach(s:G.Nodes) {
  Int _p1 = 1;
  Foreach(t: s.Nbrs)(f(t))
     _p1 *= X(t,s) @ u;
  _s0 += _p1 @ s;
}
y = _s0;
```

Loop Fusion: In the following example, two loops `s` and `t` are fused into one even though the two loops have dependencies (through property `A` and `B`), since the access pattern is *Linear*. Fusing loops in general reduces loop overhead and increases locality. Note that procedures that are written with implicit parallel constructs allow for many opportunities to apply loop fusion.

```
Foreach(s: G.Nodes)(f(s))
   s.A = X(s.B);
Foreach(t: G.Nodes)(g(t))
   t.B = Y(t.A)
```

becomes

```
Foreach(s: G.Nodes)(
   if (f(s)) s.A = X(s.B);
   if (g(s)) s.B = Y(s.A);
)
```

Hoisting Definitions: Temporary property definitions can be moved out of sequential loops, which can save repeated large memory allocations and de-allocations in some target systems.

```
For(s:G.Nodes) { //sequential loop
    Node_Prop<Int>(G) A;
    ...
}
```

becomes

```
Node_Prop<Int>(G) A;
For(s:G.Nodes) {
    ...
}
```

Reduction Bound Relaxation: Reduction bounds can be relaxed to the *outmost parallel iteration* that comes after the target symbol is defined. If there is no such iteration, the reduction is transformed back to a normal assignment. Note that in general reductions are more expensive than normal reads and writes.

```
int x = 1;
Foreach(s:G.Nodes) { // par loop
 int y = 0;
 For(t: s.Nbrs) { // seq loop
   x*= s.A @ s;
   y+= s.B + t.C @ t;
} }
```

becomes

```
int x = 1;
Foreach(s:G.Nodes) { // par loop
 int y = 0;
 For(t: s.Nbrs) { // seqloop
   x*= s.A @ s;
   y= y + s.B + t.C; // normal assignment
} }
```

Flipping Edges: Reductions that are applied with reverse edges can be replaced with ones that use forward edges as in the following example. (See Figure 2.(a) to visualize this optimization.) Currently, the compiler only applies this optimization when use of reverse-edges is discouraged via a command-line options; use of reverse edge is often disabled because reverse edges may not be available from the original graph data but would need to be generated via an extra computation step.

```
Foreach(t:G.Nodes)(f(t))
  Foreach(s:t.InNbrs)(g(s))
     t.A += s.B;
```

becomes

```
Foreach(s:G.Nodes)(g(s))
  Foreach(t:s.OutNbrs)(f(t))
     t.A += s.B;
```

3.4 Architecture Dependent Optimizations

In this phase, the compiler applies optimizations based on further available information. It utilizes specific knowledge about the target system (*Selection of Parallel Regions*) as well as about the target language(*deferred assignment* and *Saving BFS Children*). It also takes advantage of the performance characteristics of the underlying data-structures that implement Green-Marl built-in types (*Set-Graph Loop Fusion*).

In addition, architecture independent optimizations (e.g. *Relaxing Reduction Bounds*, and *Hoisting Definitions*) are re-applied since new opportunities for those optimizations can be uncovered as a result of other optimizations (e.g. *Selection of Parallel Regions*).

Set-Graph Loop Fusion: Using the uniqueness property of a set, set iteration can be fused with linear graph iteration. This optimzation is only enabled when the back-end library ensures that the Has() operation is fast (e.g. O(1)).

```
Node_Set S(G); // ...
Foreach(s: S.Items)
   s.A = x(s.B);
Foreach(t: G.Nodes)(g(t))
   t.B = y(t.A)
```

becomes

```
Foreach(s: G.Nodes)(
   if (S.Has(s)) s.A = x(s.B);
   if (g(s)) s.B = y(s.A);
)
```

Selection of Parallel Regions: The compiler determines which parallel iterations are actually going to be parallelized. Currently, the compiler flattens all the nested parallelism but selects only the inner-most graph-wide foreach iteration or BFS traversal. This decision is based on the assumption that the graph instance is large enough to consume all the processor and memory bandwidth of the given system.

```
Foreach(s:G.Nodes) {
  InBFS(x:G.Nodes)
    doX(x);
  Foreach(y:s.Nbrs)
    doY(y);
  Foreach(z:G.Nodes)
    doZ(z);
}
```

becomes

```
For(s:G.Nodes) {    // Seq
  InBFS(x:G.Nodes) // Par
    doX(x);
  For(y:s.Nbrs)     // Seq
    doY(y);
  Foreach(z:G.Nodes) // Par
    doZ(z);
}
```

Deferred Assignment: Deferred assignments are transformed into the definition of temporary properties, initializing them and copying back the final result.

```
Foreach(s:G.Nodes)(f(s))
  s.A = Sum(t:s.Nbrs){t.A}
```

becomes

```
Node_Prop<...>(G) A_new;    // define temp
G.A_new = G.A;              // init temp
Foreach(s:G.Nodes)(f(s))
  s.A_new = Sum(t:s.Nbrs){t.A}  // write to temp
G.A = G.A_new;              // copy back temp
```

However, initialization can be removed if the property is linearly and unconditionally updated inside the binding iteration.

```
Foreach(s:G.Nodes)
  s.A = Sum(t:s.Nbrs){t.A}
```

becomes

```
Node_Prop<...>(G) A_new;    // define temp
Foreach(s:G.Nodes) // linear & unconditonal
  s.A_new = Sum(t:s.Nbrs){t.A}  // write to temp
G.A = G.A_new;              // copy back temp
```

Furthermore, if the binding iteration is inside a sequential loop, the copy back operation can be replaced with pointer swaps, while a final copy back operation is required at the iteration exit. Note that the compiler can generate aliases, whereas users cannot.

```
While (...) {
  // ...
  Foreach(s:G.Nodes)(f(s))
    s.A = Sum(t:s.Nbrs){t.A}
  // ...
}
```

becomes

```
Node_Prop<..>(G) A_new;
// following syntax is for explanation only
Prop* ptr_saved = _alias_ptr(A);
While(...) {
  // ...
  Foreach(s:G.Nodes) {
    s.A_new = Sum(t:s.Nbrs){t.A}
  }
  _swap_ptr(A, A_new);
  // ...
}
If (ptr_saved != A) {
  _swap_ptr(A, A_new);
  A = A_new; // copy back before return
}
```

Saving BFS Children: Our compiler also applies a technique used in Madduri et al.'s work [28]. This optimization checks if the down neighbors are used during the reverse order traversal, in which case the compiler prepares an O(E) array named edge-marker. During forward BFS iteration, if a neighbor is identified in the next level, the edge leading to it is marked. During reverse iteration, next-level neighbors can be identified quickly by looking at the edge information rather than the nodes.

```
InBFS(v:G.Nodes; s) { ... //forward }
InRBFS { // reverse-order traverse
  Foreach(t: v.DownNbrs) { //using DownNbrs
     DO_THING(t);
} }
```

becomes

```
// before BFS
_prepare_edge_marker(); // O(E) array
{     // inside code template of
  ... // forward BFS iteration
  for (e = edges ... ) {
    index_t t = ...node(e);
     ... // normal BFS expansion here
    // [added: mark-down nbrs]
    if (isNextLevel(t)) {
        edge_marker[e] = 1;
} } } // end of forward BFS
{ ...  // reverse BFS
 // iterate Down_Nbrs
  for (e = edges ..) {
   // check on edge instead of node
   if (edge_marker[e] ==1) {
     index_t t= ...node(e);
     DO_THING(t);
} }}
```

3.5 Code Generation

In this phase, the compiler emits out target code using code-generation templates that make use of back-end libraries. Currently, we use OpenMP [31] as our threading library. Thus, during code generation, most of the parallel iterations are trivially translated into `#pragma omp parallel for` headers. We also assume gcc as our target compiler.

The graph is represented using the same data format used in a publicly available parallel graph library [9]. The format is essentially equivalent to the CSR (Compressed Sparse Row) format used in sparse matrix computation. A `Set` is implemented using both a bitmap and a vector while an `Order` is implemented using a bitmap and a list. Finally, node and edge properties are implemented as an array of length O(N) and O(E) respectively.

Graph and Neighborhood Iteration: Thus a typical neighborhood expansion iteration is translated into as following form:

```
Foreach(s:G.Nodes)
  For(t: s.Nbrs)
    s.A = s.A + t.B;
```

becomes

```
OMP(parallel for)
for(index_t s = 0; s < G.numNodes(); s++) {
  // iterate over node's edges
  for(index_t t_=G.edge_idx[s]:t_<G.edge_idx[s+1];t_++){
    // get node from the edge
    index_t t = G.node_idx[t];
    A[s] = A[s] + B[t];
} }
```

Efficient DFS and BFS traversals and **Small BFS Instance Optimization**: code generation for DFS and BFS traversals is done using efficient code-generation templates. For BFS traversal we use an efficient parallel implementation [22] as our base template with the additional optimization of delaying initialization of expensive runtime structures (e.g. an O(N) array) until the BFS traversal grows wide enough.

Note that there have been many publications on efficient parallel implementation of BFS traversal [4, 6, 22] and more are to come. Green-Marl users, however, can benefit from any future BFS implementation without modifying their program, as the compiler can simply generate target source code using new code generation templates.

Reduction on Properties: Reductions involving node properties are translated using an atomic compare and swap.

```
Foreach(s:G.Nodes)
  For(t: s.Nbrs)
    t.A += s.B @s;
```

becomes

```
OMP(parallel for)
for( s = ... )
  for( t_ = ... ) {
    t = ...
  // The follwing 4 lines are implemented with C-MACRO
    {int __old;
     int __new;
     do { __old = A[t];
          __new = __old + B[s] ;
     } while (CAS(&t[A]), __old, __new);
} }
```

Reduction on Scalars: Reductions on scalar values use privatization. In other words, the value is first reduced into a thread-local variable and a reduction is done at the end. Although this is similar to OpenMP's reduction clause, OpenMP for C does not support reduction by minimum or maximum.

```
int x = ...;
Foreach(s:G.Nodes)
  x min= s.B @s;
```

becomes

```
int x = ...;
OMP(parallel)
{  // create thread local
  int _x_prv = INT_MAX;
  OMP(for)
  for( s = ... )
    _x_prv = MIN(_x_prv, B[s]);
 // C-macro equivalent to the above example.
  REDUCE_MIN(int, x, _x_prv)
}
```

3.6 Discussion

Before we move on, let us discuss the benefit of using a compiler to apply the optimizations that have been presented in the previous sections. Each of the optimization techniques is not completely novel in itself; it is either an application of a classic compiler optimization (e.g. *Loop Fusion*) or a technique that has been discussed in previous work (e.g. *Saving BFS Children*).

However, using a compiler allows optimization without requiring significant effort from a graph algorithms expert, and allows optimizations that are difficult with fixed function libraries (those that don't participate in compilation). For example, in applying *Saving BFS Children*, the compiler takes a look at the statements that are executed during reverse BFS traversal, and inserts extra lines of codes in forward traversal only if `DownNbrs` are referred to during reverse traversal. Finally, some optimizations are difficult to apply in a low-level language compiler without domain knowledge. For example, it is challenging for a C++ compiler to merge loops in the following example, which is a possible C++ implementation of the Green-Marl source code (line 103 – 106) in the *Loop Fusion* example; C++ compiler cannot ascertain data dependencies between line 264 and line 266 without information about the uniqueness of the loop index.

```
260 Map<Node, int> A,B;
261 List<Node>& Nodes = G.getNodes();
262 List<Node>::iterator t,s;
263 for(s=Nodes.begin();s!=Nodes.end();s++)
264   if (f(*s)) A[*s] = X(B[*s]);
265 for(t=Nodes.begin();t!=Nodes.end();t++)
266   if (g(*t)) B[*t] = Y(A[*t]);
```

4. Experiments

In this section, we demonstrate the productivity benefits of using Green-Marl, and the efficiency of the target-specific implementations it generates. Table 3 lists the popular graph algorithms we used to evaluate Green-Marl. The first three of these algorithms come from a parallel graph library called SNAP [9]. BC denotes the betweenness centrality computation algorithm as explained in section 1.1. Conductance [12] evaluates a single value from a graph partition, by counting edges between nodes in a given partition and nodes in other partitions; the algorithm is frequently used to detect community structures in social graphs. Vertex Cover [17] is a well known approximation to the NP-hard minimum vertex cover problem. Note that each of the above three algorithms belongs to a different type of graph analysis task defined in section 2.1.

In order to exercise more language constructs in Green-Marl, we also used two famous algorithms that are not included in the SNAP library. PageRank [32] is a famous algorithm which evaluates the importance of each node in a graph based on (out-)degrees of its in-coming neighbors. The algorithm can be described naturally with the bulk-synchronous consistency model. Kosaraju's algorithm [17] is one way to find strongly connected components in a directed graph. The algorithm performs two DFS traversals on the graph; one traversal using the original edges and a second one using the reverse edges. Therefore the algorithm is naively sequential. However, the second DFS traversal can be replaced with a BFS traversal that can be parallelized. Green-Marl's syntax makes it easy to switch between DFS and BFS traversals.

We first consider the productivity gains in using Green-Marl. Table 3 compares the number of lines of code of the above algorithms when they are implemented in both in Green-Marl as well a general-purpose language. For a fair comparison, we counted only the relevant lines of code: we did not count lines of code responsible for data generation, time measurement, or ifdef statements. We also treated every block of comments as a single line.

Overall, Green-Marl enables a much more concise implementation than what can be achieved in a general purpose language. Note that SNAP already uses OpenMP [31], which significantly reduces the lines of code needed to parallelize programs. However, the Green-Marl implementation was much shorter. The extreme example is the BC computation, which is more than 300 lines long as implemented in the SNAP library whereas the Green-Marl implementation is only 24 lines (Figure 1). The main reason for this reduction in LOC is that the SNAP implementation cannot make use of a BFS library call, because its execution was tightly coupled with the BFS iteration code. On the other hand, Green-Marl allows a concise implementation of the algorithm, while the compiler to apply optimizations which ultimately yield better performance than the SNAP version.

Of course, fewer lines of code does not necessarily mean higher productivity. However, we believe that the Green-Marl implementations, in general, are more concise and intuitive than those written in a general-purpose language. For example, the Green-Marl description of Conductance computation (Figure 9) reflects the mathematical definition of Conductance more closely than the SNAP library's implementation. We show the Green-Marl implementations of the algorithms in Figure 9 so the reader can judge for themselves.

Name	LOC Original	LOC Green-Marl	Source
BC	350	24	[9] (C OpenMp)
Conductance	42	10	[9] (C OpenMp)
Vetex Cover	71	25	[9] (C OpenMp)
PageRank	58	15	[2] (C++, sequential)
SCC(Kosaraju)	80	15	[3] (Java, sequential)

Table 3. Graph algorithms used in the experiments and their Lines-of-Code(LOC) when implemented in Green-Marl and in a general purpose language.

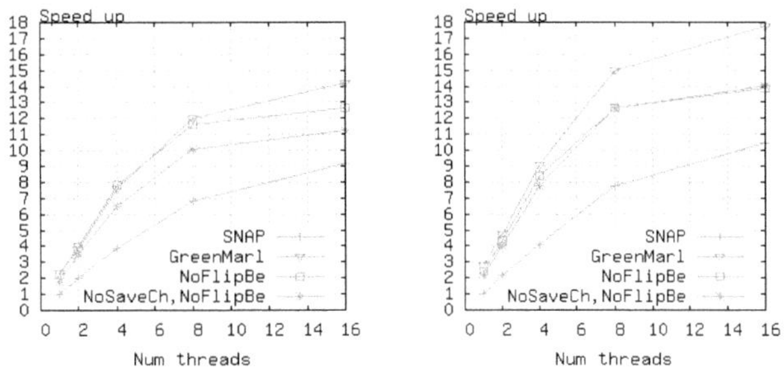

(a) RMAT (b) Uniform

Figure 4. Speed-up of Betweenness Centrality. Speed-up is over the SNAP library [9] version running on a single-thread. NoFlipBE and NoSaveCh means disabling the *Flipping Edges* (Section 3.3) and *Saving BFS Children* (Section 3.5) optimizations respectively.

Next, we measure the performance of the target-specific compiler-generated Green-Marl implementations. For these experiments, we used two kinds of widely-accepted synthetic graph generators [9]: Uniform and RMAT. Uniform generates a random graph based on a simple model where two nodes are randomly selected and edges are inserted between them. On the other hand, RMAT [15] generates a scale-free graph which has a power-law skewed degree distribution. Unless stated otherwise, we used graphs with 32 million nodes and 256 million edges which were generated using default parameters [9]. All the performance was measured on a commodity server-class machine, which has two sockets with an Intel Xeon X5550, each with 4 cores and 2 hardware threads per core. The total last-level-cache size was 16MB.

Figure 4 compares the performance of the Betweenness Centrality computation implemented in Green-Marl to the hand-optimized version included in the SNAP library. The Green-Marl implementation (denoted as GreenMarl in the plot) performs far better than the current SNAP library implementation – the improvement is up to 2.5 times when using 4 cores with the Uniform graph data set. The performance gap is diminished with higher thread counts as the memory bandwidth gets saturated.

Note that Madduri et al. proposed a more optimized implementation [28], with a reported speed-up of 2.3 over the current SNAP version. However, this implementation was developed specifically for the Cray XMT machine, and thus is not usable on commodity systems. Also note that the Green-Marl compiler applies all of the optimizations discussed in the paper automatically. Furthermore, these optimizations can be automatically applied to other algorithms. This is one of the main benefits of using a DSL; we are able to leverage the insights developed in optimizing a specific application and apply them to a whole class of similar algorithms.

To show the impact of the optimizations, the figure also shows the performance of the Green-Marl implementation when some optimizations are disabled. The NoFlipBe and NoSaveCh curves show the performance of this algorithm when the *Flipping Edges* (Section 3.3) and the *Saving BFS Children* (Section 3.5) optimizations, respectively, are not applied. Figure 4 shows that most of the

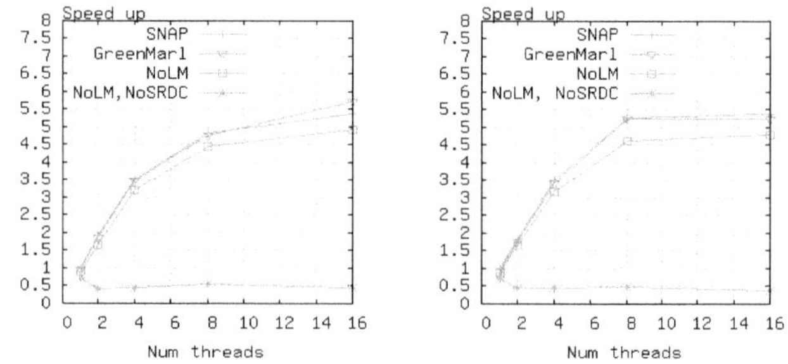

(a) RMAT (b) Uniform

Figure 5. Speed-up of Conductance. Speed-up is over the SNAP library [9] version running on a single-thread. NoLM and NoSRDC means disabling the *Loop Fusion* (Section 3.3) and *Reduction on Scalars* (Section 3.5) optimizations, respectively.

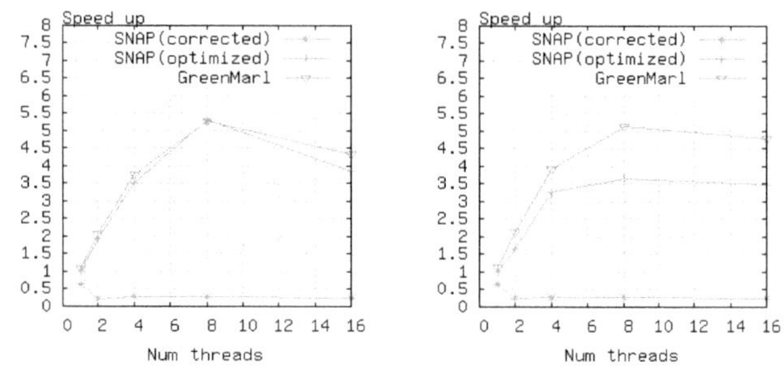

(a) RMAT (b) Uniform

Figure 6. Speed-up of Vertex Cover implemented in Green-Marl and two versions of the corrected SNAP implementation SNAP which had a data-race. The first version, SNAP(correct) utilizes a simple locking approach. The second version, SNAP(optimized), uses a more advanced test and test-and-set scheme. A small instance (100k nodes, 800k edges) was used in this experiment.

parallel speed-up is attained from using an optimized parallel BFS iteration (Section 3.5). The two optimizations mentioned above do however have a measurable contribution to overall performance.

Figure 5 shows the performance of the conductance algorithm implemented in Green-Marl compared to the implementation included in the SNAP library. In this experiment, we randomly partitioned the nodes of each graph into four sets where each set contains 10, 20, 30, and 40% of the nodes. We measured the time to compute the conductance of all these partitions in turn. The figure shows that the Green-Marl implementation performs as well as the hand-tuned SNAP library. Furthermore, we can see that the *Reduction on Scalars* optimization is critical to achieving parallel performance. Without the *Loop Fusion* optimization, we witness some performance loss due to additional synchronization overhead.

Figure 6 shows the performance result of the vertex cover algorithm. Note that the original implementation in the current version of the SNAP library (ver 0.4) is not correct – a critical region was not properly protected. One simple way to fix this issue is to protect the critical region with a simple `omp critical` pragma. However such a fix completely serializes the execution (SNAP(corrected) in the figure). While a more advanced scheme (test and test-and-set) can improve the performance of this implementation (SNAP(optimized) in the figure), Green-Marl still outperforms the more advanced version due by applying additional optimizations such as *Reduction on Scalars*(Section 3.5).

Figure 7 shows the performance results of the PageRank algorithm implemented in Green-Marl. The Green-Marl compiler successfully parallelized the original sequential algorithm. In the fig-

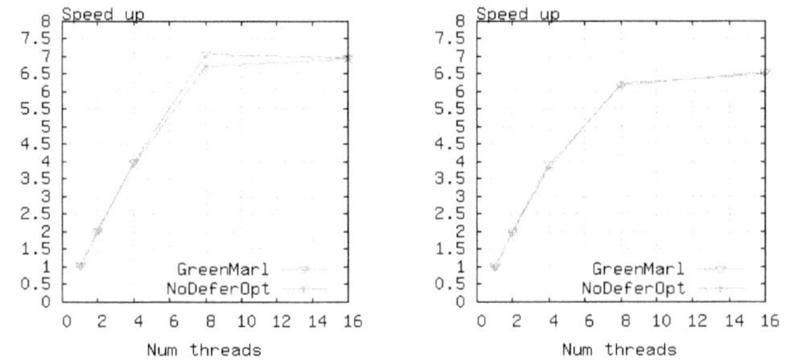

(a) RMAT (b) Uniform

Figure 7. Speed-up of PageRank implemented in Green-Marl. Speed-up is over a single-threaded implementation of the original algorithm [2]. NoDeferOpt means disabling the *Deferred Assignment* (Section 3.4) optimization. These results are based on running the implementation for 10 iterations.

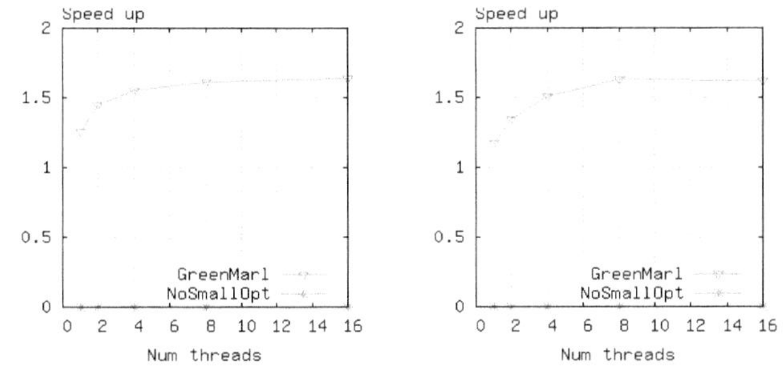

(a) RMAT (b) Uniform

Figure 8. Speed-up of Kosaraju implemented in Green-Marl. The Speed-up is measured over a single-threaded C++ implementation which performs two DFS iterations. NoSmallOpt means disabling our *Small BFS Instance Optimization*. A small instance (1M nodes, 8M edges) was used in this experiment.

ure, the curve denoted as NoDeferOpt shows the resulting performance when disabling the *Deferred Assignment* (Section 3.4) optimization. Although this optimization eliminates the initialization and copy-back of the temporary array variable, its impact on overall performance was not significant; the performance was governed by the random memory accesses during the neighborhood expansion phase of the algorithm.

Figure 8 shows the performance result of Kosaraju's algorithm implemented in Green-Marl. Note that while the original algorithm involves two DFS (i.e. sequential) traversals on the graph, only the second DFS traversal can be replaced with a BFS (i.e. parallel) traversal. Therefore, as a result of Amdahl's law, the theoretical speed-up limit is 2. The NoBFSOpt curve shows the impact of our small instance optimization which is an improvement over a recently proposed BFS scheme [4] for small sub-graphs. Real-world graphs which are mimicked by our synthetic graphs tend to be composed of a small number of large (i.e. O(N)) components and a large number of small (i.e. O(1)) components. Thus, our optimization ensures that the overhead of the BFS traversal is minimized when iterating on small sub-graphs.

5. Smoothing the Way to Green-Marl Adoption

So far, we have shown the benefits of using a DSL to achieve optimum efficiency with high productivity. However requiring users to adopt a new programming language introduces a new set of challenges. In this section, we show how most of these concerns can be addressed.

5.1 Programmer Productivity

Green-Marl doesn't require the application developer to re-write their whole application. They can isolate graph-analysis routines in their application and only rewrite these using Green-Marl. Our compiler will then generate an efficient implementation of the algorithms in the target source code (e.g. C++). The generated implementation can then be compiled along with the rest of the application with minimal changes to other modules. Any extra effort required to convert between the data types in the original application and those expected by Green-Marl would also be required when using any other graph library.

Green-Marl also allows the embedding of foreign data types and statements. In the example that follows, procedure `foo` accepts an argument with a foreign type (`my_type`). During the type-checking phase, the compiler simply treats all foreign types as equivalent (line 269)[8] Foreign statements are also easily embedded in Green-Marl through a square bracket expression (line 270).

Foreign statements are conceptually similar to the inline assembler (i.e. `asm`) in gcc. During the code generation phase, the compiler copies the text enclosed in square bracket as is, other than properly handling variables with DSL types (denoted by the $ sign inside the back-ticks). For example, '*$a.F*' would be translated to *F[a]* (in our current C++ back-end compiler). At the end of a foreign statement, the application developer may supply a *list of mutated variables*. This allows the Green-Marl compiler to correctly identify read after write (RAW) hazards and prevents it from moving any statements that read the variable beyond the point at which it will be modified. It is also up to the application developer to correctly handle data races inside a foreign function if it is called during parallel execution.

```
267  Procedure foo(G:Graph, my_var:$my_type) {
268      Int x = 0;
269      $my_type2 var2 = my_var;          \\ compiles okay
270      [$my_var->mutate($x)]::[x]; }  \\ text replacement
```

Since the Green-Marl compiler performs source-to-source translation, the application developer will still end up with code generated in a more widely-used target language such as C++. This significantly reduces the risk associated with adopting a new language. The generated source from the current Green-Marl compiler is fairly human-readable: variable names and code layouts are preserved to a reasonable degree. We also plan to preserve comment blocks in future versions of our compiler.

While one could always have manually typed in the exact same source code that was emitted by the Green-Marl compiler, the DSL approach provides additional benefits, as was shown in the previous sections. First, more concise and intuitive descriptions of graph algorithms, and secondly, a set of optimizations during translation that span multiple function calls. These optimizations across library entry points are nearly impossible to achieve using a general purpose compiler that lacks any higher level semantic knowledge of the application (Section 3 and 4).

Furthermore, users of Green-Marl may rely on the robust debugging tools of the target language. In general, using Green-Marl leads to an expression of the desired graph algorithms that makes it easy to reason about the algorithm itself, leading to fewer errors. We also plan on implementing an interpreter for Green-Marl applications that will feature step-wise code execution and a visual graph representation.

5.2 Architecture Portability

Although not the main focus of this paper, a domain-specific approach such as that adopted by Green-Marl, in fact, can greatly

[8] The behavior can be changed to treat each type distinctly, via command-line options.

improve the portability of graph analysis applications. By replacing the back-end module of the compiler without modifying the DSL source code, the user can obtain equivalent implementations tailored for systems substantially different from one another, for example GPUs or clusters rather than symmetric shared-memory machines. Each back-end would use different code-templates for the language constructs and different optimizations in order to produce high-performance code for the target platforms. In contrast, the low-level implementation required to achieve performance on one system (e.g. C++ for SMP), rarely achieves similar performance and often cannot be made to work on other systems (e.g. GPU or cluster) without significant code restructuring, such adding CUDA or MPI constructs. A Green-Marl compiler back-end for GPU systems is being developed; this version adopts recent techniques in GPU graph processing [21] which leverage the massive amount of thread-level parallelism and large memory bandwidth available on GPUs.

Green-Marl will ultimately be applicable to the analysis of very large graph instances which cannot fit in a single physical memory space. Currently, the application developer is being encouraged to use libraries such as Pregel [29], a distributed graph processing framework, which consists of a MapReduce-like API that abstracts the details of data communication in the distributed system. However, the Pregel framework also forces the user to restructure their traditional graph algorithms in terms of this API. This can yield non-intuitive expressions of such graph algorithms. We refer the readers to the original paper of Malewicz et al. [29] which shows how the PageRank algorithm is implemented with Pregel APIs. By contrast, in Figure 9 we show the same algorithm written in Green-Marl. The Green-Marl implementation closely resembles the natural way the algorithm was explained in the original PageRank publication [32]. Hence, we are investigating the possibility of adding another back-end that would translate Figure 9 into the Pregel implementation. All of this is possible because considerations for CUDA and distributed environments have influenced the Green-Marl language design. Features like relaxed-memory consistency, support for full bulk-synchronous memory consistency, rich reduction operators and a limited selection of built-in data-types are examples of such considerations.

6. Related Work

DSLs fall into two broad categories, namely external DSLs which are completely independent languages, and internal DSLs, which borrow functionality from a host language [23]. While Green-Marl is currently implemented as an external DSL, we will consider in the future the viability of implementing it as an internal DSL. Indeed there has been a lot of research into how to leverage domain-specific knowledge in the service of more optimized execution. Expression Templates [35] can produce customized generation, and are used by Blitz++ [36]. Active libraries [37], which are libraries that participate in compilation were introduced by Veldhuizen. Kennedy coined the term telescoping languages [24] for efficient DSLs created from annotated component libraries. TaskGraph [11] is a meta-programming library that supports run-time code generation in C++. Delite [14] is a more recent proposal that aims at simplifying the creation of performance oriented DSLs such as Green-Marl.

Noticeably, many features of Green-Marl are reminiscent of those found in OpenMP [31], as both programming models let the user explicitly specify parallel regions of execution. However, Green-Marl provides further performance benefits by using domain specific knowledges in applying optimizations. Previous work has also shown some of these benefits. Guyver et al. present significant performance improvements by annotating library methods with domain-specific knowledge [20], and CodeBoost [10] uses user-defined rules to transform programs using domain knowledge.

There are several publicly available libraries for graph analysis. Popular single-threaded libraries include the Boost Graph Library(BGL) [33] and igraph [18]. There are only a few libraries that support parallel or distributed execution: Parallel BGL [19] is a distributed version of BGL while SNAP [8] is a stand-alone parallel graph analysis package. GraphLab [25] is a framework for machine learning type graph algorithms. We are considering to use GraphLab as one of our future back-ends. No matter how wide the range of fixed functions supported by such libraries, the user still may need to implement a different algorithm not supplied by the library. Green-Marl allows users to implement their own algorithms and still get generated code that performs as well as hand-tuned low-level implementations. Note that Green-Marl can still make use of the efficient data structures supplied by a graph library such as SNAP [8].

The efficient implementation of parallel graph algorithms is a challenging task. The best implementation often is closely coupled to an underlying hardware architecture. For example, a simple BFS traversal has been implemented differently on commodity servers [4, 22], GPUs [21], Cray XMT machines [6] and cluster environments [38]. Techniques for efficient implementation of other algorithms such as betweenness centrality [28], shortest path [27], and minimum spanning tree [16] can be found in the research literature. Green-Marl does not obviate the need for these studies; rather these techniques can easily be reused and applied to other algorithms with similar patterns by means of the Green-Marl DSL and compiler.

Large graph instances are drawing more and more attention from the high performance computing community. Traditional HPC technologies such as vectorization do not provide satisfactory performance in processing large graph instances. Graph500 [5] is an effort to create a benchmark that captures the computational requirements of large graph applications. Pregel [29] is a MapReduce like framework that aims to bring distributed processing to graph algorithms. In Section 5.2, we discussed our plans for targetting such a framework in future versions of Green-Marl.

7. Conclusions and Future Work

The Green-Marl DSL approach to graph analysis demonstrates that developers can generate an implementation via an intuitive high-level language that has competitive performance with hand-written native code. Green-Marl allows users to get the benefit of optimizations specifically for graph data structures, without writing those optimizations directly, and without tying those optimizations to architecture-specific characteristics. The language approach provides benefits over a library approach by optimizing across the call boundaries of currently available graph libraries. Green-Marl can be linked with native C++ programs, allowing graph algorithms written in Green-Marl to be embedded in more complex, general-purpose software. The next steps for Green-Marl are to generate code for alternative architectures, such as clusters and GPUs, to provide more support for the architecture-independent benefits of this approach.

Acknowledgements

We thank Dr. Peter B. Kessler and Dr. Mario Wolczko (Oracle Labs) for reviewing this paper and making helpful suggestions. This work is supported by Army contract AHPCRC W911NF-07-2-0027-1; DARPA contract, Oracle order US1032821; DOE contract, Sandia order 1134180; SEEC: Specialized Extremely Efficient Computing, Contract HR0011-11-C-0007; Stanford PPL affiliates program, Pervasive Parallelism Lab: Oracle, NVIDIA, AMD, NEC, and Intel.

References

[1] Green-marl lanaguage specification. `http://ppl.stanford.edu/main/green_marl.html`.

[2] Pagerank c++ implementation. http://code.grnet.gr/projects/pagerank.

[3] Strongly connected component (kosaraju) java implementation. http://www.keithschwarz.com/interesting/.

[4] V. Agarwal, F. Petrini, D. Pasetto, and D. Bader. Scalable Graph Exploration on Multicore Processors. In *ACM/IEEE SC 2010*.

[5] M. Anderson. Better benchmarking for supercomputers. *Spectrum, IEEE*, 48(1), 2011.

[6] D. Bader and K. Madduri. Designing multithreaded algorithms for breadth-first search and st-connectivity on the Cray MTA-2. In *ICPP 2006*. IEEE.

[7] D. Bader and K. Madduri. Parallel algorithms for evaluating centrality indices in real-world networks. In *IEEE ICPP 2006*.

[8] D. Bader and K. Madduri. Snap, small-world network analysis and partitioning: An open-source parallel graph framework for the exploration of large-scale networks. In *IEEE IPDPS*, 2008.

[9] D. A. Bader and K. Madduri. Snap: small-world network analysis and partitioning. http://snap-graph.sourceforge.net.

[10] O. Bagge, K. Kalleberg, M. Haveraaen, and E. Visser. Design of the CodeBoost transformation system for domain-specific optimisation of C++ programs. In *Source Code Analysis and Manipulation, 2003. Proceedings. Third IEEE International Workshop on*.

[11] O. Beckmann, A. Houghton, M. Mellor, and P. H. Kelly. Runtime code generation in c++ as a foundation for domain-specific optimisation. In *Domain-Specific Program Generation*, volume 3016 of *Lecture Notes in Computer Science*. Springer Berlin / Heidelberg, 2004.

[12] B. Bollobás. *Modern graph theory*. Springer Verlag, 1998.

[13] U. Brandes. A faster algorithm for betweenness centrality. *The Journal of Mathematical Sociology*, 25(2):163–177, 2001.

[14] H. Chafi, A. Sujeeth, K. Brown, H. Lee, A. Atreya, and K. Olukotun. A domain-specific approach to heterogeneous parallelism. In *PPoPP*. ACM, 2011.

[15] D. Chakrabarti, Y. Zhan, and C. Faloutsos. R-mat: A recursive model for graph mining. In *SDM*, 2004.

[16] G. Cong and D. Bader. Lock-free parallel algorithms: An experimental study. *High Performance Computing-HiPC 2004*, 2005.

[17] T. H. Cormen, C. E. Leiserson, R. L. Rivest, and C. Stein. *Introduction to Algorithms*. MIT press and McGraw-Hill, 2001.

[18] G. Csardi and T. Nepusz. The igraph software package for complex network research. *InterJournal Complex Systems*, 1695, 2006.

[19] D. Gregor and A. Lumsdaine. The parallel bgl: A generic library for distributed graph computations. *Parallel Object-Oriented Scientific Computing (POOSC)*, 2005.

[20] S. Z. Guyer and C. Lin. An annotation language for optimizing software libraries. In *PLAN '99: Proceedings of the 2nd conference on Domain-specific languages*.

[21] S. Hong, S. Kim, T. Oguntebi, and K. Olukotun. Accelerating CUDA graph algorithms at maximum warp. In *PPoPP*, 2011.

[22] S. Hong, T. Oguntebi, and K. Olukotun. Efficient parallel graph exploration for multi-core cpu and gpu. In *IEEE PACT 2011*.

[23] P. Hudak. Building domain-specific embedded languages. *ACM Computing Surveys*, 28, 1996.

[24] K. Kennedy, B. Broom, A. Chauhan, R. Fowler, J. Garvin, C. Koelbel, C. McCosh, and J. Mellor-Crummey. Telescoping languages: A system for automatic generation of domain languages. *Proceedings of the IEEE*, 93(3), 2005.

[25] Y. Low, J. Gonzalez, A. Kyrola, D. Bickson, C. Guestrin, and J. Hellerstein. Graphlab: A new parallel framework for machine learning. In *Conference on Uncertainty in Artificial Intelligence*, 2010.

[26] A. Lumsdaine, D. Gregor, B. Hendrickson, J. Berry, and J. Guest Editors. Challenges in parallel graph processing. *Parallel Processing Letters*, 17(1):5–20, 2007.

[27] K. Madduri, D. Bader, J. Berry, and J. Crobak. Parallel shortest path algorithms for solving large-scale instances. *9th DIMACS Implementation Challenge-Shortest Paths*, 2006.

[28] K. Madduri, D. Ediger, K. Jiang, D. Bader, and D. Chavarria-Miranda. A faster parallel algorithm and efficient multithreaded implementations for evaluating betweenness centrality on massive datasets. In *IEEE IPDPS 2009*.

[29] G. Malewicz, M. H. Austern, A. J. Bik, J. C. Dehnert, I. Horn, N. Leiser, and G. Czajkowski. Pregel: a system for large-scale graph processing. In *SIGMOD '10*. ACM.

[30] NVIDIA. CUDA. `http://developer.nvidia.com/object/cuda.html`.

[31] OpenMP ARB. Openmp. `http://www.openmp.org`.

[32] L. Page. Method for node ranking in a linked database, Sept. 4 2001. US Patent 6,285,999.

[33] J. Siek, L. Lee, A. Lumsdaine, L. Lee, L. Blackford, J. Demmel, J. Dongarra, I. Duff, S. Hammarling, M. Heroux, et al. The boost graph library: user guide and reference manual. 2002.

[34] L. G. Valiant. A bridging model for parallel computation. *Commun. ACM*, 33, August 1990.

[35] T. L. Veldhuizen. Expression templates, C++ gems. SIGS Publications, Inc., New York, NY, 1996.

[36] T. L. Veldhuizen. Arrays in blitz++. In *ISCOPE*, pages 223–230, 1998.

[37] T. L. Veldhuizen. *Active Libraries and Universal Languages*. PhD thesis, Indiana University Computer Science, May 2004.

[38] A. Yoo, E. Chow, K. Henderson, W. McLendon, B. Hendrickson, and U. Catalyurek. A scalable distributed parallel breadth-first search algorithm on BlueGene/L. In *SC 2005 ACM/IEEE*.

```
//------------------------------------------------------------------------------------------------------
// Computing Conductance
//------------------------------------------------------------------------------------------------------
Procedure conductance(G: Graph, member: N_P<Int>(G), num: Int) : Double {
  Int Din, Dout, Cross;
  Din   = Sum(u:G.Nodes)(u.member==num){u.Degree()};         // Compute degree sum of inside nodes.
  Dout  = Sum(u:G.Nodes)(u.member!=num){u.Degree()};         // Compute degree sum of outside nodes.
  Cross = Sum(u:G.Nodes)(u.member==num){                      // Count number of crossing edges.
             Count(j:u.Nbrs)(j.member!=num)};                 // (Count is a syntactic sugar to Sum(..){1}
  Double m = (Din < Dout) ? Din : Dout;
  If (m ==0) Return (Cross == 0) ? 0.0 : +INF;
  Else Return (Cross / m);
}

//------------------------------------------------------------------------------------------------------
// Obtaining vertex cover
//------------------------------------------------------------------------------------------------------
Procedure vertex_cover(G: Graph, VC:Edge_Prop<Bool>(G)): Int {
  Node_Prop<Int>(G) Deg;
  Node_Prop<Bool>(G) covered;
  G.covered = False;                                          // Initialization
  G.Deg = G.InDegree() + G.OutDegree();                       // Deg: the sum of in-degree and out-degree
  G.VC = False;
  Int remain = G.NumEdges()*2;

  Do {
    Int maxVal = 0;
    Node(G) from, to;
    Edge(G) e;
    Foreach(s: G.Nodes)(!G.covered) {                         // Choose an edge that has maximum Deg
      Foreach(t: s.OutNbrs)                                   //   value among remaining nodes
         maxVal <from, to, e> max= (s.Deg + t.Deg) <s, t, t.GetEdge()> @s;
    }
    e.VC = True;                                              // Select this edge.
    from.covered = to.covered = True;                         // Node 'from' and 'to' are now covered.
    from.Deg = to.Deg = 0;
    remain = remain - maxVal;
  } While (remain > 0)                                        // Finish when there is no more edges

  Int C = Count(t:G.Nodes)(t.covered);                        // Count number of covered nodes
  Return C;
}

//------------------------------------------------------------------------------------------------------
// Computing PageRank
//------------------------------------------------------------------------------------------------------
Procedure PageRank(G: Graph, e,d: Double, max_iter: Int, PR: Node_Prop<Double>(G)) {
  Double diff =0;                                          // Initialization
  Int cnt = 0;
  Double N = G.NumNodes();
  G.PR = 1 / N;

  Do {                                                     // Main Iteration.
    diff = 0.0;
    Foreach (t: G.Nodes) {                                 // Compute PR from neighbor's current PR.
       Double val = (1-d) / N +
            d* Sum(w: t.InNbrs) (w.OutDegree()>0) {w.PR / w.OutDegree()};
       t.PR <= val @ t;                                    // Modification of PR will be visible after t-loop.
       diff += | val - t.PR |;                             // Accumulate difference (t.PR is still old value)
    }
    cnt++;                                                 // ++ is a syntactic sugar.
  } While ((diff > e) && (cnt < max_iter));                // Iterate for max num steps or difference is
}                                                          //   smaller than given threshold.

//------------------------------------------------------------------------------------------------------
// Obtaining strongly connected components using Kosarajus algorithm
//------------------------------------------------------------------------------------------------------
Procedure SCC(G: Graph, CompID: Node_Prop<Int>(G)): Int {
  G.CompID = -1;                                              // Initialization

  Node_Order(G) P;                                            // Phase 1: get reverse post-DFS order.
  For(t:G.Nodes)(!P.Has(t))  {                                // Starting from a non-visited node,
    InDFS(s: G.Nodes From t)[!P.Has(s)] {}                    // Do DFS traversal and
    InPost {P.PushFront(s);}                                  //   store nodes in reverse post DFS order.
  }

  Int numC = 0;                                               // Phase 2: get strongly connected components.
  For(s: P.Items)(s.compID==-1) {                             // Starting from a non-connected node,
    InBFS(t: G^.Nodes From s) [t.CompID == -1]                // Do BFS traversal and
    { t.CompID = numC;}                                       //   add visited node into the current component.
    numC++;                                                   // End current component.
  }
  Return numC;
}
```

Figure 9. Algorithms used in the paper

SIMD Defragmenter: Efficient ILP Realization on Data-parallel Architectures

Yongjun Park, Sangwon Seo [*], Hyunchul Park [†], Hyoun Kyu Cho, and Scott Mahlke

Advanced Computer Architecture Laboratory
University of Michigan - Ann Arbor, MI
{yjunpark, swseo, parkhc, netforce, mahlke}@umich.edu

Abstract

Single-instruction multiple-data (SIMD) accelerators provide an energy-efficient platform to scale the performance of mobile systems while still retaining post-programmability. The central challenge is translating the parallel resources of the SIMD hardware into real application performance. In scientific applications, automatic vectorization techniques have proven quite effective at extracting large levels of data-level parallelism (DLP). However, vectorization is often much less effective for media applications due to low trip count loops, complex control flow, and non-uniform execution behavior. As a result, SIMD lanes remain idle due to insufficient DLP. To attack this problem, this paper proposes a new vectorization pass called SIMD Defragmenter *to uncover hidden DLP that lurks below the surface in the form of instruction-level parallelism (ILP). The difficulty is managing the data packing/unpacking overhead that can easily exceed the benefits gained through SIMD execution. The SIMD degragmenter overcomes this problem by identifying groups of compatible instructions (subgraphs) that can be executed in parallel across the SIMD lanes. By SIMDizing in bulk at the subgraph level, packing/unpacking overhead is minimized. On a 16-lane SIMD processor, experimental results show that SIMD defragmentation achieves a mean 1.6x speedup over traditional loop vectorization and a 31% gain over prior research approaches for converting ILP to DLP.*

Categories and Subject Descriptors D.3.4 [*Processors*]: [Code Generation and Compilers]; C.1.2 [*Processors Architectures*]: Multiple Data Stream Architectures—Single-instruction-stream, multiple-data-stream processors (SIMD)

General Terms Algorithms, Experimentation, Performance

Keywords Compiler, SIMD Architecture, Optimization

1. Introduction

The number of worldwide mobile phones in use exceeded five billion in 2010 and is expected to continue to grow. The computing platforms that go into these and other mobile devices must provide ever increasing performance capabilities while maintaining low energy consumption in order to support advanced multimedia and signal processing applications. Application-specific integrated circuits (ASICs) were the most common solutions for the heavy lifting, performing the most compute intensive kernels in a high performance but energy-efficient manner. However, new demands push designers toward a more flexible and programmable solution: supporting multiple applications or variations of applications, providing faster time-to-market, and enabling algorithmic changes after the hardware is constructed.

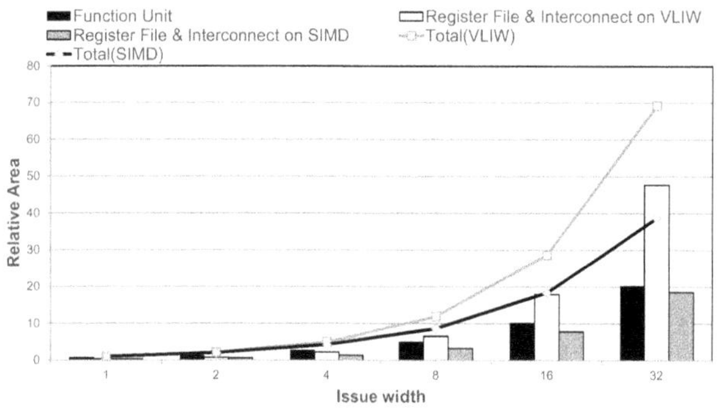

Figure 1. Scalability of datapaths that exploit instruction-level parallelism (VLIW) and data-level parallelism (SIMD). Plotted is the relative area as issue width increases from 1 to 32. Area is broken down into function unit and register file & interconnect.

Processors that exploit instruction-level parallelism (ILP) provide the highest degree of computing flexibility. Modern smart phones employ a one GHz dual-issue superscalar ARM as an application processor. Higher performance digital signal processors are also available such as the 8-issue TIC6x. However, the scalability of ILP processors is inherently limited by register file (RF) and interconnect complexity as shown in Figure 1. Single-instruction multiple-data (SIMD) accelerators have long been used in the desktop space for high performance multimedia and graphics functionality. But, their combination of scalable performance, energy efficiency, and programmability make them ideal for mobile systems as well [4, 5, 12, 20, 33]. Figure 1 shows that the area of SIMD datapaths scale almost linearly with issue width. Power follows a similar trend [33]. SIMD architectures provide high efficiency because of their regular structure, ability to scale lanes, and low control overhead.

The difficult challenge with SIMD is programming. The application developer or compiler must find and extract sufficient data-level parallelism (DLP) to efficiently make use of the parallel hardware. Automatic loop vectorization is a popular approach and is available in a variety of commercial compilers including offerings from Intel, IBM, and PGI. Applications that resemble classic scientific computing (regular structure, large trip count loops, and few data dependences) perform well on most SIMD architectures.

However, mobile applications are not limited to these types of applications. High-definition video, audio, 3D graphics, and other

[*] Currently with Qualcomm Incorporated, San Diego, CA

[†] Currently with Programming Systems Lab, Intel Labs, Santa Clara, CA

ASPLOS'12, March 3–7, 2012, London, England, UK.

Vectorization granularity

Coarser ◄······► Finer

Level	Loop	Subgraph	Superword
Scope	Loop body	Group of instructions	Instruction
Vectorization advantage	High	Middle	Small
Coverage	Small	High	High

Figure 2. A spectrum of the vectorization at different granularities.

forms of media processing are high value applications for mobile devices. These applications continue to grow in complexity and resemble scientific applications less and less. Computation is no longer dominated by simple vectorizable loops. Instead, current media processing algorithms behave more like general-purpose programs with DLP available selectively and to varying degrees in different loops. Also, significant amounts of control flow are present to handle the complexity of media coding and limits the available DLP. The overall affect is that loop-level DLP is less prevalent and less efficient to exploit in media algorithms. Due to these application-specific complexities, available SIMD resources cannot be fully utilized and a substantial portion of resources are idle at runtime. Talla [32] reports that only 1-4% performance improvement exists when scaling the SIMD components from 2-way to 16-way on the MediaBench suite [19]. Thus, an improved approach beyond simple loop level techniques is necessary in order to effectively use wide SIMD resources.

To supplement the insufficient degree of DLP from traditional vectorization, superword-level parallelism (SLP) [17] can be applied. SLP is a short SIMD parallelism between isomorphic instructions within a basic block. As shown in Figure 2, SLP can cover more code regions as compared to loop-level vectorization because SLP can be performed in non-loop regions, in loops having cross-iteration dependences, and in outer loops. For vectorizable loops, traditional vectorization is preferred because SLP misses loop-specific optimization opportunities [24]. The weakness of SLP is that the vectorization scope is too fine, resulting in a high overhead of getting data into packed format that is suitable for SIMD execution. Often, this packing overhead can exceed the benefits of parallel execution on the SIMD hardware. In addition, SLP is performed with a local scope that commonly misses opportunities for vectorization when a large number of isomorphic instructions exist.

To address the limitations of SLP, we introduce a coarser level of vectorization within basic blocks, referred to as *Subgraph Level Parallelism (SGLP)*. SGLP refers to the parallelism between subgraphs (groups of instructions) having identical operators and dataflow inside a basic block: parallel subgraphs that can execute together on separate data. SGLP has two major advantages that allow it more opportunities to convert ILP to DLP: 1) data rearrangement and packing overhead can be minimized by encapsulating the data flow inside the subgraph, 2) natural functional symmetries that exist in media applications (e.g., a sliding window of data long which computation is performed) can be exposed to enable vectorization of larger groups of instructions. The net result is SGLP leads to a combination of more SIMD execution opportunities and fewer instructions dedicated to data reorganization and inter-lane data movement.

This paper presents the design of a supplemental vectorization pass referred to as the *SIMD Defragmenter*. It automatically identifies and extracts SGLP from vectorized loops and orchestrates parallel execution of subgraphs with minimum overhead using unused resources. In the SIMD Defragmenter, a loop is first vectorized using traditional vectorization techniques. Then, vectorizable subgraphs are identified based on the availability of unused lanes in the hardware. The compiler then allocates the subgraphs to unused SIMD resources to minimize inter-lane data movement. Finally, new SIMD operations for SGLP are emitted and operations for inter-lane movements are added where necessary. Small architectural features are provided to enhance the applicability of SGLP and the configuration is statically generated during compilation.

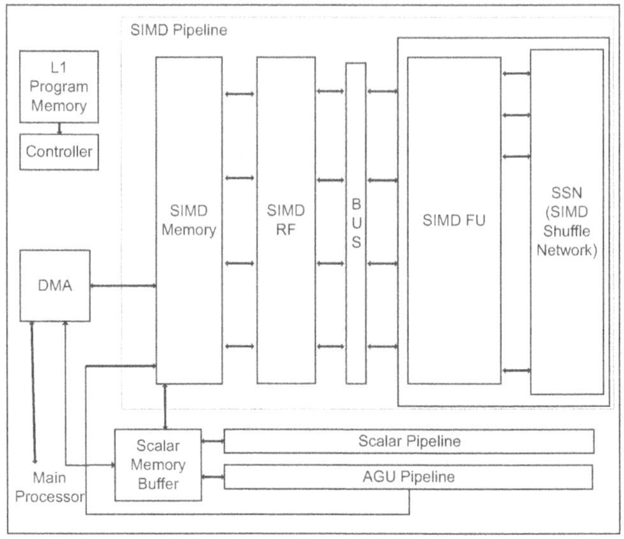

Figure 3. Baseline SIMD architecture.

This paper offers the following three contributions:

- An analysis of the difficulties of putting SIMD resources to efficient use across three mobile media applications (MPEG4 audio decoding, MPEG4 video decoding, and 3D graphics rendering).
- The introduction of SGLP that can efficiently exploit unused SIMD resources on already vectorized code.
- A compilation framework for SGLP that identifies isomorphic subgraphs and selects a mapping strategy to minimize data reorganization overhead.

2. Background and Motivation

In this section, we examine the current limitations of SIMD architectures based on an analysis of the following three widely used multimedia applications:

- AAC decoder: MPEG4 audio decoding, low complexity profile
- H.264 decoder: MPEG4 video decoding, baseline profile, qcif
- 3D: 3D graphics rendering

We then analyze why the well-known solutions are not as effective as expected. Finally, we discuss several potential approaches to overcome these bottlenecks and increase the utilization of existing resources.

2.1 Baseline Architecture Overview

A basic SIMD architecture that is based on SODA [20] (Figure 3) is used as the baseline architecture. This architecture has both SIMD and two scalar datapaths. The SIMD pipeline consists of a multiple-way datapath where each way has an arithmetic unit working in parallel. Each datapath has a two read-ports, one write-port, a 16 entry register file, and one ALU with a multiplier. The number of ways in the SIMD pipeline can vary depending on the characteristics of target applications. The SIMD Shuffle Network (SSN) is implemented to support intra-processor data movement. The scalar pipeline consists of one 16-bit datapath and supports the application's control code. The AGU pipeline handles DMA (Direct Memory Access) transfers and memory address calculations for both scalar and SIMD pipelines.

2.2 Analysis of Multimedia Applications

SIMD architectures provides an energy-efficient means of executing multimedia applications. However, it is difficult to determine the optimal number of SIMD lanes because the number depends on the algorithms that constitute the workload. In this analysis, we first categorize the innermost loops of three applications into different groups according to their vector width. Then, two types of SIMD width variance are identified and the practical difficulties of finding the optimal SIMD width and achieving high utilization are discussed.

2.2.1 SIMD Width Characterization

Multimedia applications typically have many compute intensive kernels that are in the form of nested loops. Among these kernels, we analyze the available DLP of the innermost loops and find the maximum natural vector width which is achievable. Based on the Intel Compiler [15], the rules to be selected as a vectorizable innermost loop are as follows:

- The loop must contain straight-line code. No jumps or branches, but predicated assignments, are allowed only when the performance degradation is negligible.
- The loop must be countable and there must be no data-dependent exit conditions.
- Backward loop-carried dependencies are not allowed.
- All memory transfers must have same strides over iteration.

If a loop satisfies the above four conditions, the minimum iteration count is set to the vector width of the loop.

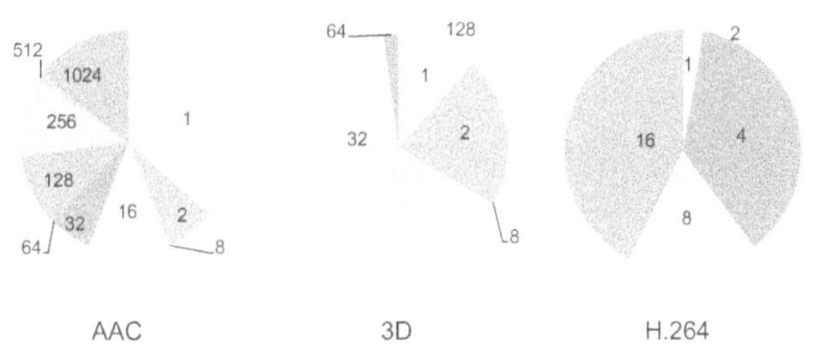

Figure 4. Scalar execution time distribution at different SIMD widths for three media applications: the maximum SIMD widths are 1024, 128, and 16, and the SIMD widths, which can be fully utilized for more than 50% execution time, are 16, 32, and 8 for AAC, 3D, and H.264 applications.

2.2.2 SIMD Width Variance

Figure 4 shows how many different natural vector widths reside in the three target benchmarks. The execution time breakdown between loops having different vector widths are shown in Figure 4. The three pie charts show the distribution of scalar execution time spent in innermost loops at various SIMD widths for three applications. From Figure 4, we can see that there are many different vector widths inside each application, hence it is quite difficult to determine the optimal SIMD width even for one application. For example, to define 16 as the SIMD width for H.264 is not desirable because the maximum vector width is 16 but the execution time ratio of loops with vector width of 16 is just 42% and some SIMD lanes are wasted for the remaining time. On the other hand, four is also not desired because the execution time of the loops with a width of four is not dominant with substantial execution occurring in loops having larger SIMD widths. Similarly, AAC and 3D applications cannot set the number of SIMD lanes as the maximum vector width due to the waste of resources, nor dominant vector width due to the low performance. Therefore, effectively supporting multiple SIMD widths is required to take advantage of the SIMD architectures.

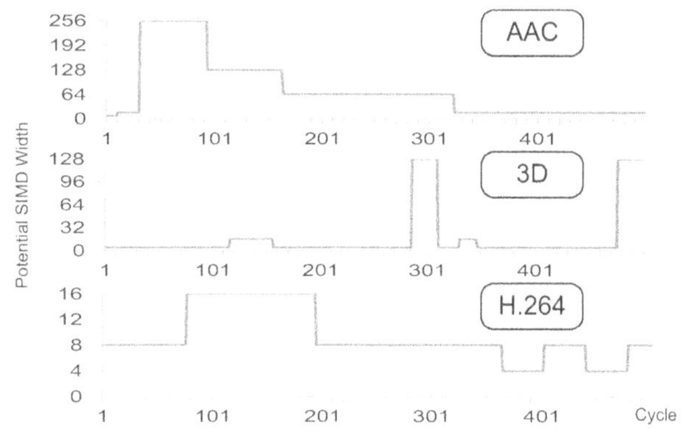

Figure 5. The SIMD width requirement changes at runtime: The X-axis indicates the execution clock cycle and the Y-axis is the maximum SIMD width assuming infinite resources. The minimum duration between width transition is 20 cycles from 311 to 330 for 3D application.

Dynamic power gating is one of the most successful energy saving techniques for the resource waste problem. Each SIMD lane can be selectively cut off from the power rails when the lane is not utilized using a MOSFET switch. This technique is attractive because it is effective for dynamic power saving and also has positive impact on leakage power savings. Although dynamic power gating achieves high energy savings, the relatively high overhead when changing modes prevents current SIMD architectures from applying it [29]. Even applying simple dynamic power gating techniques [14, 22, 23] is not effective since at least a few microseconds are required to compensate the power on/off energy overhead in current technologies. Figure 5 shows the SIMD width requirement changes over the runtime for three applications. The x-axis is the time stamp for 500 cycles when the SIMD architecture supports infinite DLP and the y-axis is the natural SIMD width that achieves the best performance. As shown, power gating cannot even compensate the transition energy overhead because of frequent power mode transitions within less than 200 cycles (1 μs at 200 Mhz) based on the different SIMD width requirements. Moreover, power gating comes with about 8% area overhead due to the header/footer power gate switch implementation. Therefore, power gating is hard to integrate into current SIMD architectures.

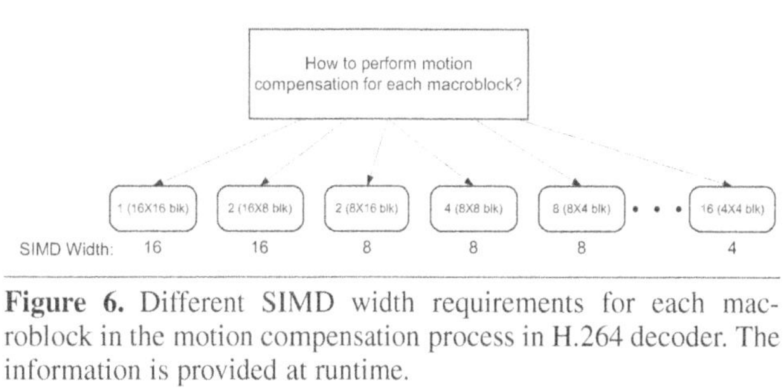

Figure 6. Different SIMD width requirements for each macroblock in the motion compensation process in H.264 decoder. The information is provided at runtime.

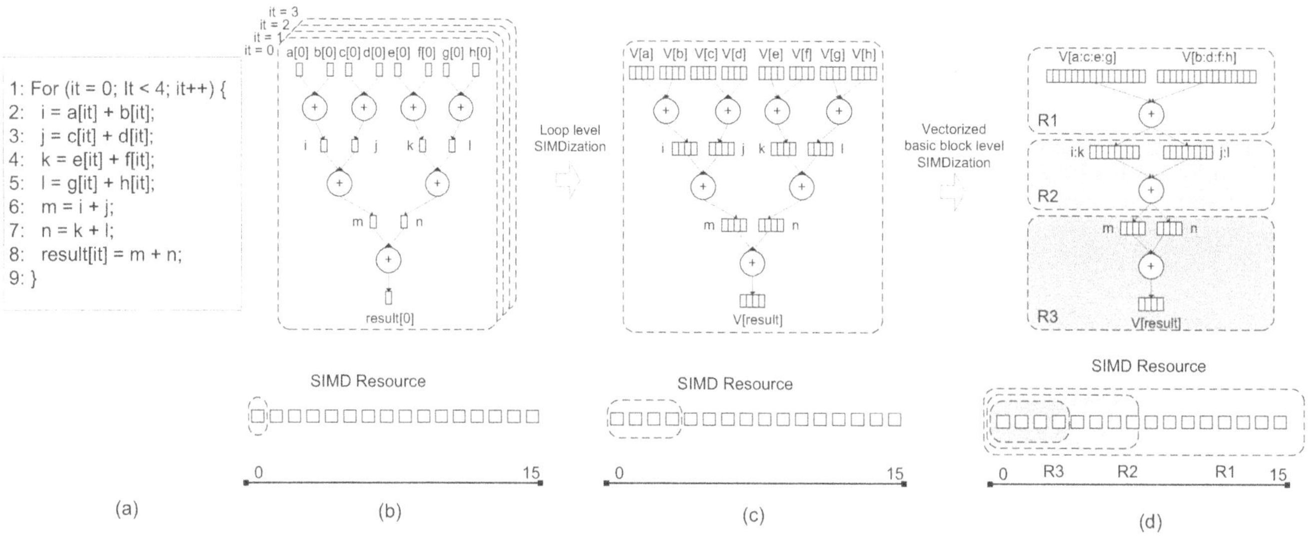

Figure 7. Different levels of parallelism: (a) an example loop's source code, (b) original multiple scalar subgraphs utilizing a single SIMD lane, (c) a vectorized subgraph using four SIMD lanes, and (d) the opportunity of partial SIMD parallelism inside the vectorized basic block (SIMD lane utilization: (R1: 16), (R2: 8), (R3: 4))

Thread-level Parallelism (TLP) for SIMD architectures has also been proposed to solve the temporal resource waste due to the small amount of DLP [34]. TLP supports running multiple threads that work on separate data on a wide SIMD machine when the SIMD width is small. By exploiting two kinds of parallelism, the SIMD lanes can be maximally utilized but the realization of TLP's potential in SIMD architectures has some critical limitations. First, TLP might not be fully exploited if parallel threads have different instruction flow. The motion compensation process for the H.264 decoder is a well-known example of this case. Figure 6 shows the various configurations of the motion compensation process for one macroblock. In this figure, the configuration of each macroblock is different so that SIMD specific restriction, which needs to execute the same instruction stream across the lanes, prohibits executing multiple processes in parallel even though the process has high TLP. Second, TLP cannot handle input-dependent control flow. For example, conditions to choose the macro block configuration in Figure 6 are decided from input header data hence TLP cannot be considered in the compilation phase. Finally, TLP generally requires more memory pressure. As a result, TLP looks appealing but the actual implementation of it is complicated.

The analysis reveals the difficulty of implementing common solutions in the real world. To further improve resource utilization, it is necessary to find a way to exploit other forms of parallelism.

2.3 Beyond Loop-level SIMD Parallelism

Most kernels have some degree of DLP, which can be easily vectorized using loop unrolling. An interesting question is how to find extra parallelism when the degree of DLP is smaller than the degree supported in the architecture. For this question, the next opportunity can be found inside the vectorized basic block. Even if the basic block is not fully vectorizable, some parts inside the block can be vectorized as a restricted form of ILP. Compared to ILP, DLP requires two more conditions: 1) the instructions should perform the same work and 2) data flow should also be in the same form. Therefore, parallel instructions with the same opcode can be executed together in a SIMD architecture. Figure 7 shows examples of additional SIMD parallelism inside the vectorized basic block for our three applications. Figure 7 (a) is a vectorizable loop to generate the sum of eight input data arrays. (b) shows the unrolled dataflow graph (DFG) that can be executed in only one lane when assuming a 16-way SIMD datapath. This loop can then be vectorized as shown in (c) and four lanes can be assigned as the trip count of the loop but still 12 lanes are idle. In this case, another opportunity for partial SIMD parallelism can be found inside the basic block as illustrated in (d). Four ADD instructions in the 'R1' region are able to execute together with 16 degrees of parallelism, two ADD instructions in the 'R2' region can also execute together using eight lanes. Based on the application analysis, more than 50% of total instructions have at least one parallel identical instruction.

2.4 Summary and Insights

The analysis of these three applications provides several insights. First, resource utilization of a wide SIMD architecture is low because multimedia applications have various degrees of SIMD parallelism, and current solutions are not effective due to the high dynamic variance and the unpredictability. Second, ILP inside the vectorized basic block can be converted to DLP in many cases. Therefore, additional partial SIMD parallelism can be added when the DLP is insufficient.

A major challenge is how to minimize the data movement across the different SIMD lanes. For loop-level DLP, inter-lane data movement does not happen, whereas partial DLP has a large number of such movements due to each part having different levels of DLP, causing the amount of the occupied SIMD lanes to change at runtime in such a manner that the data packing/unpacking/reorganizing process happens frequently. For example, two data movements across the lane need to be done when exploiting partial SIMD parallelism in Figure 7 (d): 1) 'R1' to 'R2': After the 16-wide instruction, half of the data in lanes 9 to 15 should move to 0 to 8, and 2) 'R2' to 'R3': After the 8-wide instruction, half of the data in lanes 4 to 7 should move to 0 to 3. Therefore, we can save just two total instructions due to the data movement even if we save four instructions on partial SIMD parallelism. The conclusion is that minimizing inter-lane data movements is the key challenge in getting benefits from partial SIMD parallelism.

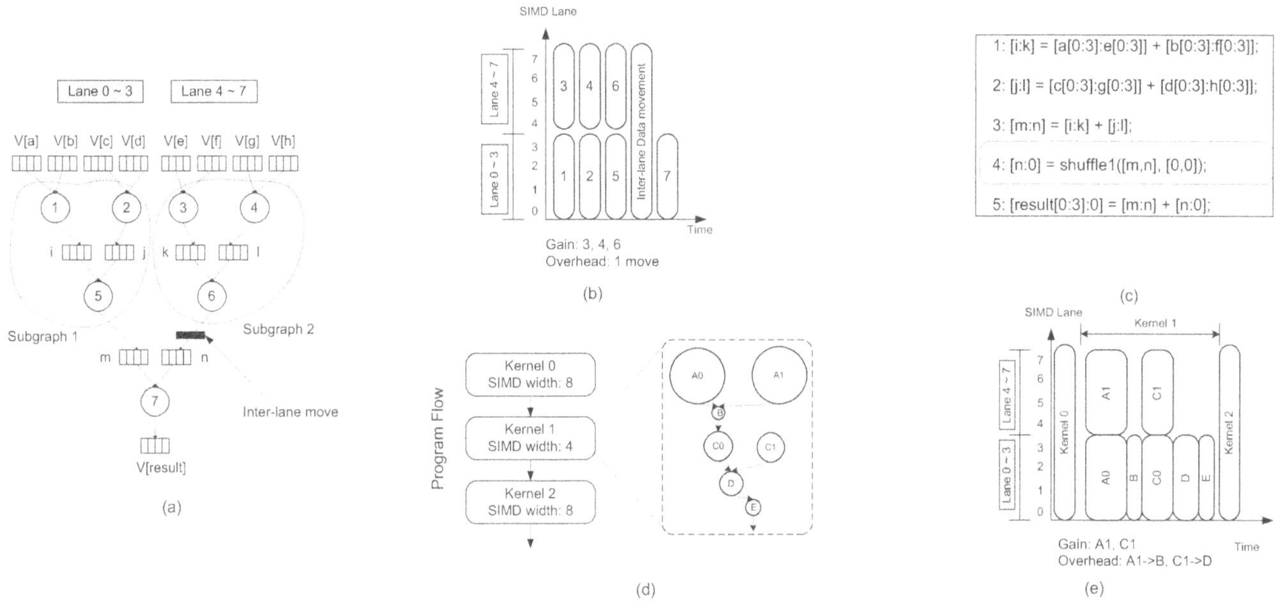

Figure 8. Subgraph level parallelism: (a) identical subgraphs are identified, and (1, 2, 5, 7) and (3, 4, 6) are executed in parallel with one overhead, (b) execution of the graph on two SIMD lane groups, (c) SGLP exploited output source code, (d) high level program flow with three sequential kernels and kernel 1 can exploit SGLP, and (e) execution of three kernels with SGLP exploration on kernel 1.

3. Subgraph Level Parallelism

This section describes a new vectorization technique. We first introduce some new terminologies and discuss its effectiveness in contrast to other related techniques. An execution model using SGLP is then proposed on the conventional wide SIMD architecture. Finally, we list practical challenges to exploit this parallelism and suggest proper solutions.

3.1 Overview

Subgraph level parallelism is defined as SIMD parallelism between *identical* subgraphs which 1) have an isomorphic form of dataflow with SIMDizable operations and 2) have no dependencies on each other inside the basic block. This parallelism is detected through the identical subgraph search inside the whole dataflow graph extracted from a basic block. These identical subgraphs can be executed in parallel in the form of a sequence of SIMD instructions inside the subgraph. There are two major advantages when searching packing opportunities at the subgraph level:

- **Packing steering:** SGLP minimizes the overall data reorganization overhead because the data movements between instructions inside a subgraph are automatically captured and assigned to one SIMD lane, and the alignment analysis between subgraphs is performed over a global scope. This benefit becomes more apparent when converting ILP to DLP in the low-DLP region such as loop-level vectorized or scalar code because the subgraph guides the instruction packing in directions that reduce or keep constant the amount of conversion overheads when the packing opportunities are not restricted by the memory alignment so that the number of possible packing combinations increase.
- **High packing gain:** Converting ILP to DLP is not common because it is hard to expect that the data reorganization process will provide enough gain to compensate for its performance loss due to the expensive nature. However, the considerable instruction savings of subgraph packing gives more chances to guarantee a positive net performance gain in spite of the substantial amount of overheads.

Figure 8 illustrates an example of SGLP realization. Using the vectorized basic block from Figure 7, Figure 8(a) identifies two identical subgraphs of (1, 2, 5) and (3, 4, 6) due to the same dataflow and same operations with no dependencies. Each corresponding instruction of two subgraphs is packed together and executed in parallel. Figure 8(b) shows the actual execution model using an 8-way SIMD datapath. Due to the insufficient degree of DLP for the original innermost loop from Figure 7(a), SGLP is applied and two isomorphic subgraphs are identified from the 4-wide vectorized basic block (Figure 8(a)). From these two subgraphs, (3, 4, 6) is chosen to be executed in the unused lanes. As a result, instructions (1, 2, 5, 7) and (3, 4, 6) are executed in lane 0-3 and 4-7 as shown in Figure 8(b). In addition to this, one cycle of overhead is incurred to move the output data of instruction 6 to lane 0-3. Figure 8(c) is the pseudo code exploiting both SIMD parallelism and SGLP. In this program, parallel instructions in the isomorphic subgraphs are packed together and data movement is enabled by the *shuffle* instruction, which moves data using the shuffle network in Figure 3. Shuffle0 extracts the left column data of two input vectors and Shuffle1 extracts the right column data of two input vectors.

Figure 8(d) and (e) illustrate the high-level execution model of this paradigm. The example scenario is three consecutive kernels having different natural SIMD widths (kernel 0:8, kernel 1:4, kernel 2:8) are executed on an 8-way SIMD architecture. Kernel 0 and 2 are executed only using SIMD parallelism by loop unrolling without any inter-lane overhead. However, the natural SIMD width of kernel 1 is smaller than the architecture allows, so SGLP is exploited as shown in (d). The SGLP compiler finds two groups of two isomorphic subgraphs as (A0, A1) and (C0, C1) and offloads two subgraphs of A1 and C1 onto lanes 4-7. As a result, the whole program can improve the total performance by the execution time of A1 and C1 as shown in (e) with some overhead. Inspired by this scenario, the total speedup achieved by SGLP over the current execution model is derived as the following equation when executing

n different kernels with iv invocations, which have t normal execution time, t_{sglp} execution time can be saved by subgraph offloading and ov inter-lane movement overhead.

$$Speedup = \frac{\sum_{k=0}^{n-1}(t(k) \times iv(k))}{\sum_{k=0}^{n-1}((t(k) - t_{sglp}(k) + ov(k)) \times iv(k))} \quad (1)$$

Based on Equation (1), the performance gain can be maximized when a program has a high number of invocations on kernels with a small degree of DLP, a high degree of SGLP and a small overhead. Therefore, an SGLP compiler needs to increase the number of instructions covered by identical subgraphs with minimum inter-lane overhead. The key algorithm to achieve this goal is explained in section 4.

3.2 Comparison with Superword Level Parallelism

Superword level parallelism [17] is the most similar paradigm to our work with respect to searching potential parallelism inside the basic block. Because SLP focuses on short SIMD instructions, isomorphic instructions are only considered and thus they cannot handle inter-lane data movement. This problem is often ignored because the overhead of data movement inside the vector is fairly small in a narrow SIMD component, however, it usually induces high performance degradation in a wider SIMD component [17]. In addition to this, the local scope of superword level parallelism may be fooled into selecting packing instructions when a large number of isomorphic instructions exists.

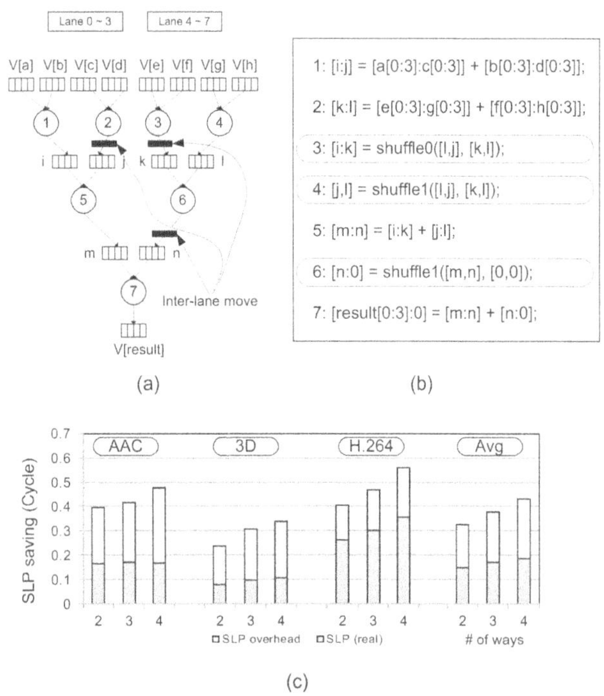

Figure 9. Superword level parallelism difficulty: (a) (1, 3, 5, 7) and (2, 4, 6) are chosen to execute in parallel and three overheads occur, (b) superword level parallelism exploited output source code, and (c) average cycle savings of SLP: Y-bar means ideal savings and it is broken down as overheads and real savings.

Figure 9 shows the result of exploiting superword parallelism from Figure 7 (a). For a fair comparison, we relax the memory alignment constraint of [17] so that all memory instructions can be packed. As the compiler searches the isomorphic instructions in program order with local scope, instructions are packed as (1, 2), (3, 4), (5, 6). Then lanes 0-3 execute (1, 3, 5, 7) and lanes 4-7 execute (2, 4, 6) as shown in Figure 9 (a). Even though total instruction savings are the same as SGLP , the overhead also increases to three instructions (Figure 9 (b)). Therefore, there is no performance gain even in this small basic block, and when the block becomes more complex the algorithm cannot ensure a good result.

Based on the above consideration, we analyze the cost of these overheads for the vectorized kernels of three media applications. Figure 9(c) shows average cycle savings when applying SLP at different SIMD ways from two to four compared to the original schedule on the baseline processor. The Y-bar shows the ideal savings assuming the SIMD overhead is free, and each bar is broken down by SLP overhead and real savings. The SLP overhead is calculated assuming all the data rearrangement instructions take one cycle. The results give two major insights: 1) SLP, the well-known SIMDization technique used inside the basic block, can ideally deliver a fair amount of performance enhancement and is also scalable as the number of ways increases, and 2) large SIMD overheads of more than 50% of ideal savings hinder the effectiveness of SLP and make SLP barely scalable as the overheads also grow dramatically at wider ways. The actual performance gain will be worse in a real situation because many SIMD overhead instructions take more than an single cycle with current technology. Section 5 shows how much SGLP improves performance by both increasing the ideal savings and decreasing the overheads when compared to SLP. In addition to this, we also show how much ILP can be converted into SGLP.

3.3 Challenges and Solutions

As discussed, SGLP introduces more potential parallelism but has many principal challenges to make this paradigm feasible. We list the four major architectural challenges and suggest possible solutions with architectural or compiler modifications. Simple architectural changes are proposed as shown in Figure 10 and compilation challenges are addressed in Section 4.

Control flow: Because SGLP is basically exploited within the basic block, control flow is not a big issue. Furthermore, as scalar pipelines are primarily responsible for handling control flow, SGLP generally does not need to consider control flow. However, basic blocks are sometimes merged using if-conversion with predication. Even in this case, SGLP is not affected because predication also can be detected in the identical subgraph identification process.

Instruction flow: When multiple SIMD lane groups execute some task in parallel, all the instructions are not covered as subgraphs, and some SIMD lane groups may not be enabled because the number of identical subgraphs is smaller than the number of SIMD lane groups. Therefore, the main SIMD lane group is necessary to cover all the instructions.

Register flow: First, data movement across or inside the SIMD lane groups can be supported by single-cycle shuffle instructions using a shuffle network. Second, although multiple SIMD lane groups execute the same instructions, their actual register names are different. Therefore, the compiler must handle register renaming, which packs multiple parallel short registers into a wide register. In addition to this, some instructions covered by multiple identical subgraphs may have different immediate values, and therefore the architecture must provide a way to support wide constant values in a cycle because it is impossible to supply multiple values in a cycle. Therefore, a small constant value memory can be added. The compiler then automatically generates the wide constants from multiple immediate values. The application study shows that these cases rarely exist, and thus the overhead incurred is trivial.

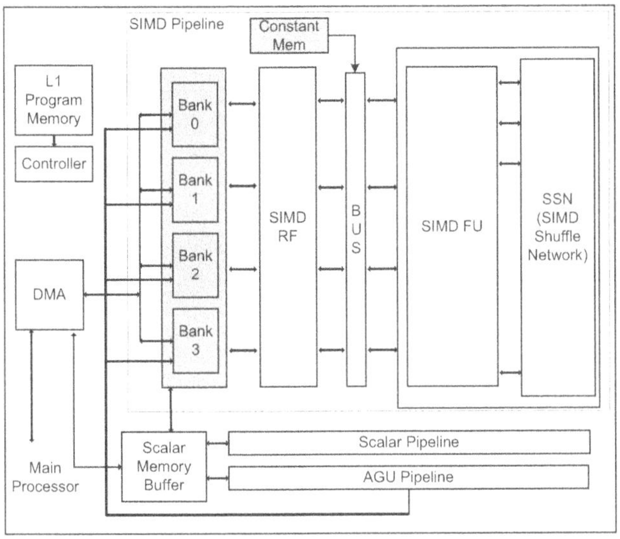

Figure 10. Architectural modifications: (1) multi-bank memory and (2) wide SIMD constant memory is supported.

Memory flow: If identical subgraphs have memory instructions, the references of the instructions may be different, and thus the architecture must provide a smart memory packing mechanism such as gather-scatter operation.

The possible architectural modification is to replace the SIMD scratchpad memory from one wide memory to a short width multiple bank memory. This change is required to relax the memory alignment constraint. The most critical reason why the basic block typically has high ILP but low DLP is that the architecture does not support unaligned memory access [17]. By supporting unaligned memory packing/unpacking from DMA using the multi-bank memory, more memory instructions can be executed in parallel. One key point is that multi-addressing is only allowed for Memory-DMA communications, while the SIMD pipeline views the memory as a single bank. Another key point is that the number of banks depends on the ratio of the number of memory instructions to normal instructions because the address calculations are the responsibility of the AGU pipeline and they are not scalable, thus the performance of the AGU may be the limiting factor.

4. Compiler Support

4.1 Overview

In this section, we describe the compiler support for SGLP. Taking the concept of subgraph identification [11], we developed a SGLP scheduler that can support both simple loop-level DLP and SGLP for wide SIMD components. The system flow is shown in Figure 11. Applications are run through a front-end compiler, producing generic Intermediate Representation (IR), which is unscheduled and uses virtual registers. The compiler also gets high-level machine specific information, including the number of SIMD lanes, and supported inter-lane movement instructions. Given the IR and hardware information, the compiler performs loop-level vectorization on the selected SIMDizable loops. The compiler then exploits SGLP if the SIMD parallelism is insufficient. After generating the DFG, the compiler iteratively discovers identical subgraphs in the DFG and assigns the subgraphs to unused SIMD lanes until no more SGLP opportunities exist. Finally, the compiler generates the final vectorized IR.

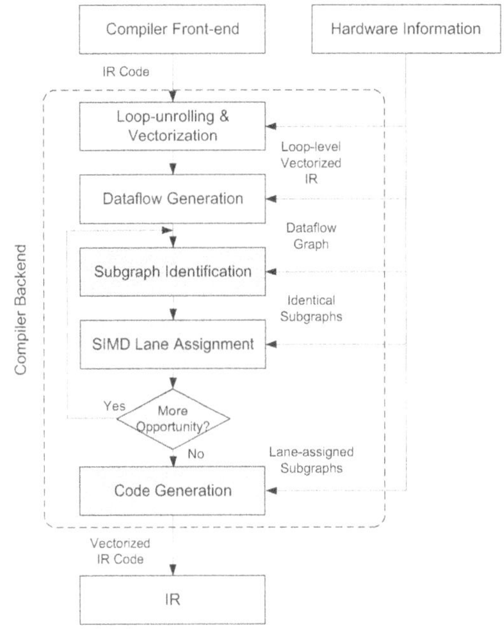

Figure 11. Compilation flow of the SIMD defragmenter: shaded regions exploit subgraph level parallelism.

4.2 Subgraph Identification

First, identical subgraphs are extracted from the given DFG. The compiler sets the maximum number of identical subgraphs as the available degree of SGLP. The compiler then iteratively searches the groups of identical subgraphs having some number of instances from maximum number down to two (the minimum degree). Heuristic discovery [11], which picks the seed node and grows the nodes, is used for DFG exploration. Exploration starts by examining each node in the DFG and using it as the seed for a candidate identical subgraph. The algorithm attempts to find the largest candidate subgraphs with n identical instances within the given DFG, where n is the degree of SGLP. If, however, the algorithm identifies m identical instances of a candidate subgraph, where $m > n$, only n instances are saved and the nodes from the remaining $m - n$ instances are "discarded" and "re-used" in the next exploration phase. This of course assumes that the current candidate subgraph could not be grown further while still ensuring that n instances could still be identified. If all the identical subgraphs with the target number of instances, n, are found, the compiler decreases the target number by one and starts the subgraph search again.

Additional conditions for the general subgraph search are that 1) the corresponding operations from each subgraph should be identical, 2) live values and immediate values should also be taken into consideration, and 3) inter-subgraph dependencies should not exist. Condition 1) enables the corresponding instructions inside the subgraphs to be packed into one opcode, and condition 2) enables packing whole operands of the instructions. Live values and immediate values are not generally considered in common subgraph pattern matching, but the SGLP compiler must take them into account because only same type of operands can be packed for SGLP. The last condition ensures that the subgraphs are parallelizable.

4.3 SIMD Lane Assignment

Once all possible groups of identical subgraphs are identified, the compiler selects the subgraphs to be packed and assigns them to SIMD lane groups. Instructions included in remaining subgraph groups lose the subgraph information and are reused in the next subgraph identification process. The objectives of SIMD lane assignment process are two-fold: 1) pack maximum number of instructions with minimum inter-lane data movement, and 2) ensure packed groups of instructions can be executed safely in parallel without any dependence violation. To achieve these goals, the compiler considers three kinds of criteria: gain, partial order, and affinity.

The gain of the subgraph is the most critical criteria and is largely calculated by the size of the subgraph. Larger subgraphs can provide higher performance with less overheads as more dataflow can be covered. The memory packing overhead is also accounted for in the gain if it incurs performance degradation. The compiler tries to assign subgraphs to specific SIMD lanes based on decreasing order of the gain.

The partial order between subgraphs inside the SIMD lane group is the next most critical issue. When assigning new identical subgraphs to different SIMD lane groups, the partial order of the subgraphs inside the SIMD lanes may be different across the SIMD lanes because identical subgraphs are only parallel with each other and the relations with other subgraph groups are not considered. If the relation between different subgraphs in some lane groups is different from the relations in other lane groups, the corresponding subgraphs cannot be executed in parallel. Figure 12 shows a simple example case of this kind of conflict. From a vectorized basic block having 3 groups of identical subgraphs with (A0, A1), (B0, B1), and (C0, C1), (A0, A1) and (B0, B1) are chosen to be parallelized using the two SIMD lane groups. After this assignment, C0 and C1 cannot execute in parallel through two SIMD lane groups because C0 must execute before B0 in the lane group 0-3 but C1 must execute after B1 in the lane group 4-7.

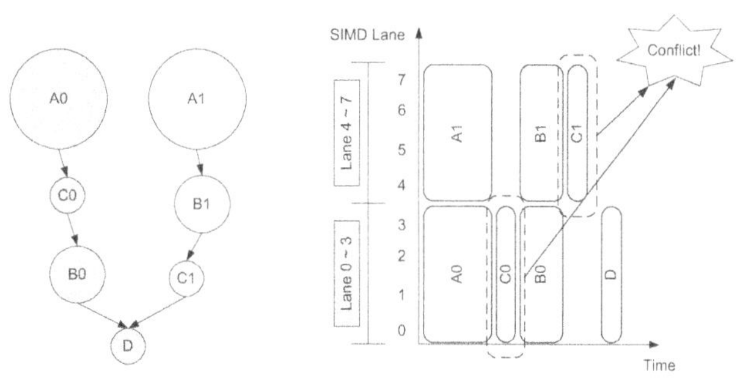

Figure 12. Subgraph partial order mismatch: when (B0, B1) is chosen to execute in different SIMD lanes, (C0, C1) cannot be chosen due to the partial order mismatch between lanes.

As the inter-lane data movement overheads inside the subgraphs are already solved by subgraph identification, the next objective is to minimize the overheads between different subgraphs. Typically, a subgraph is related to multiple other subgraphs, so the compiler must consider which combination of subgraphs can minimize the overall overhead. To address this issue, an *affinity cost* was introduced inspired by previous works [27, 28]. The affinity value for a pair of subgraphs reflects their proximity in the DFG. When a group of identical subgraphs is chosen to be parallelized, each lane group is assigned an affinity cost depending on how close the subgraph candidate is to any already placed subgraphs that have high affinity with the candidate. This gives preference for assigning a subgraph in the same lane group as other subgraphs it is likely to communicate with thus reducing inter-lane data movements.

$$
\begin{aligned}
affinity(A,B) = & \sum_{a \in nodes\_A} \Big(\sum_{d=1}^{max\_dist} 2^{max\_dist-d} \\
& \times ((N_{cons}(a,B,d) + N_{prods}(a,B,d)) \times C_0 \\
& + (N_{com\_cons}(a,B,d) + N_{com\_prods}(a,B,d)) \times C_1)\Big) \\
& , where \quad C_0 >> C_1
\end{aligned}
\quad (2)
$$

Equation (2) calculates the affinity between two subgraphs A and B. The value is determined by four different relations between nodes inside A and B: producer, consumer, common consumer, and common producer relations. Producer/consumer relation means that nodes in A have direct/indirect producer-consumer/consumer-producer relations to nodes in B. Common producer/consumer relations mean that nodes in A and nodes in B have common producer/consumer relations. The former two relations have explicit data movement between subgraphs but the latter relations just imply that they may have some data movements when merging or diverging. Therefore, we put more weight on the former two relations ($C_0 >> C_1$). Nodes within max_{dist} are used, where N refers to the number of nodes in subgraph A that have a relationship with a node in subgraph B at a distance d. The distance is the number of nodes to reach the target node.

Algorithm 1 SIMD Lane Assignment

Input: *IdSubGroups*, *G*, *SIMDGroups*
Output: *SIMDGroups*

{ Assign subgraphs into the appropriate SIMD lane group. }
1: `SortSubGraphGroupsByGain`(*IdSubGroups*);
2: **while** `HasGroup`(*IdSubGroups*) **do**
3:    *curSubGroup* ← `Pop`(*IdSubGroups*);
4:    **while** `HasGroup`(*curSubGroup*) **do**
5:       *curSubGraph* ← `Pop`(*curSubGroup*);
6:       *curSIMDGroup* ← `findSIMDGroupByMaxAffinity`(*SIMDGroups*, *curSubGraph*);
7:       *curSIMDGroup* → `addSubGraph`(*curSubGraph*);
8:    **end while**
9:    **if** (!`PartialOrderCheck`(*SIMDGroups*)) **then**
10:       `Restore`(*SIMDGroups*);
11:    **end if**
12: **end while**

{ If no more updates, find the main lane group and assign remaining nodes. }
13: **if** (!`IsUpdated`(*SIMDGroups*)) **then**
14:    *curSIMDGroup* ← `findSIMDGroupByMaxOverhead`(*SIMDGroups*);
15:    *curSIMDGroup* → `addRemainingNodes`(*G*);
16:    `SetMainSIMDGroup`(*curSIMDGroup*);
17: **end if**

Algorithm 1 shows how the SIMD lane assignment works. The inputs are the list of identical subgraph groups (*IdSubGroups*), dataflow graph (*G*) and the current list of SIMD lane groups (*SIMDGroups*). The output is the list of SIMD lane groups with new subgraph assignment (*SIMDGroups*). The algorithm starts by sorting the *IdSubGroups* by subgraph gain because we place the top priority on the gain of subgraph. Based on the sorted order of the list, the while loop assigns the subgraphs on the appropriate SIMD lane group. Lines 3-8 take one identical subgraph group and assign each of the subgraphs onto the SIMD lane group having the maximum affinity. Lines 9-11 perform the partial order check for all the SIMD lane groups and, if some conflicts occur, the latest update is cancelled. When no more subgraphs are assigned to the initial *SIMDGroups*, the compiler decides not to try the subgraph identification process again using the remaining nodes, sets the SIMD lane group with the maximum overhead as the main lane group, and assigns uncovered nodes of DFG to the main lane group in order to minimize the total overhead.

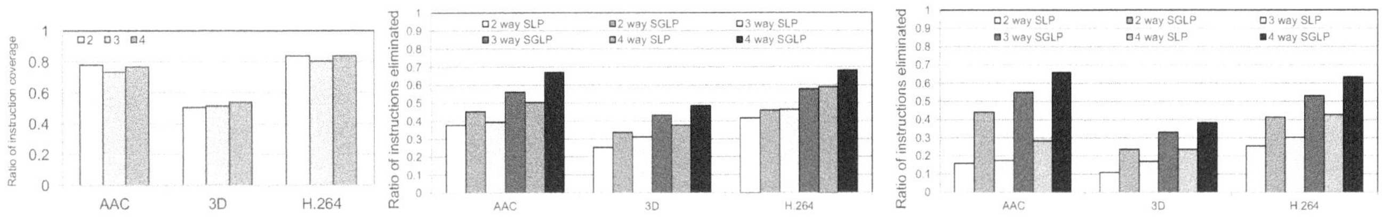

Figure 13. Ratio of instructions covered by the subgraph level parallelism and static instructions eliminated for three media applications: (a) instruction coverage, (b) static instruction elimination without inter-lane overheads, and (c) static instruction elimination with inter-lane overheads.

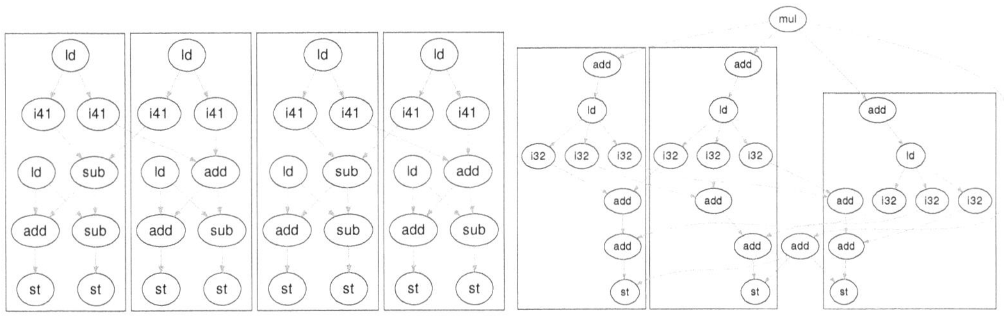

Figure 14. Example dataflow graphs: (a) FFT: two identical subgraphs ((1) ld, i41, i41, (2) ld, (sub/add), add, sub, st, st), (b) MatMul3x3: two identical subgraphs ((1) add, ld, i32 , i32, i32 (2) add, add, st). i41 and i32 are intrinsic instructions.

4.4 Code Generation

The compiler generates new vectorized IR from the lane assignment and inter-lane movement information from the previous process. When the compiler meets instructions covered by the identical subgraphs, the compiler gathers each parallel operand and converts them into one long register by remapping, a short immediate, or a wide constant. When a wide constant exists, the compiler generates the data and saves it to the constant memory. Shuffle instructions are also added if the compiler detects inter-lane data movement.

5. Experimental Results

5.1 Experimental Setup

To evaluate the availability and performance of SGLP, 144 loop kernels, varying in size from 4 to 142 operations, are extracted from three media applications in the embedded domain (AAC decoder, 3D graphics, and H.264 decoder). The iteration count per invocation of the kernels varies from 1 to 1024, and the natural SIMD widths are decided by the conditions discussed in Section 2.2.1 and memory dependence checks are performed using profile information. The IMPACT compiler [26] is used as the frontend compiler and both SGLP and SLP [17] are implemented in the backend compiler using a SODA-style [21] wide vector instruction set. The inter-lane move is performed using a single-cycle delay shuffle instruction, supporting data rearrangement in the SIMD RF as indicated by the permutation pattern similar to vperm (VMX) or vec_perm (AltiVec [30]). We also allow some similar instructions (e.g. add/sub) to be packed as common vector architectures allow this. The vectorizable kernels are automatically vectorized by loop unrolling and the evaluation is performed using the loop-level vectorized basic block. The wide SIMD architecture as discussed in Section 2.1 is used as the baseline architecture. The number of SIMD resources can vary from 16 to 64, while the number of memory banks are limited to four.

Our experiments do not apply SGLP more than 4-way. Two main reasons for this are: 1) the degree of ILP, the theoretical maximum gain of SGLP, is mostly smaller than four, and 2) only computation instructions can be SIMDized, and therefore the decreased ratio of computation to memory instructions causes the performance to be constrained by the AGU pipeline.

5.2 Subgraph Level Parallelism Coverage

We first calculate the percentage of instructions covered by identical subgraphs in order to gauge the availability of subgraph level parallelism. From the vectorized basic blocks of kernels, we found identical subgraphs ranging from 2-way to 4-way. The coverage is calculated as the number of instructions covered by the identical subgraphs. The results for three applications are shown in Figure 13(a). For H.264 and AAC, a large percentage of instructions is covered by identical subgraphs because high degrees of parallelism still exists even inside the vectorized basic block. Even though SGLP covers relatively small amount of instructions, more than 50% of instructions in the 3D application are still covered. Compared to other applications, the 3D application has a smaller degree of SIMD opportunity due to each instruction having a small number of parallel instructions with the same operation.

The interesting point here is that the coverage of the 3-way for AAC and H.264 applications is smaller than the 2- and 4-way. This is because most dataflow graphs have a tree structure and therefore 2 and 4 way are well matched but 3-way frequently misses some instructions when dataflow merges. For example, a dataflow graph of the FFT kernel is likely parallelizable in a 4-way, and thus 3-way exploration cannot find the profitable identical subgraphs in the one remaining flow as shown in Figure 14(a).

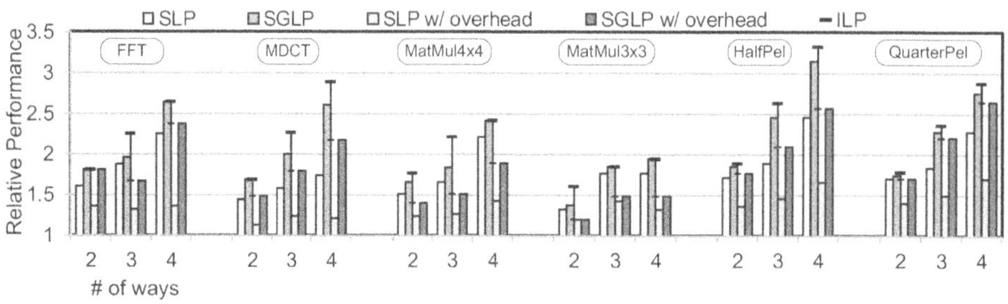

Figure 15. Performance comparison of SLP/SGLP without overhead, SLP/SGLP with overhead, and ILP for key kernels: FFT, MDCT for AAC, MatMul4x4, MatMul3x3 for 3D, and HalfPel, QuarterPel for H.264.

Figure 13(b) and Figure 13(c) show the ratio of static instructions eliminated from the vectorized basic block when applying SGLP and SLP. The configuration is expressed as: (number_of_simdization_ways) way (technique). Figure 13(b) shows the result without overhead (number of shuffle instructions) and the percentage of savings has the trend similar to that of the SGLP coverage. An interesting question is how the SGLP can eliminate more instructions than the SLP even though both techniques have a fair amount of gains. This is because 1) SLP frequently makes the wrong decision among various packing opportunities and 2) SLP cannot vectorize pure scalar codes [3]. When considering the inter-lane data movement overhead as shown in Figure 13(c), SLP performs dramatically worse than the ideal condition due to many shuffle instructions. On the other hand, SGLP was found to still deliver consistent amounts of instruction eliminations by smart data-movement control. Based on the application complexity, H.264 and 3D have a notable degradation of savings, whereas AAC is rarely affected by the overhead.

5.3 Performance

Inspired by the promising result of finding abundant opportunities for SGLP in the vectorized basic block, we compared the performance of SGLP to both SLP and ILP. Performances of SGLP and SLP are measured as the schedule length when the kernel is mapped a (a degree of loop-level vectorization $\times$ the number of ways)-wide SIMD architecture. As SGLP is the restricted form of ILP, the ILP result can be thought of as the theoretical upper bound. The performance of ILP is measured as the schedule length when the kernel is scheduled in the same sized fully-connected VLIW machine having a central register file. For example, if an example kernel is loop-level vectorized by 16 and 2-way SGLP is applied, the corresponding ILP performance is calculated when an ideal 32-wide VLIW machine executes unrolled scalar code.

Figure 15 and 16 show the individual performance enhancement results of six well-known kernels and geometric mean of gains for each application. The target ways are shown on the X-axis, relative performance normalized to the original vectorized kernel on the Y-axis. The following techniques are examined and shown as a bar form: SLP and SGLP with zero-cycle data-movement latency (SLP and SGLP) and SLP and SGLP with single-cycle data-movement latency (SLP and SGLP w/ overhead). The ILP results are also shown as a short horizontal form and the vertical line indicates the performance difference between ideal ILP and loop-level vectorization combined with practical SGLP. From these two graphs, substantial amounts of speedups exist in both ideal cases and are similarly scalable as ILP. In addition to this, gains from SGLP in real situations are also mostly prominent and scalable without large overhead increases on wider ways. In contrast, SLP with overhead has a large performance degradation due to the immense inter-lane data-movements, and increasing overheads on wider ways make it barely scalable.

Unlike most cases, a few kernels showed negligible performance improvements while applying SGLP, namely FFT in AAC and 3x3 matrix multiplication in 3D. These are due to the specific characteristics of each dataflow graph. First, as shown in Figure 14(a), the FFT kernel can have two subgraphs without inter-lane data movements in the 2-way case. In the 4-way case, each subgraph for the 2-way case is split once more with only two data movements such as (i41 $\rightarrow$ add) and (i41 $\rightarrow$ sub). In the 3-way case, three of the subgraphs for the 4-way case are identified and a remaining subgraph cannot be effectively executed in multi-lane, which has a high data-movement overhead. As a result, the gain of 3-way SGLP is worse than that of 2-way SGLP including overheads. Second, the 3x3 matrix multiplication can be split into three subgraphs as shown in Figure 14(b), and therefore a considerable increasing in overheads when applying 4-way SGLP hinder it from fully exploiting the benefits.

As shown in Figure 16, on average, SGLP without and with overheads achieve relative performance improvements of 1.42x, 1.36x at 2-way, 1.61x, 1.47x at 3-way, and 1.84x, 1.66x at 4-way. In addition to this, SGLP with overheads also provides 18-40% more performance improvement over baseline compared to SLP with the same resources. The performance difference between SGLP and SLP increases as applied on wider ways. Finally, a comparison with ILP suggests that SGLP is a cheap and powerful solution to accelerate performance, considering that SGLP only requires minimum additional hardware while a wide fully-connected VLIW architecture is impractical.

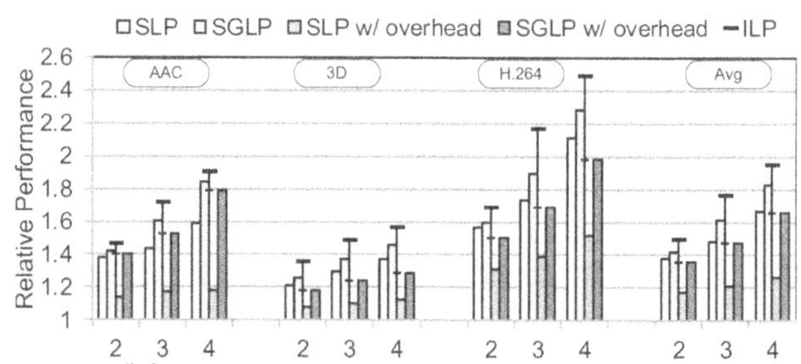

Figure 16. Average kernel performance comparison of SLP/SGLP without overhead, SLP/SGLP with overhead, and ILP for three application domains.

Based on the schedule results for kernels, we execute three applications on three wide SIMD architectures having 16, 32, and 64 lanes. When the original SIMD width of the kernel is equal or larger than the width of the architecture, SGLP or SLP is not exploited. Only when the current SIMD width of the kernel is insufficient to fully use the architecture, the available amount of SGLP, up to 4-way, is exploited. For example, 4-way SGLP is exploited if a kernel is 4-wide vectorized on the 16 way architecture and 2-way when 8-wide vectorized. The final performance is also compared to traditional ILP in the equivalent VLIW architecture and SLP. The results are provided in Figure 17 with considerable performance gains. The X-axis shows the number of SIMD lanes on the wide SIMD architecture and the Y-axis shows speedup relative to the simple SIMD execution time on the baseline architecture. The two bars of each application represent the runtime speedup of real SLP and SGLP with overheads. In a similar ways from previous Figures, ILP results are also provided. For all the applications, real SGLP still shows notable performance gain by utilizing more SIMD resources with smart overhead control. As we discussed in Section 2.2.2, kernels having smaller than 16 SIMD width are accelerated by SGLP when using 16 wide architecture, and AAC and H.264 have high gains due to the high execution time ratio of such kernels, which are more than 50% of their total execution time. As the architecture size becomes larger, the performance is saturated at some point because SGLP is constrained by maximum degree of 4. The key observation is that the real performance gain of SGLP is also fairly scalable due to the fact that the performance gain successfully compensates for the increased overheads different from SLP. Finally, on average, SGLP with overhead can have 1.61x, 1.73x, and 1.76x speedups at 16, 32, and 64 wide SIMD architectures while SLP only achieves 1.24x, 1.28x, and 1.29x speedups.

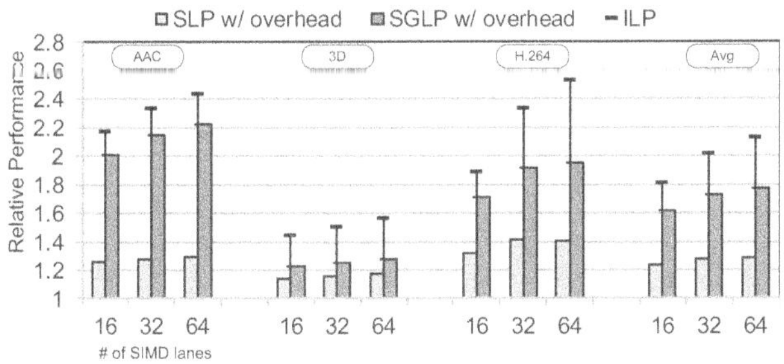

Figure 17. Overall performance comparison of SLP/SGLP with overhead and ILP for three domains on SIMD architectures.

5.4 Energy Measurement

To evaluate the energy savings of SGLP in the real world, we measured total energy consumption for running H.264 to determine the effectiveness of SGLP. We used a 32-wide SIMD architecture for SGLP, and a practical 4-way VLIW, in which each datapath supports 8-wide SIMD instructions for ILP and an 8 read-ports, 4 write-port 8-wide SIMD RF. Both architectures are generated in RTL Verilog for a 200 MHz target frequency, then synthesized with the Synopsys Design Compiler and Physical Compiler using IBM 65nm standard cell library with typical operating conditions. PrimeTime PX is used to measure power consumption. Instead of measuring power for every cycle, average activity of each component was monitored. Figure 18 shows that the SGLP is 30% more energy efficient than ILP. Even though the performance of SGLP is slightly lower, the high power overheads of VLIW implementation, such as those introduced by a multi-port register file and a complex interconnect, dominate the results. The power number for constant memory is also considered based on the standby power and read power extracted from the SRAM compiler. The constant memory power overhead is trivial because the standby power is roughly 1/250 of read power and the wide constant values are rarely read. The access timing is also smaller than 5 ns (i.e., 200 MHz), hence data can be read in one cycle.

	SGLP @ 32-wide SIMD	ILP @ 4 way 8-wide VLIW	ratio
power (mW)	54.40	93.17	58.39%
cycle(million)	13.07	10.77	121.36%
energy (mJ)	3.55	5.02	70.86%

Figure 18. Energy comparison for the SGLP on the 32-wide SIMD architecture and ILP on the 4 way 8-wide VLIW architecture.

6. Related Works

Most prior work in automatic vectorization are performed on the loop-level [2, 25] and some of the techniques have already been implemented on commercial compilers such as the Intel Compiler [15]. These types of vectorization are usually exploited by loop unrolling. Our SGLP vectorization starts after simple loop-level vectorization, and thus it is an orthogonal approach and can be helpful to enhance the overall performance of our compiler framework by finding more loop-level DLP. SGLP tries to identify opportunities for parallelism within the vectorized basic block.

Superword-level parallelism [17] is the closest related work but this work is hard to apply to long vector architectures as discussed in Section 3. To improve this technique, some research [18, 31] focuses on smart memory control such as increasing contiguous memory instructions and decreasing memory accesses. There are two key differences between SGLP and SLP: 1) SGLP tries to minimize the SIMD overheads in the scope of dataflow graph analysis, whereas most approaches do in the scope of memory management, and 2) we focus on finding groups of instructions to guarantee sufficient gain over the overheads but others usually focus on decreasing the overheads. Unroll-and-jam with SLP [25] is the most similar work and we can get 30% higher performance on average due to SLP being less effective when applied to scalar code.

Another key contribution of this work is the ability to minimize the interaction between the SIMD lanes. This scheme is highly related to the research in the area of clustering [1, 6, 7, 13]. However, general clustering techniques for VLIW machines focus on load balancing and critical path search, and thus cannot handle dataflow and instruction mismatches between clusters.

Subgraph exploration for finding identical subgraphs is also a well-known research area [8–11] but the goal of these works is mostly to generate custom accelerators for the subgraphs. We introduce a new algorithm for orchestrating sets of subgraphs at a high-level for SIMDization on existing architectures.

AnySp [34] or SCALE [16], which exploit multiple forms of parallelism, are also similar to this work. AnySp integrated DLP and TLP, and SCALE exploits both vector parallelism and TLP. However, they need substantial architectural changes like multiple AGUs, flexible functional units, and swizzle networks in AnySp, or additional multiple fetch unit, special inter-cluster network, and Atomic Instruction Block (AIB) cache in SCALE. However, we can provide SGLP with two minimal hardware modifications (a small wide-constant memory and banked memory access) that incur very little overhead.

7. Conclusion

The popularity of mobile computing platforms has led to the development of feature-packed devices that support a wide range of software applications with high single-thread performance and power efficiency requirements. To efficiently achieve both objectives, embedding SIMD components is an attractive solution. However, utilization of SIMD resources is a major limiting factor for adopting such a scheme. In response, we propose an efficient vectorization framework, called the *SIMD defragmenter*, to enhance the throughput by maximizing SIMD utilization. The *SIMD defragmenter* framework first performs simple loop-level vectorization, then tries to find more DLP within the vectorized basic block using subgraph level parallelism (SGLP). To achieve this, partially parallelizable subgraphs are identified inside the basic block, which are offloaded to the unused SIMD lanes while minimizing the number of inter-lane data movements. We introduce a new way to orchestrate the partially parallel subgraphs, which is implemented in our SGLP compiler. The SGLP compiler is able to effectively assign the SIMD lanes for each subgraph based on the relations between subgraphs. On a 16-wide SIMD processor, SGLP obtains an average 62% speedup over traditional vectorization techniques, with a maximum gain of 2x. In comparison to superword-level parallelism, the well-known basic block level vectorization technique, SGLP achieves an average 30% speedup. We believe as SIMD, or more general data-parallel, accelerators become more commonplace, new techniques to put these resources to work across a wide spectrum of applications will be essential.

8. Acknowledgments

Thanks to Anoushe Jamshidi, Mark Woh, Shuguang Feng, Griffin Wright, and Gaurav Chadha for all their help and feedback. We also thank the anonymous referees who provided good suggestions for improving the quality of this work. This research is supported by Samsung Advanced Institute of Technology and the National Science Foundation under grants CCF-0819882 and CNS-0964478.

References

[1] A. Aletà, J. Codina, J. Sánchez, and A. González. Graph-partitioning based instruction scheduling for clustered processors. In *Proc. of the 34th Annual International Symposium on Microarchitecture*, pages 150–159, Dec. 2001.

[2] R. Allen and K. Kennedy. *Optimizing compilers for modern architectures: A dependence-based approach*. Morgan Kaufmann Publishers Inc., 2002.

[3] R. Barik, J. Zhao, and V. Sarkar. Efficient Selection of Vector Instructions Using Dynamic Programming. In *Proc. of the 43rd Annual International Symposium on Microarchitecture*, Dec. 2010.

[4] K. Berkel, F. Heinle, P. Meuwissen, K. Moerman, and M. Weiss. Vector processing as an enabler for software-defined radio in handheld devices. *EURASIP Journal Applied Signal Processing*, 2005(1):2613–2625, 2005.

[5] H. Bluethgen, C. Grassmann, W. Raab, and U. Ramacher. A programmable platform for software-defined radio. In *Intl. Symposium on System-on-a-Chip*, pages 15–20, Nov. 2003.

[6] A. Capitanio, N. Dutt, and A. Nicolau. Partitioned register files for VLIWs: A preliminary analysis of tradeoffs. In *Proc. of the 25th Annual International Symposium on Microarchitecture*, pages 103–114, Dec. 1992.

[7] M. Chu, K. Fan, and S. Mahlke. Region-based hierarchical operation partitioning for multicluster processors. In *Proc. of the SIGPLAN '03 Conference on Programming Language Design and Implementation*, pages 300–311, June 2003.

[8] N. Clark et al. Application-specific processing on a general-purpose core via transparent instruction set customization. In *Proc. of the 37th Annual International Symposium on Microarchitecture*, pages 30–40, Dec. 2004.

[9] N. Clark et al. An architecture framework for transparent instruction set customization in embedded processors. In *Proc. of the 32nd Annual International Symposium on Computer Architecture*, pages 272–283, June 2005.

[10] N. Clark, A. Hormati, S. Mahlke, and S. Yehia. Scalable subgraph mapping for acyclic computation accelerators. In *Proc. of the 2006 International Conference on Compilers, Architecture, and Synthesis for Embedded Systems*, pages 147–157, Oct. 2006.

[11] N. Clark, H. Zhong, and S. Mahlke. Processor acceleration through automated instruction set customization. In *Proc. of the 36th Annual International Symposium on Microarchitecture*, pages 129–140, Dec. 2003.

[12] J. Glossner, E. Hokenek, and M. Moudgill. The sandbridge sandblaster communications processor. In *Proc. of the 2004 Workshop on Application Specific Processors*, pages 53–58, Sept. 2004.

[13] J. Hiser, S. Carr, and P. Sweany. Global register partitioning. In *Proc. of the 9th International Conference on Parallel Architectures and Compilation Techniques*, pages 13–23, Oct. 2000.

[14] Z. Hu, A. Buyuktosunoglu, V. Srinivasan, V. Zyuban, H. Jacobson, and P. Bose. Microarchitectural techniques for power gating of execution units. In *Proc. of the 2004 International Symposium on Low Power Electronics and Design*, pages 32–37, Aug. 2004.

[15] Intel. Intel compiler, 2009. software.intel.com/en-us/intel-compilers/.

[16] R. Krashinsky, C. Batten, M. Hampton, S. Gerding, B. Pharris, J. Casper, and K. Asanovic. The vector-thread architecture. In *Proc. of the 31st Annual International Symposium on Computer Architecture*, 2004.

[17] S. Larsen and S. Amarasinghe. Exploiting superword level parallelism with multimedia instruction sets. In *Proc. of the SIGPLAN '00 Conference on Programming Language Design and Implementation*, pages 145–156, June 2000.

[18] S. Larsen and S. Amarasinghe. Increasing and detecting memory address congruence. In *Proc. of the 11th International Conference on Parallel Architectures and Compilation Techniques*, pages 18–29, Sept. 2002.

[19] C. Lee, M. Potkonjak, and W. Mangione-Smith. MediaBench: A tool for evaluating and synthesizing multimedia and communications systems. In *Proc. of the 30th Annual International Symposium on Microarchitecture*, pages 330–335, 1997.

[20] Y. Lin et al. Soda: A low-power architecture for software radio. In *Proc. of the 33rd Annual International Symposium on Computer Architecture*, pages 89–101, June 2006.

[21] Y. Lin et al. Soda: A high-performance dsp architecture for software-defined radio. *IEEE Micro*, 27(1):114–123, Jan. 2007.

[22] A. Lungu, P. Bose, A. Buyuktosunoglu, and D. J. Sorin. Dynamic power gating with quality guarantees. In *Proc. of the 2009 International Symposium on Low Power Electronics and Design*, pages 377–382, Aug. 2009.

[23] N. Madan, A. Buyuktosunoglu, P. Bose, and M. Annavaram. A case for guarded power gating for multi-core processors. In *Proc. of the 17th International Symposium on High-Performance Computer Architecture*, Feb. 2011.

[24] D. Nuzman et al. Vapor simd: Auto-vectorize once, run everywhere. In *Proc. of the 2011 International Symposium on Code Generation and Optimization*, pages 151–160, Apr. 2011.

[25] D. Nuzman and A. Zaks. Outer-loop vectorization - revisited for short simd architectures. In *Proc. of the 17th International Conference on Parallel Architectures and Compilation Techniques*, pages 2–11, 2008.

[26] OpenIMPACT. The OpenIMPACT IA-64 compiler, 2005. http://gelato.uiuc.edu/.

[27] H. Park, K. Fan, M. Kudlur, and S. Mahlke. Modulo graph embedding: Mapping applications onto coarse-grained reconfigurable architectures. In *Proc. of the 2006 International Conference on Compilers, Architecture, and Synthesis for Embedded Systems*, pages 136–146, Oct. 2006.

[28] H. Park, K. Fan, S. Mahlke, T. Oh, H. Kim, and H. seok Kim. Edge-centric modulo scheduling for coarse-grained reconfigurable architectures. In *Proc. of the 17th International Conference on Parallel Architectures and Compilation Techniques*, pages 166–176, Oct. 2008.

[29] J. Park, D. Shin, N. Chang, and M. Pedram. Accurate modeling and calculation of delay and energy overheads of dynamic voltage scaling in modern high-performance microprocessors. In *Proc. of the 2010 International Symposium on Low Power Electronics and Design*, pages 419–424, Aug. 2010.

[30] F. Semiconductor. Altivec, 2009. www.freescale.com/altivec.

[31] J. Shin, J. Chame, and M. W. Hall. Compiler-controlled caching in superword register files for multimedia extension architectures. In *Proc. of the 11th International Conference on Parallel Architectures and Compilation Techniques*, pages 45–55, 2005.

[32] D. Talla, L. K. John, and D. Burger. Bottlenecks in multimedia processing with simd style extensions and architectural enhancements. *IEEE Transactions on Computers*, 52(8):1015–1031, 2003.

[33] M. Woh et al. From SODA to scotch: The evolution of a wireless baseband processor. In *Proc. of the 41st Annual International Symposium on Microarchitecture*, pages 152–163, Nov. 2008.

[34] M. Woh, S. Seo, S. Mahlke, T. Mudge, C. Chakrabarti, and K. Flautner. AnySP: Anytime Anywhere Anyway Signal Processing. In *Proc. of the 36th Annual International Symposium on Computer Architecture*, pages 128–139, June 2009.

An Update-Aware Storage System for Low-Locality Update-Intensive Workloads

Dilip N Simha
Computer Science Department, Stony Brook University
dnsimha@cs.sunysb.edu

Maohua Lu
IBM Almaden Research
lum@us.ibm.com

Tzi-cker Chiueh
Computer Science Department, Stony Brook University & Industrial Technology Research Institute
tcc@itri.org.tw

Abstract

Traditional storage systems provide a simple read/write interface, which is inadequate for *low-locality update-intensive* workloads because it limits the disk scheduling flexibility and results in inefficient use of buffer memory and raw disk bandwidth. This paper describes an *update-aware* disk access interface that allows applications to explicitly specify disk update requests and associate with such requests call-back functions that will be invoked when the requested disk blocks are brought into memory. Because call-back functions offer a *continuation* mechanism after retrieval of requested blocks, storage systems supporting this interface are given more flexibility in scheduling pending disk update requests. In particular, this interface enables a simple but effective technique called *Batching mOdifications with Sequential Commit* (BOSC), which greatly improves the sustained throughput of a storage system under low-locality update-intensive workloads. In addition, together with a space-efficient low-latency disk logging technique, BOSC is able to deliver the same durability guarantee as synchronous disk updates. Empirical measurements show that the random update throughput of a BOSC-based B^+ tree is more than an order of magnitude higher than that of the same B^+ tree implementation on a traditional storage system.

Categories and Subject Descriptors D.0 [*Software*]: GENERAL; E.2 [*Data*]: DATA STORAGE REPRESENTATIONS

General Terms Design, Performance

Keywords B+ Trees, Storage, Hard disks, Buffered writes, Fast logging, Update interface, low-locality, update-intensive, BOSC

1. Introduction

A disk update request retrieves a disk block, modifies it, and writes the resulting block back to disk. A low-locality update-intensive disk access workload is one that is dominated by disk update requests with a large working set and poor locality. Such workloads commonly result from index updates in data de-duplication, user-generated content management and on-line transaction processing applications, and have posed a major performance challenge for storage stack designers. Traditional storage systems do not perform well under these workloads and thus require higher storage stack layers to carefully schedule incoming disk requests to mitigate the performance penalty associated with such workloads. Even storage systems using flash memory-based disks perform poorly in the face of these workloads, sometimes faring ever worse when compared with magnetic disks. A large body of previous research efforts on disk buffering [4, 12], caching [16, 24, 28], and scheduling [32, 50] have attempted to solve this problem, but they are generally ineffective because low access locality leads to excessive random disk I/Os.

A well-known technique to boost the performance of workloads dominated by low-locality disk writes is to structure the storage system as a log and convert each disk write into an append to the log. However, such techniques carry hidden performance overheads in the form of metadata look-up and garbage collection. For workloads dominated by low-locality disk reads, no generally effective performance-boosting measure is available. Because a disk update is a disk read followed by a disk write, on the surface it appears that there is not much one can do to boost the performance of workloads dominated by low-locality disk updates. However, this paper describes an *update-aware* disk access interface and a novel storage system exploiting this new interface that together demonstrate that it is possible to apply the same logging technique to low-locality disk update workloads and produce one to two orders of magnitude in performance improvement as compared with conventional storage systems.

Traditional storage systems support a disk access interface for higher-layer systems software, such as a file system or a DBMS, to read or write data stored on disks. The granularity of disk reads and writes ranges from disk blocks [26, 33] to more sophisticated constructs such as objects [17, 29]. Regardless of access granularity, these simple read/write interfaces are not adequate for low-locality update-intensive workloads for two reasons. First, storage systems are typically designed to minimize the response time for disk read accesses and thus tend to service them as synchronously as possible. However, for a disk update, it's OK to service the update's leading disk read access asynchronously, like its following disk write access, because a disk update is considered completed only after its following disk write is completed. Unfortunately, the standard read/write disk access interface does not allow the storage system to distinguish between stand-alone disk reads and disk reads associated with disk updates. Second and more importantly, an ideal way to optimize the performance of a set of modifications to a disk block is to aggregate them and apply them to the disk block when it is brought into memory. This is very similar to the strategy employed in InnoDB [27] which is a standard storage engine used in most of the MySQL applications. But when multiple ap-

ASPLOS'12, March 3–7, 2012, London, England, UK.

plication processes issue update requests concurrently, the simple read/write interface prevents such aggregation, because the storage system does not know how to apply individual updates and has to rely on application processes to perform these updates.

To remove the above two problems, we propose a new disk access interface that allows applications of a storage system (a) to explicitly declare a disk access request as an `update` request to a disk block, in addition to the standard `read` or `write` request, and (b) to associate with an update request a callback function that performs the actual update on its target disk block. With disk update requests explicitly labeled, a storage system can now aggregate them, including the implicit reads contained within, in the same way as it does with disk write requests. With access to application-specific disk block update functions, a storage system can directly apply proper updates to each disk block retrieved on behalf of the processes issuing the disk update requests, thus gaining much more flexibility in disk access scheduling.

The update-aware disk access interface enables a new storage system architecture called *BOSC* (Batching mOdifications with Sequential Commit), which sits between storage applications, e.g., a DBMS process or file system, and hardware storage devices, and is specifically optimized for low-locality update-intensive workloads. In BOSC, incoming disk update requests targeted at a disk block are queued in the in-memory queue associated with the disk block; in the background, BOSC *sequentially* scans the disk(s) to bring in disk blocks whose associated queue is not empty. When a disk block is fetched into memory, BOSC applies all of its pending updates to it in one shot.

BOSC treats each disk update request as an atomic operation, and optimizes them as if they are disk write requests. The resulting throughput improvement under low-locality update-intensive workloads is quite impressive, between one to two orders of magnitude. In addition, combined with a space-efficient low-latency logging technique, BOSC is able to achieve this throughput improvement while delivering the same durability guarantee and latency as if each disk update request is serviced synchronously.

2. Related Work

A common approach to improving the performance of small disk writes is to use NVRAM to buffer writes, which provides two benefits: scheduling disk writes more flexibly and combining multiple writes with the same target. However, NVRAM is expensive, and for workloads with poor locality, high update rate, and large working set such as TPC-C [15], a small amount of NVRAM can only mask the delay for a finite number of disk writes, because eventually the sustained write performance is bottlenecked by the speed at which writes are propagated to disks. Write-only disk cache [40] mitigates the performance problem due to buffer flushing by injecting disk writes between consecutive disk reads. However, a single buffer page is still required to hold the result of each disk read and the read operations can still exhibit poor performance if the input workload has poor data locality. In contrast, BOSC's low-latency logging technique can accommodate a much larger number of disk writes, its use of sequential disk I/O to commit pending updates greatly improves the sustained disk update throughput, and it does not rely on NVRAM to ensure data durability.

There has been a long line of research on efficient file system metadata update techniques that ensure metadata consistency with minimal performance overhead. HyLog [49] further reduces the performance overhead associated with LFS's cleaning [45] by treating hot and cold pages separately. The soft update technique [18, 34] avoids synchronous metadata writes by exploiting dependencies among metadata updates and makes it possible to aggregate updates as much as possible to improve the disk I/O efficiency. One problem with soft updates is that it is metadata-specific and thus needs to be tailored to each type of file system. Also, the above metadata update techniques focused mainly on the latency but not the throughput of metadata updates.

Efficient file system metadata update techniques that ensure metadata consistency with minimal performance overhead have received significant attention in the last two decades. *WAL (Write-Ahead Logging)* [14, 22] and shadow paging [9, 10, 45, 47, 49] group relate metadata updates and commit them atomically to ensure metadata consistency. Performance benefits of *WAL* mainly come from sequential disk writes and group commit.

Much work [8, 21, 25, 35, 36, 43] has been done to optimize the disk I/O performance for inserting and querying index data structures. One particularly interesting line of research in this area is the cache-oblivious data structures and algorithms [5–8]. Take a binary tree B of height H for example. This tree is abstracted into a 2-level abstract tree AB, whose root corresponds to the first $\frac{H}{2}$ levels of B, and each of whose leaf nodes corresponds to a $\frac{H}{2}$-level subtree of B. Each node in AB is then recursively abstracted in the same way until the size of each final abstract tree node is smaller than a pre-defined threshold T. This linearization strategy for tree data structures, known as the van Emde Boas scheme, substantially reduces the number of disk accesses required in the tree look-up process if T is smaller than the cache line (page) size. The performance improvement of cache-oblivious data structures mainly comes from the fact that they put portions of a tree that are likely to be accessed together during the look-up process in the same units which are transferred in the memory hierarchy. With this set-up, when a transfer unit is brought in, it is expected to service multiple accesses to the unit before it is evicted.

There have been several research efforts on the bulk update problem, which attempts to speed up index updates in the presence of a continuous stream of inputs to a database, which require real-time updates to its indexes. Arge et al. [1, 2] proposed a bulk update mechanism for dynamic R-trees, whereas Procopiuc et al. [42] described a scalable bulk update algorithm for kd-trees. The basic idea behind these schemes is to hold the inserted input records in the internal nodes as long as possible and copy them sequentially to grow the tree when the internal nodes are filled up. In [19], Graefe proposed to add an artificial leading column to logically partition a single B^+ tree to several small B^+ trees. Similarly in the *buffer tree technique* [8], incoming updates to a B^+ tree are written to the smallest B^+ tree that can fit into the main memory. Merging is implemented as a background operation to take advantage of large sequential writes. However, read query performance again is sacrificed because multiple B^+ trees have to be queried before the final result can be computed. In [20], Graefe proposed a novel technique to improve the de-fragmentation and reorganization performance of B^+ tree. A logical pointer called *fence* instead of a physical pointer to sibling B^+ tree leaf nodes was proposed to limit the performance overhead of migrating B^+ tree leaf nodes. However, this scheme optimizes the performance of insert operations but not update-in-place operations because the latter needs to fetch target leaf nodes before modifying them.

BOSC is different from these database index optimization schemes in three ways. First, BOSC is application-independent and requires only minor modifications to the database indexes built on top of it. Second, BOSC speeds up the disk access performance through request batching and sequential commit, without requiring any additional data structure copying. Third, BOSC can handle arbitrary index modifications, i.e., insert, delete and in-place update, but most bulk update schemes are optimized for streaming inserts.

3. Update-Aware Disk Access Interface

The conventional disk access interface provides
`read(target_block_addr, dest_buf_addr)`

`write(target_block_addr, src_buf_addr)` for applications (including file system and DBMS) to read and write disk blocks, respectively. Under this interface, existing storage systems optimize disk write accesses by delaying and/or scheduling them to maximize their throughput, and optimizes disk read accesses by servicing them as soon as possible to minimize their latency.

A disk update involves a disk read of the target disk block and then a disk write of the same block after the block is brought into memory and modified. If a storage system could treat each disk update as an atomic operation, theoretically it can delay and schedule the disk reads associated with disk updates in the same way as it does with disk writes. However, to atomically service a disk update request, the storage system must be able to perform the request's intended update operation *without involving the application process issuing the disk update request.* To allow an application running on a storage system to explicitly declare a disk access request as a disk update request and supply the necessary information for the storage system to service it atomically, we propose an *update-aware* disk access primitive specific for disk updates, `modify(target_block_addr, ptr_modification, ptr_commit_function)`, which specifies the target disk block to be modified, a pointer to an application-specific data structure that includes all the information required by the requested modification, and a pointer to an application-specific call-back function that commits the actual modification to disk. This primitive is sufficiently general to accommodate disk update requests from such common storage applications as database index managers, including creating a new index entry, updating an existing index entry, and deleting an existing index entry.

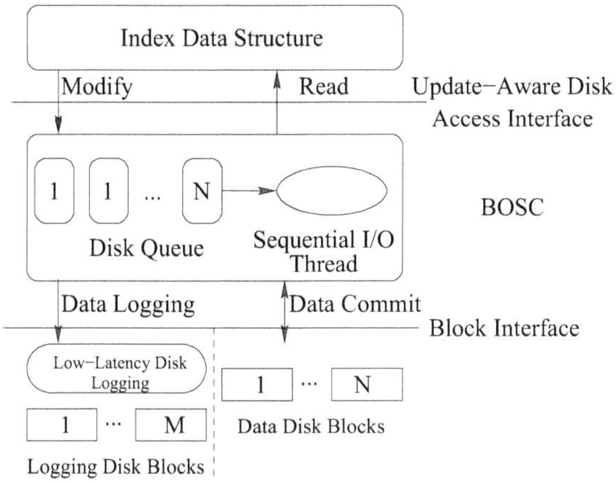

Figure 1. *BOSC associates with each disk block an in-memory update request queue. When BOSC receives a disk update request, it logs the request to disk, queues the request in the target block's associated update request queue, and performs the update operation only when the target disk block is brought into memory. BOSC brings disk blocks into memory sequentially according to their logical block addresses.*

In the proposed disk update primitive, the application-specific part of each disk update request, i.e., the internal organization of the data structure pointed to by `ptr_modification` and the internal logic of the function pointed by `ptr_commit_function`, is fully encapsulated. A storage system implementing the proposed interface carries out the requested modification of each disk update request by blindly invoking the specified function on the specified data structure, without requiring any knowledge about the data structure and function. Even the developers of BOSC's modify API do not need to know anything about BOSC's internals except following the guideline below when writing a call-back function: "It does not contain any calls to the modify API". In fact, such a storage system does not even need to differentiate among *create*, *update*, or *delete* operations. As a result, the update-aware disk access interface provides the underlying storage system the same flexibility of scheduling disk block create, disk block update, and disk block delete requests as disk block write requests, and thus the corresponding performance boost.

3.1 Caveats with Call-back Function

In the general case,running the call back functions in BOSC entails some security risks like a buggy or malicious program that mismanages system resources. However, these risks are reasonably low for our two target use cases.

1. When BOSC is used as a user-level library that allows a user-level application (e.g. DBMS) to directly manage a disk or disk partition, the background thread that invokes the call-back function runs at the user level and thus can at most compromise the user-level application itself.
2. When BOSC runs as a kernel module, only trusted software components such as file systems are allowed to use the BOSC interface, and the call-back functions they registered with BOSC are all kernel code. So, practically speaking, the fact that the background thread invokes these call-back functions in the kernel context does not really introduce any additional safety risks.

If an application calling an update function needs to receive the function's return code in order to proceed, it is NOT appropriate to implement such an update function on top of BOSC, because this use pattern is similar to a read function.In our experiences, there are many applications like dedupe and CDP that do not need the called update function to return results.

All the inputs that a call-back function in BOSC needs to run are either logged and put in the per-block queue or available on the corresponding fetched disk block. At recovery time, the per-block queues at the time of crash are reconstructed, and therefore, the call-back function for a given fetched disk block must be able to run after recovery. Here the assumption is that the registered function pointer remains valid across a system crash, which is the case because function pointers are virtual addresses and we assume application binaries are not modified and call-backed functions are all statically linked.

4. Batching Modifications with Sequential Commit

Figure 1 shows how BOSC leverages the update-aware disk access interface to aggregate disk update requests and reduce the overall physical disk I/O overhead. It applies a space-efficient low-latency disk logging technique to log each incoming disk update request, queues it in an in-memory per-block request queue, commits updates to disk asynchronously using mostly sequential disk I/O, and recovers from failures efficiently. The following subsections describe its design in more detail.

4.1 Low-Latency Disk Array Logging

Logging a disk update request to disk synchronously and then performing whatever operations triggered by the update asynchronously is a well-known technique. BOSC adopts this technique to service disk updates asynchronously and achieve high sustained disk update throughput, while delivering the same durability guarantee as synchronous disk updates.

Because the end-to-end throughput of BOSC is bounded by its synchronous disk logging performance, BOSC extends a low-latency disk logging technique called Trail [13] to be low-latency, space-efficient, and able to work on commodity disk arrays [31]. The key idea in this low-latency disk logging technique is to write an incoming disk block to where the disk head happens to be, which requires real-time knowledge of the disk head position of each log disk. To do so, BOSC statically extracts the physical disk geometry information from every log disk, and constantly keeps track of each log disk's disk head position at run time. Upon receiving a disk update request, BOSC prepares its log record, which includes the following information:

- A copy of the data structure pointed to by `ptr_modification`,
- A global sequence number for the current disk update request,
- A *back pointer* to the disk location of the log record that is temporally immediate before this record,
- A *global frontier*, which corresponds to the global sequence number of the *youngest* disk update request before which all disk update requests have been committed to disk, and
- A *local frontier*, which corresponds to the global sequence number of the *youngest* disk update request before which all disk update requests to the same target disk block of the current disk update request have been committed to disk.

To service physical disk write requests, BOSC maintains a separate disk request queue for each disk in the log disk array. At any point in time, one of the log disks serves as the *active* disk. In the beginning, BOSC randomly chooses one of the log disks as the active disk. Once a log disk becomes the active disk, it remains as the active disk until the waiting time of the oldest pending request in its disk request queue exceeds a threshold, T_{wait}. Whenever a new disk write request arrives, BOSC inserts the request to the active disk's queue as long as the waiting time of its oldest pending request is smaller than T_{wait} and there is enough free space in the current track to accommodate the new request; otherwise BOSC dispatches the request batch currently in the active disk's queue, chooses another log disk if available as the active disk and inserts the new request to the new active disk's request queue.

To select a new active disk for an incoming disk write request, BOSC considers the degree of possible batching and the write latency. When estimating a write request's write time on a log disk, BOSC takes into account the current position of the log disk's head and the possibility of batching the new request with others already in the disk's queue. For those log disks that are currently idle, BOSC only needs to consider the delay due to batching. A key design decision in BOSC is to dispatch a new write request to a log disk that allows as many disk write requests to be batched into one physical disk write operation as possible, rather than to one with the earliest write time for that request. However, BOSC uses T_{wait} to limit the size of batching and to ensure that the experienced latency of each incoming disk write request is always bounded.

Because of disk request batching, multiple log records could be merged into a physical disk write request when they are written to disk. Also, the actual disk location of each log record is only known at the last moment, i.e., right before they are written to disk, and BOSC keeps track of this information accurately to chain related log records together through their back pointers.

To track the log disks' disk head position, BOSC statically extracts the physical disk geometry information from every log disk, and constantly keeps track of each log disk's disk head position at run time. More concretely, after a physical disk write is completed, BOSC records the *LBA (Logical Block Address)* of its last sector, LBA_0, and its completion timestamp T_0. Assuming the disk head stays in the same track, when the next write arrives at T_1, BOSC estimates the disk head's current position $CurrentLBA$ using the following formula:

$$CurrentLBA = SPT \cdot \frac{(T_1 - T_0)\ mod\ RoTime}{RoTime} + LBA_0 \quad (1)$$

where SPT is the number of sectors in the current track, $RoTime$ is the disk's full rotation time. The final predicted position, $DestinationLBA$, is $CurrentLBA$ + $Lookahead$, where $Lookahead$ is an empirical value chosen to account for such delays as the controller delay and avoid a full rotation delay due to tracking errors.

4.2 Sequential Commit of Aggregated Updates

In addition to *log disks*, BOSC maintains a set of *data disks* to store application data and a set of in-memory disk update request queues, one for each data disk block. Upon receiving a disk update request, BOSC first checks if the target disk block is memory-resident; if it is, BOSC performs the update against the block immediately, otherwise BOSC appends the update request to the per-block disk update request queue associated with the request's target disk block and logs the update request to the log disk array; finally, BOSC returns control to the caller. Because of BOSC's low-latency disk logging, the perceived delay of each disk update request is relatively small, typically smaller than 1 msec. In the background a separate thread of BOSC constantly reads the data disks sequentially to fetch into memory those disk blocks whose pending request queue is non-empty. This thread goes from the beginning to the end of the data disks, and repeats the cycle. This is referred to as the *sequential commit cycle*. Every time the background BOSC thread brings in a disk block, it applies all the pending updates to the disk block and writes the block back to the disk. To further minimize the disk access overhead in this read-modify-write loop of commit processing, instead of processing one disk block at a time, BOSC physically reads and writes a continuous run of disk blocks, and commits pending updates on a run by run basis.

A disk block run corresponds to a contiguous sequence of disk blocks the percentage of which having a non-empty pending request queue is above a threshold (currently set to 0.5) and whose length is no greater than another threshold (currently set to 32 blocks). The first and last disk block in a run must have a non-empty pending request queue, and runs are disjoint. As one run is being fetched from a data disk, the background thread applies pending updates to another run that has previously been brought into memory, and pushes a third run, whose pending updates have already been applied, to another data disk. By pipelining the processing of runs, BOSC is able to eliminate unnecessary disk seek delays and reduce the number of disk rotations required to commit pending updates to a sequence of disk blocks to 2.

4.3 Recovery Processing

After a system crash, BOSC scans the log disks to discover uncommitted disk update requests, reconstructs the in-memory per-disk-block update request queues that exist immediately before the crash, and resumes its normal processing. This is similar to the idea employed in Aries [37] with some optimizations as described below. Note that BOSC chooses *not* to commit all uncommitted disk update requests to disk at recovery time. Instead, it merely aims to reconstruct the in-memory per-block update request queues and relies on BOSC's normal sequential commit mechanism to write them to disk. More concretely, BOSC's recovery procedure consists of the following steps:

1. Searching the log for the log record with the largest global sequence number,

2. Determining the *replay window* in the log that contains log records required for the reconstruction of per-disk-block update request queues, and
3. Parsing the log records in the replay window to reconstruct the per-block request queues.

To speed up Step (1), BOSC performs a binary search (rather than a sequential scan) of the tracks of the log disk array to track down the youngest log record, which is the last one to be inserted before the crash and thus corresponds to the *end* of the replay window. The binary search works because the disk logging proceeds one track by one track in a FIFO fashion.

Finding the *beginning* of the replay window is trivial because it actually corresponds to the *global frontier* field of the youngest log record, because all update requests associated with log records before the global frontier by definition have already been committed to disk. In Step (3), the log records in the replay window are traversed backwards from the end to the beginning. Given a log record, BOSC first assigns the value in its *local frontier* field to its target block's *local frontier* if the request queue associated with its target block is empty; then BOSC inserts the update request in the log record into its target block's request queue in the global sequence number order if the log record's global sequence number is larger than the target block's *local frontier*. By exploiting the global and local frontier information in log records, BOSC can avoid inserting a significant percentage of the log records in the replay window into per-block request queues.

4.4 Extensions

A straightforward way for a BOSC application like a database index manager to query if a record of a certain qualification exists in a disk block is to explicitly read in the block and scan it for records with the target qualification. However, if the desired record already exists in the disk block's pending update request queue, this approach may bring the target block into memory unnecessarily. To eliminate this unnecessary disk I/O, BOSC provides a query API that allows an application to query a specific disk block: `query(target_block_addr, ptr_query, ptr_query_function)`, where `target_block_addr` is the target disk block's ID, `ptr_query` is a pointer to a data structure containing the query's parameters, and `ptr_query_function` is a pointer to an application-specific call-back function that BOSC invokes to search the target disk block's memory-resident update requests queue and/or the target disk block itself if BOSC needs to fetch it into memory. When a disk block is read into memory because it is a target of a read request, BOSC applies all the block's pending updates to it before returning the block to the application issuing the read request. This API allows BOSC to double each in-memory per-block request queue as a cache for the associated disk block.

BOSC treats every disk update request it receives from an application as an independent I/O transaction, and is able to guarantee their durability across system failures by synchronous logging and recovery. When a system recovers from a crash, BOSC's recovery manager first restores the side effects of all the disk update requests that BOSC considers already committed, and then invokes the application's recovery logic. However, BOSC's I/O transaction is not equivalent to an application-level transaction. If a disk update request U is contained in an application-level transaction that the application's recovery manager thinks should be aborted, it should explicitly issue a compensating update request to undo U. Further, when a transaction calling a BOSC update function is committed after the called BOSC update function is ACKed, it is OK for the transaction to release all the locks and consider everything is done, even though the actual updates underlying the BOSC update function happen much later. The reason is that BOSC's recovery mechanism guarantees that all ACKed updates eventually happen.

The current BOSC design is mainly for directly attached disks. To generalize the BOSC idea to a network storage server requires leveraging the security mechanisms developed in the Active Disk [44] project.

5. BOSC-Based B^+ Tree

We have successfully ported B^+ tree index implementation from TPIE [3, 48] to the BOSC storage system prototype. TPIE is a software environment written in C++ that is designed specifically to minimize the disk I/O cost in the face of very large data sets.

The BOSC-based B^+ tree assumes all internal tree nodes and a small subset of leaf nodes are memory-resident. To service a modification query that inserts, deletes, or updates an index record, the BOSC-based B^+ tree first traverses the internal nodes to identify the leaf node containing the target index record, then constructs a disk update request record, and finally calls BOSC's disk update API using the target leaf node's disk block address, the associated update request record and the corresponding commit function as input arguments. Upon receiving such a disk update request, BOSC logs the request to the log disks first, commits the update to the target leaf node immediately if it is currently cached in memory, and queues the update request record in the corresponding in-memory request queue associated with the target leaf node otherwise.

To ensure atomicity, the BOSC-based B^+ tree acquires a lock on a leaf node before modifying it, and releases the lock after BOSC logs the associated disk update request and queues it in the associated request queue. It is safe to release the lock associated with the target leaf node of a modification query before physically committing the requested modification to disk, because BOSC *guarantees* the effects of a modification query's associated disk update request be visible to all subsequent queries that access the same leaf node, even in the presence of power failures.

An implicit assumption underlying the design of BOSC is that each disk update request modifies only its target disk block. However, this assumption does not always hold for B^+ tree, because a modification to a tree node, e.g., an insertion of a new index record, may trigger a restructuring of the tree and thus modifications to other tree nodes. If a disk update request that triggers additional disk updates is not processed immediately at the time when it is queued but deferred until the time when it is committed to disk, a disk block's in-memory request queue may grow unbounded, because the triggered restructuring may be recursive. This makes the update commit processing time of a disk block less predictable, and increases the response time of read query requests because servicing read query requests requires scanning of per-block update request queues.

To mitigate the performance overhead due to disk update requests that trigger additional disk updates, the BOSC-based B^+ tree maintains a count for the *effective* number of index records in each leaf node, including the pending delete and insert operations, and *proactively* triggers the split of a leaf or internal node when the effective number of records in a tree node exceeds a threshold, say 70%. If the leaf node to be split does not have any index records on disk, all the node's index records are in the associated update request queue and the BOSC-based B^+ tree performs the split without incurring any disk accesses. If the leaf node to be split has some index records on disk, the BOSC-based B^+ tree defers the split operation until the time when these records are brought into memory by the background BOSC thread.

6. Performance Evaluation

6.1 Evaluation Methodology

We have built a complete Linux-based BOSC prototype. This prototype supports the update-aware disk access interface as well as

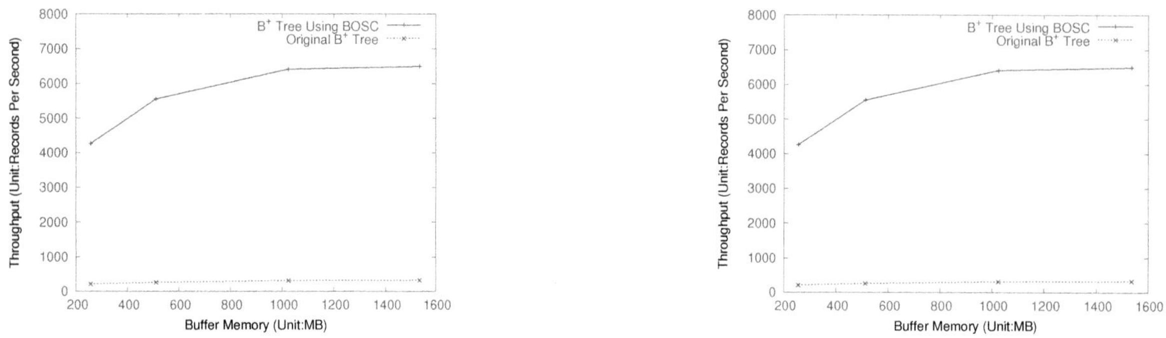

(a): BOSC vs. Vanilla for Random insert workload

(b): BOSC vs. Vanilla for Random update workload

Figure 2. *Comparison between the record insertion throughput of a BOSC-based B^+ tree implementation and a vanilla B^+ tree implementation based on the conventional disk read/write interface under the random insert workload (a) and random update workload (b) when the total amount of buffer memory is varied from 256 MB to 1.5 GB. The leaf block size is 64 KB, the record size is 64 B, and the initial index size is 16 GB.*

sequential commit of aggregated disk updates. On top of this BOSC prototype, we built a BOSC-based B^+ tree implementation, which is derived from TPIE and took about 2 man weeks.

To evaluate the efficiency of the BOSC-based B^+ tree, we used the following four synthetic workloads: (1) *sequential insert* workload, (2) *random insert* workload, (3) *clustered insert* workload, and (4) *random update* workload. In the sequential insert workload, records with sequentially increasing key values between 0 and 2^{60} are inserted into an initialized index. In the random insert workload, records with randomly generated key values, which fall between 0 and the pre-defined index size, are inserted into an initialized index. The clustered insert workload consists of a group of fixed-sized (32 by default) clusters of record insertions. Within each cluster, records with sequentially increasing key values are inserted. However, the key of the start record for each cluster is randomly generated. The random update workload updates random existing records that are inserted by the random insert workload.

The evaluation testbed for the BOSC prototype is a Dell PowerEdge 600SC machine with an Intel 2.4GHz CPU, 512KB L2 cache, 4GB memory, a 400MHz front-side bus, two Gigabit Ethernet interfaces and five 7200-RPM IBM Deskstar DTLA-307030 disks, four of which store the B^+ tree index records and one of which is dedicated to low-latency logging. We have done a separate study on the ratio of data disks to log disks, and concluded that "4 data disks and 1 logging disk" is the most performant configuration for a 5-disk storage system. Due to space constraints, the details of that study are omitted.

To be realistic, the initial B^+ tree must contain a substantial number of index records, on the order of tens of gigabytes of data. If we were to measure the throughput of the BOSC-based B^+ tree implementation against an initially empty B+ tree, then the measurement results for initial inserts/updates would be biased as they don't include such critical components as lock acquisition and tree traversal. However, it takes several hours to generate a properly initialized multi-gigabyte B^+ tree, and we need dozens of initialized B^+ trees, each with a different node or record size, in the entire evaluation study. So a fast B^+ tree initialization method is needed. The major bottleneck in the B^+ tree initialization process is the disk I/Os required to put leaf node data on disk. Because the actual contents of the leaf nodes are immaterial to our evaluation study, we could completely skip these disk I/Os in the initialization process and focus only on the creation of internal tree nodes. Therefore, when a B^+ tree is initialized this way, only its internal nodes are properly set up and its leaf nodes are only allocated on disk but not actually initialized. During the experiment run, whenever a leaf node is brought into memory for the first time, its content is filled with proper values at that point. The values filled are calculated on the fly, because the structure of the initialized B^+ tree and the key values in it are pre-determined. This B^+ tree initialization method proves invaluable to our evaluation study, because it saves us hundreds of hours, e.g., the time to initialize a 64-Gbyte B^+ tree is reduced from 36 hours to under 50 seconds.

6.2 Overall Performance Improvement

Figure 2 shows the throughputs of a vanilla B^+ tree implementation on a conventional disk read/write interface (with 5 data disks) and a BOSC-based B^+ tree implementation under the random insert and random update workload. The throughput of the vanilla B^+ tree implementation increases only slightly with the buffer memory because the poor locality in the random insert workload does not offer much room for leaf node caching to be effective. In contrast, the throughput of the B^+ tree implementation keeps improving with the increase in buffer memory size because more pending insertion requests can be accumulated in each sequential commit cycle. This improvement saturates at 1024 MB because the given buffer memory exceeds the product of the new record insertion rate and the sequential commit cycle length. When the buffer memory size is 1024 MB, the sustained throughput of the BOSC-based B^+ tree implementation under the random insert workload reaches around 6410 requests/second, which is *20 times* higher than that of the vanilla B^+ tree implementation using the conventional disk read/write interface (311 records/second). When buffer memory is not the performance bottleneck, the throughput of the BOSC-based B^+ tree implementation is mainly bound by the physical disk I/O efficiency in the sequential commit process.

The performance of the BOSC-based B^+ tree implementation under the random update workload is almost the same as that under the random insert workload, because in both workloads the accesses to the index pages are random and consequently their performance is bottlenecked by disk I/O. Figure 2(b) shows that the throughput improvement of the BOSC-based B^+ tree implementation over the vanilla B^+ tree implementation is the same as in Figure 2(a). These two results conclusively demonstrates BOSC is as efficient for an *update-in-place* workload as for an *insert-only* workload. In contrast, most previous B^+ tree optimizations [1, 6, 21] are only applicable to insert-only workloads.

The two key performance-boosting features of BOSC are low-latency logging and asynchronous sequential commit using multiple request queues. A simpler alternative to BOSC's low-latency logging is logging by appending to the end of a file. A simpler alternative to asynchronous sequential commit is to queue all update requests in a single queue and batch-commit the head N requests in the queue according to their target disk block addresses. To evaluate the performance contribution of each of these two features, we compare the throughputs of the following four B^+ tree variants. The first variant, called *One-Queue-Append*, appends each incoming update request to the end of a log file and inserts it into a single FIFO queue. The second variant, called *One-Queue-Trail*, uses low-latency logging to log each incoming update request and inserts it into a single FIFO queue. The third variant, called *Multi-Queue-Append*, appends each incoming update request to the end of a log file and inserts it into the per-block queue associated with its target block. The fourth variant is BOSC, which uses low-latency logging to log each incoming update request and inserts it into the per-block queue associated with its target block.

To demonstrate the performance benefits of BOSC under more realistic workloads, we collected a trace of access requests to the index engine of the MySQL DBMS under the TPC-C workload [39], where the number of warehouses is set to 20, 40, 60 and 80. Each trace entry includes the type (e.g. read, update, delete and insert) and the key/data information of each request issued to the index engine. For each warehouse number, we ran the TPC-C workload for three hours to generate an index of the size 16 GB, 32 GB, 48 GB, and 64 GB, respectively, and collected the corresponding access request trace. For each index access trace collected, we replayed the first half to create an initial image of the database index, and then replayed the second half and measured the throughput of the input requests in the second half of the trace.

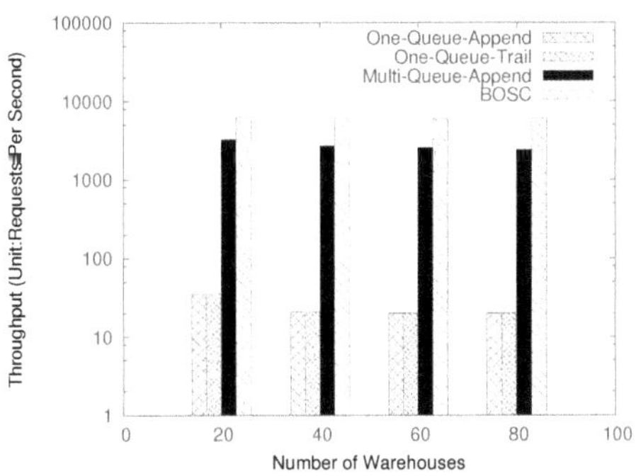

Figure 3. *Throughput comparison among the BOSC-based B^+ tree implementation, the B^+ tree implementation with multiple request queues and append-only logging, the B^+ tree implementation with one request queue and append-only logging, and the B^+ tree implementation with one request queue and low-latency logging under the four index access traces collected by running the TPC-C workload with different warehouse numbers against MySQL. The Y axis is in log scale. The leaf node size is 64 KB and the buffer memory is 1 GB.*

Figure 3 compares the throughputs of these four B^+ tree implementation variants under four different TPC-C traces. Across all warehouse parameters, as expected the BOSC-based B^+ tree implementation tops the four variants with the best throughput. For example, when the warehouse number is 80, the throughput of the BOSC-based B^+ tree is 6058 requests/second, as compared to 20 requests/second for the *One-Queue-Trail* scheme, and 2386 requests/second for the *Multi-Queue-Append* scheme. The performance gain of BOSC over the *Multi-Queue-Append* scheme comes from low-latency logging, which maximizes logging efficiency and thus the overall update throughput. The fact that the BOSC-based B^+ tree implementation is more than 2.5 times faster than the *Multi-Queue-Append* variant (the Y axis is in log scale) shows the importance of lower logging latency. The BOSC-based B^+ tree implementation is more than 300 times faster than the *One-Queue-Trail* variant, which shows the importance of sequential commit as enabled by multiple request queues is much more than low-latency logging. There is no noticeable performance difference between the *One-Queue-Trail* variant and the *One-Queue-Append* variant because both are bottlenecked by the excessive disk access overhead associated with committing pending updates to disk.

Larger warehouse number corresponds to larger database index size and lower access locality. The fact that the throughput of the BOSC-based B^+ tree implementation remains largely independent of the warehouse number suggests that BOSC enables a B^+ tree implementation to exhibit good throughput without relying on the input workload's locality characteristics. Overall, under the TPC-C workload, the BOSC-based B^+ tree implementation is 300 times faster than that of the vanilla B^+ tree implementation when there are 80 warehouses, and is 180 times faster when there are 20 warehouses.

6.3 Sensitivity Study

In this section, we evaluate the impacts of the leaf node size, the index record size, the total index size and the buffer memory size on the performance of the BOSC-based B^+ tree implementation. Each experiment run starts with a fixed-sized initial B^+ tree and continues with index record insertions/updates until the first *sequential commit cycle* is completed. At that point, we measured the total number of insertions/updates and the elapsed time.

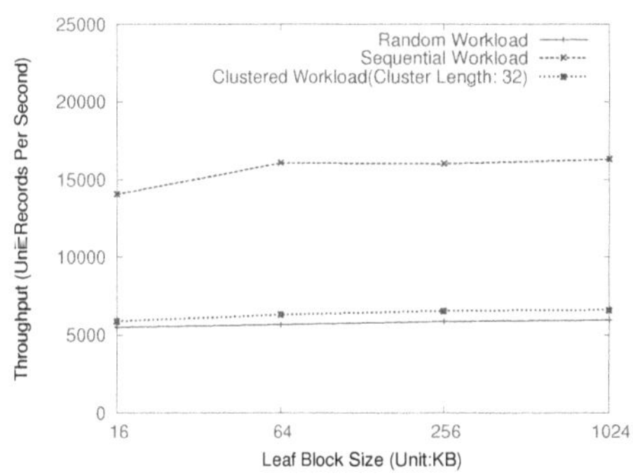

Figure 4. *Record insertion throughput of a BOSC-based B^+ tree implementation under the sequential insertion, clustered insertion, and random insertion workload when the leaf node size is varied from 16 KB to 1024 KB. The X axis is log-scale. The Y axis is the number of new records inserted per second. The memory allocated for all per-block request queues is 1 GB, the record size is 64 B, and the initial index size is 64GB.*

In evaluating the impact of different parameters on the insert/update rate, there are 3 factors to consider: (1) the disk I/O efficiency, which reflects how effectively the background commit thread removes unnecessary disk access overhead, (2) the degree of batching, which determines how many requests over which each disk I/O operation's cost is amortized, and (3) the CPU overhead associated with traversing from the B^+ tree's root to the target leaf node of a given insert/update request, and queuing pending requests.

The throughputs of the BOSC-based B^+ tree under the random insertion, sequential insertion and clustered insertion workload when the leaf node size varies are shown in Figure 4. The throughput performance of the BOSC-based B^+ tree index under the sequential insert workload is much higher than that under the random insert workload for two reasons. First, the average number of pending requests in each queue at the time of commit is higher under the sequential insert workload than that under the random insert workload. Second, the CPU overhead of processing insert/update requests is lower under the sequential insert workload than that under the random insert workload because of fewer L2 cache misses. For the random insert workload, it takes around 140

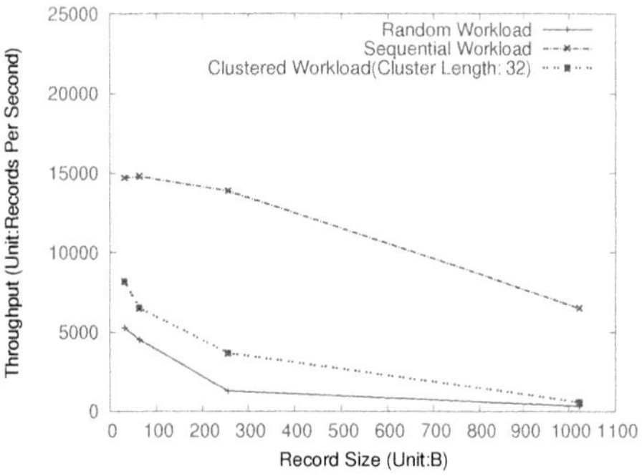

Figure 5. *Record insertion throughput of a BOSC-based B^+ tree implementation under the sequential insertion, clustered insertion, and random insertion workload when the index record size is varied from 64 B to 1024 B.*

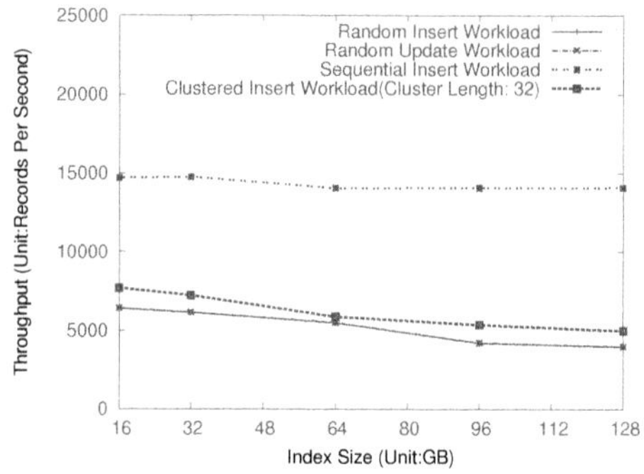

Figure 7. *Record insertion/update throughput of a BOSC-based B^+ tree implementation under the sequential insertion, clustered insertion, random insertion and random update workload when the initial index size is varied from 16 GB to 128 GB.*

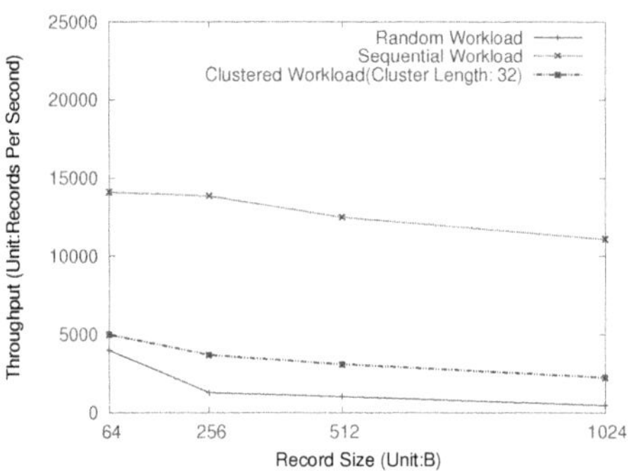

Figure 6. *Record insertion throughput of a BOSC-based B^+ tree implementation under the sequential insertion, clustered insertion, and random insertion workload when the index record size increases from 64 B to 1 KB, and the leaf node size also varies proportionally so that the ratio between the two is fixed.*

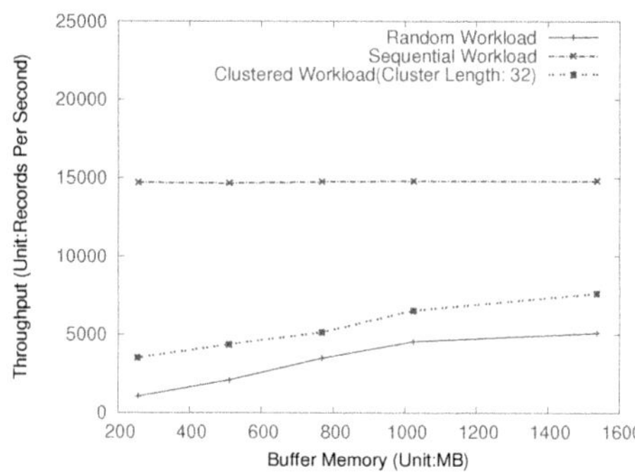

Figure 8. *Record insertion throughput of a BOSC-based B^+ tree implementation under the sequential insertion, clustered insertion, and random insertion workload when the BOSC's buffer memory is varied from 512 MB to 1536 MB.*

micro-seconds to complete an insertion request, whereas it takes only 67 micro-seconds for the sequential insert workload.

As the size of the test B^+ tree index's leaf block is increased, more index records can be packed into each leaf block, the degree of batching in terms of number of pending requests per disk block fetched is increased and so is the throughput of the BOSC-based B^+ tree index, as shown in Figure 4. This effect is more pronounced under the clustered and sequential insert workload than under the random insert workload, because there is not much batching in the random insert workload anyway.

Figure 5 shows that, as the size of the test B^+ tree's index record is increased, fewer index records can fit within each leaf block, and the degree of batching in terms of number of pending requests per disk block is decreased. The throughput degradation for the clustered insert and random insert workload is directly correlated with the decrease in the degree of batching, but that for the sequential insert workload is mainly due to additional L2 cache misses during insert request processing.

If both leaf block size and index record size are increased while keeping their ratio constant, the number of index records per leaf block remains the same, but the degree of batching in terms of number of pending requests per fixed-sized disk I/O is still decreased, e.g., the effective number of pending requests committed per 100-KB disk I/O decreases as the leaf block size is increased from 8KB to 64KB, and so is the throughput of the BOSC-based B^+ tree index, as shown in Figure 6.

As the total B^+ tree index size is increased, the average number of pending requests accumulated in each per-block queue within one sequential commit cycle becomes smaller, the degree of batching at the time of commit is thus decreased, and so is the throughput of the BOSC-based B^+ tree index, as shown in Figure 7. The throughput impact of the index size is less obvious under the sequential insert workload because the degree of batching remains largely constant regardless of the index size. Figure 7 also shows that the performance of the BOSC-based B^+ tree implementation under the random update workload is almost the same as that under the random insert workload, because in both cases accesses to the index pages are random and consequently their performance is bottlenecked by disk I/O.

As the buffer memory for per-block request queues is increased, the number of pending requests at the time of commit is increased, the degree of batching is increased, and the overall throughput under the random insert and clustered insert workload are increased, as shown in Figure 8. The performance impact of buffer memory size is minimal for the sequential insert workload because its degree of batching is already quite high and largely unaffected by the buffer memory size.

6.4 Read Query Latency

Although BOSC is designed to optimize the throughput of low-locality update-intensive workloads, it does *not* degrade the latency of read accesses to database indexes built on top it. This is unusual, because many previously proposed B^+ tree implementations opti-

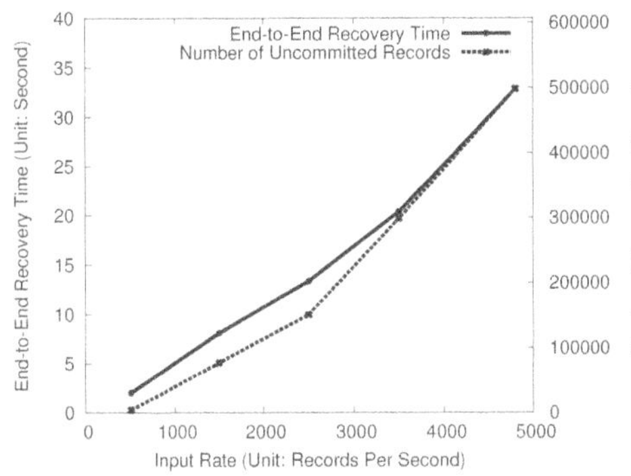

Figure 9. *The total recovery time for a 64-GB B^+ index and the number of uncommitted pending update requests in the replay window as the input update request rate is varied before the crash.*

mized for the same workload tend to trade better update throughput for longer read latency.

Index Structure	Point Query (Unit: msec)		Range Query (Unit: msec)	
	With BOSC	Without BOSC	With BOSC	Without BOSC
B^+ Tree	10.20	10.19	15.75	15.76

Table 1. *The average latency of Point and Range queries for the B^+ tree implementations with and without BOSC. The leaf block size for all index structures is 4 KB, and the buffer memory is 256 MB.*

Table 1 shows the average latency of 100 Point and Range queries against a pre-populated B^+ tree using the B^+ tree implementations with and without BOSC. For *point* queries, the key values are generated randomly from the underlying key space. For *range* queries, the starting key values are generated randomly from the key space and the maximum range size is fixed at 1,000. There is no statistically significant difference between the average read query latency of the BOSC-based B^+ tree implementation and that of the vanilla B^+ tree implementation, even though the read-path processing in BOSC requires an additional step of searching the target block's in-memory request queue. BOSC's caching has little effect on it's read performance because the locality in the input workload is relatively low, as evidenced by the relatively large average latency. This result demonstrates that the update/insert performance gain of BOSC does not come at the expense of read performance degradation, which is often the case for other B^+ tree optimizations [1, 6, 21].

6.5 Logging and Recovery Performance

BOSC relies on low-latency logging to provide the same durability guarantee as synchronous disk updates. The average latency of logging a 4-Kbyte block to an IDE disk array is under 0.5 msec, about an order of magnitude smaller than conventional disk logging implementations and the fastest ever reported in the literature. In addition, through aggressive disk request batching, BOSC is able to log more than 50000 per-insertion-request log records per second, or about 20 μs per log record. Finally, even with such high logging efficiency, BOSC is able to keep the log disks' space utilization above 70%.

There are two major steps in BOSC's recovery procedure: (1) identifying the youngest log record and (2) reconstructing the in-memory per-block request queues by analyzing the log records between the youngest log record and its associated global frontier. Because Step (1) uses a binary search through the logging disk array, it typically takes between 0.8 to 0.9 seconds to complete.

The time required by Step (2) depends on the number of uncommitted pending updates, which in turn depends on the input request rate. To evaluate how the total recovery time scales with the input rate, we ran a random update workload with varying input request rates to update records in a 64-GB B^+ tree with the following configuration: 256-MB buffer memory, and 16-byte index record. In each run, we issued about 64 million update requests, shut down the B^+ tree machine, restarted it and measured its recovery time.

Figure 9 shows that the total recovery time of a BOSC-based B^+ tree implementation indeed increases with the input request rate, because higher input request rate populates the per-block request queues faster and accumulates more uncommitted pending updates in the request queues when the system is shut down. These pending updates need to be scanned and reconstructed in Step (2) of the recovery process. As expected, increase in the total recovery time is roughly linearly proportional to increase in the number of uncommitted pending updates, as shown in the right Y axis of Figure 9.

6.6 Applications of BOSC

We have built two applications on top of BOSC: an index manager for a continuous data protection (CDP) system called *Mariner* and a garbage collector for a data de-duplication engine. This subsection shows BOSC's effectiveness in improving their performance.

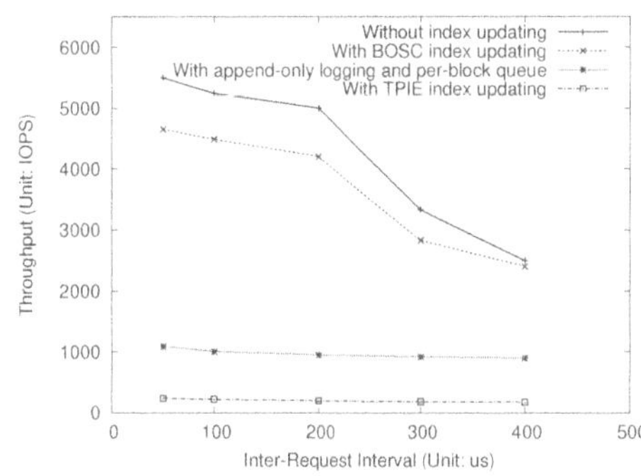

Figure 10. *The block-level logging throughputs of four* Mariner *variants: The first variant does not update any index; the second variant updates the map index using a BOSC-based B^+ tree; the third variant updates the map index using a B^+ tree that uses append-only logging and multiple per-block queues; The fourth variant updates the map index using a vanilla B^+ tree.*

6.6.1 Index Update for Continuous Data Protection

Mariner [31] is a Continuous Data Protection (CDP) system that logs every block-level disk write to a protected storage server, and creates a new version for a logical disk block whenever it is over-written. *Mariner* maintains a map between each logical block number and its physical block numbers, each corresponding to a distinct version. Upon receiving a block-level disk write request, *Mariner* logs the write request's payload to create a new version and inserts a new entry into the map.

To measure the overall disk write logging throughput of *Mariner*, we ran a kernel thread inside *Mariner* that constantly generates new 4KB block versions, with their logical block numbers uniformly and randomly distributed in $[0, 2^{41}]$. During the experiment run, there are totally 20 GB worth of new block versions logged and 935 MB ($20GB * \frac{24}{512}$) worth of indexed map entries inserted. The buffer memory for BOSC's per-block update request queuing is set to 64 MB and the leaf page cache for TPIE is also set to 64 MB.

The disk write logging performance of *Mariner* when the indexed map is not updated at all is mainly determined by the overhead of logging new block versions, and thus represents its performance upper bound. As shown in Figure 10, compared with the upper bound, the throughput degradation due to the indexed map update is up to 95% when the indexed map is implemented as a vanilla B^+ tree (i.e. TPIE), is up to 80% when the indexed map is implemented as a B^+ tree using file-level append-only logging and per-block request queuing, and is no more than 15% when the indexed map is implemented as a BOSC-based B^+ tree. This result demonstrates that the BOSC-based B^+ tree implementation successfully removes indexed map update as a performance bottleneck of *Mariner*. Across these three variants, the throughput degradation decreases with the increase in the inter-request interval, because the additional indexed map update overhead becomes less significant when the input load is less demanding. In terms of absolute performance, the disk write logging throughput of the *Mariner* version using a BOSC-based B^+ tree is more than 45 times higher than that of the *Mariner* version using a TPIE-based B^+ tree, and is more than 3 times better than that of the *Mariner* version using a BOSC-based B^+ tree without low-latency logging.

6.6.2 Garbage Collection for Data Backup

In a data backup system with data de-duplication capability, a physical block may be referenced by multiple backup snapshots. Because a backup snapshot typically has a finite retention period, the number of references to a physical block varies over time. When a physical block is no longer referenced by any backup snapshot, it should be reclaimed and reused.

When a logical block is modified, it is going to be backed up in the next backup run, and the information required to back up this logical block includes its logical block number(LBN), the physical block number (PBN) of the physical block previously mapped to this LBN (BPBN), and the PBN of the physical block currently mapped to this LBN (CPBN). The data backup system uses the logical block's payload to determine whether it is a duplicate of some existing physical block (whose PBN is DPBN) in the data backup system. Therefore, backing up a logical block triggers the updates of the GC-related metadata of up to three physical blocks. Assume a data backup system manages a 4-PB physical disk space with a 4-KB block size, then there are one billion physical blocks, and we need an array of one billion entries to record their GC-related metadata. Obviously this GC metadata array (GMA) cannot fit into the memory, and there is no reason to expect much locality in the accesses to this array.

To remove the performance bottleneck due to GMA updates, we partitioned the GMA into 128-Kbyte chunks, and queued each GMA update in the corresponding per-chunk queue after logging it. Then we used one or multiple background commit threads to commit the updates to those chunks that have enough pending updates to disk using largely sequential disk I/O. When multiple commit threads are in action, they work on disjoint but neighboring chunks simultaneously. We compared this with a vanilla GMA update implementation, which buffers GMA update requests in a queue, and uses a background thread to commit them on a first come first serve basis. The evaluation machine consists of two quad-core 3.4GHz Intel Core i-7 processor, 14GB of RAM, five 7200-RPM WD Caviar blue hard disks of 1TB each, one for the system disk, two for storing the GMA on a striped software RAID with a 64-Kbyte stripe unit size, and the remaining two for storing the deduplication fingerprints on a striped software RAID.

In Table 2, the throughput of the data deduplication engine without any GMA updates (the last column) sets an upper bound because it corresponds to a zero-cost GMA update scheme. When the BOSC-based GMA update scheme uses a single commit thread, the end-to-end throughput of the deduplication engine is decreased to 19% of the upper bound. By increasing the number of commit threads to 4 and therefore the disk I/O concurrency, it increases the end-to-end throughput to 97% of the upper bound. The number of commit threads represent a tradeoff between disk access locality and disk I/O concurrency. Empirically, the optimal number of commit threads for our experiment set-up seems to be 4. However, regardless of the number of commit threads used, the end-to-end throughput of the data deduplication engine using the vanilla GMA update scheme never exceeds 5% of the upper bound.

Commit Threads	*Dedupe + vanilla GC*	*Dedupe + BOSC-based GC*	*Dedupe without GC*
1	4441	40821	216938
2	4534	202582	216938
4	7583	209721	216938
10	6134	203363	216938

Table 2. *End-to-end throughputs(fingerprints processed/second) of a data deduplication engine with multiple garbage collector configurations.*

7. Conclusion

Conventional storage systems are seriously challenged when facing input workloads that are update-intensive and have low access locality. Such workloads are not uncommon. For example, the back-end databases in typical Internet E-commerce services are routinely bombarded with workloads with intensive update requests (e.g., due to order processing) that involve random disk accesses (e.g., due to a large number of concurrent users). As of now, no good solution can effectively handle such workloads without resorting to special caching hardware such as battery-backed DRAM. This paper describes a simple but effective solution to this problem, which consists of (1) an *update-aware* disk access interface and (2) an efficient batched processing strategy that completes pending update requests using sequential disk I/O called BOSC. We have successfully built a BOSC prototype that embodies these two ideas, and empirically demonstrated its efficiency by showing that the update request throughput of a BOSC-based B^+ tree implementations is more than an order of magnitude faster than that of a vanilla B^+ tree built on top of the conventional disk access interface. In addition, BOSC is able to deliver this performance improvement while providing the same durability guarantee as servicing update requests synchronously. In summary, the specific research contributions of this work include

- A new disk access interface that supports disk update as a first-class primitive and enables the specification of application-specific callback functions to be invoked by the underlying storage system,
- A highly efficient storage system architecture that effectively commits pending update requests in a batched fashion, and drastically improves the physical disk access efficiency by using only *sequential* disk I/O to bring in the requests' target disk blocks, and
- A complete prototype implementation of the BOSC architecture and a comprehensive evaluation of this prototype by measuring and analyzing the performance results taken on a BOSC-based B^+ tree and two applications built on BOSC.

References

[1] L. Arge. The buffer tree: A new technique for optimal i/o-algorithms (extended abstract). In *WADS '95: Proceedings of the 4th International Workshop on Algorithms and Data Structures*, pages 334–345, London, UK, 1995. Springer-Verlag.

[2] L. Arge, K. Hinrichs, J. Vahrenhold, and J. S. Vitter. Efficient bulk operations on dynamic r-trees. *Algorithmica*, 33(1):104–128, 2002.

[3] L. Arge, O. Procopiuc, and J. S. Vitter. Implementing I/O-Efficient Data Structures Using TPIE. In *ESA '02: Proceedings of the 10th Annual European Symposium on Algorithms*, pages 88–100, London, UK, 2002. Springer-Verlag.

[4] L. N. Bairavasundaram, M. Sivathanu, A. C. Arpaci-Dusseau, and R. H. Arpaci-Dusseau. X-RAY: A Non-Invasive Exclusive Caching Mechanism for RAIDs. In *ISCA '04: Proceedings of the 31st annual international symposium on Computer architecture*, page 176, Washington, DC, USA, 2004. IEEE Computer Society.

[5] M. A. Bender, G. S. Brodal, R. Fagerberg, D. Ge, S. He, H. Hu, J. Iacono, and A. Lopez-Ortiz. The cost of cache-oblivious searching. In *Proceedings of FOCS 2003*, pages p. 271–282, 2003.

[6] M. A. Bender, E. D. Demaine, and M. Farach-Colton. Cache-oblivious b-trees. In *SIAM Journal of Computing*, volume 35(2), pages p. 341–358, 2005.

[7] M. A. Bender, J. T. Fineman, S. Gilbert, and B. C. Kuszmaul. Concurrent cache-oblivious b-trees. In *Proceedings of SPAA 2005*, pages p. 228–237, 2005.

[8] L. Biveinis, S. Šaltenis, and C. S. Jensen. Main-memory operation buffering for efficient R-tree update. In *VLDB 2007: Proceedings of the 33rd International Conference on Very Large Data Bases*, pages 591–602. VLDB Endowment, 2007.

[9] D. D. Chamberlin, M. M. Astrahan, M. W. Blasgen, J. N. Gray, W. F. King, B. G. Lindsay, R. Lorie, J. W. Mehl, T. G. Price, F. Putzolu, P. G. Selinger, M. Schkolnick, D. R. Slutz, I. L. Traiger, B. W. Wade, and R. A. Yost. A History and Evaluation of System R. *Communications of the ACM*, 24(10):632–646, 1981.

[10] C. Chao, R. English, D. Jacobson, A. Stepanov, and J. Wilkes. Mime: A High-Performance Parallel Storage Device with Strong Recovery Guarantees. Technical Report HPL CSP 92 9 rev 1, HewlettPackard Laboratories Report, November 1992.

[11] Y.-Y. Chen, Q. Gan, and T. Suel. I/O-Efficient Techniques for Computing PageRank. In *CIKM '02: Proceedings of the 11th International Conference on Information and Knowledge Management*, pages 549–557, New York, NY, USA, 2002. ACM Press.

[12] Z. Chen, Y. Zhang, Y. Zhou, H. Scott, and B. Schiefer. Empirical Evaluation of Multi-level Buffer Cache Collaboration for Storage Systems. *SIGMETRICS Perform. Eval. Rev.*, 33(1):145–156, 2005.

[13] T. Chiueh and L. Huang. Track-Based Disk Logging. In *DSN '02: Proceedings of the 2002 International Conference on Dependable Systems and Networks*, pages 429–438, Washington, DC, USA, 2002. IEEE Computer Society.

[14] S. Chutani, O. T. Anderson, M. L. Kazar, B. W. Leverett, W. A. Mason, and R. N. Sidebotham. The Episode File System. In *Proceedings of the USENIX Winter 1992 Technical Conference*, pages 43–60, San Fransisco, CA, USA, 1992. USENIX Association.

[15] T. P. P. Council. *TPC Benchmark C Standard Specification*, volume 1 and 2. Waterside Associates, Fremont, CA, 1.0.a edition, Aug, 1996.

[16] A. Dan and D. Towsley. An Approximate Analysis of the LRU and FIFO Buffer Replacement Schemes. *SIGMETRICS Perform. Eval. Rev.*, 18(1):143–152, 1990.

[17] A. Devulapalli, D. Dalessandro, P. Wyckoff, and N. Ali. Attribute Storage Design for Object-based Storage Devices. In *MSST '07: Proceedings of the 24th IEEE Conference on Mass Storage Systems and Technologies*, pages 263–268, Washington, DC, USA, 2007. IEEE Computer Society.

[18] G. R. Ganger, M. K. McKusick, C. A. N. Soules, and Y. N. Patt. Soft Updates: a Solution to the Metadata Update Problem in File Systems. *ACM Transactions on Computer Systems (TOCS)*, 18(2):127–153, 2000.

[19] G. Graefe. Sorting and Indexing with Partitioned B-Trees. In *Conference on Innovative Data Systems Research*, 2003.

[20] G. Graefe. Write-optimized B-trees. In *VLDB 2004: Proceedings of the Thirtieth International Conference on Very Large Data Bases*, pages 672–683. VLDB Endowment, 2004.

[21] G. Graefe. B-tree Indexes for High Update Rates. *SIGMOD Rec.*, 35(1):39–44, 2006.

[22] R. Hagmann. Reimplementing the Cedar File System using Logging and Group Commit. In *SOSP '87: Proceedings of the 11th ACM Symposium on Operating Systems Principles*, pages 155–162, New York, NY, USA, 1987. ACM Press.

[23] T. Haveliwala. Efficient Computation of PageRank. Technical Report 1999-31, Stanford University, Stanford University, Feburary 1999.

[24] L. O. X. B. He, M. J. Kosa, and S. L. Scott. A Unified Multiple-Level Cache for High Performance Storage Systems. In *MASCOTS '05: Proceedings of the 13th IEEE International Symposium on Modeling, Analysis, and Simulation of Computer and Telecommunication Systems*, pages 143–152, Washington, DC, USA, 2005. IEEE Computer Society.

[25] J. Hirai, S. Raghavan, H. Garcia-Molina, and A. Paepcke. WebBase: a Repository of Web Pages. In *Proceedings of the 9th International World Wide Web Conference on Computer Networks : the International Journal of Computer and Telecommunications Networking*, pages 277–293, Amsterdam, The Netherlands, 2000. North-Holland Publishing Co.

[26] G. F. Hughes and J. F. Murray. Reliability and Security of RAID Storage Systems and D2D Archives using SATA Disk Drives. *Transactions on Storage*, 1(1):95–107, 2005.

[27] *The InnoDB Storage Engine*.

[28] N. P. Jouppi. Cache Write Policies and Performance. In *ISCA '93: Proceedings of the 20th annual international symposium on Computer architecture*, pages 191–201, New York, NY, USA, 1993. ACM Press.

[29] V. Y. K. Kher. Decentralized Authentication Mechanisms for Object-based Storage Devices. In *SISW '03: Proceedings of the Second IEEE International Security in Storage Workshop*, page 1, Washington, DC, USA, 2003. IEEE Computer Society.

[30] M. Lifantsev and T. Chiueh. I/O-Conscious Data Preparation for Large-Scale Web Search Engines. In *VLDB '2002: Proceedings of the 32nd International Conference on Very Large Data Bases*, pages 382–393, Hongkong, China, 2002. VLDB Endowment.

[31] M. Lu, S. Lin, and T. Chiueh. Efficient Logging and Replication Techniques for Comprehensive Data Protection. In *MSST '07: Proceedings of the 24th IEEE Conference on Mass Storage Systems and Technologies*, pages 171–184, Washington, DC, USA, 2007. IEEE Computer Society.

[32] C. R. Lumb, J. Schindler, and G. R. Ganger. Freeblock Scheduling Outside of Disk Firmware. In *FAST '02: Proceedings of the Conference on File and Storage Technologies*, pages 275–288, Berkeley, CA, USA, 2002. USENIX Association.

[33] C. Malakapalli and V. Gunturu. Evaluation of SCSI over TCP/IP and SCSI over Fibre Channel Connections. In *HOTI '01: Proceedings of the The Ninth Symposium on High Performance Interconnects (HOTI '01)*, page 87, Washington, DC, USA, 2001. IEEE Computer Society.

[34] M. K. McKusick and G. R. Ganger. Soft Updates: a Technique for Eliminating Most Synchronous Writes in the Fast Filesystem. In *ATEC'99: Proceedings of the Annual Technical Conference on 1999 USENIX Annual Technical Conference*, pages 24–24, Berkeley, CA, USA, 1999. USENIX Association.

[35] S. Melnik, S. Raghavan, B. Yang, and H. Garcia-Molina. Building a Distributed Full-Text Index for the Web. In *WWW '01: Proceedings of the 10th International Conference on World Wide Web*, pages 396–406, New York, NY, USA, 2001. ACM Press.

[36] S. Mitra, W. W. Hsu, and M. Winslett. Trustworthy Keyword Search for Regulatory-Compliant Records Retention. In *VLDB '2006: Proceedings of the 32nd International Conference on Very Large Data Bases*, pages 1001–1012. VLDB Endowment, 2006.

[37] C. Mohan, D. Haderle, B. Lindsay, H. Pirahesh, and P. Schwarz. Aries: A transaction recovery method supporting fine-granularity locking and partial rollbacks using write-ahead logging. In *ACM Transactions on Database Systems, vol. 17*, pages 94–162, 1992.

[38] E. B. Nightingale, K. Veeraraghavan, P. M. Chen, and J. Flinn. Rethink the Sync. In *OSDI'2006: Proceedings of the 7th conference on USENIX*

Symposium on Operating Systems Design and Implementation, pages 1–14, Berkeley, CA, USA, 2006. USENIX Association.

[39] Open Source Development Labs (OSDL). Database Test Suite: DBT-[1,2,3,4,5]. http://osdldbt.sourceforge.net/, 2003.

[40] C. U. Orji and J. A. Solworth. Write-Only Disk Cache Experiments on Multiple Surface Disks. In *ICCI '92: Proceedings of the Fourth International Conference on Computing and Information*, pages 385–388, Washington, DC, USA, 1992. IEEE Computer Society.

[41] L. Page, S. Brin, R. Motwani, and T. Winograd. The PageRank Citation Ranking: Bringing Order to the Web. Technical Report 1999-66, Stanford Digital Library Technologies Project, 1998.

[42] O. Procopiuc, P. Agarwal, L. Arge, and J. Vitter. Bkd-tree: A dynamic scalable kd-tree, 2002.

[43] B. Ribeiro-Neto, E. S. Moura, M. S. Neubert, and N. Ziviani. Efficient Distributed Algorithms to Build Inverted Files. In *SIGIR '99: Proceedings of the 22nd Annual International ACM SIGIR Conference on Research and Development in Information Retrieval*, pages 105–112, New York, NY, USA, 1999. ACM Press.

[44] E. Riedel, C. Faloutsos, G. A. Gibson, and D. Nagle. Active disks: Remote execution for network-attached storage. Technical Report CMU-CS-97-198, Parallel Data Lab, Carnegie Mellon University, December 1997.

[45] M. Rosenblum and J. K. Ousterhout. The Design and Implementation of a Log-Structured File System. *ACM Transactions on Computer Systems (TOCS)*, 10(1):26–52, 1992.

[46] R. Stata, K. Bharat, and F. Maghoul. The Term Vector Database: Fast Access to Indexing Terms for Web Pages. In *Proceedings of the 9th International World Wide Web Conference on Computer Networks : the International Journal of Computer and Telecommunications Networking*, pages 247–255, Amsterdam, The Netherlands, 2000. North-Holland Publishing Co.

[47] M. Stonebraker. The Design of the POSTGRES Storage System. In *VLDB '87: Proceedings of the 13th International Conference on Very Large Data Bases*, pages 289–300, San Francisco, CA, USA, 1987. Morgan Kaufmann Publishers Inc.

[48] D. E. Vengroff and J. S. Vitter. I/O-Efficient Algorithms and Environments. *ACM Computing Surveys (CSUR)*, 28(4):212, 1996.

[49] W. Wang, Y. Zhao, and R. Bunt. HyLog: A High Performance Approach to Managing Disk Layout. In *FAST '04: Proceedings of the 3rd USENIX Conference on File and Storage Technologies*, pages 145–158, Berkeley, CA, USA, 2004. USENIX Association.

[50] C. Zhang, X. Yu, A. Krishnamurthy, and R. Y. Wang. Configuring and Scheduling an Eager-Writing Disk Array for a Transaction Processing Workload. In *FAST '02: Proceedings of the 1st USENIX Conference on File and Storage Technologies*, page 24, Berkeley, CA, USA, 2002. USENIX Association.

Providing Safe, User Space Access to Fast, Solid State Disks

Adrian M. Caulfield Todor I. Mollov Louis Alex Eisner
Arup De Joel Coburn Steven Swanson

Computer Science and Engineering Department
University of California, San Diego
{acaulfie,leisner,arde,jdcoburn,swanson}@cs.ucsd.edu

Abstract

Emerging fast, non-volatile memories (e.g., phase change memories, spin-torque MRAMs, and the memristor) reduce storage access latencies by an order of magnitude compared to state-of-the-art flash-based SSDs. This improved performance means that software overheads that had little impact on the performance of flash-based systems can present serious bottlenecks in systems that incorporate these new technologies. We describe a novel storage hardware and software architecture that nearly eliminates two sources of this overhead: Entering the kernel and performing file system permission checks. The new architecture provides a private, virtualized interface for each process and moves file system protection checks into hardware. As a result, applications can access file data without operating system intervention, eliminating OS and file system costs entirely for most accesses. We describe the support the system provides for fast permission checks in hardware, our approach to notifying applications when requests complete, and the small, easily portable changes required in the file system to support the new access model. Existing applications require no modification to use the new interface. We evaluate the performance of the system using a suite of microbenchmarks and database workloads and show that the new interface improves latency and bandwidth for 4 KB writes by 60% and 7.2×, respectively, OLTP database transaction throughput by up to 2.0×, and Berkeley-DB throughput by up to 5.7×. A streamlined asynchronous file IO interface built to fully utilize the new interface enables an additional 5.5× increase in throughput with 1 thread and 2.8× increase in efficiency for 512 B transfers.

Categories and Subject Descriptors D.4.2 [*Operating Systems*]: Storage Management—Secondary storage

General Terms Design, Measurement, Performance

Keywords File Systems, IO Performance, Non-Volatile Memory, Storage Systems, Virtualization

1. Introduction

Emerging fast, non-volatile technologies such as phase change, spin-torque transfer, and memristor memories make it possible to build storage devices that are orders of magnitude faster than even the fastest flash-based solid-state disks (SSDs). These technologies will rewrite the rules governing how storage hardware and software interact to determine overall storage system performance. In particular, software overheads that used to contribute marginally to latency (because storage hardware was slow) will potentially squander the performance that these new memories can provide.

ASPLOS'12, March 3–7, 2012, London, England, UK.

Recent work describing Moneta [5], a fast, next-generation storage architecture, showed that optimizing the existing IO stack and tuning the hardware/software interface can reduce software overheads by up to 62% and increase sustained bandwidth for small accesses by up to 19×. However, even with these reduced overheads, IO processing places large demands on the system's compute resources – sustaining peak performance on Moneta for 4 KB requests requires the dedicated attention of 9 Nehalem thread contexts. Entering the kernel, performing file system checks, and returning to user space account for 30% (8 μs) of the latency of a 4 KB request. Together those costs reduce sustained throughput by 85%. However, simply removing those layers is not possible because they provide essential management and protection mechanisms.

This paper describes extensions to Moneta that remove these costs by transparently bypassing the operating and file systems while preserving their management and protection functions. The extensions provide each process with a private interface, or *channel*, to Moneta. Unlike other systems that virtualize an entire device (e.g., a graphics card or network card), Moneta's channels are virtual *interfaces* to a single device. Each process uses its channel to access Moneta directly, without interacting with the operating system for most accesses. Hardware permission verification replaces permission checks in the operating system, preserving all of the protection guarantees the operating system normally provides.

To utilize channel-based IO, unmodified applications link with an untrusted user space library that intercepts IO system calls and performs the operations directly. The library works with a trusted driver and a slightly modified file system to extract file protection information and transfer it to Moneta. The library presents a standard POSIX interface.

We refer to the new system as *Moneta Direct* (*Moneta-D*) throughout the remainder of the paper. Moneta-D's unique features eliminate file system overheads and restructure the operating system storage stack to efficiently support direct, user space access to fast non-volatile storage arrays:

- Moneta-D removes trusted code and the associated overheads from most accesses. Only requests that affect meta-data need to enter the operating system.
- Moneta-D provides a fast hardware mechanism for enforcing the operating and file system's data protection and allocation policy.
- Moneta-D trades off between CPU overhead and performance by using different interrupt forwarding strategies depending on access size and application requirements.
- Moneta-D provides an asynchronous software interface, allowing applications to leverage its inherently asynchronous hardware interface to increase performance and CPU efficiency.

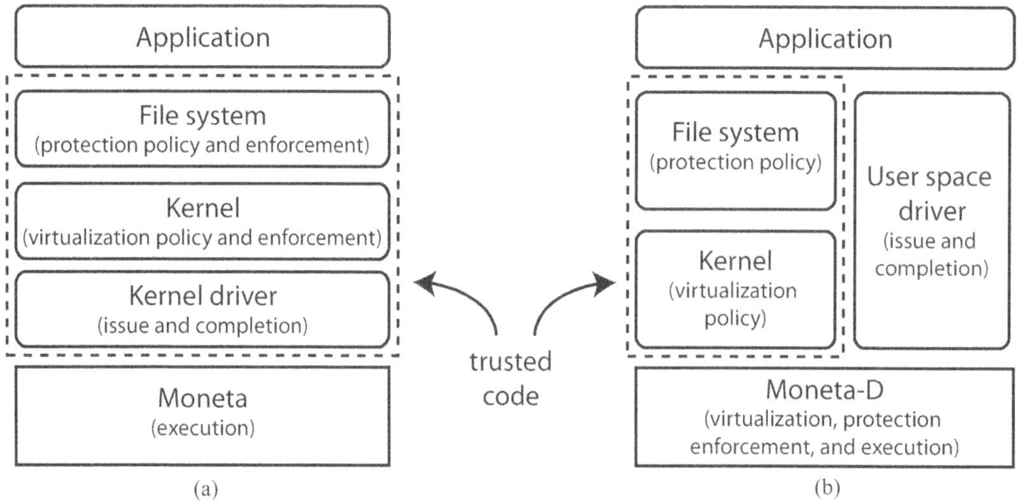

Figure 1. Changes to the high-level system architecture The operating and file systems protect storage devices like Moneta (a) by requiring a system call on every access. In Moneta-D (b), the OS and file system are only responsible for setting protection and sharing policy. Moneta-D enforces that policy in hardware, eliminating the need for most system calls and file system accesses. A virtualized hardware interface allows for an untrusted driver.

We evaluate options for key design decisions in Moneta-D and measure its performance under a collection of database workloads and direct file access benchmarks. Our results show that Moneta-D improves performance for simple database operations by between 2.6× and 5.7×. For full SQL server workloads, performance improves by between 1.1× and 2.0×. For file access benchmarks, our results show that Moneta-D can reduce the latency for a 512 byte read operation by 64% (to 4.1 μs) relative to the original Moneta design. The reduction in latency leads to a 14.8× increase in bandwidth for 512 byte requests in the presence of a file system, allowing the storage array to sustain up to 1.8 million 512 byte IO operations per second. With a single thread, Moneta-D's asynchronous IO interface improves performance by 5.5× for 4 KB accesses compared to synchronous IO. Asynchronous IO also improves efficiency by up to 2.8×, reducing CPU utilization and saving power.

The remainder of this paper is organized as follows. Section 2 describes the baseline Moneta storage array and provides an overview of the changes required to virtualize it. Section 3 places our work in the context of other research efforts. Section 4 describes Moneta-D's architectural support for virtualization. Section 5 evaluates the system. Finally, Section 6 concludes.

2. System overview

Moneta-D's goal is to remove operating system and file system overheads from accesses while maintaining the strong protection guarantees that these software layers provide. The resulting system should be scalable in that many applications should be able to access Moneta-D concurrently without adversely affecting performance. Furthermore, it should not be necessary to modify the applications to take advantage of Moneta-D.

Figures 1(a) and (b) summarize the changes Moneta-D makes to the hardware and software components of the original Moneta system. In Moneta (Figure 1(a)), all interactions with the hardware occur via the operating system and file system. Together, they set the policy for sharing the device and protecting the data it contains. They also enforce that policy by performing checks on each access. Performing those checks requires the file system to be trusted code. The driver is trusted since it accesses a shared, non-virtualized hardware resource.

Figure 1(b) shows the revised organization that Moneta-D uses. The kernel and the file system remain responsible for making policy decisions that control access to data, but the Moneta-D hardware enforces that policy. The hardware exposes a set of virtual *channels* that each provide a single process with access to storage. The kernel manages these channels, assigns them to processes, and maintains protection information associated with each channel. Since the hardware enforces protection and each process has a private channel, there is no need for a privileged driver. Instead, applications access their channels via an untrusted driver library, avoiding system call overheads.

Our intent is that this new architecture be the default mechanism for file access rather than a specialized interface for high-performance applications. To make it feasible for all applications running on a system to use the interface, Moneta-D supports a large number of virtual channels. This decision has forced us to minimize the cost of virtualization.

Below, we describe the channel interface, the user space driver library, and discuss the interactions between our system and the file system.

2.1 Channels

A channel is a virtual interface to the storage array. Each channel provides all the facilities necessary for a process to access data in the array and for the kernel to restrict access to only files that the process has successfully opened.

A channel has two interfaces, a privileged interface for configuration by the kernel and an unprivileged interface for application access. The privileged interface comprises a set of control registers that let the kernel manage the channel and install permission information. The unprivileged interface has three components: 1) a set of user registers that the user space library uses to access array data, 2) a set of tags that distinguish between outstanding requests on the channel, and 3) a DMA buffer.

Below, we describe how a process and the kernel use their respective interfaces to initialize a channel, access data, and manage permission information. Section 4 describes these mechanisms in more detail.

Channel initialization The user space driver library initializes a channel by opening the storage device's file in `/dev/` and `mmap()` ing several pages into its address space. Mapping these pages allocates a channel for the process and grants it access to the hardware and shared-memory software interfaces. The first mapped page contains the user registers that the process will use to communicate with the hardware. The next pages provide communication with the kernel via shared memory. The remaining pages make up the channel's DMA buffer. Initially, the channel does not have permission to access any of the data in Moneta-D.

Managing permissions To gain access to data in Moneta-D, the user space library issues a system call that takes a file descriptor and an offset in the file. The system call returns a description of the file system extent (i.e., the range of physical bytes in Moneta-D) containing that offset. The process uses this information to populate a user space table that maps file offsets onto physical extents. If the process does not have access to that data, the system call returns an error.

The system call also installs the permission record for the extent in the process's channel. Moneta-D's permission record storage is finite, so installing one permission record may require the kernel to evict another. This also means that the process may issue a request for data that it should be able to access and have the request fail. In this case, the process re-issues the system call to re-install the permission record and retries the request.

Issuing and completing commands Once the process has installed a permission record, it can start making requests. To initiate a command, the process writes a 64-bit command word to the channel's memory mapped command register. The command encodes the operation to perform (read or write), the portion of the DMA buffer to use, the physical location in Moneta-D to access, and a tag to differentiate between requests. After issuing the command, the thread waits for the command to complete.

When Moneta-D receives the command word, it checks the hardware permission table to determine whether the channel has permission to access the location. If it does, it performs the command and signals its completion. In Section 4 we describe several schemes for notifying the thread when a command completes.

2.2 The user space driver

The user space library for accessing Moneta-D performs the low-level driver functions including tag management, extent lookup, and command retry. The library transparently replaces the standard library calls for accessing files using LD_PRELOAD. Dynamically linked applications do not require any modification or recompilation. When the program `open()` s a file on Moneta-D, the library allocates a channel if necessary and then handles all future accesses to that file. The library forwards operations on all other files to the normal `libc` functions.

The POSIX compatibility layer implements POSIX calls (e.g. `read()`, `write()`, and `seek()`) calling Moneta-D specific read and write functions. The layer also tracks file descriptor manipulation functions (e.g. `dup()`, `dup2()`, and `close()`) to track per-file descriptor state (e.g. the file pointer's position) and file descriptor aliasing relationships.

Other, Non-POSIX interfaces are also possible. Moneta-D's hardware interface is inherently asynchronous, so a high-performance asynchronous IO library is a natural fit. In addition, since the channel's DMA buffers reside in the process's address space, an optimized application could avoid copying data to and from the DMA buffer and operate on the data in place instead. We explore both these options in Section 4.

2.3 The file system

Moneta-D changes the way applications interact with the file system to increase performance. These changes require minor modifications in the file system to support moving protection checking into hardware. They also introduce some challenges to maintaining existing functionality and consistency in the file system.

The only change required to the file system is the addition of a function to extract extent information. We implemented this change in XFS [10] and found it to be straightforward, even though XFS is a very sophisticated file system. The single 30-line function accesses and transfers file extent meta-data into Moneta-D's data structures. We expect that adding support to other file systems would also be relatively easy.

All meta-data updates and accesses use the conventional operating system interface. This requirement creates problems when the driver uses the kernel to increase a file's size and then accesses the resulting data directly. When it extends a file (or fills a hole in a sparse file), XFS writes zeros into the kernel's file buffer cache. Although the operating system writes out these dirty blocks after a short period of time, the user space library accesses the newly-allocated blocks as soon as the system call returns and that access will not "see" the contents of the buffer cache. If the application updates the new pages in Moneta-D before the operating system flushes the cached copy, a race will occur and the flushed pages will overwrite the application's changes. To avoid this problem, we flush all blocks associated with a file whenever we fill a hole or extend a file. After the first access to the file, this is usually a fast operation because the buffer cache will be empty.

Guaranteeing consistency while accessing files concurrently through Moneta-D and via the operating system remains a challenge, because of potential inconsistencies caused by the kernel's buffer cache. One solution is to detect files that applications have opened a file using both interfaces and force the application using the user space interface to switch to the system-call based interface. The library could do this without that application's knowledge. Alternatively, disabling the buffer cache for files residing on Moneta-D would also resolve the problem. Our system does not yet implement either option.

Moneta-D's virtual interface also supports arbitrarily sized and aligned reads and writes, eliminating the need to use read-modify-write operations to implement unaligned accesses.

3. Related Work

Our extensions to Moneta touch on questions of virtualization, fast protection and translation, and light-weight user space IO. Below we describe related work in each of these areas and how the system we describe differs from and extends the current state of the art.

3.1 Virtualization

Moneta-D differs from other efforts in virtualizing high-speed IO devices in that it provides virtual *interfaces* to the device rather than logically separate virtual devices. In our system, there is a single logical SSD and a single file system to manage it. However, many client applications can access the hardware directly. Creating multiple, independent virtual disks or multiple, independent virtual network interfaces for multiple virtual machines is a simpler problem because the virtual machine monitor can statically partition the device's resources across the virtual machines.

Previous work in high-speed networking [4, 21, 31] explores the idea of virtualizing network interfaces and allowing direct access to the interface from user space. DART [21] implements network interface virtualization while also supporting offloading of some packet processing onto the network card for additional performance enhancements. Our work implements similar hardware interface virtualization for storage accesses while enabling file systems protection checking in hardware.

Many projects have developed techniques to make whole-device virtualization more efficient [18, 19, 25, 29, 33], particularly for graphics cards and high-performance message-passing interconnects such as Infiniband. Virtualization techniques for GPUs are most similar to our work. They provide several "rendering contexts" that correspond to an application window or virtual machine [6]. A user space library (e.g., OpenGL) requests a context from the kernel, and the kernel provides it a set of buffers and control registers it can use to transfer data to and from the card without OS involvement. Some Infiniband cards [9] also provide per-application (or per-virtual machine) channels and split the interface into trusted and untrusted components. The work in [16] has explored how to expose these channels directly to applications running inside virtual machines. However, neither of these applications requires the hardware to maintain fine-grain permission data as Moneta-D does.

The concurrent, direct network access (CDNA) model [33] is also similar, but applies to virtual machines. In this model, the network card provides multiple independent sets of queues for network traffic, and the VMM allows each virtual machine to access one of them directly. On an interrupt, the OS checks a register to determine which queues need servicing and forwards a virtual interrupt to the correct VMs.

Recent revisions of the PCIe standard include IO virtualization (IOV) [22] to support virtual machine monitors. PCIe IOV allows a single PCIe device to appear as several, independent virtual devices. The work in [35] describes a software-only approach to virtualizing devices that do not support virtualization, assuming the devices satisfies certain constraints. In both cases the support is generic, so it cannot provide the per-channel protection checks that Moneta-D requires. Some researchers have also found the PCIe approach to be inflexible in the types of virtualized devices it can support [13].

The work in [26] and [24] present new IO architectures with virtualization as the driving concern. In [26] researchers propose a unified interface to several of the techniques described above as well as extensions to improve flexibility. [24] proposes a general approach to self-virtualizing IO devices that offloads many aspects of virtualization to a processor core embedded in the IO device.

3.2 User space IO

Efficiently initiating and completing IO requests from user space has received some attention in the high-speed networking and message passing communities. In almost all cases, the VMs issue requests via stores to PIO registers, and the VMM is responsible for delivering virtual interrupts to the VMs. We describe two alternative approaches below.

Prior work [3, 4, 31] proposed supporting user space IO and initiating DMA transfers from user space without kernel intervention. SHRIMP [3] proposes user space DMA through simple load and store operations, but requires changes to the CPU and DMA engine to detect and initiate transfers. Our work requires no changes to the CPU or chipset.

The work in [27, 28] proposes architectural support for issuing multi-word PIO commands atomically. In effect, it implements a simple form of bounded transactional memory. Moneta-D would be more flexible if our processors provided such support. The same work also suggests adding a TLB to the PCIe controller to allow the process to specify DMA targets using virtual addresses. The PCIe IOV extensions mentioned above provide similar functions. The combination of multi-word atomic PIO writes and the DMA TLB would eliminate the need for a dedicated DMA buffer and make it possible to provide a zero-copy interface on top of Moneta-D that was POSIX-compatible.

The same work also proposes hardware support for delivering interrupts to user space. The device would populate a user space buffer with the results of the IO operation, and then transmit data to the CPU describing which process should receive the interrupt. The OS would then asynchronously execute a user-specified handler. Moneta-D would benefit from this type of support as well, and one of the request completion techniques we examine is similar in spirit. More recently, researchers have proposed dedicating an entire core to polling IO device status and delivering notifications to virtual machines through memory [15]. The driver for recent PCIe-attached flash-based SSDs from Virident dedicates one processor core solely to interrupt handling.

Several papers have argued against user space IO [17]. They posit that efficient kernel-level implementations can be as fast as user-level ones and that the kernel should be the global system resource controller. However, our work and prior work [36] have found that user-level IO can provide significant benefit without significantly increasing complexity for application developers. Our work maintains the kernel as the global policy controller — only policy enforcement takes place in hardware.

3.3 Protection and translation

Moneta-D removes file system latency by copying permission information into hardware and caching the physical layout of data in user space. Some approaches to distributed, networked storage use similar ideas. The latest version of the network file system (NFS) incorporates the pNFS [20] extension that keeps the main NFS server from becoming a bottleneck in cluster-based NFS installations. Under pNFS, an NFS server manages storage spread across multiple storage nodes. When a client requests access to a file, it receives a map that describes the layout of the data on the storage nodes. Further requests go directly to the storage nodes. NASD [7] is similar in that a central server delegates access rights to clients. However, it uses intelligent drives rather than separate storage servers to provide access to data. NASD uses cryptographic capabilities to grant clients access to specific data.

Modern processors provide hardware support for translation and protection (the TLB) and for servicing TLB misses (the page table walker) in order to reduce both translation and miss costs. Supporting multiple file systems, many channels, and large files requires Moneta-D to take a different approach. Our SSD provides hardware support for protection only. Translation must occur on a per-file basis (since "addresses" are file offsets), and hardware translation would require Moneta-D to track per-file state rather than per-channel state.

Rather than addressing physical blocks in a storage device, object-based storage systems [1, 8, 32], store objects addressed by name. They provide a layer of abstraction mapping between object names and physical storage in the device. Moneta-D performs a similar mapping in its user space library, mapping between file descriptor and offset. Shifting these translations into the hardware has several drawbacks for a system like Moneta-D. First, the file system would require significant alterations, breaking the generic support that Moneta-D currently enables. Second, performing the translations directly in hardware could limit Moneta-D's performance if the lookups take more than a few hundred nanoseconds. Finally, dedicated DRAM in Moneta-D for storing lookup information might be better located in the host system where it could be repurposed for other uses when not needed for translations.

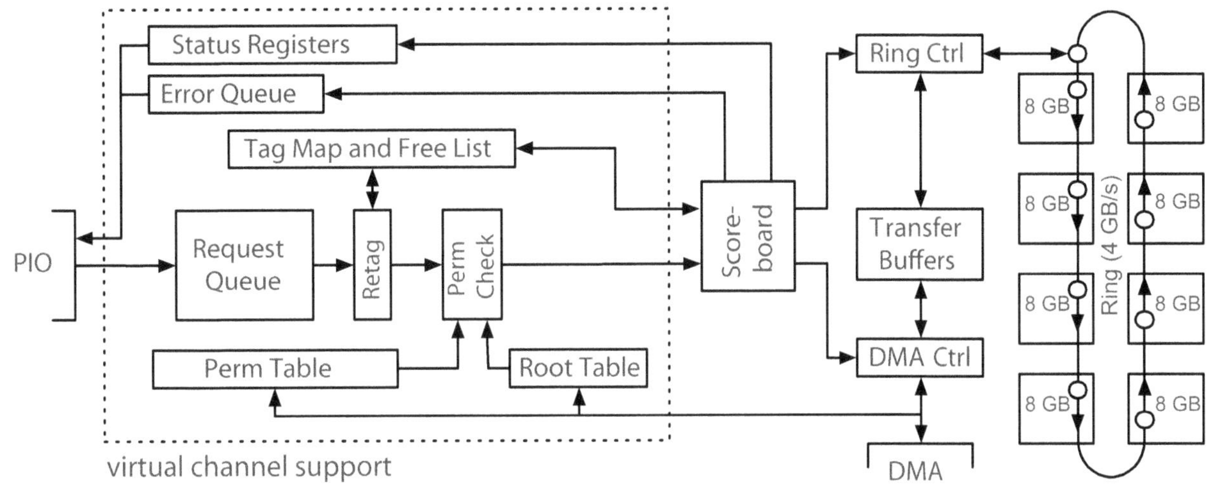

Figure 2. Controller architecture Components inside the dashed box provide support for virtualization and are the focus of this work. The other components (at right) execute storage access commands.

	Name	R/W Kernel	User	HW	Description
Kernel global registers	CHANNELSTATUS	R	-	W	Read and clear channel status and error bits
	ERRORQUEUE	R	-	W	Read and pop one error from the error queue
User per-channel registers	COMMAND	W	W	R	Issue a command to the device.
	TAGSTATUSREGISTER	R	R	W	Read and clear tag completion bits and error flag.
Per-channel mapped memory	TAGSTATUSTABLE	W	R/W	W	Tracks completion status of outstanding requests.
	COMPLETIONCOUNT	W	R	-	Count of completed requests on each channel.
	DMABUFFER		R/W	R/W	Pinned DMA buffer for data transfers.

Table 1. Moneta-D channel interfaces There are three interfaces that control Moneta-D: The kernel registers that the kernel uses to configure channels, the per-channel user registers that applications use, and the per-channel mapped memory region shared between the kernel and the application to maintain channel state.

4. Moneta-D Implementation

This section describes the changes to the Moneta [5] hardware and software that comprise Moneta-D. The baseline Moneta system implements a highly optimized SSD architecture targeting advanced non-volatile memories. The Moneta-D modifications enable the hardware and software to work together to virtualize the control registers and tags, efficiently manage permission information, and deliver IO completions to user space. We discuss each of these in turn. Section 5 evaluates their impact on performance.

4.1 The baseline Moneta hardware

The right side of Figure 2 (outside the dotted box) shows the architecture of the baseline array. It spreads 64 GB of storage across eight memory controllers connected via a high-bandwidth ring. An 8-lane PCIe 1.1 interface provides a 2 GB/s full-duplex connection (4 GB/s total) to the host system. The baseline design supports 64 concurrent, outstanding requests with unique tags identifying each. The prototype runs at 250 MHz on a BEE3 FPGA prototyping system [2].

The baseline Moneta array emulates advanced non-volatile memories using DRAM and modified memory controllers that insert delays to model longer read and write times. We model phase change memory (PCM) in this work and use the latencies from [11] — 48 ns and 150 ns for array reads and writes, respectively. The array uses start-gap wear leveling [23] to distribute wear across the PCM and maximize lifetime.

The baseline Moneta design includes extensive hardware and software optimizations to reduce software latency (e.g. bypassing the Linux IO scheduler and removing unnecessary context switches) and maximize concurrency (e.g., by removing all locks in the driver). These changes reduce latency by 62% compared to the standard Linux IO stack, but system call and file system overheads still account for 65% of the remaining software overheads.

The baseline design implements one channel that the operating system alone may access. It provides a set of configuration and command registers and targets a single DMA buffer in the kernel's address space.

Figure 3 shows the latency breakdown for 512 B reads and writes on Moneta-D. The hardware, DMA, and copy overheads are common across the baseline and the extensions we describe in this work. These, combined with the file system, system call, and interrupt processing overheads bring the total request latency in the baseline to 15.36 and 16.78 μs for reads and writes, respectively.

4.2 Virtual channels

Supporting virtual channels on Moneta-D requires replicating the control registers, tags, and DMA buffers mentioned above, while maintaining file coherency across multiple processes. This section describes the hardware and software implementation of virtual channels on Moneta-D. The dashed box in Figure 2 contains the components that implement virtual channels.

Control registers and data structures The interface for a channel comprises several memory-mapped hardware control registers and a shared memory segment. Together, these allow the kernel and the user space library to configure the channel, perform operations on it, and receive notifications when they complete.

Table 1 describes the most important control registers and the shared memory segment. The kernel's global registers allow the kernel to manage Moneta-D's functions that apply to multiple channels, such as error reporting and channel status. The user per-channel registers allow the process to access the hardware. Finally, the per-channel mapped memory shared by the kernel and user contains the channel's DMA buffer and data structures used to notify threads when operations complete. We discuss the role of these components in detail below.

In the non-virtualized system, a single set of control registers exposes Moneta's interface to the kernel. In the virtualized system, Moneta-D exposes 1024 channels, each with a private set of control registers located at a unique physical address. Reading or writing to any of these registers will send a PIO request to Moneta-D. Moneta-D uses the address bits to determine which channel the command targets. To give a process access to a particular channel, the kernel maps the registers for the channel into the process's address space. The unique mapping of physical addresses to channels allows Moneta-D to reliably know which process issued a particular request and prevents processes from accessing channels other than their own.

Request tags The baseline design supports 64 concurrent, outstanding requests. To maximize performance and concurrency, each channel needs its own set of tags. One option is to support 65,536 tags (64 tags for each of the 1024 channels) in hardware and statically partition them across the channels. In a custom ASIC implementation this might be possible, but in our FPGAs maintaining a request scoreboard of that size is not feasible at our 250 MHz clock frequency.

Instead, we provide each channel with 64 virtual tags and dynamically map them onto a set of 64 physical tags. The virtual tag number comprises the channel ID and the tag number encoded in the command word. The "retag" unit shown in Figure 2 assigns physical tags to requests by drawing physical tags from a hardware free tag list. If a physical tag is not available, the retag unit stalls until a request completes and releases its physical tag.

DMA buffer Each channel has a private 1 MB DMA buffer pinned in system DRAM that Moneta-D uses as the source and destination for writes and reads. The target DMA address for a request depends on its tag with each tag corresponding to one 16 KB slice of the channel's DMA buffer. If the process issues a command on tag k, the DMA transfer will start at the kth slice. The access that uses the tag can be larger than 16 KB, but it is the software's responsibility to not issue requests that overlap in the buffer. Moneta-D supports arbitrarily large DMA buffers, but since they must be contiguous in physical memory allocating bigger DMA buffers is challenging. Better kernel memory management would eliminate this problem.

Asynchronous interface Moneta-D's user space library provides asynchronous versions of its `pread()` and `pwrite()` calls (i.e., read/write to a given offset in a file). The asynchronous software interface allows applications to take advantage of the inherently asynchronous hardware by overlapping storage accesses with computation. For example, double buffering allows a single thread to load a block of data at the same time as it processes a different block. The asynchronous calls return immediately after issuing the request to the hardware and return an asynchronous IO state structure that identifies and tracks the request. The application can continue executing and only check for completion when it needs the data from a read or to know that a write has completed.

4.3 Translation and protection

The Moneta-D hardware, the user space library, and the operating system all work together to translate file-level accesses into hardware requests and to enforce permissions on those accesses. Translations between file offsets and physical storage locations occur in the user space library while the hardware performs permission checks. Below, we describe the role of both components and how they interact with the operating system and file system.

Hardware permission checks Moneta-D checks permissions on each request it receives after it translates virtual tags into physical tags ("Perm Check" in Figure 2). Since the check is on the critical path for every access, the checks can potentially limit Moneta-D's throughput. To maintain the baseline's throughput of 1.8 M IOPS, permissions checks must take no more than 500 ns.

Moneta-D must also cache a large amount of permission information in order to minimize the number of "misses" that will occur when the table overflows and the system must evict some entries. These *hard permission misses* require intervention from both the user space driver and the operating system to remedy, a process that can take 10s of microseconds (Figure 3).

To minimize the number of permission entries it must store for a given set of files, Moneta-D keeps extent-based permission information for each channel and merges entries for adjacent extents. All the channels share a single permission table with 16K entries. To avoid the need to scan the array linearly and to allow channels to dynamically share the table, Moneta-D arranges the extent information for each channel as a balanced red-black binary tree, with each node referring to a range of physical blocks and the permission bits for that range. The "Root Table" (Figure 2) holds the location of the root of each channel's tree. Using balanced trees keeps search times fast despite the potentially large size of the permission tree: The worst-case tree traversal time is 180 ns, and in practice the average latency is just 96 ns. With a linear scan, the worst-case time would exceed 65 μs.

To reduce hardware complexity, the operating system maintains the binary trees, and the hardware only performs look ups. The OS keeps a copy of the trees in system DRAM. When it needs to update Moneta-D's permission table, it performs the updates on its copy and records the changes it made in a buffer. Moneta-D then reads the buffer via DMA, and applies the updates to the tree while temporarily suspending protection checking.

User space translation When the user space library receives a read or write request for a file on Moneta-D, it is responsible for translating the access address into a physical location in Moneta-D and issuing requests to the hardware.

The library maintains a translation map for each file descriptor it has open. The map has one entry per file extent. To perform a translation, the library looks up the target file location in the map. If the request spans multiple extents, the library will generate multiple IO requests.

The library populates the map on-demand. If a look up fails to find an extent for a file offset, we say that a *soft permissions miss* has occurred. To service a soft miss, the library requests information for the extent containing the requested data from the operating system. The request returns the mapping information and propagates the extent's protection and physical location information to hardware.

Once translation is complete, the library issues the request to Moneta-D and waits for it complete. If the request succeeds, the operation is complete. Permission record eviction or an illegal request may cause the request to fail. In the case of an eviction,

Component		Latency R/W (μs) 1 extent	Latency R/W (μs) 1K extents
Hardware + DMA		1.26 / 2.18	
Copy		0.17 / 0.13	
SW Extent lookup		0.12	0.23
HW Permission check		0.06	0.13
Soft miss handling		7.28	29.9
Hard miss handling		14.7	38.1
Permission update		3.23	3.26
File System	Baseline	4.21/4.64	
	Moneta-D	0.21/0.29	
System call	Baseline	3.90/3.96	
	Moneta-D	0.00/0.00	
Completion	Baseline (interrupts)	5.82 / 5.87	
	OS forwarding	2.71 / 2.36	
	DMA	2.32 / 2.68	
	issue-sleep	14.65 / 14.29	

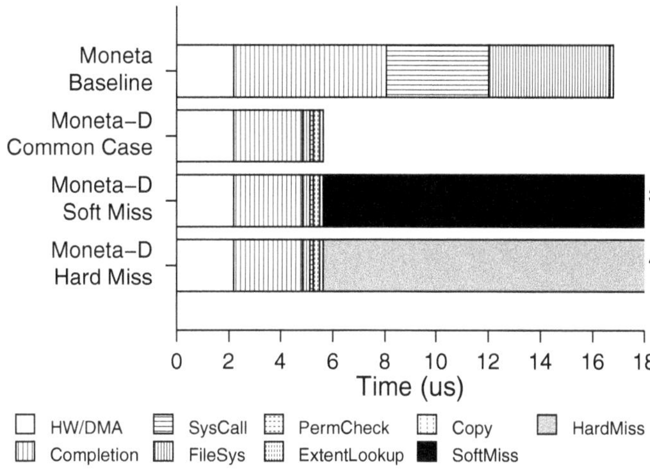

Figure 3. Component latencies Software latencies required to manage permissions, tags, and user data all contribute to operation latency. DMA and copying values are for 512 byte accesses. Cells with a single value have the same latency for both read and write accesses. The graph at right shows the latency breakdown graphically, for 1K extents and using DMA completion.

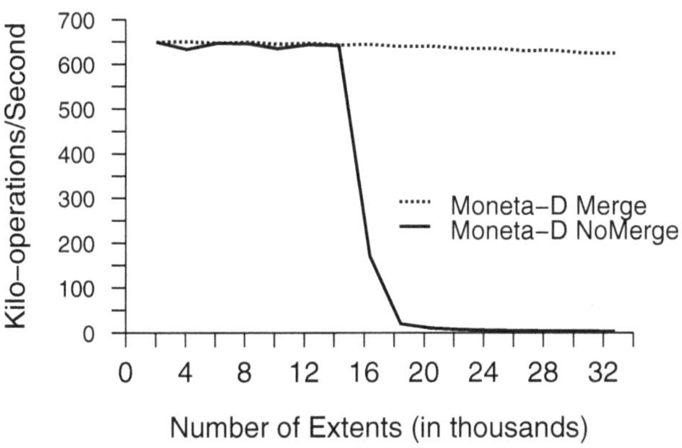

Figure 4. Extent merging to alleviate permission table contention Merging permission entries improves performance because it allows Moneta-D to take advantage of logically discontinuous file extents that the file system allocates in physically adjacent storage.

the permission entry is missing in hardware so the library reloads the permission record and tries again.

Permission management overheads Permission management and checking add some overhead to accesses to Moneta-D, but they require less time than the conventional system call and file system overheads that provide the same functions in conventional systems. Figure 3 shows the latencies for each component of an operation in the Moneta-D hardware and software. To measure them, we use a microbenchmark that performs 512 B random reads and writes to a channel with one permission record and another with 1000 records present. The microbenchmark selectively enables and disables different system components to measure their contribution to latency.

In the common case, accesses to Moneta-D incur software overhead in the user space library for the file offset-to-extent lookup. This requires between 0.12 and 0.23 μs, depending on the number of extents. The hardware permission check time is much faster – between 60 ns and 130 ns.

The miss costs are significantly higher: Handling a soft miss requires between 4.1 μs and 26.8 μs to retrieve extent information from the file system and 3.2 μs to update the permission tree in hardware. In total, a soft miss increases latency for a 512 B access by between 7.3 μs and 30 μs, depending on the number of extents in use. The hard miss adds another 7.7 μs of latency on average, because the user space library does not detect it until the initial request fails and reports an error.

In the best case, only one soft miss should occur per file extent. Whether hard misses are a problem depends on the number of processes actively using Moneta-D and the number of extents they are accessing. Since fragmented files will place more pressure on the permission table, the file system's approach to preventing fragmentation is important.

XFS uses aggressive optimizations to minimize the number of extents per file, but fragmentation is still a problem. We measured fragmentation on a 767 GB XFS file system that holds a heavily-used Postgres database [14] and found that, on average, each file contained 21 extents, and ninety-seven percent of files contained a single extent. However, several files on the file system contain 1000s of extents, and one database table contained 23,396.

We have implemented two strategies to deal with fragmentation. The first is to allocate space in sparse files in 1 MB chunks. When the library detects a write to an unallocated section of a file, it allocates space by writing up to 1 MB of zeroed data to that location before performing the user's request. This helps reduce fragmentation for workloads that perform small writes in sparse files. The second is to merge contiguous extents in the hardware permission table even if the file contents they contain are logically discontiguous in the file. This helps in the surprising number of cases in which XFS allocates discontinuous portions of a file in adjacent physical locations.

Figure 4 shows the benefits of merging permission entries. It shows aggregate throughput for a single process performing random 4 KB accesses to between 2048 and 32,768 extents. The two lines depict the workload running on Moneta-D with (labeled "Moneta-D Merge") and without ("Moneta-D NoMerge") combining permission table entries. Moneta-D Merge combines entries if they belong to the same channel, represent data from the same file,

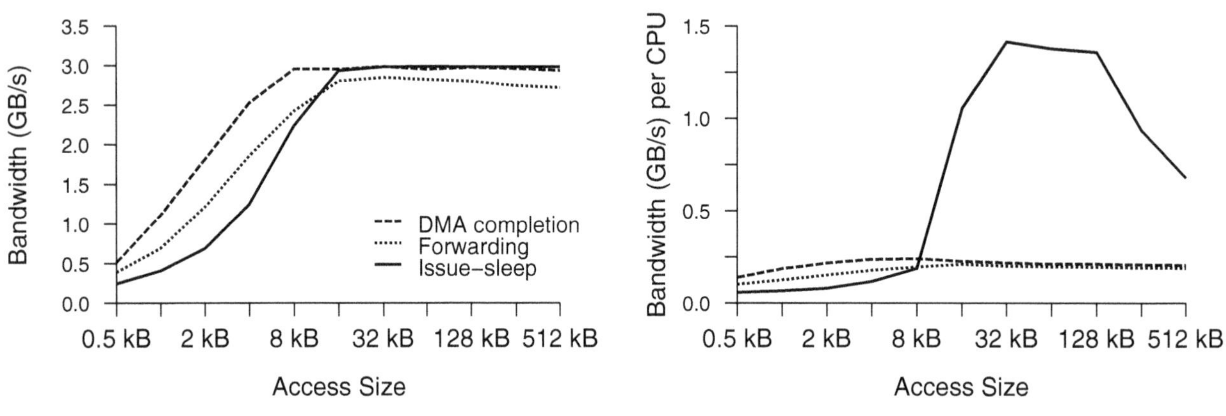

Figure 5. Completion strategies and bandwidth The graphs compare performance and CPU behavior for our three completion strategies for 32 threads performing a 50/50 mix of random reads and writes. Graph (a) measures maximum sustained bandwidth and (b) measures efficiency as the ratio of bandwidth to CPU utilization. For small accesses, DMA completion is the best alternative by both measures. For larger accesses, however, issue-sleep enjoys a large advantage in efficiency.

have the same permission bits set, and cover physically adjacent blocks. Moneta-D NoMerge does not merge extents.

Throughput remains high for Moneta-D NoMerge when there are enough permission table entries to hold all the extent information. Once all 16K permission table entries are in use, throughput drops precipitously as the hard miss rate rises. For Moneta-D Merge, performance remains high even when the number of extents exceeds the permission table size by 2×, because many extents merge into a smaller number of entries.

Avoiding hard misses requires having a sufficient number of permission table entries available for the process accessing Moneta-D directly. There are (at least) three ways to achieve this. The first is to increase the permission table size. In a custom ASIC implementation this would not be difficult, although it would increase cost. The second is to detect over-subscription of the permission table and force some processes to use the conventional system call interface by evicting all their permission table entries, refusing to install new ones, and returning an error code informing the process of the change in policy. Finally, enhancements can be made to more aggressively avoid fragmention in the file system block allocator.

4.4 Completing requests and reporting errors

Modern hardware provides no mechanism for delivering an interrupt directly to a process, so virtualizing this aspect of the interface efficiently is difficult. Moneta-D supports three mechanisms for notifying a process when a command completes that trade-off CPU efficiency and performance. Moneta-D also provides a scalable mechanism for reporting errors (e.g., permission check failures).

Forwarding interrupts The first notification scheme uses a traditional kernel interrupt handler to notify channels of request status through a shared memory page. Moneta-D's kernel driver receives the interrupt and reads the CHANNELSTATUS register to determine which channels have completed requests. The kernel increments the COMPLETIONCOUNT variable for each of those channels.

After issuing a request, the user space library spins on both COMPLETIONCOUNT and the TAGSTATUSTABLE entry for the request. Once the kernel increments COMPLETIONCOUNT one thread in the user space library sees the change and reads the per-channel TAGSTATUSREGISTER from Moneta-D. This read also clears the register, ensuring that only one reader will see each bit that is set. The thread updates the TAGSTATUSTABLE entries for all of the completed tags, signalling any other threads that are waiting for requests on the channel.

DMA completion The second command completion mechanism bypasses the operating system entirely. Rather than raise an interrupt, Moneta-D uses DMA to write the request's result code (i.e., success or an error) directly to the tag's entry in the channel's TAGSTATUSTABLE. In this case, the thread spins only on the TAGSTATUSTABLE.

Issue-sleep The above techniques require the issuing thread to spin. For large requests this is unwise, since the reduction in latency that spinning provides is small compared to overall request latency, and the spinning thread occupies a CPU, preventing it from doing useful work.

To avoid spinning, issue-sleep issues a request to hardware and then asks the OS to put it to sleep until the command completes. When an interrupt arrives, the OS restarts the thread and returns the result code for the operation. This approach incurs the system call overhead but avoids the file system overhead, since permission checks still occur in hardware. The system call also occurs *in parallel* with the access.

It is possible to combine issue-sleep on the same channel with DMA completions, since the latter does not require interrupts. This allows the user library to trade-off between completion speed and CPU utilization. A bit in the command word that initiates a requests tells Moneta-D which completion technique to use. We explore this trade-off below.

Reporting errors Moving permission checks into hardware and virtualizing Moneta's interface complicates the process of reporting errors. Moneta-D uses different mechanisms to report errors depending on which completion technique the request is using.

For interrupt forwarding and issue-sleep, the hardware enqueues the type of error along with its virtual tag number and channel ID in a hardware error queue. It then sets the error bit in the CHANNELSTATUS register and raises an interrupt.

The kernel detects the error when it reads the CHANNELSTATUS register. If the error bit is set, it extracts the error details from the queue by reading repeatedly from the ERRORQUEUE register. Each read dequeues an entry from the error queue. For interrupt forwarding the kernel copies the error codes into the TAGSTATUSREGISTERS for the affected channels. For issue-sleep completion it returns the error when it wakes up the sleeping thread. The kernel reads from ERRORQUEUE until it returns zero.

For DMA completion, the hardware writes the result code for the operation directly into the TAGSTATUSTABLE when the operation completes.

Completion technique performance The four completion method lines of Figure 3 measure the latency of each complation strategy in addition to the interrupt processing overhead for the baseline Moneta design. Interrupt forwarding and DMA completion all have similar latencies – between 2.5 and 2.7 μs. Issue-sleep takes over 14 μs, but for large requests, where issue-sleep is most useful, latency is less important.

Figure 5 compares the performance of the three completion techniques. The data are for 32 threads performing random accesses of the size given on the horizontal axis. Half of the accesses are reads and half are writes. Figure 5(a) measures aggregate throughput and shows that DMA completion outperforms the other schemes by between 21% and 171%, for accesses up to 8 KB. Issue-sleep performs poorly for small accesses, but for larger accesses its performance is similar to interrupt forwarding. We use DMA completion throughout the rest of the paper.

Figure 5(b) measures efficiency in terms of GB/s of bandwidth per CPU. The two spinning-based techniques fare poorly for large requests. Issue-sleep does much better and can deliver up to 7× more bandwidth per CPU. The drop in Issue-sleep performance for requests over 128 KB is an artifact of contention for tags in our microbenchmark: Threads spin while waiting for a tag to become available and yield the processor between each check. Since our microbenchmark does not do any useful work, the kernel immediately reschedules the same thread. In a real application, another thread would likely run instead, reducing the impact of the spinning thread.

The data show that DMA completion is a good choice for all request sizes, but that issue-sleep has a slight advantage for CPU-intensive workloads. Issue-sleep is the best choice for accesses of 8 KB or larger because it is more CPU-efficient.

5. Results

Moneta-D's virtualized interface reduces both file and operating system overhead, but it also introduces new sources of potential latency as described in Section 4. This section quantifies the overall impact of these changes on Moneta-D's performance using an IO microbenchmark and several database applications. We also evaluate the benefits of using asynchronous IO on Moneta-D rather than the conventional synchronous operations.

5.1 Operation latency

Figure 6 shows how end-to-end single thread access latency varies over a range of write request sizes from 512 B to 32 KB on the baseline Moneta design and Moneta-D. Read latencies are similar. The graph shows data for accesses running with 1000 permission table entries installed. We collect these data using XDD [34], a flexible IO benchmarking tool. Moneta-D extends the baseline Moneta's performance by a wide margin, while Moneta outperforms state-of-the-art flash-based SSDs by up to 8.7×, with a harmonic mean speedup of 2.1× on a range of file system, paging, and database workloads [5].

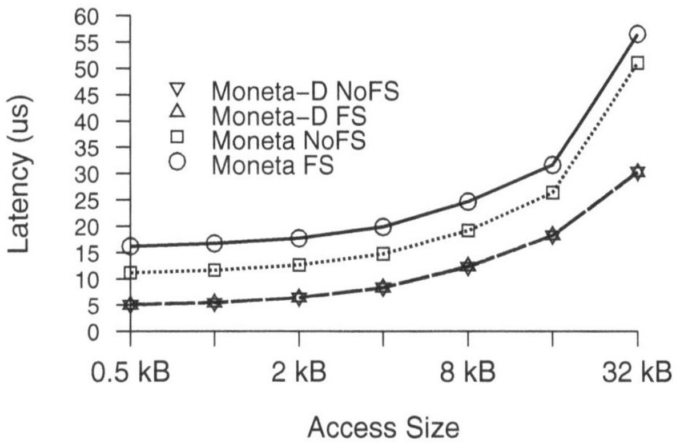

Figure 6. Write access latency Moneta-D's user space interface eliminates most of the file system and operating system overheads to reduce file system access latency by between 42% and 69%.

Figure 6 shows that Moneta-D eliminates most file system and operating system overheads from requests of all sizes, since the lines for Moenta-D FS and NoFS lay on top of each other. Figure 3 provides details on where the latency savings come from for small requests. Assuming the access hits in the permission table, Moneta-D all of this, reducing latency by 60%. Reducing software overheads for small (512 B) requests is especially beneficial because as request size decreases, hardware latency decreases and software latency remains constant.

5.2 Raw bandwidth

Since removing the operating and file systems from common case accesses reduces software overhead per IO operation, it also increases throughput, especially for small accesses. Figure 7 compares the bandwidth for Moneta-D and baseline Moneta with and without the file system. For writes, the impact of virtualization is large: Adding a file system reduces performance for the original Moneta system by up to 13×, but adding a file system to Moneta-D has almost no effect. Moneta-D eliminates the gap for reads as well, although the impact of the file system on the baseline is smaller (at most 34%).

Reducing software overheads also increases the number of IO operations the system can complete per second, because the system must do less work for each operation. For small write accesses with a file system, throughput improves by 26×, and Moneta-D sustains 1.8 M 512 B IO operations per second.

5.3 Application level performance

Table 2 describes the workloads we use to evaluate the application level performance of Moneta-D compared to the baseline Moneta design. The first two workloads are simple database applications that perform random single-value updates to a large key-value store in Berkeley-DB, backed either by a B+tree or a hash table. The six MySQL and PGSQL workloads consist of full OLTP database servers that aggressively optimize storage accesses and have strong consistency requirements. They are running the OLTP portion of the SysBench benchmark suite [30] which includes a variety of OLTP operations including read-only lookups, single-value increments, and complex transactions with multiple lookups and updates.

Table 3 shows the performance results for baseline Moneta and the Moneta-D systems for all of our workloads. We also include performance numbers from a FusionIO 80 GB Flash SSD for comparison. Moneta-D speeds up the Berkeley-DB applications by between 2.6× and 5.7× in terms of operations/second, compared to

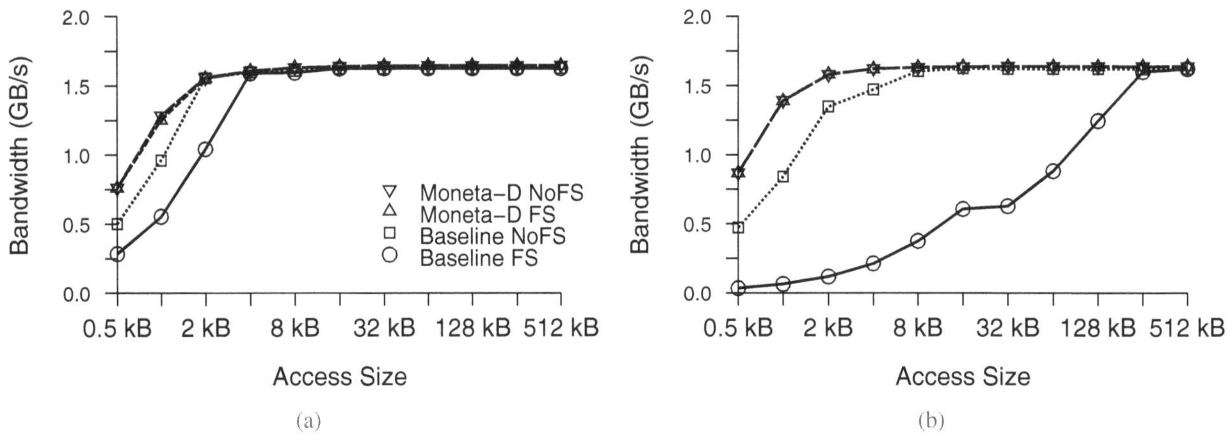

Figure 7. File system overhead Each pair of lines compares bandwidth with and without the file system for reads (a) and writes (b) for the baseline system and Moneta-D. The data show that giving the applications direct access to the hardware nearly eliminates the performance penalty of using a file system and the cost of entering the operating system.

Name	Data footprint	Description
Berkeley-DB Btree	45 GB	Transactional updates to a B+tree key/value store
Berkeley-DB Hash	41 GB	Transactional updates to a hash table key/value store
MySQL-Simple	46 GB	Single value random select queries on MySQL database
MySQL-Update	46 GB	Single value random update queries on MySQL database
MySQL-Complex	46 GB	Mix of read/write queries in transactions on MySQL database
PGSQL-Simple	55 GB	Single value random select queries on Postgres database
PGSQL-Update	55 GB	Single value random update queries on Postgres database
PGSQL-Complex	55 GB	Mix of read/write queries in transactions on Postgres database

Table 2. Benchmarks and applications We use eight database benchmarks and workloads to evaluate Moneta-D.

	Raw Performance			Speedup of Moneta-D vs.	
Workload	FusionIO	Moneta	Moneta-D	FusionIO	Moneta
Berkeley-DB Btree	4066 ops/s	8202 ops/s	21652 ops/s	5.3 ×	2.6 ×
Berkeley-DB Hash	6349 ops/s	10988 ops/s	62124 ops/s	9.8 ×	5.7 ×
MySQL-Simple	13155 ops/s	13840 ops/s	15498 ops/s	1.2 ×	1.1 ×
MySQL-Update	1521 ops/s	1810 ops/s	2613 ops/s	1.7 ×	1.4 ×
MySQL-Complex	390 ops/s	586 ops/s	866 ops/s	2.2 ×	1.5 ×
PGSQL-Simple	23697 ops/s	49854 ops/s	63308 ops/s	2.7 ×	1.3 ×
PGSQL-Update	2132 ops/s	2523 ops/s	5073 ops/s	2.4 ×	2.0 ×
PGSQL-Complex	569 ops/s	1190 ops/s	1809 ops/s	3.2 ×	1.5 ×
			Harmonic mean	2.4 ×	1.7 ×

Table 3. Workload performance Moneta-D provides significant speedups compared to baseline Moneta and FusionIO across a range of workloads. The Berkeley-DB workloads benefit more directly from the increased IO throughput, while the full SQL databases see large gains for write intensive queries. All of the data use the best performing thread count (between 1 and 16) for each workload. FusionIO performance is provided for reference.

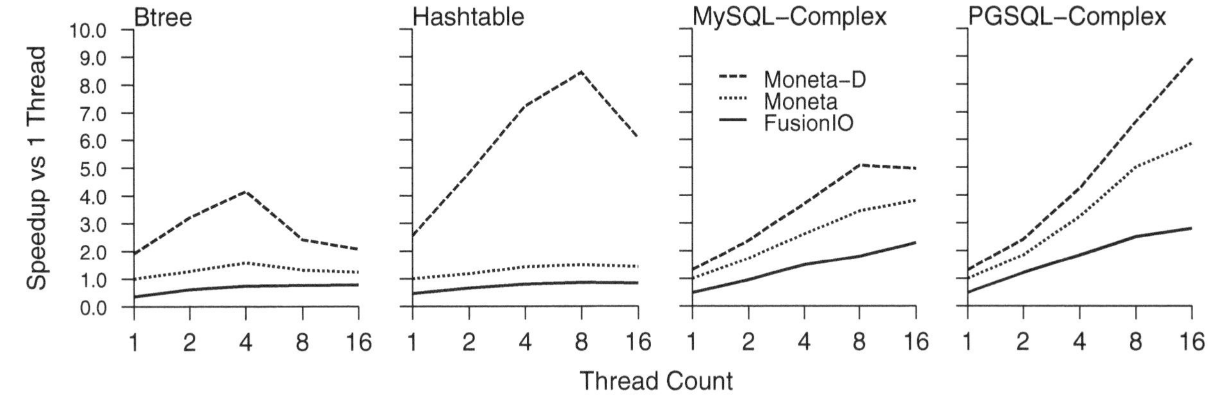

Figure 8. Workload scalability For most workloads, Moneta-D allows application performance to scale better with additional threads, especially for workloads with little inter-thread contention, like Hashtable. Changing Hashtable from 1 to 8 threads on Moneta-D increases performance by 2.2 ×more than the same change on either FusionIO or baseline Moneta.

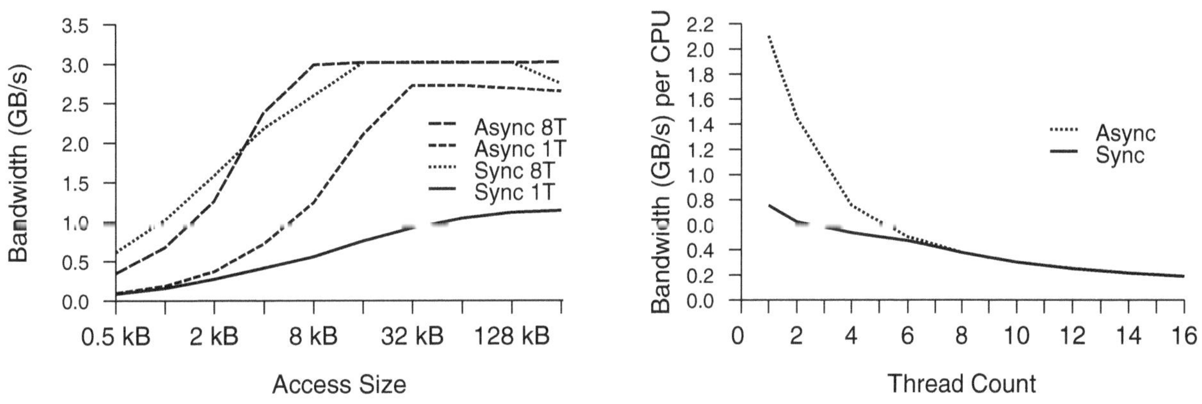

(a) (b)

Figure 9. Asynchronous performance (a) Moneta-D's asynchronous interface improves single threaded performance by up to 3.5× by eliminating time spent waiting for completions. The data in (b) measure efficiency in terms of bandwidth per CPU with synchronous and asynchronous 16 KB accesses for varying numbers of threads.

baseline Moneta and by between 5.3× and 9.8× compared to FusionIO. We attribute the difference in performance between these two workloads to higher data structure contention in the B+tree database implementation.

Figure 8 shows application performance speedup for varying thread counts from 1 to 16 for the Berkeley-DB and complex MySQL and Postgres databases. Other MySQL and Postgres results are similar. The results are normalized to 1-thread baseline Moneta performance. Baseline Moneta out-performs FusionIO for all thread counts across all of workloads, while Moneta-D provides additional speedup. Increasing thread counts on Moneta-D provides significantly more speedup than on Moneta or FusionIO for the Berkeley-DB workloads, and improves scaling on PGSQL-Complex.

The larger database applications, MySQL and Postgres, see performance improvements from 1.1× to 2.0× under Moneta-D, compared to baseline Moneta. The data show that for these workloads, write-intensive operations benefit most from Moneta-D, with transaction throughput increases of between 1.4× to 2.0×. Read-only queries also see benefits but the gains are smaller — only 1.1× to 1.3×. This is consistent with Moneta-D's smaller improvements for read request throughput.

We found that Postgres produces access patterns that interact poorly with Moneta-D, and that application level optimizations enable better performance. Postgres includes many small extensions to the files that contain its database tables. With Moneta-D these file extensions each result in a soft miss. Since Postgres extends the file on almost all write accesses, these soft misses eliminate Moneta-D's performance gains. Pre-allocating zeroed out data files before starting the database server enables Postgres to take full advantage of Moneta-D. Although Moneta-D requires no application level changes to function, this result suggests that, large performance improvements could result from additional optimizations at the application level, such as allocating large blocks in the file system rather than many small file extensions.

5.4 Asynchronous IO

Providing an asynchronous IO interface to Moneta-D allows applications to take advantage of its inherently asynchronous hardware interface. Figure 9 compares the performance of Moneta-D with and without asynchronous IO. Figure 9(a) shows sustained bandwidth for the synchronous and asynchronous interfaces with 1 and 8 threads. Asynchronous operations increase throughput by between 1.1× and 3.0× on access sizes of 512 B to 256 KB when using 1 thread. With 8 threads, asynchronous operations boost performance for requests of 4 KB or larger. Small request performance suffers from software overheads resulting from maintaining asynchronous request data structures and increased contention during tag allocation.

Figure 9(b) shows the efficiency gains from using asynchronous requests on 16 KB accesses for varying numbers of threads. The data show that for one thread, asynchronous requests are 2.8× more efficient than synchronous requests with respect to the amount of bandwidth per CPU. As the number of threads increases, the asynchronous accesses slowly lose their efficiency advantage compared to synchronous accesses. As the number of threads increases, the per-thread performance decreases because of increased contention for hardware bandwidth and tags.

To understand the application-level impact of an asynchronous interface, we modified the ADPCM codec from Mediabench [12] to use Moneta-D's asynchronous IO interface and then used it to decode a 100 MB file. Using the asynchronous IO interface results in an 1.4× speedup over the basic Moneta-D interface. By using three buffers, ADPCM can process one block while reading in another and writing out a third. ADPCM's performance demonstrates how overlapping data accesses with data processing enables significant gains. In this case, Moneta-D transformed an IO bound workload into a CPU bound one, shifting from 41% CPU utilization for one thread on the baseline Moneta system to 99% CPU utilization with the asynchronous interface.

6. Conclusion

As emerging non-volatile memory technologies shrink storage hardware latencies, hardware interfaces and system software must adapt or risk squandering the performance these memories offer. Moneta-D avoides this danger by moving file system permission checks into hardware and using an untrusted, user space driver to issue requests. These changes reduce latency for 4 KB write requests through the file system by up to 58% and increase throughput for the same requests by 7.6×. Reads are 60% faster. These increases in raw performance translate into large application level gains. Throughput for an OLTP database workload increased 2.0× and our Berkeley-DB based workloads sped up by 5.7×. Asynchronous IO support provides 5.5× better 4 KB access throughput with 1 thread, and 2.8× better efficiency for 512-B operations, resulting in a 1.7× throughput improvement for a streaming application. Overall, out results demonstrate the importance of eliminating software overheads in IO-intensive applications that will use these emerging memories and point to several opportunities to improve performance further by modifying the applications themselves.

Acknowledgements

The authors would also like to thank Geoff Voelker for his feedback and Jack Sampson for his comments. We would also like to thank the reviewers for their feedback and suggestions and the Xilinx University Program for their support. This work was supported by NSF awards CCF-1018672 and OCI-0910847.

References

[1] The lustre project. http://www.lustre.org/.

[2] http://www.beecube.com/platform.html.

[3] M. A. Blumrich, C. Dubnicki, E. W. Felten, and K. Li. Protected, user-level DMA for the SHRIMP network interface. In *Proceedings of the 2nd IEEE Symposium on High-Performance Computer Architecture*, HPCA '96, pages 154–, Washington, DC, USA, 1996. IEEE Computer Society.

[4] G. Buzzard, D. Jacobson, M. Mackey, S. Marovich, and J. Wilkes. An implementation of the hamlyn sender-managed interface architecture. In *Proceedings of the second USENIX symposium on Operating systems design and implementation*, OSDI '96, pages 245–259, New York, NY, USA, 1996. ACM.

[5] A. M. Caulfield, A. De, J. Coburn, T. I. Mollov, R. Gupta, and S. Swanson. Moneta: A high-performance storage array architecture for next-generation, non-volatile memories. In *In the Proceedings of The 43rd Annual IEEE/ACM International Symposium on Microarchitecture*, 2010.

[6] M. Dowty and J. Sugerman. Gpu virtualization on vmware's hosted i/o architecture. In *Proceedings of the First conference on I/O virtualization*, WIOV'08, pages 7–7, Berkeley, CA, USA, 2008. USENIX Association.

[7] G. A. Gibson, D. F. Nagle, K. Amiri, J. Butler, F. W. Chang, H. Gobioff, C. Hardin, E. Riedel, D. Rochberg, and J. Zelenka. A cost-effective, high-bandwidth storage architecture. In *Proceedings of the eighth international conference on Architectural support for programming languages and operating systems*, ASPLOS-VIII, pages 92–103, New York, NY, USA, 1998. ACM.

[8] G. A. Gibson, D. F. Nagle, K. Amiri, J. Butler, F. W. Chang, H. Gobioff, C. Hardin, E. Riedel, D. Rochberg, and J. Zelenka. A cost-effective, high-bandwidth storage architecture. *SIGOPS Oper. Syst. Rev.*, 32:92–103, October 1998.

[9] D. Goldenberg. Infiniband device virtualization in xen. http://www.mellanox.com/pdf/presentations/xs0106_infiniband.pdf.

[10] S. G. International. XFS: A high-performance journaling filesystem. http://oss.sgi.com/projects/xfs.

[11] B. C. Lee, E. Ipek, O. Mutlu, and D. Burger. Architecting phase change memory as a scalable dram alternative. In *ISCA '09: Proceedings of the 36th annual international symposium on Computer architecture*, pages 2–13, New York, NY, USA, 2009. ACM.

[12] C. Lee, M. Potkonjak, and W. H. Mangione-smith. Mediabench: A tool for evaluating and synthesizing multimedia and communications systems.

[13] J. LeVasseur, R. Panayappan, E. Skoglund, C. du Toit, L. Lynch, A. Ward, D. Rao, R. Neugebauer, and D. McAuley. Standardized but flexible i/o for self-virtualizing devices. In *Proceedings of the First conference on I/O virtualization*, WIOV'08, pages 9–9, Berkeley, CA, USA, 2008. USENIX Association.

[14] K. Levchenko, A. Pitsillidis, N. Chachra, B. Enright, M. Félegyházi, C. Grier, T. Halvorson, C. Kanich, C. Kreibich, H. Liu, D. McCoy, N. Weaver, V. Paxson, G. M. Voelker, and S. Savage. Click Trajectories: End-to-End Analysis of the Spam Value Chain. In *Proceedings of the IEEE Symposium and Security and Privacy*, Oakland, CA, May 2011.

[15] J. Liu and B. Abali. Virtualization polling engine (vpe): using dedicated cpu cores to accelerate i/o virtualization. In *Proceedings of the 23rd international conference on Supercomputing*, ICS '09, pages 225–234, New York, NY, USA, 2009. ACM.

[16] J. Liu, W. Huang, B. Abali, and D. K. Panda. High performance vmm-bypass i/o in virtual machines. In *Proceedings of the annual conference on USENIX '06 Annual Technical Conference*, pages 3–3, Berkeley, CA, USA, 2006. USENIX Association.

[17] K. Magoutis, M. Seltzer, and E. Gabber. The case against user-level networking. In *Proceedings of the Workshop on Novel Uses of System-Area Networks*, SAN-3, 2004.

[18] D. McAuley and R. Neugebauer. A case for virtual channel processors. In *Proceedings of the ACM SIGCOMM workshop on Network-I/O convergence: experience, lessons, implications*, NICELI '03, pages 237–242, New York, NY, USA, 2003. ACM.

[19] A. Menon, A. L. Cox, and W. Zwaenepoel. Optimizing network virtualization in Xen. In *Proceedings of the annual conference on USENIX '06 Annual Technical Conference*, pages 2–2, Berkeley, CA, USA, 2006. USENIX Association.

[20] http://www.pnfs.com/.

[21] R. Osborne, Q. Zheng, J. Howard, R. Casley, D. Hahn, and T. Nakabayashi. Dart – a low overhead atm network interface chip.

[22] Pci-sig - i/o virtualization. http://www.pcisig.com/specifications/iov/.

[23] M. K. Qureshi, J. Karidis, M. Franceschini, V. Srinivasan, L. Lastras, and B. Abali. Enhancing lifetime and security of pcm-based main memory with start-gap wear leveling. In *MICRO 42: Proceedings of the 42nd Annual IEEE/ACM International Symposium on Microarchitecture*, pages 14–23, New York, NY, USA, 2009. ACM.

[24] H. Raj and K. Schwan. High performance and scalable i/o virtualization via self-virtualized devices. In *Proceedings of the 16th interna-*

tional symposium on High performance distributed computing, HPDC '07, pages 179–188, New York, NY, USA, 2007. ACM.

[25] M. Rosenblum and T. Garfinkel. Virtual machine monitors: Current technology and future trends. *Computer*, 38:39–47, May 2005.

[26] J. Satran, L. Shalev, M. Ben-Yehuda, and Z. Machulsky. Scalable i/o - a well-architected way to do scalable, secure and virtualized i/o. In *Proceedings of the First conference on I/O virtualization*, WIOV'08, pages 3–3, Berkeley, CA, USA, 2008. USENIX Association.

[27] L. Schaelicke and A. Davis. Improving i/o performance with a conditional store buffer. In *Proceedings of the 31st annual ACM/IEEE international symposium on Microarchitecture*, MICRO 31, pages 160–169, Los Alamitos, CA, USA, 1998. IEEE Computer Society Press.

[28] L. Schaelicke and A. L. Davis. Design trade-offs for user-level i/o architectures. *IEEE Trans. Comput.*, 55:962–973, August 2006.

[29] J. Sugerman, P. Venkitachalam, and B.-H. Lim. Virtualizing i/o devices on vmware workstation's hosted virtual machine monitor. In *Proceedings of the General Track: 2002 USENIX Annual Technical Conference*, pages 1–14, Berkeley, CA, USA, 2001. USENIX Association.

[30] http://sysbench.sourceforge.net/index.html.

[31] T. von Eicken, A. Basu, V. Buch, and W. Vogels. U-net: a user-level network interface for parallel and distributed computing. *SIGOPS Oper. Syst. Rev.*, 29:40–53, December 1995.

[32] S. A. Weil, S. A. Brandt, E. L. Miller, D. D. E. Long, and C. Maltzahn. Ceph: a scalable, high-performance distributed file system. In *Proceedings of the 7th symposium on Operating systems design and implementation*, OSDI '06, pages 307–320, Berkeley, CA, USA, 2006. USENIX Association.

[33] P. Willmann, J. Shafer, D. Carr, A. Menon, S. Rixner, A. L. Cox, and W. Zwaenepoel. Concurrent direct network access for virtual machine monitors. In *Proceedings of the 2007 IEEE 13th International Symposium on High Performance Computer Architecture*, pages 306–317, Washington, DC, USA, 2007. IEEE Computer Society.

[34] Xdd version 6.5. http://www.ioperformance.com/.

[35] L. Xia, J. Lange, P. Dinda, and C. Bae. Investigating virtual passthrough i/o on commodity devices. *SIGOPS Oper. Syst. Rev.* 43:83–94, July 2009.

[36] Y. Zhou, A. Bilas, S. Jagannathan, C. Dubnicki, J. F. Philbin, and K. Li. Experiences with VI communication for database storage. In *Proceedings of the 29th annual international symposium on Computer architecture*, ISCA '02, pages 257–268, Washington, DC, USA, 2002. IEEE Computer Society.

Whole-System Persistence

Dushyanth Narayanan Orion Hodson
Microsoft Research, Cambridge
{dnarayan,ohodson}@microsoft.com

Abstract

Today's databases and key-value stores commonly keep all their data in main memory. A single server can have over 100 GB of memory, and a cluster of such servers can have 10s to 100s of TB. However, a storage back end is still required for recovery from failures. Recovery can last for minutes for a single server or hours for a whole cluster, causing heavy load on the back end. Non-volatile main memory (NVRAM) technologies can help by allowing near-instantaneous recovery of in-memory state. However, today's software does not support this well. Block-based approaches such as persistent buffer caches suffer from data duplication and block transfer overheads. Recently, user-level persistent heaps have been shown to have much better performance than these. However they require substantial application modification and still have significant runtime overheads.

This paper proposes whole-system persistence (WSP) as an alternative. WSP is aimed at systems where all memory is non-volatile. It transparently recovers an application's entire state, making a failure appear as a suspend/resume event. Runtime overheads are eliminated by using "flush on fail": transient state in processor registers and caches is flushed to NVRAM only on failure, using the residual energy from the system power supply. Our evaluation shows that this approach has 1.6–13 times better runtime performance than a persistent heap, and that flush-on-fail can complete safely within 2–35% of the residual energy window provided by standard power supplies.

Categories and Subject Descriptors D.4.2 [*Storage Management*]: Main memory

General Terms Design

Keywords NVRAM, persistence

1. Introduction

Databases and key-value stores today commonly keep their working sets entirely in main memory. In-memory operation gives high throughput and low latency by removing I/O bottlenecks and hence is used even for large datasets. Today's servers can hold hundreds of gigabytes of main memory, and larger datasets are partitioned across multiple such servers. These servers might be viewed as caches for a back-end storage layer [6, 10, 20] or as main-memory databases that integrate in-memory operation with back-end storage [19, 31, 34]. In both cases, their key feature is that they hold a copy of the entire data set in main memory.

Recovery is a concern for these large main-memory deployments. After a power outage or any failure that causes loss of in-memory state, the entire state must be read or reconstructed from the storage back end. Typically this involves reading a recent checkpoint of the state and then replaying a log of recent updates. Recovering several terabytes of state in this manner is slow and puts a heavy load on the back end. For example, a Facebook outage in September 2010 [14] caused the service to be unavailable for 2.5 hours while in-memory cache servers refreshed their state from servers. The problem is that while in-memory operation and scale-out now allow the service to sustain very high levels of load during normal operation, the recovery mechanisms are I/O bound and they are not provisioned to deal with such spikes in load.

What if servers could recover their in-memory state locally and near-instantaneously after a failure? This would significantly speed up recovery and reduce back end load, especially after a correlated failure such as a power outage. This is possible if the server state is stored in non-volatile memory (NVRAM). Of course, servers can also fail due to application software errors. In this case, we must rely on the server application to handle the error locally (e.g. by rolling back a recent update) and/or to refresh its state from the back end. However NVRAM offers significant benefits for transient crash failures, specifically power outages or UPS failures that are correlated across a large number of servers.

In this paper we argue that it is feasible to use NVRAM in servers for recovery from transient crash failures. We further argue that current models for using NVRAM have significant limitations. Persistent buffer caches [7] and RAMdisks duplicate state, doubling the memory footprint of an in-memory application. They also suffer from block transfer and system call overheads. NVRAM-based persistent heaps [8, 33] achieve better performance than these block-based approaches by allowing in-place, user-space updates of persistent state. However, they still have substantial runtime overheads and require non-trivial changes to application code.

We propose *whole-system persistence (WSP)* as an alternative. WSP relies on all system main memory being non-volatile. It presents the application with the simple abstraction that all state is recovered after a power failure. In other words, a power outage is converted into a "suspend/resume" event with heap, stack, and thread context state all being restored. This is done transparently and does not impose any runtime overheads on the application. The key idea behind WSP is *flush-on-fail*: transient state held in processor registers and cache lines is only flushed to NVRAM on a failure, using a small *residual energy window* provided by the system power supply (PSU). This is the period of time for which the power supply continues to maintain output DC voltages after signaling a power failure. The residual energy window is a result of the internal capacitance of the PSU. Flush-on-fail eliminates the runtime overhead of flushing cache lines on each update.

ASPLOS'12, March 3–7, 2012, London, England, UK.

This paper makes three contributions. First, we propose whole-system persistence as the best programming model for using NVRAM, and discuss its advantages, especially with respect to the persistent heap model. Second, we describe an efficient design and implementation of flush-on-fail: saving transient state to NVRAM on failure rather than during program execution. Third, we show both the performance advantages and feasibility of the flush-on-fail approach through an empirical evaluation. Our results show that flush-on-fail performs 13x better than a user-level persistent heap [33] for an update-intensive workload, and 6x better for a read-only workload. They also show that saving transient state takes less than 5 ms across a range of platforms. By comparison, measurements of standard PC power supplies show that they can supply power to the system for 10–300 ms after raising a power failure signal.

Section 2 provides some background for this work: the increasing importance of in-memory operation, and the feasibility of using NVRAM in servers. Section 3 describes the design considerations that led us to the WSP model, including performance considerations, programming models, and failure assumptions. Section 5 presents the experimental evaluation that validates our key claims. Section 6 discusses the implications of our results, shortcomings of NVRAM-based recovery, and directions for future work. Section 7 describes related work and Section 8 concludes with a brief summary of the key contributions of this paper.

2. Motivation and background

Main-memory servers The main motivation for this work is the increasing prevalence of main-memory operation for databases. Servers with 100s of gigabytes of DRAM are easily available, going up to 1 TB [11] at the high end. This means that many previously disk-based data sets can now reside entirely in memory, fundamentally changing the system design assumptions. This is driving main-memory designs for both traditional SQL databases [19, 26, 31] as well as the ubiquitous "no SQL" databases or key-value stores [6, 10, 20, 34]. The latter typically use a "share-nothing" architecture, which means that they can scale out to 100s or 1000s of main-memory servers. This means that they can potentially approach petabyte scale with all data stored in main memory.

Main-memory operation gives high throughput and low latency by removing I/O bottlenecks. However, large memories give rise to a new problem: recovery times. After a crash or reboot, a server must recover its state, typically from back end storage. This is limited by I/O bandwidth, which has not scaled with memory sizes. Reading 256 GB at 0.5 GB/s from a high-end storage array will take more than 8 min, even if all the storage resources were dedicated to that single recovering machine. Correlated failures such as rack-level power outages will cause 10s to 100s of servers to concurrently recover their state from a shared back end.

Ideally, servers would recover locally and near-instantaneously from such failures, without causing "recovery storms" on the back end. We briefly examine current approaches to surviving transient power failures and some trends that motivate the use of NVRAM.

Power failures and NVRAMs Power outages are particularly relevant because (without NVRAM) it is not possible today to recover in-memory state locally after a power failure; and because power failures can be correlated across a large number of machines. This means that power outages are a problematic case for recovery load, causing large correlated spikes in load on the recovery subsystem.

Hardware solutions for power outages today mainly consist of *uninterrupted power supplies (UPS)*. These use large lead-acid batteries to maintain power to the entire system for up to several hours after a power failure. An UPS allows the system to continue operation until the battery is almost completely discharged. UPSes are bulky, adding to data center space requirements, and environmentally unfriendly. Additionally, UPS failures can lead to hundreds of machines suffering power outages simultaneously. Alternative designs, such as a "distributed UPS" [16], avoid some of these problems by including a small lead-acid battery in each server. However, this still retains the space, cost, environmental problems, and unreliability of lead-acid batteries.

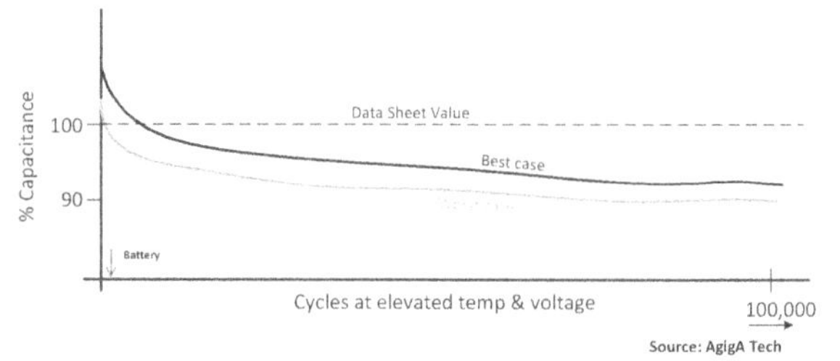

Figure 1. Effect of charge-discharge cycles on ultracapacitors

Battery-backed NVRAMs such as those used in RAID controllers typically augment DRAM (or sometimes SRAM) with rechargeable Lithium-ion batteries. When power fails the batteries maintain the memory contents while their charge lasts, up to a few hours. These batteries require frequent monitoring and replacement. Additionally they can only sustain a few hundred charge/discharge cycles before their performance degrades significantly. These disadvantages mean that battery-backed NVRAMs have been restricted to niche uses such as RAID controllers.

In the long term, *storage class memories (SCMs)* promise large capacities, low idle power consumptions, and non-volatility. Hence they seem ideal for in-memory server applications. However, they do not seem likely to replace DRAM in the near term (2–5 years). The most promising SCM candidate — phase-change memory (PCM) — requires additional additional hardware support such as fine-grained wear leveling [29] to be usable as a main memory alternative. This has only recently been proposed by the research community and it will be several years before PCM becomes commercially available as main memory. Additionally, PCM is expected to be significantly slower than DRAM, especially for writes [22] and hence will become competitive with DRAM only when the capacity benefits outweigh this disadvantage.

Battery-free NVDIMMs offer a practical and performant NVRAM option today. They are based on commodity components: DRAM, ultracapacitors and NAND flash integrated into a single module. The amount of NAND flash is equal to the amount of DRAM. The flash is not visible to the host system; it exists only as a backup and is not read or written during normal operation. When signaled by the host, the NVDIMM saves or restores the DRAM contents to/from the flash. Thus the NVDIMM gives the illusion of a non-volatile memory to the host system. The host is only responsible for flushing transient state to the NVDIMM over the memory bus and signaling the start of a save operation. After this, the NVDIMM's contents are preserved even if the system PSU and host lose power.

At least two recently developed products — AgigaRAM [1] and ArxCis-NV [2] — uses this approach to make NVDIMMs that are drop-in replacements for standard (volatile) DIMMs. The DRAM, flash, and controllers are all integrated onto the NVDIMM, which fits in a standard DDR2 or DDR3 DIMM slot. The ultracapacitor module charges from the system's 12 V DC power supply, and discharges to provide power to the NVDIMM when the system power fails. Unlike Lithium-ion batteries, ultracapacitors can tolerate hundreds of thousands of charge/discharge cycles with only a 10% loss in usable capacitance (Figure 1). Although they store much less to-

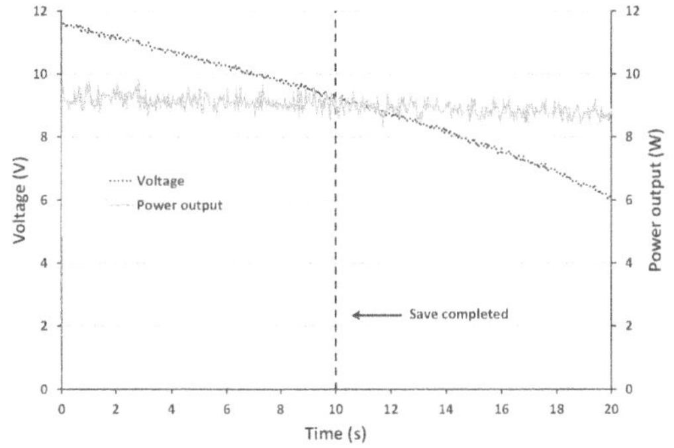

Figure 2. Voltage and power draw on ultracapacitors during NVDIMM save

tal charge than batteries, they can discharge it at a much higher rate to power the saving of DRAM contents to flash. Figure 2 shows the voltage delay and power output for a 1 GB NVDIMM. The save time is under 10 s for NVDIMMs of up to 8 GB and the ultracapacitor is able to supply power to the NVDIMM for at least twice as long[1].

Using flash-based NVDIMMs is not the same as saving system state ("hibernating") to a flash-based SSD. The latter requires the OS to suspend processes and devices, and to write out the state to a file on the SSD. This adds a long and variable latency, during which the entire system must be kept powered up. Additionally, the entire state must be written through a single shared memory bus and I/O channel. NVDIMMs by contrast save their contents off the critical path; there is no interaction with the host system during the save process, and the ultracapacitor backups ensure that the save does not rely on system power. Additionally, NVDIMMs can be saved/restored in parallel, since they do not use any shared resources.

This approach creates main-memory NVRAMs based entirely on cheap commodity components: DRAM, NAND flash, and ultracapacitors. Ultracapacitors (or supercapacitors) have achieved large economies of scale in recent years due to demand in the automotive industry, and costs are below \$0.01/F and \$2.85/kJ [15]. For comparison, the Agiga NVDIMMs require 5–50 F of capacitance and 0.1–1 kJ of energy, depending on size.

Thus the availability of commodity component based NVDIMMs today, and projected trends for storage class memories, make it likely that large main memory NVRAMs will be a viable option for servers. In the rest of this paper we assume servers where all main memory is NVRAM made up of NVDIMMs, i.e., non-volatile memory with DRAM performance.

3. Design rationale

This section gives the detailed design rationale for WSP. First, we distinguish failures that are recoverable using NVRAM from those that are not. Next we examine different programming models for using NVRAM. Finally we examine the performance implications of flushing transient state in processor caches on each update. We use these comparisons to motivate the two key features of WSP: to recover all application state rather than selected subsets of it; and to flush transient state on a failure rather than during execution.

[1] The internal voltage required by the NVDIMM is only 3.3 V, and hence a power input of 6 V is still usable.

3.1 Failure models

NVRAM is useful for recovery from crash failures, such as power outages. It cannot be used to recover from errors that corrupt state, such as software bugs. Other, software-based mechanisms exist for failures such as kernel panics [12] or application component failures [5]. Generic mechanisms, e.g. rolling back state on failure using checkpoints or software transactions, might also help in the case of software bugs.

These mechanisms work equally whether memory is volatile or non-volatile. This observation favors a design where recovery from crash failures using NVRAM is decoupled from other types of failure recovery. For the purposes of this paper we use "persistence" to mean survival of state after a crash failure rather than any other kind of failure. By decoupling persistence from other forms of recovery, it should be possible to support a wide range of programming models and recovery mechanisms, while at the same time providing resilience to crash failures.

In our model, NVRAM is the first but not the last resort for recovery after a crash failure. Recovery from a back-end storage layer such as a file system or database will always be necessary in some cases, e.g., if an entire server fails. The in-memory server is a cache, but one with a high refresh cost. Our aim is to reduce this cost by enabling local recovery in the case of power outages.

3.2 Models for persistence

There is a variety of ways in which applications can persist and recover state after a failure. We can broadly categorize them as:

1. *Block-based:* Applications propagate updates from the in-memory representation to a file, block device, or database. Typically the in-memory objects are first converted to a more suitable representation such as database records or serialized objects. On recovery, these are read back and deserialized to recreate the in-memory state.
2. *Persistent heaps:* Applications use a transactional API to allocate, deallocate, and modify persistent objects. On recovery, the application retrieves a special "root" object from which it can reach the others.
3. *Whole-system:* The application uses only in-memory objects, and does not distinguish between persistent and volatile objects. On recovery, all state is restored transparently.

In any of these cases, the state to be persisted can be stored in NVRAM, or on a disk or other back-end storage.

Block-based persistence on local NVRAM could be implemented as a persistent buffer cache [7], an NVRAM-based file system [9], or simply as a non-volatile RAMdisk. Regardless of the implementation, block-based persistence suffers from three disadvantages. First, it doubles the application's memory footprint by storing data in two locations. Second, the application must convert data between the two representations on each update and during recovery. Third, the application pays the overhead of block transfers and system calls to transfer data to the NVRAM.

NV-RAM based persistent heaps, or *NV-heaps* [8, 33] avoid these problems. Persistent objects are stored in NVRAM and mapped directly into the application's address space, and updated in-place. A transactional mechanism ensures that the persistent heap is always recovered to a consistent state after a failure. NV-Heaps thus combine three key features. First, they use *selective persistence*: the persistent heap is recovered after a failure but not volatile heap objects, stack objects, or thread contexts. Second, they use *flush-on-commit* of updates and transactional logs to NVRAM to ensure that updates are not lost after a power failure. Third, they use *software transactional memory (STM)* for isolation across threads and consistency of the persistent heap. Selective persistence is problematic for legacy applications; flush-on-commit causes significant runtime overheads; and STM, while potentially useful, is not used by all applications.

Whole-system persistence (WSP) relies on all application memory being mapped to NVRAM. With NVDIMMs, we believe this is feasible simply by replacing all server memory with NVDIMMs. Thus with WSP only transient state (processor registers and cache contents) needs to be captured when a failure occurs; we address this through a flush-on-fail mechanism that writes this state to memory when a failure occurs.

We claim that the best use of NVRAM is for whole-system persistence (WSP). This can then be combined with a block-based model for the back end storage, e.g., applications can periodically checkpoint their state to a file. This allows instantaneous local recovery of state after a power failure, with more expensive recovery from the back end for more severe failures. With WSP and flush-on-fail, we eliminate the first two disadvantages of NV-heaps and make the third (use of STM) optional. WSP can be used transparently with single-threaded, lock-based, or STM-based applications. In the rest of this section we compare WSP with NV-heaps in more detail.

Selective vs. whole-system persistence Designating only certain objects as persistent opens the door to "dangling references": persistent objects that refer to volatile ones. After a crash/recovery, such references become unsafe, since the volatile objects have disappeared.

Such dangling references are hard to avoid when porting a large legacy application and even when writing an application from scratch. They include not just pointers from persistent to volatile objects but also indirect references, e.g., array indexes or hash table keys where the array or hash table is part of the volatile state. They also include handles to OS objects. The application code must ensure that such references are never stored in a persistent object. This makes transparent persistence — re-using existing data structures as persistent ones — difficult.

Legacy applications are particularly problematic, since their state needs to be cleanly partitioned between persistent and volatile. If the original application was not written with such a separation in mind, this can involve substantial rewriting, assuming that source code is available. Any code that might obtain a reference to a persistent object must be checked to ensure that it does not then create an unsafe reference. This includes third-party libraries, for which source is often unavailable.

Even if all source code is available, aliasing in C/C++ means that dangling references cannot always be found through static analysis. Since it is impractical to check all code by hand, there is always the risk of following a unsafe pointer. Although careful restrictions on persistent object types can reduce the probability of "programmers getting it wrong" [8], selective persistence still adds to the challenges of writing (or porting) programs correctly.

The "dangling reference" problem is avoided in models that use transitive persistence [4, 27]: objects are dynamically made persistent whenever a reference is created to them from a persistent object. However this requires a garbage-collected language such as Java [4] or SML [27] and is not suitable for the many server applications that are written in C or C++.

Flush-on-commit vs. flush-on-fail Flush-on-commit refers to the fact that persistent heap updates must be propagated to the NVRAM before the update is considered persistent. Transaction logs must be similarly written to the NVRAM rather than remain in processor caches.

Transaction logs can be either redo or undo logs. We evaluated an existing NV-Heap implementation, Mnemosyne [33] which uses redo logs; in addition it also uses STM for concurrency control. As a result, each write to the persistent heap is recorded in the

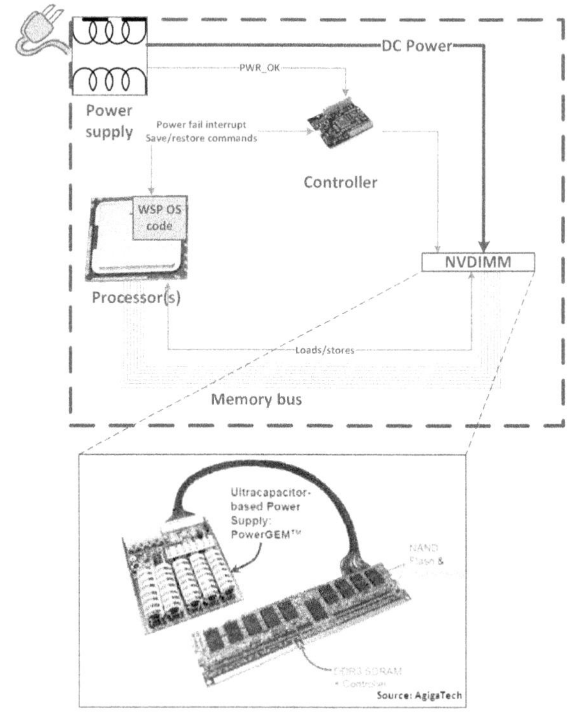

Figure 3. WSP hardware prototype

transaction's write set at write time; generates a redo log record which is written to NVRAM at commit time; and requires a cache line flush at log truncation time to ensure that updates are not lost. In addition reads must be instrumented to check the writeset for local uncommitted writes. Finally, using STM for concurrency control adds additional overheads in the form of conflict detection at commit time.

Not all the above operations are necessary for persistence; in fact Mnemosyne has significant overheads even for a read-dominated workload due to the instrumentation of reads. To remove these overheads, we implemented a minimal NV-Heap, which provides persistence (i.e. crash consistency) but not isolation (concurrency control). It uses an undo log rather than a redo log. Undo log records are written efficiently to a torn-bit raw log using non-temporal stores, as in Mnemosyne. For single-threaded operation, this performs significantly better than Mnemosyne; however, flushing of updates and log records still impose a high overhead.

The high overheads of runtime flushing motivated our "flush-on-fail" approach. Section 5.1 describes our experimental evaluation of NV-heaps in detail.

Summary Persistent heaps are an inappropriate mechanism for using NVRAM. They impose a problematic programming model and require substantial changes to legacy applications. They offer transactional consistency, which might be useful for recovery from a specific class of software failures. However, if this is desired, exactly the same recovery semantics can be enabled, with better performance, by using a non-persistent transactional heap combined with WSP. Alternatively, legacy applications can use WSP to recover from power and hardware failures, with no change in their behavior after software failures.

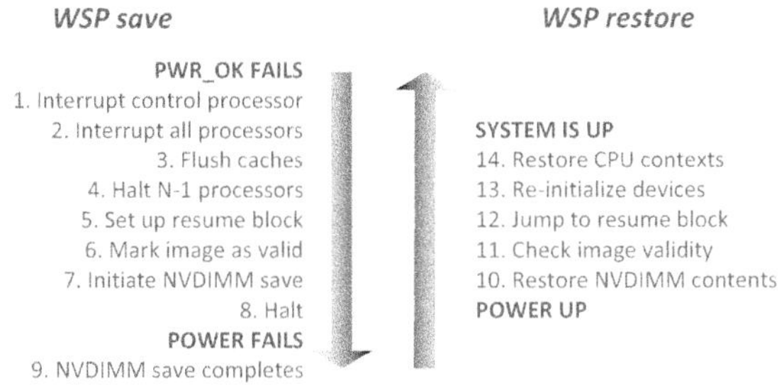

Figure 4. Save and restore steps for WSP

4. Design and Implementation

Implementing WSP requires four components. A hardware *power monitor* signals the system when a power failure is detected. A software *save routine* saves and flushes all transient state to RAM, and halts all processors, before power is actually lost. A corresponding *recovery routine* restores the saved state when power is next restored. Finally, one or more hardware *NVDIMMs* are required to implement the NVRAM functionality. Figure 3 shows a schematic of our hardware prototype. The software components are implemented on the Windows Server 2008 R2 OS running on a 64-bit PC platform.

Power monitor The power monitor is implemented using a NetDuino programmable microcontroller. It monitors the ATX power supply's PWR_OK signal [17]; the power supply drops this signal as soon as it detects an input power failure. The microcontroller then triggers an interrupt on one of the host processors via a serial line.

Save and restore routines The save routine is invoked by the interrupt handler corresponding to the serial line connected to the power monitor. The key functionality of the save routine is to implement "flush-on-fail". One of the processors — the control processor — co-ordinates the flush process. It issues an "inter-processor interrupt" — essentially a task that executes at high priority — to all the other processors. In parallel, all processors save their processor context to memory and flush their caches using the x86 `wbinvd` (Write Back and Invalidate Cache) instruction. All processors other than the control processor then halt. The control processor waits for all the tasks to complete, sets up a resume context, writes and flushes a "valid" marker to memory, signals the power failure to the NVDIMM(s), and halts. The valid marker is cleared on system startup and after a successful resume; it ensures that any failure during the save step is correctly detected.

The restore process is the inverse of the save routine, and is invoked on the next boot-up after a power failure. A modified boot loader signals the NVDIMMs to restore their saved contents. When the restore is complete it checks the valid image marker, and jumps to a resume context that is set up in a well-known location. This code in turn restores the saved contexts on other processors, and resumes normal scheduling. Figure 4 shows the save and restore steps.

Device restart The save/restore routines ensure that application and OS state (i.e. processor contexts and memory) are retained across a power failure. This means that, after a restore, the in-memory state of device drivers will be inconsistent with that of the devices, since the latter have been power-cycled. Also, kernel and/or user threads might be blocked waiting for a device operation to complete. To restore the system to a fully working state, devices and device drivers must be re-initialized, and device I/Os that were in flight at the time of failure canceled and either failed or retried.

There are multiple ways to do device restart. We have implemented and evaluated a simple strawman approach, which is to save all device state on failure using the existing support for putting the system in a sleep (S3) power state. In other words, we simply use the system's ACPI suspend/resume functionality to save and restore system and device context to memory, while relying on the NVDIMM support to retain the in-memory saved state. This approach is simple and transparent but can require significant amounts of additional time on the save path. Putting devices in a sleep state usually involves allowing all outstanding I/O to complete, which could take 100s of milliseconds or more on a heavily loaded and slow device such as a disk. Section 5, we show that the latency of using ACPI suspend significantly exceeds the residual energy window on our test systems, thus making this approach infeasible without adding a large amount of additional capacitance.

A better approach is to avoid any additional work on the save path, but instead to clean up device state on the restore path. We have investigated several ways of doing this, e.g., using plug-and-play support to "reboot" the device stack during restore. Although conceptually straightforward, this is complex to implement in a large OS such as Windows, and cannot handle all devices: e.g., legacy non plug-and-play devices, or the disk device holding the paging file which cannot be "unplugged".

A more practical approach to device restart might be to *virtualize* the devices, e.g. by using a virtual machine (VM) hypervisor. Virtualized server environments are common and increasingly so. In this approach, a fresh instance of the entire "host OS" and its physical device stack is booted after a failure. Individual VMs have their state restored from NVRAM, and the hypervisor transparently retries or fails outstanding operations on the virtualized devices. We are currently looking at implementing such I/O replay support in a VM hypervisor such as Hyper-V.

NVDIMMs The save and restore routines rely on main memory contents being preserved by the memory, i.e., the NVRAM. Our design uses AgigaRAM NVDIMMs [1], which use their own ultra-capacitor charge to save their contents to on-board flash on a power failure. Thus it is sufficient to initiate the NVDIMM save within the residual energy window; the save will be completed without system power using energy from the ultracapacitors.

In our prototype, the microcontroller communicates with Agiga NVDIMM(s) over an I^2C bus. It translates commands sent from the host processor over the serial line to NVDIMM commands, i.e. "save" and "restore". The current version of the AgigaRAM NVDIMM requires the DRAM module to be put into "self-refresh" mode before the save or the restore operation can begin. In the case of "restore", the host processor also has to bring the memory out of self-refresh, and re-initialize the memory parameters. These steps require firmware (BIOS) support not provided by standard BIOS implementations (AgigaRAM is targeted at embedded systems with custom firmware). We are currently working on modifying a standard BIOS to support this.

5. Evaluation

In this section we present experiments that answer three questions. First, what is the performance benefit of WSP's "flush-on-fail" approach over the "flush-on-commit" approach of NV-heaps, i.e., what is the performance gained from moving cache flushes out of the performance path? Second, how long is the residual energy window on typical PC power supplies? Third, how long is the "flush-on-fail" save time?

The testbed for our performance experiments was a 2.13 GHz 2-socket Intel C5528 system with 4 cores per socket and 2 hyper-

Configuration	Updates/s	
Mnemosyne	2160	(77)
WSP	5274	(139)

Means of 5 runs, with standard deviations shown in brackets.

Table 1. Update throughput for OpenLDAP

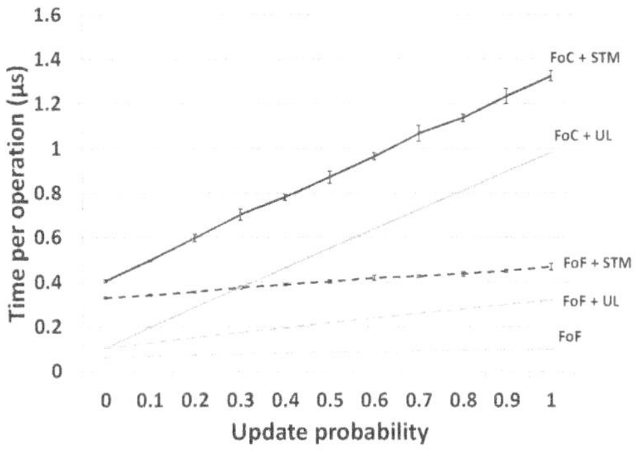

Each point is the mean of 10 runs, with min-max error bars.

Figure 5. Hash table microbenchmark performance

threads per core. The testbed has 48 GB of DDR3 DRAM (1333 MT/s). For the measurements of residual energy and save time, we measured this platform as well as a lower-powered AMD platform. This had a single 6-core AMD 4180 processor and 8 GB of DDR3 DRAM.

5.1 Performance

In our first experiment we compare the performance of an NV-heap implementation, Mnemosyne [33], with the WSP approach. We use the OpenLDAP benchmark reported by Volos et. al [33] with the same configuration parameters, on our hardware testbed running Linux 2.6.35. The benchmark inserts 100,000 randomly generated entries into an empty directory. The workload is processed by an OpenLDAP server that uses an AVL tree stored in the Mnemosyne NV-heap, rather than the default Berkeley DB, as the persistent store.

Mnemosyne ensures durability and consistency of the AVL tree by wrapping updates in transactions and logging updates in an efficient in-memory log structure. This log is written directly to memory, bypassing the processor caches, using non-temporal stores. We compared this with a WSP "flush-on-fail" version in which all transactional instrumentation and logging was disabled, i.e., a normal in-memory AVL tree. We did not undo the other modifications made to OpenLDAP to avoid dangling references; although these modifications are unnecessary with WSP, they do not add much performance overhead.

Table 1 shows the results of these experiments in terms of update throughput. This is a single-threaded, closed-loop experiment and hence operation latency is simply the inverse of throughput. We see that the WSP version is 2.4x faster than the Mnemosyne version. The overheads of Mnemosyne are partially due to the persistent log and flushing of updates; and partially due to other STM-related overheads such as tracking readsets, instrumenting reads, etc. These are not required for persistence, and since OpenLDAP is lock-based, they are not needed for concurrency control either.

To separate out these sources of overhead, we evaluated and compared five configurations using a simple hash table benchmark. The configurations are:

- *FoC + STM* (Flush-on-commit with STM): this is the default Mnemosyne configuration.
- *FoC + UL* (Flush-on-commit with undo logging): this uses flush-on-commit with an undo log (Section 3), and does not use STM.
- *FoF + STM* (Flush-on-fail with STM): uses the default Intel STM library, which instruments and logs transactional reads and writes, but does not flush logs or updates from the processor caches.
- *FoF + UL* (Flush-on-fail with undo logging): Undo logging is enabled but log appends and data writes are in-cache; they are not flushed synchronously to memory.
- *FoF* (Flush-on-fail with no transactions or logging).

As the non-STM configurations do not provide concurrency control, we ran the benchmark single-threaded: our purpose is not to compare different concurrency control mechanisms, but to measure the overheads of logging and flushing. The undo log was implemented on a Windows platform and relies on the Phoenix compiler framework [24] to instrument writes to the persistent heap, whereas the STM-based configurations use the Intel STM compiler [18] on Linux. The *FoF* configuration works on both platforms; we found that the Phoenix-based version was 11–17% slower, and we report this slower performance.

Each benchmark run pre-populated an in-memory hash table with 100,000 entries, and then measured the performance of 1,000,000 random operations on it. Each operation was either a key lookup or an update (with equal numbers of inserts and deletes). Figure 5 shows the results as the average time per operation as a function of the proportion of updates in the workload.

We can observe several things. First, the *FoC + STM* configuration is 6–13x slower than *FoF*. The penalty increases linearly with the update ratio, reflecting the cost of flushing updates and log records. By using undo logs (*FoC + UL*), the STM overheads are removed. For a read-only workload the remaining overhead (60%) is that of creating a transactional context for each operation, which is significant for short operations. For a write-intensive workload, *FoC + UL* is still almost 10x slower than *FoF*. This shows that it is synchronous flushing to memory that dominates performance, rather than other transaction-related costs.

This is confirmed if we examine the *FoF + STM* and *FoF + UL* configurations. Although slower than *FoF*, they are much faster than the flush-on-commit configurations. We conclude that even if transactions are desired for concurrency control or error recovery, it is still better to use them in-cache with a flush-on-fail approach, than to combine transactions with persistence using flush-on-commit.

5.2 Residual energy

To evaluate the feasibility of flush-on-fail, we measured the residual energy window and the time to flush-on-fail (save transient state) on both the high-end (Intel) and the low-end (AMD) testbed. We first present the residual energy measurements and then the timing measurements.

To measure the residual energy window, we used a sampling oscilloscope to monitor the PWR_OK signal as well as the voltage levels on DC output lines from the ATX power supply, with a sampling frequency of 100 kHz. When the power supply detects an input power failure, it drops the PWR_OK signal. We measured the interval from this signal dropping to the first voltage drop seen on any of the power supply's output lines. Since the samples are noisy, we define an output voltage drop as any 250 μs interval where the output voltage drops below 95% of its nominal value.

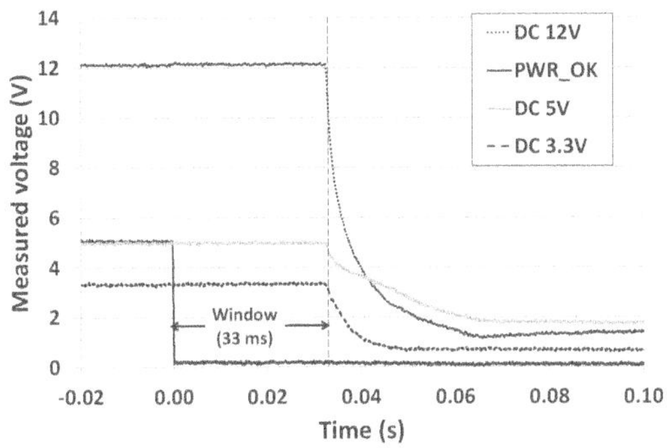

Figure 6. Residual energy window (Intel testbed)

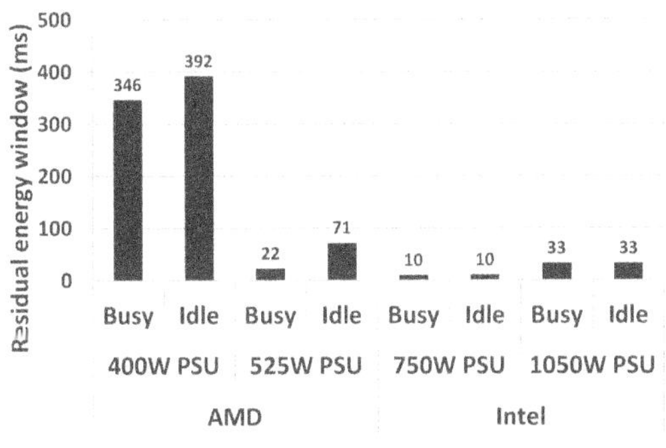

Each value is the worst (lowest) observed of 3 runs.

Figure 7. Residual energy windows across configurations

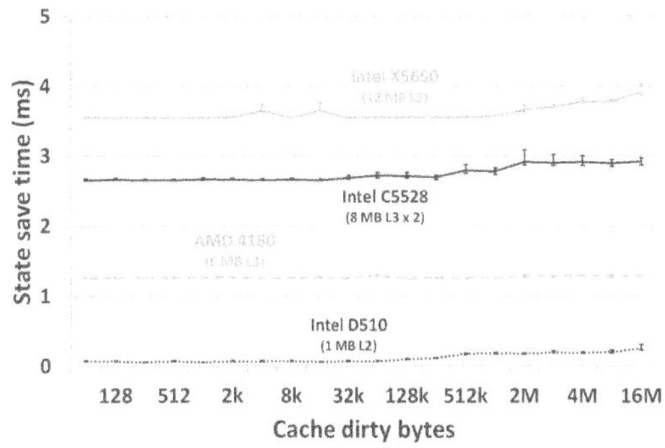

Values shown are means of 32 runs; error bars show min-max variation. Sizes in parentheses are those of the largest cache on each chip.

Figure 8. Context save and cache flush times.

	`wbinvd`	`clflush`	Theoretical best
2 x Intel C5528	2.8 ms	2.3 ms	0.79 ms
AMD 4180	1.3 ms	1.6 ms	0.65 ms

Table 2. Cache flush times using different instructions

Figure 6 shows the voltage over time for the Intel platform, before and after the power failure signal. A CPU-intensive prime number calculator and a disk stress test were used on the high-end testbed to keep all processors and block devices busy. To ensure a worst-case configuration, all stress tests continue to run even after the power failure notification, thus keeping the system busier than with WSP. The residual energy window measured in this experiment was 33 ms.

These results used a 1050 W power supply. We repeated the experiment with a lower-rated 750 W power supply. We also tested the lower-power AMD system with two power supplies rated at 400 W and 525 W. For each configuration we measured both a worst case (all stress tests running) and a best case (idle). Figure 7 shows the residual energy window for each configuration. We see residual energy windows from 10–400 ms, depending on the power supply as well as the system being tested. This variation reflects the variation in internal capacitance across different power supplies.

5.3 State save time

Figure 8 shows the time to save all processor contexts and flush all caches on our two test platforms (Intel C5528 Nehalem and AMD 4180 Opteron) as well as two other Intel processors (Intel X5650 Xeon and D510 Atom). The cache invalidate/flush time dominates the total save time; using a simple benchmark we varied the amount of dirty data in the cache, up to the size of the largest cache on any of the processors. We see that save times are consistently under 5 ms in all cases, and under 3 ms for our two testbed platforms. Interestingly, there is little dependence on the number of dirty cache lines. We believe this is an artifact of the implementation of the `wbinvd` instruction. Flushing individual dirty lines (using the `clflush` instruction) is more efficient when there are few dirty cache lines; however it is not practical to track the location of dirty cache lines in software. Table 2 shows the worst-case (all cache lines dirty) flush times for `wbinvd` and `clflush`, as well as the theoretical best achievable based on measured memory bandwidths.

Thus the measured residual energy window on our two testbed platforms is 2.5–80 times larger than the save time, even in the worst case. This shows that it is feasible to use the residual energy to save processor contexts and flush caches. Further, the worst-case time to flush the caches is a function of processor cache size and memory bandwidth, and is easily characterized and measured for a given system. Similarly the residual energy window can be conservatively estimated as a function of capacitance and the maximum rated power draw of the system, and external capacitance added to provide any desired safety margin.

Device state save time The timing measurements in Section 5.3 are from a system that saves only processor state and does not save device state. We believe that the correct approach is to re-initialize devices and restart I/Os on the recovery path, rather than quiesce devices or save device state on the save path. However, it is interesting to ask the question: what is the additional latency of saving device state on the save path?

We measured the time taken by Windows to put all system devices into the D3 sleep state for both our testbeds and in both the busy and idle configurations. Figure 9 shows the results. We see that state save times are large and variable: comparable to the residual energy windows on the AMD testbed and much larger on the Intel testbed. Additionally, the "idle" save times are substantial, showing

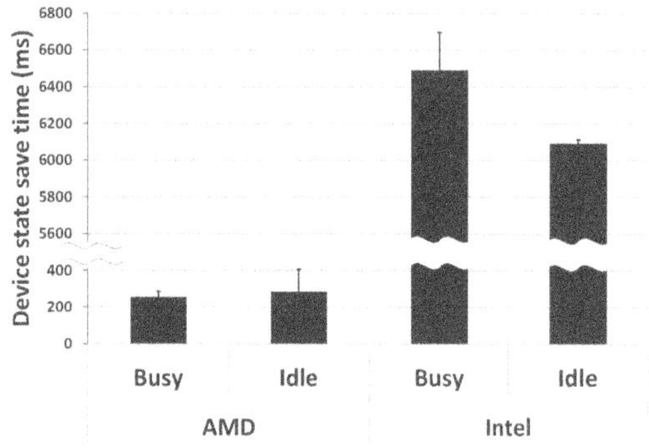

Values shown are means of 5 runs; error bars show standard deviations. Note the break in the y-axis.

Figure 9. Device state save time

that even when there are no outstanding I/Os, the state save process is slow. We further investigated the high state save times for the Intel testbed and found that they are dominated by three devices: the GPU, the disk, and the network interface (NIC). The first is not required for a server configuration: in fact the only crucial devices for a server are the disk and the NIC. These device drivers could be modified to eliminate unnecessary timeouts and delays, and speed up the save process. However we believe that a better approach is to avoid executing any device driver code on the save path, and to use virtualization to transparently restart the device stack on restore.

5.4 Summary

We have shown that there are significant performance advantages to a "flush-on-fail" approach compared to "flush-on-commit" approach to data stored in NVRAM. Unlike flush-on-commit, flush-on-fail does not require STM or transactional logging; at the same time transactional applications also benefit from improved performance with flush-on-fail.

It is clear that processor contexts and cache contents can safely be saved well within the residual energy windows of standard PSUs. If desired, this residual energy can be explicitly provisioned by using a supercapacitor. For example, the state save on our test platform could be powered by a 0.5 F supercapacitor that costs less than US$2.

However, device suspend paths are slow and potentially unbounded since they rely on draining outstanding I/Os. It is not clear that we can rely on saving device state within a fixed time and energy budget. Instead, we must recover device state on the restore path, for example by using virtualization and replaying outstanding I/Os on the virtualized devices.

6. Discussion and Future Work

Our evaluation shows that flush-on-fail has better runtime performance than a flush-on-commit approach, and that standard power supplies provide a sufficient residual energy window to make this feasible. We believe that overall our results show promise for the use of main-memory NVRAM as the first resort recovery mechanism after a power failure. However there are still many open questions and directions for future work; here we discuss the most relevant ones.

Distributed applications Data center servers are often deployed today as part of a scalable distributed system. These systems already tolerate server failures, e.g. by using replication and/or failover techniques. On a failure, these systems must pay the cost of reading in-memory state from a checkpoint in the storage tier, or re-replicating the state from a live replica. For large memory servers, the cost of this state refresh can be substantial. With NVRAM and WSP, a server that suffers a short period of unavailability will have state that is stale but still mostly relevant, allowing a more efficient state refresh by only applying the recent updates that were missed during the failure. Some distributed applications maintain versioned state and/or update logs, allowing missed updates to be efficiently recovered. For other applications that are constructed as an "all or nothing" cache, this will require some added complexity.

Long outages So far we have assumed that power outages are relatively short (seconds to tens of seconds), and hence there is benefit in rapidly recovering state locally on the failed machine. However, with longer outages, the system might be forced to instantiate a new instance of the service on a different server, thus incurring the penalty of recovering from the back end. Does NVRAM change these tradeoffs, e.g., can we delay the re-instantiation of a server to allow NVRAM-based recovery? This is particularly relevant when using state machine replication [30]. If replication is done across uncorrelated servers (e.g. with independent sources of power), then the service can be kept available after a failure, with a new replica brought online in the background. This can potentially be delayed, to reduce the recovery costs in case the failed machine is able to recover with most of the state, i.e., lacking only the most recent updates.

SCM-based NVRAMs So far we have focused on DRAM-based, rather than SCM-based, NVRAMs. SCMs (storage class memories) such as phase-change memory and memristors have only recently emerged, and it is difficult to predict exactly what their performance will be, and whether/when they will become viable as server main memory. Broadly, they are expected to have access times comparable to, but slower than, DRAM. This will increase the overhead of flush-on-commit, especially for asymmetric memories such as phase-change memory, which is expected to be 10–100x slower than DRAM for writes but only 2x slower for reads [13]. Hence we expect that these slower memories will show an even larger performance advantage for flush-on-fail. SCMs are also expected to scale to much larger capacities than DRAM, potentially allowing multi-terabyte main memories. Note that the energy costs of flush-on-fail do not scale with main memory sizes, but only with the size of processor caches.

One potential disadvantage of SCMs such as phase-change memory is that they are expected to be more energy-intensive to write than DRAM. This might require additional capacitance in power supplies as a function of processor cache size, memory bandwidth, and the power consumption of writing the memory.

Hybrid systems With SCMs, there is also the potential for hybrid DRAM-SCM systems, with a small fast DRAM alongside a larger slower SCM. WSP can be used with such systems by replacing the DRAMs with NVDIMMs, with no impact on runtime performance. Regardless of persistence, however, hybrid systems raise an interesting performance challenge: automatically mapping objects and pages to either DRAM or SCM to maximize overall performance.

NVRAM failures Flush-on-fail adds an additional failure mode to the system, which is failure during the save process. A failed save will be detected on boot-up and trigger a normal recovery from the back end. However we believe such failures will be rare. The save routine is implemented at a very low level of the OS and required changing fewer than 200 lines of code. Thus software failures are unlikely. The internal capacitance of the PSU might unexpectedly fail to provide the required residual energy. It is straightforward and cheap to provision the PSU with sufficient capacitance by using supercapacitors [23].

Process persistence So far we have assumed a model where both application and OS structures are restored after a power failure. An alternative is to save only application state process state and to restore it on a fresh instance of the OS. This still provides the same abstraction to the application as whole-system persistence: unlike the persistent heap model, thread contexts and stacks would be restored. It could also use the same fast save path for NVRAM. The recovery mechanism however would be different, since in effect application state will have to be separated out from OS state. Otherworld [12] is an implementation of process persistence for Linux. In Windows, application processes have dependencies on a variety of OS structures, making this approach complex. However, recent work on Drawbridge [28] has shown that most of these dependencies can be encapsulated into a "library OS" that can be included in the application's state, leaving a narrow and easily restartable interface to the OS kernel.

Future work Our immediate goal is to extend our prototype into a fully implemented and deployable system. This involves added firmware support for saving and restoring NVDIMM state, and hypervisor support for per-VM persistence. In the longer term, we intend to investigate failure and recovery tradeoffs for different scenarios: e.g., what are the costs/benefits of adding capacitance to a system compared to more frequent recovery from the back end.

7. Related Work

Persistence models Whole-system persistence is very similar to the orthogonal global persistence model of KeyKOS [21]. KeyKOS implemented global persistence through periodic checkpoints to disk and required extensive OS support. WSP is aimed at NVRAM-based systems and is based on flushing transient state to NVRAM on failure rather than during runtime, and operates with little or on OS modification. The persistent heap model has also been widely used in different language environments including PS-ALGOL [3], Java [4], and SML [27]. Section 3.2 provides in more detail our rationale for using whole-system or global persistence rather than heap persistence.

SCM based architectures Recent developments in SCMs have led to new designs for file systems and "on-disk" data structures optimized for these technologies. BPFS [9] is an in-kernel file system that leverages the byte-addressability of SCMs to provide fast file operations. Similarly the Rio buffer cache [7] preserves file buffer cache contents after a "warm reboot"; when used with NVRAM it means that file writes can be considered durable when they are written to the buffer cache. Both BPFS and Rio leverage non-volatile memory to speed up file writes. For an in-memory server, however, even such fast file operations cause significant runtime overheads as well as duplication of state. These overheads are reduced significantly in the persistent heap approach and eliminated in the WSP approach. CDDS B-Trees [32] are non-volatile B-Trees optimized for byte-addressable rather than block operation; they outperform traditional block-based B-Trees by 75–138%. NV-heaps allow use of a wider range of data structures such as hash tables, binary trees, and skip lists. WSP is transparent to applications and any in-memory data structures can be used.

Flash-based NVRAMs eNVy [35] proposed the use of SRAM backed by batteries and flash, to implement the abstraction of a byte-addressable non-volatile store on the main memory bus, i.e., a large NVRAM. The Agiga NVDIMMs are similar (with the use of ultracapacitors and DRAM rather than batteries and SRAM). A key difference is that in eNVy the SRAM was used to buffer only a small subset of the flash contents: with a random-access workload, the system would be bottlenecked on paging to and from the flash. NVDIMMs by contrast leverage dropping DRAM prices to store the entire contents in DRAM, with the flash layer being written/read only on failure/recovery.

Device recovery Our WSP prototype takes a simple approach to saving and recovering device state, which takes much longer than flushing processor caches and contexts. Ohmura et al. [25] propose an alternative approach: shadowing device registers in NVRAM by logging register writes on each device operation. This removes eliminates the "state save" at the cost of additional complexity in the device driver. A more device-independent approach is to re-initialize all device-related state, and replay device operations as necessary. Otherworld [12] reboots the entire operating system, transferring control to a new "crash kernel". Application state is maintained, and application threads that are in system calls have those calls aborted with a failure code; they can then retry the I/O. Although the aim of Otherworld is to recover from operating system crashes, this approach could also be used as a way to re-initialize device state after a WSP save/restore. Similarly, Drawbridge [28] allows an entire application, together with its OS "personality", to be serialized and restarted on a new kernel. This could be used after a WSP save/restore to extract application state safely, after which the OS can be restarted.

8. Conclusion

Main-memory servers are common in data centers today and will be increasingly used, driven by the need to avoid I/O bottlenecks, the availability of large-memory (up to 1 TB) DRAM systems, and the potential for even larger byte-addressable storage-class memories (SCMs). These servers introduce the problem of recovering a large amount of in-memory state from back-end storage after a failure. Non-volatile main memory (NVRAM) can alleviate this problem, but current software models for using NVRAM have limitations. In particular, user-level persistent heaps, while outperforming block-based NVRAM, still have high overheads compared to in-memory operation. They also require applications to be rewritten to a new API and memory model.

In this paper we argued for, and showed the feasibility of, an alternative approach: whole-system persistence. This allows legacy applications to run unmodified and with no overheads, by flushing transient state at failure time rather than during execution. We showed through experiments that this "flush-on-fail" can be powered using the residual energy from the system power supply, and that this gives a runtime performance benefit of 1.6–13x compared to a user-level persistent heap.

References

[1] AgigaTech. AGIGRAM (TM) Non-Volatile System. `http://www.agigatech.com/agigaram.php`, 2012.

[2] AgigaTech. ArxCis-NV (TM) Non-Volatile DIMM. `http://www.vikingmodular.com/products/arxcis/arxcis.html`, Jan. 2012.

[3] M. Atkinson, K. Chisholm, and P. Cockshott. PS-algol: an Algol with a persistent heap. *ACM SIGPLAN Notices*, 17(7):24–31, July 1982.

[4] M. P. Atkinson, L. Daynes, M. J. Jordan, T. Printezis, and S. Spence. An orthogonally persistent Java. *SIGMOD Record*, 25(4):68–75, Dec. 1996.

[5] G. Candea, S. Kawamoto, Y. Fujiki, G. Friedman, and A. Fox. Microreboot - A technique for cheap recovery. In *Proceedings of the Symposium on Operating Systems Design and Implementation (OSDI)*, pages 31–44, San Francisco, CA, Dec. 2004.

[6] F. Chang, J. Dean, S. Ghemawat, W. C. Hsieh, D. A. Wallach, M. Burrows, T. Chandra, A. Fikes, and R. E. Gruber. Bigtable: A distributed

storage system for structured data. In *Proceedings of the ACM Symposium on Operating Systems Design and Implementation (SOSP)*, Lake George, NY, Nov. 2006.

[7] P. M. Chen, W. T. Ng, S. Chandra, C. Aycock, G. Rajamani, and D. Lowell. The Rio file cache: Surviving operating system crashes. In *Proceedings of the International Conference on Architectural Support for Programming Languages and Operating Systems (ASPLOS)*, pages 74–83, Cambridge, MA, Oct. 1996.

[8] J. Coburn, A. M. Caulfield, A. Akel, L. M. Grupp, R. K. Gupta, R. Jhala, and S. Swanson. NV-heaps: making persistent objects fast and safe with next-generation, non-volatile memories. In *Proceedings of the International Conference on Architectural Support for Programming Languages and Operating Systems (ASPLOS)*, pages 105–118, Newport Beach, CA, Mar. 2011.

[9] J. Condit, E. B. Nightingale, C. Frost, E. Ipek, B. C. Lee, D. Burger, and D. Coetzee. Better I/O through byte-addressable, persistent memory. In *Proceedings of the ACM Symposium on Operating Systems Principles (SOSP)*, pages 133–146, Big Sky, MT, Oct. 2009.

[10] G. DeCandia, D. Hastorun, M. Jampani, G. Kakulapati, A. Lakshman, A. Pilchin, S. Sivasubramanian, P. Vosshall, and W. Vogels. Dynamo: Amazon's highly available key-value store. In *Proceedings of the ACM Symposium on Operating Systems Principles (SOSP)*, Oct. 2007.

[11] Dell. Dell poweredge r910 4u rack server. `http://www.dell.com/us/enterprise/p/poweredge-r910/pd?~ck=anav`, July 2011.

[12] A. Depoutovitch and M. Stumm. Otherworld: giving applications a chance to survive OS kernel crashes. In *Proceedings of the European conference on Computer systems (EuroSys)*, pages 181–194, Paris, France, Apr. 2010.

[13] E. Doller. Phase change memory and its impacts on memory hierarchy. `http://www.pdl.cmu.edu/SDI/2009/092309.html`.

[14] Facebook engineering notes: More details on today's outage. `http://www.facebook.com/note.php?note_id=431441338919`, Sept. 2010.

[15] Foresight. T2+2 (tm) market overview: Supercapacitors. `http://batteries.foresightst.com/resources/MarketOverviews/NET0007IO.pdf`, Dec. 2009.

[16] J. Hamilton. Open compute ups & power supply. `http://perspectives.mvdirona.com/2011/05/04/OpenComputeUPSPowerSupply.aspx`.

[17] Intel. Atx specification (version 2.2). `http://www.formfactors.org/developer/specs/atx2_2.pdf`, 2004.

[18] Intel. Intel C++ STM Compiler, Prototype Edition. `http://software.intel.com/en-us/articles/intel-c-stm-compiler-prototype-edition/`, Aug. 2010.

[19] R. Kallman, H. Kimura, J. Natkins, A. Pavlo, A. Rasin, S. B. Zdonik, E. P. C. Jones, S. Madden, M. Stonebraker, Y. Zhang, J. Hugg, and D. J. Abadi. H-store: a high-performance, distributed main memory transaction processing system. *PVLDB*, 1(2):1496–1499, 2008.

[20] A. Lakshman and P. Malik. Cassandra – a decentralized structured storage system. In *Proceedings of the ACM SIGOPS International Workshop on Large Scale Distributed Systems and Middleware (LADIS)*, Big Sky, MT, Oct. 2009.

[21] C. R. Landau. The checkpoint mechanism in KeyKOS. In *Proceedings of the International Workshop on Object Orientation in Operating Systems*, pages 86–91, Sept. 1992.

[22] B. C. Lee, E. Ipek, O. Mutlu, and D. Burger. Architecting phase change memory as a scalable DRAM alternative. In *Proceedings of the International Symposium on Computer Architecture (ISCA)*, Austin, TX, June 2009.

[23] Maxwell. Maxwell boostcap ultracapacitors. `http://www.maxwell.com/products/ultracapacitors`, Dec. 2011.

[24] Microsoft. Phoenix technical overview. `https://connect.microsoft.com/Phoenix/content/content.aspx?ContentID=4513`, July 2011.

[25] R. Ohmura, N. Yamasaki, and Y. Anzai. Device state recovery in non-volatile main memory systems. In *COMPSAC*. IEEE Computer Society, 2003.

[26] Oracle. Oracle TimesTen in-memory database overview. `http://www.oracle.com/technetwork/database/timesten/overview/timesten-imdb-086887.html`, July 2011.

[27] J. O'Toole, S. Nettles, and D. Gifford. Concurrent compacting garbage collection of a persistent heap. In *Proceedings of the ACM Symposium on Operating Systems Principles (SOSP)*, pages 161–174, New York, NYA, Dec. 1993.

[28] D. E. Porter, S. Boyd-Wickizer, J. Howell, R. Olinsky, and G. C. Hunt. Rethinking the library OS from the top down. In *Proceedings of the International Conference on Architectural Support for Programming Languages and Operating Systems (ASPLOS)*, pages 291–304, Newport Beach, CA, Mar. 2011.

[29] M. K. Qureshi, V. Srinivasan, and J. A. Rivers. Scalable high performance main memory system using phase-change memory technology. In *Proceedings of the International Symposium on Computer Architecture (ISCA)*, Austin, TX, June 2009.

[30] F. B. Schneider. Implementing fault-tolerant services using the state machine approach: a tutorial. *ACM Comput. Surv.*, 22:299–319, Dec. 1990.

[31] M. Stonebraker, S. Madden, D. J. Abadi, S. Harizopoulos, N. Hachem, and P. Helland. The end of an architectural era (it's time for a complete rewrite). In *Proceedings of the International Conference on Very Large Data Bases (VLDB)*, pages 1150–1160, Vienna, Austria, Sept. 2007.

[32] S. Venkataraman, N. Tolia, P. Ranganathan, and R. H. Campbell. Consistent and durable data structures for non-volatile byte-addressable memory. In *Proceedings of the USENIX Conference on File and Storage Technologies (FAST)*, pages 61–75, San Jose, CA, Feb. 2011.

[33] H. Volos, A. J. Tack, and M. M. Swift. Mnemosyne: lightweight persistent memory. In *Proceedings of the International Conference on Architectural Support for Programming Languages and Operating Systems (ASPLOS)*, pages 91–104, Newport Beach, CA, Mar. 2011.

[34] VoltDB. `http://voltdb.com/`, July 2011.

[35] M. Wu and W. Zwaenepoel. eNVy: A non-volatile main memory storage system. In *Proceedings of the Symposium on Architectural Support for Programming Languages and Operating Systems (ASPLOS)*, San Jose, CA, 1994.

ELI: Bare-Metal Performance for I/O Virtualization

Abel Gordon[1*] Nadav Amit[2*] Nadav Har'El[1]
Muli Ben-Yehuda[21] Alex Landau[1] Assaf Schuster[2] Dan Tsafrir[2]

[1]IBM Research—Haifa
{abelg,nyh,lalex}@il.ibm.com

[2]Technion—Israel Institute of Technology
{namit,muli,assaf,dan}@cs.technion.ac.il

Abstract

Direct device assignment enhances the performance of guest virtual machines by allowing them to communicate with I/O devices without host involvement. But even with device assignment, guests are still unable to approach bare-metal performance, because the host intercepts all interrupts, including those interrupts generated by assigned devices to signal to guests the completion of their I/O requests. The host involvement induces multiple unwarranted guest/host context switches, which significantly hamper the performance of I/O intensive workloads. To solve this problem, we present ELI (Exit-Less Interrupts), a software-only approach for handling interrupts within guest virtual machines *directly* and *securely*. By removing the host from the interrupt handling path, ELI manages to improve the throughput and latency of unmodified, untrusted guests by 1.3x–1.6x, allowing them to reach 97%–100% of bare-metal performance even for the most demanding I/O-intensive workloads.

Categories and Subject Descriptors C.0 [*General*]: Hardware/software interfaces

General Terms Performance

Keywords SR-IOV, I/O Virtualization, Interrupts, I/O Performance, Device Assignment

1. Introduction

I/O activity is a dominant factor in the performance of virtualized environments [32, 33, 47, 51], motivating *direct device assignment* where the host assigns physical I/O devices directly to guest virtual machines. Examples of such devices include disk controllers, network cards, and GPUs. Direct device assignment provides superior performance relative to alternative I/O virtualization approaches, because it almost entirely removes the host from the guest's I/O path. Without direct device assignment, I/O-intensive workloads might suffer unacceptable performance degradation [29, 32, 37, 51, 53]. Still, direct access does not allow I/O-intensive workloads to approach bare-metal (non-virtual) performance [9, 15, 26, 31, 51], limiting it to 60%–65% of the optimum by our measurements. We find that nearly the *entire* performance difference is induced by interrupts of assigned devices.

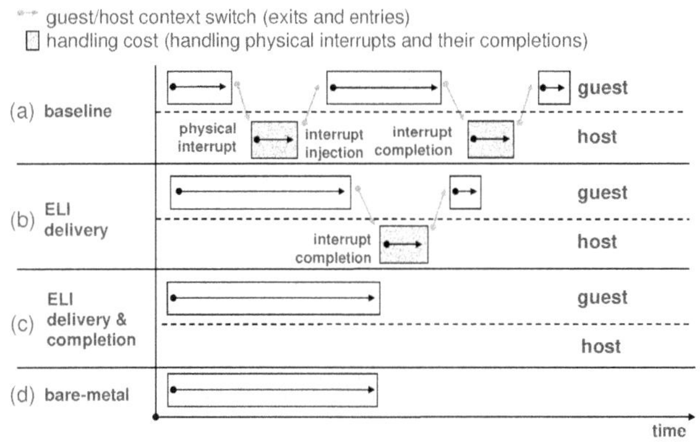

Figure 1. Exits during interrupt handling

I/O devices generate interrupts to asynchronously communicate to the CPU the completion of I/O operations. In virtualized settings, each device interrupt triggers a costly *exit* [2, 9, 26], causing the guest to be suspended and the host to be resumed, regardless of whether or not the device is assigned. The host first signals to the hardware the completion of the physical interrupt as mandated by the x86 specification. It then injects a corresponding (virtual) interrupt to the guest and resumes the guest's execution. The guest in turn handles the virtual interrupt and, like the host, signals completion, believing that it directly interacts with the hardware. This action triggers yet another exit, prompting the host to emulate the completion of the virtual interrupt and to resume the guest again. The chain of events for handling interrupts is illustrated in Figure 1(a).

The guest/host context switches caused by interrupts induce a tolerable overhead price for non-I/O-intensive workloads, a fact that allowed some previous virtualization studies to claim they achieved bare-metal performance [7, 27, 29]. But our measurements indicate that this overhead quickly ceases to be tolerable, adversely affecting guests that require throughput of as little as 50 Mbps. Notably, many previous studies improved virtual I/O by relaxing protection [6, 24, 27] or by modifying guests [7, 29], whereas we focus on the most challenging virtualization scenario of guests that are untrusted and unmodified.

Many previous studies identified interrupts as a major source of overhead [9, 28, 49], and many proposed techniques to reduce it, both in bare-metal settings [17, 43, 45, 54] and in virtualized settings [4, 15, 26, 31, 51]. In principle, it is possible to tune devices and their drivers to generate fewer interrupts, thereby reducing the

*Both authors contributed equally.

ASPLOS'12, March 3–7, 2012, London, England, UK.

related overhead. But doing so in practice is far from trivial [8, 44] and can adversely affect both latency and throughput. We survey these approaches and contrast them with ours in **Section 2**.

Our approach rests on the observation that the high interrupt rates experienced by a core running an I/O-intensive guest are mostly generated by devices assigned to the guest. Indeed, we measure rates of over 150K physical interrupts per second, even while employing standard techniques to reduce the number of interrupts, such as *interrupt coalescing* [4, 43, 54] and *hybrid polling* [17, 45]. As noted, the resulting guest/host context switches are nearly exclusively responsible for the inferior performance relative to bare metal. To eliminate these switches, we propose ELI (ExitLess Interrupts), a software-only approach for handling physical interrupts directly within the guest in a secure manner.

With ELI, physical interrupts are delivered directly to guests, allowing them to process their devices' interrupts without host involvement; ELI makes sure that each guest forwards all other interrupts to the host. With x86 hardware, interrupts are delivered using a software-controlled table of pointers to functions, such that the hardware invokes the k-th function whenever an interrupt of type k fires. Instead of utilizing the guest's table, ELI maintains, manipulates, and protects a "shadow table", such that entries associated with assigned devices point to the guest's code, whereas the other entries are set to trigger an exit to the host. We describe x86 interrupt handling relevant to ELI and ELI itself in **Section 3** and **Section 4**, respectively. ELI leads to a mostly exitless execution as depicted in Figure 1(c).

We experimentally evaluate ELI in **Section 5** with micro and macro benchmarks. Our baseline configuration employs standard techniques to reduce (coalesce) the number of interrupts, demonstrating ELI's benefit beyond the state-of-the-art. We show that ELI improves the throughput and latency of guests by 1.3x–1.6x. Notably, whereas I/O-intensive guests were so far limited to 60%–65% of bare-metal throughput, with ELI they reach performance that is within 97%–100% of the optimum. Consequently, ELI makes it possible to, e.g., consolidate traditional data-center workloads that nowadays remain non-virtualized due to unacceptable performance loss.

In **Section 6** we describe how ELI protects the aforementioned table, maintaining security and isolation while still allowing guests to handle interrupts directly. In **Section 7** we discusses potential hardware support that would simplify ELI's design and implementation. Finally, in **Section 8** we discuss the applicability of ELI and our future work directions, and in **Section 9** we conclude.

2. Motivation and Related Work

For the past several decades, interrupts have been the main method by which hardware devices can send asynchronous events to the operating system [13]. The main advantage of using interrupts to receive notifications from devices over polling them is that the processor is free to perform other tasks while waiting for an interrupt. This advantage applies when interrupts happen relatively infrequently [39], as has been the case until high performance storage and network adapters came into existence. With these devices, the CPU can be overwhelmed with interrupts, leaving no time to execute code other than the interrupt handler [34]. When the operating system is run in a guest, interrupts have a higher cost since every interrupt causes multiple exits [2, 9, 26].

In the remainder of this section we introduce the existing approaches to reduce the overheads induced by interrupts, and we highlight the novelty of ELI in comparison to these approaches. We subdivide the approaches into two categories.

2.1 Generic Interrupt Handling Approaches

We now survey approaches that equally apply to bare metal and virtualized environments.

Polling disables interrupts entirely and polls the device for new events at regular intervals. The benefit is that handling device events becomes synchronous, allowing the operating system to decide when to poll and thus limit the number of handler invocations. The drawbacks are added latency and wasted cycles when no events are pending. If polling is done on a different core, latency is improved, yet a core is wasted. Polling also consumes power since the processor cannot enter an idle state.

A **hybrid** approach for reducing interrupt-handling overhead is to dynamically switch between using interrupts and polling [17, 22, 34]. Linux uses this approach by default through the NAPI mechanism [45]. Switching between interrupts and polling does not always work well in practice, partly due to the complexity of predicting the number of interrupts a device will issue in the future.

Another approach is **interrupt coalescing** [4, 43, 54], in which the OS programs the device to send one interrupt in a time interval or one interrupt per several events, as opposed to one interrupt per event. As with the hybrid approaches, coalescing delays interrupts and hence might suffer from the same shortcomings in terms of latency. In addition, coalescing has other adverse effects and cannot be used as the only interrupt mitigation technique. Zec et al. [54] show that coalescing can burst TCP traffic that was not bursty beforehand. It also increases latency [28, 40], since the operating system can only handle the first packet of a series when the last coalesced interrupt for the series arrived. Deciding on the right model and parameters for coalescing is complex and depends on the workload, particularly when the workload runs within a guest [15]. Getting it right for a wide variety of workloads is hard if not impossible [4, 44]. Unlike coalescing, ELI does not reduce the number of interrupts; instead it streamlines the handling of interrupts targeted at virtual machines. Coalescing and ELI are therefore complementary: coalescing reduces the number of interrupts, and ELI reduces their price. Furthermore, with ELI, if a guest decides to employ coalescing, it can directly control the interrupt rate and latency, leading to predictable results. Without ELI, the interrupt rate and latency cannot be easily manipulated by changing the coalescing parameters, since the host's involvement in the interrupt path adds variability and uncertainty.

All evaluations in Section 5 were performed with the default Linux configuration, which combines the hybrid approach (via NAPI) and coalescing.

2.2 Virtualization-Specific Approaches

Using an emulated or paravirtual [7, 41] device provides much flexibility on the host side, but its performance is much lower than that of device assignment, not to mention bare metal. Liu [31] shows that device assignment of SR-IOV devices [16] can achieve throughput close to bare metal at the cost of as much as 2x higher CPU utilization. He also demonstrates that interrupts have a great impact on performance and are a major expense for both the transmit and receive paths. For this reason, although applicable to the emulated and paravirtual case as well, ELI's main focus is on improving device assignment.

Interrupt overhead is amplified in virtualized environments. The Turtles project [9] shows interrupt handling to cause a 25% increase in CPU utilization for a single-level virtual machine when compared with bare metal, and a 300% increase in CPU utilization for a nested virtual machine. There are software techniques [3] to reduce the number of exits by finding blocks of exiting instructions and exiting only once for the whole block. These techniques can increase the efficiency of running a virtual machine when the main reason for the overhead is in the guest code. When the reason is in external interrupts, such as for I/O intensive workloads with SR-IOV, such software techniques do not alleviate the overhead.

Dong et al. [15] discuss a framework for implementing SR-IOV support in the Xen hypervisor. Their results show that SR-IOV can achieve line rate with a 10Gbps network interface controller (NIC). However, the CPU utilization is 148% of bare metal. In addition, this result is achieved using adaptive interrupt coalescing, which increases I/O latency.

Like ELI, several studies attempted to reduce the aforementioned extra overhead of interrupts in virtual environments. vIC [4] discusses a method for interrupt coalescing in virtual storage devices and shows an improvement of up to 5% in a macro benchmark. Their method decides how much to coalesce based on the number of "commands in flight". Therefore, as the authors say, this approach cannot be used for network devices due to the lack of information on commands (or packets) in flight. Furthermore, no comparison is made with bare-metal performance. Dong et al. [14] use virtual interrupt coalescing via polling in the guest and receive side scaling to reduce network overhead in a paravirtual environment. But polling has its drawbacks, as discussed above, and ELI improves the more performance-oriented device assignment environment.

In CDNA [51], the authors propose a method for concurrent and direct network access for virtual machines. This method requires physical changes to NICs akin to SR-IOV. With CDNA, the NIC and the hypervisor split the work of multiplexing several guests' network flows onto a single NIC. In the CDNA model the hypervisor is still involved in the I/O path. While CDNA significantly increases throughput compared to the standard paravirtual driver in Xen, it is still 2x–3x slower than bare metal.

SplitX [26] proposes hardware extensions for running virtual machines on dedicated cores, with the hypervisor running in parallel on a different set of cores. Interrupts arrive only at the hypervisor cores and are then sent to the appropriate guests via an exitless inter-core communication mechanism. In contrast, with ELI the hypervisor can share cores with its guests, and instead of injecting interrupts to guests, programs the interrupts to arrive at them directly. Moreover, ELI does not require any hardware modifications and runs on current hardware.

NoHype [24, 48] argues that modern hypervisors are prone to attacks by their guests. In the NoHype model, the hypervisor is a thin layer that starts, stops, and performs other administrative actions on guests, but is not otherwise involved. Guests use assigned devices and interrupts are delivered directly to guests. No details of the implementation or performance results are provided. Instead, the authors focus on describing the security and other benefits of the model. In addition, NoHype requires a modified and trusted guest.

In Following the White Rabbit [52], the authors show several interrupt-based attacks on hypervisors, which can be addressed through the use of interrupt remapping [1]. Interrupt remapping can stop the guest from sending arbitrary interrupts to the host; it does not, as its name might imply, provide a mechanism for secure and direct delivery of interrupts to the guest. Since ELI delivers interrupts directly to guests, bypassing the host, the hypervisor is immune to certain interrupt-related attacks.

3. x86 Interrupt Handling

ELI gives untrusted and unmodified guests direct access to the architectural interrupt handling mechanisms in such a way that the host and other guests remain protected. To put ELI's design in context, we begin with a short overview of how interrupt handling works on x86 today.

3.1 Interrupts in Bare-Metal Environments

x86 processors use interrupts and exceptions to notify system software about incoming events. Interrupts are asynchronous events generated by external entities such as I/O devices; exceptions are synchronous events—such as page faults—caused by the code being executed. In both cases, the currently executing code is interrupted and execution jumps to a pre-specified interrupt or exception handler.

x86 operating systems specify handlers for each interrupt and exception using an architected in-memory table, the Interrupt Descriptor Table (IDT). This table contains up to 256 entries, each entry containing a pointer to a handler. Each architecturally-defined exception or interrupt have a numeric identifier—an exception number or interrupt *vector*—which is used as an index to the table. The operating systems can use one IDT for all of the cores or a separate IDT per core. The operating system notifies the processor where each core's IDT is located in memory by writing the IDT's virtual memory address into the Interrupt Descriptor Table Register (IDTR). Since the IDTR holds the virtual (not physical) address of the IDT, the OS must always keep the corresponding address mapped in the active set of page tables. In addition to the table's location in memory, the IDTR also holds the table's size.

When an external I/O device raises an interrupt, the processor reads the current value of the IDTR to find the IDT. Then, using the interrupt vector as an index to the IDT, the CPU obtains the virtual address of the corresponding handler and invokes it. Further interrupts may or may not be blocked while an interrupt handler runs.

System software needs to perform operations such as enabling and disabling interrupts, signaling the completion of interrupt handlers, configuring the timer interrupt, and sending inter-processor interrupts (IPIs). Software performs these operations through the Local Advanced Programmable Interrupt Controller (LAPIC) interface. The LAPIC has multiple registers used to configure, deliver, and signal completion of interrupts. Signaling the completion of interrupts, which is of particular importance to ELI, is done by writing to the end-of-interrupt (EOI) LAPIC register. The newest LAPIC interface, x2APIC [20], exposes its registers using model specific registers (MSRs), which are accessed through "read MSR" and "write MSR" instructions. Previous LAPIC interfaces exposed the registers only in a pre-defined memory area which is accessed through regular load and store instructions.

3.2 Interrupts in Virtual Environments

x86 hardware virtualization [5, 50] provides two modes of operation, *guest mode* and *host mode*. The host, running in host mode, uses guest mode to create new contexts for running guest virtual machines. Once the processor starts running a guest, execution continues in guest mode until some sensitive event [36] forces an exit back to host mode. The host handles any necessary events and then resumes the execution of the guest, causing an entry into guest mode. These exits and entries are the primary cause of virtualization overhead [2, 9, 26, 37]. The overhead is particularly pronounced in I/O intensive workloads [26, 31, 38, 46]. It comes from the cycles spent by the processor switching between contexts, the time spent in host mode to handle the exit, and the resulting cache pollution [2, 9, 19, 26].

This work focuses on running unmodified and untrusted operating systems. On the one hand, unmodified guests are not aware they run in a virtual machine, and they expect to control the IDT exactly as they do on bare metal. On the other hand, the host cannot easily give untrusted and unmodified guests control of each core's IDT. This is because having full control over the physical IDT implies total control of the core. Therefore, x86 hardware virtualization extensions use a different IDT for each mode. Guest mode execution on each core is controlled by the guest IDT and host mode execution is controlled by the host IDT. An I/O device can raise a physical interrupt when the CPU is executing either in host mode or in guest mode. If the interrupt arrives while the CPU is in guest mode, the

CPU forces an exit and delivers the interrupt to the host through the host IDT.

Guests receive virtual interrupts, which are not necessarily related to physical interrupts. The host may decide to inject the guest with a virtual interrupt because the host received a corresponding physical interrupt, or the host may decide to inject the guest with a virtual interrupt manufactured by the host. The host injects virtual interrupts through the guest IDT. When the processor enters guest mode after an injection, the guest receives and handles the virtual interrupt.

During interrupt handling, the guest will access its LAPIC. Just like the IDT, full access to a core's physical LAPIC implies total control of the core, so the host cannot easily give untrusted guests access to the physical LAPIC. For guests using the first LAPIC generation, the processor forces an exit when the guest accesses the LAPIC memory area. For guests using x2APIC, the host traps LAPIC accesses through an MSR bitmap. When running a guest, the host provides the CPU with a bitmap specifying which benign MSRs the guest is allowed to access directly and which sensitive MSRs must not be accessed by the guest directly. When the guest accesses sensitive MSRs, execution exits back to the host. In general, x2APIC registers are considered sensitive MSRs.

3.3 Interrupts from Assigned Devices

The key to virtualization performance is for the CPU to spend most of its time in guest mode, running the guest, and not in the host, handling guest exits. I/O device emulation and paravirtualized drivers [7, 25, 41] incur significant overhead for I/O intensive workloads running in guests [9, 31]. The overhead is incurred by the host's involvement in its guests' I/O paths for programmed I/O (PIO), memory-mapped I/O (MMIO), direct memory access (DMA), and interrupts.

Direct device assignment is the best performing approach for I/O virtualization [15, 31] because it removes some of the host's involvement in the I/O path. With device assignment, guests are granted direct access to assigned devices. Guest I/O operations bypass the host and are communicated directly to devices. As noted, device DMA's also bypass the host; devices perform DMA accesses to and from guests; memory directly. Interrupts generated by assigned devices, however, still require host intervention.

In theory, when the host assigns a device to a guest, it should also assign the physical interrupts generated by the device to that guest. Unfortunately, current x86 virtualization only supports two modes: either *all* physical interrupts on a core are delivered to the currently running guest, or *no* physical interrupts are delivered to the currently running guest (i.e., all physical interrupts in guest mode cause an exit). An untrusted guest may handle its own interrupts, but it must not be allowed to handle the interrupts of the host and the other guests. Consequently, before ELI, the host had no choice but to configure the processor to force an exit when *any* physical interrupt arrives in guest mode. The host then inspected the incoming interrupt and decided whether to handle it by itself or inject it to the associated guest.

Figure 1(a) describes the interrupt handling flow with baseline device assignment. Each physical interrupt from the guest's assigned device forces at least two exits from guest to host: when the interrupt arrives (causing the host to gain control and to inject the interrupt to the guest) and when the guest signals completion of the interrupt handling (causing the host to gain control and to emulate the completion for the guest). Additional exits might also occur while the guest handles an interrupt. As we exemplify in Section 5, interrupt-related exits to host mode are the foremost contributors to virtualization overhead for I/O intensive workloads.

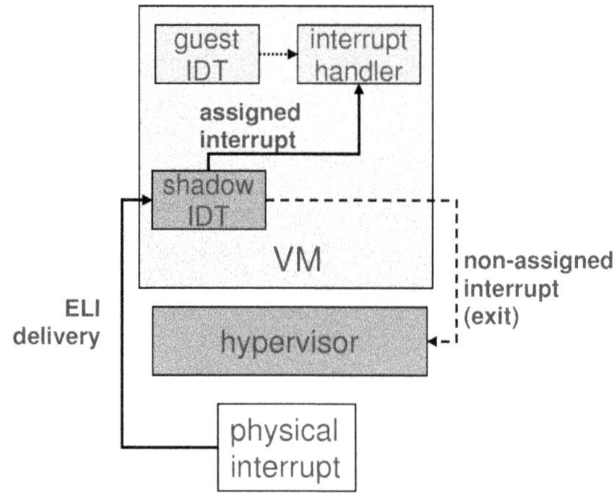

Figure 2. ELI interrupt delivery flow

4. ELI: Design and Implementation

ELI enables unmodified and untrusted guests to handle interrupts directly and securely. ELI does not require any guest modifications, and thus should work with any operating system. It does not rely on any device-specific features, and thus should work with any assigned device. On the interrupt delivery path, ELI makes it possible for guests to receive physical interrupts from their assigned devices directly while still forcing an exit to the host for all other physical interrupts (Section 4.1). On the interrupt completion path, ELI makes it possible for guests to signal interrupt completion without causing any exits (Section 4.4). How to do both securely, without letting untrusted guests compromise the security and isolation of the host and guests, is covered in Section 6.

4.1 Exitless Interrupt Delivery

ELI's design was guided by the observation that *nearly* all physical interrupts arriving at a given core are targeted at the guest running on that core. This is due to several reasons. First, in high-performance deployments, guests usually have their own physical CPU cores (or else they would waste too much time context switching); second, high-performance deployments use device assignment with SR-IOV devices; and third, interrupt rates are usually proportional to execution time. The longer each guest runs, the more interrupts it receives from its assigned devices. Following this observation, ELI makes use of available hardware support to deliver *all* physical interrupts on a given core to the guest running on it, since most of them should be handled by that guest anyway, and forces the (unmodified) guest to reflect back to the host all those interrupts which should be handled by the host.

The guest OS continues to prepare and maintain its own IDT. Instead of running the guest with this IDT, ELI runs the guest in guest mode with a different IDT prepared by the host. We call this second guest IDT the *shadow* IDT. Just like shadow page tables can be used to virtualize the guest MMU [2, 7], IDT shadowing can be used to virtualize interrupt delivery. This mechanism, depicted in Figure 2, requires no guest cooperation.

By shadowing the guest's IDT, the host has explicit control over the interrupt handlers invoked by the CPU on interrupt delivery. The host can configure the shadow IDT to deliver assigned interrupts directly to the guest's interrupt handler or force an exit for non-assigned interrupts. The simplest method to cause an exit is to force the CPU to generate an exception, because exceptions can be selectively trapped by the host and can be easily generated if the host intentionally misconfigures the shadow IDT. For our implementation, we decided to force exits primarily by generating not-present (NP) exceptions. Each IDT entry has a present bit. Before invoking an entry to deliver an interrupt, the processor checks if that entry is present (has the present bit set). Interrupts delivered to not-present entries raise a NP exception. ELI configures the shadow IDT as follows: for exceptions and physical interrupts belonging to devices assigned to the guest, the shadow IDT entries are copied from the guest's original IDT and marked as present. Every other entry in the shadow IDT should be handled by the host and is therefore marked as not present to force a not-present exception when the processor tries to invoke the handler. Additionally, the host configures the processor to force an exit from guest mode to host mode whenever a not-present exception occurs.

Any physical interrupt reflected to the host appears in the host as a not-present exception and must be converted back to the original interrupt vector. The host inspects the cause for the not-present exception. If the exit was actually caused by a physical interrupt, the host raises a software interrupt with the same vector as the physical interrupt, which causes the processor to invoke the appropriate IDT entry, converting the not-present exception into a physical interrupt. If the exit was not caused by a physical interrupt, then it is a true guest not-present exception and should be handled by the guest. In this case, the host injects the exception back into the guest. True guest not-present exceptions are rare in normal execution.

The host also sometimes needs to inject into the guest virtual interrupts raised by devices that are emulated by the host (e.g., the keyboard). These interrupt vectors will have their entries in the shadow IDT marked not-present. To deliver such virtual interrupts through the guest IDT handler, ELI enters a special *injection mode* by configuring the processor to cause an exit on any physical interrupt and running the guest with the original guest IDT. ELI then injects the virtual interrupt into the guest, which handles the virtual interrupt as described in Section 3.2. After the guest signals completion of the injected virtual interrupt, ELI leaves injection mode by reconfiguring the processor to let the guest handle physical interrupts directly and resuming the guest with the shadow IDT. As we later show in Section 5, the number of injected virtual interrupts is orders of magnitude smaller than the number of physical interrupts generated by the assigned device. Thus, the number of exits caused by physical interrupts while the guest is running in injection mode is negligible.

Instead of changing the IDT entries' present bits to cause reflection into the host, the host could also change the entries themselves to invoke shadow interrupt handlers in guest mode. This alternative method can enable additional functionality, such as delaying or batching physical interrupts, and is discussed in Section 8.

Even when all the interrupts require exits, ELI is not slower than baseline device assignment. The number of exits never increases and cost per exit remains the same. Changes in the IDT are rare and the guest OS does not normally modify the IDT content after system initialization. The processor reconfiguration to enter and leave injection mode requires only two memory writes, one to change the IDT pointer and the other to change the CPU execution mode.

4.2 Placing the Shadow IDT

There are several requirements on where in guest memory to place the shadow IDT. First, it should be hidden from the guest, i.e., placed in memory not normally accessed by the guest. Second, it must be placed in a guest physical page which is always mapped in the guest's kernel address space. This is an x86 architectural requirement, since the IDTR expects a virtual address. Third, since the guest is unmodified and untrusted, the host cannot rely on any guest cooperation for placing the shadow IDT. ELI satisfies all three requirements by placing the shadow IDT in an extra page of a device's PCI BAR (Base Address Register).

PCI devices which expose their registers to system software as memory do so through BAR registers. BARs specify the location and sizes of device registers in physical memory. Linux and Windows drivers will map the full size of their devices' PCI BARs into the kernel's address space, but they will only access specific locations in the mapped BAR that are known to correspond to device registers. Placing the shadow IDT in an additional memory page tacked onto the end of a device's BAR causes the guest to (1) map it into its address space, (2) keep it mapped, and (3) not access it during normal operation. All of this happens as part of normal guest operation and does not require any guest awareness or cooperation. To detect runtime changes to the guest IDT, the host also write-protects the shadow IDT page. Other security and isolation considerations are discussed in Section 6.

4.3 Configuring Guest and Host Vectors

Neither the host nor the guest have absolute control over precisely when an assigned device interrupt fires. Since the host and the guest may run at different times on the core receiving the interrupt, both must be ready to handle the same interrupt. (The host handles the interrupt by injecting it into the guest.) Interrupt vectors also control that interrupt's relative priority compared with other interrupts. For both of these reasons, ELI makes sure that for each device interrupt, the respective guest and host interrupt handlers are assigned to the same vector.

Since the guest is not aware of the host and chooses arbitrary interrupt vectors for the device's interrupts, ELI makes sure the guest, the host, and the device all use the same vectors. ELI does this by trapping the guest's programming of the device to indicate which vectors it wishes to use and then allocating the same vectors in the host. In the case where these vectors were already used in the host for another device, ELI reassigns that device's interrupts to other (free) vectors. Finally, ELI programs the device with the vectors the guest indicated. Hardware-based interrupt remapping [1] can avoid the need to re-program the device vectors by remapping them in hardware instead, but still requires the guest and the host to use the same vectors.

4.4 Exitless Interrupt Completion

As shown in Figure 1(b), ELI IDT shadowing delivers hardware interrupts to the guest without host intervention. Signaling interrupt completion, however, still forces (at least) one exit to host mode. This exit is caused by the guest signaling the completion of an interrupt. As explained in Section 3.2, guests signal completion by writing to the EOI LAPIC register. This register is exposed to the guest either as part of the LAPIC area (older LAPIC interface) or as an x2APIC MSR (the new LAPIC interface). With the old interface, nearly every LAPIC access causes an exit, whereas with the new interface, the host can decide on a per-x2APIC-register basis which register accesses cause exits and which do not.

Before ELI, the host configured the CPU's MSR bitmap to force an exit when the guest accessed the EOI MSR. ELI exposes the x2APIC EOI register directly to the guest by configuring the MSR bitmap to not cause an exit when the guest writes to the EOI register. No other x2APIC registers are passed directly to the guest; the security and isolation considerations arising from direct guest access to the EOI MSR are discussed in Section 6. Figure 1(c) illustrates that combining this interrupt completion technique with ELI IDT shadowing allows the guest to handle physical interrupts without any exits on the critical interrupt handling path.

Guests are not aware of the distinction between physical and virtual interrupts. They signal the completion of all interrupts the same way, by writing the EOI register. When the host injects a virtual interrupt, the corresponding completion should go to the host for emulation and not to the physical EOI register. Thus, during injection mode (described in Section 4.1), the host temporarily traps accesses to the EOI register. Once the guest signals the completion of all pending virtual interrupts, the host leaves injection mode.

Trapping EOI accesses in injection mode also enables ELI to correctly emulate x86 nested interrupts. A nested interrupt occurs when a second interrupt arrives while the operating system is still handling a previous interrupt. This can only happen if the operating system enabled interrupts before it finished handling the first interrupt. Interrupt priority dictates that the second (nested) interrupt will only be delivered if its priority is higher than that of the first interrupt. Some guest operating systems, including Windows, make use of nested interrupts. ELI deals with nested interrupts by checking the interrupt in service LAPIC register. This register holds the highest interrupt vector not yet completed (EOI pending) and lets ELI know whether the guest is in the middle of handling a physical interrupt. If it is, ELI delays the injection of any virtual interrupt with a priority that is lower than the priority of that physical interrupt.

4.5 Multiprocessor Environments

Guests may have more virtual CPUs (vCPUs) than available physical cores. However, multiplexing more than one guest vCPU on a single core will lead to an immediate drop in performance, due to the increased number of exits and entries [30]. Since our main goal is virtual machine performance that equals bare-metal performance, we assume that each guest vCPU has a mostly-dedicated physical core. Executing a guest with multiple vCPUs, each running on its own mostly-dedicated core, requires that ELI support interrupt affinity correctly. ELI allows the guest to configure the delivery of interrupts to a subset of its vCPUs, just as it does on bare metal. ELI does this by intercepting the guest's interrupt affinity configuration changes and configuring the physical hardware to redirect device interrupts accordingly.

5. Evaluation

We implement ELI, as described in the previous sections, within the KVM hypervisor [25]. This section evaluates the functionality and performance of our implementation.

5.1 Methodology and Experimental Setup

We measure and analyze ELI's effect on high-throughput network cards assigned to a guest virtual machine. Network cards are the most common use-case of device assignment, due to: (1) their higher throughput relative to other devices (which makes device assignment particularly appealing over the slower alternatives of emulation and paravirtualization); and because (2) SR-IOV network cards make it easy to assign one physical network card to multiple guests.

We use throughput and latency to measure performance, and we contrast the results achieved by virtualized and bare-metal settings to demonstrate that the former can approach the latter. As noted earlier, performance-minded applications would typically dedicate whole cores to guests (single virtual CPU per core). We limit our evaluation to this case.

Our test machine is an IBM System x3550 M2, which is a dual-socket, 4-cores-per-socket server equipped with Intel Xeon X5570 CPUs running at 2.93 GHz. The chipset is Intel 5520, which includes an IOMMU as required for device assignment. The system includes 24GB of memory and an Emulex OneConnect 10Gbps NIC. We use another similar remote server (connected directly by 10Gbps fiber) as workload generator and a target for I/O transactions. We set the Maximum Transmission Unit (MTU) to its default size of 1500 bytes; we do not use jumbo Ethernet frames.

Guest mode configurations execute with a single vCPU. Bare-metal configurations execute with a single core enabled, so as to have comparable setups. We assign 1GB of memory for both types of configurations. We disable the IOMMU in bare-metal configurations, such that the associated results represent the highest attainable performance. We use the IOMMU for device assignment in virtualized configuration, but do not expose it to guests [6]. We disable Dynamic Voltage and Frequency Scaling (DVFS) to avoid power features related artifacts. Both guest and bare-metal setups run Ubuntu 9.10 with Linux 2.6.35.

We run all guests on the KVM hypervisor (which is part of Linux 2.6.35) and QEMU-KVM 0.14.0. We run them with and without ELI modifications. To check that ELI functions correctly in other setups, we also deploy it in an environment that uses a different device (a Broadcom NetXtreme II BCM5709 1Gbps NIC) and a different OS (Windows 7); we find that ELI indeed operates correctly.

Unless otherwise stated, we configure the hypervisor to back the guest's memory with 2MB *huge pages* [35] and two-dimensional page tables. Huge pages minimize two-dimensional paging overhead [11] and reduce TLB pressure. We note that only the host uses huge pages; in all cases the guest still operates with the default 4KB page size. We later quantify the performance without huge pages, finding that they improve performance of both baseline and ELI runs.

Recall that ELI makes use of the x2APIC hardware to avoid exits on interrupt completions (see Section 4.4). x2APIC is a relatively new feature available in every Intel x86 CPU since the release of the Sandy Bridge microarchitecture. Alas, the hardware we used for evaluation did not support x2APIC. To nevertheless measure the benefits of ELI utilizing x2APIC hardware, we slightly modify our Linux guest to emulate the x2APIC behavior. Specifically, we expose the physical LAPIC and a control flag to the guest, such that the guest may perform an EOI on the virtual LAPIC (forcing an exit) or the physical LAPIC (no exit), depending on the value of the control flag. We verified that our approach conforms to the published specifications.

5.2 Throughput

I/O virtualization performance suffers the most with workloads that are I/O intensive, and which incur many interrupts. We start our evaluation by measuring three well-known examples of network-intensive workloads, and show that for these benchmarks ELI provides a significant (49%–66%) throughput increase over baseline device assignment, and that it nearly (to 0%-3%) reaches bare-metal performance. We consider the following three benchmarks:

1. **Netperf** TCP stream, is the simplest of the three benchmarks [23]. It opens a single TCP connection to the remote machine, and makes as many rapid `write()` calls of a given size as possible.
2. **Apache** is an HTTP server. We use *ApacheBench* to load the server and measure its performance. ApacheBench runs on the remote machine and repeatedly requests a static page of a given size from several concurrent threads.
3. **Memcached** is a high-performance in-memory key-value storage server [18]. It is used by many high-profile Web sites for caching results of slow database queries, thereby significantly improving the site's overall performance and scalability. We used the *Memslap* benchmark, part of the *libmemcached* client library, to load the server and measure its performance. Memslap runs on the remote machine, sends a random sequence of memcached `get` (90%) and `set` (10%) requests to the server and measures the request completion rate.

We configure each benchmark with parameters which fully load the tested machine's CPU (so that throughput can be compared), but do not saturate the tester machine. We configure Netperf to do 256-byte writes, ApacheBench to request 4KB static pages from 4

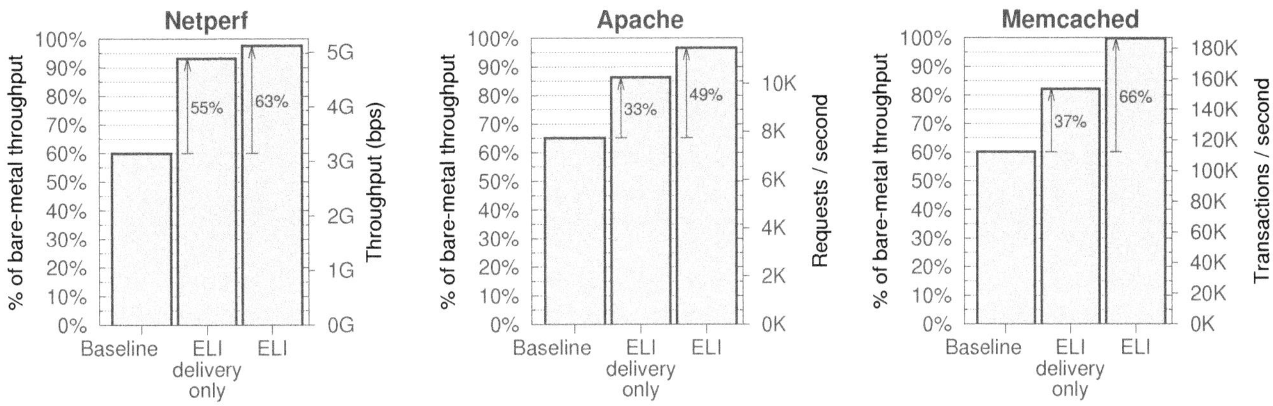

Figure 3. Performance of three I/O intensive workloads (described in the main text). We compare the throughput measured when using baseline device assignment, delivery-only ELI and full ELI, scaled so 100% means bare-metal throughput. Throughput gains over baseline device assignment are noted inside the bars.

concurrent threads, and Memslap to make 64 concurrent requests from 4 threads (with other parameters set to their default values). We verify that the results do not significantly vary when we change these parameters.

Figure 3 illustrates how ELI improves the throughput of these three benchmarks. Each of the benchmarks was run on bare metal (no virtualization) and under three virtualized setups: baseline device assignment, device assignment with ELI delivery only, and device assignment with full ELI (avoiding exits on both delivery and completion of interrupts). The results are based on averaging ten identical runs, with the standard deviation being up to 0.9% of the average for the Netperf runs, up to 0.5% for Apache, and up to 2.6% for Memcached.

The figure shows that baseline device assignment performance is still considerably below bare-metal performance: Netperf throughput on a guest is at 60% of bare-metal throughput, Apache is at 65%, and Memcached at 60%. With ELI, Netperf achieves 98% of the bare-metal throughput, Apache 97%, and Memcached 100%. As mentioned above, it is meaningful to compare the throughputs, and not CPU usage, because the CPU is fully utilized in all these setups.

It is evident from the figure that using ELI gives a significant throughput increase, 63%, 49%, and 66% for Netperf, Apache, and Memcached, respectively. The measurements also show that ELI delivery-only gives most of the performance benefit of the full ELI. For Apache, ELI delivery-only gives a 33% throughput increase, and avoiding the remaining completion exits improves throughput by an additional 12%.

As noted, these results are obtained with the huge pages feature enabled, which means KVM utilizes 2MB host pages to back guests' memory (though guests still continue to use normal-sized 4KB pages). Backing guests with huge pages gives an across-the-board performance improvement to both baseline and ELI runs. To additionally demonstrate ELI's performance when huge pages are not available, Figure 4 contrasts results from all three benchmarks with and without huge pages. We see that using ELI gives a significant throughput increase, 128%, 42%, and 59% for Netperf, Apache, and Memcached, respectively, even without huge pages. We further see that bare-metal performance for guests requires the host to use huge pages. This requirement arises due to architectural limitations; without it, pressure on the memory subsystem significantly hampers performance due to two-dimensional hardware page walks [11].

Netperf statistic	Base-line	ELI delivery	ELI	Bare metal
Exits/s	102222	43832	764	
Time in guest	69%	94%	99%	
Interrupts/s	48802	42600	48746	48430
handled in host	48802	678	103	
Injections/s	49058	941	367	
IRQ windows/s	8060	686	103	
Throughput mbps	3145	4886	5119	5245

Apache statistic	Base-line	ELI delivery	ELI	Bare metal
Exits/s	90506	64187	1118	
Time in guest	67%	89%	98%	
Interrupts/s	36418	61499	66546	68851
handled in host	36418	1107	195	
Injections/s	36671	1369	458	
IRQ windows/s	7801	1104	192	
Requests/s	7729	10249	11480	11875
Avg response ms	0.518	0.390	0.348	0.337

Memcached statistic	Base-line	ELI delivery	ELI	Bare metal
Exits/s	123134	123402	1001	
Time in guest	60%	83%	98%	
Interrupts/s	59394	120526	154512	155882
handled in host	59394	2319	207	
Injections/s	59649	2581	472	
IRQ windows/s	9069	2345	208	
Transactions/s	112299	153617	186364	186824

Table 1. Execution breakdown for the three benchmarks, with baseline device assignment, delivery-only ELI, and full ELI.

5.3 Execution Breakdown

Breaking down the execution time to host, guest, and overhead components allows us to better understand how and why ELI improves the guest's performance. Table 1 shows this breakdown for the above three benchmarks.

Intuitively, guest performance is better with ELI because the guest gets a larger fraction of the CPU (the host uses less), and/or

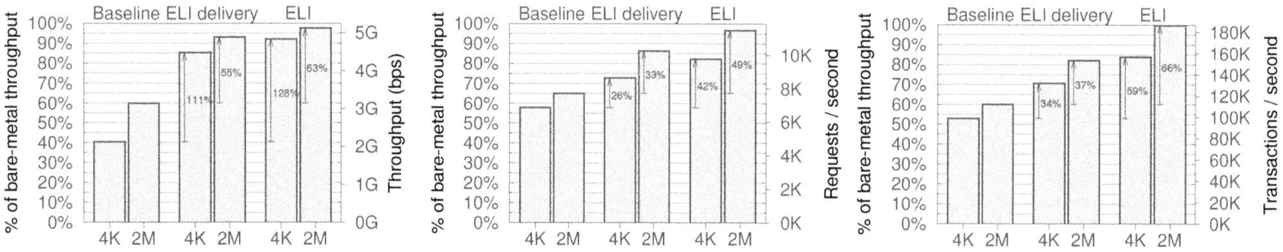

(a) Netperf (b) Apache (c) Memcached

Figure 4. ELI's improvement for each of the workloads, with normal (4K) and huge (2M) host pages. Gains over baseline device assignment with normal pages or huge pages are noted inside the respective bars.

because the guest runs more efficiently when it gets to run. With baseline device assignment, only 60%–69% of the CPU time is spent in the guest. The rest is spent in the host, handling exits or performing the world-switches necessary on every exit and entry.

With only ELI delivery enabled, the heavy "interrupts handled in host" exits are avoided and the time in the guest jumps to 83%–94%. Although EOI exit handling is fairly fast, there are still many exits (43832–123402 in the different benchmarks), and the world-switch times still add up to a significant overhead. Only when ELI completion eliminates most those exits and most world-switches, do both time in host (1%–2%) and number of world-switches (764–1118) finally become low.

In baseline device assignment, all interrupts arrive at the host (perhaps after exiting a running guest) and are then injected to the guest. The injection rate is slightly higher than interrupt rate because the host injects additional virtual interrupts, such as timer interrupts.

With ELI delivery, only the 678–2319 interrupts that occur while the host is running, or during exits, or while handling an injected interrupt, will arrive at the host—the rest will be handled directly by the guest. The number of interrupts "handled in host" is even lower (103–207) when ELI completion is also used, because the fraction of the time that the CPU is running the host or exiting to the host is much lower.

Baseline device assignment is further slowed down by "IRQ window" exits: on bare metal, when a device interrupt occurs while interrupts are blocked, the interrupt will be delivered by the LAPIC hardware some time later. But when a guest is running, an interrupt always causes an immediate exit. The host wishes to inject this interrupt to the guest (if it is an interrupt from the assigned device), but if the guest has interrupts blocked, it cannot. The x86 architecture solution is to run the guest with an "IRQ window" enabled, requesting an exit as soon as the guest enables interrupts. In the table, we can see 7801–9069 of these exits every second in the baseline device assignment run. ELI mostly eliminates IRQ window overhead, by eliminating most injections.

As expected, ELI slashes the number of exits, from 90506–123134 in the baseline device assignment runs, to just 764–1118. One might guess that delivery-only ELI, which avoids one type of exit (on delivery) but retains another (on completion), should result in an exit rate halfway between the two. But in practice, other factors play into the ELI delivery-only exit rate: the interrupt rate might have changed from the baseline case (we see it significantly increased in the Apache and Memcached benchmarks, but slightly lowered in Netperf), and even in the baseline case some interrupts might have not caused exits because they happened while the host was running (and it was running for a large fraction of the time). The number of IRQ window exits is also different, for the reasons discussed above.

As can be seen in Figures 3 and 4, the time saved by eliminating the exits due to interrupt delivery and completion varies. The host handling of interrupts is a complex operation, and it is avoided by ELI delivery. What ELI completion then avoids is the host handling of EOI, but that handling is quick when ELI is already enabled—it basically amounts to issuing an EOI on the physical LAPIC (see Section 4.4).

5.4 Impact of Interrupt Rate

The benchmarks in the previous section demonstrated that ELI significantly improves throughput over baseline device assignment for I/O intensive workloads. But as the workload spends less of its time on I/O and more of its time on computation, it seems likely that ELI's improvement might be less pronounced. Nonetheless, counterintuitively, we shall now show that ELI continues to provide relatively large improvements until we reach some fairly high computation-per-I/O ratio (and some fairly low throughput). To this end, we modify the Netperf benchmark to perform a specified amount of extra computation per byte written to the stream. This resembles many useful server workloads, where the server does some computation before sending its response.

A useful measure of the ratio of computation to I/O is *cycles/byte*, the number of CPU cycles spent to produce one byte of output; this ratio is easily measured as the quotient of CPU frequency (in cycles/second) and workload throughput (in bytes/second). Note, cycles/byte is inversely proportional to throughput. Figure 5(a) depicts ELI's improvement as a function of this ratio, showing it remains over 25% until after 60 cycles/byte (which corresponds to throughput of only 50Mbps). The reason underlying this result becomes apparent when examining Figure 5(b), which shows the interrupt rates measured during the associated runs from Figure 5(a). Contrary to what one might expect, the interrupt rate is not proportional to the throughput (until 60 cycles/byte); instead, it remains between 30K–60K. As will be shortly exemplified, rates are kept in this range due to the NIC (which coalesces interrupts) and the Linux driver (which employs the NAPI mechanism), and they would have been higher if it were not for these mechanisms. Since ELI lowers the overhead of handling interrupts, its benefit is proportional to their rate, *not* to throughput, a fact that explains why the improvement is similar over a range of computation-I/O values. The fluctuations in interrupt rate (and hence in ELI improvement) shown in Figure 5 for cycles/byte < 20 are not caused by virtualization; they are also present in bare metal settings and have to do with the specifics of the Linux NIC driver implementation.

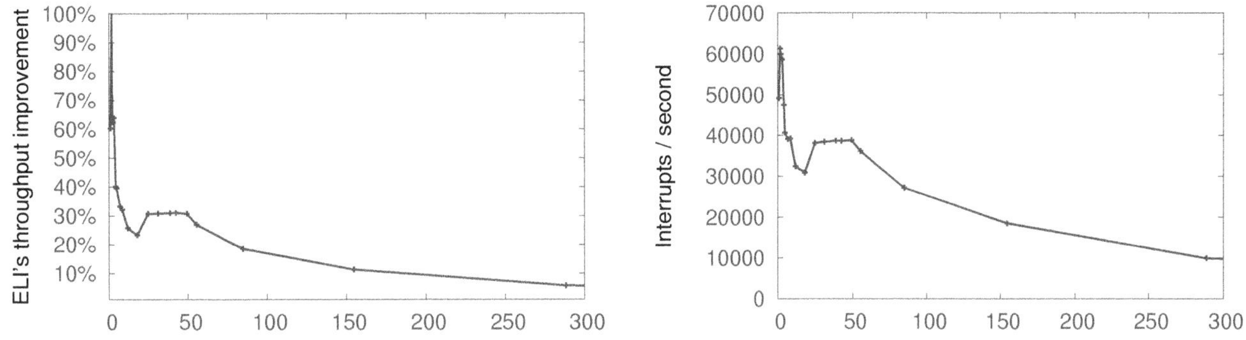

(a) ELI's throughput improvement (b) Baseline interrupt rate

Figure 5. Modified-Netperf workloads with various computation-I/O ratios.

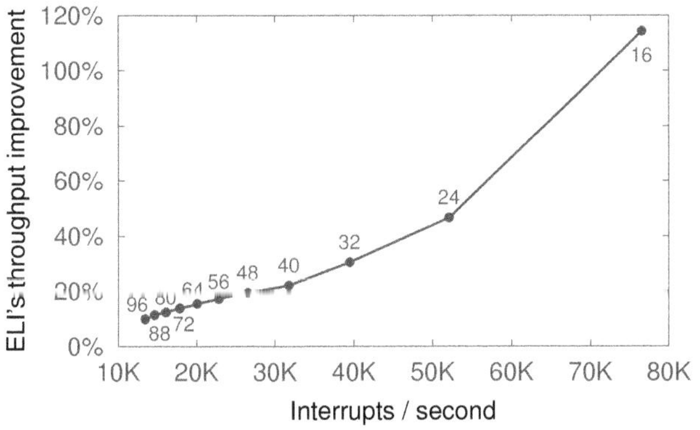

Figure 6. Throughput improvement and interrupt rate for Netperf benchmark with different interrupt coalescing intervals (shown in labels).

We now proceed to investigate the dependence of ELI's improvement on the amount of coalescing done by the NIC, which immediately translates to the amount of generated interrupts. Our NIC imposes a configurable cap on coalescing, allowing its users to set a time duration T, such that the NIC will not fire more than one interrupt per $T\mu s$ (longer T implies less interrupts). We set the NIC's coalescing cap to the following values: $16\mu s$, $24\mu s$, $32\mu s$, ..., $96\mu s$. Figure 6 plots the results of the associated experiments (the data along the curve denotes values of T). Higher interrupt rates imply higher savings due to ELI. The smallest interrupt rate that our NIC generates for this workload is 13K interrupts/sec (with T=$96\mu s$), and even with this maximal coalescing ELI still provides a 10% performance improvement over the baseline. ELI achieves at least 99% of bare-metal throughput in all of the experiments described in this subsection.

5.5 Latency

By removing the exits caused by external interrupts, ELI substantially reduces the time it takes to deliver interrupts to the guest. This period of time is critical for latency-sensitive workloads. We measure ELI's latency improvement using Netperf UDP request-response, which sends a UDP packet and waits for a reply before sending the next. To simulate a busy guest that always has some work to do alongside a latency-sensitive application, we run a busy-

Configuration	Average latency	% of bare-metal
Baseline	36.14 μs	129%
ELI delivery-only	30.10 μs	108%
ELI	28.51 μs	102%
Bare-metal	27.93 μs	100%

Table 2. Latency measured by Netperf UDP request-response benchmark.

loop within the guest. Table 2 presents the results. We can see that baseline device assignment increases bare metal latency by $8.21\mu s$ and that ELI reduces this gap to only $0.58\mu s$, which is within 98% of bare-metal latency.

6. Security and Isolation

ELI's performance stems from the host giving guests direct access to privileged architectural mechanisms. In this section, we review potential threats and how ELI addresses them.

6.1 Threat Model

We analyze malicious guest attacks against the host through a hardware-centric approach. ELI grants guests direct control over several hardware mechanisms that current hypervisors keep protected: interrupt masking, reception of physical interrupts, and interrupt completion via the EOI register. Using these mechanisms, a guest can disable interrupts for unbounded periods of time, try to consume (steal) host interrupts, and issue interrupt completions incorrectly.

Delivering interrupts directly to the guest requires that the guest be able to control whether physical interrupts are enabled or disabled. Accordingly, ELI allows the guest to control interrupt masking, both globally (all interrupts are blocked) and by priority (all interrupts whose priority is below a certain threshold are blocked). Ideally, interrupts that are not assigned to the guest would be delivered to the host even when the guest masks them, yet x86 does not currently provide such support. As a result, the guest is able to mask any interrupt, possibly forever. Unless addressed, masking high-priority interrupts such as the thermal interrupt that indicates the CPU is running hot, may cause the system to crash. Likewise, disabling and never enabling interrupts could allow the guest to run forever.

While ELI configures the guest shadow IDT to trigger an exit for non-assigned physical interrupts, the interrupts are still first delivered to the guest. Therefore, we must consider the possibility that a guest, in spite of ELI, manages to change the physical IDT. If this happens, both assigned interrupts and non-assigned interrupts will be delivered to the guest while it is running. If the guest manages to change the physical IDT, a physical interrupt might not be delivered to the host, which might cause a host device driver to malfunction.

ELI also grants the guest direct access to the EOI register. Reading EOI is prevented by the CPU, and writes to the register while no interrupt is handled do not affect the system. Nevertheless, if the guest exits to the host without signaling the completion of in-service interrupts, it can affect the host interruptibility, as x86 automatically masks all interrupts whose priority is lower than the one in service. Since the interrupt is technically still in service, the host may not receive lower-priority interrupts.

6.2 Protection

ELI's design addresses all of these threats. To protect against malicious guests stealing CPU time by disabling interrupts forever, ELI uses the *preemption timer* feature of x86 virtualization, which triggers an unconditional exit after a configurable period of time elapses.

To protect host interruptibility, ELI signals interrupt completion for any assigned interrupt still in service after an exit. To maintain correctness, when ELI detects that the guest did not complete any previously delivered interrupts, it falls back to injection mode until the guest signals completions of all in-service interrupts. Since all of the registers that control CPU interruptibility are reloaded upon exit, the guest cannot affect host interruptibility.

To protect against malicious guests blocking or consuming critical physical interrupts, ELI uses one of the following mechanisms. First, if there is a core which does not run any ELI-enabled guests, ELI redirects critical interrupts there. If no such core is available, ELI uses a combination of Non-Maskable-Interrupts (NMIs) and IDT limiting.

Non-Maskable-Interrupts (NMIs) trigger unconditional exits; they cannot be blocked by guests. ELI redirects critical interrupts to the core's single NMI handles. All critical interrupts are registered with the NMI handler, and whenever an NMI occurs, the NMI handler calls all registered interrupt vectors to discern which critical interrupt occurred. NMI sharing has a negligible run-time cost (since critical interrupts rarely happen). However, some devices and device drivers may lock up or otherwise misbehave if their interrupt handlers are called when no interrupt was raised.

For critical interrupts whose handlers must only be called when an interrupt actually occurred, ELI uses a complementary coarse grained *IDT limit* mechanism. The IDT limit is specified in the IDTR register, which is protected by ELI and cannot be changed by the guest. IDT limiting reduces the limit of the shadow IDT, causing all interrupts whose vector is above the limit to trigger the usually rare general purpose exception (GP). GP is intercepted and handled by the host similarly to the not-present (NP) exception. Unlike reflection through NP (Section 4.1), which the guest could perhaps subvert by changing the physical IDT, no events take precedence over the IDTR limit check [21]. It is therefore guaranteed that all handlers above the limit will trap to the host when called.

For IDT limiting to be transparent to the guest, the limit must be set above the highest vector of the assigned devices' interrupts. Moreover, it should be higher than any software interrupt that is in common use by the guest, since such interrupts will undesirably trigger frequent exits and reduce performance. Therefore, in practice ELI sets the threshold just below the vectors used by high-priority interrupts in common operating systems [12, 42]. Since this limits the number of available above-the-limit handlers, ELI uses the IDT limiting for critical interrupts and reflection through not-present exceptions for other interrupts.

7. Architectural Support

The overhead of interrupt handling in virtual environments is due to the design choices of x86 hardware virtualization. The implementation of ELI could be simplified and improved by adding a few features to the processor.

First, to remove the complexity of managing the shadow IDT and the overhead caused by exits on interrupts, the processor should provide a feature to assign physical interrupts to a guest. Interrupts assigned to a guest should be delivered through the guest IDT without causing an exit. Any other interrupt should force an exit to the host context. Interrupt masking during guest mode execution should not affect non-assigned interrupts. To solve the vector sharing problem described in Section 4.3, the processor should provide a mechanisms to translate from host interrupt vectors to guest interrupt vectors. Second, to remove the overhead of interrupt completion, the processor should allow a guest to signal completion of assigned interrupts without causing an exit. For interrupts assigned to a guest, EOI writes should be directed to the physical LAPIC. Otherwise, EOI writes should force an exit.

8. Applicability and Future Work

While this work focuses on the advantages of letting guests handle physical interrupts directly, ELI can also be used to directly deliver all virtual interrupts, including those of paravirtual devices, emulated devices, and inter-processor interrupts (IPI). Currently, hypervisors deliver these interrupts to guests through the architectural virtual interrupt mechanism. This mechanism requires multiple guest exits, which would be eliminated by ELI. The only requirement for using ELI is that the interrupt vector not be used by the host. Since interrupt vectors tend to be fixed, the host can in most cases relocate the interrupts handlers it uses to other vectors that are not used by guests.

ELI can also be used for injecting guests with virtual interrupts without exits, in scenarios where virtual interrupts are frequent. The host can send an IPI from any core with the proper virtual interrupt vector to the target guest core, eliminating the need for exits due to interrupt-window, interrupt delivery, and completion. The host can also inject interrupts into the guest from the same core by sending a self-IPI right before resuming the guest, so the interrupt will be delivered in the guest context, saving at least the exit currently required for interrupt completion.

ELI can also be used for direct delivery to guests of LAPIC-triggered non-critical interrupts such as the timer interrupt. Once the timer interrupt is assigned to the guest, the host can use the architectural preemption timer (described in Section 6) for preempting the guest instead of relying on the timer interrupt.

The current ELI implementation configures the shadow IDT to force an exit when the guest is not supposed to handle an incoming physical interrupt. In the future, we plan to extend our implementation and configure the shadow IDT to invoke shadow interrupt handlers—handler routines hidden from the guest operating system and controlled by the host [10]. Using this approach, the shadow handlers running host code will be executed in guest mode without causing a transition to host mode. The code could then inspect the interrupt and decide to batch it, delay it, or force an immediate exit. This mechanism can help to mitigate the overhead of physical interrupts not assigned to the guest. In addition, shadow handlers can also be used for function call injection, allowing the host to run code in guest mode.

9. Conclusions

The key to high virtualization performance is for the CPU to spend most of its time in guest mode, running the guest, and not in the host, handling guest exits. Yet current approaches to x86 virtualization induce multiple exits by requiring host involvement in the critical interrupt handling path. The result is that I/O performance suffers. We propose to eliminate the unwarranted exits by introducing ELI, an approach that lets guests handle interrupts directly and securely. Building on many previous efforts to reduce virtualization overhead, ELI finally makes it possible for untrusted and unmodified virtual machines to reach nearly bare-metal performance, even for the most I/O-intensive and interrupt-heavy workloads.

ELI also demonstrates that the rich x86 architecture, which in many cases complicates hypervisor implementations, provides exciting opportunities for optimization. Exploiting these opportunities, however, may require using architectural mechanisms in ways that their designers did not necessarily foresee.

Acknowledgments

The research leading to the results presented in this paper is partially supported by the European Community's Seventh Framework Programme ([FP7/2001-2013]) under grant agreements #248615 (IOLanes) and #248647 (ENCORE).

References

[1] ABRAMSON, D., JACKSON, J., MUTHRASANALLUR, S., NEIGER, G., REGNIER, G., SANKARAN, R., SCHOINAS, I., UHLIG, R., VEMBU, B., AND WIEGERT, J. Intel virtualization technology for directed I/O. *Intel Technology Journal 10*, 3 (2006), 179–192.

[2] ADAMS, K., AND AGESEN, O. A comparison of software and hardware techniques for x86 virtualization. In *ACM Architectural Support for Programming Languages & Operating Systems (ASPLOS)* (2006).

[3] AGESEN, O., MATTSON, J., RUGINA, R., AND SHELDON, J. Software techniques for avoiding hardware virtualization exits. Tech. rep., VMware, 2011.

[4] AHMAD, I., GULATI, A., AND MASHTIZADEH, A. vIC: Interrupt coalescing for virtual machine storage device IO. In *USENIX Annual Technical Conference (ATC)* (2011).

[5] AMD INC. AMD64 Architecture Programmer's Manual Volume 2: System Programming, 2011.

[6] AMIT, N., BEN-YEHUDA, M., TSAFRIR, D., AND SCHUSTER, A. vIOMMU: efficient IOMMU emulation. In *USENIX Annual Technical Conference (ATC)* (2011).

[7] BARHAM, P., DRAGOVIC, B., FRASER, K., HAND, S., HARRIS, T., HO, A., NEUGEBAUER, R., PRATT, I., AND WARFIELD, A. Xen and the art of virtualization. In *ACM Symposium on Operating Systems Principles (SOSP)* (2003).

[8] BEN-YEHUDA, M., BOROVIK, E., FACTOR, M., ROM, E., TRAEGER, A., AND YASSOUR, B.-A. Adding advanced storage controller functionality via low-overhead virtualization. In *USENIX Conference on File & Storage Technologies (FAST)* (2012).

[9] BEN-YEHUDA, M., DAY, M. D., DUBITZKY, Z., FACTOR, M., HAR'EL, N., GORDON, A., LIGUORI, A., WASSERMAN, O., AND YASSOUR, B.-A. The Turtles project: Design and implementation of nested virtualization. In *USENIX Symposium on Operating Systems Design & Implementation (OSDI)* (2010).

[10] BETAK, T., DULEY, A., AND ANGEPAT, H. Reflective virtualization improving the performance of fully-virtualized x86 operating systems. `http://citeseerx.ist.psu.edu/viewdoc/summary?doi=10.1.1.129.7868`.

[11] BHARGAVA, R., SEREBRIN, B., SPADINI, F., AND MANNE, S. Accelerating two-dimensional page walks for virtualized systems. In *ACM Architectural Support for Programming Languages & Operating Systems (ASPLOS)* (2008).

[12] BOVET, D., AND CESATI, M. *Understanding the Linux Kernel, Second Edition*. O'Reilly & Associates, Inc., 2002.

[13] CODD, E. F. *Advances in Computers*, vol. 3. New York: Academic Press, 1962, pp. 77–153.

[14] DONG, Y., XU, D., ZHANG, Y., AND LIAO, G. Optimizing network I/O virtualization with efficient interrupt coalescing and virtual receive side scaling. In *IEEE International Conference on Cluster Computing (CLUSTER)* (2011).

[15] DONG, Y., YANG, X., LI, X., LI, J., TIAN, K., AND GUAN, H. High performance network virtualization with SR-IOV. In *IEEE International Symposium on High Performance Computer Architecture (HPCA)* (2010).

[16] DONG, Y., YU, Z., AND ROSE, G. SR-IOV networking in Xen: architecture, design and implementation. In *USENIX Workshop on I/O Virtualization (WIOV)* (2008).

[17] DOVROLIS, C., THAYER, B., AND RAMANATHAN, P. HIP: hybrid interrupt-polling for the network interface. *ACM SIGOPS Operating Systems Review (OSR) 35* (2001), 50–60.

[18] FITZPATRICK, B. Distributed caching with memcached. *Linux Journal*, 124 (2004).

[19] GAVRILOVSKA, A., KUMAR, S., RAJ, H., SCHWAN, K., GUPTA, V., NATHUJI, R., NIRANJAN, R., RANADIVE, A., AND SARAIYA, P. High-performance hypervisor architectures: Virtualization in HPC systems. In *Workshop on System-level Virtualization for HPC (HPCVirt)* (2007).

[20] INTEL CORPORATION. Intel 64 Architecture x2APIC Specification, 2008.

[21] INTEL CORPORATION. Intel 64 and IA-32 Architectures Software Developer's Manual, 2010.

[22] ITZKOVITZ, A., AND SCHUSTER, A. MultiView and MilliPage—fine-grain sharing in page-based DSMs. In *USENIX Symposium on Operating Systems Design & Implementation (OSDI)* (1999).

[23] JONES, R. A. A network performance benchmark (revision 2.0). Tech. rep., Hewlett Packard, 1995.

[24] KELLER, E., SZEFER, J., REXFORD, J., AND LEE, R. B. Nohype: virtualized cloud infrastructure without the virtualization. In *ACM/IEEE International Symposium on Computer Architecture (ISCA)* (2010), ACM.

[25] KIVITY, A., KAMAY, Y., LAOR, D., LUBLIN, U., AND LIGUORI, A. KVM: the Linux virtual machine monitor. In *Ottawa Linux Symposium (OLS)* (2007).

[26] LANDAU, A., BEN-YEHUDA, M., AND GORDON, A. SplitX: Split guest/hypervisor execution on multi-core. In *USENIX Workshop on I/O Virtualization (WIOV)* (2011).

[27] LANGE, J. R., PEDRETTI, K., DINDA, P., BRIDGES, P. G., BAE, C., SOLTERO, P., AND MERRITT, A. Minimal-overhead virtualization of a large scale supercomputer. In *ACM/USENIX International Conference on Virtual Execution Environments (VEE)* (2011).

[28] LARSEN, S., SARANGAM, P., HUGGAHALLI, R., AND KULKARNI, S. Architectural breakdown of end-to-end latency in a TCP/IP network. In *International Symposium on Computer Architecture and High Performance Computing* (2009).

[29] LEVASSEUR, J., UHLIG, V., STOESS, J., AND GÖTZ, S. Unmodified device driver reuse and improved system dependability via virtual machines. In *USENIX Symposium on Operating Systems Design & Implementation (OSDI)* (2004).

[30] LIAO, G., GUO, D., BHUYAN, L., AND KING, S. R. Software techniques to improve virtualized I/O performance on multi-core systems. In *ACM/IEEE Symposium on Architectures for Networking and Communications Systems (ANCS)* (2008).

[31] LIU, J. Evaluating standard-based self-virtualizing devices: A performance study on 10 GbE NICs with SR-IOV support. In *IEEE International Parallel & Distributed Processing Symposium (IPDPS)* (2010).

[32] LIU, J., HUANG, W., ABALI, B., AND PANDA, D. K. High performance VMM-bypass I/O in virtual machines. In *USENIX Annual Technical Conference (ATC)* (2006), pp. 29–42.

[33] MENON, A., SANTOS, J. R., TURNER, Y., JANAKIRAMAN, G., AND ZWAENEPOEL, W. Diagnosing performance overheads in the Xen virtual machine environment. In *ACM/USENIX International Conference on Virtual Execution Environments (VEE)* (2005), pp. 13–23.

[34] MOGUL, J. C., AND RAMAKRISHNAN, K. K. Eliminating receive livelock in an interrupt-driven kernel. *ACM Transactions on Computer Systems (TOCS) 15* (1997), 217–252.

[35] NAVARRO, J., IYER, S., DRUSCHEL, P., AND COX, A. Practical, transparent operating system support for superpages. In *USENIX Symposium on Operating Systems Design & Implementation (OSDI)* (2002).

[36] POPEK, G. J., AND GOLDBERG, R. P. Formal requirements for virtualizable third generation architectures. *Communications of the ACM (CACM) 17* (1974), 412–421.

[37] RAJ, H., AND SCHWAN, K. High performance and scalable I/O virtualization via self-virtualized devices. In *International Symposium on High Performance Distributed Computer (HPDC)* (2007).

[38] RAM, K. K., SANTOS, J. R., TURNER, Y., COX, A. L., AND RIXNER, S. Achieving 10Gbps using safe and transparent network interface virtualization. In *ACM/USENIX International Conference on Virtual Execution Environments (VEE)* (2009).

[39] ROSS, T. L., WASHABAUGH, D. M., ROMAN, P. J., CHEUNG, W., TANAKA, K., AND MIZUGUCHI, S. Method and apparatus for performing interrupt frequency mitigation in a network node. US Patent 6,115,775, 2000.

[40] RUMBLE, S., ONGARO, D., STUTSMAN, R., ROSENBLUM, M., AND OUSTERHOUT, J. It's time for low latency. In *USENIX Workshop on Hot Topics in Operating Systems (HOTOS)* (2011).

[41] RUSSELL, R. virtio: towards a de-facto standard for virtual I/O devices. *ACM SIGOPS Operating Systems Review (OSR) 42*, 5 (2008), 95–103.

[42] RUSSINOVICH, M. E., AND SOLOMON, D. A. *Microsoft Windows Internals, Fourth Edition: Microsoft Windows Server(TM) 2003, Windows XP, and Windows 2000 (Pro-Developer)*. Microsoft Press, 2004.

[43] SALAH, K. To coalesce or not to coalesce. *International Journal of Electronics and Communications 61*, 4 (2007), 215–225.

[44] SALAH, K., AND QAHTAN, A. Boosting throughput of Snort NIDS under Linux. In *International Conference on Innovations in Information Technology (IIT)* (2008).

[45] SALIM, J. H., OLSSON, R., AND KUZNETSOV, A. Beyond Softnet. In *Anual Linux Showcase & Conference* (2001).

[46] SANTOS, J. R., TURNER, Y., JANAKIRAMAN, J. G., AND PRATT, I. Bridging the gap between software and hardware techniques for I/O virtualization. In *USENIX Annual Technical Conference (ATC)* (2008).

[47] SUGERMAN, J., VENKITACHALAM, G., AND LIM, B.-H. Virtualizing I/O devices on Vmware workstation's hosted virtual machine monitor. In *USENIX Annual Technical Conference (ATC)* (2001), pp. 1–14.

[48] SZEFER, J., KELLER, E., LEE, R. B., AND REXFORD, J. Eliminating the hypervisor attack surface for a more secure cloud. In *ACM Conference on Computer and Communications Security (CCS)* (2011).

[49] TSAFRIR, D., ETSION, Y., FEITELSON, D. G., AND KIRKPATRICK, S. System noise, OS clock ticks, and fine-grained parallel applications. In *ACM International Conference on Supercomputing (ICS)* (2005), pp. 303–312.

[50] UHLIG, R., NEIGER, G., RODGERS, D., SANTONI, A. L., MARTINS, F. C. M., ANDERSON, A. V., BENNETT, S. M., KAGI, A., LEUNG, F. H., AND SMITH, L. Intel virtualization technology. *Computer 38*, 5 (2005), 48–56.

[51] WILLMANN, P., SHAFER, J., CARR, D., MENON, A., RIXNER, S., COX, A. L., AND ZWAENEPOEL, W. Concurrent direct network access for virtual machine monitors. In *IEEE International Symposium on High Performance Computer Architecture (HPCA)* (2007).

[52] WOJTCZUK, R., AND RUTKOWSKA, J. Following the White Rabbit: Software attacks against Intel VT-d technology. `http://invisiblethingslab.com/resources/2011/Software%20Attacks%20on%20Intel%20VT-d.pdf`. (Accessed Jul, 2011).

[53] YASSOUR, B.-A., BEN-YEHUDA, M., AND WASSERMAN, O. Direct device assignment for untrusted fully-virtualized virtual machines. Tech. Rep. H-0263, IBM Research, 2008.

[54] ZEC, M., MIKUC, M., AND ŽAGAR, M. Estimating the Impact of Interrupt Coalescing Delays on Steady State TCP Throughput. In *International Conference on Software, Telecommunications and Computer Networks (SoftCOM)* (2002).

DejaVu: Accelerating Resource Allocation in Virtualized Environments

Nedeljko Vasić, Dejan Novaković, Svetozar Miučin *, Dejan Kostić, and Ricardo Bianchini[†]

School of Computer and Communication Sciences
EPFL, Switzerland
{firstname.lastname}@epfl.ch

[†]Department of Computer Science
Rutgers University, USA
ricardob@cs.rutgers.edu

Abstract

Effective resource management of virtualized environments is a challenging task. State-of-the-art management systems either rely on analytical models or evaluate resource allocations by running actual experiments. However, both approaches incur a significant overhead once the workload changes. The former needs to re-calibrate and re-validate models, whereas the latter has to run a new set of experiments to select a new resource allocation. During the adaptation period, the system may run with an inefficient configuration.

In this paper, we propose DejaVu – a framework that (1) minimizes the resource management overhead by identifying a small set of workload classes for which it needs to evaluate resource allocation decisions, (2) quickly adapts to workload changes by classifying workloads using signatures and caching their preferred resource allocations at runtime, and (3) deals with interference by estimating an "interference index". We evaluate DejaVu by running representative network services on Amazon EC2. DejaVu achieves more than 10x speedup in adaptation time for each workload change relative to the state-of-the-art. By enabling quick adaptation, DejaVu saves up to 60% of the service provisioning cost. Finally, DejaVu is easily deployable as it does not require any extensive instrumentation or human intervention.

Categories and Subject Descriptors D.4.8 [*Operating Systems*]: Performance; K.6.4 [*Management of Computing and Information Systems*]: System Management

General Terms Design, Measurement, Performance

Keywords Resource management, Data center, Virtualization

1. Introduction

Cloud computing is rapidly growing in popularity and importance, as an increasing number of enterprises and individuals have been offloading their workloads to cloud service providers, such as Amazon, Microsoft, IBM, and Google. One of the main reasons for the proliferation of cloud services is virtualization technology. Virtualization (1) enables providers to easily package and identify each customer's application into one or more virtual machines (VMs); (2) allows providers to lower operating costs by multiplexing their physical machines (PMs) across many VMs; and (3) simplifies VM placement and migration across PMs.

However, effective management of virtualized resources is a challenging task for providers, as it often involves selecting the best resource allocation out of a large number of alternatives. Moreover, evaluating each such allocation requires assessing its potential performance, availability, and energy consumption implications. To make matters worse, the workload of certain applications varies over time, requiring the resource allocations to be re-evaluated and possibly changed dynamically. For example, the workload of network services may vary in terms of the request rate and the resource requirements of the request mix.

A service that is provisioned with an inadequate number of resources can be problematic in two ways. If the service is over-provisioned, the provider wastes money. If the service is under-provisioned, its performance may violate a service-level objective (SLO). As an illustration of the impact of such an SLO violation, Amazon reports that it loses 1% of sales for an increase of 100 ms in response latency [15]. Thus, it is very important that the service is adequately provisioned.

Given these problems, automated resource managers or the system administrators themselves must be able to evaluate many possible resource allocations quickly and accurately. Both analytical modeling and experimentation have been proposed for evaluating allocations in similar datacenter settings [10, 12, 14, 18, 30, 33, 36, 37, 40, 42, 43]. Unfortunately, these techniques may require substantial time. Although modeling enables a large number of allocations to be quickly evaluated, it also typically requires time-consuming (and often manual) re-calibration and re-validation whenever workloads change appreciably. In contrast, sandboxed experimentation can be more accurate than modeling, but requires executions that are long enough to produce representative results. For example, [42] suggests that each experiment may require minutes to execute. Finally, experimenting with resource allocations on-line, via simple heuristics and/or feedback control [2, 8, 21, 28, 38, 41], has the additional limitation that any tentative allocations are exposed to users.

This paper addresses this set of problems by proposing DejaVu, a system that simplifies and accelerates the management of virtualized resources in cloud computing services. The key idea behind DejaVu is to cache and reuse the results of previous resource allocation decisions. When the DejaVu framework detects that workload conditions have changed (perhaps because a VM or service is

* Work done during this author's internship at EPFL.

ASPLOS'12, March 3–7, 2012, London, England, UK.

not achieving its desired performance), it can lookup the DejaVu cache, each time using a VM identification and a *workload signature*. The signature is an automatically determined, pre-defined vector of metrics describing the workload characteristics, and the VM's current resource utilization. To enable the cache lookups, DejaVu automatically constructs a classifier that uses off-the-shelf machine learning techniques. The classifier operates on workload clusters that are determined after an initial learning phase. DejaVu clustering has a positive effect on reducing the overall resource management effort and overhead, because it reduces the number of invocations of the tuning process (one per cluster).

The resource manager can use the output of DejaVu to quickly reallocate resources. The manager only needs to resort to time-consuming modeling, sandboxed experimentation, or on-line experimentation when no previous workload exercises the affected VMs in the same way. When the manager does have to produce a new optimized resource allocation using one of these methods, it stores the allocation into the DejaVu cache for later use.

Like any other cache, DejaVu is most useful when its cached allocations can be repeatedly reused. Although DejaVu can be used successfully in a variety of environments, in this paper we focus on cloud computing providers that run collections of network services (these are also known as Web hosting providers). Previous works and our own experience suggest that DejaVu should achieve high "hit rates" in this environment. For example, it is well-known that the load intensity of network services follows a repeating daily pattern, with lower request rates on weekend days. In addition, these services use multiple VMs that implement the same functionality and experience roughly the same workload (e.g., all the application servers of a 3-tier network service).

Our approach to dealing with performance interference on the virtualized hosting platform recognizes the difficulty of pinpointing the cause of interference, and the inability of cloud users to change the hosting platform itself to eliminate interference. DejaVu uses a pragmatic approach in which it probes for interference and adjusts to it by provisioning the service with more resources.

The contributions of this paper are as follows:

1. We propose DejaVu, a framework for learning and reusing optimized VM resource allocations.
2. We describe a technique for automatically profiling, clustering, and classifying workloads. Clustering reduces the number of tuning instances and thus reduces the overall resource management overhead.
3. We evaluate DejaVu using realistic network services and real-world MSN messenger and HotMail traces. Our results show that DejaVu achieves more than 10x speedup in adaptation time for each workload change, relative to the state-of-the-art. Further, DejaVu saves between 35-45% and 55-60% of the provisioning cost when scaling up and scaling out, respectively, as compared to the approach that always overprovisions the service to ensure the SLO is met. The DejaVu-achieved savings translate to about $250,000 per year for 100 large EC2 instances.

We conclude that deploying DejaVu in the field would have two key benefits. First, it would enable cloud providers to meet their SLOs more efficiently as workloads change. It would also enable providers to lower their energy costs (e.g., by consolidating workloads on fewer machines, more machines can enter a low-power state [8, 22, 39]). Second, the more efficient adaptation to workload changes would enable users to purchase fewer resources from the provider. In addition, the lower provider costs would likely translate into savings for users as well.

2. Background and Motivation

In this section, we briefly describe the background for our work, and demonstrate the need for DejaVu.

2.1 Background

We assume that the user[1] of the virtualized environment deploys her service across a pool of virtualized servers. We use the term application to denote a standalone application or a service component running within a guest operating system in a virtual machine (VM). The service itself is mapped to a number of VMs. A typical example would be a 3-tier architecture which consists of a web server, an application server, and a database server component. All VMs reserved for a particular component can be hosted by a single physical server, or distributed across a number of them. The user and the provider agree on the Service Level Objective (SLO) for the deployed service.

While DejaVu is not restricted to any particular virtualized platform, we evaluate it using Amazon's Elastic Computing Cloud (EC2) platform. EC2 offers two mechanisms for dynamic resource provisioning, namely *horizontal* and *vertical* scaling. While horizontal scaling (scaling out) lets users quickly extend their capacities with new virtual instances, vertical scaling (scaling up) varies resources assigned to a single VM. EC2 provides many server instance types, from small to extra large, which differ in available computing units, memory and I/O performance. We evaluate DejaVu with both provisioning schemes in mind.

2.2 The Case for DejaVu

The key issue in resource provisioning is to come up with the sufficient, but not wasteful, set of virtualized resources (e.g., number of virtual CPU cores and memory size) that enable the application to meet its SLO. Resource provisioning is challenging due to: (1) workload dynamics, (2) the difficulty and overhead of deriving the resource allocation for each workload, and (3) the difficulty in enforcing the resource planning decisions due to interference. As a result, it is difficult to determine the resource allocation that will achieve the desired performance while minimizing the cost for both the cloud provider and the user.

The most important problem is that the search space of allocation parameters is very large and makes the optimal configuration hard-to-find. Moreover, the workload can change and render this computed setting sub-optimal. This in turn results in underperforming services or resource waste.

Once they detect changes in the workload, the existing approaches for dynamic resource allocation re-run time-consuming modeling and validation, sandboxed experimentation, or on-line experimentation to evaluate different resource allocations. Moreover, on-line experimentation approaches (including feedback control) adjust the resource allocation incrementally, which leads to long convergence times. The convergence problem becomes even worse when new servers are added to or removed from the service. Adding servers involves long boot and warm-up times, whereas removing servers may cause other servers to spend significant time rebalancing load (as in Casandra [1]).

The impact of the state-of-the-art online adaptation on performance is illustrated by our experiment using RUBiS [6] (an eBay clone) in which we change the workload volume every 10 minutes. Further, to approximate the diurnal variation of load in a datacenter, we vary the load according to a sine-wave. As shown in Figure 1, even if the workload follows a recurring pattern, the existing approaches are forced to repeatedly run the tuning process since

[1] We use the terms "user" and "tenant" interchangeably. We reserve the term "client" for the client of the deployed service itself.

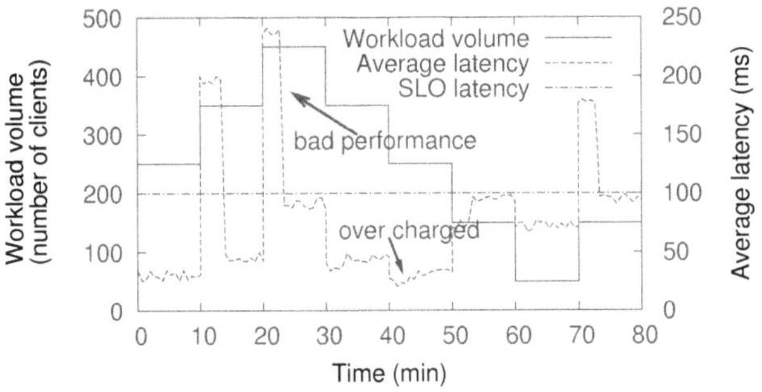

Figure 1. Every time the workload changes, the state-of-the-art approaches spend a considerable amount of time in performance retuning. During this time, the service can deliver insufficient performance due to a lack of resources. Alternatively, the service can be overprovisioned, and ultimately waste resources.

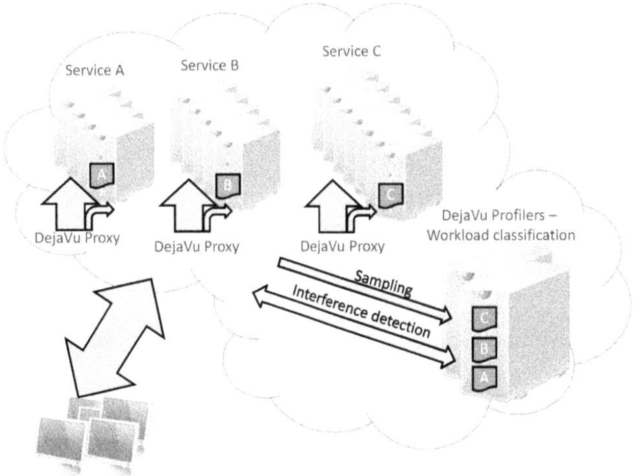

Figure 2. High-level overview of the way DejaVu's integrates with the service running in the cloud.

they cannot detect the similarity in the workload they are encountering. Unfortunately, this means that the hosted service is repeatedly running for long periods of time under a suboptimal resource allocation. Such magnitude of response latency increase (100 ms) has substantial impact on the revenue of the service [15]. Finally, computing the optimal resource allocation is an expensive task.

When faced with such long periods of unsatisfactory performance, the users might have to resort to overprovisioning, e.g., by using a large resource cap that can ensure satisfactory performance at foreseeable peaks in the demand. For the user, doing so incurs unnecessarily high deployment costs. For the provider, this causes high operating cost (e.g., due to excess energy for running and cooling the system). In summary, overprovisioning negates one of the primary reasons for the attractiveness of virtualized services for both users and providers.

Another problem with existing resource allocation approaches is that virtualization platforms do not provide ideal performance isolation, especially in the context of hardware caches and I/O. This implies that application performance may suffer due to the activities of the other virtual machines co-located on the same physical server. For instance, previous works and our own experience suggest that, due to the interference, even virtual instances of the same type might have very different performance over time.

3. Approach

In this section, we describe the DejaVu framework, starting with its high-level overview.

3.1 Overview

DejaVu operates alongside the services deployed in the virtualized environment of a cloud provider. Although other organizations are conceivable, we assume that the cloud provider itself deploys and operates DejaVu. Figure 2 highlights DejaVu's main components and the way they integrate with the cloud provider, while Figure 3 illustrates its operation. DejaVu accelerates the management of virtualized resources in datacenters by caching the results of past resource allocation decisions and quickly reusing them once it faces the same or a similar workload. For DejaVu to be effective in dealing with dynamic workloads, it first needs to learn about workloads and their associated resource allocations (e.g., the number and size of the required virtualized instances on EC2) during the learning phase (e.g., a week of service use).

To profile a workload, DejaVu deploys a proxy that duplicates the client requests directed to selected service VM instances to the DejaVu profiler. DejaVu then uses a dedicated profiling machine to compute a *workload signature* for each encountered workload. The workload signature itself is a set of automatically chosen low-level metrics. Further, DejaVu *clusters* the encountered workloads, and by doing so it reduces the resource management overhead, as well as the number of potentially time-consuming service reconfigurations to accommodate more or fewer virtual machines. The *Tuner* maps the clusters to the available virtualized resources, and populates the resource allocation repository.

After the initial learning phase, DejaVu profiles the workload periodically or on-demand (e.g., upon a violation of an SLO) using its proxy. It then uses each computed workload signature to automatically *classify* the encountered workload. If the classifier points to a previously seen workload (cache hit), DejaVu quickly reuses the previously computed resource allocation. In case of a different resource allocation, DejaVu instructs the service to reconfigure itself. In case of a failure to classify the workload (e.g., due to an unforeseen increase in service volume), DejaVu can either reinvoke the Tuner, or instruct the service to deploy its full capacity configuration. Compared to the state-of-the-art, DejaVu drastically reduces the time during which the service is running with inadequate resources. This translates to fewer and shorter SLO violations, as well as significant cost reduction for running the service itself.

To deal with interference from co-located workloads, DejaVu computes an *interference index* by contrasting the performance of the service on the DejaVu profiler with that in the production environment. It then stores this information in the resource allocation repository. Simply put, this information tells DejaVu how many more resources it needs to request to have a better probabilistic guarantee on the service performance. Using the historically collected interference information once again allows DejaVu to reduce the tuning overhead relative to the interference-oblivious case (state-of-the-art).

3.2 Workload Dispatching and Profiling

At a high level (Figure 2), DejaVu consists of two main components: *proxy* and *workload profiler*. To profile workloads under real-world conditions and traces, we introduce a proxy between the clients and the hosted services. The proxy forwards the client request to the system in production, but also duplicates and sends a certain fraction of the requests to the profiling environment for workload characterization.

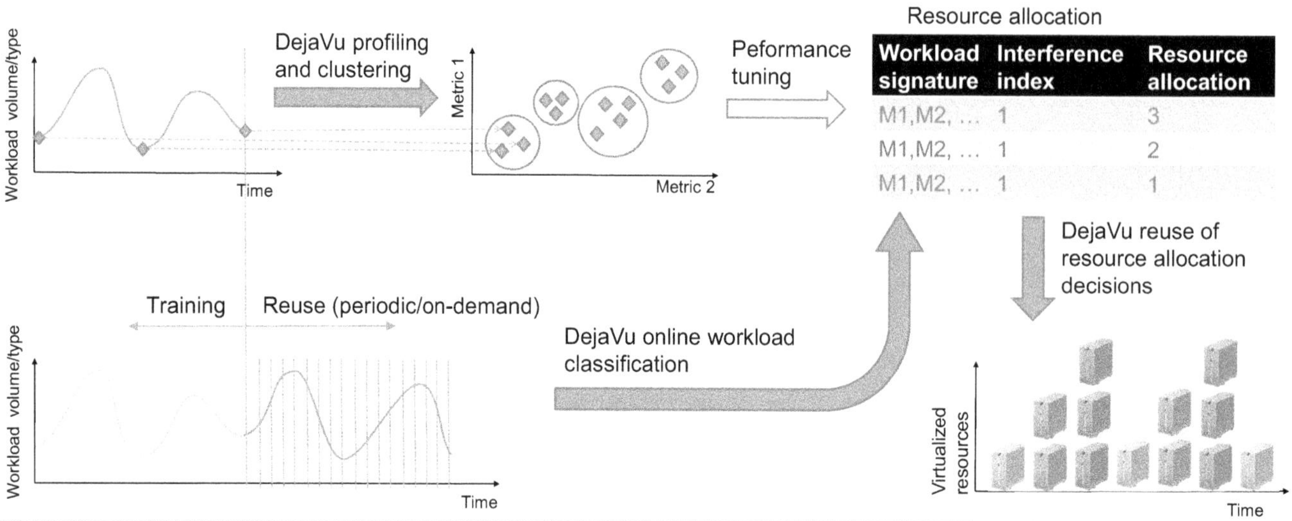

Figure 3. High-level overview of DejaVu's operation. It first profiles and clusters a dynamic workload during the learning phase. State-of-the-art performance tuning then maps the clusters to virtualized resources. Finally, DejaVu profiles workloads at runtime and reuses previous resource allocation decisions to allow the service to quickly adapt to workload changes.

3.2.1 DejaVu Proxy

The proxy needs to be careful when selecting the requests for profiling. In the case of Internet services, the sampling is done at the granularity of the client session to avoid issues with non-existent web cookies that might cause workload anomalies. Other types of applications may require more sophisticated approaches. For example, a distributed key-value storage system (e.g., Cassandra [1]) requires sampling where the dispatching needs to be aware of the node partitioning scheme, and duplicate only the requests with keys that belong to the particular server instance used for workload characterization.

Having a proxy between the service in production and the testing environment (in our case the profiling environment) has been addressed before [42]. The authors typically propose application protocol-aware proxies, ending up with numerous implementations that understand HTTP, mod-jk, jdbc, etc. In contrast, our workload characterization targets an arbitrary service; this in turn poses a need for a general proxy that can work with any service. Hence, we propose a novel proxy which which sits between the application and transport layers.

The proxy duplicates incoming network traffic (all the requests) of the server instance that DejaVu intends to profile, and forwards it to the clone. By doing so, DejaVu ensures that the clone VM serves the same requests as the profiled instance, resulting in the same or similar behavior. Finally, to make the profiling process transparent to the other nodes in the cluster, the clone's replies are dropped by the profiler. To avoid instrumentation of the service (e.g., changing the listening ports), we transparently redirect incoming traffic to the DejaVu proxy using iptables routines [19].

It is particularly hard to make the profiler behave just like the production instance in multi-tier services. For example, consider a three-tier architecture. In this architecture, it is common for the front-end web server to invoke the application server which then talks to the database server before replying back to the front-end. In this case, if DejaVu is instructed to profile only the application server (the middle tier), it is obvious that we need to deal with the absence of the database server.

DejaVu addresses this challenge by having its proxy cache recent answers from the database such that they can be re-used by the profiler. Requests coming from the clone are also sent to the proxy. Upon receiving a request from the profiler, the proxy computes its hash and mimics the existence of the database by looking up the most recent answer for the given hash. Note that the proxy's lookup table exhibits good locality since both the production and the profiler deal with the same requests, only slightly shifted in time as one of these two might be running faster. This caching scheme does not necessarily produce the exact same behavior as in the production system because the proxy can: (1) miss some answers due to minor request permutations (i.e. the profiler and the production instance generate different timestamps), or (2) feed the profiler with obsolete data. However, the scheme still generates the load on the profiler that is similar to that of the production system (recall that DejaVu does not need a verbatim copy of the production system).

3.2.2 DejaVu Profiler

During the workload characterization process, DejaVu's profiler serves realistic requests (sent by the proxy) in the profiling environment, allowing us to collect all the metrics required by the characterization process, without interfering with the system in production. DejaVu relies on VM cloning to reconstruct a subset of the monitored service that can serve the sampled requests, but makes sure that VM clones have different network identities (recall that the clone is running in our private profiling environment). To minimize the cloning cost, DejaVu profiles only a subset of the service, typically a single server instance (e.g., one VM per tier) and assumes that services balance the load evenly across its server instances.

The services with little or no state are quickly brought to an equivalent operational state to that of the system in production. In contrast, replicating a database instance might be time-consuming, and it is important to consider the cloning of the disk storage [7, 20]. However, our goal is not to exactly capture the service's complex behavior and resulting performance, but only to label the current workload which gives us additional flexibility – our VM clone does not need to be tightly synchronized with the system in production. Instead, we envision periodic synchronization and resort to the current image, as long as DejaVu manages to identify the minimal set of resources that enable the service to meet its SLO.

To avoid the VM cloning and DejaVu overhead altogether, one can perform profiling on-line, without cloning the monitored VM.

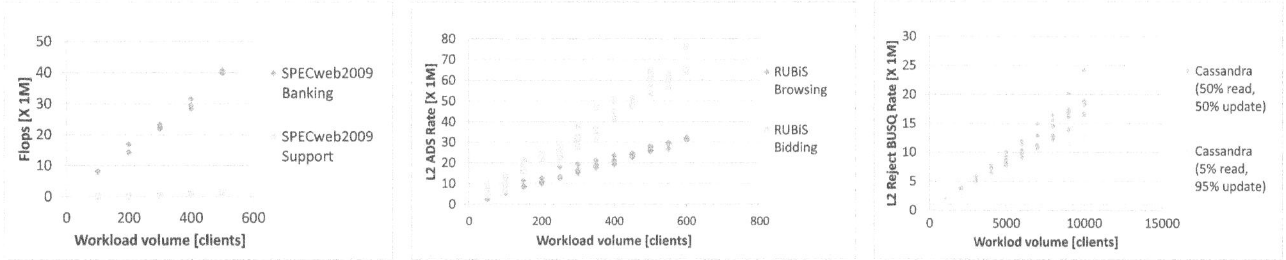

(a) SPECweb2009 (b) RUBiS (c) Cassandra

Figure 4. Low-level metrics can serve as a signature which reliably identifies workloads that differ either in their type (i.e., read/write ratio) or intensity.

This again comes with two major obstacles. First, some metrics might be disturbed by co-located tenants during the sampling period; hence one would need to carefully identify the signature-forming metrics that are immune to interference. The second obstacle is that the cloud provider would need to make all low-level metrics available for our profiling.

3.3 Choosing the Workload Signature

For any metric-based workload recognition, it is crucial that the set of metrics chosen as the *workload signature* can uniquely identify all types of workload behaviors. Before going into the details of our workload signature selection process, we discuss how we collect the workload-describing metrics.

The DejaVu framework relies on its *Monitor* to periodically or on-demand (e.g., upon a violation of an SLO) collect the workload signatures. The design of the Monitor includes several key challenges:

- *Non-intrusive monitoring.* Given the diverse set of applications that might run in the cloud, DejaVu cannot rely on any prior service knowledge, semantics, implementation details, or highly-specific logs. Further, DejaVu assumes that it has to work well without having any control over the guest VMs or applications running inside them. This is a desirable constraint given that we target hosting environments like Amazon's EC2 that provides only a "bare-bones" virtual server.
- *Isolation.* Because the DejaVu profiler (possibly running on a single machine) might be in charge of characterizing multiple services, we need to make sure that the obtained signatures are not disturbed by other profiling processes running on the same profiler.
- *Small overhead.* Since DejaVu might be running all the time, its proxy must induce negligible overhead while duplicating client requests, to avoid an impact on application performance.

Using low-level metrics to capture the workload behavior is attractive as it allows us to uniquely identify different workloads without requiring knowledge about the deployed service. The virtualization platforms are already equipped with various monitoring tools that are useful to us. For instance, Xen's `xentop` command reports individual VM resource consumption (CPU, memory, and I/O). Further, modern processors usually have a set of special registers that allow monitoring of performance counters without affecting the code that is currently running. It has been shown that these *Hardware Performance Counters (HPC)* can be used for workload anomaly detection [17] and online request recognition [29]. In addition, the HPC statistics can conveniently be obtained without instrumenting the guest VM. We only read a hardware counter value before a VM is scheduled, and right after it is preempted. The difference between the two gives us the exact number of events for which the VM should be "charged". Tools such as `Xenoprof` already provide this functionality with passive sampling.

Leveraging low-level metrics brings another practical question: given the complexity of the hosted services, can we rely on these metrics as a reliable signature to distinguish different workloads? We assume that as long as a relevant counter value lies in a certain interval, the current workload belongs to the class associated with the interval.

To validate this assumption in practice, we run experiments with realistic applications. In particular, we run typical cloud benchmarks under different load volumes, with 5 trials for each volume. Figures 4(a) - 4(c) present the results with each point representing a different trial. In the most obvious example, Figure 4(a) clearly shows that the hardware metric (Flops rate in this case) can reliably differentiate the incoming workloads. Moreover, the results for each load volume are very close. Once we change either workload type (e.g., read/write ratio) or intensity, a large gap between counter values appear. Similar trends are seen in the other benchmarks as well, but with a bit more noise. Nevertheless, the remaining metrics that belong to the signature (we are plotting only a single counter for each benchmark) typically eliminate the impact of noise.

While we can choose an arbitrary number of xentop-reported metrics to serve as the workload signature, the number of HPC-based metrics is limited in practice – for instance, our profiling server, Intel Xeon X5472, has only four registers that allow monitoring of HPCs, with up to 60 different events that can be monitored. It is possible to monitor a large number of events using time-division multiplexing, but this causes a loss in accuracy [16]. Moreover, many of these events are not very useful for workload characterization, as they provide little or no value when comparing workloads. Finally, we can reduce the dimensionality of the ensuing classification problem and significantly speed up the process by selecting only a subset of relevant events.

The task at hand is a typical feature selection process, which evaluates the effect of selected features on classification accuracy. The problem has been investigated for years, resulting in a large number of machine learning techniques. As our focus is not on inventing new models, we simply apply various mature methods from the WEKA machine learning package [13] on our datasets obtained from profiling (Section 3.4). During this phase, we form the dataset by collecting all HPC and xentop-reported metric values.

Applying different techniques on our dataset, we note that the `CfsSubsetEval` technique, in collaboration with the `GreedStepWise` search, results in high classification accuracy. The technique evaluates each attribute individually, but also observes the degree of redundancy among them internally to prevent undesirable overlap. As a result, we derive a set of N representative HPCs and xentop-reported metrics, which serve as the workload signature (WS) in the form of an ordered N-tuple:

$$WS = \{m^1, m^2, ..., m^N\} \quad (1)$$

where m^i represents the metric i. We further analyze the feature selection process by manually inspecting the chosen counters. For instance, the HPC counters chosen to serve as the workload signature in case of the RUBiS workload are depicted in Table 1 (the xentop metrics are excluded from the table). Indeed, the signature metrics provide performance information related to CPU, cache, memory, and the bus queue.

Given that the selection process is data-driven, the metrics forming the workload signatures are *application-dependent*. We however do not view this as an issue since the *metric selection process is fully automated* and transparent to the user.

To ensure that our workload signature is robust to arbitrary sampling duration, we normalize the values with the sampling time. This is important as it allows us to generalize our signatures across workloads regardless of how long the sampling takes.

3.4 Identifying Workload Classes

Given that the majority of network services follow a repeating daily pattern, DejaVu should achieve high "cache hit rates". But still a challenge remains. To achieve high hit rates, DejaVu first needs to populate preferred resource allocations for representative workloads, i.e. those workloads that will most likely reoccur in the near future and result in a cache hit.

Note that there is a tradeoff between the overhead of adjusting resource allocations (tuning) and the achieved hit rates. One can achieve high hit rates by naively marking every workload as representative. However, this would cause DejaVu to perform costly tuning for too many workloads. On the other hand, omitting some important workloads could lead to unacceptable resource allocations during certain periods.

DejaVu addresses this tradeoff by automatically identifying a small set of workload classes for a service. First, it monitors the service for a certain period (e.g., a day or week) until the administrator decides that DejaVu has seen most, or ideally all, workloads. During this initial profiling phase, DejaVu collects the low-level metrics discussed in Section 3.3. Then, it analyzes the dataset to identify workload signatures, and represent each workload as a point in N-dimensional space (N is the number of metrics in the signature). Finally, DejaVu clusters workloads into classes.

DejaVu leverages a standard clustering technique, simple k means, to produce a set of workload classes for which the Tuner needs to obtain the resource allocations. The framework can automatically determine the number of classes, as we did in our experiments, but also allows the administrators to explicitly strike the appropriate tradeoff between the tuning overhead and hit rate. As an example, Figure 5 shows the representative workload classes that we obtain from a service after replaying the day-long Microsoft HotMail trace [35]. Each workload is projected onto the two-dimensional space for clarity. DejaVu collected a set of 24 workloads (an instance per hour), and it identified only four different workload classes for which it has to perform the tuning. For instance, a workload class holding a single workload (the top right corner) stands for the peak hour.

DejaVu assumes that the workload classes obtained in the profiling environment are also relevant for the production system. This does not mean that the counter values reported by the profiler need to be comparable to corresponding values seen by the service in production. This would be too strong of an assumption, as DejaVu would then have to make the profiling environment a verbatim copy of the hosting platform, which is most likely infeasible. Instead,

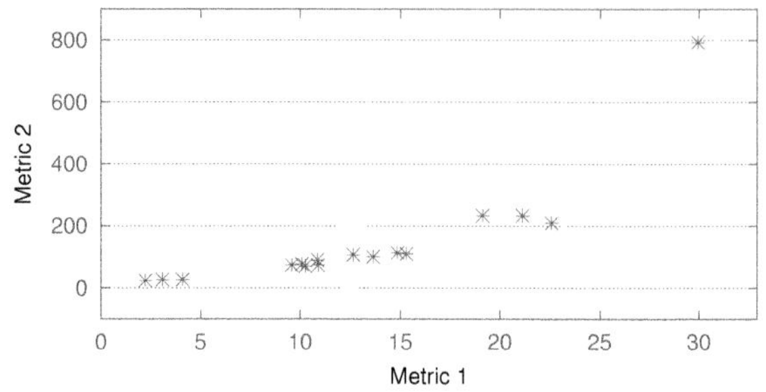

Figure 5. Identifying the representative workloads - DejaVu substantially reduces the tuning overhead by producing only 4 workload classes out of 24 initial workloads.

DejaVu only assumes that the relative ordering among workloads is preserved between the profiling and the production environment. For instance, if workload A is closer to workload B than to workload C in the profiling environment, the same also holds in the production environment. We have verified this assumption empirically using machines of different types in our lab.

After DejaVu identifies the workload classes, it triggers the tuning process for a single workload from each workload class. It typically chooses the instance that is closest to the cluster's centroid. The Tuner's job is to determine the sufficient, but not wasteful, set of virtualized resources (e.g., number and type of virtual instances) that ensure the application meets its SLO. The Tuner can use modeling or experiments for this task. Moreover, it can be manually driven or entirely automated. The choice of a tuning mechanism is orthogonal to our work. After the Tuner determines resource allocations for each workload class, DejaVu has a table populated with workload signatures along with their preferred resource allocations – *the workload signature repository* – which it can re-use at runtime.

Since our focus is not on the Tuner itself, we resort to a very simple technique – linear search – in our evaluation. In more detail, we replay a sequence of runs of the workload, each time with an increasing amount of virtual resources. We then choose the minimal set of resources that fulfill the target SLO. For instance, one can incrementally increase the CPU or memory allocation (by varying the VMM's scheduler caps) until the SLO is fulfilled. Since our experiments involve EC2, we can only vary the number of virtual instances or instance type. Note that we can accelerate the tuning process by using more sophisticated methods, as in [30]. We leave this avenue for our future work.

3.5 Quickly Adapting to Workload Changes

Since DejaVu's goal is to re-use resource allocation decisions at runtime, it needs a mechanism to decide to which cluster a newly encountered workload belongs – the equivalent of the cache lookup operation. DejaVu uses the previously identified clusters to label each workload with the cluster number to which it belongs, such that it can train a *classifier* to quickly recognize newly encountered workloads at runtime. The resulting classifier stands as the explicit description of the workload classes. We have experimented with numerous classifier implementations from the WEKA package and observe that both Bayesian models and decision trees work well for the network services we considered. We use the C4.5 decision tree in our evaluation, or more precisely its open source Java implementation – J48).

Upon a workload change, DejaVu promptly collects the relevant low-level metrics to form the workload signature of the new workload and queries the DejaVu repository to find the best match

Name	Description	Name	Description
busq_empty	Bus queue is empty	cpu_clk_unhalted	Clock cycles when not halted
l2_ads	Cycles the L2 address bus is in use	l2_reject_busq	Rejected L2 cache requests
l2_st	Number of L2 data stores	load_block	Events pertaining to loads
store_block	Events pertaining to stores	page_walks	Page table walk events

Table 1. The HPC metrics included in RUBiS's workload signature.

among the existing signatures. To do this, it uses the previously defined classification model and outputs the resource allocation of the cluster to which the incoming signature belongs. Given that the number of workload classes is typically small and the classification time practically negligible, DejaVu can adjust to workload changes on the order of a few or several seconds, as needed by the DejaVu profiler to collect the workload signatures.

Along with the preferred resource allocations, the repository also outputs the certainty level with which the repository assigned the new signature to the chosen cluster. If the repository repeatedly outputs low certainty levels, it most likely means that the workload has changed over time and that the current clustering is no longer relevant. DejaVu can then initiate the clustering and tuning process once again, allowing it to determine new workload classes, conduct the necessary experiments (or modeling activities), and update the Repository. Meanwhile, DejaVu configures the service with the maximum allowed capacity to ensure that the performance is not affected when experiencing non-classified workloads.

3.6 Addressing Interference

In the previous subsection, we described how to populate the repository with the smallest (also called *baseline*) resource allocation that meets the SLO at the time of tuning. The baseline allocation however, due to interference, may not guarantee sufficient performance at all times. DejaVu deals with this problem by estimating the *interference index* and using it, along with the workload signature, when determining the preferred resource allocation.

In more detail, after DejaVu deploys the baseline resource allocation for the current workload, it monitors the resulting performance (e.g., service latency). If it observes that the SLO is still being violated, DejaVu blames interference for the performance degradation. Workload changes are excluded from the potential reasons, because the workload class has just been identified in isolation. It then proceeds by computing the interference index as:

$$\textit{Interference index} = \frac{PerformanceLevel_{production}}{PerformanceLevel_{isolation}} \quad (2)$$

The index contrasts the performance of the service in production after the baseline allocation is deployed with that obtained from the profiler. Note that DejaVu relies on each application to report a performance-level metric (e.g., response time, throughput). This metric already needs to be collected and reported when the performance is unsatisfactory. Others have argued for computing this metric [18].

Finally, DejaVu queries the repository for the preferred resource allocation for the current workload and the interference amount. If the repository does not contain the corresponding entry, DejaVu triggers the tuning process and sends the obtained results, along with the estimated index, to the repository for later use. After this is done, DejaVu will be able to quickly lookup the best resource allocation for this workload given the same amount of interference.

Interference may vary across the VM instances of a service, making it hard to select a single instance for profiling that will uniquely represent the interference across the entire service. Inspired by typical performance requirements (e.g., the $Xth - percentile$ of the response time should be lower than Y seconds), we envision a selection process that chooses an instance at which interference is higher than in $X\%$ of the probed instances. This conservative performance estimation would give us a probabilistic guarantee on the service performance.

For the time being, DejaVu quantifies the interference impact and reacts upon it to maintain the SLO. However, we plan to further investigate this aspect of DejaVu and ensure it provides finer information about the interference. Assuming that the cloud provider collects the low-level metrics from its VM instances, it might compare the metric values imposed by the same workload class over time to reveal which resource is primarily affected by the interference (e.g., cache, I/O).

3.7 Discussion

We now discuss a few interesting questions about DejaVu.

Who should run DejaVu: the cloud provider or a third party? Although we view this choice as orthogonal to our work, we believe that it is more practical for the cloud provider to run DejaVu. In fact, this is the setup we have assumed so far. This deployment scenario eliminates the privacy and network traffic concerns with shipping code (clones of the services' VMs) and client requests to a third party.

Nevertheless, it is conceivable that a third party could run DejaVu. In this case, users would likely have to explicitly contract with both the provider and the third party. Alternatively, the DejaVu proxy could be configured to selectively duplicate the incoming traffic such that private information (e.g., e-mails, user-specific data) is not dispatched to the profiler. However, having to share the service code with the third party would still be a problem.

Regardless of who runs DejaVu, a tenant needs to reveal certain information about their service. Specifically, the proxy needs to know the port numbers used by the service to communicate with the clients and, internally, among VMs. Finally, to completely automate the resource allocation process, DejaVu assumes that it can enforce a chosen resource allocation policy without necessitating user involvement. Amazon EC2, for instance, allows us to automatically adjust the number of running instances by using its APIs.

How does DejaVu deal with unforeseen workloads? DejaVu provides no worse performance than the existing approaches when it encounters a previously unknown workload (e.g., large and unseen workload volume [4]). In this case, DejaVu has to spend additional time to identify the resource allocation that achieves the desired performance at minimal cost (just like the existing systems). To try to avoid an SLO violation by the service, the current version of DejaVu responds to unforeseen workloads by deploying the maximum resource allocation (full capacity). If the workload occurs multiple times, DejaVu invokes the Tuner to compute the minimal set of required resources and then readjust the resource allocation.

What is the scope of DejaVu? Although DejaVu primarily targets "request-response" Internet services, we believe that our interference mechanism can be useful even for long-running batch workloads (e.g., MapReduce/Hadoop jobs). In this case, DejaVu would require the equivalent of an SLO. For example, for Hadoop map tasks, the SLO could be their user-provided expected running times (possibly as a function of the input size). Upon an SLO violation, DejaVu would run a subset of tasks in isolation to determine the interference index. This computation would also expose cases in which interference is not significant and the user simply mis-estimated the expected running times. We leave the issue of applying DejaVu to other types of workloads for future work.

4. Evaluation

Our evaluation uses realistic traces and workloads to answer the following questions. First, can DejaVu produce significant savings while scaling network services horizontally (scaling out) and vertically (scaling up)? Second, how does DejaVu compare with: (1) a time-based controller (called Autopilot) which attempts to leverage the re-occurring (e.g., daily) patterns in the workload by repeating the resource allocations determined during the learning phase at appropriate times, and (2) an existing autoscaling platform, such as RightScale [24]? Third, is DejaVu capable of detecting and mitigating the effect of interference? Finally, can the profiling overhead, and to what extent, affect the performance of the production system? This section starts by describing our experimental setup.

Testbed. Our profiling environment consists of two servers: Intel SR1560 Series rack servers with Intel Xeon X5472 processors (eight cores at 3 GHz), 8 GB of DRAM, and 6 MB of L2 cache per every two cores. We use them to collect the low-level metrics while hosting the clone instances of Internet service components.

We evaluate the DejaVu framework by running widely-used benchmarks on Amazon's EC2 cloud platform. We ran all our experiments within an EC2 cluster of 20 virtual machines (both clients and servers were running on EC2). To demonstrate DejaVu's ability to scale out, we vary the number of active instances from 2 to 10 as the workload intensity changes, but resort only to EC2's large instance type. In contrast, we demonstrate its ability to scale up by varying the instance type from large to extra-large, while keeping the number of active instances constant.

To focus on DejaVu rather than on the idiosyncrasies of EC2, our scale out experiments assume that the VM instances to be added to a service have been pre-created and stopped. In our scale up experiments, we also pre-create VM instances of both types (large and extra large). Pre-created VMs are ready for instant use, except for a short warm-up time. In all cases, state management across VM instances, if needed, is the responsibility of the service itself, not DejaVu.

Internet services. We evaluate DejaVu for two representative types of Internet services: (1) a classic multi-tier web site with an SQL database back-end (SPECweb2009), and (2) a NoSQL database in the form of a key-value storage layer (Cassandra).

SPECweb2009 [32] is a benchmark designed to measure the performance of a web server serving both static and dynamic content. Further, this benchmark allows us to run 3 workloads: e-commerce, banking, and support. While the first two names speak for themselves, the last workload tests the performance level while downloading large files.

Cassandra [1] differs significantly from SPECweb2009. It is a distributed storage facility for maintaining large amounts of data spread out across many servers, while providing highly available service without a single point of failure. Cassandra is used by many real Internet services, such as Facebook and Twitter, whereas the clients to stress-test it are part of the Yahoo! Cloud Service Benchmark [11].

In Section 4.4, we also profile RUBiS [6], a three-tier e-commerce application (given its similarity to SPECweb2009, we do not demonstrate the rest of DejaVu's features on this benchmark). RUBiS consists of a front-end Apache web server, a Tomcat application server, and a MySQL database server. In short, RUBiS defines 26 client interactions (e.g., bidding, selling) whose frequencies are defined by RUBiS transition tables. Our setup has 1,000,000 registered clients and that many stored items in the database, as defined by the RUBiS default property file.

Given that these are widely-used benchmarks, client emulators are publicly available for all of them and we use them to generate client requests. Each emulator can change the workload type by varying its "browsing habits", and also collect numerous statistics, including the throughput and response time, which we use as the measure of performance. Finally, all clients run on EC2 instances to ensure that the clients do not experience network bottlenecks.

Workload traces. To emulate a highly dynamic workload of a real application, we use real load traces from HotMail (Windows Live Mail) and Windows Live Messenger from September, 2009 [35]. Figures 6(a) and 7(a) plot the normalized load from these traces. Both traces contain measurements at 1-hour increments during one week, aggregated over thousands of servers. We proportionally scale down the load such that the peak load from the traces corresponds to the maximum number of clients that we can successfully serve when operating at full capacity (10 virtual instances).

In all our experiments, we use the first day from our traces for initial tuning and identification of the workload classes, whereas the remaining 6 days are used to evaluate the performance/cost benefits when DejaVu is used.

4.1 Case Study 1: Scaling Out

Our first set of experiments demonstrates DejaVu's ability to reduce the service provisioning cost by dynamically adjusting the number of running instances (scale out) as the workload intensity varies according to our live traces. We show DejaVu's benefits with Cassandra's update-heavy workload which has 95% of write requests and only 5% of read requests.

Figure 6(b) plots how DejaVu varies the number of active server instances as the workload intensity changes according to the Messenger traces. The initial tuning produces 4 different workload classes and ultimately 4 preferred resource allocations that are obtained using the Tuner. DejaVu collects the workload signature every hour (dictated by the granularity of the available traces) and classifies the workload to promptly re-use the preferred resource allocation. While the savings compared to the fixed maximum allocation are promising, about 55% over the 6-day period, we need to ensure that the desired performance level is maintained.

Figure 6(c) shows the response latency in this case. The SLO latency is set to 60 ms. Although this is masked by the monitoring granularity, we note that Cassandra takes a long time to stabilize (e.g., tens of minutes) after DejaVu adjusts the number of running instances. This delay is due to Cassandra's re-partitioning; a well-known problem that is the subject of ongoing optimization efforts [11]. Apart from Cassandra's internal issues, DejaVu keeps the latency below 60 ms, except for short periods when the latency is fairly high – about 100 ms. These latency peaks correspond to DejaVu's adaptation time, around 10 seconds, which is needed by the profiler to collect the workload signature and deploy a new preferred resource allocation. Note that this is 18x faster than the reported figures of about 3 minutes for adaptation to workload changes by state-of-the-art experimental tuning [42].

We now conduct a similar set of experiments, but drive the workload intensities using the HotMail trace. Figures 7(b) and 7(c) visualize the cost (in number of active instances) and latency over time, respectively. While the overall savings compared to the maximum allocation are again similar (60% over the 6-day period), there are few points to note. First, the initial profiling identified 3 workload classes for the HotMail traces, instead of

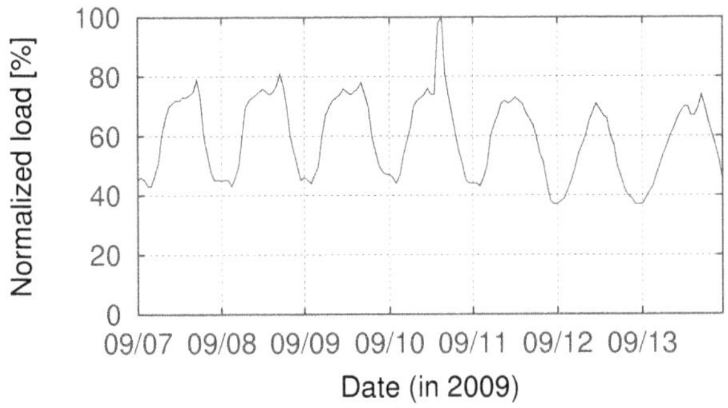

(a) Windows Live Messenger load trace.

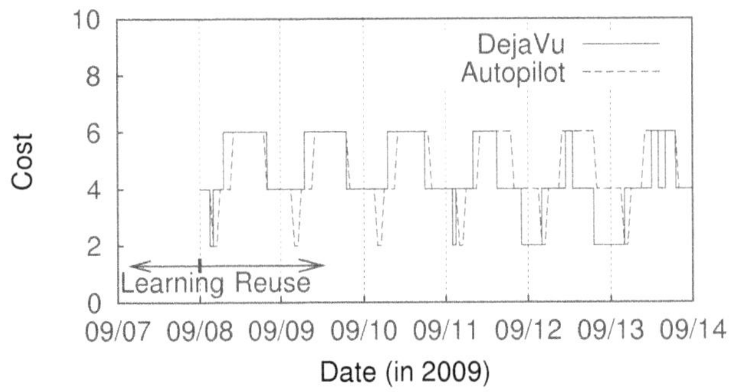

(b) Number of virtual instances used to accommodate the load.

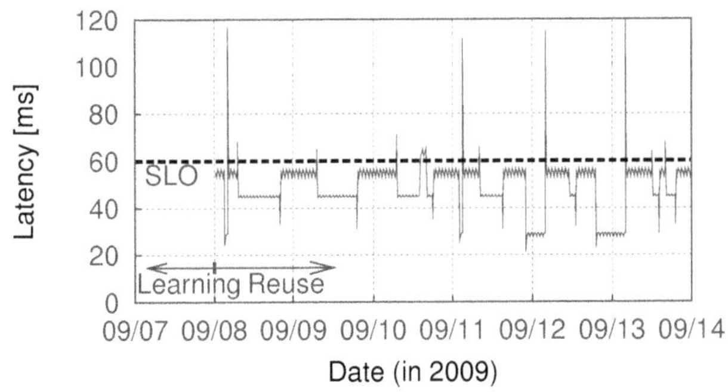

(c) Service latency as DejaVu adapts to workload changes. SLO = 60 ms.

Figure 6. Scaling out Cassandra with the Messenger trace.

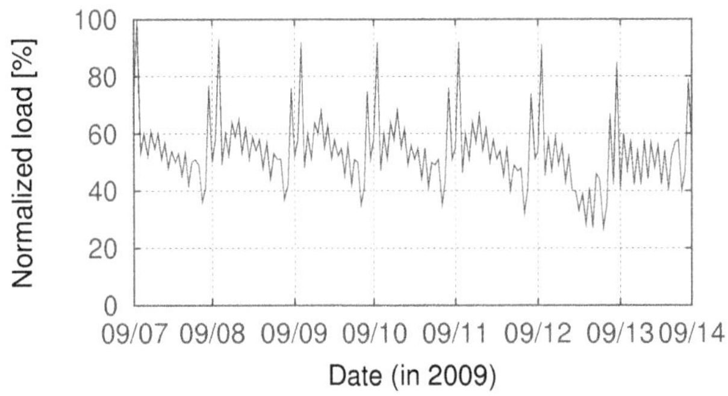

(a) HotMail load trace.

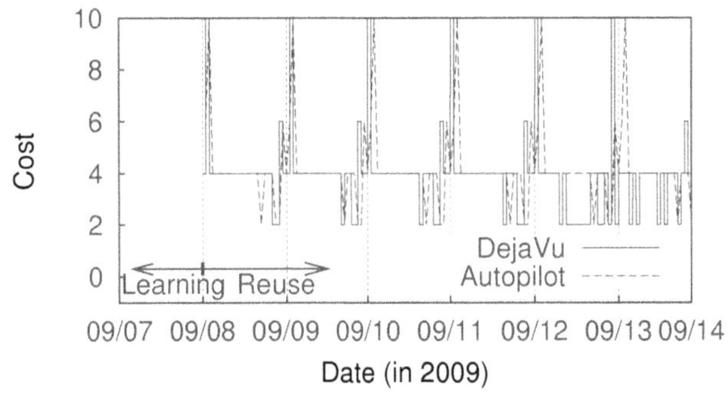

(b) Number of virtual instances used to accommodate the load.

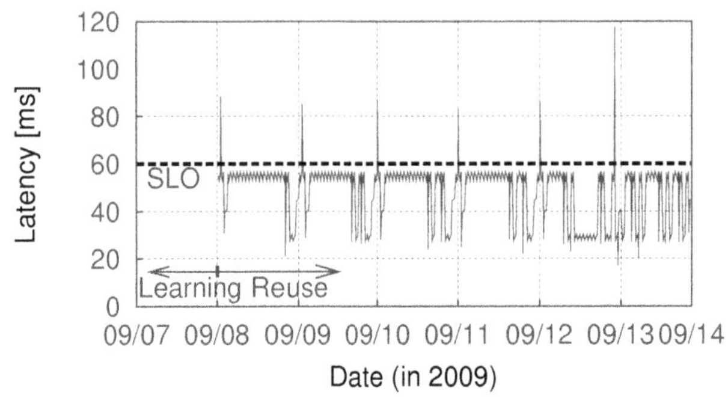

(c) Service latency as DejaVu adapts to workload changes. SLO = 60 ms.

Figure 7. Scaling out Cassandra with the Hotmail trace.

4 for the Messenger traces. Second, during the 4th day, DejaVu could not classify one workload with the desired confidence, as it differs significantly from the previously defined workload classes. The reason is that the initial profiling had not encountered such a workload in the first day of the traces. To avoid performance penalties, DejaVu decided to use the full capacity to accommodate this workload. If this scenario were to re-occur, DejaVu would resort to repeating the clustering process.

Comparison with existing approaches. Next, we compare DejaVu's behavior with that of two existing approaches. Figure 6(b) depicts the resource allocation decisions taken by Autopilot. Specifically, Autopilot simply repeats the hourly resource allocations learned during the first day of the trace. The Autopilot approach leads to suboptimal resource allocations and the associated provisioning cost increases. Due to poor allocations, Autopilot violates the SLO at least 28% of the time, in both traces. These measurements illustrate the difficulty of using past workload information blindly.

We further compare DejaVu with an existing autoscaling platform called RightScale [24]. Because we are not RightScale customers, we reproduced their approach based on publicly available information. The RightScale algorithm reacts to workload changes by running an agreement protocol among the virtual instances. If the majority of VMs report utilization that is higher than the predefined threshold, the scale-up action is taken by increasing the number of instances (by two at a time, by default). In contrast, if the instances agree that the overall utilization is below the specified threshold, the scaling down is performed (decrease the number of instances by one, by default). To ensure that the comparison is fair, we run the Cassandra benchmark which is CPU and memory intensive, as assumed by the RightScale default configuration [25].

Figure 8 shows the average adaptation time for DejaVu and RightScale (assuming its default configuration) for the HotMail and Messenger traces. In case of RightScale, we experiment with 3 (the minimum used in [25]) and 15 minutes (the recommended value) for the "resize calm time" parameter – the minimum time between successive RightScale adjustments. DejaVu's reaction time is about

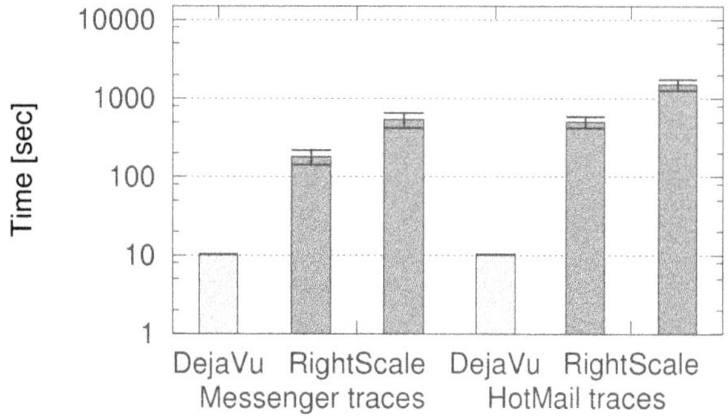

Figure 8. DejaVu and RightScale decision times (error bars show the standard error). RightScale decision times are shown for the "resize calm time" of 3 and 15 minutes in the middle and on the right for each trace, respectively.

10 seconds in the case of a "cache hit". Note that this time can vary depending on the length of the workload signature (e.g., a larger number of HPCs may take longer to collect). When a single resize operation is sufficient for RightScale, we record an instantaneous adaptation time (zero seconds). However, multiple resize operations are often needed. As a result, RightScale's adaptation time is between one and two of orders of magnitude longer than DejaVu's (note the log scale on the Y axis). This is because DejaVu can automatically jump to the right configuration, rather than gradually increase or decrease the number of instances as RightScale does. Note that the resize calm time is different in nature from the VM boot up time and cannot be eliminated for RightScale; RightScale has to first observe the reconfigured service before it can take any other resizing action.

4.2 Case Study 2: Scaling Up

We next evaluate DejaVu's ability to reduce the service provisioning cost while varying the instance type (scaling up) from large to extra-large or vice versa, as dictated by the workload intensity. Toward this end, we monitor the SPECweb service with 5 virtual instances serving at the front-end, and the same number of them at the back-end layer. We use the support benchmark which is mostly I/O-intensive and read-only to contrast with the Cassandra experiments which are CPU-, memory-, and write-intensive. Similar to the previous experiments, DejaVu uses the first day for the initial profiling/clustering, while the remaining days are used to evaluate its benefits.

Figures 9(a) plots the provisioning cost, shown as the instance type used to accommodate the HotMail load over time. Note that the smaller instance was capable of accommodating the load most of the time. Only during the peak load (two hours per day in the worst case), DejaVu deploys the full capacity configuration to fulfill the SLO. In monetary terms, DejaVu produces savings of roughly 45%, relative to the scheme that has to overprovision at all times with the peak load in mind. Figure 9(b) demonstrates that the savings come with a negligible effect on the performance levels; the quality of service (QoS, measured as the data transfer throughput) is always above the target that is specified by the SPECweb2009 standard. The standard requires that at least 95% of the downloads meet a minimum 0.99Mbps rate in the support benchmark for a run to be considered compliant.

We perform a similar set of experiments with the Messenger trace. In this case, Figures 10(a) and 10(b) show the provisioning cost and performance levels, respectively. The savings in this case are about 35% over the 6-day period. Excluding a few seconds after

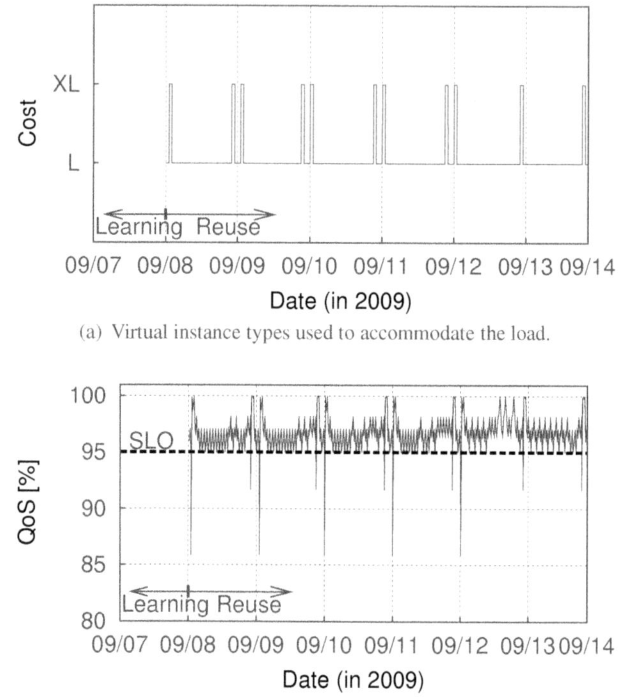

(a) Virtual instance types used to accommodate the load.

(b) Service latency as DejaVu adapts to workload changes. QoS = 95%.

Figure 9. Scaling up SPECweb with the Hotmail trace.

each workload change spent on profiling, QoS is as desired, above 95%.

4.3 Case Study 3: Addressing Interference

Our next experiments demonstrate how DejaVu detects and mitigates the effects of interference. We mimic the existence of a co-located tenant for each virtual instance by injecting into each VM a microbenchmark which occupies a varying amount (either 10% or 20%) of the VM's CPU and memory over time. The microbenchmark iterates over its working set and performs multiplication while enforcing the set limit. These amounts of interference mimic the amount of performance degradation reported in similar settings [44].

Figure 11(a) contrasts DejaVu with an alternative in which its interference detection is disabled. Without interference detection, one can see that the service exhibits unacceptable performance most of the time. Recall that the SLO is 60 ms. In contrast, DejaVu relies on its online feedback to quickly estimate the impact of interference and lookup the resource allocation that corresponds to the interference condition such that the SLO is met at all times. Figure 11(b) shows that DejaVu indeed provisions the service with more resources to compensate for interference.

4.4 Measuring DejaVu's Overhead

DejaVu requires only one or a few machines to host the profiling instances of the services that it manages. Its network overhead corresponds to the amount of traffic that it sends to the profiling environment. This overhead is roughly equal to $1/n$ of the incoming network traffic, where n is the number of service instances, assuming the worst case in which the DejaVu proxy is continuously duplicating network traffic and sending it to the DejaVu profiler. Given that the inbound traffic (client requests) is only a fraction of the outbound traffic (service responses) for typical services, the

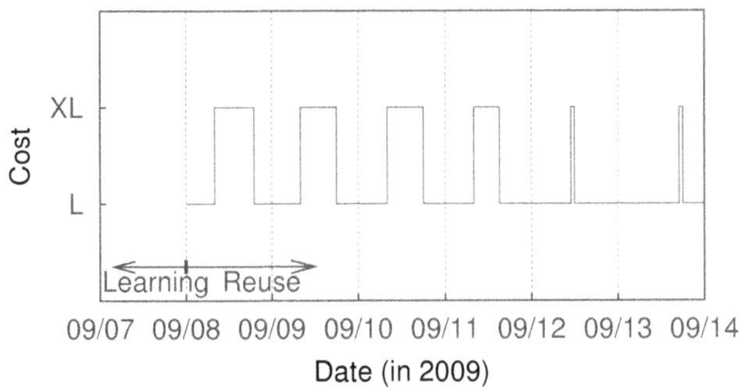

(a) Virtual instance types used to accommodate the load.

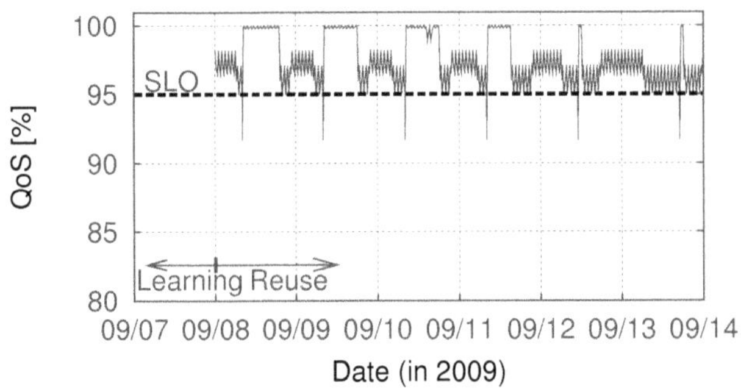

(b) Service latency as DejaVu adapts to workload changes. QoS = 95%.

Figure 10. Scaling up SPECweb with the Messenger trace.

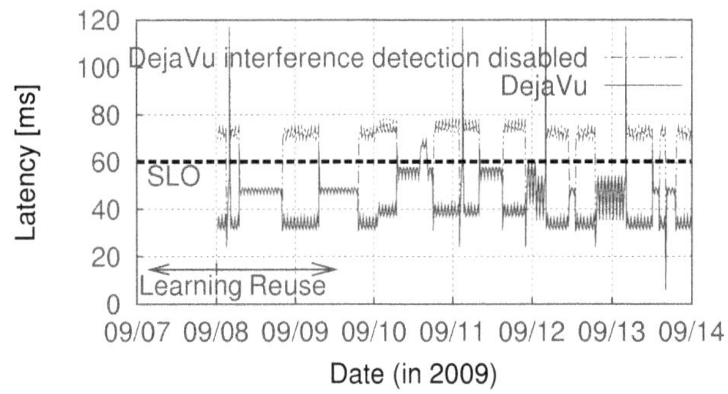

(a) Service latency as DejaVu adapts to workload changes.

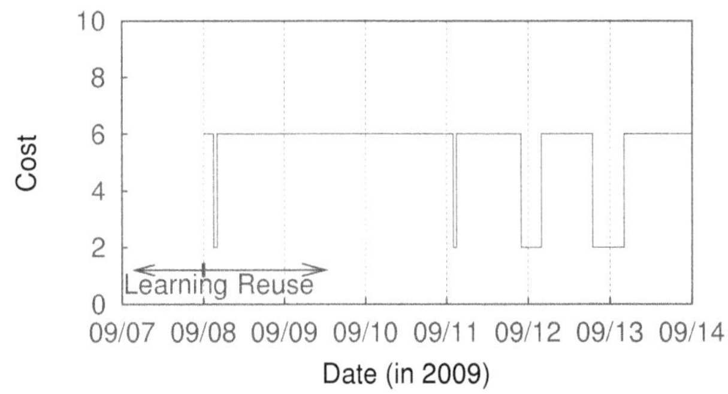

(b) Number of virtual instances used to accommodate the load.

Figure 11. Scaling out Cassandra with the Messenger trace under interference. The amount of interference varies, and is set to either 10% or 20%.

network overhead is likely to be negligible. For example, it would be 0.1% of the overall network traffic for a service that uses 100 instances, assuming a 1:10 inbound/outbound traffic ratio that is typically used for home broadband connections.

We now turn our attention to a more important question: To what extent does the DejaVu proxy affect the performance of the system in production, as it duplicates the traffic of a single service instance? To answer this question, we run a set of experiments with the RUBiS benchmark, while profiling its database server instance. We compare the service latency under a setup where the profiling is disabled against a setup with continuous profiling. To exercise different workload volumes, we vary the number of clients that are generating the requests from 100 to 500. Our measurements show that the presence of our proxy degrades response time by about 3 ms on average.

4.5 Summary

To summarize, our evaluation shows that DejaVu maps multiple workload levels to a few relevant clusters. It uses this information at runtime to quickly adapt to workload changes. The adaptation is short (about 10 seconds) and more than 10 times faster than the state-of-the-art. Having such quick adaptation times effectively enables online matching of resources to the offered load in pursuit of cost savings.

We demonstrate provisioning cost savings of 35-60% (compared to a fixed, maximum allocation) using realistic traces and two disparate and representative Internet services: a key-value store and a 3-tier web service. The savings are higher (50-60% vs. 35-45%) when scaling out (varying the number of machines) vs. scaling up (varying the performance of machines) because of the finer granularity of possible resource allocations. The scaling up case had only two choices of instances (large and extra-large) with a fixed number of instances vs. 1-10 identical instances when scaling out.

DejaVu successfully manages interference by recognizing the existence of interference and pragmatically using more resources to compensate for it.

The DejaVu-achieved savings translate to more than $250,000 and $2.5 Million per year for 100 and 1,000 instances, respectively (assuming $0.34/hour for a large instance on EC2 and $0.68/hour for extra large as of July 2011). We draw these service sizes from the available data: the Reddit aggregation web site reportedly uses about one hundred EC2 instances (218 virtual CPUs) [23], whereas the Animoto video creation site uses a few thousand EC2 instances [26].

In terms of overheads, we argue that the network traffic induced by DejaVu is negligible, while our final experiments demonstrate that DejaVu's impact on the performance of the system in production is also practically negligible.

5. Related Work

There has been a large body of recent work on various aspects of data center resource management.

Automated resource management in virtualized data centers. Industrial efforts such as Rightscale [24] use a load-based threshold to automatically trigger creation of a previously configured number of new virtual instances in a matter of minutes. This approach uses an additive-increase controller, and as such may take long to converge.

Applying modeling and machine learning to resource management in data centers. Urgaonkar *et al.* [37] propose a closed queuing network model along with Mean Value Analysis (MVA) algorithm for multi-tier applications. Watson *et al.* [40] follow a similar approach, and develop queuing-based performance models for enterprise applications, but with emphasis on the virtualized environment. Another example of explicitly using models to enhance coordinated provisioning of various computer resources was presented in [12]. Stewart *et al.* [33] significantly enhance the accuracy of models by explicitly modeling a non-stationary transaction mix; their main point is that the workload type (as in a different type of incoming requests to a service) is equally important as the workload volume itself. In general, these efforts work well for the workloads used during parameter calibration, but may require (manual) adjustment when the workload changes. Further, achieving higher accuracy requires highly skilled labor, along with a deep understanding of the application.

Running actual experiments instead of using models. Zheng *et al.* [42] advocated running actual experiments for resource management in a virtualized environment. Relative to this work, DejaVu quickly characterizes the workloads at runtime to avoid re-running experiments. In doing so, it dramatically reduces the amount of time the service is running with suboptimal parameters.

Performance counters and workload characterization. Recently, HPCs have been extensively used to characterize activities within the entire system for various purposes. For instance, Merkel *et al.* [17] leverage HPCs to predict task energy consumptions. Using these predictions, a scheduler can get the maximum performance out of a multiprocessor system, and still avoid overheating of system components. Sweeney *et al.* [34] demonstrate that HPCs are also useful in understanding the behavior of Java applications. Namely, their tool is effective in identifying performance anomalies and can help in pinpointing their cause. Finally, Shen *et al.* [29] argue that the HPCs might be used for on-the-fly prediction at the request granularity, thus enabling online system adaptation. Although related, our work is fundamentally different as we are aiming at workload classification, rather than fine-granularity recognition. For instance, our monitoring module could provide feedback such as "workload volume is medium, and the requests are mostly read requests".

Even earlier, sample-based profiling was used to identify different activities running within the system (e.g., Magpie [3] and Pinpoint [9]). For instance, Magpie uses clustering to classify requests and produce a workload model. Although such tools can be useful for post-execution decisions, they do not provide online identification and the ability to react during execution. This ability is crucial for our framework to quickly adapt to workload changes.

Automatic benchmarking. Developers devote considerable time to benchmarking to obtain insight into the performance, inter-layer interactions, and most important for our work, workload characterization. There have been a few works that automate this laborious task [30, 43]. Although this is orthogonal to our approach, our framework would greatly benefit from the existence of a tool that determines the most representative workloads to benchmark.

Automatic VM configuration and performance crisis detection. Soror *et al.* [31] address the problem of automatically configuring a database management system (DBMS) by adjusting the configurations of the VM in which they run. They use information about the anticipated workload and then compute the workload-specific configuration. However, their framework assumes help from the DBMS which describes a workload in the form of a set of SQL statements. In contrast, DejaVu does not require any information from the guest OS (VM), and very little information from the application running inside it.

Bodik *et al.* [5] propose a methodology for automatic classification and identification of performance crises, and in particular for detecting whether a given crisis has been seen before, so that a known solution may be immediately applied. As opposed to DejaVu, the focus of the work is mostly on (1) identifying performance anomalies due to bugs or unexpected behaviors, and (2) speeding up the stabilization. In contrast, DejaVu accelerates the management of virtualized resource allocations under workload changes.

Cost-aware elasticity. Sharma *et al.* [27] propose Kingfisher, a system that tries to minimize the cloud tenant's deployment cost, while being elastic to workload changes. Kingfisher takes into account the cost of each VM instance, the possibilities of scaling up and scaling out, as well as the transition time from one configuration to another. It then solves an integer linear program to derive the minimum cost configuration under each workload change. Kingfisher and DejaVu are orthogonal and can benefit from one another. Kingfisher assumes a perfect workload predictor, and it would benefit from storing its resource allocation decisions in the DejaVu cache (and avoid re-running the ILP solver every time a workload change dictates a configuration change). DejaVu could simply use Kingfisher as its Tuner.

6. Conclusion

The problem of resource allocation is challenging in the cloud, as the co-located workloads constantly evolve. The result is that system administrators find it difficult to properly manage the resources allocated to the different virtual machines, leading to suboptimal service performance or wasted resources for significant periods of the time.

In this paper we described the design and implementation of DejaVu, a framework that quickly and automatically reacts to workload changes by learning the preferred virtual resource allocations from past experience. DejaVu also detects performance interference across virtual machines and adjusts the resource allocation to counter it.

Though this work provides a solid foundation, there are multiple challenging directions that we want to pursue in the future. For example, we demonstrated that an application can significantly benefit from its own resource allocation experience. However, we believe that it can benefit from the experience of other cloud tenants as well, and we plan to further explore this potential.

Acknowledgments

This research is funded by the Swiss NSF (grant FNS 200021-130265). Dejan Novaković is also supported by the Swiss NSF (grant FNS 200021-125140). We thank the anonymous reviewers for their valuable feedback. We are grateful to Eno Thereska, Austin Donnelly, and Dushyanth Narayanan for providing us with their HotMail and Messenger traces.

References

[1] Apache Foundation. The Apache Cassandra Project. `http://cassandra.apache.org/`.

[2] M. Aron, P. Druschel, and W. Zwaenepoel. Cluster reserves: a mechanism for resource management in cluster-based network servers. In *SIGMETRICS*, 2000.

[3] P. Barham, A. Donnelly, R. Isaacs, and R. Mortier. Using magpie for request extraction and workload modelling. In *OSDI*, 2004.

[4] P. Bodik, A. Fox, M. J. Franklin, M. I. Jordan, and D. A. Patterson. Characterizing, modeling, and generating workload spikes for stateful services. In *Symposium on Cloud Computing*, 2010.

[5] P. Bodik, M. Goldszmidt, A. Fox, D. B. Woodard, and H. Andersen. Fingerprinting the datacenter: automated classification of performance crises. In *EuroSys*, 2010.

[6] E. Cecchet, J. Marguerite, and W. Zwaenepoel. Performance and scalability of ejb applications. *SIGPLAN Not.*, 2002.

[7] E. Cecchet, R. Singh, U. Sharma, and P. Shenoy. Dolly: virtualization-driven database provisioning for the cloud. In *VEE*, 2011.

[8] J. S. Chase, D. C. Anderson, P. N. Thakar, and A. M. Vahdat. Managing energy and server resources in hosting centers. In *SOSP*, 2001.

[9] M. Y. Chen, E. Kiciman, E. Fratkin, A. Fox, and E. Brewer. Pinpoint: Problem determination in large, dynamic internet services. In *DSN*, 2002.

[10] Y. Chen, A. Das, W. Qin, A. Sivasubramaniam, Q. Wang, and N. Gautam. Managing server energy and operational costs in hosting centers. In *SIGMETRICS*, 2005.

[11] B. F. Cooper, A. Silberstein, E. Tam, R. Ramakrishnan, and R. Sears. Benchmarking cloud serving systems with YCSB. In *SoCC*, 2010.

[12] R. P. Doyle, J. S. Chase, O. M. Asad, W. Jin, and A. M. Vahdat. Model-based resource provisioning in a web service utility. In *USITS*, 2003.

[13] M. Hall, E. Frank, G. Holmes, B. Pfahringer, P. Reutemann, and I. H. Witten. The weka data mining software: an update. *SIGKDD Explor. Newsl.*, 11:10–18, November 2009.

[14] T. Heath, A. P. Centeno, P. George, L. Ramos, Y. Jaluria, and R. Bianchini. Mercury and freon: temperature emulation and management for server systems. In *ASPLOS*, 2006.

[15] G. Linden. Make Data Useful. `https://sites.google.com/site/glinden/Home/StanfordDataMining.2006-11-28.ppt`.

[16] W. Mathur and J. Cook. Improved estimation for software multiplexing of performance counters. In *MASCOTS*, 2005.

[17] A. Merkel and F. Bellosa. Balancing power consumption in multiprocessor systems. In *EuroSys*, 2006.

[18] R. Nathuji, A. Kansal, and A. Ghaffarkhah. Q-clouds: managing performance interference effects for qos-aware clouds. In *EuroSys*, 2010.

[19] Netfilter. netfilter/iptables. `http://www.netfilter.org/`.

[20] F. Oliveira, K. Nagaraja, R. Bachwani, R. Bianchini, R. P. Martin, and T. D. Nguyen. Understanding and validating database system administration. In *USENIX*, 2006.

[21] P. Padala, K. G. Shin, X. Zhu, M. Uysal, Z. Wang, S. Singhal, A. Merchant, and K. Salem. Adaptive control of virtualized resources in utility computing environments. In *EuroSys*, 2007.

[22] E. Pinheiro, R. Bianchini, E. V. Carrera, and T. Heath. Load balancing and unbalancing for power and performance. In *Proceedings of the Workshop on Compilers and Operating Systems for Low Power*, 2001.

[23] Reddit. `http://www.reddit.com/r/IAmA/comments/a2zte/i_run_reddits_servers_and_do_a_bunch_of_other/`.

[24] RightScale. `http://www.rightscale.com/`.

[25] RightScale. `http://support.rightscale.com/12-Guides/Lifecycle_Management/03_-_Understanding_Key_Concepts/RightScale_Alert_System/Alerts_based_on_Voting_Tags/Understanding_the_Voting_Process`.

[26] RightScale. Animoto's facebook scale-up. `http://blog.rightscale.com/2008/04/23/animoto-facebook-scale-up/`.

[27] U. Sharma, P. Shenoy, S. Sahu, and A. Shaikh. A cost-aware elasticity provisioning system for the cloud. In *Distributed Computing Systems (ICDCS), 2011 31st International Conference on*, pages 559 –570, june 2011.

[28] K. Shen, H. Tang, T. Yang, and L. Chu. Integrated resource management for cluster-based internet services. *SIGOPS Oper. Syst. Rev.*, 2002.

[29] K. Shen, M. Zhong, S. Dwarkadas, C. Li, C. Stewart, and X. Zhang. Hardware counter driven on-the-fly request signatures. *ASPLOS*, 2008.

[30] P. Shivam, V. Marupadi, J. Chase, T. Subramaniam, and S. Babu. Cutting corners: workbench automation for server benchmarking. In *USENIX*, 2008.

[31] A. A. Soror, U. F. Minhas, A. Aboulnaga, K. Salem, P. Kokosielis, and S. Kamath. Automatic virtual machine configuration for database workloads. In *SIGMOD*, 2008.

[32] SPECweb2009. `http://www.spec.org/web2009/`.

[33] C. Stewart, T. Kelly, and A. Zhang. Exploiting nonstationarity for performance prediction. In *EuroSys*, 2007.

[34] P. F. Sweeney, M. Hauswirth, B. Cahoon, P. Cheng, A. Diwan, D. Grove, and M. Hind. Using hardware performance monitors to understand the behavior of java applications. In *VM*, 2004.

[35] E. Thereska, A. Donnelly, and D. Narayanan. Sierra: practical power-proportionality for data center storage. In *EuroSys*, 2011.

[36] R. Thonangi, V. Thummala, and S. Babu. Finding good configurations in high-dimensional spaces: Doing more with less. In *Proceedings of the International Symposium on Modeling, Analysis, and Simulation of Computer and Telecomunication Systems*, 2008.

[37] B. Urgaonkar, G. Pacifici, P. Shenoy, M. Spreitzer, and A. Tantawi. An analytical model for multi-tier internet services and its applications. In *SIGMETRICS*, 2005.

[38] B. Urgaonkar, P. J. Shenoy, and T. Roscoe. Resource overbooking and application profiling in shared hosting platforms. In *OSDI*, 2002.

[39] N. Vasić, M. Barisits, V. Salzgeber, and D. Kostić. Making Cluster Applications Energy-Aware. In *ACDC*, 2009.

[40] B. J. Watson, M. Marwah, D. Gmach, Y. Chen, M. Arlitt, and Z. Wang. Probabilistic performance modeling of virtualized resource allocation. In *ICAC*, 2010.

[41] T. Wood, P. Shenoy, A. Venkataramani, and M. Yousif. Black-box and gray-box strategies for virtual machine migration. In *NSDI*, 2007.

[42] W. Zheng, R. Bianchini, G. J. Janakiraman, J. R. Santos, and Y. Turner. Justrunit: Experiment-based management of virtualized data centers. In *USENIX*, 2009.

[43] W. Zheng, R. Bianchini, and T. D. Nguyen. Automatic configuration of internet services. In *EuroSys*, 2007.

[44] S. Zhuravlev, S. Blagodurov, and A. Fedorova. Addressing shared resource contention in multicore processors via scheduling. In *ASPLOS*, 2010.

Architectural Support for Hypervisor-Secure Virtualization

Jakub Szefer
Princeton University
szefer@princeton.edu

Ruby B. Lee
Princeton University
rblee@princeton.edu

Abstract

Virtualization has become a standard part of many computer systems. A key part of virtualization is the all-powerful hypervisor which manages the physical platform and can access all of its resources, including memory assigned to the guest virtual machines (VMs). Continuing releases of bug reports and exploits in the virtualization software show that defending the hypervisor against attacks is very difficult. In this work, we present *hypervisor-secure virtualization* – a new research direction with the goal of protecting the guest VMs from an untrusted hypervisor. We also present the HyperWall architecture which achieves hypervisor-secure virtualization, using hardware to provide the protections. HyperWall allows a hypervisor to freely manage the memory, processor cores and other resources of a platform. Yet once VMs are created, our new Confidentiality and Integrity Protection (CIP) tables protect the memory of the guest VMs from accesses by the hypervisor or by DMA, depending on the customer's specification. If a hypervisor does become compromised, e.g. by an attack from a malicious VM, it cannot be used in turn to attack other VMs. The protections are enabled through minimal modifications to the microprocessor and memory management units. Whereas much of the previous work concentrates on protecting the hypervisor from attacks by guest VMs, we tackle the problem of protecting the guest VMs from the hypervisor.

Categories and Subject Descriptors C.0 [*General*]: System Architectures

General Terms Security, Design

Keywords Computer Architecture, Cloud Computing, Security, Virtualization, Hardware Security, Hypervisor, Trust Evidence, Attestation, Confidentiality, Integrity

1. Introduction

We introduce the HyperWall architecture, which provides protections to guest VMs from attacks by a malicious hypervisor. We are interested in the increasingly popular IaaS (infrastructure-as-a-service) cloud computing model where the infrastructure provider, such as the Amazon EC2 service [1], maintains physical servers and leases VMs to the customers. While the infrastructure provider provides the hardware and the virtualization software, the customers provide their own guest operating system (OS) and applications to run inside the leased VMs.

ASPLOS'12, March 3–7, 2012, London, England, UK.

Cloud customers leasing VMs from an IaaS provider can have a more flexible computing infrastructure while also reducing their operational costs. However, adversarial parties or competitors can lease VMs from the same provider. These competitors may then have incentive to attack the hypervisor and use it to gain information about other VMs.

Past work in this area concentrated on hardening the hypervisors and protecting them from attacks. Even the hardened or minimized hypervisors, however, have memory management functionalities which they use to access the guest VM's memory. If the hypervisor is compromised, the management functions can be abused to violate the confidentiality and integrity of the guest VMs. Our work then aims to protect guest VMs from a compromised or malicious hypervisor. We call this *hypervisor-secure virtualization*.

HyperWall's key feature is the Confidentiality and Integrity Protection (CIP, pronounced "sip") tables, which are only accessible by hardware; they protect all or portions of a VM's memory based on the customer's specification. The customer can specify which memory ranges require protection from accesses by the hypervisor or DMA (Direct Memory Access). The tables essentially provide for a hardware-controlled protection of memory resources.

In HyperWall, the hypervisor is able to fully manage the platform, to start, pause or stop VMs or to change memory assignment. To cross-check that the hypervisor is not behaving maliciously, our architecture provides signed hash measurements to attest that the customer's initial VM image and specified protections were indeed instantiated at VM launch. Furthermore, trust evidence can be generated during the VM's lifetime to verify that the specified VM protections have not been violated, or indicate how many attempts at violating these protections have occurred. When the VM is terminated, its protected memory is zeroed out by the hardware to prevent leakage of data or code, and the hypervisor and DMA regain full access rights to the VM's memory.

HyperWall aims to extend a modern 64-bit shared-memory multi-core and multi-chip system. By building on a base architecture which supports virtualization, many elements can be re-used to minimize the modifications required to support hypervisor-secure virtualization. The main contributions of this work are:

- definition of *hypervisor-secure virtualization*,
- the HyperWall architecture which achieves *hypervisor-secure virtualization* by using hardware to isolate a VM's memory from malicious hypervisor or DMA accesses, in page-sized granularity as specified by the cloud customer, while allowing a commodity hypervisor to fully manage the platform,
- introduction of a general-purpose mechanism for hardware protection of memory (and other resources) that scales with memory size, e.g., used in HyperWall for the CIP tables, and
- formulation of trust evidence mechanisms which provide the cloud customer assurance that protections he or she specified were installed and are being enforced.

Table 1. Different hypervisors and OSes, their SLOC count and the components which are part of their TCB.

Hypervisor [44]	**SLOC**	**TCB**
Xen-4.0	194K	Xen, Dom0
VMware ESX	200K	VM kernel
Hyper-V	100K	Hyper-V, Windows Server
OS [25, 27, 34]	**SLOC**	**TCB**
Linux 2.6.23	13500K	OS kernel
Window XP	40000K	OS kernel
seL4	8K+	OS kernel

1.1 Excluding Hypervisor from TCB

Many of today's security problems with virtualization solutions occur because of the size of the Trusted Computing Base (TCB). Table 1 shows a number of hypervisors and OSes, their code size and the components that are part of their TCB. While hypervisors are two orders of magnitude smaller than commodity operating systems, they are still about an order of magnitude larger than seL4 [25], a formally verified micro-kernel. Hence, today's hypervisors are probably too large for formal verification for the foreseeable future. Also, in spite of developers' efforts to provide bug-free code, a search on NIST's National Vulnerability Database [7] shows a number of bugs for both Xen [14] and VMware ESX [12]: 98 and 78 were listed, respectively, when a search was performed in the summer of 2011. An example of a concrete attack on a hypervisor found in the database is a vulnerability in Xen which allowed arbitrary commands to be executed in the control domain via a specially crafted configuration file [3]. Because of difficulties in implementing bug-free hypervisors, our work concentrates on protecting guest VMs from a compromised hypervisor.

1.2 Enlisting Hardware Protections

We now discuss why software-only solutions may not be sufficient to protect VMs. In a software-only approach, the hypervisor could use encryption so that different views of the memory are presented to different entities [20]. If the protection is in the hypervisor, however, then the hypervisor has to be in the TCB. Exploits and vulnerabilities which are being constantly discovered in real-life hypervisors indicate that securing a commercial hypervisor is an open issue. If the hypervisor is subverted, the protections can not be ensured.

A number of minimized and hardened hypervisors have been designed. Such systems, however, can still be misconfigured or bypassed. For example, HyperSentry [15] shows how to use the system management mode (SMM) to bypass the hypervisor for introspection purposes, but such functionality can also be used for malicious purposes.

Nested virtualization, e.g. the Turtles project [16], could be used where there is an extra hypervisor layer below the main hypervisor. That software layer could be used for security and implement HyperWall-style protections. What is to prevent a malicious attacker from slipping in an extra layer below the current lowest layer?

Researchers have also demonstrated Ring -1 Hypervisor rootkits [38], Ring -2 SMM rootkits [47] or even Ring -3 Chipset-based rootkits [41]. These rootkits cleverly use different functionalities of hardware, highlighting the fact that software protections are vulnerable since they can be subverted if attacked from below, i.e. by using the hardware. However, these rootkits are not due to any problems with hardware, rather they are due to the problem of having protections in software while it is the hardware which is logically the lowest level in the system.

By enlisting hardware protections, we also capitalize on hardware having performance advantages over software. In addition, changing functionality implemented by hardware or probing the microprocessor chip to recover secrets are extremely difficult. Furthermore, various vendors already modify hardware to improve virtualization through extensions which are widely deployed in commodity microprocessors [2, 5]. Extensions in various hardware subsystems are also available today: the I/O MMU [13] or the SR-IOV [9] extension for virtualizing PCI devices. This indicates that the commercial vendors do not see the costs of modifying the hardware for enhancing virtualization performance and security as outweighing the benefits of the modifications.

1.3 Hypervisor-Secure Virtualization

We have made a case for hardware protection of guest VMs from compromised hypervisors in a position paper [40] which outlined a broad research agenda, but no specific solutions. In this work, *we define hypervisor-secure virtualization as protection of a VM's secret code and data from an attacker with hypervisor-level privileges, and provide a concrete architectural solution.* The focus of the protections is on the memory, as this is where code and data resides, during a VM's execution. Moreover, any keys for cryptographically securing communications and persistent storage will be placed by the VM in memory. By controlling which memory regions the hypervisor or DMA can access, the confidentiality and integrity of code, data and keys can be protected, thus protecting VM runtime execution as well as its cryptographically-secured network channels and storage.

The rest of the paper is organized as follows. Section 2 provides our threat model and assumptions. Section 3 describes the HyperWall architecture and explains the details of how a HyperWall system operates. Our implementation and evaluation is presented in Section 4, and the security analysis in Section 5. Section 6 describes related work, and Section 7 concludes the paper.

2. Threat Model and Assumptions

Consistent with the definition of hypervisor-secure virtualization, the HyperWall implementation aims to protect the confidentiality and integrity of a VM's code and data. The cloud customer is able to specify which memory pages inside the guest VM require the protection. These protections are installed in hardware on the HyperWall system where the VM is to run and the hardware enforces the protections. Throughout, however, a commodity hypervisor (with minimal additions for handling our new hardware state) is able to manage the platform. For example it can dynamically change the physical to machine memory mapping.

Considering that we enlist hardware to provide the protections, we assume that the hardware is trusted, is correctly implemented and its functionality has not been tampered with. Some of the "hardware" functionality may actually be implemented as code or microcode stored in read-only memory (ROM). This is also assumed to be correct.

It is not our goal to protect against bugs in the guest OS or the applications. Our work aims to provide a customer with a guarantee that running a VM in the cloud is as secure as running it in the customer's own facilities (if not more secure due to a cloud provider's ability to provide better physical security). It is up to the customer to verify that the OS and applications do what the customer expects. Also, we do not aim to provide protection from attacks by the OS on applications. Verifying the security of guest OS and applications are both assumed to be the responsibility of the customer.

Preventing DoS (denial-of-service) attacks by the hypervisor on a VM's availability is not covered in this work. Moreover, the cloud provider needs a method for terminating a VM if a customer does not pay for the leased resources. However, confidentiality should still be protected – hardware zeroes out the state and memory so no information is leaked when a VM is terminated.

We assume that the SMM, or similar remote management mode, is disabled in the hardware so that new security mechanisms cannot be bypassed. Incorporating security measures in SMM is an orthogonal research problem. For example, the STM (SMM Transfer Monitor) [42] has been designed for Intel microprocessors, but this is not widely deployed.

Hardware attacks (e.g. snooping on the memory bus) are not in the threat model. This assumption is consistent with the fact that the IaaS providers have an incentive to secure their facilities and deter insider attacks. Cloud providers can afford to physically secure the servers, install monitoring equipment, etc., to prevent an intruder from installing a hardware probe, for example.

We do not aim to protect against side channels such as those due to a processor's functional units, caches or I/O buses. Various work has been done on minimizing such channels (e.g. dynamically randomized caches [45]). Debug registers or performance counters could be another avenue for hypervisor or malicious VMs to glean information about a target VM. We do not protect against these covert channels and side channels in our current work.

3. HyperWall Architecture

HyperWall's objective is to protect guest VMs from a compromised hypervisor. We use standard encryption techniques to protect confidential code and data in persistent storage and during I/O and networking. We also protect the processor state, e.g. the general-purpose registers, when a VM is interrupted or suspended. The protection of memory, however, is achieved through the new hardware-controlled isolation. The isolation approach incurs less overhead than using a cryptographic approach (no extra decryption and hashing overhead when VMs access memory). Also, memory read and write paths do not need to be modified with extra cryptographic hardware. Moreover, since hardware attacks are not considered, encryption to hide contents of DRAM is not needed. Instead, the isolation of the protected VM memory from hypervisor and DMA access ensures its confidentiality and integrity.

The protections are accomplished through our architecture which:

- enables cloud customer specification of desired confidentiality and integrity protection policy (at page-sized granularity) to the cloud provider's HyperWall-enabled server,
- ties the protection policy to the VM initiated by the hypervisor on the provider's server,
- enables hardware enforcement of these policies through the addition of minor modifications of existing hardware and the re-use of existing commodity microprocessor features such as TLBs (Translation Lookaside Buffers), DRAM (Dynamic Random Access Memory), and the memory management units,
- enables the server to attest to the protections provided by the hardware to the cloud customer, and
- performs hardware-controlled cleanup of a VM's state and memory upon termination so no information is leaked.

3.1 VM Protection Mechanisms

In order to protect a VM's memory, we introduce new Confidentiality and Integrity Protection (CIP) tables to protect both the confidentiality and integrity of the VM's data and code (for the regions of memory which the customer requested to be protected).

The CIP tables are only accessible to the hardware; they store mappings of hypervisor and DMA access rights to the machine memory pages. These are used to enforce protections of the guest

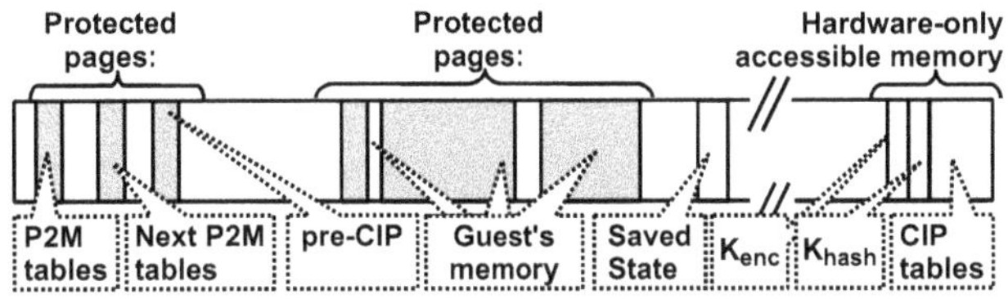

Figure 1. The main memory holds both the CIP tables (light gray) and other memory ranges (dark gray) which are protected by the CIP tables.

VM's memory. For each machine memory page, the CIP table stores protection bits which are used to encode the protection information about the page. The page can be: not assigned to any VM (not protected), assigned to a VM with hypervisor and DMA access allowed, assigned to a VM with hypervisor access denied, assigned to a VM with DMA access denied, or assigned to a VM with no hypervisor nor DMA access.

The default setting that a customer specifies for a VM can be to deny access to all pages, except for allowing the hypervisor or DMA access to the I/O buffers in a VM. At system boot up time, all bits in the CIP tables are zero, which gives the hypervisor and DMA access to all of the DRAM.

We note that it is not possible to just add additional access rights fields to the existing page tables because the hypervisor or the guest OSes need full access to their respective tables to manage memory mapping. Hence, a separate structure like our CIP tables is needed. In addition, we provide DMA protection, as a malicious hypervisor could configure a physical device to access the VM's memory through DMA and then read out that data from the device itself. Finally, if a page is not explicitly protected, it is marked as assigned to a VM but with hypervisor and DMA access allowed. This way a compromised hypervisor cannot maliciously map a machine page to two VMs so that an attacker VM could access a victim VM's memory.

CIP tables are consulted by a modified MMU (Memory Management Unit) in the microprocessor when hypervisor code is executing (or by logic in the I/O MMU on DMA accesses) to verify that a memory location can be accessed. The CIP tables are updated whenever a new VM is created or a memory assignment for a VM is changed. The CIP tables update will end with an error (a VM will not be started or new memory mapping will not be installed) if there is detection of a new VM being assigned memory already in use by other VM. The CIP tables are updated whenever a VM is terminated so pages can be reclaimed.

3.1.1 CIP Tables

We designed the architecture to use a portion of physical memory (DRAM) to store the CIP tables. This removes the need to add extra hardware storage for CIP tables in the microprocessor chip. It also allows the CIP table storage to be proportional to the amount of installed DRAM. Moreover, an important benefit of our approach of using DRAM memory for CIP tables is that it is a general-purpose, scalable, hardware mechanism that can be applied to many other uses.

When the computer boots up, the memory controller discovers the amount of physical memory and proportionally a section of it is reserved for CIP tables and made inaccessible to any software. Consequently, the memory controller announces a smaller DRAM size to the rest of the system. A single new register is needed in the memory controller to keep track of the end of visible DRAM; this register also marks the starting location of the CIP tables. The CIP logic can query this register to obtain the location of the tables so it can access them.

Figure 1 shows the host physical memory of the system. The part of the physical DRAM not accessible to any software is shaded light gray at the right of the figure. This region holds the CIP tables as well as an encryption key and a hash key, discussed below.

3.1.2 Protected Memory Regions

Other parts of DRAM are freely accessible unless they are protected by the CIP tables (sample protected regions for a VM are shaded dark gray in Figure 1). When a guest VM is running, the physical memory used by it is protected (as specified by the customer). A VM's memory does not have to be contiguous and the hypervisor is free to assign host physical memory to VMs by any algorithm, e.g. to avoid fragmentation.

Moreover, the CIP tables protect the memory which holds the page tables mapping the physical to machine memory (marked *P2M* tables) for the guest. During any memory mapping update, both the old mapping (*P2M* tables) and the new mapping (marked *next P2M* tables) are protected. A customer's requested protections are stored in the region marked *pre-CIP*. The pre-CIP specifies which pages are to be protected (hypervisor or DMA access denied) and which can be accessed by hypervisor or DMA. The pre-CIP needs to be saved so that the original requested protections can be checked each time the hypervisor attempts to update the guest's memory mapping.

The region marked *Saved State* in Figure 1 is shown to indicate that whenever the VM is interrupted, the (encrypted) general purpose registers, program counter, P2M page table pointer, and our new HyperWall register state need to be saved. Saving of VM state is already performed by today's hypervisors, and we only require that the code be updated to handle saving of the new state which we define. The saving and restoring of the new state is needed so that the CIP logic can verify the protections whenever the VM is resumed. The memory region holding the (encrypted and hashed) saved state is fully accessible to the hypervisor, e.g. so it can save it on disk when the VM is suspended.

3.1.3 Cryptographic Keys

Our CIP protection strategy is isolation through hardware access control, rather than through cryptographic methods; isolation is used to bar the hypervisor or DMA from accessing a VM's memory (as specified by the customer). We do, however, use cryptography to enable a customer to validate a genuine HyperWall server, to protect VM-related processor state as the hypervisor manages the VMs, and to protect communication between a VM and the external world, as is often done today. Hence, we discuss the cryptographic keys used in a HyperWall system.

The SK_{cpu} is a private signing key burned into the microprocessor chip and not accessible to any software (see Figure 2). If a system has multiple chip packages, each will have a different key. We envision that the hardware manufacturers would designate trusted certificate authorities which would sign the certificates of each chip's SK_{cpu}. Customers would obtain certificates for the chips of the servers where their VMs will run from the cloud provider. Customers would use the trusted certificate authority's public key to verify the certificates and thus whether the HyperWall hardware is genuine.

The K_{enc} and K_{hash} are two keys used by the HyperWall hardware and stored inside the protected memory (see Figure 1); the keys are generated during each boot up cycle. They are used whenever a VM is interrupted. Storing these keys in protected shared DRAM memory (rather than in new registers in a core) enables a VM to be paused on one core and resumed on a different core, even in a different chip package on the same HyperWall server.

Later we will also introduce a per-VM key, the PK_{vm}, which is generated inside each VM and should be unique to each VM (e.g. by using a hardware random number generator instruction, `trng` in Table 3, to ensure the hypervisor cannot orchestrate two VMs generating the same key pair by controlling inputs which affect collected randomness). This key should be stored inside the memory region that is specified as private and off-limits both to the hypervisor and to DMA.

3.2 Detailed Operation

We explain the reason for each of HyperWall's new hardware features as we describe its detailed operation at server boot up, VM initialization, VM interruption, VM runtime, and VM termination. For reference, the hardware modifications are shown in Figure 2, while Tables 2 and 3 give details about new registers and instructions. The architectural features highlighted in Figure 2 will be summarized in Section 3.4.

The HyperWall architecture is designed to incur most overhead on starting a VM and to minimize the overhead as the VMs run. Regular VM operation incurs no new overhead. There is overhead only when the hypervisor interrupts the VM, updates the VM's memory mapping or itself makes a memory access. For this purpose, we interpose on TLB updates to check the protections when a new memory address is accessed. Consequently, a load or store from the hypervisor only incurs new overhead if an address translation entry in the TLB is not found.

3.2.1 Initializing HyperWall Components

When the system boots up, the CIP logic queries the memory controller to determine the start and end address of the protected memory and issues commands (e.g. injects store instructions) to write all 0s to the memory range. This memory becomes hardware-only accessible. As initially there are no guest VMs running, this invalidates all the entries in the CIP tables since no protection is needed. In addition, the CIP logic generates encryption and hashing keys (K_{enc} and K_{hash} in Figure 1).

Once the HyperWall components are initialized, the regular boot sequence continues. This includes the BIOS zeroing out the memory which was not reserved by hardware (i.e. all memory visible to software). There is no special boot up procedure for the hypervisor.

3.2.2 Starting a VM

We assume that the initial kernel image and data sent to the IaaS provider along with the requested protections are not confidential and are visible in plaintext to the hypervisor. This allows the hypervisor to inspect the protections to make sure they match what the customer requested. The customer also needs to provide a nonce (NC, to prevent replay attacks) and the requested protections. A new VM id (VID) is issued to identify this VM.

As part of the request, the VM will be assigned some devices (e.g. network card or disk). The guest OS will access these devices via memory pages shared with the hypervisor (if the device is emulated in software) or DMA (if hardware device is used). Such pages can simply be specified as allowing hypervisor and DMA access. If more details are available about the virtualization environment (emulated devices vs. dedicated hardware devices), the customer can provide a more detailed protection request (e.g., allow only hypervisor or only DMA access for the shared pages). We do not, however, specify whether physical devices have to be dedicated to VMs or emulated by the hypervisor. The VM simply expects a device and uses shared memory pages to access it.

Enabling the protections at VM start time requires a number of steps. First, the guest OS kernel image has a certain memory layout for its physical memory. The requested protections specify which

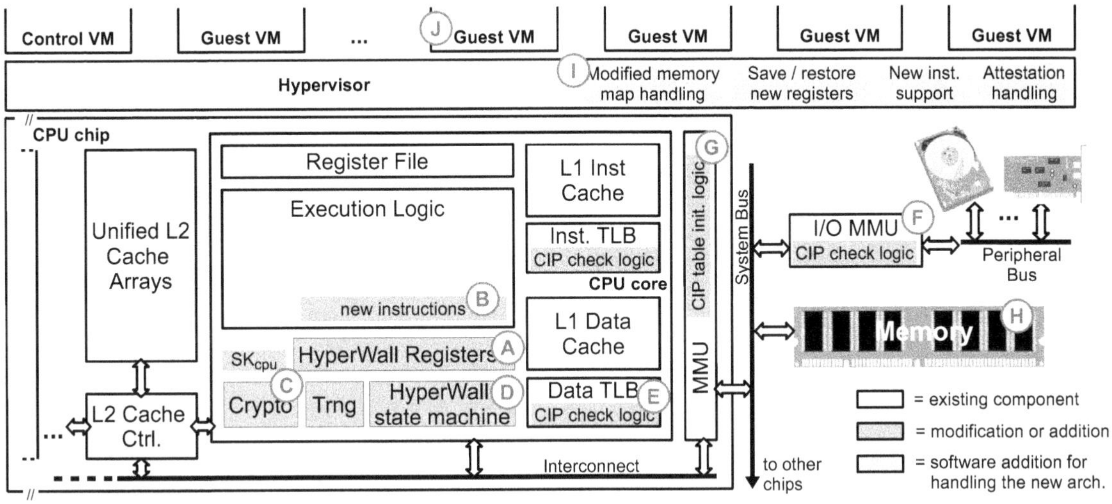

Figure 2. New hardware additions, and hypervisor updates, needed to support the HyperWall architecture.

Table 2. New HyperWall registers.

Register	Description (size)
SH	state keyed hash (32 bytes)
NC	customer's request nonce (8 bytes)
SS	initial state signature (128 bytes)
VID	VM id (8 bytes)
RPP	requested protections pointer (8 bytes)
IPH	initial protections hash (32 bytes)
IMH	initial memory hash (32 bytes)
VCNT	violation count (8 bytes)
VMAD	violation machine address (8 bytes)
VSIG	VCNT & VGPA signature (128 bytes)

Table 3. New instructions for HyperWall.

Instruction	Description
`sign_bytes`	Use CPU's private key to sign specified data.
`trng`	Access true random number generator.
`vmlaunch`	Signal hardware that a new VM is launched.
`vmresume`	Resume a VM.
`vmterminate`	Signal hardware to terminate the VM.

physical pages need to be protected. We call this specification the pre-CIP, it is provided by the customer to the cloud provider.

Second, when the VM is created, the hypervisor also sets up a mapping from the guest physical memory to the machine memory in the P2M page tables. By specifying protections for the physical memory and using the hypervisor's assigned memory mapping to obtain the corresponding machine pages requiring protections, we allow the hypervisor to freely manage physical to machine memory mapping.

Third, to enable the protections for a VM, the HyperWall architecture intercepts the `vmlaunch` instruction and updates the CIP tables with the new VM's protections. When the `vmlaunch` is intercepted, the CIP logic traverses the VM's memory mapping (the P2M tables). For each page referenced in the P2M tables, the hardware reads the pre-CIP data to check if this page requires protection. Initially all pages are marked as not assigned in the CIP tables. When the CIP logic detects that an un-assigned page is being assigned to a VM, the page's state transitions into one of the assigned states (hypervisor and DMA access allowed, hypervisor access denied, DMA access denied, or hypervisor and DMA access denied – see Figure 4), depending on the pre-CIP data. If a page being assigned does not have a corresponding entry in the pre-CIP data, it is automatically set to the state of "assigned with hypervisor and DMA access denied." If a page is already assigned in the CIP tables, it can not be assigned to more VMs and any action on that page, except freeing the page, will cause an error. If error is encountered at any time, the hardware rolls back any of the updates it did to the protections for the requested VM (i.e. the CIP tables do not hold any information about the requested VM), the VM is not started, and the `vmlaunch` instruction returns an error. The failed `vmlaunch` instruction will be detected by the hypervisor so it can attempt to remedy the problem (e.g. fix the memory mapping).

Fourth, if there has been no error during initialization, the hardware generates the hash of the initial protections and the hash of the initial memory contents (storing these in the new IPH and IMH registers in Table 2), and updates the attestation measurement signature (SS register). This SS value is a signature over all the HyperWall registers when the VM is created and uses the SK_{cpu} key:

$$SS = SIGN_{SK_{cpu}}(NC||VID||RPP||IPH||IMH ||VCNT||VMAD) \quad (1)$$

The NC is a nonce specified by the customer each time the customer requests the HyperWall system to create a new VM or do an attestation. The nonce is part of signatures and hashes and ensures freshness. The VID is an identification number used to uniquely identify each VM and is set when the VM is first created. The RPP is a pointer to the memory location where the customer's original requested protections (the pre-CIP) are stored for future reference. The VCNT and VMAD are used for trust evidence, described later in Section 3.3, and are set to 0 when the VM is created.

After the VM is launched the hypervisor will send this SS signature (along with the values of other HyperWall registers associated with the VM, see Table 2) back to the customer to attest the VM that was started. The nonce, NC, and initial protection and memory hashes, IPH and IMH, can then be verified by the customer.

3.2.3 Runtime Protections Enforcement

Whenever the hypervisor runs and attempts to access some memory there will be a TLB miss on a first access to a memory page due to the lack of a translation entry in the TLB. Before the TLB is updated, the HyperWall mechanisms traverse the CIP tables to check the access rights for the machine memory page. If no restrictions are present, a TLB entry is added as usual and there is no overhead on subsequent accesses. If there is a restriction, the TLB entry is not added and a trap to the hypervisor occurs, to signal the hypervisor that an illegal memory access was performed. The hardware will also record this violation (VCNT and VMAD in Table 2), and sign the violation record (VSIG in Table 2). The hypervisor already knows what the protected regions are so the trap conveys no new information, but allows it to make forward progress. The TLB entries need to be flushed whenever the CIP tables are updated to remove stale mappings. This can be performed via a TLB shoot-down to the remaining cores from the processor which updates the CIP tables. TLB shoot-down clears the entries in the TLBs, essentially flushing the old data held there.

A malicious hypervisor could configure a physical device to access the VM's memory and then read out that data from the device itself. To counter this in the HyperWall architecture, the I/O MMU is also modified so that the CIP tables are consulted on DMA accesses.

3.2.4 Interrupting and Resuming a VM

When the VM is interrupted and before the hypervisor begins to run, the VM's state needs to be protected: the general purpose registers are encrypted by hardware and the hash of the registers and the new HyperWall state is generated and stored in the SH register (see Table 2). This is a keyed-hash (using K_{hash} key) generated by HyperWall hardware each time the VM's execution is interrupted, to help preserve the VM's integrity.

The K_{hash} key is stored in memory (c.f. Figure 1) and thus accessible to HyperWall hardware on each core so a VM interrupted on one core can be resumed on any other core. Equation 2 describes how SH is generated.

$$SH = HASH_{Khash}(NC||SS||VID||RPP||IPH||IMH \\ ||VCNT||VMAD||VSIG||P2Mpointer \\ ||PC||E_{Kenc}(GPregisters)) \quad (2)$$

Then, the hypervisor can read out the registers and save them for when the VM is to be resumed.

When the hypervisor wants to schedule the paused VM again, it loads the saved state values back into the registers and calls `vmresume` to resume the VM. The CIP logic intercepts the instruction call and performs the inverse of the tasks performed when the VM was interrupted, i.e. it reads the saved hash of the VM state, verifies the hash and decrypts the registers before resuming the VM. The P2M pointer is included in the measurement so the hypervisor cannot restart the VM with a different memory mapping. A VM paused on one core can be resumed on any other core.

For hypercalls, whereby a guest OS requests some service from the hypervisor, the general purpose registers can not be encrypted (nor included in the SH hash). The guest OS uses the registers to pass some arguments and may return results also in the registers so the values will be different when the VM makes the call and when it is resumed. The HyperWall hardware can detect the case of a hypercall by comparing the trap number with the one associated with hypercalls (e.g. 0x100 on SPARC) and conditionally not do the encryption. For device emulation, we assume that all data copied between the hypervisor (or a driver VM emulating a device) will be copied in the shared memory. When the VM is interrupted to perform the device emulation, its register state will not need to be updated by the hypervisor. Consequently hypercalls are the only case when our hardware must not encrypt general purpose registers.

3.2.5 Runtime VM Management

During the lifetime of a VM, the hypervisor needs to perform a number of tasks. Most prominent are: scheduling VMs on different cores, memory management and VM migration.

Scheduling VMs requires the hypervisor to interrupt a VM, save the state and at some later time restore the state and resume the VM (on the same or different core). We have already discussed how the VM is protected when it is interrupted. These protections ensure that the sensitive code and data are protected when the VM is paused and resumed.

Memory management tasks involve the hypervisor updating the physical to machine memory mapping as VMs are created, the memory allocation is changed or VMs are terminated. The requested protections (the pre-CIP) are saved when the VM is created and made unreadable by the hypervisor or DMA. The pre-CIP data is consulted again whenever the memory mapping is updated. Such an update is triggered when the hypervisor writes the P2M pointer register with a new value. First, our hardware mechanisms deny access to hypervisor or DMA (set the pages as private) for the pages which occupy the *next P2M* tables (see Figure 1). Second, they traverse the new memory mapping in the *next P2M* tables and, using pre-CIP data, they update the CIP tables with the hypervisor-deny or DMA-deny protections for the machine pages corresponding to the physical pages in the new mapping. Just as when creating a mapping for the first time, if a page being assigned to the VM (as specified in the next P2M) is already assigned to some other VM in the CIP tables, the CIP table will not be updated and the memory mapping update will terminate with error. If new memory pages have been successfully assigned to the VM with no errors, our hardware mechanisms traverse the previous P2M mapping to remove from the CIP tables the memory pages not used anymore by the VM so they can be reclaimed. If a removed page was protected from hypervisor or DMA accesses, it is zeroed out by hardware, so no information leaks out, before clearing the protection bits. Finally, the machine memory pages where the old memory mapping was stored (P2M tables in Figure 1) is released back to the hypervisor, i.e., the protection bits in the CIP tables are cleared.

Through the above memory management, the HyperWall allows for the common technique of memory ballooning [43]. Memory ballooning is a technique for reserving some pages of a VM's allocated memory that can then be dynamically given to this or another VM when needed. Ballooning depends on the hypervisor's ability to dynamically change the memory mapping of a VM as it runs – as described above. To prevent information leakage, any (protected) memory reclaimed by the hypervisor will first be zeroed out by HyperWall hardware. Zeroing does not cause problems since before reclaiming memory in a VM, its balloon size is increased causing the OS to save data in any pages that will be reclaimed, so it is safe for hardware to zero them out.

To allow migration between different servers, we propose the use of guest-assisted migration [22]. For OSes which do not support such self-migration, we propose the use of a software shim to perform the migration tasks. Guest-assisted migration can be used for the majority, if not all, of the scenarios and the extra complexity of adding migration support in HyperWall hardware does not seem justified.

3.2.6 Communicating with Customer

Once the attestation measurements are verified, the customer knows that the specified VM and protections were started, and the VM's memory is isolated from the hypervisor and DMA. External communication, however, still needs to be protected. To secure communications between the customer and his leased guest VM, a cryptographically-secured channel is set up using a modified SSL

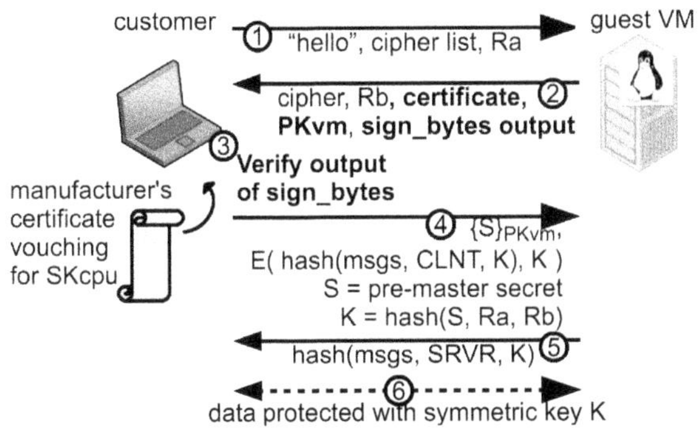

Figure 3. Establishing secure communication with the guest VM.

protocol. Note that this secure channel is between the VM (not the server) and the customer's machine. Hence, we generate a new public-private key pair for this VM, after its memory is securely isolated from the untrusted hypervisor and DMA.

The protocol is shown in Figure 3 with our modifications shown in bold. With our modifications, the servers's certificate and public key, used in standard SSL exchange, are replaced by PK_{vm} and the output of our new `sign_bytes` instruction. Initially, the VM has no public key which could be used in standard SSL exchange (recall that initial VM contents are sent in plain text so any key would be visible to the hypervisor and thus not secure). However, once the VM is started, its memory is off limits to the hypervisor, so it can generate a public-private key pair, e.g. using the OpenSSL library. Once the PK_{vm} and its associated private key is generated, the VM can use the `sign_bytes` instruction to have the hardware sign the PK_{vm} key. The PK_{vm} and the signature are sent back in our modified SSL exchange. By using the hardware manufacturer's certificate, the signature can be verified to have come from a HyperWall server. The CPU privilege level (priv_level), VM id (VID), and the nonce (NC) are included in the signature to verify that indeed the VM executed the instruction:

$$\begin{aligned} &sign\_bytes(PK_{vm}) \\ &= SIGN_{SK_{cpu}}(\,PK_{vm} \,||\, priv\_level \,||\, VID \,||\, NC\,) \end{aligned} \tag{3}$$

3.2.7 VM's Persistent Storage

If confidential data or code is sent when a VM is created, there would be a need to have hardware on the HyperWall-enabled server for doing complex mutual authentication between the customer and the hardware. Instead, the initial kernel image and protections are visible in plaintext to the hypervisor. The customer sends a vanilla VM image (with cryptographic libraries such as OpenSSL). The CIP protections are then locked in for this VM. Once a secure channel between the customer and the guest VM is established, the software inside the protected VM can perform the mutual authentication with the customer. Also, proprietary or confidential data or code can then be sent to the VM. An encrypted disk image (or remote storage) can be used to store the code or data, and the SSL connection can be used to give the VM keys to decrypt the encrypted storage. Because the communication is protected and the VM's memory is isolated from the hypervisor, the hypervisor will not be able to access the keys to decrypt the storage and see its plaintext contents.

3.2.8 VM Termination

When the VM is terminated, its memory is reclaimed by issuing our `vmterminate` instruction (see Table 3). The CIP logic intercepts the call to this instruction and traverses the P2M page table mapping to find all pages used by the VM. After each protected page is zeroed out by hardware, its entry in the CIP table is cleared so that this memory page can be freely accessed. If a hypervisor fails to issue the `vmterminate` instruction, it will remain locked out of the memory that has been assigned to the VM.

3.3 Trust Evidence

We propose trust evidence that can be used to provide a customer with information he or she can use to verify the target system, the VM that was started and the protections installed in hardware. Trust evidence is composed of two parts: attestation of the initial VM and the requested protections and attestation of the enforcement of the protection.

3.3.1 Attesting Initial VM and Protections

When the VM is created, the HyperWall hardware generates the initial state signature, SS, as defined by Equation 1. This locks in the initial VM state, and the hypervisor sends the values of the registers (including IMH and IPH) as an attestation to the customer. This attests that the requested VM started with the requested protections. Given the hardware manufacturer's certificate, the customer is able to verify the signature and compare the register state to the expected values. The measurement includes the initial memory hash to check that the provided VM image was used. It also includes the initial protections hash to check that the hypervisor did not alter the requested protections as it inspected them. If all the values are as expected, then a correct VM was started and the requested memory regions are protected.

3.3.2 Attesting Runtime Protection Enforcement

The customer may also want to verify that the protections are being enforced as the VM runs. For this purpose, HyperWall keeps track of the count of memory access violations (VCNT in Table 2) and the address where the last violation occurred (VMAD in Table 2).

To obtain the runtime attestation, the customer sends the VM id to identify the VM, a nonce for freshness and a challenge. The challenge specifies the physical address that the hypervisor or DMA should try to access so enforcement of protections can be verified. Next, the hypervisor performs the challenge (e.g., attempts to access the machine page which is mapped to the VM's physical page). If the access is in violation of protections, the hardware increments the violation count (VCNT) and saves the address that caused the violation (VMAD). At the same time, the VSIG signature is generated by the hardware using the SK_{cpu} key:

$$VSIG = SIGN_{SK_{cpu}}(NC||VCNT||VMAD) \tag{4}$$

If there was no violation, the violation count and address are not updated. Violation count, the address and signature form the trust evidence which is read by the hypervisor and sent to the customer, as the runtime attestation response.

This is one possible implementation of runtime attestation. By comparing the challenge and the response, the customer can check that the protections are enforced for the address specified in the challenge. Given this base mechanism, a customer can design different schemes for verifying the whole VM's protections: randomly spot check the protections or fully scan all protected regions, for example.

We point out that our trust evidence attests to the protections of the VM requested by the customer; it is not a measurement of the current state of the OS or hypervisor or the entire software stack (as in the Trusted Platform Module's attestation [11]). We provide evidence that the protections of the VM used in the cloud are indeed being enforced.

3.4 Architecture Summary

Figure 2 shows the hardware modifications required to implement HyperWall and highlights our re-use of existing commodity microprocessor mechanisms.

New HyperWall registers (Ⓐ in Figure 2) are introduced to store protection information about the currently executing VM. Table 2 lists these new registers for each processor core. These registers are updated by hardware and can be saved and restored by the hypervisor when it switches VMs. Two new instructions, `sign_bytes` and `trng` are added (Ⓑ), while three existing ones are modified (see Table 3 and description in previous section). A hardware random number generator block is added to support the `trng` instruction.

A cryptographic engine (Ⓒ) is needed for performing encryption, decryption, hashing and signing (for which the SK_{cpu} key will be used). The bulk of the HyperWall logic is in a state machine (Ⓓ) which is responsible for updating the CIP tables when a VM is created or terminated. Moreover, the state machine ensures the protections are maintained when the memory mapping for a guest VM is updated. This is done by the hardware mediating updates to the physical to machine (P2M) page mapping.

The TLB update logic (Ⓔ) is expanded to consult the CIP tables before inserting an address translation into the TLBs. To improve performance, the access checks are done when the address translation is performed. The address translation is cached in the TLB if there is no violation, and the CIP table check can be avoided in the future. To prevent stale mappings, the TLBs need to be flushed whenever the CIP tables are updated. Similarly to the address translation in the main processor, the I/O MMU (Ⓕ) needs to have extra logic to consult the CIP tables. The MMU (Ⓖ) is updated with 1 extra register to mark where the protected memory region starts, and CIP logic is added to walk the CIP tables on a hypervisor access. We re-use a portion of DRAM (Ⓗ) to store the CIP tables.

Although we introduce our modification only in the microprocessor and consider the hypervisor untrusted; the hypervisor (Ⓘ), as the entity in charge of the platform, will need to interact with our new architecture. In addition to the usual tasks, the hypervisor needs to perform a few additional functions. It needs to save and restore the new registers when VMs are interrupted and resumed (as it does already with other state today). It needs to handle the `vmlaunch`, `vmresume`, and `vmterminate` instructions to start, resume, or terminate a VM respectively. It needs to read attestation measurements from hardware registers. It needs to use a modified procedure for updating the memory mapping during VM runtime (i.e. swap old and new P2M tables rather than modify individual entries in old P2M mapping).

The guest OSes (Ⓙ) do not need explicit modification. The only change is the possible inclusion of a library which makes use of the new `trng` instruction. However, commodity Linux distributions already are able to use hardware random number generators found in computer chipsets (e.g. in Intel's 82802 Firmware Hub [6]) so no modification in such systems is needed. The software memory manager found in the guest OSes should never map the sensitive code or data such that it is located in the pages accessible to the hypervisor. If only pages which are used as buffers between VM and (emulated or read) devices are accessible to the hypervisor, the manager will never map any data or code to these pages as they are set to be used by the device drivers for those devices. If only a small subset of pages is protected, however, then guest OS modification may be needed so that sensitive data is never mapped into unprotected pages.

3.4.1 New Register State

Table 2 shows per processor core registers which are used to manage VM protections. These have all been described in Section 3.2 (Detailed Operation).

3.4.2 New Instructions

New or modified instructions are listed in Table 3. We add unprivileged `sign_bytes` and `trng` instructions. The `sign_bytes` is used to sign the data at the requested address. In addition to the data, the signature includes: current privilege level and the VID and NC register values. All the data are concatenated and then signed with the SK_{cpu} key. The privilege level specifies whether user software, OS, or hypervisor invoked the instruction. For user or OS invocation, the VID specifies the VM that invoked it (value is 0 for hypervisor invocation). The NC is used to ensure freshness, e.g. the customer requests the VM to sign some data and gives it the nonce to use. The `sign_bytes` is especially used when the PK_{vm} is generated by a VM so that the customer can verify that PK_{vm} indeed came from their VM. The `trng` uses a hardware random number generator and returns random bytes to the guest.

We make use of hyper-privileged instructions to start, resume and terminate a VM. Some of these are already present in many modern architectures (e.g. Intel's x86 with virtualization extensions). The `vmlaunch` signals the hardware that a new VM is launched and causes HyperWall protections for that VM to be enabled. The `vmterminate` instruction causes all of the VM's protected memory regions to be zeroed out by the hardware and their entries in the CIP tables cleared so the memory can be reclaimed. When a VM is interrupted the new HyperWall registers describing that VM are saved; the `vmresume` instruction signals that the VM is ready to be resumed, causing the hardware to check the integrity of the restored HyperWall registers.

3.4.3 Cryptographic Routines

We have included the cryptographic routines as an extra hardware unit in the microprocessor. This can be implemented as dedicated circuits (as in our simulations), microcode or software routines in on-chip ROM.

4. Simulation and Evaluation

4.1 Baseline Simulation

We have implemented HyperWall in an OpenSPARC T1 simulator. OpenSPARC is an open-source 64-bit, multi-threaded, multicore microprocessor from Sun Microsystems (now Oracle), modeled after their UltraSPARC commercial microprocessor. The whole microprocessor code (which can be synthesized to ASIC or FPGA), the code for the hypervisor, as well as a set of simulators (Legion and SAM) are available. We use the Legion simulator which is able to simulate multiple cores, boot the hypervisor, and run multiple VMs. HDL (hardware description language) code could be modified if the design is to be synthesized into a real chip or to obtain power and area measurements.

We have modified the Legion simulator with the new HyperWall functionality. We utilize the PolarSSL [8] library to simulate

Table 4. Simulator Configuration

Component	Parameter	Value
System Total	ITLB, DTLB	16 entries each
	DRAM	32 GB
	CPU cores	2
Each guest VM	CPU cores	1
	Memory, Disk	256MB, 2GB
	Guest OS	Ubuntu Linux 7.10

the cryptographic operations. We have configured Legion to simulate 2 cores and run 2 VMs (one per core), see Table 4. Each guest VM has 10 memory regions spanning 4GB of memory (e.g. RAM, memory-mapped disk image, emulated console, etc.) and the protections are consequently specified for a 4GB region in our test pre-CIP data.

For the performance evaluation we run the hypervisor, Ubuntu OS and selected SPEC 2006 benchmarks on the simulator to obtain instruction counts for various operations and events. We assume conservatively 5 cycles per instruction (CPI=5) for memory load and store instructions, CPI=1 for register-based functional instructions, and CPI=2 as average for all instructions to estimate cycle counts. We simulate: SHA-256 for hash generation with 0.13 cycles/byte [24], AES for encryption with 1.38 cycles/byte [28] and 1024-bit RSA digital signature which takes 283K cycles [36].

4.2 CIP Tables Implementation

There are many possible implementations for the CIP tables. We chose a flat table with one entry per machine page. This has simple addressing logic: the high-order bits of a machine page's address are used as an index into the CIP table.

Each CIP table entry is 4 bits. While 3 bits are enough for the 5 states currently defined per page as described in Section 3.1, we opted for 4 bits, a power of 2, see Figure 4. The extra (reserved) encodings can be used for future functionality. The first two bits of each entry are used to detect if a page has been assigned to a VM or not: 00 is unassigned, 11 is an assigned page that is private to a VM. While 01 and 10 are reserved, one future use for these encodings which we are investigating is for pages shared among VMs.

An alternative design is to use a dedicated hardware memory structure for storing the CIP tables. This, however, would impact scalability (having a dedicated hardware structure pre-determines the maximum amount of memory which can be protected, preventing installation of more memory at a later time) and increase hardware costs (having to add more hardware components). By using a hardware-only accessible portion of DRAM, we reduce the costs by using existing DRAM and provide scalability. At boot up time, the memory size is discovered and proportionally a part of DRAM is made hardware-only accessible and the tables are stored there. This allows the system to reserve exactly the size of memory needed for the tables; there is never a situation where some subset of memory cannot be protected due to insufficient hardware CIP table entries, nor are resources wasted by provisioning for the worst case. Moreover, the lost DRAM storage space is negligible (~0.012% in our evaluation).

Another alternative design for the CIP tables that we explored is a page-table-like structure. This has the advantage that existing page-table walking hardware could be reused. However, more than

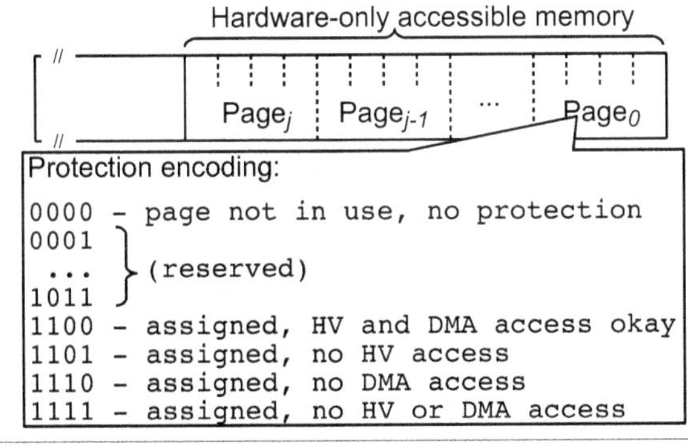

Figure 4. One design of CIP tables which uses 4 protection bits per page, all stored in hardware-only accessible memory.

Table 5. Worst-case Overhead of Accessing CIP Tables

Operation	Original System *total inst.*	Extra Memory Accesses *total (change)*
Startup (hypervisor boot)	58 M	
Init. CIP tables		524 K (0.9%)
Check CIP		21 M (36%)
VM Launch (guest OS boot)	2686 M	
Set CIP entries		2 M (<0.1%)
VM interrupt due to:		
Scheduling	~76	8 (10%)
TLB miss	~35	5 (14%)
VM terminate	- - -	
Clear CIP entries		1 M

one memory access is needed for a CIP table lookup (e.g., 2 memory accesses for a 2-level page-table structure). Also, CIP tables are located in fixed memory locations, and do not need the flexibility of locating them in arbitrary memory locations like conventional page tables. Hence, we chose the flat table structure for our CIP table implementation.

The size of the CIP tables depends on the amount of installed DRAM. For our implementation, we have chosen to simulate a system with 32 GB of addressable memory, which requires 4MB of storage (32GB $\rightarrow 2^{23}$ 4KB pages $*$ 4 bits per page $\rightarrow$ 4MB).

4.3 Storage Overhead

One benefit of storing CIP tables in DRAM is that the reserved amount of memory depends on the size of DRAM. Assuming 4KB pages and using 4 bits per page to describe the protections, 0.012% (i.e. 4MB out of the 32GB) of DRAM is made accessible only to the hardware and not usable by the rest of the system.

The new HyperWall registers in each microprocessor core sum to a total of only 392 bytes. There is also need for an extra register in the MMU to hold the start address of the hardware-only accessible memory region.

4.4 CIP Table Access Overhead

The worst case overhead of initializing the 4MB of CIP tables is ~524K 64-bit accesses, which initialize the table entries by writing all 0s. This overhead can be greatly reduced if there is support for zeroing out whole blocks of memory at a time. Once the CIP tables are initialized and the system begins to run, they are consulted (in the worst case) on each hypervisor or DMA access. In this worst case, each memory access causes 1 extra access to the CIP tables to read the protections. In the average case, this will be much less as once an address translation is placed in the TLB, the CIP lookup does not need to be performed. Table 5 shows the worst case overheads for the simulated system.

During hypervisor boot up there are ~58M instructions executed, of these 21M are memory instructions. Each memory instruction will cause in the worst case one extra access to read the CIP tables, hence the overhead of 21M extra memory accesses. During Ubuntu guest OS boot up, we observed ~2686M instructions being executed, of these 2M were hypervisor memory accesses. Again, each hypervisor access in the worst case causes one extra access due to reading CIP tables, hence the overhead of 2M extra memory accesses. During regular OS execution, the OS often is interrupted by the hypervisor. For example, when a periodic interrupt to allow the hypervisor to perform scheduling duties happens, the hypervisor executes ~76 instructions, of which 8 are memory accesses causing overhead of 8 extra memory accesses (due to reading the CIP tables). During VM termination, the CIP table entries need to be updated. In our simulation, the VMs are

Table 6. Approximate Runtime Cycle Overheads

Operation	Extra Overhead	
	Hardware (cycles)	Hypervisor (cycles)
VM Launch (5372 M cycles)		
set CIP entry	10 (per page)	
generate IMH	34900 K	
generate IPH	140 K	
generate SS	280 K	
read SS		4
VM Interrupt		
encrypt GPR	353	
generate SH	84	
save HyperWall regs.		21
VM Resume		
restore HyperWall regs.		21
verify SH	84	
decrypt GPR	353	
Runtime Attestation		
write NC		1
generate VSIG	280 K	
read VSIG		4
VM Terminate		
Zero VM memory	512 (per page)	
Clear CIP entries	10 (per page)	

assigned 4GB memory regions (1M pages) which requires 1M CIP entries to be updated.

4.5 Runtime Overhead

During runtime, a HyperWall system also experiences overhead due to cryptographic operations and updates of HyperWall registers. In addition, the hypervisor needs to perform new operations to save and restore the HyperWall registers; issue instructions to launch, interrupt, resume and terminate the VM; handle the attestation operations and handle the modified memory mapping update mechanisms. Recall, however, that the CIP tables are only consulted when the hypervisor is running and that there is no extra overhead for memory accesses from the guest OS or applications. Table 6 summarizes the different overheads and breaks them up into overheads incurred by hardware or by the hypervisor, while in the text below we highlight some important points.

Upon VM launch, most of the overhead is in updating the memory protection. We report overhead per protected page, which needs to be multiplied by the number of protected pages and will vary for each system. In our simulation setup, each VM occupies a 4GB space (memory, memory-mapped disk and memory-mapped devices) which is 1M pages. There will also be extra work in the cloud infrastructure to handle the protection specification and pass it to the hypervisor; this overhead is not reported here.

For the hash generation we emulate a hardware implementation of SHA-256 with 0.13 cycles/byte [30]. For our configuration (c.f. Table 4), hashing 256MB of memory and the pre-CIP tables takes about 35M cycles. One signature will take on the order of 280K cycles if a recent speed-optimized 1024-bit RSA design is emulated [36].

When a VM is interrupted, the overhead of encrypting the general purpose registers (GPRs) will be incurred on all VM interruptions, except due to a hypercall (when the registers are not encrypted, so information can be passed to the hypervisor). Similarly, during VM resume the decryption overhead will not be incurred if the VM is returning from a hypercall. The encryption of the 32 64-bit GPRs using a 1.38 cycles/byte AES implementation [28] takes 353 cycles. Generation of the signed hash, using a 0.13 cycles/byte [30] implementation, of the GPRs (32 64-bit registers) and our new state (392 bytes) requires hashing 648 bytes for a total of 84 cycles. The reverse of these operations is performed to verify the state when the VM is resumed.

For runtime attestation, there will also be extra work to deliver the attestation result to the customer. This is a complex process involving many software components, and the overhead is not reported. However, much similar overhead is incurred today, for example when the status of a VM executing in the cloud is reported to the customer, so the overall percentage change should be small.

When a VM is terminated, the protected memory regions need to be zeroed out by hardware and the CIP table entries removed. We report numbers per page-sized (4KB) region. Because now the hardware zeroes out the memory, the associated functionality can be disabled in the hypervisor, so the extra overhead will be partially compensated.

4.6 Impact on Memory Hierarchy Performance

Because there are extra accesses to the CIP tables, they will cause the cache hit rate to decrease. The cache hit rate changes can be used as a proxy for estimating performance impact.

To model the impact of the extra CIP table accesses on the system performance, we extended the OpenSPARC Legion simulator with a simulation of cache hierarchy. We simulate split L1 instruction and data caches, 4-way, 32KB each (there is one pair of caches per core); and a unified 12-way 3MB L2 cache. The parameters are set to match the OpenSPARC architecture. These are inclusive, write-back caches with a simple round robin replacement policy. We simulate the HyperWall state machine using the data cache to cache the CIP table entries, and hence it impacts software performance.

Our test runs included: booting the hypervisor, booting the whole guest OS, and running selected SPEC 2006 benchmarks. The cache hit rate changes were within 1 % in all cases. This suggests that HyperWall's impact should be minimal, but a more detailed cache and memory simulation is needed to get more exact estimates; this is part of our future work on optimizing a HyperWall implementation.

5. Security Analysis

We now evaluate the security of the HyperWall system. Keep in mind the goal of HyperWall is to protect the confidentiality and integrity of a VM's memory.

5.1 Protecting Confidentiality and Integrity

In any of today's virtualization solutions, the hypervisor is able to access all of a VM's memory or disk images and violate confidentiality and integrity of the code and data stored there. In HyperWall, the hypervisor has access to the initial guest VM image and the requested protections sent by the customer. Any of this data can be modified before the hardware is initialized and protections locked in. This attack is averted by the use of hardware-based attestation and sending the signed measurements when the VM is started. Moreover, during VM runtime, the customer can request trust evidence and verify that it came from a genuine HyperWall system (due to the hardware signature) and that the protections are still correctly specified for hardware enforcement.

Also, when the VM is running, the hypervisor could intercept communications between the customer and the VM. Initially, no confidential data is sent, so this does not gain anything for the attacker. Once the VM is started, customer to VM communication is protected with the modified SSL protocol. The hypervisor, which has no access to the decryption key, cannot break the SSL secure channel and extract any data sent in the SSL tunnel after the VM is running. The customer can also use this secure SSL tunnel to send the key for the VM to access and decrypt its encrypted storage where it can store proprietary code and confidential data.

Because the VM contains memory regions off-limits to the hypervisor or DMA, it can generate keys and keep them secure from a compromised hypervisor or DMA. Such keys should be used for hashing and encryption to protect the integrity and confidentiality of swap space that the guest VM may use, for example. In HyperWall, all disk storage, except for the initial VM image, should be encrypted and hashed.

5.2 Availability Considerations

HyperWall implementation of hypervisor-secure virtualization does not provide availability protection for the guest VMs. The confidentiality and integrity of the protected code and data, however, is maintained even if an untrusted hypervisor performs a denial-of-service (DoS) attack on the VM by suspending or terminating it. The memory with the code and data is protected from hypervisor or DMA access even if the VM is suspended and, moreover, it is zeroed out by hardware when the VM is terminated so that no information leaks out.

One reason we felt it was reasonable to leave out availability protection is because the IaaS cloud provider must be able to stop a VM anyway. In an IaaS hosted infrastructure cloud computing scenario, customers lease the resources and pay for them. The IaaS cloud provider (via using hypervisor mechanisms) needs to be able to stop a VM if the customer is not paying for the resources. Otherwise the customers could execute a DoS attack on the cloud provider's resources, or get to use the resources for free.

5.3 Other Security Concerns

One potential concern is the hypervisor's lack of ability to fully inspect the memory contents for the guest VM, and thus perform security checking of the VM via introspection. Allowing the hypervisor to access a VM's memory, however, is at odds with our assumption of an untrusted hypervisor. But, the infrastructure provider can still use network-based intrusion detection systems (IDS) to monitor the network for any unusual activity that may hint at a malicious VM. Also while still using the protections, a customer could use in-VM monitoring and install a security agent that monitors the state of the VM and reports back to the customer and the infrastructure provider.

Another potential concern is a set of cooperating malicious hypervisors which may start one copy of the VM on a genuine HyperWall machine and a second copy on a different server and forward the same data to both so that the second system leaks the data or code. However, after receiving the attestation measurement sent when the VM is started, the customer knows which machine the VM is executing on (due to the unique SK_{cpu}). The guest VM generates a public-private key pair and signs it using the new `sign_bytes` instruction to establish a secure connection with the customer. When the customer receives and verifies the signed PK_{vm} key, he or she knows that it came from the same server which properly attested. The copy of the VM on the non-HyperWall machine will not have the keys needed to decrypt the communication or decrypt the customer's encrypted data or code.

The ability of the customer to verify the SK_{cpu} opens up the possibility of infrastructure mapping attacks [37] as now there is an easy way to identify a particular server. While we do not protect against such attacks in the current work, ideas from direct anonymous attestation [17] could be used.

A different concern is that a malicious hypervisor could attempt to assign memory pages to a victim VM that have already been assigned to a hostile VM. If this was possible, the hypervisor access and DMA access checks would be bypassed as memory protections are not checked on VM access. This attack is not possible in HyperWall. When a VM is created, the CIP tables are updated to hold information about its pages. Even unprotected, but assigned, pages are marked in the CIP tables (recall the CIP table entry `1100` encoding in our implementation). Consequently, all pages assigned to a potentially hostile VM would be marked in the CIP tables. When a hypervisor attempts to assign the same page to the victim VM, the CIP logic detects that the page is already in use, CIP table update terminates with error and the victim VM is not started.

All the above analysis assumes correctness of the underlying hardware which implements our new mechanisms. Also, the protocols used to transfer the data back to the customer need to work correctly. Consequently, our ongoing work looks at verification of the various parts of the architecture as well as of the protocols. While full formal verification of security architectures is an open research issue, by verifying components and protocols we can significantly raise the confidence in the HyperWall architecture.

6. Related Work

We summarize some past work on aspects of our architecture: hardware support for isolation, attestation, using hypervisors to monitor VMs, hardening or minimizing hypervisors, secure processor architectures, and the homomorphic encryption approach. None of this surveyed work met our goals of hypervisor-secure virtualization with hardware support.

In the past, manufacturers such as IBM and Sun Microsystems (now Oracle) have solutions which are used to partition physical resources and enforce strong isolation between the VMs [4, 10]. They, however, include the management software in the TCB and do not protect against compromised or malicious management software which can snoop on or attack the VMs, as we do.

TPM has been deployed extensively in notebook PCs and can be used for attestation of the software stack. For example, work by Krautheim et al. [26] looks at extending the TPM to the cloud computing environment. Also, Flicker [35] uses the TPM along with a trusted hypervisor. While work which uses TPM can provide attestation by creating a measurement chain of bootloader, hypervisor, OSes, etc., we are able to provide attestation separately to each VM and without inclusion of the untrusted hypervisor in the measurements. Also, we introduced the runtime attestation of protection enforcement not present in TPM-based systems.

The majority of hypervisor-related work has been done on using the hypervisors to inspect or monitor guest VMs (introspection) and on hardening the hypervisors. Such work does not consider attacks from the hypervisor on the VMs. Introspection schemes use the hypervisor's higher privilege to secure the guest VMs. One of the first mentions of the idea was presented by Chen, et al. [19]. HookSafe [46] is a hypervisor-based system for detecting guest OS rootkits. Also, KvmSec [33], an extension to Linux's kernel virtual machine, adds the ability to check the integrity of the guest VMs. Such work on inspecting and monitoring guest VMs have a different goal than HyperWall. In HyperWall, we consider attacks from the hypervisor. Also, we aim to provide confidentiality and integrity to the VM's data and code from a potentially compromised hypervisor, rather than monitoring the VMs to discover any anomalies when they have already been compromised.

The hardening and minimizing of hypervisors has also been explored. For example, Li, et al., [31] propose protecting the hypervisor kernel from an untrusted management OS while HyperSafe [44] is a proposed prototype of a hypervisor which aims to protect a hypervisor's code and data from unauthorized modification. These and similar works modify the hypervisor's code to make it more resilient to attacks. They can be combined with HyperWall to provide defense in depth to guard against any bugs or misconfigurations in the hardened hypervisors.

Our earlier NoHype architecture [23] proposed removing the hypervisor altogether. However, NoHype still has a small trusted management software which can maliciously access a guest's memory, if it is compromised. HyperWall also allows more functionality than NoHype as it allows a hypervisor layer to run and actively manage the VMs.

A number of research projects have looked at secure processor architectures and adding hardware support to protect software. These include XOM [32], AEGIS [39], SP [29] and Bastion [18]. In Bastion, the hypervisor is trusted, and the others do not consider hypervisors at all. Unlike HyperWall, these proposals do protect against hardware attacks, but these are much less likely in physically-secured data centers for cloud computing.

Outside of hardware solutions, researchers have been exploring fully homomorphic encryption [21]. Its main advantage is that computation can be performed on encrypted data without revealing what the data is. The disadvantage is the (currently) very low performance and that only the data is protected, not the code. We offer a solution which can be realized with small modifications to today's hardware and protects both code and data.

7. Conclusions and Future Work

We presented the HyperWall architecture which relies on new Confidentiality and Integrity Protection (CIP) tables to protect the guest VM's memory from a compromised or malicious hypervisor. HyperWall allows hypervisors to freely manage the memory, processor cores and other resources of the platform. Yet, once VMs are created, CIP logic protects the memory of the guest VMs from a potentially compromised hypervisor and from DMA. The HyperWall architecture is also able to provide trust evidence attestation to the customer showing that the VM was started with the correct protections, and the protections are being enforced during runtime, in spite of a possibly malicious hypervisor. HyperWall can be especially useful in a setting such as IaaS clouds to enable customers to have the confidentiality and integrity of their VM's data and code protected while enjoying the economic benefits of cloud computing. Our evaluation shows reasonably small overheads due to the new mechanisms. Thus, HyperWall strikes a good balance between security and performance.

Our ongoing and future work includes studying HyperWall architecture's interaction with performance counters and other state which may leak information about the guest VM, protecting the code and data when it is executed outside the microprocessor chip (e.g. on GPUs), and providing nested protections where both the whole VM and some applications inside it can be protected separately. We are also investigating verification of various parts of the architecture as well as of the protocols. These issues suggest that this paper may open up many interesting and important new research topics in the new research direction that we have called *hypervisor-secure virtualization*.

Acknowledgments

We would like to thank the anonymous reviewers for their suggestions which improved this paper. We also thank Yu-Yuan Chen for his help in looking up hypervisor vulnerabilities and their statistics. This work is supported in part by NSF grants CCF-0917134 and EEC-0540832.

References

[1] Amazon Elastic Compute Cloud (Amazon EC2). http://aws.amazon.com/ec2/.

[2] AMD Virtualization (AMD-V) Technology. http://sites.amd.com/us/business/it-solutions/virtualization/Pages/amd-v.aspx.

[3] Vulnerability Summary for CVE-2007-4993. http://web.nvd.nist.gov/view/vuln/detail?vulnId=CVE-2007-4993.

[4] Introduction to the New Mainframe: z/VM Basics, section 1.9.2 and 2.4.1. IBM Redbooks, http://www.redbooks.ibm.com/abstracts/sg247316.html.

[5] Intel Virtualization Technology, . http://www.intel.com/technology/itj/2006/v10i3/1-hardware/6-vt-x-vt-i-solutions.htm.

[6] Intel 82802AB/82802AC Firmware Hub (FWH) datasheet, November 2000, . http://download.intel.com/design/chipsets/datashts/29065804.pdf.

[7] National Vulnerability Database, CVE and CCE Statistics Query Page. http://web.nvd.nist.gov/view/vuln/statistics.

[8] PolarSSL, Small Cryptographic Library. http://www.polarssl.org.

[9] PCI SIG: PCI-SIG Single Root I/O Virtualization. http://www.pcisig.com/specifications/iov/single_root/.

[10] Oracle VM Server For SPARC. http://www.oracle.com/us/oraclevm-sparc-ds-073441.pdf.

[11] Trusted Computing Group. TCG TPM Specification. http://www.trustedcomputinggroup.org/.

[12] VMWare. http://www.vmware.com/.

[13] Intel Corporation: Intel Virtualization Technology for Directed I/O. http://download.intel.com/technology/itj/2006/v10i3/v10-i3-art02.pdf.

[14] Xen. http://www.xen.org.

[15] A. M. Azab, P. Ning, Z. Wang, X. Jiang, X. Zhang, and N. C. Skalsky. Hypersentry: enabling stealthy in-context measurement of hypervisor integrity. In *Proc. of the 17th ACM Conference on Computer and Communications Security*, CCS, pages 38–49, October 2010. doi: http://doi.acm.org/10.1145/1866307.1866313. URL http://doi.acm.org/10.1145/1866307.1866313.

[16] M. Ben-Yehuda, M. D. Day, Z. Dubitzky, M. Factor, N. Har'El, A. Gordon, A. Liguori, O. Wasserman, and B.-A. Yassour. The turtles project: design and implementation of nested virtualization. In *Proc. of the 9th USENIX Conference on Operating Systems Design and Implementation*, OSDI, pages 1–6, October 2010. URL http://portal.acm.org/citation.cfm?id=1924943.1924973.

[17] E. Brickell, J. Camenisch, and L. Chen. Direct anonymous attestation. In *Proc. of the 11th ACM Conference on Computer and Communications Security*, CCS, pages 132–145, October 2004. ISBN 1-58113-961-6. doi: http://doi.acm.org/10.1145/1030083.1030103. URL http://doi.acm.org/10.1145/1030083.1030103.

[18] D. Champagne and R. Lee. Scalable architectural support for trusted software. In *16th International Symposium on High Performance Computer Architecture (HPCA)*, pages 1 –12, January 2010. doi: 10.1109/HPCA.2010.5416657.

[19] P. M. Chen and B. D. Noble. When virtual is better than real. *Workshop on Hot Topics in Operating Systems*, May 2001. doi: http://doi.ieeecomputersociety.org/10.1109/HOTOS.2001.990073.

[20] X. Chen, T. Garfinkel, E. C. Lewis, P. Subrahmanyam, C. A. Waldspurger, D. Boneh, J. Dwoskin, and D. R. Ports. Overshadow: a virtualization-based approach to retrofitting protection in commodity operating systems. In *Proc. of the 13th International Conference on Architectural Support for Programming Languages and Operating Systems*, ASPLOS, pages 2–13, March 2008. ISBN 978-1-59593-958-6. doi: http://doi.acm.org/10.1145/1346281.1346284. URL http://doi.acm.org/10.1145/1346281.1346284.

[21] C. Gentry. Fully homomorphic encryption using ideal lattices. In *Proc. of the annual Symposium on Theory of Computing*, STOC, pages 169–178, May 2009. ISBN 978-1-60558-506-2. doi: http://doi.acm.org/10.1145/1536414.1536440. URL http://doi.acm.org/10.1145/1536414.1536440.

[22] J. G. Hansen and E. Jul. Self-migration of operating systems. In *Proc. of the 11th ACM SIGOPS European Workshop*, September 2004.

[23] E. Keller, J. Szefer, J. Rexford, and R. B. Lee. NoHype: virtualized cloud infrastructure without the virtualization. In *Proc. of the 37th*

annual International Symposium on Computer Architecture, ISCA, pages 350–361, June 2010. ISBN 978-1-4503-0053-7.

[24] M. Kim, J. Ryou, and S. Jun. Efficient Hardware Architecture of SHA-256 Algorithm for Trusted Mobile Computing. In *Information Security and Cryptology*, volume 5487 of *Lecture Notes in Computer Science*, pages 240–252. 2009.

[25] G. Klein, K. Elphinstone, G. Heiser, J. Andronick, D. Cock, P. Derrin, D. Elkaduwe, K. Engelhardt, R. Kolanski, M. Norrish, T. Sewell, H. Tuch, and S. Winwood. seL4: formal verification of an OS kernel. In *Proc. of the ACM SIGOPS 22nd Symposium on Operating Systems Principles*, SOSP, pages 207–220, October 2009. ISBN 978-1-60558-752-3. doi: http://doi.acm.org/10.1145/1629575.1629596.

[26] F. Krautheim, D. Phatak, and A. Sherman. Introducing the Trusted Virtual Environment Module: A New Mechanism for Rooting Trust in Cloud Computing. In *Trust and Trustworthy Computing*, volume 6101 of *Lecture Notes in Computer Science*, pages 211–227. 2010.

[27] G. Kroah-Hartman, J. Corbet, and A. McPherson. Linux kernel development. A White Paper By The Linux Foundation, December 2010. `www.linuxfoundation.org/publications/whowriteslinux.pdf`.

[28] R. B. Lee and Y.-Y. Chen. Processor accelerator for AES. In *Proc. of the 8th IEEE Symposium on Application Specific Processors*, SASP, pages 16 –21, June 2010. doi: 10.1109/SASP.2010.5521153.

[29] R. B. Lee, P. C. S. Kwan, J. P. McGregor, J. Dwoskin, and Z. Wang. Architecture for Protecting Critical Secrets in Microprocessors. In *Proc. of the 32nd annual International Symposium on Computer Architecture*, ISCA, pages 2–13, June 2005.

[30] Y. Lee, H. Chan, and I. Verbauwhede. Iteration Bound Analysis and Throughput Optimum Architecture of SHA-256 (384,512) for Hardware Implementations. In S. Kim, M. Yung, and H.-W. Lee, editors, *Information Security Applications*, volume 4867 of *Lecture Notes in Computer Science*, pages 102–114. 2007.

[31] C. Li, A. Raghunathan, and N. K. Jha. Secure Virtual Machine Execution under an Untrusted Management OS. *Proc. of the IEEE International Conference on Cloud Computing*, pages 172–179, July 2010. doi: http://doi.ieeecomputersociety.org/10.1109/CLOUD.2010.29.

[32] D. Lie, C. Thekkath, M. Mitchell, P. Lincoln, D. Boneh, J. Mitchell, and M. Horowitz. Architectural support for copy and tamper resistant software. In *Proc. of the 9th International Conference on Architectural Support for Programming Languages and Operating Systems*, ASPLOS, November 2000.

[33] F. Lombardi and R. Di Pietro. KvmSec: a security extension for Linux kernel virtual machines. In *Proc. of the 2009 ACM Symposium on Applied Computing*, SAC, pages 2029–2034, March 2009. ISBN 978-1-60558-166-8. doi: http://doi.acm.org/10.1145/1529282.1529733.

[34] V. Maraia. *The Build Master: Microsoft's Software Configuration Management Best Practices*. Addison-Wesley Professional, 2005.

[35] J. M. McCune, B. J. Parno, A. Perrig, M. K. Reiter, and H. Isozaki. Flicker: an execution infrastructure for TCB minimization. In *Proc. of the 3rd ACM SIGOPS/EuroSys European Conference on Computer Systems*, EuroSys, pages 315–328, March 2008. ISBN 978-1-60558-013-5. doi: http://doi.acm.org/10.1145/1352592.1352625. URL `http://doi.acm.org/10.1145/1352592.1352625`.

[36] A. Miyamoto, N. Homma, T. Aoki, and A. Satoh. Systematic Design of RSA Processors Based on High-Radix Montgomery Multipliers. *IEEE Transactions on Very Large Scale Integration (VLSI) Systems*, (99):1–11, 2010. ISSN 1063-8210. doi: 10.1109/TVLSI.2010.2049037.

[37] T. Ristenpart, E. Tromer, H. Shacham, and S. Savage. Hey, you, get off of my cloud: exploring information leakage in third-party compute clouds. In *Proc. of the conference on Computer and Communications Security*, CCS, pages 199–212, Nov. 2009. ISBN 978-1-60558-894-0.

[38] J. Rutkowska. Subverting Vista Kernel for Fun and Profit. Symposium on Security for Asia Network (SyScan), July 2006.

[39] G. E. Suh, D. Clarke, B. Gassend, M. van Dijk, and S. Devadas. AEGIS: architecture for tamper-evident and tamper-resistant processing. In *Proc. of the 17th annual International Conference on Supercomputing*, ICS, pages 160–171, June 2003. ISBN 1-58113-733-8. doi: http://doi.acm.org/10.1145/782814.782838. URL `http://doi.acm.org/10.1145/782814.782838`.

[40] J. Szefer and R. B. Lee. A Case for Hardware Protection of Guest VMs from Compromised Hypervisors in Cloud Computing. In *Proc. of the Second International Workshop on Security and Privacy in Cloud Computing*, SPCC, June 2011.

[41] A. Tereshkin and R. Wojtczuk. Introducing ring -3 rootkits. Black Hat USA, July 2009.

[42] A. Vasudevan, J. M. McCune, N. Qu, L. Van Doorn, and A. Perrig. Requirements for an integrity-protected hypervisor on the x86 hardware virtualized architecture. In *Proc. of the 3rd international conference on Trust and Trustworthy Computing*, TRUST, pages 141–165, June 2010. ISBN 3-642-13868-3, 978-3-642-13868-3. URL `http://portal.acm.org/citation.cfm?id=1875652.1875663`.

[43] C. A. Waldspurger. Memory resource management in VMware ESX server. *SIGOPS Oper. Syst. Rev.*, 36:181–194, December 2002. ISSN 0163-5980. doi: http://doi.acm.org/10.1145/844128.844146. URL `http://doi.acm.org/10.1145/844128.844146`.

[44] Z. Wang and X. Jiang. HyperSafe: A Lightweight Approach to Provide Lifetime Hypervisor Control-Flow Integrity. In *Proc. of the 2010 IEEE Symposium on Security and Privacy*, S&P, pages 380 –395, May 2010. doi: 10.1109/SP.2010.30.

[45] Z. Wang and R. B. Lee. A novel cache architecture with enhanced performance and security. In *Proc. of the annual IEEE/ACM International Symposium on Microarchitecture*, MICRO, pages 83–93, Nov. 2008. ISBN 978-1-4244-2836-6.

[46] Z. Wang, X. Jiang, W. Cui, and P. Ning. Countering kernel rootkits with lightweight hook protection. In *Proc. of the conference on Computer and Communications Security*, CCS, pages 545–554, Nov. 2009. ISBN 978-1-60558-894-0. doi: http://doi.acm.org/10.1145/1653662.1653728.

[47] R. Wojtczuk and J. Rutkowska. Attacking intel trusted execution technology. Black Hat DC, Feb. 2009.

Region Scheduling: Efficiently Using the Cache Architectures via Page-level Affinity

Min Lee, Karsten Schwan

Georgia Institute of Technology
Center for Experimental Research in Computer Systems
Atlanta, GA, USA
{minlee, karsten.schwan}@cc.gatech.edu

Abstract

The performance of modern many-core platforms strongly depends on the effectiveness of using their complex cache and memory structures. This indicates the need for a memory-centric approach to platform scheduling, in which it is the locations of memory blocks in caches rather than CPU idleness that determines where application processes are run. Using the term 'memory region' to denote the current set of physical memory pages actively used by an application, this paper presents and evaluates region-based scheduling methods for multicore platforms. This involves (i) continuously and at runtime identifying the memory regions used by executable entities, and their sizes, (ii) mapping these regions to caches to match performance goals, and (iii) maintaining region to cache mappings by ensuring that entities run on processors with direct access to the caches containing their regions. Region scheduling can implement policies that (i) offer improved performance to applications by 'unifying' the multiple caches present on the underlying physical machine and/or by 'balancing' cache usage to take maximum advantage of available cache space, (ii) better isolate applications from each other, particularly when their performance is strongly affected by cache availability, and also (iii) take advantage of standard scheduling and CPU-based load balancing when regioning is ineffective. The paper describes region scheduling and its system-level implementation and evaluates its performance with micro-benchmarks and representative multi-core applications. Single applications see performance improvements of up to 15% with region scheduling, and we observe 40% latency improvements when a platform is shared by multiple applications. Superior isolation is shown to be particularly important for cache-sensitive or real-time codes.

Categories and Subject Descriptors D.4.1 [**Operating Systems**]: Process Management – Scheduling

General Terms Performance, Design, Experimentation

Keywords Virtualization, Xen, Cache, Memory, Region, Server Consolidation

1. Introduction

For modern computer architectures, memory access times and caching effectiveness are key determinants of program and system performance. This is evident not only from a rich set of research on caches in computer architecture [12, 13, 14, 15, 18, 19, 20, 21, 22, 23], but also from the wide variety of cache structures found on modern multi- and many-core platforms, ranging from single last level caches shared by from 2 (e.g., in Intel's Dual-core Xeon chips) to 8 cores (e.g., in Intel's Nehalem chips), to the distributed caches seen in the Larrabee chip [1].

Recognizing the importance of caching, modern methods for thread scheduling take into account cache affinity [9], avoid cache thrashing [10,11], and/or carefully select the threads that are permitted to share a common cache [2,3]. Leveraging such insights and in expectation of the increased importance of memory structures to the performance of future multicore platforms, our research is exploring a new approach that departs from prior process- or thread-centric scheduling methods to instead, create a memory-centric scheduler that first allocates to caches the sets of pages used by executable entities and then schedules those entities to the processors that use those caches. The schedulable sets of memory pages are termed *memory regions*, defined as the sets of physical pages within address spaces that currently exhibit 'good' locality, which means that an executable entity spends significant time within each such page set – region – before changing its locality to reside elsewhere, i.e., in another region.

Making regions first class entities states as an explicit goal the optimization of how memory is accessed, by controlling the mappings of regions to caches. *Region-based scheduling:*

- tracks the regions (and their associated physical pages) being used by each executable entity; where
- each entity can have multiple regions, but at any one time, a physical page resides in exactly one region;
- regions are mapped onto caches by system-defined mapping policies; and
- the system enforces the resulting cache-centric constraints on executable entities like processes.

This paper presents a hypervisor-level implementation of region-based scheduling in which the VMM identifies and tracks the memory regions used in each address space, estimates working set sizes and consequent cache occupancies, and then maps regions onto caches. Mapping policies can minimize duplicate cache lines and/or cache contention or interference (e.g., to lower cache misses [32] or to improve isolation or reduce interference [26]), or they can balance cache usage across multiple processes. To attain these ends, three different scheduling policies are devised and evaluated in this paper: (1) *cache-balancing*, where the system ensures high aggregate performance for the current processes running on a multi-core platform, (2) *cache unification*, in which the different regions used by a process are distributed across multiple caches to maximize the performance of cache-sensitive codes, and (3) *cache partitioning*, where software methods approximately partition the caches used by different processes to reduce interference or improve isolation. With region scheduling, it is also possible to unfairly allocate caches across different processes, perhaps to provide additional cache space to those that need it, but other than to demonstrate improvements in isolation, we do not further experiment with such techniques in this paper.

In order to make its performance advantages available to arbitrary applications and operating systems, region-based scheduling is implemented at hypervisor level, controlling VCPU to PCPU mappings and interacting with the hypervisor's page table structures (using the Xen open source hypervisor [27]). An alternative operating system-level implementation would apply region scheduling methods to the processes and their address spaces manipulated by OS schedulers and memory managers (i.e., via page tables).

The outcome is a system with the following properties:

- *cache-awareness* – the hypervisor understands the cache structure of the underlying machine, i.e., it knows which caches are associated with which P(hysical)CPUs;
- *runtime region tracking* – low overhead runtime methods identify and track the memory regions used by the address spaces in virtual machines;
- *region-based scheduling* – maps the V(irtual)CPUs used by a VM to PCPUs so as to match the VM's region mappings to caches; and performs runtime *micro-scheduling*, which forces a VCPU-PCPU switch to prevent the hardware from re-mapping a region when it is accessed from a PCPU associated with a different cache.

Finally, region scheduling strictly improves upon existing cache-unaware scheduling methods like those used in Unix or implemented in current hypervisors. This is because their implementation 'reverts' to unaware methods whenever regioning is deemed ineffective.

We evaluate the performance implications of region-based scheduling with representative multi-core and server applications. Experiments with the SPEC benchmark suite diagnose the potential utility and limitations of region scheduling, resulting in runtime conditions based on which we determine when region scheduling should revert to Xen's standard credit-based methods. Significant performance improvements are seen for VMs running memory- and cache-intensive codes, in part by mapping their regions in ways that better leverage the combined cache sizes of multiple on-chip caches, termed cache unification. More predictable levels of performance due to improved isolation are observed for server applications with strong constraints, such as parallel codes using barriers [26] and the enterprise level VoIP codes [25] (e.g., achieving up to 40% response time improvement for the latter).

We view region-based scheduling as a first step toward designing schedulers that recognize the importance, if not predominance, of cache and memory structures for the performance of future multi-core applications. Complementing prior work on NUMA awareness in operating systems or hypervisors [28], region scheduling offers system-level methods that improve and control application performance by explicitly managing their cache usage, without requiring additional hardware support [23] or inputs from applications [29]. Region scheduling can also be viewed as a first step toward systems that better support modern compiler runtimes that wish to explicitly manage the memory units – 'places' – used by applications [30].

In the remainder of this paper, Section 2 describes the software architecture underlying the region scheduling approach, called the region framework. Section 3's analysis establishes the region tracking algorithm, and working set tracking is presented in Section 4. Section 5 presents performance evaluations. Section 6 details related work. In Section 7, conclusions summarize results and future work, including speculations on potential hardware support to reduce tracking costs.

2. Regions

This section explains regions and the page touch methods used to implement region tracking, micro-scheduling, and the mapping of regions to caches.

2.1 Software Framework and Methods

A region is a set of physical pages. Regions partition memory, since at any one time; each page can belong to only one region. A region is private when its pages are accessible from only one address space, with typical private regions being those that contain heap or stack data. Shared regions, i.e., those shared among multiple address spaces, usually contain shared pages like code. Region scheduling addresses private regions, whereas shared regions are handled by standard caching hardware.

Region-based scheduling explicitly places private regions into caches. Such mappings are maintained by having the scheduler restrict 'from where' the region's pages can be accessed, in accordance with the hardware-level association of caches with PCPUs. Access restrictions are based on specifications associated with page tables, which state, for instance, that the physical frame numbers in a region, say, 10, 11, and 12, shall be accessed only through PCPUs 0 or 2 (on our machine, both of these share access to the same cache). With such specifications, we must ensure that a region can only be accessed through the cache to which it has been mapped. This is done by raising 'page touch' faults whenever this restriction is violated. When a fault occurs, the thread or process attempting the access is moved to one of the allowable PCPUs (i.e., 0 or 2 in this example) -- termed *micro-scheduling*. Of course, regions may also be unmapped, and when such unmapped regions are accessed, beyond micro-scheduling, the additional option is to once again map the region to the cache used by the PCPU in question -- termed '*opening*' the region.

Via page touch faults and with micro-scheduling, one can ensure that the memory blocks in a region, e.g., pages 10, 11, and 12, exist only on cache 0, which is private to PCPUs 0 and 2. Note that this technique also minimizes the number of duplicate cache lines found in caches and in addition, it may potentially reduce cache coherency traffic and false sharing of cache lines. Further, an understanding of page to cache mappings provides approximate information about cache load, which region-based scheduling uses to better utilize the cache resources present on multicore platforms, as discussed in more detail in Section 4.1.

Figure 1(a) depicts a sample scenario in which the physical pages of an address space are located in different regions, private and shared ones. Each private region may be mapped to a single cache. A shared region typically exists in all caches -- termed global region -- an example being R7 in the figure. When there are a large number of global regions, there are fewer restrictions concerning how executable entities are run (since they can run anywhere). This means that in the extreme case of there being only global regions, the region framework layer is not active, and region scheduling reverts to standard methods, like the credit scheduler in our Xen implementation. Figure 1(b) illustrates this

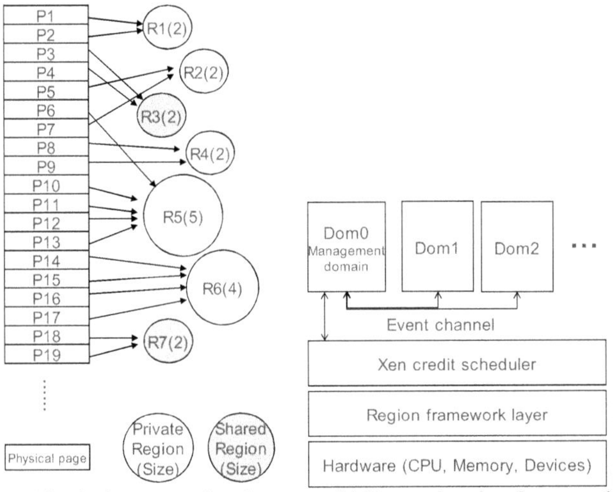

(a) Physical pages and regions (b) Xen and region framework
(Size) is the number of pages that belong to (static) or the measured working set size at run time (dynamic).

Figure 1. Region framework overview.

by showing how region scheduling is implemented in a layer residing between the hardware and the standard VMM scheduler.

Regions change over time, as address mappings (page table entries) are created or destroyed and with changes in the behaviors of the executable entities using the address space. An address space's dynamic size – its working set – is the sum of the dynamic sizes of its regions, and its cache load is the sum of the mapped regions' sizes. Working set size is measured at runtime (see Section 4). C2(11) in Figure 2 shows the working set size of C2 is measured 11, which is sum of those for R5,R6 and R7 (5,4,2 respectively in Figure 1(a)). Regions, the address spaces in which they occur, and their mappings to caches are depicted in Figure 2, which shows that regions can differ in size, that VCPU to PCPU mappings are controlled to maintain region to cache mappings, and that a single address space can be mapped across multiple caches. The latter is particularly useful for memory- and cache-intensive applications able to benefit from such cache unification.

Figure 2 also shows how region scheduling 'packs' regions into caches, where the two address spaces A1 and A2 run on cache C1, while A3 runs on C2 because its working set is larger. Cache load is shown in parentheses, the cache with a lower load being considered 'emptier' when regions are bin-packed into caches.

2.2 Region Scheduling – Implementation

Table 1 describes the data structure maintained for each region: (i)

Table 1. System-level representation of regions.

```
struct region_t {
    struct page_dir *pgd;           // address space if private region
    atomic_t vr_refcnt;                     // reference count
    struct list_head list[MAX_CACHE];  // mapping to caches
    spinlock_t lock;                        // lock
    struct list_head rmaps_list;            // reverse maps
    unsigned short int frame_count;         // static size
    unsigned short int rmap_count;          // # of reverse map
    unsigned short int flags;               // flags
    unsigned short abit[MAX_CACHE][32];  // histogram
};
```

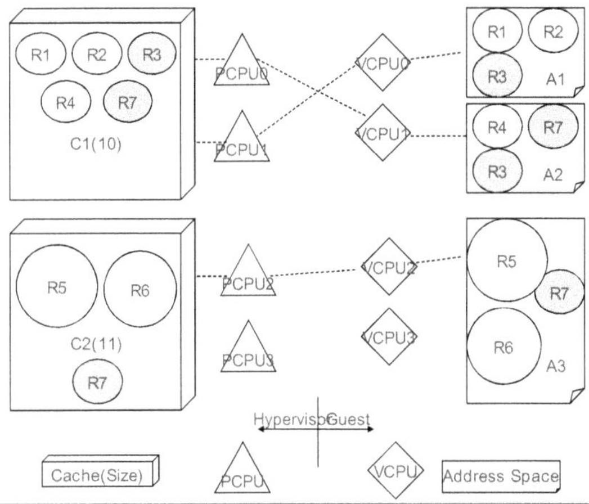

Figure 2. How regions interact with caches and address spaces.

if private, it belongs to a certain address space; (ii) it has a reference count, which is used to deallocate a region when it is no longer used; (iii) it is mapped to some number of caches (typically, to only one); (iv) it has a reverse map to the page table so that region to page mappings are easily changed; (v) there is additional information to calculate its working set size; and (vi) there are also additional counters for bookkeeping.

The reverse map is important because when a region is mapped to a cache, all page table entries to all pages in the region must be modified in order to ensure that only those address spaces running on the 'right' cores are permitted to access it. It is easy to maintain because Xen must already intercept all page table modifications. For other address spaces, we simply clear the protection bit in the page table, thereby causing an access fault when any of them attempts to use the page. Such 'page touches' are not propagated to guests, but are transparently handled by the region scheduling framework. Figure 3 depicts this. Note that without a reverse map, these actions would require an expensive complete page table scan.

2.2.1 Page touch and cache switch

As indicated in Section 2.1, upon page touch, the region scheduler has two options: (i) to allow the access, which requires mapping the touched region to the current cache, termed 'opening' the

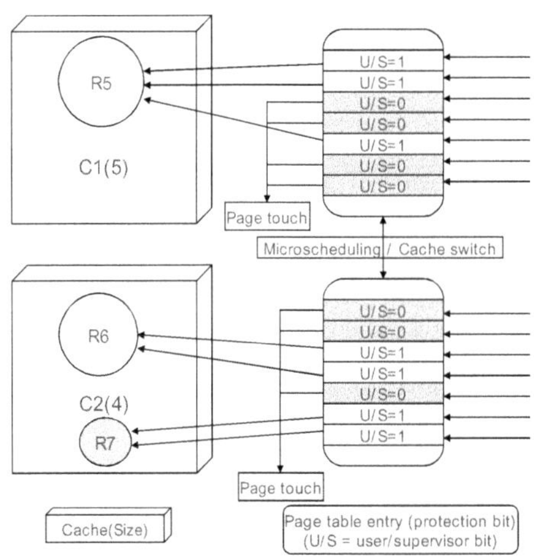

Figure 3. Page touch and cache switch.

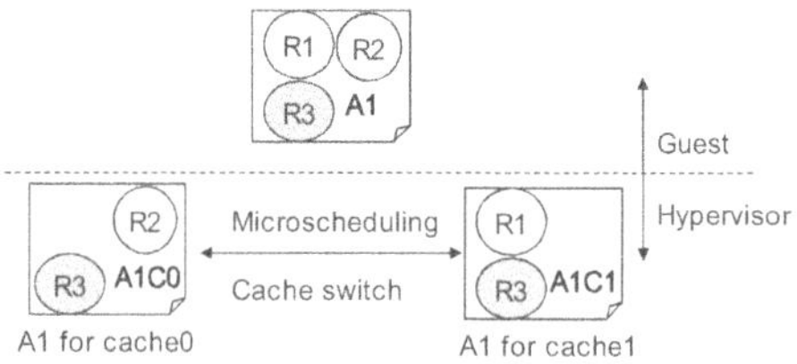

Figure 4. Per-cache page table.

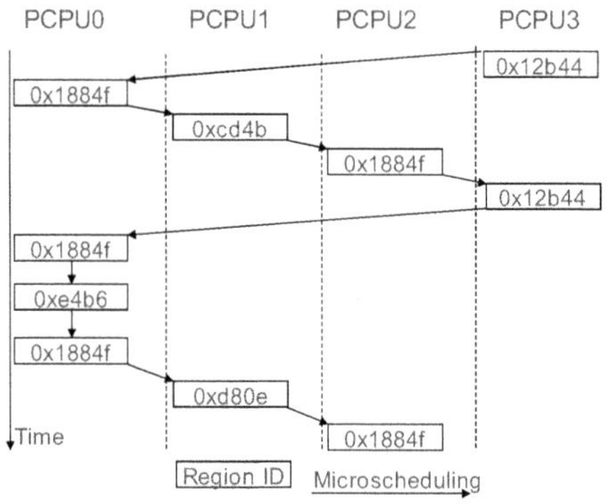

Figure 5. Microscheduling with 1VCPU.

region; or (ii) to move the executable entity to the CPU whose cache is currently allocated to the region, termed micro-scheduling. An entity is micro-scheduled in order to force it to run on a different cache. For such a cache switch, we inspect all of the regions used by that entity, set the protection bits for the mapped regions to the target cache – 'opening' the regions – and clear it for the other regions – 'closing' them. Figure 3 shows how page tables are manipulated for each cache switch. Global regions, which are already mapped into both caches, are skipped since there is no need to manipulate them.

Page table manipulations are also used to collect information about an application's behaviour in terms of memory accesses and to track its working set. By simply 'closing' a region, one can detect when a VCPU enters it, for instance, which we use to help assess working set size. By 'closing' regions that have not been accessed for a while, region management is optimized in terms of the number of open regions it must consider.

2.2.2 Micro-scheduling and cache switches

As evident from the description above, micro-scheduling involves cache switching. This could be expensive if it required the hypervisor to explicitly touch all of the address space's private regions and their page table entries. We eliminate this overhead by maintaining per-cache page tables. This is shown in Figure 4, where the hypervisor's page tables A1C0 and A1C1 jointly have the same contents as the guest's cache table A1; they differ only in the protection bits used to ensure that regions are open or closed with respect to certain caches. This also enables multiple threads in a process to run across caches.

Beyond cache switching, the other costs of micro-scheduling concern VCPU/PCPU re-mappings. Figure 5 depicts a case in which one VCPU runs on four PCPUs, where the hexadecimal in each rectangle is the unique ID for each region used by the VCPU. In this hardware configuration, Cache 0 is shared by (or local to) PCPUs 0, 2, and Cache 1 is shared by (local to) PCPUs 1, 3. Cache 0 is allocated to Regions 0x1884f, 0xe4b6, and Cache 1 is

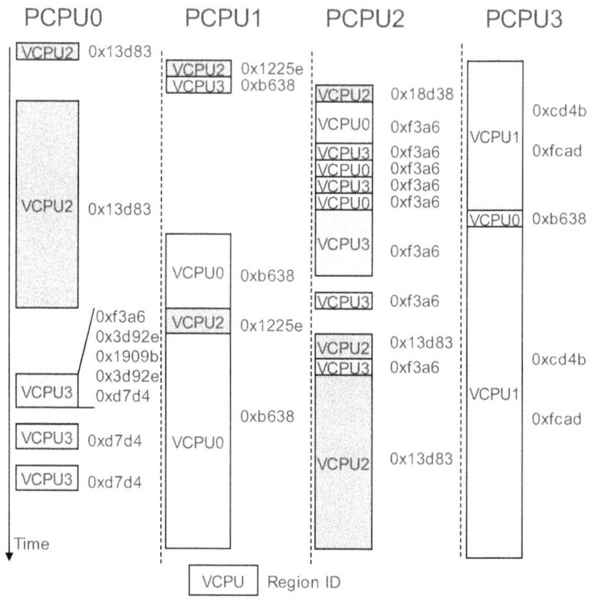

Figure 6. Microscheduling with 4 VCPUs.

allocated to Regions 0xcd4b, 0xd80e, and 0x12b44. For example, since Region 0x1884f is mapped only to Cache 0, when the VCPU tries to access this region, it is scheduled onto PCPU0 or PCPU2. Note that it is the standard scheduler (such as Xen's credit scheduler) that determines which PCPUs are allocated to them. Micro-scheduling, then, simply makes sure that VCPUs always run on those PCPUs that are associated with the caches allocated to the regions they are currently accessing. Potential performance opportunities and liabilities derived from these constraints are discussed next.

Figure 6 depicts a more complex case in which 4 VCPUs run on 4 PCPUs, where VCPUs access some regions only through PCPUs 0, 2 and others through PCPUs 1, 3. For example, the region 0x13d83 is mapped to Cache0, and 0x1225e is mapped to Cache1 (see Figure 7 for the associated region-to-cache mapping). We can see how the region framework balances cache loads from these figures. We discuss cache balancing in Section 4.

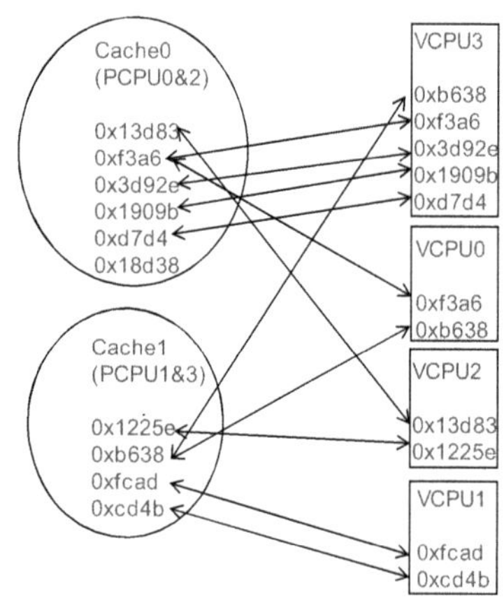

Figure 7. Mappings among regions, caches, and VCPUs.

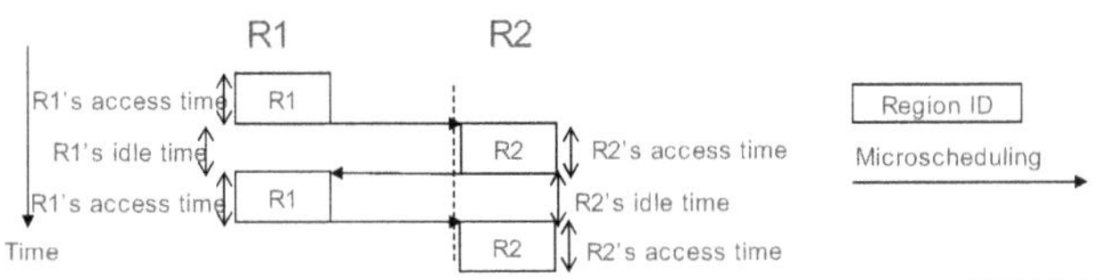

Figure 8. Two region memlat's access and idle times.

A potential side effect of cache balancing is that PCPUs may experience additional idle time. This is illustrated by the idle time observed on PCPU1 in Figure 6, which occurs because VCPUs 0, 3, 2 are running on Cache 0 (PCPU0, 2) while only VCPU1 is running on Cache 1 (PCPU1, 3). In fact, VCPUs 0, 3 are competing for PCPU2, while PCPU1 is idle. This transient imbalance of VCPUs on two caches is due to restrictive region-to-cache mappings. Such an imbalance is desirable if VCPU1 greatly benefits from its exclusive access to its cache (e.g., for cache-intensive codes), but at the same time, it may increase the latencies experienced by other VMs due to the effectively smaller cache sizes made available to them. The conflict is mitigated (1) when there are more VCPUs (due to VM-internal parallelism or consolidated VMs), so that it is likely that other VCPUs can be found to fill this gap, or (2) when there are more PCPUs per cache. Further, we use an additional method to prevent CPU idleness, in which instead of micro-scheduling VCPUs, we manage regions in order to handle this conflict between CPU and cache workload balancing. Results on such cache balancing appear in Section 5.3. Our final solution is to simply permit the region framework to make regions global (region opening) to prevent CPU idleness. Such degeneration to standard scheduling is useful for codes that do not depend much in performance on efficient cache use.

3. Regioning

This section explains region identification and tracking. At two extreme ends, all (private) physical pages in an address space could be placed (1) into a single region (too coarse-grained) or (2) into many single-page regions (too fine-grained). The first says that only entire address spaces can be mapped onto caches, whereas the second states that we have little information regarding its locality. To determine page-to-region associations, therefore, requires runtime methods that analyze the benefits and overheads of region formation and management, and of the micro-scheduling actions necessary to enforce region to cache mappings. This section identifies such regioning conditions and uses them to construct regioning algorithm.

3.1 Cache Unification

A simple single-threaded micro-benchmark, termed 'memlat' (memory latency) based on [4], is used to assess the potential utility of cache unification. This memlat has two identically sized regions, which it traverses randomly for some given number of memory references and across a given number of pages, termed region 'access time', before its execution switches to the other region, which results in a consequent value of region 'idle time' (see Figure 8).

In the experiment, instead of confining the memlat's regions and thus, its execution to one cache, we map its two regions to two different caches and micro-schedule it across the associated PCPUs, then compare it to the cache confining case. This is done for two different generations of machines (Clovertown and Westmere -- see Section 5 for additional detail)

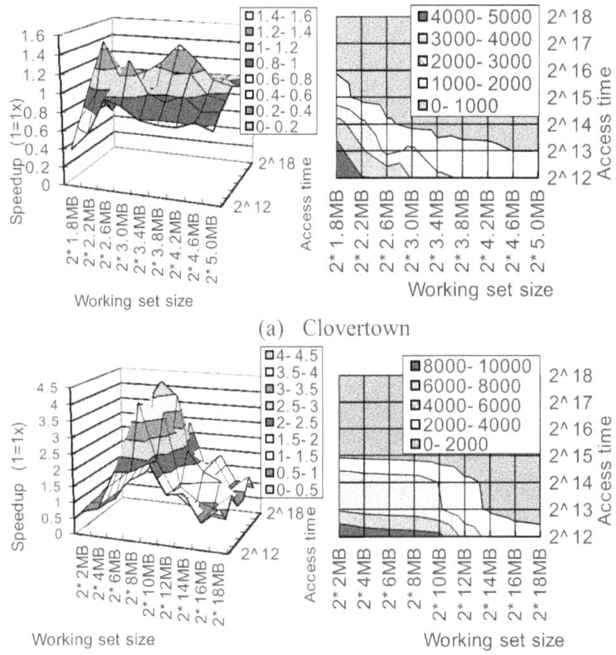

(b) Westmere

Normalized performance (3D) and

(c) microscheduling rate per second (contour view)

Figure 9. Two-region memlat across caches.

Figure 9 shows the normalized performance of the two region memlat when caches are unified, where values greater than 1 denote improved performance compared to the case of cache confinement. The x axis is working set sizes (2*2MB means two 2MB regions), and the y axis is access time in the number of elements touched before a region switch occurs. In this section, 'access time' is expressed in memory access count rather than actual time. The figure shows that improved performance appears in the center, not at the edges of the graphs.

There are several interesting insights from these simple experiments. First, substantial opportunities exist for gaining performance improvements from using cache unification, up to 45% for Clovertown and over 300% for Westmere. This is despite significant numbers of micro-scheduling actions in Figure 9, with rates ranging from 295 to 2240 per second for successful cache-unification near the center for Clovertown, and with rates ranging from 180 to 5100 per second for Westmere. Second, Westmere has a greater range in which improvements are seen (>1), and this is because of its relatively lower cost of micro-scheduling (see Section 5.1). This reflects the fact that computer architects have taken great pains to reduce the overheads of context switching on modern CPUs. Also, third, we can see that the microscheduling rate increases as region size and access time decrease.

Second, on Clovertown, performance improvements are marginal when access times are high (>= 2^16) because in those cases, there are relatively few micro-scheduling actions that permit applications to benefit from cache unification. Third, as expected, when access times are too short (<=2^12), the large number of micro-scheduling actions create overheads that outweigh the utility of cache unification. The outcome is Condition 1, which states that access time must be in some platform-specific range (i.e., these normative experiments have to be performed for each

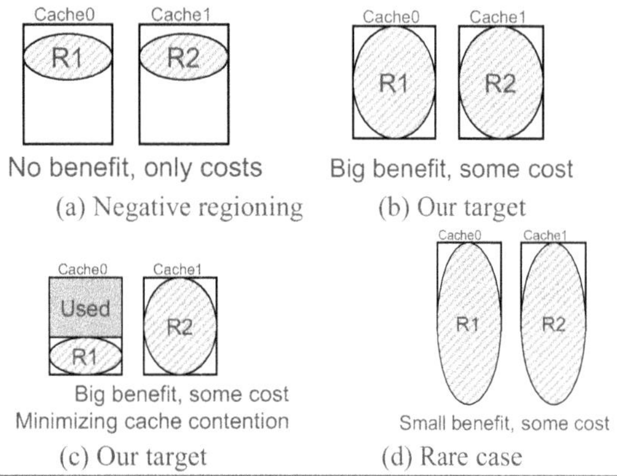

Figure 10. Cache working sets and cache sizes.

platform used) in order for region-based scheduling to benefit from cache unification.

Conditions 2 and 3 concern cache working set sizes (recall that a cache working set is defined as the sum of the sizes of all of the regions being used). First, there are negative effects when working sets are too small (<=2*1.8MB for Clovertown, <=2*4MB for Westmere), because placing working sets that would fit into a single cache into two different caches simply causes the added overheads of micro-scheduling. Second, when a working set is so large that it does not fit into the unified two caches, then again, there are no benefits from region scheduling, since there would be cache misses both with region scheduling (and the additional overheads associated with it) and without region scheduling. Condition 2, then, states that the total working set size must be larger than that of a single cache, and Condition 3 states that each working set must fit into the unified space provided by both caches. Conditions 1-3 are shown pictorially in Figure 10. As stated earlier, actual benefits and costs vary across platforms, but from the Westmere vs. Clovertown results shown here, it appears that future platforms will likely further tilt the playing field toward our more explicit methods for cache management.

3.2 Bottom-up Regioning

We are now ready to explain how regioning is performed. Regions are captured at runtime. There are two extremes: (1) 'random regioning' where physical pages are placed into regions randomly, which would cause high rates of micro-scheduling, and (2) single regioning, where all pages are placed into a single region, thereby effectively disabling region-based scheduling and entirely avoiding micro-scheduling overheads. Between these two extremes, we use Conditions 1-3 formulated above to assess the utility of regioning, and we identify and track regions using a sampling-based clustering technique, a bottom-up approach based on the notions of access and idle times.

Each address space runs for 1% of its time in regioning mode (see Figure 11), in which initially, there are only single-page regions that are then repeatedly merged to form suitably sized regions to contain application locality. In addition, at the end of each regioning phase, some regions are torn down in order to prevent them from becoming too large and/or to capture substantial changes in application behavior (e.g., phase changes). Finally, for accuracy, regioning performed across interrupt handlers and system timers is adjusted to correctly consider such system activities.

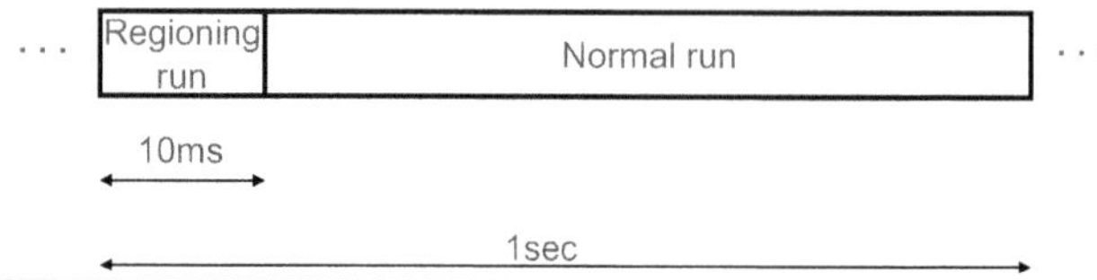

Figure 11. Regioning run (p = 1%).

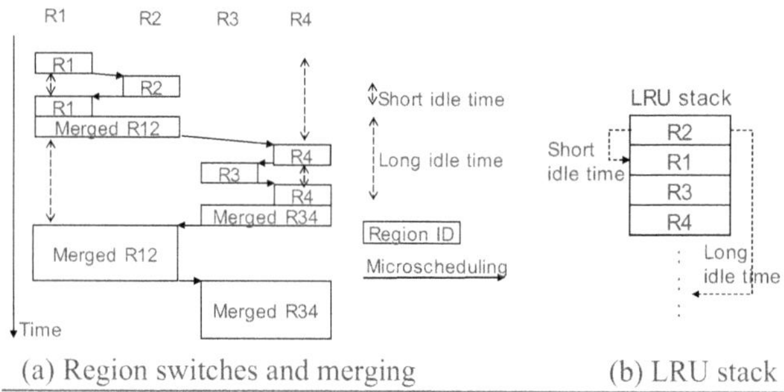

Figure 12. Regions and region merging via LRU stack.

Figure 12 depicts a scenario in which multiple smaller regions with longer vs. shorter inter-region idle times are merged into a smaller number of larger regions. This is done as follows. First, during the regioning phase, all region switches are detected because initially, all regions are closed (except for global regions). This means that entering a region causes a page touch that is visible to the system. This makes it possible to construct a stack of regions based on the (prev_region → next_region) occurrences. Second, when a new region is entered, the previous region is closed, so that only one region (the current region) is open at any given time. This makes it easy to measure the access and idle times for all regions.

Idle times correspond to the LRU distance between regions. Therefore, a long idle time indicates a locality change, whereas a short idle time between two regions is a strong indicator for merging them, both of which are shown in Figure 12. Using a threshold 'q' to determine short idle times based on the memlat measurements explained earlier, we merge regions when idle time is less than q and take no action otherwise. Note that a low threshold results in fine (small) regions, while a high threshold creates coarse (bigger) regions.

All regions are opened to resume normal execution after the regioning phase has completed. This entering/exiting of the regioning phase could be expensive, however, because all regions in the address space should be closed/opened when this occurs. This is optimized by introducing per-mode page tables in ways similar to what is discussed in Section 2.2.2. As a result, the regioning phase can be entered by simply switching to separate regioning-phase page table that already has closed entries.

3.3 Region Types

There are several types of regions. Initially, all regions are 'seed' regions. When locality is captured in the regioning phase, they become regular regions and once mapped to some cache, they are termed 'local' regions. As stated earlier, there are also 'global' regions not subject to region scheduling.

Differentiating global from other regions is done as follows. At each page-touch from a seed region, the new page is determined as 'code' if the faulting address equals the eip (program counter) register. If the faulting address is near the stack pointer, it is determined to be a 'stack' page. Both code and stack pages are classified into 'global' regions, and thus, do not further participate

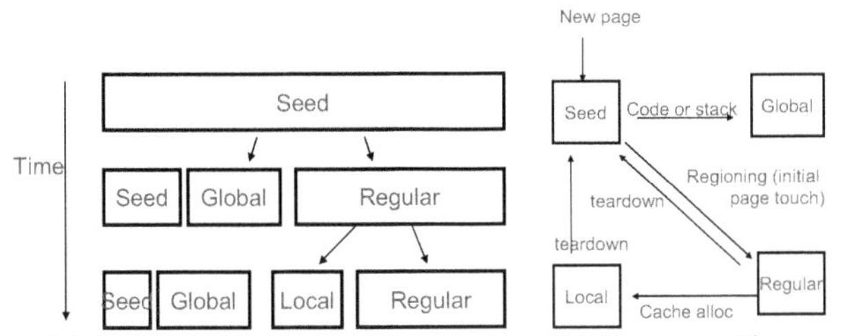

(a) Region evolution over time (b) State transition

Figure 13. Types of regions.

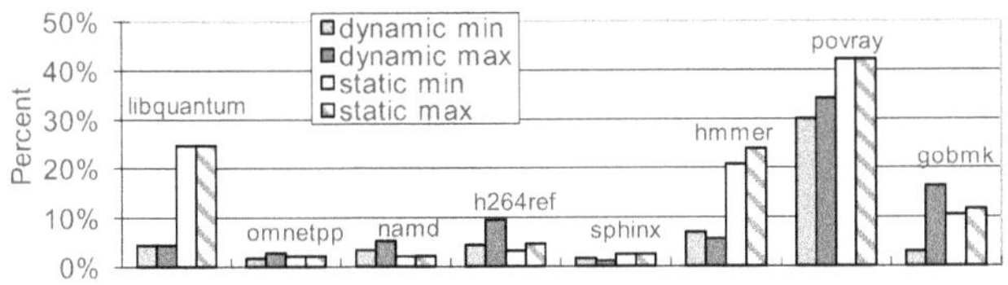

Figure 14. Portion of shared pages (observed min/max value).

Table 2. Regioning process.

(1) Start regioning (close all regions except global regions)
(2) Regioning phase (merging)
(3) End regioning (open all regions)
(4) Cache balancer does cache allocation, cache balancing.
(5) Teardown (pick largest local region from regioning phase and make it into a seed region.)

in the regioning process. The type transitions shown in Figure 13 apply to all other pages. In summary, the process in Table 2 is used for regioning.

We have not yet explained when large regions are destroyed (by turning them into seed regions). This is done in conjunction with cache allocation to regions. Specifically, cache allocation is performed after regioning is completed, by picking a regular region and making it into a local region (i.e., mapping the region to some cache). Next, we select the largest local region determined in the regioning phase (which is marked in that phase, so this is an O(1) operation), and denote it as a seed region, thereby initiating the process of tearing it down. We never consecutively tear down the same region, however. In this fashion, we incrementally build (and tear down) regions in response to observed program behavior. Finally, a region may shrink during a run when an abnormally high microscheduling rate is detected, by excluding from the region the page that causes it.

Regioning is independently conducted for each core, the current policy doing it at every 1 second of CPU time for each address space. Thus, long-lived processes will experience more regioning actions, whereas short-lived ones may not experience any regioning at all (i.e., if they live less than 1sec). For multi-threaded applications sharing an address space, each of the different threads (i.e., the cores on which they run) enter the regioning phase at a different time, thereby avoiding concurrent use of the shared page table.

3.4 Global Regions

Inappropriate placement of shared pages and stack pages can cause unnecessary micro-scheduling overheads. An example is to map the glibc code onto only one cache, which would cause virtually all processes to frequently micro-schedule to glibc's cache. To address this issue, we declare all code pages (and similarly, the

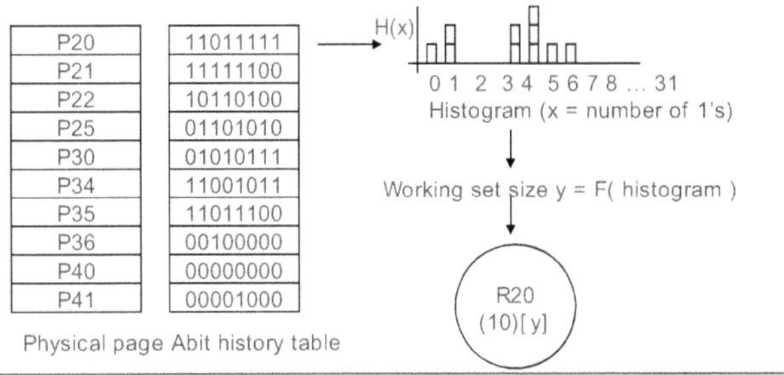

Figure 15. Access bit history and region's working set size.

stack pages) to be 'global', which causes some level of cache line duplication. The resulting overheads in terms of cache space usage are moderate, however, as shown by the measurements in Figure 14 assessing the portion of shared pages in the SPEC benchmark suite. The figure shows the percentage of observed shared pages at runtime, both actually accessed (dynamic) percentage and the static percentage seen in page tables.

4. Working Set Tracking

Working set sizes are determined dynamically, using the access bits (A-bits) in page table entries. Specifically, every 100ms (as virtual time for each address space), the page table is scanned, and the access-bit history is recorded in a 32bit word. Only currently open regions are scanned to minimize overhead. For the example shown in Figure 3, if it is running on C2, only the part of the page table corresponding to R6 and R7 would be scanned, for instance. The access bits gathered over time form an access bit history (i.e., 3.2 seconds worth of access history) for each page. This is also termed the page's 'access pattern' recorded as region histograms based on their pages' access histories.

Figure 15 shows region R20's details. From its 10 pages' access histories, it builds a histogram by counting the number of 1's, and it calculates its working set size 'y' using a heuristic moving average function F below that takes the histogram as its input. The weights are determined experimentally.

$$y = \sum_{i=26}^{31} H(i) + \sum_{i=20}^{25} \frac{3}{4} H(i) + \sum_{i=14}^{19} \frac{1}{2} H(i) + \sum_{i=8}^{13} \frac{1}{4} H(i)$$

Consistent with this function, we define cache load as the sum of the dynamic sizes of mapped regions. Interpreting this value as cache occupancy, the cache balancer uses it to determine cache imbalance; a simple greedy algorithm periodically balances cache usage in conjunction with the regioning process.

Since access bits are gathered every 100ms, and a 32bit word is used to store its history, roughly the past 3.2 seconds are reflected in the working set sizes used for region scheduling. Figure 16 shows the evolution of cache working set sizes observed over time for select benchmark codes, which the cache balancer would use.

5. Experimental Evaluation

Region scheduling is evaluated on two generations of Intel platforms. The first, labelled 'Clovertown' in all figures below, is an older machine with Intel quad-core Xeon X5365@3.00GHz cores with 1GB RAM. The caches are an 8-way L1 cache (32K Data+32K Instruction) and a 16-way 2x4MB L2 cache. The cache line size is 64bytes. The second, labelled 'Westmere' in all figures below is a newer machine with two Intel six-core Xeon X5660@2.80GHz sockets with 12GB RAM. The caches are a 4-

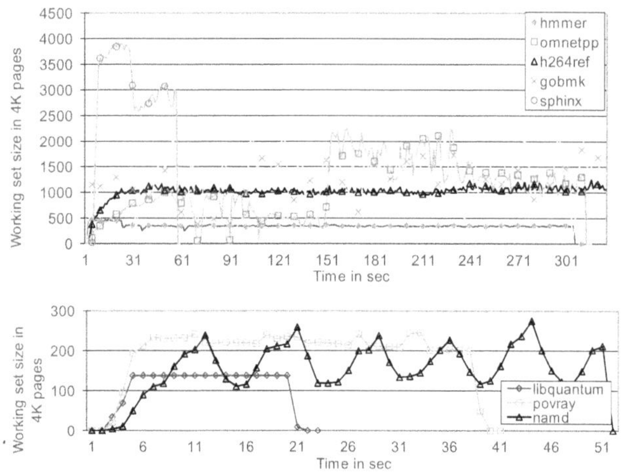

Figure 16. Tracking working set size.

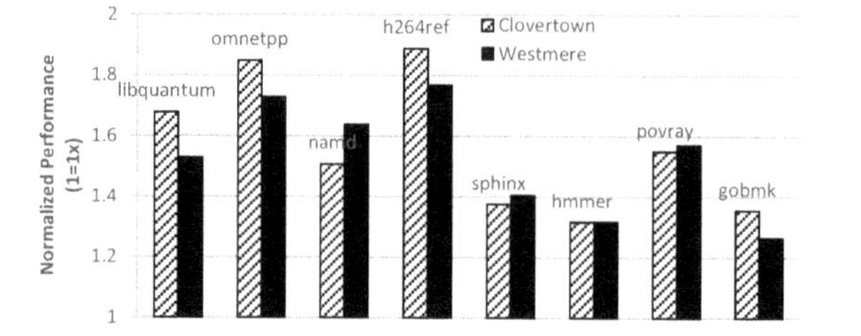

Figure 17. Speedup with cache balancing.

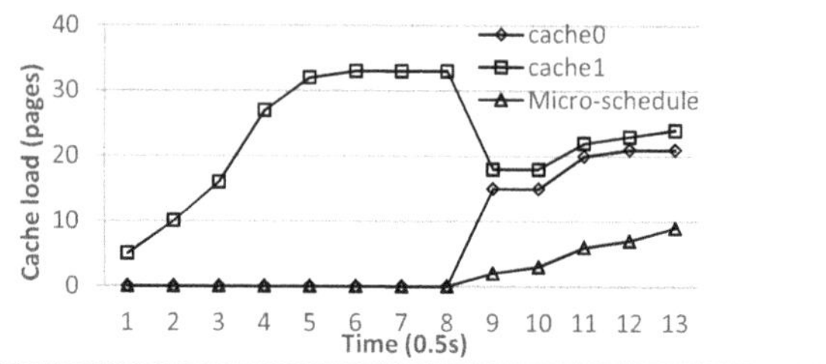

Figure 18. Cache-unification for two-region memlat.

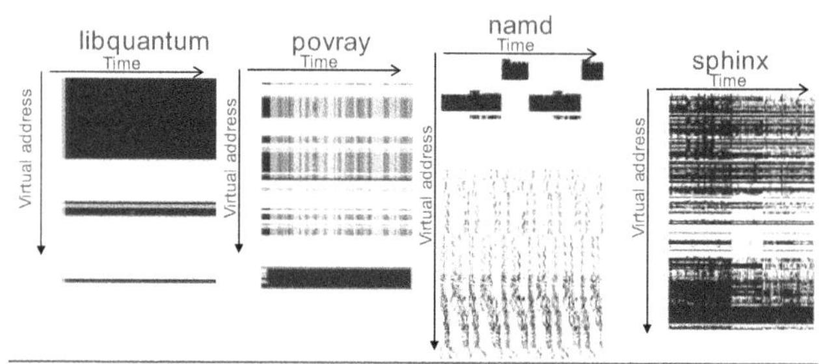

Figure 19. SPEC 2006 memory accesses.

way 32KB L1I, 8-way 32KB L1D, 8-way 256KB L2, and shared 16-way 12288KB L3.

5.1 Overhead

Regions are enforced by the hardware MMU. Once page protection bits are set during opening/closing regions, no additional runtime overheads are incurred during execution for enforcing regions. Full TLB flushes are avoided by using optimized instructions like 'invlpg'.

Four major overhead sources are the do_clock(), usched(), switch_cache(), and regioning() calls, which perform page table scanning, microscheduling, page table updates, and regioning respectively. Using the two-region memlat with a small working set size, we conduct an extreme case experiment to assess these overheads, by choosing working sets that perfectly fit into the two different machine's caches, thereby eliminating all potential benefits derived from micro-scheduling. When not using the 'per-cache page table' optimization, total overhead is measured to be roughly 5.5% with 700 microscheduling per second. Performing the do_clock() call ten times and making one regioning() call results in less than 1% overhead, but the switch_cache() call constitutes over 90% of total overhead, which is effectively eliminated using said optimization. This results in constant-time micro-scheduling, its composite time comprised of page fault, context switch, runqueue manipulation, IPI, and TLB flush. Micro-scheduling is measured as 47600 cycles (i.e., 15.86 us, 1.5% for 1000 uschedule actions) for Clovertown, and 17800 cycles (i.e. 6.357 us, 0.6% for 1000 uschedule) for Westmere. Do_clock() has some overheads depending on page table size, but it is several milliseconds in most cases (less than 1%). Regioning overheads benefit from the optimization that uses per-mode page tables, where an upper bound on these costs is defined by the sampling rate p. Naturally, overheads are even lower, close to two TLB flushes, for codes that operate with stable regions, like libquantum. That overall overhead is measured to be less than 3%, typically 2% on both machines.

5.2 Microbenchmarks

To reduce cache contention, the cache balancer dynamically remaps regions based on cache loads. For example, on machine Clovertown, when running two processes of 4MB working set size and two processes of 16KB working set size, with region scheduling, the cache balancer ensures that the cache is shared by the pair of 4MB+16KB processes. This improves performance by more than 50% for all processes compared to a region unaware mapping in which two 4MB processes share a cache. Similar results are observed on machine Westmere, using 12MB and 512KB working set sizes, respectively.

Figure 17 shows simple experiments on both machines, in which we run two 4MB memlats + 16KB memlat + a SPEC benchmark on the machine Clovertown, and two 12MB memlats + 512KB memlat + a SPEC benchmark on the machine Westmere. Depending on scheduling, the SPEC benchmark experiences different levels of cache contention. The cache balancer improves performance by correctly pairing processes onto caches and mitigating cache contention. The figure shows that there is substantial potential for performance improvement for all SPEC benchmarks. Or stated negatively, without cache balancing, SPEC programs experience significant levels of disturbance by the presence of other cache-intensive codes.

Conversely, performance can be improved for cache-intensive codes by giving them access to multiple caches, termed cache unification. The initial effects of cache unification on cache loads for the simple memlat micro-benchmark on machine Clovertown are shown in Figure 18.

The first half of the figure shows unbalanced cache loads, and the second half shows balanced loads plus micro-scheduling. Similar results are obtained on machine Westmere and for brevity, are not shown here. We evaluate the performance implications of such actions in more detail below.

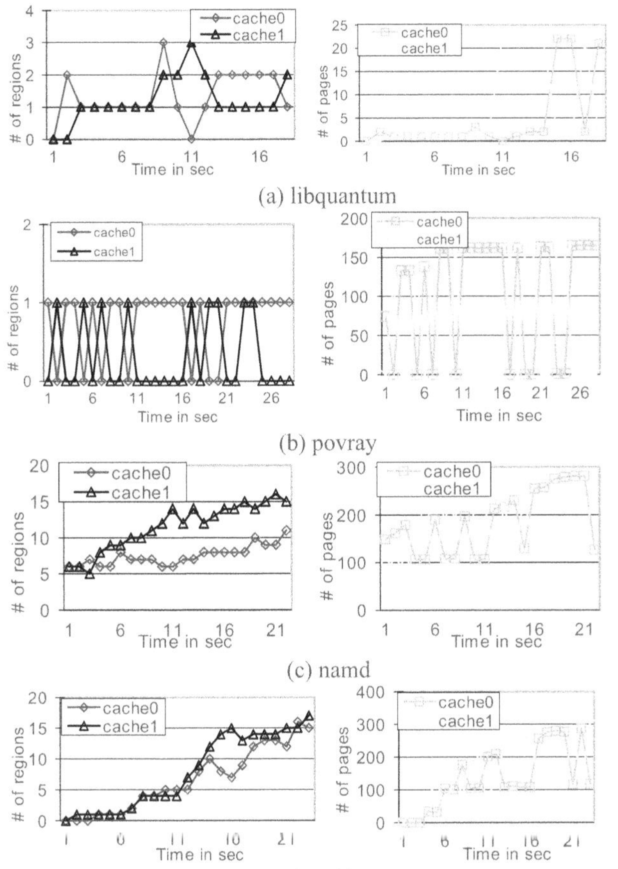

(a) libquantum

(b) povray

(c) namd

(d) sphinx

Regioning threshold = 100us on Clovertown

Figure 20. SPEC 2006 regioning.

5.3 SPEC Benchmarks

Figure 19 depicts measured results for experiments that assess the memory access pattern of the SPEC 2006 benchmark, which is obtained by collecting their access bit history over a test run (see Figure 15). From these runs, it is clear that libquantum and povray have simple access patterns, resulting in very stable regions, whereas sphinx and namd regions are more dynamic. This is verified by Figure 20, showing just a few regions in each cache for the first two, and a much larger number of regions for the latter two. Results obtained on machine Westmere are consistent, except that it tends to have bigger region sizes due to its higher performance (not reported for brevity).

Considering the access patterns depicted in Figure 19, these measurements show that the regioning methods correctly identify the memory region-based execution behavior of these codes, where e.g., libquantum and povray have few regions while namd and sphinx have many regions.

Another set of results in Figure 20 (the graphs on the right) depict the cache load (sum of region sizes for each cache) imposed by these codes. First, note that in the case of namd and sphinx, cache balancing succeeds in balancing both caches. This is in part because the number of regions for these codes is relatively large, which then permits the cache balancer to advantageously pack these regions into caches. In contrast, libquantum and povray show poor cache balancing, in part due to their small numbers of

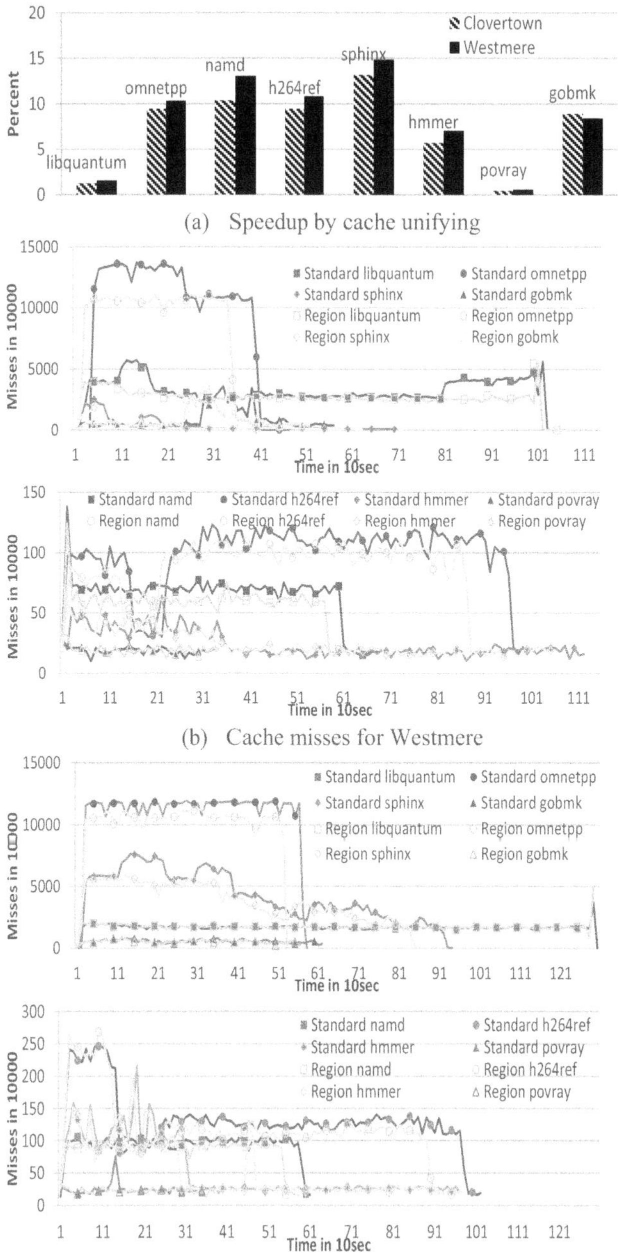

(a) Speedup by cache unifying

(b) Cache misses for Westmere

(c) Cache misses for Clovertown

Figure 21. SPEC benchmark cache unifying.

regions. Second, and as shown in Figure 21, successful cache balancing always improves performance, with an almost 15% gain for the Sphinx benchmark.

The outcome from these experiments is that regioning and cache balancing result in performance improvements even when the number of micro-scheduling actions is high. In fact and as shown in Figure 22, improved performance is seen even for very large numbers of micro-scheduling actions, e.g., the 10% improvement seen for namd on machine Clovertown is attained with up to 2000 micro-scheduling actions per second! Further, Westmere shows better performance due to its cheaper micro-scheduling. The measured cache misses in Figure 21 demonstrate why this is the case. In many workloads, such as omnetpp, sphinx,

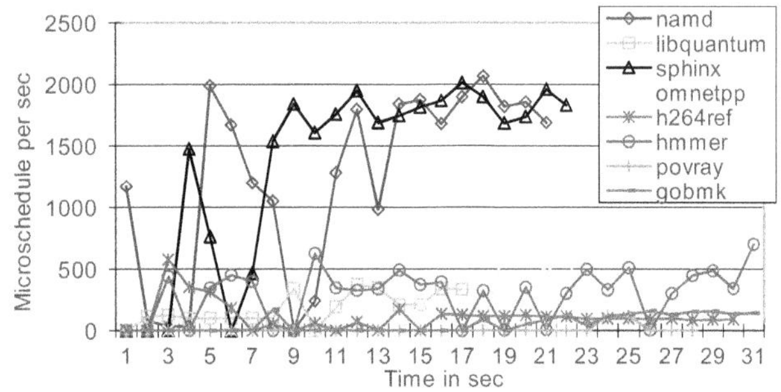

Figure 22. Micro-scheduling rates on Clovertown.

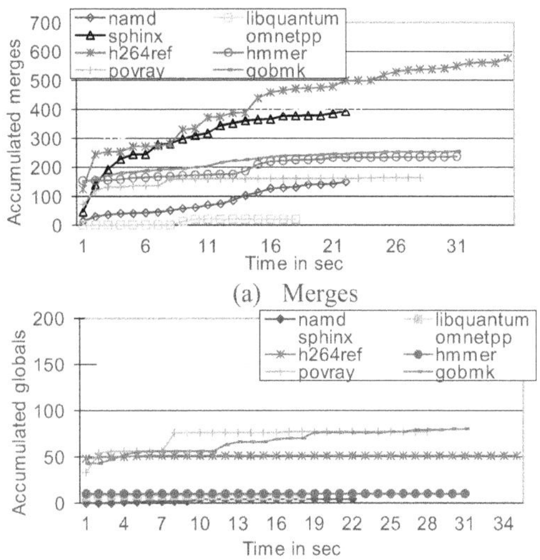

(a) Merges

(b) Globals (stack&code)

Figure 23. Regioning details (Clovertown).

h264ref, the measured cache miss rates are lower with region-based scheduling.

The fact that *performance benefits are seen even with high micro-scheduling rates (up to 2000 context switches per second)* is a key result of this research. This demonstrates that given the relatively low cost context switching on modern architectures, there is an almost overwhelming importance of caching to program performance. We view results like these as an important motivation for carrying out and continuing our research into memory- and cache-centric methods for processor scheduling.

We also note that these SPEC-based results are consistent with the memlat-based ones shown in Section 3.1, thereby demonstrating that the potential behaviors we diagnosed with the memlat micro-benchmark are realistic in that they occur in actual codes. From the memlat-based diagnostic measurements, we also note that unduly high micro-scheduling rates can reduce or eliminate the potential performance gains derived from cache unification. This places constraints on the granularities of regions and region mappings that must be observed and taken into account by region scheduling.

Finally, the results in Figure 23 confirm that the bottom-up approach to regioning used in our research is viable. First, since we start with many small regions, initially, there are many merge actions, but second, there is sufficient stability that the number of merges quickly subsides, along with the number of re-regioning actions, as evident from the number of global regions seen in these codes. We deduce that memory regions are sufficiently

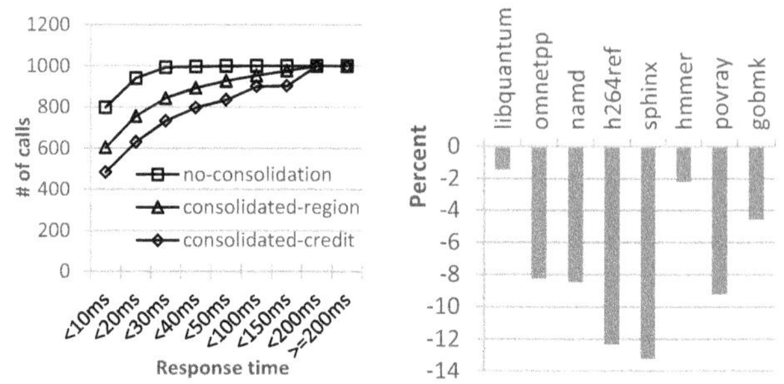

(a) Response time **(b) SPEC cost**

Figure 24. Media server+SPEC consolidation on Clovertown.

stable to warrant their runtime detection and use, even without special hardware support for doing so.

5.4 Media Benchmark

Region scheduling can help improve performance, as shown in Section 5.3, but it can also improve other important metrics, such as noise [26] for parallel codes or timing perturbation for real-time applications. We demonstrate the latter on machine Clovertown by measuring the response times seen for high performance IP telephony software, Asterisk [25].

Asterisk is a complete IP PBX, comprised of a voice communication server featuring voice mail, conference calling, interactive voice response, etc. It supports VoIP protocols such as SIP, MGCP, and H.323. It acts as a signalling server (SIP server) and a media server. When it handles signalling, it deals with call set-up/teardown, etc. When it is used as a media server, it takes a voice stream, processes it (including transcoding, if needed), and then sends the stream to the recipient. This real-time media server requires low latencies to process voice streams, and it requires that those latencies remain within certain upper bounds to protect voice quality.

Using the SIPp traffic generator for the SIP protocol, we run experiments exercising the system at 10 calls per second with RTP traffic. Signalling is initiated from SIPp, and an 8 second pcap file (RTP stream of G.711 encoded) is sent to the media server after call establishment. The call hold time is 10 seconds. The parameters above imply that there are at most 200 RTP streams flowing into the media server at any point of time (100 streams from the caller and 100 streams from the callee).

5.5 Cache Sharing

To demonstrate the utility of cache balancing, the VOIP experiment uses unfair policies that offer additional cache space to a preferred virtual machine. This is particularly important, of course, when there are multiple applications that share access to the platform's CPU and cache/memory resources.

Figure 24 shows the media server's improved response time on machine Clovertown when it is the only application running (denoted 'no consolidation'), when no region scheduling is used (denoted 'consolidated-credit'), or when region scheduling is employed and the media server is the preferred VM (denoted 'consolidated-region'). Results show that the server's response times are much more consistent for the region-based vs. credit-based scheduling approaches, and both are worse, of course, than the non-shared scenario. The figure shows the cumulative number of calls with various durations observed during the runs, with a 'flat' line being 'best'. We also note that the overall average response time is 7.765ms for no-consolidation, 19.415ms for consolidated-region, and 32.535ms for consolidated-credit, respectively. The almost 40% improvement in the average response time seen for the server comes at a moderate cost for the other applications running on the platform, with an up to 15% detriment observed for the sphinx code. Degradation occurs because the cache balancer is instructed to provide additional cache to the media server, which is known to be cache-sensitive.

5.6 Reducing Noise for Parallel Codes

We next explore the use of region scheduling to protect parallel codes (e.g., OpenMP codes) running on a shared platform from each other and/or from the effects other codes on the same platform may impose on them. This is particularly important as we move toward many-core systems where the platforms on which parallel simulation computations take place will be shared with other applications (as in consolidated and cloud computing systems) or will be shared with additional codes that analyze simulation output data as it is being produced [35]. One could, of course, strictly partition nodes and their caches, but an approach like region scheduling that explicitly understands memory usage and can better isolate codes from each other, as evident from the results shown in the previous section, should result in improved levels of node utilization and permit richer and more finer-grain ways of using and sharing the node resources of future machines.

We use two virtual machines – one virtual machine running a ray tracing parallel workload (PAR VM) and other a SPEC omnetpp workload (SPEC VM). Figure 25(a) shows the measured (worst) elapsed time and (average) CPU time for each virtual machine. In case of raytrace, elapsed time increases as more workload is added to the SPEC VM. However, its CPU time stays constant. This is because this parallel code does not reuse its data, so is not impacted by cache contention. Meanwhile, the omnetpp's performance suffers from sharing cache with PAR VM. Region scheduling improves the SPEC VM's performance by mostly isolating PAR VM onto one cache while SPEC VM runs on the other cache. Figure 25(b) shows their average cache misses. In general, with region scheduling, we observe 8.39% less cache misses in Figure 25(b).

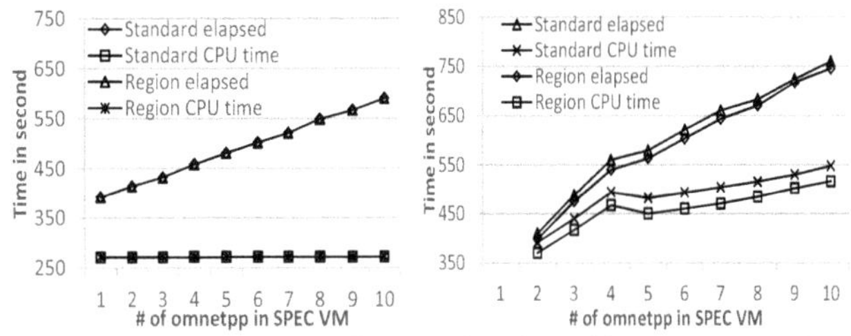

(a) Performance for two virtual machines (Westmere)

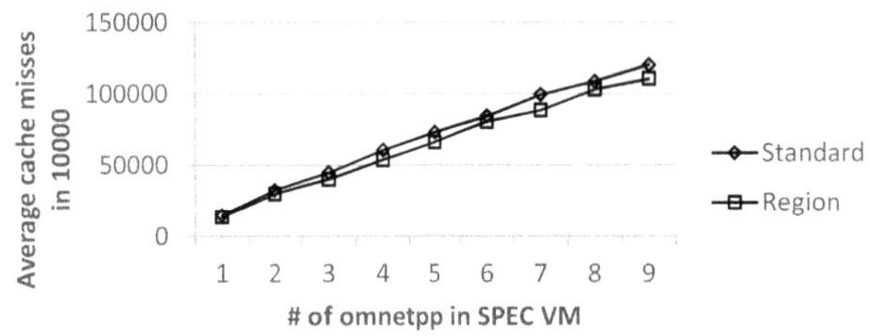

(b) Cache misses (Westmere)

Figure 25. Parallel code VM consolidated with SPEC VM.

6. Related Work

The importance of efficient cache usage is well known [12, 13, 14, and 15]. There are hardware approaches to cache partition (e.g., based on utility metrics [23] or spill/receive [24]) and software-based methods. The ones proposed in [16, 17] are similar to those used in our work, but these simulation-based results are focused on NUCA caches [12], whereas we contribute a general framework for and implementation of policies for cache management for realistic multi-cache, multi-core platforms.

Other cache-aware schedulers [5, 8] use thread migration and matching, and [6, 7] use page coloring or guided page allocation to partition shared caches, whereas we use page-table-based page-level affinity and microscheduling. Since our methods are implemented at hypervisor level, they can be used without modifying operating systems. Further, we go beyond earlier results to deal with multiple rather than the single caches addressed in prior work, and for such multiple caches, we go beyond cache partitioning to also support cache unification. Finally, we can estimate cache loads, since we track region working sets [10, 11].

Recent work at MIT has commonalities with our work, using a synthetic directory workload [31] as a demonstration. In that research, ideas similar to ours [32, 33, 34] are implemented in hardware, using instruction-level execution migration. We differ in that we extend the idea to cover all of a system's memory, and we do so in the VMM in order to make the functionality accessible to arbitrary unmodified applications and systems, without requiring any hardware changes.

Affinity scheduling [9] constitutes early work motivating the importance of caching for high performance codes. Our work can be thought as a next step in such work – page-level affinity. We have identified and demonstrated how this page-level affinity could be used.

The term 'region scheduling' also appears in [36], but that work has nothing in common with what is presented in this paper.

7. Conclusions And Future Work

This paper introduces a memory-centric approach to managing the resources of multi-core platforms, motivated by the ever-increasing importance of memory and cache resources (and their efficient use) in multi-core architectures. Indeed, we show results where improved performance is gained due to superior cache usage even at the cost of relatively high rates of context switching (e.g., up to 2000 micro-scheduling actions per second). Intuitively, this is because it is preferable to move the computational entity to where its memory is vs. moving the memory (i.e., cache lines) to where the entity currently runs.

To realize cache-centric scheduling, we introduce the novel notion of memory regions and then develop system-level support for dynamically determining these regions for mapping them to caches so as to optimize program performance. The resulting region framework is realized as a software layer in the Xen hypervisor, and beyond determining and mapping memory regions to caches, its additional task is to ensure that the entities touching memory regions are run so that region-to-cache mappings are preserved, i.e., a process is run only on a core associated with the cache in which its region is currently mapped.

Region scheduling could benefit from additional hardware support. For instance, execution migration by hardware [32, 33, 34] could reduce micro-scheduling overheads to only 100 cycles [34], thereby further broadening the usefulness of region-scheduling to applications. Further, there may be hardware-level opportunities to exploit the information about the behavior of an address space in terms of its region accesses and working set size. A particular opportunity is to use such inputs to affect the cache eviction policy used by hardware, i.e., to select victims for eviction. For example, once a region is unmapped from a cache, existing cache lines from the regions are ideal victims because they will not be accessed through that cache until opening region.

Other options include (i) not to evict cache lines from shared pages, such as those containing library codes, or (ii) to exploit the memory reference patterns detected by region scheduling to choose as victim's one-time data, e.g., one-time data such as the inputs or outputs produced by codes. Finally, (iii) rather than pursuing hardware methods for cache partitioning, one could exploit region scheduling for soft cache partitioning. Such partitioning can be used to give unfair advantages to certain codes, or even to dynamically resize codes' cache sizes to adjust them to their current working set sizes. On asymmetric multi-core architectures, this would make it possible, for instance, to isolate small workloads onto a smaller cache while giving most other cache capacity larger workloads.

This paper clearly demonstrates the promise of memory-centric scheduling, but there are several limitations in the current region framework: (i) to understand parallelism in multithreaded applications remains future work; (ii) if no region is detected, there are costs but not benefits – this should be addressed; (iii) the OS kernels in guest operating systems remain undifferentiated 'global regions' – this is being remedied in our current work.

References

[1] Larry Seiler, Doug Carmean, et al. "Larrabee: A Many-Core x86 Architecture for Visual Computing", SIGGRAPH 2008.

[2] Alexandra Fedorova, et al. "Performance Of Multithreaded Chip Multiprocessors And Implications For Operating System Design." USENIX 2005 Annual Technical Conference.

[3] Vahid Kazempour, Ali Kamali and Alexandra Fedorova, "AASH: An Asymmetry-Aware Scheduler for Hypervisors," International Conference on Virtual Execution Environments.

[4] Ulrich Drepper. "What every programmer should know about memory," www.akkadia.org/drepper/cpumemory.pdf

[5] Sergey Zhuravlev, Sergey Blagodurov, Alexandra Fedorova. "Addressing Shared Resource Contention in Multicore Processors via Scheduling". ASPLOS 2010.

[6] D. Tam, R. Azimi, L. Soares, M. Stumm. "Managing Shared L2 Caches on Multicore Systems in Software," Workshop on the Interaction between Operating Systems and Computer Architecture (WIOSCA), Jun 2007, pp. 27-33.

[7] L. Soares, D. Tam, M. Stumm, Int'l Symp. "Reducing the Harmful Effects of Last-Level Cache Polluters with an OS-Level, Software-Only Pollute Buffer," on Microarchitecture (MICRO), Nov 2008.

[8] D. Tam, R. Azimi, M. Stumm. "Thread Clustering: Sharing-Aware Scheduling on SMP-CMP-SMT Multiprocessors," European Conf. in Computer Systems (EuroSys), Mar 2007.

[9] Mark S. Squillante, and Edward D. Lazowska. "Using Processor-Cache Affinity Information in Shared-Memory Multiprocessor Scheduling," IEEE Transactions on Parallel and Distributed Systems. Vol. 4. No. 2. February 1993.

[10] P. J. Denning. "Thrashing: Its Causes and Prevention." Proceedings AFIPS, 1968 Fall Joint Computer Conference, vol. 33, pp. 915-922.

[11] P. J. Denning. "Before Memory was Virtual." From the book In the Beginning: Recollections of Software Pioneers, edited by Robert Glass, IEEE Press, 1997.

[12] Huh, Kim, Shafi, Zhang, Burger, and Keckler. "A NUCA Substrate for Flexible CMP Cache Sharing," ICS 2005.

[13] Zhang, Asanovic, "Victim Replication: Maximizing Capacity while Hiding Wire Delay in Tiled Chip Multiprocessors", ISCA 2005.

[14] Evan Speight, Hazim Shafi, Lixin Zhang, and Ram Rajamony. "Adaptive Mechanisms and Policies for Managing Cache Hierarchies in Chip Multiprocessors," ISCA 2005.

[15] Andreas Moshovos, "RegionScout: Exploiting Coarse Grain Sharing in Snoop-Based Coherence," ISCA 2005.

[16] S. Cho and L. Jin, "Managing distributed, shared L2 caches through OS-level page allocation," in Micro, 2006.

[17] Lei Jin and S. Cho, "Better than the two: Exceeding private and shared caches via two-dimensional page coloring," in Workshop on Chip Multiprocessor Memory Systems and Interconnects, 2007.

[18] D. Chandra, F. Guo, S. Kim, and Y. Solihin. "Predicting inter-thread cache contention on a chip multi-processor architecture," in HPCA, 2005.

[19] F. Guo and Y. Solihin. "An analytical model for cache replacement policy performance," in SIG METRICS, 2006.

[20] R. Iyer, "CQoS: a framework for enabling QoS in shared caches of CMP platforms," in ICS, 2004.

[21] H. Kannan, F. Guo, L. Zhao, R. Illikkal, R. Iyer, D. Newell, Y. Solihin and C.Kozyrakis, "From chaos to QoS: Case studies in CMP resource management," in dasCMP, 2006.

[22] S. Kim, D. Chandra, and Y. Solihin, "Fair cache sharing and partitioning in a chip multiprocessor architecture," in PACT, 2004.

[23] M. Qureshi and Y. Patt. "Utility-based cache partitioning: A lowoverhead, high-performance, runtime mechanism to partition shared caches," in Micro, 2006.

[24] Moinuddin K. Qureshi. "Adaptive Spill-Receive for Robust High-Performance Caching in CMPs" International Conference on High Performance Computer Architecture (HPCA) 2009.

[25] Min Lee, A. S. Krishnakumar, P. Krishnan, Navjot Singh, Shalini Yajnik. "Supporting Soft Real-Time Tasks in the Xen Hypervisor," VEE 2010, Pittsburgh, PA, March 17-19, 2010.

[26] Kurt B. Ferreira, Ron Brightwell, and Patrick G. Bridges. "Characterizing application sensitivity to OS interference using kernel-level noise injection." Supercomputing'08, November 2008.

[27] Paul Barham, et al. "Xen and the art of virtualization," In Proceedings of the nineteenth ACM symposium on Operating systems principles (2003), pp. 164-177.

[28] D. Rao and K. Schwan. "vnuma-mgr : Managing vm memory on numa platforms." In HiPC, Goa, India, 2010.

[29] Vishakha Gupta, Rob Knauerhase, Karsten Schwan, "Attaining System Performance Points: Revisiting the End-to-End Argument in System Design for Heterogeneous Many-core Systems" Sigops Operating Systems Review, January 2011.

[30] X10 Programming Language, http://x10.codehaus.org/

[31] Silas Boyd-Wickizer, Robert Morris, and M. Frans Kaashoek, "Reinventing Scheduling for Multicore Systems," HotOS '09

[32] M. Lis, K. S. Shim, O. Khan, and S. Devadas. "Shared Memory via Execution Migration", ASPLOS Ideas and Perspectives Session, March 2011.

[33] K. S. Shim, M. H. Cho, M. Lis, O. Khan, and S. Devadas, "System-level Optimizations for Memory Access in the Execution Migration Machine (EM2)," Second Workshop on Computer Architecture and Operating System co-design (CAOS), January 2011.

[34] M. H. Cho, K. S. Shim, M. Lis, O. Khan, and S. Devadas, "Deadlock-Free Fine-Grained Thread Migration," Proceedings of the 5th Network-on-Chip Symposium (NOCS), May 2011.

[35] Hasan Abbasi, Matthew Wolf, Greg Eisenhauer, Scott Klasky, Karsten Schwan, Fang Zheng, "DataStager: Scalable Data Staging Services for Petascale Applications," Proceedings of HPDC 2009.

[36] Gupta and Soffa. "Region Scheduling: An Approach for Detecting and Redistributing Parallelism" IEEE Transactions on Software Engineering Volume 16 Issue 4, April 1990.

Author Index

NOTES

NOTES

NOTES

www.ingramcontent.com/pod-product-compliance
Ingram Content Group UK Ltd.
Pitfield, Milton Keynes, MK11 3LW, UK
UKHW051413290926
15471UKWH00009B/1584

9 781450 307598